2014/15

THE GUIDE TO

MAJOR TRUSTS
VOLUME 1

FOURTEENTH EDITION

Tom Traynor, Jude Doherty, Lucy Lernelius-Tonks,
Denise Lillya & Emma Weston

DIRECTORY OF SOCIAL CHANGE

Published by the Directory of Social Change (Registered Charity
no. 800517 in England and Wales)
Head office: 24 Stephenson Way, London NW1 2DP
Northern office: Suite 103, 1 Old Hall Street, Liverpool L3 9HG
Tel: 08450 77 77 07

Visit www.dsc.org.uk to find out more about our books,
subscription funding websites and training events. You can also
sign up for e-newsletters so that you're always the first to hear
about what's new.

The publisher welcomes suggestions and comments that will help
to inform and improve future versions of this and all of our titles.
Please give us your feedback by emailing publications@dsc.org.uk.

It should be understood that this publication is intended for
guidance only and is not a substitute for professional or legal
advice. No responsibility for loss occasioned as a result of any
person acting or refraining from acting can be accepted by the
authors or publisher.

First published 1986
Second edition 1989
Third edition 1991
Fourth edition 1993
Fifth edition 1995
Sixth edition 1997
Seventh edition 1999
Eighth edition 2001
Ninth edition 2003
Tenth edition 2005
Eleventh edition 2007
Twelfth edition 2010
Thirteenth edition 2012
Fourteenth edition 2014

ISBN 978 1 906294 85 4

British Library Cataloguing in Publication Data
A catalogue record for this book is available from the British
Library

Cover and text design by Kate Bass
Typeset by Marlinzo Services, Frome
Printed and bound by Page Bros, Norwich

MIX
Paper from
responsible sources
FSC® C023114
FSC
www.fsc.org

Contents

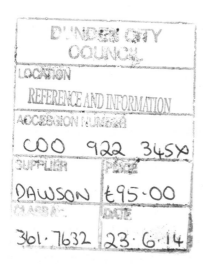

Foreword

If there is anything akin to a Fundraiser's Bible then *The Guide to Major Trusts* is it, so I was delighted to be asked to write a foreword for the 2014/15 editions. I find it incredible that it is almost 30 years since the first edition was published in 1986. It is testament to these guides' enduring worth that they are still appearing in print version in this digital age.

Despite the economic downturn in recent years, the trust market is worth an estimated £2.8 billion per year and is a fundamental source of funding for charities both large and small. These DSC guides provide clear, concise summaries of each trust's policies and preferences, detailed information on how to apply and, in many ways most importantly, what a trust *won't* fund. They are essential resources for an organisation that is looking to develop its trust fundraising from scratch and one or both guides have a place on the desk of every trust fundraiser. They represent exceptional value for money in terms of the amount of funding on offer within it!

Research is the basis of good fundraising. Without insight into our donors and prospects we cannot forget those mutually beneficial donor journeys that deliver such an impact across our communities. Once we have some understanding of our donor motivations we can cultivate strong long-term partnerships and move away from a transactional approach that is less satisfying for both parties. These DSC guides help to broker these relationships and provide a key link between funder and grantee.

I hope those new to fundraising and more experienced practitioners alike benefit from and enjoy these new editions.

Lynda Thomas
Director of Fundraising, Macmillan Cancer Support

About the Directory of Social Change

The Directory of Social Change (DSC) has a vision of an independent voluntary sector at the heart of social change. The activities of independent charities, voluntary organisations and community groups are fundamental to achieve social change. We exist to help these organisations and the people who support them to achieve their goals.

We do this by:

▶ providing practical tools that organisations and activists need, including online and printed publications, training courses, and conferences on a huge range of topics;
▶ acting as a 'concerned citizen' in public policy debates, often on behalf of smaller charities, voluntary organisations and community groups;
▶ leading campaigns and stimulating debate on key policy issues that affect those groups;
▶ carrying out research and providing information to influence policymakers.

DSC is the leading provider of information and training for the voluntary sector and publishes an extensive range of guides and handbooks covering subjects such as fundraising, management, communication, finance and law. We have a range of subscription-based websites containing a wealth of information on funding from trusts, companies and government sources. We run more than 300 training courses each year, including bespoke in-house training provided at the client's location. DSC conferences, many of which run on an annual basis, include the Charity Management Conference, the Charity Accountants' Conference and the Charity Law Conference. DSC's major annual event is Charityfair, which provides low-cost training on a wide variety of subjects.

For details of all our activities, and to order publications and book courses, go to www.dsc.org.uk, call 08450 777707 or email publications@dsc.org.uk.

Introduction

Welcome to the fourteenth edition of *The Guide to Major Trusts Volume 1*. The purpose of this book has always been to get inside the policies and practices of the largest trusts and foundations in the country, and to explain what they are doing with their money, open them up to public scrutiny, encourage transparency and provide information for charities that are seeking funding for their valuable work. In doing this, the book has had considerable success. As well as being a practical and useful resource for those seeking grants, it has also been an independent review of the work of the larger trusts and foundations. As such, it has enabled readers to compare and contrast grant-makers and how they operate.

In recent editions we have reported on the difficult economic conditions faced by grant-making trusts and foundations, the wider voluntary and community sector and society as a whole over the past six or seven years. In the twelfth edition in 2010, this book used data and financial information from the height of the worst recession for generations, and the situation looked bleak. Many trusts and foundations were hit hard, and collectively the value of the assets fell by around £4 billion on pre-recession levels. The thirteenth edition, published in 2012 using financial information from a time when the economy was slowly emerging from the recession, showed a picture of recovery, as asset value increased by £3.7 billion to around £36.5 billion.

Research for this, the fourteenth, edition shows that the value of the assets for the trusts and foundations described here totalled over £38.3 billion. This is an increase of more than £1.8 billion in comparison to the last edition. Correspondingly, income has increased by £181 million since the previous edition. Excluding the Big Lottery Fund, total grants have also increased by almost £102.3 million. If we include the substantial increase in funding from the Big Lottery Fund, the total grants of the 400 organisations featured in this book increased by £507 million.[1]

However, this overall trend towards a recovery of the finances of these larger trusts and foundations needs to be viewed in the wider context of severe cuts or 'efficiency savings' in practically every area of public expenditure, from welfare and the NHS to education and the environment, with the poorest and most disadvantaged in society being hit hardest. It is also reported that at the start of 2014, just 40% of the government's cuts in funding for public services have been implemented so far, with a further 60% to come (Marszal 2014).

Figure 1: value of the total assets of the trusts and foundations featured in the Guide to Major Trusts Volume 1

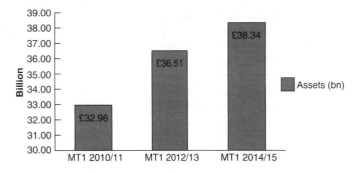

Figure 2: value of the total income and grants of the trusts and foundations featured in the Guide to Major Trusts Volume 1

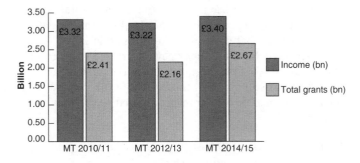

Thousands of charities across the UK provide valuable support to the most disadvantaged and vulnerable and their services are more in demand than ever before. An often vital source of funding to help them deliver their services comes from grant-making trusts and foundations. As figure 2 shows, the organisations featured in this book provided grants totalling almost £2.67 billion to a wide range of charities, community groups, social enterprises and educational institutions during the latest year for which financial information was available: in most cases

---

[1] Funding from the Big Lottery Fund increased from £374 million (2010/11) in the previous edition to over £778 million (2012/13) described here. It should be noted, however, that the figure for 2010/11 would have been £200 million higher had this amount not slipped into the 2011/12 financial year.

Top 25 trusts (excluding Big Lottery Fund and Awards for All)

	The Guide to Major Trusts Volume 1 – 2012/13	Total grants			The Guide to Major Trusts Volume 1 – 2014/15	Total grants
1	The Wellcome Trust	£551.5 million	1 (1) ^		The Wellcome Trust	£511.1 million
2	Comic Relief	£58.2 million*	2 (3)		The Leverhulme Trust	£80.4 million
3	The Leverhulme Trust	£53.4 million	3 (2)		Comic Relief	£78 million**
4	BBC Children in Need	£41.7 million	4 (9)		The Wolfson Foundation	£49.7 million
5	The Football Foundation	£40.5 million	5 (6)		The Garfield Weston Foundation	£46 million
6	The Garfield Weston Foundation	£34.2 million	6 (8)		The Monument Trust	£45 million
7	The Gatsby Charitable Foundation	£33.1 million	7 (7)		The Gatsby Charitable Foundation	£42.7 million
8	The Monument Trust	£32 million	8 (10)		Esmée Fairbairn Foundation	£32.4 million
9	The Wolfson Foundation	£28.2 million	9 (4)		BBC Children in Need	£31.2 million
10	Esmée Fairbairn Foundation	£27.6 million	10 (-)		The Gosling Foundation Limited	£27.5 million
11	The Henry Smith Charity	£24.9 million	11 (11)		The Henry Smith Charity	£27 million
12	Lloyds TSB Foundation for England and Wales	£23.4 million	12 (12)		Lloyds Bank Foundation for England and Wales	£21 million
13	The Sigrid Rausing Trust	£21.3 million	13 (16)		The City Bridge Trust	£19 million
14	The Tudor Trust	£19 million	14 (15)		Paul Hamlyn Foundation	£17.7 million
15	Paul Hamlyn Foundation	£18.7 million	15 (14)		The Tudor Trust	£17.5 million
16	The City Bridge Trust	£16.8 million	16 (-)		The Clore Duffield Foundation	£17 million
17	Age UK	£16 million	17 (13)		The Sigrid Rausing Trust	£17 million
18	Wales Council for Voluntary Action	£14.8 million	18 (5)		The Football Foundation	£16.8 million
19	The Northern Rock Foundation	£12.4 million	19 (17)		Age UK	£16 million
20	The Coalfields Regeneration Trust	£12.1 million	20 (20)		The Coalfields Regeneration Trust	£15.6 million
21	The Trust for London	£10.4 million	21 (23)		The Robertson Trust	£14.7 million
22	The Shetland Charitable Trust	£10.3 million	22 (-)		The Mercers' Charitable Foundation	£11.8 million
23	The Robertson Trust	£9.7 million	23 (18)		Wales Council for Voluntary Action	£11.5 million
24	J Paul Getty Jr Charitable Trust	£9.5 million	24 (21)		The Trust for London	£11.4 million
25	Allchurches Trust Ltd	£8.3 million	25 (22)		The Shetland Charitable Trust	£10.6 million
	Total	**£1.13 billion**			**Total**	**£1.19 billion**

* £19.7 million in the UK   ** £32.3 million in the UK   ^ figures in brackets show position in the previous edition

the 2011/12 financial year. This represents an overall increase of around 23%.[2]

But this overall increase in assets, income and total grants does not tell the whole story. Looking at the individual funders reveals that while there are those that have increased their funding, many have decreased their grant-making since last time. Figure 3 shows the percentage of the 400 trusts contained in this book and the variance in their assets, income and grants compared to the previous edition.

Figure 3: Percentage of trusts whose assets, income and grant total have increased and decreased

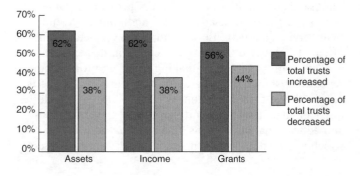

Significant reductions in grants came from funders, including:

▷ the Wellcome Trust, which again reduced its overall grant total, giving £511.1 million in 2011/12 compared to £551.5 million in 2009/10;
▷ the Football Foundation, which gave £16.8 million in 2011/12 compared to £40.5 million in 2009/10;
▷ BBC Children in Need, which gave £31.2 million in 2011/12 compared to £41.7 million in 2009/10.

As noted previously, however, decreases in funding are not necessarily due to a difficult economic climate. The Wellcome Trust, for example, again saw the value of its assets increase, this time by £498.5 million since the last edition, although conversely a relatively small decrease in income of £7.7 million. A decrease in grants of £40 million since the last edition simply reflects routine regular fluctuations from year to year, and with funding from this huge trust typically exceeding half a billion pounds each year, relatively small decreases of around 7% can distort the overall picture. In the case of BBC Children in Need, its financial year for this edition covered just nine months because the charity changed its year end to fit in with its major appeal, resulting in a lower grant expenditure. Also

---

[2] Excluding the Big Lottery Fund, total grants in this edition have risen by around 5.7%.

of note is an increase in the charity's income, helped significantly by a record appeal total in 2011.

Largely reliant on donations from the Football Association, the Premier League and the government, the Football Foundation, however, has seen a drop in income of almost £19.4 million since the previous edition and a narrowing of its focus, which is perhaps reflected in the reduction in grant-making described in this edition. Fortunately there do appear to be future commitments from the foundation's major funders which ensure it can continue its work, albeit with a reduced capacity on levels seen in previous years.

As figure 3 shows, 56% of the trusts and foundations featured here have increased the value of their grants since the last edition. These include Comic Relief, whose grant-making has increased by £18.6 million on the figure in the previous edition. This is perhaps as a result of an increase in income during the year on figures reported in the previous edition, but also because the charity had an exceptional income of £120.5 million in the intervening financial year: 2010/11. Other trusts that have shown an increase in funding in this edition include:

- the Leverhulme Trust, which again increased its donations, this time due to the funding of the Research Leadership Awards and arts scholarships during the year;
- the Clore Duffield Foundation, which saw an increase of over £12.6 million since the previous edition with grants totalling almost £17 million – however, most of this increase was due to an exceptional capital grant to JW3 Trust Limited for the development of the Jewish Community Centre for London at Finchley Road;
- the Gatsby Charitable Trust, whose total grants increased by almost £9.7 million on the previous edition – during the financial year reported on here, the trust received another substantial donation from the settlor, David Sainsbury, and the trust has also expressed its intent to spend out over the coming years.

Another example of a substantial one-off donation came from the Gosling Foundation Limited, which awarded £25 million in 2011/12 to the HMS Victory Preservation Company (an amount which was match-funded by the Ministry of Defence).

There are 28 trusts which are new to this volume, including recently registered charities and ones that have increased their charitable giving. New additions to the grant-making scene include the 101 Foundation, the Ian & Natalie Livingstone Foundation and the CML Family Foundation. It should be noted, however, that some of the recently registered trusts featured here had little or no financial information available at the time of writing and may prove to have a grant-making capacity lower than would normally make them eligible for inclusion. They are featured here as they appear to have the potential to make significant grants in the future, although this may prove not to be the case. As in previous years, responses to requests for further information were unfortunately disappointing.

As we can see from the Top 25 table, the top 25 trusts and foundations gave around £60 million more overall than the top 25 featured in the previous edition. As in previous editions, fluctuations either way can be influenced by the

variations in the giving of the very largest in this guide; however, this overall increase comes despite significant reductions by the Wellcome Trust and the Football Foundation as highlighted earlier, something which fundraisers should find encouraging.

The current environment

In summer 2013 we surveyed the trusts and foundations in this book and asked them a variety of questions, including:

- Did you receive fewer, about the same or more applications than the previous year?
- How are you reacting to any increase in demand from applicants?
- What are the most common mistakes applicants make when they apply to you for funding?

We had a response rate of 32%, which is slightly higher than for the survey conducted for the last edition. The 127 responses drew some interesting results and comments.

Of those that responded, 65% received fewer or about the same number of applications compared to the previous year, with 35% receiving more applications. Interestingly, the previous edition reported that just over half of the respondents to this question said they received more applications than the previous year, meaning that more trusts and foundations are seeing the level of applications either remaining the same or decreasing.

Figure 4: The number of applications received during the most recent financial year compared to the previous year (127 respondents)

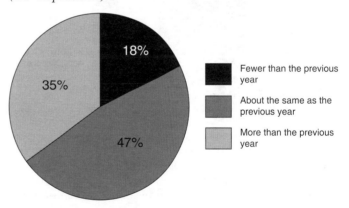

There will be many reasons why an increasing number, almost two thirds, of the trusts and foundations who responded to this question have received fewer or about the same number of applications compared to the previous year: potential applicants may be discouraged from applying, for example, because they believe there has been a dramatic drop in the general funds available; many charities may have shifted their focus towards engaging in the procurement process and tendering for contracts. Recent research conducted on behalf of the Garfield Weston Foundation also suggests that at small and medium-sized charities, a shortage of staff means that they are unable to 'make the most of funding opportunities', despite regarding income generation as a high priority (Nadeem 2014). The Garfield Weston Foundation itself states that it has seen a 40% fall in applications over the past three years (unfortunately the Garfield Weston Foundation did not respond to our survey).

It was reported that in 2011 the voluntary sector lost 70,000 jobs (Wilding 2014), and with further cuts to funding from local authorities on the horizon there is no reason to assume that this trend will not continue. The impact of this clear – fewer experienced staff able to fundraise effectively.

In our recent survey we also asked all of the trusts and foundations in this book:

▶ How many applications did you receive in the last financial year?
▶ How many of these were ineligible?
▶ How many of the applications you received resulted in a grant being awarded?

Out of the 400 trusts and foundations, 79 were able to provide figures for all three of these questions. The total number of applications received by these 79 trusts was 55,524. Some trusts appear to have included applications from individuals as well as organisations (significantly, this does not include applications to the Big Lottery Fund or Awards for All). These figures are broken down as shown in figure 5.

Figure 5: Breakdown of the total number of applications received by the 79 trusts and foundations responding to the question

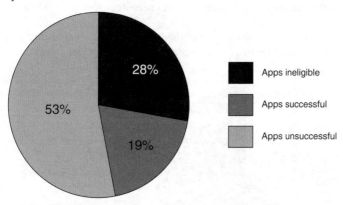

Even though this only represents less than a quarter of the funders here, it provides an interesting picture for fundraisers. Compared to the results from the previous survey when we asked this question for the last edition of this guide, ineligible applications have increased slightly (1%), successful applications have decreased by 5% and unsuccessful applications have increased by 4%.

In addition to this we again asked each trust to tell us what the most common mistakes were that applicants made when applying for funding.

Overwhelmingly, as in the previous edition, the main theme was applicants clearly not reading the trusts' guidelines, or choosing to ignore them and submitting ineligible applications. We have once again included the full comments in the entries of those that replied.

Clearly, ineligible applications are a significant issue, which is why DSC continues to campaign for an end to ineligible applications by providing detailed information on the policies and practices of trusts and foundations and making key recommendations to potential applicants, namely:

▶ Read the guidelines provided by the trust (not doing so being the most common reason for applications being ineligible given by the trusts who responded to our survey).
▶ Do your research; make sure you apply to the right funders.
▶ Seek clarification if there is anything you are unsure of in the guidelines or application process.
▶ Do not send blanket appeals: funders can tell if an application is a general mail-merged appeal sent to many organisations without due regard for their individual policies and funding priorities.
▶ Make sure that your application is clear, concise and jargon-free.

In conclusion, our research suggests that the finances of grant-making trusts and foundations are recovering and look healthy on the whole and funding from these organisations is increasing, which is good news for fundraisers. The worst effects of the recession on assets and income appear to have passed.

As we also saw in the previous edition, sources of funding have ceased to exist, but new sources are created on a regular basis. Grant-making trusts and foundations exist to give money to other organisations, but the need to put forward a strong case for why your charity or your beneficiaries should receive some of it has never been greater.

References

BBC (2014), 'George Osborne targets welfare as he warns of £25bn more cuts', www.bbc.co.uk, 4 January (accessed 6 February 2014).

Marszal, Andrew (2014) 'George Osborne warned "hugely challenging" public service cuts still to come', www.telegraph.co.uk, 5 February (accessed 6 February 2014).

Nadeem, Beena (2014) 'Two-fifths of smaller charities in north-east say they lack staff to apply for funding', www.thirdsector.co.uk, 30 January 2014 (accessed 11 February 2014).

Wilding, Karl (2014), 'The voluntary sector shed 70,000 jobs in 2011', www.theguardian.com, 11 January 2012 (accessed 11 February 2014).

DSC policy and campaigning

Over the years DSC has campaigned on a number of fronts for better grant-making. We believe that funders have a responsibility that extends far beyond providing funding. The way funders operate and develop their programmes has a huge impact on the organisations, causes and beneficiaries which their funding supports, as well as on the wider voluntary sector. Transparency is a key principle for us: by providing information about funders in this book and other DSC publications we have sought to open up their practices to greater scrutiny. Clearer and more accessible information enables fundraisers to focus their efforts effectively, and encourages open review and discussions of good practice. Our Great Giving campaign has grown out of these long-established beliefs.

We have identified some specific campaigning areas that we wish to focus on as part of an overall campaign for better grant-making.

1) A clear picture of the funding environment

We think that to enable better planning and decision making from funders and policymakers, more comprehensive information is needed about where money is going and what it supports. Many of the funders in this book are leading the way, although some fall short in terms of the level of detail they provide about their activities and effectiveness.

2) Accessible funding for campaigning

Financial support for campaigning is vital to the role organisations play in achieving social change. Greater clarity from grant-making trusts is needed so that campaigning organisations can find the support they need more easily.

3) An end to hidden small print

DSC is asking all funders to provide the terms and conditions which govern the use of the funds at the outset when people apply and to be open to negotiating terms when applicants request it.

4) No ineligible applications

We know that most funders receive applications that do not fall within the funder's guidelines. Clearer guidelines can help, but applicants also need to take more heed of funder guidelines and target their applications appropriately.

DSC has always believed that clear and open application and monitoring processes are essential for both funders and fundraisers to produce more effective applications and better eventual outcomes. The availability of such information has come a long way since the first edition of this guide. However, an important element of the funding process often remains hidden from wider scrutiny.

Some may argue that providing more information at the beginning of the application process could make things more time consuming and costly, but DSC believes the benefits of greater transparency should take precedence.

It is crucial that fundraisers have access to all the information they need to make an informed decision about whether to apply. It is also vital that such information is publicly available so that funders and others can make comparisons and share good practice. Further, in this age of digital communication, there is an ever-increasing expectation that all the relevant information, guidance and application forms will be available online. A link to a web page or a short document outlining the detailed terms and explaining their place in the application process is easy to provide and need not cost anything. Clear instructions should be provided for the fundraiser about the importance of the terms and conditions, why they are necessary and what they mean, along with exhortations to read them thoroughly.

Again the onus is not entirely on the funder – fundraisers have a responsibility to inform themselves as fully as possible and to ask for relevant information if it isn't available or is not clearly presented by the funder. Reading and evaluating the criteria, guidance and detailed terms and conditions is part of making a well-targeted application which is more likely to be successful. More crucially it is about protecting the organisation's independence and building funding relationships that will work well for both parties. The fundraiser, therefore, has an important role to play in scrutinising the conditions of the funding arrangement at the outset, and communicating their views to other decision-makers in the organisation (see www.dsc.org.uk for more advice on terms and conditions for fundraisers).

DSC's Big Lottery Refund campaign

The National Lottery occupies a unique place in the grant-making world. Whilst the various distributors are statutory bodies which distribute what is, technically speaking, public money, their activities, aims and beneficiaries have much in common with charitable grant-making trusts.

DSC's campaign will therefore be of interest to fundraisers, fundraising charities, and anyone interested in the Big Lottery Fund in particular. The aim of the campaign is for the government to refund to the Big Lottery Fund £425 million of Lottery revenue which was diverted to help pay for the London 2012 Olympics. We argue that this decision, taken in 2007, was wrong in principle, as it should have been given out in grants to voluntary and community groups across the country, not to make up the budgetary shortfall of a one-off sporting event.

Both the previous and current government have committed to refund the Lottery using proceeds from selling Olympics assets after the Games, and there have been a series of agreements between the various agencies involved. However, it is unfortunately not straightforward: asset sales are expected to take decades, which is not acceptable in our view. Learn more and stay updated with developments at www.biglotteryrefund.org.uk.

Frequently asked questions

How do you get your information?

In general we use the copy of the report and accounts on the public file at the Charity Commission. We then write a draft entry and send it to the trust via email, if necessary, inviting suggested additions as well as corrections or comments. New information provided by the trust, and not generally available, is usually put in the form 'The trust notes that . . . '. In cases where the trust or foundation has a website containing full information on its activities, including downloadable annual reports and accounts, this is the first port of call. In many cases the amount of information available on a trust's website is comprehensive, including guidelines for applicants and detailed information on current programmes, and this information is used extensively throughout this book. We also conduct a biennial survey of all of the trusts and foundations in this guide, the responses to which inform their entries, in particular the percentage of awards to new applicants and the common applicant mistakes – where a funder provided answers to these questions their responses have been incorporated into their entries.

Do you print everything the trusts say?

Generally yes, but there are two kinds of exceptions. First, if what the trust says is purely formal and could be said equally of most of the other trusts in this book, we do not feel it needs repeating. Second, some trusts, such as the Lloyds Bank foundations or the Esmée Fairbairn Foundation, now produce literature on such a scale that it has become impossible to reprint it all. Provided it is available there, we often refer to the availability of further material on the trust's website. This is particularly the case where guidelines or funding programmes are under review and liable to change soon after the publication of this book.

Do you investigate further when the information from a trust is inadequate?

No, we just report the fact that it is inadequate. We also try to ignore hearsay and anecdote, whether positive or negative.

What is your policy on telephone numbers?

When we know the telephone number we will normally print it, and will do so even if a trust doesn't want us to (provided it is an office rather than a private number). Where a trust has stated that it does not wish to receive telephone calls from potential applicants, or to have its number listed, this is noted in the text of the entry. However, when the available telephone number is simply the head office of a big professional firm that acts as a post box for the trustees, we generally leave it out.

Do you edit the 'applications' information?

No and yes. The content of this section generally comes from the trust if they have a specific document regarding making applications, and we will reproduce whatever they have available. However, we sometimes edit it to achieve a reasonable level of consistent presentation from one entry to another. If there is no specific application document available we collate information from annual reports, accounts and websites.

Why do you leave out the letters after trustees' names?

There are so many of them, and we try to present the entries in as simple and straightforward a way as we can. Besides, where do you draw the line? At Captain the Honourable A. Anthony, DSO? Or going on to MBE, D Phil, AMCEEE and so on? The additional information might be helpful in identifying one A. Anthony from another. However, we do see more and more trusts using simpler systems themselves: Arthur Anthony being more often happy nowadays to appear as such. Nevertheless, we do list titles – Lord, Lady, Dr, Professor and so on.

We are also sparing with capital letters. We use this minimalist style in the interests of clarity and correct editorial rules, but it does annoy some trusts, which go to considerable effort to try to change our usage back to what they see as proper. But reading about Trust after Foundation after Guideline after Application Form can get tiring.

Why don't the figures in the entries always add up?

There are a number of reasons.

- Unclear distinctions between grant commitments and grant payments.
- The fact that grants' lists and totals are often created by trusts quite separately from their audited figures.
- The fact that values for returned grants are included in some totals and not in others.
- The existence of small undisclosed grants: if the discrepancies are large, we go to some effort to clarify the situation. Where they are small, the figures are normally for illustration rather than being the basis for further calculation. If resources were spent on seeking perfect numerical consistency, they would have to be taken from the more useful task of trying to find out and reflect clearly what the trust is doing.
- Grant figures given in the entries are rounded up or down, which sometimes means that there may be a slight discrepancy between figures given individually and sum totals given elsewhere.

What's in a name? Trusts, foundations, funds, charities, settlements, companies, appeals: are they all the same?

The book covers organisations, usually charitable, that give grants to other charities. They may use almost any name; we judge them by what they do rather than what they are called.

Which trusts are in this book?

Roughly, those that give, or could give £300,000 or more in grants. Smaller trusts are covered in Volume 2 of this book as well as DSC's www.trustfunding.org.uk subscription website and the *Directory of Grant-Making*

Trusts. Some trusts here do fall below this threshold, however they may be newer organisations which look like they have the potential to give more, or the level of their grant-making fluctuates from year to year but their capacity make them of interest here.

Why are some grant-making charities omitted?

This book does not generally seek to cover the following grant-making charities.

▸ **Company trusts:** if they are operated by company staff on company premises, we will usually regard this as a channel for giving by the company, to be reported in our Guide to UK Company Giving and on our www.companygiving.org.uk subscription website.

▸ **Specialised grant-makers:** those that operate in a narrow field where they are likely to be well known and accessible to most applicants. Examples include trusts only funding research on specific medical conditions (these are generally accessible through the excellent website of the Association of Medical Research Charities, www.amrc.org.uk) or only supporting projects designed by themselves.

▸ **Trusts or charities only making grants for work overseas:** while some trusts included here do make grants to organisations overseas, we do not list those which do so exclusively, such as Oxfam or Christian Aid.

▸ **Statutory funders, awarding public money:** these sources are covered in our *Government Funding Guide* and on our www.governmentfunding.org.uk subscription website.

What about lottery grants?

We have difficulties about deciding what we should include and have to make compromises. We include the Big Lottery Fund and Awards for All, but we do not cover the arts councils, the sports councils or the Heritage Lottery Fund. Although all Lottery grants are part of public expenditure, subject to review by the National Audit Office and the Public Accounts Committee of the House of Commons, in many ways the Big Lottery Fund looks and acts like a grant-making trust, and a particularly big and interesting one at that.

...and community foundations?

Local community foundations are a rapidly developing part of the voluntary sector. Originally the idea was that they would build up endowments which would enable them to become important local grant-makers. They are still doing this, but only a few have generated enough income from their endowments to earn them a place in this book. However, most of them have also developed two new streams of income. Firstly, they have become a vehicle through which local philanthropists make their donations, usually using a named subsidiary fund. But this is still on a modest scale in most cases. Secondly and more importantly, they have become the vehicles for distributing local and central government money. We have included brief entries for those giving grants of £300,000 or more, even when most of this is coming from statutory sources.

Finally...

The research for this book has been conducted as carefully as possible. Many thanks to those who have made this easier, especially the trusts themselves through their websites, their trust officers who provided additional information and the trustees and others who have helped us. Also thanks to the Charity Commission for making the annual reports and accounts available online.

We are aware that some of this information may be incomplete or will become out of date. We are equally sure we will have missed some relevant charities. We apologise for these imperfections. If you come across any omissions or mistakes, or if you have any suggestions for future editions of this book, do let us know. We can be contacted at the Liverpool Office Research Department of the Directory of Social Change either by phone on 0151 708 0136 or by email: research@dsc.org.uk

How to use this guide

The trusts are listed alphabetically and the indexes are at the back of the book. As well as an alphabetical index, there are subject and geographical indexes which will help you to identify the trusts working in your field and area.

From page xviii we have ranked the trusts by the amount of money they give. This list also shows their main areas of interest. If you are looking for grants for your charity, we recommend that you start with this listing and select those trusts which might be relevant, starting with the biggest.

When you have chosen enough to be getting on with, read each trust entry carefully before deciding to apply. Very often a trust's interest in your field will be limited and precise, and may demand an application specifically tailored to its requirements or often no application at all as it may not currently be accepting applications.

Remember to cover all parts of the guide: do not just start at the beginning of the alphabet. It is surprising, but still true, that trusts near the end of the alphabet receive fewer applications.

It is particularly important to show awareness of all the information available from the trust, to acquire up-to-date guidelines where possible, and to target your applications with respect to each trust's published wishes where such information exists.

Inappropriate and ill-considered approaches, especially those that show you have not read the published guidelines, antagonise trusts and damage your organisation's reputation. Of course, many trusts publish little of use. Unfortunately this may result in a waste of your time and theirs if they reject an application which they then deem to be ineligible.

We have included a 'Dates for your diary' chart to help with the timings of your applications (see page xv). It shows, for over 100 trusts, the months when trustee meetings are usually held, or when applications need to be submitted.

For those new to raising money from trusts, following the 'How to apply to a trust' guidelines overleaf is recommended as a starting point.

Classification

Serious applicants who will be fundraising from trusts in the long term do best, we believe, if they go to the most promising entries in this book and try to establish specific links between what the trust seems to be interested in and what their organisation is trying to do. The indexes and summary headings in this book are not likely to be enough on their own to identify the trusts that are most likely to have matching interests with a particular charity.

Notes on the entries

The entry headings (see also 'A typical trust entry' on page xiv)

The main areas of funding

These categories have been chosen by the editors from an analysis of the trusts' funding. They are indicative rather than definitive, and useful in a preliminary trawl through the guide. They are no substitute for a close reading of each entry.

Grant total and financial year

The most up-to-date information available is given here. In a few cases the grants commentary in the main text is for the preceding year, as this information for the most recent year was unavailable or it was supplied at the last minute and was too late for inclusion in this guide. Sometimes the information received on a particular trust dates from two different years. For example, most of the entry may contain information from the latest published annual report, but may also include very recent information gained from consultations directly with the trust or taken from its website.

Beneficial area

This is the area or areas – when this is restricted – within which the trust operates, either legally or as a matter of policy or practice. When a trust with a UK-wide remit shows an interest in a particular locality, this is noted. While the information usually comes from the trust itself, it may also arise from a pattern of grant-making seen by the editors.

The correspondent

This is the lead person. Sometimes this is a solicitor or an accountant handling trust affairs solely on a 'postbox' basis. Other useful administrative contacts may also be given in the 'applications' section, or within the main body of text.

The main body of the entry

A summary of the trust's grant-making usually prefaces the text. Trusts' policy notes and guidelines for applicants, where these exist, are normally reprinted in full. However, there are a few instances in which these are so lengthy that some abridgement has had to be undertaken. More trusts now analyse their own funding in their annual reports and, where available, this material will also usually be quoted in full. Some analysis has also been carried out by the editors based on grants lists accompanying the accounts.

Exclusions and applications sections

These reproduce, where possible, the trust's own information or comments, though edited to suit the format of this book.

It would be useful to mention here why we include trusts and foundations which do not wish to receive unsolicited applications. These are included partly because this book is a survey of the grant-making of the largest trusts and also to try and save the time and resources of organisations that may otherwise apply for funding in vain.

Percentage of awards to new applicants
We have added the percentage of awards to new applicants where provided by respondents to our biennial survey. These are charities that have not received a grant in the past from that trust.

Common applicant mistakes
We have added comments from trusts provided to us though a survey we conducted in summer 2013. Not all trusts responded to this question but where they did this information is included in individual entries in their own words.

Information gathered from
This section notes the sources of information we have used for the entries. If there is a website, this is usually the best starting point for information, but we also use the Charity Commission's Register of Charities extensively.

How to apply to a trust

Although there are complete books on this (for example *The Complete Fundraising Handbook* and *Writing Better Fundraising Applications*, both published by DSC), there is no need to be daunted by the challenge of making effective applications. If your charity's work is good – and of a kind supported by the trust in question – a very simple letter (of one uncrowded page or less, and backed by a clear annual report and set of accounts) will probably do 90% of everything that can be done.

If there is an application form and detailed applications requirements, just follow them. However, because these sorts of trusts make the process easier, they tend to get a lot of applications. You may have even better chances with the others.

1) Select the right trusts to approach

If they fund organisations or work like yours, and if you genuinely fit within any guidelines they publish, put them on your list.

2) Ring them

If the entry makes this sound sensible, ring the trust to check that the guidelines in this guide still apply and that the kind of application you are considering is appropriate.

3) Send in an application

Unless the trust has an application form (many do not), we suggest that the main part of this should be a letter that fits easily on one side of a sheet of paper (back-up materials such as a formal 'proposal' may be necessary for a big or complex project, but are usually, in our view, secondary). We suggest that the letter contains the following points.

- A summary sentence such as: 'Can your trust give us £10,000 to develop a training programme for our volunteers?'
- The problem the work will address: This should normally be the beneficiaries' problem, not your charity's problem: 'Mothers of children with learning disabilities in our area get very little help from the statutory services in coping with their children's day-to-day needs.'
- What you are going to do about this: 'Our volunteers, who have been in the same situations themselves, support and help them, but the volunteers need and want better training, especially on home safety.'
- Details of the work: 'We want to commission an expert from our sister charity Home-Start to develop and test suitable training materials that we will be able to use.'
- Information about your charity: 'We attach one of our general leaflets explaining what we do, and a copy of our latest annual report and accounts.'
- Repeat the request: 'We would be very grateful if your trust can give us this grant.'

And that is all. Keep the style simple and informal. Where you can, handwrite the date, salutation and signature. A charity is not a business and is not impressed by applicants trying to sound like one. The best letter comes from a person involved in the proposed activity.

Making the letter longer will often reduce rather than increase its impact, but attaching compelling material is fine. You are not saying that they have to read it through. A letter of endorsement might also be nice: your local bishop saying your work is wonderful, for example.

Appearance matters. It is a great help if you have a good quality letterhead on something better than photocopy paper, and if your report and accounts and literature are of appropriately high quality for your kind of organisation. However, you don't want to give the impression that your charity spends unnecessary money on expensive materials rather than on carrying out its work.

Good luck.

A typical trust entry

The Fictitious Trust

Welfare

£1.3 million (2013)

Beneficial area
UK.

Correspondent: Ann Freeman, Appeals Secretary, The Old Barn, Main Street, New Town ZC48 2QQ

Trustees: Eva Appiah; Rita Khan; Lorraine Murphy.

CC Number: 123456

The trust supports welfare charities in general, with an emphasis on homelessness. The trustees will support both capital and revenue projects. 'Specific projects are preferred to general running costs.'

In 2013 the trust had assets of £20.3 million and an income of £1.5 million. Over 200 grants were given totalling £1.3 milliom. Grants ranged from £5,000 to £200,000, with about half given in New Town. Beneficiaries included: Homelessness UK (£200,000); Shelter (£150,000); Charity Workers Benevolent Society (£80,000); Children Without Families (£50,000); New Town CAB (£10,000); and Ex-Offenders UK (£5,000).

Smaller grants were given to a variety of local charities, local branches of national charities and a few UK welfare charities.

Exclusions
No grants to non-registered charities, individuals or religious organisations.

Applications
In writing to the correspondent. Trustees meet in March and September each year. Applications should be received by the end of January and the end of July respectively.

Applications should include a brief description of the project and audited accounts. Unsuccessful applicants will not be informed unless a stamped, addressed envelope is provided.

Percentage of awards given to new applicants: between 10% and 20%.

Common applicant mistakes
'They don't read our guidelines.'

Information gathered from:
Accounts; Charity Commission record; further information provided by the funder.

Name of the charity

Summary of main activities – what the trust will do in practice rather than what its trust deed allows it to do.

Grant total – total grants given for the most recent year available.

Geographical area of grantgiving – including where the trust can legally give and where it gives in practice.

Correspondent and contact details – including telephone and fax numbers, and email and website addresses, if available.

Trustees

Background/summary of activities – a quick indicator of the trust's policies to show whether it is worth reading the rest of the entry.

Financial information – noting the assets, ordinary income and grant total, and comment on unusual figures.

Typical grants range – indicates what a successful applicant can expect to receive.

Beneficiaries included – a list of typical beneficiaries which indicates where the main money is going. This is often the clearest indication of trust priorities. Where possible, we include the purpose of the grant. We also indicate whether the trust gives one-off or recurrent grants.

Exclusions – a list of any area, subjects or types of grant the trust will not consider.

Applications – this includes how to apply and when to submit an application.

Percentage of awards given to new applicants – the grant-maker's response to DSC's 2013 survey.

Common applicant mistakes – the grant-maker's response to DSC's 2013 survey.

Information gathered from – our researchers' sources of information.

Dates for your diary

X = the usual month of trustees' or grant allocation meetings, or the last month for the receipt of applications.

Please note that these dates are provisional, and that the fact of an application being received does not necessarily mean that it will be considered at the next meeting.

	Jan	Feb	Mar	Apr	May	Jun	Jul	Aug	Sep	Oct	Nov	Dec
The 29th May 1961 Charitable Trust		X			X			X			X	
The H B Allen Charitable Trust		X										
The Architectural Heritage Fund			X			X			X			X
The Baily Thomas Charitable Fund				X						X		
Percy Bilton Charity			X			X			X			X
The Bluston Charitable Settlement			X									
British Record Industry Trust									X			
The William A Cadbury Charitable Trust					X						X	
Calouste Gulbenkian Foundation – UK Branch			X				X				X	
Sir John Cass's Foundation			X			X					X	
The Childwick Trust	X						X					
Richard Cloudesley's Charity				X							X	
The Colt Foundation			X						X			
The Ernest Cook Trust				X						X		
The D'Oyly Carte Charitable Trust			X				X				X	
Roald Dahl's Marvellous Children's Charity			X						X			
The Daiwa Anglo-Japanese Foundation			X						X			
Baron Davenport's Charity			X						X			
The Davidson Family Charitable Trust												
Peter De Haan Charitable Trust			X			X			X			X
The Dulverton Trust		X				X				X		
The Dunhill Medical Trust			X			X			X			X
The Equitable Charitable Trust	X	X	X	X	X	X	X	X	X	X	X	X

	Jan	Feb	Mar	Apr	May	Jun	Jul	Aug	Sep	Oct	Nov	Dec
The Eranda Foundation			X				X				X	
Essex Community Foundation	X								X			
Euro Charity Trust												
The Eveson Charitable Trust	X		X			X				X		
The February Foundation	X	X	X	X	X	X	X	X	X	X	X	X
Allan and Nesta Ferguson Charitable Settlement		X							X			
The Sir John Fisher Foundation					X						X	
The Fishmongers' Company's Charitable Trust			X			X					X	
The Donald Forrester Trust					X						X	
The Freemasons' Grand Charity	X			X		X						
The Gannochy Trust	X	X	X	X	X	X	X	X	X	X	X	X
Simon Gibson Charitable Trust					X							
The G C Gibson Charitable Trust										X		
The Girdlers' Company Charitable Trust	X						X					
The Goldsmiths' Company Charity	X	X	X	X	X	X	X			X	X	X
The Great Britain Sasakawa Foundation		X			X					X		
The Grocers' Charity	X			X		X					X	
The Kathleen Hannay Memorial Charity		X										
The Harbour Foundation		X										
The Harpur Trust			X						X			X
Heart of England Community Foundation	X		X		X		X		X	X		
The Hedley Foundation	X		X		X		X		X	X		
Lady Hind Trust			X				X			X		
Sir Harold Hood's Charitable Trust										X		
The Albert Hunt Trust			X				X			X		
The Isle of Anglesey Charitable Trust				X								
John James Bristol Foundation		X			X			X			X	
Jewish Child's Day				X			X					X
The Kay Kendall Leukaemia Fund					X					X		
Ernest Kleinwort Charitable Trust			X							X		
The Leverhulme Trade Charities Trust		X										
Lloyds TSB Foundation for Northern Ireland	X			X			X			X		
The Trust for London		X				X				X		
The London Marathon Charitable Trust									X			
John Lyon's Charity			X			X					X	
The R S Macdonald Charitable Trust			X						X			
The Machkevitch Foundation												
The Mackintosh Foundation					X					X		
The MacRobert Trust			X								X	
The Manifold Charitable Trust	X	X	X	X	X	X	X	X	X	X	X	X
Marshall's Charity	X			X			X			X		

	Jan	Feb	Mar	Apr	May	Jun	Jul	Aug	Sep	Oct	Nov	Dec
The Henry Moore Foundation	X			X			X			X		
The Frances and Augustus Newman Foundation						X						X
The Ofenheim Charitable Trust			X									
The P F Charitable Trust	X	X	X	X	X	X	X	X	X	X	X	X
The Parthenon Trust	X											
The Dowager Countess Eleanor Peel Trust			X				X				X	
The Pilgrim Trust	X			X			X			X		
Polden-Puckham Charitable Foundation										X		
The Rank Foundation Limited			X			X			X			X
The Joseph Rank Trust			X			X			X			X
The Sir James Reckitt Charity					X					X		
The Robertson Trust	X		X		X		X		X		X	
Joseph Rowntree Reform Trust Limited			X				X			X		X
The Saddlers' Company Charitable Fund	X						X					
The Francis C Scott Charitable Trust			X				X				X	
Seafarers UK (King George's Fund for Sailors)							X			X		
The Archie Sherman Charitable Trust	X	X	X	X	X	X	X		X	X	X	
The Henry Smith Charity			X			X			X			X
Sparks Charity (Sport Aiding Medical Research For Kids)			X							X		
St James's Place Foundation							X					X
The Steel Charitable Trust		X			X			X		X		
Sir Halley Stewart Trust		X				X				X		
Stratford upon Avon Town Trust		X					X			X		
The Sir Jules Thorn Charitable Trust											X	
The Tolkien Trust												X
The Trusthouse Charitable Foundation		X			X		X			X		
The Douglas Turner Trust		X			X			X				X
The Garfield Weston Foundation	X	X	X	X	X	X	X	X	X	X	X	X
The Will Charitable Trust	X							X				
The Harold Hyam Wingate Foundation	X			X			X			X		
The Wixamtree Trust	X			X			X			X		

The major trusts ranked by grant total

Trust	Grants	Main grant areas
☐ The Big Lottery Fund	£778.7 million	Community, young people, welfare
☐ The Wellcome Trust	£511.1 million	Biomedical research, history of medicine, biomedical ethics, public engagement with science
☐ The Leverhulme Trust	£80.4 million	Scholarships, fellowships and prizes for education and research
☐ Comic Relief	£76.8 million (£32.3 million in the UK)	Social welfare
☐ Awards for All	£73.7 million	General charitable purposes
☐ The Wolfson Foundation	£49.7 million	Medical and scientific research, education, health and welfare, heritage, arts
☐ The Garfield Weston Foundation	£46 million	General charitable purposes
☐ The Monument Trust	£45 million	Arts and heritage, health and community care particularly HIV/AIDS and Parkinson's, social development particularly rehabilitation of offenders, general
☐ The Gatsby Charitable Foundation	£42.7 million	General charitable purposes
☐ Esmée Fairbairn Foundation	£32.4 million	Social welfare, education, environment, and arts
☐ BBC Children in Need	£31.2 million	Sport and health for people under the age of 18 who are disadvantaged
☐ The Gosling Foundation Limited	£27.5 million	Relief of poverty, education, religion, naval and service charities and general charitable purposes beneficial to the community
☐ The Henry Smith Charity	£27 million	Social welfare, older people, disability, health, medical research
☐ Lloyds Bank Foundation for England and Wales	£21 million	Social and community needs

☐ The City Bridge Trust	£19 million	Arts, culture, recreation and sports; community development; mental health; environment; older people; disability; voluntary sector
☐ Paul Hamlyn Foundation	£17.7 million	Arts, education and learning in the UK and local organisations supporting vulnerable groups of people, especially children, social justice
☐ The Tudor Trust	£17.5 million	General charitable purposes; social welfare
☐ The Clore Duffield Foundation	£17 million	Arts/museums, Jewish charities, education, older people and people who are disadvantaged
☐ The Sigrid Rausing Trust	£17 million	Human rights and justice
☐ The Football Foundation	£16.8 million	Grassroots football, community, education

☐ Age UK	£16 million	Older people
☐ The Coalfields Regeneration Trust	£15.6 million	General, health, welfare, community regeneration, education, young people, older people
☐ The Robertson Trust	£14.7 million	General charitable purposes
☐ The Mercers' Charitable Foundation	£11.8 million	General welfare, education, Christianity, heritage and the arts
☐ Wales Council for Voluntary Action	£11.5 million	Local community, volunteering, social welfare, environment, regeneration
☐ The Trust for London	£11.4 million	Social welfare
☐ The Shetland Charitable Trust	£10.6 million	Social welfare; art and recreation; environment and amenity
☐ Allchurches Trust Ltd	£9.4 million	Churches, general
☐ The Elton John Aids Foundation	£8.9 million	AIDS and related welfare
☐ ABF The Soldiers' Charity	£8.5 million (£3.2 million to organisations)	Army charities

☐ The Northern Rock Foundation	£8.5 million	Disadvantaged people
☐ Royal British Legion	£7.7 million	Armed services
☐ Achisomoch Aid Company Limited	£7.6 million	Orthodox Jewish religious charities
☐ The Helping Foundation	£7.2 million	Orthodox Jewish
☐ The Rank Foundation Limited	£7 million	Christian communication, youth, education, general
☐ Foundation Scotland	£6.9 million	Community development, general
☐ The Goldsmiths' Company Charity	£6.9 million	General, London charities, the precious metals craft
☐ Keren Association	£6.8 million	Jewish, education, general
☐ Nominet Charitable Foundation	£6.5 million	IT, education, social welfare
☐ The Charles Wolfson Charitable Trust	£6.5 million	Medical research, education and welfare

☐ The Linbury Trust	£6.4 million	Arts, heritage, social welfare, humanitarian aid, general
☐ The Joseph Rowntree Charitable Trust	£6.3 million	Equalities, rights and justice; power and accountability; peace and security; and sustainable future
☐ The National Art Collections Fund	£6.3 million	Acquisition of works of art by museums and galleries
☐ The Souter Charitable Trust	£6 million	Christian evangelism, welfare
☐ The Waterloo Foundation	£5.9 million	Children, the environment, developing countries and projects in Wales
☐ The LankellyChase Foundation	£5.7 million	Severe and multiple disadvantage particularly homelessness, substance misuse, mental and physical illness, extreme poverty and violence and abuse

THE MAJOR TRUSTS RANKED BY GRANT TOTAL

☐ Voluntary Action Fund (VAF)	£5.7 million	General, social welfare and inclusion
☐ John Lyon's Charity	£5.3 million	Children and young people in north and west London
☐ The Foyle Foundation	£5.3 million	Arts and learning
☐ The Joseph Rowntree Foundation	£5.3 million	Research and development in social policy and practice
☐ The Kay Kendall Leukaemia Fund	£5.2 million	Research into leukaemia and patient care
☐ The Nuffield Foundation	£5 million	Science and social science research and capacity development, particularly in the fields of law and justice, children and families and education
☐ The Jack Petchey Foundation	£4.9 million	Young people aged 11 – 25 in the London boroughs, Essex and the Algarve, Portugal
☐ The Stewards' Company Limited (incorporating the J W Laing Trust and the J W Laing Biblical Scholarship Trust)	£4.85 million	Christian evangelism, general
☐ The Fidelity UK Foundation	£4.8 million	General, primarily in the fields of arts and culture, community development, education and health
☐ Community Foundation Serving Tyne and Wear and Northumberland	£4.5 million	Social welfare; education; religion; community benefit
☐ The John Ellerman Foundation	£4.5 million	Welfare, environment and arts
☐ The Hintze Family Charitable Foundation	£4.5 million	Education; Christian churches; museums, libraries and galleries
☐ The Bowland Charitable Trust	£4.4 million	Young people, education, general
☐ The London Marathon Charitable Trust	£4.4 million	Sport, recreation and leisure
☐ The Stone Family Foundation	£4.4 million	Relief-in-need, social welfare, overseas aid
☐ A W Charitable Trust	£4.3 million	Jewish causes through educational and religious organisations; general charitable purposes
☐ The Clothworkers' Foundation	£4.3 million	General charitable purposes
☐ The Headley Trust	£4.3 million	Arts, heritage, health, welfare, overseas development
☐ The Liz and Terry Bramall Foundation	£4.3 million	General, social welfare
☐ The Underwood Trust	£4.3 million	Medicine and health, social welfare, education, arts, environment and wildlife
☐ Allan and Nesta Ferguson Charitable Settlement	£4 million	Peace, education, overseas development
☐ Porticus UK	£4 million	Social welfare, education, religion
☐ The London Community Foundation	£3.9 million	Community activities and social welfare
☐ Kent Community Foundation	£3.7 million	Community; education; health; social welfare
☐ St James's Place Foundation	£3.6 million	Children and young people with special needs, hospices
☐ The Community Foundation for Northern Ireland	£3.6 million	Community, peace building, social exclusion, poverty and social injustice
☐ Forever Manchester (The Community Foundation for Greater Manchester)	£3.5 million	General charitable purposes
☐ The M and R Gross Charities Limited	£3.5 million	Jewish causes
☐ The Pilgrim Trust	£3.5 million	Social welfare and the preservation of buildings and heritage
☐ The Sobell Foundation	£3.5 million	Jewish charities, medical care and treatment, education, community, environment, disability, older people and young people
☐ The 29th May 1961 Charitable Trust	£3.4 million	Social welfare, general
☐ The Zochonis Charitable Trust	£3.4 million	General, particularly youth education and welfare

☐ The Dunhill Medical Trust	£3.2 million	Medical research, elderly people
☐ Maurice and Hilda Laing Charitable Trust	£3.1 million	Promotion of Christianity, relief of need
☐ The Barrow Cadbury Trust and the Barrow Cadbury Fund	£3 million	Young adult and criminal justice, migration and Europe, and poverty and exclusion
☐ The Michael Uren Foundation	£3 million	General charitable purposes
☐ The Sir Jules Thorn Charitable Trust	£3 million	Medical research, medicine, small grants for humanitarian charities
☐ Action Medical Research	£2.9 million	Medical research, focusing on child health
☐ Quartet Community Foundation	£2.9 million	General charitable purposes
☐ The Thompson Family Charitable Trust	£2.9 million	Medical, veterinary, education, general
☐ Mayfair Charities Ltd	£2.8 million	Orthodox Judaism
☐ The Dulverton Trust	£2.8 million	Youth opportunities, conservation, welfare, general
☐ The Lord's Taverners	£2.8 million	Youth cricket, increasing participation, equipment and facilities, disability and disadvantage
☐ Amabrill Limited	£2.7 million	Orthodox Jewish
☐ Rachel Charitable Trust	£2.7 million	General charitable purposes, in practice mainly Jewish organisations
☐ The Schroder Foundation	£2.7 million	General charitable purposes
☐ The Baily Thomas Charitable Fund	£2.6 million	Learning disability
☐ The Jerusalem Trust	£2.6 million	Promotion of Christianity
☐ The Medlock Charitable Trust	£2.6 million	Education, health, welfare
☐ The Michael Bishop Foundation	£2.6 million	General charitable purposes
☐ Seafarers UK (King George's Fund for Sailors)	£2.5 million	The welfare of seafarers
☐ The Baring Foundation	£2.5 million	Strengthening the voluntary sector, arts and international development
☐ The Bernard Sunley Charitable Foundation	£2.5 million	General charitable purposes
☐ The Cadogan Charity	£2.5 million	General charitable purposes
☐ The Freemasons' Grand Charity	£2.5 million	Social welfare, medical research, hospices and overseas emergency aid
☐ The Kirby Laing Foundation	£2.5 million	Health, welfare, Christian religion, youth, general
☐ The Prince of Wales's Charitable Foundation	£2.5 million	Culture, the environment, medical welfare, education, business and enterprise, children and youth and overseas aid
☐ Dunard Fund	£2.4 million	Classical music, the visual arts, environment and humanitarian causes
☐ Euro Charity Trust	£2.4 million	Relief of poverty, education
☐ Sparks Charity (Sport Aiding Medical Research For Kids)	£2.4 million	Medical research
☐ The Childwick Trust	£2.4 million	Horse racing and breeding; welfare of and research into thoroughbred horses: health, people with disabilities and older people and Jewish charities in the UK; education in South Africa
☐ The Joseph Rank Trust	£2.4 million	The Methodist Church, Christian-based social work
☐ Cripplegate Foundation	£2.3 million	General charitable purposes
☐ The P F Charitable Trust	£2.3 million	General charitable purposes
☐ The Samuel Sebba Charitable Trust	£2.3 million	General, covering a wide range of charitable purposes with a preference for Jewish organisations
☐ The Stobart Newlands Charitable Trust	£2.3 million	Christian religious and missionary causes

☐ Ridgesave Limited	£2.2 million	Jewish, religion, education, general
☐ SHINE (Support and Help in Education)	£2.2 million	Education of children and young people
☐ Sir Siegmund Warburg's Voluntary Settlement	£2.2 million	Arts
☐ The Eranda Foundation	£2.2 million	Research into education and medicine, the arts, social welfare
☐ The Helen Hamlyn Trust	£2.2 million	Medical, the arts and culture, education and welfare, heritage and conservation in India, international humanitarian affairs and 'healthy ageing'
☐ The River Farm Foundation	£2.2 million	General, older people, young people, animal welfare and the environment
☐ County Durham Community Foundation	£2.1 million	Tackling social disadvantage and poverty, general
☐ Lloyds TSB Foundation for Scotland	£2.1 million	Social welfare
☐ Reuben Foundation	£2.1 million	Healthcare, education, general
☐ The Dollond Charitable Trust	£2.1 million	Jewish, general
☐ The February Foundation	£2.1 million	Education, heritage, community-based charities, environment, animals, medical/welfare
☐ The Hadley Trust	£2.1 million	Social welfare
☐ The Trusthouse Charitable Foundation	£2.1 million	General charitable purposes
☐ The Variety Club Children's Charity	£2.1 million	Children's charities
☐ Hobson Charity Limited	£2 million	Social welfare, education
☐ The Eveson Charitable Trust	£2 million	People with physical disabilities, (including those who are blind or deaf); people with mental disabilities; hospitals and hospices; children who are in need; older people; homeless people; medical research into problems associated with any of these conditions
☐ The Hugh Fraser Foundation	£2 million	General
☐ The Maurice Wohl Charitable Foundation	£2 million	Jewish groups and health, welfare and medical organisations
☐ The Morgan Foundation	£2 million	Children and young people, health, social welfare
☐ The Northwood Charitable Trust	£2 million	Medical research, health, welfare, general
☐ The Sir Joseph Hotung Charitable Settlement	£2 million	General
☐ The Beatrice Laing Trust	£2 million	Relief of poverty and advancement of the evangelical Christian faith
☐ Community Foundation for Merseyside	£1.9 million	General charitable purposes
☐ Lloyds TSB Foundation for Northern Ireland	£1.9 million	Social and community need, education and training
☐ The Queen's Silver Jubilee Trust	£1.9 million	General, in practice grants to organisations supporting disadvantaged young people
☐ The Royal Foundation of the Duke and Duchess of Cambridge and Prince Harry	£1.9 million	General, children and young people, armed forces and veterans, conservation and sustainability
☐ Stratford upon Avon Town Trust	£1.85 million	Education, welfare, general
☐ Hurdale Charity Limited	£1.8 million	Advancement of Jewish religion, relief of poverty and general charitable purposes
☐ The Albert Hunt Trust	£1.8 million	Health and welfare
☐ The John Swire (1989) Charitable Trust	£1.8 million	General charitable purposes
☐ The Lancaster Foundation	£1.8 million	Christian causes
☐ The Leverhulme Trade Charities Trust	£1.8 million	Charities benefiting commercial travellers, grocers or chemists
☐ The Shirley Foundation	£1.75 million	Autism spectrum disorders with particular emphasis on medical research

☐ Church Urban Fund	£1.7 million	Welfare and Christian outreach in deprived communities in England
☐ S F Foundation	£1.7 million	Jewish, general
☐ The Community Foundation in Wales	£1.7 million	Community, social inclusion, social welfare
☐ The Davidson Family Charitable Trust	£1.7 million	Jewish, general
☐ The True Colours Trust	£1.7 million	Special needs, sensory disabilities and impairments, palliative care, carers
☐ Hampton Fuel Allotment Charity	£1.7 million	Relief in need, health, education of children and young people and social welfare
☐ CHK Charities Limited	£1.6 million	General charitable purposes
☐ The Barclay Foundation	£1.6 million	Medical research, young people, the elderly, people with disabilities, the sick and the disadvantaged
☐ The Birmingham Community Foundation	£1.6 million	General charitable purposes; social welfare
☐ The Campden Charities Trustee	£1.6 million	Welfare and education
☐ The Nationwide Foundation	£1.6 million	Social welfare
☐ The Reed Foundation	£1.6 million	General, arts, education, relief of poverty, women's health
☐ The Wolfson Family Charitable Trust	£1.6 million	Jewish institutions and charities, particularly Jewish groups and Israeli institutions
☐ Entindale Ltd	£1.5 million	Orthodox Jewish charities
☐ Essex Community Foundation	£1.5 million	Social welfare, general
☐ Global Charities	£1.5 million	Disadvantaged children, young people and adults
☐ Rosetrees Trust	£1.5 million	Medical research
☐ The Burdett Trust for Nursing	£1.5 million	Healthcare
☐ The Ernest Cook Trust	£1.5 million	Educational grants focusing on children and young people for the environment, rural conservation, arts and crafts, literary and numeracy and research
☐ The Gannochy Trust	£1.5 million	General
☐ The Peacock Charitable Trust	£1.5 million	Medical research, disability, general
☐ The R S Macdonald Charitable Trust	£1.5 million	Neurological conditions, visual impairment, community, family, children and animal welfare
☐ The Rayne Foundation	£1.5 million	Arts, education, health, medicine, social welfare
☐ East End Community Foundation	£1.4 million	Community development
☐ Ernest Kleinwort Charitable Trust	£1.4 million	General charitable purposes
☐ Shlomo Memorial Fund Limited	£1.4 million	Jewish causes
☐ The Al Fayed Charitable Foundation	£1.4 million	Children, health and general
☐ The John Armitage Charitable Trust	£1.4 million	Medical, relief-in-need, education, religion
☐ The Leathersellers' Company Charitable Fund	£1.4 million	General charitable purposes
☐ The Vail Foundation	£1.4 million	General, Jewish
☐ The DM Charitable Trust	£1.35 million	Jewish, social welfare and education
☐ Cumbria Community Foundation	£1.3 million	General charitable purposes
☐ Nemoral Ltd	£1.3 million	Orthodox Jewish causes
☐ The ACT Foundation	£1.3 million	Welfare, health, housing, disability
☐ The Ashden Trust	£1.3 million	Environment, homelessness, sustainable regeneration, community arts
☐ The Geoff and Fiona Squire Foundation	£1.3 million	General, medicine, education, disability and the welfare and healthcare of children
☐ The Roddick Foundation	£1.3 million	Arts, education, environmental, human rights, humanitarian, medical, poverty, social justice

THE MAJOR TRUSTS RANKED BY GRANT TOTAL

☐ The Sir James Reckitt Charity	£1.3 million	Society of Friends (Quakers), social welfare, general
☐ The Westminster Foundation	£1.3 million	Social welfare, military charities, education, environment and conservation
☐ The Charles Dunstone Charitable Trust	£1.25 million	General charitable purposes
☐ Calouste Gulbenkian Foundation – UK Branch	£1.2 million	Cultural understanding, fulfilling potential, environment, maximising social and cultural value
☐ The Breadsticks Foundation	£1.2 million	Healthcare and education
☐ The Charles Hayward Foundation	£1.2 million	Heritage and conservation; criminal justice; overseas
☐ The Constance Travis Charitable Trust	£1.2 million	General charitable purposes
☐ The Golden Bottle Trust	£1.2 million	General with a preference for the environment, health, education, religion, the arts and developing countries
☐ The Performing Right Society Foundation	£1.2 million	New music of any genre
☐ The Peter Harrison Foundation	£1.2 million	Sports for people in the UK who have disabilities or are disadvantaged; support for children and young people in the south east of England who are terminally ill, have disabilities, or are disadvantaged; and certain educational initiatives
☐ The Polonsky Foundation	£1.2 million	Arts, social science, higher education institutions
☐ The Sir James Knott Trust	£1.2 million	General charitable purposes
☐ The Sylvia Adams Charitable Trust	£1.2 million	Disability, welfare, poverty, children and young people, social disadvantage
☐ The Wates Foundation	£1.2 million	Assisting organisations in improving the quality of life of the deprived, disadvantaged and excluded in the community
☐ Volant Charitable Trust	£1.17 million	General charitable purposes
☐ Peter De Haan Charitable Trust	£1.15 million	Social welfare, the environment, the arts
☐ The George Müller Charitable Trust	£1.15 million	Christian evangelism; children and young people; orphans
☐ Sir John Cass's Foundation	£1.12 million	Education in inner London
☐ The Vardy Foundation	£1.12 million	Christian causes, education in the north east of England, young people and general charitable purposes in the UK and overseas
☐ British Record Industry Trust	£1.1 million	Performing arts, music therapy, general
☐ Hexham and Newcastle Diocesan Trust (1947)	£1.1 million	Religion
☐ Jerwood Charitable Foundation	£1.1 million	Arts
☐ Melow Charitable Trust	£1.1 million	Jewish
☐ Mrs L D Rope Third Charitable Settlement	£1.1 million	Education, religion, relief of poverty, general
☐ The Harold Hyam Wingate Foundation	£1.1 million	Jewish life and learning, performing arts, music, education and social exclusion, overseas development, medical
☐ The Sir John Fisher Foundation	£1.1 million	General charitable purposes with a preference for the shipping industry, medicine, the navy or military and music and theatre
☐ The Sutton Trust	£1.1 million	Education
☐ Cash for Kids Radio Clyde	£1 million	Children
☐ Joseph Rowntree Reform Trust Limited	£1 million	Promoting political and democratic reform and defending of civil liberties

☐ Network for Social Change	£1 million	Developing world debt, environment, human rights, peace, arts and education
☐ The Carpenters' Company Charitable Trust	£1 million	Education, general
☐ The Gerald Ronson Foundation	£1 million	General, Jewish
☐ The H B Allen Charitable Trust	£1 million	General charitable purposes
☐ The R and S Cohen Foundation	£1 million	Education, relief in need and the arts
☐ The Steel Charitable Trust	£1 million	Social welfare; culture; recreation; health; medical research; environment; and occasionally, overseas aid
☐ The Three Guineas Trust	£1 million	Autism and Asperger's Syndrome, climate change
☐ The Drapers' Charitable Fund	£998,000	General charitable purposes including education, heritage, the arts, prisoner support, Northern Ireland and textile conservation
☐ Lloyds Bank Foundation for the Channel Islands	£998,000	General charitable purposes
☐ The Equitable Charitable Trust	£993,000	Education of disabled and/or disadvantaged children under 25
☐ The HDH Wills 1965 Charitable Trust	£987,000	General charitable purposes with particular favour towards wildlife and conservation
☐ Baron Davenport's Charity	£986,000	Almshouses; hospices; residential homes for the elderly; children and young people under the age of 25
☐ The Welton Foundation	£985,500	Principally supports projects in the health and medical fields Other charitable purposes considered include education, welfare and arts organisations
☐ 4 Charity Foundation	£975,500	Jewish
☐ The Wixamtree Trust	£958,000	General charitable purposes
☐ The Archie Sherman Charitable Trust	£956,000	Jewish charities, education, arts, general
☐ The Hedley Foundation	£956,000	Youth and health
☐ The Great Britain Sasakawa Foundation	£951,000	Links between Great Britain and Japan
☐ The Edith Murphy Foundation	£950,000	General, individual hardship, animals, children and the disabled
☐ The Maurice Hatter Foundation	£931,000	Jewish causes, general
☐ The D'Oyly Carte Charitable Trust	£930,000	Arts, medical welfare, environment
☐ The J J Charitable Trust	£929,000	Environment, literacy
☐ The John R Murray Charitable Trust	£913,000	Arts and literature
☐ The Rose Foundation	£911,500	General – grants towards building projects
☐ Six Point Foundation	£911,000	Welfare of Holocaust survivors and Jewish refugees
☐ Sutton Coldfield Charitable Trust	£906,000	Relief of need, arts, education, building conservation, general
☐ Charitworth Limited	£904,000	Religious, educational and charitable purposes In practice, mainly Jewish causes
☐ John James Bristol Foundation	£901,000	Education, health, older people, general
☐ The James Dyson Foundation	£889,000	Science, engineering, medical research and education
☐ ShareGift (The Orr Mackintosh Foundation)	£887,000	General charitable purposes
☐ The Francis C Scott Charitable Trust	£872,000	Disadvantaged young people in Cumbria and North Lancashire
☐ The Djanogly Foundation	£868,000	Jewish, general, medicine, education, the arts and social welfare
☐ The Richmond Parish Lands Charity	£867,000	General, community
☐ The Jane Hodge Foundation	£855,000	Medical care and research, education and religion

☐ The National Churches Trust	£855,000	Preservation of historic churches
☐ The Sussex Community Foundation	£829,000	Community-based projects, education, disability, health, and the relief of poverty and sickness
☐ The Daiwa Anglo-Japanese Foundation	£828,000	Anglo-Japanese relations
☐ The David and Elaine Potter Foundation	£817,000	Human rights, education, research and the arts
☐ Sir Halley Stewart Trust	£810,000	Medical, social, educational and religious activities

☐ The Architectural Heritage Fund	£809,000	Loans and grants for building preservation
☐ Tees Valley Community Foundation	£807,000	General charitable purposes
☐ Tuixen Foundation	£805,000	General charitable purposes
☐ The Girdlers' Company Charitable Trust	£802,000	Medicine and health, education, welfare, youth welfare, heritage, environment, humanities and Christian religion
☐ The Harbour Foundation	£802,000	Relief of poverty for refugees and homeless people; education; research
☐ The Yorkshire Dales Millennium Trust	£801,000	Conservation and environmental regeneration
☐ GrantScape	£800,000	Environmental and community-based projects
☐ The Donald Forrester Trust	£800,000	General charitable purposes
☐ Oglesby Charitable Trust	£797,000	General charitable purposes
☐ The Joseph Levy Charitable Foundation	£796,000	Young people, elderly, health, medical research

☐ The Haramead Trust	£770,500	Children, social welfare, education, people with disabilities, homeless people, medical assistance, victims and oppressed people
☐ Community Foundation for Surrey	£764,000	Strengthening communities
☐ The Hunter Foundation	£750,000	Education, young people, children, relief of poverty, community development
☐ The Ardeola Charitable Trust	£746,000	General charitable purposes
☐ Marshall's Charity	£745,000	Parsonage and church improvements
☐ Childs Charitable Trust	£740,000	Christian, general
☐ The Sovereign Health Care Charitable Trust	£739,000	Health, people with disabilities
☐ The Allen Lane Foundation	£732,000	Charities benefiting asylum-seekers and refugees, gypsies and travellers, lesbian, gay, bisexual or transgender people, offenders and ex-offenders, older people, people experiencing mental health problems and people experiencing violence or abuse
☐ Edward Cadbury Charitable Trust	£728,000	General; community development; education; culture; the environment
☐ The Peter Cruddas Foundation	£716,000	Children and young people

☐ The Evan Cornish Foundation	£714,500	Education, older people, health, human rights, social & economic inequality, prisons
☐ The South Yorkshire Community Foundation	£713,000	General charitable purposes
☐ The Joffe Charitable Trust	£706,000	Alleviation of poverty and protection/ advancement of human rights
☐ The 101 Foundation	£700,000	General charitable purposes
☐ The Barcapel Foundation	£700,000	Health, heritage, youth
☐ The Bluston Charitable Settlement	£699,000	Jewish, general
☐ The Henry Moore Foundation	£699,000	Fine arts, in particular sculpture, and research and development, projects and exhibitions which expand the definition of sculpture, such as film, photography and performance

☐ Jewish Child's Day	£687,000	Charitable purposes of direct benefit to Jewish children who are disadvantaged, suffering or in need of special care
☐ The Bromley Trust	£684,500	Human rights, prison reform, conservation
☐ Community Foundation for Calderdale	£681,000	General charitable purposes
☐ The Indigo Trust	£679,000	Technology in Africa
☐ The William A Cadbury Charitable Trust	£675,000	Local welfare and disability charities, environment and conservation, Quaker charities and international development
☐ Rowanville Ltd	£670,000	Orthodox Jewish
☐ The EBM Charitable Trust	£668,500	Children/youth, animal welfare, relief of poverty, general
☐ The Kathleen Hannay Memorial Charity	£666,000	Health, welfare, Christian, general
☐ Itzchok Meyer Cymerman Trust Ltd	£661,000	Advancement of the orthodox Jewish faith; education; social welfare; relief of sickness; medical research and general charitable purposes
☐ The Alliance Family Foundation	£661,000	Jewish, general
☐ The Tolkien Trust	£652,500	General charitable purposes
☐ The Mark Leonard Trust	£650,000	Environmental education, youth, general
☐ The Band Trust	£649,000	People with disabilities, children and young people, scholarships, hospices and hospitals, education, older people and people who are disadvantaged
☐ The Freshfield Foundation	£631,000	Environment, healthcare, sustainable development and overseas disaster relief
☐ Northamptonshire Community Foundation	£624,000	Education, health, poverty
☐ John Moores Foundation	£619,000	Social welfare in Merseyside and Northern Ireland, emergency relief overseas
☐ The Grocers' Charity	£616,000	General charitable purposes
☐ The Mary Kinross Charitable Trust	£614,000	Relief of poverty, medical research, community development, youth and penal affairs
☐ The Sandra Charitable Trust	£606,000	Animal welfare and research, environmental protection, social welfare, health and youth development
☐ Devon Community Foundation	£605,000	General charitable purposes
☐ Percy Bilton Charity	£603,000	People with disabilities, disadvantaged youth, older people
☐ H C D Memorial Fund	£594,000	Health, education, environment and community action
☐ Simon Gibson Charitable Trust	£583,000	General charitable purposes
☐ The George John and Sheilah Livanos Charitable Trust	£579,000	Health, maritime charities, general
☐ The Isle of Anglesey Charitable Trust	£577,000	General, community
☐ The Will Charitable Trust	£575,500	People with sight loss and the prevention and cure of blindness, cancer care, people with mental disability
☐ The James Tudor Foundation	£573,500	Relief of sickness, medical research, health education, palliative care
☐ The Harpur Trust	£556,000	Education, welfare and recreation
☐ The Kohn Foundation	£545,500	Scientific and medical projects, the arts – particularly music, education, Jewish charities
☐ The Alice Ellen Cooper Dean Charitable Foundation	£544,000	General charitable purposes

☐ The MacRobert Trust	£535,000	General charitable purposes
☐ The Valentine Charitable Trust	£532,000	General charitable purposes
☐ The Fishmongers' Company's Charitable Trust	£527,000	General, in particular education, relief of poverty and disability
☐ The Mulberry Trust	£526,000	General charitable purposes
☐ Mercaz Torah Vechesed Limited	£525,000	Orthodox Jewish
☐ Investream Charitable Trust	£518,500	Jewish
☐ Sir Harold Hood's Charitable Trust	£517,000	Roman Catholic charitable purposes
☐ Colyer-Fergusson Charitable Trust	£514,500	Social isolation, exclusion or poverty, community activity (often through churches), church maintenance, environment, the arts
☐ The Enid Linder Foundation	£511,000	Medicine, the arts, general
☐ Heathside Charitable Trust	£508,000	General, Jewish
☐ The Church and Community Fund	£506,000	Church of England, social welfare
☐ The Staples Trust	£505,000	Development, environment, women's issues
☐ The Charities Advisory Trust	£500,000	General charitable purposes
☐ The Football Association Youth Trust	£500,000	Sports
☐ The 1989 Willan Charitable Trust	£499,000	General In practice mainly organisations supporting, children, older people, people with mental and physical disabilities and medical research
☐ The AIM Foundation	£491,000	Healthcare, community development, youth, environmental matters and other charitable activities particularly related to influencing long-term social change
☐ The Charles and Elsie Sykes Trust	£489,000	General, social welfare, medical research
☐ The John Apthorp Charity	£480,000	Education, religion, social welfare
☐ The Maud Elkington Charitable Trust	£478,000	Social welfare, general charitable purposes
☐ The Mackintosh Foundation	£473,000	General; priority is given to the theatre and the performing arts
☐ Mr and Mrs J A Pye's Charitable Settlement	£471,000	General charitable purposes
☐ The G C Gibson Charitable Trust	£471,000	Art, music and education; health, hospices and medical research; community and other social projects; religion
☐ Milton Keynes Community Foundation	£466,000	Welfare, arts
☐ The Peter Stebbings Memorial Charity	£464,000	General charitable purposes
☐ The Tajtelbaum Charitable Trust	£456,000	Jewish, welfare
☐ Derbyshire Community Foundation	£454,000	Social welfare
☐ Trustees of Tzedakah	£450,000	Jewish charities, welfare
☐ The Hertfordshire Community Foundation	£447,000	General charitable purposes
☐ The Lennox and Wyfold Foundation	£447,000	General charitable purposes
☐ The Schreib Trust	£445,000	Jewish, general
☐ Brushmill Ltd	£442,000	Jewish causes, education, social welfare
☐ Queen Mary's Roehampton Trust	£438,000	Ex-service support
☐ The Glass-House Trust	£438,000	Social housing and the urban environment, art and child development
☐ Erach and Roshan Sadri Foundation	£427,500	Education, welfare, homelessness, Zoroastrian religion, general
☐ The Boltini Trust	£426,000	General, international development, music
☐ The Balcombe Charitable Trust	£423,000	Education, environment, health and welfare
☐ The Colt Foundation	£422,500	Occupational and environmental health research
☐ The Pilkington Charities Fund	£420,000	General, health, social welfare, people with disabilities, older people and victims of natural disaster or war

☐ The Neil Kreitman Foundation	**£418,000**	Arts and culture; education; health and social welfare
☐ The Tedworth Charitable Trust	**£416,000**	Parenting, child welfare and development, general
☐ The Alan and Babette Sainsbury Charitable Fund	**£414,000**	General, with a focus on scientific and medical research, youth work, projects overseas and civil liberties
☐ The Madeline Mabey Trust	**£414,000**	Medical research, children's welfare and education, humanitarian aid
☐ The Hilden Charitable Fund	**£411,000**	Homelessness, asylum seekers and refugees, penal affairs, disadvantaged young people and overseas development
☐ The Sheepdrove Trust	**£411,000**	Mainly environment, education
☐ The Privy Purse Charitable Trust	**£406,000**	General charitable purposes
☐ The Jones 1986 Charitable Trust	**£404,000**	People with disabilities, welfare of older people, welfare of younger people, education and purposes beneficial to the community
☐ Fisherbeck Charitable Trust	**£402,000**	Christian, homelessness, welfare, education, heritage
☐ The Jordan Charitable Foundation	**£397,000**	General charitable purposes
☐ The Douglas Turner Trust	**£383,000**	General charitable purposes
☐ The Rubin Foundation	**£375,000**	Jewish charities, the arts, general
☐ BC Partners Foundation	**£368,500**	General charitable purposes
☐ The Arbib Foundation	**£367,000**	General charitable purposes
☐ The Saddlers' Company Charitable Fund	**£361,000**	General, education
☐ The Crerar Hotels Trust	**£360,000**	Health, social welfare
☐ The Ofenheim Charitable Trust	**£352,000**	General, mainly charities supporting health, welfare, arts and the environment
☐ The Frances and Augustus Newman Foundation	**£347,500**	Medical research and equipment
☐ The Tompkins Foundation	**£345,500**	General charitable purposes
☐ Jay Education Trust	**£343,000**	Jewish
☐ Richard Cloudesley's Charity	**£341,000**	Churches, medical and welfare
☐ Gwyneth Forrester Trust	**£330,000**	General charitable purposes
☐ Polden-Puckham Charitable Foundation	**£327,000**	Peace and security, ecological issues, social change
☐ Lord Leverhulme's Charitable Trust	**£324,000**	Welfare, education, arts, health, young people
☐ Lady Hind Trust	**£322,000**	General with some preference for health, disability and welfare related charities
☐ The Manifold Charitable Trust	**£322,000**	Education, historic buildings, environmental conservation, general
☐ The John S Cohen Foundation	**£316,000**	General, in particular music and the arts, education and environment
☐ The Community Foundation for Wiltshire and Swindon	**£314,500**	Community welfare
☐ The Triangle Trust (1949) Fund	**£312,500**	Social welfare, health, people with disabilities, integration and general
☐ The Dowager Countess Eleanor Peel Trust	**£311,000**	Medical research, the elderly, socially disadvantaged people and general
☐ The Kennedy Leigh Charitable Trust	**£305,000**	Jewish charities, general, social welfare
☐ The Mike Gooley Trailfinders Charity	**£286,000**	Medical research, general
☐ Heart of England Community Foundation	**£284,000**	General charitable purposes
☐ Dorset Community Foundation	**£279,500**	Community; social welfare; education; health; the relief of poverty

☐ **The Goodman Foundation**	**£256,000**	General, overseas, social welfare, older people, health and disability

☐ **Autonomous Research Charitable Trust**	**£244,000**	General charitable purposes
☐ **The Manoukian Charitable Foundation**	**£230,000**	Social welfare, education, medical, the arts, 'Armenian matters'
☐ **Roald Dahl's Marvellous Children's Charity**	**£217,000**	Haematology and neurology conditions affecting children and young people up to the age of 25
☐ **The William Leech Charity**	**£204,000**	Health and welfare in the north east of England, overseas aid
☐ **The Grace Charitable Trust**	**£188,000**	Christian, general, education, medical and social welfare
☐ **The Duke of Devonshire's Charitable Trust**	**£158,500**	General charitable purposes
☐ **The Bruntwood Charity**	**£120,000**	General, social welfare
☐ **The Debmar Benevolent Trust**	**£76,500**	Jewish causes; relief of poverty

The 101 Foundation

General charitable purposes
Around £700,000 (2012/13)

Beneficial area

UK.

Correspondent: Coutts and Co., Coutts and Co., Trustee Department, 440 Strand, London WC2R 0QS (tel: 020 7663 6826)

Trustees: Angela Dawes; David Dawes; Coutts and Co.

CC Number: 1146808

Registered in April 2012, the foundation has general charitable purposes, with a particular interest in children and young people. It was established by David and Angela Dawes, who won £101 million on the EuroMillions lottery in October 2011. The foundation's first annual report and accounts were submitted to the Charity Commission towards the end of January 2014, but were not available to view as this book went to press. However, figures available from the Charity Commission record show that during its first year of operation the foundation had an income of almost £1.3 million and a total expenditure of £739,000.

Applications

In writing to the correspondent.

Information gathered from:
Charity Commission record.

The 1989 Willan Charitable Trust

General. In practice mainly organisations supporting, children, older people, people with mental and physical disabilities and medical research
£499,000 to organisations
(2011/12)

Beneficial area

Worldwide, in practice mainly the north east of England.

Correspondent: Mark Pierce, Head of Policy, Projects and Programmes, Community Foundation Tyne and Wear and Northumberland, 9th Floor, Cale Cross, 156 Pilgrim Street, Newcastle upon Tyne NE1 6SU (tel: 01912 220945; fax: 01912 300689; email: mp@communityfoundation.org.uk)

Trustees: Francis A. Chapman; Alex Ohlsson; Willan Trustee Ltd.

CC Number: 802749

The trust was established in 1989 for general charitable purposes, with a preference for benefiting organisations in the north east of England.

> In recognition of the origins of the trust fund and the economic impact that the decline of shipbuilding has had on the region, the trustees tend to concentrate their support towards causes which are active in Tyne & Wear and its immediate surrounds. The trustees favour causes which aim to ease social deprivation and/or enrich the fabric of the local community and the quality of life of individuals within that community.

In 2011/12 the trust had assets of £15.9 million and an income of £445,000. There were 143 grants made to organisations during the year totalling £499,000, with a further £7,500 also being awarded to 15 individuals. The trust's accounts give the following breakdown of how the money was distributed by category, region and size of grant:

Category

Building our children's future	64	£198,000
Taking part in community life	60	£191,000
Improving health	22	£90,000
Enjoying later life	8	£16,000
Caring for our environment	4	£12,000

Region

Newcastle	32	£143,500
Northumberland	37	£95,000
'Out of area'	21	£55,000
Sunderland	13	£45,000
Durham	19	£42,000
North Tyneside	9	£37,000
South Tyneside	8	£31,000
Gateshead	7	£25,500
Hartlepool	6	£17,000
Middlesbrough	3	£10,500
Stockton	2	£5,000
Darlington	1	£500

Size of grant

More than £10,000	1	£12,500
£5,001 – £10,000	44	£276,000
£1,001 – £5,000	70	£187,000
£1,000 or less	43	£31,000

A list of beneficiaries was not included in the accounts. Previous beneficiaries included: SAFC Foundation and Cancer Connexions; Amble Multi Agency Crime Prevention Initiative; Durham City Centre Youth Project; The Children's Society; Chester le Street Youth Centre; Different Strokes North East; Northumberland Mountain Rescue; Association of British Poles; Healthwise; and Newcastle Gang Show.

Exclusions

Grants are not given directly to individuals. Grants for gap year students may be considered if the individual will be working for a charity (in this case the grant would be paid to the charity).

Applications

In writing to the correspondent at the Community Foundation Serving Tyne and Wear.

> Applicants should provide a letter of application not exceeding 2,000 words in length (approx. 2 sides of A4).
>
> The letter of application should provide:
> - Contact details for the applicant organisation, and a named individual with whom we may discuss the funding proposal in more detail
> - A brief description of the applicant organisation, its track record and current activities
> - Details of the activities for which funding is sought and why they are needed
> - A budget for the activities and details of any match funding provided by the applicant or other funders
> - Details of the charity's bank account (a copy of a recent bank statement will suffice)
>
> Applicants should provide their charity registration number and recent accounts if these are not held on the Charity Commission website. Where the applicant is asking a registered charity to hold the grant on its behalf, details of that charity must be provided and also recent accounts or financial statements for the group itself.
>
> The trustees will meet in March, June, September and December. Applications will generally be considered at the next scheduled trustee meeting provided they are received by the 15th of the preceding month. However applicants are encouraged to submit their applications as early as possible to ensure they are considered at the next available trustees' meeting.

Percentage of awards given to new applicants: between 40% and 50%.

Common applicant mistakes

'Applying for projects that are not based in, or serving, North East England.'

Information gathered from:
Accounts; Charity Commission record; further information provided by the funder; funder's website.

The 29th May 1961 Charitable Trust

Social welfare, general
£3.4 million (2011/12)

Beneficial area

UK, with a special interest in the Warwickshire/Birmingham/Coventry area.

Correspondent: Vanni Emanuele Treves, Trustee, Ryder Court, 14 Ryder Street, London SW1 Y 6QB (tel: 020 7024 9034; email: enquiries@29may1961charity.org.uk)

Trustees: Vanni Emanuele Treves; Andrew C. Jones; Anthony J. Mead; Paul Varney.

CC Number: 200198

The trust takes its name from the date on which it was established. The trustees include Mr Vanni Treves, who is a former chair of Channel 4 and senior partner at Macfarlanes solicitors, amongst other senior positions.

The trust gives the following concise description of its grantmaking policy, aims and objectives:

The 29th May 1961 Charitable Trust is a general grant making trust. The policy of the trustees is to support a wide range of charitable organisations across a broad spectrum. Although for disclosure purposes grants are analysed into separate categories, the trustees are interested in funding initiatives which meet their selection criteria regardless of the charitable area into which the grant falls. Grants are made for both capital and revenue purposes. Some grants are one-off, some recurring and others spread over two or three years. Grants that cover more than one year are subject to annual review and the satisfaction of conditions. The majority of grants are made to organisations within the United Kingdom and preference is given, where possible, to charities operating in the Coventry and Warwickshire area. The policy of the trustees is to consider grants on an equal opportunities basis, regardless of gender, religion or ethnic background.

Grants range in size from hundreds to hundreds of thousands of pounds; most are between £1,000 and £5,000. About half appear to be for work in the Coventry and Warwickshire area. Most grants are now on a three-year basis and will not be renewed without at least some interval.

In 2011/12 the trust had assets of £99.4 million, which generated an income of £3.1 million. Grants were made to 475 organisations totalling £3.4 million. The trust's annual report gives an overview of major awards:

Major new funding during the year was given to Godiva Awakes Trust towards the costs of a Coventry arts project as part of the cultural Olympiad programme, Coventry Sports Foundation towards the costs of subsidising fitness programmes for deprived families, Monte San Martino Trust towards the costs of bringing young Italians of families who sheltered allied prisoners of war to England to learn English, English National Opera towards the costs of commissioning new opera projects and Smallpiece Trust towards the costs of running engineering courses for young people.

Further funding was given to Shelter towards a project to prevent ex-offenders becoming homeless on release and the Princes Trust towards their work with young people in the Midlands.

The charity continued to support substantially the following organisations amongst others:- University of Warwick, Coventry and Warwickshire Awards Trust, Coventry Day Care Fund, Crisis, Macmillan Cancer Support, St Basil's Centre, Abbeyfields West Midlands, Heart of England Community Foundation, NACRO, Warwickshire Association of Youth Clubs and Coventry Cyrenians.

Exclusions

Grants only to registered charities. No grants to individuals.

Applications

To the secretary in writing, enclosing in triplicate the most recent annual report and accounts. Trustees normally meet in February, May, August and November. Due to the large number of applications received, they cannot be acknowledged.

Information gathered from:

Accounts; annual report; Charity Commission record.

4 Charity Foundation

Jewish
£975,500 (2011/12)

Beneficial area

UK and Israel.

Correspondent: Jacob Schimmel, Trustee, UK I Ltd, 54–56 Euston Street, London NW1 2ES (tel: 020 7387 0155)

Trustees: Jacob Schimmel; D. Rabson; Anna Schimmel.

CC Number: 1077143

Set up in 1999, in January 2008, the charity changed its name from Les Freres Charitable Trust to 4 Charity Foundation. Grants are made to Jewish organisations for religious and educational purposes.

In 2011/12 the foundation had assets of £13.1 million and an income of £7 million, mainly from rents. Grants were made during the year totalling £975,500.

Just three beneficiaries were disclosed in the accounts; they were: American Joint Jewish Distribution Committee (£115,500); Imaginations (£97,000); and Matan – Your Way to Give (£34,500).

Previous beneficiaries include: the Millennium Trust; Keren Yehoshua V'Yisroel; Project Seed; World Jewish Relief; Menorah Grammar School; British Friends of Jaffa Institute; Friends of Mir; Heichal Hatorah Foundation; Chai Life Line Cancer Care; Jewish Care; and British Friends of Ezer Mizion.

Applications

This trust does not respond to unsolicited applications.

Information gathered from:

Accounts; Charity Commission record.

A. W. Charitable Trust

Jewish causes through educational and religious organisations, general charitable purposes
£4.3 million (2011/12)

Beneficial area

Unrestricted.

Correspondent: Rabbi Aubrey Weis, Trustee, 1 Allandale Court, Waterpark Road, Manchester M7 4JL (tel: 01617 400116)

Trustees: Rabbi Aubrey Weis; Rachel Weis.

CC Number: 283322

This trust was established in 1981 for general charitable purposes. The trust's aims are 'to support all worthy Orthodox Jewish causes' and it meets these objects by making grants mainly to Jewish education and religious organisations both in the UK and abroad. It is the charitable trust of Aubrey Weis, director of Aberdeen Estate Company, owners of land and property throughout the North West.

In 2011/12 the trust had assets of £100.2 million and an income of £29.5 million, most of which came from rental income. Grants were made totalling £4.3 million. A list of beneficiaries was not included in the accounts.

Previous beneficiaries include: TET; Asser Bishvil Foundation; Chevras Oneg Shabbos-Yomtov; Friends of Mir; CML; Toimchei Shabbos Manchester; British Friends of Kupat Hair; Purim Fund; Beenstock Home; and Zoreya Tzedokos.

Applications

In writing to the correspondent. The trust considers 'all justified applications for support of educational establishments, places of worship and other charitable actives'. Each application and request is considered on its own merit.

Information gathered from:

Accounts; Charity Commission record.

ABF The Soldiers' Charity

Army charities
£3.2 million to organisations (2011/12)

Beneficial area

Worldwide.

Correspondent: Roger Musson, Director of Finance and Resources, Mountbarrow House, 12 Elizabeth Street, London SW1W 9RB (tel: 0845 241 4820; fax: 0845 241 4821; email: rmusson@ soldierscharity.org; website: www. soldierscharity.org)

Trustees: Maj. Gen. George Kennedy; Maj. Sir Michael Parker; Stephen Clark; Guy Davies; Maj. Gen. Peter Sheppard; Maj. Gen. Richard Nugee; Brig. Andrew Freemantle; Allison M. Gallico; Damien Francis; Andrew Vernon.

CC Number: 1146420

During the year 2011/12 the charity became incorporated and was registered with the Charity Commission with the new number 1146420 (formerly 211645). The charity's mission, vision and core values have not changed and are:

Mission: ABF The Soldiers' Charity supports, soldiers, former soldiers and their families in need; *Vision:* to be the most effective and reliable charity for soldiers; *Core values:* trust, respect, inspiration and responsiveness.

The current policy set by the trustees is to support individuals through the Regimental and Corps Benevolence Funds, and to support other military and national charities which look after the needs of the serving and retired army community.

Grant areas

Grants are made for the support and benefit of people serving, or who have served, in the British Army, or their families/dependents. They fall into seven broad areas:

Annuities

To help supplement the incomes of older veterans or their widows living alone on basic pensions.

Bursaries

To help with education and training and include funding for training colleges that help retrain soldiers with disabilities and training course fees and essential equipment for individual soldiers; support for ex-soldiers taking higher education courses to start on new careers; help with funding for continuing education of children of soldiers who have died or been severely disabled in the service.

Care home fees

Modest top-up grants to help with the cost for older veterans or their widows where local authority grants are insufficient.

Holiday schemes

Short breaks for families under stress. Also, an annual grant to the Guild of St Helena allows service children with special needs to have a holiday.

Special funds

To assist soldiers who have been injured while on active service in Northern Ireland, the Falklands Campaign or the Gulf War. Dependents of those killed may also qualify. There is also provision for support to those who live in South Wales and are in need of respite care.

General needs

For a variety of purposes, as long as there is a clear need which cannot be met from other sources.

Current operations fund

Supporting soldiers injured or families of those killed as a result of their service during current operations in Iraq and Afghanistan. Grants for those requiring immediate help and covering a wide range of purposes including retraining soldiers who have a disability, to providing holiday funds for a war widow and her children.

Examples of support include: assistance to those recovering from operational injuries; the impact of bereavement and the transition of the injured to civilian life; help for the elderly (through assistance with mobility aids, home adaptations and care home fees); help in covering priority debts; help with providing retraining for civilian occupations; and support for children's education.

In 2011/12 the fund (immediately prior to transfer to the new incorporated charity), had assets of £43 million. Income for the year was £16.8 million from donations, legacies and investments. Grants to other charities totalled £3.2 million plus £5.3 million to regiments and corps for the benefit of individuals.

Around 100 organisations benefit from the fund each year with grants ranging from £250,000 to less than £1,000. In 2011/12 beneficiaries included: Scottish Veterans Residences (£250,000); Royal Commonwealth Ex-Services League (£245,000); SSAFA Forces Help (£225,500); Combat Stress (£195,000); Erskine Hospital (£150,000); Community Housing and Therapy (£64,000); Victory Services Club (£60,000); Queen Alexandra Hospital Home (£40,000); The Warrior Programme (£30,000); Timeback (£25,000); STUBS (£10,000); West Indian Association of Service Personnel (£5,000); and Ulster Defence Regiment Benevolent Fund (£500).

Applications

Individual cases should be referred initially to the appropriate Corps or Regimental Association. Charities should apply in writing and enclose the latest annual report and accounts. Also refer to the charity's website for current eligibility criteria and application processes. Initial telephone enquiries are welcome.

Percentage of awards given to new applicants: less than 10%.

Common applicant mistakes

'Not understanding the specific veteran community.'

Information gathered from:

Accounts; annual report; Charity Commission record; further information provided by the funder; funder's website.

Achisomoch Aid Company Ltd

Orthodox Jewish religious charities
£7.6 million (2011/12)

Beneficial area

Unrestricted.

Correspondent: Yitzchock Katz, Trustee, 26 Hoop Lane, London NW11 0NU (tel: 020 8731 8988; email: admin@ achisomoch.org; website: www. achisomoch.org)

Trustees: David Chontow; Jack Emanuel; Yitzchock Katz; Michael Hockenbroch.

CC Number: 278387

The trust seeks to advance religion in accordance with the Jewish faith, and also supports Jewish education and young people. The following information about how the trust operates is given on the its website:

> Achisomoch is a charity voucher agency – it is like a bank. You open an account with us and then pay money into the account. You are given a cheque (voucher) book and can then make (charitable) payments by using these vouchers. As a charity in its own right, we can reclaim the tax rebate under Gift Aid to increase the money in your account and available for distribution to charities. Donations, via vouchers can be made only to registered charities. You get regular statements and can arrange to speak to client services for any help or special instructions.

In 2011/12 the trust had assets of £2.6 million and an income of £8 million, mainly from donations and Gift Aid receipts. Grants were made during the year totalling £7.6 million.

Previous beneficiaries have included: the Ah Trust, Beis Malka Trust, Chevras Maoz Ladol, Comet Charities Ltd, Davis Elias Charitable Trust, Havenpoint Ltd, Heritage Retreats, Jewish Educational Trust, Lolev Charitable Trust, Menorah Primary School, Michlala Jerusalem College, SOFT, Tomchei Cholim Trust and Yad Eliezer – Israel.

Applications

In writing to the correspondent.

The ACT Foundation

Information gathered from:
Accounts; annual report; Charity Commission record; funder's website.

Welfare, health, housing, disability

£839,000 to organisations
(2011/12)

Beneficial area

UK and overseas.

Correspondent: James Kerr, Grants Manager, 61 Thames Street, Windsor, Berkshire SL4 1QW (tel: 01753 753900; fax: 01753 753901; email: info@ theactfoundation.co.uk; website: www. theactfoundation.co.uk)

Trustees: Paul Nield; John J. O'Sullivan; Michael Street; Christine Erwood; Robert F. White; Denis Taylor.

CC Number: 1068617

The foundation was established in 1994, and it provides grants to individuals and other charities, principally in the UK, with the aim of enhancing the quality of life for people in need, (specifically those with mental and physical disabilities).

Grants generally fall into the following areas:

▶ Building – funding modifications to homes, schools, hospices, etc.
▶ Equipment – provision of specialised wheelchairs, other mobility aids and equipment including medical equipment to assist independent living
▶ Financial assistance – towards the cost of short-term respite breaks at a registered respite centre

Projects that intend to be a platform for continuing services will be expected to demonstrate sustainability. ACT would be concerned to be a sole funder of projects that require ongoing support.

The following statement is taken from the foundation's useful and informative website:

ACT's income is derived almost entirely from its investment portfolio and in any year we receive many more applications than we can fund. As our funds are limited we have to prioritise. Not all applications for grants will be successful and some may be met only in part.

In 2011/12 the foundation had assets of £46 million and an income of £15 million. Grants totalling £1.3 million were made including £489,000 in 447 grants to individuals and £839,000 in 76 grants to organisations (including grants to partner organisations – Livability and Treloar Trust).

Grantmaking in 2011/12

From the chair's report:

I have previously reported that since 2009/10 our grant making has focused more strongly on the 'transition' that young physically and mentally disabled people make as they leave full time education move into adulthood. This is an area in which we feel more could be done to support vulnerable members of society to enable them to fulfil their potential. We work with many fine organisations to achieve our aims in this area . . . our partnerships with these organisations are a very important part of our grant making strategy and without their expert operational knowledge many of the innovative projects we help fund would not be deliverable. . . . We experienced a 20% increase in the number of grant applications received and this trend is continuing in 2012. Where we can, we have sought to help and have provided assistance to an increased number of beneficiaries, both individuals and charities. Excluding the grants to our strategic partners we made 447 (2011: 411) grants to individuals and 74 (2011: 65) institutional grants.

Beneficiaries included: Treloar Trust – grants to outreach projects (£500,000); Livability – grants towards 'Lifestyle Choices' project (£100,000); Theatre Royal Stratford East (£20,000); Aspire, Diverse Abilities Plus, HTF Kent, Outreach 3 Way and Swindon Therapy Centre for Multiple Sclerosis (£10,000 each); Build IT International – Zambia, Disability Action Yorkshire, Family Care Trust and PHAB (£5,000 each); Calvert Trust (£4,500); Scottish Huntington's Association and Special Educational Needs Families Support Group (£2,000 each); and Goldhill Adventure Playground (£1,000).

Exclusions

The foundation will not make grants:

▶ Which would replace statutory funding
▶ Which would pay for work that has already commenced or equipment already purchased, deposits paid or goods on order
▶ Towards the operating costs of other charities except in connection with setting up new services
▶ To charities that have not been registered for at least three years
▶ For projects which promote a particular religion or faith
▶ To community centres and youth clubs except where those served are in special need of help (e.g. the elderly or persons with special needs)
▶ To local authorities
▶ To umbrella or grantmaking organisations except where they undertake special assessments not readily available from the foundation's own resources
▶ To universities and colleges, and grant-maintained, private or local education authority schools or their parent teacher associations, except if those schools are for students with special needs
▶ For costs associated with political or publicity campaigns

Applications

The foundation's website provides the following information:

Application by registered charities and overseas charitable organisations has to be by way of letter on the organisation's headed paper and should:

▶ Give a brief description of your organisation including any statutory or voluntary registration
▶ Provide a summary of the work you plan to undertake with the grant, together with a cost breakdown, plans and/or specification if available and a summary of the key milestones for the work
▶ Provide information on why you need to do this work and what would happen if you were unable to do it
▶ Give details of any other UK-based support received or pledged for your project
▶ Specify what you expect the results of the work to be and the number of beneficiaries helped
▶ Explain how you plan to evaluate whether the work achieved its goals
▶ Explain if the work will require capital and/or on-going operational funding and if so how you plan to meet these costs
▶ In addition you need to attach the following financial information to the letter:
  ▶ A cash flow projection of income and expenditure budget for the work
  ▶ Details of any income already raised for the work and income outstanding and where you plan to raise it from
  ▶ Your latest annual report and accounts

When to apply

You can apply for a grant at any time. Trustees meet four times a year, but you do not need to time your application to coincide with these meetings. Procedures exist to give approvals between meeting dates, where necessary.

We do not publish the dates of trustees' meetings.

What happens to your application

We will send you an acknowledgement letter within one week of receiving your application. If your proposal is either in an unacceptable form, or ineligible, or a low priority, we will tell you in this letter.

We will assess all acceptable applications and we may contact you for further information and/or make a personal visit. In the case of charitable bodies we may also ask for a presentation.

We aim to make decisions on 95% of grant applications within one month and on all applications within three months

If the application is for an emergency you may request a faster timescale and we will do our best to assist.

Information gathered from:
Accounts; annual report; Charity Commission record; funder's website.

Action Medical Research

Medical research, focusing on child health

£2.9 million (2012)

Beneficial area
UK.

Correspondent: Martin Richardson, Administrator, Vincent House, 31 North Parade, Horsham, West Sussex RH12 2DP (tel: 01403 210406; fax: 01403 210541; email: info@action.org.uk; website: www.action.org.uk)

Trustees: Valerie Remington-Hobbs; Prof. Sarah Bray; Charles Jackson; Prof. Andrew George; Richard Price; Sir John Wickerson; David Gibbs; Mark Gardiner; Philip Hodkinson; Esther Alderson.

CC Number: 208701

Set up in 1952, Action Medical Research has more than 60 years of history in funding medical research with many notable successes. With roots in research into the polio vaccine, the charity now focuses on the health of babies, children and young people. The following information is taken from the charity's informative website:

Research strategy

We select the very best projects and research training fellows through peer review. Our research funding programme over the three years 2013–2015 will aim to:

 Attract and select the best research most likely to deliver by using peer review and an expert scientific advisory panel to recommend each year research training fellowships and project grants
 Identify the impact of research by each year analysing the potential clinical impact of recently completed grants as scored by peers and carrying out selected retrospective impact reports
 Support the work of Clinical Studies Groups in the areas of neonatology and preterm birth
 Collaborate with other organisations where this moves forward key research

The research we support focuses on child health including problems affecting pregnancy, childbirth, babies, children and young people.

Within this we support a broad spectrum of research with the objective of preventing disease and disability and of alleviating physical disability.

Our emphasis is on clinical research or research at the interface between clinical and basic science. We pride ourselves that our research is innovative and of a high standard as judged by rigorous peer review.

Within these criteria, we also support research and development of equipment and techniques to improve diagnosis, therapy and assistive technology (including orthoses, prostheses and aids to daily living) and encourage applications in the field of medical engineering.

Guidelines

The charity gives the following guidance, available from its website, on its project grants:

The principal investigator (PI) for a project grant is normally employed in a permanent position in a UK university or institution. Fixed term employees on a long-term contract may be eligible to be a PI, providing the term of employment extends at least six months beyond the duration of the proposed research project and the host research institution is prepared to give all the necessary support to the individual and the project. We would not pay the salary of a PI.

Research workers who require personal support from a project grant, and who have made a substantial intellectual contribution to the grant proposal, may be named as co-applicants with an established member of staff as the principal applicant.

Grants are provided for up to three years duration in support of one precisely formulated line of research. A two page outline of the proposed research is required before a full application can be invited. Successful applicants from the outline stage will be sent a link to our application form. Awards will be made following peer review.

Applications should be of the highest quality as the scheme is very competitive.

Our maximum project grant award is normally £200,000. We are happy to consider grant requests at a lower level of funding including grants below £50,000.

Support covers salary costs, consumables and items of dedicated equipment essential for carrying out the work. We would expect the university or research institute to provide standard laboratory equipment and standard office computers. The application should not include any indirect costs such as administrative or other overheads imposed by the university or other institutions and we would not normally pay salary costs for those already employed on salaried positions.

A research team can only apply for one grant per grant round.

Please note that there will be a limit to the number of full application forms that we can send out. Where the work is considered peripheral to our aims or in cases where demand on our funds is high, we will inform you of our decision not to request a full application.

In 2012 the charity had assets and an income of almost £7 million. Grants were made totalling £2.9 million excluding governance and administration costs.

Beneficiaries included: University Hospital Southampton and Southampton University (£200,000); Universities of Oxford and Oxford University Hospitals NHS Trust £173,000); King's College London (£170,000); University of Glasgow (£52,000); and Swansea University (£10,000). Full details of these grants and the purposes for which they were awarded can be found in the annual report and accounts.

Exclusions

The charity does not provide:
 Grants towards service provision or audit studies
 Grants purely for higher education, e.g. BSc/MSc/PhD course fees and subsistence costs
 Grants for medical or dental electives
 Grants for work undertaken outside the UK
 Any indirect costs such as administrative or other overheads imposed by the university or other institution
 Costs associated with advertising and recruitment
 'top up' funding for work supported by other funding bodies
 Costs to attend conferences and meetings (current Action Medical Research grant holders may apply separately)
 Grants to other charities – applications would normally come directly from research teams and projects need to be passed through the Action Medical Research scientific peer review system
 Grants for research into complementary/alternative medicine
 Grants on how best to train clinical staff
 Grants for psychosocial aspects of treatment
 Grants on social research, family relationships or socioeconomic research
 Grants for very basic research with little likelihood of clinical impact within the short to medium-term

Applicants based in core funded units can apply but need to demonstrate added value.

Information gathered from:
Accounts; annual report; Charity Commission record; funder's website.

The Sylvia Adams Charitable Trust

Disability, welfare, poverty, children and young people, social disadvantage

£1.2 million (2011/12)

Beneficial area

Hertfordshire; work in the UK which has a national impact; and Kenya, Tanzania and Uganda.

Correspondent: Jane Young, Director, Sylvia Adams House, 24 The Common, Hatfield, Hertfordshire AL10 0NB (tel: 01707 259259; fax: 01707 259268; email: info@sylvia-adams.org.uk; website: www.sylvia-adams.org.uk)

Trustees: Richard J. Golland; Mark Heasman; Timothy Lawler.

CC Number: 1050678

This trust was set up using the income from the sale of works of art, following Sylvia Adams' death. The trust's aim is to improve the quality of life of those who are disadvantaged, through the alleviation of disease, sickness and poverty.

Grants generally range from £5,000 to a maximum of £30,000, though occasionally a grant may be made for £50,000. Most grants will be for one or two years, although grants can be made for three.

Grants are made in the following categories:

▶ Children and young people
▶ People with a disability
▶ People living in poverty or who are disadvantaged

The trust is particularly interested in helping people to become self-supporting and self-help projects. UK focus is on enabling people to participate fully in society. Worldwide, the focus is on primary healthcare and health education, access to education, appropriate technology and community enterprise schemes. Both UK causes providing a national benefit and causes local to Hertfordshire are supported, as well as UK charities working overseas. The trust funds specific projects but will also consider core funding.

The trust reviews its priorities each year within its overall guidelines and up to date information is available on its website. Interests in Hertfordshire and the UK currently include:

Hertfordshire and the UK

Children and young people

We are looking to support organisations that are working with socially disadvantaged and excluded children and young people, and which are giving them opportunities to develop in ways that will enable them to become resilient and capable adults. We are particularly interested in:

▶ Work which addresses the needs of children at risk of neglect and who are affected by lack of appropriate parenting
▶ Work with young people that will give them the chance to acquire essential life skills such as communication, self discipline, motivation and empathy. This includes projects that focus on challenging activities, sport, the arts and access to the natural environment.

Disability

We are looking to support organisations that improve the lives of people with disabilities with a particular emphasis on:

▶ Innovations that have the potential to bring about significant improvements (excluding medical research)
▶ Sporting and cultural activities, and access to the natural environment
▶ Conditions that are less publicised or generally known and therefore attract less public support.

* We have an interest in employment issues but are not currently seeking new projects in this area

Poverty and Social Exclusion

We are interested in supporting organisations that work with people living in poverty or who are socially excluded, enabling them to access a better long-term future. This will include:

▶ Work which addresses homelessness
▶ Sporting and cultural activities, and access to the natural environment
▶ The particular problems facing some rural communities.

* We are prepared to consider local projects in England and Wales where there is the potential for impact on poverty and social exclusion within rural communities.

Overseas

For 2013/14 we will continue to support projects in Kenya, Tanzania and Uganda. We will not consider applications for work in other countries.

We will only consider applications from organisations with an average income over £50,000 a year.

We are interested in:

▶ Education
▶ Water and sanitation
▶ High impact health initiatives
▶ Initiatives to help small scale farmers

Check the trust's website for current priorities.

Grantmaking in 2011/12

In 2011/12 the trust had assets of £7.9 million and an income of £209,500. Grants were made totalling £1.2 million, and were summarised as follows:

UK	£583,000
Overseas	£314,000
Hertfordshire	£185,000
Grants under £5,000	£97,000
Trustee grants	£20,000

UK beneficiaries included: Down Syndrome Association (£50,000), for an employment project; Raleigh International (£30,000) towards its Youth Agency Partnership Programme; Jubilee Sailing Trust (£26,500), for the costs of an additional fundraiser; Stonewall (£20,000), for a youth programme; Volunteer Reading Project (£15,000), to fund reading support for an additional 90 children; Unique (£10,000), towards IT and fundraising costs; London Youth (£10,000), towards the renovation of Woodrow House (£10,000); Housing Justice (£6,000), towards project work; and Host (£5,000), core funding.

Beneficiaries in Hertfordshire included: YMCA Central Hertfordshire (£25,000), for the SPACE project in Hatfield; Groundwork Herts (£12,500), towards a summer holiday scheme; Letchworth Arts Centre (£7,500), for two arts interns; Greenside Studio (£5,000), towards the purchase of a vehicle; and React (£2,500), towards equipment.

Exclusions

The trust does not give grants to:

▶ Individuals
▶ Projects in the Middle East or Eastern Europe or the countries of the ex-Soviet Union
▶ Work that solely benefits elderly people
▶ Organisations helping animals, medical research or environmental causes

Applications

There is a two stage application process: Stage 1 can **only** be made through the trust's website; applicants who successfully get through this stage will be asked to submit a fuller Stage 2 application.

Telephone queries about the guidelines and application process are welcome in advance of applications being made.

Percentage of awards given to new applicants: between 40% and 50%.

Common applicant mistakes

'Not applying through the right medium; not reading application instructions on the trust's website in their entirety.'

Information gathered from:

Accounts; annual report; Charity Commission record; further information provided by the funder; funder's website.

Age UK

Older people
£16 million (2011/12)

Beneficial area
UK and overseas.

Correspondent: Grants Unit, Tavis House, 1–6 Tavistock Square, London WC1H 9NA (tel: 0800 169 8787; email: contact@ageuk.org.uk; website: www. ageuk.org.uk)

Trustees: Dianne Jeffrey, Chair; Patrick Cusack; Dr Bernadette Fuge; Jeremy Greenhalgh; Timothy Hammond; Chris Hughes; Glyn Kyle; Prof. Brendan McCormack; Jane Newell; Michael Vincent; Lucy Bracken; Timothy Hunter; Prof. John Williams; Prof. James Wright.

CC Number: 1128267

General

The Age UK website describes the charity's vision as:

A world in which older people flourish is a world in which older people will:
- Be equal citizens with equal rights
- Have enough money for a secure and decent life, and have access as consumers to the products and services they need at a price they can afford
- Have access to the healthcare and social care they need
- Have the opportunity to live healthier longer lives and to enjoy a sense of well-being
- Live in homes and neighbourhoods that are safe and comfortable and which enable them to lead fulfilling lives
- Have opportunities to participate and contribute as volunteers, active citizens, good neighbours, family members, and workers
- Enjoy the benefits of longer life, wherever they are in the world

To achieve this vision, the charity focuses on five core areas of work:
- Money matters
- Health and wellbeing
- Travel and lifestyle
- Home and care
- Work and learning

On 1 April 2012, Age UK and HelpAge International created a new charity – Age International. Age International will lead on ageing and international development issues in the UK and will be the UK member of the HelpAge global network. Age International will focus on poverty relief, improving healthcare, fighting for rights and emergency relief focused on older people.

The charity Age UK has continued the work of Help the Aged and Age Concern, providing several million pounds in grant funding each year for research relating to age and ageing, and organisations working with people in later life.

General grants

The charity administers a variety of grant programmes funded from its own reserves and on behalf of external providers such as government and the national lottery. All the programmes are aimed at organisations working to make life better for older people, by addressing people's immediate needs or tackling the root causes of problems they are experiencing. Small clubs, groups and forums receiving grants must be independently constituted, not-for-profit and accessible to all people in later life.

For further information on grant programmes currently open to applications, contact the charity directly. You can call free on 0800 169 8787.

Research grants
Age UK aims to improve outcomes for older people in a wide variety of areas that may affect their lives. First-class research, knowledge and research partnerships support this aim. We:
▷ Carry out research ourselves to generate authoritative evidence on age and ageing to achieve change and development in policy and services for older people
▷ Fund research carried out by others that will lead to positive solutions for later life
▷ Are a hub for knowledge about older people and issues in ageing for ourselves and others
▷ Work in partnership with others from a local to global level to support the promotion and generation of age-related research and the uptake of new knowledge

At Age UK we focus our research funds exclusively on later life.

Our research supports Age UK's vision of a world in which older people flourish.

Commissioned research
We commission social, economic and health research, often by competitive tender, to generate evidence on issues that affect older people. The research is at the heart of our work to change public policy and attitudes on ageing for the better and has supported major successes, for example, abolition of the default retirement age, increasing pensioner income and legislative change for a more age equal society.

Grant-funded research
From 1976 to 2012, we have supported over 370 research projects to improve the health and wellbeing of older people. These include projects on healthy ageing, the diseases and disabilities of ageing and the ageing process itself. As a result, significant advances have been made in the understanding, prevention, diagnosis, management and treatment of age-related health problems and in knowledge about healthy ageing.

Today grants are awarded through the Research into Ageing Fund for research to improve the health and wellbeing of older people.

The Research into Ageing Fund is a fund set up and managed by Age UK to support age-related research and is the name by which the Research into Ageing research programme is now referred. This does not affect the way in which research grants are awarded, nor the continuation or funding of current projects. Research into Ageing remains a constituent charity in Age UK.

Grantmaking in 2011/12
In 2011/12 the charity had assets of £34 million and an income of £167 million. Grants in the UK were made totalling £16 million were broken down as follows:

Support for organisations working with people in later life	£8.2 million
Well-being services	£3.1 million
Home services	£2.2 million
Information and advice	£1.1 million
Research	£861,000
Services development programmes	£339,000
Digital inclusion	£191,000
Engagement	£157,000

Note: A significant proportion of the grant total was given to local Age Concern and Age UK branches.

There are also extensive grantmaking programmes overseas, amounting to £11 million in 2011/12, which are not covered here.

Exclusions
No grants to individuals.

Applications
For further information on general grant programmes currently open to applications, contact the grants team. Applicants interested in research funding should contact the research department at Tavis House, 1–6 Tavistock Square, London WC1H 9NA or email: research@ageuk.org.uk.

Information gathered from:
Accounts; annual report; Charity Commission record; funder's website.

The AIM Foundation

Healthcare, community development, youth, environmental matters and other charitable activities particularly related to influencing long-term social change
£491,000 (2011/12)

Beneficial area
Worldwide. In practice, UK with a preference for Essex.

Correspondent: Louisa Tippett, Administrator, Whittle and Co., 15 High Street, West Mersea, Colchester, Essex C05 8QA (tel: 01206 385049; email: louisa@whittles.co.uk)

Trustees: Ian Roy Marks; Angela D. Marks; Nicolas Marks; Joanna Pritchard-Barrett; Caroline Marks; Philippa Bailey.

CC Number: 263294

Set up in 1971 as the Ian Roy Marks Charitable Trust, this trust changed its name to the AIM Foundation in 1993. The foundation stresses that grantmaking policy is highly proactive in seeking out potential partners to initiate and promote charitable projects principally in the fields of healthcare, community development, youth, environmental matters and other charitable activities particularly related to influencing long-term social change, both in the UK and overseas. Grants are made for core costs and salaries.

In 2011/12 the foundation had assets of £9.3 million and an income of over £300,000. Grants were made totalling £491,000 and were broken down as follows:

Influencing long-term social change	£190,000
Youth – care and development	£63,000
Environment	£52,000
Miscellaneous	£43,000
Healthcare	£25,000
Community development	£15,000
Small grants in the above categories	£30,500

Beneficiaries included: New Economics Foundation (£110,000); The Impetus Trust (£50,000); ChildLine NSPCC (£35,000); Health Empowerment Through Nutrition (£20,000); Friends of the Earth and the Children's Society (£15,000 each); ASHOKA (£10,000); Families in Focus, Wells for India, Freedom from Torture and Chance to Shine (£5,000 each); and Amnesty International (£3,000).

Exclusions
No grants to individuals.

Applications
It cannot be stressed enough that this foundation 'is proactive in its approach' and does not wish to receive applications. 'Unsolicited requests for assistance will not be responded to under any circumstance.'

Percentage of awards given to new applicants: less than 10%.

Common applicant mistakes
'Just applying.'

Information gathered from:
Accounts; Charity Commission record; further information provided by the funder.

The Al Fayed Charitable Foundation

Children, health and general
£1.4 million (2012)

Beneficial area
Mainly UK.

Correspondent: Susie Mathis, Administrator, 60 Park Lane, London W1K 1QE (tel: 07717 652316; email: mathissusie@aol.com; website: www.alfayed.com/philanthropy.aspx)

Trustees: Mohamed Al-Fayed; Camilla Fayed; Heini Fayed.

CC Number: 297114

The foundation was established in 1987 by Mohamed Al-Fayed. It supports a range of charities but it primarily focuses its resources on children and young people's health and hospices.

In 2012 the foundation had assets of £81,000 and an income of £1.4 million derived from Gift Aid payments entered into by Mr Al Fayed. Grants were made during the totalling £1.4 million including £8,300 in grants to individuals.

Beneficiaries included: Shooting Star (Chase) (£390,000); West Heath (£328,000); Zoe's Place (£180,000); Francis House (£175,000); Lotus Children's Centre (£77,000); WSPA (£40,000); The New School at West heath (£30,000); Spring Films (£8,400); Fauna and Flora International (£5,000); Harrods Ltd (£3,700); Opera Rara (£2,000); Thando Art (£1,400); and Bespoke Food (£1,100).

Applications
In writing to the correspondent including the following:
- Name and contact details
- An overview of why you are seeking funding
- A breakdown of funds sought
- A stamped addressed envelope

Information gathered from:
Accounts; annual report; Charity Commission record; funder's website.

Allchurches Trust Ltd

Churches, general
£9.4 million (2012)

Beneficial area
UK.

Correspondent: The Relationship and Grants Manager, Beaufort House, Brunswick Road, Gloucester GL1 1JZ (tel: 01452 873189; fax: 01452 423557; email: atl@ecclesiastical.com; website: www.allchurches.co.uk)

Trustees: Michael Chamberlain; Rt Revd Nigel Stock; Fraser Hart; Nick J. E. Sealy; The Ven. Annette Cooper; William Icaew; Philip Mawer; Christopher Smith; Denise Wilson.

CC Number: 263960

Allchurches Trust Ltd was established in 1972 its income being derived from its wholly-owned subsidiary company Ecclesiastical Insurance Office plc. Its aims are to promote the Christian religion, to contribute to the funds of any charitable institutions or associations and to carry out any charitable purpose.

Grants will be considered in response to appeals in support of Churches, Church establishments, religious charities and charities preserving UK heritage.

The trust describes its grants strategy as:
- Supporting deployment of clergy at parish level, particularly within deprived areas
- Funding other staff to support the work of the clergy
- Funding new initiatives ranging from supporting parishes to educational work in schools
- Maintaining and repairing church and cathedral buildings
- Funding specific mission and outreach activities

Grantmaking in 2012
The trust described its activities during the year in its annual report, including a list of sample beneficiaries:

Purpose	No. of grants	Amount
Dioceses	120	£6.2 million
Parishes and other charities	1,047	£1.6 million
Cathedrals	160	£1.3 million

Dioceses and cathedrals
The majority of the trust's donations are used to support the dioceses and cathedrals of the Church of England. During the year, the trust *allocated* donations of £7.6 million to those beneficiaries (2001: £7.4 million).

Anglican churches, churches of other denominations and the Christian community
The trust has a general fund which responds to requests for financial assistance from Anglican churches, churches of other denominations, the Christian community and other charitable organisations in accordance with its grant making policy. In general, the trust supports appeals from churches for building and restoration projects, repair of church fabric, church community initiatives, religious charities and charities preserving the UK heritage. During 2012, the trust made charitable distributions from its general fund in response to appeals for financial assistance as follows: Anglican Church – 69%; Other denominations 20%; and other charities 11%

Special project fund
This fund was established in 1999. Its purpose is to support a small number of projects on a larger basis. During the year, ATL provided funds to support chaplaincy at the London 2012 Olympics and Paralympics, assistance with research into the role of cathedrals in today's society, and a grant to the Archbishop's Council in relation to clergy development.

Overseas projects fund
This fund was established in 2005. During the year, the trust *allocated* funds amounting to £121,000 (2011: £54,000) to support Christian causes overseas. The increase in 2012 was due to an exceptional payment to support the cathedral in Christchurch, New Zealand. In addition, subsidiary companies operating in Australia, New Zealand and Canada donated £357,000 (2011: £535,000) to charitable causes in those countries.

In 2012 the trust's consolidated statement of financial activities shows an income of £18.7 million and assets of £376 million. Grants were made totalling £9.4 million.

Beneficiaries included: Butterwick Hospice Care – Stockton-on-Tees, Cleveland: A grant was given towards the construction of a new Family Support and Complementary Therapy Centre at the Hospice; Dobwalls United Church – Liskeard, Cornwall: A donation was given towards the re-rendering of the outside of the church, to replace the wooden porch doors with glass ones, and to install kitchen and toilet facilities; Hope Corner Community Church and Kids First – Runcorn, Merseyside: A grant was made towards furnishing and equipping a new church and community centre specifically with the needs of young people and their families in mind; Lisburn Cathedral – Northern Ireland: Financial assistance was given to help refurbish the cathedral's interior, including repairs to doors, plasterwork repairs, to electrically re-wire and to install a new audio system; St Andrew's Church – Cullompton, Devon: A grant was given towards the building of a community centre to serve both the church and the community; St Cuthbert's Church – Fir Vale, Sheffield: A donation was made towards extending the church building to provide community space, a meeting room and integral toilets to benefit both church and community; St John the Evangelist Church – Cleckheaton, West Yorkshire: Financial assistance was given towards the re-ordering of the church to provide community space, meeting rooms and kitchen facilities; Shirley Baptist Church – West Midlands: A grant was given towards the re-development of the church's halls to create modern kitchen, toilet and meeting room facilities; and

Trinity Methodist Church – East Grinstead, West Sussex: Financial assistance was given towards the building of a new multi-functional church for a growing congregation.

Exclusions
The trust is unable to support:
- Charities with political associations
- National charities
- Individuals
- Appeals for running costs and salaries

Applications cannot be considered from the same recipient twice in one year or in two consecutive years.

Information gathered from:
Accounts; annual report; Charity Commission record; funder's website.

The H. B. Allen Charitable Trust

General
£1 million (2012)

Beneficial area
Worldwide.

Correspondent: Peter B. Shone, Trustee, Homefield, Chidden Holt, Hambledon, Waterlooville, Hampshire PO7 4TG (tel: 02392 632406; email: mail@hballenct.org.uk; website: www.hballenct.org.uk)

Trustees: Helen Ratcliffe; Peter Shone.

CC Number: 802306

Background
This trust was established in 1985 by the late Heather Barbara Allen, whose family produced the famous Beefeater gin. The trust benefited from just under £10.5 million from her estate and smaller grantmaking trust in 2005 (following her death) and 2006. Miss Allen had maritime interests and was a supporter of Padstow lifeboat station, paying for the 'James Burrough' lifeboat (named after the creator of Beefeater gin in the early 1860s and founder of the company). Its replacement, 'Spirit of Padstow', was bought by the trust with a £2 million donation to the RNLI in 2006.

There is no typical grant size though the trustees make a large number at £5,000. They are made to a wide range of national and, occasionally, local charities. Many grants are to charities previously supported.

General
The trustees have no restrictions on them as to the kinds of project or the areas they can support, and are generally prepared to consider any field. They do not make grants to, or sponsorship arrangements with, individuals or to

organisations that are not UK registered charities.

Grants can be recurring or one-off, and for revenue or capital purposes. They are unlikely to be awarded to provide initial funding for newly established charities. The trustees give priority each year to those organisations to which grants have been made in the past.

The trust notes that many charities do not carry out up to date research into its activities and hopes that potential applicants will read the guidelines carefully and, if necessary, make a preliminary call to check their eligibility. The trust's guidelines are available on its website and include the current status of all the grant categories.

Grantmaking in 2012
In 2012 the trust had assets of £32.4 million and an income of £1.4 million. Grants were made during the year to 55 organisations totalling just over £1 million. Mr Shone, one of the two trustees, received £42,000 in fees. The accounts state: 'The management and administration of the charity is carried out by Peter B Shone, a solicitor and one of the trustees, in conjunction with the charity's investment managers.'

Beneficiaries were categorised under a wide range of fields: blindness; children and young people, churches; people with disabilities; education/schools; environment, wildlife and animals; general community, hospices; housing/ homeless; mental health; museums/ galleries/heritage and overseas/ international. The two largest grants were made to Exeter Cathedral – Libraries and Archives (£250,000); and St Michael and All Angels Church Bedford Park (£150,000).

Other beneficiaries included: Friends of Butser Ancient Farm (£72,000); RN Submarine Museum (£50,000); Wildlife Conservation Research Unit (£40,000); Deafness Research UK and St Botolph's – Boston Stump (£35,000 only); National Eye Research Centre (£30,000); Bowel Disease Research Foundation (£20,000); The Sobriety Project – Young Offenders Scheme (£15,000); Fauna and Flora International, Little Ouse Headwaters Project, St Wilfrid's Hospice and The Orton Trust (£10,000 each); Birmingham Pen Trade Heritage Association, Books Abroad, The Gurkha Welfare Trust and Wheelpower – British Wheelchair Sport (£5,000 each); Rural Youth Trust (£3,000); and Frontier Youth Trust and Small Woods Association (£2,500 each).

Exclusions
No grants to individuals, organisations which are not UK-registered charities or gap-year students (even if payable to a registered charity).

Applications

In writing to the correspondent: including a copy of the organisation's latest annual report and accounts. Applications should be submitted by post, not email, although enquiries prior to any application can be made by email. Read the trust's application guidelines available from its helpful and concise website.

Note the following comments from the trust:

Applicants should note that, at their main annual meeting (usually in January or February), the trustees consider applications received up to 31 December each year but do not carry them forward. Having regard for the time of year when this meeting takes place, it makes sense for applications to be made as late as possible in the calendar year so that the information they contain is most up to date when the trustees meet. It would be preferable, from all points of view, if applications were made only in the last quarter of the calendar year. Although, preferably not in December.

The trustees receive a very substantial number of appeals each year. It is not their practice to acknowledge appeals, and they prefer not to enter into correspondence with applicants other than those to whom grants are being made or from whom further information is required. Only successful applicants are notified of the outcome of their application.

Percentage of awards given to new applicants: between 10% and 20%.

Information gathered from:

Accounts; annual report; Charity Commission record; further information provided by the funder; funder's website.

The Alliance Family Foundation

Jewish, general
£313,000 to organisations
(2011/12)

Beneficial area
UK and Israel.

Correspondent: The Trustees, Spencer House, 27 St James's Place, London SW1A 1NR

Trustees: Lord David Alliance; Graham Alliance; Sara Esterkin; Joshua Alliance.

CC Number: 258721

The foundation's objectives are 'the relief of poverty, advancement of education, advancement of religion and any other charitable purpose'. Most grants are made to Jewish organisations. The settlor of the foundation, Lord David Alliance, is the founder of textile business Coats plc with Sir Harry Djangoly and former chair of N Brown

Group plc. He is a Liberal Democrat peer and a substantial donor to the party.

In 2011/12 the foundation had assets of £13.7 million and an income of £642,000. Grants were made totalling £661,000, of which £313,000 was given to organisations and £238,000 was distributed to individuals. The remaining £110,000 was classified as 'sundry general charitable donations'.

Four beneficiaries were listed in the accounts; they were: Jewish Community Secondary School Trust (£50,000); University of Manchester (£47,500); Prince Ali Reza Pahlavi Foundation Fellowship (£32,000); and the Weizmann Institute – Israel (£30,000).

Applications

The trustees review requests for financial support and make donations periodically and will continue to do so over the forthcoming twelve months.

Information gathered from:
Accounts; Charity Commission record.

Amabrill Ltd

Orthodox Jewish
£2.7 million (2011/12)

Beneficial area
UK, with a preference for north west London.

Correspondent: Charles Lerner, Trustee, 1 Golder's Manor Drive, London NW11 9HU (tel: 020 8455 6785)

Trustees: Charles Lerner; Frances R. Lerner; Salamon Noe; Israel Grossnass.

CC Number: 1078968

The principal activity of this charity is the advancement of education and religious practice in accordance with the teachings of the Orthodox Jewish faith.

Grants are made both for capital purposes – which can include buildings, equipment and educational material – and towards the general running costs of the grantee institution. Other grants are made for the relief of poverty and these are only made after appropriate certification has been seen. (An independent organisation has been set up in North West London to verify the identity and means of Orthodox Jewish persons for this purpose.)

In 2011/12 the charity had assets of £3.8 million and an income of almost £2.6 million, mostly from donations. Grants were made totalling £2.7 million.

A list of grants was not included in the most recent accounts. Previous beneficiaries include: Kahal Chassidim Bobov; YMER; BFON Trust; Beth Hamedrash Elyon Golders Green Ltd; Friends of Shekel Hakodesh Ltd; Friends of Mir and Parsha Ltd; Cosmon Belz

Ltd; United Talmudical Academy; British Friends of Mosdos Tchernobel; Mayfair Charities Ltd; Friends of Toldos Avrohom Yitzchok; Achisomoch Aid Company; the Gertner Charitable Trust; and Higher Talmudical Education Ltd.

Applications

Appeal letters are received from, and personal visits made by representatives of Jewish charitable, religious and educational institutions. These requests are then considered by the trustees and grants are made in accordance with the trustees' decisions. 'All applications receive the fullest and most careful consideration.'

Information gathered from:
Accounts; Charity Commission record.

The John Apthorp Charity (formerly Summary Ltd)

Education, religion, social welfare
£480,000 (2012)

Beneficial area
UK, with a preference for Hertfordshire.

Correspondent: John Apthorp, Trustee, The Field House Farm, 29 Newlands Avenue, Radlett, Hertfordshire WD7 8EJ (tel: 01923 855727)

Trustees: John Apthorp; Duncan Apthorp; Justin Apthorp; Kate Arnold.

CC Number: 1102472

Established in 2004, the objects of the charity are the advancement of education, the advancement of religion and the relief of poverty and suffering. In 2010 the charity received a donation to the value of £4.3 million from the Milly Apthorp Charitable Trust, which is in the process of spending out and shares two trustees from the Apthorp family. As a result of this, the grantmaking capacity of this charity has increased significantly.

In 2012 the charity had assets of £9.5 million and an income of £423,000. Grants were made to 38 organisations during the year totalling £480,000.

Beneficiaries included: Radlett Lawn and Tennis Club (£35,000); Tools for Self Reliance (£25,000); John Clements Centre (£20,000); Reach Out Plus (£15,000); The Living Room, Home Start Welwyn and Teens Unite Fighting Cancer (£10,000 each); Radlett Art Society (£7,000); Alzheimer's Society (£5,000); and the Tall Ships Youth Trust (£1,500).

Applications
In writing to the correspondent.

Information gathered from:
Accounts; Charity Commission record.

The Arbib Foundation

General
£367,000 (2011/12)

Beneficial area
Unrestricted.

Correspondent: Paula Doraisamy, Administrator, 61 Grosvenor Street, London W1K 3JE (tel: 020 3011 1100)

Trustees: Sir Martyn Arbib; Lady Arbib; Annabel Nicoll.

CC Number: 296358

The foundation's grantmaking is described as follows:

> The charity supports the philanthropy of Sir Martyn Arbib, one of the trustees, and his direct family. Much of the funds are donated to the River and Rowing Museum Foundation, and mainly charities with which the trustees have a connection.

In 2011/12 the foundation had assets of £408,000 and an income of £475,000, in the form a donation from the Arbib family. Grants were made totalling £367,000.

Grants were made during the year under the headings of social welfare, medical, education and children's welfare. Major grants during the year were made to: Langley Academy (£86,000 in total – Annabel Nichol is the sponsor and chair of governors at the academy); and the Institute of Cancer Research and the River and Rowing Museum Foundation (£50,000 each).

Other beneficiaries included: Row to Recovery (£30,000 in total); Alfred Dunhill Foundation and the Barbados Community Foundation (£25,000 each); Ramsbury Recreation Centre (£15,000); RNIB (£11,500 in total); CLIC Sargent (£10,000 in total); Community Security Trust (£5,000); and Bowel Cancer Research Fund and Movember (£1,000 each).

Exclusions
No grants to individuals.

Applications
In writing to the correspondent, although note that grants are largely made to organisations with which the trustees have a connection, and therefore unsolicited applications are unlikely to be successful.

Information gathered from:
Accounts; Charity Commission record.

The Architectural Heritage Fund

Loans and grants for building preservation
£809,000 (2011/12)

Beneficial area
UK (excluding the Channel Islands and the Isle of Man).

Correspondent: Barbara Wright, Loans and Grants Manager, Alhambra House, 27–31 Charing Cross Road, London WC2H 0AU (tel: 020 7925 0199; fax: 020 7930 0295; email: ahf@ahfund.org.uk; website: www.ahfund.org.uk)

Trustees: Colin Amery; Malcolm Crowder; Roy Dantzic; Rita Harkin; George McNeill; Philip Kirby; Merlin Waterson; Thomas Lloyd; Liz Davidson; John Townsend; Michael Hoare; John Duggan.

CC Number: 266780

The Architectural Heritage Fund promotes the permanent preservation for the benefit of the public of historic buildings, monuments or other edifices or structures of particular beauty or historical, architectural or constructional interest in the United Kingdom. The fund provides financial assistance, advice and information to building preservation trusts (BPTs) and other charities and disseminates information about the work of BPTs to statutory and non-statutory bodies, other organisations and the public at large. BPTs, (charities established to preserve historic buildings for the benefit of the nation), operate within defined geographical areas, usually a specific town or county.

The fund seeks to achieve its objects primarily by making grants and low-interest short-term loans to assist BPTs and other charities to acquire and repair buildings which merit preservation for re-use. Grants up to £20,000 are available; loans up to £500,000 (more in exceptional circumstances).

Only organisations with charitable status are eligible for financial assistance from the AHF. Any charity with a qualifying project is entitled to apply for an options appraisal grant, or a loan, but the AHF's other grants are reserved for BPTs.

Financial assistance is available only for buildings that are listed, scheduled or in a conservation area and of acknowledged historic merit. Projects must involve a change either in the ownership of a property or in its use.

In 2011/12 the fund has assets of almost £15.8 million and an income of £4.1 million, which included grants from statutory sources totalling £2.6 million. Grants were made by the AHF totalling £809,000; loans were made to the value of £69,500.

Projects supported included those initiated by: Clophill Heritage Trust; Creetown Building Preservation Trust; Four Acres Charitable Trust; Glasgow Building Preservation Trust; Heritage of London Trust Operations Ltd; Heritage Trust for the North West; Penarth Arts and Crafts Ltd; Rame Conservation Trust; The SAVE Trust; The Sheffield General Cemetery Trust; Tyne and Wear Building Preservation Trust Ltd; Ulverston Ford Park Community Group; The Vivat Trust; and West Midlands Historic Buildings Trust.

The AHF's very useful and informative website features a number of case studies of projects that have received support over the years which potential applicants may find particularly interesting.

The AHF also produces 'Funds for Historic Buildings', a comprehensive guide to funding for anyone seeking to repair, restore or convert historic buildings in the United Kingdom (excluding the Channel Islands and the Isle of Man). It includes details of virtually all substantive funding sources relevant to historic buildings, including statutory and public sources, sources for special categories of project (such as religious buildings in use, sports and the arts and village halls), and local and regional charitable trusts. As well as many (including a variety of regeneration programmes) which provide funding for historic building projects within a wider remit. Funds for Historic Buildings is available to view free at: www.ffhb.org.uk.

Guidelines
The AHF offers the following guidelines on its schemes:

Project Viability Grant
From 1 April 2013 we are offering a new scheme called Project Viability Grants.

This is intended to be a swift initial assessment of whether it is viable to restore or convert a historic building. The grant is for a maximum of £3,000, to fund a short study looking at potential uses for a building and its current condition, to be submitted within six months from the date of an offer being made by the AHF.

Successful completion of this initial stage will be used to judge whether applicants can then apply for our existing Project Development Grant funding.

The grant is administered on a rolling basis, so please contact us at any time. We aim to let you know whether you have been successful within six weeks.

Project Development Grant
The AHF's Project Development Grant scheme is only available to building preservation trusts that are on the AHF's Register of revolving fund BPTs or are members of the UK Association of

11

Preservation Trusts. To qualify the trust must have demonstrated that the end use for the project is likely to be feasible and have decided to take the project forward.

Project development grants are intended to help BPTs with the costs and expenses of developing a project once its viability has been established, and take it towards the point at which work starts on site.

The maximum amount available per project from this grant scheme is £20,000 in total and could include, for example, a combination of:

Administration costs: any reasonable administrative costs relevant to the project (e.g. printing and copying, photography, telephone etc.) may be claimed, up to a limit of £1,000.

The costs of a suitably qualified project organiser to develop and co-ordinate a viable project and take it towards the point at which work starts on site. The project organiser is usually someone appointed for a fee from outside, but could be an employee; the grant will not normally exceed 75% of the project organiser's total cost, up to a limit of £15,000;

Other development costs: a BPT can apply for assistance towards development costs of an eligible project that cannot be recovered from other funders, e.g. the fee cost of business plans. BPTs with paid staff may claim for their own staff time and overheads to produce such items at cost, up to a limit of £7,500;

The costs of a Mentor to work with a less experienced BPT to help them move their project forward up to a limit of £7,500; in some cases this help may be available before an options appraisal is commissioned. Please speak to a member of the AHF's Projects Team for more information.

There is additional grant funding available for projects in Scotland, please speak to a member of the AHF's Projects Team to find out if you are eligible for this extra funding.

Cold Spot Grants Scheme
Any not-for-profit organisation or charity with a qualifying project is eligible for the 'Cold Spot' grant but please talk to one of the members of staff mentioned in the guidance before completing the application form.

The AHF is administering grants of up to £10,000 in total per project. The grants can cover 100% of the total cost of development work – no match funding is required. However applicants are encouraged to seek donations from other sources and should demonstrate clear financial need for the grant.

Grants are intended to cover initial development costs. As long as it is directly related to a project involving the rescue of an historic building, any proposal for development work will be considered.

Low-interest loans
The AHF loan scheme is intended to assist registered charities by making short-term, low-interest loans for acquisition and/or working capital to repair historic buildings. The recipient must have, or acquire, title or a long lease for the historic building to be repaired.

Amount – loans are usually subject to a ceiling of £500,000 with interest charged at 5% for working capital and 7% for acquisition.

Duration – the normal loan period is three years, or until the building is sold, whichever is earlier. The AHF will always consider allowing extra time, if this is requested before the loan falls due for payment, but the AHF does not offer long-term finance.

Security – security can be offered in the form of a repayment guarantee from a bank, local authority or other acceptable institution, or as a first charge over any property (including that for which the loan is required) to which the borrower has a free and marketable title.

Development loans
Development loans are available for any professional work required to develop an eligible project to the point where it is ready to go on site. Under this scheme the AHF is able to make a loan of up to £50,000, secured by a repayment guarantee, for a period of up to 18 months, at an interest charge of 2.5% simpler per annum.

Amount – development loans are subject to a maximum ceiling of £50,000 with interest charged at 2.5% simple. Should a larger AHF working capital loan for the same project be contracted, the interest charged on the development loan will be waived.

Duration – a development loan will normally be for a period of up to eighteen months and will not be extended beyond its due date.

Security – a development loan must be secured by a repayment guarantee, preferably from a local authority.

More detailed guidance on all the AHF's schemes is available from the AHF website.

Exclusions
Applications from private individuals and non-charitable organisations. Applications for projects not involving a change of ownership or of use, or for a building not on a statutory list or in a conservation area.

Applications
Detailed notes for applicants for loans and grants are supplied with the application forms, all of which are available from the fund's website. The trustees meet in March, June, September and December and applications must be received six weeks before meetings.

Common applicant mistakes
'As we don't take applications without prior consultation, mistakes are virtually unknown.'

The Ardeola Charitable Trust

General
£746,000 (2011/12)

Beneficial area
Worldwide.

Correspondent: The Trustees, Coutts and Co., Trustee Dept., 440 Strand, London WC2R 0QS (tel: 020 7753 1000)

Trustees: Graham Barker; Joanna Barker; Coutts and Co.

CC Number: 1124380

This trust was established in 2008 for general charitable purposes.

In 2011/12 it had assets of just under £2.6 million and an income of £565,500, most of which was in the form of a donation from the settlors. Grants were made to three organisations during the year totalling £746,000.

As in previous years, the main beneficiary was Target Ovarian Cancer, which received £600,000 (Joanna Barker is a trustee of the charity). The other beneficiaries were: Durham University (£75,000); and Non-Profit Enterprise and Self-sustainability Team (NESsT) (£71,000).

Applications
In writing to the correspondent, although potential applicants should note that the trust's main beneficiary is connected with the trustees.

The John Armitage Charitable Trust

Medical, relief-in-need, education, religion
£1.4 million (2011/12)

Beneficial area
England and Wales.

Correspondent: John Armitage, Trustee, c/o Sampson West, 34 Ely Place, London EC1N 6TD (tel: 020 7404 5040; fax: 020 7831 1098; email: finance@sampsonwest.co.uk)

Trustees: John Armitage; Catherine Armitage; William Francklin; Celina Francklin.

CC Number: 1079688

Established in 2000, this is the trust of John Armitage, co-founder of Egerton Capital, the City-based hedge fund. 'The principal objective of the trust is to provide financial support for charitable and worthy causes at the discretion of the trustees in accordance with the trust deed.'

In 2011/12 the trust had assets of £39.5 million, an income of £1.5 million and gave grants to 42 organisations totalling £1.4 million, broken down into the following categories:

General	£447,500
Medical research/medical care	£283,000
Advancement of education	£259,500
Religion	£255,000
Poverty, disability, age religion	£208,000

Beneficiaries included: The Thames Diamond Jubilee Foundation and Westminster Abbey Foundation (£100,000 each); Marie Curie Cancer Care (£72,000); National Churches Trust and Russian Revival Project (£60,000 each); Sir John Soanes Museum Trust (£50,000); Independence at Home, Miracles, Redress and Youth Sport Trust (£36,000 each); Bibury School (£27,000); Fishmongers Company Charitable Trust and New Horizon Youth (£24,000 each); Only Connect (£17,000); Barnsley Parochial Church Council (£10,000); and Aspire (£5,000).

Applications

In writing to the correspondent. Applications received by the trust are 'reviewed by the trustees and grants awarded at their discretion'.

Information gathered from:

Accounts; annual report; Charity Commission record.

The Ashden Trust

Environment, homelessness, sustainable regeneration, community arts

£1.3 million (2011/12)

Beneficial area

UK and overseas.

Correspondent: Alan Bookbinder, Director, The Peak, 5 Wilton Road, London SW1V 1AP (tel: 020 7410 0330; fax: 020 7410 0332; email: ashdentrust@ sfct.org.uk; website: www.ashdentrust. org.uk)

Trustees: Sarah Butler-Sloss; Robert Butler-Sloss; Judith Portrait.

CC Number: 802623

This is one of the Sainsbury Family Charitable Trusts, which share a joint administration. They have a common approach to grantmaking which is described in the entry for the group as a whole.

Sarah Butler-Sloss (née Sainsbury) is the settlor of this trust and she has been continuing to build up its endowment, with donations and gifts in 2011/12 of £500,000. Total income during the year was £1.4 million including investment income. Its asset value stood at £28.5 million. Grants were paid during the year totalling £1.3 million.

Grantmaking

This trust's main areas of interest are (with the value of grants paid in 2011/12):

Ashden Awards – sustainable solutions, better lives	46.8%	£617,000
Avoiding Deforestation (Low Carbon Fund)	8.3%	£110,000
Climate Change Collaboration (Low Carbon Fund)	7.9%	£105,000
Sustainable Regeneration	7.7%	£102,000
People at Risk	6.3%	£84,000
Sustainable Development – UK	5.1%	£68,000
Arts and Sustainability	4.6%	£61,000
General	4.3%	£57,000
Green Finance (Low Carbon Fund)	4.1%	£54,000
Sustainable Development – International	3%	£40,000
Cultural Shift (Low Carbon Fund)	1.9%	£25,500

The following information about the trust's grantmaking in 2011/12 is taken from its helpful and descriptive annual report:

Ashden Awards – sustainable solutions, better lives

Since Ashden was founded in 2001 it has rewarded over 150 projects in the UK and the developing world. To date £2.7 million has been awarded in prize money and £8.5 million has been leveraged for winning projects. Collectively, Ashden winners are now benefitting over 33 million people, and reducing CO2 emissions by more than four million tonnes a year.

Ashden's experience over the past eleven years has shown that just giving organisations a prize is not enough. It is now working with winners to help them develop and grow. It also collates and disseminates knowledge on successful approaches and is actively engaged in advocacy, using winners as exemplars to influence policy and to add informed comment to debates on energy. Ashden's website is a major resource for anyone interested in sustainable energy: www. ashdenawards.org.

Award winners for 2011 included: Barefoot Power – Africa, National Trust – Wales, Parity Projects, Shri Kshethra Dharmasthala Rural Development Project – South India, Student Switch Off and University Hospital of South Manchester NHS Foundation Trust.

Preventing Deforestation

The trust recognises the vital role that forests play in sequestering and storing

carbon and also in providing 'eco-system services'. The trust has made grants to projects which address the issues from a number of perspectives; from the land rights of indigenous people to the value of carbon in forests as part of the Reducing Emissions from Deforestation and Forest Degradation (REDD) programme to highlighting and spotlighting illegal forest clearances.

Climate Change Collaboration (Low Carbon Fund)

The Collaboration was created in 2009 by four of the Sainsbury Family Charitable Trusts – the Ashden Trust, the J J Charitable Trust, the Mark Leonard Trust and the Tedworth Charitable Trust.

The primary aim of the collaboration is to identify and support projects that accelerate progress towards a low carbon society. Currently the trusts are making significant grants towards work on domestic energy efficiency in the UK guided by advice from experts in the fields of finance, economics, the environment and sustainable living. Proposals are generally invited by the trustees or initiated at their request. Unsolicited applications are not encouraged unless they are aligned with the trustees' interests.

The trustees prefer to support innovative schemes that can be successfully replicated or become self-sustaining.

Sustainable Regeneration

Funding in this category is for projects which support the development of sustainable communities especially projects that encourage greater links to the natural environment and growing food in deprived communities and with disadvantaged people.

There was one grant approved in this category: Vauxhall City Farm – £45,000 (over three years) – towards salaries for workers in the farmyard who care for the animals and support the range of education activities that take place there.

People at Risk

Grants are made to organisations which help people at risk of homelessness to obtain support, secure permanent accommodation, regain economic independence and reconnect with important family and social networks.

Over the years the trust has provided considerable help to projects where housing is seen as only part of the solution, and where there is awareness of the value for people at risk of cultivating their sense of personal identity, of aspiration for life and livelihood, and of belonging among family and friends.

In this and the Sustainable Regeneration category, the trust assists projects that pioneer fresh approaches in self-help and peer support, education and training, and opportunities leading to employment for people at risk, and other socially excluded groups, especially where social enterprise can lead to inspiration and achievement.

Approved grants for this year include:

- St Christopher's Fellowship – £28,000 – towards The Wrap Challenge and information film-making by young people at risk
- Manna Society – £5,000 – towards the set up and first year's work of an English language and literacy service for homeless foreign nationals in south central London

Sustainable Development – UK

The trust initiates and supports work that can reduce the speed and impact of climate change including energy efficiency and renewable energy technology, aviation and transport policy, and the wide ranging benefits of sustainable agriculture. In the area of climate change, sustainable energy and sustainable agriculture, the trust aims to take a broad approach supporting research, practical action, awareness-raising, education and organisations that aim to influence policy in the field.

Examples of grants approved this year include:

- World Wildlife Fund (WWF) UK – £60,000 (over three years) – towards staff time and running costs to continue the work of the 1 in 5 Challenge in which WWF works with major companies to reduce business flights by 20% and advises the UK Government on the implication of reduced business travel for UK aviation policy
- Sustainable Food Trust – £5,000 – support for review into where the grant-making activity of Ashden Trust and Mark Leonard Trust can have greatest impact to support sustainable food and farming

Arts and Sustainability

The trust continues to support the rapidly developing field of arts and sustainability, in particular initiatives that encourage artists, writers and arts organisations to engage with current environmental issues through their work. The guiding aim is to encourage people to think about climate change in as many ways as possible, to break down the idea of climate change, which has become heavily politicised, into a variety of narratives (migration, resource shortage, climate science, social justice, East/West relations) and to encourage responses that have imaginative force on the one side and academic rigour on the other.

The trust continues to fund the Ashden Directory of Environment and Performance: www.ashdendirectory.org.uk.

General

Grants approved in this category included those to: MERLIN towards its emergency response to the drought in Somalia (£10,000); and AKU Society towards medical research (£500).

Green Finance (Low Carbon Fund)

Support is given towards the development of financial products and services to support the transition to a low-carbon economy.

Sustainable Development – International

The trust continues to support community-based sustainable technology projects which aim to equip people with the knowledge and tools to help themselves in an environmentally sustainable way. These projects help to alleviate poverty by using sustainable technologies for the enhancement of income generation, agriculture, education and health.

Examples of grants approved this year include:

- ACE Africa – £15,000 (over three years) – towards community work with vulnerable people in Kenya and Tanzania and to share lessons between NGOs in the region
- Green Belt Movement – £4,000 – towards the memorial event with HRH The Prince of Wales for Wangari Maathai at Kew Gardens being organised by the Green Belt Movement for spring 2013

Cultural Shift (Low Carbon Fund)

The transition towards a low-carbon economy and low-carbon lifestyles has many cultural components. The work in this funding stream encourages projects in the arts and the media that imaginatively engage with this shift.

Grants included: Julie's Bicycle (£45,000 over three years) towards core costs of working with the arts and creative industries to cut carbon emissions and make environmental sustainability a core component of their work; and Culture and Climate Change (£1,000) towards the distribution and marketing of 'Culture and Climate Change: Recordings'.

Exclusions

The trustees generally do not make grants in response to unsolicited applications. However, see 'Applications'.

Applications

Who should apply?

If your organisation has a proven track record in supplying local, sustainable energy solutions in the UK or in the developing world then you should read the guidelines for the Ashden Awards for Sustainable Energy [available on the trust's website].

The Ashden Trust is one of the Sainsbury Family Charitable Trusts. Before applying read the guidelines below. For further, more detailed information visit the trust's website.

- We primarily support programmes which have a focus on climate change, sustainable development or on improving the quality of life in poorer communities. Generally, we do not accept unsolicited approaches, unless they are exceptional proposals which closely fit our specific areas of interest
- The trustees take a proactive approach to the work they wish to support,

employing a range of specialist staff and advisers to research their areas of interest and bring forward suitable proposals. It should therefore be understood that the majority of unsolicited proposals we receive will be unsuccessful

- The trust does not normally fund individuals for projects, educational fees or to join expeditions; support for general appeal or circular; work that is routine or well-proven elsewhere or with a low impact; or work that is the responsibility of central or local government, health trusts or health authorities, or which are substantially funded by them. We never support retrospective funding, that is, work that has already been completed.
- Do not apply to more than one of the Sainsbury Family Charitable Trusts. Each application will be considered by each trust which may have an interest in this field.

If you would like to apply to the trust you should send a brief description of the proposed project, by post, to the director, or email your application to: ashdentrust@sfct.org.uk.

The proposed project needs to cover:

- The aims and objectives of the project
- Why the project is needed
- How, where, when the project will be delivered
- Who will benefit and in what way
- How the project will continue once your funding has come to an end
- Income and expenditure budget
- Details of funding – secured, applied for
- Description of the organisation

Information gathered from:

Accounts; annual report; Charity Commission record; funder's website.

Autonomous Research Charitable Trust

General
£244,000 (2011/12)

Beneficial area
UK, mainly London, and Africa.

Correspondent: Keith Lawrence, Administrator, Moore Stephens, 150 Aldersgate Street, London EC1A 4AB (tel: 020 7334 9191; email: keith.lawrence@moorestephens.com)

Trustees: Graham Stuart; Britta Schmidt; Nathalie Garner; Neeta Atkar.

CC Number: 1137503

This trust was established in 2010 for general charitable purposes. It is the charitable trust of Autonomous Research, a company that provides intelligence on banking and insurance companies. The focus of the trust appears to be making grants to organisations working with children and young people and older people.

According to the company's website, 5% of its annual profits are donated to charitable causes, presumably through the trust, although no information on how much this amounts to was available.

The following information is taken from the trust's 2011/12 annual report and accounts:

The core aims of the charity are:
- To help disadvantaged people get a step up in life
- To empower people to improve the quality of their lives
- To focus our resources upon a small number of key partner charities – both in London and abroad – where we feel we can make a difference and establish long-term relationships.

The charity carries out these aims and objectives by:
- Providing funding to other recognised charitable institutions and
- Providing mentoring business and career advice and a variety of other hands-on roles

The charity has established its grantmaking policy to achieve its objectives for the public benefit to improve the lives of people suffering from financial hardship.

The trustees consider and agree a short-list of charities that are to be core partner charities for that year. Specific support will be directed to these organisations, with meetings and other feedback being sought, as well as considering other worthy causes that fall within the criteria and aims of the trustees. Alongside the core charity partners, the charity maintains discretional funds for ad hoc distributions.

Unsolicited applications are accepted but due to the high number of applications, most are unsuccessful. The trustees are proactive in their giving and prefer to support causes about which they have undertaken their own research and which fall in with the criteria for the year.

Grants are monitored and only continue where they satisfy the trustees' requirements.

In 2011/12 the charity had assets of £164,000 and an income of £278,500. Grants were made to 13 organisations and totalled £244,000.

Beneficiaries included: One Degree – The Adnan Jaffery Educational Trust (£95,000); Plan UK and Tusk (£63,000 each); Macmillan Cancer UK (£6,000); Group B Strep Support and Hakuna Matata (£2,000 each); and Cardiac Risk in the Young and Get Kids Going (£1,500 each).

Applications
In writing to the correspondent.

Information gathered from:
Accounts; annual report; Charity Commission record.

Awards for All (see also the Big Lottery Fund)

General
England – £55.2 million awarded to 6,698 projects; Northern Ireland – £3.9 million awarded to 487 projects; Scotland – £11.5 million to 1,638 projects; Wales – £3.1 million to 846 projects (2012/13)

Beneficial area
UK.

Correspondent: See 'General' section for full details of contacts., (See General section) (tel: BIGAdviceLine:08454102030; website: www.awardsforall.org.uk)

Awards for All is a Big Lottery Fund grants scheme funding small, local community-based projects in the UK. Each country in the UK administers its own programme. The following information is reproduced from Awards for All's website.

England
Awards for All gives groups a quick and easy way to get small Lottery grants of between £300 and £10,000.

We want to fund projects which address the issues, needs and aspirations of local communities and people. We will fund a wide range of community projects aimed at developing skills, improving health, revitalising the local environment and enabling people to become more active citizens.

You can apply to Awards for All England if you are a community group, not for profit group, parish or town council, health body, or school. You do not need to be a registered charity to apply.

You must have a bank account that requires at least two people to sign each cheque or withdrawal.

You must use the grant within one year.

See the Q&A document for more information, and read the guidance notes before applying.

We will pay for activities that will benefit the community, including:
- Putting on an event, activity or performance
- Buying new equipment or materials
- Running training courses
- Setting up a pilot project or starting up a new group
- Carrying out special repairs or conservation work

- Paying expenses for volunteers, costs for sessional workers or professional fees
- Transport costs.

You must read the guidance notes carefully before filling in the application form. We have very clear criteria as to what we can and can't fund.

Please note: There are amendments to the guidance notes and application form
- Read the Guidance notes before you apply
- Make sure you are using the latest version of Adobe Reader (you need it to fill in the form)
- Save the application form to your computer and then open it using Adobe Reader
- Email the completed form to englandapplications@awardsforall.org.uk at least 3 months before you want your project to start
- We'll let you know our decision in six weeks

Contact details
If you need more information email general.enquiries@awardsforall.org.uk or call the team for advice on 0845 410 2030

Northern Ireland
Awards for All Northern Ireland gives groups a quick and easy way to get small Lottery grants of between £500 and £10,000. You can apply if you are a voluntary or community organisation, or a statutory organisation. You do not need to be a registered charity to apply. Application may be made at any time and you will normally hear the decision in three months.

You can apply for funding for a wide range of community based projects that involve people in charitable, health, education and environmental related activities.

We want our money to make a difference by helping people to:
- Participate in their communities to bring about positive change
- Develop their skills and widen their experiences
- Work towards better and safer communities
- Improve their physical and mental health and well-being

It is hoped that these projects will improve people's lives and will strengthen community activity.

You can apply for funding for activities including:
- Developing an existing service in your area, such as a playgroup, lunch club or information centre
- Helping more people to play a fuller part in local life, for example, producing a community newsletter, talking newspapers for people who are blind or visually impaired, mobility schemes or respite services

- Helping your neighbourhood organisation to set up a new service in your community
- Small improvements to premises that you own or lease
- Developing skills for volunteers and committee members
- Creating a wildlife garden
- Start-up costs for a community composting scheme
- Encouraging activities to promote healthier lives and good mental health such as keep fit classes for older people.

We welcome applications for projects combining a range of community activities. We will give priority to applications which increase opportunities for volunteering or build community capacity. We will also give priority to projects with activities that are new or develop what you do now and to those projects which have not previously received funding from Awards for All.

Make sure you read the programme details carefully, as we have very clear criteria as to what we will and won't fund.

You can type directly into the electronic application form, but, you must save the form to your own computer first, and you must have the latest version of Adobe Reader installed to be able to save your answers.

Full details on how to apply are contained in the guidance notes which together with the application form can be downloaded from the AWA Northern Ireland website.

For enquiries relating to Awards for All Northern Ireland contact: Outreach team, Big Lottery Fund, 1 Cromac Quay, Cromac Wood, Ormeau Road, Belfast BT7 2JD; tel: 02890 551455; Fax: 02890 551445; textphone: 02890 551431; Email: enquiries.ni@biglotteryfund.org.uk. Open hours: 9am – 5pm, Monday – Friday.

Scotland

Awards for All Scotland is a quick and easy way to get small Lottery grants of between £500 and £10,000. The programme aims to help people become actively involved in projects that bring about change in their local community. This could be through a wide range of community, arts, sports, health, education and environmental activities. There are no deadlines and applications from not-for-profit/voluntary or community sector group, community council, school or health organisations, can be submitted at any time.

We want to fund projects that will achieve one or more of the following outcomes:
- People have better chances in life
- Communities are safer, stronger and more able to work together to tackle inequalities
- People have better and more sustainable services and environments
- People and communities are healthier

Our priorities are listed in more detail in the guidance notes. It should be noted that meeting one or more of these priorities is not essential to receive funding.

One of our priorities is projects taking place in areas we would like to see receive more funding from Awards for All. This is based on our analysis of where our funding has gone to date. These are different for each of the three lottery distributors involved in Awards for All.

Applications coming from arts or sports groups are mostly likely to be considered through Creative Scotland or sportscotland. Other groups will usually be considered through Big Lottery Fund. Schools will always be Big Lottery Fund even if they are running an arts or sports project.

For example, an application from a theatre group wanting to hold a performance would be considered by Creative Scotland. A school applying for football equipment would be considered by Big Lottery Fund and not sportscotland.

Big Lottery Fund	Creative Scotland	sportscotland
Aberdeen City	Aberdeen City	Angus
Aberdeenshire	Falkirk	Clackmannanshire
East Ayrshire	Inverclyde	Dundee City
East Lothian	Perth & Kinross	East Renfrewshire
North Ayrshire	Renfrewshire	Falkirk
Perth & Kinross	West Lothian	Shetland Islands

Areas that feature in the 15% most deprived data zones in the Scottish Index of Multiple Deprivation are one of our other priorities.

Small towns (those with a population of 3,000 to 10,000) are also a priority. You can check this by entering a postcode through the Scottish Neighbourhood Statistics.

Contact details:

For advice on completing the application form and any general queries you have about the scheme you can call the Information and Events Officers on 0870 240 2391 and you can also email them at scotland@awardsforall.org.uk. The postal address is: Awards for All, 4th Floor, 1 Atlantic Quay, 1 Robertson Street, Glasgow G2 8JB; Tel: 01412 421400; Fax: 01412 421401; textphone: 01412 421500.

Wales

Awards for All Wales provides voluntary and community groups with a quick and easy way to get small National Lottery grants of between £500 and £5,000 for projects which aim to help improve local communities and the lives of people most in need.

The programme encourages a wide range of community, health, educational and environmental projects from community, not for profit groups, community or town council, health bodies or schools. You do not need to be a registered charity to apply for Awards for All.

We will pay for activities including:
- Putting on an event, activity or performance
- Buying new equipment or materials
- Running training courses
- Setting up a pilot project or starting up a new group
- Educational toys and games and information technology equipment
- Paying expenses for volunteers, costs for sessional workers or professional fees
- Transport costs and refurbishment

But we won't pay for:
- Activities that happen or start before we confirm our grant
- Any costs you incur when putting together your application
- Day-to-day running costs (for example, utility bills, council tax, rent and insurance)
- Contingency costs
- Endowments
- Feasibility studies
- Fundraising activities for your organisation or others
- Items that mainly benefit individuals (for example, equipment that is not shared)
- Existing activities and repeat or regular events including those that we have funded before

Contact details: tel: 0845 410 2030; fax: 01686 622458; textphone: 0845 602 1659; email: enquiries.wales@biglotteryfund. org.uk.

Exclusions

Visit the individual country's webpages for full details of those organisations/projects/activities that Awards for All programmes exclude.

Applications

Application forms are simple and straightforward and are available from Awards for All's webpages on the Big Lottery Fund's website: www. biglotteryfund.org.uk.

Information gathered from:

All information is accessible through the useful and informative Awards for All webpages on the Big Lottery Fund website.

Backstage Trust

General, the arts

Beneficial area
UK.

Correspondent: Lady Susan Sainsbury, Trustee, North House, 27 Great Peter Street, London SW1P 3LN (tel: 020 7072 4590; email: info@backstagetrust.org.uk)

Trustees: Lady Susan Sainsbury; Dominic Flynn; David Wood.

CC Number: 1145887

The trust was established in February 2012 by Lady Susan Sainsbury for general charitable purposes. In practice, the trust's priorities are likely to be focused on the arts, particularly theatre and the performing arts. Lady Sainsbury is the deputy chair of both the Royal Shakespeare Company and the Royal Academy of Music, and she and her husband, Lord David Sainsbury of Turville, are high profile patrons of the arts.

Applications

In writing to the correspondent.

Information gathered from:

Charity Commission record.

The Baily Thomas Charitable Fund

Learning disability

£2.6 million (2011/12)

Beneficial area

UK.

Correspondent: Ann Cooper, Secretary to the Trustees, c/o TMF Management (UK) Ltd, 400 Capability Green, Luton LU1 3AE (tel: 01582 439225; fax: 01582 439206; email: info@bailythomas.org.uk; website: www.bailythomas.org.uk)

Trustees: Prof. Sally-Ann Cooper; Prof. Anne Farmer; Suzanne Jane Marriott; Kenneth Young.

CC Number: 262334

This charity is dedicated solely to the well-being of those with learning disabilities. It combines one or two major funding programmes with an extensive programme of generally one-off medium and smaller grants, which are divided between revenue and capital costs.

The fund gives the following general guidance on its useful and informative website:

The Baily Thomas Charitable Fund is a grant making registered charity which was established primarily to aid the research into learning disability and to aid the care and relief of those affected by learning disability by making grants to voluntary organisations working in this field.

We consider under learning disability the conditions generally referred to as severe learning difficulties, together with autism. In this area, we consider projects concerning children or adults. Learning disability, thus defined, is our priority for funding. We do not give grants for research into or care of those with mental illness or dyslexia.

Applications will only be considered from voluntary organisations which are registered charities or are associated with a registered charity. Schools and Parent Teachers Associations and Industrial & Provident Societies can also apply. The fund does not currently accept appeals from Community Interest Companies.

In 2011/12 the charity had assets of £77.8 million and an income of £1.7 million. There were 288 grants made during the year totalling over £2.6 million. The trustees' annual report states that the fall in grantmaking over the previous year is as a result of the projected fall in incoming resources and available reserves, and is not a reflection of a change in the trustees' grantmaking policy. All grants over £25,000 are listed in the accounts.

Beneficiaries included: Kings College London – Institute of Psychiatry (£187,000 in two grants); University of Edinburgh (£131,000); Autistica (£100,000); Rix-Thompson-Rothenberg Foundation (£70,000); Berwickshire Housing Association (£50,000); Papworth Trust (£40,000); and Grace Eyre Foundation, Hextol Foundation, National Family Carer Network and Young Epilepsy (£25,000 each).

Exclusions

Grants are not normally awarded to individuals. The following areas are unlikely to receive funding:

- Hospices
- Minibuses except those for residential and/or day care services for people with learning disabilities
- Advocacy projects
- Arts and theatre projects
- Conductive education projects
- Swimming and hydro-therapy pools
- Physical disabilities unless accompanied by significant learning disabilities

Applications

Meetings of the trustees are usually held in April and October each year and applicants are advised to visit the charity's website for details of current deadlines. The website states that late applications will not be considered. If your application is considered under the Small Grants procedure then this will be reviewed by the trustees ahead of the usual meetings. Following the meeting all applicants are contacted formally to advise on the status of their application. Feel free to submit your application whenever you are ready, rather than waiting for the deadline.

Applications must be made online via the charity's website, from which the following information is taken:

General applications

Funding is normally considered for capital and revenue costs and for both specific projects and general running/core costs.

Grants are awarded for amounts from £250 and depend on a number of factors including the purpose, the total funding requirement and the potential sources of other funds including, in some cases, matching funding.

Normally one-off grants are awarded but exceptionally a new project may be funded over two or three years, subject to satisfactory reports of progress.

Grants should normally be taken up within one year of the issue of the grant offer letter which will include conditions relating to the release of the grant.

The following areas of work normally fall within the fund's policy:

- Capital building/renovation/ refurbishment works for residential, nursing and respite care, and schools
- Employment schemes including woodwork, crafts, printing and horticulture
- Play schemes and play therapy schemes
- Day and social activities centres including building costs and running costs
- Support for families, including respite schemes
- Independent living schemes
- Support in the community schemes
- Snoezelen rooms

Research applications

We generally direct our limited funds towards the initiation of research so that it can progress to the point at which there is sufficient data to support an application to one of the major funding bodies.

How to apply

Applications will only be considered from established research workers and will be subject to normal professional peer review procedures.

Applications, limited to five pages with the type no smaller than Times New Roman 12, should be in the form of a scientific summary with a research plan to include a brief background and a short account of the design of the study and number of subjects, the methods of assessment and analysis, timetable, main outcomes and some indication of other opportunities arising from the support of such research.

A detailed budget of costs should be submitted together with a justification for the support requested. Details should be included of any other applications for funding which have been made to other funders and their outcomes, if known.

The fund does not contribute towards university overheads.

A one page curriculum vitae will be required for each of the personnel actually carrying out the study and for their supervisor together with a note of the total number of their peer reviewed publications and details of the ten most significant publications.

Evidence may be submitted of the approval of the ethics committee of the applicant to the study and approval of the university for the application to the fund.

An 80 word lay summary should also be submitted with the scientific summary.

Any papers submitted in excess of those stipulated above will not be passed to the research committee for consideration.

Before submitting a full application, researchers may submit a one page summary of the proposed study so that the trustees may indicate whether they are prepared to consider a full application.

Percentage of awards given to new applicants: between 30% and 40%.

Common applicant mistakes

'They do not answer the question in fitting to the fund's remit.'

Information gathered from:

Accounts; annual report; Charity Commission record; further information provided by the funder; funder's website.

The Balcombe Charitable Trust

Education, environment, health and welfare
£423,000 (2011/12)

Beneficial area

UK and overseas.

Correspondent: Jonathan W. Prevezer, Administrator, c/o Citroen Wells, Devonshire House, 1 Devonshire Street, London W1W 5DR (tel: 020 7304 2000; email: jonathan.prevezer@citroenwells. co.uk)

Trustees: R. A. Kreitman; Patricia M. Kreitman; Nicholas Brown.

CC Number: 267172

This trust generally makes grants in the fields of education, the environment and health and welfare. It only supports registered charities. One of the trustees, Patricia Kreitman, is a writer, broadcaster, environmental campaigner and former psychologist. She is also a trustee and fellow of the Durrell Wildlife Conservation Trust.

In 2011/12 it had assets of £25.7 million and an income of £722,000. Grants were made to 18 organisations totalling £423,000, and were broken down as follows:

Health and welfare	£300,000
Environment	£114,500
Education	£8,500

Beneficiaries included: Durrell Wildlife Conservation Trust (£114,500); Samaritans (£38,000); Brook Advisory Centres Ltd (£30,000); Oxfam (£25,000); Who Cares Trust and Christian Aid (£20,000 each); Beating Bowel Cancer (£15,000); Platform 51 (£12,500); Tel Aviv University Trust (£8,500); and the 999 Club Trust (£5,000).

Exclusions

No grants to individuals or non-registered charities.

Applications

In writing to the correspondent.

Information gathered from:

Accounts; annual report; Charity Commission record.

The Band Trust

People with disabilities, children and young people, scholarships, hospices and hospitals, education, older people and people who are disadvantaged
£649,000 (2011/12)

Beneficial area

UK.

Correspondent: Richard J. S. Mason, Trustee, Moore Stephens, 150 Aldersgate Street, London EC1A 4AB (tel: 020 7334 9191; fax: 020 7248 3408; email: richard. mason@moorestephens.com; website: www.bandtrust.co.uk)

Trustees: The Hon. Nicholas Wallop; The Hon. Nicholas Wallop; Richard J. S. Mason; Bruce G. Streather.

CC Number: 279802

The trust was established in 1976 for general charitable purposes and beneficiaries are registered charities in the UK. The trust describes its policy as follows:

[The trust] aids persons (primarily those who are residents of the United Kingdom) who are in need of education or care, whether wholly or partially, including those who are ill, disabled or injured, old and infirm or children with special needs. Such aid will be given through making grants to the providers of care such as institutions and homes. The trustees' policy is to devote the greater part of their available income to the foregoing needs with a smaller part going to particular charitable objectives chosen by the settlors of the trust personally during their lifetime or known to meet their wishes, including certain scholarships. The trustees individually identify potential recipients for donations who fall within the trust's objectives during the year. Each of the potential recipients is considered by the trustees collectively and if a grant is approved an appropriate donation is determined. Since the trustees identify sufficient potential recipients to whom to distribute the whole of the income of the trust, the trustees do not wish to receive unsolicited applications for grants. The trustees continue their policy of visiting or otherwise contacting recipients of grants to ensure that the anticipated benefit has been realised from the grant.

In 2011/12 the trust had assets of £23.3 million and an income of £783,000. There were 92 grants were made during the year totalling £649,000 broken down as follows:

Disabled	17	£232,500
Children and young people	7	£100,000
Disadvantaged	4	£42,500
Educational	4	£36,000
Scholarships*	2	£50,000
Nursing	3	£30,000
Hospice and hospital	2	£20,000
Miscellaneous (up to £2,000)	42	£18,500
Elderly	7	£53,000
Ex-employees	1	£13,000
Army	1	£35,000
Victims	2	£17,500

Beneficiaries across all categories included: NSPCC (£45,000); National Memorial Arboretum (£35,000); U Can Do It (£30,000); Victim Support (£15,000); Stanley Spencer Gallery, Norfolk Hospice and Cancer Research UK (£10,000 each); Church Housing Trust (£7,500); and the Barristers Benevolent Fund (£2,000).

*The scholarship funds were awarded to the Florence Nightingale Foundation and the Honourable Society of Gray's Inn (£25,000 each).

Exclusions

No grants are made to individuals.

Applications

The trustees do not wish to receive unsolicited applications for grants as they themselves identify sufficient potential recipients of grants who fulfil their criteria from information that is in the public domain. If they require further information, they will request this from the potential candidates identified.

Trustees' meetings are held at least three times a year.

Information gathered from:

Accounts; Charity Commission record; funder's website.

The Barcapel Foundation

Health, heritage, youth
Around £700,000 (2012)

Beneficial area

Scotland and other parts of the UK.

Correspondent: Mia McCartney, Administrator, The Mews, Skelmorlie Castle, Skelmorlie, Ayrshire PA17 5EY (tel: 01475 521616; email: admin@ barcapelfoundation.org; website: www. barcapelfoundation.org)

Trustees: Robert Wilson; Amanda Richards; Jed Wilson; Clement Wilson; Niall Scott.

SC Number: SC009211

The foundation was established in 1964 after the sale of the family business, Scottish Animal Products. The following information is taken from the foundation's website:

The three priority areas of interest for funding are:

Health
The foundation supports all aspects of health, a wide ranging remit acknowledging that 'health is a state of complete physical, mental and social well-being and not merely the absence of disease or infirmity.

Heritage
The original financiers of the foundation had a keen interest in our heritage, specifying that one of the foundation's aims was the preservation and beautification of historic properties. The foundation continues to support the built environment and will support our literary and artistic heritage as well as architectural.

Youth
The development of people is one of the principal objectives of the foundation. Whilst charitable giving can be used to alleviate problems it can also be used to empower people and this is particularly true of the young.

In 2012 the foundation had an income of £201,000 and a total expenditure of £833,000.

Grant beneficiaries for 2012 and 2013 include: Great Ormond Street Hospital (£60,000); Macmillan Cancer Support (£44,500); Innerpeffray Library (£42,500); St Mark's Hospital (£40,000); National Youth Theatre, Prince's Trust Scotland and PRIME (£25,000 each); Place2Be (£20,000); and Edinburgh Art Festival and The Beacon Centre (£15,000).

Exclusions
No support for:
- Individual applications for travel or similar
- Organisations or individuals engaged in promoting religious or political beliefs
- Applications for funding costs of feasibility studies or similar

Support is unlikely to be given for local charities whose work takes place outside the British Isles.

Applications
A preliminary application form can be downloaded from the foundation's website. Ensure that interests, aims and objectives are compatible with those of the foundation. A copy of your latest accounts must accompany the application. Applications are not accepted by email.

Information gathered from:
OSCR record; funder's website.

The Barclay Foundation

Medical research, young people, the elderly, people with disabilities, the sick and the disadvantaged
£1.6 million (2012)

Beneficial area
Not defined, in practice, UK.

Correspondent: Michael Seal, Administrator, 3rd Floor, 20 St James's Street, London SW1A 1ES (tel: 020 7915 0915; email: mseal@ellerman.co.uk)

Trustees: Sir David Barclay; Sir Frederick Barclay; Lord Alistair McAlpine of West Green; Aidan Barclay; Howard Barclay.

CC Number: 803696

The foundation was established in 1989 by brothers, Sir David and Sir Frederick Barclay who provide all of the funds. The objects of the foundation are wide and the trustees distribute the income at their own discretion for general charitable purposes.

In 2012 the trust had an income of £1.6 million from donations. Grants were made totalling almost £1.6 million.

The beneficiaries were: Great Ormond Street Children's Hospital (£1 million); the Prince's Foundation (£250,000 in two grants); University of Oxford (£147,500); the Healing Foundation (£100,000); Elton John AIDS Foundation (£50,000); and the Make-A-Wish Foundation (£18,000).

Applications
Applications should be in writing, clearly outlining the details of the proposed project, (for medical research, as far as possible in lay terms). The total cost and duration should be stated; also the amount, if any, which has already been raised.

Following an initial screening, applications are selected according to their merits, suitability and funds available. Visits are usually made to projects where substantial funds are involved.

The foundation welcomes reports as to progress and requires these on the completion of a project.

Information gathered from:
Accounts; Charity Commission record.

The Baring Foundation

Strengthening the voluntary sector, arts and international development
£2.5 million (2012)

Beneficial area
England and Wales, with a special interest in London, Merseyside, Cornwall and Devon; also UK charities working with NGO partners in developing countries.

Correspondent: David Cutler, Director, 60 London Wall, London EC2M 5TQ (tel: 020 7767 1348; fax: 020 7767 7121; email: baring.foundation@uk.ing.com; website: www.baringfoundation.org.uk)

Trustees: Amanda Jordan, Chair; Mark Baring; Geoffrey Barnett; Prof. Ann Buchanan; David Elliott; Katherine Garrett-Cox; Janet Morrison; Andrew Hind; Ranjit Sondhi; Dr Danny Sriskandarajah; Christopher Steane; Prof. Myles Wickstead.

CC Number: 258583

Established in 1969, the Baring Foundation's purpose is to improve the quality of life of people suffering disadvantage and discrimination. Its main objective is to help build stronger voluntary organisations, which serve those people, directly or indirectly, both in this country and abroad. This is achieved by making grants to voluntary and other civil society organisations and by adding value including through promoting knowledge and influencing others.

The foundation's values are:
We:
- Believe in the fundamental value of an independent and effective civil society both nationally and internationally. Civil society identifies new needs and ways to meet these. It engages citizens, giving them voice in a unique way, holding the powerful to account
- Use our funds to strengthen voluntary sector organisations, responding flexibly, creatively and pragmatically to their needs and with a determination to achieve value for money
- Aspire to help to create enduring change both in the lives of those served by the work we are funding and by building the capacity of organisations to become more sustainable and resilient
- Put high value on learning from organisations and their beneficiaries. We seek to add value to our grants by encouraging the communication of knowledge through a variety of means, including influencing others
- Seek to build positive, purposeful relationships with grant recipients, as well as with other grant makers
- Aim to treat grant-seekers and recipients with courtesy and respect,

being as accessible as possible within clear programme guidelines and maintaining consistently high standards of administrative efficiency

Grant programmes

Potential applicants are advised to check the website for current guidelines and up-to-date information on deadlines for applications. The following information was taken from the foundation's website:

Arts and Older People 2014

We will continue to fund under the theme of Arts and older people. We are supporting the Arts and Older People programme run by the Arts Council Northern Ireland and details of this can be found at: www.artscouncil-ni.org. Other decisions for 2014 have not yet been made but we may be in a position to announce a limited open programme in April [2014].

International Development Programme 2014

No grants will be made under this programme in 2014. A full review will take place and a new programme will be announced in 2015.

Strengthening the Voluntary Sector programme 2014

This will continue to fund under the theme of Future Advice. We will review this programme with several under partners in the first quarter of 2014 and it likely that we will announce a new funding round in late April [2014].

Visit the website for up-to-date information on the status of the above programmes.

Grantmaking in 2012

In 2012 the foundation had assets of £59 million and an income of £2.1 million. The Review of Activities states that 65 grants were made totalling £2.5 million. The financial statements within the Review show a figure of £3.6 million and it may be that this includes management/support costs. Grants were broken down as follows:

Strengthening the voluntary sector	£1.4 million
International programme	£756,500
Arts programme	£581,000
Special initiatives	£110,000
Other work	£31,000

Beneficiaries across all programmes included: Conciliation Resources (£166,500); Trust for Africa's Orphans (£166,000); Fauna and Flora International (£152,000); Citizens UK, Community Links Trust Ltd and Coventry Law Centre (£75,000 each); AIRE Centre and Disability Law Service (£73,000); Creative Scotland and Legal Action Group (£50,000); Cheshire Dance and Gallery Oldham (£30,000 each); Serpentine Trust (£15,000); Arts 4 Dementia (£12,000); and African Diaspora Academic Network (UK) (£4,000).

Exclusions

See individual grant programmes on the foundation's website. Generally, the foundation does not accept applications from:

▶ Appeals or charities set up to support statutory organisations
▶ Animal welfare charities
▶ Grant maintained, private, or local education authority schools or their Parent Teachers' Associations
▶ Individuals

Applications

On application forms available via the foundation's website. Potential applicants should check the foundation's website for current guidelines and application deadlines.

Information gathered from:

Accounts; annual report; Charity Commission record; funder's website.

BBC Children in Need

Sport and health for people under the age of 18 who are disadvantaged
£31.2 million (2011/12)

Beneficial area

UK.

Correspondent: Sheila Jane Malley, Director of Grants and Policy, PO Box 1000, London W12 7WJ (tel: 0345 6090015; email: pudsey@bbc.co.uk; website: www.bbc.co.uk/pudsey)

Trustees: Daniel Cohen; Susan Elizabeth; Beverley Tew; Phil Hodkinson; Luke Mayhew; Peter McBride; Robert Shennan; Ralph Rivera; Stevie Spring; Donalda MacKinnon; Gillian Sheldon.

CC Number: 802052

This charity, registered in 1989, distributes the proceeds of the BBC's annual Children in Need appeal (first televised in 1980). The BBC Children in Need's vision is that every child in the UK has a safe, happy and secure childhood and the chance to reach their potential.

The charity awards grants each year to organisations supporting disadvantaged children and young people in the UK. Grants are made for specific projects which directly help children and young people (aged 18 and under). Around 2,600 projects were supported in 2011/12. Amounts range from a few hundred pounds to a (usual) maximum of £100,000.

Grants programmes

There are two grants programmes open to charities and not-for-profit organisations; the small grants programme awarding up to £10,000 and the main grants programme giving up to £100,000 over a maximum of three years.

Grants for both programmes are awarded for children and young people of 18 years and under experiencing disadvantage through:

▶ Illness, distress, abuse or neglect
▶ Any kind of disability
▶ Behavioural or psychological difficulties
▶ Living in poverty or situations of deprivation

Organisations funded are those working to combat this disadvantage and to make a real difference to children and young people's lives.

The Children in Need website states:

The trustees are looking for projects where a relatively small amount of money can make a big difference. They are unlikely to fund applications which top up funding for salaries or larger projects where a small grant would only make a marginal impact on its success.

Who can apply?

▶ Not-for-profit organisations that work with disadvantaged children and young people of 18 years and under who live in the UK, the Isle of Man or the Channel Islands
▶ If your organisation currently has a grant from the charity, you can apply for further funding providing your current grant is coming to an end within the next 12 months. You will need to be able to provide convincing evidence of the differences the grant has made to the lives of the disadvantaged children and young people you have worked with

Comprehensive guidelines for completing both the Main Grant and Small Grant application forms are available on the charity's website – a detailed A-Z of policy advice and guidance can also be found there.

If you have a general enquiry, are unsure about anything you have read or are looking for support regarding your application please contact the helpdesk on 0345 609 0015 or at pudsey@bbc.co.uk. The helpdesk is open from 9am-5pm Monday to Friday. You can also contact your local regional or national office.

Emergency Essentials

This programme provides items that meet children's most basic needs such as a bed to sleep in, a cooker to give them a hot meal, clothing (in a crisis) and other items and services that are critical to children's wellbeing. The programme is administered by Buttle UK which, through its network of frontline partner agencies, is able to reach families who need the programme most.

In response to increased demand for essential goods from families living with severe financial, health and social difficulties which affect children's wellbeing, BBC Children in Need [gave] £2 million worth of Emergency Essentials grants for the year to October 2013. Visit Buttle UK's website for more information on how to apply.

In the nine months to June 2012, BBC Children in Need had an income of £45 million and a total expenditure of £34.8 million. A total of 862 grants were made totalling £31.2 million. These were the remainder of funds from Appeal 2010 and awards from Appeal 2011 funds made to date. For comparison, in the nine months to 30 June 2011, there were 892 grants made totalling £26.2 million. The following table gives the geographical distribution of grants:

North	163	23%	£7.3 million
London and South East	209	23%	£7.2 million
Central	145	18%	£5.4 million
South West	81	10%	£3.1 million
Total England	598	74%	£23 million
Scotland	93	12%	£3.5 million
Wales	50	7%	£2.3 million
Northern Ireland	121	7%	£2.3 million
Total Grants	**862**	**100%**	**£31.2 million**

In addition, 5,833 grants have been awarded to individual children and young people through the Emergency Essentials programme.

Beneficiaries included: Buttle UK (Emergency Essentials Programme) (£2 million); Zinc Arts – Essex (£286,000); Llamau – Wales (£164,000); Headway – Devon (£83,000); Women's Aid – Cheltenham (£82,000); Positive Action on Cancer – Somerset (£47,000); Bookbug – Leith (£26,000); and Meningitis Trust – Northern Ireland (£3,000).

Exclusions

Grants will not be given for:

▶ Relief of statutory responsibility
▶ Applications from local government or NHS bodies
▶ Building projects which are applying to us for more than £20,000
▶ The promotion of religion
▶ Trips or projects abroad
▶ Medical treatment/research
▶ Projects for pregnancy testing or advice, information or counselling on pregnancy choices
▶ General awareness-raising work
▶ Bursaries, sponsored places, fees or equivalent
▶ Individuals (unless an eligible organisation is applying on their behalf)
▶ Distribution to another/other organisation/s, for example, PTAs applying on behalf of schools
▶ General appeals or endowment funds
▶ Deficit funding or repayment of loans
▶ Retrospective funding (projects taking place before the grant award date)
▶ Projects unable to start within 12 months of the grant award date
▶ Unspecified expenditure

▶ For organisational overheads or running costs which the organisation would incur whether the project was running or not. (Although the trustees will consider funding support costs incurred as a direct result of running the project)

Applications

Straightforward and excellent application forms and guidelines are available from the charity's website. **Application forms must be completed online.** Note: incomplete or late application forms will not be assessed. If you have a general enquiry, are unsure about anything you have read or are looking for support regarding your application contact the helpdesk on 0345 609 0015 or at pudsey@bbc.co.uk. The helpdesk is open from 9am-5pm Monday to Friday. You can also contact your local regional or national office.

Information gathered from:

Accounts; annual report; Charity Commission record; funder's website.

BC Partners Foundation

General
£368,500 (2012)

Beneficial area
UK.

Correspondent: The Trustees, BC Partners Ltd, 40 Portman Square, London W1H 6DA (tel: 020 7009 4800; email: bcpfoundation@bcpartners.com)

Trustees: Nikos Stathopolous; Joseph Cronley; Lorna Parker; Michael Pritchard; Richard Kunzer.

CC Number: 1136956

Established in 2010 for general charitable purposes, this is the foundation of private equity firm BC Partners.

The foundation's annual report states:

The foundation's goal is to support a wide range of organisations that positively affect the advancement of the communities where BC Partners and its employees and alumni are active. Its mandate is intentionally broad so that it can support giving to charities of all kinds.

Donations have been made to a broad range of charities around the world, which can be divided into three areas: (i) community development (e.g., infrastructure advancements, development aid, health care improvements); (ii) environmental conservation (e.g., pollution reduction, natural preservation, clean technologies); and (iii) arts & education (e.g., educational, scholastic or artistic programs).

In 2012 the foundation had assets of £168,500 and an income of £355,500.

Grants were made to organisations totalling £368,500.

The largest grants were made to the Private Equity Foundation (£102,000), of which Nikos Stathopolous is also a trustee, and the French Education Property Trust (£100,000), now called the K T Educational Charitable Trust, which is connected the Wembley French International School.

Other beneficiaries included: Royal Opera House (£25,000); Over The Wall and the Fondation Philanthropique (£16,000 each); The Dolphin Society (£5,000); Opportunity International (£3,000); Water Aid (£2,000); and Feedback Madagascar (£1,000).

Applications

In writing to the correspondent.

Information gathered from:

Accounts; annual report; Charity Commission record.

The Big Lottery Fund (see also Awards for All)

Community, young people, welfare
£778.7 million (2012/13)

Beneficial area
UK and overseas.

Correspondent: See 'Useful contacts' at the end of this entry, (tel: 0845 410 2030; email: enquiries@biglotteryfund.org.uk; website: www.biglotteryfund.org.uk)

Trustees: Peter Ainsworth, Chair; Anna Southall; Nat Sloane; Frank Hewitt; Rajay Naik; Sir Adrian Webb; Maureen McGinn; Dr Astrid Bonfield; Tony Burton.

Summary

The National Lottery (the lottery) was launched in 1994 and rapidly established itself as a key funder of the voluntary sector. It is operated by Camelot which although responsible for generating returns for National Lottery Good Causes, plays no role in the allocation of funding, which is the responsibility of national lottery distribution bodies, each with specialist knowledge of their sectors. In the year ending 31 March 2013, 28% of total National Lottery revenue was returned to the 'good causes', while over 50% of total revenue was paid to players in prizes. Over the same period, 12% of total revenue was paid to the government in lottery duty and around 5% was paid to retailers in commission.

The income raised for good causes from ticket sales is paid by Camelot into the

National Lottery Distribution Fund (NLDF) and then allocated to the distribution bodies according to a formula set by the Department for Culture, Media and Sport. In the year to 31 March 2013, the money Camelot delivered to the NLDF for good causes was allocated as follows:

Health, education, environment and charitable causes	40%
Sport	20%
Arts	20%
Heritage	20%

General

Distribution bodies

Distribution bodies, sometimes referred to as lottery funders, are the organisations that distribute the good causes' money to local communities and national and international projects. They cover arts, heritage, sport, community and voluntary groups as well as supporting projects concerned with health, education and the environment. According to the publication 'National Lottery Distribution Fund Account 2011–12' current funding bodies are:

▶ Big Lottery Fund (including Awards for All – a BIG Lottery Fund grants scheme funding small, local community-based projects in the UK. Each country in the UK runs its own programme.)
▶ Heritage Lottery Fund
▶ Arts Council England
▶ Creative Scotland
▶ Arts Council of Northern Ireland
▶ Arts Council for Wales
▶ British Film Institute
▶ UK Film Council
▶ Scottish Screen
▶ English Sports Council
▶ Scottish Sports Council
▶ Sports Council for Wales
▶ Sports Council of Northern Ireland
▶ UK Sports Council
▶ Olympic Lottery Distribution Fund

The lottery distribution bodies are independent; however, because they distribute public funds, their policies are subject to a level of statutory control from government. Their grantmaking is also under close public and media scrutiny and is often the subject of wide-ranging debate.

Much of BIG's funding is given in grants made directly to successful applicants, particularly those in the voluntary sector, however, BIG also administers non-lottery funds.

BIG's website gives the following information on its non-Lottery funding operation:

The Big Fund

The National Lottery Act (2006) gave BIG the powers to distribute Third Party Funding (non-lottery), as well as lottery funding. The Fund's Third Party mission is to work collaboratively, putting our experience, systems and learning at the disposal of others for the benefit of communities and people most in need.

The Big Fund is the brand we use to distribute funding that does not come from the National Lottery. It is not a funding programme but can be used to deliver funding on behalf of other organisations, such as government departments. If you are interested in applying for funding from a Big Fund programme please use the funding finder or call our advice line on 084541020 30.

The Fund's experience, infrastructure and expertise mean we are perfectly positioned to deliver wider community funding programmes. We deliver funding throughout the UK, through programmes tailored specifically to the needs of communities in England, Scotland, Wales or Northern Ireland as well as programmes that cover the whole UK.

As well as the ability to distribute Third Party Funding BIG can also explore shared service opportunities or collaboration on joint funding schemes. If you would like to discuss collaboration of new initiatives contact the team at: team@bigfund.org.uk.

Big Lottery Fund

The Big Lottery Fund (BIG) is responsible for distributing the 40% of all funds raised for good causes (about 11 pence of every pound spent on a Lottery ticket) by the National Lottery. This currently totals almost £800 million.

Since June 2004 BIG has awarded over £6 billion to projects supporting health, education, environment and charitable purposes. 80%-90% of its funding is awarded to voluntary and community sector organisations. Its mission is 'to bring real improvements to communities and the lives of people most in need'.

Note: The accounts for 2012/13 state: 'In March 2007 Parliament agreed that between February 2009 and August 2012, £638 million should be transferred from the Big Lottery Fund to the Olympic Lottery Distribution Fund (OLDF). During 2012/13 transfers totalling £80 million were made.'

Directory of Social Change believes that this is totally unacceptable and has been campaigning for the return of this money since it was taken. The current government says that charities could wait until 2030 to get this money back, which DSC considers untenable – charities and communities up and down the country need this money now. Get the full picture and sign up to support the campaign at: www.biglotteryrefund.org.uk.

Funding is delivered mostly through programmes tailored specifically to the needs of communities in England,

Scotland, Wales or Northern Ireland as well as some programmes that cover the whole of the UK.

The assessment process is a rigorous and demanding one. Many organisations commit a substantial part of their fundraising resources in applying for grants from the various lottery distribution bodies.

BIG is the largest of the lottery distributors and is responsible for giving out 40% of the money for good causes raised from the lottery, which currently provides a budget of around £800 million a year. Funding covers health, education, environment and charitable purposes.

In October 2010 responsibility for the Big Lottery Fund was transferred to the Cabinet Office.

The 'About Us' section of BIG's website states:

BIG's mission is to be committed to bringing real improvements to communities and the lives of people most in need. To do this, it has identified the following values:

Making best use of lottery money
▶ To develop new programmes and make fair funding decisions
▶ By running our operations as efficiently as possible, while still providing an excellent service
▶ By being an Intelligent Funder, meaning we focus on the impact of our funding, rather than just the process.

Using knowledge and evidence
▶ To help good projects to succeed even if they aren't familiar with applying for Lottery funding
▶ To understand the needs and solutions for different communities
▶ To ensure we are meeting the needs of all our audiences including applicants and the public.

Being supportive and helpful
▶ By funding projects that are most likely to make a difference where it is needed
▶ Through excellent customer service
▶ By supporting our staff to provide help and support to all audiences
▶ Accessibility
▶ Strategic focus
▶ Involving people
▶ Innovation
▶ Enabling
▶ Additional to government

Much of BIG's funding is given in grants made directly to successful applicants, particularly those in the voluntary sector, however, BIG also administers non-lottery funds.

Funding in 2012/13

Information is taken from the 2012/13 annual report and accounts – the chair's introduction and summary:

In 2012/13 over 92 per cent of our funding was awarded to the VCS. Rising demand for services, the impact of public sector funding cuts and a fall in individual donations have contributed to a difficult funding environment. We received twice as many applications as we were able to fund; however this was against a backdrop of strong lottery ticket sales and we were able to make just over 12,000 awards totalling over £778 million to projects, organisations and partnerships working in health, education, the environment and charitable purposes.

(Note: We have used the figure of £778 million as the total amount awarded in grants).

Demand for lottery funding continues to grow: BIG received 4,516 outline proposal applications requesting almost £1.1 billion. Of those for which initial assessment was complete, 47.5% were successful in reaching stage two.

New awards made during 2012/13 – (Some of these awards relate to applications received in earlier years).

Big Lottery Fund programmes	12,300	£751.3 million
Non-Lottery funded programmes	646	£71.8 million
Totals	13,680	£823.1 million

A full analysis of BIG's activities during the year can be found in its latest annual report.

BIG programmes

Examples of 2013 funding are given below. Check BIG's website for up-to-date information on current programmes.

England

Awards for All – England

Awards for All gives groups a quick and easy way to get small Lottery grants of between £300 and £10,000. Projects which address the issues, needs and aspirations of local communities and people are considered. BIG will fund a wide range of community projects aimed at developing skills, improving health, revitalising the local environment and enabling people to become more active citizens.

Commissioning Better Outcomes and the Social Outcomes Fund

We are focusing on approaches that use payment by results (PbR) mechanisms, particularly those which involve social investment such as Social Impact Bonds (SIBs). To achieve this we have set up two funds – the Cabinet Office's Social Outcomes Fund and the Big Lottery Fund's Commissioning Better Outcomes – with a joint mission to support the development of more SIBs. Between them these funds are making up to £60 million available to pay for a proportion of outcomes payments for these types of models in complex policy areas, as well as support to develop robust proposals.

Our shared overarching aim is to grow the market in SIBs, while each fund has a specific focus that reflects the missions of the Big Lottery Fund and Cabinet Office.

For the Big Lottery Fund, this is to enable more people, particularly those most in need, to lead fulfilling lives, in enriching places and as part of successful communities. For the Cabinet Office, this is to catalyse and test innovative approaches to tackling complex issues using outcomes based commissioning.

We have appointed a support contractor to work on a one to one basis with applicants submitting an expression of interest. Social Finance will be working in partnership with the Local Government Association to deliver the contract. You can contact them by emailing: sioutcomesfunds@socialfinance.org.uk.

The Cabinet Office Centre for Social Impact Bonds provides light-touch support to SIB developers and has produced a series of tools and resources to help develop SIBs.

▶ The Knowledge Box is a modular resource containing the latest thinking on SIBs
▶ A template and guidance for developing payment by results contracts
▶ You can contact the Centre for Social Impact Bonds by emailing: sibs@cabinetoffice.gsi.gov.uk

The Big Lottery Fund has up to £40 million available through Commissioning Better Outcomes. Up to £3 million of this total has been set aside for development funding. The Cabinet Office has up to £20 million available through the Social Outcomes Fund.

International Communities

The International Communities programme helps disadvantaged communities around the world. International Communities has a budget of up to £80 million between 2010 and 2015. Grants of between £50,000 and £500,000 are available to UK based non-governmental organisations working with overseas partners.

Parks for People

£10 million available to provide funding for parks: the programme is run in partnership with the Heritage Lottery Fund, to whom further enquiries and applications should be made.

Reaching Communities

£150 million available for this programme: there are two strands to this funding.

Reaching Communities funding is for projects that help people and communities most in need. Grants are available from £10,000, upwards and funding can last for up to five years. If you think you need more than £500,000 you must call the staff at BIG before you apply to discuss why you believe a larger project is appropriate. There is no upper limit for total project costs.

Funding is available for salaries, running costs, a contribution towards core costs and equipment. BIG can also fund

£100,000 for land, buildings or refurbishment capital costs. If you need more than £100,000 for a land and/or buildings project see the Reaching Communities buildings page on BIG's website.

There is a two stage application process. You should read the Reaching Communities guidance notes to make sure your project stands a good chance of success.

Northern Ireland

Awards for All Northern Ireland

Awards for All gives groups a quick and easy way to get small Lottery grants of between £500 and £10,000. You can apply at any time and you will normally hear BIG's decision in three months.

Full details on how to apply are contained in the guidance notes. The guidance notes and application form can be downloaded from the website.

Reaching Out – Supporting Families

£25 million in projects lasting five years to help families in Northern Ireland to improve their children's lives. BIG's mission is to support people and communities most in need so the projects it funds help families facing challenges such as separation, absence of a key family member, poverty, substance abuse, disability, social isolation, homelessness, physical and/or emotional abuse.

For this programme, childhood is defined as pre-birth up to the age of 12. 'Families' is defined as children and their parents or carers, as well as wider family members, such as grandparents and siblings.

Funding will support a wide range of activities such as getting parents more involved in their children's learning, reducing family isolation from the wider community, and strengthening family relationships and communication.

Projects should complement the range of relevant strategies and activities in Northern Ireland. These include:
▶ Families Matter
▶ The Child Poverty Strategy
▶ Care Matters NI
▶ Our Children and Young People – Our Pledge United Nations Convention on the Rights of the Child

Space and Place

The Space and Place Consortium in Northern Ireland, will deliver this £15 million programme to bring communities in Northern Ireland together by making better use of local spaces and places. This programme will support local communities to connect people by developing under-used and difficult spaces, improve the health and well-being of local people and increase their opportunities to take part in activities in their area.

For more information on the Space and Place programme and how to apply for funding visit: www. communityfoundationni.org/ spaceandplace.

Scotland

2014 Communities

Building a lasting legacy for communities across Scotland. 2014 Communities offers grants of between £300 and £2,000 to encourage more people to take part in physical activity.

There are no deadlines and applications can be submitted at any time.

Awards for All Scotland

Awards for All is a quick and easy way to get small Lottery grants of between £500 and £10,000. The programme aims to help people become actively involved in projects that bring about change in their local community. This could be through a wide range of community, arts, sports, health, education and environmental activities. There are no deadlines and applications can be submitted at any time.

Celebrate

The Commonwealth community represents a third of the world's population and brings together 71 diverse cultures. Now the four Scottish Lottery distributors, Big Lottery Fund, Creative Scotland, Heritage Lottery Fund and sportscotland have come together and created Celebrate – to offer Lottery funding support to communities across Scotland as they celebrate and are inspired by this landmark event.

Celebrate has a budget of £4 million and will make grants from £500 to £10,000 to communities across Scotland to come together to hold arts, heritage, sports and local community celebrations of the 2014 Commonwealth Games. Celebrate will also support communities to celebrate the diversity of the Commonwealth and create a legacy of community and Commonwealth connections.

Investing in Ideas

A £1 million fund, renewed each year, which provides groups with an opportunity to spend time and money developing ideas that have a clear public benefit. Grants of up to £10,000 are available. There are no deadlines.

Investing in Communities

Investing in Communities: Growing Community Assets is designed to support communities to take more control and influence over their own future through ownership of assets. These are usually physical assets, such as land, buildings or equipment, but may also include other types of asset such as energy.

There are no deadlines and applications can be submitted at any time.

Wales

Awards for All – Wales

This programme provides voluntary and community groups with a quick and easy way to get small National Lottery grants of between £500 and £5,000 for projects which aim to help improve local communities and the lives of people most in need.

People and Places

People and Places will fund capital and revenue projects that encourage co-ordinated action by people who want to make their communities better places to live. Support is available for local and regional projects throughout Wales that focus on:

▶ Revitalising communities
▶ Improving community relationships, or
▶ Enhancing local environments, community services and buildings

People and Places is open for applications until further notice. Any change to this will be posted on the website.

Useful contacts

Enquiries

St James's Court, Newcastle upon Tyne NE1 4BE; tel: 0845 410 2030.

Head Office – London

5th Floor, 1 Plough Place, London EC4A 1DE; tel: 020 7842 4000; textphone: 0845 039 0204; fax: 020 7842 4010.

Applications

Full details on current programmes, contacts, application forms and guidance are available via the BLF website or by calling 0845 410 2030.

Information gathered from:

Accounts; annual report; funder's website.

Percy Bilton Charity

People with disabilities, disadvantaged youth, older people
£420,000 to organisations
(2011/12)

Beneficial area

UK.

Correspondent: Tara Smith, Charity Administrator, Bilton House, 7 Culmington Road, Ealing, London W13 9NB (tel: 020 8579 2829; fax: 020 8579 3650; website: www. percybiltoncharity.org.uk)

Trustees: Miles A. Bilton, Chair; James R. Lee; Stefan J. Paciorek; Kim Lansdown; Hayley Bilton.
CC Number: 1094720

Background

The Percy Bilton Charity was founded on 9 July 1962 by the late Percy Bilton for exclusively charitable purposes. The directors have redefined and updated the charity's grantmaking policies over time to suit changing social and economic needs. The charity makes distributions primarily in areas relating to older people, people with disabilities and children and young people who are socially or educationally disadvantaged or underprivileged. The following information is taken from the charity's website:

Percy Bilton was an entrepreneur who in the 1920s and 1930s built up a group of successful property companies which in the 1970s was listed on the London Stock Exchange. He endowed the charity with a substantial parcel of shares in Percy Bilton Ltd, which later became Bilton plc.

Although the companies were legally separate, the charity shared in the success of Bilton plc for many years receiving a steadily increasing dividend income. The investments in both Bilton plc and in the unquoted company were sold in 1998 and the total proceeds are now invested in a diversified investment portfolio.

During his lifetime, Percy Bilton took a keen personal interest in the activities of the charity retaining his involvement until his death in 1982. The directors of the charity, who are its trustees, have continued the charity's activities in accordance with the charitable objects set out by the founder.

Guidelines

The charity's website provides the following details and guidance on its grantmaking:

This is a guide to the charity's current grant policies and procedures.

We would ask you to read these notes carefully to verify that both your organisation and your project are within our policies before applying. You are welcome to contact the Grants Office at any stage of your application for advice and guidance by telephone or in writing.

Who may apply

Only registered charities in the UK whose primary objectives are to assist one or more of the following groups:

▶ Disadvantaged/underprivileged young people (persons under 25)
▶ People with disabilities (physical or learning disabilities or mental health problems)
▶ Older people (aged over 60)

We do not respond to organisations who do not meet the above criteria.

Type of grants offered
We have 2 programmes for organisations:
1 Large grants – one-off payments for capital expenditure of approximately £2,000 and over, i.e. furniture and equipment; building/refurbishment projects. Please note that we do not fund running costs
2 Small grants – donations of up to £500 towards furnishings and equipment for small projects. This programme is more suitable for smaller organisations

Amount of grant
The amount offered will usually depend on the number of applications received in relation to the funds available for distribution. You may therefore not receive the full amount requested.

Major appeals
In the case of major appeals and minibuses please apply after 75% of the funding has been secured, as offers are conditional upon the balance being raised and the project completed within one year. We also require grants to be taken up within 12 months of the offer and it is essential to ascertain that your project is likely to be completed within this time scale before applying.

Who the charity will fund
The charity will consider capital funding for the following projects and schemes:
1 *Disadvantaged/underprivileged young people (persons under 25)*: supported housing schemes and educational and training projects to encourage disadvantaged young people who may be homeless and/or unemployed away from crime, substance/alcohol misuse and homelessness; facilities for recreational activities and outdoor pursuits specifically for young people who are educationally or socially underprivileged or disadvantaged
2 *People with disabilities (physical or learning disabilities or mental health problems)*: residential, respite care, occupational and recreational establishments for children, young people and adults with physical or learning disabilities or enduring mental health problems
3 *Older people (aged over 60)*: day centres, nursing and residential homes, sheltered accommodation and respite care for the frail or sufferers from dementia or age related disorders; projects to encourage older people to maintain their independence

General
In 2011/12 the charity had assets of £19.2 million and an income of £711,000. Grants were made totalling £603,000, of which £420,000 was given to 179 organisations, £143,500 was donated to individuals and £40,000 was given in food parcels to older people.

Grants to organisations were categorised as follows:

Large grants
Young people with a disability	£149,500
Older people with a disability	£143,000
Disadvantaged young people	£55,000
Older people	£35,000

Small grants
Disability/older people	£24,500
Disadvantaged youth	£20,000

Grants in 2011/12
Beneficiaries receiving large grants included: Albert Kennedy Trust – London (£11,000); Jumbulance Trust – Hertfordshire (£10,000); Home Farm Trust – Oxfordshire (£9,500); St Raphael's Hospice – Surrey (£7,500); Age UK – Hull (£6,000); Children's Trust – Surrey, Reigate and Redhill YMCA and Sunfield – West Midlands (£5,000 each); and Cumbria Cerebral Palsy, Carlisle and Greenwich and Bexley Community Hospice – London (£2,000 each).

Small grant beneficiaries included: Barons Court Project – London, Grenfell Club – Redcar, Music Space – Bristol, Making a Difference – Tameside, STEPS – Devon, Wellspring Family Centre – Norfolk and Where Next Association – Worcester (£500 each); Eyres Monsell Club for Young People – Leicester, Phoenix Stroke Club – West Sussex and Oxfordshire Family Mediation – Oxford (£400 each); and North Somerset Crossroads (£300).

Exclusions
The charity will not consider the following (the list is not exhaustive):
- Running expenses for the organisation or individual projects
- Salaries, training costs or office equipment/furniture
- Projects for general community use e.g. community centre and church halls
- Disabled access to community buildings
- Publication costs e.g. printing/distributing promotional and information leaflets
- Projects that have been completed
- Items that have already been purchased
- Provision of disabled facilities in schemes mainly for the able-bodied
- General funding/circularised appeals
- Pre-schools or playgroups (other than predominantly for disabled children)
- Play schemes/summer schemes
- Holidays or expeditions for individuals or groups
- Trips, activities or events
- Community sports/play area facilities
- Consumables (e.g. stationery, arts and crafts materials)
- Refurbishment or repair of places of worship/church halls

- Research projects
- Mainstream pre-schools, schools, colleges and universities (other than special schools)
- Welfare funds for individuals
- Hospital/medical equipment
- Works to premises not used primarily by the eligible groups

Applications
The charity's website gives the following guidance on making an application:

Large grants (£2,000 and over)
Please apply on your organisation's headed notepaper giving or attaching the following information. 1–6 must be provided in all cases and 7 as applicable to your appeal:
1 a summary outlining the amount you are requesting and what the funding is for.
2 a brief history of your Charity, its objectives and work
3 a description of the project and what you intend to achieve
4 a copy of your most recent Annual Report and audited Accounts
5 details of funds already raised and other sources that you have approached
6 proposals to monitor and evaluate the project
7 any other relevant information that will help to explain your application
8 the following additional information that applies to your appeal:

Building/Refurbishment appeals
- A statement of all costs involved. Please itemise major items and professional fees
- Confirmation that the project has on-going revenue funding
- Confirmation that all planning and other consents and building regulations approvals have been obtained
- Details of ownership of the premises and if leased, the length of the unexpired term
- Timetable of construction/refurbishment and anticipated date of completion

Equipment appeals
- An itemised list of all equipment with estimate of costs. Please obtain at least 2 competitive estimates except where this is not practicable e.g. specialised equipment
- When you plan to purchase the equipment.

Contribution towards purchase of minibuses:
Please note that minibuses can only be considered if used to transport older and/or disabled people with mobility problems.
- Please give details of provision made for insurance, tax and maintenance etc. We require confirmation that your organisation can meet future running costs.

Small grants (up to £500)
Please apply on your organisation's headed notepaper with the following information:

- Brief details about your organisation and its work
- A copy of your most recent annual accounts
- Outline of the project and its principal aims
- Breakdown of the cost of item/s required
- The organisation's bank account name to which the cheque should be made payable if a grant is approved. (We cannot make cheques payable to individuals).
- If your organisation is not a registered charity, please supply a reference from a registered charity with whom you work or from the local Voluntary Service Council

Common applicant mistakes

'Applying for running costs and other items that are outside of our criteria.'

Information gathered from:

Accounts; annual report; Charity Commission record; further information provided by the funder; funder's website.

The Birmingham & Black Country Community Foundation

General charitable purposes, social welfare

£1.6 million (2011/12)

Beneficial area

Greater Birmingham.

Correspondent: Karen Argyle, Programmes Manager, Nechells Baths, Nechells Park Road, Nechells, Birmingham B7 5PD (tel: 01213 225560; fax: 01213 225579; email: team@bbccf. org.uk; website: www.bhamfoundation. co.uk)

Trustees: David Bucknall; John Andrews; Kay Cadman; Angela Henry; Richard Harris; John Matthews.

CC Number: 1048162

Summary

The Birmingham & Black Country Community Foundation was established in 1995 to help local people 'create, encourage and resource initiatives that would alleviate poverty and deprivation, and also promote employment within our community'.

The foundation's website provides the following overview of its activities:

We provide philanthropy services to families, companies, trusts by managing funds, building endowment and being the vital link between local donors and local needs; investing back into our communities – where we live, work and play. Most people's perception of charitable giving is to make a donation to one or a number of charities; seeing a cause and finding an organisation, that

resonates with their giving desires. Giving through Birmingham & Black Country Community Foundation is an effective way of directing your giving to the heart of our local communities, encouraging strong and vibrant community activities that benefit us all.

We empower people by:

Working with local donors and pooling the donations of philanthropically minded individuals and community-minded companies into an Endowment Fund; providing a permanent and growing fund for activities that strengthen community today and in perpetuity;

Working with the community, supporting local voluntary and community activity through a programme of constructive grant making and capacity building; we are able to award grants to grassroots groups that do not have charitable status, but do make a local impact.

The Birmingham & Black Country Community Foundation manages a number of funds which often change quickly and as such, potential applicants are advised to consult the foundation's website for the latest information before applying.

Grantmaking

In 2011/12 the foundation had assets of £790,000 and an income of £2.7 million. Grants were made totalling almost £1.6 million and distributed as follows:

Community assistance	£867,000
Other grant programmes	£481,000
ESF Community grants	£209,000

Beneficiaries included: Jerico Enterprises CIC (£50,000); Kingshurst Development Trust (£22,000); Alexandra High School and Sixth Form Centre (£20,000); The Big Clean Up (£17,500); City United (£15,000); Birmingham Friends of the Earth (£12,000); Aspire4U (£11,000); The Dean Foundation (£4,500); and Banners Gate Coffee Club (£3,000).

Exclusions

No funding is available:
- To individuals, for whatever purpose
- To statutory organisations, including PCT's and *schools
- For groups who are not constituted or do not have a set of rules
- To fund trips abroad or overseas activities
- To fund buses, mini buses or other community transport schemes (not including transport costs forming part of a project)
- To fund building costs, including access adaptations to buildings
- For projects operating outside Birmingham, Dudley, Sandwell, Walsall and Wolverhampton
- For donations towards general appeals or for an application from a large national charity

- Organisations and individuals in the promotion of political or purely religious ideology – although some faith group activities can be supported

*Note – whilst schools are not currently eligible to apply, independent groups within schools such as PTA's and before/after school clubs can apply.

**These are general exclusions to BBCCF and you are advised to read specific grant guidelines associated with funding programmes being administered by BBCCF at any one time.

Applications

Refer to the foundation's website for full details of how to apply to the various programmes currently being administered.

Information gathered from:

Charity Commission record; funder's website; SIR (published by the Commission).

The Michael Bishop Foundation

General charitable purposes

£2.6 million (2011/12)

Beneficial area

Worldwide with a preference for Birmingham and the Midlands.

Correspondent: Charlotte Newall, Administrator, Staunton House, Ashby-de-la-Zouche, Leicestershire LE65 1RW (tel: 01530 564388)

Trustees: Grahame N. Elliott; Baron Glendonbrook of Bowdon; John S. Coulson.

CC Number: 297627

Sir Michael Bishop (now Baron Glendonbrook of Bowdon) of British Midland set up the foundation in 1987 by giving almost £1 million of shares in Airlines of Britain (Holdings) plc, the parent company of British Midland. A further sum was given in 1992.

The trustees in their annual report of 2011/12 state that given the increase in the size of the funds at their disposal, they will in due course establish more formal guidelines as to the types of charitable activities they favour in order to assist those seeking support.

In 2011/12 the trust had assets of over £18 million and an income of £430,000. Grants to 29 organisations totalled £2.6 million.

Beneficiaries included: Loughborough University Development Trust (£1 million); Mill Hill School Foundation (£300,000); Glendonbrook Foundation (£231,000); Future Directions International (£189,000);

Commonwealth Youth Orchestra (£75,000); The Terrence Higgins Trust and Vipingo Village Fund (£25,000 each); the Student Entrepreneurial Fund (£15,000); Barry and Martin's Trust and Christchurch Earthquake Appeal (£2,500 each); and Autistica (£500).

Applications
In writing to the correspondent.

Information gathered from:
Accounts; annual report; Charity Commission record.

The Bluston Charitable Settlement

Jewish, general
£699,000 (2011/12)
Beneficial area
Mostly UK.

Correspondent: Martin D. Paisner, Trustee, c/o Prism Gift Fund, 20 Gloucester Place, London W1U 8HA (tel: 020 7486 7760)

Trustees: Daniel Dover; Martin D. Paisner.

CC Number: 256691

The trust has general charitable purposes, although in practice most grants are given to Jewish organisations. The level of grantmaking has been increasing over recent years, and the trust states that it intends to maintain the current level in the near future.

It is the trust's policy to support the following:
- The education of children
- Capital expenditure projects for schools and other educational establishments
- The welfare of the underprivileged
- Hospitals and medical institutions
- Universities for specific research projects

In 2011/12 the trust had assets of just over £8.5 million and an income of £465,000. Grants were made during the year to 24 organisations totalling £699,000.

Beneficiaries included: Norwood (£75,000); British Friends of Bet Medrash Gevoha, Gateshead Talmudical College, Jewish Care and Ohel Sarah (£50,000 each); Weizmann Institute Foundation (£40,000); Jaffa Institute (£31,000); Langdon Foundation and Prisoners Abroad (£25,000 each); Holocaust Educational Trust (£20,000); Golders Green Beth Hamedrash and Keren Hatorah Trust (£10,000 each); and Kisharon (£5,000). The trust has a list of regular beneficiaries.

Exclusions
No grants to individuals.

Applications
In writing to the correspondent. The trustees meet annually in the spring.

Information gathered from:
Accounts; annual report; Charity Commission record.

The Boltini Trust

General, international development, music
£426,000 (2012/13)
Beneficial area
UK, with a particular focus on Surrey and West Sussex. Some international support to developing world.

Correspondent: Anthony Bolton, Trustee, Woolbeding Glebe, Woolbeding, Midhurst, West Sussex GU29 9RR (email: boltinitrust@gmail.com)

Trustees: Anthony Bolton; Sarah Bolton; James Nelson; Emma Nelson; Oliver Bolton; Benjamin Bolton.

CC Number: 1123129

This family trust was established in 2008 and supports UK charities with a particular emphasis on Surrey and West Sussex. Organisations involved with contemporary music and international development are also supported. The trust does not offer recurrent funding.

In 2012/13 the trust had assets of £9.5 million and an income of £412,000. Grants were made totalling £426,000, and were broken down as follows:

Music	£148,000
Medical research/medical institutions	£73,000
Children and young people	£67,500
Community foundations and charities	£62,500
Disadvantaged/homeless adults	£27,500
Major disaster relief funds	£25,000
Education and training institutions	£22,000

Beneficiaries include: Royal Opera House, Breakthrough Breast Cancer and Médecins Sans Frontières (£25,000 each); Island Academy (Antigua) (£16,000); St Barnabas Hospices (Sussex) Ltd – Chestnut Tree House and Music Theatre Wales (£15,000 each); Hong Kong Academy of Performing Arts (£14,000); The Prince's Trust (£11,500); The Challenge Network and Rother Valley Together (£10,000 each); The Mary Howe Trust for Cancer Prevention (£7,500); International Spinal Research Trust, British Association for Adoption and Fostering and Drop-for-Drop (India) (£5,000 each); and Missing People Ltd and National Opera Studia (£2,500 each).

Exclusions
No grants to individuals.

Applications
Initial enquiries should be made in writing to the correspondent. Trustees meet twice a year to consider applications. Successful applicants may be visited.

Information gathered from:
Accounts; Charity Commission record.

The Bosson Family Charitable Trust

Education and training and religious activities
Beneficial area
UK.

Correspondent: Paul Bosson, Trustee, 7 Seer Mead, Seer Green, Beaconsfield, Buckinghamshire HP9 2QL (tel: 01494 680148)

Trustees: Paul Bosson; Alison Bosson; George Bosson.

CC Number: 1146096

Registered in February 2012, the trust's objects are education, training and religious activities, with capital grants being given to registered charities and churches. The settlors of the trust are Paul Bosson, chief financial officer at Sophis, and his wife.

Applications
Unsolicited applications are not considered.

Information gathered from:
Charity Commission record.

The Bowland Charitable Trust

Young people, education, general
£4.4 million (2011)
Beneficial area
North west England.

Correspondent: Carole Fahy, Trustee, Activhouse, Philips Road, Blackburn, Lancashire BB1 5TH (tel: 01254 290433)

Trustees: Tony Cann; Ruth A. Cann; Carole Fahy; Hugh D. Turner.

CC Number: 292027

This charity invites applications for funding of projects from individuals, institutions and charities in particular (but not exclusively) for the promotion of education. Although its beneficial area covers the whole of the UK, in practice grants are mainly made in north west England. 'Projects may be funded over varying periods of time, but the majority are made as one-off payments.'

Accounts for the year 2012 were overdue at the Charity Commission at the time of writing (December 2013) and we have taken our information from the most recent available – 2011. In that year the trust had assets of £10.6 million and an income of £5.9 million. According to the trustees' annual report:

> The trust's income was considerably higher in this year due to the transfer of shares from trusts in which there are trustees in common with the Bowland Charitable Trust. The shares were acquired in consideration for the assignment of certain loan debtors to these trusts. However, the value of the shares was greater than the debts assigned and therefore the difference has been treated as voluntary income in order to reflect the full market value of the shares acquired. The majority of these shares were subsequently transferred to institutions which had been awarded grants, in settlement of the amount committed to them but not yet paid.

Grants were made to organisations totalling £4.4 million and £1,000 was awarded to individuals.

Beneficiaries of grants approved in the year included: Institute for Effective Education – York (£1.4 million); The Church School Company (£1.1 million); Success for All Foundation (£644,000); National Maths Case Studies Project (£241,000); Gaskell House Restoration Project and Grindleton Recreation Ground Charity (£100,000 each); Blackburn Youth Zone (£75,000); Blackburn Cathedral (£50,000); Nazareth Unitarian Chapel (£14,000 each); Age UK (£10,000); and Cumbria Country History Trust (£2,000).

Applications
The charity invites applications for funding of projects from individuals, institutions and charitable organisations. The applications are made directly to the trustees, who meet regularly to assess the applications.

Information gathered from:
Accounts; annual report; Charity Commission record.

The Liz and Terry Bramall Foundation

General, social welfare
£4.3 million (2011/12)

Beneficial area
UK, in practice mainly Yorkshire.

Correspondent: Terry Bramall, Trustee, c/o Gordons LLP, Riverside West, Whitehall Road, Leeds, West Yorkshire LS1 4AW (tel: 01132 270100; fax: 01132 270113)

Trustees: Terry Bramall; Liz Bramall; Suzannah Allard; Rebecca Bletcher; Rachel Tunnicliffe; Anthony Sharp.

CC Number: 1121670

Registered in 2007, this is the charitable trust of Terry Bramall, former chair of Keepmoat, builders of social housing in northern and central England. It was reported that the Bramall family sold their stake in the company in 2007 for £563 million. Terry Bramall is also a director of Doncaster Rovers FC.

The specific objects and areas of interest noted in the trust's 2011/12 annual report are as follows:

> Under the terms of the trust deed dated 6 July 2007 the original areas of support are in respect of the Christian faith, for the benefit of the public in accordance with the statements of belief of the Church of England, and the promotion for the benefit of the public of urban or rural regeneration, in areas of social and economic deprivation. In the prior year, the objectives of the trust were updated during the year to include the relief of sickness and the advancement of health. On 30 December 2009 the objectives of the charity were broadened further to include education and health as well as support for arts and culture. Unsolicited requests from national charities will generally only be considered if there is some public benefit to the Yorkshire region.

> It is unlikely that the trustees would support the total cost of a project and applicants should be able to demonstrate that funds have been raised or are in the process of being raised from other sources.

The report further states that the grantmaking policy of the charity is being developed but it will include small donations (on application) to causes within the objectives and also larger long-term projects. In the short-term, additional spend, over and above the current level of income, will be employed to bring the free reserves down to £500,000.

In 2011/12 the trust had assets of over £105 million and an income of £2.2 million. Grants were made to 86 organisations totalling £4.3 million. Grants ranged from under £1,000 to £1 million.

Beneficiaries included: The Prince's Trust (£1 million); Horizon Life Coaching (£527,000); St Peter's Church Building Fund (£450,000); Neuroblastoma and Yorkshire Air Ambulance (£200,000 each); Royal College of Church Music (£140,000); Martin House Children's Hospice, St Michael's Hospice and Yorkshire Sculpture (£100,000 each); Yorkshire Historic Churches Trust (£50,000); Wakefield Cathedral (£42,000); Harrogate Theatre (£40,000); Christians Against Poverty and Ripon Cathedral

Choristers (£20,000 each); Cyclone Technology (£16,500); Bowel and Cancer Research, Chrissy's Quest, Hospital Heartbeat Appeal and Magic Breakfast (£10,000 each); and Cerebra and Listening Books (£1,000 each).

Applications
In writing to the correspondent. The trust also states that 'unsolicited requests from national charities will generally only be considered if there is some public benefit to the Yorkshire region'.

Information gathered from:
Accounts; annual report; Charity Commission record.

The Breadsticks Foundation

Healthcare and education
£1.2 million (2011/12)

Beneficial area
UK, Africa and Asia.

Correspondent: Beatrix Payne, Trustee, 35 Canonbury Square, London N1 2AN (tel: 020 7288 0667; email: info@ breadsticksfoundation.org; website: www.breadsticksfoundation.org)

Trustees: Beatrix Payne, Chair; Dr Yolande Knight; Dr Paul Ballantyne; Beatrice Roberts; Trevor Macy; Alison Burkhari.

CC Number: 1125396

The foundation was established in 2008 to support organisations involved in improving the provision of healthcare and education. The foundation supports projects based in the UK, Africa and Asia.

The following information is taken from the foundation's website:

> The Breadsticks Foundation supports programmes aimed at improving the quality of life within marginalised communities and creating a platform for long-term economic independence. We have a particular interest in health, education and child and youth development. Where necessary, we work directly with other grant-making foundations to achieve these aims.

> We aim to build close, long-term partnerships with the organisations we support. Where possible we aim to provide partner organisations with long-term core funding but will also provide project-related grants. Grant sizes vary.

> The countries in which the foundation currently works are the United Kingdom, Cote D'Ivoire, Sudan, Ethiopia, Kenya, Rwanda, Zambia, Zimbabwe, South Africa, India, Indonesia and Laos. The Breadsticks Foundation will consider programmes outside these core countries from across Africa and India but, unless the trustees judge the programme to be

outstanding, there is a low probability of success.

We participate closely in monitoring and evaluation with our partners and, in order to achieve this, require half-yearly progress reports on each grant. In assessing a grant application, we will analyse each applicant's financial reports and accounts and will conduct telephone and face-to-face interviews.

In 2011/12 the foundation had assets of £491,500 and an income of £1.7 million, most of which came from the anonymous settlor of the foundation. Grants were made to 23 organisations totalling £1.2 million.

Beneficiaries included: Hope and Homes for Children (£240,000); The Medical Foundation (£153,000); Class Act Educational Services – Johannesburg (£139,500); Kids in Need of Education – Mumbai (£85,000); St Mungo's (£70,000); International Childcare Trust (£40,000); Hanley Crouch Community Centre – London (£25,000); Christine Revell Children's Home (£15,500); and the International Children's Trust (£5,000).

Exclusions
The foundation will not sponsor individuals or fund animals, medical research or capital and building projects. It will not fund faith-based programmes unless they work with beneficiaries from all faiths and none.

Applications
Applications are by invitation only, and unsolicited applications will not be considered. The foundation does, however, welcome communication via email.

Information gathered from:
Accounts; Charity Commission record; funder's website.

British Record Industry Trust

Performing arts, music therapy, general
£1.1 million (2012)

Beneficial area
Worldwide, in practice UK.

Correspondent: Jenny Clarke, Correspondent, Riverside Building, County Hall, Westminster Bridge Road, London SE1 7JA (tel: 020 7803 1351; email: jenny.clarke@bpi.co.uk; website: www.brittrust.co.uk)

Trustees: John Craig, Andy Cleary; Derek Green; Paul Burger; David Kassner; Rob Dickins; Tony Wadsworth; Jonathan Morrish; Geoff Taylor; Korda Marshall; David Sharpe; John Deacon; Simon Robson; Emma Pike.

CC Number: 1000413

The trust's website states:

> The BRIT Trust considers applications which meet the criteria within its mission statement:
>
> To encourage young people in the exploration and pursuit of educational, cultural or therapeutic benefits emanating from music.

The following information is taken from the 2012 trustees' annual report:

Grantmaking Policy
The trust meets its objectives through the giving of grants and has a long standing relationship with a number of entities that receive funding each year. In addition, the trust will also consider grants to other charitable organisations that fit the mission statement of the trust. The trust invites grant applications from institutions through the BRIT Trust website and through word of mouth in the industry. Applicants will submit an application form, which details information about the charity, including financial requirements, aims and a description of benefit that the grant would provide.

Grant applications are considered at each trustee meeting. After meeting the larger commitments of the BRIT School and Nordoff Robbins. If possible, it is the trustees' policy to make a number of smaller donations to various charities.

In 2012 the trust had assets of £7.3 million and an income of over £1.2 million. Grants ranging from £1,000 to £350,000 were made to ten organisations totalling £1.1 million.

As in previous years, the beneficiaries of the largest grants were the BRIT School for the Performing Arts and Technology (£735,000); and Nordoff-Robbins Music Therapy (£300,000). Other beneficiaries included: Drugscope (£60,000); Chickenshed Theatre, Heart n Soul and Bigga Fish (£5,000 each); and the Paul Walter Award (£1,000).

Exclusions
No scholarships or grants to individuals. No capital funding projects are considered. Only registered charities in the UK are supported.

Applications
Taken from the trust's website:

> Please note that The BRIT Trust is only able to consider applications from fellow organisations with a charitable status. Unfortunately it is unable to consider individual grants, scholarships or capital grants or grant donations outside of the UK. For details of other organisations that may be able to assist, check-out our website.
>
> To apply for funding from The BRIT Trust, please complete the application form [on its website]. (Please note that applications are only considered annually at a trust meeting in September. All applications should be received by the trust no later

than August and should be for projects planned for the following year.)

Information gathered from:
Accounts; annual report; Charity Commission record; funder's website.

The Bromley Trust

Human rights, prison reform, conservation
£684,500 (2011/12)

Beneficial area
Worldwide.

Correspondent: Teresa Elwes, Grants Executive, Studio 7, 2 Pinchin Street, Whitechapel, London E1 1SA (tel: 020 7481 4899; email: info@thebromleytrust. org.uk; website: www.thebromleytrust. org.uk)

Trustees: Bryan Blamey; Dr Judith Brett; Peter Alan Edwards; Jean Ritchie; Anthony John Roberts; Anne-Marie Edgell; Nigel Dyson.

CC Number: 801875

In 1989 Keith Bromley set up the Bromley Trust which he termed 'the most important work of my life' committed to 'offset man's inhumanity to man'; he endowed the trust with much of his fortune. The trust supports charities concerned with human rights, prison reform and conservation and sustainability. This well organised and focused trust also offers other organisations with similar interests and objectives the chance to participate in a network of like-minded groups.

In later years, the settlor had been particularly concerned with the plight of prisoners in overcrowded prisons and the waste of public resources spent building more and more prisons. He understood the cycle of re-offending and saw the value of supporting offenders to learn a trade that would enable them to gain employment after release.

In 2004 the Bromley Trust set up three awards in memory of Keith Bromley. Three charities involved with prison reform, were chosen for this additional support. They were the Butler Trust, the Hardman Trust and the Prison Reform Trust.

Additionally, the Koestler Award Trust, which encourages and rewards a variety of creative endeavours culminating in an annual exhibition of work from prison, probation and secure psychiatric hospitals, has named a prize after Keith Bromley as he had been such a support to their work over the years. The Bromley Trust chose nature photography as this had been a great interest of the settlor's throughout his life. The Keith Bromley Award for Outstanding Nature

Photography was presented for the first time at the Koestler exhibition in 2004.

The website provides the following information:

Over the last twenty years the Bromley Trust has made many awards to charities working in the key focus areas of the trust. Our funding is broken down into three main funding streams:

 ▷ Human Rights
 ▷ Prison Reform
 ▷ Environment

Our specific focus areas within these funding streams are periodically reviewed and assessed, with the aim of responding to current areas of need.

If you are interested in applying to the Bromley Trust for support, please check that you fall within our current focus areas, and also read through our general criteria and guidelines, by selecting these from the menu on the left. You can also read through a list of all of our currently funded organisations, and read through details of the application process.

The Bromley Trust is based in London, but funds any UK-registered charities, many of whom undertake work internationally as well as in the UK.

The trust's strategy is detailed as follows:

The Bromley Trust is an independent grant-making foundation. We make grants to charities working in our designated focus areas, where we believe we can achieve the maximum impact. We tend to provide *unrestricted* funding towards organisations that wholly fall within our remit. By supporting the core costs of an organisation we can allow the charity to undertake their work to the best of their abilities. We make relatively small grants, ranging from approximately £5,000 to £20,000 per year. We fund within specific focus areas, within each of our three funding streams. This allows us to direct our funding to particular areas of need. We aim to operate in a clear and transparent fashion, and aim to make the process of applying for a grant as simple as possible. We aim to develop a close relationship with our grantees, in order to best support their work.

Guidelines

The trust's criteria for awarding grants are listed on its website as follows:

 ▷ We can only accept completed application forms – we will not consider any other form of application
 ▷ We can only make grants to UK-registered charities, and are unable to accept any applications from other organisations
 ▷ We will only support charities that fall within our remit and focus areas
 ▷ We are happy to work with other grant-making foundations to support worthwhile work within our focus areas
 ▷ We particularly encourage crossover between our different funding streams and focus areas
 ▷ We tend to provide unrestricted support to organisations that fall wholly within our remit; if you feel that you do not entirely fit within these criteria, but

wish to apply for a specific project or element of your work then please send an email to info@thebromleytrust.org.uk and we will advise you on making an application

 ▷ As we make unrestricted grants, please do not request a specific amount, the size of our grants is made at the discretion of the trustees
 ▷ We are a small grantmaker with limited funds and a high demand. We are only able to support a fraction of the applications that we receive

The trust's website contains full information on recent grants to organisations, many of which are supported on a regular basis. One-off grants are occasionally made, but are infrequent. The trust prefers to give larger amounts to fewer charities rather than spread its income over a large number of small grants.

Grantmaking in 2011/12

In 2011/12 the trust had assets of £15 million and an income of £620,000. Grants were made to 60 organisations totalling £684,500 and were distributed as follows:

Human rights	33	£340,000
Prison reform and prison awards	14	£179,500
Sustainability and conservation	13	£165,000

Beneficiaries included: The Clink (£30,000); Prison Reform Trust (£25,000); Ashden Awards and Redress Trust (£20,000 each); Anti-Slavery International, Landlife and World Pheasant Association (£15,000 each); Cape Farewell, Gatwick Detainees Welfare Group and Wave Trust (£10,000 each); Koestler Award Trust (£8,000); Birdlife Human Rights, Detention Forum and National Working Group for Sexually Exploited Children and Young People (£5,000 each); and PRT – Women's Justice Taskforce (£2,000).

Exclusions

Grants are only given to UK registered charities. The following are not supported:

 ▷ Individuals
 ▷ Expeditions
 ▷ Scholarships, although in certain cases the trust supports research that falls within its aims (but always through a registered charity)
 ▷ Statutory authorities, or charities whose main source of funding is via statutory agencies
 ▷ Overseas development or disaster relief
 ▷ Local conservation projects or charities that work with single species
 ▷ Drug rehabilitation programmes

Applications

New applicants are directed, where possible, to the trust's website where the

trust's criteria, guidelines and application process are posted.

An application form can be accessed from the website for charities that fit the trust's remit, and should be completed and returned via email to: applicant@thebromleytrust.org.uk. There is no strict page limit on completed application forms but the average length is approximately eight to ten pages. Applicants are asked not to return applications which are significantly larger than this.

The trust aims to notify applicants within four to six weeks as to whether or not they are eligible for the next stage of the process, although this may vary. No feedback is given to unsuccessful applicants. All charities are visited before a grant is made. Note: the trust asks that organisations who have previously submitted an application do not submit any further requests for funding. Applicant details are held on the trust's database and if any assistance can be provided in the future, they will make contact.

Percentage of awards given to new applicants: between 10% and 20%.

Common applicant mistakes

'They are not positioned in our focus areas.'

Information gathered from:

Accounts; annual report; Charity Commission record; further information provided by the funder; funder's website.

The Bruntwood Charity

General, social welfare
£120,000 (2011/12)

Beneficial area
UK.

Correspondent: Sally Hill, Trustee, Bruntwood Ltd, City Tower, Piccadilly Plaza, Manchester M1 4BT (tel: 01612 373883)

Trustees: Katharine Vokes; Andy Allan; Rob Yates; Sally Hill; Kathryn Graham; Jane Williams.

CC Number: 1135777

The charity was established in 2010 for general charitable purposes. It is the charity of Bruntwood Ltd, a company which owns and manages commercial property and offices space in Birmingham, Leeds, Manchester and Liverpool. The founder of Bruntwood is Michael Oglesby of the Oglesby Charitable Trust.

From 2011–13 the charity focused on fundraising for five charities; they were: Onside and the Factory Youth Zone (Manchester); St Gemma's Hospice (Leeds); Claire House Children's

Hospice (Liverpool); The Prince's Trust (Birmingham). St Gemma's Hospice is being supported through to March 2015.

In 2011/12 the charity had an income of £105,000 from its fundraising activities. Grants totalling £120,000 were paid to the five nominated charities.

Applications
In writing to the correspondent, although potential applicants should be aware that the relationships with the nominated charities may continue.

Information gathered from:
Accounts; Charity Commission record.

Brushmill Ltd

Jewish causes, education, social welfare
£442,000 (2011/12)

Beneficial area
Worldwide.

Correspondent: Mrs M. Getter, Secretary, 76 Fairholt Road, London N16 5HN

Trustees: C. Getter, Chair; J. Weinberger; E. Weinberger.

CC Number: 285420

Established in 1982, the trust gives grants for education, the relief of poverty and to Jewish causes.

In 2011/12 the trust had an income of £404,000, entirely from donations. Grants were made totalling £442,000, although a list of beneficiaries was not available.

Previous beneficiaries have included Bais Rochel, Friends of Yeshivas Shaar Hashomaim and Holmleigh Trust.

Applications
In writing to the correspondent.

Information gathered from:
Accounts; Charity Commission record.

The Burdett Trust for Nursing

Healthcare
£1.2 million to organisations
(2012)

Beneficial area
Mostly UK.

Correspondent: Rachel Iles, Administrator, SG Hambros Trust Company, Norfolk House, 31 St James's Square, London SW1Y 4JR (tel: 020 7597 3065; email: administrator@btfn.org.uk; website: www.btfn.org.uk)

Trustees: Alan Gibbs, Chair; Dame Christine Beasley; Jack Gibbs; Bill

Gordon; Andrew Martin-Smith; Lady Henrietta St George; Eileen Sills; Jo Webber; Evy Hambro.

CC Number: 1089849

The Burdett Trust for Nursing is an independent charitable trust named after Sir Henry Burdett KCB, the founder of the Royal National Pension Fund for Nurses. The trust was set up in 2002 and established with the following charitable objects:

> To promote and advance education, research and training within the nursing and other healthcare professions for the benefit of the public and to promote public awareness of nursing and health issues; provide for the relief of hardship and mental or physical ill-health among nurses and other health-care professionals, and their dependents; and promote and advance the provision of nursing and other health services for the benefit of the public.

The following is taken from the trust's helpful website and explains the grantmaking policy.

> Currently Burdett Trust for Nursing Trustees focus their funding on three key areas:
> - *Building nursing research capacity:* to support clinical nursing research and research addressing policy, leadership development and delivery of nursing care
> - *Building nurse leadership capacity:* supporting nurses in their professional development to create a cadre of excellent nursing and allied health professionals who will become leaders of the future and foster excellence and capacity-building in advancing the nursing profession
> - *Supporting local nurse-led initiatives:*to support nurse-led initiatives that make a difference at local level and are focused explicitly on improving care for patients and users of services

Grant programmes

To maximise the impact of their funding the trustees work in partnership with other organisations to deliver some of their grant programmes. Details of these programmes can be found on the 'Our Partners' page of the website.

The trust also makes grants and bursaries within other targeted grant programmes, the details of which are set out below.

Delivering Dignity through Empowered Leadership
The Delivering Dignity through Empowered Leadership programme is now closed. [Potential applicants should check the trust's website for current information on the status of this programme.]

Burdett Bursaries
Over the last two years the Burdett Trust has made a series of bursary awards to nurses, midwives and allied health professionals undertaking post-graduate study.

PLEASE NOTE: This programme is currently closed and applicants are advised to revisit [the trust's website] for news about when the programme will be reopened.

International Grants
From time to time the Burdett Trust for Nursing will consider applications from UK registered charities working overseas to build nurse leadership capacity or to empower nurses to make significant improvements to the patient care environment.

Guidance notes are available to download from the website.

Proactive Grants
Burdett Trust for Nursing aims to be more than a reactive grant-making charity. It strives to be a catalyst for change, an active player in improving the health and well-being of patients. To this end the trustees participate in dialogue and share new ideas with grantee organisations, service providers, other funders and government agencies. The trust aims to create opportunities to engage nursing stakeholders in collaborative problem-solving and program development. Through the Proactive Grants programme trustees work with a wide range of public and private partners to advance the foundation's long-term goals. All proactive grants are initiated by the Burdett Trust for Nursing and the trustees do not accept unsolicited applications within this programme.

Grants in 2012
In 2012 the trust had assets of £66.9 million and a consolidated income of almost £1.5 million. Grants approved during the year totalled £1.5 million, of which £307,000 was given to 134 individuals in grants and bursaries.

Beneficiaries included: Tenovus (£188,500); Terrence Higgins Trust (£180,000); Pennine Care NHS Foundation Trust (£116,500); Age Cymru (£168,000); QNIS (£87,000); Hospices of Hope (£50,000); University of Hull (£40,000).

Exclusions
Consult the relevant programme guidance for information on the funding criteria.

Applications
See the trust's website for further information on how to apply for funding. Applicants interested in the 'Funding Partners' programme should consult the appropriate partner website.

Information gathered from:
Accounts; annual report; Charity Commission record; funder's website.

C. M. L. Family Foundation

General charitable purposes

Beneficial area

UK.

Correspondent: Martin Pollock, Administrator, c/o Moore Stephens, 150 Aldersgate Street, London EC1A 4AB (tel: 020 7651 1707)

Trustees: Alexander Lemos; Constantine Lemos; Michael Lemos.

CC Number: 1151765

Registered in April 2013, the foundation's objects are general charitable purposes. The Lemos family are involved in shipping and maritime insurance.

Applications

In writing to the correspondent.

Information gathered from:

Charity Commission record.

Edward Cadbury Charitable Trust

General, community development, education, culture, the environment
£728,000 (2011/12)

Beneficial area

Worldwide, in practice mainly UK with a preference for the Midlands region.

Correspondent: Sue Anderson, Trust Manager, Rokesley, University of Birmingham, Bristol Road, Selly Oak, Birmingham B29 6QF (tel: 01214 721838; fax: 01214 721838; email: ecadburytrust@btconnect.com; website: www.edwardcadburytrust.org.uk)

Trustees: Andrew Littleboy; Charles R. Gillett; Nigel Cadbury; Hugh Marriott; Dr William Southall.

CC Number: 227384

The trust was established in 1945 for general charitable purposes. The trust supports charities which encourage community development, empowerment of the individual and inclusiveness, provide compassionate support to those in need and promote educational, cultural and environmental projects. Support is for charities in the Midlands area including: Herefordshire, Shropshire, Staffordshire, Warwickshire and Worcestershire.

Grants usually vary in size between £500 and £5,000 and are normally awarded on a one-off basis for a specific purpose or part of a project. Larger grants are occasionally made on an exceptional basis. A few grants are awarded to UK groups working overseas and to overseas charities. Grants are rarely made to local charities outside the Midlands region.

In 2011/12 the trust had assets of £30 million. Income for the year totalled £881,000 and there were 65 grants made totalling £728,000. Grants were distributed as follows:

Conservation and the environment	£307,500
Arts and culture	£256,000
Education and training	£75,000
Compassionate support	£37,000
Community projects and integration	£35,000
Research	£14,000
Ecumenical mission and interfaith relations	£5,000

The trust gives the following description of the larger grants made during the year in its annual report:

Larger grants this year have included a grant of £250,000 to Woodbrooke Quaker Study Centre towards its Garden Lounge Development project to improve community facilities; £250,000 to the Birmingham Royal Ballet to set up an Endowment Fund to train young ballet dancers, £35,000 to Birmingham Museum and Art Gallery to purchase specialist equipment to enable the structure and composition of the Staffordshire Hoard to be fully explored; £25,000 to Aston University's Woodcock Sports Centre which included the restoration of the Edwardian swimming baths; £20,000 to Fircroft College of Adult Education, Birmingham, towards the costs of running a residential 'New Directions' programme for priority and prolific offenders; £10,000 to the Youth Hostel Association's centre at Wilderhope Manor, £10,000 towards the costs of setting up a new Marie Curie Cancer Care Hospice in the Midlands and £10,000 to Arthritis Research UK.

Other beneficiaries included: Action Centres UK, Birmingham Museum and Art Gallery – Soho House, Samaritans – Birmingham and Sunfield Children's Home (£5,000 each); Cruse Bereavement Care – Birmingham and Black Country Living Museum (£2,500 each); and Birmingham City Mission, Carrs Lane Counselling Centre, Home from Hospital Care, Marine Conservation, No Panic and St John Ambulance (£1,000 each).

Exclusions

Grants to registered charities only. No student grants or support for individuals.

Applications

The Edward Cadbury Charitable Trust (Inc.) only makes grants to registered charities and not to individuals.

An application for funding may be made at any time and should be submitted in writing to the Trust Manager either by post or email. Trustees request that the letter of application should provide a clear and concise description of the project for which the funding is required as well as the outcomes and benefits that it is intended to achieve. They also require an outline budget and explanation of how the project is to be funded initially and in the future together with the latest annual report and accounts for the charity.

Applications for funding are generally considered within a three month timescale. Note that applications which fall outside the trust's stated areas of interest may not be considered or acknowledged.

Before awarding a grant, trustees assess applications against the trust's objectives and the Charity Commission's public benefit guidelines to check that public benefit criteria are met.

Information gathered from:

Accounts; annual report; Charity Commission record; funder's website.

The William A. Cadbury Charitable Trust

Local welfare and disability charities, environment and conservation, Quaker charities and international development
£675,000 (2011/12)

Beneficial area

West Midlands, especially Birmingham and, to a lesser extent, UK, Ireland and overseas.

Correspondent: Carolyn Bettis, Trust Administrator, Rokesley, University of Birmingham, Bristol Road, Selly Oak, Birmingham B29 6QF (tel: 01214 721464; email: info@wa-cadbury.org.uk; website: www.wa-cadbury.org.uk)

Trustees: Victoria Salmon; Rupert Cadbury; Katherine van Hagen Cadbury; Margaret Salmon; Sarah Stafford; Adrian Thomas; John Penny; Sophy Blandy; Janine Cobain.

CC Number: 213629

This trust was established in 1923 for general charitable purposes. It describes its origins as follows:

William was the second son of Richard Cadbury, who, with his younger brother George, started the manufacture of chocolate under the Cadbury name. He came from a family with strong Quaker traditions which influenced his whole life. It was this Quaker ethos which underpinned his commitment to the advancement of social welfare schemes in the city of Birmingham.

William Cadbury established the trust soon after his two years as lord mayor of Birmingham from 1919 to 1921, wishing to give more help to the causes in which he was interested. One such was the building of the Queen Elizabeth Hospital, a medical centre with the space and facilities to bring together the small specialised hospitals scattered throughout Birmingham [...] He did much to encourage the city library and art gallery and a wide circle of Midland artists who became his personal friends. Through this charity, he also secured several properties for the National Trust.

As time went on, members of his family were brought in as trustees and this practice has continued with representatives of the next three generations becoming trustees in their turn, so that all the present trustees are his direct descendants.

The trust's website outlines a clear grantmaking policy:

▶ The William Cadbury Charitable Trust supports charitable organisations based in the UK. If you do not have a UK base, are not registered with the Charity Commission or are applying as an individual we will not be able to help

▶ Please review the Grant Programmes page [on the trust's website] in order to establish whether your project qualifies for our support. The West Midlands grant programme is sub divided into sectors which may overlap. Please select the sector which best fits your project

▶ Please ensure that your application is brief, concise and to the point. Trustees are required to undertake a large volume of reading prior to a meeting and if you have exceeded the equivalent of three sides of A4 you may be asked to re-submit a shortened application

▶ Trustees will consider applications for core costs as well as for development/project funding

▶ if the trust has supported you in the past, please briefly describe the outcome of the most recent project to receive our support

▶ Grant applications can be submitted online or, if preferred, by post

▶ Applications are considered by trustees on a regular basis and small grants (up to a maximum of £2,000) are awarded monthly

▶ Trustees meet in May and November to award approximately twenty large grants at each meeting, ranging in value from £10,000 to £20,000 with an occasional maximum of £50,000

▶ Grants are normally awarded on a one-off basis and repeat applications are not usually considered within two years of the award

▶ UK bodies legally exempt from registration with the Charity Commission can apply and small grants are occasionally made to unregistered groups in the West Midlands (who must nevertheless have a constitution, an elected committee and a bank account controlled by two or more committee members)

▶ We normally respond to appeals within six weeks of submission. If at that stage your appeal has been shortlisted for a large grant you may be asked to provide additional information and, if

you have not already done so, to complete our online application form. Trustees may also ask to visit certain shortlisted applicants

▶ Applicants selected from the shortlist for consideration at the next half yearly meeting will be notified in the month prior to the meeting

▶ Successful applicants are asked to provide a receipt so that we can meet the requirements of our auditors and it is very much appreciated if this can be done promptly

▶ All applicants will receive a response from the trust whether or not their application has been successful

Birmingham and the West Midlands

▶ *community action* – community based and organised schemes (which may be centered on a place of worship) aimed at solving local problems and improving the quality of life of community members

▶ *vulnerable groups* – vulnerable groups include the elderly, children and young people, the disabled, asylum seekers and similar minorities

▶ *advice, mediation and counselling* – applicants must be able to point to the rigorous selection, training and monitoring of front line staff (particularly in the absence of formal qualifications) as well as to the overall need for the service provided

▶ *education and training* – trustees are particularly interested in schemes that help people of working age develop new skills in order to re-enter the jobs market

▶ *environment and conservation* – projects which address the impact of climate change and projects to preserve buildings and installations of historic importance and local interest

▶ *medical and healthcare* – covers hospices, self-help groups and some medical research which must be based in and be of potential benefit to the West Midlands

▶ *the arts* – music, drama and the visual arts, museums and art galleries

United Kingdom

▶ *the religious society of friends* – support for groups with a clear Quaker connection and support for the work of the Religious Society of Friends in the UK

▶ *penal affairs* – restorative justice, prison based projects and work with ex-offenders aimed at reducing re-offending

Ireland

▶ *peace and reconciliation*

international development

▶ *Africa* – the international development programme is concentrated on West Africa and work to reduce poverty on a sustainable basis in both rural and urban communities – schemes that help children access education are also supported

▶ *Asia and Eastern Europe*

▶ *South America.*

Note: The international development programme is heavily oversubscribed

and unsolicited applications are unlikely to be successful.

Grantmaking

In 2011/12 the trust had assets of £25 million and an income of £902,000. Grants were made totalling £675,000. Grants were broken down as follows:

West Midlands	75%
International development	18%
United Kingdom	5%
Ireland	2%

Beneficiaries across all categories receiving £2,000 or more included: Concern Universal (£90,000); Youth Hostel Association – Wilderhope Manor (£50,000); Birmingham Royal Ballet Trust (£24,000 each); Ideal for All and The Patients Association (£15,000 each); Age Concern and Royal Birmingham Society of Artists (£10,000 each); Castle Gates Family Trust (£8,000); Britain Yearly Meeting of The Religious Society of Friends (Quakers) (£5,000); and Birmingham Settlement (£3,000).

Exclusions

The trust does not fund:

▶ Individuals (whether for research, expeditions, educational purposes or medical treatment)

▶ Projects concerned with travel, adventure, sports or recreation

▶ Organisations which do not have UK charity registration (except those legally exempt)

Applications

Applications can be submitted via the trust's online application form. Alternatively, they can be made in writing to the correspondent, including the following information:

▶ Charity registration number

▶ A description of the charity's aims and achievements

▶ The grant programme being applied to

▶ An outline and budget for the project for which funding is sought

▶ Details of funds raised and the current shortfall

▶ If the organisation has received funding from the trust before, provide brief details of the outcome of this project

There is no requirement to send your charity's annual report and accounts as the trust will refer to the accounts held online by the Charity Commission. Applications are considered on a continuing basis throughout the year. Small grants are assessed each month. Large grants are awarded at the trustees' meetings held twice annually, normally in May and November. Applicants whose appeals are to be considered at one of the meetings will be notified in advance.

Information gathered from:

The Barrow Cadbury Trust and the Barrow Cadbury Fund

Young adult and criminal justice, migration and Europe, and poverty and exclusion

£3 million (2011/12)

Beneficial area

Unrestricted, with a preference for Birmingham and the Black Country (Wolverhampton, Dudley, West Bromwich, Smethwick or Sandwell).

Correspondent: Mark O'Kelly, Company Secretary, Kean House, 6 Kean Street, London WC2B 4AS (tel: 020 7632 9075; email: info@barrowcadbury.org.uk; website: www.barrowcadbury.org.uk)

Trustees: Ruth Cadbury, Chair; Anna Southall; Erica Cadbury; Nicola Cadbury; Tamsin Rupprechter; Gordon Mitchell; Harry Serle; Helen Cadbury.

CC Number: 1115476

Background

The Barrow Cadbury Trust was set up in 1920 as the Barrow and Geraldine S Cadbury Trust and merged with the Paul S Cadbury Trust in 1994. Barrow Cadbury was the eldest son of Richard Cadbury, one of the two brothers who established the Cadbury chocolate factory. His main interest lay in the Quakers, peacetime reconstruction and the relief of war victims after the First World War. He believed that the profits from industry should be diverted into social causes that would safeguard the true welfare of people. In later life, he took a great personal interest in the administration of his trust fund, personally overseeing accounts, writing cheques himself, and addressing envelopes in his own hand.

Barrow's wife, Geraldine Southall, was a thinker and innovator, descended from a family of inventors and entrepreneurs. She campaigned for reform of the penal system and the treatment of children and young adults in the criminal justice system. Geraldine was an early believer in working with the policy-makers and opinion-formers of her day to achieve social change.

The trust aims to encourage a fair, equal, peaceful and democratic society. The income generated from the endowment left by Barrow Cadbury and his wife Geraldine is used to make grants to support groups, (usually registered charities) that are working to achieve the trust's objectives. Grants are made to enable groups to act as catalysts of social change.

The trust was incorporated as a company limited by guarantee in June 2006. In August 2006, the trustees of the unincorporated separate charity the Barrow Cadbury Trust (registered charity number: 226331) transferred the assets, subject to their liabilities, and activities of that charity to this trust.

The company, the Barrow Cadbury Fund, administered and managed by the trustees of the trust, is not a registered charity and supports non-charitable activity where this meets the trust's priorities. Note: it is not possible to apply to the fund.

The trust aims to work in partnership with groups it funds to:

- Build bridges between policy makers and grassroots activity
- Find ways of identifying best practice from projects to help social change
- Encourage new solutions to old problems

General

The trust promotes social justice through grantmaking, research, influencing public policy and supporting local communities. The following themes are prominent across the trust's work:

- Supporting the independence and diversity of the voluntary sector
- Addressing gender-based disadvantage
- Addressing disadvantage based on race and ethnicity
- Funding groups, projects and programmes in Birmingham and the West Midlands

The trust seeks to develop partnerships with the many projects it supports and its main priority is to fund grassroots, user-led projects. Projects that are likely to have a high impact on social change at a policy or practice level are favoured. The trust looks for visionary proposals, often those that are considered radical or risky and great emphasis is placed on projects that are backed by strong leadership. Detailed examples of previously funded projects are available under each programme stream on the trust's website.

The trust is willing to provide match-funding for projects. Organisations should make it clear in their initial proposal if they require match-funding or a contribution to a large project and state whether or not they have secured other funding already. If not, the trust may still consider the application but the final award may depend on securing all of the funding. Funding for core costs is considered but the amount applied for should reflect the amount of funding the organisation is applying for compared to the total organisational budget.

Proposals must explain and justify what costs are being applied for. If the proposal passes the initial assessment the trust will work with the organisation to understand what the full cost of the project delivery will be, including a percentage of the overhead costs for the organisation.

The availability of funds generally dictates what grants the trust is able to make but it does try to ensure a fair geographic spread. The primary focus is on Birmingham and the West Midlands but applications from elsewhere are considered under some programmes. Refer to the specific grant programme criteria below to see which geographic areas are covered.

The trust always receives more applications than it is able to fund. Even if the organisation is eligible and the project meets the criteria, the application may not be successful. Assessments are based on the grant criteria but decisions will be influenced by the finance available and the overall profile of the trust's grantmaking through the year.

Strategic objectives and programmes

The programme priorities are based on social objectives that are of particular concern to the trust. These are based on the existing strengths of work previously funded and current or possible areas of policy development. Projects will be chosen that the trust believes will help to achieve tangible shifts in policy and practice.

The trust aims to develop clusters of activity around each social objective. This means identifying complementary projects, that is, those that add value to the efforts of other groups supported by the trust. It also aims to find ways of connecting them across community sectors and with people involved at different levels of decision-making (including policy officials, practitioners and leaders of statutory and mainstream organisations). This approach means that it is unlikely that the trust will support more than one of the same type of project in any cluster.

The trust aims to stay flexible and respond to current circumstances and will monitor and regularly review its objectives. Any amendments will be highlighted on the trust's website and published each year but this should not affect any projects that it is already considering.

The trust's work is divided into three main areas of interest:

- Criminal justice
- Migration
- Poverty and exclusion

Funding is given through policy and research grants and grassroots funding – under each area of interest.

The following information has been largely taken from the trust's detailed website:

Criminal justice

The trust's current criminal justice work includes:

▶ Transition to adulthood (T2A) alliance
▶ Young adults and criminal justice grassroots
▶ Women offenders and women at risk of offending

The Barrow Cadbury Trust's Criminal Justice Programme aims to support people who are within or at risk of entering the criminal justice system to improve their life chances, with a particular focus on young adults and women. We convene and support the Transition to Adulthood (T2A) Alliance, a coalition of 12 of the leading organisations in criminal justice, youth and health sectors. T2A identifies best practice and campaigns for a more effective criminal justice system for young adults.

The trust is also a member of the Corston Independent Funders Coalition (CIFC), a group of funders who support best practice in relation to women and criminal justice.

Under the Criminal Justice programme, the trust funds:

▶ Projects in Birmingham and the Black Country that support young people in the transition to adulthood to move away from the criminal justice system
▶ Projects in Birmingham and the Black Country that demonstrate effective interventions for girls and women at risk of entering (or who are already in) the criminal justice system
▶ Policy and research work that provides evidence for the T2A campaign

Migration

The Barrow Cadbury Trust's Migration Programme aims to ensure that migration is managed in a way that does not disadvantage vulnerable groups of refugees, asylum seekers and migrants or established residents. It supports groups working with vulnerable migrants and campaigning for their fair treatment.

The trust also works in partnership with think-tanks, policy-makers, academics and campaigners on research and policy work. One important current priority is to help generate a more constructive, balanced and inclusive public and policy debate on migration and integration.

Under this programme, the trust will fund:

▶ Organisations working with the most vulnerable groups of refugees, asylum seekers and migrants, particularly in Birmingham and the Black Country. This includes undocumented migrants, who often face considerable hardship and discrimination
▶ Projects that provide a platform for migrants to speak out at local, national or international level
▶ Campaigning organisations and grassroots groups seeking to influence the public and policy debate on migration
▶ Work promoting greater understanding within communities and countering xenophobia
▶ Work that broadens and deepens the public debate on migration and integration and ensures that it draws on shared values as well as evidence
▶ Policy research that promotes workable and fair policies in relation to immigration and integration

Poverty and exclusion

The Barrow Cadbury Trust's *Resources and Resilience Programme* aims to support people or communities experiencing financial or social exclusion.

We want to help people to build their economic security and overcome barriers to financial inclusion. We also want to support communities to tackle and find solutions to their own problems and have an active role and voice in the structures and services that affect them – we call this 'Community-Led Change.' The trust wishes to achieve change at both a community and structural level and to encourage learning to be shared across these areas.

This programme funds:

▶ Projects in Birmingham and the Black Country that are seeking to build financial inclusion and/or people's ability to participate and influence at a local level to improve their resilience
▶ Projects in Birmingham and the Black Country that are supporting effective and sustainable approaches to building community-led social change at a local level in communities
▶ Policy and research work that support effective approaches to building sustainable and socially just economic systems
▶ Community led mutual aid and enterprise projects in Birmingham and the Black Country, under the Small Change programme

Small Change

Through the Small Change initiative, the trustees want to support mutual aid activities at a local level in Birmingham and the Black Country, where local people both give and receive help from each other. One-off grants of up to £3,000 are available that will either help mutual aid initiatives to start, or that will expand existing activities.

Small Change projects must be:

▶ Mutual – those involved in the project must both give and receive support
▶ Member-led – members of the group must lead the project, services that are provided by a paid worker will not be considered
▶ Sustainable – projects will need to show how they will continue after funding ends without the need for further grants from the trust or another funder
▶ Local – Small Change is intended help people in local neighbourhoods improve life for themselves and others

What type of projects does Small Change support?

The following are examples of ideas that might be eligible for Small Change. There are plenty of others – this list is not exhaustive and any new ideas which fit the programme criteria can be considered:

▶ *Bulk buying schemes and food co-ops* – where a group of local people want to save money by buying in bulk and sharing the costs. Or they might want to take the idea a step further and set up a co-op. Small Change could help with start-up funding to buy initial stocks, but after that, sales would provide the income required to keep the bulk buying scheme or co-op going
▶ *Time banks* – where local people exchange their time with others. Just like a high street bank, they 'pay in' by helping someone else and withdraw' by getting the same number of hours back from another member of the time bank. Small Change could help by, for example, paying for publicity materials to attract new members to the time bank
▶ *Allotments/community gardens* – where a group of volunteers want to grow food for themselves or others in their local neighbourhoods. Small Change could help with funding to buy seeds and equipment, and the project could be sustained through sales of plants, fruit and vegetables
▶ *Collectives* – where a group of local people want to start a small social enterprise that will help other local people and become self-sustaining

You can read case studies of projects funded by Small Change on the trust's website.

It is expected that most applications for Small Change will be from groups with little or no income. However, the trustees will consider applications from larger organisations wishing to support the setting up or expansion of mutual aid projects. If you are not sure if your project is eligible, contact the trust for advice before submitting an application.

Is my project eligible for funding?

To be eligible for Small Change funding, you must be able to say 'yes' to the following questions:

◗ Are you asking for a grant of up to £3,000?
◗ Is your organisation based in Birmingham or the Black Country (Dudley, Sandwell, Walsall or Wolverhampton)?
◗ Is your project designed to help local people help each other?
◗ Will those involved in your project both give and receive support?
◗ Will your project help people who are on low incomes or are isolated?
◗ Is your project able to either continue without further funding once your Small Change grant ends OR do you have realistic plans to generate the income you will need to continue it without applying to Barrow Cadbury or another funder for a grant?
◗ Is your group formally constituted and have you been operating under your constitution for at least six months?
◗ Does your governing body have at least three unrelated people on it?
◗ Do you have a bank account in the name of the organisation?

Ineligible projects

Common reasons for the trustees turning down applications for Small Change are:

◗ One individual is being paid to provide support to others (for example a training course on web design)
◗ The project will need further grant funding after the grant ends
◗ Services are being run on a for-profit basis (projects will be funded where earned income is used to sustain the activities, but not where it is creating a profit to be used elsewhere)
◗ There is little or no element of mutual aid
◗ The service depends on a paid worker

If you can answer all the questions above then visit the website for the Small Change application form. If you are not sure whether your project is suitable for funding through Small Change, you and ring the trust for advice on 020 7632 9068.

Grantmaking in 2011/12

In 2011/12 the trust had assets of £63.5 million and an income of £2.6 million. Grants made during the year totalled £3 million including research and policy grants and excluding all support costs.

Previous beneficiaries include: Castle Vale Tenants' and Residents' Alliance (CVTRA), St Margaret's Community Trust, Young Foundation, IPPR, Centre for Crime and Justice Studies, Revolving

Doors Agency, Stechford Youth Network, Key Birmingham, Migrants' Rights Network, Transatlantic Trends – Immigration Survey, Women for Refugee Women and Refugee Youth.

Detailed examples of funded projects are available under each programme stream on the trust's website.

Exclusions

The trust does not fund:

◗ Activities that the public sector is responsible for
◗ Animal welfare
◗ Arts and cultural projects
◗ Capital costs for building, refurbishment and outfitting
◗ Endowment funds
◗ Fundraising events or activities
◗ General appeals
◗ General health projects
◗ Individuals
◗ Housing
◗ Learning disability
◗ Medical research or equipment
◗ Mental health
◗ Children under 16 and older people
◗ Physical disability
◗ The promotion of religion or belief systems
◗ Schools
◗ Sponsorship or marketing appeals
◗ Unsolicited international projects

The trust will not consider funding the following areas unless they are part of a broader project:

◗ *counselling drug and alcohol services* – will only be considered under the criminal justice programme, and must be part of a broader project that meets the aims of the programme
◗ *environmental projects* – will only be considered under the poverty and inclusion programme, and must be as part of a broader project that meets the aims of the programme
◗ *homelessness and destitution* – will only be considered for those leaving the criminal justice system or in relation to the migration programme
◗ *IT training*
◗ *sporting activities*

The trust asks that organisations planning a proposal that includes one of these services contact the grants team before submitting any application.

Colleges and universities can only apply under the policy and research funding streams.

Applications

The trust asks that potential applicants first contact the grants team, either by calling 020 7632 9068 or completing the online enquiry form on its website.

Note: applicants for policy and research grants under the Criminal Justice and Migration categories are asked to email general@barrowcadbury.org.uk with their proposal or call 020 7632 9068.

If the trust is not able to support the project, it will notify the applicant within one month. It can take three to six months for proposals that the trust wishes to take forward to be assessed and presented to trustees, but the trust will be in contact during this period. Grants are approved by trustees at quarterly meetings throughout the year.

Information gathered from:

Accounts; annual report; Charity Commission record; funder's website.

The Cadogan Charity

General charitable purposes, in particular, social welfare, medical research, service charities, animal welfare, education and conservation and the environment

£2.5 million (2011/12)

Beneficial area

Worldwide. In practice, UK with a preference for London and Scotland.

Correspondent: P. M. Loutit, Secretary, 18 Cadogan Gardens, London SW3 2RP (tel: 020 7730 4567)

Trustees: Earl Cadogan; Countess Cadogan; Viscount Chelsea; Lady Anna Thomson; The Hon. William Cadogan.

CC Number: 247773

The trust was established in 1966 for general charitable purposes and operates two funds namely, the general fund and the rectors' fund. The rectors' fund was created with a gift from Cadogan Holdings Company in 1985 to pay an annual amount to one or any of the rectors of Holy Trinity Church – Sloane Street, St Luke's Church and Chelsea Old Church. The general fund provides support for registered charities in a wide range of areas (see below).

In 2011/12 the trust had assets of £37.6 million and an income of £2.1 million. 79 grants were made totalling almost £2.5 million and were categorised as follows:

Social welfare in the community	37	£1.9 million
Military charities	5	£148,000
Education	7	£143,000
Medical research	19	£89,000
Animal welfare	8	£65,000
Conservation and the environment	3	£40,000

Beneficiaries included: Holy Trinity Church – Sloane Street (£800,000); St George's Cathedral – Perth (£390,000); Royal Horticultural Society (£250,000); Historic Royal Palaces (£200,000); In-Pensioners Mobility Fund (£100,000); Eton College (£50,000); Home of Horseracing Trust (£25,000);

Blue Cross and Priors Court Fountain £20,000 each); Alzheimer's Research Trust, Meningitis Research Foundation Oatridge Agricultural College, Scottish Countryside Alliance Educational Trust and Scottish Uplands Appeal (£10,000 each); Guild of Air Pilots (£9,000); Haven, New Astley Club, Royal Hospital for Neuro-disability, Samaritans and Skin Treatment and Research Trust (£5,000 each); Action for Blind People and Songbird Revival (£2,000 each); and Atlantic Salmon Trust and Epilepsy Research Foundation (£1,000 each).

Exclusions

No grants to individuals.

Applications

In writing to the correspondent. However, note that we have received information stating that the trust's funds are fully committed until 2016.

Information gathered from:

Accounts; annual report; Charity Commission record.

CAF (Charities Aid Foundation)

Capacity building for small and medium sized charities

Beneficial area

Worldwide, in practice mainly UK.

Correspondent: Ms Ann Doan, Correspondent, 25 Kings Hill Avenue, Kings Hill, West Malling, Kent ME19 4TA (tel: 0300 012 3000; fax: 0300 012 3001; email: companysecretary@ cafonline.org; website: www.cafonline. org)

Trustees: Dominic Casserley, Chair; Saphy Ashtiany; Robin Creswell; Philip Hardaker; Alison Hutchinson; Martyn Lewis; David Locke; Stephen Lovegrove; Iain Mackinnon; Matthew Hammerstein; Tina Lee.

CC Number: 268369

In 1924, the National Council of Social Service (now the NCVO) set up a charities department to encourage more efficient giving to charity. In 1958 the charities department began administering deeds of covenant – the first ever means of charities receiving untaxed donations. The following year, the department was re-named the Charities Aid Fund, the purpose of which was to distribute large sums of money for charitable purposes. In 1968, the fund published the first Directory of Grant Making Trusts – a pioneering effort to find new donors and new funding sources, (now researched and published by the Directory of Social Change).

The fund, under the new title, Charities Aid Foundation became an independent registered charity in 1974 and its objectives are to benefit any charitable organisation anywhere in the world. In practice, it works to raise the profile of charitable giving, lobby for tax breaks and provide an increasingly broad suite of services to charities and their supporters. The foundation helps both individual and company donors as well as charities.

CAF also provides banking and investment services to charities, as well as a fundraising support service to help organisations process and manage donations.

CAF's Mission

Motivating society to give ever more effectively, helping to transform lives and communities around the world.

To put this mission statement into action, we:

- Facilitate the most effective support to charities from individual donors, whether through regular donations or a more strategic giving plan
- Support companies' work with charities and communities, and help them engage their employees in charitable activity to achieve greater impact
- Provide tailored solutions for charities' funding and finance needs, across banking, investments, fundraising and social investment
- Help individual and company donors to maximise their support to charities across borders worldwide
- Work to secure supportive legal, fiscal and regulatory conditions for donors, charities and social enterprises.

Programmes

Note the following statement taken from CAF's website:

CAF runs grant programmes on a periodic basis. We do not currently have an open programme and we are unable to accept grant applications or appeals for support.

Each of our funding programmes will have its own theme. We use our data, research and understanding of the sector to develop the theme, then invite organisations who fit the programme theme and criteria to apply for grants. We do not accept unsolicited appeals for grants.

We also manage grant programmes for companies, trusts and foundations to support civil society organisations in the UK and worldwide.

If you would like a list of grants that CAF have awarded, please contact [the advisory team].

Venturesome

Venturesome, a social enterprise initiative, operates where a charity needs finance but its requirements may be too risky for a bank loan or outside the criteria of a grantmaker. It offers loans and investment support to charities and

other social enterprises, to suit the needs of individual organisations. This support might take the form of underwriting, unsecured loans or equity type investments and it is anticipated that the money loaned will be repaid over time.

The programme will only invest in social purpose organisations that:

- Are registered in the UK
- Can clearly state their charitable purpose and social impact (organisations do not have to be registered charities but do need to be of charitable purpose)
- Can provide evidence of at least one year of income (whether from donations or trading)
- Are looking for between £25,000 and £250,000
- Have a legal structure which allows them to take on debt/equity funding

Venturesome manages a fund of £10 million on behalf of CAF and other external investors, including individual philanthropists, foundations and banks. In 2011/12 Venturesome approved £4.6 million in loans and investments to 47 charities, social enterprises and community land trusts.

Technically, CAF made grants worth £331 million in 2011/12 (exclusive of direct, support and governance costs), but almost all of these are 'donor directed' payments where the foundation administers the funds of other donors who are using its financial services. These include separate trusts set up within CAF by donors seeking to use the administrative and grant payment services of CAF while keeping for themselves the decisions about where those grants should go.

Previous beneficiaries include: London Business School, City Centre for Charity Effectiveness Trust – CASS Business School, Nottingham Law Centre, Kairos in Soho, UK Youth Parliament, People in Action, Northern Ireland Childminding Association, Scottish Adult Learning Partnership and African and Caribbean Voices Association.

Applications

In the first instance, applicants to Venturesome should contact the trust directly to discuss their requirements.

Common applicant mistakes

'They assuming that we operate open grant programmes on an appeals response basis.'

Information gathered from:

Accounts; annual report; Charity Commission record; further information provided by the funder; funder's website.

Community Foundation for Calderdale

General charitable purposes
£681,000 (2011/12)

Beneficial area
Calderdale, with ability to manage funds outside of this area.

Correspondent: Danni Bailey, Senior Grants Administrator, The 1855 Building (first floor), Discovery Road, Halifax HX1 2NG (tel: 01422 438738; fax: 01422 350017; email: enquiries@cffc.co.uk; website: www.cffc.co.uk)

Trustees: Leigh-Anne Stradeski; Rod Hodgson; Russell Earnshaw; Juliet Chambers; Roger Moore; Clare Townley; Stuart Rumney; Wim Batist; Susannah Hammond; Spencer Lord; John Mitchell.

CC Number: 1002722

The foundation, as a registered charity, was established for the support or promotion of any charitable purposes; the relief of poverty; the advancement of education (including training for employment or work); the advancement of religion; or any other charitable purpose for the benefit of the community in the area of the Metropolitan Borough of Calderdale and its immediate neighbourhood. Support is also available for other charitable purposes in the United Kingdom with a preference for those which are in the opinion of the executive committee beneficial to the community in the area of benefit.

By raising money through its network of supporting 'members' and donors, and holding a long-term investment fund, the Community Foundation for Calderdale is able to address local need indefinitely – the interest gained on the invested money is given out in grants. This gives local people the opportunity to give to local causes, see where their money has gone and be able to contribute to a permanent pot of cash to benefit the community.

Grants have been given to support causes as varied as social clubs for elderly people, community recycling schemes, children's after-school clubs, community bands, sports clubs, refugee centres, and individuals in crisis.

Grants Programmes

In 2013 the funding programmes listed on the foundation's website were:

General Grants Programme

This funding is available to community groups and charitable bodies working in Calderdale. The General Grants Programme is funded with the income from the foundation's invested endowment. Small grants of up to £900 are available as well as larger grants from £901 to £5,000.

Applications should be made via the foundation's website.

Donor Interest Programme

Awards from this are usually small, from £200 to £3,000. Donors specify their interests and areas of work so that applicants can read about them on the website, and apply via the community foundation if they feel they match their needs.

Health Connections Programme

This programme is managed by the Community Foundation for Calderdale on behalf of NHS Calderdale. There is particular interest in projects that will improve and make a real and sustained difference to people's health locally. The programme aims to provide the opportunity for organisations to be a part of the national drive to improve people's health. Ensure that you read the guidelines, which you can download from the website.

Calderdale College Educational Fund 2013–14

This programme is managed by The Community Foundation for Calderdale on behalf of Calderdale College. It encourages applications that will improve and make a real and sustained difference to the educational attainment of students at Calderdale College. You can see full details of the scheme and how to apply on the foundation's website.

Comic Relief Local Communities Programme 2013–2015

Application deadlines and full details of the scheme are available on the foundation's website. Note that the foundation is currently only processing applications from groups in Calderdale. Groups in Kirklees should contact One Community Foundation and groups in Bradford should contact Leeds Community Foundation.

Yorkshire Venture Philanthropy Programme

This new initiative is supported by the Community Foundations in Leeds, Calderdale and South Yorkshire in partnership with the Key Fund, part-financed by the European Regional Development Fund Programme 2007–13. It consists of a number of different elements: a small grants programme up to £5,000; a combined grants/loan programme for investments over £5,000; pro bono mentoring support and access to a specialist consultancy fund.

For further details, visit the foundation's website.

The Individual Fund

This fund is available to referring bodies working with individuals in crisis or emergency need, particularly those who cannot be supported by statutory agencies.

Referring agencies are authorised organisations and other charities directly supporting individuals (e.g. Calderdale Smartmove, Citizens Advice, Social Services, certain housing associations and some health visitors/health professionals). In some instances, a referring agency may be allocated a pot of money from which to make its own awards within the various criteria set by the Community Foundation.

Referring agencies wishing to apply should, in the first instance, contact the foundation for the current application form.

Noel John Greenwood Halifax Children's Trust

Funds from this trust are available to children and young people (up to the age of 18) in the parliamentary constituency of Halifax who are facing disadvantage in their lives and in accessing education. Grants of up to £130 are available. Support may be granted directly to an individual applicant but is generally granted through a referring agency.

Referring agencies and individuals wishing to apply should, in the first instance, contact the foundation for the relevant application form

Halifax Older Persons Holiday Fund

Funds are available to individuals and couples over the age of 60 in need of support due to economic disadvantage, towards the cost of a short break away from home. The fund provides grants of up to £500 for a couple (or a single person with carer) and £300 for a single person.

Details of the fund and of the application process are available from the foundation's website.

Upper Valley Flood Fund

As part of the flood relief measures the foundation is now also operating a Flood Protection and Resilience Scheme inviting applications from affected householders who wish to make alterations or additions to their properties to make them more resistant to flooding in the future or to make them easier to dry out or repair should flooding occur again. You can see details of the scheme and download an application form on the trust's website.

In case of flooding the foundation has available some FREE Emergency Flood Kits available that can be delivered to flood affected households. To request a flood kit email steve@cffc.co.uk

To make an online donation to the Flood Relief Fund visit www.localgiving.com/cffc

Other Managed Programmes

As recognised, independent experts, the foundation's staff deliver award schemes on behalf of other bodies (e.g. national charities, national and local public sector organisations and grantmaking trusts). Details of schemes will be updated as they come on stream. Schemes currently open for applications are:-

Henry Smith Charity – This charity has a number of different grant programmes available with varying eligibility criteria. You can see further information on their website www.henrysmithcharity.org.uk.

Applications are NOT made through the Community Foundation but directly through the Henry Smith Charity.

In 2011/12 the foundation had an income of £1.3 million, assets of £8.1 million and made grants totalling £681,500. Support costs were £97,500.

Beneficiaries from all categories included: Mirfield Community Trust (£37,000); Healthy Minds (£29,000); Noah's Ark Centre and Relate Pennine Keighley and Craven (£11,000 each); Pavilion in the Park and St Andrew's Youth Centre (£5,000 each); British School Trust (£2,500); Make A Dream £1,000); Rastrick Local History Group (£850); and Halifax Irish JFC and Handmade Parade CIC (£300 each).

Exclusions

The foundation will not fund any of the following:

- General appeals
- Projects which have already taken place or for retrospective funding
- Projects which would normally be funded from statutory sources, i.e., Calderdale MBC, the local education authority, social services or central government
- Projects for the advancement of religion
- Projects where the main beneficiaries are animals
- Projects that do not directly benefit people living in Calderdale
- Political activities
- Applications made up entirely of core and/or running costs (exceptions may be made in extraordinary circumstances)

Applications

The foundation's website has details of the grant schemes currently being administered. Application packs for all of the programmes are available to download from the website. Alternatively, contact the foundation directly and they will send a pack in the post.

If you wish to discuss your project before applying, the grants team are always happy to answer any queries. The foundation also runs a monthly drop-in, where groups can go for advice and support on their applications.

Information gathered from:

Accounts; annual report; Charity Commission record; funder's website.

Calouste Gulbenkian Foundation – UK Branch

Cultural understanding, fulfilling potential, environment, maximising social and cultural value

£1.2 million (2012)

Beneficial area

UK and the Republic of Ireland.

Correspondent: Barbara Karch, Grants Administrator, 50 Hoxton Square, London N1 6PB (tel: 020 7012 1400; fax: 020 7739 1961; email: bkarch@ gulbenkian.org.uk; website: www. gulbenkian.org.uk)

Trustee: The foundation's board of administration is in Lisbon. UK resident trustee: Martin Essayan.

Background

The following information is taken from the foundation's website:

Calouste Sarkis Gulbenkian was an Armenian born in the Ottoman Empire in 1869, his father was a trader and banker in Scutari, just south of Istanbul. Gulbenkian graduated in engineering at King's College London and in 1902 became a British citizen, conducting much of his work from London and then Paris, but finally settling in Portugal. He was both multicultural and multilingual and spent a lifetime bringing together people from different cultures and nationalities. In his will he left his collection – a unique mixture of Eastern and Western art – and almost his entire fortune to a foundation to be headquartered in Lisbon and to bear his name. He wanted his foundation to reflect his interests in arts, science, education and social welfare and told his primary trustee that it should benefit not just Armenian causes but 'all humanity'. The Calouste Gulbenkian Foundation was established in Lisbon in 1956.

The following is taken from the Strategy Leaflet available from the foundation's UK website:

The purpose of the UK branch is to help enrich and connect the experiences of individuals in the UK and Ireland and secure lasting beneficial change. We have a special interest in those who are most disadvantaged and we place a particular emphasis on maximising the beneficial impact of our work through encouraging cross-border exchanges of lessons and experiences.

The UK branch of the foundation is concerned with three key issues:

- Cultural understanding
- Fulfilling potential
- Environment

The values that characterise all the foundation's work include 'aspiring to be innovative, international, independent yet involving'.

Funding Programme

The majority of the foundation's work is proactive. It does however, maintain a small funding stream open to R&D proposals closely related to its three key aims.

The foundation publishes a useful *Strategy Leaflet* from which this information is taken:

The foundation's strategic aims and objectives
Cultural understanding
To help improve people's perceptions of each other by providing opportunities through culture and between cultures.

- Promotion of Portuguese visual art – to support strategic arts initiatives which promote new international arts practice, particularly work from Portugal that has had insufficient exposure in the UK

Fulfilling potential
To assist the most disadvantaged in society to fulfil their potential by building connections and developing opportunities.

- Ageing and Social Cohesion – to support and develop more meaningful connections for older people and across generations

We are interested in receiving proposals specifically for social innovations which have potential for significant impact in reducing loneliness in later life by building connections and relationships. In particular, ideas which engage hard-to-reach groups will be viewed favourably. At the moment we are unlikely to support any new intergenerational initiatives under this strand but please check our website later in the year.

- Multiple needs – to support coordinated, collaborative services for adults facing multiple needs and exclusions

As this programme nears conclusion of its first phase, we are concentrating on reviewing our impact to date and developing plans for how to scale this impact in the next phase. As such, we will not be undertaking any new projects under this theme for the time being but please check our website later in the year.

Environment
To help in the development of a society which benefits from a more sustainable relationship with the natural world and understands the value of its resources.

- Valuing nature – to identify strategies that have impact in promoting the value of the environment and help to drive change to more sustainable lifestyles, through a creative engagement with the natural world

We are currently interested in supporting new ideas or approaches that will help to measure the impact of engagement with the natural world and/or promote a better understanding of the value of the marine environment.

▸ Greening the economy – to identify and promote some effective strategies to help green the economy

We may fund a small number of innovative initiatives to share the learning and/or maximise the impact of the work we have supported to promote 'green and decent' jobs for disadvantaged communities.

Guidelines:
The foundation in the UK is looking to fund projects that:

▸ Scope a new idea to address a specified need or implement new approaches that are already successfully applied in other sectors or outside the UK

▸ Are relevant to our programme of work and meet one or more of the objectives in our strategic aims

▸ Have a clearly articulated vision of how the work will impact beyond the project lifetime

▸ Address and evidence a clearly identified need

What can organisations apply for?

▸ As a guide, grants are likely to average between £10,000 and £30,000

▸ Funding is given for the specific activity proposed and not for general core costs

▸ Although we may occasionally give further funding for projects that are developed as a result of the R&D support, we stress that we do not guarantee continued support

▸ We are open to co-funding projects but not where our contribution is a small part of a much larger budget

▸ Please note that the budget allocated for unsolicited proposals is modest and we approve only a small number of projects each year

Who can apply?

▸ We only accept proposals from not-for-profit organisations based in the UK or Republic of Ireland. If you are not a registered charity or a community interest company, you must be able to demonstrate not-for-profit status and that your constituting document does not allow for any surplus to be distributed to members. We do not fund individuals

▸ We only fund projects that take place in the UK or Republic of Ireland and directly benefit people in those countries. However, we are particularly interested in proposals that may also involve international partners or that emulate good practice in other countries

In 2012 the UK Branch of the foundation made 52 grants totalling £1.2 million awarded as follows:

Social change	£1.1 million
Arts	£418,500
Education	£394,000

Beneficiaries included: Homeless Link (£250,000); Independent Age (£100,000); Battersea Arts Centre and Manchester International Festival (£75,000 each); Climate Outreach and Information Network (COIN) (£50,000); The Geffrye – Museum of the Home (£35,000); British Trust for Conservation Volunteers (£30,000); Capacity Global (£25,000); And Other Stories and Norwood School (£15,000 each); and Planning Aid for Scotland and WWF – UK (£10,000 each).

Exclusions
The UK Branch of the foundation gives grants only for proposals of a charitable kind, from registered charities or similar not-for-profit organisations in the UK or Ireland. It does not fund:

▸ Work that does not have a direct benefit in the UK or the Republic of Ireland
▸ Individuals
▸ Curriculum based activities in statutory education
▸ Student grants or scholarships for tuition and maintenance
▸ Vocational training
▸ Teaching or research posts or visiting fellowships
▸ Educational resources and equipment
▸ Gap year activities
▸ Group or individual visits abroad, including to Portugal
▸ Core services and standard provisions
▸ Routine information and advice services
▸ Capital costs for housing or the purchase, construction, repair or furnishing of buildings
▸ Equipment, including vehicles, IT, or musical instruments
▸ Scientific or medical research
▸ Medicine or related therapies such as complementary medicine, hospices, counselling and therapy
▸ Promoting religion or belief system
▸ Publications
▸ Website development
▸ Sports
▸ Holidays of any sort
▸ Animal welfare

Historically we have supported the arts, arts and science and arts education but we will not any longer consider arts applications unless they meet our current strategic aims. We never make loans or retrospective grants, nor help to pay off deficits or loans, nor can we remedy the withdrawal or reduction of statutory funding. We do not give grants in response to any capital, endowment or widely distributed appeal.

Applications
How and when to apply:

Please use the Initial Enquiry Form to submit your proposal [available on the foundation's website].

▸ Initial enquiries can be submitted at any time of the year but please allow at least three months between submission and the proposed starting date
▸ Proposals are assessed at monthly meetings in the context of other applications
▸ If proposals are short-listed, fuller information will be requested and applicants invited to discuss their project
▸ Final applications will be considered at one of the three annual trustee meetings

Email any queries to the Grants Administrator, Barbara Karch, at: bkarch@gulbenkian.org.uk.

Information gathered from:
Annual review; funder's website. As the foundation is not a charity registered in the UK there are no files at the Charity Commission.

The Campden Charities Trustee

Welfare and education
£388,000 to organisations
(2012/13)

Beneficial area
The former parish of Kensington, London; a north-south corridor, roughly from north of the Fulham Road to the north of Ladbroke Grove (a map can be viewed on the website).

Correspondent: Chris Stannard, Clerk to the Trustees, 27a Pembridge Villas, London W11 3EP (tel: 020 7243 0551; fax: 020 7229 4920; website: www. campdencharities.org.uk)

Trustees: Revd Gillean Craig, Chair; David Banks; Elisabeth Brockmann; Dr Chris Calman; Dr Kit Davis; Robert Atkinson; Susan Lockhart; Tim Martin; Terry Myers; Ben Pilling; Michael Finney; Richard Walker-Arnott; Ms M. Rodkina; Sam Berwick.

CC Number: 1104616

Summary
The Campden Charities were founded by endowments in the wills of Baptist Viscount Campden and Elizabeth Viscountess Dowager Campden who died in 1629 and 1643 respectively. The endowments were '…for the good and benefit of the poor of the parish forever …' and '… to put forth one poor boy or more to be apprentices …'. The charities' area of benefit remains the old parish of Kensington.

The current scheme interprets the original objects in terms of providing grants for the relief of need and for the advancement of education. Grants are made directly for the benefit of individuals and to organisations that assist individuals.

During the course of the financial year to 31 March 2006 the management of the assets of the Campden Charities was transferred to the Campden Charities Trustee. The Uniting Order granted by the Charity Commissioners in a letter dated 25 January 2005 came into effect on 1 April 2005. This order united the Campden Charities Trustee and the Campden Charities under the former's charity number. Since then there has been aggregated accounts and reporting.

The charity is focused on supporting relief in need and education in the former parish of Kensington and the former Royal Borough of Kensington. It must spend at least half of its income available for grant giving on relief in need and up to half on the advancement of education. The trustees' ambition is to make a real impact upon poverty within the area of benefit.

The charity's website states:

Our four main areas of grant giving:
- To assist those of working age to obtain employment with grants for course fees, travel, childcare and equipment
- To support students at university
- Help for older people including cash grants to help with bills and replacement of household appliances
- Grants for not-for-profit organisations that help us with our work with individuals

Grantmaking in 2012/13

In 2012/13 the charity had assets of over £124 million and an income of £3 million. Grants to 19 organisations totalled £388,000. Nine of these organisations were funded under partnership agreements to support individual beneficiaries in particular ways, the remaining ten were supported through referral funding. A further £1.2 million was awarded to individuals.

The following extract from the 2012/13 annual report describes the current grantmaking policy (figures have been rounded to the nearest £1,000):

The trustees' objective is to help financially disadvantaged individuals and families towards financial independence. They seek to do this by identifying the needs of individuals and tailoring packages of support to help them overcome the obstacles they face in improving their circumstances. This help is not restricted to a single payment, trustees want to continue to help people until their circumstances change; this may mean making a number of grants, sometimes over a period of years.

The trustees make incentive payments to non-statutory not for profit organisations that refer and support individuals. After twelve months of receiving such referrals trustees may enter into partnership arrangements to fund work delivered by these organisations to enhance the support offered to individuals. The trustees do not accept unsolicited applications from organisations.

The trustees are guided in their grant giving by two fundamental principles:

Independence
Grants will not be made to support statutory services; neither are the trustees party to local or central Government initiatives or political priorities. The trustees value their position as an independent local grant maker.

Fairness
Trustees seek to make the application process fair to all potential beneficiaries. All grant applications are made and considered in the same manner. There are no privileged applicants and individual trustees are required to declare an interest where appropriate.

Distribution of grants
The scheme governing the charities directs the trustees to apply one half of the charities' income to the relief of need and the other half to the advancement of education save that if in so far as income in any one year is not required for application for the advancement of education, it may be applied to the relief of need.

The young people whom the trustees wish to assist with educational support are those from impoverished backgrounds. Often those young people in greatest need have at some stage become disenfranchised from formal education and they find it difficult to re-engage without extensive professional advice and support. Independent applications made by these young people to the charities are often inappropriate or ill advised. Whilst it is relatively straightforward to make substantial grants to academically able scholars, it is more challenging to provide appropriate financial support directly to those individuals who may need it most.

Similarly adults who have experienced long periods of unemployment often become demoralised; occasionally they find themselves in a 'benefits trap' where they would be financially worse off in low paid employment. Lone parents often cannot finance childcare that would enable them to train. Many of the poorest people have also accumulated significant debt. In recognition of these and many other issues, the trustees employ an unusually large grants officer team so that instead of funding individuals at arm's length, grants officers can build up a relationship with families in need and work with them to tailor individual packages of assistance. Grants Officers also actively seek ways to work with other not-for-profit partners to support the charities' beneficiaries.

The trustees believe that the resources of the charities are well deployed not only in

making grants but also in funding a team of grants officers that can bring 'added value' to the grants made.

Direct grants to individuals
Grants are made in response to direct applications from individuals responding to the charities' publicity and referrals are also welcomed and encouraged from all not for profit organisations and statutory agencies.

This year grants totalling £223,000 were made in support of vocational education. Grants totalling £92,000 were given to families of working age for child-care, fares, goods and services to assist them towards financial independence. In addition 45 grants totalling £131,000 were awarded to encourage academically able young people from disadvantaged backgrounds to attend university.

£784,000 in total was awarded to 752 pension age beneficiaries. 607 were awarded grants in a programme to assist the financially worst off. The number of beneficiaries remaining in the now closed Campden Pensioners scheme reduced from 145 to 115 during the year.

Leaflets were circulated to those in receipt of housing benefit in 2012/13 to ensure that all eligible pension age residents in the area are aware of the opportunity to apply for pension age grants.

Grants to Organisations
The aim of funding not for profit organisations has been to assist those organisations that are supporting individuals receiving direct grants. The focus is on outcomes for individual beneficiaries rather than responding to organisation requests. Organisations operating within the area of benefit are funded where their work directly supports the work of the charities.

In 2012/13 organisations were funded that provided youth work, debt and money management advice, employment advice and counselling as well as direct training providers. The funding of organisations is considered in two ways, partnerships and referral funding.

In 2012/13 grants officers negotiated and renewed individual partnership agreements to support and train individuals with nine organisations, £341,000 was awarded in this way. These organisations provide direct assistance with the plans developed by grants officers for each individual.

Referral funding is intended to help organisations working in a more general way with individual beneficiaries but still within the charities' objects. Referral funding may lead to future partnership funding. Any not for profit organisation working within the charities' broader objects receives funding for each successful referral of an individual to any of the charities' grants programmes; £47,000 was awarded for such referrals during the year.

Beneficiaries of partnership funding included: NOVA and Westway Community Transport (£72,000 each);

Nucleus Legal Advice Centre (£68,000); Volunteer Centre (£50,000); Blenheim Project (£30,000); St Mungo's Housing (£10,000); and North Kensington Women's Textile Workshop (£6,000).

Beneficiaries of referral funding included: Earls Court YMCA (£23,000); Age UK (£8,000); Notting Hill Housing Trust (£3,000); and Harrison Housing, London Cyrenians, St Christopher's Fellowship and St Clements (£1,000 each).

Exclusions

No grants for:

- UK charities or charities outside Kensington, unless they are of significant benefit to Kensington residents
- Schemes or activities which are generally regarded as the responsibility of the statutory authorities
- UK fundraising appeals
- Environmental projects unless connected with education or social need
- Medical research or equipment
- Animal welfare
- Advancement of religion or religious groups, unless they offer non-religious services to the community
- Commercial and business activities
- Endowment appeals
- Projects of a political nature
- Retrospective capital grants

Applications

The charity's website provides the following information:

We are trying to target our resources where they can be of the most direct benefit to financially disadvantaged individuals. **We therefore do not receive unsolicited applications from organisations.**

However, the charities' officers are eager to meet with colleagues from other not-for-profit organisations to explore ways in which we can work together to help individuals to end dependency on benefits or improve a low wage. We make incentive payments to any not-for-profit non-statutory organisations that successfully refer individuals and families to us. The best way to show us that you are working with the people that we want to help is to refer individuals to us and at the same time you will benefit your organisation.

Referrals: Non-statutory not-for-profit organisations that are working directly with low-income residents of Kensington are eligible to receive £1,000 for each individual or family that they refer successfully (i.e. each individual or family that is awarded a grant or pension).

If you have contact with individuals whom you would like to refer, telephone the correspondent:

Working age and students: 020 7313 3797; older people: 020 7313 3794 or 020 7313 3796.

Percentage of awards given to new applicants: less than 10%.

Information gathered from:

Accounts; annual report; Charity Commission record; further information provided by the funder; funder's website.

The Carpenters' Company Charitable Trust

Education, general
£1 million (2011/12)

Beneficial area

UK.

Correspondent: The Clerk, Carpenters' Hall, 1 Throgmorton Avenue, London EC2N 2JJ (tel: 020 7588 7001; email: info@carpentersco.com; website: www. carpentersco.com/charitable_ccct.php)

Trustees: Peter A. Luton; Michael Matthews; Michael I. Montague-Smith; Guy Morton-Smith.

CC Number: 276996

The trust's website provides the following information:

The Carpenters' Company is a City of London Livery Company. It received its first royal charter in 1477, and was granted a coat of arms in 1466.

The Company was originally established as a medieval trade guild to safeguard the welfare and interests of carpenters in the City of London. Today, charitable activities and support for the craft of woodworking through scholarships, competitions and the Building Crafts College are the two cornerstones of its work.

The Carpenters' Company is the senior construction trade company amongst the City Livery Companies, and maintains close links with the carpentry profession and other building trades.

The trust's income is derived from a capital sum gifted by the company's corporate fund, supplemented when warranted by further grants from that fund. The majority of the trust's income each year goes to the Building Crafts College, but the trust also maintains long-standing commitments to numerous other organisations, mainly in the Greater London area. Craft causes receive a high priority when awards are considered. Other charitable causes benefiting from grants include organisations supporting older people, youth and children and people who are homeless.

In 2011/12 the trust had assets of £20 million and an income of £1 million. Grants were made totalling £1 million. Grants were broken down as follows:

Craft activities	£920,000*
Miscellaneous	£80,000
Youth and children's organisations	£20,000
City of London	£20,000
Religious organisations	£6,000

*The Building Crafts College received a grant of over £880,000.

Other beneficiaries included: Carpenters and Docklands Centre (£25,000); Carpenters Road School (£15,000); Wood Awards (£13,000); and Institute of Carpenters (£6,000).

Exclusions

Grants are not normally made to individual churches or cathedrals, or to educational establishments having no association to the Carpenters' Company. No grants (except educational grants) are made to individual applicants. Funds are usually only available to charities registered with the Charity Commission or exempt from registration.

Applications

The consideration of grants is delegated to the Charitable Grants Committee which meets three times each year. Day to day management is the responsibility of the Clerk to whom applications should usually be addressed. However, the trust's website states: 'In normal years the Carpenters' Company Charitable Trust disburses grants to a wide range of charitable causes but all funds for 2013 and 2014 are already committed. We will not be considering new applications until 2015 at the earliest.'

Information gathered from:

Accounts; annual report; Charity Commission record; funder's website.

Cash for Kids – Radio Clyde

Children
£1 million (2012)

Beneficial area

Radio Clyde transmission area, i.e. west central Scotland.

Correspondent: Trust Administrator, Radio Clyde, 3 South Avenue, Clydebank Business Park, Glasgow G81 2RX (tel: 01412 041025; fax: 01415 652370; email: lesley.cashforkids@radioclyde.com; website: www.clydecashforkids.com)

Trustees: J. Brown; Ewan Hunter; Ian Grabiner; Lord Jack McConnell; Sir Tom Hunter; Brenda Ritchie.

SC Number: SCO03334

Set up in 1984, Cash for Kids continues to have as its overall objective: the relief of poverty amongst children in West Central Scotland and South West Scotland who are in need due to ill-health, disability or special needs, financial hardship or other disadvantage – particularly at Christmas. The trustees seek to provide assistance for those children in this community who are most in need of support. In addition to the support given at Christmas, the charity awards financial support throughout the year to groups and organisations that serve the needs of vulnerable children.

Types of Grant

Group grants are paid to groups that help support the health, welfare and educational needs of children, e.g. Gingerbread, Brownies, homeless centres. These are allocated on a per capita basis based on need within the group.

Individual family grants are paid to the supporter (usually a council social work department or recognised voluntary organisation) of the application. It is the supporter's responsibility to ensure that the award is used to benefit the child or children named in the application.

Special grants or sustainable grants are paid to the group or organisation to help support children facing physical, emotional or educational challenges.

For further information, contact the trust directly or go to its website.

We have taken information for this entry from the brief details given on the OSCR's website and also the charity's website. Unfortunately we were unable to view a copy of the full accounts for 2012.

In 2012 the charity had an income of £1.41 million and a total expenditure of £1.47 million. We have estimated the total grant figure for this year to be in the region of £1 million.

Previous beneficiaries include: Aberlour Bridges Project – Royston: supporting children affected by addiction; and Centre for Under 5s Toy Library: supporting children with physical disabilities through a novel 'Toys on the Road' mobile library.

Exclusions

The trust does not fund:
- Trips or projects abroad
- Medical treatment/research
- Unspecified expenditure
- Deficit funding or repayment of loans
- Retrospective funding (projects taking place before the grant award date)
- Projects unable to start within six months of the grant award date
- Distribution to another/other organisation/s
- General appeals or endowment funds
- Relief of statutory responsibility
- The promotion of religion

No funding for capital expenditure except in very special circumstances that must be made clear at the time of applying. Organisations whose administration costs exceed 15% of total expenditure will not be supported.

Applications

Application forms and guidelines are available from the charity's website.

Percentage of awards given to new applicants: less than 10%.

Common applicant mistakes

'Not providing sufficient information as to how they will spend the grant; not showing a true reflection of their organisation's current state of affairs; and applying for the wrong type of grant for the ask.'

Information gathered from:

Accounts; annual report; OSCR record; further information provided by the funder; funder's website.

Sir John Cass's Foundation

Education in inner London
£968,500 (2011/12)

Beneficial area

The inner London boroughs – Camden, Greenwich, Hackney, Hammersmith and Fulham, Islington, Kensington and Chelsea, Lambeth, Lewisham, Newham, Southwark, Tower Hamlets, Wandsworth, Westminster and the City of London.

Correspondent: Tony Mullee, Clerk/Chief Executive, 31 Jewry Street, London EC3N 2EY (tel: 020 7480 5884; fax: 020 7488 2519; email: contactus@sirjohncass.org; website: www.sirjohncass.org)

Trustees: Kevin Everett; HH. Judge Brian Barker; Graham Forbes; David Turner; Mervyn Streatfeild; Helen Meixner; Dr Ray Ellis; Sarah Dalgarno; David Hogben; Prof. Michael Thorne; Inigo Woolf; Revd Laura Jorgensen; Right Revd Bishop Christopher Chessun; Trevor Critchlow; Paul Bloomfield; Jennifer Moseley; Sophie Fernandes.

CC Number: 312425

The principal objective of this foundation is the promotion of education of young people in attendance at Sir John Cass's Foundation and Red Coat Secondary School, Sir John Cass's Foundation Primary School, the London Metropolitan University or resident in the City of London, the Royal Borough of Kensington and Chelsea, and the London Boroughs of Camden, Greenwich, Hackney, Hammersmith and Fulham, Islington, Lambeth, Lewisham, Newham, Southwark, Tower Hamlets, Wandsworth and the City of Westminster.

The following information is taken from the foundation's annual report:

The Sir John Cass Foundation dates formally from 1748. The foundation takes its name from its founder who was born in the City of London in 1661 and, during his lifetime, served as both Alderman and Sheriff. He was also MP for the City and knighted in 1713. In 1710 Cass set up a school for 50 boys and 40 girls in buildings in the churchyard of St Botolph-without-Aldgate. Intending to leave all his property to the school, when he died in 1718 of a brain haemorrhage, Cass had only initialled three pages of his will. The incomplete will was contested, but was finally upheld by the Court of Chancery 30 years after his death. The school, which by this time had been forced to close, was re-opened, and the foundation established.

The history of the foundation touches upon education in and around the City of London at almost every level, ranging from primary education to postgraduate study and representing an historical microcosm of the development of English education over more than three centuries. Today, the foundation has links in the primary, secondary and tertiary sectors of education. It provides support to its primary school in the City of London and its secondary school in Tower Hamlets, as well as the Sir John Cass Department of Art, Media and Design (part of London Metropolitan University) and the Cass Business School (part of City University).

In addition, the foundation supports three academies; St Mary Magdalene and the City of London Academies in Islington, and St Michael and All Angels Academy in Camberwell. It has also awarded grants to 34 secondary schools across inner London towards their bids to become designated as Specialist Schools, including a grant to Elmgreen School in Lambeth, which is the first parent promoted school in the country.

The foundation gives its name to Cass Housing Estate located in and around Cassland Road in Hackney.

Grants are made to organisations for educational work with children and young people in inner London. The majority of grants are revenue funding for projects, though capital grants are occasionally made.

There is also a substantial programme of support for individual students with priority to those aged 19–24. (see *The Guide to Educational Grants* also published by the Directory of Social Change).

The foundation continued to provide support in the form of rent free accommodation to the Sir John Cass's Foundation Primary and Secondary Schools, Cass and Claredale Halls of

Residence and London Metropolitan University, equating to a significant benefit to each of these educational institutions.

The foundation will only consider proposals from schools and organisations that benefit:

- Children or young people under the age of 25, who are permanent residents of named *inner* London boroughs (Camden, Greenwich, Hackney, Hammersmith and Fulham, Islington, Kensington and Chelsea, Lambeth, Lewisham, Newham, Southwark, Tower Hamlets, Wandsworth, Westminster and the City of London) and from disadvantaged backgrounds or areas of high deprivation

Priorities

The foundation has four areas of focus for grant giving, which are as follows:

- Widening participation in further & higher education
- Truancy, exclusion and behaviour management
- Prisoner education
- New initiatives

There are one or more priorities for each area of focus. Details of the priorities and our aims and objectives for each area of focus are:

Widening Participation in Further and Higher Education

Aim

To promote access to further and higher education for disadvantaged young people in inner London.

Objective

To increase the number of inner London students from disadvantaged backgrounds successfully participating in further and higher education.

Priorities

Work with communities currently under-represented in further and higher education and/or hard to reach learners (e.g. care leavers or young people with learning difficulties). Applications could involve work with secondary school pupils as well as those in further education and universities.

Truancy, Exclusion and Behaviour Management

Aim

To encourage and support children and young people's attainment through initiatives that help them engage with, and stay in, education.

Objectives

- To reduce truancy levels amongst pupils attending primary and secondary schools
- To reduce levels of exclusions and expulsions
- To improve pupil motivation, behaviour and achievement through initiatives that promote children and young people's emotional well being and social development

Priority

Work with primary and secondary schools in challenging circumstances and/or those with higher than average truancy, exclusion or expulsion rates. Challenging circumstances could include, for example, schools in areas of high social deprivation or in special measures, as well as schools that have higher than average rates of truancy, exclusion or expulsion.

Prisoner Education

Aim

To reduce re-offending through education and initiatives that promote employability.

Objectives

- To improve the literacy and numeracy skills of prisoners and ex-offenders
- To help prisoners and ex-offenders gain skills and education qualifications that will help them into employment

Priority

Work with prisoners and ex-offenders that helps secure employment and prevent re-offending.

New Initiatives

Aim

To influence and improve education policy and practice, both within the foundation's area of benefit and more widely.

Objectives

i) To test new and ground breaking approaches to learning that have the potential to enhance and influence education policy and practice.

ii) To support work that focuses on identified needs and gaps in statutory provision.

Priorities

- Projects that are pioneering and original in their approach to teaching or learning and are strategic (relates to objective i)
- projects addressing an identified need within a geographical area or learning establishment that are new and innovative in context i.e. must be a new initiative for the school or borough, but need not be a completely new approach to education (relates to objective ii)
- Projects that focus on addressing under-achievement in literacy and numeracy in primary and secondary schools (relates to objectives i and ii)
- Projects seeking to attract greater numbers of young people into the teaching profession (relates to objectives i and ii)

Applicants should say which priority their project addresses as well as describing how their project meets that priority. Applications need not meet more than one priority but, for those that do, applicants are welcome to describe how their application meets each of the priorities.

Grantmaking in 2011/12

In 2011/12 the foundation had assets of £119.4 million and an income of £6 million. Grants were made to organisations and schools totalling £968,500, with a further £153,500 being awarded in grants to individuals.

Grantmaking to organisations and schools was broken down as follows:

Organisations	£342,500
Foundation's schools	£338,500
Institutions bearing the founder's name	£224,500
Organisation's working with the foundation's schools	£63,000

Beneficiaries included: British Schools Exploring Society (£50,000); Music First (£44,000); Pitch Perfect (£30,000); East London Business Alliance (£22,000); University of the Arts (£16,500); New Bridge (£10,000); and the Specialist Schools and Academies Trust (£5,000).

Exclusions

There are many activities and costs that the foundation will not fund. The following list gives a sample of the type of activities the foundation does not support:

- Projects that do not meet a foundation priority
- Conferences, seminars and academic research
- Holiday projects, school journeys, trips abroad or exchange visits
- Supplementary schools or mother tongue teaching
- Independent schools
- Youth and community groups, or projects taking place in these settings
- Pre-school and nursery education
- General fundraising campaigns or appeals
- Costs for equipment or salaries that are the statutory responsibility of education authorities
- Costs to substitute for the withdrawal or reduction of statutory funding
- Costs for work or activities that have already taken place prior to the grant application
- Costs already covered by core funding or other grants
- Curriculum enhancing projects
- Capital costs, that are exclusively for the purchase, repair or furnishing of buildings, purchase of vehicles, computers, sports equipment or improvements to school grounds

Applications

The foundation operates a two stage application process – an initial enquiry and a full application stage.

The following information has been taken from the foundation's website:

Stage 1

Complete and submit the initial enquiry form which is available from the foundation's website and on request from the correspondent. The form asks for:

- Outline information about your proposed project
- Information about how the project meets the foundation's priorities
- A summary of the project that includes the following information: the aims of the project including outputs and

outcomes, how the project will be delivered; the duration of the project, including when and where it will take place; and a budget covering project costs

We will consider your enquiry and inform you, within three weeks, whether or not you may proceed to Stage 2. If we have any queries we may contact you during this time to discuss details of your project submitted in the initial enquiry form. We receive a large number of applications. Unfortunately, this means that good projects sometimes have to be refused even if they meet a priority. If we invite you to proceed to Stage 2 and submit a full application, we will send you a copy of our Stage 2 application guidelines for schools and organisations.

Stage 2

Complete your detailed application and send it to us with copies of your memorandum and articles of association (or constitution) and your organisation's latest annual report and accounts.

Assessment and decision making process

On receipt of your application our staff may meet with you as part of our assessment process. After we have received responses to any queries and any further information requested, a report on your application will be considered by the foundation's grants committee, whose decision is final. The grants committee meets in March, June and November each year. It normally takes between two and four months from receipt of a full application until a decision is made.

Notification of the decision

All applicants will be sent formal notification of the outcome of their applications within two weeks of the committee decision.

Successful applicants

Those who are offered a grant will be sent a formal offer letter and copies of our standard terms and conditions of grant. Copies of our standard terms and conditions of grant are available on our website. Additional conditions are sometimes included depending on the nature of the grant.

Monitoring and evaluation

Staff will contact you to clarify and agree how the outputs and outcomes for your project will be monitored and evaluated. Your project will be visited at least once during the lifetime of the grant. If your grant covers more than one year you will be asked to submit a progress report for each year. Continuation of multi-year grants is dependent upon satisfactory progress towards agreed outputs and outcomes. At the end of the grant you will be asked to provide a final report. The foundation provides guidance on the structure and content of these reports.

Unsuccessful applicants

Applying for funding is a competitive process and the foundation's grants budget is limited. Because of the high volume of applications received, good projects sometimes have to be refused, even if they meet a priority. All applications are assessed on merit. If your application is refused you can apply again twelve months after the date you submitted your last application.

Information gathered from:

Accounts; annual report; Charity Commission record; funder's website.

The Charities Advisory Trust

General

£500,000 (2011/12)

Beneficial area

UK and overseas.

Correspondent: Dame Hilary Blume, Director, Radius Works, Back Lane, London NW3 1HL (tel: 020 7794 9835; fax: 020 7431 3739; email: people@ charitiesadvisorytrust.org.uk; website: www.charitiesadvisorytrust.org.uk)

Trustees: Prof. Cornelia Navari; Dr Carolyne Dennis; Brij Bhasin; Dawn Penso.

CC Number: 1040487

Summary

In 1979, by way of Home Office funding, Dame Hilary Blume started the Charity Trading Advisory Group to provide impartial information on all aspects of trading and income generation for charities. The charity's stated aim is to find practical methods of redressing inequalities and injustice.

The trustees' annual report for 2011/12 states:

> The objects of the charity are to relieve poverty throughout the world; advance education; preserve buildings and monuments of architectural merit; assist charities so that they may make better use of their assets and resources both generally and in relation to trading and/or fundraising activities; and advance any other charitable purposes.

The charity's main objectives for the year were:

▶ Strive and maintain Card Aid, in a falling market, as a service to charities
▶ Improve IT; this is an ongoing process
▶ Expand Knit for Peace, particularly in the UK
▶ Explore new ways of generating income using the internet

Plans for future periods:
▶ Nurture Card Aid and Good Gifts Catalogue through difficult economic circumstances
▶ Make sure charities (and their beneficiaries) continue to receive support, particularly those in most need
▶ Expand Knit for Peace

▶ Scale back on costs so as to protect the amounts available for the beneficiaries

Grantmaking policies

The charity is willing to consider applications for any charitable purpose throughout the year, but rarely responds to unsolicited applications for projects of which it knows nothing (in such cases, where support is given the amounts are usually £200 or less). Nearly all grants are made because the charity has a prior knowledge of the project or area of concern. In most cases the idea for the project comes from the charity itself; it works with suitable organisations to achieve its objectives. The charity very rarely gives grants directly to individuals in need, and does not support missionary work of any religion.

Current Projects are listed on the charity's website as:

Card Aid

In 1980 we established Card Aid and revolutionized the charity Christmas card market in 3 ways: (a) by providing charities with a tailor-made service plus pragmatic advice, (b) by supplying Christmas cards to companies who welcome the ability to support charity and (c) helping charities access new markets through the Card Aid chain of charity Christmas card shops, the largest in London, selling high quality cards for over 100 charities and good causes. Over the years, Card Aid has raised tens of millions.

Scrooge Awards

2013 [was] our 12th Scrooge Awards. We have run a very successful campaign to highlight the small amount going to charity on so called charity cards sold on the high street. Commercial card companies and retailers try to cash in on the charity card market. The Scrooge Awards highlight bad practice.

Good Gifts Catalogue

In autumn 2003, we launched the Good Gifts Catalogue, a radical concept in giving, employing charitable donations to buy imaginative gifts like 'goats for peace' and acres of threatened rain forest. The soaring success of the idea has not only generated many millions of pounds, but also a slew of imitations. However, Good Gifts remains the catalogue uniquely committed to the principle of actually buying the gifts stated, rather than using the income for general purposes.

Grant Giving

The trust gives has been giving over £500,000 a year, eclectically and nearly all pro-actively. We find the projects and the people and help them develop their ideas.

The Green Hotel

We established The Green Hotel, in Mysore, South India as a model of sustainable tourism with all profits given to charitable and environmental projects in India. Green in both name and operation, our hotel has been garlanded with numerous travel accolades and awards, with the most satisfying comment coming from Time magazine (Asia): 'the best place in Asia to improve your karma.

Peace Oil

Peace Oil, a Charities Advisory Trust initiative, is produced in Israel by Jews, Arabs, Druze and Bedouins working together. The olives, grown in the foothills of the Carmel Mountains, are pressed within hours of picking to produce a prize winning extra virgin oil. By encouraging co-operation between communities and helping to market their produce, we hope that Peace Oil will deliver economic prosperity, encouraging others to follow its example.

Grantmaking in 2011/12

In 2011/12 the trust had assets of £2.5 million and an income of £1.4 million. Charitable activities are also listed at £1.4 million. The trust states on its website that £500,000 is given in grants each year and this is the figure we have used.

The main beneficiaries listed in the accounts included: Survivors Fund (£112,000); Africa Education Trust (£50,000); Ashwini (£14,000); Ikamva Labantu (£79,000); Shuhada Organisation (£27,000); and Life for African Mothers (£18,000).

Smaller grants were made to a wide range of organisations through the Card Aid and Good Gifts schemes.

Exclusions

The trustees rarely respond to unsolicited applications for projects of which they have no knowledge. In such cases where support is given, the amounts are usually £200 or less. No support for individuals, large fundraising charities or missionary work.

Applications

The trustees are pro-active in looking for causes to support. They are though 'happy for charities to keep us informed of developments, as we do change our support as new solutions to needs emerge'.

Unsolicited applications for projects about which the trust know nothing are rarely responded to.

To apply, simply send details of your proposal (no more than two pages in length) in the form of a letter. You might try to include the following information:

▶ The aims and objectives of your organisation
▶ The project for which you need money
▶ Who benefits from the project and how
▶ Breakdown of the costs and total estimated costs
▶ How much money you need from the trust
▶ Other funding secured for the project
▶ A summary of your latest annual accounts

If we refuse you it is not because your project is not worthwhile – it is because we do not have sufficient funds, or it is simply outside our current area of interest.

Percentage of awards given to new applicants: between 10% and 20%.

Information gathered from:

Accounts; annual report; Charity Commission record; further information provided by the funder; funder's website.

Charitworth Ltd

Religious, educational and charitable purposes. In practice, mainly Jewish causes

£904,000 (2011/12)

Beneficial area

Worldwide, mainly UK and Israel.

Correspondent: David Halpern, Trustee, Cohen Arnold and Co., New Burlington House, 1075 Finchley Road, London NW11 0PU (tel: 020 8731 0777; fax: 020 8731 0778)

Trustees: David Halpern; Reilly Halpern; Sidney Halpern; Samuel J. Halpern.

CC Number: 286908

This trust was set up in 1983 and its objects are the advancement of the Jewish religion, education, relief of poverty and general charitable purposes. It is particularly interested in supporting Jewish charities.

In 2011/12 the consolidated statement for the year declared assets of £25.2 million (charitable funds over £10 million) and an income of £782,000. Grants were made during the year totalling £904,000. There was no list of beneficiary organisations included in the annual report and accounts.

Previous beneficiaries include: Zichron Nahum; British Friends of Tshernobil; Cosmon Belz; Chevras Maoz Ladal; Dushinsky Trust; Centre for Torah Education Trust; Finchley Road Synagogue; Friends of Viznitz; Beer Yaakov; and Beis Soroh Schneirer.

Applications

In writing to the correspondent.

Information gathered from:

Accounts; annual report; Charity Commission record.

The Childs Charitable Trust

Christian, general
£740,000 (2011/12)

Beneficial area

Worldwide.

Correspondent: Melanie Churchyard, Secretary, 3 Cornfield Terrace, Eastbourne, East Sussex BN21 4NN (tel: 01323 417944; email: info@childstrust. org; website: childscharitabletrust.org)

Trustees: Derek N. Martin; John Harris; Chris Large; Andrew B. Griffiths; Steve Puttock.

CC Number: 234618

The objects of the trust are the furtherance of Christian Gospel, education, the relief of poverty and other charitable causes. The principal object is the furtherance of the Christian Gospel and the trustees are actively involved in supporting and encouraging Christian charities to achieve this goal. There is a preference for large-scale projects in the UK and abroad and ongoing support is given to some long-established Christian organisations.

In 2011/12 the trust had assets of £9.1 million and an income of £409,000. Grants were made totalling over £740,000 which included £70,000 to organisations outside the UK and £750 to individuals.

Beneficiaries included: Amano Christian School (£67,000); Redcliffe College (£58,000); Mission Aviation Fellowship (£38,000); Memralife Group (£33,000); LAMA Ministries (£27,000); Institute for Bible Translation and Outreach UK – Home Evangelism (£25,000 each); Cross Teach (£21,000); Slavic Gospel Association (£14,000); Scripture Gift Mission (£13,000); Moorlands College (£10,000); Operation Mobilisation (£9,000); People Matter (£7,000); Christian Institute, Elam Ministries, Frontiers, Hope FM, London City Mission and Shared Hope (£5,000 each); and Sports Reach (£2,000).

Applications

In writing to the correspondent. The trust states that 'all applications are considered but, unfortunately, not all charitable causes can be supported'. Funds may also be committed for long-term projects.

Information gathered from:

Accounts; annual report; Charity Commission record; funder's website.

The Childwick Trust

Horse racing and breeding, welfare of and research into thoroughbred horses: health, people with disabilities and older people and Jewish charities in the UK, education in South Africa

£2.4 million (2011/12)

Beneficial area

UK; South Africa.

Correspondent: Karen Groom, Trust Administrator, 9 The Green, Childwick Bury, St Albans, Hertfordshire AL3 6JJ (tel: 01727 844666; email: karen@childwicktrust.org; website: www.childwicktrust.org)

Trustees: John Wood, Chair; Anthony Cane; Peter Glossop; Sarah Frost; Peter Anwyl-Harris.

CC Number: 326853

The trust was established in 1985 by the settlement of assets of the late founder, Mr H J Joel. The principal objects of the trust under which grants are awarded are as follows:

▶ To assist older people in need including the former employees of the settlor and of companies associated with the settlor and the families of such former employees
▶ To make payments to charities or for charitable objects connected with horse racing or breeding within the United Kingdom or people involved with horse racing or horse breeding who shall be in need
▶ To make payments to Jewish charities within the United Kingdom or support Jews in need within the United Kingdom
▶ To support charities and charitable objects for the education and benefit of people and the families of people who intend to work, are working, or have worked in the mining industry in the Republic of South Africa
▶ To support the education of people resident in the Republic of South Africa
▶ To make payments for the benefit of charities for the promotion of health and relief of people with disabilities within the United Kingdom

The Childwick Trust controls a subsidiary charity in South Africa, The Jim Joel Education and Training Fund, through which it conducts its South African based charitable objects.

The bulk of the grants awarded each year are made to charities that promote health and relief of people with disabilities in the UK. The next largest proportion of grants goes to charities in

South Africa via the subsidiary charity. Charities connected with thoroughbred racing and breeding are next in line and Jewish charities follow. These funding preferences were set by Mr Joel in the Trust Deed in 1985 and are not changed by the trustees.

Summaries of the main grant categories, taken from the trust's website, are given below:

Disability, the elderly and serious illness

The trust has a strong emphasis on helping charities which offer care and support for people who are terminally ill, or have a serious illness, the elderly, adults and children who have mental health problems or a learning disability. We give help to both children and adults with physical disabilities and offer funding towards specialist equipment, respite care, holidays, education and core costs.

We support both adult and children's hospices specifically those based in the South East of the UK and funding is given to all aspects of hospice care including running costs.

We help the elderly who are vulnerable and isolated and in need. Funding is offered towards respite for carers, general care and support plus specialist equipment.

Please note that applications from national organisations and charities will only be considered for the benefit of people in the South East of England.

We are happy to consider funding from organisations who offer care and support for ex-servicemen and women who have been injured or traumatised from past and recent conflicts.

Medical research projects form only a small part of what we fund.

Within the above criteria we will consider support for specialist equipment, salaries which are related to nursing and general care. We will consider funding towards some building and refurbishment costs but only once the appeal has reached at least half of the total budget.

N.B. Around half the trust's grants are distributed under this object. Typically grants range from £5,000 – £30,000.

South Africa

The trust also operates in South Africa. This area of our objects reflects the Joel family's long involvement in the mining industry in South Africa. Predominantly funds are given to early childhood development projects and applications are administered on behalf of the directors by Mrs Giuliana Bland at The Childwick Trust's Jim Joel Fund in South Africa.

Mrs Bland can be contacted at jimjoel@iafrica.comor by telephone on (0027) 01170 46539. Office hours are Monday and Tuesday mornings between 8am-1pm.

The trust also provides funding for South African residents to promote education

through charitable institutions in South Africa or the U.K.

Horseracing

The major portion of funding under this object is given to the welfare of those in need within the racing industry. This is generally aimed at people who are elderly and retired, injured and those on a low income plus young people who need support.

Other applications outside this area may be considered as long as it is related to either the welfare of people in the industry or connected to the welfare of thoroughbred race horses.

Jewish Charities

Mr Joel (the founder) was Jewish and his wish was to benefit charities which promote the Jewish faith and to help Jewish people in need. We consider applications from Jewish charities throughout the UK that help the elderly, adults with disabilities and children and young people. Please note payments are only made to benefit charities in the UK and not in Israel.

Grants in 2011/12

In 2011/12 the trust had assets of £70.4 million and an income of nearly £2 million. 249 grants were made totalling almost £2.4 million.

UK

Grants were made totalling £2.2 million. Beneficiaries included: Racing Welfare – Newmarket (£200,000); British Racing School – Newmarket (£100,000); Early Learning Resource Unit (£40,000); Iain Rennie Grove House Hospice – St Albans (£30,000); Deafblind UK – Peterborough and St Elizabeth's Centre – Hertfordshire (£20,000 each); J's Hospice – Chelmsford (£18,000); and Hop, Skip and Jump – Gloucestershire and Not Forgotten Association – London (£15,000 each).

A further £9,000 was given in welfare payments to pensioners.

South Africa

Grants were made totalling £145,000. Beneficiaries included: Ntataise Trust (£65,500); Tree – South Africa (£41,000); Little Elephant Training Centre (£29,000); Sekhukhune Educare Project (£21,000); Thusanang Association (£20,000); and Sego Monene and Sunshine Centre Association (£16,000 each).

Exclusions

Grants to registered charities only. No funding for:

▶ Complementary health and therapy projects
▶ Charities offering legal advice
▶ Charities offering counselling
▶ Hospices outside the South East of England
▶ NHS Hospitals and other statutory bodies

- Universities – academic research, scholarships and bursaries
- Homeless charities
- Projects related to drugs or alcohol addiction
- HIV/Aids related projects
- Charities which are part of a wider network i.e. Age UK, Mind, Mencap etc., only those who are based within the South East can apply
- Individuals or organisations applying on behalf of an individual (other than in relation to South African educational grants)
- Students seeking sponsorship for educational or gap year projects
- Animal charities unless they are connected to thoroughbred racehorses
- Larger charities with widespread support are less likely to be considered unless they support local causes in Hertfordshire/Bedfordshire
- National appeals
- Conferences, Seminars and workshops
- Organisations that have received a grant within the previous two years
- Apart from South Africa, funding outside the UK

Applications

In writing to the correspondent. Note: the trust welcomes initial enquiries by email or telephone, but asks that formal applications are sent by post.

There is no official application form but the trust does provide the following guidelines for potential applicants:

- Applications should be written, with a fully completed cover sheet (available from the trust's website)
- Applications should be no longer than two pages of A4
- Applications must clearly and concisely describe the project for which funding is being sought
- Applications should include breakdown of costings for the project
- Applications SHOULD NOT include charity accounts
- Applications SHOULD NOT include DVDs, newsletters or bulky reports

Applications that do not meet these requirements will not be considered for funding – should the trust require any further documentation, staff will request it.

Post to Karen Groom after following the guidelines given in the PDF document 'Guidelines for Applicants' available from the trust's website. This should include a fully completed 'cover sheet', also available from the website. The trustees meet in January and July to consider applications which can be submitted between the months of April – May and October – November. Applications are assessed before each meeting to check that they meet the trust's objectives. Applicants will be informed of the outcome within six weeks following the meeting.

Note: Applications for funding in South Africa should be made to Mrs G. Bland (Fund Director) at jimjoel@iafrica.com.

Percentage of awards given to new applicants: between 10% and 20%.

Common applicant mistakes

'They write to us at the wrong time; they don't read the guidelines; and inappropriately addressed or wrongly addressed applications.'

Information gathered from:

Accounts; annual report; Charity Commission record; further information provided by the funder; funder's website.

CHK Charities Ltd

General charitable purposes
£1.6 million (2011/12)

Beneficial area
UK, with a special interest in national charities and the West Midlands.

Correspondent: Nick Kerr-Sheppard, Administrator, Kleinwort Benson Trustees Ltd, 14 St George Street, London W1S 1FE (tel: 020 3207 7338; fax: 020 3207 7655; website: www.chkcharities.co.uk)

Trustees: David Peake; Charlotte Percy; David Acland; Joanna Prest; Katharine Loyd; Lucy Morris; Rupert Prest; Serena Acland; Susanna Peake.

CC Number: 1050900

CHK Charities Ltd was established in 1995. The origin of the charity derives from the wish of Sir Cyril Kleinwort and his descendants, who constitute the members of the company, to devote some of their time and resources to charitable activities. The charity normally makes grants totalling up to £2 million a year for a wide range of purposes across the UK, though preference is given to West Midlands and national charities.

Grantmaking

The trust's set meetings are held twice a year. Consideration of appeals received is undertaken by small groups of trustees who have the authority to make grants in specific fields up to individual amounts of £25,000. These groups meet roughly bi-monthly, so appeals can be dealt with quickly and their decisions are reviewed and ratified at the next trustee meeting.

Ad hoc meetings of the trustees are convened as and when applications exceeding £25,000 have to be considered between regular meetings. The trust seeks to provide support to a significant number of charitable organisations working in the fields on which it concentrates its activities. Included in this are national or West Midlands charities working in countryside matters, drug prevention, education, youth matters, job creation, population control, culture, conservation, care of the elderly, care of the sick, crime prevention, homelessness, deafness, blindness, and the provision of treatment and care for people with disabilities. The trust's current policy is to consider all written appeals received within these broad guidelines.

Types of grant
One-off Grants
The trust aims to 'make a difference'; it does not support individuals or very small and narrowly specialised activities but, on the other hand, it tries to avoid 'bottomless pits' and unfocused causes. Therefore grants made on a one-off basis will be towards core costs for a specific project. This could include specialist equipment for a project or help with running costs.

Conditionally Renewable Grants
Grants made for more than one year can be towards start-up costs, for a specific item in the applicant's budget (i.e. a salary) or towards the costs of a particular project. These are subject to annual progress reports.

Large Grants (over £25,000)
These are approved as a result of close knowledge of specific charities by a trustee.

Further information on the trust's funding guidelines is available on its website.

In 2011/12 the trust had a total income of £2.2 million and assets of £77.6 million. Grants were made totalling £1.6 million and were broken down into the following areas:

Miscellaneous	£257,000
Youth care	£233,000
Education	£216,000
Treatment and care for people with disabilities	£195,000
General welfare and social problems	£193,000
Artistic causes	£127,000
Reproductive health control	£70,000
Blindness	£57,000
Employment and job creation	£50,000
Countryside matters and animal welfare and disease	£46,000
Care of the elderly	£46,000
Crime prevention	£40,000
Conservation/preservation	£33,000
Homelessness/housing	£31,500
Hospices	£20,500
Drug prevention and treatment	£20,000
Hospital/nursing home building and equipment	£5,000
Medical care and research	£5,000
Deafness	£5,000

Beneficiaries included: Charities Aid Foundation and Marie Curie Cancer Centre (£105,000 each); Home-Start UK (£75,000); Margaret Pyke Trust (£60,000); Calvert Trust, Skill Force Development and St Clement and St James' Community Development Project (£50,000 each); Reeds School (£20,000); Academy of Ancient Music,

Beechen Cliff School, Chipping Norton Theatre Trust, Hospital of St Cross and Almshouse of Noble Poverty, House of Illustration, Interact Worldwide, Support Parents Autistic Children Everywhere, Royal National College for the Blind, Well Child and Winston's Wish (£10,000 each); Almshouse Association, Chaos Theory, Great Oaks Dean Forest Hospice, Listening Post, Motobility, Nordoff-Robbins Music Therapy, Peach, Royal Opera House, Sportsaid South West and YMCA (£5,000 each); Volunteer Reading Help (£4,000); Children's Country Holidays Fund and Woodland Heritage Ltd (£3,000 each); Leys Youth Programme (£2,000); and Garsington Opera Ltd (£1,000).

Exclusions

The following will not normally be considered for funding:

 ▷ Organisations not registered as charities or those that have been registered for less than a year
 ▷ Pre-school groups
 ▷ Out of school play schemes including pre-school and holiday schemes
 ▷ 'bottomless pits' and unfocused causes
 ▷ Very small and narrowly specialised activities
 ▷ Community centres
 ▷ Local authorities
 ▷ Umbrella or grantmaking organisations
 ▷ Universities and colleges and grant maintained private or local education authority schools or their Parent Teachers Associations, except if these schools are for students with special needs
 ▷ Individuals or charities applying on behalf of individuals
 ▷ General requests for donations
 ▷ Professional associations and training of professionals
 ▷ Projects which are abroad even though the charity is based in the UK
 ▷ Expeditions or overseas travel
 ▷ 'campaigning organisations' or Citizens Advice projects providing legal advice
 ▷ Community transport projects
 ▷ General counselling projects, except those in areas of considerable deprivation and with a clearly defined client group

Applications

The following information is taken from the trust's website:

 Preference is given to National or West Midlands charities, and the organisation will normally be based within the United Kingdom. The trust does not have an application form, but suggests that the following guidelines be used when making an application which should be in writing to the secretary:

 ▷ Applications should be no longer than four A4 sides, and should incorporate a short (half page) summary
 ▷ Applications should also include a detailed budget for the project and the applicant's most recent audited accounts. If those accounts show a significant surplus or deficit of income, please explain how this has arisen

 Applicants should:

 ▷ State clearly who they are, what they do and whom they seek to help
 ▷ Give the applicant's status, e.g., registered charity
 ▷ Confirm that the organisation has a Child Protection Policy (where appropriate) and that Criminal Record Bureau checks are carried out on all staff working with children
 ▷ Describe clearly the project for which the grant is sought answering the following questions: What is the aim of the project and why is it needed? What practical results will it produce? How many people will benefit from it? What stage has the project reached so far? How will you ensure that it is cost-effective?
 ▷ If the request is for a salary, enclose a job description
 ▷ Explain how the project will be monitored, evaluated and, how its results will be disseminated
 ▷ State what funds have already been raised for the project, and name any other sources of funding applied for
 ▷ Explain where on-going funding (if required) will be obtained when the charity's grant has been used
 ▷ If the request is for revenue funding for a specific item, please state the amount needed

 Please keep the application as simple as possible and avoid the use of technical terms, acronyms and jargon. If you are sending videos or CD Roms, please provide a stamped address envelope so that they may be returned.

Additional information on the application process can be found on the trust's website.

Information gathered from:

Accounts; annual report; Charity Commission record; funder's website.

The Church and Community Fund

Church of England, social welfare
£506,000 (2012)

Beneficial area
England and Wales.

Correspondent: Andrew Hawkings, Grants Manager, Church House, Great Smith Street, London SW1P 3AZ (tel: 020 7898 1541; email: ccf@ churchofengland.org; website: www. centralchurchfund.org.uk)

Trustee: The Archbishop's Council.

CC Number: 1074857

Established in 1915, the Church and Community Fund is an excepted charity but its trustee, the Archbishop's Council, is registered under the above number. The fund exists to promote the charitable work of the Church of England primarily by making grants to church and community projects. It encourages the church to engage with their local communities by funding effective and innovative community outreach projects. Brief accounting details for the fund were included in the notes to the accounts for the Archbishops' Council, of which the fund is a subsidiary.

The following information is taken from the trust's website:

 The Church and Community Fund aims to grow the Church of England and develop its capacity to engage with the whole community.

Objectives

By making grants to the national church and local projects the Church and Community Fund will assist the Church of England to:

 ▷ Develop its capacity to engage with the whole community through supporting innovative use of resources
 ▷ Help transform areas of greatest need and opportunity and
 ▷ Grow spiritually and numerically

Strategic Funding Themes

In 2012 – 2014 the CCF will support projects that:

1 significantly expand the Church's engagement with neighbourhood renewal
2 seek innovative ways of developing established community projects so that they either a) grow existing or b) evolve into new communities of Christian Faith, and
3 replicate models of successful community engagement across the wider church

The CCF awards grants to projects run by local Anglican Churches in England or other organisations who are working in close partnership with the Church of England on the ground.

In 2012 the fund had assets of £17.3 million and an income of £90,000. Grants were made totalling £506,000. Types of project supported include the salary costs for youth, children's and community workers, the running costs for homeless centres, conversion of church buildings to enable use by the wider community, funding towards street outreach.

The most recent beneficiaries displayed on the fund's website included: Chapel Street Community Arts – Salford and Luton Roma Church – St Albans (£15,000 each); CHAT Trust – Newcastle (£13,000); Three Spires Tots – Coventry (£12,000); and Narthex Centre –

Sparkhill and YeovilNET – Bath and Wells (£10,000 each).

Exclusions

The fund will not support:

- Projects that are essentially insular and inward looking
- Projects which are primarily about maintaining the nation's architectural heritage
- Projects which are primarily about liturgical reordering
- Restoration works to bells or organs
- Research projects or personal grants
- The repayment of debts or overdrafts
- Projects which are not directly connected with the Church of England, ecumenical or other faith partnerships in which the Church of England element is small and projects which are predominantly secular in nature
- Anything for which the Church Commissioners' funds or diocesan core funding are normally available, including stipend support
- Feasibility studies (the fund is able to offer limited support towards the preliminary costs of projects, for example professional fees, but where a grant is awarded at this stage, no further funding will be available for the main body of the work)

Applications

Full details of how to apply can be found on the fund's website and applicants are advised to refer to these before applying. If you feel that your project meets the aims of the funding themes and match the criteria detailed in the guidelines, then complete the eligibility quiz and online application form.

Percentage of awards given to new applicants: 85%.

Common applicant mistakes

'Not supplying the correct supporting documentation; providing out of date financial statements.'

Information gathered from:

Accounts; annual report; Charity Commission record; further information provided by the funder; funder's website.

Church Urban Fund

Welfare and Christian outreach in deprived communities in England

£1.7 million (2012)

Beneficial area

The most deprived areas of England.

Correspondent: Revd Canon Paul Hackwood, Trustee, Church House, 27 Great Smith Street, Westminster, London SW1P 3AZ (tel: 020 7898 1090;

email: enquiries@cuf.org.uk; website: www.cuf.org.uk)

CC Number: 297483

The Church Urban Fund was set up in 1988 in response to the Church of England's Faith in the City report which drew attention to the increasing levels of poverty in urban areas and to the widening gap between rich and poor. The report suggested that the church should set up a fund to help churches work more closely with their local communities to help people tackle poor housing, poor education, unemployment and poverty. An initial capital sum was raised from what was presented at the time as a one-off appeal.

The trustees' report for 2012 states that 'the aim of Church Urban Fund is to tackle poverty by transforming the lives of the poorest and most marginalised'. The fund 'gives people opportunities, restoring their dignity and enabling them to feel they belong to and contribute to their community'.

> Church Urban Fund seeks to work with all faiths and denominations. Beneficiaries are not restricted by faith, gender, ethnic origin, disability, age or sexual orientation. Our goal and approach flow from our charitable purpose – the relief of poverty. Through our joint ventures with local Anglican dioceses we help to grow, equip and resource local responses to poverty.

The fund tackles extreme poverty in England and helps local people to restore relationships and transform lives in their own communities. They do this by supporting, resourcing and working alongside people in the most deprived parts of England. They identify churches, projects and local people already at work in their own communities to offer funding, collaboration, advice and support.

The fund's main priority areas are as follows:

- Offenders/ex-offenders
- Refugees and asylum seekers
- Deprived people aged 14–19 years
- Homelessness
- Substance misuse

The objectives of Church Urban Fund, according to the trustees' report for 2012, are as follows:

> Joint Action. Creating communities of action. These communities will bring together those living in poverty, members of local churches (and other religious groups) and other people of good will to seek the transformation of lives. This is the active building of civil society

> Providing resources and support for practical action. Sometimes this is money but often it is encouragement and support (occasionally it is a call to action!). Though local churches are active in their community they often need help to mobilise their assets for action. We want to act as a resource for this practical local action

> Making connections, raising the profile of this local work and connecting it with the public arena. This is about connecting with the media, politicians and the general public and bringing to their attention the work local churches are engaged in across the country. We want to mobilise their support

In 2012 the fund had an income of £4.5 million and an expenditure of £4.7 million. Grants were made totalling around £1.7 million.

Addiction/substance abuse	£9,000
Advice/advocacy/counselling	£22,000
Community	£135,000
Criminal justice	£15,000
Debt/financial advice	£39,000
Education	£22,000
Employment/training	£47,000
Health/mental health	£4,000
Homeless/housing	£42,000
Interfaith	£5,000
Prostitution/people trafficking	£24,000
Refugees/asylum seekers	£44,000
Social welfare	£15,000

Previous beneficiaries included: Project Freedom Trust, Sussex Pathways; Faith Drama Productions, Housing Justice, Community Money Advice, Reading Refugee Support Group, The Bridge Pregnancy Crisis Centre and All Saints Hanley (£5,000 each); Church Action on Poverty and Bristol Inter Faith Group Keeping Health in Mind (£4,500); Youth Project @ Apostles and Cuthbert's (£4,200); and St Andrews Community Network (£4,000).

Exclusions

The fund's website states that it will not fund the following:

- Projects outside England
- Individuals
- Projects not directly tackling profound poverty
- Projects without faith links
- Organisations with an annual turnover of over £150,000
- Salary costs, except where there is a significant increase in hours in order to expand an existing project or begin new work
- Core costs
- Repeated activities
- Work that has already been completed or started
- Campaigning and fundraising activity
- Revenue and capital for national voluntary/community organisations and public and private sector organisations
- Activities open only to church members
- Evangelistic activity not part of a response to poverty
- Clergy stipends including church army posts
- General repairs and refurbishment

General appeals

Those that fall outside of the priority groups, which are: offenders/ex-offenders; refugees and asylum seekers; deprived young people aged 14–19 years; homelessness; and substance misuse are unlikely to be funded. The fund is also unable to fund health and wellbeing projects, general family work, or work addressing shorter term aspects of poverty such as food banks.

Applications

The trust has produced a detailed and helpful grants policy and procedure manual and applicants are advised to read this before making an application. The manual is available from the trust's website, as is detailed guidance on application procedures and guidelines.

Percentage of awards given to new applicants: over 50%.

Common applicant mistakes

'Not reading the grant criteria closely enough.'

Information gathered from:

Accounts; annual report; Charity Commission record; further information provided by the funder; funder's website; Summary Information Return (SIR).

The City Bridge Trust

Arts, culture, recreation and sports, community development, mental health, environment, older people, disability, voluntary sector

£19 million (2011/12)

Beneficial area

Greater London.

Correspondent: Steven Reynolds, Administrator, PO Box 270, Guildhall, London EC2P 2EJ (tel: 020 7332 3710; email: citybridgetrust@cityoflondon.gov. uk; website: www.citybridgetrust.org.uk/cbt)

Trustee: The Mayor and Commonalty and Citizens.

CC Number: 1035628

The City Bridge Trust is the grantmaking arm of Bridge House Estates. The purpose of the charity is the maintenance of the river bridges plus charitable activities that benefit Greater London, which it has chosen to do so far by making grants to charitable organisations. The trust particularly supports charitable activities that contribute towards the provision of transport, and access to it, for elderly or disabled people in the Greater London area.

According to the trustees' report for 2011/12, the trust's mission is as follows:

> The City Bridge Trust aims to reduce disadvantage by supporting charitable activity across Greater London through quality grant-making and related activity within clearly defined priorities.

In 2011/12 the trust had an income of £45 million and assets of £870 million. 230 grants were made totalling £19 million.

Grants are given for capital or revenue costs, although no usually both at the same time. Core costs are also considered. The majority of grants are for revenue and are awarded over two or three years. There is no minimum or maximum revenue grant. However, it is not in the trust's policy to award large grants to small organisations. A grant cannot be more than 50% of the organisation's income.

The trust offers a range of grants programmes, which span from improving Londoners' mental health to making London safer and reducing poverty to working with offenders towards resettlement and rehabilitation. For all of the current programmes available, visit the trust's website.

The trust occasionally makes exceptional grants outside its priority areas. Consideration may be given to applications from organisations which demonstrate that they are. Note, the trust states that only a small number of grants are likely to be made in this category.

Of the 230 grants awarded during the year, around 175 were two or three year revenue funding.

Grants were distributed as follows:

Arts, culture, recreation and sport	23	£1.19 million
Access to buildings	20	£706,000
Access to transport	3	£125,000
Community development	32	£2 million
Mental health	34	£3 million
Environment and animals	17	£4.2 million
Older people	36	£1.9 million
Independent Living	31	£2.5 million
Strengthening the third sector	21	£2 million

Beneficiaries included: Hampstead Heath Charitable Trust (£3 million); London Wildlife Trust (£169,000); Campaign Against Living Miserably – CALM and Thames 21 Ltd (£150,000 each); Bromley by Bow Centre (£149,000); Learn English at Home (£132,000); Refugee Action Kingston (£126,000); Haringey Shed (£107,000); Heart n Soul and Fashion Awareness Direct (£90,000 each); City of London Sinfonia (£86,000); Westway Community Transport (£80,000); East European Advice Centre and Mayhew Animal Home (£75,000 each); Art in Perpetuity Trust, Charles Dickens Museum and Thrive (£50,000 each);

Jewish Community Centre (£46,000); All Saints Church – Ealing Common (£37,000); Afghanistan and Central Asian Association (£33,000); Alternatives to Violence Project and JAN Trust (£25,000 each); Russian Immigrants Association (£21,000); Vocaleyes, Creekside Education Trust, Kisharon and Beyond Youth (£20,000 each); Artangel (£15,000); St Christopher's Hospice (£11,000); In-Deep Community Task Force (£5,000); and Battersea Arts Centre (£3,500).

Exclusions

The trust cannot fund:
- Political parties
- Political lobbying
- Non-charitable activities
- Work which does not benefit the inhabitants of Greater London

The trust does not fund:
- Individuals
- Grantmaking bodies to make grants on its behalf
- Schools, PTAs, universities or other educational establishments (except where they are undertaking ancillary charitable activities specifically directed towards one of the agreed priority areas)
- Medical or academic research
- Churches or other religious bodies where the monies will be used for religious purposes
- Hospitals
- Projects which have already taken place or building work which has already been completed
- Statutory bodies
- Profit making organisations (except social enterprises)
- Charities established outside the UK

Grants will not usually be given to:
- Work where there is statutory responsibility to provide funding
- Organisations seeking funding to replace cuts by statutory authorities, except where that funding was explicitly time-limited and for a discretionary (non-statutory) purpose
- Organisations seeking funding to top up on under-priced contracts
- Work where there is significant public funding available (including funding from sports governing bodies)

Applications

Application forms are available from the trust or downloadable from its website, along with full and up-to-date guidelines. Applications are assessed by a member of the grants team and then considered by the grants committee. Most programmes do not have deadlines. Applications aim to be processed within four months. Applications are encouraged to contact the trust for initial guidance before making an application. Applications for grants of £5,000 and over must be accompanied by a detailed proposal. The trust expects applicants to work to its principles of good practice. These include: involving beneficiaries in the planning, delivery and management of services; valuing diversity; supporting volunteers; and taking steps to reduce the organisation's carbon footprint. The trust requires all grants to be monitored and evaluated. Details of the trust's monitoring and evaluation policy can be found on the website.

Percentage of awards given to new applicants: between 30% and 40%.

Common applicant mistakes

'Not sufficiently meeting the funding priorities, which are fairly specific, and making an application which would make us their largest single funder.'

Information gathered from:

Accounts; annual report; Charity Commission record; further information provided by the funder; funder's website.

The Clore Duffield Foundation

Arts/museums, Jewish charities, education, older people and people who are disadvantaged

£17 million (2012)

Beneficial area

UK, the larger grants go to London-based institutions.

Correspondent: Sally Bacon, Executive Director, Studio 3, Chelsea Manor Studios, Flood Street, London SW3 5SR (tel: 020 7351 6061; fax: 020 7351 5308; email: info@cloreduffield.org.uk; website: www.cloreduffield.org.uk)

Trustees: Dame Vivien Duffield, Chair; Caroline Deletra; David Harrel; Michael Trask; Sir Mark Weinberg; James Harding; Melanie Clore.

CC Number: 1084412

The Clore Foundation was founded in 1964 by the late Sir Charles Clore, one of Britain's most successful post-war businessmen and one of the most generous philanthropists of his day. Sir Charles was born in Whitechapel, the son of Jewish immigrants from Riga. After his death in 1979, his daughter, Vivien Duffield, became chair of the foundation and created her own foundation in 1987 with the aim of continuing and consolidating her family's history of philanthropy. The two charities were merged in 2000 to become the Clore Duffield Foundation.

The foundation is a grantmaking charity which concentrates its support on cultural learning, creating learning spaces within arts and heritage organisations, leadership training for the cultural and social sectors, social care, and enhancing Jewish life. The trustees have awarded more than £50 million to charitable purposes over the past decade.

The trustees state in their 2012 annual report that the foundation does not adopt a rigid approach in terms of the criteria for its grantmaking. It does not fund individuals but it can fund capital re-developments and has a particular emphasis on supporting Clore Learning Spaces within cultural organisations. It can also provide project, programme and revenue funding. The foundation's application procedures are straightforward and it continues to maintain a balance between supporting large-scale projects with far-reaching effects, and small-scale local community endeavours (the latter largely through its small grants programme which currently has a focus on poetry and literature for under 19s).

The foundation makes grants mainly in the fields of:

- Museums, galleries and heritage sites (particularly for learning spaces)
- The arts
- The performing arts
- Heritage
- Education
- Literature
- Leadership training
- Health, social care and disability
- Jewish charities with interests in any of the above areas

The foundation's website states that it has:

two distinct grant-making strands: the Main Grants Programme and a new Small Grants Programme, the Clore Poetry and Literature Awards for children and young people. When making an application to either of these programmes, please make sure you read all the information and follow the guidelines carefully. We are a small team, and try to keep things simple: we have made the application process as straightforward as we can and all the information you need should be on this site.

Main Grants Programme

This offers grants ranging from below £5,000 to in excess of £1 million and the foundation continues to maintain a balance between supporting large-scale projects, with far-reaching effects, and small-scale community endeavours. All grants are awarded at a meeting of the trustees, held twice a year. As there is no fixed schedule for these meetings, applications are reviewed on an ongoing basis.

Whilst the foundation does occasionally make donations to the health and social care sectors, it should be noted that the majority of its support is directed towards the cultural sector, and in particular to cultural learning and to museum, gallery, heritage and performing arts learning spaces. Support for enhancing Jewish life is largely directed towards the new Jewish Community Centre for London.

Note that organisations must be registered charities to be eligible for the Main Grants Programme.

The Clore Poetry and Literature Awards (Small grants programme)

These awards fund poetry and literature initiatives for children and young people, under the age of 19, across the UK. The Awards are worth a total of £1 million over five years, 2011 to 2015, with individual awards ranging from £1,000 to £10,000. The Clore Duffield Foundation has created these Awards with the aim of providing children and young people with opportunities to experience poetry and literature in exciting and compelling ways, in and out of school. For full details, download the guidance leaflet from the website.

Grantmaking in 2012

In 2012 the foundation had assets of £77 million and an income of £14 million. Grants were made to 86 organisations totalling almost £17 million, excluding support and governance costs, and were broken down as follows:

Jewish causes	£13.6 million
Arts, heritage and education	£2.1 million
Leadership training	£981,000
Health and social care	£180,000

Beneficiaries included: Jewish Community Centre (£13 million); Royal Shakespeare Company (£275,000); University Church of St Mary the Virgin – Oxford (£215,000); Holburne Museum and Turner Contemporary Art (£125,000 each); Ballet Boyz and Historic Royal Palaces (£100,000 each); Aldeburgh Foundation, Jewish Museum and NSPCC (£50,000 each); Maggie Keswich Jencks Cancer Caring Centre and Motivation Charitable Trust (£25,000 each); Afghan Connection, Amber Foundation, Anglo-Israeli Association, the Art Room, Grange Park Opera, Hampstead Theatre and Whitworth Gallery (£10,000 each); and Apples and Snakes and Quintessentially Foundation (£5,000 each).

Exclusions

Potential applicants should note that their organisation must be a registered charity to be eligible. Unfortunately, the foundation does not fund projects retrospectively and will not support applications from the following:

- Individuals
- General appeals and circulars

It should also be noted that the following are funded only very rarely:

▶ Projects outside the UK
▶ Staff posts
▶ Local branches of national charities
▶ Academic or project research
▶ Conference costs

Applications

Refer to the foundation's guidance leaflet which can be downloaded from its website. You are invited to contact the foundation, before making application if you have any queries regarding criteria set or the process itself.

Information gathered from:

Accounts; annual report; Charity Commission record; funder's website.

The Clothworkers' Foundation

General charitable purposes, in particular social inclusion, young people, older people, disability, visual impairment, alcohol/substance misuse, prisoners, ex-offenders, homelessness and textiles

£4.3 million (2011/12)

Beneficial area

UK.

Correspondent: Andrew Blessley, Chief Executive, Clothworkers' Hall, Dunster Court, Mincing Lane, London EC3R 7AH (tel: 020 7623 7041; fax: 020 7397 0107; email: foundation@ clothworkers.co.uk; website: www. clothworkers.co.uk)

Trustees: Michael Howell; Joanna Dodd; Alexander Nelson; Andrew Clarke; Robin Booth; Thomas Clark; Philip Portal; Michael Jarvis; Richard Jonas; Michael Maylon; Christopher McLean May; Dr Carolyn Boulter; Melville Haggard.

CC Number: 274100

The Clothworkers' Company is an ancient City of London livery company, founded in 1528 and the twelfth of the 'Great Twelve' companies. One of the functions of livery companies was to support their members in times of need. As they grew wealthier, they were also able to benefit outsiders. The Clothworkers' Company acquired a number of trusts, established by individual benefactors for specific charitable ends. These totalled over 100 by the twentieth century. In addition, the company has always made payments to good causes from its own funds.

The Clothworkers' Foundation was set up in 1977 by the company as the independent arm for the whole of its charitable work.

The foundation's early income came from a leasehold interest in a City of London property, 1 Angel Court. Subsequent funding from the company, together with the sale of the long leasehold interest in Angel Court in 1994, represents the assets of the foundation which are substantially invested in stocks and shares. Income from these investments, together with unrestricted donations from the company, is given away each year to a wide range of charities. During its first 35 years, the foundation has made grants totalling around £100 million.

The objects of the foundation are for general charitable purposes and the foundation seeks to improve quality of life, particularly for people and communities that face disadvantage.

Grant programmes

The following information is taken from the trust's website:

The foundation has two programmes that are open to unsolicited applications: the Main Grants Programme and the Small Grants Programme. If you are not a registered charity, please consult the FAQ section of the trust's website.

Main Grants Programme (decision within 6 months, no maximum grant)

▶ UK registered charities with an annual operating income of less than £15m. Operating income is the normal day to day income of the organisation, such as money received from donations, grants, contracts, investments etc. Exceptional income (such as money received for a major, one-off, fundraising initiative) is deducted from the total income, to calculate the operating income total
▶ No maximum project cost
▶ Grants of up to £100,000 (larger grants awarded on very rare occasions)
▶ Average grant size of £20,000, grants size is relative to project size – smaller projects usually receive smaller grants and vice versa.

Building and vehicle projects rarely fully funded – we advise you to apply to other funders in addition to the foundation

Small Grants Programme (decision within 8 weeks, £10,000 maximum grant)

▶ UK registered charities with an annual turnover of less than £250,000. Total income must be less than £250,000 pa, regardless of any exceptional income (see definition above) or one-off grants
▶ Maximum total project cost of £100,000
▶ Grants of between £500 and £10,000 for capital costs

Organisations that have been awarded a grant cannot apply again (under either programme) for five years.

The trust will consider applications from eligible charities for projects in the areas listed below.

The organisation must work with these groups/in these areas of focus the majority of the time. If, for example, the organisation normally works with the general public, but occasionally works with a disabled person or a blind person, it is not eligible to apply under the Disability or Visual impairment programme areas.

Alcohol and substance misuse
Projects supporting people affected by drug and/or alcohol dependency, and their families.

People with disabilities
Projects providing services for people with physical and/or learning disabilities, and/or for people with mental health issues (We will not fund projects which focus solely on meeting the requirements of the Disability Discrimination Act).

Disadvantaged minority communities
Projects that work with minority communities facing both disadvantage (e.g.: economic or cultural) AND discrimination (e.g.: due to ethnicity, sexuality, faith) to:
▶ Promote integration between minority communities and mainstream society, and/or
▶ Provide specialist services, and/or
▶ Provide access to mainstream services

Disadvantaged young people
Projects which support disadvantaged young people, particularly (but not limited to) those in or leaving care, or not in employment, education, or training.

Domestic and sexual violence
Projects supporting people affected by domestic or sexual violence or abuse.

Elderly people
Projects providing services for elderly people, in particular those living in areas of high deprivation and/or where rural isolation is an issue.

Homelessness
Projects providing services for people who are homeless or at risk of becoming homeless.

Prisoners and ex-offenders
Projects supporting prisoners and/or ex-offenders, or those at risk of offending, and their families.

Visual impairment
Projects providing services for blind or visually impaired people.

Proactive Grant Programmes

Note: These programmes are **not** open to applications. Potential grant beneficiaries are selected by the foundation, and unsolicited applications are **not** accepted.

The Proactive Grants Programme funds specific fields in which the foundation aims to make a significant impact over a period of time. The themes and priorities of the programme change over time, and grants can be strategic and/or tactical. The first Proactive Grants Programme to be set up was the Mathematics initiative, in 2007. This initiative has now ended. Visit the foundation's website for current initiatives.

Grantmaking policy

We award one-off grants for capital costs such as building refurbishments, buying vehicles, and office equipment. Our grants are only for UK-registered charities (or equivalent) with an annual turnover of less than £15m.

What are capital costs?

To us, capital costs are tangible items or work; things that can be seen and used. This includes:

- Buildings – purchase, construction, renovation, refurbishment, redecoration
- Equipment – office, sports, gym, furnishings, digital, camping, kitchen, furniture, garden, specialist therapeutic (but not purely medical)
- IT equipment, for example computers, printers, phones
- Vehicles – for example minibus, car, caravan, people-carrier, 4X4. Please note that it is rare for us to fully fund brand new vehicles so you will need to apply to other funders, in addition to us, if this is your project

The list above is not exhaustive, but should give an indication of what we consider to be capital costs. We do not fund non-capital costs.

What are non-capital costs?

To us, non-capital costs are the normal everyday costs of running your organisation, and any one-off costs which are not for tangible items. They include:

- Salaries
- Overheads
- Training
- Rent
- Lease of equipment
- Volunteer expenses
- Professional fees
- Websites
- Databases
- Software
- Any other running costs

For charities which, by their nature, have no capital requirements, we will consider funding one-off projects such as production of publications (not ongoing publications such as newsletters), or the creation of training materials. This option is only available for charities which can demonstrate that they do not have any capital costs (at all, not just at that particular time) and that capital development is unlikely in the future. Usually this option is only available to charities which do not provide tangible services, and therefore do not have a building from which they operate, and do not use any equipment. An example of this would be a charity which provides information about a particular disability for sufferers and carers. Such an organisation would not need capital help with buildings or equipment and would be eligible to apply for funding towards a publication.

Grantmaking in 2012

The following information is taken from the Annual Review for 2012:

We have historically awarded between 150 and 200 grants each year. However, the introduction of the Small Grants Programme in 2007 resulted in an increase, with a range of 255 to 313 from 2007 to 2011. In 2012, 225 grants were awarded, 44 fewer than the 269 awarded the previous year. We cannot attribute this to any one factor, but do not believe that the drop is cause for concern. Our policy remains for our grant to be meaningful to the overall project.

Most of our grants by number (over 51%) were for £10,000 or less, a similar pattern to previous years, with grants between £20,000 and £50,000 representing 26% of the total. Larger grants continued to be few in number, accounting for 7%, although four grants comprised 29% of total commitments. Notable amongst these were £720,000 to the University of Leeds, the first instalment of a £1.75 million commitment to create the Clothworkers' Centre for Textile Materials Innovation for Healthcare, and £366,000 to Vision Aid Overseas for a project in Sierra Leone.

Although application numbers were also slightly down on previous years, we believe this is due to improved guidance and clarity on our new website and new, more focused programme areas, all of which were introduced in 2012. We are pleased with the continuing increase in our success rate which was 58% compared to 50% in 2011.

In 2012 the foundation and associated trusts had assets of £89.2 million and an income of £5.1 million. There were 225 grants made totalling £4.3 million.

Grants were distributed across all of the priority areas as follows:

Disability	£1 million
Textiles	£883,000
Encouragement of young people	£503,000
Visual impairment	£384,000
Homelessness	£297,000
Conservation	£278,000
Autism	£217,000
Elderly	£216,000
Other	£180,000
Disadvantaged minority communities	£143,500
Prisoners and ex-offenders	£63,500
Domestic violence	£61,500
Alcohol and substance misuse	£50,500

Beneficiaries across all categories included: Vision Aid Overseas (£366,000); North of England Refugee Service (£60,000); Ashley Foundation (£65,000); Julian House (£45,000); Blind Aid, Fine Cell Work, Hope for Tomorrow, LifeLine Community Projects and South Tyneside Churches' KEY Project (£40,000 each); Wester Hailes Youth Agency (£33,000); Bury Hospice, Exodus Project, RedR (Register of Engineers for Disaster Relief), UCL Medical School (£30,000 each); Preshal Trust (£25,000); Age UK Lancashire, Caldecott Foundation and Citizens Advice West Lothian (£20,000); It's Your Choice, Ray's Playhouse and Young

Devon (£15,000 each); Oxfordshire Motor Project (£13,000); Parkinson's Self Help Group and Survive South Gloucestershire and Bristol (£12,000 each).

Exclusions

The foundation does not fund:

- Salaries
- Overheads
- Training
- Rent
- Lease of equipment
- Volunteer expenses
- Professional fees
- Websites
- Databases
- Software
- Any other running costs
- In the Main Grants programme: IT equipment which will only be used by staff/volunteers and not by service users
- Hospices
- Arts and education projects, unless they are focused on disadvantaged young people, elderly people, or disabled people
- Educational establishments, other than schools specifically for disabled children/children with learning difficulties or special educational needs
- Emergency response appeals
- Environmental organisations or projects
- Events (including exhibitions)
- General or mass appeals
- Grantmaking organisations
- Heritage projects
- Individuals (other than CPD Bursaries for conservators)
- Medical research or equipment
- Non UK-registered charities
- Organisations that have received a grant from the foundation in the last five years
- Organisations with an annual operating income of more than £15 million (read the FAQ for more information)
- Overseas work/projects
- Political, industrial, or commercial projects
- Projects that do not fall within the programme areas
- Projects where the item(s) funded will be used for religious purposes, or projects or organisations which promote a particular religion
- Work which is needed to meet the requirements of the Disability Discrimination Act
- Projects that we have already declined to fund

Applications

Refer to the foundation's very helpful and detailed guidelines on how to apply, available on its website.

Percentage of awards given to new applicants: 60%-70%.

Common applicant mistakes

'Not reading guidelines. Not describing project clearly and having a clear understanding of outcomes.'

Information gathered from:

Accounts; annual report; Charity Commission record; further information provided by the funder; funder's website.

Richard Cloudesley's Charity

Churches, medical and welfare

£341,000 to organisations

(2011/12)

Beneficial area

North Islington, London.

Correspondent: Melanie Griffiths, Director, Reed Smith LLP, 26th Floor, Broadgate Tower, 20 Primrose Street, London EC2A 2RS (tel: 020 3116 3624; email: kwallace@reedsmith.com; website: www.richardcloudesleycharity.org.uk)

Trustee: Richard Cloudesley Trustee Ltd.

CC Number: 205959

Summary

The charity was founded in 1518 by the will of Richard Cloudesley. He left the rent from a 14 acre field in Islington, London, to be used for the benefit of residents of Islington parish. The field was in Barnsbury and its centre was what is now Cloudesley Square. The significant endowment of the charity derives from the original piece of land left by Richard Cloudesley.

The governing document is now a Charity Commission Scheme of 2 July 1980 which says that half of the net income from the original endowment is to be applied for the 'relief in sickness' of people in need by providing items, services or facilities which are calculated to alleviate suffering or assist their recovery. The other half of the income is to be used for making grants towards 'the upkeep and repair of the fabric of, and the maintenance of services in, the Parish Church of the Ecclesiastical Parish of St Silas Pentonville and any churches of the Church of England in the area of the Ancient Parish of Islington'.

Church Grants

The beneficiaries of the Richard Cloudesley's Charity Church Grant programme are 21 Church of England churches in the area.

Grants are made towards: 'The upkeep and repair of the fabric of, and the maintenance of the services in any

Churches of the Church of England in the Ancient Parish of Islington and the Parish Church of the Ecclesiastical Parish of St Silas, Pentonville'.

The charity holds two rounds of applications each year, in spring and autumn.

Guidance notes, available from the charity's website, set out the principal criteria used to assess applications, the general policy and the application process. There is also a FAQ section.

To make a grant application any qualified church has to complete an application form.

Health Grants

Grants are made to organisations that:
- Work with people affected by illness or disability who are living on benefits or a low income
- And operate within the area of benefit

Welfare Grants

Since 2 April 2013, there has been a new local scheme in place in Islington to help individuals called the Resident Support Scheme with a budget of approximately £3 million. Details of the scheme are available on the Cripplegate Foundation and Islington Council websites.

In the light of these changes, Richard Cloudesley's Charity is carrying out a review of its grant programme to find the best way to offer support to individuals and complement the Resident Support Scheme. During 2013/14, the charity will work with a number of Cloudesley Partners to deliver its support for individuals.

The charity remains committed to supporting the most vulnerable Islington residents in the years to come.

Grants ranging from £100 to around £40,000 are given to Church of England churches and to charities supporting a range of beneficiaries, for the 'sick poor in the ancient parish of Islington'. As part of its help to the 'sick poor' the trust operates a welfare fund making quick and modest grants to needy individuals.

The charity can only assist in activities in the ancient parish of Islington which is now the northern part of the modern London Borough of Islington – roughly everything north of Chapel Market and City Road. 'It is clear that there are few bodies that confine their work to such a small area and the charity does help charities in Islington as a whole, or Islington and nearby London boroughs.' The charity requires applicants to provide an assessment of the proportion of what they do that can be said to be related to people living in the ancient parish. This limited geographical scope makes for difficulties in granting funds to nationally organised charities. Some of these have locally accounted branches

– and others have locally identifiable projects – but without some restriction like this, the charity will be unable to assist.

The charity's policy tends to be to make grants that are free of conditions. Feedback from grantees suggest that this gives much needed flexibility in helping to fill gaps caused by the more rigid terms that other funders are constrained to adopt. The charity though is aware of the need for accountability and is able to exercise some monitoring through accounts, information, trustee contact and the occasional visit.

Most grants are given to charities previously supported, though the amounts are clearly reassessed each year as they frequently vary.

Grantmaking in 2011/12

In 2011/12 the charity had assets of over £23.4 million and an income of £1.2 million. Grants were made in three categories totalling £488,000 as follows:

Churches	19	£290,000
Medical and welfare needs	9	£51,000
Welfare fund grants	unknown	£147,000

The above welfare fund grants refers to grants made to individuals in need in the Islington area [see *The Guide to Grants for Individuals in Need* published by Directory of Social Change].

Grants to organisations included those made to: St David's – Lough Road (£50,000); St Mary's – Islington (£29,000); St Jude and St Paul – Mildmay Park (£23,500); Claremont Park, Maya Centre and St Andrew Whitehall Park (£10,000 each); Angel Shed Theatre Company, CARIS – Islington and Community Language Support Services (£6,000 each); Islington Bangladesh Association (£3,000); and EAGLE Recovery Project (£1,000).

Applications

Applicants should write to the correspondent requesting an application form.

Applications should be in time for the trustees' meetings in April and November and should be accompanied by the organisation's accounts. The following information should be supplied:
- Details of the work your organisation undertakes
- How it falls within the geographical area of the trust
- Details of what the grant will fund

If you would like acknowledgement of receipt of your application send an sae.

Block grants are considered twice a year, in late April, and early November, at a grants committee meeting. Recommendations are made by the grants committee at these meetings and are reviewed and authorised by the trustees two weeks later. The charity will give brief reasons with any application that is not successful.

Percentage of awards given to new applicants: between 10% and 20%.

Information gathered from:
Accounts; annual report; Charity Commission record; further information provided by the funder; funder's website.

The Coalfields Regeneration Trust

General, health, welfare, community regeneration, education, young people, older people

£15.6 million (2011/12)

Beneficial area
Coalfield and former coalfield communities in England (North West and North East, Yorkshire, West Midlands and East Midlands, Kent), Scotland (West and East) and Wales.

Correspondent: Louise Dyson, Head of Finance and Corporate Services, 1 Waterside Park, Valley Way, Wombwell, Barnsley S73 0BB (tel: 01226 270800; fax: 01226 272899; email: info@coalfields-regen.org.uk; website: www.coalfields-regen.org.uk)

Trustees: Peter McNestry, Chair; Jim Crewdson; Prof. Anthony Crook; Dawn Davies; John Edwards; Vernon Jones; Wayne Thomas; Fran Walker; Sylvia Wileman; Nicholas Wilson; Michael Clapham; Bill Skilki; Roger Owen; Thomas McAughtrie.

CC Number: 1074930

Summary
Set up in 1999, the Coalfields Regeneration Trust is an independent charity dedicated to the social and economic regeneration of coalfield communities in England, Scotland and Wales. It was set up in response to a recommendation by the government's Coalfields Task Force Report. The report highlighted the dramatic effects that mine closures had, and continue to have, on communities in coalfield areas.

The trust provides advice, support and financial assistance to community and voluntary organisations which are working to tackle problems at grassroots level within coalfield communities. It is closely connected with the areas it serves, operating through a network of staff based at offices located within coalfield regions themselves.

The trust's mission is: To work closely with partners and be the key agency to deliver, champion and broker social and economic regeneration for the benefit of former coalfield communities in Britain. In addition to grantmaking, the trust has invested and acted strategically where a more structured intervention is necessary.

The annual report for 2011/12 states:

> Despite improvements, lower income persists in the coalfields with coalfield wards remaining amongst the most deprived in England, Scotland and Wales. A lack of skills, employment, poor health and low income are inextricably linked to lack of progress and on-going economic problems are compounded by geographical isolation and poor public transport. To add to this, these severely deprived former mining communities have not necessarily had their fair share of structural, charitable or lottery funding. The current recession and credit crunch have impacted on these communities, damaging the fragile recovery progress previously made. The trust tries, with limited resources, to impact on these major issues.

> Our grants programme is about helping groups to respond to local need but we are also pro-active in developing ideas and projects that address key issues such as worklessness, isolation, skills sector development and sustainability. The trust has continued to explore areas where it can work in partnership and maximise the benefits that will contribute to the regeneration of coalfields communities. Across England, Scotland and Wales the trust is working in partnership with numerous government agencies, local authorities, primary care trusts, community partnerships and the voluntary sector.

Programmes
The trustees' annual report for 2011/12 states that in terms of strategic objectives, the funding is committed to four main themes:

Access to Employment
This theme aims to connect people living in deprived neighbourhoods to mainstream opportunities rather than job creation.

Education and Skills
This theme aims to support people in accessing learning opportunities and developing their skills through added value activity rather than statutory mainstream provision.

Health and Well Being
This theme aims to improve the health and lifestyles of people living in coalfield communities through community based approaches and preventative projects.

Access to Opportunities
This theme aims to improve access to services in coalfield communities recognising that limited community infrastructure and geographical isolation can prevent people from taking up opportunities.

The following extracts are taken from the trust's website, refer to this for more detailed information and guidelines:

Coalfields Community Grants (England)
The Coalfields Community Grants Programme in England can award grants from £500 up to £5,000. This programme is for community and voluntary organisations who can demonstrate that a grant will impact positively on people living in the former coalfield communities of England. At the trust we believe that communities should define their own solutions to respond to local needs and issues. However, sometimes there is the requirement to secure additional resources to meet any challenges and enable new activities to take place. Our grant programme can help provide funding to turn these aspirations into a reality.

Download our application form and information booklet which will help to get you started. You can also contact our Head Office on 01226 270800 to speak to our team or email at info@coalfields-regen.org.uk

Community Enterprise Network (Wales)
The Community Enterprise Network is a Community Economic Development project, backed by the European Regional Development Fund through the Welsh Government, which aims to forge an enterprising culture and ignite an entrepreneurial spark in the valleys; raising prosperity amongst communities in Bridgend, Merthyr Tydfil and Rhondda Cynon Taff. The Community Enterprise Network explores the wealth of under-used skills and talents in communities; encouraging individuals to engage in active citizenship and actively explore possibilities that will benefit themselves and their local area, by fostering a sense of community through network membership and sharing best practice.

The project also helps new social enterprise start-ups and link emerging and established social enterprises; as well as providing on-going access and referral to a wealth of resources, creating a sustainable enterprise culture and long-term change.

To find out more, to become a member of the network, the Enterprise Fund, or to discuss other opportunities with CEN in RCT, please contact Hayley Doorhof at The Coalfields Regeneration Trust on 01443 404455 or email hayley.doorhof@coalfields-regen.org.uk

Coalfields Community Investment Programme (Scotland)
The Coalfields Community Investment Programme has been developed to support voluntary organisations, community groups and social enterprises operating in the Scottish coalfields. We want to help them unlock the potential of their communities by supporting new ideas which develop social cohesion,

community enterprise and regeneration activity. We will invest between £500 and £10,000 in capital, revenue or a blend of both for projects that complement the CRT's activities in Scotland.

Our investments will:

- Encourage community led capacity, innovation and services
- Create an environment in which people can participate and encourage local growth
- Support the community outcomes identified within the Coalfields Community Futures and Challenge programmes
- Increase partnership between players which can act as a catalyst for levering in other funds

An organisation can only receive one investment in any twelve month period.

Contact us using the details below and our team will be happy to help. Tel: 01259 272127 or email: david.wright@coalfields-regen.org.uk

Coalfields Capacity Building (Scotland)

The Coalfields Regeneration Trust was set up as a vehicle to enable community-led regeneration, recognising that strong, engaged and empowered communities are vital to the future of fragile coalfield areas. We have supported 130 organisations to attract over £750,000 of funding into their communities.

For further information about this programme of work contact the Scottish team on 01259 272127.

Coalfields Community Futures (Scotland)

The Coalfields Community Futures Programme is delivering in partnership and has worked with three local communities with a total population of 17,000. The initiative has supported 38 local community groups and assisted them through improved capacity to make prioritised and positive change to their own communities.

Community Futures is an approach to local community planning and sustainable community development that aims to encourage active citizenship and build local democracy.

The programme involves:

- Working with local residents and groups to identify local needs and priorities and develop a common sense of purpose and a deliverable community action plan
- Making use of a small seed corn fund for each area, that can be allocated by residents to initiate small-scale improvements through a *Participatory Budgeting Process*
- Providing tailored capacity building support, working with local residents and groups to establish skills/structures and secure external funding for agreed projects
- Where possible support the development of a new community 'anchor' organisation to provide a focus or hub for continued community regeneration

- Helping organisations to 'make the right connections' with other successful organisations to encouraging learning, pooling of resources and ongoing mentoring and support

For further information about this programme of work contact the Scottish team on 01259 272127.

Coalfields Community Grants (Wales)

The Coalfields Community Grants Programme in Wales can award grants from £500 up to £10,000. This programme is for community and voluntary organisations who can demonstrate that a grant will impact positively on people living in the former coalfield communities of Wales.

Grants will be made which can show an impact on the lives of people living within the former coalfield areas within the following themes:

- Increasing prosperity and wellbeing for the whole community
- Moving towards low carbon communities
- Improving the life chances for children and young people

Please contact us at the Wales office if you would like to discuss a potential project for this programme by emailing wales@coalfields-regen.org.uk or telephoning 01443 404455

Grantmaking in 2011/12

In 2011/12 the trust had an income of £22.3 million and assets of £9.1 million. There were 568 grants approved in the financial year totalling £15.6 million (this figure excludes community support and development activities, development and governance costs).

All grant approvals are intended to support the regeneration of coalfield communities and contribute towards the implementation plans agreed with the trust's principal funders. Across England, Scotland and Wales grants are approved under our social investment templates that contribute to the following objectives:

- Building new or improving community
- Facilities helping people into work
- Increasing childcare provision
- Supporting existing or creating new social enterprises
- Assisting people to access training and gaining qualifications

The trust has grants teams working in the coalfield areas of England, Scotland and Wales. These teams continue to provide essential support, application forms, advice and guidance to help applicants with their project and represent the trust's ongoing commitment to grass-roots regeneration of coalfield communities.

Grants were broken down in the annual report by country and amount:

	England	Scotland	Wales
under £10,000	£1 million	£368,000	£146,000
£10,000 – £30,000	£1.1 million	£286,000	£97,000
£30,000 – £60,000	£3 million	£312,000	£440,000
£60,000 – £300,000	£8 million	£281,000	£153,000
over £300,000	£401,000	–	–
Total	**£13.5 million**	**£1.2 million**	**£836,000**

Previous beneficiaries included: Aylesham Neighbourhood Project (£210,000); Haswell and District Mencap Society – The Community Anchor (£98,000); Derbyshire Rural Community Council – Wheels to Work (£89,000); The Cornforth Partnership – The Reach Project (£75,000); Nottinghamshire Independent Domestic Abuse Link Workers (£66,000); Stoke On Trent and District Gingerbread Centre Ltd – Peer Mentoring (£37,000); St Johns Church – A Building in Which to Serve Our Community (£10,000); Mansfield and Dukeries Irish Association – Luncheon Club (£5,000); City of Durham Air Cadets – Achieving Duke of Edinburgh's Awards (£3,800); and Thornycroft Art Club – Christmas Tree Exhibition (£520).

Exclusions

The following organisations are not eligible to receive support:

- Individuals
- Private businesses
- Statutory bodies
- National organisations
- Parish, town and community councils
- Organisations with total annual income (from all sources) above £100,000
- Organisations that the trust believes are in a poor financial position or whose financial management systems are not in good order
- 'friends of' groups where the end beneficiary will clearly be a statutory body
- Pigeon (flying) clubs
- Organisations not established in the UK

Applications

Application details are different for each programme. The trust has produced very comprehensive information booklets that should be read before applying to any fund. Applicants are advised to contact their regional manager before making an application, details of which are also on the trust's website. The staff will be able to advise on the trust's application process and an appointment can be made with a member of the development team to discuss the application in more detail.

Percentage of awards given to new applicants: between 40% and 50%.

Common applicant mistakes

'Incomplete application forms; missing information; not reading the guidance and document checklist.'

Information gathered from:

Accounts; annual report; Charity Commission record; further information provided by the funder; funder's website.

The John S. Cohen Foundation

General, in particular music and the arts, education and environment
£316,000 (2011/12)

Beneficial area

Worldwide, in practice mainly UK.

Correspondent: Mrs Diana Helme, Foundation Administrator, PO Box 21277, London W9 2YH (tel: 020 7286 6921)

Trustees: Dr David Cohen, Chair; Imogen Cohen; Olivia Cohen; Veronica Cohen.

CC Number: 241598

The objectives of the foundation are general charitable purposes in the UK or elsewhere and it is particularly active in supporting education, music and the arts and the environment, both built and natural.

In 2011/12 the foundation had assets of £6.9 million and an income of £442,000. Grants were made to 97 organisations totalling £316,000.

Beneficiaries included: Royal Opera House (£25,000); the National Gallery (£20,000); British Museum and Public Catalogue Foundation (£10,000 each); Wigmore Hall Trust (£7,000); Chatham House, Garsington Opera and Poetry Book Society (£5,000 each); Mayor of London's Fund and Truro Cathedral (£4,000 each); Eden Trust and The Sixteen (£3,000 each); British Film Institute and Jewish Museum (£2,000 each); 45' Aid Society, Alzheimer's Society, Birmingham Repertory Theatre and World Jewish Relief (£1,000 each); Musical Brain (£500); and Tait Memorial Trust (£100).

Applications

In writing to the correspondent.

Grants are awarded after the submission of applications to the trustees. The trustees review the application to judge if the grant falls within the charity's objectives and whether the application meets its requirements in terms of the benefits it gives. Each application is discussed, reviewed and decided upon by the trustees at their regular meetings.

Information gathered from:

Accounts; annual report; Charity Commission record.

The R. and S. Cohen Foundation

Education, relief in need and the arts
Around £1 million (2012)

Beneficial area

Worldwide.

Correspondent: Martin Dodd, Administrator, 42 Portland Place, London W1B 1NB

Trustees: Lady Sharon Harel-Cohen; Sir Ronald Cohen; Tamara Harel-Cohen; David Marks; Jonathan Harel-Cohen.

CC Number: 1078225

The foundation was established for general charitable purposes in 1999 by Sir Ronald Cohen, chair of Bridges Ventures Investment Company.

The trust states that its objectives are:
- The advancement of education
- The relief of persons who are in conditions of need, hardship or distress as a result of local, national or international disaster or by reason of their social and economic circumstances
- In promoting and encouraging for the public all aspects of the arts, including painting, sculpture, theatre and music
- Other deserving causes as the trustees see fit

In 2012 the foundation had an unusually low income of £15,500 (2011: £1.17 million). Total expenditure was £1.25 million. Grants are likely to have totalled around £1 million.

We do not have details of the year's beneficiaries but previous organisations have included: UJIA (£50,000); Design Museum (£40,000); Muscular Dystrophy, Royal National Institute for the Blind (£25,000 each); Jewish Care (£20,000); Tel-Aviv University Trust (£15,000); British Museum (£13,000); New Israel Fund (£8,000); Tate Foundation (£5,000); Royal Academy of the Arts (£4,500); and WLS Charitable Fund (£1,200).

Applications

In writing to the correspondent.

Information gathered from:

Charity Commission record.

The Colt Foundation

Occupational and environmental health research
£422,500 to institutions (2012)

Beneficial area

UK.

Correspondent: Jacqueline Douglas, Director, New Lane, Havant, Hampshire PO9 2LY (tel: 02392 491400; fax: 02392 491363; email: jackie.douglas@uk. coltgroup.com; website: www. coltfoundation.org.uk)

Trustees: Prof. David Coggon; Clare Gilchrist; Prof. Sir Anthony J. Newman Taylor; Peter O'Hea; Alan O'Hea; Jerome O'Hea; Natasha Heydon; Patricia Lebus.

CC Number: 277189

This foundation was established in 1978 and its primary aim is to promote and encourage research into social, medical and environmental problems created by commerce and industry.

The foundation considers applications for funding high quality research projects in the field of occupational and environmental health, particularly those aimed at discovering the cause of illnesses arising from conditions at the place of work. The work is monitored by the foundation's scientific advisers and external assessors to achieve the maximum impact with available funds. The trustees prefer to be the sole source of finance for a project.

The foundation also makes grants through selected universities and colleges to enable students to take higher degrees in subjects related to occupational and environmental health. PhD Fellowships are awarded each year, and the foundation is committed to support the MSc course in Human and Applied Physiology at King's College, London. More than 80 students have been supported since the inception of the foundation and grants to students account for over one-quarter of the foundation's annual grants.

Donations to organisations vary from a few thousand pounds to over £100,000 and may be repeated over two to five years. Beneficiaries are well-established research institutes (awards to individuals are made through these). The foundation takes a continuing interest in its research projects and holds annual review meetings.

In 2012 the foundation had assets of £15 million and an income of £559,500. Grants were made during the year totalling £583,000, which included 16 grants to institutions amounting to £422,500 and £161,000 to students.

Some institutions received more than one grant during the year. Beneficiaries included: University of Oxford (£75,000); Heriot-Watt University (£59,500); Edinburgh University (£56,500 in total); City University (£27,000); Imperial College (£14,000); and Colt Foundation Day 2012 (£8,000).

Exclusions

Grants are not made for the general funds of another charity, directly to individuals or projects overseas.

Applications

The foundation provided the following information on its website:

The trustees meet twice a year to review applications, in the spring and in the autumn, and applications normally need to be received at the beginning of April and October to be considered at the meetings. Applicants can submit a single sheet lay summary at any time during the year prior to working on a full application, so that advice can be given on whether the work is likely to fall within the remit of the foundation. The trustees are particularly keen to fund research that is likely to make a difference to government policy or working practices.

What needs to be in an application

Applications should contain sufficient information for the Scientific Advisers to be able to comment, and should include a lay summary for the trustees' first appraisal. This lay summary is essential as the majority of the trustees do not have a medical or scientific background. This summary will help them in their decision between the different applications under consideration. Applications are not expected to exceed 3,000 words, excluding references, the lay summary and justification of resources. Brief CVs, not exceeding two sides of A4 paper, should be attached for each of the major applicants. Please read the following questions carefully and bear them in mind when preparing your application.

1 What is the work you would like to do? Explain the background and its relevance for occupational health
2 Explain the specific research question and why it is important
3 What are you proposing to do to answer the research question? Why do you think this is the right approach? How will it answer the research question? What potential problem (e.g. biases) do you see with this study design, and how will they be addressed?
4 What do you think will be the potential ultimately to influence policy or practice for the benefit of workers or the wider public? Who else is doing or has done work in the same area, and how will your work complement theirs?
5 What resources will you need to do the work, and to what extent are these resources already available? How much money do you need to complete the work? You will need to

demonstrate that the study is good value for money
6 Who will do the work, and how much time will each of the people, including yourself as PI, involved devote to it?
7 How long will the work take and when do you plan to start?

Notes

Applications involving research on people and/or on human tissues must receive the approval of an ethics committee. As a charity, the Colt Foundation will only pay the Directly Incurred Costs of a project, together with some categories of necessary Directly Attributable Costs. Universities are reimbursed by HEFCE for the majority of Directly Attributable and Indirect Costs. In addition to funding, the foundation takes a continuing interest in its research projects and holds annual review meetings. The trustees may appoint an external assessor to report on project progress. Grants are not made to the general funds of other charities, or directly to individuals, or to projects based outside the UK. Details of recent projects supported are shown on the website under 'Projects.

Applicants are advised to visit the foundation's helpful website.

Information gathered from:

Accounts; Charity Commission record; funder's website.

Colyer-Fergusson Charitable Trust

Social isolation, exclusion or poverty, community activity (often through churches), church maintenance, environment, the arts

£514,500 (2011/12)

Beneficial area

Kent.

Correspondent: Jacqueline Rae, Director, Hogarth House, 34 Paradise Road, Richmond, Surrey TW9 1SE (tel: 020 8948 3388; email: grantadmin@cfct.org.uk; website: www.cfct.org.uk)

Trustees: Jonathan Monckton, Chair; Nicholas Fisher; Robert North; Ruth Murphy.

CC Number: 258958

The following information is available from the trust's website:

The Colyer-Fergusson Charitable Trust is delighted to announce its new funding programmes focused on supporting young people with 'poverty of opportunity'. The trust will make grants to support organisations working with this target group and use its funds to expand opportunities for apprenticeship and vocational learning. It will also continue to make grants through its hardship awards programme working in partnership with its referral partners.

Disadvantaged and vulnerable young people in Kent face enormous challenges. The recession has impacted on every community across the county, but none more so than Kent's young people who have suffered disproportionately from a lack of employment opportunities. Colyer-Fergusson Charitable Trust plans to use its funds to support disadvantaged young people and help them navigate the difficult journey into adulthood. The trust will allocate its funds through three funding programmes:

Hardship Award Programme

The hardship grants are aimed at disadvantaged young people living in Thanet, Shepway, Swale and Medway and are intended to meet the costs of practical items such as: interview clothes; course fees; tools or equipment; travel costs to a new job etc. All applicants must be referred by an approved CFCT referral partner. If your organisation believes it may be in a position to refer young people for a hardship award please email jrae@cfct.org.uk for more information about applying to become a partner.

Approved Referral Partners will be able to make a hardship grant application online [via the trust's website].

Investing in Young People Programme

The trust is interested in hearing from organisations that work with young people with 'poverty of opportunity'. The trust recognises that there are many excellent organisations in Kent working with young people. However, we are interested in hearing from those where a grant of between £25,000 and £75,000 from the trust would allow them to make a significant and demonstrable difference to these young people. The trust expects to receive a great deal of interest for this programme and therefore applicants are asked to download and read the guidance material [on the trust's website] before completing a brief expression of interest form online. Projects of interest will be contacted and invited to provide more information in due course.

Funding for Apprenticeships and Vocational Learning Programme

The trust is interested hearing from organisations that can deliver apprenticeships and/or vocational education for young people with 'poverty of opportunity'. Organisations may be offering these in house or they may have the ability to unlock employer engagement. The trust is particularly interested in organisations that are able to meet the needs of very vulnerable and disadvantaged young people, including ex-offenders. Grants of up to £100,000 may be available for outstanding and innovative projects. Applicants are asked to download and read the guidance material [on the trust's website] before completing a brief expression of interest form online. Projects of interest will be invited to provide more information in due course.

Grantmaking 2011/12

In 2011/12 the trust had assets of £17.1 million and an income of £122,000. Grants were made to 32 charities and churches in Kent and in addition 29 small grants were made from the trustees' discretionary funds together totalling £514,500. In 2011/12, under previous criteria, grants were broken down as follows:

Young people leaving care	2	£90,500
Trustees discretionary grants	29	£89,500
Church fabric repair	9	£89,000
Encouraging active living	7	£76,500
Safer communities	7	£74,000
Caring for carers	4	£58,000
Older vulnerable people	3	£37,000

Beneficiaries from all categories included: The Caldecott Foundation (£75,000); Kings Church Medway (£30,000); Herne Bay Sea Cadets and Special Needs Advisory and Activities Project (£20,000 each); Caring All Together on Romney Marsh and Cerebral Palsy Care – Kent (£15,000 each); Listening Books (£12,000); Eastbridge Hospital (£10,000); and Cliffe Memorial Hall (£5,000).

Exclusions

No grants are considered for the following:

▶ Individuals directly
▶ Animal welfare charities
▶ Events such as conferences, seminars and exhibitions
▶ Expeditions and overseas travel
▶ Fee-charging residential homes, nurseries and care facilities
▶ Festivals, performances and other arts and entertainment activities
▶ Fundraising events
▶ Hospitals, NHS trusts, medically related appeals and medical equipment
▶ Loans or repayment of loans
▶ Commercial ventures or publications
▶ National charities – unless they have a project located and operating within Kent
▶ Mini-buses other than community transport schemes
▶ Research – academic and medical
▶ Retrospective grants
▶ Schools other than pre-school and after school clubs
▶ Work that duplicates existing local provision
▶ Sponsorship – organisations and individuals
▶ Large capital, endowment or widely distributed appeals

Applications

Full guidance and application forms are available on the trust's website.

Information gathered from:

Accounts; annual report; Charity Commission record; funder's website.

Comic Relief

Social welfare

£32.3 million in the UK (2011/12)

Beneficial area

UK and overseas.

Correspondent: Judith McNeill, Grants Director, 5th Floor, 89 Albert Embankment, London SE1 7TP (tel: 020 7820 2000; fax: 020 7820 2222; email: ukgrants@comicrelief.com; website: www.comicrelief.com)

Trustees: Tim Davie, chair; Richard Curtis; Lenny Henry; Suzi Aplin; Peter Salmon; Cilla Snowball; Colin Howes; Diana Barran; Harry Cayton; Imelda Walsh; Joe Cerrell; Mike Harris; Robert S. Webb; Theo Sowa; Tristia Clarke; Danny Cohen.

CC Number: 326568

Since 1985 Comic Relief has raised around £500 million to tackle poverty and social injustice in the UK, Africa, and more recently in some of the poorest countries in other parts of the world. This entry is primarily concerned with grantmaking in the UK.

In 2002, Comic Relief started a second initiative, Sport Relief. Half of its income goes to the International Children and Young People's programme, the other half to projects in the UK that are using sport to increase social cohesion and inclusion.

The charity also administers Robbie Williams' Give It Sum Fund for community-based projects in his home area of North Staffordshire.

The charity principally receives its income through the generosity of the public via its Red Nose Day fundraising event. This is held every two years in partnership with the BBC, and the extent of the grantmaking depends entirely on the success of the preceding event.

The charity's UK and international grantmaking strategy is based on five themes:

Better Futures

Improving the lives of vulnerable young people in the UK, and enabling some of the world's poorest people to gain access to vital services such as health and education.

Healthier Finances

Tackling financial poverty, and enabling economic resilience in families and communities, as well as supporting enterprise and employment.

Safer Lives

Reducing violence, abuse and exploitation.

Stronger Communities

Empowering people, organisations and networks to play an effective role in their communities and society, as well as nurturing talent and leadership.

Fairer Society

Helping people overcome inequality and have a say in decisions that affect their lives, whoever and wherever they are.

The following information on the grantmaking in the UK is taken from the charity's website:

UK Grantmaking

In the UK, Comic Relief funds work that aims to achieve at least one of our five themes. We do this by supporting organisations with the people, ideas and ability to tackle complex problems and create positive social change across the UK. Young people and older people are important to us, as are others who face disadvantage, particularly in areas with high levels of deprivation. We also welcome proposals from projects that use sport to transform lives.

Our UK grants team follows a flexible and responsive funding strategy, allowing organisations to select the approaches they feel are most effective in tackling pressing issues.

Principles and priorities

We have a set of principles that guide our grant making and management in the UK and internationally, based on over 25 years of working with others to create social change. They inform how we work with partners and, as part of our commitment to improving how we, ourselves, work, we aim to 'live' these principles too. Whilst our principles underpin our grant making, we're also interested in a number of priority areas in the UK. We'll favour proposals which demonstrate how they meet one or more of these priorities.

Our principles

▶ Demonstrating a proven and significant gap: for example, for a particular user group or in an underfunded geographical location
▶ Building on effective practice: with well-supported evidence of change from existing work and clear plans for building on that knowledge in the future
▶ People with direct experience at the heart of the organisation: where people with personal and 'lived' experience play a lead role in running, managing and shaping the organisation
▶ Supporting new ways of working: where there is a strong case for new approaches with the 'right' people to do it
▶ Commitment to partnerships: with others that can help resources go further and deliver a better service or project

Our priorities

▶ Understanding the context and good practice
▶ Consulting and engaging others

- Understanding change and applying lessons learned
- Being responsive
- Building effective organisations and their leadership
- Valuing diversity
- Using resources effectively
- Making change last

How we fund

Potential applicants should the eligibility checker on the charity's website to determine if they are eligible to apply. Further information is given as follows:

The types of grants we make
UK Main Fund

The majority of our grants are awarded through the UK Main Fund and we welcome proposals from organisations working within our five themes [see above].

Special Initiatives

We work in partnership with a range of organisations and other funders to create long-term change for specific groups of people, issues and sectors.

UK Small Grants

We provide smaller, mostly community-based, grants in partnership with UK Community Foundations. They have the networks and local expertise to make decisions closer to the ground [see below].

Who can apply

We make grants to organisations based in England, Scotland, Wales, Northern Ireland, the Channel Islands and the Isle of Man. We welcome proposals from registered charities and other eligible not-for-profit organisations.

New and emerging or small not-for-profit groups who are not registered are eligible to apply as long as they have a constitution.

We can only fund legally charitable work that your constitution allows you to do.

We can only accept one proposal from an organisation at any one time.

How much and for how long

The minimum grant you can apply for in our UK Main Fund is £10,000 but we do not set an upper limit. We expect to make grants across a fairly wide spectrum of sizes but most will be between £20,000 and £40,000 per annum. We only make a small number of larger grants and, where this is the case, you'll need to demonstrate that your work has either regional or national significance, is delivered by a number of partners or is clearly breaking new ground.

Comic Relief makes smaller grants through UK Community Foundations. To apply for a grant of £10,000 or less, [visit the UK Community Foundations website: ukcommunityfoundations.org/programmes/comicrelief]

Although we're willing to fund up to 100% of the cost of the proposal, you are encouraged to seek other sources of funding as well. We would usually expect to fund a minimum of 25% of the total costs of the proposed activities, to ensure

that it's involved in the work in a meaningful way.

We make grants for a maximum of three years.

When you can apply

You can apply at any time. There are no cycles or closing dates. You do not need to rush your proposal as we make funding decisions every two months throughout the year.

Where we fund

We fund work which benefits people in England, Scotland, Wales, Northern Ireland, the Channel Islands and the Isle of Man.

We fund across urban and rural areas and are especially keen to fund areas of the UK with high levels of deprivation.

We want to ensure a good spread of funding around the UK and make sure that areas which often miss out are encouraged to apply.

Costs we cover and those we don't

We will fund revenue costs, such as salaries, and are willing to fund small capital items, such as office furniture and computers. We won't usually fund building costs, the purchase of vehicles and land or heavy equipment unless it can be clearly shown that such expenditure is proportionately small, in relation to the overall budget, and adequately justified as essential to the proposed activity. Additionally you must be able to demonstrate how you would effectively manage the asset for the duration of the project or over its lifetime. We're committed to covering the reasonable wider organisational costs of running your programme as part of a 'full cost recovery' approach.

Grantmaking

In 2011/12 the charity had assets of £134.5 million and an income of £89.5 million. (Red Nose Day 2013, the charity's main fundraising event, raised over £100 million.) Grants were made in the UK during 2011/12 totalling £32.3 million. A further £45.7 million was awarded in international grants.

The charity's annual report highlighted some achievements and developments in the UK during the year:

Particular highlights this year include the Mental Health Impact Study, which revealed that our support over the last 5 years had helped over 500,000 people to get their needs met more effectively and have a voice in decisions about their lives.

Since 2007 UnLtd (for social entrepreneurs) and Comic Relief have awarded £4m to 850 young people who are using sport to tackle community tensions and improve cohesion. In the last year, 23% of those young people secured employment, 28% gained a qualification and 55% improved their hopes for the future.

83% of the 11,500 children that Kids Company works with across 40 schools in London, achieved a positive education

outcome – many of these young people have profound difficulties caused by traumatic events in their lives.

We have made a number of other key advances this year including: A review of the Young People and Sexual Exploitation programme during 2011/12 revealed that our support had helped over 120,000 young people who were either victims of abuse, or at serious risk. This is also linked to work to prevent young people being lured into situations where they are trafficked from their home countries in Eastern Europe. This includes a project in Albania, where the Government is using a Comic Relief funded film Two Little Girls, as a teaching resource that is integrated it into the school curriculum. It is now being widely used across the country, ensuring that many more young people will be aware of the dangers of trafficking in order to help prevent it.

The findings from Comic Relief's Alcohol Hidden Harm cohort study – one of the very few studies in this area that we are aware of – were included in the Children's Commissioner for England's study into parental alcohol/substance misuse, Silent Voices.

The 'Card Before You Leave' Campaign, instigated by a Comic Relief funded organisation in Northern Ireland, ensures that no-one experiencing mental health issues leaves hospital without having appropriate follow up support in place. The campaign was so successful that that the government signed up to the policy bringing about a lasting change across Northern Ireland.

Grants in the UK were awarded as follows:

Local Communities	£7.4 million
Older People	£3.7 million
Sport for Change	£3.6 million
Young People with Alcohol Problems	£3.3 million
Domestic and Sexual Abuse	£2.7 million
Sexually Exploited and Trafficked Young People	£2.6 million
Mental Health	£2.2 million
Young People with Mental Health Problems	£2 million
Refugees and Asylum Seekers	£1.9 million
Special Applications	£1.2 million
Give it Sum	£542,000
Steve Redgrave Fund	£202,000
Elder Abuse Initiative	£18,000
Other Restricted Funds	£1.8 million

Exclusions

There are certain types of work and organisations that Comic Relief does not fund. If your proposal falls into one of these categories, do not apply.

- Grants to individuals
- Medical research or hospitals
- Churches or other religious bodies where the monies will be used for religious purposes
- Work where there is statutory responsibility to provide funding
- Projects where the work has already taken place
- Statutory bodies, such as local authorities or Primary Care Trusts or

organisations seeking funding to replace cuts by statutory bodies

▶ Profit-making organisations, except social enterprises

▶ Where your 'free' (unrestricted or designated) reserves are more than one year's running costs, 'we may not provide the full amount you ask for – or may not fund at all – if we feel you have enough to pay for the work yourself'

▶ Funding for minibuses

Applications

Applications are made online via the charity's website, where full guidance is also provided. Potential applicants must register and complete Stage 1 of the process, an initial proposal. Applicants are shortlisted from those successfully completing Stage 1.

Information gathered from:

Accounts; annual report; Charity Commission record; funder's website.

The Ernest Cook Trust

Educational grants focusing on children and young people for the environment, rural conservation, arts and crafts, literary and numeracy and research

£1.5 million (2011/12)

Beneficial area

UK.

Correspondent: The Grants Administrator, Fairford Park, Fairford, Gloucestershire GL7 4JH (tel: 01285 712492; fax: 01285 713417; email: grants@ernestcooktrust.org.uk; website: www.ernestcooktrust.org.uk)

Trustee: This charity has been given a dispensation by the Charity Commission from publishing the names of its trustees.

CC Number: 313497

The following information on the trust's background, interests and activities is taken from its annual report of 2011/12:

Ernest Edward Cook, the founder of the trust which bears his name, died in 1955 at the age of 89. Following the sale of his family business (the travel agent Thomas Cook & Sons) in 1928, Mr Cook devoted his wealth and energy to the purchase of country houses and estates, and the collections of works of art which they contained, thus preserving them from fragmentation. Mr Cook made significant bequests and donations to the National Art Collections Fund and to the National Trust; as a result of those donations, the National Trust turned its attention to country houses, at that time a new activity for the Trust.

Mr Cook founded his Trust in 1952 as an educational charity, initially deriving its income from the 14,462 acres of agricultural estate land he put into trust which still continues to form part of the endowment.

The overall management of the Trust's affairs is carried out by a chief executive, whose title is 'Agent and Director, Secretary to the Trustees'; he is supported by professional and administrative staff, and by a relevant range of external advisors. Decisions are made at the appropriate management level; day-to-day matters are decided by the managers, with reference as necessary to the Agent. More important decisions are taken by the Agent: matters requiring a decision by the Trustees are referred to them either at one of their meetings or, in between such meetings, by correspondence (by letter or email) and telephone calls.

Objectives and activities

The Ernest Cook Trust is an educational charitable foundation which makes grants to provide financial assistance to suitable educational projects run by other charities or not-for-profit organisations and runs educational visits to its estates. The document setting out the strategy for the operation and management of the Trust, which was adopted in July 2008 and reviewed in 2011, contains the following statement of purpose: 'The aim of the Ernest Cook Trust is to make educational grants and to carry out other educational work so as to be highly effective in pursuit of its charitable objective whilst, subject to that, maintaining its investment in its estates in ways that ensure their value, excellence and preservation'. Whilst the majority of beneficiaries are school-children, this is not exclusively the case.

Grant-Making

The trust's grants policy was reviewed in January 2006; it is influenced by Mr Cook's two great passions, namely art and country estates but includes support to increase standards of literacy and numeracy. Grants, which must always be for clearly educational purposes, aim principally to focus upon the needs of children and young people. To that end the trustees are keen to support applications from registered charities or other not-for-profit organisations within the United Kingdom in three main areas of activity, being the environment and the countryside, the wide spectrum of arts, crafts and architecture, and literacy and numeracy. All applications are expected to link in with either the National Curriculum or recognised qualifications.

It is appreciated that sometimes a contribution will be required towards the salary of an education officer, but the ECT always expects to be a part-funder. Funds are not usually committed for more than one year: successful applicants are normally asked to wait three years before applying for further help.

Research grants are occasionally awarded if the work links in to the above interests: suitable projects which do not

fall into any of the main categories are also considered.

All applications are processed by the Grants Administrator in consultation with the Agent and Director. Applications which meet the trust's criteria are passed to the trustees, who make all decisions relating to awards and the size of grant. The Small Grants programme is administered by the Education Trustee, with the help of the other trustees by rotation, six times per year: the full board of trustees considers applications for main grants twice per year. All recipients of grants are required to report on the use of the award, within one year of it being made. By making grants in this way, the trust enables numerous charitable organisations to carry out a wide variety of work benefiting diverse sections of the public; without such grant support these organisations would not have the necessary funding and would therefore not be able to carry out their enriching work.

Programmes

The following information is taken from the trust's website:

Small Grants Programme

The small grants programme supports state schools and small registered charities which would like to undertake projects which meet the trust's objectives and require a small amount of pump-priming in order for such projects to take place. The programme is a rolling one, with meetings at two-monthly intervals throughout the year – but it is wise to think well ahead. Suitable applications are allocated to the next available meeting, however **due to high demand you are advised to submit an application at least six months ahead of your project start date**.

Large Grants Programme

The large grants programme is aimed at more comprehensive education programmes: these sometimes require support for the salary of an education officer; in such cases the ECT would always expect to be a part-funder. The range of the programme is wide; over the years education projects linked to theatres, art galleries and orchestras have been supported, as have those covering a wide range of environmental and countryside projects.

In 2011/12 the trust had assets of £112.7 million and an income of £3.4 million. There were 460 grants made totalling £1.5 million, categorised as follows:

Environment	£618,500
Arts, crafts and architecture	£542,000
Literacy and numeracy	£311,000
Other	£52,000

Details of individual beneficiaries were not included in the trust's 2011/12 annual report, however recipients of grants from the previous year were detailed at the time of writing, on the trust's website, with more recent examples no doubt available in due course.

Beneficiaries in September 2012 included: Canterbury Cathedral and Opera North (£10,000 each); Watts Gallery (£8,000); Conservation Volunteers Northern Ireland (£7,000); Edward Peake Middle School (£5,000); Read for Life CIC (£4,000); and Making Places (£2,000).

Exclusions

Applicants must represent either registered charities or not-for-profit organisations. Grants are normally awarded on an annual basis and will not be awarded retrospectively.

Grants are not made:

- To pre-school groups, individuals, agricultural colleges, independent schools or local authorities
- For building work, infrastructure or refurbishment work
- For youth work, social support, therapy and medical treatment, including projects using the arts, environment or literacy and numeracy for these purposes
- For projects related to sports, outward bound type activities or recreation
- For overseas projects
- For wildlife trusts and for farming and wildlife advisory groups other than those which are based in counties in which the ECT owns land (Buckinghamshire, Dorset, Gloucestershire, Leicestershire and Oxfordshire)

Applications

The ECT aims to have a 'light-touch' application process with a view to enabling small regional or local organisations to apply for support. All applicant organisations must be based and working in the UK and should be either state schools, registered charities or other recognised not-for-profit organisations. It is very important however to read the exclusions before applying. Grants are normally awarded for one year only.

There are no application forms. All applicants are asked to post a covering letter on the official headed paper of the applicant organisation and also include:

- Up to two additional sheets of A4 describing the organisation, outlining the project and specifying its educational elements and the way in which it fits in with the interests of the ECT
- A simple budget for the project, outlining the way in which the grant would be spent
- A list of any other funding applications
- The latest annual report and accounts for the organisation (schools are not required to send one)

Do not send further supporting material or email applications, which are not accepted. It is advisable to read the examples of projects supported before making an application. **Questions** (not applications) can be addressed to the grants administrator. Applications must be posted.

When to apply

Applicants who have been successful previously are asked to wait for **three years** before re-applying.

Large Grants programme:

The full board of trustees meets twice a year, in April and September, to consider grants in excess of £4,000. At the spring meeting only projects related to arts, crafts and architecture and literacy and numeracy are considered while at the autumn meeting only projects covering environment and countryside and literacy and numeracy are considered. Apart from a few larger awards to projects especially close to the interests of the trustees, most awards are in the range of £4,000 to £10,000.

Applications for the spring meeting (which usually takes place in mid-April) must be received by the trust by 31 January of that year. Applications for the autumn meeting (which takes place in September) must be received by the trust by 31 July of that year.

Small Grants Programme:

Meetings to consider applications for the small grants programme take place bi-monthly throughout the year. This programme deals mainly, but not exclusively, with requests for support from state schools and small charitable organisations.

There is no specific closing date; suitable applications are allocated to the next available meeting though it is always wise to think well ahead of the start date of your project. Although the full range of the small grants programme is up to £4,000, due to the huge pressure on the available resources most awards are in the region of £1,000 to £1,500.

Information gathered from:

Accounts; annual report; Charity Commission record; funder's website.

The Alice Ellen Cooper Dean Charitable Foundation

General charitable purposes
£544,000 (2011/12)

Beneficial area

Mainly local organisations in Dorset and west Hampshire as a top priority.

Correspondent: Rupert Edwards, Trustee, Edwards and Keeping, Unity Chambers, 34 High East Street, Dorchester, Dorset DT1 1HA (tel: 01305 251333; fax: 01305 251465; email: office@edwardsandkeeping.co.uk)

Trustees: John Bowditch; Linda Bowditch; Rupert Edwards; Douglas Neville-Jones; Emma Blackburn.

CC Number: 273298

The foundation was established for general charitable purposes in 1977 with an initial gift by Ellen Cooper Dean and supplemented by a legacy on her death in 1984. Donations are only made to registered charities with a preference for local organisations in Dorset and west Hampshire. Grants usually range from £1,000 to £10,000 each.

In 2011/12 the foundation had assets of £24.3 million and an income of £1 million. There were 121 grants made totalling £544,000.

In addition to supporting local and national charities in the areas of health, social disadvantage, education, religion, community, arts and culture, amateur sport and disability, mainly on a regular basis, the foundation has made overseas grants to advance education, relieve poverty, sickness, and suffering caused by conflict and disasters.

Beneficiaries included: Sheltered Work Opportunities (£30,000); The Crumbs Project, Dorset Archives Trust, Marie Curie Cancer Care, Shelter and Youth Resources Services Ltd (£10,000 each); Eventide Homes Bournemouth (£8,000); Families for Children Trust Inspire Foundation and Listening Books (£5,000 each); Forest Forge Theatre Company and Motivation Charitable Trust (£3,000 each); British Liver Trust and Talking Newspapers Association (£2,000 each); and Moving On and Samaritans – Hampshire Projects (£1,000 each).

Exclusions

No grants to individuals. Grants to registered charities only.

Applications

In writing to the correspondent. Telephone calls are not welcome. Applications are considered from both local and national charitable organisations, with local charities given top priority and national charities only supported occasionally as funds permit.

Each application should include:

- Name and address of the organisation
- Charity registration number
- Details of the project
- Details of the community, including area covered and numbers who will benefit from the project
- Details of fundraising activities and other anticipated sources of grants
- A copy of the latest financial accounts

Percentage of awards given to new applicants: between 10% and 20%.

Common applicant mistakes

'They fail to provide last annual accounts.'

Information gathered from:

Accounts; annual report; Charity Commission record; further information provided by the funder.

The Evan Cornish Foundation

Education, older people, health, human rights, social and economic inequality, prisons

£714,500 (2011/12)

Beneficial area

UK and overseas.

Correspondent: Rachel Cornish, Trustee, The Innovation Centre, 217 Portobello, Sheffield S1 4DP (email: contactus@ evancornishfoundation.org.uk; website: www.evancornishfoundation.org.uk)

Trustees: Rachel Cornish; Barbara Ward; Sally Cornish.

CC Number: 1112703

The Evan Cornish Foundation was created by the widow and four daughters of businessman Evan Cornish who died in 2002. According to the 2011/12 trustees' report, the foundation aims to reach the marginalised both in the UK and overseas.

The foundation has six central areas of work:

▶ Education – to work with children who cannot access mainstream education
▶ Elderly – to support the wellbeing of older people through the provision of services by supporting charities which provide care in order to improve quality of life
▶ Health – to support and promote mental health, women's health and sight related disorders
▶ Human rights – to fight injustice by combating human rights violations and support victims of such violations
▶ Social and economic inequality – to reach the most marginalised and to address inequality through empowerment
▶ Prisons – to promote and ensure that the prison service is just, humane and effective

In 2011/12 the foundation had assets of £12.9 million and an income of £7 million, £6.9 million of which was a donation from the estate of the late Ethel Cornish – Evan Cornish's wife. A total of

133 donations were made ranging from £200 to £13,000 totalling £714,500.

Beneficiaries included: Unicef – City of Joy (£13,000); Christ Church Armley, Sheffield Together Women and Angels International (£10,000 each); Artlink (£8,500); Ambitious About Autism, Everychild and Lippy People (£7,500 each); Emmaus (£6,500); Hope Foundation, CAFOD and Kickstart (£5,000 each); Find Your Feet, Hope and Homes for Children and NOEL (£3,000 each); Sheffield Conversation Club and Notting Hill Churches Homeless Concern (£2,000 each); and Friends of the Elderly (£1,000).

Exclusions

The foundation is unable to support the following activities:

▶ Religious activities
▶ Animal welfare
▶ Individuals/gap year students
▶ Political activities
▶ Medical research
▶ Holiday club providers

Applications

The trustees will consider applications as well as seeking out causes to support. They have a three step application process which can be found on its website.

First time applicants should complete the standard application form, which can be obtained from the foundation's website. Applicants who wish to apply again should complete the re-application form, which can also be found on the foundation's website.

The trustees have two meetings per application deadline. One for UK based projects and one for overseas projects. This allows trustees to compare applications which are focused in similar areas.

Applicants can re-apply for additional funding one year from the date of the last grant, however a one year progress report must be provided.

Recipients of support are expected to provide feedback on the use of any grant and the achievements from it, through a six month update and a one year progress report.

Information gathered from:

Accounts; annual report; Charity Commission record; funder's website.

The John and Barbara Cotton Charitable Foundation

General charitable purposes

Beneficial area

UK, with a preference for West Yorkshire.

Correspondent: John Cotton, Trustee, c/o John Cotton Group Ltd, Nunbrook Mils, Huddersfield Road, Mirfield, West Yorkshire WF14 0EH (tel: 01924 496571; email: saraha@johncotton.co.uk)

Trustees: John Cotton; Barbara Cotton.

CC Number: 1145865

The foundation was registered in February 2012 and has general charitable purposes. The settlors and trustees of the foundation are directors of John Cotton Group Ltd, which includes 'Europe's leading manufacturer of pillows, duvets and mattress protectors'.

Applications

In writing to the correspondent.

Information gathered from:

Charity Commission record.

County Durham Community Foundation

Tackling social disadvantage and poverty, general

£2.1 million to organisations (2011/12)

Beneficial area

County Durham, Darlington and surrounding areas.

Correspondent: Barbara Gubbins, Chief Executive, Victoria House, Whitfield Court, St Johns Road, Meadowfield Industrial Estate, Durham DH7 8XL (tel: 01913 786340; fax: 01913 782409; email: info@cdcf.org.uk; website: www.cdcf.org.uk)

Trustees: Mark I'Anson, Chair; David Watson; Michele Armstrong; Ada Burns; George Garlick; Christopher Lendrum; Andrew Martell; David Martin; Lady Sarah Nicholson; Gerry Osborne; Kate Welch; Ruth Thompson.

CC Number: 1047625

The aim of the County Durham Foundation is to build up endowment funds so as to provide long-term income that is used to provide grants to approved projects within County Durham and Darlington (and in specified circumstances across the north east). The foundation supports and promotes charitable purposes in these areas and has focused on combating social disadvantage and poverty in its grant distribution. It receives donations and manages funds for individuals, companies, trusts and government departments who want to support the local community.

The foundation currently holds over 160 different funds all of which have their own policy and criteria. The majority of endowment-based funds are now donor advised, where the foundation works with the fund holder to determine potential recipients.

Grant programmes

All information taken from the foundation's helpful website:

Standard applications

Community groups, non-registered and registered charities are all able to apply for funds using just one main application form. Foundation staff mix-and-match applications when received and find the most appropriate fund for you. With the exception of the Banks Community Fund, ESF Community Grants and Surviving Winter, which have their own bespoke application forms, all of the foundation's funds can be accessed using the standard application form available online.

Note: To apply for a grant you need to read the general guidelines on the foundation's website before filling in an application form.

Armed Forces Community Covenant Grant Scheme

The Community Covenant grant scheme has been set up to fund local projects which strengthen the ties or the mutual understanding between members of the armed forces community and the wider community in which they live.

Successful projects will be able to demonstrate that they benefit both the armed forces community and their local community, for example:
- Fun days for service families
- Serving and ex-service personnel helping disabled and elderly people
- Mentors for service personnel and veterans who want to set up their own business
- Support for service families dealing with long periods of separation

Banks Community Fund

Read the guidelines available from the foundation's website:

Funding will be awarded to projects that aim to:
- Bring land back into use
- Reduce or prevent pollution
- Provide information on sustainable waste management
- Build, improve or maintain public parks or amenities
- Build, improve or maintain community buildings or amenities
- Improve quality of life in a local environment
- Promote or conserve biological diversity through the provision, conservation, restoration or enhancement of a natural habitat or the maintenance or recovery of a species in its natural habitat

Community Games

The Community Games programme will provide support and resources which include a national accredited e-training

and mentoring programme, designed to create a lasting legacy of community volunteers with the skills and confidence to activate social change. This new partnership will provide support and resources for the local communities of County Durham to organise their own local sporting and cultural events as a legacy of the London 2012 Olympic and Paralympic Games.

ESF Community Grants

Visit the foundation's website to find out about, and apply to, ESF Community Grants.

North East Fund for the Arts

The North East Fund for the Arts was established at the Community Foundation in May 2012 and will be built over the next three years with match funding from the Arts Council England's Catalyst scheme. The aim of the fund is to support arts activity in communities across the North East (Northumberland, Tyne & Wear, County Durham, Tees Valley) through building greater arts philanthropy to support those activities.

Projects could address a range of social issues but ultimately the aim is to strengthen community engagement in the arts. Projects could therefore engage a community in arts activity for the first time, develop their engagement, or inspire participants to seek further opportunities in the arts. The project may lead to the creation of a piece of art but an 'end product' is not a requirement. It is likely that for these founding grants we will support projects which are planned but not yet funded, or which have previously been tested and require support for continuation, expansion or application in a new area.

The fund is open to artists and arts organisations but we would especially welcome applications from non-arts community and voluntary groups who wish to work with professional artists/arts organisations. Applications from artists/arts organisations must show a real understanding of the community needs/interests and address them.

A community for the purpose of grant-making is a group of people who will benefit as a result of the grant. They could be a geographical community or have a shared background, identity or interest.

Priority Health

The aim of the Priority Health fund is to help address three key health issues that have been identified as priorities by the Health and Wellbeing Partnerships within County Durham and Darlington through their Needs Assessments. Projects will be considered that address the following three priority issues:
- Mental health resilience/wellbeing – front-line organisations addressing depression, stress-related problems and prevention of suicide
- Obesity in children – of primary school age. Projects that support and work with families, provide after school education and cookery and healthy eating clubs

- Alcohol awareness – emphasis will be on awareness-raising, especially with teenagers, although consideration will also be given to supporting cessation groups

Grant schemes change frequently. Consult the foundation's website for details of current programmes and their deadlines.

The foundation's publication 'Building Thriving Communities' states that in 2011/12 the foundation had assets of £8.5 million and an income of £2.8 million. Grants were made from all funds totalling £2.1 million. An additional £166,000 was awarded to individuals. The foundation approved 59.9% of applications received, rejected 28.3% and 11.8% were withdrawn. We have been unable to access the foundation's annual report and accounts, however, in 2010/11 the foundation categorised its grantmaking as follows:

Education and training	£586,000
Community support and development	£446,000
Sport and recreation	£269,500
Other	£241,000
Environment	£239,000
Health and Wellbeing	£145,000
Employment and labour	£80,000
Poverty and disadvantage	£75,000
Disability and access issues	£53,000
Housing	£50,000
Art, craft and drama	£40,000
Social inclusion	£32,000
Volunteering	£26,000
Social services and activities	£20,500
Supporting family Life	£16,000
Rural issues	£16,000
Social enterprises	£10,000
Crime	£2,500
IT/technology	£2,000
Counselling, advice and mentoring	£1,500
Religion	£1,000

Exclusions

The foundation will not fund:
- Projects outside County Durham and Darlington
- National or regional charities with no independent office in County Durham or Darlington
- Groups that have more than one year's running costs held as free reserves
- Projects which should be funded by a statutory body
- Sponsored events
- Improvements to land that is not open to the general public at convenient hours
- Projects promoting political activities
- Deficit or retrospective funding
- Faith groups promoting religious, non-community based activities

Funding is not normally given for:
- Medical research and equipment
- Grants for more than one year
- School projects
- General contributions to large appeals (but specific items can be funded)

> Building or buying premises and freehold or leasehold land rights
> Minibuses or other vehicles
> Overseas travel
> Animal welfare

Some of the programmes have other exclusions. If your project is at all unusual contact the foundation to discuss your application before submitting it.

Applications

The trust gives the following guidance:

Community groups, non-registered charities and registered charities are all able to apply to our many funds using just one main application form. We mix-and-match applications to the most appropriate fund behind the scenes, so you don't need to worry about which fund is right for you.

With the exception of the Banks Community Fund, ESF Community Grants and Surviving Winter, which have their own bespoke application forms, all our funds can be accessed using our standard application form.

To apply for a grant you need to read our general guidelines before filling in an application form.

The full guidelines are available from the foundation's website.

Information gathered from:

Annual review; Charity Commission record; funder's website.

The Crerar Hotels Trust (formerly the North British Hotel Trust)

Health, social welfare
£360,000 (2011/12)

Beneficial area
Scotland.

Correspondent: Claire Smith, Clerk, c/o Crerar Management Ltd, 1 Queen Charlotte Lane, Edinburgh EH6 6BL (tel: 08430502020; email: crerarhotelstrust@samuelston.com)

Trustees: Patrick Crerar; Graham Brown; Jeanette Crerar; Mike Still; James Barrack; John Williams; Claire Smith; Tarquin De Burgh.

CC Number: 221335

The trust was established with shares from the company formerly known as North British Hotels Group, for general charitable purposes. Giving is concentrated in areas where the company operates, mainly Scotland, although one hotel is located in Otley, North Yorkshire. The trust's only source of income is from its investment in Crerar Hotels Group Ltd.

The trust has a non-trading subsidiary trust, the North British Hotel Cancer

and Leukaemia in Childhood Edinburgh Trust.

In 2011/12 the trust had assets of £9.8 million and an income of £390,000. Grants were made during the year totalling £360,000.

Beneficiaries included: Euan MacDonald Microscope (£61,000 in total); Hospitality Industry Trust (£25,000); Autistica and the Scottish Book Trust (£15,000 each); Music in Hospitals and the Wellchild Trust (£10,000 each); Action Medical Research (£7,000); Happy Days (£6,000); Argyll Piping Trust and Motability (£5,000 each); Guide Dogs for the Blind (£4,000); Rape and Abuse Scotland (£3,000); Moray Arts Centre and Pain Association Scotland (£2,000 each).

Exclusions
No grants to individuals.

Applications
On an application form available from the correspondent.

Information gathered from:
Accounts; annual report; Charity Commission record.

Cripplegate Foundation

General
£2 million to organisations (2012)

Beneficial area
London borough of Islington and part of the City of London.

Correspondent: Kristina Glenn, Director, 13 Elliott's Place, Islington, London N1 8HX (tel: 020 7288 6940; email: grants@cripplegate.org.uk; website: www.cripplegate.org)

Trustee: Cripplegate Foundation Ltd – Sole Corporate Trustee.

CC Number: 207499

Summary

The first recorded gift to the Church of St Giles Without Cripplegate was by the Will of John Sworder dated 2 April 1500. Cripplegate Foundation was established in 1891 by a Charity Commission scheme which amalgamated all the non-ecclesiastical charitable donations previously administered as separate trusts. The early governors of the foundation built an institute on Golden Lane, containing reading and reference libraries, news and magazine rooms, classrooms, a theatre and even a rifle range. The institute was run until 1973, when it was closed and the foundation became a grant giving charity.

The original beneficial area of the foundation was the ancient parish of St Giles, Cripplegate, to which was

added in 1974 the ancient parish of St Luke's, Old Street. On 1 April 2008, a Charity Commission Scheme extended the foundation's area of benefit. This now covers the Parish of St Giles, Cripplegate in the City of London and the former parish of St Luke, Old Street (both as constituted by the Act of Parliament of the year 1732–3), and the London Borough of Islington.

Note: although the foundation's area of benefit has been extended to cover the whole of Islington, the governors have agreed that the foundation will need to develop partnerships and significantly increase its income before it can fully fund new initiatives in north Islington.

The following information is taken from the foundation's website:

Cripplegate Foundation identifies and targets important local needs. Around 30% of the foundation's funding is currently allocated this way. This is central to the foundation's approach to funding.

In 2008 Cripplegate Foundation commissioned research to shine a light on the hidden poverty in Islington. The report Invisible Islington: Living in Poverty in Inner London tells the stories of Islington's residents. It examines the inter-connected factors that makes their deprivation so entrenched. The report reveals that:

> Debt is a fact of life for many residents
> Being out of work is the norm
> Family, friends and community are crucial
> Ill health causes isolation and unhappiness

In response to these findings we have helped to set up:

> Help on Your Doorstep, a charity to run the 'Connect' door-knocking services in Islington.
> It identifies the poorest residents and brings advice, information and support directly to their homes. It knocks on the doors of residents and steers them to services, education and opportunities for employment and volunteering. Help on Your Doorstep works in EC1, Canonbury, Finsbury Park and Caledonian
> Access to a Wider Life – to link ESOL to wider opportunities.
> The project is testing what support residents need to increase their successful participation on English language courses and to improve their prospects of employment
> Catalyst.
> In January 2009 the Catalyst Programme was set up to provide one-off grants of up to £500 to residents. Grants are for training and employment, life skills, hobbies and confidence building and are to help people achieve their personal goals
> Islington Debt Coalition – IDC.
> IDC aims to: support individuals in debt; improve access to good quality local advice; promote financial inclusion and capability amongst Islington residents through skills development in schools and voluntary

and statutory organisations; help the poorest residents access affordable credit

Grant giving programmes

Cripplegate Foundation currently administers six funds for Islington. This includes grants for organisations and residents.

The foundation's grantmaking is informed by:

- A knowledge of available funding streams
- Its links with other funders and organisations
- Its knowledge of Islington

This can mean directing organisations to more appropriate funding or providing match funding. The foundation ensures it is not replacing or duplicating statutory funding. Grantmaking aims to help organisations meet their aims.

The foundation runs the following programmes:

- Grants to organisations
- Pro-activity programme
- Resident Support Scheme
- Islington Council's Community Chest
- *Islington Giving* grants
- Richard Cloudesley's Charity health grants
- Richard Cloudesley's Charity welfare grants

For more information contact the Programme Team:

The following programme information is drawn largely from the foundation's detailed website which includes details of all the foundation's grant-giving, services and activities.

Current priorities

The following is taken from the Guidelines for the Main Grants Programme available to download from the foundation's website:

All of the foundation's work focuses on tackling inequality and improving people's lives, particularly the most vulnerable residents and those living in poverty. We currently categorise this into three main areas: reducing poverty and addressing inequality; increasing access to opportunities and making connections; and social cohesion.

Our current priorities for the Main Grants Programme are shown below. All applicants must show how their work will address at least one of these themes. We recognise there will be inevitable crossover between themes and are happy to receive applications which address a number of different areas.

- *Financial Inclusion and Capability* – our work in this area aims to address economic inequalities and maximise incomes for those living in poverty
- *Advice and Access to Services* – this area of work helps connect residents to the information, advice, services and support they need to address their

problems – including financial, housing, welfare, child support, and employment issues – and to take control of their lives in the long term
- *Supporting Families* – this area of work aims to limit the long-term effects of poverty and inequality by supporting parents with young children and during the early years
- *Investing in Young People* – we want to remove barriers to young people accessing activities and opportunities and to build young people's resilience, capabilities and aspirations for the future
- *Mental Health and Well-being* – our work in this area aims to strengthen the psychological resources of vulnerable and low income residents so they are more resilient to the effects of poverty and inequality and are able to take advantage of available opportunities
- *Confronting Isolation* – this area of work aims to address the social dimensions of poverty and inequality to improve social well-being and strengthen residents' connections to friends, family and their wider community

Grantmaking in 2012

In 2012 the foundation had assets of £31 million and an income of £2.6 million. Grants were made totalling £2.3 million (including £327,000 to individuals).

Beneficiaries across all themes and approved in 2012 included: Islington Giving (£100,000); Friendship Works (£60,000); The New Economics Foundation and The Women's Therapy Centre (£50,000 each); Children Our Ultimate Investment (UK) (£44,000); Angel Shed Theatre Company and CASA Social Care (£30,000 each); Freightliners Farms Ltd (£20,000); and CARIS – Islington (£15,000).

Exclusions

In the main grants programme no funding is given for:

- National charities or organisations outside the area of benefit
- Schemes or activities which would relieve central or local government of their statutory responsibilities
- Grants to replace cuts in funding made by the local authority or others
- Medical research or equipment
- National fundraising appeals
- Advancement of religion unless the applicant also offers non-religious services to the community
- Animal welfare
- Retrospective grants
- Commercial or business activities
- Grants for events held in the church of St Giles-without Cripplegate
- For students at City University
- To organisations recruiting volunteers in Islington for work overseas

Applications

Each programme has a different application form and deadline dates. Applicants are encouraged to telephone or email the foundation to discuss their project before making a full application.

Full details of the application process are available on the foundation's website.

Percentage of awards given to new applicants: between 10% and 20%.

Common applicant mistakes

'Not contacting to discuss their project before applying; lack of knowledge of local area.'

Information gathered from:

Accounts; annual report; Charity Commission record; further information provided by the funder; funder's website.

The Peter Cruddas Foundation

Children and young people
£716,000 (2011/12)

Beneficial area

UK, with a particular interest in London.

Correspondent: Stephen Cox, Administrator, 133 Houndsditch, London EC3A 7BX (tel: 020 3003 8360; fax: 020 3003 8580; email: s.cox@ pcfoundation.org.uk; website: www. petercruddasfoundation.org.uk)

Trustees: Lord David Young, Chair; Peter Cruddas; Martin Paisner.

CC Number: 1117323

Established in December 2006, this is the charitable foundation of Peter Cruddas, founder of City financial trading group CMC Markets, who has pledged to donate at least £100 million to good causes during his lifetime. Since December 2006 in excess of £13 million has already been donated and/or committed to numerous charitable causes.

The foundation provides the following information in the 2011/12 accounts about its funding priorities:

The foundation gives priority to programmes calculated to help disadvantaged young people to pursue their education (including vocational) and more generally develop their potential whether through sport or recreation, voluntary programmes or otherwise. Preference will be given to the support of projects undertaken by charitable organisations for the benefit of such people, but consideration will also be given in appropriate circumstances to applications for individual support.

The foundation adopts a priority funding programme scheme that is available to be scrutinised on the web site. The programmes are subject to trustee review at any time.

In addition to financial funding given by the foundation, the foundation has provided mentoring support to many organisations through the foundation administrator's experience in the third sector.

Ways of meeting the foundation's aims are listed on its website as:

▶ Pathways/support for young disadvantaged or disengaged young people in the age range 14 to 30 into education, training or employment

▶ Work experience/skills projects for young people aged 16 to 30

▶ Youth work in London; particularly evening work for disadvantaged young people aged 16 to 30

In 2011/12 the foundation had assets of £274,000 and an income of £6,000. Grants were made to 42 organisations totalling £716,000.

Beneficiaries included: Royal Opera House Foundation (£105,000); The White Ensign Association (£50,000); Jewish Care and The Institute for Policy Research (£25,000 each); The Prince's Trust (£20,000); ARK, Mayor's Fund for London, Guildhall School Development Fund and British Cardiac Research Trust (£10,000 each); English National Opera and Royal Ballet School (£5,000 each); and Water Aid (£1,000).

Applications

On an application form available to download from the foundation's website.

The foundation provides guidance on how to complete the application form, also available on the website.

Information gathered from:

Accounts; annual report; Charity Commission record; funder's website.

Cumbria Community Foundation

General charitable purposes in Cumbria, in particular grantmaking to children and young people, older people and their carers, people with disabilities, the unemployed and people on low incomes

£1.3 million (2011/12)

Beneficial area

Cumbria.

Correspondent: Andrew Beeforth, Director, Dovenby Hall, Dovenby, Cockermouth, Cumbria CA13 0PN (tel: 01900 825760; fax: 01900 826527; email: enquiries@cumbriafoundation.org; website: www.cumbriafoundation.org)

Trustees: W. Slavin; S. Snyder; C. Tomlinson; J. Whittle; Ian Brown; June Chapman; David Brown; James Carr; Rob Cairns; Robin Burgess; Catherine Alexander; Mike Casson; James Airey; T. Knowles; Dawn Roberts; Dr A. Naylor; J. Humphries; T. Foster; C. Giel; Lyndsay Aspin.

CC Number: 1075120

Established in 1999, with the funding support of the local authorities and a founding donation of £1 million from British Nuclear Fuels Ltd., the foundation focuses on improving the community life of people in Cumbria, (and is able to make limited grants immediately outside the principal area of benefit, subject to the majority of funds being spent in Cumbria). The foundation particularly supports those in need by reason of disability, age, financial or other disadvantage.

The foundation's main activities are grantmaking and promoting giving. In addition to making grants from its own funds, it manages and administers grants programmes on behalf of individual donors, companies, trusts and central and local government. The foundation also runs the Cumbria ProHelp scheme. This allows volunteers with professional qualifications to undertake time limited pieces of work on a 'pro bono' basis with voluntary groups.

The foundation also responds to local disasters, such as floods, storms and Foot and Mouth to help those people affected. Grant levels differ from programme to programme but awards are mostly under £10,000.

Grant programmes

Programmes have been created by donors to the foundation. Each has its own criteria and area of interest. Most support locally based community and voluntary groups and there are a number of funds to support individuals.

Make sure you read each of the fund guidelines carefully before applying. If you are applying online you will receive an email from the foundation with the second part of your application. You must print and complete this form before returning it to the foundation's office.

Applications will be considered for all relevant funds. However, if you are unsure if you qualify to apply, or would like any advice then contact the foundation's staff on 01900 825760 or email enquiries@cumbriafoundation.org

Check the deadline dates published on the website to find out when your application will be considered.

Successful applicants are expected to publicise their project and tell the foundation how the grant has been spent

and what difference it has made. Sometimes foundation staff may visit the project as part of their monitoring procedure.

Grantmaking 2011/12

In 2011/12 the foundation had assets of £7 million and an income of £2.6 million. Grants were awarded totalling over £1.3 million. Grants are normally made to small, local charities and voluntary groups but have also been made to individuals in response to community need. The total grant figure includes £115,000 paid to 217 individuals; £102 spent in distributing flood bags to households and £174,000 awarded from funds managed for others.

The foundation manages a variety of separate funds, each with different criteria and geographical interests. Distribution of grant awards reflects the money available through those funds – potential applicants should check the foundation's website for information on current programmes.

The foundation is currently targeting its grants to meet the following strategic aims:

▶ Rural community regeneration
▶ Urban deprivation
▶ Children and young people
▶ Mental health
▶ Hidden and emerging need
▶ Other aims

Total grants distributed through the funds operated by the foundation were as follows:

Children and young people	180	£430,000
Hidden and emerging need	116	£186,000
Rural generation	68	£159,000
Other aims	47	£150,500
Urban deprivation	81	£141,500
Flood recovery appeal	77	£105,500
Mental health	20	£30,500

In addition the foundation also provides administrative and assessment support services for another seven funds and 209 grants awarded from these were as follows:

Mary Grave Trust	£55,000
Holehird Trust	£48,000
Joyce Wilkinson Trust	£29,000
Cumberland Building Society Charitable Foundation	£24,000
Cumberland Educational Foundation	£7,000
Crag House Charitable Trust	£6,000
Edmund Castle Educational Trust	£5,500

Beneficiaries included: Warm Homes Healthy People (£234,000); Bridging the Gap (£61,500); Robin Rigg West Cumbria Fund (£40,500); High Sheriff's Crimebeat Fund (£16,000); BNFL Live the Dream Fund (£11,000); John Winder Fund (£10,000); Youth Work Aid Fund (£9,000); Barrow Community Trust (£7,500); High Pow Community Fund (£3,000); Kipling Fund for Older People

(£2,000); Cumbria Cultural Fund £1,250); and AMW Environment Fund (£750).

Exclusions

The following are not supported:

▶ Animal welfare
▶ Deficit funding
▶ General large appeals
▶ Boxing clubs
▶ Medical research and equipment
▶ Non-Cumbrian projects
▶ Sponsored events
▶ Replacement of statutory funding
▶ Projects that have already happened
▶ Applications where a grant from that fund has been received within the last year (except Grassroots Grants)
▶ Individuals (except for specific funds)

Contact the foundation for further information on individual restrictions on any of the grant programmes.

Applications

Application forms and clear and full guidelines for each of the foundation's programmes are available to download on the foundation's website or by contacting the correspondent directly. The foundation prefers to receive applications via email, even if supporting documents have to be sent by post. Applicants are encouraged to contact the foundation prior to making an application in order to confirm their eligibility. Applications are accepted throughout the year and decisions are usually taken within two months. Some programmes offer a faster process for small urgent projects.

Information gathered from:

Accounts; annual report; Charity Commission record; funder's website.

Itzchok Meyer Cymerman Trust Ltd

Advancement of the Orthodox Jewish faith, education, social welfare, relief of sickness, medical research and general charitable purposes
£661,000 (2011/12)

Beneficial area

UK and Israel.

Correspondent: Ian Heitner, Trustee, 497 Holloway Road, London N7 6LE (tel: 020 7272 2255)

Trustees: H. F. Bondi; M. D. Cymerman; S. Cymerman; S. Heitner; L. H. Bondi; Ian Heitner; R. Cymerman.

CC Number: 265090

The trust was established in 1972 and its objectives are the advancement of the Orthodox Jewish faith and general

charitable purposes. Almost all the trust's grants are to Jewish charitable organisations although occasional grants to individuals in need are made. Many grants are made to the same organisations each year.

In 2011/12 the trust had assets of just under £11.5 million and an income of £2 million. Grants were made totalling £661,000, and were categorised as follows:

Advancement of religion	£319,000
Advancement of education	£195,000
Relief of poverty	£134,500
Medical care and research	£12,500

Beneficiaries included: M D and S Charitable Trust (£125,000); Dencommon Ltd (£105,000); Russian Immigrant Aid Fund (£104,000); and Trumart Ltd (£84,000).

Applications

In writing to the correspondent.

Information gathered from:

Accounts; annual return; Charity Commission record.

The D'Oyly Carte Charitable Trust

Arts, medical welfare, environment
£930,000 (2011/12)

Beneficial area

UK.

Correspondent: Jane Thorne, Secretary, 1 Savoy Hill, London WC2R 0BP (tel: 020 7420 2600)

Trustees: Jeremy Leigh Pemberton, Chair; Francesca Radcliffe; Julia Sibley; Henry Freeland; Andrew Jackson; Michael O'Brien.

CC Number: 1112457

Summary

The trust was founded in 1972 by Dame Bridget D'Oyly Carte, granddaughter of the founder of both the Savoy Theatre and the Savoy Hotel. Its distributable income increased significantly on her death in 1985, when it inherited her shareholding in The Savoy Hotel plc, and again in 1998 following the company's sale.

The trust supports general charitable causes connected with the arts, medical welfare and the environment. Certain charities in which the founder took a special interest continue to be supported on a regular basis.

The D'Oyly Carte Charitable Trust is entirely separate from the aims and objectives of The D'Oyly Carte Opera Trust.

Grants start at around £500. The majority are for amounts under £5,000 although some can be for larger amounts. Most funding goes to the arts and medical welfare.

The majority of grants made by the trust are on a one-off basis although term grants are also agreed from time to time for a maximum period of three years, particularly in respect of bursary funding for educational establishments, mainly in the arts sector, and to help newly created charities become established. Recipients of these grants are required to report regularly to the trust for monitoring purposes.

The trustees have continued their commitment to make grants to charities that do not enjoy a high profile in order to create significant impact on the work of the charity concerned, and, recognising the day-to-day funding needs of charities, the trustees continue to consider applications for core costs.

Guidelines for applicants
The Arts

▶ Promotion of access, education and excellence in the arts for young people to increase their opportunities to become involved outside school and to build future audiences with special emphasis on choral singing for children and young people to encourage recruitment into choirs
▶ Access to the arts for people who least have access to them
▶ Performance development of graduates in the performing arts in the early stages of their careers and to encourage their involvement in the community through performances and workshops for the benefit of those with special needs and those who would otherwise have no opportunity to hear or participate in a live performance
▶ Support for charities seeking to engage with young people on the fringes of society through music and drama projects to improve their employability and diminish the risk of social exclusion

Medical/Welfare

▶ Promotion and provision of music and art therapy to improve the quality of life for the elderly and the disabled, and in the palliative care of children
▶ Support for charities concerned with alleviating the suffering of adults and children with medical conditions who have difficulty finding support through traditional sources
▶ Support and respite for carers with emphasis on the provision of holidays for those carers who wouldn't normally have a break from their responsibilities – and with special emphasis on projects and schemes that allow young carers to enjoy being children
▶ Support for charities seeking to rehabilitate young people on the fringes of society to improve their employability and diminish the risk of social exclusion

The Environment
- Preservation of the countryside and its woodlands -with emphasis on the encouragement of voluntary work and active involvement in hands-on activities
- Protection of species within the United Kingdom and their habitats under threat or in decline
- Conservation of the marine environment and sustainable fisheries around the UK
- Heritage conservation within the United Kingdom based on value to, and use by the local community – the trust favours projects that seek to create a new use for fine buildings of architectural and historic merit to encourage the widest possible cross-section of use. (The trust does not normally support major restorations unless a specific element of the work can be identified as appropriate to the aims of the trust.)
- Rural crafts and skills in heritage conservation, with emphasis on increasingly rare skills that would otherwise be lost

Grantmaking in 2011/12

In 2011/12 the trust had assets of £41.7 million and an income of £1.1 million. There were 271 grants made during the year totalling £930,000. Grants were broken down as follows:

Arts	122	£461,500
Medical welfare	112	£388,000
Environment	37	£126,500

Beneficiaries included: Royal Academy of Dramatic Art (£20,000); Anthony Nolan Trust, Ashgate Hospice, BREAK, Cahoots NI, Grasslands Trust, Leicestershire Chorale, Polka Theatre for Children, SignHealth and Whale and Dolphin Conservation Society (£5,000 each); Bach Choir, Bournemouth Symphony Orchestra, British Stammering Association, CHICKS, Gabriele, Live Music Now, Spinal Injuries Association, Two Moors Festival and Wirral Society for the Blind and Partially Sighted (£4,000 each); Action Transport Theatre, Artlink Central, Buglife, Children's Aid Team, Sickle Cell Society, St John's Hospice and Wigmore Hall Trust (£3,000 each); Leicester Theatre Trust, New English Ballet Theatre and YMCA Sutton Coldfield (£2,000 each); and Swaledale Festival and Young Dementia UK (£1,000 each).

Exclusions

The trust is unlikely to support the following:
- Animal welfare
- Campaigning or lobbying projects
- Community transport organisations or services
- Conferences and seminars
- Exhibitions
- Expeditions and overseas travel
- Friend/Parent Teacher Associations
- General appeals
- Individuals or applications for the benefit of one individual
- Large national charities enjoying wide support
- Local authorities and areas of work considered a statutory requirement
- Medical research
- NHS hospitals for operational and building costs
- Projects taking place or benefiting people outside the UK
- Recordings and commissioning of new works
- Religious causes and activities
- Requests from charities that have had an application turned down (until two years have elapsed after the date of rejection)
- Routine maintenance of religious buildings
- Salaries and positions, though the trustees will consider contributing to core operating costs of which they recognise general salary costs will be a part
- Support and rehabilitation from drug abuse or alcoholism
- Universities, colleges, schools, nurseries, playgroups (other than those for special needs children)

Applications

Potential applicants should write to the correspondent with an outline proposal of no more than two A4 pages. This should cover the work of the charity, its beneficiaries and the need for funding. Applicants qualifying for consideration will then be required to complete the trust's application form. The form should be returned with a copy of the latest annual report and accounts. Applications for specific projects should also include clear details of the need the intended project is designed to meet and an outline budget.

Information gathered from:

Accounts; annual report; Charity Commission record.

Roald Dahl's Marvellous Children's Charity

Haematology and neurology conditions affecting children and young people up to the age of 25

£107,000 to organisations

(2011/12)

Beneficial area

UK.

Correspondent: Richard Piper, Chief Executive, 81a High Street, Great Missenden, Buckinghamshire HP16 0AL (tel: 01494 890465; fax: 01494 890459; email: grants@ marvellouschildren'scharity.org; website: www.marvellouschildren'scharity.org)

Trustees: Felicity Dahl, Chair; Martin Goodwin; Roger Hills; Georgina Howson; Virginia Fisher; Graham Faulkner.

CC Number: 1137409

Roald Dahl is one of the world's best-known children's authors. During his life time he took steps to improve the lives of those around him who suffered from medical problems, even pioneering new treatment methods or encouraging others to find new solutions. This charity was established in 2010 to supersede the Roald Dahl Foundation following a strategic review, although the focus of the charity remains the same. The charity focuses on severe, complex or rare problems of the blood and the brain (haematology and neurology) in the UK.

The charity's website states:

> Roald Dahl's Marvellous Children's Charity exists to help seriously ill children and young people live a fuller and happier life. We believe that every child has the right to a good quality of life, no matter how ill they are. So we raise money to support individuals and organisations so that sick children can receive the highest quality care, advice and support.

> We do this through our amazing Roald Dahl Nurses, our hugely valued Family Grants, and our innovation programmes that identify new needs and new ways to meet them.

> We think that's a marvellous thing to do. We hope you agree.

The trustees' annual report for 2011/12 states that in that financial year it undertook five types of activity in order to help children and young people achieve better health, a fuller Life and a happier family. These activities were:
- Grants to families
- Grants for projects
- Specialist nurses
- Research
- Influence

The charity provides excellent information about its work on its website, some of which is reprinted here.

> Roald Dahl's Marvellous Children's Charity cares about children with lifelong neurological and blood conditions. These rare conditions receive very little funding, even though they have a huge impact on both the child and the family around them.

> We work in partnership with organisations who share our belief that all children have the right to the best possible quality of life. We raise money to help support children in the UK living with conditions like acquired brain injury, neuro-degenerative conditions, rare forms of epilepsy and long-term blood diseases (excluding cancer).

> We help these children by: funding specialist nurses and carers; supporting

parent groups and charities that help families with information, activities and all-important fun; making grants to hospitals to help improve children's facilities.

Giving direct assistance to families with grants to help pay for things like expensive equipment – wheelchairs for example – or activities such as weekends away with other children and families experiencing the same illnesses.

Grants to charitable organisations
Our grants to charitable organisations are made through a series of programmes, each designed to achieve specific impacts. We do not operate a reactive grants programme and therefore do not accept unsolicited applications. We currently have one active programme.

Family Resilience Programme
Aims: to increase knowledge and understanding about new ways to help families improve their emotional resilience, when they have a child with a serious, long-term condition.

Parameters: This is a two year, £100k programme, looking to support 8 to 12 innovation projects.

Who can apply: This is, in the first instance, a closed programme. We have encouraged over 60 organisations to assess their eligibility using our online initial assessment. If we do not have enough high quality applications from this first round we will look at the option of opening this up to all eligible charities.

At the time of writing (November 2013) there were no grants programmes open.

Grants to individuals
Family Grants Programme
The aim of our Family Grants programme is simple: to provide assistance to help families cope with financial difficulties when living with and caring for a sick child. To be eligible, children must be living with one of the specific conditions of the blood or brain that we support – and the family must be on a low income (see our application form for more details).

PLEASE NOTE that from 1 Dec 2013 we are temporarily closing the Family Grants programme and will not be accepting applications. This is to enable us to research and implement improvements to the programme, including new criteria and a swifter application process. Applications received after 1 Dec 2013 will unfortunately have to be discarded.

We hope the revised programme will re-open by April 2014.

Dates will be published on the charity's website.

In 2011/12 the charity had assets of £1.5 million and an income of £639,000. Grants awarded totalled £217,000 and were broken down as follows:

Grants to organisations	£107,000
Grants to individuals	£63,000
Burdett nurse awards	£43,500
Nurse training grants	£3,000

Beneficiaries included: Child Brain Injury Trust NI (£50,000); Sickle Cell

and Young Stroke Survivors (£38,000); OSCAR – Sandwell (£15,000); Batten Disease Family Association (£12,500); Meningitis Trust NI (£11,000); Cerebra and Sickle Cell Society (£10,000 each); and Huntington's Disease Association and Matthew's Friends (£9,000).

Exclusions
The charity will not fund:
- General appeals from large, well-established charities
- National appeals for large building projects
- Arts projects
- Any organisations which do not have charitable status or exclusively charitable aims (other than NHS organisations under the charity's specialist nurses programme)
- Statutory bodies (other than NHS organisations under the charity's specialist nurses programme)
- School or higher education fees
- Organisations outside the UK
- Organisations for people with blood disorders which are cancer related due to the relatively large number of charities helping in the oncological field

Applications
Visit the charity's website for full and current information on how to apply.

Percentage of awards given to new applicants: between 40% and 50%.

Information gathered from:
Accounts; annual report; Charity Commission record; further information provided by the funder; funder's website.

The Daiwa Anglo-Japanese Foundation

Anglo-Japanese relations
£342,000 to organisations
(2011/12)

Beneficial area
UK, Japan.

Correspondent: Jason James, Director General and Secretary, Daiwa Foundation, Japan House, 13/14 Cornwall Terrace, London NW1 4QP (tel: 020 7486 4348; fax: 020 7486 2914; email: office@dajf.org.uk; website: www.dajf.org.uk)

Trustees: Sir Michael Perry; Hiroaki Fujii; Takafumi Sato; Mami Mizutori; Masahiro Dozen; Christopher Everett; Merryn Somerset Webb; Lord Brittan; Sir Peter Williams; Andrew Smithers; Akira Kyota.

CC Number: 299955

The Daiwa Anglo-Japanese Foundation is a UK charity, established in 1988 with a benefaction from Daiwa Securities Co.

Ltd. The foundation's purpose is to support closer links between Britain and Japan. It does this by:
- Making grants available to individuals, institutions and organisations to promote links between the UK and Japan in all fields of activity
- Enabling British and Japanese students and academics to further their education through exchanges and other bilateral initiatives
- Awarding of Daiwa Scholarships for British graduates to study and undertake work placements in Japan
- Organising a year-round programme of events to increase understanding of Japan in the UK

Daiwa Foundation Japan House, the London-based headquarters, acts as a centre for UK-Japan relations in Britain by offering a wide programme of lectures, seminars, book launches, courses and exhibitions as well as meeting rooms for Japan-related activities and facilities for visiting academics.

The foundation is represented in Japan by its Tokyo office, which provides local assistance to Daiwa scholars and administers grant applications from Japan. It also handles general enquiries and forms part of the network of organisations supporting links between the UK and Japan.

The foundation awards grants to individuals and organisations in the UK and Japan in all areas of the visual and performing arts, the humanities, the social sciences, science and engineering, mathematics, business studies and education, including schools and universities, and grass roots and professional groups.

The foundation's website provides a useful summary of its grantmaking programmes:

Daiwa Foundation Small Grants
Grants of £3,000–£7,000 are available to individuals, societies, associations or other bodies in the UK or Japan to promote and support interaction between the two countries. Daiwa Foundation Small Grants can cover all fields of activity, including educational and grassroots exchanges, research travel, the organisation of conferences, exhibitions, and other projects and events that fulfil this broad objective. New initiatives are especially encouraged.

Daiwa Foundation Awards
Awards of £7,000–£15,000 are available for collaborative projects that enable British and Japanese partners to work together, preferably in the context of an institutional relationship. Daiwa Foundation Awards can cover projects in most academic, professional, arts, cultural and educational fields. (Support for scientific collaborations is separately provided through The Royal Society-

Daiwa Anglo-Japanese Foundation International Exchanges Scheme.)

The Royal Society – Daiwa Anglo-Japanese Foundation International Exchanges Scheme

These grants support travel, subsistence and research for collaborative projects between British and Japanese researchers in the field of science. They are funded by the foundation and administered by The Royal Society.

Daiwa Adrian Prizes

Daiwa Adrian Prizes are awarded in recognition of significant scientific collaboration between British and Japanese research teams in the field of pure science or the application of science. They acknowledge those research teams who have combined excellence in scientific achievement with a long-term contribution to UK-Japan relations.

Daiwa Foundation Art Prize

The Daiwa Foundation Art Prize is an open submission prize which offers a British artist a first solo exhibition at a gallery in Tokyo, Japan. The winner is awarded a £5,000 participation fee plus travel and accommodation costs for a period in Japan to coincide with the opening of the exhibition. S/he is also offered introductions to key individuals and organisations in the Japanese contemporary art world.

In 2011/12 the foundation had assets of £37.7 million and an income of nearly £418,000. Charitable expenditure totalled £1.4 million, including £486,000 given in scholarships and £342,000 given in grants, awards and prizes (excluding support costs).

Grants (including support costs the amounts of which we were unable to determine) were awarded as follows:

Daiwa Foundation Awards	£145,000
Daiwa Foundation Small Grants UK – side	£87,000
Daiwa Adrian Prizes	Not listed
Royal Society Joint Project Grants	£69,000
Daiwa Foundation Small Grants – Japan side	£24,000
Daiwa Foundation Art Prize	£21,000

Beneficiaries include: De Montfort University (£13,000); Clifton Scientific Trust and Tokyo College of Music (£10,000 each); Ruthin Craft Centre (£7,500); Sadler's Wells (£7,000); Shakespeare's Globe (£5,000); Barbican Centre Trust, Bridgewater Hall, and English Speaking Union of Japan (£3,000 each).

Exclusions

Daiwa Foundation Small Grants cannot be used for:
- General appeals
- Capital expenditure (e.g., building refurbishment, equipment acquisition, etc.)
- Consumables (e.g., stationery, scientific supplies, etc.)
- School, college or university fees

- Research or study by an individual school/college/university student
- Salary costs or professional fees
- Commissions for works of art
- Retrospective grants
- Replacement of statutory funding
- Commercial activities

Daiwa Foundation Awards cannot be used for:
- Any project that does not involve both a British and a Japanese partner
- General appeals
- Capital expenditure (e.g., building refurbishment, equipment acquisition, etc.)
- Salary costs or professional fees
- Commissions for works of art
- Retrospective grants
- Replacement of statutory funding
- Commercial activities

Applications

Application forms are available to download from the foundation's website.

Details of deadlines and criteria for grants, awards and prizes, together with the relevant application forms and guidelines are also available on the foundation's website.

Percentage of awards given to new applicants: between 40% and 50%.

Common applicant mistakes

'They don't realise we have a minimum grant request budget of £3,000 or they apply for ineligible costs or for retrospective funding.'

Information gathered from:

Accounts; annual report; Charity Commission record; further information provided by the funder; funder's website.

Baron Davenport's Charity

Almshouses, hospices, residential homes for the elderly, children and young people under the age of 25.
£605,500 to organisations (2012)

Beneficial area

Warwickshire, Worcestershire, Staffordshire, Shropshire and West Midlands.

Correspondent: Marlene Keenan, Administrator, Portman House, 5–7 Temple Row West, Birmingham B2 5NY (tel: 01212 368004; fax: 01212 332500; email: enquiries@ barondavenportscharity.org; website: www.barondavenportscharity.org)

Trustees: Christopher Hordern; Sue M. Ayres; William M. Colacicchi; Paul Dransfield; Lisa Bryan; Rob Prichard.

CC Number: 217307

Established in 1930 by Mr Baron Davenport, the charity is now governed by a Charity Commission Scheme dated 16 April 1998. The income of the charity is distributed as follows:
- £2,500 for each trustee (other than the ex-officio trustee) to nominate for charitable purposes
- £10,000 to the Bishop of Birmingham
- £10,000 to the Chief Minister of the Birmingham Hebrew Congregation

Of the remaining income:
- 40% goes in grants for individuals, specifically for widows, spinsters, divorced women (of 60 years and over) and women deserted by their partners together with their children, who are under 25 and in financial need
- 60% is distributed in Birmingham and the counties of the West Midlands, equally to: almshouses, residential homes for the elderly and hospices; charities that assist children and young people under 25

Grants are made to a large number of organisations each year – some organisations are funded in consecutive years, but every grant must be separately applied for each year; there is no automatic renewal.

In 2012 the charity had assets of almost £30 million and an income of £1.1 million. Grants were made to 407 organisations totalling £605,500.

Beneficiaries included: Marie Curie Hospice (£20,000); Stonehouse Gang (£12,000); Compton Hospice, Donna Louise Trust and St Richard's Hospice (£9,000 each); and Age Concern Birmingham, James and Ada Robb Charity and Laslett's Charities (£8,000 each).

The charity also awarded grants to 1,671 individuals totalling £408,000.

Exclusions

There are no exclusions, providing the applications come within the charity's objects and the applying organisation is based within the charity's beneficial area, or the organisation's project lies within, or benefits people who live in, the beneficial area.

Applications

In writing to the correspondent, accompanied by the latest accounts and any project costs. Distributions take place twice a year at the end of May and November and applications should be received at the charity's office by 15 March or 15 September. All applications are acknowledged and those not within the charity's objects are advised.

Information gathered from:

Accounts; annual report; Charity Commission record; funder's website.

The Davidson Family Charitable Trust

Jewish, general
£1.7 million (2011/12)

Beneficial area

UK.

Correspondent: Eve Winer, Trustee, c/o Queen Anne Street Capital, 58 Queen Anne Street, London W1G 8HW (tel: 020 7224 1030; email: ewiner@ wolfeproperties.co.uk)

Trustees: Gerald A. Davidson; Maxine Y. Davidson; Eve Winer.

CC Number: 262937

Established in 1971, this is the trust of Gerald Davidson, director of Queen Anne Street Capital and Wolfe Properties, and his family.

In 2011/12 the trust had assets of £418,000 and an income of £1.3 million. After very low governance costs of just £300, grants totalled almost £1.7 million.

Grants were awarded as follows:

Medical	£737,000
Religious	£363,000
Arts	£260,000
Welfare	£249,000
Educational	£86,000

Beneficiaries included: United Synagogue (£351,000); Holburne Museum (£210,000); Jewish Care (£205,000); The Hertford House Trust (£50,000); Emunah Child Resettlement Fund and Treehouse (£20,000 each); Cystic Fibrosis (£15,000); British Ort Foundation, Centre for Jewish Life, Magen David Adom UK and Peterhouse Development Fund (£10,000 each); and Kisharon and UK Branch of Meir Panim (£1,000 each).

Applications

In writing to the correspondent.

Information gathered from:

Accounts; annual report; Charity Commission record.

Peter De Haan Charitable Trust

Social welfare, the environment, the arts
£705,000 to organisations (2011/12)

Beneficial area

UK.

Correspondent: Simon Johnson, Finance Director, Wool Yard, 54 Bermondsey Street, London SE1 3UD (tel: 020 7232 5465; email: sjohnson@pdhct.org.uk; website: www.pdhct.org.uk)

Trustees: Peter Charles De Haan; Janette McKay; Dr Rob Stoneman; Carol Stone; Opus Corporate Trustees Ltd.

CC Number: 1077005

The trust's grantmaking currently focuses on three areas:

- The arts
- The environment
- Social welfare

The trust also operates *Under One Roof* – an innovative new model of collaborative working for charities sharing premises, human and physical resources, and creative new ways of thinking and working.

The trust's website states:

> The Peter De Haan Charitable Trust was constituted in 1999. The trust aims to improve the quality of life for people and communities in the UK through its work with arts, environmental and community welfare organisations. Some of the projects the trust supports combine these themes to maximise the impact of its funding.
>
> Led by businessman and philanthropist Peter De Haan, the trust operates under a venture philanthropy model, working closely with the organisations it supports financially and organisationally to increase their capacity and impact.
>
> Since 1999 the trust has donated £21,340,500 to the benefit of over 540 organisations. Currently the trust is targeting a significant proportion of its resources towards IdeasTap, the creative network for emerging creative people, UK wildlife trusts and community projects surrounding its South London offices.
>
> The trust will not exist in perpetuity, as the founding trustees planned for its reserves to be gradually spent over a 20 year period from its date of constitution.

In 2011/12 it had assets of £13 million and an income of £516,000. Grants totalled £1.1 million of which £705,000 were made to organisations and £453,000 to young adults. The majority of grants went to support work in the arts.

Guidelines

The following information is taken from the trust's website and 2011/12 annual report and accounts:

The Arts

The PDHCT arts programme is now delivered through IdeasTap – the leading online youth arts hub for young creative people, founded by PDHCT in winter 2008.

> On the 10th of November 2009 Ideas Tap Ltd became a charity registered with the Charity Commission under the registered number 1132623. On the 6 April 2010 the company commenced its activities within the trust's arts programme. The company's primary objects are:

- To advance education, particularly but not exclusively, for young people up to the age of 25
- To provide or assist in the provision of facilities, items and services to enable young people up to the age of 25 to engage in the arts and education and to do so in the interests of social welfare and with the object of improving their condition of life
- To advance in life and relieve the needs of young people up to the age of 25, through providing support and activities which develop their skills, capacities and capabilities to enable them to participate in society as mature and responsible individuals
- To further such other exclusively charitable purposes as the trustees shall in their absolute discretion from time to time determine

The Environment

The trust has been a strong supporter of UK Wildlife Trusts since 2004. The trust's environmental programme is informed by an over-arching theme of climate change, whilst remaining sensitive to the needs of its partner charities: Yorkshire Wildlife Trust and Leicestershire & Rutland Wildlife Trust, who currently receive ongoing support.

The trust has also supported a number of arts projects incorporating environmental themes and continues to do so through its arts programme IdeasTap.

Social Welfare

The trust began supporting social welfare work by making traditional grants to organisations, before evolving into making more conditional grants as the trustees narrowed its focus towards young people and projects which are aimed at early intervention. Projects providing continuity which sought to help beneficiaries back into mainstream society were given priority.

Since then, the trust has worked in this field in long-term partnerships with delivery organisations in a venture philanthropy model. This approach evolved through years of work and investment in social welfare and enables the trust to achieve a focused and sustainable impact.

Alongside its social inclusion work, in recent years the trust has also increased the amount of community-based projects it has supported, in the area surrounding its South London headquarters. This has included supporting young people from disadvantaged backgrounds, business start-ups, careers advice for young creative people and community environmental action and festivals.

The trust has often supported projects that combine community welfare work with its other core themes, arts and the environment, in order to maximise the impact of its funds.

Beneficiaries/those supported in partnerships across all three areas include: Chickenshed Theatre; City Hope Church; Cumbria Wildlife Trust; Leicestershire and Rutland Wildlife

Trust; Old Vic New Voices; RashDash; South Bank Mosaics; Southwark Sea Cadets; Steam Industry Free Theatre; Ulster Wildlife Trust; and Yorkshire Wildlife Trust.

Exclusions

The trust will not accept applications for grants:

▶ That directly replace or subsidise statutory funding
▶ From individuals or for the benefit of one individual
▶ For work that has already taken place
▶ Which do not have a direct benefit to the UK
▶ For medical research
▶ For adventure and residential courses, expeditions or overseas travel
▶ For holidays and respite care
▶ For endowment funds
▶ For the promotion of a specific religion
▶ That are part of general appeals or circulars
▶ From applicants who have applied to within the last 12 months

In addition to the above, it is unlikely to support:

▶ Large national charities which enjoy widespread support
▶ Local organisations which are part of a wider network of others doing similar work
▶ Individual pre-schools, schools. out-of-school clubs, supplementary schools, colleges, universities or youth clubs
▶ Websites, publications, conferences or seminars

Applications

The PDHCT website states: 'Historically we made traditional grants in support of social welfare, the environment and the arts. Funding for our arts programme is now channelled through IdeasTap. Our previous grant programmes are now fully assigned. We are not open to unsolicited applications.'

For IdeasTap funding visit: www. ideastap.com.

Information gathered from:

Accounts; annual report; Charity Commission record; funder's website.

The Debmar Benevolent Trust

Jewish causes, relief of poverty
£76,500 (2011/12)

Beneficial area

UK and Israel.

Correspondent: Hilary Olsberg, Trustee, 16 Stanley Road, Salford M7 4RW

Trustees: Gella Klein; Hilary Olsberg; Rosalind Halpern; Vivienne Lewin.

CC Number: 283065

Grants are given towards the advancement of the Orthodox Jewish faith and the relief of poverty.

In 2011/12 the trust had assets of £6 million and an income of £1 million. Grants were made during the year totalling £76,500. This was lower than in previous years due to the fact that the company received fewer donations and was committed to make capital repayments off its bank loan.

A list of beneficiaries was not provided by the trust in its accounts. Previous beneficiaries included: Beis Hamedrash Hachodosh, Chasdei Belz, Chevras Mauous Lador, Gevurath Ari, Telz Talmudical Academy, Friends of Assos Chesed, Pardes Chana, ATLIB, Bobov Institutions, Ohr Akiva Institute, Tomchei Shaarei Zion, Ponivitch Institutions, Yeshiva Shaarei Zion, Beis Yoel High School, Format Charity Trust and Manchester Kollel.

Applications

In writing to the correspondent.

Information gathered from:

Accounts; annual report; Charity Commission record.

Derbyshire Community Foundation

Social welfare
£454,000 (2011/12)

Beneficial area

Derbyshire and the city of Derby.

Correspondent: The Grants Team, Foundation House, Unicorn Business Park, Wellington Street, Ripley, Derbyshire DE5 3EH (tel: 01773 514850; fax: 01773 741410; email: info@derbyshirecommunityfoundation.co.uk; website: www.derbyshirecommunityfoundation.co.uk)

Trustees: Dr Ranjit Virma; Michael Hall; Arthur Blackwood; David Coleman; Nicola Philips; Nick Mirfin; Matthew Montague; Sir Alan Jones; Lucy Palmer; David Walker; Robin Wood; Rt Revd Alastair Redfern; Janet Birkin; Louise Pinder; Simon Ingham; Helen Bishop.

CC Number: 1039485

Derbyshire Community Foundation is an independent charity, building an endowment fund to provide grants to voluntary and community groups across the county. It supports the most vulnerable in society and helps enrich the lives of people living in Derbyshire communities by funding a wide range of groups, including those involved in supporting carers, survivors of domestic abuse, children, young people and isolated elderly residents.

Grant Programmes

The foundation distributes funds on behalf of companies, individuals and local, regional and national government agencies, through a variety of grantmaking programmes. The average grant is around £1,000 and grants usually cover a 12 month period. Most grants will cover equipment and general running costs. Each of the programmes is different and applicants need to decide which one is best suited to their particular project/organisation. There are currently (August 2013) 11 main grant programmes and a selection is given below:

Embrace Derbyshire Fund (formerly General Fund)

This fund supports a broad range of small community and voluntary groups with a variety of different costs. As with all of the foundation's funds the overarching purpose of each grant we make is to enhance the quality of life for people living in Derbyshire communities and to tackle disadvantages and inequalities faced by people living in the county today. The following funding is provided:

▶ Capital (any items of equipment) although it is unlikely to fund building works
▶ Revenue (any non-equipment costs) including on-going running costs for a project or group
▶ One off events and one-off projects

This fund has additional exclusions:

▶ If you have received a grant for your group's core/on-going running costs (i.e. rent, transport etc.) you will need to wait a period of 18 months before re-applying for the same costs
▶ The fund will not consider contributing to projects costs exceeding £5,000

Comic Relief Fund

The fund is designed to be used to support work where there is clear evidence of a sustained beneficial impact on people's lives that are excluded or disadvantaged through low income, rural or social isolation, age disability, race, sexuality or gender. It aims to empower local people, enabling them to create lasting change in their communities; projects should be run by people directly affected by the issues they are dealing with.

50% of the funds available will be used on sports projects that increase access to sport and exercise for people who face genuine social exclusion and isolation – individuals who would otherwise find it difficult to join mainstream sports clubs, gyms or exercise programmes, either due to low confidence, lack of role models, accessibility, opportunity.

The remaining 50% will be used to fund projects working towards the following outcomes:

- Increasing locally led services – spotting a gap in local provision
- Building the skills of local people
- Increasing community cohesion (projects that bring communities together, allowing people a chance to get to know each other, working together to improve the community, a sense of pride in where they live)
- Responding to local economic needs – tackling local problems with unemployment, low income, housing issues etc

More information on all of the funds listed above including grant priorities, types of project costs funded, application documents and deadlines, can be found on the foundation's website.

Grants in 2011/12

In 2011/12 the trust had assets of £6.3 million and an income of £462,000. Grants were made to 286 organisations and totalled £454,000 which was £510,000 lower than 2010/11. According to the trustees' report, this was 'primarily due to the continued absence of large flow through programmes such as the OTS's Grassroots Small Grants Programme which ended on 31 March 2011'.

Grants in excess of £7,000 included those made to: SNAP (Project Fairshare) (£34,000); Fairshare Derby Community Safety Officers (£12,000); The Laura Centre – Derby, Repton Foundation Bursary and Sinfonia Viva (£10,000 each); and Derby Academy of Performing Arts (£7,500).

Exclusions

The foundation's general exclusions are:
- Profit making organisations
- Medical equipment
- Animal charities
- Any project which promotes faith or involves the refurbishment/building of a place of worship
- Statutory bodies including schools, hospitals, police etc
- Any project which directly replaces statutory obligations
- Any project which promotes a political party
- Projects which benefit people outside of Derbyshire
- Retrospective funding (grants for activities which have already taken place)
- Sponsored events

Applications

The grants team are always willing to discuss applications before they are formally submitted, this saves both the applicant and the foundation time. Call them on: 01773 514850.

The foundation offers several different funds, each with a specific focus or set of criteria. Visit the foundation's website for full details of the current grant programmes and the relevant application documents.

Applicants should download and complete the appropriate application form from the website and send it to the correspondent.

Applications are passed to a member of the grants team for assessment and to prepare all of the information ready to present to the award making panel. During this time, applicants are likely to be contacted by the grants team for an informal chat about their application and their group, which helps the foundation to understand the background of the project and gives the best chance of a successful bid.

Applicants will be informed of the decision date for their application and are invited to call the grants team or check the website to find out the decision two days after the panel date. You will also receive the panel decision in writing within one week of the panel date.

The foundation states that it is willing to provide full, honest feedback on all decisions and is happy to discuss any outcome with applicants.

Information gathered from:

Accounts; annual return; Charity Commission record; funder's website.

Devon Community Foundation

General charitable purposes
£605,000 (2011/12)

Beneficial area
Devon.

Correspondent: Martha Wilkinson, Chief Executive, The Factory, Leat Street, Tiverton, Devon EX16 5LL (tel: 01884 235887; fax: 01884 243824; email: grants@devoncf.com; website: www. devoncf.com)

Trustees: Dr Katherine Gurney; Steve Hindley; Mike Bull; Arthur Ainslie; Peter Keech; John Glasby; Caroline Marks; Nigel Arnold; James Bullock; James Cross; Steven Pearce; Robin Barlow; Christine Allison.

CC Number: 1057923

Devon Community Foundation is an independent local charity that aims to promote and support local charitable and community organisations throughout Devon to tackle disadvantage. This is achieved by channelling funds to grass roots organisations within the community to support a wide variety of causes. It acts as a conduit for a variety of funds, including those from the statutory, voluntary and corporate sectors, and for donations and income from its own endowed funds.

A key aim of the foundation is to develop and encourage philanthropy in the county of Devon, facilitating people to give money and other resources to help make stronger and more caring communities.

Grants go to support a wide range of projects tackling social exclusion and building better communities. The foundation always has a variety of grant programmes running and new ones are regularly added. Each scheme tends to have a different application procedure and size of award. Organisations can hold more than one grant at a time from the different funds available. It is not necessary to be a registered charity to receive a grant from the foundation, but you must be a not-for-profit organisation that is benevolent, charitable or educational and established to alleviate disadvantage in your local community.

Grant schemes change frequently. Consult the foundation's website for details of current programmes and their deadlines. Two programmes listed on the website at the time of writing were:

Devonian Fund
The Devonian Fund helps groups or individuals to alleviate mobility in relation to disability or ill-health. This fund aims to help people overcome or relieve mobility problems, such as contributing towards the cost equipment that significantly improves individuals' quality of life. It can also help with specialised transport needs, such as accessible coaches or taxis.

The average grant for individuals is between £500 – £1,000, but groups may apply for up to £5,000. Each grant is assessed individually.

Comic Relief Local Communities Programme
There are still many communities in the UK that suffer from economic and social deprivation and the current economic climate may make this situation worse. For this reason, Comic Relief has decided that £4.5 million should be available to fund projects across the UK which are addressing these issues through the 'Local Communities' programme. Comic Relief is pleased to be working with UK Community Foundations and Community Foundations across the UK, to deliver this local programme. Devon Community Foundation is one of the delivery partners.

The Local Communities programme will run for two years and during this time, grants of between £1,000 and £10,000 will be available.

The programme aims to empower local people, enabling them to create lasting change in their communities. Projects should be run by people directly affected by the issues they are dealing with and priority will be given to small, locally based groups or organisations in areas of disadvantage that have a clear understanding of the needs of their community.

Under the programme, organisations can apply for funding to:
- Increase local services
- Build skills of local people
- Increase community cohesion
- Respond to local economic needs

Organisations which have received a community cash grant or any other grant from a community foundation **can** apply for a local communities grant. However organisations which hold a grant directly from Comic Relief, **cannot** apply for a local communities grant.

In 2011/12 the foundation had assets of £3.3 million and an income of £695,000. According to the foundation's annual report for that accounting year:

From April 2011 to March 2012 Devon Community Foundation distributed £569,500 [accounts show £605,000] in a total of 504 grants (300 of which were grants awarded through localgiving.com) to local voluntary and community groups helping people in need in Devon. This represents a considerable increase in activity on last year. These grants have been used to fund an amazing variety of projects and ideas and the foundation's grants fall into three categories:

- Community Glue – the activities and events that bring communities together and keep them together like playgroups, luncheon clubs and befriending schemes, village halls and community celebration events
- Crisis interventions – work with families in crisis, debt and housing advice, counselling, work with the homeless, helping the unemployed into work and foodbanks
- Prevention – including opportunities for young people, work with the elderly on health issues or early intervention with families

Beneficiaries included: Grow 4 Good South West Ltd (£35,000); Exeter YMCA (£23,000); Cornwall Community Foundation (£22,500); Young Devon (£15,000); Plymouth Cricket Club, Shout it Out Learning Project and Time Out For All (£5,000 each); Coast Net and Community Housing Aid (£4,500); Plymouth Foodbank (£2,000); and Devon and Cornwall Refugee Support, Play Torbay and Tavistock Street Pastors (£1,000 each).

Exclusions

The foundation does not fund:
- More than one application to the same fund in a 12 month period
- Non-constituted organisations
- Grantmaking organisations
- Commercial organisations
- Groups that have funded before but have not returned an evaluation form when requested
- Major building works or their associated costs

- Organisations that are regional or national charities (unless locally led and run)
- Organisations that have substantial unrestricted funds
- Activities that promote political or religious beliefs (groups that are based in a religious building can apply, providing the activity/project is open to all people in the community)
- Statutory bodies e.g. schools/colleges, local councils. However, 'Friends of' or Parents' Associations may be eligible to apply
- Organisations or activities that primarily support animals or plants
- 100% of the project costs
- Retrospective funding – this includes activities that have already taken place or repayment of money that you have already spent
- Consultancy fees or feasibility studies
- Sponsorship and/or fundraising events
- Contributions to an endowment
- Minibuses or other vehicle purchases
- Activities or organisations that are for personal profit or are commercial
- Grants for IT and associated equipment will be limited to no more than £400
- Overseas travel
- Never 100% of the project costs
- Capital purchases over £1,000
- Projects outside Devon
- No funding individuals (except from the Devonian Fund)

Individual programmes may have further eligibility criteria. Check the foundation's website or contact the foundation directly to confirm that your organisation is eligible to apply.

Applications

The foundation's website has details of the grant schemes currently being administered and how to apply. The website also has a 'grant alert sign-up' which emails information about new grant programmes as they are available.

Information gathered from:

Accounts; annual report; Charity Commission record; funder's website.

The Duke of Devonshire's Charitable Trust

General
£158,500 (2011/12)

Beneficial area
UK.

Correspondent: Mollie Moseley, Correspondent, Chatsworth, Bakewell, Derbyshire DE45 1PP (tel: 01246 565437; website: ddct.org.uk)

Trustees: Duke of Devonshire; Duchess of Devonshire; Earl of Burlington; Sir Richard Beckett.

CC Number: 213519

The Duke of Devonshire's Charitable Trust is a small independent family charity established by the 11th Duke of Devonshire in 1949. It supports a wide range of charitable organisations by way of grants and loans.

In 2011/12 the trust had assets of £11.3 million and an income of £238,000. Grants of between £250 – £25,000 were made to 48 organisations totalling £158,500. The donations figure has fallen significantly in this accounting year. According to the latest accounts, this is because in 2009, the trustees received a donation of £5.4 million from the liquidation of funds in the 'Bermuda Settlement'. These funds were used to assist Chatsworth House Trust over a period of two years. Income has now reverted to the more usual figure of between £200,000 – £300,000.

Beneficiaries included: St Wilfred's Hospice (£25,000); St Peter's Church (£20,000); Fine Cell Trust (£10,000); Hertford House Trust (£5,000); Sight Support Derbyshire (£4,000); Good News Family Care, Helen's Trust, Help for Heroes and Medway Centre Community Association (£2,000 each); and Northern Racing College, On Side and The School of Artisan Food (£1,000 each).

Exclusions

The following information is taken from the trust's concise and helpful website:
- The trust will not normally consider any funding request made within 12 months of the outcome of a previously unsuccessful application or 5 years of a successful one. This is to ensure that the trust can assist as wide a spread of worthwhile organisations as possible
- The trust only considers applications from UK registered charities and your registration number is required (unless you have exempt status as a church, educational establishment, hospital etc.)
- The trust does not typically fund projects outside the UK, even if the organisation is a registered charity within Britain
- The trust is not able to accept applications from individuals or for individual research or study. This includes gap year activities, study trips, fundraising expeditions and sponsorship
- The trust does not normally make funding commitments over several years – grants made are typically for a single year with few exceptions
- The trust does not normally fund specific salaries and positions. This is primarily because grants are single-year commitments and the trustees would not wish a specific job to become unsustainable

- It is unusual for the trust to consider making a grant to organisations who cannot demonstrate significant progress with fundraising, so please bear this in mind when considering the timing of your application
- Applications will not be considered until all the information we have requested has been being provided. Please keep your answers concise and avoid including protracted Mission Statements, jargon and acronyms. Failure to do so may result in your application being overlooked

Applications

In writing to the correspondent. The trust's website provides guidelines and details of current application deadlines.

Percentage of awards given to new applicants: over 50%.

Common applicant mistakes

'Not reading guidelines to assess their organisation/project's suitability. Omitting accounts for their current/most recent financial year; omitting grant payee details.'

Information gathered from:

Accounts; annual report; Charity Commission record; further information provided by the funder; funder's website.

Deymel Charitable Trust

General

Beneficial area

UK.

Correspondent: The Trustees, Rathbone Trust Company Ltd, 4th Floor, Port of Liverpool Building, Pier Head, Liverpool L3 1NW (tel: 01512 366666)

Trustees: W. R. Morgan; T. Morgan.

CC Number: 1145305

The trust was registered in January 2012 for general charitable purposes. The trustees are descendants of David Morgan, founder of the David Morgan department store in Cardiff which closed in 2005 after 125 years. The store was operated by the Morgan family through the holding company, Deymel Investments Ltd, which also went into liquidation at the end of 2009.

The trust's first set of accounts, for the financial year 2012/13, show an income of £65,500 and a total expenditure of £2,000. No grants were made during the year and the trust has expressed its intention to build up its funds.

Applications

In writing to the correspondent.

Information gathered from:

Charity Commission record.

The Djanogly Foundation

Jewish, general, medicine, education, the arts and social welfare

£868,000 (2011/12)

Beneficial area

UK and overseas, mainly Israel.

Correspondent: Christopher Sills, Secretary, 3 Angel Court, London SW1Y 6QF (tel: 020 7930 9845)

Trustees: Sir Harry Djanogly; Michael S. Djanogly; Lady Carol Djanogly.

CC Number: 280500

The foundation was established in 1980 by Sir Harry Djangoly, a wealthy businessman from Nottingham who made his fortune in the textile industry. He is a well-known benefactor of the arts and has made substantial donations to art institutions from his personal fortune.

The foundation supports developments in medicine, education, social welfare, the arts, Jewish charities and welfare of older and younger people, and is particularly concerned with funding projects that are new and may require a number of years to become established. In such cases the grantmaking activity will be related to the development phases of these projects.

In 2011/12 the foundation had assets of £6.4 million and an income of £55,000. Grants were made to 43 organisations totalling £868,000.

Beneficiaries of the largest grants were: University of Nottingham (£211,500); Jerusalem Foundation (£203,500); Victoria and Albert Museum (£125,000); and Great Ormond Street Children's Hospital and Nottingham Trent University (£100,000 each).

Other beneficiaries included: Mencap (£25,000); Nottingham City Academy – (now called Djangoly City Academy) (£12,000); Israel Philharmonic Orchestra and the Oxford Centre for Hebrew and Jewish Studies (£10,000 each); Churchill Centre and Tate Foundation (£5,000 each); Institute of Jewish Policy Research and Southwell Minster (£2,000 each); and Chicken Shed Theatre Trust and Wellington Hospital (£1,000 each).

There were 15 grants for less than £1,000.

Applications

In writing to the correspondent. 'The charity achieves its objectives receiving and evaluating grant applications.'

Information gathered from:

Accounts; annual report; Charity Commission record.

The DM Charitable Trust

Jewish, social welfare and education

£1.35 million (2011/12)

Beneficial area

UK and Israel.

Correspondent: Stephen J. Goldberg, Trustee, Sutherland House, 70–78 West Hendon Broadway, London NW9 7BT (tel: 020 8457 3258)

Trustees: Stephen J. Goldberg, Chair; David Cohen; Patrice Klein.

CC Number: 1110419

The trust was established in 2005 for the relief of poverty and sickness, educational purposes and the support of Jewish organisations.

In 2011/12 the trust had assets of £6.1 million and an income of £986,000, most of which came from donations. Grants were made totalling £1.35 million, however a list of beneficiaries was unavailable in this year's accounts. Previous attempts to obtain a list of grants have been unsuccessful.

Applications

In writing to the correspondent.

Information gathered from:

Accounts; Charity Commission record.

The Dollond Charitable Trust

Jewish, general

£2.1 million (2011/12)

Beneficial area

UK and Israel.

Correspondent: Jeffrey Milston, Trustee, c/o FMCB, Hathaway House, Popes Drive, Finchley, London N3 1QF (tel: 020 8346 6446; email: gwz@fmcb.co.uk)

Trustees: Adrian Dollond; Jeffrey Milston; Melissa Dollond; Brian Dollond; Rina Dollond.

CC Number: 293459

The trustees' annual report for 2011/12 states: 'Although the constitution of the charity is broadly based, the trustees have adopted a policy of principally assisting the Jewish communities in Britain and Israel. The trustees aim to maximise the grants that it pays taking into account the return on its investments and likely infrastructure projects.'

In 2011/12 the trust had assets of almost £36 million and an income of £1.1 million, including £547,000 from the estate of the settlor, Arthur Dollond. There were 137 grants made totalling nearly £2.1 million, broken down as follows:

Education/training	34	£615,000
Religious education	45	£420,000
Medical/health/sickness	33	£390,500
Relief of poverty	44	£362,000
Disability	12	£186,000
Religious activities	12	£120,000

A list of specific beneficiary organisations was not published within the annual report and accounts.

Applications

In writing to the correspondent.

Information gathered from:

Accounts; annual report; Charity Commission record.

Dorset Community Foundation (formerly known as Community Foundation for Bournemouth, Dorset and Poole)

Community, social welfare, education, health, the relief of poverty

£279,500 to organisations (2011/12)

Beneficial area

The county of Dorset, including the authorities of Bournemouth and Poole.

Correspondent: Mr Ashley Rowlands, Trustee, Abchurch Chambers, Dorset, Bournemouth BH1 2LN (tel: 01202 292255; email: Philanthropy@dorsetcf. org; website: www. dorsetcommunityfoundation.org)

Trustees: Christopher Beale; Ashley Rowlands; Gwyn Bates; Christopher Morle; Gordon Page; Richard Cossey; Christopher Mills; Jeffrey Hart; Henry Digby.

CC Number: 1122113

The Dorset Community Foundation (formerly known as the Community Foundation for Bournemouth, Dorset and Poole) is a charitable trust and was founded in 2000. The foundation changed its name and rebranded to Dorset Community Foundation to reflect its work across the whole area of Dorset.

According to the 2011/12 trustees' report, the objectives of the Dorset Community Foundation are:

The promotion of any charitable purpose for the benefit of the community of the borough of Bournemouth, county of Dorset and borough of Poole including its immediate neighbourhood. In particular the advancement of education, the protection of good health, both mental and physical and the relief of poverty and sickness.

Correspondence with the foundation's administrator at the time of writing (August 2013) revealed that 'Dorset Community Foundation is one of the biggest grant makers in the county of Dorset. Grants of up to £10,000 are available from various funds the foundation manages on behalf of Dorset County Council.'

In common with other community foundations, Dorset Community Foundation administers a number of funds which are subject to change. Check the website for current availability.

In 2011/12 the foundation had assets of £1.2 million and an income of £405,000. Grants were made totalling £284,500.

Beneficiaries included: West Howe Neighbourhood Worker (£40,500); Action for Children (£12,500); Youth Resources Services – the Rendezvous Sherborne (£10,000); Victim Support, Corfe Mullen Sports Association and Shaftesbury Town Council (£7,500 each); Frampton Village Hall and Age Concern – Christchurch (£6,000 each); Moving On and Diverse Abilities Plus (£5,000 each); Club Bournemouth and Poole, Bournemouth Fellowship of Clubs and Active Games for All (£2,000 each); Age Concern – North Dorset, Match Patch and Bourne Spring Trust (£1,000 each); Dorset Blind Association, Dorset Fire and Rescue Service and Beaminster Festival (£500 each); Walkford Youth Club (£250); and St Luke's Church Hall (£50).

Exclusions

Each fund has different criteria, consult the website for up to date eligibility.

General exclusions, as stated in the 2011/12 trustees' report, are as follows:

- Projects operating outside Bournemouth, Dorset and Poole
- Individuals
- Direct replacement of statutory obligation and public funding
- General large appeals
- Medical research and equipment
- Statutory work in educational institutions
- Projects that are about the promotion of political causes
- Sponsored events
- Retrospective grants
- Groups with more than one year's unrestricted reserves
- Animal welfare
- Projects that are primarily about the promotion of religion.

However these may not apply to every fund the foundation represents.

Applications

Contact the foundation for details of up-to-date programmes. An online contact form is available on the foundation's website.

Information regarding criteria and eligibility for each individual fund can be found on the foundation's website. For any further advice and guidance contact the grants team on 01202 292255 or email: grants@dorsetcf.org.

According to the foundation's website, most of the grant schemes require the completion of an online application form. This is a two stage application, which should then be posted to the grants team along with the following documentation:

- A signed copy of your organisation's rules/constitution/governing document
- A copy of your last year's accounts (or any other years accounts this will be specified on the application)
- A copy of your safeguarding: child protection/vulnerable persons policy (if appropriate)
- Quotes (as appropriate)
- A list of your management committee/ trustee names with any relationships to one another and cheque signatories identified
- Any other material you consider relevant to your application (please do not send material you want returned) e.g. leaflets, flyers, press cuttings

Information gathered from:

Accounts; annual report; Charity Commission record; funder's website.

The Drapers' Charitable Fund

General charitable purposes including education, heritage, the arts, prisoner support, Northern Ireland and textile conservation

£998,000 to organisations from non-designated funds (2011/12)

Beneficial area

UK, with a special interest in the City and adjacent parts of London and County Derry.

Correspondent: Andy Mellows, Head of Charities, The Drapers' Company, Drapers' Hall, Throgmorton Avenue, London EC2N 2DQ (tel: 020 7588 5001; fax: 020 7628 1988; email: charities@ thedrapers.co.uk; website: www. thedrapers.co.uk)

Trustee: The Drapers' Company.

CC Number: 251403

The Drapers' Company is a City livery company, one of those descended from the guilds of London, and the charity has a trail of historical connections, the most important of which are with Queen Mary College, University of London and Bancroft's School in Essex, but which also includes Adam's Maintained Comprehensive School in Wem, Shropshire and various Oxford and London university colleges.

The charity awards grants to help improve the quality of life for people and their communities. Disadvantaged and socially excluded people are targeted, through grants in the fields of education and relief of need. Grants are also awarded in support of textiles, heritage and the arts, and for projects in Northern Ireland. In directing its grantmaking, the trust applies criteria such as geographical area, particular types of project, beneficiary group or specific areas of charitable activity.

Grantmaking policy

The charity will normally only accept applications from UK registered charities. Support is focused on small to medium sized organisations whose total income is less than £5 million per annum. Funding is primarily provided for core costs although appeals from charities requiring support to get new initiatives off the ground will be considered, providing that sustainability of the initiative is clearly demonstrated. There is no minimum or maximum grant size, but the majority of grants awarded are normally for sums under £10,000. Awards are seldom made for sums in excess of £20,000.

Most of the grants awarded are one-off payments, but recurring grants for up to three years may be made subject to specific conditions. These conditions include an annual progress review where payment of subsequent years' grants is dependent on the satisfactory outcome of the progress review. Further appeals from organisations will not normally be considered for three years from the date of the final grant award.

Regular contact is maintained with recipients of grants, including an annual evaluation report, for monitoring purposes. A copy of the Guidelines for Applicants, which includes details of the application procedure and information required in the application, is available on the company's website or from Drapers' Hall on request.

The trust's current priorities for funding are:

Relief of need
Homelessness
- Funding will only be considered for structured programmes aimed at breaking the cycle of homelessness

- Area of operation should be based in inner city London
- Projects offering temporary outdoor relief will not be funded

Causes and effects of social exclusion
- Beneficiaries should be young people under 25 years old
- Projects should be based in inner city London
- Projects should be focused on returning young people to education, employment or training

Prisoners
- Preference will be given to projects assisting young offenders
- Projects should aim to improve the opportunities for offenders on release or to reduce reoffending

Ex-Servicemen and women
- Projects should support or aid the rehabilitation of, injured or incapacitated ex-services personnel; or
- Charities should improve the welfare of ex-servicemen and women, particularly those disadvantaged by need, hardship or distress

Welfare, particularly the provision of support services to the following beneficiaries in areas of high deprivation:
- Older people e.g. befriending services and day centre services
- Community or family services e.g. furniture recycling services, debt advice, community centres
- Carers, particularly young carers

Disability
- Projects should provide support and improve the quality of life for adults with less visible disabilities such as hearing impairment, dyslexia, mental health, chronic fatigue syndrome, learning disabilities
- Charities addressing children's disabilities, physical disabilities or medical conditions will not be funded

Education and Training
Outreach programmes
- In particular encouraging young people from disadvantaged backgrounds to continue or further their education

Leadership and volunteering for young people from the UK
- Either in the UK or overseas and as part of a structured programme
- Applications from individuals will not be considered

Promotion of the learning of science
Textiles
Technical Textiles/Smart materials
- Projects which support the study of technical textiles or the encouragement of young people to pursue careers in the sector

Textile conservation
Northern Ireland
- Projects falling under the company's other themes for support in the area of historic involvement for the Drapers' Company, in and around County Londonderry, particularly in and around Draperstown and Moneymore

Heritage and Arts
Support for the preservation of the nation's heritage and the provision of public access to the arts and heritage, particularly in Greater London, in one of the following areas:
- City of London and the Mayoralty
- Museums, memorials and monuments related to former exploits of the armed forces, the history of London or the textile trade
- Public access to the arts for young people in inner city London

Grantmaking in 2011/12

In 2011/12 the charity had assets of almost £43 million and an income of £10 million, which included £7.5 million from the transfer of funds in 2012, from two other charities which were under the trusteeship of the Drapers' Company. The accounts state that grants were awarded to 137 charities totalling £998,000 from general funds. This figure excludes grants awarded to individuals totalling £8,500.

The table below gives details of the grants awarded in 2011/12 (excluding designated funds).

Education	62	£470,000
Relief of need in the following six categories:		
Disability	17	£96,500
Prisoner support	14	£96,500
Social exclusion	5	£43,500
Homelessness	7	£43,000
Ex-servicemen and women	2	£29,500
Welfare	1	£5,000
Textiles	4	£97,000
Heritage and arts	10	£63,000
Miscellaneous	92	£62,000
Northern Ireland	1	£1,000

The trust's annual report provides a detailed analysis of how its funds were spent and what it has achieved with those funds during the year.

Beneficiaries included: Bancroft's School (£75,000); Industrial Trust (£70,000); Kirkham Grammar School (£53,000); Centre of the Cell (£42,000); Pembroke College – Cambridge (£35,000); Poppy Factory, Shannon Trust and St Anne's College – Oxford (£25,000 each); Boxing Academy, Fields in Trust and Futureversity (£15,000 each); Baytree Centre, Fine Cell Work and Shelter from the Storm (£10,000 each); Living Paintings, Somerset Sight and Unicorn Theatre (£8,000 each).

Exclusions

Grants are not usually made for:
- Individuals
- Schools, colleges and universities (except in certain circumstances)
- Churches
- Almshouses
- Animal welfare
- Medical research/relief, hospitals or medical centres

- Children's disabilities, physical disabilities or medical conditions
- Holidays or general respite care
- Organisations that are not registered charities, unless exempt from registration
- Funds that replace or subsidise statutory funding
- Local branches of national charities, associations or movements
- Work that has already taken place
- General appeals or circulars
- Loans or business finance

Applications

We would advise that for full details of the application process and the trust's current priorities, applicants refer to the trust's website. The Charities Committee meets five times a year to review all applications which fall within the current priorities for funding. The charity aims to deal with each application within three months of its being received. Applications can be made at any time during the year. Applicants should complete the 'application summary sheet' (available to download from the website) and submit it together with a document on proposed funding. This should include detailed information about the organisation and the project/activity to be funded; full costings and project budget for the proposed work for which the grant is requested, or the organisation's income and expenditure budget for the current year (whichever is appropriate); and the most recent audited financial statements and trustees report. Applications should be submitted by post only.

Percentage of awards given to new applicants: between 40% and 50%.

Common applicant mistakes

'Failing to read and adhere to the guidelines which are published.'

Information gathered from:

Accounts; annual report; Charity Commission record; further information provided by the funder; funder's website.

The Royal Foundation of the Duke and Duchess of Cambridge and Prince Harry

General, children and young people, armed forces and veterans, conservation and sustainability

£1.9 million (2011/12)

Beneficial area

UK and overseas.

Correspondent: Miss Victoria Hornby, St James's Palace, London SW1A 1BS (tel: 020 7101 2963; email: info@ royalfoundation.com; website: www. royalfoundation.com)

Trustees: Anthony James Lowther-Pinkerton; Guy Monson; Sir David Manning; Edward Harley; Lord Janvrin; Fiona Shackleton; Theresa Green.

CC Number: 1132048

Registered in late 2009 with broad, general charitable purposes the foundation became fully operational in 2011. Specific interests include: the armed forces, young people and conservation.

The following information is provided by the foundation:

> The Royal Foundation of The Duke and Duchess of Cambridge and Prince Harry is the patrons' primary charitable vehicle, and hopes to become a leading philanthropic investor, using its time and resources to create lasting change in targeted areas and geographies, based on need and on the interests of The Duke and Duchess of Cambridge and Prince Harry.

Areas of focus

The foundation is carrying out work under three areas at this early stage. Currently organisations can apply for grants from the Endeavour Fund, the others areas are not open to unsolicited applications at this time.

Veterans and Military Families

Organisations can apply for grants under the Endeavour Fund. There are three tiers of grants available:

- Development Grants – Up to £10,000 for an individual or team to explore the feasibility of a major endeavour, for costs such as salaries, research or travel and transport
- Team Grants – Larger grants to enable teams of veterans and Servicemen to take part in UK based sporting events and international competitions
- Venture Grants – Much larger grants which may involve underwriting the costs of a major endeavour in advance of sponsorship. The aim is to have a small number of grants so the foundation can also provide advice and guidance, pro bono expertise and sponsorship

Disadvantaged Children and Young People

Work focuses on sport, coaching and outdoor education for young people, particularly those who are disengaged from education. Funding also goes towards secondary education in Uganda.

Conservation and Sustainable Development

Supporting communities to protect and conserve their natural resources for future generations.

Grantmaking in 2011/12

During the year the foundation had assets of £4.8 million and an income of £3.8 million, being particularly high due to donations received as gifts from the royal wedding in 2011. Grants to 12 organisations totalled £1.9 million, broken down as follows:

Disadvantaged children and young people	£1.8 million
Military veterans and their families	£127,000
Conservation and sustainable development	£50,000

The beneficiaries during the year were: PEAS (£830,000); ARK UK Programmes (£400,000); Fields in Trust (£330,000); Race 2 Recovery (£100,000); Greenhouse Charity (£97,000); Skillforce (£51,000); The Zoological Society of London (£50,000); Sentebale (£35,000); Together for Short Lives (£22,000); Help for Heroes (£20,000); and Army Widows Association (£7,000).

Applications

To apply for an Endeavour Fund grant email a proposal no longer than four sides of A4 with the following criteria in mind:

For distributing any size of grant:

- The applicants and/or beneficiaries should be wounded, injured or sick (including psychological illness) servicemen or women. They may or may not have been injured or become ill whilst on active duty but must have been in service at the time
- The activity must be either a sporting or adventurous challenge and must represent a significant challenge for the applicant
- Applicants should be able to demonstrate clear outcomes from the activity and should have the formal backing of their medical or rehabilitation team

For the Development and Venture grants:

- The activity must contribute to personal recovery and must contribute to a successful transition to civilian life
- The activity must contribute to raising awareness of wounded, injured and sick servicemen and women
- The activity must contribute to inspiring others, either other wounded, injured or sick servicemen and women, or members of the community, such as schoolchildren
- There must be a clear and credible plan both for raising awareness and inspiring others
- The applicant must demonstrate an ability to secure additional funding for the activity

Currently the foundation is unable to accept unsolicited requests for support apart from through this fund.

Information gathered from:

Accounts; annual report; Charity Commission record; funder's website.

The Dulverton Trust

Youth opportunities, conservation, welfare, general

£2.8 million (2012/13)

Beneficial area

Unrestricted. Mainly UK in practice. Limited support to parts of Africa. No grants for work in Greater London or Northern Ireland.

Correspondent: Anna de Pulford, Grants and Administration Manager, 5 St James's Place, London SW1A 1NP (tel: 020 7629 9121; fax: 020 7495 6201; email: grants@dulverton.org; website: www.dulverton.org)

Trustees: Christopher Wills, Chair; Sir John Kemp-Welch, Vice Chair Finance; Tara Douglas-Home; Lord Dulverton; Lord Gowrie; Dr Catherine Wills; Richard Fitzalan Howard; Sir Malcolm Rifkind; Dame Mary Richardson; Lord Hemphill.

CC Number: 1146484

This is one of the trusts deriving from the tobacco-generated fortune of the Wills family. It has an endowment worth £85 million and a body of trustees which combines family members and others.

Grantmaking

The trust's grantmaking activity focuses on: general charitable purposes; education and training; the prevention or relief of poverty; the environment, conservation and heritage. Beneficiary groups are: children and young people; older people; other charities or voluntary bodies; and the general public/mankind. The area of benefit is the UK and Africa.

The trust largely makes one-off grants, however, receipt of a grant will not prohibit organisations from applying again in the future. Many grants are single-year although multi-year grants (usually up to three years) can be made for projects which the trustees feel have particular merit.

The trust supports national, regional and local charities operating in England, Scotland and Wales, especially in areas where there is a significant amount of deprivation, and particularly where a grant would make a real difference to the recipients. Priority will be given to projects which are open to all members of the community. A few grants are also made overseas, particularly in Eastern Africa.

The trust makes two types of grant:

- *Major* – for charities that operate nationally or across the geographical regions of the UK, particularly in areas where there is significant deprivation and where a grant would make a real difference. Support will normally be restricted to charities whose annual income is below £25 million. Grants will *generally* be in the region of £10,000 – £30,000 under the categories detailed in the table below
- *Minor* – for smaller charities working in the North East of England, Cornwall, Devon or Wales. Note that the trust no longer administers its minor grants. Applications should therefore be made through the local community foundations in these areas, namely the Community Foundation Tyne and Wear and Northumberland, Cornwall Community Foundation, Devon Community Foundation and the Community Foundation in Wales respectively. The maximum size of a minor grant is £5,000

Grants in 2012/13

In 2012/13 the trust had assets of £86.5 million and an income of £3.2 million. During the year the trust received 401 appeals for funding, 83 of which received a grant. With multi-year grants awarded in previous years, the trust paid out a total of 119 grants which totalled £2.8 million (which includes £270,000 which was distributed as minor grants by various community foundations), and were distributed amongst the following categories:

Youth opportunities	48	45%	£1.2 million
General welfare	29	25.5%	£584,000
Minor grants	not known	10%	£270,000
Africa	12	10%	£246,500
Preservation	9	5%	£135,000
Conservation	5	5%	£135,000
Peace and humanitarian support	4	1%	£76,000
Local appeals	not known	1%	£25,000

The following beneficial area information is taken from the trust's excellent website. Information on grant recipients has been selected from the 2012/13 accounts.

Youth Opportunities

This is our largest category and aims to support charities that help disadvantaged children and young people, including offenders, to adopt a more positive attitude to their lives, raise their aspirations and realise their full potential. We support a wide range of charities working in this area, including those providing advice and skills training, help with finding employment, engagement with local communities and volunteering opportunities. We are particularly interested in those charities using early-intervention initiatives to ensure children

from significantly disadvantaged backgrounds are given a fairer chance to develop their social, employment and life skills. We also believe in the character-building value of challenging outdoor activities, such as adventure training, that encourage leadership and team spirit and we have long supported charities that give children from deprived urban areas the opportunity to experience and value the countryside.

General Welfare

We support a wide range of activities that benefit disadvantaged people and communities, with particular interest in:

- Strengthening and supporting family relationships
- Early intervention to support the welfare of children in disadvantaged families and looked-after children [children in care]
- Helping young homeless people to move forward
- Maintaining active living and independence for older people (Note: this does not include help with medical and mental health problems or disability)
- The welfare of those who care for others
- Prevention of re-offending, the rehabilitation of prisoners and ex-offenders and help for their families to rebuild their lives
- Developing tolerance and understanding between faiths and communities

Conservation

The trust is keen to support the general conservation and protection of wildlife habitats within the United Kingdom. We also encourage projects concerning the protection and sympathetic management of trees and native woodlands. Projects concerned with single species are rarely considered.

Peace & Humanitarian Support

This is a restricted category concerned with:

- Peace intervention
- Infrastructure for disaster relief

Like the Africa grants programme this category is currently closed to new applicants.

Preservation

We are interested in the preservation of outstanding historic artefacts and buildings of national importance. We encourage the development of craftsmanship in the traditional techniques of repair and restoration. Because we give annual grants to the National Churches Trust and the Scottish Churches Architectural Heritage Trust for churches in the United Kingdom, we are very rarely able to consider applications from individual churches.

Africa

Unless there are exceptional circumstances, we will support only a very small number of organisations operating in East Africa, or occasionally Southern Africa, which already have a long association with the trust. These usually operate in the fields of education and conservation. At present only organisations which have previously received a grant in this category may apply.

Beneficiaries across all areas included: Dulverton Scholarships (£450,000); The Community Foundation in Wales, The Cranfield Trust, Home Start UK and The Place2Be (£90,000 each); Rendcomb College (£75,000); Forgiveness Project and MapAction (£60,000 each); Devon Community Foundation (£45,000); Beatbullying and Endeavour Training (£30,000 each); Countryside Learning and Women in Prison (£25,000 each); Peace Direct, Peterhouse Appeal (UK) and West-Eastern Divan Trust UK (£15,000 each); Anna Plowden Trust (£10,000); and The Nelson Trust and Three Choirs Festival (£2,500 each).

Exclusions

The trust will not usually give grants for the following:

- Individuals (grants are given only to registered charities or organisations with officially recognised charitable status)
- Museums, galleries, libraries, exhibition centres and heritage attractions
- Individual churches, cathedrals and other historic buildings (except for limited support under the preservation category)
- Individual schools, colleges, universities or other educational establishments
- Hospices, hospitals, nursing or residential care homes
- Activities outside the stated geographical scope
- Support for charities whose main beneficiaries live within Greater London or in Northern Ireland

The trust will not normally support the following areas of activity:

- Health, medicine and medical conditions including drug and alcohol addiction, therapy and counselling
- Specific support for people with disabilities
- The arts, including theatre, music and drama (except where used as a means of achieving one of its funding priorities)
- Sport, including sports centres and individual playing field projects
- Animal welfare or projects concerning the protection of single species
- Expeditions and research projects
- Individuals volunteering overseas
- Conferences, cultural festivals, exhibitions and events
- Salaries for specific posts (however funding salaries in the context of a multi-year grant will be considered)
- Major building projects, including the purchase of property or land
- Endowments

- Work that has already taken place (retrospective funding)

Applications

How to apply

Note: The trust has asked us to emphasise that they do not accept applications via post. You should apply only through the trust's website.

Read the guidelines carefully, making sure that none of the exclusions apply to your charity or project. Applications for minor grants should be submitted to the appropriate Community Foundation, see 'general' section.

1   Complete the online eligibility quiz. Only eligible organisations will be able to progress their application further

2   If your organisation passes the eligibility quiz, you will be provided with a link to the online application

If you wish to make initial enquiries, establish eligibility, discuss time scales or need to seek further guidance about an application, please telephone the trust's office.

When to apply

Our trustees meet three times a year to consider grant proposals: in February, June and October. There are no deadlines or closing dates. The selection process can take between three to six months so it is advisable to apply in plenty of time, especially if funding is required by a certain date.

Assessment process

Each application is considered on its merits and all will receive a reply as soon as possible, although research and consultation may delay a response from time to time. All rejected applications will receive notification and an outline explanation for the rejection will usually be given.

Applications under consideration for a grant will normally receive a visit from one of the trust's staff who will subsequently report to the trustees.

Following the trustees' meeting, we will notify successful applicants by letter. The trustees' decisions are final.

Percentage of awards given to new applicants: between 10% and 20%.

Common applicant mistakes

'Applying via post – we only accept applications through our website; applying when they are outside our guidelines.'

Information gathered from:

Accounts; annual report; Charity Commission record; further information provided by the funder; funder's website.

Dunard Fund

Classical music, the visual arts, environment and humanitarian causes

£2.4 million (2011/12)

Beneficial area

UK with a particular interest in Scotland.

Correspondent: Carol Colburn Grigor, Trustee, 4 Royal Terrace, Edinburgh EH7 5AB (tel: 01315 564043; fax: 01315 563969)

Trustees: Carol Colburn Grigor; Dr Catherine Colburn Høgel; Erik Colburn Høgel; Colin Liddell.

CC Number: 295790

The charity, established in 1986, is funded annually by Marlowe Holdings Ltd, of which the correspondent is both a director and a shareholder. The funds are committed principally in Scotland, to the training for and performance of classical music at the highest standard and to education in and display of the visual arts at an international standard; and the rehabilitation of endangered architectural masterpieces and the design and construction of new architectural masterpieces. A small percentage of the fund is dedicated to environmental and humanitarian projects. The charity is also registered with the Office of the Scottish Charity Regulator.

In 2011/12 the charity had assets of £4.7 million and an income of just over £2.2 million, most of which came from the charity's benefactor. The total amount in grants listed in the accounts under 'charitable activities' was £2.4 million which includes grants paid and grants committed in the year. They were broken down as follows:

Music	£1.4 million
Culture and the arts	£919,000
Humanitarian, environmental and architectural	£72,500

Beneficiaries across all categories included: London Philharmonic Orchestra (£151,000); Edinburgh International Festival (£110,000); Edinburgh Sculpture Workshop and Anglia Ruskin University (£100,000 each); National Galleries Scotland and Refuge (£50,000 each); Ludus Baroque (£40,000); Royal Scottish National Orchestra (£30,000); Rosslyn Chapel (£25,000); The Public Catalogue Foundation (£10,000); Perth Festival of Arts and Pitlochry Festival Theatre (£5,000 each); Maritime Rescue Institute (£3,000); and The Salvation Army (£1,000).

Exclusions

Grants are only given to charities recognised in Scotland or charities registered in England and Wales. Applications from individuals are not considered.

Applications

No grants to unsolicited applications.

Information gathered from:

Accounts; annual report; Charity Commission record.

The Dunhill Medical Trust

Medical research, elderly people

£3.2 million (2011/12)

Beneficial area

UK.

Correspondent: Claire Large, Administrative Director, 3rd Floor, 16–18 Marshalsea Road, London SE1 1HL (tel: 020 7403 3299; fax: 020 7403 3277; email: info@dunhillmedical. org.uk; website: www.dunhillmedical.org. uk)

Trustees: Ronald E. Perry, Chair; Prof. Sir Roger M. Boyle; The Rt Revd Christopher T. J. Chessun; Kay Glendinning; Prof. Roderick J. Hay; Prof. James McEwen; Richard A. H. Nunneley; Timothy W. Sanderson; Prof. Martin P. Severs; John Ransford; Peter Lansley.

CC Number: 1140372

Summary

The Dunhill Medical Trust (DMT) was established in 1950 by the will left by Herbert Dunhill. The trust, which was formally registered as a charity in the 1980s, was established with charitable objects focused on medical research, care and facilities and specifically the research into care of the elderly and the provision of accommodation and care for older people.

In 1999, the trustees agreed that, in the light of the demographic changes towards an increasingly ageing population, the main priority for support should be research and other activities and developments related to older people and ageing. This focus has increasingly informed decision-making on grants over the last few years and the trustees have now formulated a formal research funding strategy.

Information relating to the trust's grantmaking is complex and too detailed to reproduce here. However, the following information is taken from the trust's very informative and helpful website which applicants will need to visit before making application:

The charitable objects of the trust are:

- The furtherance of medical knowledge and research and the publication of the results arising from the research
- Provision of medical care and facilities
- Research into the care of older people and
- The provision of care and accommodation for older people

Within these objects the trust supports four main areas of activity:

- The development of new and innovative projects
- Support for pilot research studies that could establish whether major funding is justified
- Pump-priming projects that have the potential to develop and attract other sources of funding
- Developing research capacity within the medical, clinical and scientific community, particularly where this relates to issues of ageing and older people

The main focus for support is research into ageing and older people, and other activities which reflect the national demographic of an increasingly ageing population.

Grant categories

To be eligible for consideration, applications should fall within one of the following categories:

- Furtherance of medical knowledge and research
- Provision of medical facilities
- Provision of accommodation for older people
- Services (provision of medical care/ care for older people)

All requests for funding are first appraised against criteria set out within DMT's Grant Making Policy which is available to download from the trust's website.

Grantmaking policy

The following extract is taken from the trust's grantmaking policy document which applicants should read carefully before making application.

In awarding grants, the trust will apply the following principles to all grants:

- Applications can only be considered from organisations or groups which are charitable as defined by UK charity law. This includes UK registered charities and relevant exempt charities such as universities. Proposals from non-charitable organisations (such as the NHS or social enterprises) may only be considered in exceptional circumstances and where the purposes for which the grant is sought are: charitable; for the public benefit; and not for private benefit that is more than nominal or incidental to the charitable purposes. Such proposals must have due regard to the exclusions listed (see 'exclusions' section)
- Applications from any geographical area within the UK are eligible for consideration and will be considered on merit alone
- As a general rule applicant organisations will be expected to have a policy of inclusiveness, equality and non-discrimination (i.e. applications should not be unduly restrictive)
- All applications from previous grant holders will be considered on their own merits. Although the outcome of any previous grant will be taken into account, any new application will in no way receive preferential consideration
- Applications for grants in medical areas which are already supported by large dedicated charities (e.g. cancer, heart disease) will not normally be considered
- DMT will not normally support applications from large national charities (i.e. those with an annual income in excess of £10 million or with £100 million assets)
- DMT will not normally consider applications from charities dedicated to issues deemed by the trust to be already well funded with the UK (e.g. cancer, heart disease)
- DMT will willingly work in partnership with other organisations to fund initiatives beyond the financial scope of a single organisation, where this would be appropriate

Research and research-related grants

In addition to the above, the following principles will apply to research and research-related grants:

Priority will be given to: clinical and applied research; health services research; public health research; research carried out on a multidisciplinary basis; activities that will expand research capacity in these areas.

Applicants will be expected to provide a clear demonstration of what the research is expected to achieve within a reasonable time frame, in terms of patient benefit/improving the health and well-being of older people.

- Lead research applicants will be expected to demonstrate that they are based in a strong research environment with a suitable skill mix in the research team (with other members of the team being named co-applicants), and to specify clearly the role of each member of the team in the research

All research and research-related applications will be subject to rigorous peer review and grants awarded on the basis of their scientific quality and relevance to DMT's research strategy. The opinion of appropriate external referees will be sought, in addition to scrutiny of applications by the Grants and Research Committee (which includes both scientifically qualified trustees and external advisers with expertise relevant to DMT's priority areas)
- Research will be supported directly with the institution in which the research is carried out, rather than through a third party (such as a fundraising charity supporting research)
- DMT will only support the use of protected animals in research where no viable alternative exists, and the applicant must have regard to animal welfare and advances in the refinement, replacement and reduction of animal use, including compliance with guidelines published by the National Centre for the Replacement, Refinement and Reduction of Animals in Research (NC3Rs)
- DMT supports an open access policy with regard to peer reviewed (primary) publications arising from research funded by the trust
- As a charity, DMT will not pay the full economic costs of research: directly incurred costs **will** be met; some directly allocated costs **may** be met and will be considered on a case-by-case basis (having regard to information on eligible costs included in the Guidelines for Research Applicants) providing that full justification is included in the grant application); DMT **will not** contribute towards indirect costs underpinning research

Grantmaking 2011/12

During 2011/12 the trust had assets of £98.6 million and an income of £102 million. (This unusually large income includes £99 million received from the transfer of funds from The Dunhill Medical Trust, which was an unincorporated charity, on the formation of a new charitable company of the same name which replaced it in April 2011). Grants were made totalling £3.2 million, with £2.6 million going to research and research related awards and £593,000 to non-research/general grants.

The distribution of grants by category was broken down as follows:
- Research project and programme grants – 53%
- Research training fellowships – 22%
- Services relating to medical care or care for older people – 13%

- Serendipity awards – 7%
- Provision of accommodation for older people – 5%

During the year the trust received approximately 380 grant applications of which 72% met the basic criteria for funding. Of these, 58% were either within the priority areas designated by the trustees, or were applications for Serendipity Awards (which may be in any area of medicine/medical science/health) or applications for Research Training Fellowships.

Beneficiaries included: University of Southampton (£80,000); University of Glasgow (£50,000); University of Leeds (£37,000); Integrated Neurological Services and Lost Chord – South Yorkshire (£30,000 each); Age Concern Halton and St Helens (£29,000) Alzheimer's Support (£23,000); Neighbourly Care Southall (£26,000); Green Candle Dance Company (£18,000); Fair Shares Gloucestershire £13,000); Manor Gardens Welfare Trust – London (£10,000); and RADICLE (£5,000).

Note: all requests for funding are first appraised against criteria set out within DMT's Grant Making Policy, available to download from the trust's website. The Dunhill Medical Trust is a member of the Association of Medical Research Charities.

Exclusions

The trust will not fund:
- Organisations based outside the UK, or whose work primarily benefits people outside the UK
- Large national charities, with an income in excess of £10 million, or assets exceeding £100 million
- Issues that are already well-funded in the UK, such as heart disease, cancer or HIV/AIDS
- Sponsorship of individuals
- Sponsorship of conferences or charitable events
- Services or equipment that would be more appropriately provided by the National Health Service
- Grants to cover the revenue or capital costs of hospices*
- Travel or conference fees (except where these items are an integral part of a project)
- New or replacement vehicles (unless an integral part of a community-based development)
- General maintenance
- Institutional overheads associated with research activity (i.e. the trust will not pay the full economic cost of research activities)
- Research via a third party (such as a fundraising charity supporting research)
- Continuation/replacement funding where a project or post has been

previously supported from statutory sources or similar

*Although the trust does not award grants to cover the revenue or capital costs of hospices, research undertaken within a hospice setting is eligible for consideration.

Applications

Taken from the trust's website: 'You are strongly advised to visit the DMT website before making an application to ensure that your proposal falls within the trust's criteria for funding. If after so doing you still require specific advice regarding your application, please contact the DMT office.'

Applicants to the Research, Research-related and Serendipity funding programmes should complete the appropriate online *outline application form* available in the 'policies and documents' section of the trust's website.

Applicants to the General Grants programme are asked to provide an initial outline (approximately two sides of A4) by post or email, including the following information:
- A brief description of the organisation and its status (e.g. whether it is a registered charity); who you are and what you do within the organisation
- A description of the project for which funding is being sought, where it will take place and who it will involve
- An outline of who will benefit from the work and why
- The key outcomes and timescales
- The total cost of the project/work and the specific amount being applied for from the trust

Outline applications for all programmes can be submitted at any time and those which are eligible will be invited to submit a formal application.

The formal application requirements differ depending upon the type of grant being applied for and applicants are strongly advised to visit the trust's website before making an application to ensure that they have all the relevant information.

Full applications are considered by the Grants and Research Committee which meets quarterly (normally in February, May, July and November). The committee makes recommendations on whether applications should be supported and decisions are then referred to the board of trustees for approval at their quarterly meetings (normally held in March, June, September and December). Successful applicants are normally notified within two weeks of the meeting. Generally, decisions are made within three to four months.

Percentage of awards given to new applicants: between 40% and 50%.

Common applicant mistakes

'Not bothering to read the detailed guidelines which are available on our website and therefore submitting applications which are clearly ineligible.'

Information gathered from:

Accounts; annual report; Charity Commission record; further information provided by the funder; funder's website.

The Charles Dunstone Charitable Trust

General
£1.25 million (2011/12)

Beneficial area
UK.

Correspondent: The Trustees, H. W. Fisher and Company, Acre House, 11–15 William Road, London NW1 3ER (tel: 020 7388 7000)

Trustees: Denis Dunstone; Adrian Bott; Nicholas Folland; John Gordon.

CC Number: 1085955

Established in 2001 for general charitable purposes, this is the charitable trust of Charles Dunstone, co-founder of the Carphone Warehouse.

The following information on future activities is taken from the trust's annual report:

In September 2009 the trustees began funding the development and improvement of the Fulwood Academy in Preston, Lancashire [Charles Dunstone is the sponsor of the new academy]. This represents a substantial commitment of time and funds over the coming 5 years at least and is likely to be the focus for much of the trust's work.

The trustees will continue to make a small number of grants in the following areas:

- Making lasting improvements to the lives of children with disabilities and their families
- Improving the prospects of prisoners on release, especially through the provision of better opportunities and services whilst in prison
- Making lasting improvements to the education and wellbeing of those living in disadvantaged communities, particularly young people
- Improving the availability of support and service for young carers

Grants are likely to be made to a small number of organisations which have entrepreneurial leadership and have potential to create significant impact, either at local or national level.

In 2011/12 the trust assets of £2.34 million and an income of £1.6 million. Grants were made totalling £1.25 million, broken down into the following categories:

Children and youth	£314,000
Community care and ethnic organisations	£251,500
Education and training	£176,000
Medical and disability	£169,500
Arts and culture	£151,500
Social welfare	£109,000
Conservation	£50,000
Sport	£28,000
Other	£500

During the year the Fulwood Academy received an instalment of £75,000. Other beneficiaries during the year included: Community Links and the Family Fund (£100,000 each); Prince's Trust (£80,000 for the Fairbridge merger; a further £70,000 was given for the enterprise fellowship); Dance United and Churches Conservation (£50,000 each); Kingwood Trust (£30,000); and Royal Marsden Cancer Research (£25,000).

Exclusions
The trustees do not normally make grants to individuals.

Applications
Proposals are generally invited by the trustees or initiated at their request. Unsolicited applications are not encouraged and are unlikely to be successful. The trustees prefer to support innovative schemes that can be successfully replicated or become self-sustaining.

Information gathered from:
Accounts; annual report; Charity Commission record.

The James Dyson Foundation

Science, engineering, medical research and education
£889,000 (2012)

Beneficial area
Mainly UK, local community around the Dyson company's UK headquarters, in Malmesbury, Wiltshire.

Correspondent: Lydia Beaton, Foundation Manager, Tetbury Hill, Malmesbury, Wiltshire SN16 0RP (tel: 01666 828001; email: jamesdysonfoundation@dyson.com; website: www.jamesdysonfoundation.com)

Trustees: Sir James Dyson; Lady Deirdre Dyson; Valerie West; Prof. Sir Christopher Frayling.

CC Number: 1099709

This company foundation was set up in 2002 to promote charitable giving, especially to charities working in the fields of science, engineering, medicine and education.

The annual trustees' report states:

The objects of the foundation, as stated in its governing document, are as follows:

- To advance education and training, particularly in the fields of design and technology – this work can take a number of forms including the free provision of support resources for teachers of design and technology in schools, the running of design engineering workshops and lectures in schools and universities, as well as bursary schemes and collaborative projects
- To support medical and scientific research
- To support charitable and educational projects in the region in which the foundation operates

Each year, the foundation donates a number of Dyson vacuum cleaners (for raffle prizes) to charitable causes which fall within its objectives. The cost of these is included in the total grants figure. Small grants may also be made to charitable projects that share the philosophies and objectives of the foundation.

The accounts for year 2012 were overdue at the Charity Commission at the time of writing (November 2013) and we have taken our information from the latest available – 2011. In the year to December 2011, the foundation's income and assets were listed as £2.1 million. Grants totalled £889,000 and were distributed in three categories as follows:

Education and training	£840,000
Science and medical research	£45,000
Social and community welfare	£4,000

Beneficiaries included: James Dyson Award (£106,000); Japan Education Programme (£26,000); Malmesbury Schools Project (£22,000); Dyson Centre for Neonatal Care (£16,500); Sparks (£7,000).

Applications
Applications in writing on headed paper to the correspondent. Organisations can also apply through the 'get in touch' section of the foundation's website.

Information gathered from:
Accounts; annual report; Charity Commission record; funder's website.

East End Community Foundation (formerly the St Katharine and Shadwell Trust)

Community development
£1.4 million (2012)

Correspondent: Tracey Walsh, Director, Jack Dash House, 2 Lawn House Close, London E14 9YQ (tel: 020 7345 4444; email: grants@eastendcf.org; website: www.eastendcf.org)

Trustees: Eric Sorensen; Revd P. David Paton; Denise Jones; Angela Orphanou; Dan Jones; David Hardy; Mark Gibson; Rosemary Ryde; Ian Fisher; Dr Tobias Jung; Christopher Martin; Jonathan Norbury.

CC Number: 1147789

This is a newly formed community foundation. In October 2012 the St Katharine and Shadwell Trust ceased to operate as an independent charity and merged with a neighbouring charity, the Isle of Dogs Community Foundation (IDCF) to form East End Community Foundation (EECF). The area of benefit remains the same and all trustees of both charities have joined the board of the new charity for its first year of operation. At the end of that year board membership is to be reduced to 15 trustees appointed in accordance with the categories of membership for the EECF.

The charity's website describes the new foundation as follows:

> Working across Tower Hamlets, Hackney, Newham and the City of London, the East End Community Foundation is dedicated to improving the quality of life and opportunities for people living in the East End.
>
> By funding grass roots organisations and directly delivering projects we aim to raise educational achievement, enhance employability and increase social cohesion. Our deep understanding of the needs of local communities and unique partnership with residents, frontline services and businesses enables us to provide targeted support and create real lasting change.

As well as its funding provision, the foundation uses local knowledge and expertise to deliver a range of successful projects, including employment schemes, mentoring for young people and activities for older people and young people which directly improve the educational and employability prospects of local residents, and reach out to those groups within the community affected by poverty and isolation.

Grantmaking

The foundation distributes grants to voluntary and community sector organisations and offers funding to secondary schools in Tower Hamlets for study support weekends. Community based projects and small-to-medium sized organisations are prioritised for funding.

The grant programmes and projects may vary from year to year so check the foundation's website for up-to-date information.

The grants programmes aim to:
- Improve life, social and transferable skills
- Raise educational achievement
- Enhance employability
- Increase social cohesion

Maximum grants are £10,000. Each programme has its own criteria and guidelines, which you are advised to read carefully before submitting an application. There are three application deadlines per year and details are given on the foundation's website.

Standard grants
Up to £10,000, covering at least one of the themes of employment and training, education or community wellbeing and inclusion.

Small grants
Up to £800, for one-off items of expenditure or events.

Poplar Housing and Regeneration Community Association Community grants
Up to £3,000 for projects benefiting Poplar HARCA residents. Funding covers Local Area Partnerships 6 and 7 (Bromley by Bow, Mile End East, Limehouse and East India and Lansbury wards).

Study support weekends
For secondary schools across Tower Hamlets, to take students on a residential weekend focused on increasing levels of attainment.

Comic Relief – Local communities
The Local Communities programme which address issues of economic and social deprivation has been re-released and East End Community Foundation is one of the delivery partners. Grants from the programme will be between £1,000 and £10,000 and are for projects in the City of London, Hackney, Newham or Tower Hamlets.

Under the programme, organisations can apply for funding to:
- Increase local services
- Build skills of local people
- Increase community cohesion
- Respond to local economic needs

For full guidance notes and to apply visit the foundation's website.

EECF states that it is building on the legacy of the grantmaking programmes of both the Isle of Dogs Community Foundation and St Katharine and Shadwell Trust. At the time of writing (August 2013), no accounts were due or received at the Charity Commission and so we are unable to give examples of current beneficiary organisations. However, the foundation's website states that in the last year the foundation has supported over 150 community groups and distributed £1.4 million in grants.

Previous beneficiaries (of Isle of Dogs Community Foundation and St Katharine and Shadwell Trust) include: Common Ground East, Futureversity, Shadwell Basin Outdoor Activity Centre and Tower Hamlets Education Business Partnership (£10,000 each); London Borough of Tower Hamlets (summer holiday programme) (£8,500); Summer Holiday Programme for Pensioners (£7,000); Wellington Way Sports Project, Somali Development Association, Kudu Arts Project and Banglatown Association (£5,000 each); ADEEG Community Centre (£4,000); Providence Row (£2,000); Vital Arts (£1,500); and Science in Schools – Hermitage Primary School and Mulberry School for Girls (£1,000 each).

Exclusions
Individuals.

Applications
See the trust's website or contact the trust directly for details and criteria of up-to-date schemes.

Information gathered from:
Charity Commission record; funder's website.

The EBM Charitable Trust

Children/youth, animal welfare, relief of poverty, general
£668,500 (2011/12)

Beneficial area
UK.

Correspondent: Keith Lawrence, Secretary, Moore Stephens, 150 Aldersgate Street, London EC1A 4AB (tel: 020 7334 9191; fax: 020 7651 1953)

Trustees: Richard Moore; Michael Macfadyen; Stephen Hogg; Francis Moore.

CC Number: 326186

The trustees report, as has been the case in previous years, stated simply that 'beneficiaries included charities involved in animal welfare and research, the relief of poverty and youth development'. Furthermore, that resources would be maintained at a reasonable level in order continue funding general charitable purposes.

In 2011/12 the trust had assets of £44.7 million and an income of nearly £1.2 million. Grants were made to 30 organisations totalling £668,500.

The trust manages two funds, the general fund and the Fitz' fund. The Fitz' fund was established following the death of Cyril Fitzgerald, one of the original trustees of the charity who left the residue of his estate to the trust. The money is held as a designated fund for animal charities.

Beneficiaries included: The Prostate Cancer Charity (£100,000); Fairbridge (£70,000); Animal Health Trust

(£50,000); Prior's Court Foundation (£40,000); Cardinal Hume Centre (£35,000); Marie Curie Cancer Care, Worshipful Company of Shipwrights Charitable Fund and Youth at Risk (£20,000 each); Ingwood, Macmillan Cancer Support, Royal Veterinary College and SeeAbility (£10,000 each); The Cirdan Sailing Trust and I Can (£5,000 each); and New Astley Club (£3,500).

Applications

The trustees have previously stated:

Unsolicited applications are not requested as the trustees prefer to support donations to charities whose work they have researched and which is in accordance with the wishes of the settlor. The trustees do not tend to support research projects as research is not a core priority but there are exceptions. The trustees' funds are fully committed. The trustees receive a very high number of grant applications which are mostly unsuccessful.

Information gathered from:

Accounts; annual report; Charity Commission record.

The Maud Elkington Charitable Trust

Social welfare, general charitable purposes
£478,000 (2011/12)

Beneficial area
Mainly Desborough, Northamptonshire and Leicestershire.

Correspondent: Paula Fowle, Administrator, c/o Shakespeares LLP, Two Colton Square, Leicester LE1 1QH (tel: 01162 545454; fax: 01162 554559; email: paula.fowle@shakespeares.co.uk)

Trustees: Roger Bowder, Chair; Michael Jones; Katherine Hall.

CC Number: 263929

The principle aim of the trust is to distribute grants, particularly, but not exclusively in Desborough and Northamptonshire; grants are also made in Leicestershire. Grants are made to rather small projects, where they will make a quantifiable difference to the recipients, rather than favouring large national charities whose income is in millions rather than thousands. It is the usual practice to make grants for the benefit of individuals through referring agencies such as social services, NHS Trusts or similar responsible bodies.

In 2011/12 the trust had assets of £21.5 million and an income of £577,500. Grants were made totalling £478,000. Unfortunately, unlike previous accounts, a list of beneficiaries was not included.

Previous beneficiaries include: Nottinghamshire County Council; Leicester Grammar School – Bursary; Bromford Housing Association; Cynthia Spencer Hospice; Launde Abbey; Cancer Research UK; CARE Shangton; Multiple Sclerosis Society; Elizabeth Finn Care; Voluntary Action Northants; and Phoenix Furniture.

Exclusions
No grants directly to individuals.

Applications
In writing to the correspondent – there is no application form or guidelines. The trustees meet every seven or eight weeks.

Percentage of awards given to new applicants: between 20% and 30%.

Common applicant mistakes
'Not enough information.'

Information gathered from:
Accounts; Charity Commission record; further information provided by the funder.

The John Ellerman Foundation

Welfare, environment and arts
£4.5 million (2011/12)

Beneficial area
Mainly UK; East and Southern Africa.

Correspondent: Barbra Mazur, Head of Grant Grants, Aria House, 23 Craven Street, London WC2N 5NS (tel: 020 7930 8566; fax: 020 7839 3654; email: enquiries@ellerman.org.uk; website: www.ellerman.org.uk)

Trustees: Sarah Riddell, Chair; Dominic Caldecott; Tim Glass; Brian Hurwitz; Hugh Raven; Diana Whitworth; Vivien Gould.

CC Number: 263207

The foundation was established on the death of Sir John Ellerman in 1970 as a generalist grantmaking trust. John Ellerman had inherited his substantial wealth from the business interests set up by his father, especially in shipping – the family business was called Ellerman Lines. Sir John and his wife Esther had throughout their lives developed a profound interest in philanthropy.

Today the foundation uses Sir John's legacy to make grants totalling around £4 million a year to about 150 different charities, mostly in the United Kingdom. The foundation makes grants to UK registered charities which work nationally, not locally. In 2011/12 the trustees noted that the average grant was £55,000 paid over two years, 'which has been pretty consistent for some time.' For historical reasons it continues to

support a few charities operating in Southern and East Africa.

The foundation's mission is 'to be and be seen as a model grant-maker to the charitable sector.' It aims to achieve its mission by managing its funds in such a way that it can both maintain its grantmaking capacity and operate in perpetuity, funding nationally-registered charities so as to encourage and support those which make a real difference to people, communities and the environment.

Guidelines
The following guidelines are taken from the foundation's website:

The grants we make reflect our interest in wellbeing and excellence. Our funding is in three categories, and we aim to allocate it broadly as follows:
- Arts 25%
- Environment 25%
- Welfare 50%

We remain flexible within these targets.

We are a responsive funder, so will listen to what you judge is important. We are happy to fund core costs and you can use our grant as matched-funding. This trust means we attach great importance to the quality of the charities we support, seeking those which are well run and aspirational.

The 2011/12 accounts note that:

Almost two thirds of new grants in 2011/12 were for core costs.

We want our grants to have a practical outcome, so your application should tell us what you want to achieve and how you will do this. In order for our funds to have as wide an impact as possible we fund work with a national footprint. We also list some features which could demonstrate the potential for far-reaching change.

We are keen to learn about the difference you have made as a result of the grant so you should be able to tell us how you will monitor and evaluate progress.

Welfare
We aim to help people facing poverty, hardship or disadvantage to lead fuller, more independent lives.

We expect a variety of people to benefit from our funding. They might include: young people in care or at risk of getting into trouble; carers; vulnerable or isolated adults; those with chronic ill health; disabled people; families (in the broadest sense) living with serious difficulties, perhaps because they have disabled children, are affected by a relationship breakdown or have a history of disadvantage.

What we fund
We concentrate our funding in two main areas:
1 Enabling individuals to realise their potential by:
- building self-confidence and skills to improve opportunities

helping people gain greater control over their lives and the practicalities of daily living
encouraging a greater voice for those who are less easily heard

2 Strengthening and building relationship to improve people's lives by:

creating dependable personal and social networks
bringing together diverse individuals, groups and communities

What we look for
We prioritise charities that:

Actively involve beneficiaries in their work
Focus on those in greatest need or most excluded
Provide compelling evidence of the positive impact of their work
Meet immediate needs with an eye to reducing future needs

Arts
We believe that art has the potential to enrich and transform lives. That is why we help make the highest quality art available to all. We do this by supporting arts organisations that represent excellence in their field at a national level.

What we fund
We concentrate our funding in two main areas:

1 regional museums and galleries. We aim to strengthen these institutions, with a focus on using curatorial skills to enhance collections for public benefit

2 the performing arts, mainly theatre, music and dance. We may support other performing art forms if the organisation and its work are exceptional

What we look for
Performing arts organisations should demonstrate some of the following:

National significance in the nature or quality of the work
Bringing the performing arts to people who would not otherwise attend
Involvement of emerging talent
Innovative approaches

The aim of the museums and galleries fund is to:

Help strengthen regional museums and galleries in the UK. We want to help organisations enhance and sustain curatorial development to attract a broader public.

Our budget is around £300,000 a year and we expect to make three to four grants annually. Grants may be for periods of two to three years.

Who can apply?
We focus on visual and decorative arts and social and natural history collections.

Applicants should demonstrate:

Excellence in their field at a national level
National significance, usually through a unique or high quality collection

In line with our general policy, we favour applicants with an income between £100,000 and £10m, but we may fund a larger institution if it is uniquely placed to meet our aim. While our priority is regional museums and galleries, large national institutions are eligible to apply if their project benefits the regions.

What we fund
To help us achieve our aim, we are particularly interested in funding museums and galleries that plan to:

Support new ways of working both for established curators and those just starting out
Work in partnership with others to develop and share good practice
Ensure that the experience is integrated into any future plans

What we look for
We are looking for organisations that can show the following:

An emphasis on the value of curatorial skills
A commitment to excellence, innovation and audience development
Strong leadership at board and senior management level
Effective financial management
A lasting legacy

What we do not fund:

Individual conservation projects (but we may consider conservation work as part of a wider request)
Education and outreach work

How to apply: the museum and gallery fund has a two stage application process. Check the website for future deadlines.

Environment
We aim to contribute to greater harmony between people and the planet.

We are particularly interested in organisations that integrate the needs of communities, habitats and species.

What we fund
We concentrate our funding in two main areas:

1 **Managing habitats**
Helping to create richer, sustainable places where nature and people can thrive. We welcome your application if it aims to extend, improve, create, better manage, protect, experiment with or link together habitats, including work on a landscape scale. Here we fund work in the *UK only,* but please see the point below about UK Overseas Territories

2 **Protecting the sea**
Replenishing and supporting marine ecosystems. We welcome your application if it:

ensures that UK marine protected areas (MPAs) are well planned, implemented and maintained. We will also consider an application to protect marine areas other than MPAs if it is convincing, or
uses market forces to reduce overfishing. This could mean certification schemes, developing markets for the most sustainable fisheries, and working with restaurants, wholesalers and retailers to increase sustainable sourcing of seafood

Here we prioritise work in UK waters. However, we will consider exceptional proposals for overseas work from UK-based NGOs when directly relevant to the UK.

We want to help reduce the human impact on the most significant and threatened habitats in *UK Overseas Territories*. We welcome applications from UK-based NGOs with local partners for work in these areas. Here we only expect to make a small number of grants.

What we look for
Organisations that do some of the following:

Appreciate the importance of habitats to human wellbeing, as well as the impact of people on their habitats
Promote livelihoods or employment for local communities
Use natural resources in a sustainable way

Overseas
Since 2004 the foundation has been working with the Baring Foundation on its sub-Saharan Africa programme. This was put on hold in 2012 for two years with no applications being accepted. Continue to check the website for updates.

Grants in 2011/12
In 2011/12 the foundation had assets of £115.6 million and an income of almost £1.6 million. Grants made totalled £4.5 million, with some organisations receiving instalments of multi-year awards. Grants were broken down by category as follows:

Social Welfare	46	£1.35 million
Health and Disability	56	£1.27 million
Arts and Heritage	43	£598,500
Conservation	26	£524,500
Overseas	15	£473,500

Beneficiaries across all categories included: British Liver Trust (£35,000) – towards core costs; Freedom From Torture (£32,000) – towards the work of one of the Adult Therapy and Assessment team members who helps survivors of torture; Contact a Family (£30,000) – towards core costs to increase their ability to respond efficiently and effectively to the needs of families with disabled children; British Film Institute (£30,000) – towards the salary of a conservation specialist; FoodCycle (£30,000) – towards the Hubs Programme, combining volunteers, surplus food and under-utilised kitchen space to create nutritious meals; Friends of the Earth Trust (£30,000) – towards the Get Serious About CO2 project; Chance UK (£30,000) – towards the salary of the Training and Communications Manager will recruit more mentors to work closely with children between 5 and 11 with serious behavioural problems; Leap Confronting Conflict (£30,000) – towards the 'Improving Prospects' project which aims to work with 150 NEET and vulnerable young people; Derwent Initiative (£20,000) – towards core costs, helping to reduce the risk and incidence of sexual offending; Mid-Wales Opera (£20,000) – towards core costs; Spike Island (£20,000) – towards core costs, in particular to support marketing and audience development; Birdlife International (£20,000) – towards supporting the implementation of BirdLife's climate change programme; AfriKids (£16,000) – towards capacity building of AfriKids Ghana and local partners to prevent north-south migration in Ghana, including direct resettlement and rehabilitation of displaced children and Pallant House Gallery (£10,000) – towards core costs enabling the continuation of the Gallery's exhibitions and community programmes.

Many of these grants were single instalments of multi-year commitments. The foundation's excellent annual report also provides informative case studies written by a selection of grant recipients which potential applicants may find interesting.

Exclusions

Grants are not made for the following purposes:

- For or on behalf of individuals
- General and round-robin appeals
- Capital developments and individual items of equipment
- Promotion of religion and places of worship
- Replacement or subsidy funding, or for work we consider should be funded by government
- Individual campaigns
- One-off events, such as conferences, trips, seminars, single commissions, productions or festivals
- Sport, leisure or individual holiday schemes
- Education, such as initiatives linked to the curriculum, arts or environmental educational projects
- Medical research or treatment, including drug and alcohol rehabilitation services
- Prisons and offenders
- Counselling and psychotherapy services

Please do not apply if:

- Your application has been turned down within the previous 12 months
- Your grant ended less than 12 months ago
- You focus on a single medical area, such as an individual disease, organ or condition; this is explained in the FAQs [available on the foundation's website]
- You are a hospital, hospice, school, college or university, unless you are a leading university specialist unit

The foundation will only consider applications from registered and exempt charities with a UK office. Most of our grants are for one and two years, but we will give grants for three years if a very strong case is made. Our minimum grant is £10,000. We aim to develop relationships with funded charities.

We will only support charities that work – or have reach and impact – across England/UK. Those operating within a single locality, city, borough, county or region will not be considered. We believe other trusts and funders are better placed to help individuals and local or regional charities. For this reason also, applications operating exclusively in Wales, Scotland or Northern Ireland will NOT be considered.

Applications

Information taken from the foundation's website:

If you are unsuccessful, we will ask you to wait for one year before you reapply. It is therefore important to make the best case you can at the first stage. The foundation encourages informal phone calls to discuss projects and eligibility before applications are submitted. Only one application per organisation can be considered at any one time.

Stage 1

Your first-stage application should include:

1. A description of what you are seeking funding for, on no more than two sides of A4. Please include: a brief summary of your organisation and relevant track record; where your work takes place, as we only support work with a national footprint; what you would like us to fund and why you are well placed to do this work and how your proposal fits our guidelines for this category.

2. A copy of your most recent annual accounts. If your accounts show a significant surplus or deficit, high or low reserves, please explain this briefly. If the year-end date of your accounts is more than 10 months old, please include your latest management accounts.

First stage applications can be submitted by post or email. Applications can be submitted at any time, unless you are applying for the museums and galleries fund. Applications are acknowledged and decisions made within ten weeks.

Stage 2

If we invite you to the second stage, we will ask for a more detailed application. Then we will arrange to meet you to find out more about your work.

At this second stage we aim to make a decision within three months. If your application takes longer we will be in touch.

Information gathered from:

Accounts; annual report; annual review; Charity Commission record; funder's website.

Entindale Ltd

Orthodox Jewish charities
£1.5 million (2011/12)

Beneficial area

Unrestricted.

Correspondent: Barbara Bridgemen, Trustee, 8 Highfield Gardens, London NW11 9HB (tel: 020 8458 9266; fax: 020 8458 8529)

Trustees: Allan Becker; Barbara Bridgeman; Dov Harris; Jonathan Hager.

CC Number: 277052

This trust aims 'to advance religion in accordance with the Orthodox Jewish faith'. Grants are typically less than £10,000.

In 2011/12 it had assets of £14 million and an income of £1.6 million, derived mainly from rent. Grants were made to around 144 organisations totalling £1.5 million.

Beneficiaries included: Yesamach Levav Trust (£80,000); Rachel Charitable Trust (£50,000); Doughty Charitable Trust (£37,000); Chevrat Maoz LaDol (£34,000); Beis Yaacov Primary School Foundation (£25,000); British Friends of Nadvorne (£15,000); Baer Avrohom UK Trust (£10,000); Project Seed (£8,000); Tora Ernes Primary School (£6,000); British Friends of Igud Hakolelim B'Yerushalayim (£5,000); William and Iboja Carrant Charitable Trust (£4,000); Whitefield Community Kollel (£2,500); and Golders Charitable Trust (£1,000).

Applications

In writing to the correspondent.

Information gathered from:

Accounts; Charity Commission record.

The Equitable Charitable Trust

Education of disabled and/or disadvantaged children under 25
£993,000 (2012)

Beneficial area

Mainly UK: overseas projects can sometimes be supported.

Correspondent: Jennie Long, Grants Officer, Sixth Floor, 65 Leadenhall Street, London EC3A 2AD (tel: 020 7264 4993; fax: 020 7488 9097; email: jennielong@equitablecharitabletrust.org.uk; website: www.equitablecharitabletrust.org.uk)

Trustees: Brian McGeough; Roy Ranson; Peter Goddard.

CC Number: 289548

EQUITABLE

This trust was established in 1984 to receive and distribute, for charitable purposes, a portion of the profits from a commercial school fee investment plan scheme. This scheme is now winding down therefore it is not anticipated that the trust will continue indefinitely. The trust website notes that they are **in the process of spending out** and expects to wind up having spent all available funds during 2015. Therefore, the grants programme is likely to close at the end of 2014. Until then the trust is currently able to make grants totalling around £1 million each year towards projects for young children and young people under the age of 25 who are from disadvantaged backgrounds or are disabled.

Demand for our funds is high. Trustees have therefore identified three specific priorities for the types of projects they wish to support:

- Education projects or services that support the learning and development of disabled children and young people in the UK. This is the broadest of our priorities and a wide range of education projects can be supported…Services that provide advice and support with formal education can be supported. However, services or projects that provide more general advice and guidance (e.g. a helpline providing advice about a particular disability) will not be funded.

- Formal education projects for disadvantaged children and young people in the UK that support delivery of the National Curriculum (i.e. curriculum enrichment projects) or that deliver accredited vocational learning that will increase employability. By 'curriculum enrichment projects' we mean work that is directly linked to delivery of the National Curriculum (or the Curriculum for Excellence in Scotland). In practice this normally means that work will be taking place as part of the school day (a literacy support project, for instance, that takes place in a youth or community setting during evenings or weekends, although relevant to the English curriculum, would *not* be considered a curriculum enrichment project). Under the second part of this priority ('accredited vocational learning') precedence will be given to projects that deliver accredited employment-related training (e.g. trade training courses) and to accredited vocational projects that include support, and can demonstrate success in, moving young people on into employment, work experience or further training

- Education projects that will help increase participation in, or improve the quality of, education for disadvantaged or disabled children and young people in developing countries. We particularly wish to support projects with potential to deliver benefits over the medium to long-term. Grassroots projects without a strategic element, such as those that support

students by paying their school fees or the purchase of school uniforms, are unlikely to be funded. Only UK registered charities are eligible to apply for overseas projects and they must have an Anti-Bribery Policy.

- Projects which relate to PSHE and Citizenship subjects are unlikely to be funded as they are a low priority

Types of grant
Grants can be made for project costs, capital expenditure, equipment and/or the salary costs of a post.

Area of benefit
The majority of projects funded by the trust take place within the UK at local or regional level, though national projects and those benefiting children or young people overseas (in developing countries only) are also supported.

Note that grants for overseas projects are only made through UK registered charities.

Types of organisations funded
We support a broad range of organisations; from small and medium sized not-for-profit organisations to large charities. However, priority is normally given to organisations and charities with annual incomes of under £5 million. We tend not to fund very large organisations or charities. You do not need to be a UK registered charity to apply unless you are applying for a grant towards a project or work that will take place outside the UK.

Length of Grants
The maximum length of funding you can request is one year. Grants are usually paid in annual instalments.

Size of Grants
The size of grants ranges from £3,000 to £30,000. The minimum you can request is £3,000 per year. Most of our grants are for sums between £5,000 and £20,000.

The 2012 accounts note that 'the charity is only occasionally the sole funder of a project; more commonly its grant will be one part of a funding jigsaw that, collectively, helps an organisation to achieve its aims.'

Grants in 2012
In 2012 the trust held assets of £4 million, had an income of £180,000 and a total expenditure of £1.2 million. Grants were paid totalling £993,000 to 103 organisations. During the year 329 applications were received with 62 new grants made. Most grants were for £10,000 or less, but beneficiaries of larger grants included:

Mary Hare Foundation, St John's Catholic School for the Deaf and Prior's Court Foundation (£30,000 each); National Literacy Trust (£25,000); Futureversity (£20,000); Area 51 Education and Care International UK (£18,000 each); and Afghan Connection (£15,000).

Recipients of smaller grants included: Unitas, Young Vic Theatre Company, Tir Coed, Prior's Court Foundation, Living Paintings Trust, Gwent Wildlife Trust, Construction Youth Trust and British Stammering Association (£10,000 each); AfriKids (£9,600); Artburst (£8,000); Dhaka Ahsania Mission (£6,000); Camden Arts Centre and London Philharmonic Orchestra (£5,000 each); and Stick 'n' Step (£4,300).

Exclusions
The trust does not make grants towards the following:

- General appeals or mail shot requests for donations
- Informal education projects and those that are only loosely educational (we include projects in youth work settings such as money management, drug and alcohol awareness and healthy eating in our definition of informal education, whether or not the activities are accredited)
- Projects felt to be more akin to social work than education
- Therapeutic treatments (including music and play therapy)
- Supplementary schooling and homework clubs
- Mother tongue language classes
- Local authorities
- The only schools eligible to apply to us are independent special schools with registered charity status. State-maintained or voluntary aided schools, academies, public schools, independent schools that are not exclusively for disabled children or young people, colleges and universities are not eligible to apply, either directly or via a related charity (e.g. Friends, PTAs). We are also unable to fund groups of schools (whether set up via a partnership agreement or as a registered charity) which are seeking funding for services that were previously provided by their local authorities
- Sports education, facilities or activities (e.g. playing fields, sports clubs, or projects that are delivered through the medium of sport)
- Salaries for posts that are not directly related to service delivery (we would not make a grant towards the salary of a fundraiser or book-keeper, for instance)
- Project/salary costs that will benefit only a single child (we would not fund the cost of an additional worker to support a disable child attending a mainstream or integrated nursery, for instance)
- Minibuses or vehicles
- Pre-school education projects (unless these are solely for the benefit of children with disabilities or special needs)
- Individuals
- Bursary schemes
- Projects that promote religious belief or practice
- Holidays, recreational activities or overseas trips

- Capital applications for equipment or facilities that will be only partly used for education or by under 25s from disadvantaged or disabled backgrounds (e.g. outdoor education centres that also deliver recreational activities, or that are not exclusively for the use of disadvantaged or disabled children and young people)
- Retrospective requests for work that has already taken place
- Sole traders or organisations such as companies limited by shares such as companies limited by shares whose constitutions allow the distribution of profits (whether or not this happens in practice)
- Grassroots projects without a strategic element, such as those which support students by paying their school fees or purchasing school uniforms, are also unlikely to be funded
- Projects in the UK that are primarily to deliver training to adults, staff or teachers (even if children and young people will be the ultimate beneficiaries of this work)

Applications

There is no form but there are very comprehensive application guidelines available on the trust's website. Audited or independently inspected accounts must be included. If your organisation is new and does not yet have accounts, the trust will not be able to consider your application. Trustees meet monthly. Decisions are usually made within eight weeks.

The website states that demand is high and the success rate for applications is around one in six. If you are unsure of whether your project meets the requirements the trust welcomes informal contact prior to the submission of a formal application.

Percentage of awards given to new applicants: between 40% and 50%.

Common applicant mistakes

'Not reading the full guidelines (or list of exclusions). Not demonstrating impact of effectiveness – absence of info about outcomes to date (from an existing or similar project). Not describing their fundraising strategy.'

Information gathered from:

Charity Commission record; further information provided by the funder; funder's website.

The Eranda Foundation

Research into education and medicine, the arts, social welfare

£2.2 million (2011/12)

Beneficial area

UK and overseas.

Correspondent: Gail Devlin-Jones, Secretary, PO Box 6226, Wing, Leighton Buzzard, Bedfordshire LU7 0XF (tel: 01296 689157; email: eranda@btconnect.com)

Trustees: Sir Evelyn de Rothschild; Renée Robeson; Jessica de Rothschild; Anthony de Rothschild; Sir Graham Hearne; Lady Lynn de Rothschild; Sir John Peace.

CC Number: 255650

Established in 1967, this is one of the foundations of the de Rothschild finance and banking family. The foundation supports the promotion of original research, and the continuation of existing research into medicine and education, fostering of the arts and promotion of social welfare. Grants are made to organisations in the UK, as well as Africa, Israel and the USA.

In 2011/12 the foundation had assets of £85 million and an income of £3.9 million. There were 160 grants made during the year totalling £2.2 million.

Beneficiaries included: Franklin D Roosevelt Four Freedoms Park – New York (£158,000); Peterson Institute for International Economics (£154,500); Forum for Jewish Leadership, Cancer Research UK and the Eden Project (£100,000 each); Exploring the Arts (£94,500); Fund for Refugees (£75,000); Prince's Foundation for Children and the Arts (£65,000); Young Vic (£50,000); Alzheimer's Drug Discovery Foundation (£31,000); St John of Jerusalem Eye Hospital (£30,000); Arabian School of Gymnastics (£20,000); National Association for Gifted Children (£16,000); London School of Economics (£10,000); and Friends of Africa Foundation (£5,000).

Exclusions

No grants to individuals.

Applications

In writing to the correspondent. Trustees usually meet in March, July and November and applications should be received two months in advance.

Information gathered from:

Accounts; Charity Commission record.

Essex Community Foundation

Social welfare, general

£1.5 million (2011/12)

Beneficial area

Essex, Southend and Thurrock.

Correspondent: Grants Team, 121 New London Road, Chelmsford, Essex CM2 0QT (tel: 01245 355947; email: general@essexcf.org.uk; website: www.essexcommunityfoundation.org.uk)

Trustees: John Spence; Peter Blanc; Jason Bartella; John Barnes; Carole Golbourn; Peter Heap; Rhiannedd Pratley; Martin Hopkins; Jonny Minter; Owen Richards; Jackie Sully; Kate Barker.

CC Number: 1052061

The foundation was set up in 1996 and manages funds on behalf of individuals, companies, charitable trusts and public agencies in order to give grants to voluntary and community organisations working to improve the quality of life for people living in Essex, Southend and Thurrock. Grants are usually for £250 to £10,000, although up to £250,000 in exceptional circumstances and generally fall under the broad heading of social welfare. They cover core costs/revenue costs, new or continuing projects, one-off initiatives and capital costs. The foundation is particularly interested in small grass-roots groups.

Applications should meet the following criteria:

- Have clear project aims and objectives
- Demonstrate that the grant will make a real difference to people in the community
- Involve local participation and support self-help wherever possible

The foundation administers a variety of different funds of all sizes which change availability throughout the year. Although they give details of these different funds on their website, they are likely to change throughout the year and as such, have not been reproduced here. Further information on the different funds that are available and the foundation's grant guidelines can be found on the foundation website.

In 2011/12 the foundation had assets of £19 million, an income of £4.5 million and gave grants to 274 organisations and 11 individuals totalling £1.5 million.

Beneficiaries included: 2nd Witham Boys' Brigade (£117,000); Basildon Women's Aid (£20,000); Tendring CVS (£12,000); Opportunities Through Technology and Victim Support (£10,000 each); Support 4 Sight (£6,000); Uttlesford Carers (£5,000); Colchester Furniture Project (£4,000); Dedham

Youth Club and Saffron Walden Youth Outreach Project (£3,500 each); Essex Wildlife Trust (£3,400); Essex Young Peoples Drug and Alcohol Service (£1,300); Colchester MIND (£1,000); ASD Support (£500).

Exclusions

The foundation does not support the following:

- Political or religious activities
- Statutory bodies undertaking their statutory obligations (including schools and parish councils)
- General appeals
- Activities which solely support animal welfare
- Projects that operate outside of Essex, or benefit non-Essex residents
- Retrospective funding

Applications

Essex Community Foundation manages a number of funds, many of which are tailored to the individual wishes of the donors. Applicants should use the general applications forms (for either under or over £1,000), along with application guidelines.

Applicants for Comic Relief, High Sherriff's Award or funding for individuals should use the specific application forms, also available from the foundation.

Application forms are available from the foundation's office or can be downloaded from its website; they can be submitted at any time throughout the year.

The foundation welcomes initial enquires to discuss an application.

Information gathered from:

Accounts; annual report; annual review; Charity Commission record; funder's website.

Euro Charity Trust

Relief of poverty, education
£2.4 million (2012)

Beneficial area

Worldwide, mainly India, Africa, Bangladesh and the UK.

Correspondent: Nasir Awan, Trustee, 51a Church Road, Edgbaston, Birmingham B15 3SJ (email: info@ eurocharity.org.uk)

Trustees: Nasir Awan; Abdul Malik; Abdul Alimahomed.

CC Number: 1058460

The trust receives the majority of its income from Euro Packaging Holdings Ltd. Donations are made to both organisations and individuals worldwide. Euro Packaging has grown from a small paper bag merchants into a large

diversified packaging group. Paper bag production commenced in 1984 and today the firm is the UK's largest manufacturer. It has its own facilities for polythene bag manufacture, and also recycles both plastic and paper products.

The trust's objects are as follows:

- Relief of poverty
- Relief of the elderly, the vulnerable (such as young children or anyone with special needs) or hardship, including orphans and widows
- The provision of basic necessities and amenities to those in need wheresoever such as water, electricity and medical facilities
- The advancement of education
- General charitable purposes

In 2012 the trust had assets of £751,500 and an income of £2.9 million, which included £453,000 from Euro Packaging. Grants were made totalling £2.4 million. Over two thirds of the trust's grantmaking is concentrated in India. It is also likely grants are made to organisations in the local area around Euro Packaging sites (in the UK in Birmingham and in Malaysia) and Malawi, where the settlor is originally from. Grants were broken down as follows:

	Amount*
Welfare including the provision of food, water, clothing and healthcare	£1 million
Education and sponsorship	£919,500
Construction and land	£385,000
Medical provision	£79,000
Other activities	£70,500

*this includes £51,000 to individuals.

The largest donations, listed in the trust's accounts, were made to: Nathani Charitable Trust (£1.4 million); Maulana Hussain Ahmad Madani Charitable Trust and Charitable Society (£464,500); and Imdadul Muslimeen (£140,000).

Applications

In writing to the correspondent.

Information gathered from:

Accounts; Charity Commission record.

The Eveson Charitable Trust

People with physical disabilities, (including those who are blind or deaf), people with mental disabilities, hospitals and hospices, children who are in need, older people, homeless people, medical research into problems associated with any of these conditions
£2 million (2012/13)

Beneficial area

Herefordshire, Worcestershire and the county of West Midlands (covering Birmingham, Coventry, Dudley, Sandwell, Solihull, Walsall and Wolverhampton).

Correspondent: Alex D. Gay, Administrator, 45 Park Road, Gloucester GL1 1LP (tel: 01452 501352; fax: 01452 302195)

Trustees: David Pearson, Chair; Bruce Maughfling; Rt. Revd Anthony Priddis, Bishop of Hereford; Martin Davies; Louise Woodhead; Bill Wiggin; Richard Mainwaring.

CC Number: 1032204

The trust was established in 1994 by a legacy of £49 million from Mrs Violet Eveson to support the following causes:

- People with physical disabilities (including those who are blind or deaf)
- People with mental disabilities
- Hospitals and hospices
- Children in need, whether disadvantaged or have mental or physical disabilities
- Older people
- People who are homeless
- Medical research in any of these categories
- General charitable purposes

It is the policy of the trust to support many charities on an annual basis provided such beneficiaries satisfy the need for continued support. Many capital and specific projects are also supported.

Grants are restricted to the geographical areas of Herefordshire, Worcestershire and the county of West Midlands, as a policy decision of the trustees. The trust does not instigate programmes of its own, but responds to the applications which it receives. Grants vary in amount but the average size of grants is around £7,000 to £8,000.

In 2012/13 the trust had assets of £67.9 million and an income of £1.4 million. Grants were made to 272 organisations totalling almost £2 million, and were categorised as displayed in the box below.

Beneficiaries included: Birmingham Children's Hospital Charities (£100,000), towards a major improvement in facilities at the Hospital's Children's Cancer Unit; Age UK Hereford and Localities (£75,000), towards running costs; Acorns Children's Hospice Trust (£55,000), towards running costs of their hospices in Birmingham, Walsall and Worcester that provide support to life limited or life threatened children; St Paul's Hostel – Worcester (£40,000 in total), towards care farm project and counselling service to benefit homeless people; Martha Trust Hereford Ltd (£25,000), towards new furniture and equipment for Sophie House which provides specialised care for people with profound disabilities; Birmingham City Mission (£15,000), towards cost of renovating care centre that will benefit homeless people; British Heart Foundation (£10,000), towards medical research being carried out at the University of Birmingham; Basement Youth Trust (£8,000), towards running costs; and Dorothy Parkes Centre (£7,000), towards running costs.

Exclusions

Grants are not made to individuals, even if such a request is submitted by a charitable organisation.

Applications

The following guidance is provided by the trust in its annual report:

The trustees meet quarterly, usually at the end of March and June and the beginning of October and January.

Applications can only be considered if they are on the trust's standard, but very simple, 'application for support' form which can be obtained from the administrator at the offices of the trust in Gloucester. The form must be completed and returned (together with a copy of the latest accounts and annual report of the organisation) to the trust's offices at least six weeks before the meeting of trustees at which the application is to be considered, in order to give time for

necessary assessment procedures, often including visits to applicants.

Before providing support to statutory bodies (such as hospitals and schools for people with learning difficulties), the trust requires written confirmation that no statutory funds are available to meet the need for which funds are being requested. In the case of larger grants to hospitals, the trust asks the district health authority to confirm that no statutory funding is available.

Where applications are submitted that clearly fall outside the grantmaking parameters of the trust, the applicant is advised that the application cannot be considered and reasons are given. All applications that are going to be considered by the trustees are acknowledged in writing. Applicants are advised of the reference number of their application and of the quarterly meeting at which their application is going to be considered. The decisions are advised to applicants in writing soon after these meetings. Funded projects are monitored.

Percentage of awards given to new applicants: less than 10%.

Common applicant mistakes

'Failure to read guidelines, though the standard of applications submitted has improved over the years.'

Information gathered from:

Accounts; annual report; Charity Commission record; further information provided by the funder.

Esmée Fairbairn Foundation

Social welfare, education, environment, and arts

£32.4 million (2012)

Beneficial area

UK.

Correspondent: Caroline Mason, Chief Executive, Kings Place, 90 York Way, London N1 9AG (tel: 020 7812 3700; fax: 020 7812 3701; email: info@ esmeefairbairn.org.uk; website: www. esmeefairbairn.org.uk)

Trustees: James Hughes-Hallett, Chair; Tom Chandos; Beatrice Hollond; Thomas Hughes-Hallett; Kate Lampard; Baroness Linklater; William Sieghart; John Fairbairn; Jonathan Phillips; Joe Docherty.

CC Number: 200051

Background

Ian Fairbairn established the foundation in 1961 (renamed Esmée Fairbairn Foundation in 2000). He was a leading city figure and his company, M&G, was the pioneer of the unit trust industry. Ian Fairbairn endowed the foundation with the greater part of his own holding in M&G, and in the early years the majority of grants were for economic and financial education.

His interest in financial education stemmed from his concern that most people had no access to stock exchange investment, and were therefore precluded from investing their savings in equities and sharing in the country's economic growth. It was precisely this concern that had led him into the embryonic unit trust business in the early 1930s.

The foundation was set up as a memorial to Ian Fairbairn's wife Esmée, who had played a prominent role in developing the Women's Royal Voluntary Service and the Citizens Advice before being killed during an air raid towards the end of the Second World War. Her sons Paul and Oliver Stobart contributed generously to the original trust fund, as co-founders.

General

In 2012 the foundation had assets of £779.6 million (£776.1 million in 2011) and an income of £12 million, mostly from investments. Grants were made during the year totalling £32.4 million.

Guidelines

The following guidelines are provided by the foundation:

The Esmée Fairbairn Foundation aims to improve the quality of life throughout the UK. We do this by funding the charitable activities of organisations that have the ideas and ability to achieve change for the better. We take pride in supporting work that might otherwise be considered difficult to fund.

Funding is channelled through two routes.

Main Fund

The Main Fund distributes about two-thirds of funding.

What areas do we support?
The Main Fund is open to applications for support from across our sectors, which are:

▶ Arts
▶ Education and learning

THE EVESON CHARITABLE TRUST

Social Care and Development	To organisations that provide human and social services to a community or target population, including services for children, young people, physically and mentally disabled, elderly people and homeless people.	175	£983,000
Health Care	To organisations that focus on the prevention or treatment of specific diseases, the prevention or treatment of diseases generally and/or health problems, the rehabilitation of disabled individuals, residential nursing homes for the frail, elderly, severely disabled and those offering terminal care.	73	£812,000
Accommodation	To organisations providing non-health related accommodation and respite/holiday accommodation.	24	£174,000

- Environment
- Social change

In depth discussion of each of these sectors and the foundation's preferences and priorities is available on the website.

While the foundation assesses each application on its individual merits, we receive around 3,000 applications a year so we choose to prioritise certain types of work.

We prioritise work that:

- Addresses a significant gap in provision
- Develops or strengthens good practice
- Challenges convention, taking risks in order to address a difficult issue
- Tests out new ideas or practices
- Takes an enterprising approach to achieving your aims
- Sets out to influence policy or change behaviour more widely

We welcome applications from registered charities and other not-for-profit organisations. We can only fund legally charitable work, that your constitution allows you to do.

What type of funding do we offer?
At Esmée Fairbairn we are happy to receive applications for core or project costs, and this includes staff salaries and overheads. Last year [2012], over half of our funding supported the core costs of organisations.

We do not usually make grants to large UK wide charities but make rare exceptions when their size or reach allows them, uniquely, to achieve an outcome that resonates strongly with our interests. They may, for example, have the credibility to pool the efforts of a large number of stakeholders towards a shared goal and/or exert influence at a political level to press home policy change. We may also consider applications from large charities where their project ideas are particularly innovative or risky and carry the potential for substantial impact.

We very rarely fund research.

If you ask for our assistance, you should tell us how much you need.

Around 80% of the grants we make are multi-year grants, usually for up to three years, although we will consider applications for longer periods (but rarely beyond five years).

Other Funds

The trust allocates funding to specific areas known as streams. The following topics are identified for more detailed attention. These will develop over time, and allow the foundation to make a more focused contribution in an area of interest. Others may come on stream in due course. Check the foundation's website for up-to-date information.

Merger Fund – to support organisations in the early phases of thinking about a merger.

Applications requesting funding for the following types of pre-merger feasibility work will be considered including:

- Consultation with staff/beneficiaries/ members/other stakeholders
- Facilitation of discussions with the potential merger partner/s
- Governance, planning, financial, legal, HR or communications advice

This is not an exhaustive list and we will consider any reasonable request for work that helps to make the decision whether or not to merge easier. If successful organisations require external assistance but do not have a particular consultant in mind, we may be able to help identify the most appropriate support.

Applicants to the fund need to be at, or close to, the preliminary stage of discussions with an identified potential merger partner (or partners). The fund is *not* intended to meet any costs associated with a merger once a firm decision is made to proceed. It is for organisations uncertain about what the decision might involve or those who need reassurance that a proposed merger makes sense.

Please note that the focus of the merging organisations must come under our Main Fund areas of interest; the arts, education and learning, the environment and social change. The foundation's Main Fund Exclusions still apply. Organisations applying to the Merger Fund must also demonstrate that they have unrestricted reserves equivalent to at least three months' running costs. This applies to all parties involved with the merger feasibility investigations.

Food – Our Food Strand supports work that demonstrates the important role food plays in wellbeing and that connects people to the food that they eat. As part of this primary aim the strand seeks to bring about more sustainable food production and consumption policies and practices.

The strand is open to both large-scale strategic interventions and innovative local work.

Its budget is £5 million over three years, from January 2013 although it may be extended for a further two years pending a review during 2015.

For detailed guidelines on applying to this stream check the website for the latest information.

The Esmée Fairbairn Collections Fund – The Fund, run by the Museums Association, focuses on time-limited collections work outside the scope of an organisation's core resources. Through this fund the MA will award approximately £800,000 per year to museums, galleries and heritage organisations with two grant rounds per year. This fund has been developed from the Esmée Fairbairn Museum and Heritage Collections strand and the MA's Effective Collections programme.

More information, including application guidelines, are available on the Museum Association website: www. museumsassociation.org.

In addition the trust also has the following other funds open:

Finance Fund – Aims to complement the foundation's grant making with loans and other investments to charities and social enterprises in our areas of interest.

TASK Fund – Trustees' Areas of Specialist Knowledge (TASK) Fund supports organisations known to individual trustees.

Grants in 2012
The Main Fund

Social Change	160	£14.5 million
Arts	97	£7.9 million
Education and learning	46	£5.3 million
Environment	36	£2.8 million
Total	**339**	**£30.5 million**

The average grant size from the Main Fund was £90,000; there were a total of 2,655 applications made to the Main Fund, with 339 grants approved. The following is a sample of beneficiaries from the Main Fund and the purposes for which grants were given:

Teach First (£568,000), to develop a programme of tailored leadership and development support for social entrepreneurs amongst Teach First's ambassadors; Aldeburgh Music (£500,000), to support a new initiative aimed at nurturing artistic development; Federation of London Youth Clubs (£298,000), towards core costs to support members to strengthen their evidence-base, embed conflict resolution in their practices and build the capacity of disadvantaged young people; SHINE: Support and Help In Education (£284,000), towards the Let Teachers Shine campaign, which will support local and collaborative solutions to raising attainment in literacy and numeracy; Coalition for the Removal of Pimping (£275,000), to provide one-to-one support, information and advocacy to parents whose children are sexually exploited by pimps and organised criminal gangs; London Wildlife Trust (£167,000), towards the salary of a volunteer officer and other related project costs to create a new infrastructure that effectively supports and nurtures local action and advocacy; 20 Stories High (£120,000), towards arts projects particularly for BME and socially-excluded young people in Liverpool and across the UK; Africans Unite Against Child Abuse (£102,000), towards the cost of safeguarding African children and young people from trafficking and ritual abuse; Incredible Edible Growing Ltd (£90,000), towards core costs for work reconnecting young people to the land and creating training and opportunities in business, food-growing and preparation; Spark and Mettle (£50,000), towards a programme that improves the well-being, employment skills and networks of disadvantaged young people through social media and Greenwich and Docklands Festivals (£25,000), towards a large-scale performance by deaf and disabled artists which aims to contribute to the development of high-quality disability arts in the UK.

Strands

TASK Fund	111	£959,000
Food Strand	10	£887,000
Grants Plus	0	£163,000
Total	**68**	**£2 million**

TASK Fund – The foundation also makes grants from its TASK (Trustees' Areas of Special Knowledge) Fund to support organisations known to individual trustees. Beneficiaries included: Youth Empowerment Crime Diversion Scheme (£15,000); The Royal Horticultural Society (£12,000); Support in Mind Scotland (£10,000); The George Orwell Memorial Trust and Anna Freud Centre (£5,000 each); and The Bridport Literary Festival Ltd (£1,000).

Food Strand: City University (£241,000) towards the establishment of a Food Research Hub that will enable collaboration across academia, the food sector and food industry to influence food policy and practice; Community Food Initiatives North East (£147,000), towards the development of a collective purchasing initiative for its members and Pasture-Fed Livestock Association (£20,000), towards core costs of an organisation that promotes sustainable and resilient livestock farming systems based wholly on pasture.

Grants Plus – Through our 'Grants Plus' programme we provide a range of support to grantee organisations, to run alongside a grant. By identifying and providing the extra help an organisation might need at a difficult or opportune moment. We want to enable their work to have a greater impact, to make our money go further, and to make more of a difference as a Foundation. Examples of Grants Plus support include providing expert advice – e.g. on business planning, financial management, communications and evaluation. We have a pool of experts whose work we recommend, but also fund organisations directly to work with consultants they know and trust.

Finance Fund (£6.8 million) – Loans to and investments in the following organisations: Social Impact Bond for children in care – Essex County Council (£500,000), to provide intervention services to prevent young people going into care and Fair Finance Ltd (£400,000), to create an equity buffer to enable the micro-business loans scheme to grow. Five of the 13 investments went to various Wildlife Trusts throughout the country totalling £3.3 million.

Exclusions

The foundation does not support applications for:

- Individuals or causes that will benefit only one person, including student grants or bursaries
- Support for a general appeal or circular
- Work that does not have a direct benefit in the UK
- The promotion of religion
- Capital costs, including building work, renovations, and equipment
- Work that is routine or well-proven elsewhere or with a low impact
- Healthcare or related work such as medical research, complementary medicine, hospices, counselling and therapy, education and treatment for substance misuse
- Work that is primarily the responsibility of central or local government, health trusts or health authorities. This includes residential, respite and day care, housing provision, individual schools, nurseries and colleges, and vocational training
- The independent education sector
- Animal welfare, zoos, captive breeding and animal rescue centres
- Energy efficiency or waste reduction schemes unless they have exceptional social benefits
- Retrospective funding, meaning support for work that has already taken place
- Recreational activities including outward bound courses and adventure experiences
- We will not normally replace or subsidise statutory income although we will make rare exceptions where the level of performance has been exceptional and where the potential impact of the work is substantial
- Retrospective funding
- Work that is not legally charitable
- General appeals

Applications

Applying for a grant from the Main Fund

Follow these three steps:

1. Carefully read through the guidance notes, supported areas and exclusions
2. You may find it useful to take the eligibility quiz on the foundation's website before applying
3. If you are eligible you must create an account on the site and complete the application form

If your application is successful at first stage we will contact you to invite you to make a second stage application and inform you of what further information is required.

If your first stage application is unsuccessful we will notify you by email.

We make funding decisions throughout the year so you can apply at anytime, but we only consider one application per organisation at a time.

We usually only make one Main Fund grant to an organisation at a time.

You do not need to have matched funding in place before applying but where the total cost of the work you propose for

funding is high you should indicate other sources of funding or specific plans to apply elsewhere.

Our final decisions are based on an assessment of the quality of the work proposed, the importance of the issue, the strength of your idea, the difference the work is likely to make and the match to at least one of our priorities.

The first stage application form and full guidance notes is available from the foundation's website. There is a different application process for the funding strands. To learn more about the strands and how to apply, visit the foundation's website.

Percentage of awards given to new applicants: between 40% and 50%.

Common applicant mistakes

'Not reading information in the guidance. Thinking that their work is distinctive or innovative in some way when in fact it is (from our perspective because we have a wide view) a routine activity being delivered up and down the country.'

Information gathered from:

Accounts; annual report; annual review; Charity Commission record; guidelines for applicants; further information provided by the funder; funder's website.

The February Foundation

Education, heritage, community-based charities, environment, animals, medical/welfare

£2.1 million (2011/12)

Beneficial area

UK.

Correspondent: Richard Pierce-Saunderson, Trustee, Spring Cottage, Church Street, Stradbroke, Suffolk IP21 5HT (email: rps@ thefebruaryfoundation.org; website: www.thefebruaryfoundation.org)

Trustees: James Carleton; The February Foundation (Cayman).

CC Number: 1113064

The foundation was established in 2006 for general charitable purposes and has a broad range of interests. This grantmaking policy is taken from the foundation's accounts:

The foundation will consider the following organisations for the receipt of grants, equity investment or loans:

- Charities which are for the benefit of persons who are making an effort to improve their lives
- Charities which are for the benefit of persons no longer physically or mentally able to help themselves

- Charities which have a long-term beneficial impact on the future of individuals, groups of individuals, or organisations
- Charities which protect the environment
- Small or minority charities where small grants will have a significant impact, and
- Companies where the acquisition of equity would be in line with the trust's charitable objectives

In 2011/12 the foundation had assets of just over £25.5 million and an income of £14 million. Income was particularly high as the foundation merged with The C Charitable Trust in February 2012 and received a total of £3.4 million as a consequence. There were 17 grants made to 12 organisations (of almost 600 applications received) totalling almost £2.1 million, and were broken down as follows:

Education	6	£1.4 million
Heritage	2	£400,000
Life skills development	1	£250,000
Patient support and treatment	4	£35,000
End-of-life care	4	£23,000

Although no individual beneficiaries are listed in the accounts, the foundation does offer some insight into its grantmaking objectives:

Education
The foundation's objective in its education grant strategy is to enable universal access. However, it will focus on managing its existing grant commitments in this area rather than accepting applications for new grants.

Heritage
[The accounts note that the matched funding commitment to the heritage organisation supported has now ended.] The foundation will not be accepting any new applications from the heritage sector.

Life skills development
The foundation will continue to manage its existing commitments in this area, and is not planning any new grants.

End-of-life care
The foundation remains committed to supporting end-of-life care at the grassroots level.

Patient support and treatment grants were paid to three organisations providing sporting opportunities and support for the disabled.

Exclusions
The foundation will not consider applications from the following:
- Child care
- Citizens Advice
- Community centres
- Higher education
- Housing associations
- Individuals
- Medical research
- Minibuses
- NHS trusts
- Non-departmental government bodies
- Overseas projects
- Primary education
- Scouts, Guides, Brownies, Cubs, and similar organisations
- Secondary education
- Single-faith organisations
- Sports clubs, unless for the mentally or physically disabled
- Village halls
- Youth centres

Applications
The following concise information is taken from the foundation's website:

The February Foundation makes grants to selected charities. It monitors and supports the effective management of grants made. The foundation is focused on managing its current commitments, although applications from some charities are still being accepted.

The accounts also note that:

the trustees will normally award grants to registered charities. Exceptions to this policy will be reviewed on a case-by-case basis in the light of the status of the applicant, its organisational structure (for example, was it established for philanthropic and benevolent purposes), and the requested purpose of the grant.

Email applications are preferred.

Please send details and budget of the proposed project, how many people would benefit, how those benefits might be measured (not just financially), and what the estimated cost of raising funds for the project is. It is important to include in your email application full accounts for your most recent completed financial year, and, if your accounts do not contain it, what your total fundraising costs annually are.

Please note that hardcopy applications take significantly longer to process than email applications. Please do not send DVDs, CDs, glossy brochures or other additional information.

It normally takes 12 weeks from application to applicants being informed of the trustees' decision. There are no application deadlines as trustees make grant decisions on a monthly basis.

Please note that less than 5% of all applications are successful.

Percentage of awards given to new applicants: less than 5%.

Common applicant mistakes
'Sending hard copy; not including accounts; not checking website for eligibility before applying.'

Information gathered from:
Accounts; annual report; Charity Commission record; further information provided by the funder.

The Allan and Nesta Ferguson Charitable Settlement

Peace, education, overseas development
£4 million to organisations (2012)

Beneficial area
UK and overseas.

Correspondent: James Richard Tee, Trustee, Stanley Tee Solicitors, High Street, Bishops Stortford, Hertfordshire CM23 2LU (tel: 01279 755200; email: jrt@stanleytee.co.uk; website: www.fergusontrust.co.uk)

Trustees: Elizabeth Banister; Prof. David Banister; James Richard Tee; Letitia Glaister.

CC Number: 275487

The Allan and Nesta Ferguson Charitable Trust was set up in memory of two generations of the Ferguson family to promote their particular interests in education, international friendship and understanding, and the promotion of world peace and development.

Grants are given to charitable organisations involved in projects supporting the interests of the trust, and also to individual students who are undertaking a gap year or studying for a PhD.

The trust gives the following information for organisations on its website:

Charitable organisations can be situated either in the UK or overseas but must be registered as a charity with the Charity Commission and will principally be educational bodies or aid organisations involved in projects supporting educational and development initiatives, including the promotion of world peace and development. All grants made by the trust are project based and must have an educational aim, element or content. In general the trustees will not consider applications for core funding or the construction of buildings in the UK. Overseas, however, the trustees will consider funding aid projects e.g. water treatment, food and medical supplies or the provision of basic facilities that are the pre-requisite of an educational or development initiative.

Grants made to charities during the year will vary both in size and amount, and will probably total between £5 million and £6 million. The amount of the grant is entirely at the discretion of the trustees and no reason for giving, withholding or offering a partial grant will be made.

Please note:
- Grants to charities will be on a matching funding basis only so that if the applicant has raised 50% of their budget the trustees will consider awarding matching funding up to a maximum of 50%. However, if the

applicant has raised less than 50% of their budget the trustees will only consider awarding a maximum of 30% funding
- Evidence of actively seeking funds from other sources is seen by the trustees as being a beneficial addition to any application

In 2012 the trust had assets of almost £24.5 million and an income of £869,500. Grants were made to organisations totalling £4 million.

Grants were categorised as follows:

Educational projects	£3.65 million
Overseas development	£338,500

Beneficiaries included: Open University (£1 million); University of Manchester and the School of Oriental and African Studies, University of London (£150,000 each); London School of Hygiene and Tropical Medicine (£110,000); Homeless International (£45,000); Mission Aviation Fellowship and Farm Africa (£30,000 each); The Baynards Zambia Trust (£20,000); and the Latin American Mining Monitoring Programme and Third Hope (£15,000 each).

Applications
On an application form available from the trust's website. The following guidance is given by the foundation:

When to apply
- Applications by charities for small to medium grants (up to a maximum of £50,000) may be submitted at any time and will be considered on a regular basis
- Applications for larger grants will be considered at bi-annual meetings held in March and October and applications should be submitted at the very latest in the previous months, i.e. February or September

Please note: No repeat applications will be considered within three years of the conclusion of the grant term.

How to apply
- We prefer where possible that you complete and submit the on-line application form on [the trust's] website and email it to us. Alternatively you may download and print out the application form, complete it and send it by letter post
- Please do not extend the length of the forms, or add any attachments. Applications **MUST NOT** exceed 3 pages. Please use text size 12
- Please do not apply for more than one project

All applications by email will be acknowledged and considered by the trustees within 6 to 8 weeks. If you do not hear further, after the acknowledgement, then unfortunately your application has not been successful. If the trustees do decide to award you a grant then they will contact you. No progress reports will be given and no correspondence will be entered into in the meantime.

Information gathered from:
Accounts; annual report; Charity Commission record; funder's website.

The Fidelity UK Foundation

General, primarily in the fields of arts and culture, community development, education and health

£4.8 million (2012)

Beneficial area
Particular preference is given to projects in Kent, Surrey, London and continental Europe.

Correspondent: Head of Foundations, Oakhill House, 130 Tonbridge Road, Hildenborough, Tonbridge, Kent TN11 9DZ (tel: 01732 777364; website: www.fidelityukfoundation.org)

Trustees: Edward Johnson; Barry Bateman; Anthony Bolton; Richard Millar; John Owen; Sally Walden.

CC Number: 327899

This foundation was established in 1988 to strengthen not-for-profit organisations primarily in regions surrounding Fidelity International's major corporate locations. Particular preference is given to projects in Kent, Surrey and London. Grants from the foundation are made only for charitable purposes and are designed to encourage the highest standards of management and long-term self-reliance in non-profit organisations. Taking an investment approach to grantmaking, it funds organisations where it can add lasting, measurable value. The aim is to support major initiatives that charitable organisations undertake to reach new levels of achievement.

The foundation's charitable giving is mainly in the areas of:
- Arts and culture
- Community development
- Education
- Health

The following information is provided by the foundation on its website:

Investment is typically directed to specific projects in the following categories:
- **Capital improvements** such as new construction, renovations, expansions and equipment which are central to sustainability and the strategic vision of the organisation
- High impact **information technology upgrades** which substantially increase an organisation's efficiency, effectiveness and sustainability
- **Organisational development** projects which seek to establish a new, transformational strategic path. This

can include helping charities to investigate and proceed with mergers
- **Planning initiatives**, including those that use expert/external consultants

Grants will not normally cover the entire cost of a project. We see an organisation's ability to attract support from a broad range of funders as a key sign of its strength and sustainability. Applicants should have significant funding in place prior to application... The foundation typically invests when the majority of required funding has been raised from other sources.

Grants for applicants in London, Kent and Surrey are normally made towards projects with a total budget in excess of £50,000. Applications from Birmingham and Manchester will only be considered for substantial projects. Applicants must normally have annual revenue in excess of £1 million and be applying for a grant of £150,000 or more.

How we assess an applicant
Beyond our basic grant guidelines, we review the organisation to determine whether our investment can add value. Among the factors we consider are the organisation's financial health, the strength of its management team and board, and the quality of its strategic and operational plans.

We also look at the size and scope of the organisation, evaluating its position within the context of its market and the needs of the people and stakeholders it serves. We look for leverage and wider impact. This analysis helps us evaluate if a grant has the realistic potential to measurably improve a charity's impact in its sector, and its sector's potential to bring about fundamental, lasting change.

How we assess a project
We view each project in the context of the organisation's strategy and long-term goals. Funded projects tend to be those which transform the organisation's ability to achieve its mission.

As an investor, we ultimately seek to understand a project's potential social return. We want to understand if it will work and what it will achieve. In evaluating its potential for success, we seek evidence of:
- The extent and nature of the need
- A realistic, transformational uplift in quantitative and qualitative outcomes
- A costed project budget which demonstrates value for money
- A thorough implementation plan, including a plan for performance measurement and evaluation
- Growth in value to the organisation and the community it serves
- Significant support from other funders

Some international grants are made outside the UK by the FIL Foundation, which shares some administration with the Fidelity Foundation. The priorities and restrictions are similar and grants are made to established charities serving beneficiaries in Continental Europe, Australia, Japan, China, Hong Kong, Korea and Taiwan.

Grantmaking in 2012

During the year the foundation held assets of £135 million and had an income of £7.3 million. Grants totalled £4.8 million which was broken down into the following areas:

Arts, Culture and Heritage	13	£1.6 million
Health	6	£1.2 million
Education	8	£1.2 million
Community development	12	£841,000
Other	1	£50,000

Beneficiaries included: Impetus Trust (Early Years Initiative) and Great Ormond Street Hospital Children's Charity (£500,000 each); English Heritage (Stonehenge) (£400,000); The Design Museum and The Shakespeare Globe Trust (£300,000 each); Royal Opera House Foundation (£270,000); City and Guilds of London Art School Property Trust (£150,000); National Council for Voluntary Organisations and New Philanthropy Capital (£50,000 each); FareShare (£47,000); Southbank Centre (£40,000); and Greenhouse Schools Project Ltd (£31,000).

The foundation also gives a helpful breakdown of the type of grants awarded:

Building acquisition/ development/restoration	17	£2.2 million
Equipment	7	£1.2 million
Information technology	9	£725,000
Organisational development/ planning	6	£695,000
Other	1	£10,000

Exclusions

Grants are not generally made to:
▶ Charities that have been in existence for less than three years
▶ Sectarian or political organisations
▶ Schools, colleges, universities or playgroups
▶ Individuals
▶ Community centres
▶ Sports clubs
▶ General appeals and circulars

Grants are not made for:
▶ Salaries or general running/core costs
▶ Training projects
▶ The replacement of dated or out-of-warranty IT equipment
▶ Marketing costs
▶ The promotion of religion
▶ Sponsorships or benefit events
▶ University/college fees, research projects or gap year expeditions

Grants will not normally cover the entire cost of a project. Grants will not normally be awarded to an organisation in successive years. Grants are one-off investments; they will not normally be awarded for or across multiple years. Grants are for planned expenditure; they will not normally cover costs incurred prior to application and/or the grant being awarded.

Applications

In writing to the correspondent. Applicants should enclose a summary form (which can be downloaded from the foundation's website) as well as a separate document outlining:
▶ Organisation history and key achievements
▶ An overview of the organisations forward strategy and key objectives

Project details including:
▶ An indication and evidence of the need for the project that requires funding
▶ An outline of the proposed project, and how it fits into the wider strategic plan
▶ The project's objectives and forecast outcomes
▶ An indication of how the project's success will be monitored and evaluated
▶ An implementation plan/timeline
▶ An itemised budget
▶ The fundraising plan, including a list of other actual/potential funders and the status of each request
▶ An indication of what a grant would allow your organisation to achieve, and how a grant will change or improve the long-term potential and sustainability of your organisation

You should also attach the following:
▶ A list of the directors and trustees with their backgrounds
▶ The most recently audited annual financial statements
▶ The most recent monthly management accounts

There are no deadlines for submitting grant proposals. All applications will normally receive an initial response within three months. The review process can take up to six months, which should be factored into the applicant's funding plan. The foundation may request additional information or a site visit to better familiarise themselves with the organisation, its management team and the project. The foundation welcomes informal phone calls prior to the submission of a formal application.

Applicants for international grants should not use the application form. Instead you should post a brief outline of your organisation and funding proposal. If appropriate the foundation will respond and advise you whether you should make a full application.

Information gathered from:

Accounts; annual report; Charity Commission record; funder's website.

The Sir John Fisher Foundation

General charitable purposes with a preference for the shipping industry, medicine, the navy or military and music and theatre

£1.1 million (2011/12)

Beneficial area

UK, with a preference for charities in the Furness peninsula and adjacent area and local branches of national charities.

Correspondent: Dr David Jackson, Trust Secretary, Heaning Wood, Ulverston, Cumbria LA12 7NZ (tel: 01229 580349; email: info@sirjohnfisherfoundation.org. uk; website: www. sirjohnfisherfoundation.org.uk)

Trustees: Daniel P. Tindall, Chair; Diane S. Meacock; Sir David Hardy; Rowland F. Hart Jackson; Michael J. Shields.

CC Number: 277844

The foundation was established by a deed of settlement made in 1979 by the founders, Sir John and Lady Maria Fisher. The foundation gives grants to charities concerned with the Furness peninsula and local branches of UK charities.

It supports charitable causes and projects in six main categories; these are:
▶ Maritime
▶ Medical and disability
▶ Education
▶ Music
▶ Arts
▶ Naval and military causes
▶ Community projects in and around Barrow-in-Furness

The foundation gives priority to applying its income to community projects and causes based in Barrow-in-Furness and in the surrounding Furness area. Exceptionally, occasional community projects from the remainder of Cumbria and North Lancashire will be considered. Some projects are supported nationally and worldwide, particularly in the fields of music, art and maritime projects. A limited number of high quality medical research is also supported at a national level.

Capital and revenue funding is available for up to three years. Most grants are for less than £10,000.

In 2011/12 the foundation had assets of £47 million and an income of £1.3 million. During the year there were 146 grants made totalling £1.1 million. Grants were broken down as follows:

Local beneficiaries included: Lancaster University (£185,000 in 5 grants); Hospice of St Mary of Furness (£25,000);

The Wordsworth Trust (£20,000); Blackwell Sailing and Lakeland Arts Trust (£15,000 each); Walney Community Trust (£12,000); Citizens Advice – Barrow (£10,400); Age Concern Barrow and District (£10,000); North West Air Ambulance (£9,000); The Mayor's Relief Fund (£4,000); and West Lakeland Orchestral Society (£1,000).

National beneficiaries included: National Maritime Museum (£40,000); Skin Treatment and Research Trust (£37,500); Mary Rose Trust (£25,000); London Handel Society Ltd (£20,000); The English Concert (£15,000); Tall Ships Youth Trust (£8,000); Elizabeth Finn Care (£5,000); Asthma Relief (£3,800); Imperial College (£1,000); and Children in Need (£475).

Exclusions

The trustees will generally not fund:

- Individuals
- Sponsorship
- Expeditions
- Promotion of religion
- Places of worship
- Animal welfare
- Retrospective funding
- Pressure groups
- Community projects outside Barrow-in-Furness and the surrounding area (except occasional projects in Cumbria or North Lancashire or if they fall within one of the other categories supported by the foundation)

Applications

Applications should be made by submitting a completed application form, available on the foundation's website, either by email or post, together with all relevant information (set out on the application form) to the secretary at least six weeks in advance of the trustees' meeting. The trustees meet at the beginning of May and the beginning of November each year. Precise deadline dates are published on the website.

Urgent grants for small amounts (less than £4,000) can be considered between meetings, but the trustees would expect an explanation as to why the application could not be considered at a normal meeting.

Applicants are welcome to contact the secretary for an informal discussion before submitting an application for funding.

The trustees expect to receive feedback from the organisations they support, to help in their decision making process. Organisations are asked to provide a brief one page report about nine months after receipt of a grant (or when the specific project assisted has been completed). A feedback form is also available from the foundation's website.

Information gathered from:
Accounts; annual report; Charity Commission record; funder's website.

Fisherbeck Charitable Trust

Christian, homelessness, welfare, education, heritage
£402,000 (2011/12)

Beneficial area

Worldwide.

Correspondent: Ian Cheal, Trustee, Home Farm House, 63 Ferringham Lane, Ferring, Worthing, West Sussex BN12 5LL (tel: 01903 241027)

Trustees: Ian R. Cheal; Jane Cheal; Matthew Cheal.

CC Number: 1107287

This trust was registered with the Charity Commission in December 2004, and it is the vehicle for the charitable activities of the Cheal family, owners of Roffey Homes developers. The trust's accounts state:

> The charity's objects are to encourage charitable giving from the extended Cheal family and to apply these funds to the making of grants for the following charitable objects:
>
> - The advancement of the Christian religion
> - Support the provision of accommodation for the homeless and meeting their ongoing needs
> - The relief of poverty
> - The advancement of education
> - To encourage conservation of the environment and the preservation of our heritage
> - Such other charitable objects in such manner as the trustees shall from time to time decide

In 2011/12 the trust had assets of £313,000 and an income of £483,000, mostly from donations and gifts. Grants were made to 69 organisations totalling £402,000.

There were 20 grants of £5,000 or more listed in the accounts, with most beneficiaries receiving support each year. Beneficiaries included: Christian Viewpoint for Men (£45,000); Tear Fund (£41,000); Urban Saints (£40,000); Worthing Churches Homeless Project (£30,000); Breakout Trust (£22,000); St Paul's Centre (£20,000); Youth for Christ (£10,000); and Alpha International (£8,000).

Other grants to organisations of under £5,000 totalled £59,000. One individual received a grant of £5,300.

Exclusions

Grants are only made to individuals known to the trust or in exceptional circumstances.

Applications

In writing to the correspondent, although note: 'This is a family run charitable trust. We have a list of charities supported on an annual basis. There is no money available for new applicants – only occasionally, but not very often.'

Percentage of awards given to new applicants: less than 10%.

Common applicant mistakes
'No sae.'

Information gathered from:
Accounts; annual report; Charity Commission record; further information provided by the funder.

The Fishmongers' Company's Charitable Trust

General, in particular education, relief of poverty and disability
£527,000 (2012)

Beneficial area

UK, however this refers to charities whose objects extend throughout England. Special interest in the City of London and its adjacent boroughs.

Correspondent: Peter Woodward, Assistant Clerk, The Fishmongers' Company, Fishmongers' Hall, London Bridge, London EC4R 9EL (tel: 020 7626 3531; fax: 020 7929 1389; email: ct@ fishhall.org.uk; website: www.fishhall.org.uk)

Trustees: The Worshipful Company of Fishmongers; Peter Woodward.

CC Number: 263690

The trust was established in 1972 for general charitable purposes and its focus is in the areas of education, relief of poverty and disability, fishery related organisations, the environment and heritage.

The trust provides the following guidelines for applicants:

- Applications will be accepted only from charities operating within the City of London and the boroughs of Camden, Hackney, Islington, Lambeth, Southwark, Tower Hamlets and Westminster
- Applications will be accepted from charities concerned with education, the relief of hardship and disability, heritage and the environment. Preference will be given to education
- Applications will normally be accepted only from charities whose annual income does not exceed £500,000

▶ Preference will be given to applications where the Company's donation would make a significant impact

▶ Preference will be given to charities seeking to raise funds for a specific project rather than for administration or general purposes

▶ Applications from individual educational establishments will be accepted only if they are either of national importance or if their principal purpose is to cater for disabled students

▶ Donations will normally be made on a one-off basis, although successful applicants may re-apply after three years

Grants for fishermen's welfare charities, promoting the Christian faith among people engaged in the fish and fishing industries and for medical scholarships are also made.

The 2012 accounts note that:

A review of the policy for smaller grants means that there is more of a focus on funding small organisations in the boroughs immediately adjoining the City of London. During 2013 the trustees expect to merge around forty small trusts, which share the Fishmongers' Company as a common trustee, into the charitable trust.

At the end of 2012 the trust took control of the assets (£731,000) of the Elizabeth Garrett Anderson Trust which is now held as a restricted fund with the aims of the EGA Trust. These are:

◗ The payment of bursaries of selected amounts to enable suitable women of insufficient means to receive training for the medical profession at recognised medical colleges or institutions

◗ In assisting such women to attend colleges, institutions or classes by paying their fees or travelling or other incidental expenses or by providing them with maintenance allowances

◗ For other such charitable purposes in connection with the education of women as the trustee in its absolute discretion from time to time thinks fit

In 2012 the trust had assets of £19.2 million and an income of £1.5 million. Grants were made to organisations totalling £527,000, and were broken down as follows:

Education	£437,000
Hardship	£32,000
Heritage and environment	£25,000
Fisheries	£24,000
Disability and medical	£9,700

The largest beneficiary was The Gresham Foundation which received a grant of £205,000. The Gresham Foundation has been a regular recipient of support for the last five centuries and Gresham's School also received a grant of £38,000.

Other beneficiaries included: New Model School (£34,000); Thames Diamond Jubilee Foundation and Redlands Primary School (£10,000 each); Sustainable Eel group (£9,000); London Youth Rowing (£8,400); Countryside Alliance Foundation and Fishermen's' Mission (£5,000 each); Pavilion Opera Education Trust (£3,000); Corda and The Liver Group (£1,750 each); and Mission to Seafarers, Shadwell Basin Outdoor Activity Centre and Southwark Cathedral Development Trust (£1,000 each).

The trust also made grants totalling £750 to individuals.

Exclusions

No grants to individuals except for educational purposes. Ad hoc educational grants are not awarded to applicants who are over 19 years old.

Applications

In writing to the correspondent. Meetings take place three times a year in March, June/July and October/November, and applications should be received a month in advance. No applications are considered within three years of a previous grant application being successful. Unsuccessful applications are not acknowledged.

Information gathered from:

Accounts; annual report; Charity Commission record; funder's website.

The Football Association Youth Trust

Sports
£500,000 (2011/12)

Beneficial area

UK.

Correspondent: Richard McDermott, Secretary, Wembley National Stadium Ltd., PO Box 1966, London SW1P 9EQ (tel: 0844 980 8200 ext. 6575; email: richard.mcdermott@thefa.com)

Trustees: Raymond Berridge; Barry Bright; Geoff Thompson; Mervyn Leggett; Brian Adshead.

CC Number: 265131

The principal activity of the trust continues to be the organisation or provision of facilities which will enable pupils of schools and universities and young people under the age of 21 in the UK to play association football or other games and sports including the provision of equipment, lectures, training colleges, playing fields or indoor accommodation.

In 2011/12 the trust had an income of £10,400 and a total expenditure of £591,000. No more information was available for this year. However, previous research suggests the grant total was about £500,000.

In the previous financial year grants were made totalling £1.3 million and were broken down as follows:

Girls Centre of Excellence	1	£1 million
Schools and universities	4	£204,500
County Football Associations	48	£77,500
Other	2	£1,300

Applications

In writing to the correspondent. Grants are made throughout the year. There are no application forms, but a copy of the most recent accounts should be sent.

Information gathered from:

Charity Commission record.

The Football Foundation

Grassroots football, community, education
£16.8 million (2011/12)

Beneficial area

England.

Correspondent: Effie Chrysanthou, Whittington House, 19–30 Alfred Place, London WC1E 7EA (tel: 0845 345 4555; fax: 0845 345 7057; email: enquiries@ footballfoundation.org.uk; website: www. footballfoundation.org.uk)

Trustees: Richard Scudamore; Roger Burden; Peter McCormick; Philip Smith; Richard Caborn; Jonathan Hall; Gary Hoffman.

CC Number: 1079309

The Football Foundation is the UK's largest sports charity funded by the Premier League, The FA, Sport England and the Government. Funds are occasionally provided by corporate partners.

The foundation's objectives are:

◗ To put into place a new generation of modern facilities in parks, local leagues and schools

◗ To provide capital/revenue support to increase participation in grassroots football

◗ To strengthen the links between football and the community and to harness its potential as a force for good in society

Programmes

The foundation aims to achieve its objectives through a number of programmes, short descriptions of which are included below. However, **note that these are not full descriptions**. These can be found on the foundation's website along with detailed application instructions and terms. New schemes often open and usually due to popularity schemes can close at short notice so check the website for further details.

Facilities Scheme

The facilities scheme gives grants for projects that:

- Improve facilities for football and other sport in local communities
- Sustain or increase participation amongst children and adults, regardless of background age, or ability
- Help children and adults to develop their physical, mental, social and moral capacities through regular participation in sport

The types of facilities we give money for include:

- Grass pitches drainage/improvements
- Pavilions, clubhouses and changing rooms
- Artificial turf pitches and multi-use games areas
- Fixed floodlights for artificial pitches

The maximum grant available from the foundation for each facilities project is £500,000. Applicants must demonstrate a financial need for grant aid and contribute all of their available money to the project. We also expect financial

The latest accounts also note:

The facilities programme aims to target 40% of total investment into 20% of the most disadvantaged communities in the country. It also seeks to ensure that at least a third of funded sites are multi-sport environments, defined as a third of participants taking part in a sport other than football.

Build the Game

The Build the Game scheme provides grants for small facility projects.

The scheme has flexible criteria and there are many eligible items, so long as it is the right project for the right applicant. All projects must demonstrate they can support the growth and retention of grassroots football.

A project that is considered to be an annual running cost, does not have appropriate insurance or meet basic child protection or health and safety requirements will not be eligible for grant aid.

The maximum grant available is £100,000 and there is no limit to the total cost of a project this could contribute towards. Applicants must demonstrate a financial need for grant aid and contribute all of their own available money to the project. Financial contributions from other funding organisations are also expected.

All applicants must receive advice and support from their County Football Association before applying, or they will be returned.

Grow the Game

Grow the Game provides funding up to £5,000 for projects that use football to increase participation by both players and volunteers. This is done by

supporting the costs associated with providing **new** activity.

Applications are welcome from organisations that are 'not for profit' and planning to set up two new football teams over the next two years. We will not fund individuals or educational establishments.

Organisations must have a signed constitution, child protection policy, equal opportunities policy and income/expenditure records.

Please note organisations that have an existing Community Small Grant or Grow the Game grant are not eligible to apply for a Grow the Game grant.

Grow the Game provides funding to contribute towards a combination of the following essential costs associated with providing new football activity:

- Facility hire
- Hire of FA qualified coaches
- Referees fees
- CRB checks
- Affiliation fees
- League entry
- First aid kits
- Promotion and publicity
- FA coaching courses
- Additional courses

Check the foundation's website for the current status of the scheme and application deadlines.

Football Stadia Improvement Fund

The Football Stadia Improvement Fund (FSIF) provides grant aid to clubs in the Football League, National League System and Women's National League System that want to improve their facilities for players, officials and spectators.

The Football Stadia Improvement website (separate from the Football Foundation site: www.fsif.co.uk/funding) offers highly detailed advice, including guidance on what is and is not funded as well as maximum eligible amounts per club (dependant on step). Consult the relevant page on the website before applying.

Also see 'Accessible Stadia', a good practice guide to the design of facilities that meet the needs of disabled spectators and other users. The publication has been funded by the FSIF supporter of the Football Foundation, and the Football Licensing Authority (FLA).

Mayor of London: Facility Fund

The Mayor of London: Facility Fund is part of the Mayor's commitment to deliver a sporting legacy from the 2012 Olympic and Paralympic Games aiming to raise participation levels in sport in London through the funding of new or refurbished sports facilities. The money is provided by the Mayor of London and provides grants which help to develop affordable, good quality local facilities within local communities in London, and is delivered by the Foundation.

The Facility Fund is an integral part of 'A Sporting Future for London', the Mayor's

2012 legacy plan, which was unveiled in 2009 by the London Mayor Boris Johnson and his Commissioner for Sport, Kate Hoey. The plan sets out four key goals:

1. to get more people active
2. to transform the sporting infrastructure
3. to build capacity and skills
4. to maximise the benefits of sport to our society

Eligible projects

- The fund is only open to organisations termed 'not for profit', which includes Community Interest Companies (CIC) and Social Enterprises (SE)
- Facilities must be located within the boundary of the 32 London Boroughs/City of London
- Facilities must be utilised by the local community who reside within the 32 London Boroughs/City of London.

Premier League Community Facility Fund

The Premier League (PL) has committed £6 million per year for the next three years into a ring fenced facility pot, called the Premier League Community Facility Fund (PLCFF), to be accessed by professional clubs through their community organisations and managed and administered by the Football Foundation (FF).

The PLCFF will have the overall aim of providing facilities aligned to professional club community-led inclusion schemes which will serve to increase sports participation and physical activity in deprived, inner city areas.

Premier League Creating Chances has four domestic strands and the PLCFF will contribute to meeting strategic objectives under each of these areas:

- **Community Cohesion** – bring communities together, creating inclusive environments and opportunities that channel the energy and potential of hard to reach (young) people into positive activities that contribute to safer and stronger communities
- **Education** – provide inspirational learning and personal development opportunities that motivate, improve skills, and enhance self-esteem, encouraging educational and entrepreneurial achievement
- **Health** – promote healthy lifestyles, increase physical activity, tackle sensitive health issues and improve wellbeing, changing lives for good in our communities
- **Sports Participation** – widen access to sport and provide pathways that enable (young) people to realise their full potential, experience the sheer enjoyment of taking part and benefit from a more active lifestyle

Youth Football Goalposts

The Foundation's Youth Football Goalposts grants are available to football clubs to cover 50% towards the total cost of purchasing the new smaller goals recommended by the FA for Under-11 and Under-12 matches, which become mandatory for season 2013–14, with money provided by The FA and delivered by the Foundation.

Respect

The FA and Foundation's Respect barriers and Respect packs (made up of captains' armbands, marshals' bibs and Respect Signage) are available to football leagues and clubs to ensure there is good behaviour by players and parents alike in the grassroots game, with money provided by The FA and vouchers supplied by the Foundation.

Grantmaking in 2011/12

In 2011/12 the foundation had a total income of £27.5 million, which included unrestricted income of: £10 million from Sport England; £9.4 million from the Football Association; and £6 million from the Premier League. Grants were made across all programmes totalling £16.8 million (£40.5 million in 2009/10).

Beneficiaries of the largest 100 grants from the following schemes were listed in the accounts, including:

Grassroots grants: FC United of Manchester (£500,000); The Abbey School (£390,000); Stafford Borough Council Civic Centre (£337,000); Glenfield Parish Council (£291,000); Telford College of Arts and Technology (£200,000); The London Playing Fields Foundation (£178,000); Norfolk County FA (£67,000); Norton Cricket Club and Miners Welfare (£51,000); and Gateshead Cleveland Hall Community Football (£26,000).

Premier League Community Facility Fund: Cardiff City FC Community and Education, Manchester United Football Club and Wigan Athletic Community Trust (£350,000 each); and Tottenham Hotspur Community (£259,000).

Mayor of London: Facility Fund: London Borough of Richmond upon Thames (£250,000); University of East London (£200,000); Twickenham Rowing Club (£165,000); St Pancras ABC (£130,000); The Ahoy Centre (£100,000); Stock Exchange Rifle Club (£75,000); Homes for Islington (£50,000); Tottenham Community Sports Centre (£36,000); and Kingston Riding School (£24,000).

Barclays Spaces for Sports: Preston Pirates BMX Club and Silverdale Cricket Club (£25,000); and Coventry City Football Community Scheme and Pompey Sports and Education Foundation (£24,000 each).

Applications

Detailed guidance notes are available on the foundation's website. Applications are submitted online.

Information gathered from:

Accounts; annual report; Charity Commission record; funder's website(s).

Forever Manchester (The Community Foundation for Greater Manchester)

General

£3.5 million (2011/12)

Beneficial area

Greater Manchester.

Correspondent: Awards Team, 2nd Floor, 8 Hewitt Street, Manchester M15 4GB (tel: 01612 140940; fax: 01612 140941; email: info@forevermanchester. com; website: www.forevermanchester. com)

Trustees: Philip Hogben; Simon Webber; Jo Farrell; Han-Son Lee; Sandra Lindsay; Rosamund Hughes; Andrea Harrison; Roushon Siddika Ahmed; Rachel Smith; Shefali Talukdar Henry.

CC Number: 1017504

The foundation's income originates, as with many community foundations, from a range of sources and each fund has its own criteria and conditions. With over 60 funding streams the foundation distributes grants to community groups, projects and social entrepreneurs across Greater Manchester. Many of the groups supported by the foundation have never applied for funding before and are run by volunteers. For easy accessibility to the process, a dedicated grants team has been established. The team gives advice, processes applications and monitors the impact the foundation's grants have in the local community to ensure real needs are met and lives improved.

> Our role is to take calculated risks and invest money from the private, public and statutory sectors into the local communities that make up Greater Manchester, encourage new ideas and provide lasting and sustainable support to the most effective projects. To make real change happen CFGM places its trust in the people who live their lives in these communities and who are best placed to make a difference.

The foundation serves the metropolitan borough areas of Bury, Bolton, Manchester, Oldham, Rochdale, Salford, Stockport, Tameside, Trafford, and Wigan. There are over 12,000 grassroots community projects in the area.

The foundation gives priority to projects which:

▶ Are run by local volunteers who wish to improve the circumstances of individuals and communities in economically/socially excluded and/or deprived areas of Greater Manchester
▶ Have no access to a professional fundraiser and experience difficulty in attracting funding from other sources

▶ Encourage involvement of local residents in improving, designing, identifying and implementing community activities
▶ Promote voluntary participation and social inclusion as well as community involvement and self-help
▶ Meet and demonstrate an emerging or immediate need and serve to build the community's awareness
▶ Do not duplicate an existing provision or service (if the project resembles an existing provision, you will be expected to explain why your services are needed in addition to existing provision or clarify how they are different)

During the year, the foundation had an income of £4.4 million (2010/11: £8.6 million, the reduction due in large part to the Grassroots programme finishing) and assets of £9.4 million. Grants were made totalling £3.5 million (2010/11: £4.5 million).

The foundation manages a large number of different funds, some of which cover the whole of Greater Manchester, such as the Seed Fund, and some of which are specific to separate boroughs. Organisations should check that they fulfil the eligibility conditions before applying and contact the trust if they are unsure. The foundation encourage potential applicants to call and advise that they do not advertise all funds on their website and may therefore be able to advise on other options.

As there are so many different funds, and they are regularly opening and closing for applications or finishing, they are not detailed here. Instead, applicants should check the foundation's website which has straightforward details of each fund.

Grantmaking in 2011/12

During the year, the foundation distributed £3.5 million in grants to 600 community groups and projects with the average grant being £2,700. 64% of funding was in the top 30% of areas in Greater Manchester identified as suffering from high levels of deprivation. Over one third of projects created positive activities for young people.

No grants list was included in the annual report which is disappointing, especially for a fund of this size, however some case studies were available on the website. This is in part a reflection of the ethos of the foundation, which is stated in the CEO's introduction to the 2011/12 accounts:

> CFGM is primarily in the business of building stronger, self-directing communities; accordingly our legacy will be measured not by how many grants we award, but by the increase in the number of people newly involved in community

activity, mutual support and collective community planning.

Beneficiaries included: Shaw Gas Explosion Disaster Relief Fund (£125,000); and Mad Hat Hatters, Singing With Dementia, St Willibrord's Primary School Breakfast Club, Great Lever Voice, Lostock Skate Park, MaD Theatre Company and The Life Centre.

Exclusions

The foundation will not support the following:

▶ Organisations and projects outside the Greater Manchester area
▶ Organisations trading for profit or intending to redistribute grant awards
▶ Major capital requests, i.e. building and construction work
▶ Requests that will replace or enhance statutory provision
▶ Academic or medical research and equipment
▶ Overseas travel
▶ Promotion of religious or political beliefs
▶ Retrospective grants
▶ Projects that fall within statutory sector responsibility
▶ Sponsorship or fundraising events
▶ Contributions to large/major appeals (where the application sum would not cover at least 75% of the total project cost)
▶ Holidays and social outings (except in cases of specific disablement or proven benefit to a community or group of people)
▶ Local branches of national charities unless locally managed, financially autonomous and not beneficiaries of national marketing or promotion
▶ More than one application at a time for the same project
▶ Organisations with an income of over £150,000 per annum
▶ Organisations without a governing document/constitution

Applications

The foundation have now changed policies and ask that interested parties contact them via telephone to discuss eligibility and project ideas. They can also send out application packs.

Decisions are almost always given within three months but the exact time will often depend on a number of factors and not just when the appropriate committee next meets.

One of the grants administrators may contact you for further information or to discuss your application. Contact the foundation directly for up-to-date information on deadlines for programmes and the dates of panel meetings.

Information gathered from:

Accounts; annual report; annual review; Charity Commission record; funder's website.

The Donald Forrester Trust

General charitable purposes
£800,000 (2011/12)

Beneficial area

UK and overseas.

Correspondent: Christopher A. Perkins, Trustee, Lancaster House, 7 Elmfield Road, Bromley, Kent BR1 1LT (tel: 020 8461 8014)

Trustees: Wendy J. Forrester, Anthony J. Smee; Michael B. Jones; Hilary J. Porter; Christopher A. Perkins.

CC Number: 295833

When Donald Forrester, a successful London business man and company director, died in 1985, his widow Gwyneth set up the Donald Forrester Charitable Trust which was established in 1986. The trust's grantmaking now covers a wide range of categories. Most grants go to well known (and often, though not exclusively, national) charities.

The trust is, for the most part, reliant on income from Films and Equipments Ltd and the increased gift aid and the maintained dividend from the company has allowed the trust to continue to increase total charitable giving.

In 2011/12 the trust had assets of £7.7 million and an income of £807,000. Grants totalled £800,000 (£745,000 in 2010/11) awarded to 103 organisations.

Grants were broken down as follows:

Special 25h Anniversary Grant	1	£250,000
Overseas	15	£90,000
Physical and mental disability	14	£70,000
Children and youth (social welfare and education)	9	£60,000
Community care and social welfare	11	£55,000
Medical relief and welfare	11	£55,000
Hospices and hospitals	7	£40,000
Medical research	8	£40,000
Services and ex-services	8	£40,000
Culture, heritages, environment and sport	3	£20,000
Blind and deaf	3	£15,000
Children and youth (medical)	3	£15,000
Maritime	3	£15,000
Elderly welfare	3	£15,000
Other	3	£15,000
Animals and birds	1	£5,000

Most of the beneficiaries received grants for £5,000; however, one significantly large grant of £250,000 was given as a special 25th Anniversary Grant to The Stroke Association for their Life After Stroke Centre near Birmingham. Other beneficiaries across all categories included: Churcher's College 1722 Society (£20,000); Agents of Change (£15,000); The Blue Cross, Hearing Link, Catch 22, Royal Masonic School for Girls, Church Army, FareShare, Peace Hospice, The Music Therapy Charity, Remedi, MIND, Age UK Hillingdon, Mary's Meals, Royal Star and Garter Home and Small Charities Coalition (£5,000 each).

Exclusions

No grants to individuals.

Applications

The trust supports a substantial number of charities on a regular basis. We are informed that regrettably, detailed applications, which place 'an intolerable strain' on administrative resources, cannot be considered. It is suggested that very brief details of an application should be submitted to the correspondent on one side of A4. Do not send accounts or other information.

The trustees normally meet twice a year to consider and agree on the grants which are paid half yearly. Applications should be submitted before 15 January and 15 August to be considered. There are no specific requirements under the trust deed and over the years the trustees have supported a wide range of national and international charities and endeavoured to achieve a balance between the large institutions and the smaller charities that experience greater difficulty in fundraising. The trustees have developed a fairly substantial list of charities that are supported on a regular basis, but new proposals, both regular and 'one-off' are considered at each meeting.

Percentage of awards given to new applicants: less than 10%.

Common applicant mistakes

'Sending too much information and using impenetrable business jargon.'

Information gathered from:

Accounts; annual report; Charity Commission record; further information provided by the funder.

Gwyneth Forrester Trust

General
£330,000 (2011/12)

Beneficial area

England and Wales.

Correspondent: Christopher Perkins, Trustee, Lancaster House, 7 Elmfield Road, Bromley, Kent BR1 1LT (tel: 020 8461 8014)

Trustees: Wendy J. Forrester; Anthony J. Smee; Michael B. Jones; Christopher Perkins.

CC Number: 1080921

Established in May 2000, the trustees support a specific charitable sector each year.

In 2011/12 the trust had assets of £21.1 million and an income of £366,000. Grants were made to six organisations during the year totalling £330,000. During the year the trust focused on organisations helping deaf and blind people. Previously they have assisted Age related causes (2010/11) and research into strokes and heart disease and charities helping sufferers of those conditions (2009/10). Beneficiaries were: Hearing Dogs for Deaf People, Mary Hare Foundation and Sense (£60,000 each); and Fight for Sight, Royal London Society for the Blind and The Macular Disease Society (£50,000 each).

No information was available on the future focus of the trust's grantmaking as 'once the charitable sector is chosen, we research that sector and produce a list of possibles and then contact the individual charities to discuss with them their particular needs and any specific projects they have in hand. These are then discussed and the final grant list is decided'.

Exclusions
No grants to individuals.

Applications
The trust has previously stated that 'applications for aid cannot be considered'.

Information gathered from:
Accounts; annual report; Charity Commission record.

The Foyle Foundation

Arts and learning
£5.3 million (2012)

Beneficial area
UK.

Correspondent: David Hall, Chief Executive, Rugby Chambers, 2 Rugby Street, London WC1N 3QU (tel: 020 7430 9119; fax: 020 7430 9830; email: info@foylefoundation.org.uk; website: www.foylefoundation.org.uk)

Trustees: Michael Smith; Kathryn Skoyles; Sir Peter Duffell; Roy Amlot; James Korner.

CC Number: 1081766

Summary
The foundation was formed under the will of the late Christina Foyle. She was the daughter of William Foyle who, with his brother, founded the family owned bookshop Foyles in Charing Cross Road, London, which she managed after her father's death. The foundation is an independent charity and there is no connection with Foyle's Bookshop.

The foundation makes around 200 grants each year, most of which are for between £10,000 and £50,000, in the fields of arts and learning.

Guidelines
The foundation has a main grants scheme and a small grants scheme, and provides the following guidelines:

Main Grants Scheme
Arts

The foundation seeks applications that make a strong artistic case for support in either the performing or visual arts. Our Arts programme has a twofold purpose to help sustain the arts and to support projects that particularly help to deliver artistic vision. We look for value for money and sustainability in projects that we support. Typical areas of support include:

▷ Helping to make the arts more accessible by developing new audiences, supporting tours, festivals and arts educational projects
▷ Encouraging new work and supporting young and emerging artists
▷ Building projects that improve or re-equip existing arts venues (rather than construction of new facilities, although this will not be excluded)
▷ Projects that reduce overheads or which help generate additional revenue

Generally, we make grants for specific projects/activities. We will consider applications for core funding (but generally only from smaller organisations or from those not receiving recurrent revenue funding from the Arts Council or local authorities).

Please note that community arts activity will not generally be supported.

Learning
The foundation will support projects which facilitate the acquisition of knowledge and which have a long-term strategic impact. Key areas for support are:

▷ Libraries, museums and archives
▷ Special educational needs and learning difficulties
▷ Projects that reduce overheads or which help generate additional revenue will also be considered

For state funded schools our main initiative will be The Foyle School Libraries Scheme [special guidance notes are available from the foundation's website]. Dedicated schools catering for those with Special Educational Needs (SEN) may also be supported. Private schools will not generally be supported.

Citizenship, esteem-building, training, skills acquisition to aid employment, independent living, early learning projects or playgroups will not generally be considered.

Small Grants Scheme
Our Small Grants Scheme is designed to support smaller charities in the UK, especially those working at grass roots and local community level, in any field, across a wide range of activities. Please note we are not able to support individuals.

Applications are welcomed from charities that have an annual turnover of less than £100,000 per annum. Larger or national charities will normally not be considered under this scheme. Nor will the Scheme generally support charities that are able consistently to generate operational surpluses or which have been able to build up unrestricted reserves to a level equivalent to three months turnover.

If applying on behalf of a state school please refer to the foundation's website.

Please note that competition for funding is intense and we receive many more applications that we are able to fund.

Grantmaking in 2012
In 2012 the foundation had assets of £72.2 million and an income of £3.4 million. There were 341 grants made during the year totalling £5.3 million. Grants paid during the year and those committed to future years were broken down as follows:

Arts	£2.52 million
Learning	£2.46 million
Small grants	£515,000

Beneficiaries included: Chichester Festival Theatre (£300,000), towards the theatre's 50th Anniversary capital redevelopment; Battle of Britain Memorial Trust (£200,000), towards the construction and development costs of 'The Wing', a new visitor centre at the national memorial; York Museums Trust (£150,000), towards the redevelopment of York Art Gallery; Square Chapel Trust, Halifax (£100,000), towards the Cornerstone capital development project to expand facilities at the arts venue, including a new 108 seat multi-purpose auditorium; Chichester Harbour Trust (£10,000), towards the ongoing improvement and maintenance of land; National Hospital for Neurology and Neurosurgery Development Foundation (£10,000), towards the National Brain Appeal as part of its participation in the Big Give Christmas Challenge 2011; New Belve Youth and Community Sports Centre Ltd, Liverpool (£8,000), to fund a new part-time Leisure Assistant post for 12 months; Association for Post Natal Illness (£7,500), towards running costs to support women suffering with post-natal depression; Norfolk Concerts (£6,000), towards an expansion of the music programme for young people; Boreland Village Hall (£5,000), towards phase 2 of a refurbishment project; Fairway Fife (£5,000), towards the cost of one of the Activity Coordinators; Purbeck Art Week Festival (£3,500), towards a workshop and performance by Gabrieli Consort and Players as part of the Festival; The Penytrip Project, Porthmadog (£2,000), towards core costs; and Westminster Division Guide Association (£1,000), to cover the costs of renting a school premises for two evenings a week.

Exclusions

No grants to individuals, organisations which are not registered charities or for international work. No retrospective funding.

Applications

The foundation provides the following information on its website:

Please note that competition is intense; we receive many more applications than we are able to fund. Also the foundation only supports charities and is not able to support individuals.

Guidelines and application forms are available [from the foundation's website]. Charities wishing to make an application for funding should download and read the appropriate guidelines for applicants before completing and signing the appropriate application form and sending this together with the supporting information requested.

Applications are acknowledged by email or by post within two weeks of receipt. If you do not receive this acknowledgement, please contact the foundation to confirm safe receipt of your request.

When to Apply

Applications are accepted all year round. We have no deadlines. Except for capital projects, it may take up to four months, occasionally longer, to receive a decision from the trustees, so please apply well in advance of your funding requirements.

Capital Projects

Please note for capital projects seeking more than £50,000 the foundation will now only consider these twice per year in the spring and autumn. Therefore it could be six months or more before we take a decision on your project.

Small Grants Scheme

How much can you apply for?
We plan to make one year grants of between £1,000 and £10,000 to charities which can demonstrate that such a grant will make a significant difference to their work. If you cannot demonstrate this, your application will be declined. No multi-year funding awards will be made.

Other Information

There are no deadlines for submission. Applications will be received at all times but it may take up to four months to obtain a decision from trustees. Please apply well in advance of your requirements.

All applications will be acknowledged but in order to reduce administration, usually we will not send declination letters. If you have not heard from the foundation within four months of your application being

acknowledged, you should assume that your application has been unsuccessful.

Percentage of awards given to new applicants: between 40% and 50%.

Common applicant mistakes

'They do not answer the questions we ask in our guidelines. They do not send financial information.'

Information gathered from:

Accounts; annual report; Charity Commission record; further information provided by the funder; funder's website.

The Hugh Fraser Foundation

General

£2 million (2011/12)

Beneficial area

UK, especially western or deprived areas of Scotland.

Correspondent: Katrina Muir, Trust Administrator, Turcan Connell, Princes Exchange, 1 Earl Grey Street, Edinburgh EH3 9EE (tel: 01312 288111)

Trustees: Dr Kenneth Chrystie; Patricia Fraser; Belinda Hanson; Gordon Shearer; Heather Thompson.

SC Number: SC009303

This foundation was established in 1960 with general charitable purposes. It was founded by Hugh Fraser, responsible for developing his father's shop into the retail chain now known as House of Fraser. Its annual accounts give the following guidance on the general grantmaking policy:

It is the aim of the trustees to help where possible mainly in the areas where the local economy and/or other circumstances make fundraising for charitable purposes difficult.

The trustees' policy is to support a broad range of charitable projects particularly in Scotland but also elsewhere at the discretion of the trustees.

The trustees consider that grants to large, highly publicised national appeals are not likely to be as effective a use of funds as grants to smaller and more focused charitable appeals.

The trustees also consider that better use of the funds can be made by making grants to charitable bodies to assist them with their work, than by making a large number of grants to individuals.

The trustees are prepared to enter into commitments over a period of time by making grants in successive years, often to assist in new initiatives which can maintain their own momentum once they have been established for a few years.

The foundation makes donations to charities working in many different sectors principally hospitals, schools and universities, arts organisations and

organisations working with the disabled, the underprivileged and the aged.

Note: In 2007 the Hugh Fraser Foundation merged with the Emily Fraser Trust, a related charity. As a result, the trustees will, in exceptional circumstances, help individuals and the dependents of individuals who were or are engaged in the drapery and allied trades and the printing, publishing, books and stationery, newspaper and allied trades in the UK.

In 2011/12 the foundation had assets of £57.9 million and an income of £1.9 million. Grants paid during the year totalled £2 million; this included £32,000 paid to 12 individuals. Consultancy fees of £10,900 were paid to a company directed by one of the trustees.

The foundation provided the following analysis of grants to institutions which includes future commitments and pledges:

Education and training	40	£581,000
Disadvantaged and disabled	145	£459,000
Medical research facilities	39	£355,000
Musical, theatrical and visual arts	40	£141,000
Elderly, homeless and hospices	35	£113,000
Youth organisations	24	£93,000
Conservation and environment	20	£49,000
Religion	12	£40,000
Miscellaneous	18	£141,000

The beneficiaries listed in the accounts were: Riverside Museum Appeal (£250,000); Inspiring Scotland (£200,000); University of Strathclyde and Beatson Pebble Appeal (£100,000 each); National Museums Scotland (£50,000); and Miss Margaret Kerr Charitable Trust (£40,000).

Exclusions

Grants are only awarded to individuals in exceptional circumstances (see 'general'). No grants to organisations which are not registered charities or non-profit making.

Applications

In writing to the correspondent describing the project and including a budget, if appropriate. Applications should also include either a copy of your latest formal accounts if prepared or a copy of your most recent balance sheet, income and expenditure account or bank statement if formal accounts are not prepared. If you are not a registered charity you should also enclose a copy of your constitution or policy statement. The trustees meet quarterly to consider applications in March, June, September and December. Applications should be received early in the preceding month in order to be considered.

Information gathered from:

Annual report and accounts provided by funder.

The Freemasons' Grand Charity

Social welfare, medical research, hospices and overseas emergency aid

£2.5 million in non-Masonic grants (2011/12)

Beneficial area

England, Wales and overseas.

Correspondent: Laura Chapman, Chief Executive, Freemasons Hall, 60 Great Queen Street, London WC2B 5AZ (tel: 020 7395 9261; fax: 020 7395 9295; email: info@the-grand-charity.org; website: www.grandcharity.org)

Trustees: Grahame Elliott; Roderic Mitchell; Peter Griffiths; Sir Stuart Hampson; Ian MacBeth; Charles Assad Akle; Dr Richard Dunstan; Geoff Tuck; Terry Baker; Dr Kevin Williams; Nigel Pett; Anthony Wood; Timothy Dallas-Chapman; Judge Hone; Roger Needham; Alexander Stewart; Christopher Grove; Michael Daws; Ian Johnson; Roy Skinner; Ryland James; Simon Duckworth; Anthony Wood; Ernest Skidmore; Wayne Smith; Guy Elgood; Nigel Buchanan.

CC Number: 281942

This is the central charity of all freemasons in England and Wales. It provides grants for four purposes:

▶ The relief of 'poor and distressed freemasons' and their dependents
▶ The support of other Masonic charities
▶ Emergency relief work worldwide
▶ The support of non-Masonic charities in England and Wales

Guidelines

The following guidance is provided by the charity:

Charities can apply for grants in the following areas:
▶ Medical research
▶ Support for vulnerable people
▶ Youth opportunities

The organisations supported by the Grand Charity are chosen because they aim to make a significant difference to people in need, provide maximum impact by benefitting as many people as possible and support issues that individual Freemasons and their families are concerned about and will be glad to help.

The charity also provides funding to:
▶ Hospice services
▶ Air ambulance charities
▶ Worldwide disaster relief

Vulnerable People

The Support for Vulnerable People category encompasses organisations that help people with a wide variety of problems including: disability, care for the seriously ill, care for older people, deprivation, homelessness and poverty. Grants might fund a salary or deliver a specific project. Grants may be made for capital projects provided that the application is for an identifiable element of the project.

Any request for project funding will need to include a detailed project plan, budget, timetable, objectives, milestones and intended outcomes. Evidence of successful outcomes will need to be provided with applications for on-going projects. Funding may be granted for up to three-year periods in certain circumstances where there is evidence of an on-going need for charitable grant funding.

Youth Opportunities

Youth Opportunities Grants are focused on disadvantaged young people, usually between the ages of 16 and 25, in rural and urban areas. Grants might fund a salary or deliver a specific project. Grants may be made for capital projects provided that the application is for an identifiable element of the project. Any request for project funding will need to include a detailed project plan, budget, timetable, objectives, milestones and intended outcomes.

Evidence of successful outcomes will need to be provided with applications for on-going projects. Funding may be granted for up to three-year periods in certain circumstances where there is evidence of an on-going need for charitable grant funding.

Grants to support youth opportunities and vulnerable people are made as follows:

Major Grants

Major grants are usually between £10,000 – £50,000.

Major grants are made for a specific purpose only and are given to well established, nationwide charities.

Reasons to apply for a major grant include funding salary costs or to deliver a specific project, including capital development projects.

Funding may be granted for up to three-year periods in certain circumstances, where there is evidence of an on-going need for charitable grant funding.

Minor Grants

Minor grants can be between £500 – £5,000.

These grants are for smaller, nationwide charities whose annual income does not exceed approximately £1 million.

Minor grants can be used for general running and/or overhead costs of the charity – core funding.

Medical Research

Preference is given to medical research applications from charities that are members of the Association of Medical Research Charities (AMRC). A grant will only be made for a specific research project that has been peer reviewed in accordance with the AMRC guidelines.

The institution carrying out the research project must be located in England or Wales. Funding may be granted for up to three-year periods in certain circumstances. The purpose of the grant might be to fund the salary of a researcher, such as a PhD student, and may include consumables. Generally separate grants are not made to fund pieces of equipment, unless they form part of a larger research project.

An increasing number of university or hospital research departments are making applications for medical research grants. The Freemasons' Grand Charity does not usually fund individual researchers or university research departments directly. However, if you do wish to apply, please use the medical research application form and ensure that you include evidence of external peer review from at least two or three other universities.

Grantmaking in 2011/12

In 2011/12 the charity had assets of £61.4 million and an income of £15.8 million. Grants were made to 419 non-Masonic organisations totalling just over £2.5 million, and were broken down as follows:

Vulnerable people (inc. Air Ambulances)	47	£974,000
Hospices	239	£600,000
Youth opportunities	9	£566,000
Medical research	5	£195,000
Small grants	116	£160,000
Emergency grants	3	£30,000

Beneficiaries included: The Prince's Trust (£250,000); Tomorrow's People (£90,000); Diabetes UK (£60,000); Help for Heroes (£50,000); Outward Bound and the Rainbow Trust Children's Charity (£30,000 each); Jubilee Sailing Trust (£25,000); East Anglian Air Ambulance (£16,000); Addington Fund (£15,000); North West Air Ambulance (£12,000); St Christopher's Hospice (£8,000); Earl Mountbatten Hospice and Envision (£3,000 each); Disability Law Service (£2,000); Shelter Cymru (£1,500); and the Dwarf Sports Association (£1,000).

Exclusions

Local charities (i.e. serving an individual city or region) should apply to the provincial grand lodge of the region in which they operate, (these are listed in telephone directories, usually under 'freemasons' or 'masons').

Those not eligible for a grant are:

▶ Individuals (other than for the relief of 'poor and distressed freemasons and their poor and distressed dependents')
▶ Charities that serve an individual region or city, for example, a regional hospital, local church, day centre or primary school
▶ Organisations not registered with the Charity Commission, except some exempt charities

- Activities that are primarily the responsibility of central or local government or some other responsible body
- Organisations or projects outside of England and Wales
- Animal welfare, the arts or environmental causes
- Charities with sectarian or political objectives
- Charities that are deemed to hold funds in excess of their requirements

Applications

Application forms are available from the charity's office or from its website. This form must be completed in full accompanied by a copy of the latest annual report and full audited accounts; these must be less than 18 months old.

Hospice grant applications are made on a separate form, available from either the appropriate provincial grand lodge or the trust's office.

Applications may be submitted at any time throughout the year and are considered at meetings held in January, April and July. Acknowledgement of receipt will be made by post.

Applications are not accepted for 'emergency grants' which are made as 'the need arises' and at the trustees' discretion.

Common applicant mistakes

'They do not read the guidelines and they forget to sign their applications.'

Information gathered from:

Accounts; annual report; Charity Commission record; further information provided by the funder; funder's website.

The Freshfield Foundation

Environment, healthcare, sustainable development and overseas disaster relief
£631,000 (2011/12)

Beneficial area

UK and overseas.

Correspondent: Paul Kurthausen, Trustee, BWMacfarlane LLP, Castle Chambers, 43 Castle Street L2 9SH (tel: 01512 361494; fax: 01512 361095; email: paul.k@bwm.co.uk)

Trustees: Paul Kurthausen; Patrick A. Moores; Elizabeth J. Potter.

CC Number: 1003316

The foundation was established in 1991, and aims to support organisations involved in sustainable development and overseas disaster relief.

In 2011/12 the foundation had assets of £7.3 million and an income of

£1.8 million, which included a donation of almost £1.6 million from the settlor, Patrick Moores. Grants were made totalling £631,000.

The foundation's annual report includes the following information about the trustees' plans for the future:

- Limit the donations to United Kingdom charities involved in sustainable development to £500,000 per annum
- Giving between £100,000 and £500,000 per annum to overseas disaster relief

Further to this, in 2011/12 the foundation made to following commitments:

As described above, the trustees decided to explore the idea of donating to overseas disaster relief. To this end, a grant of £500,000 was made to the Disaster Emergency Committee in May 2011 in response to their appeal for Pakistan.

In the fields of health and education, the charity continued to support the work of Afghan Connection and the Osteopathic Centre for Children for another year by committing grants to them of £10,000 and £40,000 respectively after the year end. The scope of this activity has been broadened considerably to include the making of grants to organisations supporting local communities and those providing assistance to the terminally or mentally ill, the homeless, victims of domestic violence and those with learning disabilities.

Applications

In writing to the correspondent, although the trust states that 'the process of grantmaking starts with the trustees analysing an area of interest, consistent with the charity's aims and objectives, and then proactively looking for charities that they think can make the greatest contribution'. With this in mind, a letter of introduction to your organisation's work may be more appropriate than a formal application for funding.

Information gathered from:

Accounts; annual report; Charity Commission record.

The Gannochy Trust

General
£1.5 million (2011/12)

Beneficial area

Scotland, with a preference for the Perth and Kinross area.

Correspondent: Fiona Russell, Secretary, Kincarrathie House Drive, Pitcullen Crescent, Perth PH2 7HX (tel: 01738 620653; email: admin@gannochytrust.

org.uk; website: www.gannochytrust.org. uk)

Trustees: Dr James H. F. Kynaston, Chair; Mark Webster; Ian W. Macmillan; Stewart N. Macleod; Dr John Markland.

SC Number: SC003133

The Gannochy Trust was founded in 1937 by Arthur Kinmond Bell, known as A K Bell, for charitable and public purposes for the benefit of the community of Perth and its immediate environs as a direct result of his family's successful whisky distilling business.

A K Bell's philanthropy has been developed into one of the more substantial grant-making trusts in Scotland. Originally, the trust contributed to worthy charitable causes solely within Perth and its immediate environs. In 1967 a Scheme of Alterations was approved by the Court of Session to expand its grant-making footprint to the whole of Scotland, but with a preference for Perth and its environs. The trust has made significant contributions to a wide variety of projects across Scotland over many years, ranging from major national flagship projects to smaller, but nonetheless important, community projects.

The trust has four grantmaking themes:
1 Inspiring young people
2 Improving the quality of life of the disadvantaged and vulnerable
3 Supporting and developing community amenities
4 Care for the natural and man-made environment

Note: Themes 3 and 4 are restricted to Perth and Kinross.

In 2011/12 the trust had assets of £128 million and an income of £5.9 million. Grants paid during the year totalled £1.5 million with a further £2.3 million committed for future payment.

Beneficiaries of grants paid or agreed during the year included: Pert and Kinross Heritage Trust and Black Watch Museum Trust (£300,000 each); Perth and Kinross Council Living Communities Project (£247,000); Perth and Kinross Countryside Trust (£200,000); Scottish Opera (£150,000); and Friends of the Birks Cinema (£50,000). The majority of grants (just over £1 million) were made in smaller grants of less than £40,000.

Exclusions

- General applications for funds will not be considered – applications must be specific, and preferably for a project with a defined outcome, not general running costs
- Donations will not be made to individuals.
- Donations will only be made to organisations which meet the OSCR Charity Test.

- Projects where the benefit of a donation will be realised outside Scotland.
- Donations will rarely be made to projects that do not demonstrate an element of self or other funding.
- Donations will not be made that contribute to an organisation's healthy reserves or endowments.
- Applications will seldom be considered for more than a 3-year commitment.
- Applications will not be considered for holidays, with the exception of those for the disabled and disadvantaged living in Perth & Kinross where the project has a tangible recreational or educational theme.
- Applications will not be considered for animal welfare projects, with the exception of wildlife projects within Perth & Kinross that meet the sub-themes within theme 4.
- Applications will not be considered from schools for recreational facilities unless there will be a demonstrable and sustained community involvement, preferably for the disadvantaged or vulnerable.
- Applications from pre-school groups, play schemes, after school clubs and parent-teacher associations.
- Applications will not be considered from cancer and other health-related charities unless they demonstrate that their project directly provides tangible relief from suffering and direct patient benefit.
- Applications from places of worship will not be considered unless there is a distinct community benefit through use as a community centre or village hall, and where there is not a similar facility nearby.
- Applications will not be considered from charities re-applying within a year of their previous appeal or award, or instalment thereof.
- Applications will not be considered where funding would normally be provided by central or local government.
- Waste disposal/landfill, pollution control and renewable energy projects will not be considered if they are the sole purpose of the project, and unless they meet the criteria within theme 4.
- Applications will not be considered for political or lobbying purposes
- Applications will not be considered from higher or further education establishments unless the project has been initiated by the trustees

Applications

On a form which can be downloaded from the trust's website. The application form also contains detailed guidance notes.

Percentage of awards given to new applicants: between 10% and 20%.

Common applicant mistakes

'Project does not meet current criteria or themes. Do not read guidance notes on information to provide.'

Information gathered from:

Accounts; annual report; OSCR record; further information provided by the funder; funder's website.

The Gatsby Charitable Foundation

General
£42.7 million (2011/12)

Beneficial area
Unrestricted.

Correspondent: Peter Hesketh, Director, The Peak, 5 Wilton Road, London SW1V 1AP (tel: 020 7410 0330; fax: 020 7410 0332; email: contact@gatsby.org.uk; website: www.gatsby.org.uk)

Trustees: Bernard Willis; Sir Andrew Cahn; Judith Portrait.

CC Number: 251988

Summary

This is one of the Sainsbury Family Charitable Trusts, which share a joint administration. It supports organisations that aim to advance policy and practice within its selected areas.

The foundation is proactive and seldom responds to conventional short-term applications – 'trustees generally do not make grants in response to unsolicited appeals' – but it does expect organisations to respond to its published long-term priorities: 'the trustees identify first the areas where they sense that something needs to be done. They hope organisations will respond to these priorities and propose projects.'

Background

This is one of the largest and most interesting grantmaking trusts in the UK, with assets of £291 million and an income of £46.7 million in 2011/12 (£37.3 million in 2010/11), made up of significant donations from the settlor and Lady Sainsbury. It allocates large sums to long-term programmes and so the figure for yearly grant approvals fluctuates considerably. In 2011/12 *grant expenditure given in the statement of accounts*, totalled £42.7 million. The 2011/12 trustees' report states: 'Gatsby has significant unpaid forward commitments totalling £185.4 million. Trustees approved grants amounting to £149.1 million, but made payments of £42.7 million covering some of these

grants, together with others approved in earlier years.'

The foundation was set up in 1967 by David Sainsbury, created life peer and Lord Sainsbury of Turville in 1997. He was a Labour minister with the Department of Trade and Industry until November 2006. He himself has never been a trustee of Gatsby but is still contributing massively to the endowment of the trust (£27 million in 2011/12), and it is generally supposed that the trustees pay close attention to the settlor's wishes. Since leaving his ministerial office, Lord Sainsbury has been able to 're-engage' with the foundation. A substantial part of the foundation's investments are in the form of shares in the Sainsbury company. In over 40 years of grantmaking the Gatsby Charitable Foundation has distributed around £700 million; Lord Sainsbury has stated his intention to give away £1 billion in his lifetime.

General

The following (abbreviated) statement by the settlor, David Sainsbury, is taken from the foundation's 2011/12 annual review:

[2011 saw] the official opening of the Sainsbury Laboratory at Cambridge University. It is now more than eight years since my life-long friend Roger Freedman first fired my enthusiasm for this project with his idea of a laboratory to understand plant development using the power of DNA analysis, genetics, advanced microscopy and computation. That idea has now been realised in Cambridge, in a cutting-edge laboratory housed in a beautiful building elegantly complementing its surroundings in the Botanic Gardens. They have created the perfect conditions for scientists to make exciting discoveries in plant science that could also potentially help the world meet the challenge of feeding nine billion people in 2050.

My involvement with the Cambridge laboratory has left me under no illusion about the scale of the task facing those attempting to bring another of Gatsby's ambitious ideas into reality: our partnership with the Wellcome Trust to develop a new research centre in neural circuits and behaviour. In 2011 the Sainsbury-Wellcome Centre received planning permission and construction began on our largest project to date. The Centre is attempting to meet the challenge of understanding exactly how the brain's neural circuits carry out the information processing that directly underlies behaviour. It is hugely exciting to think of the possible discoveries that await us and might be accelerated by the Centre's opening in 2014.

In 2011 I was particularly pleased to attend the first meeting in Gatsby's history of all of our current neuroscience grantees, and was struck by the diversity of disciplines, nationalities and characters ultimately striving for a common goal. I hope the participants found the three-day symposium as interesting as I did, and that it results in partnerships that may not have happened otherwise.

Elsewhere, economic conditions in the UK in 2011 added an even greater sense of urgency to Gatsby's efforts to strengthen science and engineering skills in the UK workforce. The recession has demonstrated the dangers of an unbalanced economy, while we are also threatened with losing a generation of young people to unemployment. We must ensure that we have an education system capable of supplying individuals with the skills to design, develop and manufacture the high-tech products and services we will need to sell to the rest of the world in the future.

I have been encouraged by productive discussions with John Hayes, the Minister for Further Education, Skills and Lifelong Learning, and look forward to Gatsby working with the Department for Business, Innovation and Skills to explore this area further in the coming year. I am also pleased that Gatsby will be partnering with the Department for Education to provide support for the STEM Clubs Network, an initiative we have long been supportive of, which encourages children to explore science, technology, engineering and maths in a stimulating environment away from the constraints of a prescribed curriculum.

Such partnerships with government remain crucial to Gatsby's programmes in Africa, which are ultimately focused on providing employment and relieving poverty. In 2011 I was delighted to have the opportunity to visit Tanzania to gauge progress on our programme in the cotton and textile sector and to meet the Ministers of Agriculture and Industry to discuss next steps.

In the UK, the changing political and economic landscape highlighted the importance of the two institutions we support through our governance programme. In a time of coalition government, public sector spending cuts and economic uncertainty, the Institute for Government (IfG) and Centre for Cities' non-partisan research and policy advice greatly added to, and informed, public debate.

Finally, I am extremely proud that Gatsby supports the Sainsbury Centre for Visual Arts which my parents established in 1978 and which continues to give such pleasure to the public. It is my great hope that in all the areas in which Gatsby operates we can make similar lasting contributions.

Objectives

The trustees' objectives within their current fields of interest include:

- **Plant Science** – to develop basic research in fundamental processes of plant growth and development and molecular plant pathology, and to encourage researchers in the field of plant science in the UK

- **Neuroscience** – to support world-class research in the area of neural circuits and behaviour, and theoretical neuroscience; and to support activities which enhance our understanding in these fields
- **Science and Engineering Education** – to strengthen science and engineering skills in the UK by developing and enabling innovative programmes and informing national policy
- **Africa** – to promote economic development in East Africa that benefits the poor through support to the growth and sustainability of key sectors
- **Public Policy** – to support: the Institute for Government as an independent institute available to politicians and the civil service, focused on making government more effective; and the Centre for Cities, which provides practical research and policy advice that helps cities understand how they can succeed economically
- **The Arts** – to support the fabric and programming of institutions with which Gatsby's founding family has connections

The trustees occasionally support other charitable work which falls outside their main fields of interest.

The foundation's 2010 annual review states: 'Choosing to focus our support on some areas inevitably means that, over time, we must withdraw from others. In 2009 we decided to bring gradually to a close our support for the Sainsbury Centre for Mental Health (since renamed the Centre for Mental Health). Our commitment to the Centre dates back to its foundation in 1985 and we will continue to support it for the next few years to help ensure its long-term future.'

Within these categories the trustees make grants in support of work which they judge to have particular merit. Many of their grants fund projects which the foundation has helped to initiate. It is the policy of the trustees to evaluate programmes and projects rigorously and carefully, and to assess when the evaluations should most usefully take place.

Generally, the trustees do not make grants in response to unsolicited applications or to individuals.

Grantmaking in 2011/12

Specific areas of support come under the headings shown in the table (with payments from new and previous grants):

Plant Science	£8.9 million
Science and Engineering Education	£2.7 million
Africa	£6.1 million
Neuroscience	£12.7 million
Public Policy	£3.3 million
General	£791,000
The Arts	£5 million
Mental Health	£899,000

Beneficiaries included: Sainsbury-Wellcome Centre for Brain Circuitry (£7.9 million); University of Cambridge (£6.5 million); Institute for Government (£2.5 million); Aquifier Ltd (£1.5 million); Harvard University (£598,000); The Sainsbury Institute for the Study of Japanese Arts and Cultures (£568,000); New Engineering Foundation (£424,000); Rwandan Governance Initiative (£366,000); Society for Neuroscience (£161,000); and the Academy of Ancient Music (£100,000).

There are big annual fluctuations in the size of its new awards each year to different categories of work because of the large multi-year funding commitments decided by the foundation.

Exclusions

No grants to individuals.

Applications

See the entry for the Sainsbury Family Charitable Trusts. Generally, the trustees do not make grants in response to unsolicited applications, although a single application will be considered for support by all the trusts in the group. 'Rather than awaiting proposals from third parties, trustees identify areas for action and build hypotheses for action which can then be tested in the field.'

Information gathered from:

Annual review; accounts; Charity Commission record; funder's website.

The G. C. Gibson Charitable Trust

Art, music and education, health, hospices and medical research, community and other social projects, religion

£471,000 (2011/12)

Beneficial area

UK.

Correspondent: The Trustees, c/o Deloitte, 5 Callaghan Square, Cardiff CF10 5BT (tel: 02920 460000; email: enquiries@gcgct.org; website: www.gcgct.org)

Trustees: Simon Gibson; Jane Marson Gibson; Robert D. Taylor; Martin Gibson; Lucy Kelly; Anna Dalrymple.

CC Number: 258710

The trust was established in 1969 by G C Gibson, now deceased, for general charitable purposes. Grants are given mainly for art, music and education; health, hospices and medical research; community and other social projects and religion.

Whilst the trust will consider donations for capital projects, the average donation of £3,000 is more suited for meeting the revenue commitments of an organisation. Applications are considered from charities working throughout the United Kingdom and preference is given to applications from charities who have already received donations from the trust as the trust recognises the importance of providing recurring donations wherever possible. The website notes: 'funding is provided for many years and the trustees put no restrictions on expenditure. Each year a few appeals are supported and new charities introduced.'

The trust's priorities are described on their website and change every year.

In 2011/12 the trust had assets totalling just under £13 million and an income of £578,000. Grants were made to 151 organisations totalling £471,000, categorised under the following headings (note: grants totalling £484,000 were committed with £13,000 subsequently written back):

Community and other social projects	67	£194,000
Health, hospices and other medical research	43	£159,000
Art, music and education	21	£66,000
Religion	20	£65,000

Beneficiaries included: St Nicholas Hospice – Bury St Edmunds and Leuchie House (£10,000 each); King Edward VII Hospital (£8,000); Marie Curie Cancer Care (£6,000); St David's Cathedral, Campbell Blair Drummond and Riding for the Disabled Mid-West Region (£5,000 each); Arts Active Trust and Bristol Old Vic Theatre (£3,000 each); Jo's Cervical Cancer Trust (£2,000); and Worshipful Company of Pattern Makers Educational Fund (£1,000).

Exclusions
No grants to individuals.

Applications
Online applications open in late summer and stay open for two months, usually August and September. Check in case the criteria have been amended to reflect the new funding round. Initial online applications are assessed and the trustees will contact a shortlist of charities to make a full application via email. Trustees will provide this email address – no postal or telephone applications will be considered.

Charities that have already received support from the trust do not need to reapply.

Payments are made in early December in each year and not at any other time of the year. Payments will be made direct to bank accounts.

Information gathered from:
Accounts; annual report; Charity Commission record; funder's website.

Simon Gibson Charitable Trust

General
£583,000 (2011/12)

Beneficial area
UK, with a preference for East Anglia, South Wales and Hertfordshire.

Correspondent: Bryan Marsh, Trustee, Wild Rose House, Llancarfan, Vale of Glamorgan CF62 3AD (tel: 01446 781459; email: marsh575@btinternet.com)

Trustees: Bryan Marsh; Angela Homfray; George Gibson; Deborah Connor; John Homfray.

CC Number: 269501

The Simon Gibson Charitable Trust was set up by a settlement in 1975 by George Simon Cecil Gibson of Exning, near Newmarket, Suffolk. The trust is a general grantmaking charity and therefore makes grants to the full range of charitable causes, including religious and educational causes. National charities are helped but local charities applying are restricted to East Anglia, South Wales and Hertfordshire. Grants can vary from £1,000 to £25,000 but most grants fall in the range £3,000 to £5,000.

In 2011/12 the trust had assets of almost £13.9 million and an income of £618,500. Grants were made to 120 organisations totalling £583,000.

Beneficiaries included: Royal Welsh College of Music and Drama (£25,000); Sherman Cymru (£15,000); Ely Cathedral Appeal Fund (£10,000); New Astley Club Endowment Fund (£6,000); Army Benevolent Fund, Bumblebee Conservation Trust, Papworth Hospital, Welsh National Opera and the Whale and Dolphin Conservation Society (£5,000 each); Bobath Children's Therapy Centre Wales, Dyslexia Action, Listening Books and West Suffolk Association for the Blind (£3,000 each); and Exning Methodist Church Trustees (£1,000).

Exclusions
No grants or sponsorships for individuals or non-charitable bodies.

Applications
'There are no application forms. Charities applying to the trust should make their application in writing in whatever way they think best presents their cause.' The trust acknowledges all applications but does not enter into correspondence with applicants unless they are awarded a grant. The trustees meet in May and applications should be received by the end of March.

Percentage of awards given to new applicants: between 20% and 30%.

Common applicant mistakes
'Do not follow our criteria; many send far too much information.'

Information gathered from:
Accounts; Charity Commission record; further information provided by the funder.

The Girdlers' Company Charitable Trust

Medicine and health, education, welfare, youth welfare, heritage, environment, humanities and Christian religion
£802,000 (2011/12)

Beneficial area
UK, with a preference for City and East End of London, and Hammersmith and Peckham.

Correspondent: John Gahan, Charities Manager, Girdlers' Hall, Basinghall Avenue, London EC2V 5DD (tel: 020 7638 0488; fax: 020 7628 4030; email: charitiesmanager@girdlers.co.uk; website: www.girdlers.co.uk/html/charitable-giving)

Trustee: Court of the Company of Girdlers.

CC Number: 328026

Established in 1988, the trust's main areas of interest are: medicine and health, education, welfare, youth welfare, heritage, environment, humanities and Christian religion, throughout the UK, with a preference for the City and East End of London, Hammersmith and Peckham. In 2009 the trust received the assets of the Geoffrey Woods Foundation and this was merged with The Girdlers' Company Charitable Trust.

To achieve its objectives the trust donations are made under the following headings:
- Principal, Selected Appeals, Hammersmith and Peckham and General Applications
- New Zealand Scholarship and Fellowship
- Irish Guards
- Jock French Charitable Fund
- Christmas Court Donations
- Master's Fund Donations

The focus of the trust's donations is with its Principal Charities many of which it maintains longstanding and close relationships. This represents around half of the trust's annual donations.

Selected Appeals are one of grants to charities proposed by a member of the Girdlers' Company who has a close personal involvement.

The trust operates an open application process for circa £20,000 of its total grantmaking. Up until April 2013 priority was given to organisations in Hammersmith and Peckham. The trustees are now working with ten organisations who they wish to support on a longer term basis instead of running the open grants programme. Around 20 awards are made, of approximately £1,000, to charities in England and Wales where the charity has an annual income less than £1 million. The guidelines advise that the applicant success rate is around 3% and around half of the general grants are awarded outside London. These general grants can cover core costs, salaries or capital costs.

The trust continues to support New Zealand undergraduate scholarships at Cambridge University and a medical research fellowship at Oxford University.

An annual donation goes to support the Irish Guards' Benevolent Fund and an amount is spent at the direction of the 1st Battalion's Commanding officer to support guardsmen's welfare, adventurous training and sporting activities.

The Jock French Charitable Fund encourages charitable donations from members of the Livery of the Company. The subscribing members are invited to nominate charities to receive donations. The total sum allocated is distributed in November and May each year.

The Master's Fund is allocated an amount each year for the Master to donate to charities of his own choice. A sum is also allocated to Christmas Court Donations for members to nominate donations to charities of their individual choice at Christmas time.

In 2011/12 the trust had assets of £6.6 million and an income of £1.4 million. Grants were made totalling £802,000, and were broken down as follows:

Principal Charities	£413,000
Jock French Charitable Fund	£105,000
New Zealand Scholarships and Fellowship	£105,000
Selected Appeals	£54,000
Christmas Court Charity	£33,000
Irish Guards	£30,000
Hammersmith and Peckham Charities	£26,000
General donations	£21,000
Other	£12,000
Master's Fund	£3,000

Beneficiaries included: Leyton Orient Community Sports Programme

(£60,000); London Youth (£40,000); St Giles Trust (£19,000); Royal School of Needlework (£15,000); Crown and Manor Club – Hoxton, Habitat for Humanity – Southwark and Macmillan Cancer Support (£10,000 each); The Oxford Kilburn Club (£8,000); Disabled Sailors Association (£2,000); The Coldstream Guards Charitable Fund (£1,700); ActionAid – Ethiopia and The Urology Foundation (£1,200 each); Bath Institute of Medical Engineering (£1,100); Vitalise, Institute of Economic Affairs, St Mary's Church – Brook and Lynn Athletic Club (£1,000 each); and Jubilate Choir (£500).

Exclusions

Applications will only be considered from registered charities.

Applications

Applicants should write to the correspondent on letter headed paper. Exempt charities must provide audited accounts. To be considered for a donation cover each of the following points:

> The beneficial area (which trustees support) under which a grant is sought
> A brief summary of the organisation's background and aims
> The specific nature of the request, highlighting the change you wish to bring about
> How you will know if you have achieved these changes
> Your charity registration number

Each April and November the trustee considers general applications with ten donations of approximately £1,000 being made on each occasion. The closing dates are the last Friday in January and August. Successful applicants are unlikely to be awarded a further donation within the following five years.

Successful applicants will be informed in May and December.

The trust states that only around 3% of applicants are successful.

Percentage of awards given to new applicants: over 50% (of awards in the open application process).

Common applicant mistakes

'Not having read the 1-page guidelines beforehand.'

Information gathered from:

Accounts; annual report; Charity Commission record; guidelines for applicants; further information provided by the funder; funder's website.

The Glass-House Trust

Social housing and the urban environment, art and child development
£438,000 (2011/12)

Beneficial area

Unrestricted, but UK in practice.

Correspondent: Alan Bookbinder, Director, The Peak, 5 Wilton Road, London SW1V 1AP (tel: 020 7410 0330; fax: 020 7410 0332; website: www.sfct. org.uk)

Trustees: Alexander Sainsbury; Elinor Sainsbury; Judith Portrait.

CC Number: 1017426

This is one of the Sainsbury Family Charitable Trusts, which share a joint administration. They have in common an approach to grantmaking which is described in the entry for the group as a whole.

It is the trust of Alexander Sainsbury and three of the four other trustees are his brother and sisters, who each have trusts of their own.

In 2011/12 the trust had assets of £11.1 million and income of £475,000. Grants paid during the year totalled £438,000. Grants payable during the year were slightly higher suggesting that not all grants were paid or taken up by the end of the financial year. The breakdown of grants below refers to grants paid:

Built environment	1	£187,500
Child development	4	£100,000
Art	3	£81,000
Older people	1	£35,000
Overseas	1	£18,600
Social Policy	1	£15,000
General	1	£1,300

Beneficiaries included: Glass-House Community Led Design (£200,000); Mayday Rooms (£97,000); A Space (£75,000); Money for Madagascar (£37,000); HACT: The Housing Action Charity (£35,000); Transform Drug Policy Foundation and Resonance FM (£30,000 each); Birkbeck College (£18,000); and Birth Companions (£10,000).

The trust does not consider applications and many of the beneficiaries have been supported on an ongoing basis.

Exclusions

Grants are not normally made to individuals.

Applications

See the guidance for applicants in the entry for the Sainsbury Family Charitable Trusts. A single application will be considered for support by all the trusts in the group. However, in the case of this trust, 'proposals are generally invited by the trustees or initiated at their request. The trustees prefer to support innovative schemes that can be successfully replicated or become self-sustaining.'

Information gathered from:

Accounts; annual report; Charity Commission record; funder's website.

Global Charities

Disadvantaged children, young people and adults

£1.5 million (2011/12)

Beneficial area

Greater London; UK.

Correspondent: Leah Hayden, Administrator, 30 Leicester Square, London WC2H 7LA (tel: 020 7054 8391; website: www.thisisglobal.com/charities-and-communities)

Trustees: Martin George, Chair; Nigel Atkinson; Moira Swinbank; Paul Soames; John McGeough; Darren Henley; Gareth Andrewartha; Annabel Sweet.

CC Number: 1091657

Capital Charities Ltd was incorporated on 23 January 2002 and began trading on 29 June 2002. On May 2006 the charity changed its name to GCap Charities Ltd. The charity changed its name again to Global Charities Ltd on 16 October 2008 following the acquisition of GCap Media plc by Global Radio Ltd in June 2008.

Global Charities is the grant giving charity of Global Radio, the UK's largest commercial radio company. Its mission is to improve the lives of the people in the communities in which its radio stations broadcast.

Guidelines

The charity aims to achieve its objectives through the distribution of grants to charities running projects that help to make a real difference to the lives of children, young people and adults who:
- Experience poverty and disadvantage
- Have experienced or are experiencing abuse, neglect, homelessness, violence or crime
- Have an illness or disability

Global Charities has three charity appeals:

Help a Capital Child

In London, 95.8 Capital FM's Help a Capital Child (and 97.3 LBC's Help a London Child) invites charities and voluntary and community organisations (not statutory bodies) working with less advantaged children and teenagers, aged 18 or under, in Greater London only to apply for project based funding. Groups can request grants of up to £5,000,

although the average grant given is around £2,200. HACC in London also runs bespoke large grants programmes from time to time. New applicants and/or all organisations not registered as a charity (including a company limited by guarantee, social enterprise or CIC) must enclose a letter from an independent referee with their application. Each year the fund has a number of priority themes for funding, check the website for details before applying. In the regions the Global radio stations all raise money for Teenage Cancer Trust.

Heart FM's **Have a Heart** is currently raising funds for three charities (Starlight Children's Foundation, Make-A-Wish Foundation and Rays of Sunshine Children's Charity) which make wishes come true for seriously ill children.

In recent years **The Classic FM Foundation** has been supporting music therapy sessions for children and young people delivered by Nordoff Robbins.

The grant giving strategy has been to focus on awarding small and major grants to charities and voluntary groups in London. The charity invites applications for grants through application forms which are regularly reviewed and updated by the grants panel to ensure applications comply with the funding criteria.

The trustees have delegated to a panel of experts from the voluntary sector, and radio station representatives the task of assessing application forms and making recommendations on what grants the charity should make. They are guided in their recommendations by a list of conditions as to what the charity will fund to ensure that the money is used in the best interests of the intended beneficiaries. Groups that are successful with their applications are required to complete a project report form and provide receipts to show how the grant money has been spent.

In London there are two rounds of small grant giving in the year in order to improve accessibility of funding and cash management of the charity. Operationally, in order to reduce the pressure on the volunteer grant panel, Global Charities staff have and will continue to undertake more sifting of applications prior to panel consideration.

The charity's funding categories are:
- Community, playgroups and toy libraries
- Youth
- Social and leisure
- Disability, health, illness and counselling
- Refuge and homeless projects
- Language and literacy

Grantmaking 2011/12

In 2011/12 the charity has assets of £1 million and an income of just over £3 million. During the year the charity awarded 334 grants throughout the UK totalling £1.5 million and were categorised as follows:

Disability, health, illness and counselling	111	£997,000
Social and leisure	74	£196,000
Community, playgroups and toy libraries	70	£141,000
Youth projects	43	£89,000
Refuge and homeless projects	19	£43,000
Language and literacy	17	£35,000

Beneficiaries included: Together for Short Lives (£200,000); ChildLine (£150,000); Nordoff Robbins (£90,000); London Youth Games (£20,000); and Havering Women's Aid (£1,100).

It is estimated by the charity that nearly 598,000 disadvantaged, disabled or ill children and young people, or those affected by abuse, crime, neglect or homelessness (and another 11,000 disadvantaged adults) will directly benefit from grants awarded across the country making a real difference and positive impact on their lives.

Exclusions

Each individual branch has specific exclusions, generally however the charities will not fund:
- Individual children or families
- Retrospective funding
- Statutory funding, such as schools and hospitals
- Salaried posts
- Deficit funding
- Medical research
- Purchase of minibuses
- Trips abroad
- Distribution to other organisations
- Distribution to individuals
- Religious activities
- Political groups
- General structural changes to buildings
- Projects which are part of a larger charity organisation and not separately constituted
- Core funding for a national or regional charity

Applications

Application forms and guidelines are available via email. Applicants should fill out the request form on the website or they can also request a paper copy by writing to the correspondent.

As always, we encourage groups to contact us before submitting an application to Help a Capital Child, if they have any queries on our guidelines and/or would like to discuss a project idea. For repeat applicants, please treat every application as your first, even if you've been successful before, providing as much detail as in a previous application form.

Information gathered from:
Accounts; annual report; Charity
Commission record; funder's website.

The Golden Bottle Trust

General with a preference for
the environment, health,
education, religion, the arts
and developing countries

£1.2 million (2011/12)

Beneficial area
Worldwide.

Correspondent: The Trustees, C. Hoare
and Co., 37 Fleet Street, London
EC4P 4DQ (tel: 020 7353 4522; email:
enquiries@hoaresbank.co.uk)

Trustees: Hoare Trustees (H. C. Hoare;
Sir D. J. Hoare; R. Q. Hoare;
A. S. Hoare; V. E. Hoare; S. M. Hoare;
A. S. Hopewell.)

CC Number: 327026

The trust was established in 1985 for
general charitable purposes, by C Hoare
and Co. bankers, the oldest remaining
private bank in the UK. The trust is
managed by the company, Hoare
Trustees, and continues to receive most
of its income from C Hoare and Co.

The objective of the trust is the
continuation of the philanthropic
commitments and ideals of the Hoare
family. Traditionally the charity has
supported causes including the arts,
religion, environment, health, education,
the developing world and also many
charities with whom the Hoare family is
familiar.

Grants range from £250 to £10,000 with
larger amounts occasionally being
granted, usually to the same charities
that the Hoare family has funded
regularly.

In addition to grantmaking the charity
has invested in a number of PRIs
(Programme Related Investments) in the
UK and the developing world.

During the year 2011/12 the charity held
assets of £8.8 million and had an income
of £1.5 million. Grants were made
totalling £1.2 million and were
distributed in the following areas:

Related charities*	£496,000
Health	£111,000
Arts, culture, heritage and science	£101,000
Staff match funding	£95,000
Religion and beliefs	£88,000
Education	£69,000
Environment	£61,000
Relief in need	£59,000
Emergency services and armed forces	£37,000
Citizenship, community development	£34,000
Ending poverty	£28,000
Sporting Activities	£15,000
Other	£6,500
Human rights and conflict resolution	£1,000
Animal welfare	£500
Water projects	£500

*Related charities include those
associated with the Hoare family and
with which the trust has long standing
relations: The Master Charitable Trust
(£312,000); The Bulldog Trust
(£115,000); The Henry C Hoare
Charitable Trust (£60,000); and West
Country Rivers Trust (£9,000).

Other beneficiaries, receiving £10,000 or
more, were: Future for Religious
Heritage (£93,000); Leader's Quest
Foundation (£25,000); Intermission
Youth Theatre and National Literacy
Trust (£20,000 each); Migratory Salmon
Foundation (£15,000); Wildfowl and
Wetlands Trust (£12,000); St Brides
Church (£11,000); and Heritage of
London Trust (£10,000).

Exclusions
No grants for individuals or
organisations that are not registered
charities.

Applications
The trustee does not normally respond
to unsolicited approaches.

Information gathered from:
Accounts; annual report; Charity
Commission record.

The Goldsmiths'
Company Charity

General, London charities, the
precious metals craft

£6.9 million (2010–12)

Beneficial area
UK, with a special interest in London
charities.

Correspondent: Mr R. Melly, Clerk,
Goldsmiths' Hall, 13 Foster Lane,
London EC2V 6BN (tel: 020 7606 7010;
fax: 020 7606 1511; email: the.clerk@
thegoldsmiths.co.uk; website: www.
thegoldsmiths.co.uk/charities)

Trustees: Goldsmith's Company Trustee:
Tim Schroder; Scott Shepherd; Bruno
Schroder; Sir John Rose; David Peake;
Lord Sutherland; Bryan Toye; Michael
Wainwright; Richard Vanderpump;
William Parente; Richard Came; Dame
Lynne Brindley; The Hon. Mark Bridges;
Richard Agutter; Lord Roger Cunliffe;
Martin Drury; George MacDonald; Prof.
Richard Himsworth; Rupert Hambro;
Hector Miller; Arthur Galsworthy; Sir
Jerry Wiggin; Sir Anthony Touche; Sir
Paul Girolami; Lord Tombs of Brailes;
Sir Huntington-Whiteley; C. Aston.

CC Number: 1088699

Each year the charity gives over 300
small grants of between £500 and £5,000.
Most of these are in response to
applications received, and can be for
almost any purpose, including
supporting core costs. A dozen or so
large grants are also given annually,
generally up to a maximum of £100,000.
These are usually to organisations
proactively sought out by the charity
rather than as a result of applying for a
grant.

The following information is taken from
the charity's website:

General
- Grants are made to London and
national charities with a turnover of
less than £10 million. Where charities
are members, branches or affiliates of
an association, appeals are normally
accepted from the governing body or
head office only. In the case of church
restoration, block grants are made to
the National Churches Trust and
therefore appeals from individual
churches will not normally be
considered. Similarly a block grant is
made to Children's Hospices UK, and
therefore appeals from individual
hospices will not normally be
considered.
- The Goldsmiths' Company Charity's
normal policy is to give small grants:
the average grant last year was
approximately £3,000. Recurring grants
are not normally given, however where
grants are payable in stages over a
period of more than one year, then
each payment will be considered on its
own merit and payment cannot be
assumed for subsequent years
- Requests for financial assistance by
individuals are only considered if they
are members of the Goldsmiths'
Company. The charity, however, does
make grants to other trusts who
administer grants to individuals on our
behalf.
- Appeals for specific projects are
preferred, but requests for core funding
will be considered

Education
- To foster aspects of education
considered to be in most need of
encouragement
- To fill gaps in educational provision
- To help in situations where the
company's limited finances can have
most impact through the multiplier
effect

The [charity] currently funds four major
proactive projects:

Science for Society Courses
Providing science teachers with free
residential courses, aimed at broadening
their perspective on subjects allied to the
A-level syllabus.

More details of the available courses are
listed on the charity's website.

Goldsmiths' Grant for Teachers
Providing primary and secondary school
teachers with the opportunity to take time

out from the classroom for personal and professional development.

Projects must have a long-term aim of disseminating results/research back to the school and/or wider audience. Examples of projects that would be looked on favourably include:

- Comparisons of best practice in teaching and school administration at home or abroad
- Personal development projects – e.g. creative writing, arts, music, languages and coaching
- Study tours at home or abroad

Primary School Projects
Assisting six selected primary schools to raise their standards of literacy and numeracy.

Post-Graduate Medical Students
Providing bursaries to promising but needy students who have switched to medicine as their second degree. This is carried out through the BMA who have a close association with the [Goldsmiths'] Company. Please note that we do not offer medical grants for individual applications.

The Royal Geographic Society Goldsmiths' Teaching Grants are awarded to five teachers each year to support them in developing educational resources linked to five field projects/expeditions mounted by the RGS each year. This scheme is administered by the RGS.

Grants in 2010–12

In the 18 months to March 2012 the charity had assets of £93.8 million and an income of £6.7 million, over two thirds of which was from investments. Grants were made totalling £6.9 million. Income and expenditure are higher than usual as the accounts cover an 18 rather than 12 month period. Grants can be broken down as follows:

General charitable work	£1.4 million
Support of the craft – other	£1.7 million
Goldsmith's Centre	£3.45 million
Education	£349,000

379 grants were made for general charitable work were and are divided into the categories of general welfare, medical welfare and people with disabilities, culture, youth and church.

Previous beneficiaries included: University of Cambridge – Department of Material Science and Metallurgy (£173,000); National Churches Trust (£50,000); London Borough of Lambeth – for the support of individuals (£25,000); Refugee Council and School Home Support (£15,000 each); Children's Hospices UK (£10,000); Royal Air Force Disabled Holiday Trust (£6,000); Changing Faces, The Young Vic and Country Holidays for Inner City Kids (£5,000 each); and New Horizon Youth Centre (£3,000).

Exclusions

Applications are not normally considered on behalf of:

- Medical research
- Animal welfare
- Memorials to individuals
- Overseas projects
- Individual housing associations
- Endowment schemes
- Individual churches
- Individual hospices
- Charities with a turnover of more than £10 million

Applications

Applications should be made by letter, no more than two sides of A4 in length, highlighting the case for the company to give its support.

The letter should be accompanied by:

- The completed application form, which can be downloaded from the company's website. The form may be retyped, but should follow the same format and length (no more than four sides of A4). All questions should be answered. Do not cut and paste information on the form. Legible handwritten applications are acceptable
- The charity's most recent annual report and audited accounts

Applications are considered monthly, except in August and September, and there is usually a three to four month delay between receipt of an appeal and a decision being made. Applications from any organisation, whether successful or not, are not normally considered more frequently than every three years.

Any enquiries should be addressed to the correspondent.

Common applicant mistakes

'Asking for too much; applications addressed to wrong person; inconsistencies between application form and cover letter.'

Information gathered from:

Accounts; annual report; Charity Commission record; further information provided by the funder; funder's website.

The Goodman Foundation

General, overseas, social welfare, older people, health and disability
£256,000 (2011/12)

Beneficial area

UK and overseas.

Correspondent: The Trustees, c/o Anglo Beef Processors, Unit 6290, Bishops Court, Solihull Parkway, Birmingham Business Park, Birmingham B37 7YB

Trustees: Laurence Goodman; Catherine Goodman; Richard Cracknell; Lesley Tidd.

CC Number: 1097231

This trust was registered in April 2003 for general charitable purposes. It is the foundation of Larry Goodman, an Irish businessman at the head of a beef and agribusiness empire.

In 2011/12 the trust had assets of £22.2 million and an exceptionally high income of £10.7 million, mostly due to one large donation of £10.5 million. Grants to 31 organisations totalled £256,000, broken down as follows:

Overseas and disasters	6	£97,000
Poverty, older people and people with disabilities	14	£69,000
Children's charities	5	£19,000
Other	6	£71,000

A list of beneficiaries was not included in the accounts. Given the significant increase in the foundation's funds an increase in grantmaking is likely in future years.

Applications

In writing to the correspondent.

Information gathered from:

Accounts; annual report; Charity Commission record.

The Mike Gooley Trailfinders Charity

Medical research, general
£286,000 (2011/12)

Beneficial area

UK.

Correspondent: Michael Gooley, Trustee, 9 Abingdon Road, London W8 6AH (tel: 020 7938 3143; email: trailfinders@trailfinders.com; website: www.trailfinders.com)

Trustees: Mark Bannister; Tristan Gooley; Michael Gooley; Bernadette Gooley; Fiona Gooley; Louise Breton.

CC Number: 1048993

The charity supports medical research, community projects which encourage young people in outdoor activities and armed forces veteran organisations.

In 2011/12 the charity had assets of £10.3 million and an income of £1.1 million. Grants were made during the year totalling £286,000.

No beneficiaries were listed in the charity's accounts. Previous beneficiaries have included: Alzheimer's Society (£400,000); Prostate Cancer Charity (£100,000); and the Second World War Experience Centre (£40,000).

Exclusions

Grants are not made to overseas charities or to individuals.

Applications

In writing to the correspondent.

Information gathered from:

Accounts; annual report; Charity Commission record.

The Gosling Foundation Ltd

Relief of poverty, education, religion, naval and service charities and general charitable purposes beneficial to the community

£27.5 million (2011/12)

Beneficial area

Worldwide. In practice UK.

Correspondent: Miss Anne Yusof, Secretary, 21 Bryanston Street, Marble Arch, London W1H 7PR (tel: 020 7495 5599)

Trustees: Sir Donald Gosling; Sir Ronald F. Hobson; Cmdr Gosling.

CC Number: 326840

The foundation was established in 1985 by Sir Donald Gosling, co-founder of NCP car parks and former seafarer. The foundation's endowment derives from his personal fortune and its objects are the relief of poverty, education, religion and general charitable purposes beneficial to the community. Grants are given each year to a wide range of charities, with naval and other service related charities receiving substantial support.

In 2011/12 the foundation had assets of £71.2 million and an income of £4.5 million. There were 162 grants made to 154 organisations totalling £27.5 million. Expenditure was swelled in the year by a substantial one-off grant of £25 million to the HMS Victory Preservation Company. Grant expenditure is never usually this high, with total expenditure usually averaging between two and three million each year.

Grants were broken down into the following broad categories:

Other purposes beneficial to the community	129	£26.15 million
Advancement of education	23	£1.15 million
Relief of poverty	23	£182,000
Advancement of religion	5	£27,000

Beneficiaries included: HMS Victory Preservation Company (£25 million); Duke of Edinburgh's Award (£1 million); Rowbarge and Thames Diamond Jubilee Foundation (£100,000

each); Food Fortnight Ltd (£75,000); Westminster Abbey and SSAFA Forces Help (£50,000 each); Queen Elizabeth Castle of Mey Trust (£20,000); Soldiering on Trust, Centre of the Cell, FAA Memorial Church Fund, Worshipful Company of Shipwrights and HMS Liverpool Central Fund (£10,000 each); Macmillan Cancer Support (£7,000); Smile Support Care (£5,000); Professor Cunningham Research Fund (£2,000); and Turner Syndrome, Young Epilepsy and Variety Club Children's Charity (£1,000 each).

Exclusions

Grants are made to individuals only in exceptional circumstances.

Applications

In writing to the correspondent. The grantmaking policies of the foundation are 'regularly reviewed' and currently are:

- Applications should fall within the objects of the charity
- There is no minimum limit for any grant
- All grants will be approved unanimously

Trustees meet quarterly.

Information gathered from:

Accounts; annual report; Charity Commission record.

The Grace Charitable Trust

Christian, general, education, medical and social welfare

£188,000 to organisations (2011/12)

Beneficial area

UK.

Correspondent: Mrs G. J. R. Payne, Trustee, Swinford House, Nortons Lane, Great Barrow, Chester CH3 7JZ (tel: 01928 740773)

Trustees: G. Payne; E. Payne; G. Snaith; R. Quayle; M. Mitchell.

CC Number: 292984

Established in 1985, the trust generally gives grants of £1,000 to £10,000 each with a preference for Christian organisations.

In 2011/12 the trust had assets of £2.1 million and an income of £300,000. Grants were made to organisations totalling £195,000, which were broken down as follows:

'Christian based activities'	£93,000
Social and medical causes	£45,000
Education	£31,000
General charitable purposes	£26,000

Previous beneficiaries included Alpha, the International Christian College and Euroevangelism. Of the total grant figure, £7,700 was distributed in grants to individuals.

Applications

The trust states that 'grants are made only to charities known to the settlors and unsolicited applications are, therefore, not considered'.

Information gathered from:

Accounts; annual report; Charity Commission record.

GrantScape

Environmental and community-based projects

£800,000 (2011/12)

Beneficial area

UK.

Correspondent: Grants team, Office E, Whitsundoles, Broughton Road, Salford, Milton Keynes MK17 8BU (tel: 01908 247630; email: helpdesk@grantscape.org. uk; website: www.grantscape.org.uk)

Trustees: Dave Bramley; Alastair Singleton; Michael Clarke; Anthony Cox.

CC Number: 1102249

GrantScape is a company limited by guarantee and is enrolled with ENTRUST as a Distributive Environmental Body. Its vision is 'to improve the environment and communities by the channelling and management of charitable funding towards deserving and quality projects.'

Its generic grantmaking policy is as follows:

- GrantScape will only make grants in line with its charitable objectives
- Grants will be made on a justifiable and fair basis to projects which provide best value
- Grants will be made to projects that improve the life of communities
- GrantScape will make available specific criteria for each of the grant programmes that it manages
- All grants are subject to meeting the generic grantmaking criteria as well as the specific grant programme criteria

The accounts also note that: 'all of our community grant-making continues to be based on two main considerations: the level of community support for and involvement in the projects and the local community benefit and enjoyment which will result from the projects.'

Programmes

Grants are available in specific geographical areas. Applicants are advised to check the charity's website for up-to-date information on current programmes before applying.

Landfill Communities Funds

GrantScape distributes its grants through the Landfill Communities Fund. The following criteria, taken from GrantScape's website, apply to all the following funds listed:

Contributing Third Party Donation

Each grant awarded will require a donation to be made to [the fund in question] so that the grant can be released by GrantScape. This is called a Contributing Third Party (CTP) donation. The CTP donation covers [the fund in question's] costs in providing monies for the grant through the Landfill Communities Fund, plus associated fees.

In their applications, groups will therefore need to identify an individual or organisation who would be willing to make this CTP donation if they are awarded a grant. If desired, the CTP donation can be made by the group themselves.

In simple terms, each £11 of CTP donation will release £100 of funding for the project.

[If you require further information, please refer to the charity's website. Alternatively, contact the Grant Support Team on 01908 545780.]

Projects must comply with the requirements of the Landfill Communities Fund (LCF). If you are in any doubt whether your project meets these requirements, please contact GrantScape.

Public access requirements:

Projects must be available and open to the general public – as a minimum, for 4 evenings a week, or 2 days a week, or 104 days a year.

Judging criteria:

The main criteria used when assessing applications received will be:

- The level of community support for and involvement in the project
- The local community benefit (social, economic and environmental) and enjoyment which will result from the project

Other factors will also be considered which must be demonstrated in the application:

- The ability of the applicant to deliver the project
- How the work will be continued after the project has been completed, i.e. its sustainability and legacy
- Value for money

Caird Peckfield Community Fund

Fund overview:

- Approximately £300,000 is available
- Grants of between £5,000 and £50,000 are available
- Match Funding is not required

Project location: projects must be located within a Leeds Metropolitan District ward.

Project purpose: grants will be available for community and environmental projects.

Ineligible applicants:

- Individuals
- Commercial organisations
- Membership-based sports clubs and facilities (e.g. bowls and golf clubs); unless membership is open to the general public without undue restriction

Project exclusions. In addition to the exclusions common to all schemes, pay attention to the following:

Grants will not be available for:

- Projects at schools
- Bus services, minibus services, or vehicles
- Projects at hospitals, or hospices, or day care centres unless the public access requirements, above, are met
- Any works to public highways
- Staff posts and costs where they are not based, or specifically undertaking works, at the actual project site
- Projects to deliver visual enhancements (i.e. 'a view'), as this does not improve, maintain or provide a general public amenity
- Village or town centre enhancements, such as walkways, street works or signage
- CD's, web-sites or remote interpretation about a site
- Public car parks, unless they are specific to the general public amenity
- Public conveniences
- Allotments, or fruit growing projects
- Charity buildings, offices of charities, Citizens' Advice Bureau and advice centres
- Large scale perimeter/security fencing programmes that do not directly enhance the public amenity

CWM Community and Environmental Fund

Fund overview:

- £200,000 approximately per year
- Grants are awarded between £5,000 and £50,000
- Match funding is not required
- A maximum of 15% of the fund is available for qualifying projects from religious organisations
- A maximum of 15% of the fund is available for qualifying projects involving playgrounds on council owned land
- There are two funding rounds each year

Project location: projects must be located in Carmarthenshire and be within 10 miles of a licensed landfill site.

Project purpose: grants are available for community and environmental projects, particularly those which can demonstrate the enhancement of biodiversity.

Grants will be available for capital improvement works to public amenity projects, for example:

- Village halls
- Village greens
- Public playgrounds (see note below)
- Sports fields and facilities
- Nature reserves
- Community centres
- Cycle paths
- Country parks

(Applications involving playgrounds on Council owned land will only be funded if applicants can demonstrate significant community fundraising efforts to help financially support the project. Management, administration and professional costs will only be considered for funding if they form part of a wider application for a capital project and can only constitute a maximum of 10% in total of the amount applied for.)

Priority will be given to applicants that clearly understand and can demonstrate the social, economic and environmental benefits the project will provide.

Ineligible applicants:

- Organisations operating for the purpose of making and distributing profit
- Schools
- Individuals
- Single user sports facilities

Project exclusions. [In addition to the exclusions common to all schemes, grants will not be available for projects that are located on private land.]

Mick George

Location: Northamptonshire, Cambridgeshire and Lincolnshire. Total grants available: Approximately £200,000 each year.

Fund provided by: Mick George Ltd through the Landfill Communities Fund (LCF).

The Mick George Community Fund provides grants of between £5,000 and £50,000, although it is unlikely that individual grants over £35,000 will be made.

Projects located within 5 miles of the Mick George Operations in Northamptonshire, Cambridgeshire and Lincolnshire can apply (providing the project location is also within 10 miles of any license landfill site). [A map is available on the Grantscape website to assess whether your project may qualify.]

At each funding round, a minimum of 25% of the available money is ring fenced for worthy applications received from within the Parish of Rushton. However, if applications from Rushton are not received, the funding will be available to other applications.

Project exclusions. In addition to the exclusions common to all schemes:

Grants will not be available for:

- Membership-based sports clubs and facilities (e.g. bowls and golf clubs), unless membership is open to the general public without undue restriction
- Commercial Organisations
- Individuals
- Costs towards the fabric of new buildings (but internal fixtures and fittings are acceptable)
- Projects that are considered statutory requirements
- Projects that are solely aimed to meet the requirements of the Disability Discrimination Act
- Revenue funding and core cost funding

- Retrospective funding (i.e. projects that have already been completed)
- Projects at schools where the general public cannot benefit from the project
- Bus services, minibus services, or vehicles
- Projects at hospitals, or hospices, or day care centres
- Any works to public highways
- Staff posts and costs where they are not based, or specifically undertaking works, at the actual project site
- Projects to deliver visual enhancements (i.e. 'a view'), as this does not improve, maintain or provide a general public amenity
- Village or town centre enhancements, such as walkways, street works or signage
- CD's, web-sites or remote interpretation about a site
- Public car parks, unless they are specific to the general public amenity
- Public conveniences
- Allotments, or fruit growing projects
- Charity buildings, offices of charities, Citizens' Advice Bureau and advice centres
- Large scale perimeter/security fencing programmes that do not directly enhance the public amenity
- Land or building purchase

Whitemoss Community Fund

Location: Skelmersdale, Lancashire. Total grants available: Approximately £50,000 each year.

Fund provided by: Whitemoss Landfill Ltd through the Landfill Communities Fund (LCF).

This fund provides grants of between £5,000 and £20,000 to fund community and environmental projects located in the West Lancashire Borough Council area and that are within 5 miles of Whitemoss landfill site in Skelmersdale.

A map is available on the Grantscape website to assess whether your project may qualify.

Project exclusions. In addition to the exclusions common to all schemes:

Grants will not be available for:
- Commercial organisations
- Individuals
- Membership-based sports clubs and facilities (e.g. bowls and golf clubs), unless membership is open to the general public without undue restriction
- Bus services, minibus services, or vehicles
- Any works to public highways
- Projects to deliver visual enhancements (i.e. 'a view'), as this does not improve, maintain or provide a general public amenity
- CD's, web-sites or remote interpretation about a site
- Public car parks, unless they are specific to the general public amenity
- Public conveniences
- Charity buildings, offices of charities, Citizens' Advice Bureau and advice centres
- Projects at schools (unless the general public can also access the facilities at agreed times)

- Projects at schools, hospitals, hospices and day care centres unless the Public Access Requirements, above, are met (please contact GrantScape if your project is at one of these locations)

Renewables Funds

Partnerships for Renewables Community Benefit Fund

Partnerships for Renewables (PfR) was set up by the Carbon Trust in 2007 to develop, construct and operate renewable energy projects, primarily on public sector land.

PfR is committed to donating money into a Community Benefit Fund for each of its wind energy sites. To apply for a grant, your project will need to be in close proximity to a PfR wind energy project. Each Fund will have slightly different criteria so it is important you read these carefully before you apply.

Isle of Sheppey

Two schemes are currently open (at the time of writing) under the PfR fund, both of which apply to projects within the vicinity of the HMP Standford Hill wind turbines in the Parish of Eastchurch on the Isle of Sheppey in Kent. Approximately £10,000 will be available each year for the operational life of the turbine project (20–25 years).

Eligible groups that can apply include:
- Voluntary, community groups, community, parish and town councils
- Schools and educational establishments
- Social enterprises (including credit unions, co-operatives, social firms, community owned enterprises, community interest companies and developments trusts) provided they operate on a not-for-profit basis

A Community Advisory Panel (CAP) of local people has been established to help decide how to spend the fund. If you have any questions about the Fund, please call Alan Melrose in the first instance on 07756 029019 or email amelrose101@sky.com. If Alan is unavailable, then you can call us on 01908 247630.

If you wish to apply you will need to complete an application form and submit it to the CAP for them to consider.

As well as the PfR turbine scheme the charity hopes to launch a range of local funds in partnership with **Airvolution Energy Ltd** in the near future. The first schemes expected to launch are for communities near Ysgellog Farm in Anglesey and Garlenik Estate in Cornwall. Check the website for details of when the funds are opening.

In 2011/12 Grantscape held assets of £1.9 million and had an income of £1 million. Grants were made totalling £1.1 million, although £315,000 of this was returned as no longer required; grants approved were as follows:

Caird Bardon Community Programme	£492,000
Community Greenspace Challenge	£241,000
CWM Environmental Funds	£192,000
Mick George Funds	£87,000
Woodford Waste Management Funds	£84,000
Whitemoss Funds	£18,000

Beneficiaries across all programmes included: Oxford Preservation Trust (£73,000); Rushton Parish Council (£70,000); Llannon Community Council (£50,000); Middleton Park Equestrian Centre Riding for the Disabled (£35,000); Leeds City Council – Skateboard/BMX park and Stanwick Pocket Park (£30,000 each); 2nd Otley Scout Group (£25,500); Leeds Rugby Foundation and Llanelli Gymnastics Club (£20,000 each); Amor Baptist Chapel (£10,000); Earith Town Estate (£8,000); and The Wildlife Trust BCN Ltd and Broughton Village Hall Management Committee (£5,000 each).

Exclusions

None of the Landfill Communities Funds will fund:
- Projects that are considered statutory requirements
- Projects that are solely aimed to meet the requirements of the Disability Discrimination Act
- Core costs
- Retrospective funding (i.e. projects that have already been completed)
- Solar photovolactic cells and wind turbines unless: (i) these will be used solely to provide power and/or heat for the community amenity where they will be installed; and (ii) no income will be received from Government Feed-In Tariffs (FITs) or from any similar tariffs introduced in the future

Applications

All applications are made online via the charity's website. Some funds have two grant rounds per year but others only have one. Each fund has different deadlines, so ensure to check the website for up-to-date deadline dates before applying. Should you have any problems completing the application form you are asked to contact the charity. The website lists different contacts for each programme. The charity has previously run training courses on making applications to their Landfill Community Funds, check the website for details of future courses.

Information gathered from:

Accounts; annual report; Charity Commission record; guidelines for applicants; funder's website.

The Great Britain Sasakawa Foundation

Links between Great Britain and Japan

£951,000 (2012)

Beneficial area

UK, Japan.

Correspondent: Stephen McEnally, Chief Executive, Dilke House, 1 Malet Street, London WC1E 7JN (tel: 020 7436 9042; email: grants@gbsf.org.uk; website: www.gbsf.org.uk)

Trustees: Jeremy Brown; Michael French; Prof. Shoichi Watanabe; Sir John Boyd; Hiroaki Fujii; Earl of St Andrews; David Cope; Prof. Nozomu Hayashi; Tatsuya Tanami; Joanna Pitman; Dr Yuichi Hosoya.

CC Number: 290766

The following information is taken from the foundation's website:

The Great Britain Sasakawa Foundation was established as a result of a visit to London in 1983 by the late Ryoichi Sasakawa during which he met a number of senior British figures to discuss the international situation and, in particular, UK-Japanese relations. It was agreed at these discussions that it would be in the interest of both countries if more could be done to enhance mutual appreciation and understanding of each other's culture, society and achievements and that a non-governmental, non-profit making body should be established for this purpose.

A donation of almost £10 million was subsequently made by The Sasakawa Foundation (now called The Nippon Foundation), founded in 1962, and the Great Britain Sasakawa Foundation was inaugurated in May 1985, in parallel with similar initiatives in Scandinavia, France and the United States.

The Chairman of The Great Britain Sasakawa Foundation is the Earl of St Andrews. The Trustees are drawn from distinguished individuals in the UK and Japan, including Mr Yohei Sasakawa, Chairman of the Nippon Foundation

Foundation aims

The foundation's aim is to develop good relations between the United Kingdom and Japan by advancing the education of the people of both nations in each other's culture, society and achievements.

It seeks to promote mutual understanding and cooperation through financial support for activities in the following fields:

- Arts and culture
- Humanities and social issues
- Japanese language
- Medicine and health
- Science, technology and environment
- Sport
- Youth and education

Whilst encouraging applications in each of the above fields, the foundation particularly wishes to support activities/ projects in science and technology; medicine and health; environment and social issues; Japanese studies; and in the Japanese language.

The foundation's awards are intended to provide 'pump-priming' and not core funding of projects, but even small grants have enabled a wide range of projects to reach fruition, such as:

- Visits between the UK and Japan by academics, professionals, creative artists, teachers, young people, journalists and representatives of civic and non-governmental organisations
- Research and collaborative studies, seminars, workshops, lectures and publications in academic and specialist fields
- Teaching and development of Japanese language and cultural studies in schools, further education colleges and universities
- Exhibitions, performances and creative productions by artists, musicians, film-makers, writers and theatre groups

Criteria for awards

- Grants are intended to be 'pump-priming' or partial support for worthwhile projects which would not otherwise be realised, and evidence of core funding should be available before any application is made for an award
- There are no set budgets for any category of activity, but emphasis is placed on innovative projects and on those involving groups of people in both countries (especially young people) rather than individuals
- Trustees greatly appreciate acknowledgment of the foundation's support in any published material resulting from a grant
- Applications are not normally accepted from individuals seeking support for personal projects. However, an organisation may apply for a grant in support of the work of an individual which advances the aims of the foundation, and an application from an individual may be considered if there is clear evidence of organisational support
- The foundation does not make grants for student fees or travel in connection with study for a qualification, but might do so for research purposes
- Projects originating in the UK should be submitted through the London office and those originating in Japan through, the Tokyo office
- Projects for UK-Japan collaborations or exchanges should be submitted as a single project through Tokyo or London, and not as separate applications from the UK and Japanese partners
- No grants are made for consumables, salaries, for purchase of materials, nor for capital projects such as the purchase, construction or maintenance of buildings
- For projects designed to extend over more than one year, the foundation is prepared to consider requests for funding spread over a period of not more than three consecutive years

- We welcome applications from previous recipients for new projects
- In assessing applications for awards, the trustees will take into account any unique or innovative aspects of the project and the extent to which it will have a wide and lasting impact
- Awards average £1,500 to £2,000 and do not normally exceed £5,000–£6,000 for larger-scale projects

In 2012 the foundation had assets of £23 million and an income of £1.2 million. Grants totalled £951,000, although £507,000 was paid in restricted grants to fund the Sasakawa Lectureship Programme for Japanese Studies at UK universities and for a conference programme at Chatham House. The £444,000 of unrestricted grants were broken down as follows:

Arts and culture	73	£120,000
Medicine and health	36	£115,000
Humanities and social issues	51	£80,000
Youth and education	21	£71,000
Science, technology and environment	11	£27,000
Japanese language	8	£18,000
Sport	5	£13,000

The accounts, available on the foundation's website, contain a full list of grants and recipient organisations.

Exclusions

Grants are not made to individuals applying on their own behalf. The foundation will consider proposals from organisations that support the activities of individuals, provided they are citizens of the UK or Japan.

No grants are awarded for: retrospective funding; the construction, conservation or maintenance of land and buildings; student fees or travel in connection with study for a qualification; consumables; salaries.

Applications

The foundation expresses a strong preference for emailed applications. A form will be emailed on request, and is also available from the foundation's website where detailed information is given about the foundation's grant giving and application procedures. Application forms are also available from both the London headquarters or from the Tokyo office at: The Nippon Foundation Bldg. 4F, 1–2–2 Akasaka Minato-ku, Tokyo 107–0052.

The application form requires the following information:

- A summary of the proposed project and its aims, including dates, its likely impact and long-term sustainability
- The total cost of the project and the amount of the desired grant, together with a note of other expected sources of funds
- A description of what elements of the project grant funding has been requested for (the foundation prefers

to support identifiable activities rather than general overheads)

Organisations should be registered charities, recognised educational institutions, local or regional authorities, churches, media companies, publishers or other bodies that the foundation may approve.

Telephone enquiries or personal visits are welcomed by the foundation's staff to discuss eligibility in advance of any formal application. The awards committee meets in London in March, May and November. Applications should be received by 15 December, 31 March and 15 September. Awards meetings in Tokyo are held in April and October, with applications to be submitted by the end of February and September.

All applicants are notified shortly after each awards committee meeting of the decisions of the trustees. Those offered grants are asked to sign and return an acceptance form and are given the opportunity to say when they would like to receive their grant.

Note: the foundation receives requests for two to three times the amount of money it actually has available for grants. About 75% of applicants receive grants, but often much less than requested.

Information gathered from:

Accounts; annual report; Charity Commission record; funder's website.

The Grocers' Charity

General

£616,000 (2011/12)

Beneficial area

UK.

Correspondent: Lucy-Jayne Cummings, Charity Administrator, Grocers' Hall, Princes Street, London EC2R 8AD (tel: 020 7606 3113; fax: 020 7600 3082; email: lucy@grocershall.co.uk; website: www.grocershall.co.uk)

Trustee: The Grocers' Trust Company Ltd administers the Charity and the Directors of that company are the Master and Second Warden of the Grocers' Company, together with the Chairmen of the Education and Charities Committee and the Finance Committee. The Master and Second Warden together with eight other Members of the Court of Assistants, all of whom are elected for a fixed term of office, form the Education and Charities Committee which is responsible for grantmaking.

CC Number: 255230

The Grocers' Charity was established in 1968, and has general charitable aims. It describes its work as follows in its 2011/12 accounts:

> The charity was established as a trust with general charitable aims, which enables it to support a broad range of UK registered charities. Historically, areas supported have included education, the Church, relief of poverty, medicine, support for the arts, heritage, the elderly, young people and those with disabilities.
>
> Each year, the charity sets a budget that establishes expected income for the period and sets a target for the distribution of income and reserves through grants to charities. There is a broad categorisation of the nature of the budgeted grants, but this is advisory, and does not restrict the types of grant allocated. Once the overall financial parameters have been set, the policy on awarding grants is flexible, allowing due consideration of the worthiness of applications received from charities during the year. Over a period of time, this may result in different categories of need attracting a greater level of support, although there are certain charities to which the charity contributes on a regular basis. Amongst these, education continues to be a high priority and a significant proportion of the charity's expenditure is committed to this category in the form of scholarships and bursaries at schools and colleges with which the Grocers' Company has historic links. Donations to churches under the patronage of the Grocers' Company and payments to their respective Parochial Church Councils also feature annually.
>
> The amounts awarded per grant vary considerably. Excluding the grants provided to institutions with which there is an historic connection, 100 (2011 – 159) grants were awarded in 2011/12 from a total of 717 (20 – 1,034) applications received. Of these, 30 were for £1,000 or less and the remainder, with the exception of major grants, ranged between £1,000 and £10,000.
>
> Major grants are awarded each year. Each year a different area of charitable activity is chosen for major grant support, and every member of the company has the opportunity to nominate a charity. The nominations are then reviewed and a short-list produced. Charities on the short-list are invited to give a presentation to the Education and Charities Committee, after which the awards are decided. This year, the chosen area was disability. Two major grants were awarded, totalling £65,000. The Matched Funding Scheme initiative launched in 2007 continued in 2011/12, with the company sponsoring 32 members who raised a combined sum of £122,500. It is the trustee's intention that this worthwhile scheme be encouraged to develop.

The main open scheme is the Memorial Grants scheme – the charity tends to offer regular support to a fixed group of educational establishments and has patronages with thirteen churches across the UK. Memorial grants of up to £2,000 can be awarded in the following categories to charities meeting the associated criteria:

Relief of poverty – youth:

- Charity to support children and young people (0–25 years old) as the main beneficiary
- Working in areas of high deprivation
- Working to increase social mobility for example through training courses, better facilities or parenting support

We recognise the 'London Youth Quality Mark' when assessing applications.

The elderly

- Charities that are working towards Ending Loneliness in Old Age (www. campaigntoendloneliness.org.uk)
- Charities supporting ending social exclusion for elderly people
- Working in rural and urban settings in geographic areas linked to the Grocers' Company (Central London or in the vicinity of our schools or churches)

Disability

- Charities providing innovative projects and programmes for disabled people
- Charities providing front line support for disabled people.

Medicine

- Have a turnover of no more than £15 million
- Research into specific medical conditions
- Grant given for a piece of equipment, printing materials or tangible project
- Support sufferers of rare medical conditions

Heritage and the arts

- Conservation of historic buildings (though not places of worship)
- Conservation of historic objects and paintings
- Improving accessibility to arts projects, performances or exhibitions

Grant guidelines

- The charity will consider requests to support both capital and revenue projects
- It is usual practice for successful applicants to be advised that a further request for support will not be entertained until at least two years have elapsed from the date of the successful application
- Unsuccessful applicants are advised that a further request will not be considered until at least one year has elapsed from the date of the relevant application
- Donations are made by way of a single payment and are of a non-recurring nature (although occasionally a commitment to fund a project for a limited period will be agreed)
- Public acknowledgement of the charity's support is allowed, although it is preferred that it is undertaken in an unobtrusive manner

Grantmaking in 2011/12

During the year the charity had assets of almost £12.9 million and an income of £663,000. Grants totalled £616,000 and were summarised as follows:

Education	£302,000
Disability	£90,000
Relief of poverty	£58,000
Arts	£51,000
Churches	£51,000
Heritage	£35,000
Medicine	£23,000
Elderly	£6,200

Beneficiaries of grants of £1,000 or more are listed in the annual report and annual review. Some examples of recipients are given below.

Oundle School (£185,000); Motor Neurone Disease (£40,000); Only Connect (£26,000); Peterborough Cathedral Development and Preservation Trust (£10,000); VSO (£7,500); St John the Baptist – Stone (£7,000); Reed's School (£6,600); Royal College of Art (£6,000); St Paul's Cathedral Foundation Fabric Fund (£5,000); National Theatre (£3,000); Ulysses Trust, Bush Theatre and National Osteoporosis Society (£2,000 each); New Forest Disability Information Service (£1,250); and Royal London Society for Blind People (£1,100).

Exclusions

Only UK-registered charities are supported. Individuals cannot receive grants directly. Support is rarely given to the following unless there is a specific or long-standing connection with the Grocers' Company:
- Cathedrals, churches and other ecclesiastical bodies
- Hospices
- Schools and other educational establishments

Applications

Applications for grants can be considered from UK registered charities only and must comply with current guidelines, including restrictions, as detailed in the Grocers' Charity Annual Review and on the Grocers' Company website.

Applicants should complete the online enquiry form on the charity's website.

Please do not send any further information at this stage. We will review your enquiry and contact you if we wish to take your application further. We regret we are unable to acknowledge receipt of enquiries.

Applications are considered three to four times a year.

Unsolicited applications are not accepted for the major grants programme:

To apply for a Major Grant you must be supported by a member of the Grocers' Company and fit the criteria decided by the committee each year. Please do not contact the Grocers' Charity directly and please note the Grocers' Company are unable to provide details of members of the Company.

Percentage of awards given to new applicants: between 40% and 50%.

Common applicant mistakes

'Not reading the criteria; not making their case strong enough.'

Information gathered from:

Accounts; annual report; Charity Commission record; further information provided by the funder; funder's website.

The M. and R. Gross Charities Ltd

Jewish causes
£3.5 million (2011/12)

Beneficial area

UK and overseas.

Correspondent: Mrs Rifka Gross, Secretary, Cohen Arnold and Co., New Burlington House, 1075 Finchley Road, London NW11 0PU (tel: 020 8731 0777; fax: 020 8731 0778)

Trustees: Rifka Gross; Sarah Padwa; Michael Saberski; Leonard Lerner.

CC Number: 251888

This trust makes grants to educational and religious organisations within the Orthodox Jewish community in the UK and overseas.

In 2011/12 the trust had assets of £30.4 million and an income of £7.7 million. Grants were made totalling over £3.5 million. A list of recent beneficiaries was not included in the latest accounts.

Previous beneficiaries, many of whom are likely to be supported each year, include: Atlas Memorial Ltd; United Talmudical Associates Ltd, a grantmaking organisation which distributes smaller grants made by the trust; Chevras Tsedokoh Ltd; Kolel Shomrei Hachomoth; Telz Talmudical Academy; Talmud Torah Trust; Gevurah Ari Torah Academy Trust; Friends of Yeshivas Brisk; Beis Ruchel Building Fund; Beth Hamedresh Satmar Trust; Kehal Chareidim Trust; Daas Sholem; Craven Walk Beis Hamedrash; Union of Orthodox Hebrew Congregations; and Yetev Lev Jerusalem.

Applications

In writing to the organisation. Applications are assessed on a weekly basis and many of the smaller grants are dealt with through a grantmaking agency, United Talmudical Associates Ltd.

Information gathered from:

Accounts; annual report; Charity Commission record.

H. C. D. Memorial Fund

Health, education, environment and community action
£135,500 to organisations in the UK (2011/12)

Beneficial area

Worldwide.

Correspondent: Harriet Lear, Secretary and Trustee, Knowlands Farm Granary, Barcombe, Lewes, East Sussex BN8 5EF (tel: 01273 400321; email: hcdmemorialfund@gmail.com)

Trustees: Nicholas Debenham, Chair; Bill Flinn; Harriet Lear; Joanna Lear; Jeremy Debenham; Catherine Debenham; Susannah Drummond.

CC Number: 1044956

The trust was established in 1995 for general charitable purposes and principally makes grants to organisations in the UK and abroad engaged in the fields of health, education, environment and community action.

The grants policy is to make grants as determined by the trustees at twice-yearly meetings. The policy is flexible as regards donees, but currently:
- Maintains a balance between home and overseas grants
- Directs grants mainly towards (1) the relief of human need, whether due to poverty, ill-health, disability, want of education, or other causes, and (2) projects which aim to mitigate the effects of climate change
- Prefers projects which are small or medium-sized
- Permits the taking of risks in an appropriate case

During 2011/12 the trust made grants to a variety of charitable organisations. The organisations concerned support work in the fields of development, health and education in Africa, Central and South America, India, Pakistan, Palestine, Sri Lanka, Cambodia, Peru and Nepal; work in the environmental field, particularly in relation to climate change and other work in the UK and Ireland for environmental and community projects, including refugees, prisoners and the unemployed.

The charity also owns a freehold woodland property in the Republic of Ireland which is held for charitable purposes, including amenity value and recreational access for the community.

In 2011/12 the trust had assets of £626,000 and an income of £712,000.

Grants were made to 35 organisations totalling £594,000. Grants ranged from £3,000 to £66,000.

Organisations operating overseas – 23 grants totalling £458,500

Beneficiaries included: San Carlos Hospital – Mexico (£66,000); Impact Foundation – Cambodia (£40,000); Health Poverty Action (£35,000); Arpana Charitable Trust – India and Lifegate Rehabilitation – Palestine (£20,000 each); Tools for Self reliance – Africa/UK (£15,000); Tanzania Development Trust (£10,000); and Tigre Trust – Eritrea (£5,000).

Organisations operating in the UK – 12 grants totalling £135,500

Beneficiaries included: Whitehawk Inn (£20,000); Green Light Trust (£17,000); Sussex Pathways (£12,500); People and Planet (£10,000); Resurgo Trust (£5,000); and Friends First (£3,000).

Exclusions

The following are not supported:
- Evangelism or missionary work
- Individuals
- Nationwide emergency appeals
- Animal, cancer and children's charities

The fund stresses that it receives applications for gap year funding which are always unsuccessful as grants are never made to individuals.

Applications

In writing to the correspondent, although note that the trust has a preference for seeking out its own projects and only very rarely responds to general appeals.

'Unsolicited applications are not encouraged. They are acknowledged, but extremely rarely receive a positive response. No telephone enquiries, please.'

Information gathered from:

Accounts; annual report; Charity Commission record.

The Hadley Trust

Social welfare

£2.1 million (2011/12)

Beneficial area

UK, especially London.

Correspondent: Carol Biggs, Administrator, Gladsmuir, Hadley Common, Barnet, Hertfordshire EN5 5QE (tel: 020 8447 4577; fax: 020 8447 4571; email: carol@hadleytrust.org)

Trustees: Janet Hulme; Philip Hulme; Janet Love; Thomas Hulme; Katherine Prideaux; Sophie Hulme.

CC Number: 1064823

The trust was established in 1997 for welfare purposes. Its annual report gives an overview of its objects and activities:

[The objects of the trust] are primarily, but not exclusively, to assist in creating opportunities for people who are disadvantaged as a result of environmental, educational or economic circumstances, or [disability], to improve their situation, either by direct financial assistance, involvement in project and support work or research into the causes of, and means to alleviate, hardship.

The trustees' approach is to further the trust's objects by engaging with and making grants to other registered charities. In general, the trustees prefer to work with small to medium-sized charities and establish the trust as a reliable, long-term funding partner.

In recent years the trust has become increasingly focused on some core areas of activity where the trustees feel the trust is able to have the greatest impact. Consequently the trust has tended to establish more in-depth relationships with a smaller number of selected partners.

The result of this policy is that the trust does not take on many new funding commitments. Nevertheless the trustees will always consider and respond to proposals which might enhance the effectiveness of the trust.

Grantmaking in 2011/12

In 2011/12 the trust had assets of £90.6 million and an income of £6.3 million, which included a donation of over £4.4 million from the settlor. Grants were made to 69 organisations totalling £2.1 million, and were broken down in the following categories during the year. The trust also provides further information about grantmaking within several categories, and a brief analysis of its relationship with the five largest recipients of grants during the year, although a full breakdown of beneficiaries was not included.

Crime and justice	£851,000
Young people	£371,000
Social investment	£242,000
Medical	£184,000
Welfare reform	£161,000
Disability	£152,000
Hospices	£92,000
International	£90,000

Criminal justice is clearly the trust's single biggest area of activity. It has been growing as a proportion of total spending for several years. The trust has now established valuable, long-term working relationships with a number of dedicated criminal justice charities including Prison Reform Trust, Centre for Court Innovations, Centre for Crime and Justice Studies, Prisoners' Education Trust and Prisoners' Advice Service. It also funds think tanks such as Policy Exchange and the New Economics Foundation (NEF) to carry out research into crime and justice policy issues. By these means the trust

engages in a mixture of service provision and policy work.

The primary focus of the trust's work with young people has been on young people in care. This accounted for 72% of spend in the category for 2011/12 . . . For many years the trust worked with NEF to develop techniques to measure social return with the intention of facilitating better policy making. The methodology has now become well established. The trust still funds individual pieces of work which help to develop and embed SROI and the trust has a modest involvement with the SROI Network which aims to assure quality and share best practice.

New Economics Foundation

In 2010/11 New Economics Foundation (NEF) conducted a review of the cost and outcomes of the North Liverpool Community Justice Centre on behalf of the Ministry of Justice and funded by the Hadley Trust. In the current year NEF has started to work with the only remaining 'second generation' community court in the UK, in Plymouth. The trust is providing financial support to ensure the 'problem-solving' capability is able to continue. We are anxious to learn how Plymouth have successfully adapted to the justice environment in England and will continue to provide support as required.

NEF has successfully increased its capacity to contribute to the trust's overall criminal justice programme. Early phases of work include reviews of women's centres and drug courts. NEF also started work on a study of potential volunteer mentoring, or 'buddy' mentoring, for looked-after young people. This complements our work with Voice.

Prison Reform Trust

The Hadley Trust is the principle funder of the Prison Reform Trust's advice and information service. Each year the service provides support to over 5,000 prisoners and their families. The information gathered by the service provides an important input to PRT's policy and lobbying activity. Because of the strong link between the advice and information service and policy development the Hadley Trust also supports PRT's policy work directly.

Policy Exchange

Policy Exchange has continued to make a major contribution to the trust's work in criminal justice, looked-after children and welfare reform.

In criminal justice, Policy Exchange continued its research into ways to reduce re-offending and built a powerful case for restoring more local control over criminal justice. Policy Exchange also carried out several pieces of work on innovation in policing and championed the role of the new Police and Crime Commissioners.

At the end of the year Policy Exchange was preparing to publish Fostering Aspirations, a report which set out recommendations for the reform of the foster care system. It also continued its very influential series of reports on the reform of the welfare system.

Centre for Justice Innovation

The Centre aims to improve the implementation, evaluation and dissemination of new ideas and practices throughout the criminal justice system. The Centre supports and champions front-line innovators in their efforts to reduce crime, aid victims and improve community confidence in the justice system.

Notable in the first year of activity was the Centre's engagement with the North Liverpool Community Justice Centre which is the most established example of a problem-solving community court in the UK.

Voice

For many years the trust has contributed to Voice's core costs to enable them to provide professional advocacy series to young people in the care of the state. More recently the trust has also stepped in to help fund Voice's policy team. Recently the team has been working on a Blueprint for Advocacy in the UK.

Voice also overlaps with the trust's interest in criminal justice as Voice has been actively involved in the design of the resettlement programme for young offenders at Cookham Wood Young Offenders Institute.

Applications

In writing to the correspondent.

Information gathered from:

Accounts; annual report; Charity Commission record.

Paul Hamlyn Foundation

Arts, education and learning in the UK and local organisations supporting vulnerable groups of people, especially children, social justice

£17.7 million (2011/12)

Beneficial area

UK and India.

Correspondent: Grants Team, 5–11 Leeke Street, London WC1X 9HY (tel: 020 7812 3300; fax: 020 7812 3310; email: information@phf.org.uk; website: www.phf.org.uk)

Trustees: Jane Hamlyn, Chair; Michael Hamlyn; James Lingwood; Baroness Estelle Morris; Lord Claus Moser; Anthony Salz; Peter Wilson-Smith; Tim Bunting; Lord Anthony Hall; Baroness Kidron of Angel; Tom Wylie.

CC Number: 1102927

Paul Hamlyn was a publisher and philanthropist. He established the Paul Hamlyn Foundation in 1987 for general charitable purposes and on his death in 2001 he bequeathed the majority of his estate to the foundation so that it

became one of the UK's largest independent grant-giving organisations. He was committed to opening new opportunities and experiences for the less fortunate members of society. The following information is taken from the foundation's website:

> The foundation is one of the larger independent grant-making foundations in the UK. Grants are made to organisations which aim to maximise opportunities for individuals to experience a full quality of life, both now and in the future. In particular it is concerned with children and young people, and others who are disadvantaged. Preference is given to supporting work which others may find hard to fund, perhaps because it breaks new ground, is too risky or is unpopular. We also take initiatives ourselves where new thinking is required or where we believe there are important unexplored opportunities.

> Below are the values that underpin the Paul Hamlyn Foundation in how it operates as an independent grant-making foundation. They very much mirror the values of the founder. He believed there was a 'better way', that way being 'a society that is fair, allows people to realise their potential, fights prejudice, encourages and assists participation in and enjoyment of the arts and learning, and understands the importance of the quality of life for all communities.

> ▶ Strategic – wanting to make changes to policy and opinion
> ▶ Enabling – giving opportunities and realising potential
> ▶ Courageous – fighting prejudice and taking risks
> ▶ Focused and flexible – through targeted and open grants schemes
> ▶ Supportive – giving advice to applicants who need help
> ▶ Fair – clear application processes, equality of opportunity
> ▶ Value for money – controlling costs and expecting money to be well used

The foundation also runs a 'Grants Plus' scheme:

> We want to have impact beyond the funding we provide, so we seek to learn, share and influence others with our work. There are also some practical things we can do to help grantee and applicant organisations more and to contribute to the development of the philanthropic sector.

The funding programmes are: arts; education and learning; and social justice. The foundation also works in India supporting vulnerable groups of people, especially children.

According to the website, the foundation's strategic aims since 2006 have been:

1 Enabling people to experience and enjoy the arts
2 Developing people's education and learning
3 Integrating marginalised young people who are at times of transition

In addition, we have three related aims:

> ▶ Advancing through research the understanding of the relationships between the arts, education and learning and social change
> ▶ Developing the capacity of organisations and people who facilitate our strategic aims
> ▶ Developing the foundation itself to be an exemplar foundation, existing in perpetuity

> We tend to make grants that help fund specific activities and, as part of these grants, we will consider funding elements of core running costs (including staff salaries) and overheads as per full-cost recovery principles, provided we are told how these costs are calculated. Occasionally, we will also support organisations through core grants, though we then need to know how our funding would be spent and how it will help develop the work and the capacity of the organisation.

> We are unlikely to fund 100 per cent of the costs. We prefer to make grants where you and/or another funder are also contributing, preferably in cash, towards the cost of the activity you are asking us to fund.

Grants can be for up to three years, occasionally longer in some instances although this usually requires a primary and then a subsequent application.

Grantmaking in 2011/12

In 2011/12 the foundation had assets of £559.6 million and an income of £14.3 million. 156 grants were made totalling £17.7 million, exclusive of support costs and broken down in each area of interest as follows:

Arts	£6 million
Education and learning	£4.9 million
Social justice	£4.3 million
India	£400,000
Other grants	£2.1 million

The following selected information is taken from the trust's website and most recent accounts to give an idea of the work supported by the trust:

Arts programme

The Arts programme supports the development and dissemination of new ideas to increase people's experience, enjoyment and involvement in the arts in the UK.

Our funding benefits organisations and groups through our Open Grants and Special Initiatives. Our Open Grants scheme receives applications from organisations proposing innovative activities that we think will have a valuable impact for individuals and communities, organisations, and policy and practice. We work closely with applicants to develop high-quality proposals for consideration by the arts committee and board of trustees.

We also operate Special Initiatives. Some of these, such as Awards for Artists and the Breakthrough Fund, seek to support individuals and organisations, and others, such as our new work on Artists working in participatory settings, focus on developing a sector within the arts.

We also seek to further the understanding of the relationships between the arts and our other programmes. We are interested in how participation in the arts contributes to education and learning processes, and how the arts and/or education and learning affect social change.

The accounts record the performance of the programmes:

The **Breakthrough Fund** aims to unlock significant developments and outcomes in the arts that would otherwise not be achieved. It responded to the compelling visions of outstanding individuals working across art forms and contexts in the role of 'cultural entrepreneur', offering transformational and timely support to them and their organisations to pursue these visions. There were three annual selection processes (2008, 09 and 10), which resulted in 15 grants totalling £3,879,765.

Two further cycles of the Breakthrough Fund are planned worth a total of £3 million. The first selection process will announce decision in late spring 2014. The second will announce decisions in early 2016.

The **Awards for Artists** scheme supports individual artists to develop their creative ideas by providing funding with no strings attached over three years. The awards are made on the basis of need, talent and achievement. In 2011, awards of £45,000, paid in three annual instalments, were made to eight recipients. [In September 2012 the trustees agreed] to continue the scheme for a further five years and to increase each of the eight annual awards to £50,000.

Through the **ArtWorks** programme the foundation is helping deliver training to artists:

That will develop not only their own practice, but also the skills required to work in participatory settings such as prisons or schools. ArtWorks therefore aims to achieve a significant shift in provision, infrastructure and opportunity that will directly affect quality.

Our Museum: Communities and Museums as Active Partners

Paul Hamlyn Foundation is delivering a new Special Initiative to facilitate a process of development and organisational change within museums and galleries that are committed to active partnership with their communities, with the ambition of affecting the museum sector more widely.

This initiative will:

- Support and develop museums and galleries to place community needs, values, aspirations and active collaboration at the core of their work
- Involve communities and individuals in core decision-making processes and to implement the decisions taken
- Ensure that museums and galleries play an effective role in developing community skills, through volunteering, training, apprenticeships, etc.
- Share exemplary new models with the broader museum sector

Our Museum offers support for organisations to manage significant structural change. It is not about short-term project funding, but about facilitating organisational change so that participatory work becomes core, embedded, sustainable and less at risk of being marginalised when specific funding streams run out.

Feedback on Arts programme applicants in 2011/12

Given the financial circumstances, we had expected to see more applications from organisations that were re-thinking their operating models or considering merging with others. Interestingly, whilst numbers of applications to our Open Grants scheme have remained stable compared with last year, we saw relatively few innovative ways of tackling issues of resilience – let alone of growth – in the current climate. Obviously, this thinking did happen, but we did not see enough applications reflecting it and we have been somewhat disappointed not to find out about more people's ideas on these issues.

A notable exception was the Lincolnshire One Venues approach to joining forces and sharing resources to empower young people to become more involved in the artistic programming and running of the ten venues involved. The LOV application showed a refreshing and bold approach to genuine partnership-working and we hope that our funding will enable them to unlock the potential they think they can un-tap. We very much hope that we will see more requests that show this type of resourcefulness. We also continue to look forward to receiving applications for work taking place outside of London, particularly in Wales, Scotland and Northern Ireland.

Beneficiaries included: National Museum Wales (£149,000); Belfast Exposed (£144,000); Philharmonia Ltd (£100,000) – core support towards the development of a virtual Philharmonia Orchestra performing Holst's The Planets, enabling the public to explore the orchestra from inside; Carousel Project (£50,000) – for learning-disabled and marginalised artists to create work comprising music, film and visual art elements, to be experienced live, online and as a touring installation and Kielder Partnership Initiative (£40,000) – 'Testing Ground' will bring together the public, students and practitioners in a programme of experimental architectural education and activity at Kielder Water and Forest Park.

Education and Learning programme

The strategic aim underpinning the work of the Education and Learning programme since 2006 has been 'to support innovative ways of increasing people's education and learning'. In particular we have aimed to 'support the development and dissemination and diffusion of new ideas that work in improving education and increasing the learning of people of all ages'. Due to shifts in government policy and public sector cost-cutting measures, the sector has lost a number of key networks and agencies that previously helped to foster the sharing of best practice, particularly for schools. We remain committed to ensuring that the new thinking and practices that we are helping to develop are accessible to as many people as possible.

Beneficiaries included: Learning Futures (£393,000) – to complete the development and piloting phase of their student engagement project; Institute for Philanthropy (£154,000) – launch of the Youth and Philanthropy Initiative in Northern Ireland, to pilot in 15 schools over three years, giving young people a 'hands-on' experience of giving whilst developing their communication and presentation skills; Musical Futures (£148,000) – to continue the music learning initiative in secondary schools and extend it to Scotland, Wales and Northern Ireland; Al-Haqq Supplementary School (£122,000) – structured supplementary provision to enhance the employability and post-16 progression to further and higher education for young people of Pakistani and Kashmiri descent; Dandelion Time (£74,000) – delivery and dissemination of an experiential programme for traumatised children with emotional or behavioural difficulties facing risk of exclusion or withdrawal from school and What Works? Student Retention and Success Programme (£22,500) – to understand the best ways to support students once they arrive at university.

Social Justice programme

The Social Justice programme has a focus on supporting innovative responses to the challenges faced by young people at a time of economic uncertainty and rapid social change. It aims both to help those who are more marginalised and unable to access appropriate support, and to elevate their voices to have more influence over local and national decision-making.

Our funding is not limited to a particular sector, client group or approach, but spans employability, education and training, refugees and migrants, gangs, youth offending, health and disability. It is intended to help people experiencing discrimination, violence, intolerance or limited opportunity.

Although [the environment is] challenging, one response is to consider innovation – either by changing ways of doing things, or by doing different things entirely. We wish to help with this, and have supported organisations, through our Open Grants and Special Initiatives, to develop new forms of service or business models, or collaborative approaches.

We launched a Special Initiative designed to provide support for children and young people with irregular immigration status. The foundation has supported refugee and migrant organisations for many years, but recently we have become more concerned about those young people who come to the UK and – often through no fault of their own – find themselves unable to return to their home countries, yet unable to work, study or even access the most basic services here.

Beneficiaries included: Supported Options Initiative (£714,000) – for children and young people with irregular immigration status, in partnership with Unbound Philanthropy; Right Here (£231,000) – mental health special initiative in partnership with the Mental Health Foundation to develop new approaches to supporting the mental health and wellbeing of 16–25 year olds; User Voice England UK wide (£146,000) – provision of a staff training and support programme to develop the capacity of an ex-offender workforce to develop and promote service-user participation in criminal justice policy and practice; Islington Law Centre (£120,000) – as a service provider in the supported options initiative; Clore Social Leadership Programme UK wide (£105,000) – funding for up to three specialist Paul Hamlyn Foundation Clore Social Fellowships. Each fellow will have a particular interest in supporting excluded young people, and/or be drawn from a marginalised community and Special Initiative in development (£10,000) – girls and young women in the criminal justice system: looking at addressing the challenges facing girls and young women in the youth justice system or at risk of entering it.

India programme

In 2011/12 the programme has supported eight different social development initiatives with eight different NGOs across the country. This is lower than last year, due to there being only a single round of grant-making, rather than the customary two . . . Our open grants were made across development sectors, maintaining our philosophy of supporting well-though-through and relevant project ideas. The grants were made in the broad areas of governance, education, health and disability, violence against women and ensuring rights and entitlements of poor communities.

Beneficiaries included: Digantar (£72,000) – to undertake the base research and knowledge generation for setting up the Centre for Participatory Research and Action on Teacher Knowledge; Independent Commission for People's Rights and Development (£69,000) – continued support to the 'Men as Partners against Gender Based Violence' initiative and Chaupal Gramin Vikas Prashikshan Evam Shodh Sansthan (£27,000) – to set up health and nutrition surveillance committees to

monitor food and health entitlement in 200 villages.

Four other grants were made including a substantial grant of £2 million to the Helen Hamlyn Trust.

Exclusions

In the UK the foundation does not support:

◗ Individuals or proposals for the benefit of one individual
◗ Funding for work that has already started
◗ General circulars/appeals
◗ Proposals about property or which are mainly about equipment or other capital items
◗ Overseas travel, expeditions, adventure and residential courses

The foundation is unlikely to support:

◗ The continuation or expansion of existing provision, unless there are significant elements of innovation and change
◗ Applications which primarily benefit the independent education sector
◗ Endowments
◗ Organisations wishing to use the foundation's funding to make grants
◗ Websites, publications, seminars unless part of a wider proposal
◗ Market or academic research – unless part of a wider activity

In India, the foundation does not support:

◗ Individuals or proposals for the benefit of one individual
◗ Retrospective funding for work that has already started
◗ General circulars/appeals
◗ Proposals that solely concentrate on the purchasing of property, equipment or other capital items
◗ Overseas activities, including travel, expeditions, adventure and residential courses

Applications

Applications should be completed online via the foundation's website. The following guidelines are provided:

We have a two-stage application process. At the first stage, applicants are required to show that the work for which they are seeking funding fits with the themes and priorities of the programme they are applying to. We also require that applicants show how their proposal meets our criteria for Change and Outcomes, Innovation and Participation.

If taken forward, at the second stage we ask for more detailed information as we work with you to put together a proposal for decision by the Programme Committees or Board of Trustees.

The process takes at least four months, so be sure that your work is not due to start imminently when you apply. We do not support applications for work that has already started by the time it reaches the final approval stage.

After a short eligibility quiz, if you are eligible, you will be asked to provide details about your organisation, and some specific questions about the nature of the work you would like supported.

Alongside details of the proposed activity, we will ask for information on three particular areas that we consider to be important. We are interested in:

◗ The impact of your work: how your work will effect change, and how you propose to measure its outcomes
◗ How innovative your work is: we want to help organisations find new ways of doing things
◗ Participation: We believe that the people we are trying to help should have a role in shaping their own destiny by being involved in developing activities that will affect them

We will ask specific questions on each of these areas during the first stage of your application so it is essential that you consider each of them carefully when planning your application.

We understand that these issues can be confusing and we want to help all applicants to address them. We have published guidance on each of the areas which you can refer to during your application.

We try to respond to all first-stage applications within 28 days. [After this, if successful] our grants programme teams will work closely with you to shape your application and make it as strong as possible before putting it to the programme committee or board of trustees for a final decision.

We will need you to provide further evidence during this stage of all the areas we ask about during the first stage of the application, as well as going into greater detail about the project budget. We also have processes of due diligence, where we look at your organisation's credentials and the environment you are working in, that we need to carry out. This stage can take several months, and the timings of final decisions will depend on the schedule of our programme committees and board meetings.

Not all applications that reach the second stage will definitely progress to being considered by the programme committee or board; many will be declined during this stage.

India programme

India grants have a separate application form on the website which works differently from the other programmes.

Applicants must submit a 'Concept Note' online.

After you have submitted your 'Concept Note' it will be considered by the India team. If appropriate, one of the programme advisors will be in touch and request more information, or arrange to make an on-site assessment. Before an application is taken forward, the advisors in India will have a discussion with the Foundation's Director in the UK.

Please note that the applications process takes at least four months from receipt of your Concept Note. Therefore, please do not apply for funding for work that is due to commence in less than four months, or for work that has already started.

Information gathered from:
Accounts; annual report; Charity Commission record; funder's website.

The Helen Hamlyn Trust

Medical, the arts and culture, education and welfare, heritage and conservation in India, international humanitarian affairs and 'healthy ageing'
£2.2 million (2011/12)

Beneficial area
Worldwide.

Correspondent: John Roche-Kuroda, Trust Administrator and Secretary, 129 Old Church Street, London SW3 6EB (tel: 020 7351 5057; fax: 020 7352 3284; email: john.rochekuroda@ helenhamlyntrust.org)

Trustees: Lady Hamlyn; Dr Kate Gavron; Dr Shobita Punja; Brendan Cahill; Margaret O'Rorke; Dr Deborah Swallow; Mark Bolland.

CC Number: 1084839

Registered with the Charity Commission in January 2001, in April 2002 the assets and activities of the Helen Hamlyn 1989 Foundation were transferred into this trust.

The trust has wide powers to make grants. The trustees bring forward recommendations for projects to support and these recommendations are subject to approval by the board.

The current strategy for grant making is concentrated on the following areas of activity: medical, the arts and culture, education and welfare, heritage and conservation in India, international humanitarian affairs and healthy ageing.

Additionally, small grants of up to £10,000 are made to a wide variety of small local and regional charities where a grant of this size can make a significant difference. All small grants support the trust's charitable objectives.

The trust's core aim is to initiate and support innovative medium to long-term projects, which will effect lasting change and improve quality of life.

Individual projects aim to:
- Support innovation in the medical arena
- Increase access to the arts and support the professional development of artists from the fields of music and the performing arts
- Increase intercultural understanding; provide opportunities for young people to develop new interests and practical skills which will contribute to their education and their future lives and to create opportunities for young offenders to acquire practical skills which will support their personal development for their future lives
- Conserve heritage in India for public access and cultural activities
- Support examples of good practice in the humanitarian sector
- Provide practical support to enable the elderly to maintain their independence for as long as possible

In 2011/12 it had assets of £2.8 million and an income of £2.6 million, mainly from donations. Grants were made totalling £2.2 million, £487,000 of which was paid to the Open Futures Trust, a subsidiary trust, which carries out direct educational work on behalf of the trust. Grants were broken down into the following categories:

Medical	£1 million
Education and welfare	£315,000
Arts and culture	£266,000
Heritage and conservation in India	£79,000
Healthy ageing	£9,600

The largest beneficiary was the Hamlyn Centre for Robotic Surgery at Imperial College, London which received £1 million. It has received a similar amount in the last number of years.

Other beneficiaries included: London Symphony Orchestra – Panufik (£159,000); Museum of London – FilmIt in Museums (£129,000); The University of York (£92,000 in two grants); Royal Opera House -Paul Hamlyn First Night (£85,000); Reis Magos Fort – INTACH (£79,000); Wells Cathedral School Foundation (£10,000); Volunteer Reading Help (£9,000); St Wilfred's Care Home (£6,800); Hackney Music Development Trust (£500); and Meningitis Trust (£100).

Applications
The trust's website notes: 'our energies are focused on the initiation of projects and we do not accept unsolicited applications for major grants.'

Information gathered from:
Accounts; Charity Commission record.

Hampton Fuel Allotment Charity

Relief in need, health, education of children and young people and social welfare
£885,000 to organisations
(2011/12)

Beneficial area
Hampton, the former borough of Twickenham, and the borough of Richmond (in that order).

Correspondent: David White, Clerk to the Trustees, 15 High Street, Hampton, Middlesex TW12 2SA (tel: 020 8941 7866; email: david@hfac.co.uk; website: www.hfac.co.uk)

Trustees: David Parish, Chair; Revd Derek Winterburn; Jonathan Cardy; David Cornwell; Stuart Leamy; Jamie Mortimer; Paula Williams; Dr Jane Young; Hilary Hart; Richard Montgomery.

CC Number: 211756

General
The trust was created following the 1811 Enclosure Act by the granting of 10.14 acres of land for producing a supply of fuel for the poor of the ancient parish of Hampton. Subsequently the land was rented out for nurseries. In 1988 the land was sold for development and the sale proceeds formed the financial base for the current work of the trust.

Historically, the trust's area of benefit was the ancient town of Hampton, now the area covered by the parishes of St Mary's Hampton, All Saints Hampton and St James's Hampton Hill. In 1989 the area was widened. In brief the primary, secondary and tertiary areas of benefit are:
1 Hampton and Hampton Hill
2 Hampton Wick, Teddington, Twickenham and Whitton
3 The rest of the London Borough of Richmond upon Thames. However, trustees are unlikely to support a project in this area unless there are also a significant number of beneficiaries from areas 1 or 2

As the name of the trust suggests, its original purpose was to make grants of fuel to those in poverty. The trust has continued to fulfil its original purpose, while assuming many other roles and tasks.

The objects of the trust are:
- The relief of need, hardship or distress of those within the area of benefit

▌ Improving the conditions of life for the inhabitants in the interest of social welfare

The trust funds the following:

▌ Individuals, their social welfare and individual support
▌ Young people, through youth training organisations and clubs
▌ Education, through nurseries, play groups, schools and colleges
▌ The community, through community based organisations
▌ People with disabilities, as individuals and through disability organisations
▌ Older people, through old people's welfare organisations and clubs
▌ Housing, through housing associations and trusts
▌ Caring for the sick, through hospitals and hospices
▌ Recreation and leisure, through social and sporting clubs

Grants are given towards fuel costs and essential equipment and to not for profit organisations which support those in need or education or social welfare. The charity undertakes regular reviews of the cost of fuel, state benefits and other needs of the beneficiaries. £500,000 has been set aside for the purpose of loans to not for profit organisations.

The trustees see the merit of being able to give loans to 'not-for-profit' organisations where they are developing their facilities and need support with capital costs but are able to repay the loan out of future income. Trustees have set aside up to £200,000 for this purpose.

Grantmaking in 2011/12

During the year the trust held assets of £46.6 million and had an income of £1.8 million. Grants were made totalling £1.7 million.

Over 2,000 individuals received grant support and 82 grants were awarded to organisations, distributed into the following categories:

Social welfare	33	£437,000
Disability organisations	30	£196,000
Community organisations	11	£181,000
Educational support	7	£51,000
Hospitals and hospices	1	£20,000
Total	**82**	**£885,000**

The trust states in its annual report that:

The charity provides grant aid to organisations on the basis of an annual application and makes no commitment concerning future support. However, over the years a number of organisations have received a grant every year. These organisations provide valuable services for those in need within the area of benefit and further the objectives of the charity

The most significant beneficiaries were: Richmond Citizens Advice (£55,000); Hampton Hill Cricket Club, Twickenham Brunswick Club for Young People and Age UK Richmond (£50,000 each); Hampton and Hampton Hill Voluntary Care Group and Richmond Youth Partnership (£40,000 each); and SPEAR (£39,000).

Other beneficiaries included: Linden Hall Day Centre (£22,000); Alzheimer's Society (£16,000); Three Wings Trust and Richmond Furniture Scheme (£15,000 each); LBRUT Specialist Children's Services Leaving Care Team and Orange Tree Theatre (£10,000 each); South West London Stroke Club (£5,000); Learn English at Home (£3,000); and Richmond upon Thames College (£1,500).

Exclusions

The charity is unlikely to support:

▌ Grants to individuals for private and post compulsory education
▌ Adaptations or building alterations for individuals
▌ Holidays, except in cases of severe medical need
▌ Decoration, carpeting or central heating
▌ Anything which is the responsibility of a statutory body
▌ National general charitable appeals
▌ Animal welfare
▌ Advancement of religion or religious groups, unless offering a non-religious service to the community
▌ Commercial and business activities
▌ Endowment appeals
▌ Projects of a political nature
▌ Retrospective capital grants
▌ Organisations whose free reserves exceed 12 months' running costs
▌ Non-charitable social enterprises

Applications

Once applicants are satisfied that they meet the criteria they should contact the clerk to discuss their funding request, or preferably send a brief outline by email (david@hfac.co.uk or 020 8979 5555). If the clerk determines that you meet the criteria and have a reasonable chance of success then he will either invite you to submit an application which will be followed up by a telephone assessment or arrange an assessment visit to your organisation.

Detailed application and eligibility guidelines, as well as application forms, are available on the website. Trustees meet to consider applications every two months and feedback can be given to unsuccessful applicants.

Information gathered from:

Accounts; annual report and review; Charity Commission record; funder's website.

The Kathleen Hannay Memorial Charity

Health, welfare, Christian, general

£666,000 (2011/12)

Beneficial area

UK.

Correspondent: Martin Betts, R. F. Trustee Co. Ltd, 15 Suffolk Street, London SW1Y 4HG (tel: 020 7036 5685)

Trustees: Simon Weil; Christian Ward; Jonathan Weil; Laura Watkins.

CC Number: 299600

The trust was established by the Reverend Robert Fleming Hannay in 1988. The trust supports a wide variety of UK and overseas charitable causes. In furtherance of its objectives, the trust continues to make a substantial number of grants to charitable organisations both on a one-off and recurring basis.

In 2011/12 the trust had assets of £12.3 million and an income of £353,000. Grants were made to 32 organisations totalling £666,000. Grants were broken down as follows:

Relief of poverty	6	£69,000
Education	4	£63,000
Religion	8	£168,000
Health	7	£253,000
Arts, culture, heritage and science	4	£53,000
Amateur sport	1	£4,000
Environment	1	£30,000
Relief in need	3	£31,000

The beneficiaries listed in the accounts were: Network Training and Counselling and Hullavington Parochial Church Council (£140,000 each); Ripon College – Cuddesdon (£52,000); Save the Children (£50,000); and Children's Burn Trust (£33,000).

Exclusions

No grants to individuals or non-registered charities.

Applications

In writing to the correspondent. The trustees' report states that 'the trustees consider and approve grants annually and although many are made to the same charities each year none are promised or guaranteed'.

Information gathered from:

Accounts; annual report; Charity Commission record.

The Haramead Trust

Children, social welfare, education, people with disabilities, homeless people, medical assistance, victims and oppressed people

£770,500 (2011/12)

Beneficial area

Worldwide, in practice developing countries, UK and Ireland, locally in the East Midlands.

Correspondent: Michael J. Linnett, Trustee, Park House, Park Hill, Gaddesby, Leicestershire LE7 4WH

Trustees: Simon P. Astill; Winifred M. Linnett; Michael J. Linnett; Robert H. Smith; David L. Tams; Revd Joseph A. Mullen.

CC Number: 1047416

The Haramead Trust was established in 1995 for general charitable purposes. The trust focuses its grant giving on the relief of those suffering hardship or distress, children's welfare and education in relation to the advancement of health.

The trustees may visit funded projects, both in the UK and overseas, for monitoring purposes or to assess projects/organisations for future grants. Travel and administration costs are borne by the settlor; only audit costs are met by the trust.

In 2011/12 the trust had assets of £107,500 and an income of £628,000, most of which was in the form of a regular donation from the settlor. Grants were made to 76 organisations (following 1,015 applications) totalling £770,500, which were split geographically as follows:

UK and Ireland	£304,000
Developing world	£249,500
East Midlands	£217,000

Grants of £10,000 or more included those to: Scope and Let Children Live (£75,000 each); Leicestershire and Rutland Community Fund (£30,000); NSPCC (£25,000); Leonard Cheshire Disability (£20,000); De Montford University and Project Trust (£15,000 each); and Compassion Africa, Housing Justice, Macmillan Cancer Support and Sense International (£10,000 each).

Grants between £5,000 and £9,999 totalled £196,500; grants of less than £5,000 totalled £29,000.

Applications

In writing to the correspondent. The trustees meet every two months.

Percentage of awards given to new applicants: less than 10%.

Common applicant mistakes

'Supplying too little financial information if a small charity.'

Information gathered from:

Accounts; annual report; Charity Commission record; further information provided by the funder.

The Harbour Foundation

Relief of poverty for refugees and homeless people, education, research

£802,000 (2011/12)

Beneficial area

Worldwide.

Correspondent: The Trustees, 1 Red Place, London W1K 6PL (tel: 020 7456 8180)

Trustees: Rex Harbour; Susan Harbour; Dr Daniel Harbour; Edmond Harbour.

CC Number: 264927

The Harbour Foundation was established in 1970. According to the trustees' report for 2011/12:

> The charity's activities consist of the making of grants to charitable organisations which are based in the UK and abroad. Its objects, laid down in the governing document, are:
>
> ▸ The relief of poverty, suffering and distress among refugees and other homeless people
> ▸ The advancement of education, learning and research and the dissemination of the results of such research
> ▸ To make donations to any institution established for charitable purposes according to the law of England and Wales

In 2011/12 the trust had assets of £49 million and an income of £1.4 million. There were 83 grants made totalling £802,000, of which 74 were to charities in the UK. Grants were broken down as follows:

Education	13	£483,500
Music	22	£92,500
Medical	13	£69,000
Social organisation	20	£65,000
Religious bodies	5	£62,500
Relief	10	£29,000

A list of beneficiaries was unavailable, however previous beneficiaries have included: Royal College of Music, London and the Tel Aviv Foundation, Israel (£15,000 each).

Applications

In writing to the correspondent. Applications need to be received by February, as trustees meet in March.

Information gathered from:

Accounts; annual report; Charity Commission record.

The Harpur Trust

Education, welfare and recreation

£556,000 to organisations (2011/12)

Beneficial area

The borough of Bedford.

Correspondent: Lucy Bardner, Grants Manager, Princeton Court, Pilgrim Centre, Brickhill Drive, Bedford MK41 7PZ (tel: 01234 369500; fax: 01234 369505; email: grants@harpur-trust.org.uk; website: www.bedfordcharity.org.uk)

Trustees: David Palfreyman; Rae Levene; Michael Womack; Ian David McEwen; Rosemary Wallace; Philip Wallace; Anthony Nutt; Justin Phillimore; Susan Clark; Tina Beddoes; Prof. Stephen Mayson; Hugh Murray Stewart; Peter Budek; Richard O'Quinn; David Meghen; Sally Peck; Dr Deirdre Anderson; David Dixon; Kate Jacques; Dr Jennifer Sauboorah; Dr Anne Egan.

CC Number: 1066861

This charity is one of the oldest described in this resource, and probably one of the oldest in the country. The Harpur Trust (also formerly known as the Bedford Charity), has been in existence since 1566 when it was founded by Sir William Harpur (1496–1573) a tailor from Bedford and later Lord Mayor of London, who created an endowment to sustain a school he had established in Bedford. The trust provides the following information:

> We are a local foundation that uses the legacy of Sir William Harpur, our founder in 1566, to benefit the inhabitants of the Borough of Bedford through the promotion of education; the relief of poverty, sickness, hardship or distress; and the provision of recreational facilities with a social welfare purpose.
>
> We make grants in support of all three of our charitable objects and mission areas. Organisations and individuals are encouraged to contact us informally for initial guidance on their applications and much advice is given verbally.

The trust owns and runs four independent schools in Bedford – Bedford School, Bedford Girls' School, Bedford Modern School and Pilgrims Preparatory School. The trust is also a co-sponsor, along with Bedford College of the new Bedford Academy. It also owns and manages almshouses which provide secure, affordable accommodation for a number of the borough's less advantaged, older citizens.

Grantmaking Policy

Our responsive programme

Approximately £500,000 is awarded from our responsive programme each year. Grants within this category cover education, relief and recreation.

Our themed grants programmes

An additional £500,000 per year is available from our themed grants programmes. These enable us to focus resources on topics of particular interest which still fit within our three objects of education, relief and recreation. Our aim is to increase the impact and benefits of our funding through specific, targeted interventions. Each of the themed programmes has its own specific criteria and all projects funded through this programme must be able to demonstrate the potential to influence policy and practice in the field or be replicated in other locations.

We reviewed our themed programmes following the publication of 'Sinking and Swimming – understanding Britain's unmet needs' a report by the Young Foundation which the trust co-funded.

As a result, we have launched three new themed programmes based on the report's recommendations. Our new programmes are broader in scope than the old ones, with the aim of being accessible to a wider range of Bedford projects.

The programme we have maintained is:

The Education Challenge Fund

This is a partnership programme for state schools in the Borough of Bedford wishing to conduct research in school. Please contact the grants manager for more information.

The three new programmes are:

Transitions

This programme is for projects which provide preparation, bridges and support for people undergoing difficult life transitions in Bedford.

Resilience or Psychological Fitness

This programme is for projects which will help Bedford residents manage and cope with traumatic changes positively, learning to adapt and prosper despite setbacks.

Isolation

A programme for projects which reduce loneliness and lack of social networks amongst Bedford's most vulnerable residents.

For detailed information about each programme and examples of the type of project it might fund, please contact the Grants Manager.

More in-depth descriptions of each programme are also available on the trust's website.

Who can apply?

The organisation making the application must be a registered charity or other non-profit making body. Non statutory groups must have a constitution or other governing document or rules. The organisation must be based in the Borough of Bedford, and/or be conducting specific activities aiming to meet the needs of people who live in the Borough. The Borough comprises the town of Bedford and the surrounding area of North Bedfordshire.

Grantmaking in 2011/12

In 2011/12 the charity had assets of £110 million and a consolidated income of £50.4 million, which included £44.3 million from school fees. There were 39 grants to organisations totalling £556,000; grants, awards and bursaries to individuals totalled £94,000.

Beneficiaries during the year included: Autism Bedfordshire (£74,000); St John's Foundation Special School (£50,000); Family Groups Bedford (£41,000); The Cranfield Trust (£37,000); Alzheimer's Society (£30,000); Full House Theatre Company (£22,000); Road Victims Trust (£15,000); Show Racism the Red Card (£12,000); YMCA Bedfordshire (£10,000); Fun 4 Young People and Anglia Ruskin University (£5,000 each); Pilgrims Oakley Cricket Club (£2,500); and Queens Park Allotment Association (£1,700).

Exclusions

Grants are not made:

- In support of commercial ventures
- For any project that promotes religion, although the trust does fund faith groups for secular work
- In support of projects that do not benefit the residents of the borough of Bedford
- To cover costs already incurred
- For trips, except in very limited circumstances. Contact the grants manager for specific guidance
- For services which are the responsibility of the local authority, for example, a school applying for a grant to cover the cost of employing a teacher is unlikely to be successful. However, the trust could consider an application from a school for a creative arts project that involved paying a voluntary organisation to deliver lunch time or after school workshops

Applications

First, read the guidance notes to make sure your project is eligible. These are available on the charity's website upon completion of a short eligibility questionnaire.

The trust is open to informal contact with potential applicants. If you are in doubt about your project or whether you are eligible you are encouraged to call to discuss before applying formally.

The first stage of the formal application process is to submit a preliminary proposal form. Proposals are first considered by trustees before the trust writes to applicants to discuss the outcome, offer feedback and make an invitation to submit a formal, second stage application if applicable.

The second stage application may be completed online or by filling out a hard copy form, downloadable from the website, and posting it back to the trust. Be careful to include the required additional information. The trust guidelines detail what information is required depending on the size and type of grant requested.

Applications requesting amounts of up to £5,000 are normally considered within two to three months. Grants of up to £50,000 for a single project in any one year and up to £150,000 for a project over a three year period will be considered by the full grants committee which meets every three months. Decisions for these grants are usually made within three to six months. The trust advises:

> Please allow more time if you are submitting a request that will be processed during the summer months as there are no committee meeting in July and August. Grants awarded by the committee above £50,000 per year will need to be endorsed by the full trustee body of the Harpur Trust, which meets three times a year. These meetings usually take place in March, July and December. Awards of this size are rare, and the decision making process will almost certainly be longer than for more modest requests.

The trust has produced helpful 'how-to' documents on full cost recovery applications and dealing with outcomes and monitoring which are available on the website. Application deadlines are also published online.

Percentage of awards given to new applicants: 52%.

Common applicant mistakes

'Failing to clarify aims and outcomes; lack of proper costing of work; failing to answer questions; failing to read guidelines, e.g. applying when outside our area of benefit.'

Information gathered from:

Accounts; annual report; annual review; Charity Commission record; guidelines for applicants; further information provided by the funder; funder's website.

The Peter Harrison Foundation

Sports for people in the UK who have disabilities or are disadvantaged, support for children and young people in the south east of England who are terminally ill, have disabilities, or are disadvantaged, and certain educational initiatives

£1.2 million to organisations
(2011/12)

Beneficial area
UK; south east of England.

Correspondent: Julia Caines, Administrator, Foundation House, 42–48 London Road, Reigate, Surrey RH2 9QQ (tel: 01737 228000; fax: 01737 228001; email: enquiries@ peterharrisonfoundation.org; website: www.peterharrisonfoundation.org)

Trustees: Sir Peter Harrison, Chair; Julia Harrison-Lee; Peter Lee; Nicholas Harrison.

CC Number: 1076579

The foundation was established for general charitable purposes by Peter Harrison in April 1999. The aims of the foundation are to:

- Help disabled people or disadvantaged children/young people, principally through sport and education
- Support charitable activities which are well planned and demonstrate a high level of community involvement
- Fund projects where their grant will make a substantial difference to the charity funded
- Support projects that are likely to have a sustainable impact

Peter Harrison is a keen and active sportsman and believes that education and sport provide the key stepping stones to self-development, creation of choice, confidence building and self-reliance. A businessman, entrepreneur and sportsman he wishes to share his success by making these stepping stones more readily available to those who have disabilities or who are disadvantaged and who may not otherwise have the opportunity to develop their self-potential.

In 2009 the foundation celebrated its 10th anniversary. At this point over £19.6 million had been distributed to 375 charities throughout the United Kingdom; this has been achieved through the foundation's grants programmes. An exceptional investment return in 2011/12 has allowed the

trustees to found another trust, the Peter Harrison Heritage Foundation (Charity Commission no. 1148808), which will:

> Promote objectives which have previously been outside the Foundation's guidelines or which have been catered for under the trustees' discretionary programme of the foundation. The PHHF will be able to fund significant capital projects in order to make a lasting impact, with a particular focus on advancing the heritage, national history and traditions of Great Britain at home and in its current and former dominions and protectorates abroad (projects of particular interest to Peter Harrison CBE)...It should be noted, however, that the PHHF will not accept applications for grants.

Grant programmes
Opportunities through sport
This programme is [the foundation's only] nationwide [programme] and applications are accepted from charities throughout the United Kingdom. The trusts wish to support sporting activities or projects which provide opportunities for people who have disabilities or who are otherwise disadvantaged are supported in order to fulfil their potential and to develop other personal and life skills.

Grants will often be one-off grants for capital projects. We will, however, also consider revenue funding for a new project or if funding is key to the continuing success or survival of an established project. Applications are welcomed for projects that:
- Provide a focus for skills development and confidence building through the medium of sport
- Have a strong training and/or educational theme within the sporting activity
- Provide sporting equipment or facilities for people with disabilities or disadvantaged people
- Have a high degree of community involvement
- Help to engage children or young people at risk of crime, truancy or addiction

Special needs and care for children and young people
This programme is for charities in the south east of England and applications are accepted only from charities in: Berkshire; Buckinghamshire; Hampshire; Isle of Wight; Kent; Oxfordshire; Surrey; East Sussex; and West Sussex. Applications from charities based in or operating in London are not accepted, but the foundation may consider funding charities based in London for a specific project taking place in the south east area that meets its criteria. Applications are welcomed for projects that:
- Work with or benefit children with disabilities, chronically or terminally ill children or provide support for their parents and carers
- Help to engage children or young people at risk of crime, truancy or addiction
- Are organised for young people at risk of homelessness or that provide new

opportunities for homeless young people

Opportunities through education
This programme supports education initiatives, primarily in the south east of England, which are of particular interest to the trustees. Through this programme bursary places for children from the Reigate and Redhill areas in Surrey are funded.

Applications are not invited for this programme.

Trustees' discretion
This programme supports projects that are of particular interest to the trustees and external applications are not invited.

Guidelines for applicants
The foundation accepts applications from registered charities, community amateur sports clubs, friendly societies or industrial provident societies and organisations in Northern Ireland recognised by the HM Revenue and Customs. The foundation also accepts applications from local branches of national charities but only if they have either a separate legal constitution or have the endorsement of their national head office.

The foundation wishes to support those charitable activities that demonstrate an existing high level of voluntary commitment, together with well-planned and thought-out projects.

Grantmaking in 2011/12
In 2011/12 the foundation had assets of almost £53 million and an income of £2.4 million. Grants paid totalled £1.3 million, broken down as follows:

Opportunities through sport	19	£750,000
Trustees' discretion	13	£281,000
Special needs and care for children and young people	4	£167,000
Opportunities through education*	5	£139,000

Beneficiaries included: Loughborough University (£150,000); British Paralympic Association and the National Maritime Museum (£125,000 each); the Scout Association, Watford Grammar and St Michael's Church (£50,000 each); Dwarf Sports Association (£38,000); the Shakespeare Globe Trust (£36,000); and the Outward Bound Trust (£13,000).

*Education grants were paid as bursaries to individuals to enable them to attend Reigate Grammar School.

A full list of grant awards can be found on the foundation's website.

Exclusions
The foundation does not fund:
- General fundraising appeals
- Retrospective funding
- Other grantmaking bodies to make grants on the foundation's behalf
- Projects that directly replace statutory funding or activities that are primarily

the responsibility of central or local government

- Individuals
- Holidays or expeditions in the UK or abroad
- Outdoor activity projects such as camping and outward-bound expeditions
- Overseas projects
- Projects that are solely for the promotion of religion

Applications

The foundation has a two stage application process.

Step 1: Initial enquiry

Potential applicants are asked to first read the information on eligibility and grant programmes available on the foundation's website. If your project meets the criteria for one of the open programmes (i.e. Opportunities through Sport or Special Needs and Care for Children and Young People), then complete the online initial enquiry form. This can be found in the 'application process' section of the foundation's website.

Applications are processed as quickly as possible, but be aware that the foundation receives a large number of applications and it may sometimes take up to two months for an initial enquiry form to be considered.

Applications are first assessed by the foundation's staff. If it is felt the project will be of interest, they will arrange either to visit the project or to conduct a telephone discussion with the applicant about it. Depending on the outcome of these discussions, you may then be invited to submit a full application.

If your initial enquiry is not successful you will be notified by email. The foundation receives many more applications than it is able to support and unfortunately have to turn down many good proposals, even though they meet the criteria. No feedback is given on unsuccessful applications.

Step 2: Full application

You will only be asked to complete a full application if your initial enquiry has been successful. The application form will be sent to you by email. Trustees meet regularly to consider applications.

If an application is successful the applicant will normally be contacted by telephone followed by a grant offer letter. The letter will explain the conditions which apply to all grant awards and also set out any special conditions which apply to your organisation. It will also confirm details of how and when you will receive the grant and how payment is made.

If an application is unsuccessful the applicant will be informed by letter. The

main reason for not funding projects is the volume of applications received.

Organisations supported by the foundation are required to show how they have used the grant and, depending on the grant amount and the nature of the project, may be asked to undertake a review and evaluation of the project being funded. This will normally be on completion of the project, but for charities receiving their grant in several instalments, interim reports may be requested. Full details of the monitoring information required are given in the foundation's grant offer letter.

The foundation aims to ensure that all grant applications that are eligible for consideration within the foundation's grants criteria are given equal consideration, irrespective of gender, sexual orientation, race, colour, ethnic or national origin, or disability.

Information gathered from:

Accounts; annual report; annual review; Charity Commission record; Guidelines for applicants; funder's website.

The Maurice Hatter Foundation

Jewish causes, general
£931,000 (2011/12)

Beneficial area
Unrestricted.

Correspondent: Jeremy S. Newman, Trustee, Smith and Williamson, 1 Bishops Wharf, Walnut Tree Close, Guildford, Surrey GU1 4RA (tel: 01483 407100)

Trustees: Sir Maurice Hatter; Ivor Connick; Jeremy S. Newman; Richard Hatter.

CC Number: 298119

The foundation was established in 1987 for general charitable purposes, mainly for Jewish causes.

In 2011/12 it had assets of £4.7 million and an income of £486,000. Grants were made during the year totalling almost £931,000.

Grants were categorised as follows:

Education	£663,000
Culture and environment	£118,000
Social welfare	£80,000
Religion	£36,000
Medical research	£24,000
International policy research	£10,000

The largest grant was made to World ORT (£350,000) which has also received substantial support in previous years (£188,000 in 2010/11).

Other beneficiaries included: South of England Foundation (Charlton Athletic Community Trust) (£100,000);

University College Hospital Charity Fund – towards the Hatter Cardiovascular Institute (£80,000); Ambitious About Autism (£55,000); Jewish Community Secondary School Trust (£25,000); Community Security Trust (£15,000); Norwood Ravenswood (£10,000); Churchill Centre UK, Chief Rabbinate Trust and Social Mobility Foundation (£5,000 each); and Prostate Action (£3,000).

Applications

Unsolicited applications will not be considered.

Information gathered from:

Accounts; annual report; Charity Commission record.

The Charles Hayward Foundation

Heritage and conservation, criminal justice, overseas
£1.2 million (2012)

Beneficial area

Unrestricted, in practice mainly UK with some overseas funding.

Correspondent: Dorothy Napierala, Hayward House, 45 Harrington Gardens, London SW7 4JU (tel: 020 7370 7063; website: www.charleshaywardfoundation. org.uk)

Trustees: J. M. Chamberlain; Sir Jack Hayward; S. J. Heath; B. D. Insch; N. van Leuven; R. Hayward; A. J. Heath.

CC Number: 1078969

Sir Charles Hayward was born in 1893 in Wolverhampton, Staffordshire. In 1911 he started his own business making wooden patterns for the developing engineering trade. His early involvement in the motor industry proved to be a springboard for his later success culminating in the formation of Firth Cleveland Ltd. He was Chair from its inception in 1953 until 1973 when he retired.

Sir Charles used his personal fortune to establish and endow two charitable trusts, the Hayward Foundation and the Charles Hayward Trust. The two charities were combined on 1 January 2000, to become the Charles Hayward Foundation. The accounts note that: 'The Foundation seeks to find and support projects are preventative or provide early intervention and particularly those that increase people's capacity for self-reliance.'

In 2012 the foundation had assets of £49.4 million and an income of £1.5 million. Grants were made totalling £1.2 million, and were broken down as follows:

Hospices	£243,000
Criminal justice	£217,000
Older people	£217,000
Overseas	£190,000
Heritage and conservation	£154,000
Small grants	£137,000
Miscellaneous	£22,000

The foundation currently has a focus on the following priorities:

Current categories:
- Heritage and conservation
- Criminal justice
- Overseas
- Older people

The foundation does change priorities on a regular basis, for example hospices and younger people's causes have been discontinued as main categories in recent years. Check the website for current priorities before applying.

Beneficiaries during 2012 included: Les Bourgs Hospice (£30,000); St Barnabas House (£20,000); Age UK Norwich and Sutton Women's Aid (£15,000 each); Build Africa (£13,000); International Refugee Trust London (£11,000); Street Child Africa, Heritage Trust for the North West and Wildlife Trust Hampshire and Isle of Wight (£10,000 each); HANDS Volunteer Bureau (£5,000); Lifecycle UK (£4,500); Llanrumney Community Church (£4,000); YMCA North Somerset (£2,000); and St Breward Village Hall (£1,100).

The following details are provided on the foundation's website:

General Guidelines
The following information is intended to provide a general overview. After which, it is important that you refer to our funding categories for specific information and guidance.

Grant Programmes
We run both a main and small grant programme, and currently make grants in the following categories:

Main grant programme
Criminal Justice, Heritage & Conservation and Overseas (for charities with an income of more than £350,000).

Small grant programme
Criminal Justice, Heritage & Conservation and Older People (for charities with an income of less than £350,000).

Within all of the above categories we fund project costs and capital expenditure. For guidance on the types and size of grants we make, please refer to specific category guidelines, also downloadable click here.

Our Funding Priorities
Generally, when funding projects, we value projects that develop, expand and replicate a tried and tested approach but we are also interested in supporting creative solutions to problems which seem to be entrenched and elude resolution.

We value projects that are preventative and provide early intervention. We favour projects that respond to a well researched and clear need, provide intervention based on evidence of what works, are able to demonstrate value for money and have a clear understanding of short-term effects and long-term impact of the intervention they propose.

The website has a helpful 'Which category is right for me?' section where you click on a category which then poses a question about your organisation's annual income and then points you in the right direction, depending on your answer.

Exclusions
Individual categories have their own additional exclusions (check the website for details).

However, generally the foundation does not fund:
- Endowments
- General appeals
- Grant making charities
- Individuals
- Loan and deficits
- Retrospectively, i.e. costs already incurred prior to receiving a decision from the Foundation
- Running costs

Applications
The foundation's website provides the following information on when to apply:

Main Grants
Our main grant programme has a two stage grant process as follows:

Stage 1: A Grants Committee meets on a quarterly basis. The Committee's role is to put applications forward to stage 2.

Stage 2: Applications recommended by the Grants Committee are considered at one of the Trustees' meetings which take place on a quarterly basis and are usually held in: February, April, July and November.

Small Grants
Our small grant programme is a rolling grant programme and applications are considered every two to three months.

Re-applying:
Charities that have previously received a grant or applied unsuccessfully are asked to wait two years before applying. Unsuccessful applicants may not re-apply with the same project.

Conditions attached to grant offers:
The grant offer may be withdrawn after 12 months if it is not taken up.

The full guidelines for the Main Grant programme can be downloaded at the foundation's website (the foundation states that the guidelines should be treated as a whole and only distributed in full form).

The Small Grants programme guidelines also contains an application form which

should be used if you qualify to apply for a small grant.

The trust states that if you need clarification on whether your project fits within the foundation's policy, you are invited to discuss it with Dorothy Napierala, Kate Fawcett or Sheila Ebsworth before sending in your application. They can be telephoned at the foundation's office.

Percentage of awards given to new applicants: 59%.

Common applicant mistakes
'They do not read our guidelines.'

Information gathered from:
Accounts; annual report; Charity Commission record; guidelines for applicants; further information provided by the funder; funder's website.

The Headley Trust

Arts, heritage, health, welfare, overseas development
£4.3 million (2012/13)

Beneficial area
Unrestricted.

Correspondent: Alan Bookbinder, Director, The Peak, 5 Wilton Road, London SW1V 1AP (tel: 020 7410 0330; fax: 020 7410 0332; website: www.sfct. org.uk)

Trustees: Lady Susan Sainsbury; Judith Portrait; Timothy Sainsbury; Sir Timothy Sainsbury; J. Benson; Camilla Sainsbury.

CC Number: 266620

Summary
This is one of the Sainsbury Family Charitable Trusts which share a joint administration. Like the others, it is primarily proactive, aiming to choose its own grantees, and its annual reports state that 'proposals are generally invited by the trustees or initiated at their request'. The extent to which readers should in general be deterred by this is discussed in the separate entry, under the Sainsbury name, for the group as a whole.

In this particular case, the statement and the general sentiment that unsolicited applications are unlikely to be successful seems to be contradicted in the same document where, under the 'health and social welfare' heading the trust notes that '[the trustees] will consider applications which deal with educational and psychological support for pre-school families and] homelessness projects]'

The trust has a particular interest in the arts and in artistic and architectural heritage and has made large grants to museums, galleries, libraries and theatres.

There are ongoing programmes for the repair of cathedrals and medieval churches and other conservation projects in the UK and overseas. The trust also supports a range of social welfare issues. Its support for activities in developing countries is focused on sub-Saharan Anglophone countries and Ethiopia. There is also a small Aids for Disabled Fund. Like many of the others in the Sainsbury group, the Headley Trust prefers to support 'innovative schemes that can be successfully replicated or become self-sustaining'.

The settlor of this trust is Sir Timothy Sainsbury. His co-trustees include his wife, eldest son and legal adviser. The trust's staff includes the director of the Sainsbury family's charitable trusts, Alan Bookbinder.

The following information is taken from the trust's website:

Funding Priorities

Arts & Heritage UK
- Arts, heritage and conservation projects in the UK of outstanding importance, including industrial and maritime heritage; grants for regional museums/galleries, particularly for supporting curatorship; national museums and libraries; rural crafts; archaeological projects
- Support for principally regional museums to purchase unusual or exceptional artefacts
- Headley Museums Archaeological Acquisition Fund (www.headley-archaeology.org.uk)

Cathedrals & Major Churches
- Restoration or repair work to the fabric of ancient cathedrals, parish church cathedrals and large churches of exceptional architectural merit

Parish Churches
- Fabric repairs to listed medieval parish churches in sparsely populated and less prosperous rural areas

Arts & Heritage Overseas
- Conservation and recording of heritage (including ecclesiastical and vernacular architecture, archaeology and cultural artefacts), primarily in South Eastern Europe (Slovenia, Croatia, Albania, Macedonia, Bulgaria, Romania, Serbia, Montenegro, Bosnia-Herzegovina, Turkey)
- Raising awareness of heritage issues in these countries, supporting the capacity of new heritage NGOs, and training the next generation of conservation and heritage professionals

Developing Countries
- Development projects in sub-Saharan Anglophone Africa, and Ethiopia, under the following general headings:
  - Water (sanitation, access, better use of water resources)

- Environment (sustainable energy, farming, forestry)
- Education and literacy
- Healthcare (maternal, disability, trachoma prevention and treatment)
- Emergency appeals (at the discretion of trustees)

Education
- Bursaries for vocational training in traditional crafts, conservation and heritage skills
- Bursaries for mainly postgraduate studies in music and dance

Health & Social Welfare
- Support for elderly people of limited means and dementia sufferers to maintain their independence
- Housing provision for older people
- Music therapy for older people
- Support for older carers of an ill or disabled relative
- Family and parenting support and access for the disabled
- Occasional research projects on medical conditions of particular interest to the trustees
- Small grants providing practical aids for disabled people

Grantmaking in 2012/13

In 2012/13 the trust had assets totalling £74 million and an income of £3 million. Grants were paid during the period totalling £4.3 million, which included commitments from previous years. These figures are higher than usual as the period covered 15 months due to a change in the financial year end of the trust.

Grants approved were categorised with the number of grants and their value as follows:

Arts and Heritage – UK	43	£1.14 million
- Cathedral Programme	6	£285,000
- Parish Churches Programme	55	£197,000
- Museums Archaeological Acquisition Fund	21	£61,500
Health and Social Welfare	33	£768,000
- Aids for People with a Disability	52	£43,500
Education	24	£575,500
Developing Countries	8	£197,500
Arts and Heritage – Overseas	10	£169,000

Beneficiaries of grants of £5,000 or more across all categories included: Lakeland Arts Trust (£210,000); Peabody Trust (£118,000); National Museum of the Royal Navy and Remap (£90,000 each); Art Fund (£75,000); Canterbury Cathedral and the Royal Academy of Music (£60,000 each); Action On Elder Abuse (£58,000); Great Ormond Street Hospital Children's Charity (£50,000); Fight for Sight (£49,000); Council for British Archaeology (£45,000); Ethiopian Heritage Fund (£40,000); Halifax Minster (£30,000); Groundwork Wakefield (£25,000); Central School of Ballet and the Imperial Society of

Teachers of Dancing (£20,000 each); Penarth Pier Pavilion (£15,000); and Pontefract Museum and the Wessex Children's Hospice Trust (£10,000 each).

Exclusions
Individuals; expeditions.

Applications
See the guidance for applicants in the entry for the Sainsbury Family Charitable Trusts. A single application will be considered for support by all the trusts in the group. However, for this as for many of the trusts, 'the trustees take an active role in their grantmaking, employing a range of specialist staff and advisers to research their areas of interest and bring forward suitable proposals. Many of the trusts work closely with their chosen beneficiaries over a long period to achieve particular objectives. It should therefore be understood that the majority of unsolicited proposals we receive will be unsuccessful', however, the trust states that the 'trustees are prepared to consider unsolicited proposals so long as they closely match one of [its] areas of interest' (see general section).

Applications should be sent by post with a description (strictly no more than two pages please, as any more is unlikely to be read) of the proposed project, covering:
- The organisation – explaining its charitable aims and objectives, and giving its most recent annual income and expenditure, and current financial position. Please do not send a full set of accounts
- The project requiring funding – why it is needed, who will benefit and in what way
- The funding – breakdown of costs, any money raised so far, and how the balance will be raised

All applications will receive our standard acknowledgement letter. If your proposal is a candidate for support from one of the trusts, you will hear from us within 8 weeks of the acknowledgement. Applicants who do not hear from us within this time must assume they have been unsuccessful.

Information gathered from:
Accounts; annual report; Charity Commission record; funder's website.

Heart of England Community Foundation

General
£284,000 (2012/13)

Beneficial area
The city of Coventry and Warwickshire.

Correspondent: Kat Venton, PSA Peugeot Citroën , PO BOX 126, Torrington Avenue, Tile Hill, Coventry

CV4 0UX (tel: 02476 883262; email: info@heartofenglandcf.co.uk; website: www.heartofenglandcf.co.uk)

Trustees: Brian Clifford Holt; Sally Carrick; David Green; Susan Ong; Peter Shearing; John Taylor; Paul Belfield; Derek Cake; Philip Gordon Ewing; Sandra Garlick; Michelle Vincent.

CC Number: 1117345

In general, the foundation seeks to promote any charitable purposes for the benefit of the community in the city of Coventry, the county of Warwickshire and, in particular, the advancement of education, the protection of good health, both mental and physical, and the relief of poverty and sickness.

The Heart of England Community Foundation has a portfolio of grantmaking programmes for use by local community and voluntary groups. This enables benefactors to support community projects according to their own geographical or thematic criteria, and to have as much or as little involvement as they like in the awarding process.

Funds are held on behalf of individuals, families, trusts, companies and statutory bodies, investing them to get maximum returns. The foundation can engage with groups on behalf of the funders – promoting their criteria, making awards and collecting feedback.

Potential applicants should contact the foundation directly or check its website for details of current funds as these may change frequently.

In 2012/13 the foundation held assets of £5 million and had an income of £2.4 million. Grants totalled £284,000 and were made to 148 projects across the beneficial area. While more grants were given this year, the grants were smaller. The average grant size fell from £3,429 in 2011/12 to £1,920 in 2012/13.

Education and training	£95,000
Community support and development	£62,000
Sport and recreation	£47,000
Health and wellbeing	£43,000
Arts and culture	£24,00
Environment/Recycling	£10,200
Tackling crime	£3,500

Beneficiaries included: Coventry Somali Women's Network (£11,500); Hub @ Blackwell (£10,700); Positive Youth Foundation (£10,000); Friendship Project (£6,000 in two grants); The Open Theatre Company Ltd (£5,000); Support Sport Ltd (£4,500); Write Here Write Now CiC (£3,000); Lower Ford Street Baptist Church (£1,000); and Welford Junior Football Club (£700).

Exclusions

Grants will not usually be considered for the following:

- Statutory provision
- Activities that promote religious activity
- Activities that are not socially inclusive
- Organisations with a turnover of over £100,000 excluding restricted funding
- Grantmaking bodies
- Mainstream activities of schools and colleges
- Medical research
- Animal welfare
- Political activities
- Organisations with substantial reserves
- General and major fundraising appeals
- Continuation funding

The foundation does not usually provide part-funding, preferring to be the majority funder.

Applications

Applications should be completed online via the foundation's website. Some schemes have online applications while others have forms which can be downloaded from the site.

Applicants are encouraged to telephone the foundation to discuss their project in advance of applying. Grants Officers, who cover specific geographical areas and funds, will be pleased to assist you. Applicants should hear the outcome of their application within 12 weeks.

Information gathered from:

Accounts; annual report; Charity Commission record; guidelines for applicants; funder's website.

Heathside Charitable Trust

General, Jewish
£508,000 (2012)

Beneficial area

UK.

Correspondent: Sir Harry Solomon, Trustee, 32 Hampstead High Street, London NW3 1QD (tel: 020 7431 7739)

Trustees: Sir Harry Solomon; Lady Judith Solomon; Geoffrey Jayson; Louise Jacobs; Daniel Solomon; Juliet Solomon.

CC Number: 326959

This trust has general charitable purposes, with a preference for Jewish organisations. The trustees tend to identify organisations and projects they wish to support and this generally arises from direct contacts rather than speculative applications.

In 2012 the trust had assets of almost £2.8 million and an income of £598,000. It made grants totalling £508,000.

A list of beneficiaries was not given, however previous beneficiaries have included: Joint Jewish Charitable Trust (£141,000); Jewish Education Defence Trust and Community Security Trust (£25,000 each); Jewish Care (£15,000); and British Friends of Jaffa Institute, GRET and Motivation (£10,000 each).

Other previous beneficiaries have included Holocaust Educational Trust, First Cheque 2000, Royal London Institute, Royal National Theatre, Jewish Museum, CancerKin, King Solomon High School, Babes in Arms, Marie Curie Cancer Care and Weitzmann Institute.

Applications

In writing to the correspondent, at any time. Trustees meet four times a year.

Information gathered from:

Accounts; annual report; Charity Commission record.

The Hedley Foundation

Youth and health
£956,000 (2011/12)

Beneficial area

UK.

Correspondent: Pauline Barker, Appeals Secretary, 1–3 College Hill, London EC4R 2RA (tel: 020 7489 8076; email: pbarker@hedleyfoundation.org.uk; website: www.hedleyfoundation.org.uk)

Trustees: John F. Meadows Rodwell, Chair; Patrick R. Holcroft; George R. Stratton Broke; Lt Col. Peter G. Chamberlin; Lorna B. Stuttaford; Angus Fanshawe; Lt. Col. Andrew Ford; David Byam-Cook.

CC Number: 262933

Summary

The Hedley Foundation was set up in 1971 and endowed from a family trust of which the principle asset was the compensation received on nationalisation of the family mining concerns.

The main objective of the trustees' grantmaking is to assist and encourage development and change. Grants are for specific projects only and are mostly one off, though the trustees sometimes agree to help fund the introduction of new and innovative projects with a series of up to three annual grants. Few grants exceed £5,000 and most of them go to charities where they can make an impact. The foundation does not support large or national appeals or appeals from cathedrals and churches.

Currently about 70% of the foundation's budget goes towards supporting young people; specifically, their education, recreation, support, training and health. Its subsidiary objective is to support people with disabilities and the terminally ill through the provision of specialist equipment and support for carers.

Trustees individually have visited many charities to which the foundation might make or has made grants.

Recent grants

During the year the foundation had assets of £28.3 million and an income of over £1.4 million. Grants were made to 376 organisations totalling nearly £956,000.

The foundation was able to supply us with a list of grant recipients without grant totals. Beneficiaries of grants in 2013 included: Adventure Unlimited, Aspatria Dreamscheme, Barnet Community Projects, BASIC (Brain and Spinal Injury Centre), Brain Tumour Research Campaign, Community Action North Devon, Derby Kids Camp, Durham Wildlife Trust, Enable NI, Famous Trains Model Railway, Happy Days Children's Charity, Neuromuscular Centre Midlands, Scout Holiday Homes Trust, Warwickshire Association for the Blind, West Edinburgh Time Bank and Young Musicians Symphony Orchestra.

Exclusions

Grants are made to UK registered charities only. No support for individuals, churches and cathedrals, core revenue costs, salary or transport funding, or for very large appeals. Scouts, Guides and similar organisations will be considered but not for building or re-building projects.

Applications

Application forms are downloadable from the foundation's website. Once completed in typescript, the form should be printed off and sent by post to the appeals secretary named above, accompanied by a recent copy of your accounts and your email address. Note that the foundation is unable to return any enclosures that are sent in with applications.

The trustees meet six times a year. The closing date for a meeting is three weeks beforehand. All applications will be acknowledged, but, in the case of those short-listed, not until after they have been considered by the trustees. The trustees usually meet in January, March, May, July, September and November. A list of meeting dates for the current year is published on the foundation's website.

The foundation receives many more applications than it can fund and urges that applicants should not be surprised, or too disappointed, if they are unsuccessful.

Percentage of awards given to new applicants: between 40% and 50%.

Information gathered from:

Accounts; annual report; Charity Commission record; further information provided by the funder; funder's website.

The Helping Foundation

Orthodox Jewish
£7.2 million (2012)

Beneficial area
Greater London and Greater Manchester.

Correspondent: Benny Stone, Trustee, 1 Allandale Court, Waterpark Road, Salford M7 4JN (tel: 01617 40116)

Trustees: Rachel Weis; Rabbi Aubrey Weis; David Neuwirth; Benny Stone.

CC Number: 1104484

Registered with the Charity Commission in June 2004:

> The objects of the charity are the advancement of education according to the tenets of the Orthodox Jewish Faith; the advancement of the Orthodox Jewish Religion and the relief of poverty amongst the elderly or persons in need, hardship or distress in the Jewish Community.

In 2012 the foundation had assets of £77 million and an income of £13.7 million, which include properties gifted to the foundation to the value of £4.5 million and investment income of £9.2 million. Grants were made during the year totalling £7.2 million.

Previous beneficiaries have included: Asser Bishvil Foundation (£2 million); British Friends of Ezrat Yisrael (£670,000); Notzar Chesed (£236,500); New Rachmistrivka Synagogue Trust (£201,000); TTT (£198,500); Emuno Educational Centre (£163,000); United Talmudical Associates (£160,000); BCG CT (£105,000); Friends for the Centre for Torah Education Centre (£57,000); Toimchei Shabbos Manchester (£30,000); Gateshead Kollel (£20,000); Beis Naduorna (£10,000); and Law of Truth (£5,500).

Applications
In writing to the correspondent.

Information gathered from:
Accounts; annual report; Charity Commission record.

The Hertfordshire Community Foundation

General
£447,000 to organisations and individuals (2011/12)

Beneficial area
Hertfordshire.

Correspondent: Christine Mills, Grants Manager, Foundation House, 2–4 Forum Place, Fiddlebridge Lane, Hatfield, Hertfordshire AL10 0RN (tel: 01707 251351; email: grants@hertscf.org.uk; website: www.hertscf.org.uk)

Trustees: J. Stuart Lewis, Chair; Kate Belinis; Jo Connell; Gerald Corbett; David Fryer; Pat Garrard; Mike Master; Caroline McCaffrey; Brig John Palmer; John Peters; Penny Williams; Cllr Christopher Hayward.

CC Number: 299438

Launched in 1989, the foundation is one of a number of community trusts in the UK, which supports and provides funds to local charities and voluntary groups that serve the local community and benefit the lives of the people they serve. The foundation is able to support a wide range of charitable activities, in and around Hertfordshire. The foundation advises, therefore, that it is always worth contacting them to discuss the project, in case they can help or direct you to someone else who can.

Foundation Grants
The maximum amount any group can apply for from foundation funds is £5,000. However, most of our grants are for less than the maximum. We do not generally make repeat grants, although the same group can apply for something different. However, it is best to wait for at least 18 months between applications. Priority will be given to small, local groups rather than large, national charities or those with paid fundraisers.

Other programmes
From time to time the foundation also administers external funds, such as Comic Relief. As with other community foundations funds may open and close at short notice so applicants are advised to consult the foundation's website for more information.

Grantmaking
In 2011/12 the foundation had assets of £6.5 million, an income of nearly £1.8 million and made grants to individuals and organisations totalling £447,000. This included 161 grants to organisations and 392 grants to individuals. The main area of the foundation's grantmaking activity is in the field of social welfare.

The majority of grants awarded from the foundation's unrestricted funds are made to local charities and voluntary groups for work within these areas. Priority is given to small, community-based organisations. The foundation aims to develop community capacity and:

- Reach people who are disadvantaged and isolated
- Enable people to take opportunities that would otherwise not be available to them
- Involve local people in improving their community
- Reflect the concerns and priorities of people living and working in the area
- Reflect the needs identified in foundation research

Eligibility

Grants can be given to any local charity or voluntary group; you do not have to be a registered charity. Project, equipment and running costs are covered. The following guidelines are taken from the website:

- Your group must have a governing document which shows the name, aim/ purpose, objects of the group and which includes a dissolution clause – what happens if your group ceases to function. This clause should show that you are a not-for-profit group by confirming that any assets remaining after all debts are paid will be given to another charity or voluntary group with similar aims. This document should also include a list of your group's trustees or management committee
- The group should have some volunteer input
- The group must be able to show that it is engaged in meeting the needs of a sector of the community including:
  - Disadvantaged children and families
  - Young people at risk
  - People with disabilities
  - Older people
  - People with mental ill health or addictions
  - People who are homeless or victims of domestic violence

Exclusions

No grants are made towards:

- Individuals
- Political groups
- Animal welfare
- Projects that are solely environmental
- Statutory agencies
- Medical research
- Religious activities

Applications

Ideally, applications should be made online via the foundation's website. However, if it is not possible to apply online, contact the foundation and they will send an application pack by post or email. An initial telephone call or email to check eligibility is also welcomed. Applicants may be contacted by telephone to discuss their work and if it is your first application to the foundation a site visit may be arranged.

For amounts of £500 or more the grants committee meets quarterly to review applications.

Information gathered from:

Accounts; annual report; Charity Commission record; funder's website.

Hexham and Newcastle Diocesan Trust (1947)

Religion
£1.1 million (2011/12)

Beneficial area

Diocese of Hexham and Newcastle, overseas.

Correspondent: Kathleen Smith, Secretary, St Cuthberts House, West Road, Newcastle upon Tyne NE15 7PY (tel: 01912 433300; fax: 01912 433309; email: office@rcdhn.org.uk; website: rcdhn.org.uk)

Trustees: Very Revd Seamus Cunningham; Revd Gerard Lavender; Revd James O'Keefe; Revd Martin Stempczyk; Revd Christopher Jackson; Revd John Butters; Msgr Philip Carroll.

CC Number: 235686

This trust supports the advancement of the Roman Catholic religion in the Diocese of Hexham and Newcastle and other charitable works promoted by the church outside of the diocese. Usually this is done by initiating its own projects, but occasionally grants are given to other organisations to carry out this work. 'All of our work is underpinned and reflects the ethos of the Roman Catholic tradition through prayer, worship, a commitment to community and a sense of mission.'

The trust aims to achieve its objects through four main areas of charitable activity which are:

- To provide support to the clergy in their ongoing work
- To provide and support pastoral work in parishes and local communities
- To provide support and direct lifelong Christian education in parishes and schools
- To preserve and invest in the property infrastructure of the Diocese and parishes, facilitating worship and enabling the charitable work of the church to take place

In 2011/12 the trust held assets of £63.3 million had an income of £21.9 million. Grants were made totalling just under £1.1 million, as a share of the £18.7 million in charitable expenditure.

Funds were distributed in the following areas:

Clergy support		£1.3 million
Pastoral work	Diocese/parishes	£7.2 million
	St Cuthbert's Care	£7.3 million
Education		£664,000
Property	Diocese/parishes	£2.2 million
	School building work	£101,000
Total		£18.7 million

Grants were distributed in the following areas:

Clergy support	£25,000
Pastoral	£979,000
Education	£46,000

Beneficiaries included: CAFOD Development and emergency aid (£203,000); Papal Visit (£119,000); National Catholic Fund (£86,000); Catholic Education Service (£46,000); Holy Places (£28,000); Sick and Retired Priests NBF (£25,000); Apostleship of the Sea (£21,000); Day for Life (£13,000); Peter's Pence (£20,000); and Day for Life (£13,000).

Applications

Contact the correspondent. The accounts note the following about the grantmaking policy:

Each year the Bishop, assisted by guidance from the Catholic Bishops' Conference of England and Wales, decides which organisations will benefit from special collections to be taken in the parishes. At a local level, parish priests and their finance committees decide which additional causes they will support to further the work of the Church, by means of special appeals. The amounts raised from such appeals and paid over to charities are sometimes supplemented from general offertory income, where this is approved by the parish priest and the parish finance committee.

Information gathered from:

Accounts; annual report; Charity Commission record.

The Hilden Charitable Fund

Homelessness, asylum seekers and refugees, penal affairs, disadvantaged young people and overseas development
£411,000 (2011/12)

Beneficial area

UK and developing countries.

Correspondent: Rodney Hedley, Secretary, 34 North End Road, London W14 0SH (tel: 020 7603 1525; fax: 020 7603 1525; email: hildencharity@ hotmail.com; website: www. hildencharitablefund.org.uk)

General

This grantmaking trust was established in 1963 by an initial gift from Anthony and Joan Rampton. Priorities in the UK are homelessness, asylum seekers and refugees, penal affairs and disadvantaged young people. For projects in developing countries, priorities are projects which focus on community development, education, and health. These priorities are reviewed on a three year cycle and may change from time to time, as dictated by circumstances. The trust has also allocated a small budget to help community groups run summer playschemes for disadvantaged communities.

The aim of the fund is to address disadvantage, notably by supporting causes which are less likely to raise funds from public subscriptions. Both the UK and overseas funding policy is directed largely at supporting work at community level.

Whilst the trust's policy is to address needs by considering and funding specific projects costs, the trustees are sympathetic to funding general running, or core costs. In awarding these types of grants, they believe that great value can be added, as most charities find fundraising for core costs most difficult.

All grant recipients are expected to send a report on how they have made use of their grant. The trust's staff team ensure adequate grant monitoring. Feedback is given to the trustees via regular mailings as well as at the quarterly meetings. Similarly the secretary produces briefings on all aspects of grantmaking and policy development within the priority areas.

In establishing a secretariat for the trust in 1992, the trust aimed not only to effectively administer the grantmaking process but also to provide a helpful service to applicants on funding and good practice and applicants are encouraged to telephone the trust's offices for this service. The trustees and the staff team look to network with other funding and voluntary sector organisations, to identify new needs, improve standards and to prevent duplication.

Guidelines

UK grants

The main interests of the trustees of the Hilden Charitable Fund are:

▶ Homelessness
▶ Asylum seekers and refugees
▶ Penal affairs
▶ Disadvantaged young people aged 16 to 25

Grants are rarely given to well-funded national charities. Fund policy is directed largely at supporting work at a community level within the categories of interest stated above.

Preference is given to charities with an income of less that £500,000 per year. Priorities given to different types of work within the main categories may change from time to time, as dictated by circumstances.

Overseas grants

Funds are available for capital and revenue funding. The funding programme is designed to help small and medium size initiatives. Trustees will consider applications from any countries within the developing world. Trustees wish to fund community development, education and health initiatives. Trustees will particularly welcome projects that address the needs and potential of girls and women.

Trustees will be pleased to hear from UK Non-Governmental Organisations/ charities and hope that UK NGOs/ charities will encourage their local partners, if appropriate, to apply directly to Hilden for grant aid.

Summer playscheme grants

The fund has allocated a small budget to help community groups run summer play schemes for disadvantaged communities. Some priority will be given to projects which show they are inclusive of children from refugee families, and show BME involvement.

Trustees look to fund:

▶ Projects for children aged 5 to 18 years
▶ Locally based schemes lasting from 2 to 6 weeks
▶ Schemes with strong volunteer support

Applications are accepted from voluntary agencies with an income of less than £150,000. Trustees will accept applications from across the UK.

Trustees will not support:

▶ Playschemes with a budget of over £12,000
▶ Club or family holidays
▶ Day care costs
▶ Agencies with an income of over £150,000

Grantmaking

In 2011/12 the trust had assets of £11.2 million and income of £429,000. There were 89 grants made (average grant of £4,600) totalling £411,000, broken down as follows:

Asylum seekers and refugees	20	£112,000
Overseas	19	£101,000
Disadvantaged Young People	10	£51,000
Homelessness	8	£44,000
Scottish Community Foundation	1*	£36,000
Penal Affairs	7	£35,000
Playschemes	22	£20,000
Other	2	£12,000

to the Scottish Community Foundation for onward distribution

Beneficiaries included: Tanzania Development Trust – Tanzania (£30,000 in three grants); Joint Council for the Welfare of Immigrants – London (£15,000); Furniture Recycling Project – Gloucester and St Cuthbert's Centre – London (£7,000 each); Baynards Zambia Trust – Zambia (£6,000); Birmingham Friends of the Earth, 999 Project – Deptford and Irene Taylor Trust – London (£5,000 each); Devon and Cornwall Refugee Support Council (£4,500); Lena Gardens Primary School (£3,500); and Recyke Y'Bike – Newcastle upon Tyne (£3,000).

Exclusions

Grants are not normally made for well-established causes or to individuals, and overseas grants concentrate on development aid in preference to disaster relief.

Applications

Applications are made via the application form, available on the trust's website. When making an application, grant seekers should note the following guidance from the trust.

We expect all applicants to complete our application form. Your case for funds should be concise (no more than 2 sides of A4), but supporting documentation is essential. Please ensure your application includes enclosures of:

▶ Your most recent independently inspected accounts
▶ Your most recent annual report
▶ Projected income and expenditure for the current financial year

Be clear in your application form about when the proposed work is to commence, and give the relevant timetable.

Applicants from the UK applying for funds for their project partners must complete both the UK application form and the overseas partner profile form.

Application forms, including one for Summer Playschemes, are available from the trust's website or offices. Note that forms must be submitted to the secretary by post as hard copies; forms submitted by email or other electronic means will not be considered. Applicants are advised to ensure that they have read the application guidelines at the top of the form prior to completion.

For applicants to the Summer Playschemes fund: applications should be sent by post, along with a brief plan or timetable for the scheme and a copy of the applicant's most recent annual report and accounts which should include details of their management committee.

Potential applicants in Scotland should contact the Scottish Community Foundation, 22 Calton Road, Edinburgh EH8 8DP; Tel: 01315 240300; website: www.scottishcf.org.

Percentage of awards given to new applicants: between 40% and 50%.

Information gathered from:

Accounts; annual report; Charity Commission record; further information provided by the funder; funder's website.

Lady Hind Trust

General with some preference for health, disability and welfare related charities

£322,000 (2012)

Beneficial area

England with a preference for Nottinghamshire and Norfolk.

Correspondent: John Thompson, Administrator, c/o Shakespeares Solicitors, Park House, Friar Lane, Nottingham NG1 6DN (tel: 01159 453700; fax: 01159 480234; email: ladyhind@btinternet.com)

Trustees: Charles W. L. Barratt; Tim H. Farr; Nigel R. Savory; John D. Pears.

CC Number: 208877

The trust was established in 1951 for general charitable purposes. The trust gives widely but has a strong preference for health, disability, medical and social welfare charities.

In 2012 the trust had assets of almost £12.4 million and an income of £430,000. Grants were made totalling £322,000, with most being for £5,000 or less, and were broken down as follows:

Welfare	£94,000
Medical and disability	£92,000
Education	£29,000
Churches	£27,000
Other	£21,000
Environment	£12,000
Arts	£9,500
Accommodation	£7,000
Groups/Clubs	£5,000
Heritage	£3,000
Services	£2,000

The above table only details grants of £1,000 or more. A further £22,000 was distributed in small grants of less than £1,000 across all categories.

Beneficiaries of larger grants were: Royal Norfolk Agricultural Association (£12,500); The Norfolk and Norwich Association for the Blind, The

Nottinghamshire Hospice and Notts Mind Network (£10,000); The Benjamin Foundation, Southwell Care Project, Norfolk Wildlife Trust, The Norfolk Churches Trust, Nottingham High School for Boys – Bursary and NSPCC Nottinghamshire (£7,500 each).

More typical grants of £5,000 or less included those to: The National Association of Almshouses, Pintsize Theatre Ltd, Friends of Brancaster Church, Rutland House School for Parents, Zibby Garnett Travelling Fellowship, British Trust for Ornithology, ABF The Soldiers Charity, 1st Norwich Sea Scouts Group, Norfolk Historic Buildings Trust, The Anthony Nolan Trust, East Anglia Children's Hospices, Calibre Audio Library, Keeping Abreast, Asthma UK, The Leeds Teaching Hospitals Charitable Foundation, Pregnancy Choices Norfolk, National Search and Rescue Dog Association, Citizens Advice Broxtowe, Blue Sky Development and Regeneration, Friary Drop-In, Sailors Society and Waveney Stardust.

Exclusions

Applications from individuals are not considered.

Applications

Applications, in writing and with latest accounts, must be submitted at least one month in advance of trustee meetings held in March, July and November. Unsuccessful applicants are not notified.

The trustees consider all written applications made to them by charitable organisations. Such applications are reviewed by every trustee prior to the trustees' four-monthly meetings and are discussed at such meetings. Grants are awarded at such meeting to those organisations which the trustees collectively consider to be worthy of their support. Grants are awarded principally to institutions based on their level of need and with a geographical bias towards Nottinghamshire and Norfolk.

Percentage of awards given to new applicants: between 10% and 20%.

Common applicant mistakes

'They do not supply a copy of last audited accounts.'

Information gathered from:

Accounts; annual report; Charity Commission record; further information provided by the funder.

The Hintze Family Charitable Foundation

Education, Christian churches, museums, libraries and galleries

£4.5 million (2012)

Beneficial area

England and Wales.

Correspondent: Dorothy Hintze, Chief Executive, CQS, 5th Floor, 33 Grosvenor Place, London SW1X 7HY (tel: 020 7201 6862)

Trustees: Michael Hintze; David Swain; Brian Hannon.

CC Number: 1101842

Established in 2005 by UK based Australian businessman, philanthropist and political patron Sir Michael Hintze. He is the founder and head of CQS Management, a London hedge fund. He holds a number of prominent trusteeships including the National Gallery and The Prince's Foundation for Building Community. Since inception almost 200 charities have been supported. Many of the organisations receiving larger grants are those which the founder is closely connected to.

The main objects of the foundation are providing support for:

- Christian churches in England and Wales, particularly the Diocese of Southwark
- Relief of sickness and people with terminal illnesses
- Resources and equipment for schools, colleges and universities (in particular to enable the acquisition and retention of antiquarian books to be used as a learning resource)
- Promoting access to museums, libraries and art galleries

In 2012 the foundation had assets of £3.5 million and an income of £5.9 million, mostly from donations. Grants were made to 42 organisations during the year totalling £4.5 million, and were broken down as follows:

Education – core	£2.4 million
Education – cultural	£1.1 million
Religion	£884,000
Health	£188,000

Grants of £50,000 or more were listed in the accounts. Beneficiaries included: The Prince's Foundation for the Built Environment (£1.3 million) towards unrestricted funding 'for a charity with which [the foundation] has very strong ties'; Patrons of the Arts in the Vatican Museum (€1 million) for the restoration of the Scale Sancta; Friends of Harvard University ($1 million over five years) to support the Cultural Entrepreneurship Challenge; Old Vic Theatre (£500,000 over two years) in support of their endowment and building campaigns; Wandsworth Museum (£385,000) to provide funding since the local council decided they could no longer support it; Institute of Economic Affairs (£250,000) in support of their outreach programme; Museum of London (£150,000); St George's Chapel – Windsor (£75,000); Macmillan Cancer Support and The Prince's Teaching Institute (£50,000 each).

Applications

The trust offers the following application guidance in its latest accounts:

The foundation invites applications for grants or commitments from charities which serve the objects of the foundation. No specific format is required for applications. Applications, along with potential donations and commitments identified by the Chief Executive and the trustees, are considered in formal trustee meetings.

Percentage of awards given to new applicants: between 30% and 40%.

Common applicant mistakes

'No background research; formulaic applications; too much information in first instance; geographical irrelevance.'

Information gathered from:

Accounts; annual report; Charity Commission record; further information provided by the funder.

The Hobson Charity Ltd

Social welfare, education
£2 million (2011/12)

Beneficial area

UK.

Correspondent: Deborah Hobson, Trustee, Hildane Properties Ltd, 7th Floor, 21 Bryanston Street, Marble Arch, London W1H 7PR (tel: 020 7495 5599)

Trustees: Deborah Hobson; Sir Donald Gosling; Sir Ronald F. Hobson; Lady Hobson; J. Richardson.

CC Number: 326839

Established in 1985, the Hobson Charity Ltd is the charitable vehicle of Sir Ronald Hobson, founder of Central Car Parks and later co-owner of NCP car parks with business partner, Sir Donald Gosling, also a trustee (see also the Gosling Foundation). Both charities are administered from the same address.

In 2009/10 the charity had assets of £28.5 million and an income of £8.1 million, mainly from donations. Grants were made to 110 organisations, some of whom received multiple awards, totalling almost £2 million.

Grants were awarded in the following categories:

Other purposes beneficial to the community	87	£1.4 million
Advancement of education	20	£594,500
Advancement of religion	24	£179,000
Relief of poverty	7	£103,000

Beneficiaries during the year included: Historic Royal Palaces (£150,000); Royal Hospital for Neurodisability (£100,000 in 3 grants); Queenswood School and Great Ormond Street Hospital (£100,000 each); Food Fortnight Ltd (Cook for the Queen) Jubilee (£75,000); Hornsey Trust (£67,000); British School of Osteopathy (£55,000); SSAFA, Classics for All, Almshouse Association and the Police Foundation (£50,000 each); Changing Faces (£40,000); Skills Force Development and the Alnwick Garden Trust (£30,000 each); Army Benevolent Fund (£26,000 in 2 grants); Muscle Help Foundation (£20,000 in 2 grants); Eden Trust Project and the Anglican Space Appeal (£15,000 each); Scottish Veterans Garden City Association, Guildhall School of Music, St Peter's Church – Harrogate, British Heart Foundation and Wellbeing of Women (£10,000 each); St Mungo's (£7,000); Concord Prison Trust, Museum of Jurassic Marine Life, St Paul's Church Covent Garden, Oxford Radcliffe Hospitals Charitable Fund and Inner London Scope Nor-West Club (£5,000 each); Canadian Cancer Foundation (£4,000); Open Country (£2,000); and Rotary Club of London Charitable Trust, Hope Centre and WIZO UK (£1,000 each).

Exclusions

No grants to individuals, except in exceptional circumstances.

Applications

In writing to the correspondent. The trustees meet quarterly.

Information gathered from:

Accounts; annual report; Charity Commission record.

The Jane Hodge Foundation

Medical care and research, education and religion
£855,000 (2011/12)

Beneficial area

UK and overseas with a preference for Wales.

Correspondent: Jonathan Hodge, Trustee, 31 Windsor Place, Cardiff CF10 3UR (tel: 02920 787693; email: Marion.Pepperell@janehodgefoundation.co.uk)

Trustees: Joyce Harrison; Derek Jones; I. Davies; Margaret Cason; Eric Hammonds; Jonathan Hodge.

CC Number: 216053

The foundation was established in 1962 and its objective is to apply its income in the following areas:

▶ The encouragement of medical and surgical studies and research, and in particular the study of and research in connection with the causes, diagnosis, treatment and cure of cancer, poliomyelitis, tuberculosis and diseases affecting children
▶ The general advancement of medical and surgical science
▶ The advancement of education
▶ The advancement of religion

In 2011/12 the foundation had assets of £28 million and an income of just over £815,000. 213 grants were made, which totalled £699,000. Support costs totalled £156,000. The foundation describes its grantmaking in the 2011/12 accounts: 'The level of grants made each year can vary since there is a process of assessment and approval before grants can be made and grants may cover a period of more than one year.'

Education	33	£273,000
Medical	68	£226,000
Religion	25	£48,000
Other	87	£151,000

Beneficiaries included: Cardiff Business School (£132,000); Royal Welsh College of Music and Drama and George Thomas Memorial Trust (£50,000 each); TENOVUS (£30,000); Ty Hafan (£10,000); Leukaemia and Lymphoma Research and Aberystwyth University (£6,000 each); Race Equality First, the United World College and Welsh National Opera (£5,000 each); Plan International UK (£4,000); PDSA and the Owl Fund (£3,000 each); and the River and Corpus Christie High School (£2,500 each).

Exclusions

Applications are only considered from exempt or registered charities. No grants to individuals.

Applications

In writing to the correspondent. Applications for grants are considered by the trustees at regular meetings throughout the year. Applications are acknowledged.

The trustees' report for 2011/12 states that 'trustees invite applications for grants from charitable institutions who submit a summary of their proposals in a specific format. Institutions are required to report on completion of the project for which the grant was made'.

Percentage of awards given to new applicants: between 40% and 50%.

Information gathered from:

Accounts; annual report; Charity Commission record; further information provided by the funder.

Sir Harold Hood's Charitable Trust

Roman Catholic charitable purposes
£517,000 (2011/12)

Beneficial area
Worldwide.

Correspondent: Margaret Hood, Trustee, Haysmacintyre, Fairfax House, 15 Fulwood Place, London WC1V 6AY (tel: 020 7722 9088)

Trustees: Dom James Hood; Lord Nicholas True; Lady True; Margaret Hood; Christian Elwes.

CC Number: 225870

The trust was established in 1962 by the late Sir Harold Hood, who died in 2005. Sir Harold was an influential editor and director of several Catholic publications during his lifetime, a philanthropist who was involved in a number of charities and an early investor in an electronics company that later evolved into Vodafone. The trustees include Lord Nicholas True, Conservative leader of Richmond council. The trust supports Roman Catholic charities.

In 2011/12 it had assets of £30.1 million and an income of £555,000. Grants were made to 80 organisations totalling £517,000.

Beneficiaries included: Downside Fisher Youth Club and the Prison Advice and Care Trust (£30,000 each); Craig Lodge Trust (£25,000); Duchess of Leeds Foundation (£20,000); Diocese of Brentwood (£17,000); San Lorenzo School – Chile and Westminster Cathedral (£14,000 each); Venerable English College – Rome and the Ace of Clubs – Clapham (£10,000); Maryvale Institute (£8,000); HCPT (£7,000); Housing Justice (£5,000); Ten Ten Theatre (£3,000); Young Christian Workers (£2,000); and the Right to Life Charitable Trust (£1,000).

Exclusions
No grants for individuals.

Applications
In writing to the correspondent. The trustees meet once a year to consider applications, usually in November.

Information gathered from:
Accounts; Charity Commission record.

The Sir Joseph Hotung Charitable Settlement

General
£2 million (2011/12)

Beneficial area
Worldwide.

Correspondent: Sir Joseph Hotung, Trustee, HSBC Private Bank Ltd, 78 St James' Street, London, SWIA 1JB

Trustees: Sir Joseph E. Hotung; Sir Robert D. H. Boyd; Victoria F. Dicks.

CC Number: 1082710

Set up in 2000, in 2011/12 this trust had assets of £760,000 and an income of £1.4 million, mainly from donations from Sir Joseph Hotung. Grants totalled £2 million.

The trust tends to support a small number of organisations, often on a regular basis. St George's Hospital Medical School received a grant of £1.8 million. Six grants totalling £175,000 were made to the School of Oriental and African Studies – of which the settlor is an honorary fellow and ambassador – towards their programme of law, human rights and peace building in the Middle East). Other grants went to the Council for Assisting Refugee Academics (£50,000); and Spinal Research (£1,200).

Applications
The trust has previously stated that 'the trustees have their own areas of interest and do not respond to unsolicited applications'.

Information gathered from:
Accounts; annual report; Charity Commission record.

The Albert Hunt Trust

Health and welfare
£1.8 million (2011/12)

Beneficial area
UK.

Correspondent: The Manager, Coutts and Co., Trustee Department, 440 Strand, London WC2R 0QS (tel: 020 7663 6826)

Trustees: Breda McGuire; Richard Collis; Coutts and Co.

CC Number: 277318

The Albert Hunt Trust was established in 1979. The trustees' report for 2011/12 states that the trust's mission is as follows:

> To promote and enhance the physical and mental welfare of individuals, or groups of individuals, excluding research or the diagnosis of specific medical conditions...

A very large number of modest grants are given to a wide range of organisations, both national and local, each year. Most grants are for between £1,000 and £2,000 and many seem to go to new beneficiaries. There are around 50 grants for £5,000 or slightly more each year and many of these tend to go to regularly supported, national charities.

In 2011/12 the trust had assets of £45 million and an income of £1.6 million. Grants were made to 582 institutions totalling £1.8 million.

Beneficiaries of the largest grants were: Ambitious About Autism (£35,000); Bury Hospice, Sunfield Children's Homes Ltd, Cornwall Hospice Care Ltd, Home Farm Trust, Hollybank Trust and Chescombe Trust (£25,000 each); Botley Alzheimer's Home, Stroud Court Community Trust and Elizabeth Fitzroy Support (£20,000 each); Cancer Link Aberdeen and North (£15,000); and Douglas Macmillan Hospice (£13,000).

Beneficiaries of grants of £10,000 or less included: Ruskin Mill Educational College Ltd, Tagsa Uibhist and St Barnabas Hospice Ltd (£10,000 each); Abbeyfield Society, the Norfolk Hospice and Alexander Devine Children's Hospice Service (£9,000 each); Julian House (£7,000); and the Peace Hospice (£6,000).

Beneficiaries of grants of £5,000 or less included: Action on Hearing Loss, Aspire, Bath Institute for Medical Engineering, Birmingham St Mary's Hospice, Combat Stress, Clatterbridge, Community Campus 87, County Air Ambulance Trust, the Eric Lidell Centre, the Fire Fighters Charity, and Hestia Housing and Support.

Beneficiaries of grants of £2,000 or less included: Advocacy Matters, Action for Kids, Arcos, Asperger East Anglia, Barnstondale Centre, British Liver Trust, the Bridge Trust, British Wireless for the Blind Fund, Child Brain Injury Trust, Child Victims of Crime, Down's Heart Group, Dyspraxia Foundation, Friends First Farm, EDP Drug and Alcohol Services, Friends of Priestley Smith School, and Guildford Action.

Exclusions
No grants for medical research or overseas work.

Applications
In writing to the correspondent. All appeals should be by letter containing the following:

- Aims and objectives of the charity
- Nature of appeal
- Total target if for a specific project
- Contributions received against target
- Registered charity number

▶ Any other relevant factors

The correspondent has stated that no unsolicited correspondence will be acknowledged unless an application receives favourable consideration.

Information gathered from:

Accounts; annual report; Charity Commission record.

The Hunter Foundation

Education, young people, children, relief of poverty, community development
Around £750,000

Beneficial area

UK and overseas.

Correspondent: Sir Tom Hunter, Trustee, Marathon House, Olympic Business Park, Drybridge Road, Dundonald, Ayrshire KA2 9AE (email: info@thehunterfoundation.co.uk; website: www.thehunterfoundation.co.uk)

Trustees: Sir Tom Hunter, Chair; Lady Marion Hunter; Jim McMahon; Vartan Gregorian; Ewan Hunter.

SC Number: SC027532

The following information is taken from the foundation's website:

The Hunter Foundation (THF) is a proactive venture philanthropy that seeks to invest in determining model solutions, in partnership with others, to troubling systemic issues relating to poverty eradication and educational enablement.

However it is our strong belief that those geographical factors can be overcome to afford every child an equal opportunity to succeed regardless of location; Kigali, Rwanda or Kilmarnock, Scotland.

Strategy

The foundation's strategy is to pilot, prove and, where possible, have the relevant Government or Agencies adopt solutions to significant societal challenges.

To do so we generally work in strategic partnerships with fellow funders, Governments and Agencies and like-minded individuals; on the odd occasion we go it alone but our strong view is partnerships are a significant lever for change.

THF has a twin focus of domestic, that is UK, investment predominantly in educational initiatives and internationally in attempting to develop a sustainable model of economic and social development in partnership with African Government's i.e. enabling their vision not ours.

In the UK we partner with Children in Need on specific investments aimed at establishing a solution to the NEET challenge and with Cash for Kids in the West of Scotland.

Internationally amongst many other things our core focus is on delivering in partnership with the Clinton Foundation a model for economic and social enablement with the Rwandan and Malawian Governments. In doing so we are applying part of a joint funding pot we established with Comic Relief to leverage this activity.

Partnerships

We do not distinguish between funding partners and programme partners – as far as we see it we are all in this together, either as funders or programme deliverers. We have many partners, but as an indication they include:

▶ University of Strathclyde
▶ Prince's Scottish Youth Business Trust
▶ Cash for Kids
▶ STV Appeal
▶ Children in Need
▶ Comic Relief
▶ Clinton Foundation
▶ Ethel Mutharika Maternity Hospital

As in previous years, our requests for accounts from the foundation were ignored.

Applications

The foundation has previously stated that it is 'pro-active' and does not seek applications. However, in response to our regular survey the foundation indicated that unsolicited applications are considered, so we repeat previous guidance from the foundation on how to make an approach:

The Hunter Foundation proactively sources programmes for investment, or works with partners to develop new programmes where a gap or clear need is identified. As such it is very rare indeed for THF to fund unsolicited bids, however if you wish to apply please complete a maximum two page summary outlining how your project fits with our aims and objectives and email it to info@thehunterfoundation.co.uk. This summary should include: summary of project; impact of project; any independent evaluation undertaken of your project/programme; if this is a local programme how it could be scaled to become a national programme; current sources of funding; and funding sought from the Hunter Foundation. Please note: we do not have a large staff and thus we will not consider meetings in advance of this information being provided. If your project appears to be of initial interest, we will then contact you to discuss this further.

Percentage of awards given to new applicants: less than 10%.

Common applicant mistakes

'Inapplicable projects.'

Information gathered from:

OSCR record; further information provided by the funder; funder's website.

Hurdale Charity Ltd

Advancement of Jewish religion, relief of poverty and general charitable purposes
£1.8 million (2011/12)

Beneficial area

Worldwide.

Correspondent: Abraham Oestreicher, Trustee, Cohen Arnold and Co., New Burlington House, 1075 Finchley Road, London NW11 0PU

Trustees: Eva Oestreicher; Pinkas Oestreicher; David Oestreicher; Abraham Oestreicher; Jacob Oestreicher; Benjamin Oestreicher.

CC Number: 276997

The trust supports charitable activities mostly concerned with religion and education. Almost all of the support is given to Jewish organisations that are seen to uphold the Jewish way of life, both in the UK and overseas.

In 2011/12 the trust had assets of £16 million and an income of £1.2 million. Total charitable activities totalled just under £1.8 million, however a list of beneficiaries was unavailable with this year's accounts.

Although a full list of beneficiaries was not available, the following grants were listed as the recipient charities share trustees with the trust: Springfield Trust Ltd (£750,000); Harofeh Donations Ltd (£300,000); and Moundfield Charities Ltd (£200,000).

Applications

In writing to the correspondent.

Information gathered from:

Accounts; annual report; Charity Commission record.

Impetus – The Private Equity Foundation

Children and young people

Beneficial area

UK.

Correspondent: Barbara Storch, Portfolio Director, 20 Flaxman Terrace, London WC1H 9PN (tel: 020 3747 1001; email: info@impetus-pef.org.uk; website: impetus-pef.org.uk)

Trustees: Johannes Huth; Louis Elson; Marc Boughton; Craig Dearden-Phillips; Stephen Dawson; Charles Green; Andy Hinton; Carl Parker; Karl Peterson; Andrew Sillitoe; Nat Sloane; Ramez Sousou; Nikos Stathopoulos; Chris Underhill.

CC Number: 1152262

This foundation was formed from the merger of the Impetus Trust and Private Equity Foundation, bringing together 16 years of experience supporting charity sustainability, effectiveness and growth through its venture philanthropy model. Their mission is to support disadvantaged children and young people from cradle to career, to help unlock their full potential.

The foundation offers packages of support to charities and social enterprises that work with economically disadvantaged children and young people. Organisations must be able to demonstrate clear outcomes and have ambitious growth plans. The foundation calls the organisations it supports 'the portfolio' and the themes are:

- Early years
- Primary school years
- Secondary school years
- Re-engage

Packages of support are built upon a venture philanthropy approach which consists of funding, management support from the investment team and specialist expertise from pro bono professionals. Funding is not given for specific items or projects, the packages of support are designed to develop and grow organisations that have ambitions to build their capacity. Support is given in three areas:

- Strategic Funding – Long-term core funding to build capacity which is linked to meeting pre-agreed milestones, tracked on a quarterly basis
- Hands-on management support – given to the chief executive and senior management by the foundation's in-house investment team who have consulting, financial and voluntary sector experience
- Specialist expertise – Pro-bono expertise for specific, mutually agreed capacity-building activities, agreed before a project starts, for example: business model review and business planning; financial planning and reporting; development of performance measures; senior management team coaching

As the foundation is newly registered there are no accounts published yet, however there are some key figures provided on the website:

- In 2011/12 the foundation had an income of £7.6 million. This is a combined total of the incomes of the two previous organisations for the corresponding year
- There are currently 48 organisations receiving support from the foundation, each receiving on average £500,000 – £1 million, non-financial support

- There were 566,000 people helped by the organisations in the combined portfolio in 2011/12

Beneficiaries include: Family National Nurse Partnership; Unitas; Greenhouse; Oxford Parent-Infant Project; Business in the Community; Working Chance; HHM and Bundesnetzwerk; I CAN; Ripplez; Resurgo Trust; ThinkForward; Prison Radio Association and Teens and Toddlers.

Exclusions

No funding for particular projects or buildings, or for organisations that are not focused on working with economically disadvantaged young people.

Applications

Potential applicants can sign up to the foundation's newsletter online and receive a notification when the application process is open.

Previously applicants would complete an eligibility checker then a short expression of interest form if they were deemed eligible which would then be assessed by the foundation.

Information gathered from:

Charity Commission record; funder's website; accounts and annual reports.

The Indigo Trust

Technology in Africa
£679,000 (2011/12)

Beneficial area
Primarily Africa, some UK.

Correspondent: Fran Perrin, Director, The Peak, 5 Wilton Road, London SW1V 1AP (tel: 020 7410 0330; fax: 020 7410 0332; email: info@sfct.org.uk; website: indigotrust.org.uk)

Trustees: Dominic Flynn; Francesca Perrin; William Perrin.

CC Number: 1075920

Summary

This is one of the Sainsbury Family Charitable Trusts, which share a joint administration. They have a common approach to grantmaking which is described in the entry for the group as a whole, and which is generally discouraging to organisations not already in contact with the trust concerned, but some appear increasingly open to unsolicited approaches.

General

The trust's 2011/12 accounts offer the following analysis of its grantmaking policy:

> For the second year, the trustees have continued to focus on exploring ways of promoting information equality in Africa.

The trust now funds technology-driven projects to bring about social change, largely in African countries. The trust focuses mainly on innovation, transparency and citizen empowerment. We believe that if people have the ability to access, share and create information, then they are empowered to make positive changes in their own lives and communities.

The trust is interested in supporting interventions which provide citizens with access to information on parliamentary proceedings and elected officials, and enable citizens to report challenges in service delivery and demand change. We are interested in supporting organisations in replicating the approach of projects like Mzalendo, Fix My Street and They Work For You (the latter two are projects run by one of our grantees, mySociety) across Africa.

We also support innovative projects which utilise information technologies to stimulate development in any sector, including the health, education, human rights and agricultural spheres.

A small proportion of Indigo Trust's budget has been allocated to supporting local organisations in London. The trustees do not accept unsolicited proposals in this area. Rather, they reach out to charities which they have personally identified.

Grantmaking in 2011/12

In 2011/12 the trust had assets of £7.4 million and income of £167,000 (down from a recent high of £5.8 million in 2006/07). However, the high income in 2006/07 was mainly due to a large gift of £5.5 million from the settlor. This has since been invested by the trust.

Grants payable during the current year totalled £679,000. Grants were heavily focused on technology in Africa with just 10% of the grant expenditure going to UK based projects. For more detail on the nature of projects supported see the trust's website. Beneficiaries listed below are those who were listed as awarded although not necessarily paid at the time of reporting, as this offers a more up-to-date view of the trust's priorities.

Beneficiaries included: Co-Creation Hub Nigeria (£47,000 in four separate project grants); Copenhagen Youth Project (£45,000); iCow and KINU Group (£30,000 each); iLab Liberia (£20,000); Amnesty International (£16,000); SHM Foundation (£15,000); One World UK (£13,000); Map Kibera (£11,000); Wikimedia (£10,000); TEDx Dzorwulu (£4,000); and Institute for Philanthropy (£3,500).

Exclusions

No support for infrastructure, general equipment costs or generic ICT training.

Applications

The trust provides the following helpful information:

As a flexible funder, we recognise that conditions vary from country to country and organisation to organisation and so the following criteria should be seen more as guidelines than absolute rules. It's also important to stress here that this is very much a work in progress and we welcome feedback and input on the following points. In general, however, when considering proposals we look for some or all of the following elements:

1   the applicant should be operating wholly or partly in at least one African country or else specifically seeking to benefit those who do work and live in Africa
2   they must be implementing or hoping to implement a technology-driven project or seeking to raise the profile/efficiency of technology as a development tool in Africa
3   technology must be integrated into a well-devised project, which will have a social impact
4   the project must be well researched and tackling an unmet need
5   any technology used must be appropriate, i.e. available and usable by the target population
6   projects ought to be sustainable, replicable and/or scalable
7   there should be a robust evaluation mechanism in place that enables the impact of the project to be measured
8   any organisation must be willing to be transparent and open about their work, unless security concerns mean that such openness would present a credible risk of harm to people involved in the project
9   we generally only provide approximately £10,000 to projects. The project budget can be higher, although it's very unlikely that we would be able to cover the full cost

We also have a soft spot for the following:
▶ Local organisations (or strong collaboration with local organisations)
▶ Open source projects
▶ Small organisations (with a budget of less than £500,000)
▶ Interoperable solutions
▶ Two way interactivity
▶ Innovation

We also actively encourage collaboration and, in addition to acting as funders, we see one of our key roles as making connections between grantees, other organisations and funders.

If you think your project/organisation could be suitable for consideration by us, please contact us in the first instance to tell us a little more about it. If you would prefer to submit a concept note or proposal directly, please email [us]. We strongly recommend that applicants submit brief proposals and concept notes of **between two and four sides A4** where possible. Remember, if we require further information to be able to come to an assessment or decision, we will be in touch to ask you. By asking applicants to keep proposals brief, we hope to reduce the burden both on them and on us. We do not want applicants to spend lots of time creating proposals or concept notes for us, especially if we are unlikely to fund them. In any event, a typical proposal should contain:

▶ Brief background information on your organisation, the country/countries it operates in, approximate size etc
▶ If appropriate, an overview of the project for which you are seeking funding, including details of the technology involved, the numbers/types of people it aims to reach, current status etc
▶ A statement of need, i.e. what problem does this project address
▶ A rough budget for the project
▶ Details of how you will evaluate and monitor the project including Milestones or Objectives
▶ Any other information, which you think we should know or may be helpful, such as details of partners you'll be working with

The trust welcomes contact to discuss applications or to answer any questions you may have about applying or eligibility.

Information gathered from:

Accounts; annual report; Charity Commission record; guidelines for applicants; funder's website.

Investream Charitable Trust

Jewish
£518,500 (2011/12)

Beneficial area
In practice the UK and Israel.

Correspondent: The Trustees, Investream Ltd, 38 Wigmore Street, London W1U 2RU (tel: 020 7486 2800)

Trustees: Mark Morris; Graham S. Morris.

CC Number: 1097052

Established in 2003, the trust's income is derived from Investream Ltd and its subsidiary undertakings.

The trustees intend for the foreseeable future, to continue their policy of distributing income within a short period of time from its receipt rather than accumulating reserves for future projects.

The trustees have adopted a policy of making regular donations to charitable causes, having regard to the level of the trust's annual income. They regularly appraise new opportunities for direct charitable expenditure and from time to time make substantial donations to support special or capital projects.

In 2011/12 the trust had assets of £70,500 and an income of £455,000. Grants were made during the year totalling just over £518,500, and were categorised as follows:

Education	£391,000
Poor, needy and others	£46,500
Community and elderly care	£43,000
Medical	£38,500

Beneficiaries included: Jewish Care, UCL, Moreshet Hatorah, Cosmon Belz, Chana, Project Seed, Menorah High School for Girls, Torah and Chessed, Beis Yaakov Primary School and Woodstock Sinclair Trust. Individual grant amounts were not disclosed in the accounts.

Applications
In writing to the correspondent.

Information gathered from:
Accounts; Charity Commission record.

The Isle of Anglesey Charitable Trust

General, community
£577,000 (2011/12)

Beneficial area
The Isle of Anglesey only.

Correspondent: Head of Function (Resources), Isle of Anglesey County Council, County Offices, Llangefni, Anglesey LL77 7TW (tel: 01248 752610)

Trustee: Isle of Anglesey County Council.

CC Number: 1000818

The trust, independent in law from, but administered by the Isle of Anglesey County Council was set up with an endowment from Shell (UK) Ltd when the company ceased operating an oil terminal on Anglesey, according to the terms of the 1972 private Act of Parliament which had enabled the terminal to be set up in the first place.

The objects of the trust are:
▶ The provision of amenities and facilities
▶ The preservation of buildings
▶ The conservation and protection of the land
▶ The protection and safeguarding of the environment

Grantmaking

Allocations of grants are made annually to the following categories of projects:
▶ Community and sporting facilities (small capital projects)
▶ Village halls (annual running costs)
▶ Other grants (mainly one-off small grants)

In 2011/12 the trust had assets of £16 million, an income of £460,000 and gave grants totalling £577,000.

Beneficiaries included: Isle of Anglesey County Council – Oriel Ynys Môn (£250,000); Holyhead and Anglesey Wellbeing and Fitness Centre (£180,000); The Castle Players Amateur Dramatic Society (£6,000); Talwn Village Hall

(£4,600); Bodedem Cricket Club (£2,900); Treaddur Bay Community Centre (£2,300); Rhosneigr Boys Institute (£2,000); Menai Bridge Community Heritage Trust (£1,600); Almlwch Port Hall (£1,300); and Brynteg Community Hall (£1,100).

The trust's accounts provide information as to the distribution of its income to various organisations in Anglesey; however, it is not possible to ascertain from the accounts whether any of the grants awarded are used to subsidise the county council by providing facilities and/or services which should be provided by the local authority.

Exclusions
No grants to individuals or projects based outside Anglesey.

Applications
In writing to the correspondent with an application form, following advertisements in the local press in February. The trust considers applications once a year: 'We will take details of any prospective applicants during the year, but application forms are sent out annually in February.'

Information gathered from:
Accounts; annual report; Charity Commission record.

The J. J. Charitable Trust

Environment, literacy
£929,000 (2011/12)

Beneficial area
Unrestricted.

Correspondent: Alan Bookbinder, Director, The Peak, 5 Wilton Road, London SW1V 1AP (tel: 020 7410 0330; fax: 020 7410 0332; email: info@sfct.org. uk; website: www.sfct.org.uk)

Trustees: John Julian Sainsbury; Mark Sainsbury; Judith Portrait; Lucy Guard.

CC Number: 1015792

Summary
This is one of the Sainsbury Family Charitable Trusts, which share a joint administration. They have a common approach to grantmaking which is described in the entry for the group as a whole.

A relatively small number of grants are made. Few of them are for less than £5,000 and occasional grants can be for more than £100,000. The trust has previously stated that: 'Proposals are generally invited by the trustees or initiated at their request. Unsolicited applications are discouraged and are unlikely to be successful, even if they fall within an area in which the trustees are interested. The trustees prefer to support innovative schemes that can be successfully replicated or become self-sustaining.'

The settlor of this trust is Julian Sainsbury and he is still building up the endowment, which included making a donation of £1.6 million in 2009/10. The main areas of interest are:

▸ Literacy – to improve the effectiveness of literacy teaching in primary and secondary education for children with learning difficulties including dyslexia, and for ex-offenders or those at risk of offending

▸ Environmental education in the UK, particularly projects involving children and young adults, energy efficiency and renewable energy

▸ Environmental projects overseas, especially community-based agriculture initiatives, which aim to help people help themselves in an environmentally sustainable way

Grantmaking in 2011/12
In 2011/12 the trust had assets of £33 million and an income of £956,000. Grants paid during the year totalled £929,000, distributed as follows:

Literacy support	3	£318,000	34%
Environment – UK	10	£355,000	38%
Environment – overseas	7	£201,000	22%
General	2	£57,000	6%

Beneficiaries included: Ashden Sustainable solutions, better lives (£90,000); British Academy of Film and Television Awards (BAFTA) (£74,000); Shannon Trust (£70,000); Open Book (£60,000); Jolibe Trust (£52,000); Ecofin Research Foundation (£49,000); Lyndhurst Primary School and Ministry of Stories (£40,000 each); National Energy Foundation (£32,000); and Africa Innovations Institute (£25,000).

Exclusions
No grants for: individuals; educational fees; or expeditions. The trust only funds registered charities or activities with clearly defined charitable purposes.

Applications
See the guidance for applicants in the entry for the Sainsbury Family Charitable Trusts. A single application will be considered for support by all the trusts in the group.

However, for this as for many of the trusts, the following statement from the trust's website should be noted: 'the trustees take an active role in their grantmaking, employing a range of specialist staff and advisers to research their areas of interest and bring forward suitable proposals. Many of the trusts work closely with their chosen beneficiaries over a long period to achieve particular objectives. It should therefore be understood that the majority of unsolicited proposals we receive will be unsuccessful'.

Information gathered from:
Accounts; annual report; Charity Commission record; funder's website.

John James Bristol Foundation

Education, health, older people, general
£901,000 (2011/12)

Beneficial area
Worldwide, in practice Bristol.

Correspondent: Julia Norton, Chief Executive, 7 Clyde Road, Redland, Bristol BS6 6RG (tel: 01179 239444; fax: 01179 239470; email: info@johnjames. org.uk; website: www.johnjames.org.uk)

Trustees: Joan Johnson; David Johnson; Elizabeth Chambers; John Evans; Andrew Jardine; Andrew Webley; John Haworth; Peter Goodwin.

CC Number: 288417

The foundation was established in 1983 and its objects are the relief of poverty or sickness, the advancement of education or other charitable purposes amongst the inhabitants of Bristol, and other charitable purposes with no defined beneficial area. The foundation's main aim is to benefit as many residents of the city of Bristol as possible by granting money as diversely as they can within the foundation's key focus areas of education, health and the elderly. This may include making grants to organisations carrying out the following work:

▸ Encouraging young people, through grants to schools, youth organisations and other charities, to make the most of their educational opportunities

▸ Improving health care through grants for medical research, equipment in hospitals, specialist equipment, holidays and care at home for individuals whose health needs are recognised by a registered charity

▸ Assistance, through organisations, to older residents of Bristol in ways which will encourage them and help improve their quality of life

In 2011/12 the foundation had assets of £54 million and an income of £1.5 million. Grants made totalling £901,000 were categorised as follows:

Education	£502,000
Health	£273,000
Elderly	£126,000
General	£2,000

Beneficiaries included: Barton Hill Settlement (£33,000); The Red Maids' School and Redland High School

(£30,000 each); Barnardo's Bristol BASE Project (£25,000); Badminton School (£20,000); University of Bristol – Bowel Cancer Research (£18,000); Crisis Centre Ministries (£10,000); Deafblind UK (£5,000); Bristol Amateur Operatic Society (£4,200); St Dunstan's (£3,000); Huntington FoodCycle (£2,000); Huntington's Disease Association (£2,000); and Relate Avon (£1,000).

Exclusions

No grants to individuals.

Applications

The trustees meet quarterly in February, May, August and November to consider appeals received by 15 January, April, July and October as appropriate. There is no application form and appeals **must be submitted by post**, to the chief executive on no more than two sides of A4. Supporting information, sent by the applicant with their appeal, is available to the trustees at their meeting.

All appeal applications are acknowledged, stating the month in which the appeal will be considered by the trustees. If further information is required it will be requested and a visit to the applicant may be made by a representative of the foundation. Grants are normally only given to charitable bodies who can clearly show that they are benefiting Bristol residents, and working within the foundation's key focus areas of education, health and the elderly.

Percentage of awards given to new applicants: less than 10%.

Common applicant mistakes

'Not saying how much they want; not applying for the city of Bristol.'

Information gathered from:

Accounts; annual report; Charity Commission record; further information provided by the funder.

Jay Education Trust

Jewish
£343,000 (2011/12)

Beneficial area

Worldwide.

Correspondent: Rabbi Alfred Schechter, Trustee, 37 Filey Avenue, London N16 6JL

Trustees: Rabbi Alfred Schechter; Gabriel Gluck; Shlomo Z. Stauber.

CC Number: 1116458

'The objects of the charity are: the relief of poverty in the Jewish Community worldwide; the advancement of religious education according to the beliefs and values of the Jewish Faith worldwide and any charitable purpose at the discretion of the trustees for the benefit of the community.'

In 2011/12 the trust had assets of £925,000 and an income of £1.4 million. Grants were made totalling £343,000.

Beneficiaries included: Chevras Mo'oz Ladol (£276,500); Notzar Chesed (£10,000); Centre for Torah Education Trust (£5,500); Yeshiva Torah Chaim (£5,000); and TTT (£1,500).

Applications

In writing to the correspondent.

Information gathered from:

Accounts; Charity Commission record.

The Jerusalem Trust

Promotion of Christianity
£2.6 million (2011)

Beneficial area

Unrestricted.

Correspondent: Alan Bookbinder, Director, The Peak, 5 Wilton Road, London SW1V 1AP (tel: 020 7410 0330; fax: 020 7410 0332; email: jerusalemtrust@sfct.org.uk; website: www.sfct.org.uk)

Trustees: Rt Hon. Sir Timothy Sainsbury; Lady Susan Sainsbury; Dr V. E. Hartley Booth; Phillida Goad; Dr Peter Frankopan; Melanie Townsend.

CC Number: 285696

This is one of the Sainsbury Family Charitable Trusts, which share a joint administration. Their approaches to grantmaking have aspects in common which are described in the entry for the group as a whole. The trust is primarily proactive, aiming to choose its own grantees, and it discourages unsolicited applications.

The trust supports a wide range of evangelical organisations, across a broad though usually moderate spectrum of Christian activity.

Unfortunately at the time of writing (November 2013) the trust's accounts for 2012 were not yet available. In 2011 the trust had assets of £77.9 million and an income of £2.7 million. Grants were paid totalling £2.6 million. The number and value of grant approvals in 2011 (including future payments) were categorised as follows:

Evangelism and Christian Mission in the UK	65	£854,000
Christian Education	19	£656,500
Christian Evangelism and Relief Work Overseas	26	£559,500
Christian Media	10	£435,000
Christian Art	8	£118,000

Grants paid included those to: National Society for Promoting Religious Education (£150,000); Tear Fund (£110,000); Churches and Media Network (£82,000); Salmon Youth Centre (£60,000); Bible Reading Fellowship (£50,000); Religious Education Movement in Scotland (£40,000); Churches' National Adviser in Further Education (£30,000); African Enterprise (£20,000); and Transform Newham (£15,000).

Exclusions

Trustees do not normally make grants towards building or repair work for churches. Grants are not normally made to individuals.

Applications

See the guidance for applicants in the entry for the Sainsbury Family Charitable Trusts. A single application will be considered for support by all the trusts in the group.

However, for this as for many of the trusts, 'proposals are generally invited by the trustees or initiated at their request'.

Information gathered from:

Accounts; annual report; Charity Commission record; funder's website.

Jerwood Charitable Foundation

The arts
£1.1 million to organisations (2012)

Beneficial area

UK.

Correspondent: Ms Shonagh Manson, Director, 171 Union Street, Bankside, London SE1 0LN (tel: 020 7261 0279; email: info@jerwood.org; website: www.jerwoodcharitablefoundation.org)

Trustees: Tim Eyles, Chair; Katherine Goodison; Juliane Wharton; Anthony Palmer; Thomas Grieve; Rupert Tyler; Phyllida Earle.

CC Number: 1074036

The Jerwood Charitable Foundation (the foundation) was established in 1998 with general charitable purposes. In 1999 it took over the administration of a number of initiatives of the Jerwood Foundation (the parent company), including the Jerwood Applied Arts Prize, Jerwood Choreography Award and Jerwood Painting Prize.

In 2005 the charitable foundation became completely independent after receiving the final endowment donation from the Jerwood Foundation. However, as the foundation has previously stated, it retains close ties with all of the Jerwood family. 'We continue to see ourselves as closely linked with, and will continue to seek guidance from, the Jerwood Foundation on our activities and of course, as ever, will work closely with other Jerwood family members especially the Jerwood Space.' (The Jerwood Space is a major initiative of the company, offering affordable rehearsal spaces for dance and theatre companies to develop their work.)

The aims of the foundation are the distribution of funds to individuals and organisations for the promotion of visual and performing arts and education in the widest sense. It has four main objectives:

- To support artists in the early stages of their careers
- To support the wider infrastructure of arts organisations
- To respond positively to those taking artistic risks
- To explore the opportunity of identifying small programme related investment opportunities

Funding policy

The foundation is a major sponsor of all areas of the performing and visual arts, particularly projects which involve rewards for excellence and the encouragement and recognition of outstanding talent and high standards, or which enable an organisation to become viable and self-financing. It rarely sponsors single performances or arts events, such as festivals, nor does it make grants towards the running or core costs of established arts organisations.

The following information is taken from the foundation's website:

> We are dedicated to imaginative and responsible funding of the arts across the UK, with a particular focus on supporting emerging talent and excellence. We aim for funding to allow artists and art organisations to thrive; to continue to develop their skills, imagination and creativity with integrity.

> Where we are able, and it is appropriate, we may wish to be sole funder of a project, but we also provide partnership funding and run co-commissioned projects with other funders. We aim to monitor chosen projects closely and sympathetically, and are keen to seek visible recognition of our support.

> The JCF has the benefit of association with capital projects of the Jerwood Foundation. These include the Jerwood Space, the Jerwood Theatres at the Royal Court Theatre, the Jerwood Gallery at the Natural History Museum and the Jerwood Sculpture Park at Ragley Hall, Warwickshire. The support for these initiatives by the Jerwood Foundation will be a factor when considering any applications.

> The foundation will fund individuals, organisations and companies who are not registered charities (providing the project meets the foundation's charitable aims).

Types of Grants

Grant levels vary between the lower range of up to £10,000 (often plus or minus £5,000) and more substantial grants in excess of £10,000. The foundation states that there should be no expectation of grant level as all applications will be assessed on merit and need.

Projects and awards

The foundation actively pursues and develops initiatives in the arts world as well as receiving unsolicited applications for funding. Projects and awards cover a wide range of arts activities currently in the following areas:

- Music
- Dance
- Theatre
- Literature
- Visual arts
- Film
- Multi-disciplinary
- Mission Models Money (action research programme)

The foundation will rarely commit to repeat funding over a number of years, preferring to make revenue donations on a one-off basis. However, it is prepared, in many cases, to maintain support if the partnership has been successful and consistency will help to secure better results.

> The JCF also provides 'challenge funding', whereby the foundation will make a grant provided the recipient or other interested party can match the remaining shortfall.

> **Jerwood Visual Arts** – a year round contemporary gallery programme of awards, exhibitions, and events at Jerwood Space, London, which then tours the UK. JVA is developed and run by the Jerwood Charitable Foundation; as a major initiative it represents about a third of our work and resources. The programme currently comprises the Jerwood Drawing Prize, Jerwood Makers Open, Jerwood Painting Fellowships and the Jerwood Encounters series. We also run a talks and events programme, host a writer in residence placement and support a rolling Traineeship in gallery management.

> **Large Grants –** grant partnerships made over a number of years, or single awards of £10,000 or more. These partnerships tend to be developed proactively or through ongoing conversation with potential applicants, responding to key needs and issues within arts sectors. This fund allows us to develop strategic approaches to supporting artists through nurturing or professional development programmes founded and run by established arts organisations. Through this fund we also support research and development initiatives supporting experimentation or to generate new work or new collaborations, investigation into sectoral or policy provision, and commissioning initiatives.

> **Small grants –** We also support a broader number of small grants for one-off projects, generally under £10,000. This fund allows us to explore new relationships, work directly with individual artists, take risks and support research or development of future ideas. At the heart of every small grant is a targeted or particular professional or sectoral development opportunity to be explored.

> Due to the limitations of our funding, we do not offer general support for production costs, touring or staging exhibitions.

> The majority of our partnerships and initiatives are proactively sought and developed, however we do accept unsolicited proposals. Please note that we very rarely fund projects which are put forward in this way and are seeking specific, targeted, tangible professional development opportunities in the work that we take on.

Grantmaking in 2012

In 2012 the foundation had assets of £26 million, an income of £987,000 and made grants totalling £1.2 million of which £1.1 million went to organisations and £94,000 to individuals. Funding was provided in 44 grants of between £1,500 and £100,000. Grants were categorised as follows:

Visual arts	38%
Theatre	21%
Music	18%
Dance	10%
Small grants	9%
Cross-disciplinary projects	2%
Literature	2%

Beneficiaries included: Royal Court Theatre: Jerwood New Playwrights (£75,000); Jerwood Space re Jerwood Visual Arts (£63,000); Sadler Wells: Summer University (£43,000); Arts Admin: Develop and Create (£25,000); Chris Goode and Company: Monkey Bars (£20,000); National Theatre Wales: Online Artists' Platform (£15,000); OTO Projects: Grassroots Promoters/Emerging Artists Fund (£10,000); Undercurrent Festival: Commissions and Development (£7,500); New School House Gallery: Transformation (£5,000); and Owl Project: Organisational Development (£2,000).

Exclusions

The foundation will not consider applications for:

- Building or capital costs (including purchase of equipment)
- Projects in the fields of religion or sport
- Animal rights or welfare
- Study fees or course fees
- General fundraising appeals which are likely to have wide public appeal
- Appeals to establish endowment funds for other charities
- Appeals for matching funding for National Lottery applications

- Grants for the running and core costs of voluntary bodies
- Projects which are of mainly local appeal or identified with a locality
- Medical or mental health projects
- Social welfare, particularly where it may be considered a government or local authority responsibility
- Retrospective awards
- Projects outside Great Britain
- Schools which are trying to attain 'Special Schools Status'
- General touring, production or staging costs
- Environmental or conservation projects
- Musical instruments
- Informal education or community participation projects
- Education or participation projects for those who have not yet left formal education

The foundation may, where there are very exceptional circumstances, decide to waive an exclusion.

Applications

Initial applications should include:

- A short proposal, not more than two sides of A4, outlining a description of the organisation's aims or a short biography for individuals, and a description of the specific project for which funding is sought and the opportunity it seeks to fulfil
- A detailed budget for the project, identifying administrative, management and central costs details of funding already in place for the project, including any other trusts or sources which are being or have been approached for funds, and
- If funding is not in place, details of how the applicant plans to secure the remaining funding

The trustees may decide to contact the applicants for further information including:

- Details of the management and staffing structure, including trustees
- The most recent annual report and audited accounts of the organisation, together with current management accounts if relevant to the project

However, the foundation asks that this information is **not** sent unless it is requested.

Applications may be made online via the website which is the foundation's preferred method. Alternatively applicants can send proposals by post. The foundation may wish to enter into discussions and/or correspondence with the applicant which may result in modification and/or development of the project or scheme. Any such discussion or correspondence will not commit the foundation to funding that application.

Applications are assessed throughout the year. Successful applicants will be invited to report to the foundation at the completion of their project and to provide photographs of the work or project supported.

As the foundation receives a large number of applications, it is not always possible to have preliminary meetings to discuss possible support before a written application is made.

> The majority of our partnerships and initiatives are proactively sought and developed, however we do accept unsolicited proposals. **Please note** that we very rarely fund projects which are put forward in this way and are seeking specific, targeted, tangible professional development opportunities in the work that we take on.

Percentage of awards given to new applicants: between 20% and 30%.

Common applicant mistakes

'Failure to read the guidance on our website. Poorly written applications that do not clearly outline the project or the activity for which they are requesting funding – we do not make grants in response to general requests for funding. Applicants do not make contact with us first to check eligibility and our preferred method of working.'

Information gathered from:

Accounts; annual report; Charity Commission record; further information provided by the funder; funder's website.

Jewish Child's Day

Charitable purposes of direct benefit to Jewish children who are disadvantaged, suffering or in need of special care
£687,000 (2011/12)

Beneficial area

Worldwide. In practice, mainly Israel, UK and Eastern Europe.

Correspondent: Jackie Persoff, Grants Administrator and PA to the Executive Director, 5th Floor, 707 High Road, North Finchley, London N12 0BT (tel: 020 8446 8804; fax: 020 8446 7370; email: info@jcd.uk.com; website: www.jcd.uk.com)

Trustees: Joy Moss, Chair; June Jacobs; Stephen Moss; Virginia Campus; Francine Epstein; Susie Olins; Amanda Ingram; Gaby Lazarus; David Collins.

CC Number: 209266

The trust was established in 1947 to encourage Jewish children in the UK to help less fortunate Jewish children who were survivors of the Nazi holocaust. The trust exists to improve the lives of Jewish children, in the UK, Israel or elsewhere overseas, who for any reason are suffering, disadvantaged or in need of special care.

The trust gives grants to registered charities running programmes which help these children, giving grants for items of equipment or specific projects. All grants must directly benefit children up to the age of 18. Grants are generally for £500 to £5,000. Jewish Child's Day will support projects from all sections of the Jewish Community.

In 2011/12 the charity had assets of £640,000 and an income of £1.1 million, mostly from donations. Grants totalled £687,000.

Beneficiaries included: Friends of Givat Ada (£100,000); Beit Uri (£33,000); Friends of Neve-Kineret (£20,000); Manchester Jewish Federation (£15,000); Haifa Centre (£10,000); Schechter Institute of Jewish Studies, Yated – Downs Syndrome Society of Israel and The Jerusalem Therapeutic Riding Center (£3,000); Micha Tel Aviv and Youth Direct (£1,100).

Exclusions

Individuals are not supported. Grants are not given towards general services, building or maintenance of property or staff salaries.

Applications

To apply for a grant contact the correspondent to discuss in the first instance.

Applications must be supported by audited accounts in English or with the main heading translated into English. Applications should be submitted by 31 December, 30 April and 31 August for consideration in March, June and October respectively. Organisations with dedicated UK fundraising operations must disclose this in the application.

Percentage of awards given to new applicants: less than 10%.

Common applicant mistakes

'They do not complete application form correctly; they do not enclose all documentation requested.'

Information gathered from:

Accounts; annual report; Charity Commission record; further information provided by the funder; funder's website.

The Joffe Charitable Trust

Alleviation of poverty and protection/advancement of human rights

£706,000 (2011/12)

Beneficial area

The Gambia, Kenya, Malawi, Mozambique, South Africa, Tanzania, Uganda, Zambia and Zimbabwe.

Correspondent: Linda Perry, Trust Manager, Liddington Manor, 35 The Street, Liddington, Swindon SN4 0HD (tel: 01793 790203; email: joffetrust@lidmanor.co.uk; website: www.joffecharitabletrust.org)

Trustees: Lord Joel Joffe, Chair; Lady Vanetta Joffe; Deborah Joffe; Dr Nick Maurice; Mark Poston; Alex Jacobs.

CC Number: 270299

The Joffe Charitable Trust was established in 1968 by the settlor, Lord Joffe and Vanetta Joffe. The objectives of the trust are widely drawn but in reality most grants are made for the relief of poverty and the advancement of human rights in the Anglophone sub Saharan Africa.

The trust conducts its activities through grantmaking and loans and the trustees have an ongoing relationship with a large number of charities, (the settlor is a former chair of Oxfam and the Giving Campaign). The decisions made as to which organisations/projects to support are based on the trustees' assessment of the quality of leadership within an organisation and the impact that the initiatives which they support are likely to have.

Guidelines

The following information on funding policy is taken from the trust's website:

Our broad approach

We will fund international development institutions that have:

- A clear strategic purpose rooted in strong analysis and experience
- Realistic plans for contributing to long-term change
- Where our limited funds can make a real difference
- Are hard to fund from other sources
- Strong leadership with a track record of successful development programmes

Geographical Focus

Projects which mainly focus on or have an impact on development in Anglophone Africa.

What we will normally fund within our geographic focus

Campaigns with a realistic prospect of success in relation to human rights, corruption and economic systems that favour the poor (examples of charities we have funded in this category include Transparency International, Stamp out Poverty, Global Witness and World Development Movement).

Narrowly focused initiatives which aim to fill a specific gap in efforts to assist poor people (examples of charities we have funded in this category are Tourism Concern, ASTI – Acid Survivors Trust International, Mango – Management accounting for NGOs, Orchid – Female Genital Mutilation).

What we will occasionally fund outside our geographic and normal focus

Initiatives which we judge to have the potential to make a disproportionate impact on poor people in the developing world. These grants are very seldom made to unsolicited applications and will only be considered if they are truly exceptional.

The trust normally funds UK registered charities or organisations with equivalent not-for-profit status that have annual income of less than £5m per year.

Grant Size: the trust makes grants of between £5,000 and £40,000 per year, and very occasionally more, for up to three years.

In addition to making grants, the Trust invests a proportion of its assets in social investments which generate jobs and social benefits in sub Saharan Africa as well as a financial return for investors.

Assessment Criteria

All grant applications are assessed against the following criteria:

- Strong leadership with a successful track record
- Capacity to deliver
- Clear and focused objectives
- Realistic budgets and fundraising plans
- Strategic purpose
- Measurable results
- Strong partnerships with African organisations and/or other NGOs working in a related field
- Value for money
- Activities that are hard to fund from other sources

Which charities we will fund: Normally only charities registered with and controlled by the UK Charity Commission or its equivalent in other countries.

Grants in 2011/12

In 2011/12 the trust had assets of £11 million and an income of £387,000. Grants were made totalling £706,000.

Beneficiaries included: Ububele Educational and Psychotherapy Trust (£137,000); AFIDEP (£50,000); Acid Survivors International (£44,000); Charities Aid Foundation (£38,000); Transparency International (£25,000); Earth Security Initiative CIC (£18,000); Global Giving (£15,000); and University of California San Francisco Foundation (£12,500). Grants of £10,000 or less totalled £85,000.

Exclusions

No grants for: emergency relief, the arts, conflict resolution, formal academic education, micro credit, work directly in the field of HIV/AIDS, individuals, physical infrastructure, large charities with income of over £5 million per annum.

Applications

Firstly, applicants must complete an online application form available through the trust's website. The trust aims to respond to applicants within one month if they have been successful. If so, they will be asked to submit a more detailed proposal, including:

- Introduction to the issues you are working on
- Strategic goals
- Objectives and specific targets
- Information on how they will measure results, specified for each year of the grant
- The major external stakeholders who will have to be involved to achieve success: their roles, commitment to the work and capacity to deliver
- Your approach to measuring results, including feedback from external stakeholders
- Sustainability: how your work will contribute to long-term results after the end of this funding period
- CV of the chief executive or key operational managers
- The latest audited accounts and annual review

Limit your full proposal to seven to ten sides in length. As part of the evaluation of your application, the trust may telephone or arrange to meet you with you to discuss it further.

The trust aims to let all stage two applicants have a decision within four months of receiving their proposal.

Percentage of awards given to new applicants: between 40% and 50%.

Common applicant mistakes

'They fall outside our published remit.'

Information gathered from:

Accounts; annual report; Charity Commission record; further information provided by the funder; funder's website.

The Elton John Aids Foundation

Aids and related welfare

£8.9 million (2012)

Beneficial area
Unrestricted.

Correspondent: Mr Mohamed Osman, Head of Grants, 1 Blythe Road, London W14 0HG (tel: 020 7603 9996; fax: 020 7348 4848; email: grants@ejaf.com; website: www.ejaf.com)

Trustees: Sir Elton John, Founder; David Furnish, Chair; Lynette Jackson; Frank Presland; Anne Aslett; Marguerite Littman; Johnny Bergius; James Locke; Rafi Manoukian; Scott Campbell.

CC Number: 1017336

Summary

This foundation was established in 1993 by Sir Elton John to empower people infected, affected and at risk of HIV/AIDS and to alleviate their physical, emotional and financial hardship, enabling them to improve their quality of life, live with dignity and exercise self-determination. Their mission is to provide focused and sustainable funding to frontline programmes that help alleviate the physical, emotional and financial hardship of those living with, affected by or at risk of HIV/AIDS and continue to fight against this world pandemic.

Since its establishment the Elton John AIDS Foundation (EJAF) UK has raised over £100 million to provide grants in 25 countries over four continents to support more than 1,300 projects.

Areas of Work

The foundation funds a range of services for those living with or affected by HIV/AIDS including education, peer support, medical care, income generation, counselling and testing. It supports operational research but not pure medical research. Particular emphasis is given to the most disadvantaged or high risk groups, both nationally and internationally, and to community driven programmes that place people living with HIV/AIDS at the centre of service provision. There are two main areas of work:

Prioritising Vulnerable Populations
Support is targeted at people who are at higher risk such as men who have sex with men, sex workers and people who inject drugs. This comprises of two funds:

▶ **Pioneer Grants** – to support a specific initiative focusing on an individual key population at higher risk within an individual country.

Grants may be multi-year and there is no limit on the amount. The following criteria must be fulfilled:

▶ Focus on service delivery
▶ Catalytic in nature
▶ Scalable in design
▶ Innovative
▶ Operate within one of the programme countries
▶ Able to track changes for example access to condoms

▶ **Flagship Programmes** – to target a specific vulnerable group through a number of related initiatives within an individual country. These programmes look to genuinely 'close a gap' for a specific vulnerable group by engaging in a number of activities ranging from service delivery to advocacy. Due to the complex nature of this programme it is not open for applications; the foundation will proactively identify partners

Large Scale and Grassroots Initiatives
To complement the focus on key populations at risk, the foundation will also support regional and global initiatives that impact large numbers of people living with or at risk of HIV. In line with this there are two programmes:

▶ **Support Grants** – to be targeted at groups within the general population that the foundation has been invested in for a long time, namely vulnerable girls, women and children. The following criteria must be fulfilled:

▶ Aligned with the UNAIDS elimination agenda (Getting to Zero) and/or the UNAIDS Global Plan
▶ Allow for a unique EJAF contribution
▶ Already be working at scale
▶ Applications for this programme are by invitation only

▶ **Robert Key Memorial Fund** – Robert Key MBE (1947–2009) co-founded the UK arm of the EJAF with Sir Elton. This fund was established in his memory with the following features:

▶ Open to organisations that can demonstrate an immediate, tangible benefit for individuals living with HIV
▶ Applications can be made for awards of up to £10,000 per year on a rolling basis, for single or multi-year programmes
▶ Must operate in one of the foundation's programme countries

Grantmaking in 2012

In 2012 the foundation had assets of £27 million, an income of £12 million and gave grants totalling £8.9 million.

Some larger beneficiaries mentioned in the accounts include: Habitat for Humanity; Terrence Higgins Trust; Riders for Health; partners in Health; the Children's Society; Liverpool VCT;

Familia Salmada; Simelela Rape Crisis; All Ukrainian Network of People Living with HIV/AIDS; Romanian Angel Appeal; Nwamitwa Community Centre; Paediatric Palliative Care, Zambia; Fair Play – Tackling HIV in Ukraine and Red Badges – Tanzania.

Exclusions

For both UK and international grants the foundation will not fund:

▶ Academic or medical research
▶ Conferences
▶ Grants to individuals
▶ Repatriation costs
▶ Retrospective funding

Applications

There are two funds that accept applications:

Pioneer Grants
Available in: Cameroon, Cote D'Ivoire, Ghana, India, Kenya, Lesotho, Malawi, Myanmar (Burma), Nigeria, Russian Federation, South Africa, Tanzania, Thailand, Uganda, Ukraine, United Kingdom, Zambia and Zimbabwe.

Robert Key Memorial Fund
Applicants must be applying on behalf of an organisation that is a registered not-for-profit or charitable organisation. Available in the countries listed above under Pioneer Grants, **plus:** Botswana, Democratic Republic of the Congo, Ethiopia, Mozambique, China, Indonesia and Vietnam.

These programmes may change or open and close throughout the year so applicants are advised to check the website before making an application. Applications are made through the online form. The grants panel meets up to five times a year. Funding decisions are made by way of a majority vote and are ratified by the board.

Percentage of awards given to new applicants: between 30% and 40%.

Common applicant mistakes

'Proposals that did not demonstrate how the project fits EJAF's country specific strategy and funding priorities. Insufficient focus on specific and vulnerable populations (often proposals were too broadly targeted on general populations). Not truly integrated – e.g. proposals that aimed to integrate sexual and reproductive health (SRH) and HIV services, but did not include evidence of comprehensive sexual and reproductive health services/care/support. Proposed budgets that exceeded the capacity/ history of the organisation to deliver (using previous years funding/turnover provided). Proposals that did not explain how results would be measured. Results solely focused on inputs and outputs, as opposed to outcomes. Budgets with insufficient detail or which did not seem to relate to the activities that were set out in the project. Extensions of existing projects unrelated to EJAF's funding priorities. A lack of community focus or meaningful involvement of people living with and/or affected by HIV. Proposals that represented poor value per intervention – e.g. a very high cost for a small population served. No evidence that a plan existed to make the project sustainable beyond funding requested.'

Information gathered from:

Accounts; annual report; Charity Commission record; further information provided by the funder; funder's website.

The Jones 1986 Charitable Trust

People with disabilities, welfare of older people, welfare of younger people, education and purposes beneficial to the community

£404,000 (2011/12)

Beneficial area

UK, mostly Nottinghamshire.

Correspondent: Nigel Lindley, Trust Co-ordinator, Smith Cooper LLP, 2 Lace Market Square, Nottingham NG1 1PB (tel: 01159 454300)

Trustees: Robert Heason; John David Pears.

CC Number: 327176

The charity was established in 1986 with very wide charitable purposes. The trust primarily supports causes in the Nottingham area and much of its grant giving goes to charities assisting people with disabilities or for medical research into disabilities and the welfare of older people. The trust also supports charities supporting the welfare of the young, education and purposes beneficial to the community. The trust prefers to develop a relationship with the organisations funded over an extended period of time.

In 2011/12 the trust had assets of £18 million, an income of £487,000 and gave grants totalling £404,000, broken down as follows:

Community	£144,000
Illness and disability – general	£109,000
Illness and disability – young	£61,000
Older people	£41,000
Welfare of the young	£24,000
Education	£15,000
Medical research	£12,000

Beneficiaries included: Riding for the Disabled – Highland Group (£50,000); Cope Children's Trust (£40,000); Age UK and Kirkby Community Advice Centre (£25,000 each); The Archbishop of York's Southwell Palace Project (£15,000); I CAN and Combat Stress (£10,000 each); Platform 51 (£6,000);

Family Care Nottingham, Radford Care Group and Tree Tops Hospice (£5,000 each); Community Concern Erewash (£3,000); Relate (£2,500); Deafblind UK (£1,000); and Happy Days (£500).

Exclusions

No grants to individuals.

Applications

In writing to the correspondent. The trust invites applications for grants by advertising in specialist press. Applications are considered for both capital and/or revenue projects as long as each project appears viable.

Information gathered from:

Accounts; annual report; Charity Commission record.

The Jordan Charitable Foundation

General charitable purposes

£397,000 (2012)

Beneficial area

UK national charities, Herefordshire and Sutherland, Scotland.

Correspondent: Ralph Stockwell, Trustee, Rawlinson and Hunter, 8th Floor, 6 New Street Square, New Fetter Land, London EC4A 3AQ (tel: 020 7842 2000; email: jordan@rawlinson-hunter.com)

Trustees: Sir George Russell; Ralph Stockwell; Christopher Jan Andrew Bliss; Anthony Brierley; Snowport Ltd; Parkdove Ltd.

CC Number: 1051507

The Jordan Charitable Foundation was established in 1995. The grantmaking policies are guided by the original intentions of the founders. Grants are made to UK national charities and also to charities that are local to the county of Herefordshire, and in particular, charities operating within the city of Hereford and to a much lesser extent, charities in Sutherland, Scotland, as there is a connection between the founders and this area. The trustees assist towards funding of a capital nature and towards defraying revenue costs.

Grants are made in the following areas:

- Medical equipment
- Medical research
- Grants to elderly people
- Grants to help people with disabilities including children
- Grants for animal welfare
- Grants to assist in the maintenance of Hereford Cathedral

In 2012 the foundation had assets of £44 million, an income of £940,000 and made 52 grants totalling £397,000, broken down geographically as follows:

UK	£231,000	58%
Hereford	£153,000	39%
Sutherland	£12,500	3%

Around 60% of funding was given to organisations working throughout the UK, 38% in Hereford and 2% in Sutherland. Most grants are for between £5,000 and £10,000.

Beneficiaries included: Martha Trust – Hereford (£50,000); County Air Ambulance Trust (£15,000); Brooke Hospital for Animals, Marie Curie Cancer Care and The Special Air Service Regimental Association (£10,000 each); National Trust for Scotland, Royal National Mission for Deep Sea Fishermen and The Royal Start and Garter Home (£5,000 each); Tykes – The Young Karers East Sutherland (£1,000); and Dunrobin Castle Piping Championship (£500).

Applications

In writing to the correspondent.

Information gathered from:

Accounts; annual report; Charity Commission record.

The Kay Kendall Leukaemia Fund

Research into leukaemia and patient care

£5.2 million (2011/12)

Correspondent: Alan Bookbinder, Director, The Peak, 5 Wilton Road, London SW1V 1AP (tel: 020 7410 0330; email: info@kklf.org.uk; website: www.kklf.org.uk)

Trustees: Judith Portrait; Timothy J. Sainsbury; Charles Metcalfe.

CC Number: 290772

This is one of the Sainsbury Family Charitable Trusts, which share a joint administration. They have a common approach to grantmaking which is described in the entry for the group as a whole.

This trust is solely concerned with funding research into the causes and treatment of leukaemia, which is done on the advice of an expert advisory panel.

The trust's website offers a clear and simple summary of its grantmaking:

Project Grants
Research grants are normally awarded for projects of up to 3 years' duration. It is intended that the KKLF funding should not be the 'core' funding of any research group. Applicants should state clearly how their proposal relates to their core funding.

What will be funded
Grants will be awarded for research on aspects of leukaemia and for relevant

studies on related haematological malignancies. Requests for support for basic science programmes may be considered. Phase 3 Clinical trials will not normally be supported but applications for phase 1 or 2 studies may be considered. Proposals which are closely related to the prevention, diagnosis, or therapy of leukaemia and related diseases are particularly encouraged.

Grants are usually awarded to give additional support to programmes already underway, the aim being to further strengthen activities which are already of high quality. It follows that the KKLF will accept proposals from groups which already have support from other agencies.

The trustees will consider proposals from both UK and non-UK based organisations where the work to be funded is based primarily within the UK.

A preliminary letter or telephone call to the administration offices of the Kay Kendall Leukaemia Fund, or to one of its scientific advisers, may be helpful to determine whether or not a proposal is likely to be eligible.

Research proposal
Applicants should complete the approved Application Form and include a research proposal (aims, background, plan of investigation, justification for budget.) The research proposal should be 3-5 single-spaced pages for project grants (excluding references, costings, and CVs). Applications should be submitted by email in addition to providing a hard copy with original signatures. The trustees will take account of annual inflation and of salary increases related to nationally negotiated pay scales and these should not be built into the application.

Salaries should generally be on nationally agreed scales.

Tenured or non time-limited appointments will not be supported.

The trustees may, from time to time, set special conditions for the award of a grant.

Final decision on the award of a grant is made by the trustees, having taken into account advice from their scientific advisers.

Other Awards
Capital funding
Requests for capital grants for leukaemia research laboratories or for clinical facilities for leukaemia will be considered either alone or in conjunction with proposals for the support of research and/or patient management. Capital requests must give a budget estimate of costs, together with a full justification.

Equipment grants
Requests for single large items of equipment will be considered. Requests must give detailed cost estimates and a full scientific justification.

Clinical care
Requests for clinical support must give full costing and a detailed explanation of how this support will enhance the existing service and/or research activities.

Patient Care programme
The patient care programme is separate from the Scientific Research programme. Full details are available from the Fund's Administration Offices.

Fellowships
The KKLF Fellowship Programme offers support for highly-motivated first-class clinicians and scientists who wish to pursue a career in haematological research into leukaemia and associated malignancies. The Fellowships are designated according to the level of research experience already obtained.

The trust also describes future plans as follows:

The trustees previously agreed to a spend-out of the charity's capital which is expected to be completed by about 2022. As a result, trustees are planning to spend in total about £4.5 million per annum; £3 million on scientific research grants and £1.5 million on its patient care programme.

In 2011/12 the trust had assets of £34 million, an income of £1.3 million and made grants totalling £5.2 million.

Beneficiaries included: Institute of Cancer Research (£489,000); University College London Hospitals Charitable Foundation (£300,000); Paterson Institute for Cancer Research, School of Cancer and enabling Sciences (£233,000); The Teenage Cancer Trust (£150,000); Churchill Hospital (£120,000); Lingen Davies Cancer Research Fund (£100,000); Cardiff University, Department of Haematology (£62,000); and Royal Marsden NHS Trust (£60,000).

Exclusions
Circular appeals for general support are not funded.

Applications
A preliminary letter or telephone call to the administration offices of the Kay Kendall Leukaemia Fund may be helpful to determine whether or not a proposal is likely to be eligible. Application forms are available by contacting the trust's office.

The trustees consider proposals twice each year, normally May and October. To allow for the refereeing process, new full proposals for the May meeting should be received by 28 February and for the October/November meeting by 15 July. Late applications may be deferred for six months.

Information gathered from:
Annual report and accounts; Charity Commission record; funder's website.

Kent Community Foundation

Community, education, health, social welfare
£3.7 million (2011/12)
Beneficial area
Kent.

Correspondent: Carol Lynch, Chief Executive, 23 Evegate Park Barn, Evegate, Smeeth, Kent TN25 6SX (tel: 01303 814500; email: admin@kentcf.org. uk; website: www.kentcf.org.uk)

Trustees: Arthur Gulland; Bella Coltrain; Peter Lake; Peter Williams; Ann West; Tim Bull; Vicki Jessel; Georgina Warner; Sarah Hohler.

CC Number: 1084361

A member of the Community Foundation Network, this foundation was established in 2001. Its stated objects are:

The promotion of any charitable purposes for the benefit of the community in the County of Kent and the Borough of Medway and in particular the advancement of education, the protection of good health, both mental and physical, and the relief of poverty and sickness. Other exclusively charitable purposes in the United Kingdom and elsewhere which are, in the opinion of the trustees, beneficial to the community including those in the area of benefit.

Information is taken from the annual report and accounts for 2011/12.

Kent Community Foundation encourages and enables a culture of local charitable giving, primarily for the benefit of the communities of Kent and Medway. The foundation aims to improve the lives of local people, particularly the most disadvantaged and vulnerable, through the raising and distribution of funds given by individuals and organisations with the means and commitment to support their local community.

In addition to dedicated funds established by individuals, families and companies, the foundation has its own General Fund which enables it to support some of the many voluntary groups and organisations who approach the foundation for funding but fall outside the criteria of the dedicated funds.

Note: Grant schemes change frequently. Consult the foundation's website for details of current programmes and their deadlines.

In 2011/12 the foundation had assets of £8.6 million, an income of £6 million and grants payable were £3.7 million.

Applications
Further information on applications can be obtained from the grants team: admin@kentcf.org.uk.

Information gathered from:
Accounts; annual report; Charity Commission record; funder's website.

Keren Association

Jewish, education, general
£6.8 million (2010/11)

Beneficial area
UK and Israel.

Correspondent: Mrs S. Englander, Trustee, 136 Clapton Common, London E5 9AG

Trustees: E. Englander, Chair; S. Englander; Pinkus Englander; S. Z. Englander; Jacob Englander; H. Z. Weiss; N. Weiss.

CC Number: 313119

The trust has general charitable purposes, supporting the advancement of education and the provision of religious instruction and training in traditional Judaism. Support is also given to needy Jewish people.

Unfortunately at the time of writing (November 2013) the trust's latest accounts were almost a year overdue with the Charity Commission. In 2010/11 the trust had assets of £42.6 million and an income of almost £11 million. Grants were made totalling £6.8 million. A list of grant recipients was not included in the accounts.

Previous beneficiaries include: Beis Aharon Trust, Yeshivah Belz Machnovke, U T A, Yetev Lev Jerusalem, Lomdei Tom h Belz Machnovke, Friends of Beis Yaakov, Yeshivat Lomdei Torah, Friends of Arad, Kupat Gmach Vezer Nlsuin, Clwk Yaakov and British Heart Foundation.

Applications
In writing to the correspondent.

Information gathered from:
Accounts; Charity Commission record.

The Mary Kinross Charitable Trust

Relief of poverty, medical research, community development, youth and penal affairs
£614,000 (2012/13)

Beneficial area
UK.

Correspondent: Mrs Fiona Adams, Trustee, 36 Grove Avenue, Moseley, Birmingham B13 9RY

Trustees: Elizabeth Shields, Chair; Fiona Adams; Neil Cross; Jonathan Haw; Gordon Hague.

CC Number: 212206

This trust makes grants in the areas of medical research, community development, youth, penal affairs, health and mental health. Grants made under the heading 'youth' tend to be made with crime prevention in mind.

The trust prefers to work mainly with a group of charities with which it develops a close connection, led by at least one of the trustees. It describes its grant policy as follows:

Trustees wish to continue the policy of the founder which was to use the trust income to support a few carefully researched projects, rather than to make many small grants. The fields of work chosen reflect the particular interests and knowledge of trustees and at least one trustee takes responsibility for ensuring the trust's close involvement with organisations to which major grants are made.

When the trust makes a major grant core office costs are often included, which may enable the recipients to apply for other sources of funding. Unfortunately, the trust has to disappoint the great majority of applicants who make unsolicited appeals.

In 2012/13 the trust had assets of £31 million and an income of £758,000. There were 41 grants made totalling £614,000, of which 23 were for more than £10,000 and 18 smaller grants which totalled £70,000. Grants were broken down in the accounts as follows:

Medical research	6	£286,000
Youth	9	£132,000
Health	2	£40,000
Penal affairs	10	£120,00
Mental health	6	£56,000
Community development	5	£27,000
Miscellaneous	3	£23,000

Beneficiaries included: Department of Oncology, University of Oxford (£76,000); Scottish Centre for Regenerative Medicine, University of Edinburgh (£50,000); Greenhouse Schools Project (£36,000); Barry and Martin's Trust (£30,000); Centre for Education in the Justice System (£20,000); The Bendrigg Trust (£19,000); Woking YWCA (£10,000); Ballsall Heath Church Centre (£8,000); Gospel Oak Action Link (£5,000); Warstock Community Centre (£1,500); and Edinburgh Global Partnerships (£500).

Exclusions
No grants to individuals.

Applications
Because the trustees have no office staff and work from home, they prefer dealing with written correspondence rather than telephone calls from applicants soliciting funds. Note: unsolicited applications to this trust are very unlikely to be successful.

The majority of new grants are recommended by the chair and the secretary who can authorise small grants of up to £25,000. Other grants are discussed and agreed at trustee meetings.

Percentage of awards given to new applicants: between 20% and 30%.

Common applicant mistakes
'Over the years I've noticed that most applicants have become much more professional and have obviously read our annual report before trying to apply – the number of unsolicited applications we receive has gone down.'

Information gathered from:
Accounts; annual report; Charity Commission record; further information provided by the funder.

Ernest Kleinwort Charitable Trust

General purposes. In practice, mainly to wildlife and environmental conservation both nationally and overseas, disability, medical research, welfare of older and young people
£1.4 million (2011/12)

Beneficial area
UK, in particular Sussex; overseas.

Correspondent: Nick Kerr-Sheppard, Secretary, Kleinwort Benson Trustees Ltd, 14 St George Street, London W1S 1FE (tel: 020 3207 7008; website: www.ekct.org.uk)

Trustees: Sir Simon Robertson, Chair; Richard Ewing; Alexander Kleinwort; Lady Madeleine Kleinwort; Marina Kleinwort; Sir Richard Kleinwort; Sir Christopher Lever.

CC Number: 229665

The trust was established in 1964 by Sir Ernest Kleinwort, former chair of Kleinwort, Sons and Co. bank. He was actively involved in setting up what was to become the World Wildlife Fund UK, and the trust continues to provide support for conservation of wildlife and the natural environment, both nationally and internationally. Funding is also given for: care of the elderly, disability, general welfare, hospices, medical research, miscellaneous, family planning and youth care. More than half of the trust's funds go to Sussex based charities.

The following information on the types of grants made is provided by the trust:

In general, the trust aims to 'make a difference'; it does not support individuals or very small and narrowly specialised activities and, equally, it tries to avoid unfocused causes. Charities considered for grants will be notified and asked to complete an 'Account Summary' form taking various information from their latest Annual Accounts.

In approved cases, the trustees will provide one of the following four types of grant support:

One-off grants

Grants made on a one-off basis will be approved approximately every four months, and awarded to start up costs, core costs or for a specific project for which applicants have requested support. This could include a contribution towards a building/refurbishment project, purchase of specialist equipment or other similar capital expenditure, or assistance with running costs.

Conditionally renewable grants

Applications for annual support are not encouraged, but conditionally renewable grants might be awarded in exceptional circumstances for up to three years, following which support may be withdrawn to enable resources to be devoted to other projects.

Grants can be towards start-up costs, or for a specific item in the applicant's budget such as a salary, core costs or towards the costs of a particular project. Such grants are subject to satisfactory annual progress reports and only released at the trustees' sole discretion.

Annual subscriptions

A proportion of the trustees' annual spend is currently set aside to pay annual subscriptions, predominantly to charities operating in Sussex. Charities added or removed from this list of payments will be notified accordingly, and all payments are subject to satisfactory annual progress reports and submission of annual accounts prior to being released at the trustees' sole discretion.

Large grants (over £10,000)

Large grants are approved by the full board of trustees twice a year (normally April and October), and are typically agreed upon when the trustees have a deep understanding and/or a close relationship with the charity, which may have developed over a period of several years.

General guiding principles are:
- The trustees should be satisfied with the purpose and objectives of the charity, and that they are able to deliver a superior/pre-eminent service
- The trustees have confidence in the trustees and management of the charity, and are therefore satisfied as to its quality, efficiency, financial stability and income/expense ratios

In 2011/12 the trust had assets of £52 million and an income of £1.4 million. Grants were made totalling £1.4 million, broken down as follows:

Wildlife and conservation	£369,000
Disability	£290,000
General welfare and social problems	£158,000
Youth care	£108,000
Family planning	£92,000
Miscellaneous	£89,000
Hospices	£75,000
Medical	£62,000
Care for the elderly	£24,000

Beneficiaries included: WWF UK (£100,000); River Trust (£70,000); Tusk Trust (£50,000); Chailey Heritage School (£40,000); Crawley Open House and Resource Centre (£30,000); Blond McIndoe Centre for Medical Research (£15,000); Latitude Global Volunteering (£6,600); Adventure Unlimited (£5,000); Bat Conservation Trust (£3,000); Hope in the Valley RDA (£1,000); and Neighbourly Care (£500).

Exclusions

The trust will not consider funding:
- Large national charities having substantial fundraising potential, income from legacies and or endowment income
- Organisations not registered as charities or those that have been registered for less than a year
- Pre-school groups
- Out of school play schemes including pre-school and holiday schemes
- Projects which promote a particular religion
- Charities not funded by any other charity
- Very small and narrowly specialised activities
- Local authorities
- Individuals or charities applying on behalf of individuals
- General requests for donations
- Expeditions or overseas travel
- Campaigning organisations
- Charities whose main aim is to raise funds for other charities
- Charities with substantial cash reserves

Applications

In writing to the correspondent. Applications should be no longer than two A4 sides, and should incorporate a short (half page) summary.

Applications should also include a detailed budget for the project and the applicant's most recent audited accounts. If accounts show a significant surplus or deficit of income, explain how this has arisen.

Applicants must also complete and include an Accounts Summary form, which is available on the trust's website.

Information gathered from:

Accounts; annual report; Charity Commission record; funder's website.

The Sir James Knott Trust

General charitable purposes, in practice, support for people who are disadvantaged, the young, the elderly, the disabled, education and training, medical care, historic buildings, the environment, music and the arts and seafarers' and services' charities

£1.2 million (2011/12)

Beneficial area

Tyne and Wear, Northumberland, County Durham inclusive of Hartlepool but exclusive of Darlington, Stockton-on-Tees, Middlesbrough, Redcar and Cleveland.

Correspondent: Vivien Stapeley, Secretary, 16–18 Hood Street, Newcastle upon Tyne NE1 6JQ (tel: 01912 304016; email: info@knott-trust.co.uk; website: www.knott-trust.co.uk)

Trustees: Prof. Oliver James; John Cresswell; Sarah Riddell; Ben Speke.

CC Number: 1001363

This trust is established for general charitable purposes; in practice its primary objective is to help improve the conditions of people living and working in the North East of England.

Background

James Knott was one of the merchant giants of the nineteenth century. The Prince Line Ltd was a major shipping company that was held in the highest regard by all who sailed in their ships and by passengers voyaging on the round the world service. The Prince Line gave Knott enormous wealth and over the years he and his wife became well-known on Tyneside for their philanthropy. In 1920 and in order that his charitable giving could continue after his death he provided funds for the James Knott Settlement. The focus of his charitable interest was to support charitable bodies and organisations mainly connected with the north east of England.

The Sir James Knott Trust aims to help improve the conditions of people living and working in the North East of England allocating grants to charities working for the benefit of the population and environment of Tyne and Wear, Northumberland and County Durham, including Hartlepool. The main donations are in the fields of community issues and events, service charities, historic buildings and heritage, education, arts and culture, health, environment, public services and housing.

General

Grants are normally only made to registered charities specifically operating in or for the benefit of the North East of England (Tyne and Wear, Northumberland, County Durham inclusive of Hartlepool but exclusive of Darlington, Stockton-on-Tees, Middlesbrough, Redcar and Cleveland).

The trustees have wide discretion on the distribution of funds and meet to consider grant applications three times a year. Grants totalling about £1 million a year are made, funded out of income. The trustees try to follow the wishes and interests of the trust's founder where this is compatible with the present day needs of the north east. Charitable works known to have been of particular interest to Sir James are given special consideration, for example, Army Benevolent Fund, Northumberland Playing Fields Association, Mission to Seafarers, Royal British Legion, the YMCA and YWCA, Barnardo's, RUKBA, Historic Churches Trust, schools and universities.

In recent years, grants have been given in support of the welfare of people who are disadvantaged, the young, the elderly, people with disabilities, education and training, medical care, historic buildings, the environment, music and the arts and seafarers' and services' charities.

In 2011/12 the trust had assets of £38 million and an income of £1.4 million. There were 409 grants made totalling £1.2 million, broken down into categories as follows:

Community issues/events	162	£387,000
Health/sport and human services	65	£205,000
Arts and culture	47	£159,500
Service charities	34	£96,000
Conservation/horticultural/ biodiversity/environmental	23	£74,000
Historic buildings/heritage	19	£112,000
Homeless/housing	20	£85,000
Public services	23	£69,000
Education/training	16	£49,000

Most grants were for £5,000 or less. Beneficiaries included: Sage Gateshead (£30,000 in total); North East Autism Society (£25,000); Northumbria Historic Churches Trust (£20,000); Bowes Museum (£10,000); Disability North and Chillingham Wild Cattle Association (£5,000 each); Embleton Cricket and Football Trust, Red Squirrel Survival Trust and Army Cadet Force – Northumbria (£3,000 each); and Bubble Foundation UK and Independent Age (£2,000 each).

Exclusions

Individuals, the replacement of funding withdrawn by local authorities or organisations that do not have an identifiable project within the beneficial area.

Applications

In writing to the correspondent, giving a brief description of the need, with relevant consideration to the following points:

- The type of organisation you are and how you benefit the community
- How you are organised and managed
- How many staff/volunteers you have
- If a registered charity, your registered number, if not you will need to submit the name and registered number of a charity which is prepared to administer funds on your behalf
- Your relationship, if any, with similar or umbrella organisations
- Your main funding source
- The project you are currently fundraising for, including the cost, the amount required and when the funds are needed
- Give details of who else you have approached and what response have you had
- Confirm whether you have you applied to the Big Lottery Fund (if not, state why not)
- Enclose a copy of your latest trustees' report and accounts (if you are a new organisation then provide a copy of your latest bank statement)

Not all of these points may apply to you, but they give an idea of what the trustees may ask when considering applications. Applicants may be contacted for further information.

Trustees normally meet in spring, summer and autumn. Applications need to be submitted at least three months before a grant is required, see the trust's website for deadlines. However, if your application is for a grant of less than £1,000, this can usually be processed outside meetings and usually within one month.

The trust welcomes initial enquires by phone or email.

Percentage of awards given to new applicants: between 10% and 20%.

Common applicant mistakes

'Omitting their charity name and registration number.'

Information gathered from:

Accounts; annual report; Charity Commission record; further information provided by the funder; funder's website.

The Kohn Foundation

Scientific and medical projects, the arts – particularly music, education, Jewish charities

£545,500 (2012)

Beneficial area

UK and overseas.

Correspondent: Sir Ralph Kohn, Trustee, c/o Wilkins Kennedy and Co., Bridge House, 4 Borough High Street, London SE1 9QR (tel: 020 7403 1877; email: enquiries@wilkinskennedy.com)

Trustees: Sir Ralph Kohn, Chair; Lady Zahava Kohn; Anthony A. Forwood.

CC Number: 1003951

The foundation supports advancement of scientific and medical research, promotion of the arts – particularly music, general educational projects and Jewish charities.

In 2012 the foundation had assets of £981,500 and an income of £386,000. Grants were made to 110 organisations totalling £545,500, and were broken down as follows:

Performing arts	19	£206,500
Medical and scientific organisations and charities	20	£204,500
Advancement of the Jewish religion, education and charitable institutions	71	£134,500

Beneficiaries included: Royal Academy of Music (£100,000); Jesus College Oxford (£80,000); University of Manchester (£25,500); Jerusalem Foundation (£15,000); Foundation for Liver Research and Jewish Care (£10,000 each); Rudolf Kempe Society (£7,500); Foundation for Science and Technology (£5,000); Daniel Tumberg Memorial Trust (£2,000); and Sense about Science (£1,000).

Applications

In writing to the correspondent.

Information gathered from:

Accounts; Charity Commission record.

The Neil Kreitman Foundation

Arts and culture, education, health and social welfare

£418,000 (2011/12)

Beneficial area

Worldwide, in practice UK, USA and Israel.

Correspondent: Gordon C. Smith, Trustee, Citroen Wells and Partners, Devonshire House, 1 Devonshire Street, London W1W 5DR (tel: 020 7304 2000)

Trustees: Neil R. Kreitman; Gordon C. Smith.

CC Number: 267171

The foundation was established in 1974 and makes grants to registered or exempt charities for the arts and culture, education, health and social welfare. The foundation has also given to Jewish charities in previous years. In 2005/06 the foundation received £15 million from the Kreitman Foundation when it ceased operating.

In 2011/12 the trust had assets of £23 million, an income of £68,000 and made grants totalling £418,000. Grants were categorised as follows:

Arts and culture	£444,000
Health and welfare	£158,000
Education	£48,000

Beneficiaries included: Crocker Art Museum (£219,000); The British Museum (£68,000); International Campaign for Tibet and Médecins Sans Frontières (£50,000 each); Sierra Club Foundation (£30,000); Pacific Asia Museum, Pasadena (£25,000); The Ancient India and Iran Trust (£22,000); Release – Legal Emergency and Drugs Service (£16,000); Los Angeles County Museum of Art (£15,000); and School of Oriental and African Studies (£1,600).

The accounts also noted £421,000 governance costs due to 'foreign exchange losses'.

Amounts were converted from dollars at a rate of 0.6436.

Exclusions

No grants to individuals.

Applications

In writing to the correspondent.

Information gathered from:

Accounts; annual report; Charity Commission record.

Maurice and Hilda Laing Charitable Trust

Promotion of Christianity, relief of need

£3.1 million (2011/12)

Beneficial area

UK and overseas.

Correspondent: Elizabeth Harley, Trusts Director, 33 Bunns Lane, Mill Hill, London NW7 2DX (tel: 020 8238 8890; website: www.laingfamilytrusts.org.uk/maurice_hilda_laing.html)

Trustees: Andrea Currie; Peter Harper; Simon Martle; Paul van den Bosch; Ewan Harper; Charles Laing; Stephen Ludlow.

CC Number: 1058109

This trust was established in 1996 and is mainly concerned with the advancement of the Christian religion and relieving poverty, both in the UK and overseas. The trust is administered alongside the Beatrice Laing Trust, the Martin Laing Foundation and the Kirby Laing Foundation with which it shares members of staff and office space; collectively they are known as the Laing Family Trusts.

In practice grants awarded fall into three main categories:

- To organisations seeking to promote Christian faith and values through evangelistic, educational and media activities at home and overseas
- To organisations seeking to express Christian faith through practical action to help people in need, for example, those with disabilities, the homeless, the sick, young people, prisoners and ex-offenders
- To organisations working to relieve poverty overseas, with a particular emphasis on helping children who are vulnerable or at risk. In most cases these grants to overseas projects are made through UK registered charities who are expected to monitor and evaluate the projects on behalf of the trust, providing progress reports at agreed intervals

In 2006 the trustees made the decision to work towards winding up the trust by 2020. As such, there will be a controlled increase in the level of future grant expenditure. The trustees are making a number of significant investments to a small number of organisations that they will proactively invite to apply. Charities can still apply for the small grants programme.

During 2012 the trust had assets of £36 million, an income of £1.6 million and gave grants totalling £3.1 million, broken down as follows:

Religion	40	£1.2 million
Overseas aid	31	£700,000
Social welfare	31	£506,000
Children and youth	9	£397,000
Health and medicine	2	£20,000
Miscellaneous	4	£210,000

Beneficiaries included: Ethiopian Graduate School of Theology (£350,000); The Reculver Trust (£300,000); The Lambeth Fund (£200,000); Mission Aviation Fellowship (£150,000); Mildmay Mission Hospital (£40,000); Caring for Life (£25,000); Prison Fellowship England and Wales (£15,000); Hope UK (£10,000) St Michael and All Angels Church, Amersham and Hope Debt Advice (£5,000 each).

Exclusions

No grants are made for:

- General appeals or circulars
- Campaigning or lobbying activities
- Umbrella, second tier or grantmaking organisations
- Professional associations or projects for the training of professionals
- Feasibility studies and social research
- Individual sponsorship requirements
- Grants to individuals for educational, medical or travel purposes including gap year projects and overseas exchange programmes
- Summer activities for children/young people or after-school clubs
- State maintained or independent schools other than those for pupils with special educational needs
- Uniformed groups such as Scouts and Guides
- Costs of staging one-off events, festivals or conferences
- Animal welfare
- Core running costs of hospices, counselling projects and other local organisations
- Church restoration or repair (including organs and bells)

Applications

In writing to the correspondent. One application only is needed to apply to this or the Kirby Laing Foundation, Martin Laing Foundation or Beatrice Laing Charitable Trust. Multiple applications will still only elicit a single reply, even then applicants are asked to accept non-response as a negative reply on behalf of all these trusts, unless an sae is enclosed. After the initial sifting process, the Maurice and Hilda Laing Trust follows its own administrative procedures.

These trusts make strenuous efforts to keep their overhead costs to a minimum. As they also make a very large number of grants each year, in proportion to their income, the staff must rely almost entirely on the written applications submitted in selecting appeals to go forward to the trustees.

Application is by letter including the following information:

- Contact details
- Confirmation of charitable status
- A clear overview of the charity's aims and objectives
- Precise details of the project for which funding is sought including:
  - Project activities
  - Proposed start and end date
  - A detailed budget breakdown
  - Fundraising strategy: anticipated sources of funding, funds already secured, plans for securing the shortfall
  - Arrangements for monitoring and evaluating the project
- A copy of the charity's most recent annual report and audited accounts

Applicants can include a list of other supporting documents that can be provided upon request such as business plans or architectural drawings for building projects.

The trustees meet four times a year to consider the award of grants of over £20,000. Decisions on smaller grants are made on an ongoing basis.

Information gathered from:

Accounts; annual report; Charity Commission record; funder's website.

The Kirby Laing Foundation

Health, welfare, Christian religion, youth, general

£2.5 million (2012)

Beneficial area

Unrestricted, but mainly UK.

Correspondent: Elizabeth Harley, Trust Director, 33 Bunns Lane, Mill Hill, London NW7 2DX (tel: 020 8238 8890; website: www.laingfamilytrusts.org.uk)

Trustees: Lady Isobel Laing; David E. Laing; Simon Webley; Revd Charles Burch.

CC Number: 264299

Summary

Along with the other Laing family trusts, this is a general grantmaker, with a Christian orientation and awarding almost all kinds of grants, few of them very large. It is unusual in the group for having a small number of artistic and cultural grants. The foundation was established in 1972 for general charitable purposes.

General

The foundation is administered alongside, and shares its three staff with, the Beatrice Laing Trust, the Martin Laing Foundation and the Maurice and Hilda Laing Charitable Trust. An application to any one of these four trusts, collectively known as the Laing Family Trusts, is treated as an application to all although, after the initial 'sorting' process, applications considered suitable for further consideration by the Kirby Laing Foundation follow the foundation's own administrative and decision making process. The trust makes grants based upon applications but may occasionally adopt a more proactive approach where there is evidence of a particular need in an area of interest to the trustees.

Charities can apply for grants of up to £5,000; anything over this amount is by invitation only. The foundation states that it intends to increase the level of grant expenditure with a view to the likely winding down of the foundation in five to ten years.

Grants are made in the following areas:
- The promotion and expression of the evangelical Christian faith and values
- Education (particularly in the fields of theology, science and engineering) and youth development
- Medical research with a particular emphasis on dementia and stroke
- Social and medical welfare projects particularly where the beneficiaries include people who are elderly or disabled and ex-servicemen
- The preservation of cultural and environmental heritage and improving access to the arts for young people and people who are disabled
- Overseas development projects (supported by UK registered charities)

Grantmaking in 2012

In 2012 the trust had assets of £46 million and an income of £1.9 million. Grants were made totalling £2.5 million, and were broken down as follows:

Religion	20	£1.3 million
Health and medicine	19	£480,000
Cultural and environmental	25	£249,000
Education and youth development	14	£231,000
Social welfare	6	£80,000
Charities Aid Foundation		£75,000
Overseas aid	6	£60,000

Beneficiaries included: University of Oxford (£600,000); Royal Society of Medicine (£125,000); Moorfields Eye Hospital Development and The Education Fellowship (£100,000 each); Restoration of Appearance and Function Trust (£50,000); Queen Elizabeth Hospital Birmingham Charity (£40,000); Wakefield Cathedral (£20,000); Mines Advisory Group and Urban Saints (£10,000 each); and Welsh National Opera (£5,000).

Exclusions

No grants are made for:
- General appeals or circulars
- Campaigning or lobbying activities
- Umbrella, second tier or grantmaking organisations
- Professional associations or projects for the training of professionals
- Feasibility studies and social research
- Individual sponsorship requirements
- Grants to individuals for educational, medical or travel purposes including gap year projects and overseas exchange programmes
- Summer activities for children/young people or after-school clubs
- State maintained or independent schools other than those for pupils with special educational needs
- Uniformed groups such as Scouts and Guides
- Costs of staging one-off events, festivals or conferences
- Animal welfare
- Core running costs of hospices, counselling projects and other local organisations
- Church restoration or repair (including organs and bells)

Applications

One application only is needed to apply to this or the Beatrice Laing Trust or Maurice and Hilda Laing Charitable Trust. Multiple applications will still only elicit a single reply.

These trusts make strenuous efforts to keep their overhead costs to a minimum. As they also make a very large number of grants each year, in proportion to their income, the staff must rely almost entirely on the written applications submitted in selecting appeals to go forward to the trustees.

Application is by letter including the following information:
- Contact details
- Confirmation of charitable status
- A clear overview of the charity's aims and objectives
- Precise details of the project for which funding is sought including:
  - Project activities
  - Proposed start and end date
  - A detailed budget breakdown
  - Fundraising strategy: anticipated sources of funding, funds already secured, plans for securing the shortfall
  - Arrangements for monitoring and evaluating the project
- A copy of the charity's most recent annual report and audited accounts

Applicants can include a list of other supporting documents that can be provided upon request such as business plans or architectural drawings for building projects.

The trustees meet four times a year to consider the award of grants of over £20,000. Decisions on smaller grants are made on an ongoing basis.

For all grants above £5,000 the foundation asks for a report from the charity one year after the grant has been made, describing briefly how the grant has been spent and what has been achieved. For larger and multi-year grants more detailed reports may be required. Where a grant is paid in instalments the usual practice is not to release the second and subsequent instalments until a review of progress has been satisfactorily completed.

Information gathered from:

Accounts; annual report; Charity Commission record; funder's website.

The Beatrice Laing Trust

Relief of poverty and advancement of the evangelical Christian faith

£2 million (2011/12)

Beneficial area

UK and overseas.

Correspondent: Elizabeth Harley, Trusts Director, c/o Laing Family Trusts,

33 Bunns Lane, Mill Hill, London NW7 2DX (tel: 020 8238 8890; website: www.laingfamilytrusts.org.uk)

Trustees: Sir Martin Laing; David E. Laing; Christopher M. Laing; Charles Laing; Paula Blacker; Alexandra Gregory.

CC Number: 211884

General

This trust was established in 1952 by Sir John Laing and his wife, Beatrice, both now deceased. The trust's objects are the relief of poverty and the advancement of the evangelical Christian faith in the UK and abroad.

The Beatrice Laing Trust is administered alongside the Maurice and Hilda Laing Charitable Trust, the Martin Laing Foundation and the Kirby Laing Foundation with which it shares members of staff and office space; collectively they are known as the Laing Family Trusts. The Beatrice Laing Trust concentrates mainly on small grants for the relief of poverty in its broadest sense, both throughout the UK and overseas.

In the UK grant recipients include organisations working with children, young people and the elderly, the homeless and those with physical, mental or learning difficulties. Grants to projects overseas are concentrated on building the capacity to provide long-term solutions to the problems faced by countries in the developing world rather than providing emergency aid.

In addition to the trust's own funds, the trustees are invited to make nominations to the grants committee of the J W Laing Trust, for donations totalling 20% of that trust's income up to a maximum of £550,000 per annum. The trustees use these funds to support the advancement of the evangelical Christian faith through projects of new church building or extension or church mission activities.

Grantmaking guidelines

Grants are usually only made to UK registered charities. A very small number of individuals are supported, mostly for retired missionaries who were known to the founders and who receive an annual grant.

The trust notes in its latest accounts that:

> The grant-making process is largely reactive rather than proactive and it should be noted that any fluctuation in the level of grants funded across the categories shown [. . .] is therefore, a reflection of the applications received rather than a change in the trustees' priorities. This is also true of the geographical spread of grants made.

The vast majority of grants fall into the £500 to £5,000 range. Most of these represent either modest annual grants towards the core costs of selected

national organisations working with the trust's priority groups, or small capital grants to local organisations working to relieve poverty in their local communities.

Grants of over £5,000 are awarded by the trustees at meetings held three times a year. Grants of under £8,000 are made on a monthly basis by the trust director and are ratified at the trustees' meetings.

The trustees have stated that they wish to increase grant expenditure to align it more closely with income, therefore it rose by 26.8% during the year.

Grantmaking in 2011/12

In 2011/12 the trust had assets of £46 million and an income of £2.2 million. Grants totalled £2 million and were broken down as follows:

Social welfare	95	£502,000
Health and medicine	60	£380,000
Overseas development	46	£290,000
Children and youth, including education	35	£290,000
Religion	14	£48,000

Beneficiaries included: Together Trust (£50,000); Calvert Trust Exmoor (£50,000); Lurgan YMCA (£50,000); Echoes of Service (£30,000); Emmaus UK (£23,000); Age UK Leeds (£20,000); Crime Diversion Scheme (£10,000); Community Service Volunteers (£5,000); Autism Sussex (£4,000); Doctors of the World (£2,500); Kenyan Orphan Project and Deaf Connections (£2,000 each); and Young People Taking Action (£500).

Exclusions

No grants are made for:

▶ General appeals or circulars
▶ Campaigning or lobbying activities
▶ Umbrella, second tier or grantmaking organisations
▶ Professional associations or projects for the training of professionals
▶ Feasibility studies and social research
▶ Individual sponsorship requirements
▶ Grants to individuals for educational, medical or travel purposes including gap year projects and overseas exchange programmes
▶ Summer activities for children/young people or after-school clubs
▶ State maintained or independent schools other than those for pupils with special educational needs
▶ Uniformed groups such as Scouts and Guides
▶ Costs of staging one-off events, festivals or conferences
▶ Animal welfare
▶ Core running costs of hospices, counselling projects and other local organisations
▶ Church restoration or repair (including organs and bells)

Applications

One application only is needed to apply to this or the Beatrice Laing Trust or Maurice and Hilda Laing Charitable Trust. Multiple applications will still only elicit a single reply.

These trusts make strenuous efforts to keep their overhead costs to a minimum. As they also make a very large number of grants each year, in proportion to their income, the staff must rely almost entirely on the written applications submitted in selecting appeals to go forward to the trustees.

Application is by letter including the following information:

▶ Contact details
▶ Confirmation of charitable status
▶ A clear overview of the charity's aims and objectives
▶ Precise details of the project for which funding is sought including:
  ▶ Project activities
  ▶ Proposed start and end date
  ▶ A detailed budget breakdown
  ▶ Fundraising strategy: anticipated sources of funding, funds already secured, plans for securing the shortfall
  ▶ Arrangements for monitoring and evaluating the project
▶ A copy of the charity's most recent annual report and audited accounts

Applicants can include a list of other supporting documents that can be provided upon request such as business plans or architectural drawings for building projects.

The trustees meet three times a year to consider the award of grants of over £8,000. Decisions on smaller grants are made on an ongoing basis.

For all grants above £5,000 the foundation asks for a report from the charity one year after the grant has been made, describing briefly how the grant has been spent and what has been achieved. For larger and multi-year grants more detailed reports may be required. Where a grant is paid in instalments the usual practice is not to release the second and subsequent instalments until a review of progress has been satisfactorily completed.

Information gathered from:

Accounts; annual report; Charity Commission record; funder's website.

The Lancaster Foundation

Christian causes

£1.8 million (2011/12)

Beneficial area

UK and Africa, with a local interest in Clitheroe.

Correspondent: Mrs Rosemary Lancaster, Trustee, c/o Text House, 152 Bawdlands, Clitheroe, Lancashire BB7 2LA (tel: 01200 444404)

Trustees: Rosemary Lancaster; Dr John Lancaster; Steven Lancaster; Julie Broadhurst.

CC Number: 1066850

The object of the charity is to financially support Christian based registered charities across the world. Grants are awarded at the absolute discretion of the trustees. Although many applications are received, the administrative structure of the charity does not allow for the consideration of unsolicited requests for grant funding.

In 2011/12 the foundation had assets of £51 million, an income of £4.2 million and made grants totalling £1.8 million.

As in previous years the largest grant was made to the Grand at Clitheroe (£615,000), with which it shares three trustees. Other beneficiaries included: Message Trust (£212,000); Mary's Meals (£122,000); Saltmine Trust (£96,000); Sparrow Ministries (£60,000); Association Cristiana Manos En Accion (£48,000); Christians against Poverty (£38,000); Revelation life (£25,000); Urban Saints (£10,000); Vision (£5,000); and Bethany Project, United Christian Broadcasters and Stoneyhurst Charity Day (£1,000 each).

Applications

The trust has previously stated: 'We do not consider applications made to us from organisations or people unconnected with us. All our donations are instigated because of personal associations. Unsolicited mail is, sadly, a waste of the organisation's resources.'

Information gathered from:

Accounts; annual report; Charity Commission record.

The Allen Lane Foundation

Charities benefiting asylum-seekers and refugees, gypsies and travellers, lesbian, gay, bisexual or transgender people, offenders and ex-offenders, older people, people experiencing mental health problems and people experiencing violence or abuse

£732,000 (2011/12)

Beneficial area

UK.

Correspondent: Gill Aconley, Grants Officer, 90 The Mount, York YO24 1AR (tel: 01904 613223; fax: 01904 613133; email: info@allenlane.org.uk; website: www.allenlane.org.uk)

CC Number: 248031

Summary

The Allen Lane Foundation is a grantmaking trust set up in 1966 by the late Sir Allen Lane, founder of Penguin Books, to support general charitable causes. The foundation has no connection now with the publishing company, but five of the trustees are members of the founder's family.

The foundation wishes to fund work which will make a lasting difference to people's lives rather than simply alleviating the symptoms or current problems, is aimed at reducing isolation, stigma and discrimination and which encourages or enables unpopular groups to share in the life of the whole community.

As the foundation's resources are modest, it prefers to fund smaller organisations where small grants can have more impact. Organisations should be not-for-profit, but need not be registered charities (provided their activities are charitable) and work to benefit groups of people who are unpopular in UK society today. The foundation makes grants in the UK but does not make grants for work in London.

The Allen Lane Foundation is interested in funding work which benefits people in the following groups, or generalist work which includes significant numbers from more than one such group:

- Asylum-seekers and refugees (but not groups working with a single nationality)
- Gay, lesbian, bi-sexual or transgender people
- Gypsies and travellers
- Offenders and ex-offenders
- Older people
- People experiencing mental health problems
- People experiencing violence or abuse

'If the beneficiaries of your work do not include a significant proportion of people from one or more of these groups it is very unlikely that your application will be successful.'

A recent review has concluded that people from black and minority ethnic communities should be removed as a separate priority. Groups and organisations working with BME communities are still encouraged to apply within the other priorities. The trustees are keen to make the foundation's criteria as clear as possible to save applicants from wasted effort and disappointment, although this does mean that the guidelines list an ever increasing list of exclusions.

Guidelines for applicants

The following summary has been taken largely from the foundation's website:

The foundation will make grants for start-up, core or project costs. The grants are relatively small and are likely therefore to be appropriate for costs such as:

- Volunteers or participants expenses
- Venue hire
- Part-time or sessional staffing costs
- Work aimed at strengthening the organisation such as trustee or staff training

Examples of the kind of activities which might be suitable for funding are:

- Provision of advice or information
- Advocacy
- Arts activities where the primary purpose is therapeutic or social
- Befriending or mentoring
- Mediation or conflict resolution
- Practical work, such as gardening or recycling, which benefits both the provider and the recipient
- Self-help groups
- Social activities or drop in centres
- Strengthening the rights of particular groups and enabling their views and experiences to be heard by policy-makers
- Research and education aimed at changing public attitudes or policy
- Work aimed at combatting stigma or discrimination
- Work developing practical alternatives to violence

These lists are not exhaustive and there will be many other appropriate items/activities which could be funded.

While recognising (and being willing to support) on-going, tried and tested projects, the foundation is particularly interested in unusual, imaginative or pioneering projects which have perhaps not yet caught the public imagination.

Size and length of grants

The grants are relatively modest. The foundation has no maximum grant, but most single award grants range from £500 up to £15,000. Grants repeated for more than one year vary from about £500 per annum up to £5,000 per annum, for a maximum of three years.

The foundation will make single grants, or grants for two or three years. It is unlikely to make a second grant immediately after one has finished and if an application is refused, we ask applicants to wait a year before applying again.

Organisations who can apply

Registered charities and other organisations which are not charities but which seek funding for a charitable project.

To be eligible for a grant you should be able to answer yes to the following questions:

- Does your work benefit people from one or more of our priority groups?
- Are you confident that your application is not subject to any of the exclusions listed?
- If your work relates to a relatively local area – for example a town, village or

local community, was your income last year less than about £100,000? or

▷ If your work covers a wider area – for example a county, region or nation, was your income last year less than about £250,000?

▷ Is it more than a year since you last applied?

▷ Does your work take place in the UK?

▷ Does your work take place outside London

Allen Lane Lecture

Each year the foundation hosts a lecture in memory of Sir Allen Lane. Past lecturers have included Mary Robinson, former President of the Irish Republic, The Bishop of Oxford the Rt. Rev Richard Harries and The Rt. Hon. Frank Field MP. In 2009, Kathleen Duncan OBE was the guest lecturer with the title 'Hard Times, but Great Expectations' at the Ismaili Centre in London. Since 1999 the text of each lecture each year has been published on the foundation's website.

Grants in 2011/12

In 2011/12 the foundation had assets of £16.6 million and an income of £553,000. Grants were made to 152 organisations totalling £732,000, broken down into the following categories:

Older People	49	£181,000
Refugees and asylum seekers	18	£113,000
Beneficiaries from more than one unpopular group	17	£94,000
Mental health	29	£130,000
People experiencing violence or abuse	13	£84,000
Offenders and ex-offenders	12	£81,000
Migrant workers	4	£23,000
Lesbian, gay, bisexual and transgender	7	£33,000
Travellers and gypsies	3	£11,000

Beneficiaries included: Refugee Survival Trust (£15,000); Rape and Abuse Line (£12,000; Hope Housing (£10,000); Mind Shropshire (£7,500); Cambridge Money Advice Centre and Lanarkshire Rape Crisis Centre (£5,000 each); Art Beyond Belief and UK Association of Gypsy Women (£3,000 each); Lesbian Immigration Support Group (£1,500); Senior Citizens Lunch Club and Rainbow Families (£1,000 each); Rebound Self Harm Support (£600); and Young at Heart Club (£500).

Exclusions

The foundation does not currently make grants for:

▷ Academic research

▷ Addiction, alcohol or drug abuse

▷ Animal welfare or animal rights

▷ Arts or cultural or language projects or festivals

▷ Children and young people or families

▷ Endowments or contributions to other grantmaking bodies

▷ Health and healthcare

▷ Holidays or holiday play schemes, day trips or outings

▷ Housing

▷ Hospices and medical research

▷ Individuals

▷ Museums or galleries

▷ Overseas travel

▷ Particular medical conditions or disorders

▷ Physical or learning disabilities

▷ Private and/or mainstream education

▷ Promotion of sectarian religion

▷ Publications

▷ Purchase costs of property, building or refurbishment

▷ Refugee community groups working with single nationalities

▷ Restoration or conservation of historic buildings or sites

▷ Sports and recreation

▷ Therapy e.g. counselling

▷ Vehicle purchase

▷ Work which the trustees believe is rightly the responsibility of the state

▷ Work outside the United Kingdom

▷ Work which will already have taken place before a grant is agreed

▷ Work by local organisations with an income of more than £100,000 per annum or those working over a wider area with an income of more than £250,000

The foundation will not normally make grants to organisations which receive funding (directly or indirectly) from commercial sources where conflicts of interest for the organisation and its work are likely to arise.

Applications

There is no formal application form, but there is a short registration form, available from the foundation's website. The registration form should accompany the application. An application should be no more than four sides of A4 but the project budget may be on extra pages. It should be accompanied by your organisation's last annual report and accounts if you produce such documents and the budget for the whole organisation (and the project budget if they are different) for the current year.

The application should include the following information:

▷ The aims of your organisation as a whole

▷ How these aims are achieved

▷ How your proposals make a lasting difference to people's lives rather than simply alleviating the symptoms or current problem

▷ How the proposals reduce isolation, stigma and discrimination or encourage or enable unpopular groups to share in the life of the whole community

▷ Why your cause or beneficiary group is an unpopular one

▷ What you want the grant to pay for

▷ What difference a grant would make to your work

▷ The cost of the work

▷ Whether you are asking the foundation to meet the whole cost of the work

▷ Details of any other sources of funding you are approaching

▷ Details of how you know if the work has been successful

▷ Details of how the work, and the way it is done, promotes equal opportunities. If you do not think equal opportunities are relevant to your work please say why

If further information is needed this will be requested and a visit may be arranged when the application can be discussed in more detail.

All applications should be made to the foundation's office and *not* sent to individual trustees. If you have any queries about making an application you are encouraged to phone the staff for clarification.

Information gathered from:

Accounts; annual report; Charity Commission record; funder's website.

The LankellyChase Foundation

Severe and multiple disadvantage particularly homelessness, substance misuse, mental and physical illness, extreme poverty and violence and abuse

£5.7 million (2011/12)

Beneficial area

UK.

Correspondent: Julian Corner, Chief Executive, First Floor Greenworks, Dog and Duck Yard, Princeton Street, London WC1R 4BH (tel: 020 3747 9930; email: grants@lankellychase.org.uk; website: www.lankellychase.org.uk)

Trustees: Suzi Leather, Chair; Hilary Berg; Morag Burnett; Paul Cheng; Martin Clarke; Bobby Duffy; Victoria Hoskins; Marion Janner; Peter Latchford; Clive Martin; Jane Millar; Andrew Robinson; Kanwaljit Singh; Simon Tucker.

CC Number: 1107583

The Chase Charity and the Lankelly Foundation were established through the generosity of two separate entrepreneurs who successively developed a complex of property companies which operated in and around London. The Chase Charity was founded in 1962 and the Lankelly Foundation six years later and both reaching out to the most isolated in society.

As time went by the two trusts adopted similar grantmaking policies and whilst recognising that their differences of scale and emphasis were positive qualities; they reflected, particularly in the case of the Chase Charity, the founders' love of England's heritage and the arts, and these differences caught the attention of different needy groups, enabling the trusts to be more effective together than if they operated separately.

After so many years of working together, jointly employing the staff team, in 2005 the two trusts resolved to take the next natural step and amalgamate to form the LankellyChase Foundation.

The foundation's mission is to bring about change that will transform the quality of life of people who face severe and multiple disadvantage, meaning the persistent clustering of severe social harms, particularly homelessness, substance misuse, mental and physical illness, extreme poverty and violence and abuse.

At the end of 2013 the foundation launched a new funding programme. The following information is taken from the foundation's website:

Funds Available – Open Call for Project Ideas

LankellyChase Foundation's mission is to bring about change to improve the lives of people facing severe and multiple disadvantage. By this we mean people who are experiencing a combination of severe social harms such as homelessness, substance misuse, mental illness, extreme poverty, and violence and abuse.

We are not interested in sticking plaster solutions, even if they make people's lives better in the short term, but in changing the fundamentals. We think that:

- Many of the services that are supposed to help people operate in 'silos' (looking at each need on its own) rather than responding to the 'whole person' and that this needs to change
- Services are too often set up to respond to crisis rather than preventing problems developing in the first place
- There is a need to address the lack of power and influence in the hands of people facing severe and multiple disadvantage
- People facing severe and multiple disadvantage are often excluded from the market – the services and activities most of us take for granted, including employment, finance and leisure
- Certain discriminated-against groups face even greater disadvantage and this needs to be brought to light and addressed

We have some ideas about what might make change happen (set out in our Theory of Change: A Summary) but we are clear that we do not have all the answers and we certainly cannot do this alone.

These are really thorny issues and success in this area has so far been limited. We are all working in an environment that has changed drastically in recent times. We are convinced that new, radical and even daring ideas are needed and we want to find and support the very best of these as well as working out which current approaches are working well and why.

If you think your project (large or small, short or lengthy) can help us towards our mission, we would like to hear from you. We strongly suggest you read our Theory of Change before applying. We are looking for proposals that offer something new in addition to the work we are already supporting through our Promoting Change Network.

We do not make a large number of grants so every one has to give us something really valuable and different in terms of our overall objectives. If you read these guidelines and our website and think that there is a clear match between your ideas and ours then we want to hear from you.

Who can apply?

We are less interested in the type of organisation than the work taking place – we mainly fund charities but we can fund non-charitable organisations as long as the work itself has charitable purposes and there is no 'private benefit' to non-charitable interests.

We are especially keen to hear about work led by people with lived experience of severe and multiple disadvantage.

We are open to funding any sort of work – it does not have to be service delivery and can include things like campaigning, journalism, film making or research.

In all cases we are looking for people willing to work in an open way and to share ideas with us and the other projects we support.

Grantmaking in 2011/12

In 2011/12 the foundation had assets of £119 million, an income of £4.9 million and gave grants to 234 organisations totalling £5.7 million, broken down as follows:

Local people, local places	£1.15 million
Women's diversionary fund	£1.13 million
Breaking the cycles of abuse	£1.01 million
Custody and community	£987,000
Free and quiet minds	£874,000
Arts	£538,000
Annual grants	£192,000

Beneficiaries across all programmes included: Family Action – London (£135,000); Afiya Trust – London (£75,000); Creation Community Development Trust – South Wales (£60,000); Off the Hook/York Boxing Club and Blackpool Women's Centre (£50,000 each); New Step for African Community, Rochdale (£45,000); Together Women Project – Bradford, Small World Cultural Arts Collective – Keighley and Argyll and Bute Rape Crisis (£36,000 each); Kirckman Concert Society – London (£35,000); Amina – The Muslim Women's Research Centre – Glasgow and National Coalition of Anti-Deportation Campaigns – London (£30,000 each); The Foundation for Families – Yorkshire (£25,000); Female Prisoners Welfare Project – London

(£20,000); Artichoke Trust, London (£12,000); Ethex – Oxford (£10,000); and New Harmonie – West Sussex (£5,300).

Exclusions

The foundation states:

Our focus is always on people who are experiencing a combination of severe social harms, and we are therefore very unlikely to fund work that is about a single issue, such as mental illness alone. Please also note that we don't fund work that is focused exclusively on the following:

- A particular health condition
- Disability issues
- Imprisonment and/or prisoner resettlement
- Issues affecting asylum seekers

Applications

The following information is taken from the foundation's website:

How to apply

We have a two-stage application process:

Stage 1: Check if we are the right funder for you and send an Expression of Interest

- Please check if we are the right funder for you
- Read our Theory of Change [available on the foundation's website] to understand the problems we want to address and the type of change we want to see and support
- Email us, write to us, phone us or send us a video of yourself talking about your project or idea, whichever works best for you. When telling us about the work you would like to do, please tell us the following:
  1. what is the change that you are aiming for as a result of your project?
  2. how will you make that change happen?
  3. how will you know that you have succeeded?
  4. in what way will your project shift power to people who face severe and multiple disadvantage?
  5. how will you ensure that your ideas influence and reach beyond your organisation, e.g. locally and/or nationally?

Alongside this, you will also need to complete and submit our brief registration form.

Your letter/email should be up to a maximum of 1,000 words; and if you are applying by submitting a video, this should be between 3 and 5 minutes long.

We will send you an email to let you know that we have received your application. We will not share your project ideas with anyone else outside LankellyChase at this stage.

Stage 2: Work with us to build a full proposal

We will contact you within six weeks to let you know whether we think your idea offers something really valuable in the context of our mission. If it does, we will invite you to move forward to stage two. We will then work with you to develop your idea to the point where we can put it to our trustees in the form of a fully developed proposal and ask for funding. This is a process that may take some months and will involve meeting you, probably more than once. Our grants committee, made up of our trustees meets twice a year though we can sometimes make decisions on funding in between meetings.

Where do I send my Expression of Interest and registration form?

- You can email us at: grants@lankellychase.org.uk
- You can send your video to grants@lankellychase.org.uk, or you can use Dropbox by sharing your link or your folder
- You can call us on 020 3747 9930. We will ask you the questions listed above and write down what you say
- You can write to us

If you are successful, we will call or visit you regularly; we will support you if necessary or get you together with people from other projects we fund. We are keen to bring people together to share ideas and learn what does and doesn't work to improve the lives of people facing severe and multiple disadvantage.

Information gathered from:

Accounts; annual report; Charity Commission record; funder's website.

The Leathersellers' Company Charitable Fund

General
£1.4 million to organisations
(2011/12)

Beneficial area
UK, particularly London.

Correspondent: David Santa-Olalla, Clerk, 21 Garlick Hill, London EC4V 2AU (tel: 020 7330 1444; fax: 020 7330 1445; email: enquires@ leathersellers.co.uk; website: www. leathersellers.co.uk)

Trustee: The Leathersellers Company.

CC Number: 278072

Summary
The following is taken from the Fund's website:

The Leathersellers' Company is one of the ancient livery companies of the City of London, ranked fifteenth in the order of precedence. It was founded by royal charter in 1444 with authority to control the sale of leather within the City. The company no longer has this regulatory role, and instead devotes its energies to support for charity, education and the British leather trade.

The areas of priority are:
- Education
- Disability

- Children and young people
- Relief of need

The Company particularly welcomes applications that support the use of leather within the fashion industry, education in leather technology and the leather trade, and those working for the benefit of people in Greater London.

Core costs and specific projects can both be supported.

Types of grant
Small grants programme
This is a fast track application process for small one-off grants. The value of the grant awarded could be up to a maximum of £3,000; however the average level of grant is £500 – £1,500. A decision should be made within 6 weeks of receiving your application.

Main grants programme
The Main Grants programme awards Multi-Year Grants for a period of up to four years and large Single Year Grants. Multi-Year Grants can be offered as unrestricted revenue, for core costs or for established projects. Large Single Year Grants are normally awarded for capital costs or to cover crucial short-term development costs.

Grants in 2011/12
In 2011/12 the Company had assets of £41 million and an income of £1.5 million. Grants to 235 institutions totalled £1.4 million, broken down as follows:

Education	36	£343,000
Disability	54	£256,000
Advice and support	27	£156,000
Recreational	21	£138,000
Homeless	15	£128,000
Creative arts	16	£64,000
Leather associated	14	£105,000
Uniformed organisations	10	£70,000
Creative arts	11	£66,000
Heritage and the environment	17	£30,000

Beneficiaries of over £15,000 included: The Message Trust and National Memorial Arboretum Appeal (£50,000); Colfe's School (£38,000); Research Autism and Leather Conservation Centre (£30,000 each); St Catherine's College (£27,000); Bendrigg Trust and Widehorizons Outdoor Education Trust (£25,000 each); The London Pathway, Edmonton Eagles Amateur Boxing Club and Cancer and Bio Detection Dogs (£20,000 each); Guildhall School Trust (£18,000); and Friendship Works, Me2 Club and New Horizon Youth Centre (£15,000 each).

Grants of less than £15,000 totalled £657,000. A further 79 grants individuals for education totalled £167,000.

Applications
Applications can be made using the online form on the company's website. Successful applicants to the main grants programme will typically have to pass through a four stage process, which can

take up to nine months: Initial assessment – applicants will hear whether they have been successful or unsuccessful within six weeks; consideration by the grants committee; possible visit by committee working group for a detailed assessment; and grants committee final decision.

Only one application can be made in a year. If a charity is in receipt of a multi-year grants or a large single year grant cannot apply for another grants until four years has passed.

Percentage of awards given to new applicants: between 40% and 50%.

Common applicant mistakes
'Fail to answer all questions or mis-read question so give wrong answers. Figures that do not add up or correlate to their annual accounts'

Information gathered from:
Accounts; annual report; Charity Commission record; further information provided by the funder; funder's website.

The William Leech Charity

Health and welfare in the north east of England, overseas aid
£204,000 (2011/12)

Beneficial area
Northumberland, Tyne and Wear, Durham and overseas.

Correspondent: Kathleen M. Smith, Secretary, Saville Chambers, 5 North Street, Newcastle upon Tyne NE1 8DF (tel: 01912 433300; email: enquiries@ williamleechcharity.org.uk; website: www.williamleechcharity.org.uk)

Trustees: Adrian Gifford; Roy Leech; Richard Leech; N. Sherlock; David Stabler; Barry Wallace.

CC Number: 265491

William Leech started out as an apprentice, and went on to lead large scale building operations, providing affordable housing for sections of society who had not been able to contemplate home ownership previously. In 1972 Sir William Leech set up The William Leech Property Trust (now The William Leech Charity) and donated to it some 300 tenanted properties, the income from which was to be distributed in accordance with his guidelines.

Types of Grant
Main Fund
This fund makes grants of £100–£100,000 and interest free loans for up to £10,000 to registered charities in the North East of England. The majority of grants are given to support

community welfare in particular youth projects, medical care, projects to assist people with disabilities and the maintenance of churches.

Loans are often made when an unexpected crisis occurs, usually to allow an organisation, often a church, to get on with building work avoiding inflation. They are repayable over five years by annual instalment and are for up to £10,000 or 10% of the building costs. The following conditions apply:

- The loan offer is open for two years. If it has not been accepted within this time it will be withdrawn
- Supply a copy of the minute of the extraordinary meeting called to consider the loan offer clearly showing the amount of the loan, proposed dates and signed by the chairperson and trustee
- The loan should be shown in the accounts as 'interest free loan from the William Leech Charity'
- Loans can be made available at short notice but there must be reassurance that all other resources have been used first
- If early repayment was possible the trust would be disappointed if the recipient organisation did not repay and was found to be keeping money in the bank

Volunteer Support is given to assist volunteers in small registered charities where at least two thirds of the work is done by volunteers. Grants are usually for £500–£1,000.

Lady Leech Fund

The Lady Leech fund was created within the charity at the bequest of Lady Leech using the residue from her estate upon her death. Grants are made to charities, usually with a North East of England connection which assist projects in the developing world which focus on the needs and welfare of disadvantaged children. Emergency aid to natural disasters is also given.

Volunteer Support

This fund is designed to assist volunteers in small registered charities where at least two thirds of the work is done by volunteers. Grants are usually for £500–£1,000.

The charity also was involved in the establishment of the Northumberland Community Foundation and still has a strong connection with it, continuing to fund projects through the foundation.

Grantmaking in 2011/12

Grants were made to 78 organisations totalling £204,000 including £172,000 from the main fund and £31,000 from the Lady Leech fund. Over half of the grants made were for less than £1,000.

Beneficiaries included: St Nicholas Cathedral Trust (£50,000); Maggie's (£20,000); CAFOD and The Alnwick Playhouse Trust (£10,000); The Alnwick Garden Trust (£6,000); Central Palz and Team Kenya (£5,000 each); Northumberland Association of Clubs for Young People (£4,000); South Tyneside Asylum Seeker and Refugee (£2,000); Wallsend Sea Cadets and North Tyneside Disability Forum (£1,000 each); Shine a Light on Aniridia (£500); and Hartlepool Rugby Football Club (£250).

Exclusions

The following will not generally receive grants. The chair and secretary are instructed to reject them without reference to the trustees, unless there are special circumstances:

- Community care centres and similar (exceptionally, those in remote country areas may be supported)
- Running expenses for youth clubs (as opposed to capital projects)
- Running expenses of churches – this includes normal repairs, but churches engaged in social work, or using their buildings largely for 'outside' purposes may be supported
- Sport
- The arts
- Applications from individuals
- Organisations which have been supported in the last 12 months. It would be exceptional to support an organisation in two successive years, unless the charity had promised such support in advance
- Holidays, travel, outings
- Minibuses (unless over 10,000 miles per annum is expected)
- Schools
- Housing associations

Applications

The Main Fund

The following guidance is taken from the trust's website:

As it is the intention of the trustees to favour support for those charities who help others by utilising the generous time and skills of volunteers, they accept applications in the short form of a letter, rather than expecting the completion of a complicated application form, which may seem daunting to some applicants.

In order to safe-guard our charity status, it is important that we are accountable for how funds are distributed. As such, the following protocols exist for making and investigating applications.

Please note we only accept applications from registered charities, and the registered charity address must be included in the application process. For large grants and multiple grants, trustees would like to see as much supporting information as possible, and in rare cases, they may wish to interview the applicant.

Your applications must include:

- A description of the project that the charity is undertaking, who it hopes to help, and any evidence which will support the need for this particular project
- How much the project will cost, capital and revenue, with an indication of the amounts involved
- How much the charity has raised so far, and where it expects to find the balance
- The type of support sought; i.e. small grant, multiple grant, loan, etc
- How much does it cost to run the charity each year, including how much of the revenue is spent on salaries and employees. Where does the revenue come from? How many paid workers are there, how many volunteers are there

The Lady Leech Fund

Applications to this fund should be submitted in a letter containing:

- The name, address and registration number of the charity
- The name and contact details of the person who is authorised by the charity to apply for funding
- A description of the project that the charity is undertaking, who it hopes to help, and any evidence which will support the need for this particular project
- How much the project will cost, capital and revenue, with an indication of the amounts involved
- How much the charity has raised so far, and where it expects to find the balance
- A description of the connection between the Developing World Project, and the people in the North East of England
- How much does it cost to run the charity each year, including how much of the revenue is spent on salaries and employees. Where does the revenue come from? How many paid workers are there? How many volunteers are there?

Volunteer Support

Send a one page letter detailing:

- Organisation's name and charity registration number
- Name and address of correspondent
- Project aims, progress, funds raised to date, how much is needed and for what
- Number of paid workers, total annual salary cost, total annual administration overheads and how many unpaid volunteers

Application letters can be written and submitted on the charity's website, or sent by post.

Trustees meet every two months to consider applications.

Information gathered from:

Accounts; annual report; Charity Commission record; funder's website.

The Kennedy Leigh Charitable Trust

Jewish charities, general, social welfare

£305,000 (2011/12)

Beneficial area
Israel and UK.

Correspondent: Naomi Shoffman, Administrator, ORT House, 126 Albert Street, London NW1 7NE (tel: 020 7267 6500; email: naomi@klct.org)

Trustees: Anthony Foux; Geoffrey Goldkorn; Angela L. Sorkin; Michael Sorkin; Carole Berman; Benjamin Goldkorn.

CC Number: 288293

The trust's objects require three-quarters of its grantmaking funds to be distributed to charitable institutions within Israel, with the remainder being distributed in the UK and elsewhere. The trust's 'mission statement' reads as follows:

> The trust will support projects and causes which will improve and enrich the lives of all parts of society, not least those of the young, the needy, the disadvantaged and the underprivileged. In meeting its objectives the trust expects to become involved in a wide range of activities. The trust is able to provide several forms of support and will consider the funding of capital projects and running costs. The trust is non-political and non-religious in nature.

Capital projects and running costs are given. Usually up to three years, with the possibility of renewal.

In 2011/12 the trust had assets of £18 million and an income of £495,000. Grants were made totalling £305,000.

Beneficiaries included: Sajur Israel Tennis Centre (£50,000) St John Eye Hospital (£27,000); CHAI Lifeline, Dental Volunteers Israel, Oxford Centre for Hebrew Studies and Jewish Association for the Mentally Ill (£25,000 each); Yad Vashem (£19,000); Jerusalem Print Workshop (£11,000); Community Security Trust and Jewish Care (£10,000 each); Krembo Wings (£9,600); Jewish Arab Community Centre (£9,300); and Hand in Hand (£4,800).

Exclusions
No grants for individuals.

Applications
The trust has informed us that they are not currently giving outside Israel apart from previous commitments.

Percentage of awards given to new applicants: less than 10%.

Common applicant mistakes
'Misspell my name. Not check criteria i.e. most of our money goes to Israel.'

Information gathered from:
Accounts; annual report; Charity Commission record; further information provided by the funder.

The Lennox and Wyfold Foundation

General

£447,000 (2011/12)

Beneficial area
Worldwide.

Correspondent: Karen Wall, Fleming Family and Partners Ltd, 15 Suffolk Street, London SW1Y 4HG (tel: 020 7036 5000; fax: 020 7036 5601)

Trustees: Lennox Hannay; Adam Fleming; Christopher Fleming; Caroline Wilmot-Sitwell.

CC Number: 1080198

This foundation was established in 2000 for general charitable purposes and was formerly known as the Wyfold Foundation. In September 2005, the foundation received all the assets of the Lennox Hannay Charitable Trust which has now been wound up. Grants are made to a wide variety of UK registered charities ranging from medical research to welfare of the young and the old, from the arts to animal welfare and in some cases whilst the donations have been made to a relevant UK organisation, some of the ultimate beneficiaries are overseas.

In 2011/12 the foundation had assets of £36 million, an income of £510,000 and gave 94 grants totalling £447,000, categorised as follows:

Health	23	£103,000
Relief of disadvantage	24	£100,000
Education	10	£56,000
Religion	7	£31,000
Arts, culture, heritage and science	5	£30,000
Armed forces and emergency services	6	£30,000
Citizenship or community development	5	£29,000
Environment	3	£25,000
Sport	5	£23,000
Animal welfare	1	£10,000
Relief of poverty	1	£5,000
Human rights and conflict resolution	1	£1,000
Other	1	£10,000

The largest beneficiaries were The Maggie Keswick Jencks Cancer Caring Centres Trust (£27,000); and The Eden Trust (£20,000). There were 92 other grants made for less than £11,000 which were not listed in the accounts.

Previous beneficiaries included: Breakthrough Breast Cancer; Absolute Return for Kids; RNIB; Deafblind UK; Amber Foundation; Tusk Trust; Elephant Family; St George's Chapel – Windsor; Bucklebury Memorial Hall; Chipping Norton Theatre and Friends Trust; Gloucestershire Air Ambulance; Mary Hare Foundation; and Reform Research Trust.

Applications
In writing to the correspondent. Trustees meet once a year to discuss applications.

Information gathered from:
Accounts; annual report; Charity Commission record.

The Mark Leonard Trust

Environmental education, youth, general

£650,000 (2011/12)

Beneficial area
Worldwide, but mainly UK.

Correspondent: Alan Bookbinder, Director, Sainsbury Family Charitable Trusts, The Peak, 5 Wilton Road, London SW1V 1AP (tel: 020 7410 0330; email: info@sfct.org.uk; website: www.sfct.org.uk)

Trustees: Zivi Sainsbury; Judith Portrait; John Julian Sainsbury; Mark Sainsbury.

CC Number: 1040323

This is one of the 18 Sainsbury Family Charitable Trusts, which collectively give over £60 million a year. It mostly supports environmental causes and youth work, although it also gives towards general charitable purposes. Grants are made to support innovative schemes through seed-funding with the aim of helping projects to achieve sustainability and successful replication. The following descriptions of its more specific work are taken from its annual report:

Environment
Grants are made for environmental education, particularly to support projects displaying practical walls of involving children and young adults. The trustees do not support new educational resources in isolation from the actual process of learning and discovery. They are more interested in programmes which help pupils and teachers to develop a theme over time, perhaps combining IT resources with the networks for exchanging information and ideas between schools.

The trustees are particularly interested in projects that progressively enable children and young people to develop a sense of ownership of a project, and that provide direct support to teachers to deliver exciting and high quality education in the classroom.

The trustees are also interested in the potential for sustainable transport, energy efficiency and renewable energy in wider society. In some cases the trustees will consider funding research, but only where there is a clear practical application. Proposals are more likely to be considered when they are testing an idea, model or strategy in practice.

Youth Work
Grants are made for projects that support the rehabilitation of young people who have become marginalised and involved in anti-social or criminal activities. Trustees wish to apply their grants to overcome social exclusion. They are also interested in extending and adding value to the existing use of school buildings, enhancing links between schools and the community, and encouraging greater involvement of parents, school leavers and volunteers in extra-curricular activities.

An essential part of the youth work which the trustees wish to support will be a sense of realising the personal choice and responsibility of young people, building identity through taking their views and plans seriously and offering the tools to translate their aspirations and talents into practice. Above all, grants will be made towards work which gives young people, with the support and guidance they need, the autonomy and permission to be themselves and to be creative and enterprising. The trustees believe that creating this culture in young people in contemporary Britain will be essential for the future health of society.

In 2011/12 the trust had assets of £14 million, an income of £1 million and gave grants totalling £650,000.

The beneficiaries were: Global Action Plan (£180,000); Sustainable Restaurant Association (£100,000); BioRegional Development Group (£90,000); Ashden: Sustainable solutions, better lives (£60,000); Ecofin Research Foundation (£49,000); National Energy Foundation (£32,000); Only Connect (£25,000); Kaizen Partnership (£23,000); Behaviour Change Ltd (£20,000); Lyndhurst Primary School (£15,000); City University, Rambert School of Ballet and Dance and Centre for Sustainable Energy (£10,000 each).

Exclusions
Grants are not normally made to individuals.

Applications
'Proposals are generally invited by the trustees or initiated at their request. Unsolicited applications are discouraged and are unlikely to be successful, unless they are closely aligned to the trust's areas of interest.' A single application will be considered for support by all the trusts in the Sainsbury family group.

Information gathered from:
Accounts; annual report; Charity Commission record; funder's website.

The Leverhulme Trade Charities Trust

Charities benefiting commercial travellers, grocers or chemists

£1 million to organisations (2012)

Beneficial area
UK.

Correspondent: Paul Read, Secretary, 1 Pemberton Row, London EC4A 3BG (tel: 020 7042 9883; email: pdread@ leverhulme.ac.uk; website: www. leverhulme-trade.org.uk)

Trustees: Sir Iain Anderson; Niall Fitzgerald; Patrick Cescau; Dr Ashok Ganguly; Paul Polman.

CC Number: 288404

The Leverhulme Trade Charities Trust derives from the will of the First Viscount Leverhulme, who died in 1925. He left a proportion of his shares in Lever Brothers Ltd upon trust and specified the income beneficiaries to include certain trade charities. In 1983, the Leverhulme Trade Charities Trust itself was established, with its own shareholding in Unilever, and with grantmaking to be restricted to charities connected with commercial travellers, grocers or chemists, their wives, widows or children. The trust has no full-time employees, but the day-to-day administration is carried out by the director of finance at The Leverhulme Trust.

Grants are only made to:
▶ Trade benevolent institutions supporting commercial travellers, grocers or chemists
▶ Schools or universities providing education for them or their children
▶ The Royal Pharmaceutical Society for pharmacy research and education

In 2012 the trust had assets of £57 million and an income of £2 million. Grants to institutions were made totalling £1 million. A further £754,000 was given to institutions for undergraduate and postgraduate bursaries.

Beneficiaries included: UCTA Samaritan Fund (£255,000); The Girls' Day School Trust (£216,000); The Royal Pharmaceutical Society – Research Fellowships (£180,000); Royal Pinner School Foundation (£160,000); United Reformed Church Schools (£128,000); and The Royal Pharmaceutical Society – The Pharmacy Practice Research Trust (£68,000).

Exclusions
No capital grants. No response is given to general appeals.

Applications
On a form available from the charity's website. Deadlines are 1 November and 1 March.

Undergraduate and postgraduate bursary applications should be directed to the relevant institution.

Information gathered from:
Accounts; annual report; Charity Commission record; funder's website.

The Leverhulme Trust

Scholarships, fellowships and prizes for education and research

£80.4 million (2012)

Beneficial area
Unrestricted.

Correspondent: Ms Reena Mistry, Administrator, 1 Pemberton Row, London EC4A 3BG (tel: 020 7042 9881; email: enquiries@leverhulme.org.uk; website: www.leverhulme.org.uk)

Trustees: Sir Michael Perry, Chair; Patrick J. P. Cescau; Niall W. A. Fitzgerald; Dr Ashok S. Ganguly; Paul Polman.

CC Number: 288371

This trust derives from the will of William Hesketh Lever, the first Viscount Leverhulme. A businessman, entrepreneur and philanthropist who supported a variety of educational, religious, civic, community and medical causes. On his death in 1925, Lord Leverhulme left a proportion of his interest in the company he had founded, Lever Brothers, in trust for specific beneficiaries: to include first certain trade charities and secondly the provision of 'scholarships for the purposes of research and education', thus the Leverhulme Trust was established. In November 1983 a redefinition of the trust's objectives was brought about and subsequently, the Leverhulme Trust has concentrated its attention solely on research and education.

The trust continues to combine the direct initiatives of the trustees made in the light of specialist peer review advice with a portfolio of awards made by a research awards advisory committee, itself comprising eminent research colleagues drawn predominantly from the academic world.

The awarding of scholarships for research and education continues to be represented by awards for the conduct of research and awards and bursaries for educational purposes. In terms of support, there are five main patterns of award, namely:

▶ Research grants
▶ Fellowships
▶ Academic collaboration
▶ Prizes
▶ Arts initiatives

Awards for education are predominantly bursaries for students in fine and performing arts although there is a small involvement with innovative educational approaches in these disciplines.

Programmes

The following guidelines on grant programmes are taken from the trust's website. **Note this is a summary of the funding schemes, full details including eligibility and application procedures are available on the website.**

1. Research grants

(a) Research project grants

The aim of these awards is to provide financial support for innovative and original research projects of high quality and potential, the choice of theme and the design of the research lying entirely with the applicant (the Principal Investigator). The grants provide support for the salaries of research staff engaged on the project, plus associated costs directly related to the research proposed.

Proposals are favoured which:

▶ Reflect the personal vision of the applicant
▶ Demonstrate compelling competence in the research design
▶ Surmount traditional disciplinary academic boundaries
▶ Involve a degree of challenge and evidence of the applicant's ability to assess risk

(b) Research Leadership Awards

To support those who have succeeded in beginning a university career but are confronted with the task of building a research team adequately able to tackle an identified but distinct research problem.

(c) Research programme grants

In the one major departure from its policy of operating in the responsive mode, the trust selects on an annual basis two themes of research for which bids are invited. Normally one grant is awarded for each theme. The grants provide funds to research teams for up to five years to enable them to explore significant issues in the social sciences, in the humanities and, to a lesser extent, in the sciences. The scale of the awards (each one at a sum of up to £1.75 million) is set at a level where it is possible for a research team to study a significant theme in depth by conducting a group of interlinked research projects which taken together can lead to new understanding. The themes are selected not to exclude particular disciplines from the competition but rather to encourage research teams to look upon

their established research interests from a set of refreshing viewpoints.

The themes for the 2013 cycle were: The Nature of Knots or Innovation for Sustainable Living

2. Fellowships

Full details on the range of fellowships and studentships available to individuals can be found in the trust's website.

3. Academic collaborations

(i) International Networks

These collaborations enable a Principal Investigator based in the UK to lead a research project where its successful completion is dependent on the participation of relevant overseas institutions. A significant research theme must be identified at the outset which requires for its successful treatment international collaboration between one or more UK universities, and two or more overseas institutions (normally up to a maximum of seven institutions in total). Networks should be newly constituted collaborations. Full justification should be given for the involvement of all participants, with each participant bringing specific – and stated – expertise which can directly contribute to the success of the project. Details of the proposed methodology for the research project should be provided at the outset, as well as a clear indication of the anticipated outcomes (publications, websites), and of the dissemination strategy to be adopted.

Value and duration

The value of an award is normally up to £125,000, the activities involved lasting for up to three years.

Topics

Applications for research on any topic within the entire array of academic disciplines are eligible for support. However, an exception is made for areas of research supported by specialist funding agencies and in particular for medicine. In such cases, applicants should consider an application to these alternative funding bodies as being more appropriate. Specific attention is paid to the reasons given by applicants in justifying their choice of the trust as the most appropriate agency for the support of their project.

Institutions

The Principal Investigator should be employed at a university or other institution of higher or further education in the UK. The award is made to that institution, which must agree to administer the grant, for allocation among the participating institutions.

(ii) Visiting Professorships

The objective of these awards is to enable distinguished academics based overseas to spend between three and ten months inclusive at a UK university, primarily in order to enhance the skills of academic staff or the student body within the host institution. It is recognised that Visiting Professors may also wish to use the opportunity to further their own academic

interests. The over-riding criteria for selection are first the academic standing and achievements of the visitor in terms of research and teaching, and secondly the ability of the receiving institution to benefit from the imported skills and expertise. Priority will be given to new or recent collaborative ventures.

Value

The sum requested should reflect the individual circumstances of the visitor and the nature and duration of the proposed activities. A maintenance grant up to a level commensurate with the salary of a professor in the relevant field at the receiving institution may be requested. Economy travel costs to and from the UK will also be met. Requests for associated costs, if justified by the programme, may include, for example, travel within the UK, consumables, and essential technical assistance.

4. Philip Leverhulme Prizes

Philip Leverhulme Prizes are awarded to outstanding scholars (normally under the age of 36) who have made a substantial and recognised contribution to their particular field of study, recognised at an international level, and whose future contributions are held to be of correspondingly high promise. Approximately 25 Prizes are available each year across the five topics which are offered.

The Prizes commemorate the contribution to the work of the trust made by Philip Leverhulme, the Third Viscount Leverhulme and grandson of the Founder.

Topics

For the 2013 competition the selected disciplines were:

▶ Astronomy and Astrophysics
▶ Economics
▶ Engineering
▶ Geography
▶ Modern languages and Literature
▶ Performing and Visual Arts

The disciplines selected are intentionally broad, and nominations will be considered irrespective of a nominee's departmental affiliation.

Value

Each Prize has a value of £70,000; use should be made of the award over a two or three year period. Prizes can be used for any purpose which can advance the Prize holder's research, with the exception of enhancing the Prize holder's salary.

5. Art Initiatives

Applicants should note that any activities supported under this strand should offer an opportunity for a fresh and original educational approach to be initiated in the proposed project/activity:

(a) Artists in Residence

These awards are intended to support the residency of an artist in a UK institution in order to foster a creative collaboration between the artist and the staff and/or students of that institution. The maximum total cost can be up to £15,000 overall for a typical residency.

(b) Arts Scholarships
Applications and details for the next competition will be available in spring 2015.

Grantmaking in 2012

In 2012 the trust had assets of £1.9 billion and an income of £64 million. Grants were made totalling £80.4 million, broken down as follows:

Responsive Mode Projects	£29 million
Research Leadership Awards	£12 million
Research Awards Advisory Committee	£11.6 million
Arts Scholarships/Bursaries	£11.3 million
Exceptional Awards	£4.3 million
Major Research Fellowships	£3.8 million
Designated Programmes	£3.1 million
Leverhulme Prizes	£2.1 million
Visiting Fellows and Professors	£2.1 million
Academy Fellowships/ Scholarships	£1.1 million

Beneficiaries included the following institutions, all of whom received multiple awards: University of Cambridge (£5 million); University of Oxford (£4.8 million); University of Manchester (£3.2 million); Durham University (£2.7 million); Newcastle University (£2.2 million); School of Oriental and African Studies (£1.8 million); British Museum (£1.8 million); University of Edinburgh (£1.4 million); University of Liverpool (£1.1 million); Guildhall School of Music and Drama (£892,000); University of Southampton (£762,000); Royal Academy of Music (£717,000); and University of Strathclyde (£512,000).

In total there were 701 awards made in 2012.

Exclusions

When submitting an application to the trust, applicants are advised that the trust does not offer funding for the following costs, and hence none of these items may be included in any budget submitted to the trust:

- Core funding or overheads for institutions
- Individual items of equipment over £1,000
- Sites, buildings or other capital expenditure
- Support for the organisation of conferences or workshops, which are not directly associated with International Networks, Early Career Fellowships; Visiting Fellowships or Philip Leverhulme Prizes
- Contributions to appeals
- Endowments
- A shortfall resulting from a withdrawal of or deficiency in public finance
- UK student fees where these are not associated with a Research Project Grant bid or Arts Scholarships

Applications

Each programme, scholarship and award has its own individual application deadline and procedure. Full guidelines and application procedures for each award scheme are available from the trust directly or via its website.

Information gathered from:

Accounts; annual report; Charity Commission record; funder's website; Summary Information Return.

Lord Leverhulme's Charitable Trust

Welfare, education, arts, health, young people
£324,000 (2011/12)

Beneficial area
UK especially, Cheshire, Merseyside and South Lancashire.

Correspondent: Sue Edwards, Administrator, Leverhulme Estate Office, Hesketh Grange, Manor Road, Thornton Hough, Wirral CH63 1JD (tel: 01513 364828; fax: 01513 530265)

Trustees: A. E. H. Heber-Percy; Anthony H. S. Hannay.

CC Number: 212431

The trust was established in 1957 by the late Lord Leverhulme. Both of the restricted funds have now expired but the trust has informed us that they are still supporting the beneficiaries of these funds: the Lady Lever Art Gallery and the Youth Enterprise Scheme for the Princes Youth Trust in Merseyside and Shropshire.

In 2011/12 the trust had assets of £27 million, an income of £544,000 and made grants totalling £324,000, categorised as follows:

Community	£68,000
Arts	£65,000
Health	£64,000
Religious establishments	£58,000
Animal welfare	£33,000
Education	£22,000
Environmental	£14,000

Only grants of over £20,000 were listed in the accounts, these were: Shrewsbury Abbey Renaissance and Royal College of Surgeons (£50,000 each); Lady Lever Art Gallery Annuity and Chester Zoo (£30,000 each); Lady Lever Art Gallery (£27,000); and Community Foundation for Shropshire and Telford (£25,000).

Exclusions
No grants to non-charitable organisations.

Applications

The following is taken from the trust's annual report:

> Priority is given to applications from Cheshire, Merseyside and South Lancashire and the charities supported by the settlor in his lifetime. Others who do not meet those criteria should not apply without prior invitation but should, on a single sheet, state briefly their aims and apply fully only on being asked to do so. A handful of charities have heeded this warning and telephoned our administrator but the continuing volume of applications from charities which plainly do not meet the stated criteria suggests that many applicants do not concern themselves with their target's policies.

Information gathered from:
Accounts; annual report; Charity Commission record; further information provided by the funder.

The Joseph Levy Charitable Foundation

Young people, elderly, health, medical research
£796,000 (2011/12)

Beneficial area
UK and Israel.

Correspondent: Roland Gyallay-Pap, Grants Administrator, 1st Floor, 1 Bell Street, London NW1 5BY (tel: 020 7616 1200; fax: 020 7616 1206; email: info@jlf.org.uk; website: www.jlf.org.uk)

Trustees: Jane Jason; Peter L. Levy; Melanie Levy; Claudia Giat; James Jason.

CC Number: 245592

The foundation was established in 1965 by the late Joseph Levy, property developer and philanthropist, who helped to rebuild post-war London in the 1950s and 60s. The trust website notes:

> He worked tirelessly all his life for many charitable causes and in particular had a deep concern for the welfare of young people. His longstanding interest in youth began as a member and manager at Brady Boys' Club. He subsequently became a Vice-President of the London Federation of Boys' Clubs, now London Youth. In 1963 he became a founder trustee of the Cystic Fibrosis Research Trust, now the Cystic Fibrosis Trust, acting as Chairman for almost twenty years till his retirement in 1984. He was awarded the MBE in 1976 and the CBE eight years later for his dedication to charitable causes.

As noted below, the amount committed each year varies considerably.

In 2011/12 the foundation had assets of £16 million and an income of £796,000. There were 44 grants made to 23 charities totalling £944,000 for both capital and revenue costs, broken down as follows:

Arts, culture and sport	9	£370,000
Health and community care	13	£307,000
Education and training	10	£145,000
Social welfare	9	£107,000
Other	3	£16,000

Beneficiaries included: St Andrews University (£46,000); Dementia UK (£35,000); Jewish Community Secondary School and Target Ovarian Cancer (£25,000 each); Hammerson Home Chantable Trust (£10,000); Shluvim (£7,500); Different Strokes (£3,000); and Sussex Wildlife Trust (£1,000).

Exclusions

No grants to individuals, under any circumstances.

Applications

The foundation states on the website that due to current commitments it is no longer able to accept unsolicited applications.

Percentage of awards given to new applicants: less than 10%.

Common applicant mistakes

'They do not look at our website first, which clearly states we do not accept unsolicited applications.'

Information gathered from:

Accounts; annual report; Charity Commission record; further information provided by the funder; funder's website.

The Linbury Trust

Arts, heritage, social welfare, humanitarian aid, general
£6.4 million (2011/12)

Beneficial area

Unrestricted.

Correspondent: Alan Bookbinder, Director, The Peak, 5 Wilton Road, London SW1V 1AP (tel: 020 7410 0330; fax: 020 7410 0332; website: www. linburytrust.org.uk)

Trustees: John Sainsbury; Anya Sainsbury; Martin Jacomb; James Spooner.

CC Number: 287077

Summary

This is one of the Sainsbury Family Charitable Trusts, which share a joint administration. They have a common approach to grantmaking which is described in the entry for the group as a whole, and which is generally discouraging to organisations not already in contact with the trust concerned, but some appear to be increasingly open to unsolicited approaches.

The trust makes grants very selectively; it gives priority to charitable causes where it has particular knowledge and experience. In past years the trust has supported major capital projects such as the National Gallery and the Royal Opera House, as well as other museums and galleries. It also has a special interest in dance and dance education, Lady Sainsbury being the well-known ballerina Anya Linden. However, while the trust is particularly associated with supporting the arts, it also gives more than half of the grants for other causes.

General

The trust takes a proactive approach towards grantmaking and, consequently, unsolicited applications are not usually successful. However, the trust will consider proposals which fall within its guidelines and gives grants to a wide range of charities. The sums awarded may be small or may amount to many millions, either on a once-only basis or as a commitment over a number of years.

Within the UK, priority is given to causes that are either national in scope, or that are based in regions of which trustees have a particular knowledge or interest. Preferred causes are as follows (not in order of priority):

- Arts
- Education: promoting the study of history, support for organisations that work with those suffering from poor literacy skills or dyslexia and education in the arts
- Museums and heritage: generally large museums with major development projects
- Environment: supporting the Ashden Awards, promoting the use of renewable energy in the UK and developing countries
- Medical: research projects
- Social welfare: organisations that work with people who are socially excluded and disadvantaged particularly work with young people to reduce or prevent offending
- Overseas: particularly medical causes in Palestine and education in South Africa

Grantmaking in 2011/12

In 2011/12 the trust had assets of £145 million and an income of £6.5 million. Grants to 69 organisations totalled £6.4 million, broken down into the following categories:

Museums and heritage	£3.5 million	56%
Arts	£1.2 million	19%
Education	£557,000	10%
Social Welfare	£632,000	9%
Developing countries and humanitarian aid	£271,000	2%
Environment	£138,000	2%
Medical	£47,000	2%

Beneficiaries included: British Museum (£2.25 million); Rambert Dance Company (£250,000); Linbury Prize for Stage Design (£158,000); University of Buckingham (£150,000); Salisbury Cathedral (£100,000); Ashden (£75,000); Shakespeare Schools Festival, Medical Aid for Palestinians, Merlin, PSS and Action for Prisoners Families (£50,000 each); University of Bristol (£46,000).

Exclusions

No grants to individuals.

Applications

See the guidance for applicants in the entry for the Sainsbury Family Charitable Trusts. A single application will be considered for support by all the trusts in the group.

Note: 'the trustees take a proactive approach towards grantmaking; accordingly, unsolicited applications to the trust are not usually successful'.

Information gathered from:

Accounts; annual report; Charity Commission record; funder's website.

The Enid Linder Foundation

Medicine, the arts, general
£511,000 (2011/12)

Beneficial area

UK.

Correspondent: Martin Pollock, Secretary, c/o Moore Stephens LLP, 150 Aldersgate Street, London EC1A 4AB (tel: 020 7334 9191; fax: 020 7651 1953; email: info@enidlinderfoundation.com; website: www.enidlinderfoundation.com)

Trustees: Jack Ladeveze; Audrey Ladeveze; Michael Butler; C. Cook; Jonathan Fountain.

CC Number: 267509

Registered in 1974, this foundation benefitted from the fortune of the Linder family, who ran a marine chandler business for many years.

There are often no more than ten new grants each year, with most money going to a mixed group of regularly supported beneficiaries, mainly in the fields of health and social welfare, particularly of children and disabled people, medical education and research. Local (normally London and the south), national and international charities are supported.

The grantmaking priorities are:

- Medicine: To fund research, education and capital projects related to all areas of medicine through grants to selected medical universities, institutions and charities
- The Arts: To fund projects which aim to develop and encourage individual

and group talent in musical, theatre and illustrative art

▶ General: To make donations to projects through other registered UK charities which support and care for the benefit of the public as a whole

Grants are usually one-off for around £10,000. Multi-year grants are only considered in exceptional circumstances. The trust also funds research scholarships and medical electives directly to universities.

In 2011/12 the foundation had assets of £13 million, an income of £540,000 and gave grants totalling £511,000.

Beneficiaries included: Royal College of Surgeons (£110,000); National Children's Orchestra Bursary (£50,000); Imperial College and Victoria and Albert Museum (£30,000 each); Médecins Sans Frontières (£25,000); Moto Neurone Disease Association (£13,000); Bath Intensive Care Baby Unit and Help for Heroes (£10,000 each); Beatrix Potter Society (£7,000); and Prospect Hospice and Water Aid (£5,000 each).

Exclusions

No grants to individuals.

Applications

Apply using the online form on the foundation website. The deadline is 1 January for the March trustee meeting and 1 September for the December meeting. Grants will be made in April and January.

From the foundation's website:

> Unsolicited applications are accepted, but the trustees do receive a very high number of grant applications which, in line with their grantmaking policy, are mostly unsuccessful. The trustees prefer to support donations to a charity whose work they have researched and which falls within their guidelines.

Information gathered from:

Accounts; annual report; Charity Commission record; funder's website.

The George John and Sheilah Livanos Charitable Trust

Health, maritime charities, general

£579,000 (2012)

Beneficial area

UK.

Correspondent: Philip N. Harris, Trustee, Jeffrey Green Russell, Waverley House, 7–12 Noel Street, London W1F 8GQ (tel: 020 7339 7000)

Trustees: Philip N. Harris; Timothy T. Cripps; Anthony S. Holmes.

CC Number: 1002279

The trust gives grants from its income of about £100,000 a year but has also been making substantial awards from capital. Grants are widely spread and the previously reported interest in maritime causes, while still existing, is not as prominent as it was.

In 2012 the trust had assets of £1.9 million, an income of £102,000 and gave grants totalling £579,000.

Beneficiaries included: Ovarian Cancer Action (£170,000); Fight for Sight (£126,000); SPARKS (£54,000); Parkinson's Disease Society (£50,000) London Youth and Martlets Hospice (£10,000 each); Brainwave, The Bletchley Park Trust and Listening Books (£5,000 each); Whitechapel Mission (£2,500); Bath Institute of Medical Engineering and Children's Heart Foundation (£2,000 each); and Group B Strep Support (£1,000).

Exclusions

No grants to individuals or non-registered charities.

Applications

'Unsolicited applications are considered but the trustees inevitably turn down a large number of applications.'

Information gathered from:

Accounts; annual report; Charity Commission record.

The Ian and Natalie Livingstone Charitable Trust

General, children and young people

Beneficial area

UK.

Correspondent: Mark Levitt, Trustee, c/o Hazlems Fenton LLP, Palladium House, 1–4 Argyll Street, London W1F 7LD (tel: 020 7437 7666; fax: 020 7734 0644; email: marklevitt@ hazlemsfenton.com)

Trustees: Ian Livingstone; Natalie Livingstone; Mark Levitt.

CC Number: 1149025

Registered in September 2012, the trust's objects are general charitable purposes, with a focus on organisations working with children and young people. Ian Livingstone and his brother, Richard, own property company London and Regional, one of Europe's largest private property groups, which has a portfolio of properties with a value of around £4 billion. The company also owns the David Lloyd health club chain. The Livingstone brothers have an estimated personal wealth of around £1.3 billion. Natalie Livingstone is a journalist and

columnist for magazines and newspapers including OK!, Tatler and the Daily Express, and also a trustee of the Mayor's Fund for London.

Further research shows that Mr and Mrs Livingstone have supported organisations such as Ovarian Cancer Action and the Serpentine Gallery.

Applications

In writing to the correspondent.

Information gathered from:

Charity Commission record.

Lloyds Bank Foundation for England and Wales

Social and community needs

£21 million (2012)

Beneficial area

England and Wales.

Correspondent: Tina Claeys, Grant Administration Manager, Pentagon House, 52–54 Southwark Street, London SE1 1UN (tel: 0870 411 1223; fax: 0870 411 1224; email: enquiries@ lloydstsbfoundations.org.uk; website: www.lloydstsbfoundations.org.uk)

Trustees: Prof. Ian Diamond, Chair; Janet Bibby; Rob Devey; Pavita Cooper; Alan Leaman; Philip Grant; Mohammad Naeem; Lord Sandy Leitch; Sir Clive Booth; Dame Denise Platt; Prof. Patricia Broadfoot; Helen Edwards.

CC Number: 327114

On 15 January 2014 the foundation released the following statement on its website:

> The Lloyds Bank Foundation for England and Wales has today announced its intention to launch a new funding strategy. The new strategy – to be launched in April [2014] – reflects discussions with charities and other funders, and will reinforce the foundation's ongoing commitment to support small and medium sized charities in a challenging economic funding environment.

> **Creating a flexible and responsive approach to grant making:**
> Following the recent signing of a nine year rolling funding agreement with Lloyds Banking Group and a change of name, the Lloyds Bank Foundation for England and Wales will launch two new funding programmes, along with an optional support programme for successful applicants.

> These new programmes demonstrate the foundation's ongoing commitment to support charities that have the greatest impact upon improving the lives of disadvantaged people and their communities.

- Invest – A flexible, long-term core funding programme for organisations delivering clear, targeted outcomes for disadvantaged people
- Enable – A smaller and shorter grants programme for organisations that have identified clear development needs
- Enhance – A programme working alongside the Invest or Enable programme providing an option of tailored in kind support to strengthen and develop charities' effectiveness.

The foundation will continue to process grant requests under the current Community Programme over the coming months. However, to ensure a smooth transition between the programmes, [the programme closed] to new enquiries on 14 February 2014. Further information about the new programmes will be published in April [2014] when they will be open for new enquiries.

A trusted partner and respected voice:

As part of the new strategy, the foundation also announced its intention to partner with other funders to identify issues and contribute to policy and practices in the voluntary sector, at a national and local level, to lever positive change.

The following information on previous grantmaking under the previous strategy is provided for reference.

Grantmaking in 2012

In 2012 the foundation had assets of £39 million, an income of £27 million and gave 841 grants totalling £21 million.

During the year, grants made through the Community programme to 826 charities totalled £18.4 million. Grants made to 15 charities through the Older People Issue based programme (which is no-longer accepting applications) totalled £2.1 million. There was a total of £1.8 million given through the matched funding for staff fundraising scheme. Grants were broken down geographically as follows:

London	131	£3.5 million
North West	134	£3 million
Yorkshire and the Humber	94	£2.2 million
West Midlands	73	£2.1 million
East of England	55	£1.4 million
South East	58	£1.4 million
South West	79	£1.4 million
East Midlands	65	£1.3 million
Wales	79	£1.1 million
North East	58	£1 million

The following summary analysis of grantmaking is taken from the foundation's 2012 annual report, the full version of which is available from the foundation's website.

Over 50% of our funding is targeted towards the top 20 most deprived areas in England and Wales. Over the past three years, the foundation has invested over £8.5 million in charities within the ten most deprived areas of England.

Funding by the ten most deprived areas in England in the last three years.

Liverpool	£980,000
Hackney	£1 million
Tower Hamlets	£1 million
Manchester	£780,000
Knowsley	£240,000
Newham	£820,000
Co. Durham	£650,000
Islington	£1.3 million
Middlesbrough	£230,000
Birmingham	£1.5 million

Over the past three years, the Foundation has invested over £600,000 in the top four most deprived areas in Wales: Merthyr Tydfil, Blaenau Gwent, Rhondda Cynon Taff and Neath Port Talbot.

During 2012, our top funded issues across all geographies in the Community programme were:

Support for people with disabilities	£3.1 million
Support for children and young people	£2.6 million
Community support	£2.6 million
Advice and advocacy	£2 million
Health including mental health	£1.8 million
Victim support	£1.1 million
Ethnicity and language	£900,000
Relationships and caring	£900,000
Support for older people	£900,000
Training, employment and lifelong learning	£900,000

Beneficiaries included: Hackney CVS (£250,000); Age Concern in Cornwall and The Isles of Scilly (£188,000); Working With Men (WWM) (£38,000); Norfolk Community Law Service and Sexual Abuse and Rape Advice Centre (£30,000 each); Rainbow Services and Greenwich Mencap (£28,000 each); CVS Tamworth (£27,000); Burnley and Pendle CAB (£22,000); MIND in West Cumbria (£20,000); Hodan Somali Community (£19,000); Broxlow Youth Homelessness (£18,000); Pakistan Association Liverpool (£15,000); Downs Syndrome Association (£12,000); Halton Disability Advice and Appeals Centre (£14,000); and Children and Families in Grief (£8,000).

Exclusions

The foundation does not fund the following types of organisations and work:

Organisations

- Organisations that are **not** registered charities
- Second or third tier organisations (unless there is evidence of direct benefit to disadvantaged people)
- Charities that mainly work overseas
- Charities that mainly give funds to other charities, individuals or other organisations
- Hospitals, hospices or medical centres
- Rescue services
- Schools, colleges and universities

Types of work

- Activities which a statutory body is responsible for
- Capital projects, appeals, refurbishments
- Environmental work, expeditions and overseas travel
- Funding to promote religion
- Holidays or trips
- Loans or business finance
- Medical research, funding for medical equipment or medical treatments
- Sponsorship or funding towards a marketing appeal or fundraising activities
- Work with animals or to promote animal welfare

Applications

Refer to the foundation's website for current information.

Information gathered from:

Accounts; annual report; Charity Commission record; guidelines for applicants; funder's website; summary information return.

Lloyds Bank Foundation for the Channel Islands

General

£998,000 (2012)

Beneficial area

The Channel Islands.

Correspondent: Mr John Hutchins, Executive Director, PO Box 160, 25 New Street, St Helier, Jersey JE4 8RG (tel: 01534 845889; email: john.hutchins@ lloydstsbfoundations.org.uk; website: www.ltsbfoundationci.org)

Trustees: Pauline Torode; John Boothman; Stephen Jones; Dr John Furguson; Patricia Tumelty; Martin Fricker; Sarah Bamford; Simon Howitt; Andrew Dann.

CC Number: 327113

The foundation's mission is to 'support charitable organisations which help people, especially those who are disadvantaged or disabled, to play a fuller role in communities throughout the Channel Islands'. Income is from the Lloyds TSB banking group and is subject to ongoing discussions for 2014 onwards.

The overall policy of the trustees is to support underfunded charities which enable people, especially disadvantaged or disabled people, to play a fuller role in the community. The trustees are keen to support organisations which contribute to local community life at the grass-roots level. The trustees are also keen to encourage the infrastructure of the voluntary sector and encourage applications for operational costs. This includes salary costs, which may be funded over two or three years, and training and education for managers and staff.

Donations for one-off projects are generally in the region of £2,500 to £25,000, but there is no minimum amount set by the trustees. Applications for larger amounts will be considered where there is a wider benefit. The trustees generally make donations towards specific items rather than making contributions to large appeals, for example, building costs. The majority of donations are made on a one-off basis. Successful applicants are advised to leave at least one year before reapplying.

The foundation provides the following information on its website:

Social Partnership Initiative

In 2001 we launched the Social Partnership Initiative, designed to encourage real working partnerships to be set up between the voluntary sector and the relevant States departments' in the Islands, to stimulate the voluntary sector into seeking out opportunities to develop new services, increase knowledge and key skills.

Our funding goes mainly to charities working in Social and Community Needs and Education and Training. The trustees regularly review changing social needs and identify specific areas they wish to focus on within their overall objectives. Current priorities are:

- Creating Positive Opportunities for Disabled People – enabling people with either learning or physical disabilities to live independently
- Family Support – including the development of relationship skills for young people, and encouraging good relationships between generations
- Homelessness – in particular helping homeless people back into mainstream society, including support after temporary or permanent accommodation has been secured
- Promoting Effectiveness in the Voluntary Sector – Supporting the training of trustees, managers, staff and volunteers and encouraging the sector to communicate and work together
- Prevention of Substance Misuse – including both education and rehabilitation
- The Needs of Carers – for example, information and support services, and the provision of respite care
- Challenging Disadvantage and Discrimination – Promoting understanding and encouraging solutions which address disadvantage, discrimination or stigma

In 2012 it had assets of £1.5 million, an income of £1.2 million and approved grants totalling £998,000 (not including matched giving) broken down as follows:

Jersey	£378,000
Guernsey	£595,000
Matched Giving	£41,000
Channel Islands-wide and UK	£25,000

Beneficiaries included: Brighter Futures (£120,000); Guernsey Arts Commission (£90,000); The Bridge Project Guernsey (£75,000); Jersey Youth Trust (£65,000); St Mark's Church (£30,000); Jubilee Sailing Trust (£25,000); Guernsey Voluntary Service (£11,000); Guernsey Bereavement Service (£7,400); Chernobyl Children life line (£5,000); and Helping Wings (£1,700).

Exclusions

No grants for:

- Organisations which are not recognised charities
- Activities which are primarily the responsibility of the Insular authorities in the Islands or some other responsible body
- Activities which collect funds to give to other charities, individuals or other organisations
- Animal welfare
- Corporate subscription or membership of a charity
- Endowment funds
- Environment – conserving and protecting plants and animals, geography and scenery
- Expeditions or overseas travel
- Fabric appeals for places of worship
- Fundraising events or activities
- Hospitals and medical centres (except for projects which are clearly additional to statutory responsibilities)
- Individuals, including students
- Loans or business finance
- Promotion of religion
- Schools and colleges (except for projects that will benefit disabled students and are clearly additional to statutory responsibilities)
- Sponsorship or marketing appeals
- International appeals – trustees may from time to time consider a limited number of applications from UK registered charities working abroad

Applications

Applications are only accepted on the foundation's own form which should be submitted with:

- A copy of your latest report and accounts (or draft accounts if more recent). These should be signed as approved on behalf of your Management Committee or equivalent
- A photocopy of your most recent bank statement
- If you are applying to fund an employee post: a copy of the job description
- Income Tax letter of exemption if you are a CI-based organisation and not part of a UK registered charity

The form and guidelines are available from the foundation's website or from the foundation's office in Jersey and can be returned at any time. They must be returned by post as the foundation does not accept forms that have been emailed or faxed.

All applications are reviewed on a continual basis. The trustees meet three times a year to approve donations in March, July and November and deadlines are usually the middle of the preceding month. Decision-making processes can therefore take up to four months. Applications up to £5,000 are normally assessed within one month and all applicants are informed of the outcome of their application.

Applicants are encouraged to discuss their project with one of the foundation's staff before completing an application form. This will help ensure that your project is within its criteria and that you are applying for an appropriate amount. You will also be informed of when you should hear a decision.

Information gathered from:

Accounts; annual report; Charity Commission record; funder's website.

Lloyds Bank Foundation for Northern Ireland

Social and community need, education and training

£1.9 million (2012)

Beneficial area

Northern Ireland.

Correspondent: Sandara Kelso-Robb, Executive Director, 2nd Floor, 14 Cromac Place, Gasworks, Belfast BT7 2JB (tel: 02890 323000; fax: 02890 323200; email: info@ lloydstsbfoundationni.org; website: www. lloydstsbfoundationni.org)

Trustees: Tony Reynolds; Paddy Bailie; Angela Colhoun; Brian Scott; Hugh Donnelly; Carmel McGukian; Lord Leitch; Janet Leckey; Jim McCooe; Janine Donnelly; Robert Agnew; Sandara Kelso-Robb.

IR Number: XN72216

Summary

The foundation allocates its funds in support of underfunded, grassroots charities that enable people, especially disabled and disadvantaged people, to be active members of society and to improve their quality of life.

Most donations are said to be one-off, with a small number of commitments made over two or more years. The trustees say that they prefer to make donations towards specific items rather than contributions to large appeals, though the trust will consider core funding for small local charities. Applications which help to develop voluntary sector infrastructure are encouraged.

Programmes
Community Grant Programme
This is the main focus of the foundation and aims to support special and community welfare and education and training. The average grant is for £2,000 to £4,000. Applicants must have an income of less than £1 million in Northern Ireland.

International Grant Programme
For work in poor communities overseas which are supported by organisations with a significant presence in Northern Ireland. The scheme particularly invites applications:

▷ For costs associated with volunteering programmes that focus particularly on the development and transfer of skills to poor entities and communities overseas

▷ Which support sustainable indigenous projects overseas that enhance local, social and economic autonomy. Projects encouraging social enterprise and entrepreneurism will be particularly favoured

▷ Which help build the capacity of civil society representative organisations overseas that are working in areas of local basic social and economic rights

Collaboration
The Foundation is involved in a number of Collaboration Projects across Northern Ireland. These include:

▷ First Steps to Funding – Age NI: A two year programme (2011–13) providing fundraising training for age sector groups with an annual income of less than 20,000 delivered jointly by Age NI and Community Foundation NI. The programme also provides training for community workers supporting age sector groups in fundraising

▷ Partners In Power – Northern Ireland Youth Forum: This programme targets community and voluntary organisations that wish to improve their capacity to involve young people in decision making

▷ Social Entrepreneurship Programme: Social economy projects that have a Northern Ireland remit only can apply for grants of up to £3,000 to support their start-up work

The **Creating Change Programme** is now in its final stage of funding and will not be accepting any applications. The **Matched Giving Scheme** allows any employee of Lloyds Bank to claim up to £1,000 in matched giving for

volunteering time and fundraising efforts.

Alongside the main community grant programme, other programmes open and close therefore potential applicants are advised to visit the foundation's website or contact them directly to ensure that they keep up-to-date with the latest programme information.

Guidelines for applicants
The guidelines for applicants, detailed on the foundation's website, read as follows:

The overall policy of the charity is to support underfunded charities which enable people, especially disadvantaged or disabled people, to play a fuller role in the community.

The foundation has two main target areas to which it seeks to allocate funds:
▷ Social and community needs
▷ Education and training

Social and Community Needs
A wide range of activities are supported and the following are meant as a guide only.

▷ *Community services*: Family centres, women's centres, youth and older people's clubs, after school clubs, play schemes, help groups, childcare provision

▷ *Advice services*: Homelessness, addictions, bereavement, family guidance, money advice, helplines

▷ *Disabled people*: Residences, day centres, transport, carers, information and advice, advocacy

▷ *Promotion of health*: Information and advice, mental health, hospices, day care, home nursing, independent living for older people

▷ *Civic responsibility*: Juveniles at risk, crime prevention, promotion of volunteering, victim support, mediation, rehabilitation of offenders

▷ *Cultural enrichment*: Improving participation in and access to the arts and national heritage for disadvantaged and disabled people

Education and Training
The objective is to enhance educational opportunities for disadvantaged people and those with special needs.

▷ Projects which help socially excluded people develop their potential and secure employment.

▷ Employment Training (for disadvantaged people and those with special needs)

▷ Promotion of life skills, independent living skills for people with special needs

▷ Enhancing education for disabled pre-school children and young people (where no other support is available).

Grantmaking in 2012
In 2012 the foundation had assets of £2.4 million and an income of £2 million. There were 565 grants given totalling £1.9 million. Most of the grants made were for social welfare purposes.

Grants were distributed across various programmes:

Standard grant (now Community grant)	346	£1.2 million
Creating change	18	£270,000
Collaborative	18	£216,000
International grant	17	£104,000
Matched giving	165	£63,000
Special initiatives	1	£5,000

Grants were broken down geographically as follows:

Belfast	197
County Antrim	98
County Down	84
County Tyrone	36
Derry/Londonderry	34
UK based	33
County Armagh	30
County Derry/Londonderry	26
County Fermanagh	10

Grants approved by programme area in the Standard Grants Programme (now Community Grants Programme) were as follows:

Community services	149
Advice services	42
Disability	41
Promotion of health	46
Civic responsibility	23
Cultural enrichment	28
Education and training	17

Beneficiaries included: Northern Ireland Community Addiction Services Ltd (£5,300); Allergy NI and New Belfast Community Arts Initiative (£5,000 each); Foyle Women's Aid (£4,300); Ligoniel Amateur Boxing Club (£3,500); Northern Walking Project (£2,500); Shopmobility Lisburn and Stroke Association (£2,000 each); Windyhall Community Association (£1,650); Donaghmore Open Door Club and Killyleagh Early Years Playgroup (£1,000 each); and Alphabet Playgroup (£450).

Exclusions
Grants are not usually given for:
▷ Organisations that are not recognised as a charity by HM Revenue and Customs
▷ Individuals, including students
▷ Animal welfare
▷ Environmental projects including those that deal with geographic and scenic issues – however, the trustees may consider projects that improve the living conditions of disadvantaged individuals and groups
▷ Activities that are normally the responsibility of central or local government or some other responsible body
▷ Schools, universities and colleges (except for projects specifically to benefit students with special needs)
▷ Hospitals and medical centres
▷ Sponsorship or marketing appeals
▷ Fabric appeals for places of worship
▷ Promotion of religion
▷ Activities that collect funds for subsequent redistribution to others

- Endowment funds
- Fundraising events or activities
- Corporate affiliation or membership of a charity
- Loans or business finance
- Expeditions or overseas travel
- Construction of and extension to buildings
- Salary or training costs for the pre-school sector

Applications

Applications can be made using the online application form, available on the foundation's website. Once registered you will receive a username and password which you can use to access the online grants portal and view and apply for open programmes. Applicants are welcome to contact the foundation or make an appointment to discuss an application. As part of the assessment process the foundation may contact or visit the applicant. If you have not heard from the foundation within four weeks contact them. Guidelines, advice on completing the form, supporting document checklist and monitoring factsheets are all available from the website.

For the Community Grants Programme the closing dates are early January, April, July and October, see the website for exact dates.

Percentage of awards given to new applicants: 25%.

Common applicant mistakes

'Not showing clear disadvantage of beneficiaries; not reading our guidelines.'

Information gathered from:

Accounts; annual report; guidelines for applicants; funder's website; further information provided by the funder.

Lloyds TSB Foundation for Scotland

Social welfare

£2.1 million (2012)

Beneficial area

Scotland.

Correspondent: Ms Karen Brown, Administrator and Secretary, Riverside House, 502 Gorgie Road, Edinburgh EH11 3AF (tel: 01314 444020; fax: 01314 444099; email: enquiries@ ltsbfoundationforscotland.org.uk; website: www.ltsbfoundationforscotland. org.uk)

Trustees: Christine Lenihan, Chair; Prof. Sir John P. Arbuthnott; Prof. Sandy Cameron; James G. D. Ferguson; Jane Mackie; Maria McGill; Ian Small; Iain Webster; Tim Hall.

SC Number: SC009481

This foundation is run entirely separate from Lloyds Bank and TSB Bank but like the other Lloyds foundations receives a share of 1% of the bank's pre-tax profits. The Lloyds TSB Foundation for Scotland has been involved in a court case with the bank over how much money they are owed from 2010 and 2011. In 2013 the bank's appeal was upheld, effectively meaning that they did not have to pay the foundation £5.25 million from 2010 and 2011. This may have an effect on the amount of future funds available for distribution.

Grants are given to registered charities working in Scotland which focus on improving the quality of life for people in Scotland who are disadvantaged or at risk of becoming disadvantaged.

Programmes

The following programmes are available from the foundation:

Henry Duncan Awards

In 2010 our main grant programme was renamed the 'Henry Duncan Awards' in honour of The Reverend Henry Duncan who founded the first Trustee Savings Bank, which ultimately led to the establishment of the foundation, just over 200 years ago.

This programme was previously called the Standard Grants Scheme, so you will find that statistics and case studies from previous years refer to this name.

The majority of our grants are made through our Henry Duncan Awards, funding a huge variety of organisations to carry out an even wider range of work. Many of the organisations we fund are small grassroots charities working in their own local communities.

Registered charities with an annual income of less than £500,000 can apply to us for funding through this programme.

We have two application forms and accompanying guidance notes: one for amounts up to £3,000 for organisations with a turnover of up to £50,000, and one for grants over £3,000. You must choose which one of these forms you wish to submit, as we can only accept one application from you.

You might benefit from attending one of our surgeries, which are designed to help applicants through the application process. Please take a look at our schedule of surgeries to see if we will be in your area.

Partnership Drugs Initiative

The Partnership Drugs Initiative (PDI) promotes voluntary sector work with vulnerable children and young people affected by substance misuse. It has been running since 2000 and is funded by the foundation and the Scottish Government. Groups targeted are:

- Children and young people in families in which parents misuse drugs or alcohol

- Pre-teen children who are at higher risk of developing problems with substance misuse
- Young people who are developing or who have established problems with substance misuse

How the programme works

As we work with voluntary and statutory groups, the projects we fund gain strength from the partnership approach used.

We are also really interested in making sure the projects we fund will be accessible to the children and young people they are trying to help. So, a group of young people assess potential projects, making sure they are relevant to the children and young people who will be using them.

There are many different things to think about when we consider how effective projects will be at addressing issues around drugs and alcohol, and a steering group who have a wide range of expertise in this area gives us confidence that all aspects of projects have been looked at.

Alcohol & Drug Partnerships (ADPs) are a key group in co-ordinating work locally, and charities develop two-stage applications with them. This makes sure all the projects we fund are linked into other work going on locally.

How to apply

There is a two-stage application process for our Partnership Drugs Initiative (PDI) awards. You will need to work with your local Alcohol & Drug Partnership (ADP) to complete an initial outline application. Your ADP will send us the completed form, which needs to reach us by our deadline date [check the foundation's website for upcoming deadlines]. It will also be useful to read our 'Using the Learning to Develop a Proposal' document before you fill out your application form. If you would like to discuss your outline application before you submit it, call us on 01314 444020 and ask to speak to one of our PDI team.

You can also apply for funding for up to three years.

Once we have received your application form, it will be considered by an expert steering group and a panel of young people. If the proposal is successful at this stage you will be invited to develop a full application. Feedback from both groups is available to successful and unsuccessful projects.

You can find out more about what happens next or request us to send you one. If you would like to have a chat with someone about this award programme please call us on 01314 444020.

Capacity Building Support

Following a review of the Foundation's capacity building programme, we are very pleased to announce that we will be working in partnership with Evaluation Support Scotland and Pilotlight to deliver capacity building support. Charities will be considered for capacity building support as a result of successfully applying for funding through the Foundation's other award programmes – the Henry Duncan

Awards and the Partnership Drugs Initiative. A limited number of charities will be put forward to receive this support as a result of needs being identified during the assessment process for whichever award programme they have applied to. It is entirely up to the charities selected whether they want to proceed with this, and if they decide not to it will have no impact on any other award they may receive.

Recovery Initiative Fund

We are also working in partnership with the Scottish Recovery Consortium to deliver the Recovery Initiative Fund. Awards through this programme are being made by the Scottish Recovery Consortium and are being administered by the Foundation. You can find out more about the Scottish Recovery Consortium on the foundation's website and also how to apply to the Recovery Initiative Fund.

Grantmaking in 2012

In 2012 the foundation had assets of £6.3 million, an income of £904,000 and gave grants totalling £2.1 million, broken down into the following schemes:

Henry Duncan Awards	£978,000
Partnership Drugs Initiative	£832,000
Standard Grant Scheme	£250,000
Capacity Building Grant Scheme	£50,000

Beneficiaries included: Inspiring Scotland (£250,000); Barnardo's Perth and Kincross (£80,000 in two grants); Befriend a Child (£72,000); Tayside Council on Alcohol (£57,000); Pilotlight Scotland (£30,000); Children 1st (£27,000); PLUS (Stirling) Ltd (£8,000); Reality Adventure Works in Scotland Ltd (£7,000); Orkney Alcohol Counselling and Advisory Service (£6,000); Loanhead Community Learning Association (£5,000); Getting Better Together (£4,000); Cruse Bereavement Care Scotland (£3,000); and Scottish Minority Deaf Children's Society (£900).

Exclusions

The foundation will not support:

- Charities with an income of more than £500,000 per annum
- Organisations which are not formally recognised as charities in Scotland
- Charities which pay their board members or have paid employees who also hold a position as Director on the Board. This principle also applies to charities operating as collectives
- Individuals – including students
- Animal welfare
- Initiatives that are focused on sport, the arts or the environment, except where the subject is being used as a vehicle to engage with at risk or disadvantaged groups to increase life skills
- Conservation and protection of flora and fauna
- Mainstream activities and statutory requirements of hospitals and medical centres, schools, universities and colleges
- Sponsorship or marketing appeals
- Establishment/preservation of endowment funds
- Activities that collect funds for subsequent grantmaking to other organisations and/or individuals
- Expeditions or overseas travel
- Major building projects/capital appeals
- Historic restoration/historic publications
- Retrospective funding
- Promotion of religion/church fabric appeals
- Hobby groups
- One-off events such as gala days

Applications

Application forms for all programmes, complete with comprehensive guidance notes, are available from the foundation. These can be requested by telephone, by email, or through its website. Foundation staff are always willing to provide additional help. Check the foundation's website for details of upcoming application deadlines.

Percentage of awards given to new applicants: between 10% and 20%.

Information gathered from:

Accounts; annual report; Charity Commission record; further information provided by the funder.

The Trust for London (formerly the City Parochial Foundation)

Social welfare
£11.4 million (2012)

Beneficial area

Greater London.

Correspondent: Mubin Haq, Director of Policy and Grants, 6–9 Middle Street, London EC1A 7PH (tel: 020 7606 6145; email: info@trustforlondon.org.uk; website: www.trustforlondon.org.uk)

Trustee: Trust for London Trustee Board.

CC Number: 205629

The trust's website states:

> Trust for London is the largest independent charitable foundation funding work which tackles poverty and inequality in the capital. We support work providing greater insights into the root causes of London's social problems and how they can be overcome; activities which help people improve their lives; and work empowering Londoners to influence and change policy, practice and public attitudes.
>
> We are particularly interested in work that develops new and imaginative ways of addressing the root causes of London's social problems, especially work which has the potential to influence and change policy, practice and public attitudes. We are willing to take risks by supporting unpopular causes and activities that government is unlikely to fund. Annually we provide around £7 million in grants and fund approximately 120 organisations.

Funding is focused in four areas for 2013–17:

- Employment
- Advice
- Social Justice
- Violence
- Small community groups

What is funded:

We fund voluntary and community organisations undertaking charitable activities. You do not need to be a registered charity. This may be for a specific project or on-going costs. This includes staff salaries and overheads. We encourage organisations to include a reasonable amount of core costs to cover their overheads when they apply for funding. The majority of our funding is for revenue costs, though we can also fund small capital items. The purpose of our funding is to benefit people who are living in poverty. This includes work to increase their income as well as addressing other issues that may affect them such as inequality, discrimination or violence. We will fund work that benefits a large number of people living in poverty e.g. a campaign to make housing more affordable in London; as well as specific issues affecting smaller numbers e.g. work to prevent female genital mutilation.

Funding available:

There is no minimum or maximum size of grant and the amount you request should be the amount you need. However, the average grant (not including funding we award under our small groups priority) will be around £75,000 in total, although a number of grants will be for a lesser amount, while some will be for more. The amounts may be spread over one, two or three years. For example, if you are awarded a grant of £75,000, this could be £25,000 over three years, or £40,000 in the first year and £35,000 in the second.

We will not normally make grants that exceed £100,000. You may therefore need to apply to other funders to fund your proposed work jointly with us and we encourage you to do this, as we cannot always provide the total costs that you require.

Grants made under our small groups priority will not normally exceed £30,000 with an average grant being £20,000 in total, although many grants will be less than this. You may apply over one, two or three years.

We support long-term strategies for dealing with poverty and inequality. Therefore organisations that have received funding may return for support for work which is particularly effective and continues to meet our criteria and priorities. However, you should not assume we will award further funding and should also apply to other funders. If you wish to apply again for the same or different work, you should contact your relevant officer at least eight months before your current funding expires. Generally we do not provide more than one grant at a time.

We may occasionally fund work to tackle poverty and inequality which falls outside our priorities. Organisations will need to demonstrate clearly how the work is exceptional or how your organisation is developing genuinely innovative approaches to address these issues; or that an exceptional need has arisen. You will need to speak to us if you wish to apply under this heading. Generally we will only make a few grants under this category each year.

We have a strong tradition of supporting small community groups as we believe they are often well-placed to identify needs and find potential solutions. We are therefore keen to fund small community groups that have an emphasis on user involvement and self-help. We will fund activities that tackle poverty and inequality in London by empowering people to advocate for themselves and which build stronger communities. We define small groups as those that have an annual income of under £75,000.

For specific guidelines and criteria of funding in the four main areas see the trust's website.

City Church Fund

Grants must be for purposes that are essentially religious in nature with one third given to the City churches within the City of London and the remaining two-thirds to the six Dioceses of the Church of England which are within the area of benefit. This is distributed by the City Churches Grants Committee.

Grantmaking in 2012

In 2012 the trust had assets of £235 million, an income of £9.4 million and made grants totalling £11.4 million. This included £7.1 million through the Central Fund and £4.3 million through the City Churches Fund.

Beneficiaries included: Zacchaeus 2000 Trust (£120,000); Evelyn Oldfield Unit (£110,000); Latin American Women's Rights Service (£90,000); Africans Unite Against Child Abuse (£85,000); Roma Support Group (£60,000); Kensington and Chelsea Social Council (£56,000); London Tenants Federation (£48,000); Harrow CAB (£32,000); WinVisible (£30,000); Community Language Support Service (£20,000); Changing Minds (£15,000); Safety Net People First (£14,000); and Just for Kids Law (£5,000).

Exclusions

The foundation will not support proposals:

▸ Which do not benefit Londoners
▸ That directly replace or subsidise statutory funding (including contracts)
▸ That are the primary responsibility of statutory funders such as local and central government and health authorities
▸ From individuals, or which are for the benefit of one individual
▸ For mainstream educational activity including schools
▸ For medical purposes including hospitals and hospices
▸ For the promotion of religion
▸ For umbrella bodies seeking to distribute grants on the trust's behalf
▸ For work that has already taken place
▸ For general appeals
▸ For large capital appeals (including buildings and minibuses)
▸ From applicants who have been rejected by us in the last six months

The foundation is unlikely to support proposals:

▸ From large national charities which enjoy widespread support
▸ For work that takes place in schools during school hours
▸ Where organisations have significant unrestricted reserves (including those that are designated). Generally up to six months expenditure is normally acceptable
▸ Where organisations are in serious financial deficit

Applications

The trust's application form and funding guidelines for 2012–17 are available to download from its website. It is strongly recommended that potential applicants read the guidelines before making an application. The trust does not accept application forms by email or fax. The following information is taken from the trust's website.

> We have three closing dates for applications. They are: 4 February for the June Grants Committee; 28 May for the October Grants Committee; 8 October for the February Grants Committee.
>
> Applications must be received by 5pm on the closing date. Applications received after the deadline will not be considered until the next closing date.
>
> Once a closing date has passed, we will read and consider all the applications we have received. On some occasions we may contact you for further clarification regarding your proposed work. We aim to contact you within six weeks of the relevant closing date to let you know whether you have been rejected or shortlisted. Please avoid contacting us during this period to find out about your application as this takes up our time and resources. If you are unsuccessful we will

give you feedback. However, please understand our funding decisions are final.

All shortlisted organisations will be visited by one of our grants staff. At the visit we will discuss your application in more detail and how we will proceed. However, it is important to remember that not all organisations that we visit will receive funding. We take forward more applications than funding available can support. This is to ensure that we are funding the best work put forward to us.

If we agree to proceed to the next stage, your application will be presented to our Grants Committee which will then make the final decision about your request. We will ring you with the outcome soon after the meeting. This will be confirmed in writing generally within ten working days of the meeting. If you are successful in securing funding, the whole process will take no more than five months from our closing date.

Information gathered from:

Accounts; annual report; Charity Commission record; guidelines for applicants; funder's website.

The London Community Foundation (formerly Capital Community Foundation)

Community activities and social welfare
£3.9 million (2011/12)

Beneficial area
The London boroughs including the City of London.

Correspondent: Kath Sullivan, Grants and Monitoring Manager, Unit 7, Piano House, 9 Brighton Terrace, London SW9 8DJ (tel: 020 7582 5117; fax: 020 7582 4020; email: enquiries@londoncf.org.uk; website: www.londoncf.org.uk)

Trustees: Carole Souter; Gordon Williamson; Clive Cutbill; Stephen Jordan; Donovan Norris; Martin Richards; Davina Judelson; Francis Salway; Rhys Moore; Grant Gordon; Juliet Wedderburn; Tajinder Nijjar; Sanjay Mazumder; Jesse Zigmund.

CC Number: 1091263

The London Community Foundation provides grants to small community groups and charities in London. Registered charities, community groups, companies limited by guarantee without share capital, social enterprises and community interest companies can all be supported.

The foundation manages and distributes funds on behalf of several donors, including companies, individuals and government programmes and is able to offer a number of grant programmes which cover different areas and type of activity. Contact the foundation directly or visit its website for up-to-date information on current programmes.

Eligibility requirements:

At a minimum, to apply for a grant from LCF, your group must have the following in place, but please do read the guidance notes for each fund as there may be additional requirements:

▶ At least three trustees, directors or management committee members (If you are a community organisation, you must have this as a minimum. Registered charities and other bodies' constitutions may allow for less – in this instance, please contact us prior to making an application)

▶ A governing document e.g. constitution or memorandum & articles of association

▶ Accounts or a record of income and expenditure for your group, and sound plans for managing your money (if you are a new group you will need to provide a bank statement and a spending plan)

▶ A safeguarding policy if you are working with children or young people (under 18) or if you are working with vulnerable adults

During 2011/12 the foundation had assets of £13.6 million and an income of £6.9 million. Grants to 634 organisations totalled £3.9 million.

Beneficiaries across all programmes included: Participle (£150,000); Oasis Children's Venture (£50,000); Women like Us (£32,000); Food Cycle (£25,000); Lambeth Mind (£7,500); Camden Plus Credit Union Ltd (£5,000); Voluntary Associations Support (£3,500); Kongolese Centre for Information and Advice (£2,300); Biggin Hill Community Association (£1,500); Southside Young Leaders Academy and Race on the Agenda (£1,000 each); and Hammersmith and Fulham Older Persons Project (£750).

During the year the foundation made grants to individuals for the first time in recent years. There were 137 grants to individuals made totalling £140,000.

Exclusions

Generally, no grants for political groups or activities which promote religion.

Applications

As the foundation offers funds on behalf of different donors, you may apply to each and every programme for which your group is eligible. However, the criteria do vary for each grant programme, so be sure to read the guidance carefully. If you are unsure about your eligibility, call the grants team on Tel: 020 7582 5117 before making an application.

What the foundation looks for in an application:

▶ Demonstration of need
▶ Sound governance
▶ Sound financial management
▶ Sound project planning
▶ Good partnership working
▶ Strong capacity and ability to deliver

Application forms, guidance notes and deadlines specific to each programme are available from the foundation's website.

Information gathered from:

Accounts; annual report; Charity Commission record; funder's website; guidelines for applicants.

The London Marathon Charitable Trust

Sport, recreation and leisure
£4.4 million (2011/12)

Beneficial area

London and any area where London Marathon stages an event (South Northamptonshire).

Correspondent: David Golton, Secretary, Kestrel House, 111 Heath Road, Twickenham TW1 4AH (tel: 020 8892 6646; email: lmct@ffleach.co.uk)

Trustees: Ruth Dombey; Simon Cooper; Dame Mary Peters; Joyce Smith; John Graves; James Dudley Henderson Clarke; John Austin; John Disley; Sir Rodney Walker; John Bryant; Richard Lewis; John Spurling.

CC Number: 283813

The trust was formed to distribute the surplus income donated to the charity by its subsidiary, the London Marathon Ltd, which organises the annual London Marathon and other such events each year. Funds are given for much-needed recreational facilities across the city, as well as in areas where London Marathon Ltd stages an event. This currently includes South Northamptonshire – Silverstone.

Note: the trust has no connection to the fundraising efforts of the individuals involved in the race, who raise over £40 million each year for their chosen good causes.

In 2011/12 the trust had assets of £16 million, an income of £20 million and gave grants totalling £4.4 million.

Most of the grants made during the year were in Greater London, with around half being made through borough councils.

Beneficiaries include: LM Playing Field – Greenford (£263,000); London 2012 Legacy – Aquatic Lift (£243,000); LB Waltham Forest – London Playing Fields Foundation (£176,000); LB Enfield – Queen Elizabeth Stadium (£150,000); LB

Southwark – Camberwell Baths (£100,000); LB Lambeth – Clapham Common Skate Park (£75,000); LB Richmond – Putney Town Rowing Club (£50,000); RB Kingston – Dickerage Adventure Playground (£45,000); LB Richmond – Royal Deer Park (£30,000); and Chance to Shine – cricket markings in schools (£9,000).

The charity also spent £1.8 million on staff costs including the payment of eight employees earning £60,000 to £250,000 during the year.

Exclusions

Grants cannot be made to 'closed' clubs or schools, unless the facility is available for regular public use. No grants are made for recurring or revenue costs. Individuals are not supported.

Applications

On a form available from the correspondent. Applications are welcomed from London Boroughs and independent organisations, clubs and charities. The trustees meet once a year; the closing date is usually the end of August.

Information gathered from:

Accounts; annual report; Charity Commission record.

The Lord's Taverners

Youth cricket, increasing participation, equipment and facilities, disability and disadvantage
£2.8 million (2011/12)

Beneficial area

Unrestricted, in practice, UK.

Correspondent: Nicky Pemberton, Head of Foundation, 10 Buckingham Place, London SW1E 6HX (tel: 020 7821 2828; fax: 020 7821 2829; email: contact@ lordstaverners.org; website: www. lordstaverners.org)

Trustees: John Ayling; John Barnes; Leo Callow; Mike Gatting; Robert Powell; Sally Surridge; Tom Rodwell; Robert Griffiths; Christine Colbeck; Martin Smith; Marilyn Fry.

CC Number: 306054

The Lord's Taverners started life as a club founded in 1950 by a group of actors who used to enjoy a pint watching the cricket from the old Tavern pub at Lord's. In the early days, the money raised each year was given to the National Playing Fields Association (now the Fields in Trust), whom the Taverners still support, to fund artificial cricket pitches. Since then the Taverners has developed into both a club and a charity. There are now three fundraising groups

– Lord's Taverners, Lady Taverners and Young Lord's Taverners. The trust has 28 regional groupings (all volunteer) throughout the UK and Northern Ireland. The Lady Taverners has 24 Regions.

The principal activities and charitable mission continue to be 'to give young people, particularly those with special needs, a sporting chance'.

Activities

The trust distributes funding on the following basis: around 50% of the funds awarded by the trust are given to cricket projects for equipment and competitions for those young people playing the game at grass roots level in schools and clubs. £47,000 is to be granted to Fields in Trust, whose mission is to ensure that everyone across the country has access to outdoor space for sport, play and recreation. The balance of funds is then to be distributed as follows: 70% to supplying minibuses to special needs organisations; and 30% to provide sports and play equipment to organisations looking after young people with special needs.

The trust's mission is carried out by using specially adapted forms of cricket and cricket equipment to engage with young people and enable the delivery of a variety of youth development programmes:

- Delivery, management and support of inner city, disability and other youth cricket activities and competitions
- Supporting the installation of non-turf pitches to increase the opportunities for young people to play and donation of hundreds of cricket equipment bags to communities, clubs and school teams across the UK
- Pathways for young people into employment, education and training and other positive activities including mainstream cricket

And, supporting sporting and recreational activities for young people with special needs:

- Supplying specially adapted minibuses and sport wheelchairs, giving young people vital transportation and access to sport and recreation
- Creating new pathways for their participation, development and competition in sport
- Providing play, sports and sensory equipment

The Lord's Taverners is recognised by the England and Wales Cricket Board (ECB) as the official national charity for recreational cricket. Most cricket grants are distributed in association with the ECB. An annual grant is also made to the English Schools Cricket Association.

The trust's charitable giving is channelled through five key funds:

- Youth cricket at grass roots level
- The supply of specially adapted minibuses
- Sports wheelchair sponsorship scheme
- Disability sport and play
- The Brian Johnston Memorial Trust

See the website for more details of specific programmes.

Grantmaking in 2011/12

In 2011/12 the charity had assets of £3.4 and an income of £6.2 million. 'Grant aid' totalled £2.8 million, broken down in the accounts as follows:

Minibuses	£1.3 million
Grants to youth cricket	£937,000
Sports and recreation for young people with disabilities	£273,000
Disability Sports Appeal Grants	£156,000
Kit Aid	£105,000
Brian Johnston Memorial Fund	£41,000

A list of beneficiaries was not included in the accounts.

Exclusions

Youth cricket

Only one application in any 12 month period. The following is not normally grant aided:

- Building or renovation of pavilions
- Sight screens
- Bowling machines
- Mowers/rollers
- Overseas tours
- Clothing
- Refreshments
- Trophies

Sport for young people with special needs

The following will not normally be considered for a grant:

- Capital costs
- General grants
- Running costs including salaries
- Individuals (although applications will be considered for equipment to enable an individual to participate in a team/group recreational activity)
- Holidays/overseas tours

Minibuses

Homes, schools and organisations catering for young people with special needs under the age of 25 years, are entitled to only one minibus per location, although applications are accepted for a replacement.

Applications

The trust committee meets regularly to review applications for grant aid. All applications must be presented on the appropriate application forms and should be submitted to the secretary. See the grantmaking section for further information on individual programmes.

Application forms with detailed application instructions are available from the secretary or on the trust's website.

Information gathered from:

Accounts; annual report; Charity Commission record; funder's website.

John Lyon's Charity

Children and young people in north and west London
£5.3 million (2011/12)
Beneficial area

The London boroughs of Barnet, Brent, Camden, Ealing, Kensington and Chelsea, Hammersmith and Fulham, Harrow and the Cities of London and Westminster.

Correspondent: S. Whiddington, Chair of Grants Committee, The Grants Office, 45 Cadogan Gardens, London SW3 2TB (tel: 020 7591 3330; fax: 020 7591 3412; email: info@johnlyonscharity.org.uk; website: www.johnlyonscharity.org.uk)

Trustee: The Governors of the John Lyon School, Harrow.

CC Number: 237725

This is one of the largest local educational charities in the country, supporting both formal and informal educational activities of every sort. Its budgets vary greatly from year to year for historical reasons, and from one part of its beneficial area to another. There are, however, significant cross-borough grants.

The charity began in the late 16th century when John Lyon donated his 48 acre Maida Vale farm as an endowment for the upkeep of two roads from London to Harrow and Kenton. In 1991, the charity was given discretion to use the revenue from the endowment to benefit the inhabitants of the London boroughs through which these roads passed.

The charity is an independent branch of the larger Harrow Foundation which also governs Harrow and the John Lyon schools. The charity makes over 60 substantial new grants a year, for amounts normally between £2,000 and £50,000 and there are a further 50 or so for amounts of £2,000 or less under its small grants programme. Larger awards may be for periods of up to three years.

The following guidelines are offered by the charity:

John Lyon's Charity gives grants to groups and organisations for the benefit of children and young people up to the age of 25 who live in nine boroughs in northwest London: Barnet, Brent, Camden, Ealing, Hammersmith & Fulham, Harrow, Kensington & Chelsea and the Cities of London and Westminster.

Grants from the charity are restricted to these areas and are made in accordance with certain rules covering allocation and consultation with these local authorities.

In general the charity only gives grants to groups and organisations which are registered charities or who have automatic charitable status. Occasionally grants are awarded to local authorities in the charity's beneficial area who are working with voluntary sector partners. The charity does not give grants to individuals.

We give grants to:
▷ Support education and training, particularly for young adults
▷ Broaden horizons and encourage an appreciation of the value of cultural diversity through activities such as dance, drama, music, creative-writing and the visual arts
▷ Provide child-care, support for parents, help where parental support is lacking
▷ Enhance recreation through sport, youth clubs and play schemes
▷ Help young people achieve their full potential
▷ Develop new opportunities for young people

What we fund
▷ Core costs
▷ Salary costs
▷ Direct project costs
▷ Apprenticeships
▷ Equipment
▷ Buildings & refurbishments
▷ Bursaries

Main Grants Programme
Grants can be up to three years in length, subject to monitoring reports and the specific approval of the Trustee. There is no maximum grant amount. Applications for Main Grants are considered by the Trustee three times a year in March, June and November.

Access to Opportunity
Applications are invited from groups of schools, in partnership with local voluntary organisations where appropriate, for programmes aimed at supporting their most challenged pupils, strengthening links with home life and co-coordinating the support of other available professionals. We anticipate that a typical application might centre on a key worker, based at the lead school, whose brief would be to project manage support for a caseload of named individual young people. A typical proposal might cost £25,000–£50,000. Funding will be available for a **maximum of three years**.

Small Grants Programme
There are no deadlines for applications made under the Small Grants Programme. Requests are considered up to six times per year. The maximum amount awarded under the Small Grants Programme is £5,000 for one year only. If a repeat request is expected in the following year applicants may be referred to the Main Grants Programme.

Access to the Arts Fund
The Access to the Arts Fund is open to all state primary schools in the charity's nine boroughs.

Grants awarded under this programme are available to assist primary schools in accessing and taking part in arts activities at the many high class institutions in London. Activities could include visits to the theatre, a musical experience or to a museum or art gallery. To be eligible the school must provide a clear rationale for the activity, explain how it will add value to the school experience and demonstrate an existing commitment to the arts.

Successful applications must include the following:
▷ Evidence that this activity is in addition to, and not a replacement of, existing annual arts activities
▷ A clear rationale for taking part in the activity
▷ Details of how it will add value to the children's school experience

In 2011/12 the charity had assets of £243 million and an income of £6.5 million. Grants were given totalling £5.3 million and were broken down by programme area as follows:

Arts in education	£1.1 million
Education and learning	£842,000
Youth clubs	£761,000
Bursaries	£654,000
Children and families	£626,000
Emotional wellbeing	£358,000
SEN and disability	£353,000
Sport	£226,000
Training	£221,000
Youth Issues	£168,000
Other	£5,000

The charity also gives a helpful breakdown of its grants by the purpose for which they were made:

Direct project costs	£2.2 million
Salaries	£1 million
Core costs	£914,000
Bursaries	£694,000
Buildings and refurbishment	£455,000
Other	£5,000
Arts fund	£3,000
Equipment	£3,000

The charity's website lists the beneficiaries of the 20 largest grants during the year. They were: London Sports Trust and Brent Play Association (£70,000); Harrow Club W10 (£65,000); Skillforce (£53,000); Donmar Warehouse Projects Ltd and HAFPAC (£50,000); St Gregory's Catholic Science College (£48,000); National Numeracy Trust (£46,000); Royal Opera House (£44,000); Carlton primary School (£39,000); HAFAD (£36,000); Tricycle Theatre Company, Mousetrap Theatre Projects and Royal Institution of Great Britain (£35,000 each); Drayton Green Primary School (£34,000); Place2Be, Wigmore Town Hall, Brandon Centre, Tender and Local Employment Access Projects (£30,000 each).

Exclusions
Grants are restricted to the London boroughs of Harrow, Barnet, Brent, Ealing, Camden, City of London, City of Westminster, Hammersmith and Fulham and Kensington and Chelsea.

Grants are not made:
▷ To individuals
▷ To national organisations
▷ To not-for-profit organisations that are not registered charities
▷ To schools that have not yet been inspected by Ofsted
▷ To hospitals, hospices or primary care trusts
▷ To faith schools with a closed admissions policy
▷ For research, unless it is action research designed to lead directly to the advancement of practical activities in the community
▷ For lobbying or campaigning
▷ For endowment funds
▷ For mother tongue teaching
▷ For feasibility studies
▷ For medical care and resources
▷ In response to general charitable appeals, unless they can be shown to be of specific benefit to children and young people in one or more of the geographical areas listed
▷ As direct replacements for the withdrawal of funds by statutory authorities for activities which are primarily the responsibility of central or local government
▷ To umbrella organisations to distribute to projects which are already in receipt of funds from the charity
▷ For the promotion of religion or politics
▷ For telephone helplines
▷ For advice and information services
▷ To housing associations
▷ For school journeys or trips abroad
▷ For capital for educational institutions
▷ For IT equipment
▷ For bursaries for higher education
▷ For programmes which fall under PHSE, Citizenship or Social Enterprise
▷ For conservation, environmental projects and therapeutic gardens
▷ For core costs for umbrella bodies or second tier organisations
▷ For grants to registered charities that have applied on behalf of organisations that are not registered with the Charity Commission

Applications
The charity's main and small grants and access to opportunity programmes have a two stage application process:

Stage One – Initial Proposal
Write to the Grants Office with the following information:

- A summary of the main purpose of the project
- Details of the overall amount requested
- The timescale of your project
- Some indication of how funds from the charity would be allocated

The trust has produced guidelines on how best to write the initial proposal which can be accessed on its website.

Trustees meet to decide three times a year in March, June and November. There is no stage two for small grants of less than £2,000. Applications are made by initial proposal letter and the grants team will be in touch if more information is required.

Stage Two – Application Form
If your Initial Proposal is assessed positively, you will be advised whether you will need to complete an application form. Forms are required for all applications to the Main Grants Programme, Access to Opportunity and for requests of over £2,000 to the Small Grants Programme.

If you qualify for Stage Two you will be advised by your Grants Officer when your application form must be returned.

The John Lyon's Access to the Arts Fund

The John Lyon Access to the Arts Fund has a **single stage** application process and requests are made by application form. Applications can be made at any time.

Application forms are available via the charity's website.

Information gathered from:

Accounts; annual report; Charity Commission record; guidelines for applicants; funder's website.

The Madeline Mabey Trust

Medical research, children's welfare and education, humanitarian aid
About £414,000 (2011/12)

Beneficial area
UK and overseas particularly Asia.

Correspondent: Joanna Singeisen, Trustee, Madeline Mabey Trust, Woodview, Tolcarne Road, Beacon, Camborne TR14 9AB (tel: 01209 710304; website: www.mabeygroup.co.uk/about/heritage/the-madeline-mabey-trust)

Trustees: Alan G. Daliday; Bridget A. Nelson; Joanna L. Singeisen.

CC Number: 326450

This trust was established in 1983 and is supported by the Mabey Group, a family owned British engineering company.

The principal areas of benefit continue to be the education and welfare of children both in the UK and overseas, humanitarian aid and medical research into the causes of and cures for life threatening illnesses. The trust favours identifying organisations itself, although it is willing to consider applications for grants. The intention is to fund organisations rather than individuals directly. The trust favours locations where Mabey companies operate.

In 2011/12 the trust had assets of £167,000 and an income of £225,000. 'Direct charitable expenditure' totalled £414,000.

A breakdown of the expenditure and a list of grants were not included in the accounts. There were 170 grants made during the year.

Beneficiaries have included: Cancer Research UK, the Education Engineering Trust, Save the Children, UNICEF, Barnardo's, the Disasters Emergency Committee, Help for Heroes and Great Ormond Street Children's Hospital.

Exclusions
No grants to individuals.

Applications
In writing to the correspondent. Note, unsuccessful applications are not acknowledged.

Information gathered from:
Accounts; annual report; Charity Commission record; company website.

The R. S. Macdonald Charitable Trust

Neurological conditions, visual impairment, community, family, children and animal welfare
£1.5 million (2011/12)

Beneficial area
Scotland.

Correspondent: Douglas Hamilton, Director, 21 Rutland Square, Edinburgh EH1 2BB (tel: 01312 284681; email: Dhamilton@rsmacdonald.com; website: www.rsmacdonald.com)

Trustees: Richard Sweetman; Richard K. Austin; Donald Bain; Fiona Patrick; John Rafferty.

SC Number: SC012710

Established in 1978, this is the trust of the late R S MacDonald, whose family founded the famous whisky distiller Glenmorangie plc in 1893. The value of the trust increased substantially in

2005/06 due to the realisation of shares in the company, which were sold to LVMH (Moët Hennessy Louis Vuitton), the proceeds of which having been reinvested.

The trust supports charities concerned with the following:
- Neurological conditions
- Visual impairment
- Child welfare
- Animal welfare

Six organisations are mentioned in the trust deed and these are often, but not always, supported. The trust is prepared to give very large grants to enable organisations to carry out major projects or develop ideas. The trust stated in its 2011/12 annual report that due to the cuts in national and local government funding and the consequent difficulties that the charity sector is facing:

> Trustees have agreed to use income which, in the period up to the judicial re-statement of its charitable objects, the Trust has been unable to disburse. The intention is that, all other things being equal, the Trust will maintain its awards to a total value of £1.5 million in each of the next two/three years.

In 2011/12 the trust had assets of £57 million and an income of £1.8 million. Grants totalled £1.5 million

Beneficiaries included: Capability Scotland (£60,000); Muir Maxwell Trust (£40,000); Visability (£36,000); Deafblind Scotland and University of Edinburgh (£25,000 each); Sense Scotland (£15,000); Alcohol Focus Scotland (£13,000); Hidden Gardens Trust and Whizz-Kidz (£10,000 each); Rock Trust (£8,000); National Galleries of Scotland (£4,300).

Exclusions
Grants are not given to non-registered charities, individuals, for projects which have already started or been completed or for charitable organisations which are unable to demonstrate that they are delivering benefit in Scotland.

Applications
Applicants are invited to apply by letter; there is no application form. The trustees request that, except in relation to medical or social research, the application letter should not exceed two pages in length. It should explain (as appropriate) what and how the need to be addressed has been identified, the costs involved and the extent to which support has been sought from other sources, the outcome hoped for and how that outcome is to be measured. It should also demonstrate how the subject of the application meets the charitable objects of the trust. Where an application is for help with revenue costs for a particular service there should be an explanation of how this will continue

following the expiry of the award. Application guidelines, information and award conditions are available from the website.

Along with your letter you may enclose separate papers, providing background information and/or more detailed financial information. If there is a current DVD providing an insight into the work of your organisation you may wish to submit this.

In addition to the application letter you are required to complete and submit (a) a copy of the applicant's most recently audited accounts and (b) an Organisation Information Sheet. This can be downloaded from the trust's website or obtained from the trust's secretary.

Applications will normally be considered at trustee meeting in May and November. Applications must be received no later than 31 March or 30 September for these meetings.

Percentage of awards given to new applicants: 53%.

Common applicant mistakes

'Failure to sign information sheet; failure to provide copy of their last accounts and failure to reflect the guidance for applicants which the trust has set out.'

Information gathered from:

Accounts; annual report; OSCR record; further information provided by the funder; funder's website.

The Machkevitch Foundation

General charitable purposes

Beneficial area

Worldwide.

Correspondent: Irina Alekseeva, Administrator, c/o ALM Services UK Ltd, 22 Bruton Street, London W1J 6QE (tel: 020 7758 9672; email: info@themachkevitchfoundation.org; website: www.themachkevitchfoundation.org)

Trustees: Anna Machkevitch; Alla Machkevitch; Yacoub-Frayem Boukhris.

CC Number: 1144156

Registered in October 2011, the foundation's objects are general charitable purposes. Anna Machkevitch is the daughter of Jewish billionaire Alexander Machkevitch, who has major mining interests in Africa and Europe. Unfortunately at the time of writing (December 2013) the foundation's first set of accounts were overdue with the Charity Commission.

Applications

In writing to the correspondent.

Information gathered from:

Charity Commission record.

The Mackintosh Foundation

Priority is given to the theatre and the performing arts. Also funded are children and education, medicine particularly research into cancer and HIV and AIDS, homelessness, community projects, the environment, refugees, and other charitable purposes

£473,000 (2011/12)

Beneficial area

Worldwide. In practice, mainly UK.

Correspondent: Richard Nibb, 1 Bedford Square, London WC1B 3RB (tel: 020 7637 8866; email: info@camack.co.uk)

Trustees: Sir Cameron Mackintosh, Chair; Nicholas Mackintosh; Nicholas Allott; D. Michael Rose; Robert Noble; Bart Peerless; Thomas Schonberg; F. Richard Pappas.

CC Number: 327751

The foundation was established in 1998 by the settlor, Sir Cameron Mackintosh, to advance education in the arts, particularly the performing arts of music and drama; to establish and maintain scholarships, bursaries and awards for proficiency in drama, music or ancillary performing arts; to promote research into the causes and treatment of HIV and AIDS and to relieve poverty, hardship and distress.

The foundation has endowed Oxford University at a cost of well over £1 million with a fund known as *The Cameron Mackintosh Fund for Contemporary Theatre*, part of which has been used to set up a Visiting Professorship of Contemporary Theatre at the university. It also provided a fund of £1 million over a period of ten years, to the Royal National Theatre, for revivals of classical stage musical productions under the auspices of the RNT.

Partnership funding of £500,000 over five years, has been provided by the foundation in respect of theatres and other organisations under the Art Council's *Arts for Everyone* scheme.

The foundation has also provided financial support to a number of projects in the United States including a major grant of US$1.5 million over five years to The Alliance of New American Musicals to support the creation and production of new plays by American writers and artists.

In 2011/12 the foundation had assets of £9.3 million, an income of £59,000 and gave grants totalling £473,000, broken down as follows:

Theatre and the performing arts	
Theatrical training and education	£103,000
Promotion of new theatrical and musical works	£100,000
Theatre buildings	£18,000
Theatre company development	£16,000
Theatre related pastoral care	£10,000
Children's theatre	£7,800
	£256,000
Medical	
Medical – general	£46,000
Medical – cancer	£39,000
Medical – HIV/AIDS	£7,700
	£93,000
Community projects	**£57,000**
Children and education	**£30,000**
Homelessness	**£21,000**
The Environment	**£17,000**

Beneficiaries during the year included: Mercury Musical Developments (£75,000); Royal Conservatoire of Scotland (£75,000); Charles Dickens Museum (£30,000); Soho Theatre Company (£16,000); Macmillan Cancer Support (£10,000); The Royal Theatrical Fund (£6,000); National Student Drama Festival Ltd (£5,000); Mayor of London's Fund for Young Musicians (£4,000); Leukaemia and Lymphoma Research (£3,000); The Amber Foundation, RSPB – Scotland and Sun and Moon Foundation (£2,500 each); and The Prince's Youth Business International (£2,200).

Exclusions

Religious or political activities are not supported. Apart from the foundation's drama award and some exceptions, applications from individuals are discouraged.

Applications

In writing to the correspondent outlining details of the organisation, details of the project for which funding is required and a breakdown of the costs involved. Supporting documentation should be kept to a minimum and an sae enclosed if materials are to be returned. The trustees meet in May and October in plenary session, but a grants committee meets weekly to consider grants of up to £10,000. The foundation responds to all applications in writing and the process normally takes between four to six weeks.

Information gathered from:

Accounts; annual report; Charity Commission record.

The MacRobert Trust

General

£535,000 (2011/12)

Beneficial area

UK, mainly Scotland.

Correspondent: Air Comm. R. W. Joseph, Administrator, Cromar, Tarland, Aboyne, Aberdeenshire AB34 4UD (tel: 01339 881444; email: vicky@themacroberttrust.org.uk; website: www.themacroberttrust.org.uk)

Trustees: S. Campbell; C. D. Crole; K. Davis; J. D. Fowlie; C. W. Pagan; J. C. Swan; J. H. Strickland; P. J. Hughesdon; C. Stevenson.

SC Number: SC031346

Summary

Originally several trusts established by Lady MacRobert in memory of her three sons who were all killed as aviators, the eldest in a civil air accident in 1938 and the middle and youngest as officer pilots in the Royal Air Force on operational sorties in 1941.

This trust was established on 6 April 2001 when the assets of the no longer operating MacRobert Trusts, a collection of four charitable trusts and two holding companies were merged into the new, single MacRobert Trust. The merging of these trusts has led to a decrease in management and administration cost and a general increase in grantmaking.

The trust has assets comprising of Douneside House (a holiday country house for serving and retired officers of the armed forces and their families) and an estate of 1,700 acres of woodland and 5,300 acres of farmland and associated residential properties let by the trust. The surplus income generated from these assets, following management and administration costs, is donated in grants.

Guidelines

The following guidelines are taken from the trust's website:

Lady MacRobert recognised that new occasions teach new duties and therefore the new trust deed gives wide discretionary powers to the trustees. The trust is reactive so, with very few exceptions, grants are made only in response to applications made through the correct channels.

The trustees reconsider their policy and practice of grant giving every five years. The beneficial area is United Kingdom-wide but preference is given to organisations in Scotland. Grants are normally made only to a recognised Scottish Charity or a recognised charity outside Scotland.

The current grantmaking themes are:

- Services and sea – support for the armed forces and mercantile marine, particularly accommodation and leisure facilities at Douneside House
- Education and training – educational grants to individuals and grants to schools, colleges, universities and other training institutions
- Children and youth – health, welfare and wellbeing of young people in particular charities addressing addiction, crime, homelessness, disadvantage and disability
- Science, engineering and technology – awards for engineering, grants for research and to support the study and practice of science engineering and technology
- Agriculture and horticulture – farming scholarships, horticultural and agricultural charities and sustainability research
- Tarland and the local area – environmental protection, public access to the countryside and the promotion of sport and health locally. Education, citizenship and community development locally and youth movements

The trust offers a very detailed breakdown of these categories on a document available from the trust's website.

Most grants are between £5,000 and £25,000 but larger awards, including capital grants, are sometimes given.

A small grants programme facilitates awards of up to £5,000. Occasionally recurring grants are made for periods of up to three years. The administrator also operates a small delegated fund which enables donations to be made quickly, currently with an upper limit of £1,000 per donation.

Grantmaking in 2011/12

In 2011/12 the trust had assets of £73 million and an income of £2.5 million. During the year the trust made grants totalling £535,000, broken down into the following categories:

Disability	£156,000
Services and sea	£78,000
Youth	£74,000
Science and technology	£57,000
Medical care	£51,000
Education*	£39,000
Community welfare	£23,000
Arts and music	£19,000
Ex-servicemen's housing and hospitals	£16,000
Tarland and Deeside	£13,000
Agriculture and horticulture	£11,000

Beneficiaries across all categories included: Northern Police Convalescent and Training Centre (£60,000); University Hospital Birmingham Charities (£50,000); L'Arche Edinburgh (£35,000); Community Service (£20,000); Alzheimer's Research UK and Gamelea Countryside Training Trust (£10,000 each); The National Deaf Children's Trust (£5,000); British Schools Exploring Society (£3,400) Cleveland Housing Advice Centre (£3,000); Girlguiding Scotland (£2,500); Royal Caledonian Horticultural Society (£1,000); St Thomas' Church, Aboyne (£800); Forces Help – Aberdeen (£570); and Fife Opera (£500).

*The education total includes £21,000 given in educational grants to individuals.

Exclusions

Grants are not normally provided for:

- Religious organisations (but attention will be given to youth/community services provided by them, or projects of general benefit to the whole community)
- Organisations based outside the United Kingdom
- Individuals
- General appeals or mailshots
- Political organisations
- Student bodies as opposed to universities
- Fee-paying schools, apart from an Educational Grants Scheme for children who are at, or who need to attend, a Scottish independent secondary school and for which a grant application is made through the Head Teacher
- Expeditions, except those made under the auspices of recognised bodies such as the British Schools Exploring Society (BSES)
- Community and village halls other than those local to Tarland and Deeside
- Departments within a university, unless the appeal gains the support of, and is channelled through, the principal

Applications

The application form and full guidelines can be downloaded from the trust's website. Application forms must be posted along with a cover letter and a full set of audited accounts.

The trustees meet to consider applications twice a year in March and November. To be considered, applications must be received for the March meeting by 31 October previously and for the October meeting by 31 May previously.

Time bars:

- Unsuccessful applicants must wait for at least one year from the time of being notified before re-applying
- Successful applicants must wait for at least two years from the time of receiving a donation before re-applying
- When a multi-year donation has been awarded, the time bar applies from the date of the final instalment

▶ Withdrawn applications do not normally face a time bar

The trust stresses the importance of including an informative covering letter; completing *all* sections of the application form and asks that applicants maintain a process of dialogue with the trust: 'We deal with many hundreds of worthy applications each year. If we have to chase you for information, you will understand that our interest might wane.'

A further list of additional guidance and feedback on the application procedure is available on the trust's website.

Applicants are informed of the trustees' decision, and if successful, payments are made immediately after each meeting.

Percentage of awards given to new applicants: between 10% and 20%.

Common applicant mistakes

'Not completing (or signing) application form; not reading guidelines on our website; not providing an informative covering letter; not enclosing annual report or accounts/financial statements; not providing regular fundraising updates.'

Information gathered from:

Accounts; annual report; OSCR record; guidelines for applicants; further information provided by the funder; funder's website.

The Manifold Charitable Trust

Education, historic buildings, environmental conservation, general

£322,000 (2012)

Beneficial area
UK.

Correspondent: Helen Niven, Studio Cottage, Windsor Great Park, Windsor, Berkshire SL4 2HP (email: themanifoldtrust@gmail.com)

Trustee: Manifold Trustee Company Ltd.

CC Number: 229501

This trust was established in 1962 for general charitable purposes. It had previously focused much attention on the preservation of churches, however following the death in 2007 of its founder, Sir John Smith, the trust is now allocating most of its grants for educational purposes. Grants to Eton College, the largest beneficiary, are provided to 'enable boys whose families otherwise would not be able to support the fees to be educated at Eton College.' The trust still makes grants to the Historic Churches Preservation Trust for

onward distribution to churches; however it would seem that the amount has been reduced on previous years.

As noted in the past, the trust continues to make grants in excess of its income, preferring to 'meet the present needs of other charities rather than reserve money for the future'.

In 2010 the trust had assets of £8.6 million and an income of £490,000. There were 39 grants made totalling £322,000, distributed as follows:

Education, research and the arts	87%
Repairs to churches and their contents	10%
Other causes	3%

92% of grants were of £1,000 or less, and only 5% were for £10,000 by number.

Unfortunately a full list of beneficiaries was not included in the accounts. However, the trustees do acknowledge that most of the grant total was given to Eton College. Eton College has also been a beneficiary in previous years and other past recipients have included: Historic Churches Preservation Trust; Thames Hospice Care; Imperial College; Berkeley Castle Charitable Trust; Maidenhead Heritage Trust; Berkshire Medical Heritage Centre; Gislingham Parochial Church Council; Household Cavalry Museum Trust; Brompton Ralph Parochial Church Council; Morrab Library; Richmond Building Preservation Society; Askham Parochial Church Council and Westray Heritage Trust.

Exclusions

Applications are not considered for improvements to churches as this is covered by a block grant to the Historic Churches Preservation Trust. The trust regrets that it does not give grants to individuals for any purpose.

Applications

The trust has no full-time staff, therefore general enquiries and applications for grants should be made in writing only, by post or by fax and not by telephone. The trust does not issue application forms. Applications should be made to the correspondent in writing and should:

▶ State how much money it is hoped to raise
▶ If the appeal is for a specific project state also (a) how much it will cost (b) how much of this cost will come from the applicant charity's existing funds (c) how much has already been received or promised from other sources and (d) how much is therefore still being sought
▶ List sources of funds to which application has been or is intended to be made (for example local authorities, or quasi-governmental sources, such as the national lottery)
▶ If the project involves conservation of a building, send a photograph of it

and a note (or pamphlet) about its history
▶ Send a copy of the charity's latest income and expenditure account and balance sheet

Applications are considered twice a month, and a reply is sent to most applicants (whether successful or not) who have written a letter rather than sent a circular.

Information gathered from:

Accounts; annual report; Charity Commission record.

The Manoukian Charitable Foundation

Social welfare, education, medical, the arts, 'Armenian matters'

£230,000 (2012)

Beneficial area
Worldwide.

Correspondent: Anthony Bunker, Trustee, c/o Berwin Leighton Paisner, Adelaide House, London Bridge, London EC4R 9HA (tel: 020 7760 1000)

Trustees: Tamar Manoukian; Anthony Bunker; Steven Press; Armen Sarkissian.

CC Number: 1084065

Set up in 2000, the foundation has received donations from sources associated with the Manoukian family.

The following extract is taken from the foundation's 2012 accounts:

The objects of the charity are the promotion of general charitable purposes; the trustees give particular emphasis to projects with medical, educational or cultural aspects and those that relate to Armenian matters, although they consider applications for other charitable purposes.

Applications are considered on the basis of whether they meet the general aims of the foundation and the nature of the project concerned. The foundation will consider providing assistance to projects that may be partly funded by others if this will enable the project to proceed. The trustees have tended to give greater consideration to educational and cultural projects as well as those which are intended to relieve poverty, illness and suffering.

Funding is given in the following areas:
▶ Social services and relief
▶ Education and training
▶ Medical research and care
▶ Culture and the arts

In 2012 the foundation has assets of £6,000 and an income of £275,000 from donations. Grants were made to eight organisations totalling £230,000.

The grant recipients were: Cherie Blair Foundation for Women (£100,000);

Elton John Aids Foundation (£55,000); Give a Child a Toy (£30,000); Mission Enfance (£7,600); Our Lady of Lebanon Church and English Heritage (£5,000 each); and NSPCC and The Eve Appeal (£1,000 each).

£25,000 was given in individuals grants for 'religious, cultural and educational purposes'.

Applications

'Requests for grants are received from the general public and charitable and other organisations through their knowledge of the activities of the foundation and through personal contacts of the settlor and the trustees.' The trustees meet at least once per year.

Information gathered from:

Accounts; annual report; Charity Commission record.

Marshall's Charity

Parsonage and church improvements
£745,000 (2011/12)

Beneficial area
England and Wales with preference for Kent, Surrey, Lincolnshire and Southwark.

Correspondent: Catherine Dawkins, Clerk to the Trustees, Marshall House, 66 Newcomen Street, London SE1 1YT (tel: 020 7407 2979; fax: 020 7403 3969; email: grantoffice@marshalls.org.uk; website: www.marshalls.org.uk)

Trustees: Anthea Nicholson; Colin Bird; David Lang; Michael Dudding; Colin Stenning; Stephen Clark; Gina Isaac; Bill Eason; Jeremy Hammant; John Heawood; Surbhi Malhotra; Revd Jonathan Rust; Ven. Christine Hardman; Tony Guthrie; Lesley Bosman.

CC Number: 206780

The charity supports parsonage buildings throughout England and Wales, helps with the upkeep of Anglican churches and cathedrals in Kent, Surrey and Lincolnshire (as the counties were defined in 1855), supports the parish of Christ Church, Southwark and makes grants for education to Marshall's Educational Foundation. Special consideration is given to parishes in urban priority areas. Further information on the types of grant available can be found on the charity's website.

Grants to churches are usually between £3,000 and £5,000, though they can be higher. The majority of grants to parsonages are for up to £4,000. Loans are also sometimes made to churches, at an interest rate of 3%.

In 2012 the charity had assets of £16 million and an income of £1.2 million. 230 Grants were made totalling £745,000, distributed as per the settlors' will:

Parsonages	£419,000
Repair of churches	£156,000
Christ Church, Southwark	£59,000
Marshall's Educational Foundation	£30,000

Churches receiving grants included: Boughton under Blean – SS Peter and Paul; Canterbury Cathedral; Holmwood – St Mary Magdalene; Loose – All Saints; Spalding – St Paul; Sutton – Christ Church; Utterby – St Andrew and Welton – St Mary (£5,000 each); Hernhill – St Michael (£4,000); Mereworth – St Lawrence (£2,000); and Goodnestone – Holy Cross (£1,000). A full list of churches receiving grants can be found on the charity's website.

Exclusions
No grants to churches outside the counties of Kent, Surrey and Lincolnshire, as defined in 1855. No church funding for the following:

▶ Cost of church halls and meeting rooms
▶ Kitchens
▶ Decorations, unless they form part of qualifying repair or improvement work
▶ Furniture and fittings
▶ Work to bells, brasses or clocks
▶ Private chapels or monuments
▶ Stained glass, although work to repair ferramenta can be supported
▶ Grounds, boundary walls and fences
▶ External lighting

Applications
Applicants should write a letter or send an email to the correspondent, giving the name and location of the Church and a brief (30 – 40 words maximum) description of the proposed work. If appropriate the charity will then send out an application form which should be completed and returned within three months. Applicants will also be visited by the surveyor who will submit a report which will be submitted to the committee along with the completed application form. Applications for parsonage grants should be made by the relevant Diocesan Parsonage Board. Trustees usually meet in January, April, July and October. Application forms become available in January for each year.

Percentage of awards given to new applicants: between 40% and 50%.

Common applicant mistakes
'Not eligible – wrong denomination or geographical area.'

Information gathered from:
Accounts; annual report; Charity Commission record; further information provided by the funder; funder's website.

Mayfair Charities Ltd

Orthodox Judaism
£2.8 million (2011/12)

Beneficial area
UK and overseas.

Correspondent: Mark Jenner, Secretary, Freshwater House, 158–162 Shaftesbury Avenue, London WC2H 8HR (tel: 020 7836 1555)

Trustees: Benzion S. E. Freshwater, Chair; D. Davis; Solomon I. Freshwater.

CC Number: 255281

Established in 1968, the trust makes grants to Orthodox Jewish colleges and institutions for the advancement of religion and education and to other organisations for the Relief of poverty, in the UK and Israel. It largely appears to be a vehicle for the philanthropic activities of property investor Benzion Freshwater, who is closely connected with the management of some of the major beneficiary organisations.

'In recent years, the trustees have decided to support certain major projects which, during the year under review and subsequently, have received substantial financial grants from the company. At the present time the trustees have entered into commitments for the financial support of colleges and institutions which would absorb approximately £7 million over the next five years.' This statement has been in the trust's accounts for several years, presumably indicating that major commitments are made each year on a rolling basis.

In 2011/12 the trust had assets of £70 million and an income of £13 million, mostly from donations. Grants were made to over 300 organisations totalling £2.8 million, broken down as follows:

There are no set amounts for sizes of grants – several substantial donations are made and many organisations received small grants for a little as a few hundred pounds. A list of beneficiaries was unavailable.

Advancement of religion and education	£2.1 million
Relief of poverty	£838,000

Previous beneficiaries include: SOFT; Beth Jacob Grammar School For Girls Ltd; Merkaz Lechinuch Torani; Ohr Akiva Institute; Kollel Chibas Yerushalayim; Mesivta Letzeirim; Chevras Maoz Ladal; Congregation

Ichud Chasidim; Chaye Olam Institute; United Talmudical Association; Talmud Torah Zichron Gavriel; Friends of Bobov; Regent Charities Ltd; Comet Charities Ltd; Woodstock Sinclair Trust; Yesodei Hatorah School; Beis Aharon Trust; Ezer Mikodesh Foundation; Gateshead Jewish Teachers Training College; Edgware Foundation; Heritage House; Kiryat Sanz Jerusalem; and PAL Charitable Trust.

Applications

In writing to the correspondent.

Information gathered from:

Accounts; annual report; Charity Commission record.

The Medlock Charitable Trust

Education, health, welfare

£2.6 million (2011/12)

Beneficial area

Overwhelmingly the areas of Bath and Boston in Lincolnshire.

Correspondent: David Medlock, Trustee, c/o Hebron and Medlock Ltd, St Georges Lodge, 33 Oldfield Road, Bath, Avon BA2 3ND (tel: 01225 428221)

Trustees: Leonard Medlock; Jacqueline Medlock; David Medlock; Mark Goodman.

CC Number: 326927

The trust describes its grantmaking policy as follows:

> The trustees have identified the City of Bath and the borough of Boston as the principal but not exclusive areas in which the charity is and will be proactive. These areas have been specifically chosen as the founder of the charity has strong connections with the City of Bath, the home of the charity, and has family connections of long standing with the borough of Boston.
>
> To date the charity has supported and funded a number of projects in these areas by making substantial grants. These grants have been made to fund projects in the areas of education, medicine, research and social services all for the benefit of the local community. During the year, the trustees also receive many applications for assistance from many diverse areas in the United Kingdom. These are all considered sympathetically.

In 2011/12 the trust had assets of £27 million and an income of £832,000. Grants were made to organisations totalling £2.6 million.

A grant of £1 million was given to the Royal University Hospital in Bath towards the £5 million fundraising target for improved oncology facilities.

Other beneficiaries included: King Edward's School (Junior) (£400,000); The Boston Stump Restoration Trust (£180,000); The Forever Friends Appeal (£50,000); Kind Edward's School, Bath (£106,000); Somerset Masonic Charity (£50,000); Bristol Rugby Community Foundation (£20,000); The Central Amenities Fund, HMS Drake (£10,000); Bath Mencap and Avon Wildlife Trust (£5,000 each); Housing, Training and Support Ltd and Furniture Re-Use Network (£1,000 each); and Daylight Plus Club (£500).

Exclusions

No grants to individuals or students.

Applications

In writing to the correspondent.

Percentage of awards given to new applicants: between 10% and 20%.

Common applicant mistakes

'Individuals apply despite not qualified or out of our geographical area.'

Information gathered from:

Accounts; annual report; Charity Commission record; further information provided by the funder.

The Melow Charitable Trust

Jewish

£1.1 million (2011)

Beneficial area

UK and overseas.

Correspondent: Mr J. Low, Administrator, 21 Warwick Grove, London E5 9HX (tel: 020 8806 1549)

Trustees: Miriam Spitz; Esther Weiser.

CC Number: 275454

The trust makes grants to Jewish charities both in the UK and overseas. At the time of writing (December 2013) the trust's 2012 accounts were overdue with the Charity Commission.

In 2011 the trust had assets of £12 million, an income of £1.7 million and gave grants totalling £1.1 million, broken down as follows:

Needy persons	£346,000
Religious institutions	£344,000
General	£243,000
Education	£83,000
Schools	£60,000
Publication of religious books	£25,000
Talamundical colleges	£21,000
Synagogues	£17,000
Integrated school	£250

The largest grants were listed in the accounts: Ezer V'Hatzalah Ltd (£314,000); Lolev Charitable Trust (£179,000); Friends of Kollel Samtar (Antwerp) Ltd (£107,000); and

Rehabilitation Trust and Asser Bishvil Foundation (£100,000 each).

Applications

In writing to the correspondent.

Information gathered from:

Accounts; Charity Commission record.

Mercaz Torah Vechesed Ltd

Orthodox Jewish

£525,000 (2011/12)

Beneficial area

Worldwide.

Correspondent: Joseph Ostreicher, Secretary, 28 Braydon Road, London N16 6QB (tel: 020 8880 5366)

Trustees: Joseph Ostreicher; Mordche David Rand.

CC Number: 1109212

The charity was formed in 2005 for the advancement of the Orthodox Jewish faith, Orthodox Jewish religious education, and the relief of poverty and infirmity amongst members of the Orthodox Jewish community.

In 2011/12 the charity had an income of £491,000 from donations. Grants were made totalling £525,000. Unfortunately further information was not available in the charity's accounts.

Applications

In writing to the correspondent.

Information gathered from:

Accounts; annual report; Charity Commission record.

The Mercers' Charitable Foundation

General welfare, education, Christianity, heritage and the arts

£11.8 million (2011/12)

Beneficial area

UK; strong preference for London and the West Midlands. The foundation is keen to stress that it currently has geographical restrictions on its welfare and educational grantmaking. See individual programme information for details.

Correspondent: The Clerk, Mercers' Hall, Ironmonger Lane, London EC2V 8HE (tel: 020 7726 4991; email: info@mercers.co.uk; website: www. mercers.co.uk)

Trustee: The Mercers' Company.

CC Number: 326340

The Mercers' Company has several trusts, the main one being the Mercers' Charitable Foundation. The foundation was established in 1983 to make grants and donations for the benefit of a wide range of charitable purposes including welfare, education, the arts, heritage and religion. Its primary source of income is gift aid donations from the Mercers' Company. On 1 August 2008 the Mercers' Company Educational Trust Fund transferred all of its assets and liabilities to the foundation.

The foundation seeks to support a range of organisations with the common theme of providing effective services and facilities to those in need and to strengthen communities. Whist continuing to support small grass roots organisations, the foundation has developed relationships with some much larger organisations, complementing work that is funded by statutory bodies.

The foundation runs a number of responsive grantmaking programmes, each with agreed guidelines and each year identifies a small number of organisations working within the key programme areas who are then invited to submit proposals for the larger grants. In most cases the work takes place in London or the West Midlands. These proposals are subject to detailed scrutiny by the specialist committees and the executive staff. The grantmaking committees each meet a minimum of four times a year to discuss applications and recommend grants to the trustees.

The company has several categories of grantmaking. The following descriptions of funding categories are taken from guidance available on the foundation's website.

Guidelines

The following guidelines are taken from the trust's website:

General Welfare

The Mercers' Company supports inclusive grassroots and front-line charities that work to improve the lives of disadvantaged and marginalised people.

What we fund:

Social Welfare projects that:
- Provide help for those with special needs and
- Support the carers and families of those with special needs

Family Welfare projects that:
- Support vulnerable families by helping to improve parenting skills and develop more resilient children

Youth Support work that:
- Promotes the effective development of young people outside school, particularly through local youth clubs
- Prepares disadvantaged young people, able bodied or with special needs, for adult life by offering positive activities

that enable them to reach their full potential
- Supports young people through important transitions: leaving school, leaving care, entering and sustaining employment

Care for the Elderly projects that:
- Provide care and support for older people
- Develop improved services for older people, particularly the frail and isolated
- Improves health outcomes for older people

Assistance in this area is restricted to a geographical area within the M25, particularly the inner London Boroughs.

Education

The Company makes a number of grants to improve the availability and quality of education for children and young adults. These grants are focused on young people from the ages of 5–25, particularly in London, and in the West Midland areas of Walsall, Sandwell and Telford & Wrekin. Applicants must be UK registered charities, UK exempt charities, or state schools and colleges.

The Company gives priority to work that:
- Encourages participation in science, maths and technology
- Improves educational achievement, particularly for young people aged 5–19;
- Offers educational opportunities for underachieving groups
- Enriches educational opportunity through innovative projects that use art, drama, dance, music and sport; and
- Builds students' social capital, confidence and life skills
- Encourage the study of languages, particularly for children aged 5–11

The trust may also support work that:
- Promotes the effective management of schools and colleges, for the direct benefit of pupils
- Provides help for children and young adults with special educational needs, including the development of gifted and talented young people
- Provides ways of increasing parental and community support for learning; and
- Encourages educational progression, the acquisition of vocational skills and participation in Higher Education.

Advancement of the Christian Religion

In its work to advance and support the Christian faith, the Mercers' Company invites grant appeals from a wide variety of sources. These need not be exclusively from Anglican organisations, but we discourage appeals from overseas unless there is a UK charitable involvement. Appeals may be broadly grouped into those relating to buildings and those connected with people.

Buildings

We consider appeals from:
- Churches in the City of London

- Churches with a Mercer connection – historic (church patronage) or a present Mercer closely involved
- Cathedrals, specifically those with close links to Mercer churches

People

We aim to contribute to deepening understanding and acceptance of the Christian religion, and to developing its relationships between its denominations and with other world faiths. We seek appeals that:
- Help young people to learn about the Christian faith and develop their spiritual lives
- Support clergy and help them to develop their outreach work
- Provide spiritual training for clergy and lay people
- Provide respite, recuperation and spiritual nourishment for clergy and their families

Heritage and the arts

Heritage appeals are considered for:
- Material or fabric conservation and refurbishment
- Library/archive conservation
- Wildlife/environment conservation

Arts:

We have a modest budget for the performing arts and priority is given to supporting young professional performers at the start of their careers. There is a preference for organisations based in London but occasionally we support national organisations that are centres of excellence.

Further information about these grant programmes is available on the website including programme specific information about exclusions, application procedures and deadlines.

Grantmaking 2011/12

In 2011/12 grants totalled £11.8 million, largely due to two very large grants for education (see beneficiaries). Further financial information was not available. Grants were broken down into the following categories:

Education	£9.6 million
Welfare	£1 million
Heritage and arts	£410,000
Church and faith	£372,000
Other	£408,000

Beneficiaries included: St Paul's School London (£4.2 million); Hammersmith Academy London (£1 million); Guildhall School of Music and Drama (£250,000); London Schools Network (£139,000); Hexham Abbey Northumberland (£100,000); R L Glasspool Charity Trust (£30,000); Quaker Social Action London and Sue Ryder Care (£15,000 each); National Churches Trust and Water City Festival London (£12,000 each); London Sports Trust, Peace Direct, Age UK Camden, Calvert Trust and Contact the Elderly (£10,000 each).

Exclusions

These should be read alongside the specific exclusions for the particular category into which an application falls.

▶ Animal welfare charities
▶ Endowment appeals
▶ Campaigning work and projects that are primarily political
▶ Activities that are the responsibility of the local, health or education authority or other similar body
▶ Activities that have already taken place
▶ Other grantmaking trusts
▶ Sponsorship or marketing appeals and fundraising events
▶ Loans or business finance
▶ General or mailshot appeals

Capital projects: 'This is restricted to appeals that are within the last 20 % of their target. No capital projects are funded under the Education programme.'

Applications

Applications can be made online via the foundation's website. In addition applicants are required to post:

▶ A Project Plan for the funding proposal
▶ Your organisation's most recent statutory report and accounts (produced no later than ten months after the end of the financial year

Grants officers are happy to give advice by telephone or email. Check the website for contact details for the relevant programme.

Applicants must submit applications four weeks prior to committee meetings. Applications will be acknowledged within ten working days. Committees meet regularly throughout the year. For up to date committee meeting dates consult the foundation's website for each grant programme. Approval of successful applications may take up to four weeks from the date of the meeting at which your applications is considered.

According to the most recent accounts: 'Where possible, applicants awarded, or being considered for, a grant over £10,000 will receive a visit either from staff or from members of the Mercers' Company.'

Note: This foundation is under the trusteeship of the Mercers' Company and one application to the Company is an application to all its trusts including the Charity of Sir Richard Whittington and the Earl of Northampton's Charity.

Percentage of awards given to new applicants: between 30% and 40%.

Common applicant mistakes

'Outside the guidelines which are posted on the our website; applying within three years of their first application.'

Information gathered from:

Annual report; Charity Commission record; Summary Information Return; further information provided by the funder; funder's website.

Community Foundation for Merseyside

£1.9 million (2011/12)

Beneficial area

Merseyside, Halton and Lancashire.

Correspondent: Cathy Elliott, Chief Executive, Third Floor, Stanley Building, 43 Hanover Street, Liverpool L1 3DN (tel: 01512 322444; fax: 01512 322445; email: info@cfmerseyside.org.uk; website: www.cfmerseyside.org.uk)

Trustees: Michael Eastwood; Abi Pointing; Andrew Wallis; Robert Towers; William Bowley; Sally Yeoman; David McDonnell.

CC Number: 1068887

The Community Foundation for Merseyside connects donors with local causes in Merseyside. By providing grants to local communities, the foundation helps them focus on building a better stronger Merseyside for future generations.

At present the foundation's main function of distributing grants to local communities is supported by distinct funds, confined to specific objectives within time-limited periods. However, its long-term vision is to be sustainable; to be the biggest funder of the voluntary sector on Merseyside and to have substantial endowment – enabling the foundation to utilise unrestricted funds in creative gran making.

The foundation's values are:
▶ Community leadership
▶ Pride
▶ Transparency
▶ Working together

The foundation delivers a range of grantmaking programmes across Merseyside, Halton and Lancashire. The number and type of grants available from the foundation can vary considerably over time. Grants are typically for up to £10,000

Visit the foundation's website to find out what funds are currently available. The guidelines and criteria for each fund can also be found here. As the foundation manages a wide range of funds which open and close regularly, they are not detailed here and applicants are advised to visit the website instead to see the most up to date information.

Standard Merseyside Community Foundation guidelines apply for groups and individuals; these may be accessed on the foundation's website.

Grantmaking in 2011/12

The foundation states in its 2011/12 annual report:

Our 2011/12 financial year was a year of transition for the organisation with major Government funding programmes ending in March 2011. In 2010/11 we operated and administered public funding in the majority with only 25% of our funding from private sources at an overall level of £3.5 million, (compared to £3.9 million in 2009/10 at the same ratio). In 2011/12 this ratio switched with 25% of our funding being from public sources and 75% from private. Our funding levels for communities reduced from £3.5 million in 2010/11 to £2 million in 2011/12.

During the year the foundation had assets of £6.3 million, an income of £3.2 million. Grants to 372 organisations totalled £1.9 million. The foundation has also informed us that in 2012/13 they made 80 grants.

There were a further 64 grants totalling £19,000 were awarded to individuals. Neither a breakdown of grants nor a list of beneficiaries was included in the accounts.

Previous beneficiaries have included: Halton Voluntary Action; Jo Jo Mind and Body; The Zero Centre; Liverpool Academy of Art; Fire Support Network; and Liverpool Greenbank Wheelchair Basketball Club.

Exclusions

Each of the separate funds has separate guidelines and exclusions, see the general tab for an outline. Full lists of exclusions are available with guidance notes from the foundation's website.

Applications

Most of the trust's funds can now be applied for online using a standard form. Forms for the other funds are also available online. Once you have submitted the form the foundation will determine which fund the proposal meets. The foundation has a membership scheme available which keeps members up to date on the latest grant schemes. Applications must also include the following documents:

▶ Constitution
▶ Accounts
▶ Bank statement
▶ Safeguarding policy (where applicable)

Unless your organisation has received a grant from the foundation in the last 12 months you *must* submit these documents, otherwise your application will not be considered.

Full guidelines and application forms for individual funds are available from the foundation's website.

Percentage of awards given to new applicants: between 10% and 20%.

Common applicant mistakes

'They don't read guidelines.'

Information gathered from:

Accounts; annual report; Charity Commission record; guidelines for applicants; further information provided by the funder; funder's website.

Milton Keynes Community Foundation

Welfare, arts
£466,000 (2011/12)

Beneficial area

Milton Keynes Unitary Authority.

Correspondent: Bart Gamber, Grants Director, Acorn House, 381 Midsummer Boulevard, Central Milton Keynes MK9 3HP (tel: 01908 690276; fax: 01908 233635; email: info@ mkcommunityfoundation.co.uk; website: www.mkcommunityfoundation.co.uk)

Trustees: Judith Hooper; Fola Komolafe; Francesca Skelton; Jane Matthews; Michael Murray; Peter Kara; Peter Selvey; Richard Brown; Roger Kitchen; Ruth Stone; Stephen Norrish; Philip Butler; John Moffoot.

CC Number: 295107

Established in 1986, the foundation is a local grantmaking charity that helps to improve the quality of life for people living within the unitary authority area of Milton Keynes. It awards around 150 grants each year to local voluntary organisations and charities, supporting projects that benefit the whole community, including; public health, the needs of children and young people, older people, people with special needs, arts and culture and projects providing services to the community.

The foundation helps to build stronger communities by encouraging local giving and raises a large part of its funds through a membership scheme, supported by local people and companies who make an annual donation.

The foundation has a range of different funds and accepts applications from not-for-profit organisations working for the benefit of the community of Milton Keynes. They also offer space from their property portfolio at subsidised rates to the voluntary sector.

The foundation has three main grant programmes.

- *Jubilee Grants* – up to £200
- *Small Grants* – up to £1,500. These grants are considered monthly
- *Community Grants* – up to £5,000
- *Arts/Crafts Bursaries* – varying amounts year on year for artists resident in Milton Keynes

- *Extraordinary Grants* – 'We sometimes have the ability to fund projects that do not fit within our ordinary grant schemes, either because they require a larger amount than the normal maximum or because they arise with urgent need that cannot wait until the next deadline. We will only accept applications for Extraordinary Grants if we agree that the circumstances justify it, if we can identify potential funds available to make the grant should it be successful and if you have been given permission by our Grants Team to submit it'

The foundation's website notes that it has:

A special interest in projects that are led and driven by local people, as well as projects that utilise partnerships between different organisations.

When reviewing grant applications, we look for projects that have been carefully thought through and planned.

Due to the limited funds available for grants, we also appreciate applicants who submit frugal applications – those that only ask for the minimum amount needed to deliver the intended impact.

Examples of what may be funded:
- Start-up costs
- Extension of existing projects
- Pilot projects and extension funding for successful pilots
- Equipment and resources
- Leverage
- Conservation projects
- Total core costs related to the wider project

It is important to note that grant schemes can change frequently. For full details of the foundation's current grant programmes and their deadlines consult its website.

In 2011/12 the foundation had assets of £10 million and an income of £2.8 million. Grants were made to 162 organisations totalling £466,000. There was a further £21,000 given in 16 grants to individuals through the Arts Bursaries programme.

Recent beneficiaries have included: Age UK Milton Keynes (£9,600); Church of Council of All Saints Emberton and Milton Keynes YMCA (£5,000 each); Arabian School of Gymnastics (£4,500); Special Needs Unit Gymnastics (SNUGS) (£4,200); The Children's Society (£3,800); MK Cheerleading Academy (£3,000); Desperate 2 Dance (£2,400); Conniburrow Community Association (£2,100); Saahil Support Group (£1,400); Tattenhoe Youth Football Club (£1,000); City Discovery Centre (£800); and Age UK MK (£500).

Exclusions

No grants are made to the following types of organisation:

- Statutory organisations – including schools, hospitals and borough councils (applications from parish councils for community projects are accepted)
- Political parties or groups affiliated to a political party
- Individuals
- For-profit companies

Grants are normally not given for:
- Sponsorship and fundraising events
- Projects involving political or campaigning activities
- Projects connected with promoting a religious message of any kind
- Work which should be funded by health and local authorities or government grants aid
- The purchase of equipment that will become the property of a statutory body
- Animal welfare
- Medical research or treatment
- Grants to be distributed to other groups or individuals
- Ongoing core costs not related to a particular service or activity
- Retrospective grants, nor grants to pay off deficits or loans

Applications

Application forms and guidelines are available on the foundation's website or can be requested by telephoning the office. The grants staff can be contacted to assist with any queries or help with applications.

Deadlines for small grants programme is the last working Friday of each month and the community grants programme has five deadlines per year, see the website for the exact dates. Small grant applications are usually processed within two weeks and community grants, five weeks.

Percentage of awards given to new applicants: less than 10%.

Common applicant mistakes

'They fail to answer all questions on their application; they do not address sustainability of projects/proposals.'

Information gathered from:

Accounts; annual report; Charity Commission record; guidelines for applicants; further information provided by the funder; funder's website.

The Mittal Foundation

General charitable purposes, children and young people

Beneficial area

UK and India.

Correspondent: The Trustees, c/o Mittal Investments Ltd, Floor 3, Berkeley Square House, Berkeley Square, London W1J 6BU (tel: 020 7659 1033)

Trustees: Sudhir Maheshwari; Bhikham Chand Agarwal; Usha Mittal.

CC Number: 1146604

Registered in March 2012, this foundation is one of the charitable endeavours of steel magnate Lakshmi Mittal, one of the richest people in the world, and his wife Usha, who is a trustee. The remaining trustees, Sudhir Maheshwari and Bhikham Chand Agarwal, hold senior management and directorship positions respectively at ArcelorMittal.

The foundation has general charitable purposes, with a particular interest in children and young people. It is likely that the foundation will have a significant grantmaking capacity when it is fully operational.

Applications

In writing to the correspondent.

Information gathered from:

Charity Commission record.

The Monument Trust

Arts and heritage, health and community care particularly HIV/AIDS and Parkinson's, social development particularly rehabilitation of offenders, general

£45 million (2011/12)

Beneficial area

Unrestricted, but UK and South Africa in practice.

Correspondent: Alan Bookbinder, Director, The Peak, 5 Wilton Road, London SW1V 1AP (tel: 020 7410 0330; fax: 020 7410 0332; website: www.sfct. org.uk)

Trustees: Stewart Grimshaw; Linda Heathcoat-Amory; Charles Cator.

CC Number: 242575

Summary

This is one of the Sainsbury Family Charitable Trusts, which share a joint administration, but are otherwise independent of each other. They have a common approach to grantmaking which is described in the entry for the group as a whole.

The trust makes grants under four categories:

▶ Health and community care: areas of public health and social care which struggle to find support elsewhere. HIV/AIDS charities in the UK and southern Africa and Parkinson's Disease are priorities; homelessness, drug addiction and teenage pregnancy are examples of other areas which receive help

▶ Social development: criminal justice especially youth offending and rehabilitation, homelessness

▶ Arts and heritage: major arts and heritage institutions including museums, galleries, historic houses and gardens, and theatres. Projects to increase the public appreciation of arts and gardens

▶ General

The trust gives the following indication of its current particular area of interest: 'In the arts and heritage category [the trustees] particularly wish to be made aware of significant appeals. [They] continue to support a number of arts projects of national or regional importance. In other areas they prefer to help prove new ideas or methods that can be replicated widely and where possible become self-sustaining.' The trustees anticipate continuing to make substantial grants over the coming years, in excess of the trust's income, which will be funded using the trust's expendable endowment.

In 2011/12 the trust had assets of £175 million and an income of £9.2 million. Grants paid during the year totalled £45 million. Grants approved during the year totalled £31 million, broken down as follows:

Arts and heritage	60	£19 million
Health and community care	77	£7.8 million
Social development	28	£4.5 million
General	1	£390,000

Beneficiaries included: British Museum (£6 million); Tate Britain (£3 million); Parkinson's Disease Society (£1.2 million); Foyer Federation (£750,000); African Solutions to African Problems (ASAP) (£451,000); Landmark Trust (£400,000); Ashden Sustainable Solutions Better Lives (£390,000); BalletBoyz (£260,000); Children's HIV Association (CHIVA) (£249,000); National Communities Resource Centre (£150,000); Home-Start MAJIK (£60,000); Apples and Snakes (£30,000); and Community Media Trust (£24,000).

During the year the trust invested £850,000 in a Social Impact Bond and is now receiving payments from the Department for Justice based upon the reconviction rates of people leaving Peterborough Prison.

Exclusions

Grants are not normally made to individuals.

Applications

See the guidance for applicants in the entry for the Sainsbury Family Charitable Trusts. A single application will be considered for support by all the trusts in the group.

The trust 'will consider unsolicited proposals, as long as they demonstrably and closely fit their specific area of

interest. However, it should be understood that the majority of unsolicited proposals are unsuccessful.'

Information gathered from:

Accounts; annual report; Charity Commission record; funder's website.

The Henry Moore Foundation

Fine arts, in particular sculpture, and research and development, projects and exhibitions which expand the definition of sculpture, such as film, photography and performance

£887,000 (2011/12)

Beneficial area

UK and overseas.

Correspondent: Alice O'Connor, Grants Programme Secretary, Dane Tree House, Perry Green, Much Hadham, Hertfordshire SG10 6EE (tel: 01279 843333; email: admin@henry-moore.org; website: www.henry-moore.org)

Trustees: Marianne Brouwer; Greville Worthington; Dawn Ades; Simon Keswick; Malcolm Baker; Duncan Robinson; Laure Genillard; Henry Channon; David Wilson; Celia Clear.

CC Number: 271370

The foundation was established in 1977 to promote the public's appreciation of the fine arts and in particular the works of Henry Moore. It concentrates most of its support on sculpture. The aims of the foundation are achieved through specific projects initiated within the foundation both at Perry Green and in Leeds, particularly exhibitions and publications, and by giving grant aid to other suitable enterprises.

The foundation's grantmaking programme has been revised to provide additional financial resources to support the work of living artists and contemporary art practice. Special consideration is given to projects outside London and to venues with limited opportunities to show contemporary art. The foundation is willing to support projects in the UK which involve artists from another country but overseas projects must include a British component.

Grant categories

New projects

This includes exhibitions, exhibition catalogues and new commissions. Grants will be awarded as follows, up to a maximum of: £20,000 for a large museum exhibition; £10,000 for an exhibition catalogue; £30,000 for a commission.

Cubitt Gallery, London: Exhibition and Exhibition Booklet/Publication, *The City is a Burning, Blazing Bonfire*, 29 October-23 December 2011 – £6,000

Whitechapel Art Gallery, London: Commission, *Whitechapel Gallery Façade*: Tree of Life by Rachel Whiteread – £12,500

Collections

This is designed to provide minor capital grants help public institutions acquire, display and conserve sculpture. The maximum grants available will be around £15,000 for acquisition and £20,000 for conservation and/or display.

Ashmolean Museum, Oxford: Acquisition, *The Crucifixion with the Virgin Mary and St John*, terracotta, 1785 by Clodion (Claude Michel, 1738–1814) – £15,000

Scottish National Portrait Gallery, Edinburgh: *Sculpture display in the Library*, from November 2011 – £10,000

Research and development

For sculptural projects whether creative (e.g. contemporary commissions), academic (e.g. permanent collection catalogues of sculpture) or practical (e.g. a long-term conservation project) that require funding for more than one year. Maximum grants are likely to be in the region of £20,000 per annum.

Glasgow Sculpture Studios Redevelopment Programme, April 2012-March 2015 £15,000

Small research grants: Up to £2,500 for research on the history and interpretation of sculpture.

Fellowships

For artists: grants of up to £6,000 each are available to artists, who are supported by host institutions, for fellowships or residences of two to six months.

For postdoctoral research: two year fellowships available to scholars who have recently finished their PhD to allow them to develop publications. Three or four fellowships will usually be awarded in the spring. Applications must be supported by an appropriate UK university department.

Conferences, lectures and publications

Grants of up to £5,000 are available. Note a publication can be a book or a journal but not an exhibition catalogue or a permanent collection catalogue. If applying for a publication, specify within the application, how and where the publication will be distributed.

Art Licks, London: Publication, *Art Licks* magazine, Issues 6–13 (January 2012-December 2013) – £2,500

University of Pennsylvania, Philadelphia in collaboration with l'Institute National d'Histoire de l'Art, Paris and the Philadelphia Museum of Art: Conference, *Working Group for the Study of Medieval Sculpture (1100–1550): A Transatlantic Collaboration*, January-November 2012 – £5,000

In 2011/12 the foundation had assets of £96 million, an income of £1.5 million and gave grants totalling £887,000, broken down into:

Exhibitions and new projects	85	£691,000
Collections	9	£73,000
Fellowships	6	£59,000
Conferences, publications and workshops	17	£44,000
Research	1	£20,000

See grant categories for beneficiaries in 2011/12.

Exclusions

No grants for revenue expenditure. No grant (or any part of grant) may be used to pay any fee or to provide any other benefit to any individual who is a trustee of the foundation.

Applications

Applicants should complete an application form which is available on the foundation's website. Applications must be posted to the grants administrator. Applications will be acknowledged by letter.

The grants committee meets quarterly; consult the foundation's website for exact dates as the trust advises that applications received late will not be considered until the next meeting. It is advised to leave six months between the grants committee meeting and the project start date as funds cannot be paid for retrospective projects.

Applicants should also advise the foundation whether it is envisaged that any trustee will have an interest in the project for which a grant is sought.

Information gathered from:

Accounts; annual report; Charity Commission record; guidelines for applicants; funder's website.

John Moores Foundation

Social welfare in Merseyside and Northern Ireland, emergency relief overseas

£619,000 (2011/12)

Beneficial area

Primarily Merseyside (plus Skelmersdale, Ellesmere Port and Halton); Northern Ireland; and overseas.

Correspondent: Phil Godfrey, Grants Director, 7th Floor, Gostins Building, 32–36 Hanover Street, Liverpool L1 4LN (tel: 01517 076077; email: info@ johnmooresfoundation.com; website: www.jmf.org.uk)

Trustees: Barnaby Moores; Kevin Moores; Nicola Eastwood; Alison Navarro; Christina Mee.

CC Number: 253481

Summary

The foundation was established in 1964 with aims and objectives that were widely drawn at the beginning to allow for changing patterns of need. During the last twenty years the foundation has confined giving to four main categories:

⬧ Merseyside – this is the priority area and receives 60–80% of the annual grant total
⬧ Northern Ireland – usually receives around 15% of annual grants
⬧ World crises – including man-made or natural disasters such as famine, flood or earthquake, which by definition require large one-off grants to prevent loss of life. These donations are usually made to major relief agencies
⬧ One-off exceptional grants to causes that interest the trustees

Note: the foundation does not respond to unsolicited applications in the last two categories.

The foundation aims to enable people who are marginalised, as a result of social, educational, physical, economic, cultural, geographical or other disadvantage, to improve their social conditions and quality of life by making grants. It prefers to assist small, grass-roots and volunteer driven organisations and new rather than long-established groups, particularly those groups that find it more than usually difficult to raise money.

In line with the foundation's commitment to equal opportunities, it supports projects which aim to counter racism, sexism or discrimination of any kind. Projects which particularly focus on such anti-discrimination would be expected to have substantial input from the discriminated groups concerned.

Grantmaking

Consideration is given to organisations working in the foundation's target areas for giving, which are:

⬧ Grass roots community groups
⬧ Black and minority ethnic organisations
⬧ Promotion of equal opportunities
⬧ Women including girls
⬧ Second chance learning
⬧ Advice and information to alleviate poverty
⬧ Grassroots social health initiative
⬧ Support and training for voluntary organisations

And, in Merseyside only:
⬧ People with disabilities

- Carers
- Refugees
- Children and young people
- Homeless people
- Child care
- Complementary therapies

Further details of these areas are available on the foundation's website. The foundation is an enabling funder and would like to help groups achieve their targets and outcomes in their own way. Groups can be given advice with setting up monitoring and evaluation systems that best meet their needs and capacity.

Grants are made for the following:
- Start-up and running costs
- Volunteer and programme costs
- Education and training costs
- One-off project costs
- Equipment
- Salaries

Grants in 2011/12

In 2011/12 the foundation had assets of £24 million and an income of £1.1 million. There is a helpful breakdown of grantmaking in the 2011/12 annual report:

In 2011/12, 126 grants were made totalling £618,500 (compared with 145 grants totalling £684,000 in 2010/11). Of these 41 were revenue grants of more than one year (35 in 2010/11). Approximately 63% of grants given in Merseyside were for £5,000 or less (65% in 2010/11). In Northern Ireland 97.5 % of grants were for £5,000 or less (100% in 2010/11), with the average being £4,000 (£4,500 in 2010/11).

Grants were broken down into the areas shown in the displayed table below.

Beneficiaries in Merseyside included: Wirral Resource Centre and Toy Library (£11,000); The Debt Advice Network (£10,000); Granby Somali Women's Group (£7,500); Wirral Holistic Care Services (£4,800); Support for Asylum Seekers (3,800); Church Road Neighbourhood Resource Centre (£3,000); Women's Enterprise Breakthrough (£2,500); Kirkby Senior Collaborative (£1,200); Southport Access for Everyone (£1,000); and Stella Marks Social Enterprise (£650).

Beneficiaries in Northern Ireland included: Ardoyne Association and Foyle Sign Language Centre (£5,000 each); Omagh Independent Advice Services and Dialogue for Diversity (£4,500 each); Community Focus Learning (£3,300); Loup Women's Group (£3,200); Roundabout Playgroup (£2,000); and Belfast Butterfly Club (£1,800).

Exclusions

Generally the foundation does not fund:
- Individuals
- Projects that are not substantially influenced by their target beneficiaries
- National organisations or groups based outside Merseyside even where some of the service users come from the area
- Statutory bodies or work previously done by them
- Mainstream education (schools, colleges, universities)
- Faith-based projects exclusively for members of that faith, or for the promotion of religion
- Capital building costs – except to improve access for disabled people
- Festivals, carnivals and fêtes
- Medicine
- Holidays, expeditions and outings
- Gifts, parties, etc.
- Conferences
- Sport
- Vehicles
- Animal charities
- Arts, crafts, heritage, or local history projects
- Conservation and environmental projects
- Employment and enterprise schemes
- Academic or medical research
- Credit Unions – except for the training of management committee members or the development of a new business plan
- Uniformed groups (e.g. scouts, cadets, majorettes)
- Sponsorship, advertising or fundraising events

Applications may be refused where the foundation considers that the organisation concerned is already well funded or has excessive reserves.

Unsolicited applications which fall outside the policy criteria are not considered. Unsolicited applications for the categories World Crises and One-off exceptional grants are not responded to.

Applications

Refer to the foundation's website and make sure your project falls within the criteria. If you are unsure, or if you would like to discuss your application before submitting it, telephone the foundation staff who will be happy to advise you.

Apply by letter of no more than four sides of A4 plus an application form. Application forms and guidance notes can be obtained by letter, phone or email or from the foundation's website.

Decisions about which projects to fund are made by the trustees who meet five to six times a year to consider Merseyside applications and four times a year to consider Northern Ireland applications. As a general rule, Merseyside applicants should allow three to four months for a decision to be made, and applicants from Northern Ireland should allow four to five months. Applicants are welcome to telephone the foundation to find out at which meeting their application will be considered. Unsuccessful applicants are advised to wait at least four months before reapplying.

Information gathered from:

Accounts; annual report; Charity Commission record; guidelines for applicants; funder's website; further information provided by the funder.

JOHN MOORES FOUNDATION

		Merseyside		Northern Ireland
Advice	3	£24,000	2	£9,500
Black and ethnic minority organisations	13	£67,000	3	£10,000
Carers	4	£18,000		
Childcare	1	£9,800	6	£15,000
Community organisations	17	£71,000	11	£46,000
Disabled people	6	£28,000	2	£10,000
Family Support	7	£40,000	3	£13,000
Grassroots social health	5	£17,000		
HIV/AIDS	1	£9,900		
Homeless people	1	£3,000	1	£5,500
Refugees/asylum seekers	1	£3,800		
Second chance learning			2	£7,500
Social welfare	2	£11,000	3	£11,000
Training for community groups	1	£5,800	1	£2,600
Women	11	£60,000	4	£17,000
Young people	13	£89,000	3	£12,000
Total		**£458,000**		**£161,000**

The Morgan Foundation

Children and young people, health, social welfare

£2 million (2012/13)

Beneficial area

North Wales, Merseyside, West Cheshire and North Shropshire.

Correspondent: Jane Harris, Administrator, PO Box 3517, Chester CH1 9ET (tel: 01829 782800; fax: 01829 782223; email: contact@ morganfoundation.co.uk; website: www. morganfoundation.co.uk)

CC Number: 1087056

The foundation was established in 2001 with an endowment of over £2 million from Stephen Morgan, founder of Redrow plc and chair of Wolverhampton Wanders FC. The following outline of the foundation's aims and objectives is given on its website:

Our aim is to provide funding for small to medium-sized organisations who are addressing specific needs in [North Wales, Merseyside, West Cheshire and Shropshire]. We are particularly keen to support those who have already begun to make an impact, but need a helping hand to expand their work and increase their effectiveness.

We focus our help mainly on those who work directly with children and families, but we recognise that many wider issues may also affect their welfare so we are interested in any project which contributes to the quality of life of the people in our region.

Guidelines

The foundation gives the following information about its funding policy:

Where we fund
We operate only within the areas of North Wales, Merseyside, West Cheshire and Shropshire, so applications should be from charities, organisations and projects which are based in these regions.

Who we fund
The Morgan Foundation specialises in supporting organisations helping children and families and we will consider any work which has a positive effect on their welfare and quality of life, or which expands the opportunities and life choices for young people in this region.

Areas of support to date have included physical and learning disability, physical and mental health, plus social challenge and deprivation.

Though the majority of the recipients of our grants are registered charities, we will also consider applications from other types of organisations which are pursuing charitable causes and where aims and objectives are 'not for profit'. Whilst we recognise the need for specialist, professional care in some circumstances, preference is given to organisations with a high volunteer input.

Generally we do not support national charities or large organisations.

What we fund
Grants may be considered for a range of purposes and could include:
- Single awards for capital projects
- Start-up and/or ongoing running costs for specific projects
- Multi-year revenue grants for core funding

The type, size and time period of the award is decided on the basis of the perceived 'difference' that our support will make to the organisation, to the project and to the targeted beneficiaries.

We feel it is important that you tell us in your application the full extent of the funding you really need to achieve your aims and objectives, in order for us to assess how best we can contribute.

In 2012/13 the foundation had assets of almost £13.9 million and an income of £1.7 million. Grants were made during the year to organisations totalling £2 million.

Beneficiaries include: OnSide (£500,000); Children Today (£333,000); Wolves Aid (£125,000*); Steps to Freedom (£54,000); Christ Church Youth Club (£51,000); Five Children and Families Trust (£45,000); Norris Green Youth Centre (£42,000); Home-Start Flintshire (£36,000); Netherton Park Community Association (£31,000); Cheshire Asperger's Parent Support (£26,000); Clare Mount School (£20,000); Longmynd Adventure Camp (£16,000); Greenbank School Cycle Track (£15,000); St Peters Collegiate Church (£5,000); North Wales Superkids (£950); Oxfam (£500); and Rett Syndrome Research Trust (£200).

* The foundation has committed to giving 10% of its total grant expenditure to Wolves Aid, the charity of Wolverhampton Wanders.

The foundation also made 19 entrepreneurial awards to individuals totalling £117,500.

Exclusions
The foundation will not give grants for the following:
- Animal welfare
- Arts/heritage
- Conservation/environment
- Expeditions and overseas travel
- General fundraising appeals
- Individual and sports sponsorship
- Large national charities
- Mainstream education
- Promotion of specific religions
- Retrospective funding

Applications
The foundation gives the following guidance about making an application on its website:

First, please ensure that you are eligible under our policy:
- Check that your organisation/project is based within our geographic area
- Check that your organisation/project is not listed in our exclusions
- Ring us for an informal chat and request an application form

Before finalising or submitting an application please telephone for an informal chat to check that your proposed application falls in line with current policy. We understand that it can be daunting to pick up the phone, but we believe that an initial chat can save you and us lots of wasted time, and we will be happy to give you guidance as to what specific information we need to process your application.

Once you have contacted us by phone and it has been agreed that your application is appropriate, we will ask you to send in a description of your organisation, its history, activities, volunteers, beneficiaries, achievements to date and current funding needs. Please enclose copies of most recent reports and accounts. If you have a project in mind, describe its purpose, targets, budget, and timescale.

All applications will be acknowledged and we will contact you for any further information we require. All charities and projects will be visited before a grant is approved.

Timing of Applications: Trustee Meetings are held regularly throughout the year and there are no specific dates for applications to be received. However, organisations should be aware that applications are considered in chronological order and it can take up to six months for the process to be completed.

Percentage of awards given to new applicants: between 40% and 50%.

Common applicant mistakes
'Not reading eligibility criteria; not phoning for informal preliminary chat as directed.'

Information gathered from:
Accounts; Charity Commission record; further information provided by the funder; funder's website.

The George Müller Charitable Trust

Christian evangelism, children and young people, orphans
£400,000 to organisations
(2012/13)

Beneficial area
Worldwide.

Correspondent: Tony Davies, Company Secretary, Muller House, 7 Cotham Park, Bristol BS6 6DA (tel: 01179 245001; email: admin@mullers.org; website: www.mullers.org)

CC Number: 1066832

In 2012/13 the trust had assets of £9.3 million and an income of £2.5 million. Grants to organisations totalled £400,000.

The majority of grants (£338,000) were for amounts over £5,000 and beneficiaries include: Rwandan Orphan

Project (£80,000); Haven Home Orphanage (£52,000); 25:40 Romania (£31,000); Hebron Hostel Trust (£25,000); Helping Them to Smile Project (£10,000); Ebenezer Children's Fund (£7,000); and House of Hope (£6,000).

The remaining £61,000 was made in grants below £5,000.

Grants are also made to individual Christian workers (£756,000 in 2012/13).

Applications

In writing to the correspondent.

Information gathered from:

Accounts; Charity Commission record; funder's website.

The Mulberry Trust

General

£526,000 (2011/12)

Beneficial area

UK, with an interest in Harlow, Essex and surrounding areas, including London.

Correspondent: John Marks, Trustee, Farrer and Co., 66 Lincoln's Inn Fields, London WC2A 3LH (tel: 020 7242 2002)

Trustees: Ann M. Marks; Charles F. Woodhouse; Timothy J. Marks; Chris Marks; Rupert Marks; William Marks.

CC Number: 263296

The trust states in its annual report:

> The trust has a particular focus on parenting, children and the family, in order to strengthen family life and the general wellbeing of families from the very
>
> young to the very old; the elderly; the disadvantaged; homelessness; health; debt relief and counselling; the Christian Church and leadership and the
>
> promotion of interfaith work. The trust also supports education research and the arts, provided that this contributes to the aims set out above. The trust also
>
> supports certain community and environmental organisations and areas of specific interest to individual trustees.

Around 70 grants are made each year, most being for amounts of £5,000 or less. Grants go to a wide range of causes, with both local institutions, including hospices and universities, and national charities receiving funding. Around half the grants seem to go to regularly supported recipients. In 2012 the trustees made a £1 million commitment to Cambridge University.

In 2011/12 the trust had assets of £5.9 million and an income of £208,000. Grants were made totalling £526,000, broken down as follows:

Health	17	£109,000
Education and research	8	£105,000
Disadvantage	17	£101,000

Older people	3	£69,000
Parenting, the family and children's work	7	£61,000
The Christian Church and leadership	12	£25,000
The arts	6	£21,000
The community and environment	4	£14,000
Homelessness	2	£6,000
Other material grants	3	£12,000
Grants of £500 or less	7	£2,700

Beneficiaries included: Cambridge Interfaith Project (University of Cambridge (£50,000); Age UK (£49,000); Harlow Parochial Church Council (St Mary's Church) Calm Centre (£20,000); Parents Like Us (£12,000); Harlow Alzheimer's Society (£10,000); Hope UK (£5,000); Youth for Christ (£3,000); Bag Books (£2,000); St George's House, Windsor, Clare College, Harlow Rotary and Sailability (£1,000 each).

Applications

The trust has stated that it 'will not, as a matter of policy, consider applications which are unsolicited'.

Percentage of awards given to new applicants: between 10% and 20%.

Common applicant mistakes

'Not reading the eligibility criteria; sending out repeat mass mailings.'

Information gathered from:

Accounts; annual report; Charity Commission record; further information provided by the funder.

The Edith Murphy Foundation

General, individual hardship, animals, children and the disabled

£950,000 (2011/12)

Beneficial area

UK with some preference for Leicestershire.

Correspondent: Richard F. Adkinson, Trustee, c/o Crane and Walton, 113–117 London Road, Leicester LE2 0RG (tel: 01162 551901; email: richard.adkinson@btinternet.com)

Trustees: David L. Tams; Pamela M. Breakwell; Christopher P. Blakesley; Richard F. Adkinson.

CC Number: 1026062

The foundation was set up in 1993 by the late Mrs Murphy in memory of her late husband, Mr Hugh Murphy, with the following objectives:

- To assist those who by reason of their age, youth, infirmity, disablement, poverty or social and economic circumstances are suffering hardship or distress or are otherwise in need

- To provide relief of suffering of animals of any species who are in need of care and attention and the provision and maintenance of facilities of any description for the reception and care of unwanted animals and the treatment of sick or ill-treated animals
- To make donations for general charitable purposes

Following the death of Mrs Murphy in 2005, her will provided for the foundation to receive certain benefits including a proportion of the residue of her estate. The value of the benefits received the following year amounted to £28.2 million. A further £1.8 million was added in 2007. This has resulted in the level of grant giving increasing substantially in recent years.

In 2011/12 the foundation had assets of £31 million, an income of £777,000 and gave grants totalling £950,000, broken down as follows:

Welfare	£790,000
Children's charities	£91,000
Disability	£31,000
Animal charities	£27,000
Education	£10,000

Beneficiaries included: De Monfort University (£200,000); Build IT International (£30,000); The Stroke Association and The Harley Staples Cancer Trust (£20,000 each); Marie Curie Cancer Care (£19,000); Vista (£15,000); Leicester Hospitals Charity, Livability, Leeds Mencap and De Montfort University (£10,000 each).

Grants of less than £10,000 totalled £512,000.

Applications

In writing to the correspondent. The foundation states in its annual report: 'the foundation considers every application received and where there is a need covered by the foundation's objectives the trustees will consider making a grant.'

Percentage of awards given to new applicants: 65%.

Information gathered from:

Accounts; annual report; Charity Commission record; further information provided by the funder.

The John R. Murray Charitable Trust

Arts and literature
£913,000 (2012)

Beneficial area
UK.

Correspondent: John Murray, Trustee, 50 Albemarle Street, London W1S 4BD (tel: 020 7493 4361)

Trustees: John R. Murray; Virginia G. Murray; Hallam J. R. G. Murray; John O. G. Murray; Charles J. G. Murray.

CC Number: 1100199

Established in 2003, the trust supports organisations promoting the arts and literature. The following extract is taken from the trust's 2010 accounts:

> The trustees will normally only make grants or loans to other registered charities in area in which the trustees have an interest in the arts an literature (although not strictly limited to such areas) and where the award of a grant will have an immediate and tangible benefit to the recipient in question.

> In the medium-term the trustees' principal aim will be the continued support of the National Library of Scotland (as the ownership of the John Murray Archive) and its curatorial and preservation responsibilities for the archive as well as developing its support of the arts and in particular literature.

In 2012 the trust had assets of £23.7 million and an income of £879,000. Grants to 32 organisations totalled £913,000.

Beneficiaries included: National Library of Scotland (£313,000); Wordsworth Trust (£120,000); Bodleian Library (£60,000); Only Connect (£25,000); Lakeland Arts Trust (£20,000); Academy of Ancient Music (£15,000); British School at Athens (£11,000); Fine Cell Work (£10,000); Gilbert White's House (£7,500); Stoke Pages Society (£5,000); John Buchan Heritage Museum (£3,000); and Kings Corner Project (£200).

Applications
The trustees will not consider unsolicited applications for grants.

Common applicant mistakes
'There is no basic common mistake apart from sending an unsolicited application when we make it clear we do not accept them.'

Information gathered from:
Accounts; annual report; Charity Commission record; further information provided by the funder.

The National Art Collections Fund

Acquisition of works of art by museums and galleries
£6.3 million (2012)

Beneficial area
UK.

Correspondent: Sarah Philip, Head of Programmes, Millais House, 7 Cromwell Place, London SW7 2JN (tel: 020 7225 4822; fax: 020 7225 4848; email: programmes@artfund.org; website: www.artfund.org)

Trustees: David Verey; Paul Zuckerman; Dr Wendy Baron; Prof. Michael Craig-Martin; Christopher Lloyd; Jonathan Marsden; Dr Deborah Swallow; Prof. William Vaughan; Sally Osman; James Lingwood; Richard Calvocoressi; Caroline Butler; Prof. Chris Gosden; Antony Griffiths; Prof. Lisa Tickner; Michael Wilson; Philippa Glanville; Liz Forgan; Alastair Laing.

CC Number: 209174

Known simply as The Art Fund, this fundraising and membership charity believes that everyone should have the opportunity to experience great art at first hand, and it works to achieve this by: enriching museums and galleries throughout the UK with works of art of all kinds; campaigning for the widest possible access to art; promoting the enjoyment of art through its membership scheme. The fund has two grants programmes:

Art Fund Acquisitions Programme
For the purchase of works of art and other objects of aesthetic interest, dating from antiquity to the present day. UK public museums, galleries, historic houses, libraries and archives that are accredited under the Arts Council Scheme and are open for at least half the week for at least six months of the year. Under this programme there are three grants schemes:

- Main grants: Grants of £5,000 or more
- Small grants: Of less than £5,000
- Auctions: Applications can be fast-tracked for items at Auctions (see applications information below)

The fund sometimes operates time-limited programmes with their own criteria which aim to address specific collecting needs within the museum sector. These will be advertised on the fund's website.

The Jonathan Ruffer Curatorial Grants
For individual UK curators, scholars and researchers to undertake travel or other activities to extend and develop their curatorial expertise, collections-based knowledge and art historical interests. There are two categories:

- Grants of £200 – £1,500
- Grants of more than £1,500
- Costs that may be supported include: travel and accommodation; training courses/programmes of study; books and subscriptions to add to a museum's research resources or library; translation and transcription; temporary administrative cover to enable time away from work to undertake research. They welcome adventurous applications and will not always expect material outcomes to be an immediate consequence of the support

Grantmaking in 2012
In 2012 the fund had assets of £37 million, an income of £15 million and gave grants totalling £6.3 million.

Beneficiaries included: National Gallery (£2 million); Oxford Ashmolean Museum (£855,000); National Maritime Museum (£302,000); London Tate (£270,000); Cambridge Fitzwilliam Museum (£242,000); Towner Contemporary Museum (£135,000); National Museum Cardiff (£115,000); Scottish National Gallery (£78,000); Ben Uri Gallery (£54,000); Wrest Park (£30,000); Touchstones Rochdale (£21,000); The Creative Foundation (£15,000); Hunterian Art Gallery (£10,000); Walker Art Gallery (£8,600); Portsmouth City Museum and Records Office (£5,000); and Essex Collection of Art from Latin America (£2,300).

Exclusions
- Objects that are primarily of social-historical interest; scientific or technological material; letters, manuscripts or archival material with limited artistic or decorative inscription
- Applications where the applicant has already purchased or made a commitment to purchase the object, or made a financial commitment
- Other costs associated with acquisitions such as the conservation and restoration of works, transport and storage costs, temporary or permanent exhibitions and digitisation projects
- Applications from individuals, artist's groups, commercial organisations, hospitals, places of worship, schools or higher education institutions
- Funding towards professional development, travel or research

Applications
Firstly discuss the application with a member of the programmes office then register on the website to access the online application form. The Art Fund 'actively encourages strong applications

from national and designated museums for objects which will enrich their collections and supports their effort s to expand into new collecting areas when appropriate. The Art Fund considers applications for whatever amount is needed. Applicants are expected also to apply for any public funding for which they might be eligible, and to raise funds from other sources if they can'.

There are six deadlines a year for the main grants scheme, telephone the fund for these. Small grants applications can be submitted at any time. Potential applicants for auctions grants should contact the fund at the earliest opportunity. They need a minimum of seven working days notice for an auction in London or ten working days for an auction outside of London.

Applications for the small curatorial grants can be submitted at any time. There are three deadlines a year for curatorial grants of more than £1,500; these can be obtained by telephoning the fund.

Application forms and deadlines can be downloaded from the fund's website.

Information gathered from:

Accounts; annual report; annual review; Charity Commission record; funder's website.

The National Churches Trust (formerly the Historic Churches Preservation Trust with the Incorporated Church Building Society)

Preservation of historic churches

£855,000 (2012)

Beneficial area

UK.

Correspondent: Alison Pollard, Grants and Local Trusts Manager, 31 Newbury Street, London EC1A 7HU (tel: 020 7600 6090; fax: 020 7796 2442; email: info@ nationalchurchestrust.org; website: www. nationalchurchestrust.org)

Trustees: Charlotte Cole; Richard Carr-Archer; John Readman; John Drew; Revd Nicholas Holtam; Jennifer Page; Alastair Hunter; Andrew Day; Nicholas Holtam; Luke March.

CC Number: 1119845

Summary

The National Churches Trust was launched in 2007 as a national, non-profit organisation dedicated to

supporting and promoting places of worship used by Christian denominations in the UK. The trust promotes the use of these buildings by congregations and the wider community. It also advocates the conservation of places of worship of historic value for the use and enjoyment of future generations.

The trust was formed to act as a catalyst within the sector and to consolidate and expand the role played by its two predecessor charities, the Historic Churches Preservation Trust and the Incorporated Church Building Society (see below).

Its key roles are to:

▷ Encourage good management practices and regular maintenance by providing advice on access to funding, support and training and by developing and implementing practical solutions to the needs of the sector

▷ Provide an annual grants programme of £2 million that allocates funds for both building restoration and modernisation

▷ Encourage projects that benefit communities, integrate places of worship fully into their local areas and enable buildings to be open to the wider public

▷ Work to enhance the public and governmental perception of and support for Christian places of worship

General

In 2008 the Charity Commission appointed the National Churches Trust (NCT) as the sole trustee of the Historic Churches Preservation Trust (HCPT) and also granted a 'uniting direction'. Consequently, the NCT and HCPT are treated as a single charity for administrative, accounting and regulatory purposes. They will however, remain legally distinct so that the HCPT will operate as restricted funds within the NCT. A similar process is envisaged for the Incorporated Church Building Society (ICBS), which has been managed by the HCPT since 1983.

Founded in 1953, the HCPT, now the National Churches Trust (NCT), is the leading fundraising body involved in the restoration of architecturally and historically significant parish churches. Over the decades, work that was originally begun to reverse the neglect brought about by the socio-economic changes of the late 19th and early 20th centuries and to repair the damage of World War II has become increasingly important and far-reaching.

Spreading awareness of the needs of churches and encouraging participation in their restoration and revival at both

national and local level is also an important part of the trust's remit. Six local county trusts – in Cheshire, Essex, Kent, Lincolnshire, Staffordshire and Wiltshire were active when the trust was established. Since then, most of England has been covered.

The trust has often helped with the first essential tranche of money to get things under way, but the county trusts are all individual and independent. Representatives from the local trusts have always been members of the trust's grants committee and their ground level knowledge is considered essential in understanding the situation and pressures facing the local area.

The NCT receives no government funding, other than via the Gift Aid scheme and relies entirely on voluntary giving. The majority of income comes from legacies and grantmaking trusts and foundations, with the remaining balance made up from donations from places of worship, members of the public, subscriptions from 'Friends' and investment income.

Guidelines

To help those applying for grants, the trust has developed detailed guidelines on how to apply. The funds and the corresponding guidelines change frequently so it is advisable to check the trust's website before applying.

The trust advises that before applicants complete an application pack, it is important for them to make sure that their project will be eligible by checking it meets the following criteria:

▷ The building must be open for regular public worship – the trust does not currently have grants available for cathedrals, but any other Christian places of worship can apply if they meet the eligibility criteria

▷ It must be sited in England, Northern Ireland, the Isle of Man, Scotland or Wales

▷ The congregation must belong to a denomination that is a member or associated member of Churches Together in Britain and Ireland

▷ All projects must be overseen by an architect who is either ARB, RIBA or AABC accredited, or by a chartered surveyor who is RICS accredited

Grants Programmes

The following grants programmes open and close throughout the year, check the website for dates.

▷ **Repair Grants** – Between £10,000 and £40,000 to help places of worship to become wind and watertight. Funding is concentrated on the most urgent structural repairs and for projects with a total cost of at least £50,000

▷ **Community Grants** – Grants of between £5,000 and £25,000 for the cost of installing facilities such as kitchens and toilets, improving access for people with special needs or disabilities

▸ **Partnership Grants** – Working with local churches trusts to fund urgent repair projects with estimated costs of less than £50,000 with grants £2,500 to £10,000. The aim is to increase the grant giving capacity of local churches trusts

▸ **Waste Recycling Environmental (WREN) Heritage Fund** – grants for urgent structural repair projects for places of worship within ten miles of an active registered landfill site in a county where WREN operates

Grantmaking in 2012

In 2012 the trust had assets of £4.2 million, an income of £2.1 million and paid grants totalling £855,000. Grants committed totalled £1.5 million, broken down as follows in the annual review:

Repair grants	12	£392,000
WREN Heritage Fund	8	£322,000
Cornerstone grants	8	£320,000
Community grants	12	£309,000
Partnership grants	48	£159,000
Luke Trust	4	£20,000
Other miscellaneous grants	5	£25,000

Beneficiaries included: St Botoloph, Boston (£50,000) St Vincent, Caythorpe, St Michael and the Holy Angels, West Bromwich and St Wilfred, Halton (£40,000 each); Dunlop Parish Church, Dunlop (£35,000); North Shields Baptist Church (£20,000); St David, Llanddewi Aberarth (£10,000); and St John the Baptist, Little Maplestead (£5,000).

Exclusions

Be aware that the trust cannot make grants for certain purposes including:

▸ Non-church buildings (such as church halls and vicarages)
▸ Bell repairs
▸ Organ repairs
▸ Repairs to internal furnishings
▸ Redecoration, other than after structural repairs
▸ Clock repairs
▸ Buildings that were not originally built as places of worship
▸ To congregations that are not members or associated members of Churches Together in Britain and Ireland
▸ Monument repairs

Applications

Applicants are advised that each fund has different application procedures. Applications to the Partnership Grants Programme must be made through a local Church trust, a list of which can be found on the trust's website.

New guidelines and the online application form were due to be available from February 2014 – check the trust's website for current information.

Information gathered from:

Accounts; annual report; Charity Commission record; funder's website.

The Nationwide Foundation

Social welfare
£1.6 million (2011/12)

Beneficial area
UK.

Correspondent: Lorna Mackie, Grants Officer, Nationwide House, Pipers Way, Swindon SN38 2SN (tel: 01793 655113; fax: 01793 652409; email: enquiries@ nationwidefoundation.org.uk; website: www.nationwidefoundation.org.uk)

Trustees: Ben Stimson, Chair; Richard Davies; Simon Law; Karen McArthur; Dr Michael McCarthy; Chris Rhodes; Fiona Ellis; Graeme Hughes; Martin Coppack; Juliet Phommahaxay.

CC Number: 1065552

This foundation is funded principally from contributions from Nationwide Building Society, which donates a proportion of 1% of its pre-tax profit.

On 1 May 2013 the foundation launched its Empty Homes funding programme. The following information is available from the foundation's website:

Despite the current lack of housing stock, the UK has around 300,000 long-term empty homes and many more commercial properties that could be used as homes. The foundation will fund organisations turning such properties into safe, decent homes for people in need.

Who can apply
Organisations bringing empty properties into use for people in need with priority given to schemes including one or more of the following:
▸ Projects which are financially sustainable, or which are working towards financial sustainability
▸ Projects incorporating training for NEETS and others who are out of work or low skilled
▸ Live/work schemes
▸ Environmentally friendly practices
▸ Asset transfer

What costs will be funded?
Funds will considered towards the costs of refurbishment and can include a fair contribution towards organisational core costs where this is required to bring empty properties into use as homes for people in need. Funds will also be considered towards legal and other such costs associated with obtaining the empty properties (including landlord

negotiation and asset transfer). Funds are limited so the foundation's support is expected to complement other sources of funding which the organisation has.

Applicants can apply for grant funding or programme related (social) investment loans depending on which is the most appropriate for the scheme. Amounts of £15,000 to £140,000 will be considered.

In 2011/12 the foundation had assets of £1.8 million and an income of £868,000. 'Donated services' from Nationwide Building Society amount to £78,500. Grants were made totalling £1.6 million, although this may not be indicative of future funding levels given the foundation's strategic review and new funding programme.

Exclusions
The foundation will not consider funding:
▸ Charities with 'unrestricted reserves' which exceed 50% of annual expenditure, as shown in their accounts
▸ Charities which are in significant debt as shown in their accounts
▸ Promotion of religion or politics
▸ Charities which have been declined by the foundation within the last 12 months
▸ Applications which do not comply with the foundation's funding criteria/guidelines

Applications
On an application form available from the foundation's website.

Information gathered from:
Accounts; Charity Commission record; funder's website.

Nemoral Ltd

Orthodox Jewish causes
£1.3 million (2012)

Beneficial area
Worldwide.

Correspondent: Mrs Rivka Gross, Trustee, c/o Cohen Arnold and Co., New Burlington House, 1075 Finchley Road, London NW11 0PU (tel: 020 8731 0777)

Trustees: Ellis Moore; Rivka Gross; Michael Saberski.

CC Number: 262270

The trust supports the promotion of the Jewish religion, Jewish education and the relief of poverty in the Jewish community in the UK and abroad.

In 2012 it had assets of £2.4 million, an income of £133,000 and gave grants totalling £1.3 million. A list of grant beneficiaries was not included in the trust's accounts.

Applications

In writing to the correspondent.

Information gathered from:
Accounts; annual report; Charity Commission record.

Network for Social Change

Developing world debt, environment, human rights, peace, arts and education

£1 million (2011/12)

Beneficial area
UK and overseas.

Correspondent: Ms Tish McCrory, Administrator, BM 2063, London WC1N 3XX (tel: 01647 61106; email: thenetwork@gn.apc.org; website: thenetworkforsocialchange.org.uk)

Trustees: Sue Gillie; Bevis Gillett; Tom Bragg; Anthony Stoll; P. Boase; C. Freeman; S. Rix; A. Robbins.

CC Number: 295237

Summary

Network for Social Change, formerly the Network Foundation, is a group of philanthropic individuals who have come together to support progressive social and ecological change. Grants typically go to organisations addressing such issues as environmental sustainability and economic and social justice.

Funding is given in the UK and overseas to projects which are likely to affect social change, either through research, public education, innovatory services and other charitable activities. The network tends to favour structural change, rather than relief work, but there is no set policy on the specific types of organisations it will fund.

Grants are usually for up to £20,000 but major and longer-term projects can also be funded with much higher donations.

Organisation

The network is unusual in its organisation and offers the following information about how it operates:

Network members are each personally active in sponsoring, assessing, selecting and commending projects to fellow members. Our funding processes are designed to encourage members to find worthwhile projects, assess their potential and evaluate their achievements. Those without previous experience of such an undertaking work alongside more experienced members.

Funding

There are three funding streams:

▶ Pools – Members sponsor projects from one of six pools, currently: Green Planet; Human Rights; Economic Justice; Health and Wholeness; Peace; Arts and Education. Around half of the funding is given through pools
▶ Major Projects – Initiated and driven by a small group of members these typically focus on a neglected area of social change. Funding is normally provided for three to six years with £50,000–£100,000 given per year per project
▶ FastTrack – Grants of up to £5,000

Charities are allocated 90% of the funding but 10% is given to other organisations in order to allow the network to fund new or more radical campaigning organisations.

Grantmaking in 2011/12

In 2011/12 the trust had assets of £205,000, an income of £1.2 million and gave grants totalling £1 million. Unrestricted funds were broken down into the following categories:

General	£50,000
Arts and education for change	£64,000
Economic justice	£113,000
Green planet	£75,000
Health and wholeness	£84,000
Human rights	£112,000
Peace	£108,000
Unallocated	£0

Three major projects were also supported: New Economics Foundation – Great Transition (£155,000); One Society (£120,000); and Asylum (£29,000). Fast Track funding totalled £176,000 and anonymous donations £2,000.

Other beneficiaries included: The Joseph Rowntree Charitable Trust (£125,000); War on Want (£48,000); STAR (Student Action for Refugees) (£28,000); The Gaia Foundation (£19,000); The Children's Parliament (£16,000); Karma Nirvana Peace and Enlightenment Project for Asian Men and Women, The Holly Hill Charitable Trust, Friends of the Earth Trust Ltd and Manchester Environmental Resource Centre (£15,000 each); New Israel Fund (£13,000); Business and Human Rights Resource Centre (£13,000); Hamlin Fistula UK (£12,000); Civil Liberties Trust (£11,000); and Kanaama Interactive Community Support (£11,000).

Applications

The network chooses the projects it wishes to support and does not solicit applications. Unsolicited applications cannot expect to receive a reply.

However, the network is conscious that the policy of only accepting applications brought by its members could limit the range of worthwhile projects it could fund. To address this, the network has set up a 'Project Noticeboard' on its website to allow outside organisations to post a summary of a project for which they are seeking funding. Members of the network can then access the noticeboard and, if interested, contact the organisation for further information with a view to future sponsorship. Projects are deleted from the noticeboard after about six months. Note only 1–2% of project noticeboard entries result in sponsorship and funding.

Information gathered from:
annual report and accounts; Charity Commission record; funder's website.

The Frances and Augustus Newman Foundation

Medical research and equipment

£347,500 (2011/12)

Beneficial area
UK.

Correspondent: Hazel Palfreyman, Administrator, c/o Baker Tilly Chartered Accountants, Hartwell House, 55–61 Victoria Street, Bristol BS1 6AD (tel: 01179 452000; email: hazel. palfreyman@bakertilly.co.uk)

Trustees: David Sweetnam; Hugh Rathcavan; John Williams; Stephen Cannon.

CC Number: 277964

The foundation aims to advance the work of medical professionals working in teaching hospitals and academic units, mostly (but not exclusively) funding medical research projects and equipment, including fellowships of the Royal College of Surgeons. Grants range from £1,000 to £100,000 a year and can be given for up to three years.

In 2011/12 the trust had assets of £11.7 million and an income of £350,500. Grants were made to 14 organisations totalling £347,500.

The beneficiaries during the year included: Peterhouse College – Cambridge (£100,000 towards a new building); University of Cambridge (£100,000); Royal College of Surgeon (£50,000 towards a one-year fellowship); University College London – Institute of Ophthalmology (£24,000 towards the costs of a gene therapy technical assistant); St Wilfred's Hospice (£23,500); Alzheimer's Research UK (£10,000 for a gene analysis machine); Wellbeing of Women (£10,000); Royal College of Surgeons – Museum (£5,500 for the facial reconstruction of the Irish Giant); and the Dream Team (£1,000).

Exclusions

Applications are not normally accepted from overseas. Requests from other charities seeking funds to supplement their own general funds to support medical research in a particular field are seldom supported.

Applications

Applications should include a detailed protocol and costing and be sent to the correspondent. They may then be peer-reviewed. The trustees meet in June and December each year and applications must be received at the latest by the end of April or October respectively. The foundation awards for surgical research fellowships should be addressed to the Royal College of Surgeons of England at 35–43 Lincoln's Inn Fields, London WC2A 3PE, which evaluates each application.

Percentage of awards given to new applicants: between 20% and 30%.

Common applicant mistakes

'Applications for ineligible projects.'

Information gathered from:

Accounts; annual report; Charity Commission record; further information provided by the funder.

Nominet Charitable Foundation

IT, education, social welfare
£6.5 million (2011/12)

Beneficial area

UK and overseas.

Correspondent: Vicki Hearn, Head of Project Management, Nominet, Minerva House, Edmund Halley Road, Oxford Science Park, Oxford OX4 4DQ (tel: 01865 334000; email: enquiries@ nominettrust.org.uk; website: www. nominettrust.org.uk)

Trustees: Nora Nanayakkara; Ian Ritchie; Peter Gradwell; Millie Banerjee; Elaine Quinn; Marcus East; Charles Leadbeater; Louise Ainsworth.

CC Number: 1125735

Established in 2008, this is the charitable trust of Nominet, the company which runs the registry for all.uk domain names. The Nominet Trust, the working name of the foundation, was set up with a £5 million donation from the company.

There are five investment criteria:
- Impact
- Innovation
- Sustainability
- Capacity
- Openness

The trust aims to achieve the greatest impact by making grants and providing extra support such as mentoring and events to the projects they fund. There are currently three investment programmes:

Grant Programmes

Social Tech, Social Change

A £1 million fund to inspire entrepreneurs to develop new ventures using digital technology for social impact. The trust is looking for projects that demonstrate the potential of digital technology, experience of the social issue to be addressed and an early prototype of the idea. Funding and support will last for one year.

The Digital Edge

This programme funds innovative, tested ideas for using digital technology to improve young people's economic and social participation. The trust is looking for projects which have been co-designed with young people, to be delivered by teams that include young people and that build the skills young people require. Projects must have evidence of an early prototype and be able to demonstrate viability. Funding is typically for over £50,000 and support will last for up to two years.

Life Transitions

Funding for innovative adventures using digital technology to support people through periods of transition such as moving in and out of employment, a healthcare environment or experiencing bereavement. Projects could also be for those who are helping others in these situations including transitions in later life. Projects must have a tested prototype and be able to demonstrate viability. Funding is typically for over £50,000 and support will last for up to two years.

Eligibility

The following eligibility criteria are taken from the trust website:

The majority of ventures we invest in are UK-based. However, overseas applications will be considered if they align with our programmes of investment and can clearly demonstrate how they will address social challenges faced in the UK.

We will consider applications from entrepreneurs, teams, start-ups or organisations who want to apply their talent and technology to address UK social issues.

If you are an individual, you can apply for funding but if you are successful you will be required to form a registered legal entity.

Typical organisations we invest in include:
- Charitable or not-for-profit organisations
- Commercially-run organisations that act as social enterprises
- Community groups, schools, PTAs
- Universities
- Statutory bodies, such as local authorities

Grantmaking in 2011/12

In 2011/12 the trust had assets of £7 million, an income of £7.1 million and gave grants totalling £6.5 million.

Beneficiaries included: Online Centres Foundation (£350,000); Sidekick Studios (£300,000); DigitalMe (£258,000); We Are What We Do (£209,000); Campaign for Learning (£128,000); UK Youth (£105,000); Alzheimer's Society (£92,000); Cambridge and District CAB (£78,000); and Tyze Personal Networks and Walsall Deaf People's Centre (£50,000 each).

Grants of less than £50,000 totalled £654,000.

Exclusions

The foundation will not fund the following:
- Hardware infrastructure projects, e.g. a project to equip a school with PCs, or to install Wi-Fi for a community
- Website improvements where no new functional or service delivery innovations are delivered
- Website development unless the project and organisation delivers against one of the foundation's areas of focus and meets its funding guidelines
- Organisational running costs
- Political parties or lobbying groups

Applications

Application processes vary for each programme so potential applicants should check the information on the trust's website. Firstly fill in the online self-evaluation checklist. Then applicants must submit the short online application form and if the project is judged to be suitable for the programme they will be invited to submit stage two of the application. Applications processes involve submitting short videos explaining the project.

There are various deadlines for the various stages of application; these can be found on the website. Final investment decisions are made in October, December and April.

The trust also runs pre-application events across the country and online web chats.

Information gathered from:

Accounts; annual report; Charity Commission record; guidelines for applicants; funder's website.

Northamptonshire Community Foundation

Education, health, poverty
£624,000 (2012/13)

Beneficial area
Northamptonshire and surrounding areas.

Correspondent: Victoria Miles, Chief Executive, c/o Royal and Derngate, 19 Guildhall Road, Northampton NN1 1DP (tel: 01604 230033; email: enquiries@ncf.uk.com; website: www.ncf.uk.com)

Trustees: David Laing; John Bruce; Wendi Buchanan; Anne Burnett; Linda Davis; Sandra Bell; Robert Tomkinson; Alan Maskell; Sarah Banner; David Knight; Sally Robinson.

CC Number: 1094646

This foundation was established for general charitable purposes in the county of Northamptonshire in 2001. Its aim is to help build stronger communities by encouraging local giving by providing a cost-effective way for donors to make a long-term difference in their local area. The foundation in particular works to advance education and health and relieve poverty and sickness in its area of benefit. The following information is taken from the foundation's website:

> We deliver a variety of funding for the local voluntary and community sector in the region of £600,000 per year. As the leading independent grant-making charity in the area we are proud to have delivered vital support to our communities for the last 11 years.
>
> We are dedicated to funding community-based action which improves the lives of our county's most disadvantaged people and communities. Child poverty, unemployment, homelessness, domestic violence and social isolation are just some of the issues we strive to tackle each year.
>
> With the help and support of our donors and partners we are able to help the communities where we live, work and play. This foundation is for the county of Northamptonshire. All funding raised stays right here.
>
> Whether it's offering resources to support the vital work of our voluntary sector or providing the solution for donors who want to give back to this community, our focus is about enriching lives and making Northamptonshire even better, both today and for the future.
>
> We strive to make our grants process simple and easy for you. Our grants team are always available to talk to you about your project idea and we will match your project to our most relevant fund.
>
> In most cases, if you apply for up to £3,000 your application will be considered at our monthly grants panel. Applications

for £3,001- £5,000 will go to our bi-monthly Community Grants panel.

Visit the foundation's website for more details about making an application or call the grants team on 01604 230033 or email Rachel@ncf.uk.com

The foundation currently facilitates a number of grant schemes, including those for individuals and you should visit the website for current programmes, deadlines and grants awarded.

In 2012/13 the foundation had assets of £3.1 million and an income of £1.3 million. Grants were made to organisations totalling £624,000.

Beneficiaries included: Springs Family Centre (£11,000); Serve (£10,000); Deep Roots Tall Trees, Thomas' Fund, Wallaston Cricket Club and Wriggle Dance Theatre (£5,000 each); Blackthorn Good Neighbours and Vineyard Churches – Northampton (£4,000 each); Oundle Cinema Ltd (£3,000); Pattishall Parish Hall Association and Rotary Club of Rushden (£2,000 each); and Corby VCS (£1,000).

Exclusions
General exclusions apply as follows:
- General and major fundraising appeals
- Statutory work in educational institutions
- Overseas travel or expeditions for individuals and groups
- Direct replacement of statutory and public funding
- Organisations that aim to convert people to any kind of religious or political belief
- Medical research and equipment
- Projects operating outside Northamptonshire
- Animal welfare
- Large national charities (except for independent local branches working for local people)
- Work that has already finished
- Grantmaking bodies applying for funding to redistribute to individuals or groups

Applications
The foundation accepts online applications only. Application forms for each funding programme can be downloaded from the foundation's website, where criteria and guidelines are also available. If you wish to discuss your application then the grants team welcomes calls on 01604 230033.

Information gathered from:
Accounts; annual report; Charity Commission record; funder's website.

The Community Foundation for Northern Ireland

Community, peace building, social exclusion, poverty and social injustice
£3.6 million (2011/12)

Beneficial area
Northern Ireland and the six border counties of the Republic of Ireland.

Correspondent: Avila Kilmurray, The Director, Community House, Citylink Business Park, Albert Street, Belfast BT12 4HQ (tel: 02890 245927; fax: 02871 371565; email: info@communityfoundationni.org; website: www.communityfoundationni.org)

Trustees: Tony McCusker; Les Allamby; Maurna Crozier; Geraldine Donaghy; Brian Dougherty; Conal McFeely; Anne McReynolds; Colin Stutt; John Healy; Kevin Kingston.

IR Number: XN45242

The Community Foundation for Northern Ireland, formerly the Northern Ireland Voluntary Trust, was established in 1979 with a grant of £500,000 from government. It is an independent grantmaking organisation that manages a broad portfolio of funds and programmes, aiming to tackle social exclusion, poverty and social injustice, as well as developing communities and promoting peace and reconciliation.

The five strategic areas of activity are:
- Building community infrastructure
- Increasing social inclusion
- Building peace
- Increasing social justice
- Promoting active citizenship

The foundation is responsible for many programmes and grants that are subject to open and close for applications throughout the year. New funds are also established and some end, therefore it is important to contact the foundation or check their comprehensive website for the most recent information.

A large proportion of grantmaking is directed towards tackling disadvantage, social exclusion and improving community cohesion. Funding is also often available for grassroots and inclusive arts projects, tackling deprivation or providing education/training opportunities. Other areas funded include improving the lives of people with physical and learning disabilities, and illness, social justice, grassroots environment projects. The foundation runs a lot of peace and community cohesion programmes. The foundation states that its current priority areas are:

- Projects that support self-help amongst minority groups affected by social need
- Projects that will increase inclusive and resilient communities
- Community environmental initiatives
- Work that enhances active ageing
- Community-based Women's projects that promote participation and well-being
- Initiatives that address rural isolation
- Projects that promote health and well-being by addressing specific issues
- Community arts that promote participation
- Projects that work to enhance the involvement of marginalised groups of young people
- Projects that can increase learning and that can influence policy
- Applications for work in notably deprived areas of Northern Ireland

Grants tend to range from £500 to £10,000, although are mostly for less than £5,000.

In 2011/12 the foundation had assets of £15 million, an income of £5.2 million and gave grants totalling £3.6 million.

Beneficiaries included: Conflict Resolution Services and Ballymena Inter-Ethnic Forum (£5,000 each); Roe Valley Residents association (£3,000); Foyle Down Syndrome Trust (£2,800); Feeny Community Association and British Red Cross (£2,000 each); Crafts With Love (£1,800); Fall Women's Centre and Newington Day Centre (£1,500 each); Lisburn Sea Cadets (£1,000); Burnfoot Seniors Group (£920); Scotch Youth Group (£450); and Citizens Advice Fermanagh (£280).

Exclusions

The foundation will not fund:

- Applicants not based in Northern Ireland, national charities and appeals
- Activities that duplicate existing services and substitution for statutory funding
- Retrospective funding
- Capital build projects and large equipment purchases
- Vehicles
- Promotion of religion or party political activity
- Trips outside NI, holidays, residential costs
- Dinners, fundraising promotions or other ticketed events
- Shopping trips, parties or food (except where food forms a small but essential part of a project)
- Housing associations
- Individuals (unless a new fund is specifically aimed at helping individuals)
- Projects where the Foundation's contribution is a minor part of a larger funded initiative
- Organisations that did not comply with reporting requirements of previous grant aid

Applications

Applications to any of the funds are made through the same online process. The foundation will match the application with the most suitable fund. There are comprehensive guidelines available on the website for applications. A turnaround time of 12 weeks should be allowed for all applications.

There are two parts to the application process:

- Part A – complete the short online form to answer the questions about the project, beneficiaries and budget
- Part B – you will be a unique link to your own application form in an email along with guidelines on how to fill it out. This part must be printed off and signed by two members of the organisation

Both parts should then be posted to the foundation together with the following documentation:

- A copy of the governing document
- A copy of the most recent accounts or income and expenditure statement
- A list of the management committee members and their contact details
- A recent original bank statement for the organisation's bank account

The foundation will normally only fund groups located in Northern Ireland however some funds will make grants in the Republic as well. Applicants should check the fund specifications.

Applications are assessed by the foundation's staff and recommendations are considered by the trustee's grants subcommittee.

Successful applicants will be required to submit both qualitative and quantitative monitoring information for the benefit of both the grant holder and the foundation.

Information gathered from:

Accounts; annual report; guidelines for applicants; funder's website.

The Northern Rock Foundation

Disadvantaged people
£8.5 million (2012)

Beneficial area

Cumbria, Northumberland, Tyne and Wear, County Durham and the Tees Valley.

Correspondent: Penny Wilkinson, Chief Executive, The Old Chapel, Woodbine Road, Gosforth, Newcastle upon Tyne NE3 1DD (tel: 01912 848412; fax: 01912 848413; email: generaloffice@nr-foundation.org.uk; website: www.nr-foundation.org.uk)

CC Number: 1063906

Summary

This foundation is funded by Northern Rock plc and aims to tackle disadvantage and improve quality of life in the North East and Cumbria. It gives grants to organisations which help people who are vulnerable, disadvantaged, homeless, living in poverty or are victims of crime and discrimination. They also support training, research and demonstration work and share what they learn from the activities they fund. The foundation is also involved in seeking to inform and influence wider regional and national policies.

Recent Developments

From January 2011 the Foundation was supported by Northern Rock plc through a funding agreement to provide 1% of pre-tax profits. As part of the sale of Northern Rock plc to Virgin Money, which completed on 1 January 2012, it was confirmed that Virgin Money would extend the existing commitment, in respect of the Northern Rock business, until the end of 2013. There is also a commitment between the foundation and Virgin Money to see how they could work together beyond that date.

From the foundation's 2012 annual report:

> During 2012 the Foundation carried out an interim review of its five year strategy 2011–2015 and trustees intend to close the current grant programmes at the end of 2014, as part of the completion of this strategy. From January 2013 Trustees have also decided only to accept bids for funding by invitation for the next two years. The Foundation has adequate funds in reserves to deliver its current plans to 2015. The Foundation's future plans will be reviewed in due course in the light of its remaining reserves and the outcome of on-going discussions with Virgin Money plc. on future support and funding for the Foundation.

It is not yet clear if the foundation will be able to continue after 2015 when the current programmes end and reserves are spent. The future of the foundation depends upon the outcome of discussions between the foundation and Virgin Money, who now own Northern Rock plc.

Grant programmes

Note the update from the foundation in 'applications'.

Enabling Independence and Choice

This aims to give people with mental health problems, people with learning disabilities, older people and carers a

197

choice of excellent services that help them to become or remain independent.

Safety and Justice for Victims of Abuse

Reducing the incidence and impact of domestic abuse, sexual violence, prostitution, child abuse and hate crimes, by investing in better support for victims.

Managing Money

Helps people who are in debt or have other financial problems and needs.

Having a Home

Helps vulnerable people who are homeless or are at risk of becoming homeless.

Changing Lives

This programme helps young offenders and young people within the criminal justice system, refugees and asylum seekers and people who misuse drugs or alcohol.

Fresh Ideas Fund

Supports organisations to help them grow, explore new ways of generating income and, by doing so, achieve greater impact.

Grantmaking in 2012

In 2012 the foundation had assets of £29 million and an income of £493,000. Grants totalled £8.5 million and were awarded under the following programmes:

Changing lives	£1.9 million
Managing money	£1.9 million
Enabling Independence and Choice	£1.8 million
Having a Home	£1.2 million
Safety and Justice for Victims of Abuse	£1.1 million
Fresh Ideas	£400,000
Training and Development grants	£122,000
Policy grants	£1,000
Other awards	£117,000
Total	**£8.5 million**

The annual report also illustrated grants by geographical spread:

Cumbria	22	£1.1 million
Durham	19	£698,000
North East	32	£2.7 million
North East and Cumbria	4	£235,000
Northumberland	13	£334,000
Tees Valley	29	£1.5 million
Tyne and Wear	55	£2 million

Beneficiaries included: Addaction (£134,000); Middlesbrough First (£114,000); Barrow and District Credit Union Study Group (£99,000); My Sister's Place (£90,000); The Lawnmowers Independent Theatre Company (£80,000); Impact Housing (Eden Rural Foyer) (£75,000); Methodist Asylum Project, Middlesbrough (£66,000); Regional Youth Work Unit (£50,000); North Tyneside Art Studio Ltd (£42,000); Age UK Newcastle upon

Tyne (£27,000); Against Violence and Abuse (£25,000); and Teesside Homeless Action Group (£20,000).

Applications

Applications can now be made by invitation only. The following information is taken from the foundation's website:

> The foundation only makes grants on an invitation to bid basis. The trustees want to maximise the impact of the funds available and for that reason we are working closely with grant holders we already have a relationship with, with a particular focus on helping organisations to become more resilient.

Information gathered from:

Accounts; annual report; Charity Commission record; funder's website.

The Northwood Charitable Trust

Medical research, health, welfare, general
Around £2 million (2011/12)

Beneficial area
Scotland, especially Dundee and Tayside.

Correspondent: Brian McKernie, c/o William Thomson and Sons, 22 Meadowside, Dundee DD1 1LN (tel: 01382 201534)

Trustees: Brian Harold Thomson; Andrew Francis Thomson; Lewis Murray Thomson.

SC Number: SC014487

The Northwood Trust is connected to the D C Thomson Charitable Trust, D C Thomson and Company and the Thomson family. It was established by Eric V Thomson in 1972 and has received additional funding from other members of the family.

Previously the trust has stated in its brief annual report that 'the trustees have adopted the principle of giving priority to assisting Dundee and Tayside based charities' and says 'unsolicited applications for donations are not encouraged and will not normally be acknowledged'. Other than this there is little indication of the trust's grantmaking policy, beyond what can be deduced from the partial, uncategorised grants lists, and there was no review of the trust's grantmaking in previous reports.

In 2011/12 the trust had an income of £2.2 million and an expenditure of £2.4 million. No further information was available.

Previous beneficiaries include: Tenovus Medical Projects; Tayside Orthopaedic and Rehabilitation Technology Centre; Macmillan Cancer Relief Scotland;

Brittle Bone Society; Dundee Repertory Theatre; Dundee Samaritans; Dundee Age Concern; Couple Counselling Tayside; and Tayside Association for the Deaf.

Applications

The trust has previously stated that funds are fully committed and that no applications will be considered or acknowledged.

Information gathered from:
OSCR record.

The Nuffield Foundation

Science and social science research and capacity development, particularly in the fields of law and justice, children and families and education
£5 million (2012)

Beneficial area
UK and Commonwealth.

Correspondent: See contacts for separate programmes, 28 Bedford Square, London WC1B 3JS (tel: 020 7631 0566; fax: 020 7232 4877; email: info@ nuffieldfoundation.org; website: www. nuffieldfoundation.org)

Trustees: Prof. Genevra Richardson; Lord Krebs; Prof. Sir David Watson; Prof. David Rhind; Dr Colette Bowe; Prof. James Banks; Prof. Terrie Moffitt.

CC Number: 206601

Summary

The Nuffield Foundation is one of the UK's best known charitable trusts which was established in 1943 by William Morris (Lord Nuffield), the founder of Morris Motors. Lord Nuffield wanted his foundation to 'advance social well being', particularly through research and practical experiment. The foundation aims to achieve this by supporting work which will bring about improvements in society, and which is founded on careful reflection and informed by objective and reliable evidence.

The foundation's income comes from the returns on its investments. It does not fundraise, or receive money from the government. The foundation's financial independence and lack of vested interests helps to ensure an impartial and even-handed approach to problems in the projects it funds. Most of the foundation's income is spent on grants some of which are for research and others support practical innovation or development, often in voluntary sector organisations. In both cases the preference is for work that has wide significance, beyond the local or routine. The foundation looks to support projects that are imaginative and innovative, take a thoughtful and rigorous approach to problems, and have the potential to influence policy or practice.

Grantmaking

The foundation's grantmaking reflects its aim of bringing about improvements in society through research and practical experiment. The wide range of activities supported by the foundation fall into two main categories:

- Funding research and innovation in education and social policy
- Increasing the proliferation and quality of research and professional skills – both in science and social sciences – through capacity building programmes

Project grants are made to organisations and institutions to support research, developmental or experimental projects that meet a practical or policy need. Grants generally range in size from £5,000 to £150,000 although increasingly larger grants for over £200,000 are made. The preference is for work that has wide significance, beyond the local or routine.

The foundation has four grant programmes that support research and innovation; these are:

Law in Society

We are interested in how law functions in society, and in law as a social institution. We fund research that is likely to shed light on policy or practice; and we fund practical innovation for evaluation and experiment.

We focus on three types of work:

- Critical reviews to summarise what is known about how law functions in a particular area. These reviews are not solely doctrinal or conceptual, but evaluate empirical evidence, assessing findings and their robustness
- Empirical research to establish descriptive information or look for evidence about causes
- Evaluations of programmes or experiments. These may be formative evaluations or evaluations of outcomes, in which case a comparison group or randomised-design is likely to be needed

Children and Families

Our Children and Families programme supports work to help ensure that the laws and institutions governing family life in the UK are operating in the best interests of children and families.

We are particularly interested in applications in the following areas:

- Links between education and child development, either in the case of adolescent mental health or younger children
- Consideration of policies relevant to child welfare in a broader institutional context: parents' paid working

patterns; childcare and early years provision
- Consideration of the well-being of children growing up in adverse conditions, and what institutional responses may be appropriate
- Family law, including cohabitation, child contact and child support
- Child protection and placement (adoption and fostering), but only when it raises significant issues

Open Door

The foundation keeps an 'open door' to proposals of exceptional merit for research projects or practical innovations that lie outside our main programme areas, but that meet trustees' wider interests. These must have some bearing on our charitable objective to improve social well-being.

We are particularly interested in projects which identify change or interventions which will have practical implications for policy or practice, or that will improve the quality of research evidence in areas of public debate. Through the Open Door, the foundation may also identify emerging areas that justify more sustained attention.

Current areas of interest
- The financial circumstances of older people and economic planning for later life. Recent projects include: work on pensions; work on innovative models of financing care; a study of employers' perspectives on the ageing workforce; and a study of public attitudes to providing for old age
- Government, law making and the constitution. Recent projects include studies of: the governance of Parliament; and the audit, inspection and scrutiny of government
- Poverty and disadvantage: including work on incomes and work, and intergenerational transmission of wealth, opportunity and life chances. Recent projects include a review of the UK tax system, a study of inheritance and a study of the compliance costs of benefits and tax credits
- The UK and Europe, including cross-country comparative research. Recent projects include; education and migrant families; Chatham House commission on the UK's future role in Europe; a study of the role of migrant health and social care workers in ageing societies

Education

We are committed to improving education opportunities and outcomes for all. We have supported innovative research and development in education for over 60 years.

We consider applications for education and research grants in the following areas:
- Foundations for learning
- Mathematics education
- Science education
- Secondary education transitions
- Student parents and women's education

The foundation offers very detailed breakdowns of specific funding priorities within each category on its website.

Grants are mainly for research (usually carried out in universities or independent research institutes) but are also made for practical developments or innovation, often in voluntary sector organisations.

As an independent foundation, we are well placed to deal with sensitive issues, to challenge fashions and tacit assumptions. We support people with creative ideas to identify change or interventions which will have a practical impact for researchers, policy makers and practitioners.

We do not fund the ongoing costs of existing work or services, or provide core funding for voluntary sector bodies.

Development of research and professional capacity

We believe policy and practice should be influenced by independent and rigorous evidence. We aim to ensure these qualities are maintained in the future by funding programmes to build research and professional capacity in science and social science.

In science and social science, the foundation's grants for the development of research and professional capacity are targeted mainly at people in the early stages of their career.

The foundation is currently running the following programmes for capacity building:

- Nuffield Research Placements: For students in the first year of a post-16 STEM course to work alongside professionals in a research environment. Students get their expenses paid and may also be eligible for a weekly bursary
- Quantitative Methods Programme: The centres for this programme have now been selected
- Africa Programme: Investing in UK/ Africa partnerships to increase the professional and academic training available for people in eastern and southern Africa. This programme is not open to applications
- Oliver Bird Rheumatism Programme: Four year PhD training programmes in biosciences at five universities to build research capacity in rheumatic disease

These programmes may open and close and new ones may be added, therefore applicants interested in the capacity building arm of the foundation should check the website.

The foundation also runs the Nuffield Council on Bioethics, which identifies, examines and reports on the ethical questions raised by recent advances in biological and medical research.

Grantmaking in 2012

During the year the foundation had assets of £238 million and an income of £4.9 million. Grants were made totalling £5 million. Aside from expenditure on grants the foundation spent an additional £5 million on support costs. This total includes staffing, hosting seminars and conferences, commissioned research and evaluations of research.

Grants were categorised/broken down in the annual report as follows:

Social policy	
Open Door	£1.3 million
Children and Families	£1 million
Law in Society	£294,000
Education	
Education grants	£1.5 million
Capacity Building	
Nuffield Research Placements	£423,000
Undergraduate Research Bursaries	£331,000
Oliver Bird Rheumatism Programme	£250,000
Africa Programme	(£1,200)
New career development fellowships	(£38,000)
Social Science small grants	(£44,000)

The table shows some minus amounts due to cancelled grants outweighing grants made in those categories.

Beneficiaries included: University of Cambridge (£339,000); Institute for Fiscal Studies (£296,000); London School of Economics (£219,000); CHIVA Africa (£150,000); King's College London (£117,000); University of Oxford (£101,000); Institute for Public Policy Research (£68,000); University of Stirling (£39,000); ASA Advice Now (£25,000); and Lexicon Ltd (£20,000).

Full details of the grants made are available in the foundation's annual report and accounts.

Exclusions

The foundation normally makes grants only to UK organisations, and supports work that will be mainly based in the UK, although the trustees welcome proposals for collaborative projects involving partners in European or Commonwealth countries.

Several of our funding programmes are open to applications. There are different exclusions for different programmes so please consult the full guidelines for each area before applying.

There are a number of things that **we do not fund under any of our funding programmes.** These include:

- General appeals
- Buildings or capital costs
- Applications solely for equipment – grants for equipment are allowed when they are part of a project that is otherwise acceptable
- Support or attend conferences or seminars
- Projects that could be considered by a government department, a Research Council or a more appropriate charity
- The establishment of Chairs, or other permanent academic posts
- Grants for the production of films or videos, or for exhibitions
- Funding for school fees, a university course, or a gap year project
- Requests for funding for financial help from or on behalf of individuals in distress

Applications

The application process is the same for all of the research and innovation grant programmes, that is: Law in Society; Children and Families; Education and Open Door.

The foundation publishes the extensive 'Grants for Research and Innovation – Guide for Applications' available to download from the foundation's website, which should be read by any potential applicant.

The first stage is to submit an outline application which will be considered and then the proposal may be shortlisted for consideration by trustees. In this case applicants will be asked to submit a full application. Trustees meet three times a year to consider applications, in March, July and November. Deadlines for these meetings are four months before for outline applications then two months before for full applications; exact deadlines are available on the website.

We welcome cross-disciplinary collaborations or applications that straddle our own areas of interest. If your application meets the criteria of more than one programme, then submit the outline to the most suitable category and note if you think there is an overlap. You do not need to submit it to more than one programme.

The contacts for the four funding programmes are:

Children and Families and **Law in Society**: Alison Rees – arees@nuffieldfoundation.org

Education: Kim Woodruff – kwoodruff@nuffieldfoundation.org

Open Door: Rocio Lale-Montes – rlale-montes@nuffieldfoundation.org

Applicants for the Nuffield Research Placements should contact their local contact, a list of which can be found on the website.

Information gathered from:

Accounts; annual report; Charity Commission record; guidelines for applicants; funder's website.

The Ofenheim Charitable Trust

General, mainly charities supporting health, welfare, arts and the environment
£352,000 (2011/12)

Beneficial area
Worldwide, in practice UK with some preference for East Sussex.

Correspondent: The Trustees, Baker Tilly, The Pinnacle, 170 Midsummer Boulevard, Milton Keynes MK9 1BP (tel: 01908 687800; email: geoff.wright@bakertilly.co.uk)

Trustees: Roger Jackson Clark; Rory McLeod; Alexander Clark; Fiona Byrd.

CC Number: 286525

Established in 1983 by Dr Angela Ofenheim, it is the policy of the trust to 'provide regular support for a number of charities in East Sussex because of the founder's association with that area'. High-profile organisations in the fields of health, welfare, arts and the environment are supported with many of the same organisations benefiting each year.

In 2011/12 the trust had assets of just over £11.8 million and an income of £318,000. Grants were made to 60 organisations totalling £352,000.

Beneficiaries included: Trinity Hospice and Barnardo's (£12,000 each); Stroke Association and Friends of the Elderly (£10,000 each); National Youth Orchestra of Great Britain (£9,000); Toynbee Hall (£5,500); Wallace Collection (£4,000); Centrepoint (£3,300); Greenwich, Deptford and Rotherhithe Sea Cadet Unit (£3,000); and the Koestler Trust (£2,000).

Exclusions
No grants to individuals.

Applications
In writing to the correspondent. 'The trustees' policy has been to provide regular support for a number of charities and to respond to one-off appeals to bodies where they have some knowledge. They will consider all applications for grants and make awards as they see fit.'

Information gathered from:
Accounts; Charity Commission record.

Oglesby Charitable Trust

General charitable purposes
£797,000 (2011/12)

Beneficial area
The North West of England.

Correspondent: The Trustees, PO Box 336, Altrincham, Cheshire WA14 3XD (email: oglesbycharitabletrust@bruntwood.co.uk; website: www.oglesbycharitabletrust.co.uk)

Trustees: Jean Oglesby; Michael Oglesby; Robert Kitson; Kate Vokes; Jane Oglesby; Chris Oglesby; Peter Renshaw.

CC Number: 1026669

The Oglesby Charitable Trust was established in 1992. The funding of the trust comes from annual contributions from Bruntwood Ltd, part of a group of North West based property investment companies owned by the founding trustees that has a net worth of approximately £300 million. The trust has been established to support charitable activities across a broad spectrum, and these reflect the beliefs and interests of the founding trustee family.

The following information is taken from the trust's website:

It is accepted that the trust will be relatively modest in it resources and the trustees will be looking to place funds where they can make a real and measurable impact. They acknowledge that there already exists a large number of charitable and government backed organisations operating across all fields and it is not the trustees intention of compete with, or supplement, these. Although funding grants are made to organisations following unsolicited cold applications, increasingly these are reducing in number. The trustees are now making the majority of their grants based on areas of direct interest into areas of need which they have personally identified.

When appropriate the trustees are looking to form associations with organisations over a number of years in order that a longer-term project can be supported and the trustees can better understand an individual charity. A maximum of three years is normally placed on their associations to avoid the funding becoming core of an organisation's activities.

Who do we help?
Primarily applicants whose activities are based in the North West of England.

Organisations that can demonstrate that the funds are making a real difference, rather than being absorbed into an anonymous pool, no matter how significant the end result may appear to be.

Organisations that demonstrate both the highest standards of propriety and sound business sense in their activities. This does not mean high overheads but it does mean focused use of funds, where they are needed.

Funding that is to be operated as an individual project that can be ring-fenced as far as possible. Although preferred activities will be those that do not form part of current core operations, and which can be demonstrated to make a real difference, it is accepted that, in certain cases, they may be considered in exceptional circumstances. It is most unlikely that a new start up project will be funded if it has already commenced.

Grants are made mainly in the following areas:
- Artistic development, both on an individual and group level
- Educational grants and building projects
- Environmental improvement projects
- Improving the life and welfare of the underprivileged, where possible, by the encouragement of self-help
- Medical aid and research

Acorn Fund

We do have a fund set aside each year for smaller donations, which we call our Acorn Fund and donations from this fund will be between £200 and £1,000. This fund is administered by Forever Manchester (previously Community Foundation) and applications can be obtained from the foundation's website at: www.forevermanchester.co.uk.

In 2011/12 the trust had assets of £1.3 million and an income of £1 million, largely from donations. Grants were made totalling £797,000.

Beneficiaries over the years have included: Action for Kids, Alcohol Drug Abstinence Service, Centre for Alternative Technology, Cheadle Hulme School, Cheetham's School, Fairbridge – Family Contact Line, Halle Youth Orchestra, Manchester City Art Gallery, Manchester University Arts and Drama, Motor Neurone Disease, National Asthma Campaign, National Library for the Blind, Stroke Research, and Whitworth Art Gallery.

Exclusions
The trust will not support:
- Non registered charities
- Those whose activities are for the purpose of collecting funds for redistribution to other charities
- Animal charities
- Charities whose principal operation area is outside the UK
- Church and all building fabric appeals
- Conferences
- Continuing running costs of an organisation
- Costs of employing fundraisers
- Expeditions
- General sports, unless strongly associated with a disadvantaged group
- Holidays
- Individuals
- Loans or business finance
- Religion
- Routine staff training
- Sectarian religions
- Sponsorship and marketing appeals

Applications
In January 2014 the trust's website stated:

Due to an unprecedented number of applications for funding over recent months, caused by the economic downturn, the trustees have decided to close the fund to new applications for the next few months until the current backlog has been attended to.

To apply when the trust is open for applications complete the Stage 1 Application Form on its website. The trustees undertake to respond to this in six weeks. If this response is positive, then applicants will be required to complete a more detailed form under Stage 2.

By Stage 2, wherever possible, the trustees will require a proper Financial Plan prepared by the applicant. This should contain clear and measurable goals, which will be reviewed at regular intervals by the parties. In cases where the applicant does not possess either the skills or the resources to prepare such a Plan, the Trust may be prepared to assist.

Finally, the trustees will want to interview the applicant(s) at their place of operation or project site, both prior to the granting of funds and during the lifetime of the project, to monitor its progress. In addition the trustees will expect regular communication from the applicant, either verbal or by letter, to keep them informed of how the project is moving forward.

Information gathered from:
Accounts; annual report; Charity Commission record; funder's website.

The P. F. Charitable Trust

General charitable purposes
£2.3 million (2011/12)

Beneficial area
Unrestricted, with local interests in Oxfordshire and Scotland.

Correspondent: The Secretary, c/o Fleming Family and Partners, 15 Suffolk Street, London SW1Y 4HG (tel: 020 7036 5685)

Trustees: Robert Fleming; Philip Fleming; Rory D. Fleming.

CC Number: 220124

The trust was established in 1951 to assist religious and educational charities and for general charitable purposes. The trust makes grants to a wide range of causes and states that its policy is to continue to make a substantial number of small grants to charitable organisations both on a one-off and recurring basis.

In 2011/12 the trust had assets of £94 million, an income of £2.6 million and made grants totalling £2.3 million, broken down as follows:

Health or the saving or lives	139	£680,000
Arts, culture, heritage and science	43	£321,000
Education	38	£299,000
Relief of need	62	£202,000
Armed forces and emergency services	25	£177,000
Amateur sport	5	£112,000
Citizenship and community development	31	£84,000
Environment	9	£24,000
Religion	8	£13,000
Animal welfare	6	£8,5000
Relief of poverty	2	£6,000
Human rights, conflict resolution, religious or racial harmony, equality and diversity	2	£4,000
Other charitable purposes	4	£229,000

Beneficiaries of the largest grants of £50,000 or more, listed in the accounts, were: Eton College Appeal and Soldiers of Oxfordshire Trust (£100,000 each); Charities Aid Foundation (£96,000); Scottish Community Foundation (£58,000); and Blind Veterans UK, Prior's Court Foundation, Oxford Radcliffe Hospitals Charitable Funds, Oxfordshire Community Foundation and Queen Elizabeth Fields Challenge (£50,000 each).

Grants of less than £50,000 each totalled £1.6 million.

Exclusions
No grants to individuals or non-registered charities.

Applications
Applications to the correspondent in writing. Trustees usually meet monthly to consider applications and approve grants.

Information gathered from:
Accounts; annual report; Charity Commission record.

The Parthenon Trust

International aid, medical research, assistance to the disadvantaged including people with disabilities, culture and heritage, medical treatment and care, education, promotion of civil society and research on current affairs

Beneficial area
Unrestricted.

Correspondent: John Whittaker, Secretary, Les Mouriaux House, St Anne, Alderney, Channel Islands GY9 3UD (tel: 01481 823821)

Trustees: Dr J. M. Darmady; J. E. E. Whittaker; Y. G. Whittaker.

CC Number: 1051467

This trust was established in 1995 for general charitable purposes. The giving is international, with the organisations, as well as the activities, being based in a number of countries. Although geographically distant for UK charities, the trust is not unapproachable but applicants are urged to contact the secretary informally before submitting their applications. The trust is based in Switzerland, the home of the chair, Geraldine Whittaker and the secretary, her husband John Whittaker and is a UK registered charity.

The areas which the trust focuses on are:
▶ International aid organisations
▶ Medical research
▶ Assistance to the disadvantaged including people with disabilities
▶ Cultural and heritage purposes
▶ Medical treatment and care including supporting services, preventative medicine and assistance to those with disabilities
▶ Education
▶ Promotion of civil society and research on current affairs

The trust states that 'No grant giving or other charitable activities were undertaken in 2012, but it is expected that activities will resume in the coming months.'

In 2012 the trust had an income of £15,000 and an expenditure of £7,800.

Previous beneficiaries have included: Cancer Research UK; Friends of Diva Opera; Mont Blanc Foundation; Ungureni Trust; International Committee of the Red Cross; UNICEF UK; Ashoka Africa; Downside Up; Cecily's Fund; Andover Young Carers; Basingstoke-Hoima Partnership for Health; Esther Benjamins Trust; Leprosy Mission; North Hampshire Medical Fund; Trinity Winchester; United Aid for Azerbaijan; Feet First World Wide;

Kariandusi School Trust and Langalanga Scholarship Fund.

Exclusions
No grants for individuals, scientific/geographical expeditions or projects which promote religious beliefs.

Applications
In writing to the correspondent. Anyone proposing to submit an application should telephone the secretary beforehand. Unsolicited written applications are not normally acknowledged. Most grants are awarded at a trustees' meeting held early in the new year, although grants can be awarded at any time.

Information gathered from:
Charity Commission record.

The Peacock Charitable Trust

Medical research, disability, general
£1.5 million (2011/12)

Beneficial area
UK with a possible preference for London and the south of England.

Correspondent: The Administrator, c/o Charities Aid Foundation, Kings Hill, West Malling, Kent ME19 4TA (tel: 01732 520081)

Trustees: Charles Peacock; Bettine Bond; Dr Clare Sellors.

CC Number: 257655

This family trust was administered personally by Mr and Mrs Peacock for almost 35 years, with the assistance of Mr D Wallace who prepared reports on the majority of applicants to the trust for presentation to the trustees. Following the retirement of Mr Wallace the administration was taken over by the Charities Aid Foundation (CAF). No changes to grantmaking policy or practice have occurred with the main aims and objects being to advance the education of poor and deserving young boys and girls, and the relief of poverty, hardship, suffering and distress.

The trust has also previously commented that many of the repeated grants go towards the running costs of organisations, in recognition of the fact that charities need, and sometimes lack, continuity. It says its newer grants are often for capital purposes. Some of its recent grants have also helped organisations to pay off their debts.

The trustees rely on CAF to present charities requiring grants to them; although we note the majority of present beneficiaries are recipients of recurrent grants. As such, the opportunity for new applicants to be successful appears limited.

In 2011/12 the trust had assets of £39 million, an income of £402,000 and made grants to organisations totalling £1.5 million. Only £29,000 of this was given to new applicants.

Beneficiaries included: The Prince's Youth Business Trust (£103,000); Cancer Research UK (£95,000); Marie Curie Cancer Care (£75,000); The Jubilee Sailing Trust (£50,000); British Heart Foundation (£36,000); SENSE (£20,000); Cruse Bereavement Care (£9,000); The National Trust (£6,000); Centrepoint 8:59 (£5,000); and Royal Academy of Arts (£4,000).

Exclusions

No donations are made to individuals and only in rare cases are additions made to the list of charities already being supported.

Applications

In writing to the correspondent. The trustees meet three times a year with representatives from the Charities Aid Foundation (CAF) to decide on the grants to be made. The trust makes a lot of recurring grants therefore new applications are unlikely to be successful.

Information gathered from:

Accounts; annual report; Charity Commission record.

The Dowager Countess Eleanor Peel Trust

Medical research, the elderly, socially disadvantaged people and general
£311,000 (2011/12)

Beneficial area

Worldwide, in practice UK, with a preference for Lancashire (especially Lancaster and District), Cumbria, Greater Manchester, Cheshire and Merseyside.

Correspondent: Allan J. Twitchett, Secretary, Trowers and Hamlins LLP, 3 Bunhill Row, London EC1Y 8YZ (tel: 020 7423 8000; email: secretary@ peeltrust.com; website: www.peeltrust. com)

Trustees: Sir Robert Boyd; John W. Parkinson; Michael Parkinson; Prof. Richard Ramsden; Prof. Margaret Pearson; Julius Manduell.

CC Number: 214684

The Dowager Countess Eleanor Peel Trust was established by trust deed in 1951 in accordance with the terms of her will. The objects of the trust are for general charitable purposes but with a preference for medical charities, charities

for older people and those who are disadvantaged. There is a schedule to the trust deed listing 'scheduled charities' the trust may also support. The trustees receive payment for their services ranging from £1,000 to £8,000 per year.

Grants are made to:

- Medical care charities (specifically aimed at benefitting older people including Alzheimer's, macular disease, prostate cancer and Parkinson's disease
- Charities in connection with old people (old age, homes, carers)
- Charities assisting people who have fallen upon hard times (disability, hospices and hospitals, ex-services, relief after natural or man-made disasters, mental health, addiction and homelessness)
- Various charitable bodies specified in the Trust Deed

Medical Research Grants

Major – Grants of £10,000 to £50,000 for a defined research project for up to three years. The trustees are keen to support innovative and high quality research projects that do not fall within the areas of focus of major funding organisations.

Minor – Grants of up to £10,000 for areas such as pilot study costs or equipment.

The trust also supports individuals pursuing research, advanced study or the acquisition of a new clinical skill through The Peel and Rothwell Jackson Postgraduate Travelling Fellowship.

The trustees have a clear preference for supporting charities and projects in the North West of England, from where the trust fund monies originally emanated.

Grantmaking in 2011/12

In 2011/12 the trust had assets of £15.1 million and an income of £575,000. The trust received 357 applications during the year, 88 of which were ineligible, and made 48 grants totalling £311,000, which were categorised as follows:

Charities assisting people facing hardship	£142,000
Medical charities and medical research	£92,500
Charities in connection with older people	£22,000
Charities listed in the trust deed	£4,000
Other charitable purposes	£50,000

Beneficiaries included: Peel Studentship Trust – University of Lancaster (£35,000); University of Manchester (£28,000); Mood Swing Network and the British Red Cross (£10,000 each); Genesis Breast Cancer Prevention Appeal (£9,500); Marfan Trust (£8,000); Tax Help for Older People (£4,000); Coalition for the Removal of Pimping, FareShare and Relate Lancashire and

Cumbria (£5,000 each); and the Olive Branch (£1,500).

Exclusions

Grants are not made to charities substantially under the control of central or local government or charities primarily devoted to children. Applications from individuals are not considered, except for medical research grants and annual travelling fellowship awards.

Applications

General Grants

The following information is required:

- A general outline of the reasons for the application
- The amount of grant applied for
- The latest annual report and audited accounts
- If the application is for a major capital project, details of the cost of the project together with information regarding funds already in hand or pledged

A grant application form can be downloaded from the trust's website or completed online.

Applications for Medical Research Grants

Apply using the form available on the website.

Applications for medical research grants will be categorised as appropriate for a 'minor grant' (£10,000 or less) or a 'major grant' (greater than £10,000 per annum for a defined research project for 1–3 years). Applications to be considered for a major grant will be assessed en-block annually at the trustee's March meeting. Applications will be competitive and will be met from funds set aside for this purpose. The following additional information is required:

- Aims, objectives and direction of the research project
- The institution where the research will be carried out and by whom (principal researchers)
- An outline of costs and of funding required for the project and details of any funds already in hand

A brief (but not too technical) annual report on the progress of projects receiving major grants will be requested from the research team.

Minor medical grants

Apply using the form available on the website. 'Applications for Minor Grants are considered at each of the trustees meeting which are ordinarily held in March, July and November each year.'

Percentage of awards given to new applicants: 57%.

Common applicant mistakes

'Not fully considering the trustees' grantmaking strategy on the trust's website before submitting an application, including applications from charities primarily concerned with children, which are prohibited by the terms of the trust deed from receiving funds from the trustees.'

Information gathered from:

Accounts; annual report; Charity Commission record; further information provided by the funder; funder's website.

The Performing Right Society Foundation

New music of any genre

£1.2 million (2012)

Beneficial area

UK.

Correspondent: Fiona Harvey, Operations Director, 29–33 Berners Street, London W1T 3AB (tel: 020 7306 4233; fax: 020 7306 4814; email: info@ prsformusicfoundation.com; website: www.prsformusicfoundation.com)

Trustees: Prof. Edward Gregson; Simon Platz; Baroness Estelle Morris; Sally Millest; Paulette Long; Mick Leeson; Stephen McNeff; Simon Darlow; Ameet Shah; Vanessa Swann; John Reid.

CC Number: 1080837

The PRS for Music Foundation (PRSMF) is the UK's largest independent funder purely for new music of any genre. The principle objectives of the foundation are to support, sustain and further the creation and performance of new music and to educate the public in order to augment its appreciation in the UK.

According to the trustees' report for 2012:

The foundation supports creators, performers and promoters who are involved in creatively adventurous or pioneering musical activity. In particular, support is focused on music creators (composers/song-writers/producers) who live and work in the UK and on not-for-profit performers, festivals and promoters who are based in the UK. The foundation supports a huge range of new music activity – from unsigned band showcases to residencies for composers and performers, from ground breaking commissions to the training of music producers and audience development initiatives.

Full details of the foundation's activities are available on its website, including grantmaking policies, priorities for each scheme and application forms.

In 2012 the foundation had assets of £662,000 and an income of £2 million. Grants were made totalling £1.2 million. The foundation offers the following analysis of its grantmaking during the year:

Organisations	£665,500
Partnerships	£125,500
Performance groups	£102,500
Women Make Music	£100,500
Individuals	£92,500
Festivals	£72,500
Promoters	£41,000

A list of grant recipients was not included in the accounts. However, details of previously funded projects are available on the foundation's website, though without information on the individual grant awards. They included: Arts and Refugees Network Yorks and Humber; Brass Band Heritage Trust; Contemporary Music East (CME); 2 for the Road; Focus Wales; Get it Loud in Libraries; Hackney Music Development Trust; London Contemporary Orchestra; Metta Theatre; Oh Yeah Music Centre; Orange Hill Productions; and Workers Union Ensemble.

Bands and artists supported include: Among Brothers; Matthew Bourne; Field Music; James Bulley and Daniel Jones; Kinnie the Explorer; and Melt Yourself Down.

Exclusions

The foundation will not offer funding for:

- Companies limited by shares
- Recording costs (recording costs can only be supported through Momentum Music Fund)
- Projects that contain no element of live performance
- Technological development if it does not contain a significant aspect of new music creation
- The purchase of vans and cars
- Bursaries, tuition/education costs, or scholarships
- Capital projects (e.g. building work)
- Any project raising funds for another charity
- Buying equipment/building a studio
- Organisations or projects that have been running for less than 18 months and musicians that have not been active for 18 months
- Retrospective activity
- Activity that falls before the foundation's decision date
- Organisations based outside the UK
- Artists and music creators based outside of the UK
- British artists no longer permanently resident in the UK
- International tours/recording internationally
- Radio stations/broadcasting costs
- Start-up companies or labels
- A roster of artists on a record label
- Editing, mastering or distribution of work

Applications

Apply via the trust's website. The application forms for each programme also include full guidelines for applicants. Deadlines for applications vary from programme to programme. Contact the foundation or go to the website for further information. The foundation stresses that it funds NEW music.

Information gathered from:

Accounts; annual report; Charity Commission record; funder's website.

The Jack Petchey Foundation

Young people aged 11 – 25 in the London boroughs, Essex and the Algarve, Portugal

£4.9 million (2012)

Beneficial area

London, Essex and the Algarve, Portugal.

Correspondent: Gemma Dunbar, Head of Grants, Exchange House, 13–14 Clements Court, Clements Lane, Ilford, Essex IG1 2QY (tel: 020 8252 8000; fax: 020 8477 1088; email: mail@ jackpetcheyfoundation.org.uk; website: www.jackpetcheyfoundation.org.uk)

Trustee: Jack Petchey Foundation Company.

CC Number: 1076886

This foundation was established in 1999 by Jack Petchey and gives grants to programmes and projects that benefit young people aged 11 – 25. Jack Petchey was born in July 1925 in the East End of London. From a background with very few advantages he became a prominent entrepreneur and businessman. The foundation aims to enable young people to achieve their potential by inspiring, investing in and developing activities that increase their personal, social, emotional and physical development.

In the UK the foundation benefits all London boroughs and Essex. In 2004, the foundation introduced a programme in the Algarve, Portugal. It focused initially on the Albufeira District. In July 2005 the Loulé District was included and in January 2006, Silves District. The objectives of the work in Portugal are the same as those established in the UK.

As well as the various grant schemes that the foundation runs it also supports various large projects that it has established, including a school called Petchey Academy, a training ship – the TS Jack Petchey, Panathlon Challenge for young people with disabilities, the Step into Dance programme and a public speaking challenge – Jack Petchey's Speak Out! that over 20,000 young people a year participate in.

Achievement Award Scheme

The Jack Petchey Achievement Award Scheme is run in over 2,000 schools, colleges and clubs throughout London and Essex, contributing millions of pounds to youth organisations. The scheme is a reward and recognition initiative which enables schools and clubs to celebrate the achievements of young people and receive additional funding for the organisation.

Over £2 million is allocated to this scheme each year. The benefits of these awards are that they:

- Enable schools/colleges/youth clubs etc., to recognise the effort, endeavour and achievement of young people in a practical and positive way
- Provide additional funds for schools/colleges and youth clubs worth £2,300 plus, a year, including the leader awards' small grant scheme
- Enable young people to nominate an adult to win a leader award (for a youth worker, volunteer, teacher, non-teaching member of staff and so on)

Each month participating youth clubs, schools, colleges etc. select one young person to receive an achievement award. The month's winner receives a framed certificate and a cheque for (payable to the school/college/club) to be spent on a school, club or community project of the recipient's choice.

Registered charities working with young people, secondary schools, colleges and youth clubs are all eligible to apply.

Small Grants Fund

Organisations that are running the achievement awards effectively can apply for up to £500 to enhance their work with young people once a year. The total project cost must not be more than £5,000 and the project must not run for longer than 12 months. The project must benefit groups of young people who are most in need of support.

Individual grants for volunteering

The foundation will consider sponsoring young people (11–25 years old) living in London and Essex who are undertaking voluntary projects that will benefit other young people or specific charities. The normal support from the foundation will be £300 (maximum of 50% of the costs).

A sponsorship form is available from the foundation's website.

School Planners

Up to £500 is available for recipients of the Achievement Award towards the cost of producing School Planners for the coming academic year. Schools should contact the School Planner company directly, visit: www.school-planners.co.uk.

Future First

This is not a grant programmes, rather it provides infrastructure to schools and colleges to help them keep in touch with departing students. It is open to organisations involved in the Achievement Award Scheme. Participation costs £500 but the foundation pays 50% of the cost, bringing it to £250. Visit www.futurefirst.org.uk to find out more or apply.

Educational Visits

Organisations participating in the Achievement Award Scheme can apply for two small grants of up to £600 per year to enhance their educational visit programme.

These funds may change and others may be added so potential applicants should always check the foundation's website.

In 2012 the foundation had assets of £68,000 (not including liabilities) and an income of £5.6 million. Grants totalled £4.9 million, broken down as follows:

School (including out of school hours)	£1.5 million
Training and courses	£1.2 million
Sports clubs	£645,000
Youth clubs/youth projects	£561,000
Uniformed organisations	£489,000
Volunteering	£117,000
Medical/hospice/hospital	£113,000
Advice/support/counselling/ mentoring	£113,000
Disability	£111,000
Housing/homelessness	£24,000
Residential and holiday activity programmes	£21,000
General	£17,000
Addiction – alcohol/drugs/food etc.	£200

Exclusions

The foundation will not accept applications:

- From private schools
- From profit making companies
- That directly replace statutory funding
- From individuals or for the benefit of one individual (unless under the Individual Grants for Volunteering)
- For work that has already taken place
- Which do not directly benefit people in the UK
- For medical research
- For animal welfare
- For endowment funds
- That are part of general appeals or circulars
- Building or major refurbishment projects
- Conferences and seminars
- Projects where the main purpose is to promote religious beliefs

Applications

Application forms for each of the grant schemes can be downloaded from the foundation's website. A typical application process takes six to eight weeks and applicants may be visited by a grants officer. Organisations must have in place:

- Constitution/memorandum and articles of association
- Bank or building society accounts
- Public liability insurance
- Child protection policy
- Income and expenditure records (applicants may direct assessors to their Charity Commission record)

There are no deadlines for the achievement awards. There are two application round a year for small grants – one in the spring and one in the autumn, see the website for exact dates.

Applications for individual volunteering awards have no deadline and take around eight weeks to process.

Percentage of awards given to new applicants: between 10% and 20%.

Common applicant mistakes

'Not reading the guidance on the foundation's website.'

Information gathered from:

Accounts; annual report; Charity Commission record; further information provided by the funder; funder's website.

The Pilgrim Trust

Social welfare and the preservation of buildings and heritage

£3.5 million (2012)

Beneficial area

UK, but not the Channel Islands and the Isle of Man.

Correspondent: Georgina Nayler, Director, 55a Catherine Place, London SW1E 6DY (tel: 020 7834 6510; email: info@thepilgrimtrust.org.uk; website: www.thepilgrimtrust.org.uk)

Trustees: Sylvia Jay; Tim Knox; Paul Richards; Mark Jones; Alan Moses; John Podmore; James Fergusson; David Verey; Prof. Colin Blakemore; Lady Riddell; Sarah Staniforth; Michael Baughan.

CC Number: 206602

The Pilgrim Trust was founded in 1930 by the wealthy American philanthropist Edward Stephen Harkness. Inspired by his admiration and affection for Great Britain, Harkness endowed the trust with just over £2 million. Harkness did not want the charity named after him, so the decision was taken to name the charity The Pilgrim Trust to signify its link with the land of the Pilgrim Fathers. It was Harkness's wish that his gift be given in grants for some of Britain's 'more urgent needs' and to 'promote her future well-being'. The first trustees decided that the trust should assist with social welfare projects, preservation (of buildings and countryside) and the promotion of art and learning. This has remained the focus of The Pilgrim Trust and the current Board of Trustees follows Harkness's guidelines by giving grants to projects in the fields of Preservation and Scholarship and of Social Welfare. Trustees review these objectives every three years.

General

The trust aims to distribute £2 million a year with 60% directed towards preservation and conservation and 40% towards social welfare.

There are two grant schemes:
- **Main Grant Fund**: 90% of the annual grant budget is allocated to this scheme, for grants of over £5,000
- **Small Grant Fund**: the remainder of the grants budget is distributed through this scheme in grants of £5,000 or less

These grants are available to UK registered charities including exempt charities, recognised public bodies and registered Friendly Societies for revenue costs, project costs, costs of initial exploratory work for organisations seeking to rescue important buildings and monuments and capital costs.

The following is taken from a funding guideline document available in full on the trust's website, with the main points reproduced here:

Programmes

Preservation and scholarship
- Preservation of and repairs to historic buildings and architectural features. Special consideration is given to projects that give new use to buildings of outstanding architectural or historic importance
- Conservation of monuments or structures that are important to their surroundings, including buildings designed for public performance
- Conservation of works of art, books, significant ephemera, museum objects and records associated with archaeology, historic buildings and the landscape. Note: funding for such work is considered only if normal facilities are not available
- Promotion of knowledge through academic research and its dissemination, including cataloguing within museums, galleries and libraries and institutions where historic, scientific or archaeological records are preserved. Note: funding is restricted to works for which public funds are not available. Costs for preparing the work for publication will be considered but not those for the publication itself
- Cataloguing of archives and manuscripts: The Pilgrim Trust is currently funding the cataloguing of archives and manuscripts through the National Cataloguing Scheme administered through the National Archives. Please visit the National

Archives website for more information: www.nationalarchives.gov.u
- Conservation of manuscripts is funded through the National Manuscripts Conservation Trust. Please visit the National Archives website for more information
- Places of Worship. To apply under our block grant allocation scheme please contact the relevant administering organisation directly:
  - The Pilgrim Trust is currently funding repairs to the historic fabric of cathedrals through a programme administered by the Cathedrals Fabric Commission for England (CFCE). For information on eligibility and how to apply, please visit the CFCE website: www.churchcare.co.uk
  - Appeals for fabric repairs to churches in England and Wales should be sent to: National Churches Trust, 31 Newbury Street, London EC1A 7HU
  - Appeals for fabric repairs to churches in Scotland should be sent to: Scottish Churches Architectural Heritage Trust, 15 North Bank Street, The Mound, Edinburgh EH1 2IP
  - Appeals for fabric repairs to churches in Northern Ireland should be sent directly to the Pilgrim Trust
  - Appeals for historic contents of Church of England churches should be directed to: Church Buildings Council, Cathedral and Church Buildings Division, Church House, Great Smith Street, London SW1P 3NZ, enquires.ccb@chruchofengland.org
  - Appeals for historic contents of non-Church of England establishments (including Northern Ireland, Scotland and Wales should be sent directly to the Pilgrim Trust

Social Welfare
- Projects supporting people who misuse drugs or alcohol that fall within the following themes. Applications that fall outside this thematic area will not be considered.
  - Projects to support the families and/or carers of people who have been or are misusing drugs or alcohol, trustees include an interest in projects which assist the individual substance misuser where support for the family is integral part of the package or care delivered, as well as evidence led approaches to support the families and carers of substance misusers
  - Projects to support substance misusers with complex social needs. Trustees have an interest in supporting projects which incorporate a robust, integrated approach to the treatment of substance misuse where issues such as domestic violence, care for children, prostitution, or homelessness may feature as additional difficulties
  - Evidence driven projects will be prioritised

- Projects in prisons and projects providing alternatives to custody that fall within the following themes:
  - Projects that seek to reduce the use of custody for women. Trustees will include work with women with extreme vulnerabilities which are likely to lead to offending. Organisations applying in this area will be expected to have considerable experience and expertise in work with women with multiple and complex needs
  - Projects that seek to support women who are leaving custody and that assist them to reintegrate with society and their families. Trustees have an interest in projects that assist female offenders and ex-offenders families, particularly their children

Proposals for small academically robust research projects that meet the Trust's priority themes and that provide tangible outputs in either policy or practical terms will also be accepted. Projects that link to our priorities in both prisons and substance misuse are particularly welcome.

Please note that for all research projects that a full specification will need to be submitted at second stage.

Applications regarding the above will be considered for:
- Revenue costs such as staff salaries but generally not equipment costs
- Project costs
- The costs of initial exploratory work for organisations seeking to rescue important buildings, monuments, etc.
- Capital costs

Grantmaking in 2012

During the year the trust had assets of £54 million and an income of £1.6 million. Grants were made totalling £3.5 million, including payment of grants committed in previous years.

The trust offers this analysis of grantmaking in 2012 in their annual report for the year: Trustees committed £1.5 million for spending in 2012 with £1.2 million and £524,000 forward commitments for 2013 and 2014 respectively. They awarded 84 grants with the main grants averaging just under £43,500. Trustees have been aiming to increase the average size of grants awarded so as to make more of an impact with their funds.

Beneficiaries included: National Cataloguing Scheme (£500,000); Association of Independent Museums (£323,000); Prison Reform Trust (£300,000); Church Building Council (£150,000); SPODA (£105,000); City and Guilds of London Art School (£50,000); The University of Oxford Development Trust (£43,000); Action on Addiction (£30,000); The Mavisbank Trust (£24,000); Up-2-Us (£17,000); Dunfermline Heritage Trust (£9,000);

and Female Prisoners Welfare Project Hibiscus (£5,000).

Exclusions

Grants are not made to:

- Individuals
- Non UK registered charities or charities registered in the Channel Islands or the Isle of Man
- Projects based outside the United Kingdom
- Projects where the work has already been completed or where contracts have already been awarded
- Organisations that have had a grant awarded by us within the past two years. Note: this does not refer to payments made within that timeframe
- Projects with a capital cost of over £1 million pounds where partnership funding is required
- Projects where the activities are considered to be primarily the responsibility of central or local government
- General appeals or circulars
- Projects for the commissioning of new works of art
- Organisations seeking publishing production costs
- Projects seeking to develop new facilities within a church or the re-ordering of churches or places of worship for wider community use
- Any social welfare project that falls outside the trustees' current priorities
- Arts and drama projects – unless they can demonstrate that they are linked to clear educational goals for prisoners or those with drug or alcohol problems
- Drop in centres – unless the specific work within the centre falls within one of the trustees' current priority areas
- Youth or sports clubs, travel or adventure projects, community centres or children's play groups
- Organisations seeking funding for trips abroad
- Organisations seeking educational funding, e.g. assistance to individuals for degree or post-degree work or school, university or college development programmes

- One-off events such as exhibitions, festivals, seminars, conferences or theatrical and musical productions

Applications

Applications for both the small grants fund and the main grants can be made using the trust's online form. Applicants should read the application guidelines available on the trust's website in full before applying. There are no deadlines; applications are considered at quarterly trustee meetings. The trust welcomes informal contact prior to an application via phone or email.

Information gathered from:

annual report; accounts; Charity Commission record; guidelines for applicants; funder's website.

The Pilkington Charities Fund

General, health, social welfare, people with disabilities, older people and victims of natural disaster or war

£420,000 (2011/12)

Beneficial area

Worldwide, in practice mainly UK with a preference for Merseyside.

Correspondent: Jennifer Jones, Trustee, Rathbones, Port of Liverpool Building, Pier Head, Liverpool L3 1NW (tel: 01512 366666; email: sarah.nicklin@rathbones.com)

Trustees: Neil Pilkington Jones; Jennifer Jones; Arnold Philip Pilkington.

CC Number: 225911

The trust was established in 1950 to assist employees or former employees of Pilkington's or any associated companies. It now mainly supports registered charities in the areas of social welfare, disability, health, medical research and overseas aid. A small proportion is reserved for the benefit of present or former employees of the Pilkington Glass Company.

Grants are awarded twice a year, in November and April. Most range from £1,000 to £8,000, though larger grants for up to £100,000 are sometimes made, and typically go to national or international charities.

In 2011/12 the trust had assets of £19 million, an income of £668,000 and gave grants to 106 organisations totalling £420,000.

Beneficiaries included: Action for Addiction and UK Neurology Research Campaign (£10,000 each); Church Housing Trust and Medical Aid for Palestinians (£5,000 each); Wirral Autistic Society (£4,000); Fairbridge and Toxteth Town Hall Community Resource Centre (£3,000 each); St Johns Hospice and The Florence Institute Trust (£2,000 each); and Blood Pressure Association (£1,000).

Exclusions

Grants are only made to registered charities. No grants to individuals.

Applications

In writing to the correspondent. Applications should include the charity registration number, a copy of the latest accounts and details of the project for which support is sought.

Percentage of awards given to new applicants: between 10% and 20%.

Common applicant mistakes

'Applying for support from areas other than Merseyside.'

Information gathered from:

Accounts; annual report; Charity Commission record; further information provided by the funder.

Polden-Puckham Charitable Foundation

Peace and security, ecological issues, social change

£327,000 (2011/12)

Beneficial area

UK and overseas.

Correspondent: Bryn Higgs, Secretary, BM PPCF, London WC1N 3XX (tel: 020 7193 7364; email: ppcf@polden-puckham.org.uk; website: www.polden-puckham.org.uk)

Trustees: Harriet Gillett; Bevis Gillett; Val Ferguson; Angela Seay; Jonathan Gillett.

CC Number: 1003024

Established in 1991 with Quaker family roots, the foundation gives the following information about its areas of interest:

> In the limited areas described below we support projects that seek to influence values and attitudes, promote equity and

THE PILGRIM TRUST

	Preservation and scholarship	Social welfare	Total	Percentage split by region
National organisation	£1.3 million	£362,000	£1.7 million	46%
Scotland	£229,000	£47,000	£276,000	7%
Wales	£36,000	£0	£36,000	1%
Northern Ireland	£0	£153,000	£153,000	4%
London	£207,000	£92,000	£299,000	8%
'Home counties'	£135,000	£99,000	£234,000	6%
Rest of England	£197,000	£497,000	£994,000	27%
Total by subject area	**£2.4 million**	**£1.2 million**	**£3.5 million**	**100%**

social justice, and develop radical alternatives to current economic and social structures.

Peace and Sustainable Security
We support the development of ways of resolving violent conflicts peacefully, and of addressing their underlying causes.

Environmental Sustainability
We support work that addresses the pressures and conditions leading towards global environmental breakdown; particularly national initiatives in UK which promote sustainable living.

Our resources are limited and we receive a huge number of applications. In order to make informed grant decisions we have to focus our grant-giving in a number of ways. For this reason we fund organisations in UK that are working to influence policy, attitudes and values at a national or international level. These may be single issue groups working to achieve a particular change, or organisations with a broader remit. We give particular consideration to small pioneering headquarters organisations.

We only support practical projects when they are clearly of a pioneering nature, with potential for influencing UK national policy.

Size of grants and supported organisations
We usually give grants of between £5,000 and £15,000 per year, for up to three years. We usually support organisations for whom this would represent between 5% and 50% of their annual income (organisations with an annual income of between £10,000 and £300,000 approximately).

In 2011/12 the foundation had assets of £13 million, an income of £495,000 and gave grants totalling £327,000, broken down as follows:

Peace and security	18	£196,000
Environmental sustainability	15	£131,000

Beneficiaries during the year included: European Leadership network (£40,000); Quaker United Nations Office (£22,000); British American Security Information Council (£20,000); Carbon Tracker Initiative (£15,000); Protect the Local Globally (£11,000); Localise West Midlands and SpinWatch (£10,000); Campaign Against Arms trade (£9,000); Mines and Communities (£6,000); Oil Depletion Analysis Centre (£5,000); UK Without Incineration Network (£4,000); and Environmental Funders Network (£2,000).

Exclusions
The foundation does not fund:
- Organisations that are large (see general section)
- Organisations that are outside UK (unless they are linked with a UK registered charity and doing work of international focus)
- Work outside the UK (unless it is of international focus)

- Grants to individuals
- Travel bursaries (including overseas placements and expeditions)
- Study
- Academic research
- Capital projects (e.g. building projects or purchase of nature reserves)
- Community or local practical projects (except innovative projects for widespread application)
- Environmental/ecological conservation
- International agencies and overseas appeals
- General appeals
- Human rights work (except where it relates to peace and environmental sustainability)

Applications
The trustees meet twice a year in spring and autumn. Application forms and guidance notes can be downloaded from the foundation's website and must be submitted via email. There is also an eligibility questionnaire that potential applicants should complete before they apply. Applicants are also asked to submit their latest set of audited accounts and an annual report, preferably via email. Applications will be acknowledged within two weeks, or one week after the deadline.

Note: the foundation is happy to provide brief feedback on applications one week after the trustees have made a decision.

Percentage of awards given to new applicants: between 20% and 30%.

Common applicant mistakes
'No reading our website or guidelines or believing that we will not apply our criteria (because their work is so good – which of course it often is).'

Information gathered from:
Accounts; annual report; Charity Commission record; guidelines for applicants; further information provided by the funder; funder's website.

The Polonsky Foundation

Arts, social science, higher education institutions
£1.2 million (2011/12)

Beneficial area
UK, Israel and the USA.

Correspondent: The Trustees, 8 Park Crescent, London W1B 1PG

Trustees: Dr Georgette Bennett; Dr Leonard Polonsky; Valarie Smith; Marc Polonsky.

CC Number: 291143

Established in 1985, this is the foundation of Dr Leonard Polonsky,

executive chair of Hansard Global plc, a global financial services company based in the Isle of Man and listed on the London Stock Exchange. Its aims and objectives are as follows:

To support higher education internationally, principally in the arts and social sciences, and programmes favouring the study and resolution of human conflict. Much of this work is part of ongoing programmes being undertaken in conjunction with various Departments of the Hebrew University of Jerusalem and the Bezalel Academy of Art and Design, as well as other organisations within the United States and the United Kingdom.

In 2011/12 the foundation had assets of £44.9 million and an income of £1.1 million. Grants were made to 35 organisations totalling £1.2 million.

Beneficiaries included: British Friends of the Hebrew University (£251,500); New York Public Library (£162,500); University of Cambridge (£74,000); University of Oxford (£48,000); Royal Academy of Music (£20,000); Open Book Publishers (£15,000); Guildhall School Trust (£6,000); Guy's and St Thomas' Charity (£2,000); and The Jewish Museum (£1,000).

Applications
In writing to the correspondent.

Information gathered from:
Accounts; Charity Commission record.

Porticus UK

Social welfare, education, religion
Around £4 million each year.

Beneficial area
UK.

Correspondent: Jane Leek, Secretary, 4th Floor, Eagle House, 108–110 Jermyn Street, London SW1Y 6EE (tel: 020 7024 3503; fax: 020 7024 3501; email: porticusuk@porticus.com; website: www.porticusuk.com)

Trustees: Louise A. Adams; Mark C. L. Brenninkmeyer; Stephen R. M. Brenninkmeijer; Bert Brenninkmeijer.

CC Number: 1069245

The charity was previously called Derwent Charitable Consultancy, which administered the Waterside Trust, whose grantmaking has now been succeeded by other sources in the Netherlands advised by Porticus UK.

It is believed to be one expression of the philanthropy of the Brenninkmeyer family, founders of the C&A clothing stores in Europe. Long-term fundraisers will remember organisations such as the Marble Arch Trust. The family always sought the minimum of publicity for their energetic and much admired work.

Though the family's Catholic interests were always apparent, the range of their philanthropic interests have been wide and enterprising over the years.

Porticus UK is not in itself a grantmaker – it advises and assesses grants on behalf of several foundations in the Netherlands, including Stichting Porticus.

Porticus UK has four areas of interest and recommends in the region of 170 grants each year. Grants are normally in the range £10,000 to £25,000 but occasionally larger projects are funded. Total funds available amount to around £4 million each year.

The following information on the charity's programmes and guidelines is taken from its website:

Porticus UK's mission is to have solidarity with the poor and the marginalised, reflecting our Christian responsibility and support for the social teaching of the Roman Catholic Church. We do this through the provision of high quality charity advice, grant assessment and administration, and services to our donors and partners that promote organisational effectiveness.

We aim to offer a dynamic service, providing both effectiveness and initiative whilst remaining an organisation in touch with people's needs.

The success of our work is judged, ultimately, by how much long-lasting and tangible impact is made on people's lives; whilst producing changes which ensure the respect of our network partners, beneficiaries and donors.

We have no set funding limits and instead prefer to fund at a variety of levels.

Although our values are based in the Catholic faith, we welcome applications from all organisations, whether or not they have a faith basis.

We understand that a charity's funding priorities are not always specific project costs, and so welcome applications for developing policy, advocacy and research.

We put particular emphasis on organisations which have a proven model and wish to expand.

Strengthening Family Relationships

Encouraging and cherishing the family relationship that is so often central to people's lives, is at the centre of what we do. The support we offer aims to strengthen those family relationships that are most vulnerable and strained. We, therefore, look for applications which are focused on:

▶ Building networks and connections that tackle family isolation, especially where there is disability or illness
▶ Offering respite for families with a member who is terminally ill or disabled
▶ Encouraging family cohesion through drop-in centres and intensive family

support, particularly among families who have been under considerable stress from issues of violence and abuse
▶ Tackling isolation of the elderly, especially through intergenerational work

Enriching Education

We recognise that a well-rounded, holistic education is crucial in allowing a person to shape their future. Our funding, therefore, is aimed at educational projects which deal with the disadvantaged and vulnerable, with a particular interest in Catholic schools and education based on Catholic social teaching. We are particularly interested in projects which focus on:

▶ Pastoral care in education focused on projects which deal with character building, conflict resolution and values
▶ Educational opportunities for groups who have missed out on traditional learning, especially prisoners and ex-offenders
▶ The professional development of teachers

Transformation through Faith

As the roots of our philanthropy are in the Catholic faith, we are keen to support projects which nourish and develop that faith in a complex world. We look to fund the following particular areas:

▶ The development of Church and lay leadership capacities
▶ Projects which encourage ecumenical collaboration
▶ Organisations and projects which focus on inclusion
▶ The promotion of exploration and discussion around difficult issues, both within the Christian family and in dialogue with other Faiths

Ethics in Practice

Porticus UK sees moral formation and ethical decision making as crucially important in today's complex societies. We, therefore, support work guided by Catholic Social principles and directed at the development of the values and virtues of professionals and leaders. Since ethics cannot be considered in isolation, we are particularly interested in interdisciplinary and applied approaches. We will consider applications for:

▶ Developing courses, case studies and training
▶ Facilitating constructive public or private debates
▶ Research projects on the ethical problems encountered in specific professions
▶ Business ethics and medical ethics
▶ Initiatives that enhance understandings of Catholic social teaching

In 2012 the charity assessed 443 applications resulting in 209 new grants.

Exclusions

No grants to non-registered charities.

Applications for the following will not be considered:

▶ High profile appeals
▶ Major capital projects or restoration of buildings

▶ Grants to individuals
▶ Endowment appeals
▶ Overseas projects (including travel)

Applications

On an application form available from the charity's website. Applications can be submitted at any time.

The charity also says that: 'if you are unsure whether your project/organisation fits in with our guidelines, you are welcome to submit an initial brief outline of your organisation and funding requirements'.

Information gathered from:

Accounts; annual report; Charity Commission record; funder's website.

The David and Elaine Potter Foundation

Human rights, education, research and the arts
£817,000 (2012)

Beneficial area

UK and overseas with particular emphasis on the developing world.

Correspondent: Kathryn Oatey, Director, 6 Hamilton Close, London NW8 8QY (tel: 020 7289 3911; fax: 020 7286 3699; email: info@potterfoundation.com; website: www.potterfoundation.com)

Trustees: Michael S. Polonsky; Michael Langley; Dr David Potter; Elaine Potter; Samuel Potter.

CC Number: 1078217

Established in 1999, the foundation has general charitable purposes but focuses on supporting education, human rights, the arts and the general strengthening of civil society. The following description of the settlor's motivations are given on the foundation's website:

The David and Elaine Potter Foundation is motivated to use philanthropy to encourage the values and beliefs of the founders within society in its largest definition. The Potters believe in 'the constructs of the rational mind – the great edifice of human thought – science, philosophy, the social sciences, the arts and ethics'. The underpinnings of their views are intellectual and moral without being oriented towards religions or nationalism. They believe passionately in the power of reason and in the significance and importance of all individuals in society. By extension, their principles embrace tolerance and an 'intolerance to intolerance.

Areas of Interest

The foundation makes grants under the following categories:

Civil Society

A strong civil society holds governments accountable, enhances democratic institutions and the quality of life of its citizens, helping to strengthen and sustain economic, civil and legal rights.

One of our most important aims as a foundation is to help to create societies – both locally and worldwide – that are driven by equality and fairness. The means by which we and others can foster civil society are varied. We support projects that give people opportunities to take part in and to shape society; which enable the most disadvantaged people to play a full role in developing a fair civil society; and which foster dialogue across national and cultural boundaries. We do this by investing in a diverse array of projects: supporting education with an emphasis on commitment to civil society at the University of Cape Town; by funding the Centre for Investigative Journalism in its training of investigative journalists and other independent journalism efforts; by funding Global Witness in its efforts to highlight corruption and misuse of natural resources and many others.

Human Rights

Global society cannot be fair or equal while human rights are abused. We provide grants to organisations that defend human rights, protect individuals and campaign for change.

Because of the nature of human rights work, many of the organisations we support are international, though we also support smaller, local projects. We may fund specific projects within a large organisation. For example we have supported Amnesty International's annual Greetings Card Campaign for a number of years – and recently made a large general grant to underpin the whole range of the organisation's work.

Education

At the root of a strong civil society is an educated populace with access to good quality information. Without education, people struggle to participate in decision-making and change: the Foundation therefore supports projects which promote education for all people and particularly ones that give opportunities to those who would otherwise be excluded.

Whilst in the past the Foundation made occasional grants to individuals, today we focus our support on organisations and institutions. These bodies offer educational opportunities which will enable students to develop their skills and abilities. We hope that these students will become leaders and opinion formers and will make real contributions towards a fairer civil society.

A prime example of this ethos is our grants scheme at the University of Cape Town. Each year we offer a number of scholarships to high achieving students to enable them to pursue their studies – a requirement of the grant is that they share their research within the university and use it to contribute to wider society.

Research

A fair and strong civil society makes rational decisions and plans based on sound, well-researched information. Our grants enable academic institutions to carry out high quality research that will underpin these rational choices and suggest new, fairer ways of organising society.

A number of our educational grants will also produce significant research. For example, the new Centre of Governance and Human Rights at the University of Cambridge will certainly produce exciting new work, bringing together as it does researchers and practitioners across a range of disciplines.

Arts

The Potters feel strongly that the performing arts contribute to civil society and to quality of life in general, enhancing individual understanding and promoting independent thought. The Foundation supports a range of London-based organisations and one in New York City. The foundation tends to provide small grants for its funding in the arts; it is not a primary area of focus.

Grantmaking in 2012

In 2012 the foundation had assets of £20 million and an income of £657,000. Grants were made totalling £817,000, categorised as follows:

Education	£537,000
Human Rights	£110,000
Arts	£83,000
Community	£51,000
Other	£55,000

Beneficiaries included: UCT Trust (£151,000); Reprieve (£60,000); Business Bridge Project and Birmingham Centre for the Rule of Law (£50,000 each); Philharmonia Orchestra Trust Ltd (£39,000); Room to Read (£30,000); London Youth Support Trust (£25,000); Kasslesbai Project (£21,000); and The Almeida Theatre (£5,000).

Exclusions

No grants to individuals, animal welfare charities or humanitarian aid. Requests for endowment, capital campaigns, construction, equipment purchases and debt reduction will not be considered.

Applications

The trust has informed us that they have temporarily stopped accepting unsolicited applications. Potential applicants should check the foundation's website for current information.

Information gathered from:

Accounts; annual report; Charity Commission record; funder's website further information provided by the funder.

The Prince of Wales's Charitable Foundation

Culture, the environment, medical welfare, education, business and enterprise, children and youth and overseas aid

£2.5 million (2011/12)

Beneficial area

Unrestricted.

Correspondent: David Hutson, Administrator, The Prince of Wales's Office, Clarence House, St James's, London SW1A 1BA (tel: 020 7930 4832 ext. 4788; website: www. princeofwalescharitablefoundation.org. uk)

Trustees: John Varley; Michael Rake; William James; Amelia Fawcett.

CC Number: 1127255

The Prince of Wales's Charitable Foundation was established by trust deed in 1979 for general charitable purposes. The foundation principally continues to support charitable bodies and purposes in which the founder has a particular interest, including culture, the environment, medical welfare, education, children and youth and overseas aid. The trust wishes to focus on grass-roots community-based projects in order that awards will make a significant difference to people and their communities.

Eligibility criteria:

▶ UK registered charities, social enterprises, community interest companies and other groups exempt from registering
▶ Priority is given to charities of which the Prince of Wales is a patron
▶ Applicants must have completed two years of activity and be able to submit audited accounts
▶ Applicants must be an independent organisation

Major Grants

The major grants programme awards grants in excess of £5,000. The Foundation is unfortunately unable to accept unsolicited requests for the major grants programme.

Small Grants

The small grants programme awards grants to a maximum value of £5,000.

Grantmaking in 2011/12

During the year the foundation had assets of £18 million and an income of £14 million. Grants were made totalling £2.5 million from both restricted and unrestricted funds, and were broken down as follows:

Culture	£1 million
Environment	£579,000
Education	£238,000
Children and young people	£195,000
Overseas	£141,000
Medical welfare	£13,000
Other	£286,000

There were 22 grants made over £10,000 each listed in the accounts. Many of the larger grants were awarded to other Prince of Wales charities.

Beneficiaries of over £10,000 included: The Great Steward of Scotland's Dumfries House Trust (£1.1 million); The Soil Association (£200,000); The Princes Foundation for Building Community (£144,000); The Prince of Wales Foundation and The Prince's Trust (£100,000); The Prince's Regeneration Trust (£90,000); Scottish Business in the Community (£47,000) Children and the Arts (£45,000); The Princes countryside Fund (£25,000); United World Colleges (£23,000); The British Horse Loggers (£11,000); and The Environmental Law Foundation (£10,000).

Exclusions

No grants to individuals.

Applications

Fill out the online eligibility form in the first instance which will give you access to the full online application form, should you be eligible. The main grants programme is not open to unsolicited applications.

Information gathered from:

Accounts; annual report; Charity Commission record; funder's website.

The Privy Purse Charitable Trust

General
£406,000 (2011/12)

Beneficial area
UK.

Correspondent: Michael Stevens, Trustee, Buckingham Palace, London SW1A 1AA (tel: 020 7930 4832)

Trustees: Michael Stevens; Sir Alan Reid; Christopher Geidt.

CC Number: 296079

This trust supports a wide range of causes, giving grants to UK-wide and local charities. 'The main aims of the trustees are to make grants to charities of which The Queen is patron and to support ecclesiastical establishments associated with The Queen.'

In 2011/12 the trust had assets of £2.6 million, an income of £518,000 and made 357 grants totalling £406,000, broken down as follows:

Ecclesiastical	£227,000
Other	£125,000
Education	£55,000

Grants of over £10,000 listed in the accounts were: Chapel Royal – Hampton Court Palace (£87,000); Chapel Royal – St James Place (£53,000); Chapel Royal – Windsor Great Park (£25,000); and Game and Wildlife Conservation Trust (£10,000).

Applications

The trust makes donations to a wide variety of charities, but states that it does not respond to unsolicited applications.

Information gathered from:

Accounts; annual report; Charity Commission record.

Mr and Mrs J. A. Pye's Charitable Settlement

General
£471,000 (2012)

Beneficial area
UK, with a special interest in the Oxfordshire region and, to a lesser extent, in Reading, Cheltenham and Bristol.

Correspondent: David S. Tallon, Trustee, c/o Mercer and Hole Chartered Accountants, Gloucester House, 72 London Road, St Albans, Hertfordshire AL1 1NS (tel: 01727 869141; email: pyecharitablesettlement@ mercerhole.co.uk; website: www. pyecharitablesettlement.org)

Trustees: Simon Stubbings; David S. Tallon; Patrick Mulcare.

CC Number: 242677

The trust was endowed in 1965 by the Pye family of Oxford for general charitable purposes. The trust emphasises that it is currently concentrating its funding in the Oxfordshire region.

The following information is taken from the trust's website:

In making grants the trustees seek to continue the settlors' interests while expanding them to encompass other causes. Although the trustees have a wide discretion they will mainly entertain applications from causes in, or relating to, projects in Oxfordshire and its surrounds.

The following list is by no means exhaustive and is given for guidance only:

Environmental
This subject particularly deals with organic farming matters, conservation generally and health-related matters such as pollution research and some wildlife protection.

Adult Health and Care
Especially causes supporting the following; post-natal depression, schizophrenia, mental health generally and research into the main causes of early death.

Children's Health and Care
For physical, mental and learning disabilities, respite breaks etc.

Youth Organisations
Particularly projects encouraging self-reliance or dealing with social deprivation.

Education
Nursery, Primary, Secondary or Higher/ Institutions (not individuals).

Heritage and the Arts
Under this category, the Trustees will consider applications relating to heritage and the arts generally.

The overall policy of the trustees is to support under-funded charities in their fields of interest in order to assist those charities to play a fuller role in the community. Unfortunately, due to the demands made it is not possible to support all applications even though they may meet the charity's criteria. However, the trustees particularly recognise the difficulty many smaller charities experience in obtaining core funding in order to operate efficiently in today's demanding environment.

In 2012 the trust had assets of £11 million and an income of £654,000. Grants were made totalling £471,000 with a further £163,000 given in loans. About half the grants given were for £1,000 or less including £34,000 given in grants of less than £500 each.

Beneficiaries of loans included: Oxford Brookes University Rowing Club (£40,000); Harris Manchester College Oxford (£20,000); and Headington School (£10,000).

Beneficiaries of grants included: Organic Research Centre (£75,000); University College Oxford (£50,000); Association for Post Natal Illness (£20,000); Children with AIDS Charity (£12,000); Falcon Rowing and Canoeing Club (£5,000); St John's Family Resource Unit (£4,000); English Music Festival (£2,500); Crisis, Guide Association, The Willow Trust and Wolvercote Young People's Club in Oxford (£1,000 each.

Exclusions

Applications will not normally be considered in relation to:

- Organisations which are not registered charities
- Individuals
- Activities which are primarily the responsibility of central or local government
- Appeals for funds for subsequent redistribution to other charities-this would also preclude appeals from the larger national charities
- Endowment funds
- Fabric appeals for places of worship, other than in Oxford, Reading, Cheltenham and Bristol

Fundraising events
Hospitals and medical centres (except for projects which are clearly additional to statutory responsibilities)
Overseas appeals
Promotion of religion

Applications

All applications should be sent to the administrative office (and not to individual trustees). These are reviewed on a continual basis and the trustees meet quarterly to make their decisions. Any decision can therefore take up to four months before it is finally taken. However, all applicants are informed of the outcome of their applications and all applications are acknowledged. Telephone contact will usually be counter-productive.

There are no application forms but the following information is essential:

The registered charity number or evidence of an organisation's tax exempt status
Brief description of the activities of the charity
The names of the trustees and chief officers [**Note:** more important than patrons]
Details of the purpose of the application and where funds will be put to use
Details of the funds already raised and the proposals for how remaining funds are to be raised
The latest trustees report and full audited or independently examined accounts (which **must** comply with Charity Commission guidelines and requirements)
Details of full name of the bank account, sort code, and number into which any grant should be paid
The charity's email address

Percentage of awards given to new applicants: less than 10%.

Information gathered from:

Accounts; annual report; Charity Commission record; further information provided by the funder; funder's website.

Quartet Community Foundation (formerly the Greater Bristol Foundation)

General

£2.9 million (2011/12)

Beneficial area

West England – Bristol, North Somerset, South Gloucestershire, Bath and North East Somerset.

Correspondent: Alice Meason, Grants Director, Royal Oak House, Royal Oak Avenue, Bristol BS1 4GB (tel: 01179 897700; fax: 01179 897701; email: info@quartetcf.org.uk; website: www.quartetcf.org.uk)

Trustees: John Kane; Alexander Hore-Ruthven; Tim Ross; William Lee; Richard Hall; Lin Whitfield; John Cullum; Jane Moss; Hilary Neal; Vernon Samuels; David Harvey; Christopher Sharp; Lesley Freed.

CC Number: 1080418

Quartet Community Foundation supports small, community-based charities and voluntary groups in the West of England whose work benefits local people. It gives grants to a broad range of causes and welcomes applications from both new and established groups. Through their grants programme they aim to:

Help people who are most disadvantaged and isolated
Encourage people to get involved in improving their own community
Give people opportunities others take for granted
Respond to the needs and concerns of people living in local communities

The foundation manages a range of funds each with their own criteria, closing dates and maximum amounts (see grants programmes). Programmes open and close throughout the year and new ones may be added whilst others end. Therefore it is advisable that applicants check the website for the most up to date information.

The foundation states that organisations must:

Be sure there is a need for their group's activity by researching local need, and making sure other organisations are not already running similar organisations
Have a clear idea of what they want to achieve, with a short-term and long-term strategy
Consider ways in which they can increase the effectiveness of the activities whilst reducing the cost, possibly through community resources, other charitable organisations or local businesses
Have a structure in place that will ensure the effective delivery of their strategy including a management team and written constitution, training and CRB checks

Grantmaking in 2011/12

In 2011/12 the foundation had assets of £18 million, an income of £4 million and made grants totalling £2.9 million. During the year 1,080 grants were made and 67% of grants went to organisations with an annual turnover of less than £50,000. The average grant was £2,700.

Grants to institutions were broken down into the following areas:

Community	262	£949,000
Young people	358	£842,000
People with disabilities	187	£520,000
Black and minority ethnic groups	53	£182,000
Older people	106	£174,000
Families	53	£147,000
People who are homeless	12	£51,000

Beneficiaries included: Voluntary Action North Somerset (£120,000); Moonstone Therapy Centre Appeal (£100,000); Arnosvale (£95,000); Somerset Wood Recycling (£50,000); Easton Community Children's Centre (£40,000); Second Step Housing Association (£20,000); Oxford Food Bank (£10,000); St John's Hospice (£7,800); Swindon Bats Sport and Social Club (£6,000); and Room 13 Hareclive and Chiltern CAB (£5,000 each).

Exclusions

The foundation does not give grants to:

Individuals
General appeals
Statutory organisations or the direct replacement of statutory funding
Political groups or activities promoting political beliefs
Religious groups promoting religious beliefs
Arts projects with no community or charitable element
Sports projects with no community or charitable element
Medical research, equipment or treatment
Animal welfare
Projects that take place before an application can be processed

Applications

Before you apply to the foundation check that your group or project meets the following requirements:

You must be a small charity, community group or local voluntary organisation operating in the West of England i.e. Bath and North East Somerset, Bristol, North Somerset or South Gloucestershire
You do not need to be a registered charity but you must be able to provide a copy of your group's constitution or set of rules
Your group must be managed by a board of trustees or management committee
You must be able to provide the foundation with up-to-date financial information for your group

Applicants should refer to the foundation's website for details on how to apply to each grants programme. The funding team can be contacted for any help or advice concerning grants applications.

Percentage of awards given to new applicants: between 20% and 30%.

Common applicant mistakes

'Not reading the guidelines/criteria.'

Information gathered from:
Accounts; annual report; Charity Commission record; guidelines for applicants; further information provided by the funder; funder's website.

Queen Mary's Roehampton Trust

Ex-service support
£438,000 (2011/12)

Beneficial area
UK.

Correspondent: Col Stephen Rowland-Jones, Clerk to the Trustees, 2 Sovereign Close, Quidhampton, Salisbury, Wiltshire SP2 9ES (tel: 01722 501413; email: qmrt@hotmail.co.uk)

Trustees: Simon Brewis; Cathy Walker; James Macnamara; Gordon Paterson; Colin Green; Paul Cummings; Stephen Farringdon; Beverley Davies; Debbie Bowles; Stephen Coltman; Barry Thornton.

CC Number: 211715

The trust is established for the benefit of people who served in the armed forces or services established under the Civil Defence Acts 1937 and 1939 who have suffered a disability in that service and their widows/widowers or dependents.

The trust's objectives are met by making grants to any charities or organisations whose objects include the reception, accommodation, treatment or after-care of persons who come within the charity's objects. Grants are also made in aid of medical or surgical research having particular regard to the needs of people with disabilities who served in the armed forces of the crown.

During 2010/11 the trust carried out a major review of its activities, as described in its annual report:

> Against the background of a continuing fall in investment income and the high level of demand, a fundamental review was undertaken on the trust's Grant Making Policies and Strategy. The trustees concluded that the needs of a significant number of war pensioners would remain a high priority for the foreseeable future. It was decided to adopt a more robust approach to applications with due emphasis on the number of war pensioners assisted and the financial need of each organisation. Accordingly, the balance of grants between larger and smaller charities would be redressed in favour of the latter. Furthermore, the trustees would continue to give high priority to Service care homes and housing for the disabled. The trustees would also continue to consider applications for grants towards medical and surgical research which has a specific regard to the needs of disabled members of the Armed Forces. As a result of this

review a new compilation of the trust's Working Practices and Policies was established with effect from January 2011.

In 2011/12 the trust had assets of £11.7 million and an income of £508,000. Grants were made to 34 organisations totalling £438,000.

Beneficiaries included: Royal Naval Benevolent Trust (£35,000); Erskine Hospital (£30,000); Haig Homes (£25,000); Combat Stress (£20,000); British Ex-Services Wheelchair Sports Association (£17,000); Scottish Veterans' Garden City Association (£15,000); Veterans Aid (£10,000); Royal Navy and Royal Marine Children's Fund (£7,500); William Simpson's Home, Stirling (£5,000); Spinal Injuries Association (£3,000); and Women's Naval Service Benevolent Trust (£2,000).

Exclusions
No grants to individuals.

Applications
On a standard application form available from the correspondent. Representatives of the trust may visit beneficiary organisations.

Information gathered from:
Accounts; annual report; Charity Commission record.

The Queen's Silver Jubilee Trust

General, in practice grants to organisations supporting disadvantaged young people
£1.9 million (2011/12)

Beneficial area
UK, Channel Islands, Isle of Man, Commonwealth, Canada.

Correspondent: Anne Threlkeld, Administrator, Buckingham Palace, London SW1A 1AA (tel: 020 7930 4832; email: anne.threlkeld@royal.gsx.gov.uk; website: www.queenssilverjubileetrust. org.uk)

Trustees: Rt Hon Christopher Geidt; Sir Fred Goodwin; Stephen Hall; Sir Alan Reid; Peter Mimpriss; Michael Marks.

CC Number: 272373

The Queen's Silver Jubilee Trust was established in 1977 following a fundraising appeal based around the Queens Silver Jubilee. While its objects are wide, it is especially concerned with young people who are disadvantaged.

The following information is available on the trust's website. Note that the trust is in the process of spending out and therefore funds are unlikely to be available for new applicants:

We fund registered charities that enable and encourage young people to help others. We are spending out our funds over the next few years and will be particularly keen to work with charities to enable them to scale up work that is proven to be effective. We focus our charitable giving in the UK although we will also support charities at work in the Commonwealth.

Wherever possible, we aim to work in partnership with other funders in order to maximise the amount of money available for the causes we support. As a result, we are usually keen to work with other donors, organisations, trusts and foundations.

In 2011/12 the trust had assets of £36 million and an income of £226,000. Grants were made totalling £1.9 million.

The beneficiaries during the year were: The Prince's Trust (£1.2 million); Sentebale (£142,000); Canadian Youth Foundation/Memorial University (£100,000); Rock YK (£80,000); Create (Arts) Ltd (£62,000); Youth United (£60,000); Dance United Northern Ireland (£53,000); Southbank Sinfonia and The Lyric Theatre Belfast (£50,000 each); and Educate Girls and The Schola Foundation (£35,000 each).

Exclusions
Grants are only made to registered charities. No grants to individuals.

Applications
In choosing beneficiaries, the trust will not normally accept unsolicited applications but will identify and build trusted, strategic relationships with its charity partners, usually through multi-year grants.

Information gathered from:
Accounts; annual report; Charity Commission record; funder's website.

Rachel Charitable Trust

General charitable purposes, in practice mainly Jewish organisations
£2.7 million (2011/12)

Beneficial area
Unrestricted.

Correspondent: Robert Chalk, Secretary, F. and C. Reit Asset Management, 5 Wigmore Street, London W1U 1PB (tel: 020 7016 3549)

Trustees: Leopold Noe; Susan Noe; Simon Kanter.

CC Number: 276441

This trust was established in 1978 for general charitable purposes and focuses on the relief of poverty and the advancement of religion and religious education. In practice the trust gives mainly to Jewish organisations.

In 2011/12 the trust had assets of £5 million and an income of £3.7 million. Grants were made totalling £2.7 million. A separate list of donations made during the year was available from the trustees for £25.

Previous beneficiaries include: British Friends of Shuut Ami, Children's Hospital Trust Fund, Cometville Ltd, Encounter – Jewish Outreach Network, Chosen Mishpat Centre, Gertner Charitable Trust, Hertsmere Jewish Primary School, Jewish Learning Exchange, London Millennium Bikeathon, Manchester Jewish Grammar School, Project Seed, Shaarei Zedek Hospital, Shomrei Hachomot Jerusalem, Yeshiva Ohel Shimon Trust and Yeshiva Shaarei Torah Manchester.

Applications

In writing to the correspondent.

Information gathered from:

Accounts; annual report; Charity Commission record.

The Rank Foundation Ltd

Christian communication, youth, education, general

£7 million (2012)

Beneficial area

UK.

Correspondent: Rosamond McNulty, Administrator, 12 Warwick Square, London SW1V 2AA (tel: 020 7834 7731; email: rosamond.mcnulty@ rankfoundation.co.uk; website: www. rankfoundation.com)

Trustees: Lord St Aldwyn; James Cave; Andrew Cowan; Mark Davies; Lindsay Fox; Joey Newton; Lucinda Onslow; Lord Shuttleworth; Hon. Caroline Twiston-Davies; Johanna Ropner; Rose Fitzpatrick; Daniel Simon; Nicholas Buxton; Jason Chaffer.

CC Number: 276976

The charity was established in 1953 by the late Lord and Lady Rank (the founders). It was one of a number established by the founders at that time and to which they gifted their controlling interest in The Rank Group plc (formerly The Rank Organisation plc), best known as a film production company, though this was but one of its commercial interests. The Rank trusts and foundations all share a Christian ethos.

This is a heavily proactive foundation, with offices around the country. It concentrates on:

- The promotion of Christian principles through film and other media
- Encouraging and developing leadership amongst young people
- Supporting disadvantaged young people and those frail or lonely through old age or disability

Major grants are typically part of a three or five year commitment and very seldom result from an unsolicited application as the projects in this area are mainly identified by staff who have considerable experience and contacts within the field. Small grants (less than £7,500) are usually one off. Local charities are unlikely to get recurrent funding or multi-year awards.

The following information about grant programmes was taken from the trust's website:

> Please note that all our funding streams are only for the benefit of UK residents in UK communities. We do not accept overseas applications.

> *Youth Projects*
> If you are interested in applying for our YAP or GAP schemes of work, please see the Youth Projects pages on our website. Brochures are available to download on that page with further information, and if you have any queries please contact Helen Stockdale (helen.stockdale@rankfoundation.com) in our Penrith office.

> *Community Care Projects*
> If you are interested in applying for one of our Time to Shine internships, please contact Helen Stockdale in our Penrith office. Due to our current commitments tied to our proactive research driven work, we are not able to consider unsolicited applications for other community care projects. This will be reviewed in January 2014.

> *Special Projects*
> We very much regret that we no longer accept any new applications for Special Projects, which remains part of our researched, proactive work. Please do not send any unsolicited applications.

> *Small Appeals*
> This is a small funding stream for registered charities and recognised churches which are raising money for projects which are costed at under £1 million. If you are raising money for a particular project for which the mainstay is capital costs (building work, refurbishment or the purchase of long-term equipment) or a one-off short-term activity (such as an annual respite break or holiday for disadvantaged young people) and have already raised a third of the total costs, you may be eligible for this. Please use the application form [on the foundation's website] to confirm your eligibility and apply. Please note that we do not fund running costs or salaries through our small appeals programme.

In 2012 the foundation had assets of £207 million and an income of £1.4 million. Grants were made totalling nearly £7 million, distributed in the following areas:

Promotion of Christian religion (CTVC)	24%
Youth and education	37%
Community service programme	39%

Beneficiaries included: Gap Scheme (£358,000); Time to Shine (£235,000); Arthur Rank Centre (£60,000); Essex Boys' and Girls' Clubs (£38,000); Mersey Youth Support Trust (£30,000); Lower Wensleydale Youth Project (£28,000); Scripture Union Mission Trust (£27,000); Music in Hospitals, Special Olympics Great Britain and Blackburn Cathedral (£20,000 each); Macular Disease Society and Caring for Ex-Offenders (£15,000 each); Changing Faces (£12,000); and Counselling Prayer Trust (£10,000).

Exclusions

Grants to registered charities only. Appeals from individuals or appeals from registered charities on behalf of named individuals will not be considered; neither will appeals from overseas or from UK-based organisations where the object of the appeal is overseas. In an endeavour to contain the calls made upon the foundation to a realistic level, the directors have continued with their policy of not, in general, making grants to projects involved with:

- Agriculture and farming
- Cathedrals and churches (except where community facilities form an integral part of the appeal)
- Cultural projects
- Advocacy services
- University/school building and bursary funds
- Medical research

Unsolicited appeals are extremely unlikely to attract a grant for salaries, general running costs or major capital projects.

Applications

Grant programmes have different application processes, and some may not be open at times. See the trust's website for open programmes and how to apply. The trust encourages potential applicants to contact the administrator if they have any queries.

Information gathered from:

annual report and accounts; Charity Commission record; funder's website.

The Joseph Rank Trust

The Methodist Church, Christian-based social work

£2.4 million (2011/12)

Beneficial area

Unrestricted. In practice, UK and Ireland.

Correspondent: Dr John Higgs, Secretary, Worth Corner, Turners Hill Road, Crawley RH10 7SL (tel: 01293 873947; email: secretary@ranktrust.org; website: www.ranktrust.org)

Trustees: Tony Reddall; Colin Rank; David Cruise; Gay Moon; James Rank; Mike Shortt; Sue Warner; John Irvine; Darren Holland; Carole Holmes.

CC Number: 1093844

This trust was established in 2002 for the advancement of the Christian faith and represents an amalgamation of a number of charities established by the late Joseph Rank, or members of his family, during the period from 1918 to 1942. The original trusts represented a practical expression of the strong Christian beliefs of their founder and his desire to advance the Christian faith and to help the less fortunate members of society.

The trust's two main areas of interest are:

- The adaptation of Methodist Church properties with a view to providing improved facilities for use both by the church itself and in its work in the community in which it is based
- Projects that demonstrate a Christian approach to the practical, educational and spiritual needs of people

The strategy is to provide a grants-plus approach in dealings with charities and to collaborate with other trusts and organisations with similar objectives. The trust also owns CTCV which produces television and radio programmes, and the distribution of films and videos for Christian and educational purposes.

The trust offers the following information on its grantmaking preferences:

In considering all appeals, the trustees take into account the primary objective of the trust, which is to advance the Christian faith. After earmarking funds to support their main areas of interest the trustees are prepared to consider other unsolicited appeals, although resources remaining to support such appeals are limited. Unsolicited appeals are selected for consideration by the trustees that demonstrate, in their view, a Christian approach to the practical, educational and spiritual needs of people.

In 2012 the trust had assets of £76 million and an income of £2.6 million. Grants were made totalling £2.4 million, broken down into the following categories:

Community service	43%	£1 million
Youth projects	29%	£692,000
Church property schemes	24%	£558,000
Education	3%	£70,000
Elderly people	1.3%	£30,000

The trust gives a geographical breakdown of its grants:

North East	14%	£325,000
North West	13%	£309,000
South East	12%	£272,000
Northern Ireland and Republic of Ireland	11%	£256,000
South West	10%	£244,000
Anglia	10%	£236,000
Scotland	9%	£214,000
London	8%	£190,000
South Central	6%	£146,000
Midlands	6%	£140,000
Wales	1%	£22,000

Beneficiaries included: The Exodus Project, Barnsley (£60,000); Battle Methodist Church (£60,000); Bradford Court Chaplaincy Service and The Retreat Association (£45,000 each); Churches Together in Herald Green Youth Initiative (£42,000); SMART Community Project, St Martins Church (£30,000); Hull Civic Society (£25,000); Youth Link Northern Ireland (£24,000); Heaton Methodist Church (£20,000); Department of Youth and Children's Work – Methodist Church in Ireland (£7,600); and West Orchard United Reformed Church (£5,000).

Exclusions

The trust does not consider applications for delayed church maintenance (for example roof repairs), overseas projects, organ appeals, for completed capital projects, to repay loans, from individuals, for educational bursaries, for medical research, gap years, intern placements, from individual hospices, from social enterprises that have no charitable status, community interest companies, organisations registered under the Industrial and Provident Societies Act 1965, or from registered charities for the benefit of named individuals.

Applications

Ongoing commitments, combined with the fact that the trustees are taking an increasingly active role in identifying projects to support, means that uncommitted funds are limited and it is seldom possible to make grants in response to unsolicited appeals.

If applicants consider that their work might fall within the areas of interest of the trust the following basic information is required:

- Charity name and charity registration number
- An outline of the project for which funding is sought
- Details of the total amount required to fund the project in its entirety
- Details of the amount already raised, or irrevocably committed, towards the target
- A copy of the most recent annual report and audited accounts

Applicants should endeavour to set out the essential details of a project on no more than two sides of A4 paper, with more detailed information being presented in the form of appendices. Applications must be sent in hard copy.

If a Methodist Church is applying funding they should read the further information on the trust's website.

In normal circumstances, papers received before the beginning of February, May and August may be considered in April, July and October respectively. Visits to appeals may be made by the secretary and trustees. All appeals are acknowledged and the applicants advised that if they do not receive a reply by a specified date it has not been possible for the trustees to make a grant.

Percentage of awards given to new applicants: 100%.

Common applicant mistakes

'Not reading the criteria.'

Information gathered from:

Accounts; annual report; Charity Commission record; further information provided by the funder; funder's website.

The Sigrid Rausing Trust

Human rights and justice

£17 million (2012)

Beneficial area

Unrestricted.

Correspondent: Ms Sheetal Patel, Administrator, 12 Penzance Place, London W11 4PA (tel: 020 7313 7727; email: info@srtrust.org; website: www.sigrid-rausing-trust.org)

Trustees: Dr Sigrid Rausing; Joshua Mailman; Susan Hitch; Andrew Puddephatt; Geoff Budlender; Jonathan Cooper.

CC Number: 1046769

Summary

The trust was set up in 1995 by Sigrid Rausing and takes as its guiding framework the United Nations' Universal Declaration of Human Rights. Its vision is 'A world where the principles of the Universal Declaration of Human Rights are implemented and respected and where all people can enjoy their rights in harmony with each other and with the environment.'

The trust made its first grants in 1996 and, from the beginning, has taken a keen interest in work that promotes international human rights. It was originally called the Ruben and Elisabeth Rausing Trust after Sigrid's grandparents. In 2003 the trust was renamed the Sigrid Rausing Trust to identify its work more closely with the aims and ideals of Sigrid Rausing herself.

General

The trust currently has nine grants programmes for 2013 onwards:

- Advocacy, research and litigation
- Detention, torture and death penalty
- Human rights defenders
- Free expression
- Transitional justice
- Women's rights
- LGBTI rights
- Xenophobia and intolerance
- Transparency and accountability

The trust also has its own regional programme to encourage democracy and human rights in the MENA region; the Middle East and North Africa Strategic Fund. There are two other regional programmes -

The trust has five main principles which guide its grantmaking:

- The essential role of core funding
- Good and effective leadership
- Flexibility and responsiveness to needs and opportunities
- The value of clarity and brevity in applications and reports
- Long-term relationships with grantees

In late 2010, the trust discontinued the open enquiry system for applications. **It no longer accepts unsolicited applications for funding**. The trust has limited resources and enters into long-term relationships with its partners. There is, therefore, a limit to how many new organisations the Trust can take on.

Types of Grant

Grants may be ear-marked, or given as general support. There is no minimum or maximum level for a grant; however, it would be unusual for the trust to support more than 25% of the costs of an organisation or a project.

The trust may also exceptionally consider supporting existing grantees with an advancement grant, designed to support a major infrastructure change for an organisation.

Emergency funding is available in response to a sudden human rights crisis, or for the protection of human rights defenders. Emergency grants must be given via an existing or previous grantee, who can apply directly to their programme officer.

Trustees may bring small grant applications from organisations they know well to meeti9ngs. there is no application process for these grants.

A detailed breakdown of grantees under each funding stream is available on the trust's website.

Grantmaking in 2012

In 2012 the trust had assets of £3.7 million and an income of £13 million. Grants totalled £17 million with £16.8 million given in main grants and £135,000 in small grants. Grants in 2012 were broken down into the previous four funding categories as follows:

Civil and political rights	£7.9 million
Women's rights	£3.9 million
Social justice	£2 million
Minority rights	£1.6 million

All of the current beneficiaries are listed on the website. They include: Peace Brigades International (£450,000); Zero Mercury Campaign (£480,000 over three years); Reporters Without Borders (£390,000 over three years); Central American Women's Fund (£285,000); Women's Legal Centre (£210,000 over three years); Hotline for Migrant Workers (£195,000 over three years); Adalah (£180,000 over three years); African Refugee Development Center (£120,000 over three years); Council for Assisting Refugee Academics (£100,000 over one year); and London Mining Network (£60,000 over three years).

Exclusions

No grants are made to individuals or faith based groups. Funds are not normally given for building projects.

Applications

The trust does not accept unsolicited applications for funding. The trust's website does, however, offer the following advice:

From time to time, they may request proposals from organisations working in particular fields. Details of requests will be made available on the trust's website.

If you have not been invited to apply, but wish to let the trust know about your work, you can send an email describing your organisation to: research@srtrust.org. Programme officers review emails regularly, but are unlikely to be able to meet with you in person.

Information gathered from:

Accounts; annual report; Charity Commission record; funder's website.

The Rayne Foundation

Arts, education, health, medicine, social welfare

£1.5 million (2011/12)

Beneficial area

UK.

Correspondent: Morin Carew, Grants Administrator, 100 George Street, London W1U 8NU (tel: 020 7487 9656; email: info@raynefoundation.org.uk; website: www.raynefoundation.org.uk)

Trustees: The Hon Robert Rayne, Chair; Lord Claus Moser; Lady Jane Rayne; Lady Hilary Browne-Wilkinson; Prof. Dame Margaret Turner-Warwick; Prof. Anthony Newman Taylor; The Hon Natasha Rayne; The Hon Nicholas Rayne; Sir Emyr Jones Parry.

CC Number: 216291

The foundation provides the following description of its activities on its excellent website.

Background

The Rayne Foundation was established in 1962 by Lord Rayne, who was Life President of London Merchant Securities plc, a diversified property and venture capital business, which he built up and of which he was chairman for forty years until 2000. Lord Rayne was also chairman, trustee or council member of numerous arts, education, medical and social welfare charities. These included Chairman of the National Theatre and St Thomas' Hospital. He remained chairman of the Rayne Foundation until his death in 2003.

Over more than forty years at the Rayne Foundation we have given to many different causes and organisations. As well as being a traditional philanthropist, Lord Rayne took great efforts to ensure that the Rayne Foundation was actively engaged with the needs of society. Examples of the foundation's early work along these lines are the Rayne Institutes – created in London, Edinburgh and Paris in the 1960s and 1970s to build a bridge between medical research and hospitals. Lord Rayne worked with the government, universities and hospitals, drew on his property development expertise and experience and, with contributions from the foundation, he encouraged this new approach and provided buildings where medical researchers and doctors could work alongside each other. This kind of active engagement is now being revived.

Summary

Here at the Rayne Foundation our theme is bridge building. The aims and outcomes of our work are of utmost importance to us, and we measure the success of our own work, our partnerships and our investments by the degree to which they satisfy these two areas:

The 'bridge building' outcomes of our work such as:

- 'enlarged sympathies' – increased understanding and/or tolerance
- Reduced exclusion
- Reduced conflict
- New productive relationships which benefit the public

The aims of our work:

- It can have wider than just local application or is of national importance
- It helps the most vulnerable or disadvantaged
- It provides direct benefits to people and communities
- It tackles neglected causes
- It levers other funds and encourages the involvement of other organisations
- It strives to achieve excellence

Guidelines

We work within four sectors:

- Arts
- Education
- Health and medicine
- Social welfare and development

Our areas of special interest

Within our four sectors we encourage applications which apply to our evolving list of areas of special interest, which are listed below. Excellent applications outside these areas are also welcomed.

- Art in deprived communities
- Developing numeracy skills
- Improved quality of life for older people
- Improved palliative care in the community

What we support

These are the specific types of costs the foundation will fund:

- Salaries and all types of project costs plus a reasonable contribution to overheads (there is no fixed percentage)
- General running or core costs (normally for a maximum of three years)
- Capital costs of buildings and equipment (unless specifically stated in certain sectors)

We do not specify minimum or maximum amounts [for grants]. You can apply for a specific amount or a contribution to the total cost. Please note we are rarely able to fund a project completely and urge you to approach others to part-fund alongside The Rayne Foundation.

You can apply for a grant towards a programme of any duration, although a period of greater than three years is rare.

Check the foundation's website for full details and up-to-date information.

Grantmaking in 2011/12

In 2011/12 the foundation had assets of £74 million and an income of £1.2 million. Grants to 87 organisations totalled £1.5 million. The average award was £17,000 and the maximum grant was £150,000.

Grants were distributed as follows:

Arts	£26,000
Education	£370,000
Health and medicine	£68,000
Social welfare and development	£741,000
Areas of special interest	
Arts in deprived communities	£137,000
Improved numeracy skills	£36,000
Improved quality of life for older people	£194,000
Improved palliative care in the community	£44,000

Beneficiaries included: Kenilworth Children's Centre and Nursery School (£60,000); Emmaus UK (£50,000); Leap Confronting Conflict (£40,000); Turner Contemporary (£30,000); Youth Dementia UK (£21,000); Pro Contact Expert Services (£15,000); ArtsEkta (£12,000); Stonewall Equality Ltd (£10,000); London International Festival of Theatre (£5,000); North Derbyshire Stroke Support Group (£4,000); and Dance Umbrella (£3,000).

Exclusions

Grants are not made:

- To individuals
- To organisations working outside the UK
- For work that has already taken place
- For repayment of debts
- For endowments
- For general appeals
- To those who have applied in the last twelve months

  Generally speaking, we do not support organisations whose levels of free reserves are higher than 75% of annual expenditure. However, we may make an exception if your organisation makes a contribution from free reserves to the area of work for which you are seeking funding – and if this reduces your free reserves to below 75% of your annual expenditure.

Do not send 'round robin' or general appeals.

Applications

Applying for a grant is a two-stage process. First you must fill in the Stage One Application Form available from the foundation's website, which you can complete and email to: applications@raynefoundation.org.u. If it is not possible for you to access the first stage application online you should call the trust on 020 7487 9650.

If the trust is satisfied that its aims will be met, they will contact you to make a more detailed application. The aim is to respond to all Stage One proposals within one month of receipt.

Continuation funding – if you have previously received a grant from the foundation, you must complete a satisfactory monitoring report before reapplying. Organisations can only hold one grant at a time. Use the two-stage process for all applications, even if you

are asking the foundation to continue funding the same project.

Information gathered from:

annual report; accounts; Charity Commission record; funder's website.

The Sir James Reckitt Charity

Society of Friends (Quakers), social welfare, general

£1.3 million (2012)

Beneficial area

Hull and the East Riding of Yorkshire, UK and occasional support of Red Cross or Quaker work overseas.

Correspondent: James McGlashan, Administrator, 7 Derrymore Road, Willerby, East Yorkshire HU10 6ES (tel: 01482 655861; email: charity@ thesirjamesreckittcharity.org.uk; website: www.thesirjamesreckittcharity.org.uk)

Trustees: William Upton; James Harrison Holt; Caroline Jennings; Philip James Harrison Holt; Robin James Upton; Sarah Helen Craven; Charles Maxsted; Simon J. Upton; Simon E. Upton; James Marshall; Edward Upton; Rebecca Holt; Dr Karina Mary Upton; Andrew Palfeman; James Atherton.

CC Number: 225356

Background

This charity was founded in 1920 by Sir James Reckitt who endowed trust with a large number of shares in the family manufacturing business of Reckitt and Sons Ltd.

Summary

The charity gives grants to a wide range of local charities in Hull and the East Riding of Yorkshire as well as to some national charities. Quaker organisations and those in line with Quaker beliefs are supported, and there is an emphasis on those concerned with current social issues. Some of the charity's grants are awarded over a period of years and many organisations are regular recipients. It has a list of regular beneficiaries which it supports on an annual basis, although the recipients are informed that the grant may end at any time at the discretion of the trustees. Most grants are for £5,000 or less.

Guidelines

Support is given to:

- Community based groups and projects in the city of Hull and the county of East Yorkshire
- Quaker causes and organisations throughout the UK

- National or regional charities focused on social welfare, medicine, education or the environment, particularly in Hull and East Yorkshire
- Individuals or groups from Hull or East Yorkshire

Grants are made for:
- Start-up and core costs
- Purchase of equipment and materials
- Building improvements
- Training costs
- Project development costs

Over 50% of grants each year are made in Hull and the East Riding of Yorkshire.

Grantmaking in 2012

In 2012 the charity had assets of £30 million, an income of £1.3 million and made grants totalling £1.3 million, broken down as follows:

Children	£25,000
Education	£355,000
Elderly	£14,000
Environment	£7,100
Medical	£75,000
Religion	£157,000
Social Work	£581,000
Youth	£64,000

The table includes 226 grants to individuals totalling £58,000 for social work.

Beneficiaries included: Friends School Lisburn (£100,000); Britain Yearly Meeting (£90,000); Mount School York Foundation (£19,000); Pickering Quaker Meeting (£9,000); Home Start Hull and Woodlands Home (£4,000 each); Multiple Sclerosis Society (£3,000); Field Studies Council (£2,500); Yorkshire Quaker Arts Projects and Yorkshire Friends Holiday School (£2,000 each).

Exclusions

Grants are normally made only to registered charities. Local organisations outside the Hull area are not supported, unless their work has regional implications. Grants are not normally made to individuals other than Quakers and residents of Hull and the East Riding of Yorkshire. Support is not given to causes of a warlike or political nature.

No replacement of statutory funding or activities which collect funds to be passed on to other organisations, charities or individuals.

Applications

In writing to the correspondent. The application should include the following key points:
- The name and address of your organisation; telephone number and email address
- The nature of your organisation; its structure, aims and who it serves; and its links with other agencies and networks
- The project or funding need. What is the grant to be used for and who will benefit from it
- When is the funding required; the date of the project or event
- The bank account payee name of your organisation
- Any links to the Hull and East Yorkshire region, or the Quakers (which together are the charity's funding priorities)
- A copy of your latest annual report and accounts or equivalent

Applications are measured against the charity's guidelines and decisions are taken at a twice-yearly meeting of trustees in May and October. Applications should be submitted by 31 March and 30 September respectively.

Percentage of awards given to new applicants: between 10% and 20%.

Common applicant mistakes

'They have not read the guidelines which clearly exclude them; key details omitted, e.g. date of project, bank payee name or funding amount required.'

Information gathered from:

Accounts; annual report; Charity Commission record; guidelines for applicants; further information provided by the funder; funder's website.

The Reed Foundation

General, arts, education, relief of poverty, women's health

£1.6 million (2011)

Beneficial area

UK and developing countries.

Correspondent: Sir Alec Reed, Trustee, 6 Sloane Street, London SW1X 9LE (tel: 020 7201 9980; email: reed.foundation@reed.co.uk)

Trustees: Alec Reed; James A. Reed; Richard A. Reed; Alex M. Chapman.

CC Number: 264728

This trust has general charitable purposes. There has historically been an interest in women's causes in developing countries. The settlor is Alec Reed, entrepreneur, philanthropist and founder of several successful and high profile charitable ventures.

The Reed Foundation donated £50,000 as a loan in 2007 to set up The Big Give, an online charity comparison site for high-level donors. A further £289,000 was donated in 2011 to continue and develop the site. There were 24,827 donations processed through the site totalling £6.2 million during the year.

At the time of writing (November 2013) the trust's 2012 accounts were overdue with the Charity Commission. In 2011

the foundation had assets of £14 million, an income of £1 million and gave grants totalling £1.6 million.

Beneficiaries included: The Prince's Trust (£45,000); Classical Opera (£20,000); Bluebell Railway Trust (£15,000); Pop Up Tai Chi (£10,000); Birmingham Royal Ballet (£7,100); Zambia Orphans of Aid UK (£5,000); London Youth Support Trust (£3,800); Supporting Dalit Children (£3,200); Autism Plus (£1,700); Workaid (£1,300); and Intercountry Adoption Centre (£1,000).

Applications

In writing to the correspondent. The trust states that it does not respond to unsolicited applications.

Information gathered from:

Accounts; annual report; Charity Commission record.

The John and Sally Reeve Charitable Trust

General charitable purposes

Beneficial area

UK and overseas.

Correspondent: Ian Wyatt, Administrator, Royal Bank of Canada Trust Corporation Ltd, Riverbank House, 2 Swan Lane, London EC4R 3BF (tel: 020 7653 4146)

Trustees: John Reeve; Sally Reeve; Emily Sullivan; Royal Bank of Canada Trust Corporation Ltd.

CC Number: 1150448

Registered in January 2013, the trust's objects are wide ranging, including education, social welfare, the arts, conservation, children and young people and older people and overseas aid. John Reeve is a former chief executive of Family Investments and former chair of the Association of Financial Mutuals, amongst other roles in the insurance and financial industries.

Applications

In writing to the correspondent.

Information gathered from:

Charity Commission record.

Reuben Foundation

Healthcare, education, general
£2.1 million to organisations
(2012)

Beneficial area
UK and overseas.

Correspondent: Patrick O'Driscoll, Trustee, 4th FloorMillbank Tower, 21–24 Millbank, London SW1P 4PQ (tel: 020 7802 5000; fax: 020 7802 5002; email: contact@reubenfoundation.com; website: www.reubenfoundation.com)

Trustees: Richard Stone; Simon Reuben; Malcolm Turner; Annie Benjamin; Patrick O'Driscoll; James Reuben; Dana Reuben.

CC Number: 1094130

This trust was established in 2002 as an outlet for the charitable giving of billionaire property investors David and Simon Reuben. The foundation was endowed by the brothers with a donation of $100 million (£54.1 million), with the income generated to be given to a range of charitable causes, particularly to healthcare organisations and for educational purposes. It is likely that organisations in India and Iraq, where the brothers have their roots, may benefit as well as organisations in the UK and Israel.

The charitable objectives are:
▌ Education, particularly for young people
▌ The relief of need due to social or economic circumstances, illness or age
▌ The relief of need due to local, national or international unrest or disorder
▌ Medical research and the development of medical facilities
▌ Other charitable purposes

During 2012 the foundation launched the Reuben Scholarship Programme which will become one of the core areas of focus. This is run in association with the University of Oxford and University College London and assists pupils from disadvantaged backgrounds to continue their education to degree level.

In 2012 the foundation had assets of £66 million and an income of £4 million. Grants to 415 organisations totalled £2.1 million with a further £73,000 being given in 20 grants to individuals.

Beneficiaries included: Lyric Theatre (£850,000); University College London (£400,000); Oxford University (£300,000); Nancy Reuben Primary School (£300,000); ARK (£160,000); British Film Institute (£150,000); Impact Scholarships (£31,000); Community Security Trust (£25,000); Leaders Magazine (£15,000); and Jewish Care,

Mayo Clinic and Princess Royal Trust for Carers (£10,000 each).

Applications
The foundation's website states that applications for grants are made by invitation only. The latest accounts however state that 'The trustees welcome applications from any institution or individual which meets the criteria [of the objectives] without geographical restriction.' Potential applicants are therefore advised to contact the foundation to discuss an application.

Information gathered from:
Accounts; annual report; Charity Commission record; funder's website.

The Richmond Parish Lands Charity

General, community
£867,000 to organisations
(2011/12)

Beneficial area
Richmond, Kew, North Sheen, East Sheen, Ham, Petersham and Mortlake.

Correspondent: Jonathan Monckton, Director, The Vestry House, 21 Paradise Road, Richmond, Surrey TW9 1SA (tel: 020 8948 5701; fax: 020 8332 6792; email: grants@rplc.org.uk; website: www.rplc.org.uk)

Trustees: Ashley Casson; Niall Cairns; Rita Biddulph; Vivienne Press; Susan Goddard; Sue Jones; Ian Durant; Paul Cole; Ros Sweeting; Rosie Dalzell; Tim Sketchley; Kate Ellis; Lisa Blakemore; Gill Moffett; Roger Clark.

CC Number: 200069

Established in 1786, the charity supports a wide range of causes in specified parts of the borough of Richmond upon Thames, as outlined under 'Beneficial area'. A map of the beneficial area is available on the charity's website.

The charity describes its objectives as:
▌ The relief of poverty in the London Borough of Richmond upon Thames
▌ The relief of sickness and distress in the borough
▌ The provision and support of leisure and recreational facilities in the charity's beneficial area
▌ The provision educational facilities and support for people in Richmond wishing to undertake courses
▌ Any other charitable purpose for the benefit of the inhabitants of Richmond

Strategic priorities are reviewed periodically – currently the priority for strategic funding is social inclusion. Check the charity's website for current priorities.

The charity makes the following types of grants:
▌ Grants of more than £500
▌ Grants of less than £500
▌ Regularly Funded Organisations
▌ Strategic Funding – Social Inclusion Projects: funding for up to three years
▌ Education grants for schools, PTAs and other educational organisations

There is some cross-over within these types. As well as grant giving to organisations, the charity also gives crisis grants, fuel grants and educational grants to individuals within the beneficial area. The charity also maintains some 90 properties available for affordable rented housing.

In 2011/12 the charity had assets of £65 million and an income of £1.9 million. Grants were made totalling £1.1 million including £228,000 to 1,021 individuals and £867,000 to 98 organisations. A further £833,000 was spent on rent subsidies relating to the charity's social housing.

Beneficiaries included: Citizens Advice (£56,000); Integrated Neurological Services (£46,000); Cambrian Community Centre (£30,000); Addiction Support and Care Agency (£24,000); Three Wings Trust (£19,000); Richmond Good Neighbours (£11,000); Trans-generational Change and Ethnic Minority Advisory Group (£7,000 each); Kingston and Richmond Advocacy (£4,400); Marshgate After School Club (£2,300); Young Science Events Richmond (£1,000); and Community Mental Health Team (£500).

Exclusions
Projects and organisations located outside the benefit area, unless it can be demonstrated that a substantial number of residents from the benefit area will gain from their work. UK charities (even if based in the benefit area), except for that part of their work which caters specifically for the area.

Applications
There are separate application forms and guidelines available on the website for the various types of grants. Be sure that you fill in each section and provide the required documents.

Regularly funded organisations must apply by specific deadlines which are available on the website.

One-off unsolicited applications for funding for more than £500 will be considered in December and March. Application forms should arrive at the RPLC office by 15 November and 15 February. Potential applicants should check the charity's website to be sure of the deadlines.

Eligible applications must be received at least ten working days before the meeting at which they will be considered

– check the charity's website for upcoming deadlines.

You will be advised by letter within fourteen days of the meeting whether or not your application has been successful. Following agreement for a grant you will be sent a conditions of grant form setting out the terms and conditions of the grant. Payment will be arranged on receipt of a signed agreement. A monitoring and evaluation form will also be required on completion of your next application form.

Percentage of awards given to new applicants: between 10% and 20%.

Common applicant mistakes

'Failure to provide up-to-date management accounts or recent financial statements.'

Information gathered from:

Accounts; annual report; Charity Commission record; guidelines for applicants; further information provided by the funder; funder's website.

Ridgesave Ltd

Jewish, religion, education, general
£2.2 million (2011/12)

Beneficial area
UK and overseas.

Correspondent: Zelda Weiss, Trustee, 141b Upper Clapton Road, London E5 9DB

Trustees: Joseph Weiss; Zelda Weiss; E. Englander.

CC Number: 288020

The trust is largely focused on supporting organisations engaged in education, the advancement of the Jewish religion and the giving of philanthropic aid.

In 2011/12 the trust had assets of £2.1 million and an income of £1.3 million, most of which came from donations. Grants were made totalling £2.2 million. Information on recent beneficiaries was not available.

Previous beneficiaries include: Keren Associates Ltd, BAT, UTA, CM L, TYY, Square Foundation Ltd, Ateres Yeshua Charitable Trust, Side by Side, My Dream Time, British Friends of Rinat Aharon, Chanoch Lenaar, and All in Together Girls.

Applications

In writing to the correspondent. 'The trustees consider all requests they receive and make donation based on the level of funds available.'

Information gathered from:
Accounts (without a list of grants); Charity Commission record.

The River Farm Foundation

General, older people, young people, animal welfare and the environment
£2.2 million (2011/12)

Beneficial area
UK.

Correspondent: Deborah Fisher, Trustee, The Old Coach House, Sunnyside, Bergh Apton, Norwich NR15 1DD (tel: 01508 480100; email: info@willcoxlewis.co.uk)

Trustees: Mark Haworth; Nigel Jeremy Langstaff; Deborah Fisher.

CC Number: 1113109

The foundation was set up in February 2006. The trustees aim to fund academic institutions, museums and charities providing support to children, the homeless and other disadvantaged groups. They have stated that they are aiming to increase the number and level of grants to enable those recipient organisations to provide better and ever more appropriate levels of support.

In 2011/12 the foundation had assets of £30 million and an income of £588,000. Grants to organisations totalled £2.2 million. £2 million of this was given in one grant to The River Farm America Foundation, an American grantmaking organisation.

Other beneficiaries included: The Busoga Trust (£30,000); The University of Oxford (£20,000); Centrepoint (£15,000); Microloan Foundation, Water Aid and Richard House Trust (£9,000 each); NSPCC (£6,000); Cats Protection and Oxford Infant Parent Project (£3,000 each); Royal British Legion and Prisoners Abroad (£2,000); and Skidmore College (£900).

Applications

Trustees meet at least twice a year to review applications made and consider grantmaking.

> This strategy will continue to be implemented for as long as the number of applications remains small. As the activities of the foundation expand in the future, it is envisaged that a more refined administrative process of assessment will be put in place.

Information gathered from:
Accounts; annual report; Charity Commission record.

The Robertson Trust

General
£14.7 million (2011/12)

Beneficial area
Scotland.

Correspondent: Lesley Macdonald, Head of Assessment, 152 Bath Street, Glasgow G2 4TB (tel: 01413 537300; email: enquires@therobertsontrust.org.uk; website: www.therobertsontrust.org.uk)

Trustees: Sir Ian Good; Richard Hunter; Dame Barbara Kelly; Shonaig Macpherson; David Stevenson; Ian Curle; Mark Laing; Sandy Cumming; Andrew Walls; Heather Lamont; Judy Cromarty; Kintail Trustees Ltd.

SC Number: SC002970

General

The trust was established in 1961 by the Robertson sisters, who inherited a controlling interest in companies in the Scotch Whiskey Industry (now the Edrington Group) from their father and wished to ensure the dividend income from the shares would be given to charitable purposes.

Guidelines

There are four priority areas with the following guidelines:

Health
This category includes activities which promote health, as well as those which seek to prevent or treat sickness and disease. Examples include projects which work with children who are at risk of misusing drugs or alcohol or are affected by parental substance misuse, and with people recovering from addictions to assist them in rebuilding their lives.

Care
This category is broadly defined. Examples include palliative care, care for older people, people with disabilities, people with mental health issues, people who are homeless and offenders and their families. Support is given to charities working at both local and national level. The category includes sports and arts projects which have a specifically therapeutic purpose.

Education and training
This category includes support for community-based education activities, capital projects at Universities and F.E. Colleges and provision for people with special educational needs. The Trust is particularly interested in supporting projects which increase access and opportunity, develop recognised Centres of Excellence and contribute to the growth of the Scottish economy.

Community arts and sport
This category is primarily aimed at encouraging young people to participate in artistic and sporting activities within their local community. Projects should

demonstrate that they provide access and opportunity and/or support emerging talent. The Trust is particularly interested in supporting activities which increase the use of existing facilities; however, capital projects which seek to widen opportunity, access and participation, as well as improve provision, will also be considered.

These priority areas account for approximately two-thirds of the trust's expenditure each year. However, applications will be considered from most other areas of charitable activity, including:

- Animal conservation and welfare
- Community facilities and services
- Heritage
- Culture and science
- Environment
- Saving lives

It should be noted that overall priority will be given to those projects and posts which relate to direct service delivery. There are no minimum or maximum donations. Donations are classified according to four main types, to which different guidelines apply.

Major Awards comprise capital donations in excess of £100,000, for which the overall project costs will normally be in excess of £1 million. Major capital donations will contribute specifically to one of the Trust's priority areas other than under exceptional circumstances. Major capital applications will be considered in January, May and September

Main Awards comprise revenue donations of between £1,000 and £20,000 per annum and capital donations of up to £100,000. Capital donations will normally be for a maximum of 10% of the total project cost.

Small Awards comprise revenue donations up to £10,000. Applications for Main and Small donations will be considered six times a year and a suggested format for all applicants is provided on the Trust's website which is designed to make the process as simple as possible for all applicants.

Development Awards seek to undertake a proactive role by investigating specific areas or issues where the Trustees believe there is a need for the provision of services. They also seek to inform national policy through the commissioning and sharing of external evaluations. In these areas of work a more significant contribution to the total project cost, whether revenue or capital, may be

considered. The Trust's support in this area is currently focused on support for offenders and their families; alcohol misuse and community sport.

Grantmaking in 2011/12

During the year the trust had assets of £418 million and an income of £14 million. Grants totalled £14.7 million to 746 charities, distributed among the categories as displayed in the box below.

Beneficiaries included: Border Health Board Endowment Funds (£250,000); Scottish Opera (£200,000); Crossroads Caring Scotland (£150,000); Glasgow School of Art (£100,000); Citizens Advice (£80,000); Factory Skatepark (£45,000); REACH Community Health Project (£30,000); St Andrew's Hospice (£20,000); Wigtownshire Animal Welfare Association (£14,000); Kyle Public Hall (£10,000); Depression and Anxiety Support and Help Group (£4,000); Clann An Latha An De (£2,000); and Friends of Elmbank (£500).

Exclusions

The trust does not support:

- Individuals or organisations which are not recognised as charities by the Office of the Scottish Charity Regulator (OSCR)
- General appeals or circulars, including contributions to endowment funds
- Local charities whose work takes place outside Scotland
- Generic employment or training projects
- Community projects where the applicant is a housing association
- Core revenue costs for playgroups, nurseries, after school groups, etc.
- Projects which are exclusively or primarily intended to promote political beliefs
- Students or organisations for personal study, travel or for expeditions whether in the United Kingdom or abroad
- Medical research
- Organisations and projects whose primary object is to provide a counselling, advocacy, advice and/or information service

The trust is unlikely to support:

- Charities which collect funds for onward distribution to others

- Umbrella groups which do not provide a direct service to individuals e.g. CVS
- Feasibility studies and other research
- Charities already in receipt of a current donation from the trust

Applications

Applicants are advised to read the guidelines available to download on the trust's website.

There are two ways to apply:

By application form which is available on the trust's website, to be returned with the supporting documents, or by letter which should include the following details:

- A brief description of the organisation, including past developments and successes
- A description of the project – what you want to do, who will be involved, where will it take place and how it will be managed
- How you have identified the need for this work
- What you hope will be the outputs and outcomes of this work and the key targets you have set
- How you intend to monitor and evaluate the work so that you know whether or not you have been successful
- The income and expenditure budget for this piece of work
- How you propose to fund the work, including details of funds already raised or applied for
- The proposed timetable

In addition the trust will also require three supporting documents. These are:

1 A completed copy of the Organisation Information Sheet, which is available from the trust's website or the trust office
2 A copy of your most recent annual report and accounts. These should have been independently examined or audited
3 A job description, if you are applying for salary costs for a specified worker

The trust requests that applicants do not send a constitution or memorandum and articles. If there is any other bulky information which you feel may be relevant, such as a feasibility study, business plan or evaluation, then you should refer to it in your application, so that the assessment team can request it if required. The trust welcomes enquires from potential applicants and wishes to provide the support required by charities in order to make applications.

Information gathered from:

Accounts; annual report; annual review; Charity Commission record; guidelines for applicants; funder's website.

THE ROBERTSON TRUST

Type	No. of grants	Total	% of total	Average grant
Main	206	£5.1 million	35	£24,500
Small	424	£2.7 million	18	£6,300
50th Anniversary	46	£2.5 million	17	£54,000
Development	61	£2 million	14	£33,300
Major	8	£1.3 million	9	£166,000
Scholarship	1	£1 million	7	n/a

The Roddick Foundation

Arts, education, environmental, human rights, humanitarian, medical, poverty, social justice

£1.3 million (2012/13)

Beneficial area
Worldwide.

Correspondent: Karen Smith, Administrator, PO Box 112, Slindon Common, Arundel, West Sussex BN18 8AS (tel: 01243 814788; email: karen@theroddickfoundation.org; website: www.theroddickfoundation.org)

Trustees: Justine Roddick; Samantha Roddick; Gordon Roddick; Christina Schlieske.

CC Number: 1061372

The foundation was established in 1997 by the late Dame Anita Roddick, founder of the Body Shop. It has the following objects:

- ▶ The relief of poverty
- ▶ The promotion, maintenance, improvement and advancement of education for the public benefit
- ▶ The provision of facilities for recreation or other leisure time occupations in the interests of social welfare provided that such facilities are for the public benefit
- ▶ The promotion of any other charitable purpose for the benefit of the public

In 2012/13 the foundation made 60 grants totalling £1.3 million. Grants were broken down as follows:

Human rights	19	£462,000
Social rights	15	£251,000
Arts and culture	9	£209,500
Environment	9	£204,000
Education	3	£95,500
Medical and health	3	£56,000
Media	1	£15,000
Humanitarian	1	£6,500

Beneficiaries included: Arundel Festival; The Basement; Chestnut Tree Hospice; ClientEarth; Community Action Fund for Women in Africa; Get Paper Industries; The Marine Foundation; Red Rag Productions; Shine Trust; Slow Food UK; SumOfUs; and Transition Chichester. Information is taken from the foundation's website, which does not give the amount given to individual grant recipients.

Exclusions
The trust states that it is 'particularly not interested in the following:'

- ▶ Funding anything related to sport
- ▶ Funding fundraising events or conferences
- ▶ Sponsorship of any kind

Applications
The foundation does not accept or respond to unsolicited applications.

'Grants made by the foundation are at the discretion of the board of trustees. The board considers making a grant and, if approved, notifies the intended recipient.'

Information gathered from:
Charity Commission record; funder's website.

The Gerald Ronson Foundation

General, Jewish

£1 million (2012)

Beneficial area
UK and overseas.

Correspondent: Jeremy Trent, Secretary, H. W. Fisher and Company, Acre House, 11–15 William Road, London NW1 3ER (tel: 020 7388 7000; email: jtrent@hwfisher.co.uk)

Trustees: Gerald Ronson, Chair; Dame Gail Ronson; Alan Goldman; Jonathan Goldstein; Lisa Ronson; Nicole Ronson Allalouf; Hayley Ronson.

CC Number: 1111728

The foundation was registered with the Charity Commission in September 2005. 'The trustees' grantmaking policy is to make donations to registered charitable organisations undertaking a wide range of charitable activities.' It is the foundation of businessman and philanthropist Gerald Ronson, chief executive of Heron International, a UK-based property developer.

In 2012 the foundation had assets of £11.1 million and an income of £951,000. Grants were made totalling £1 million, and were broken down as follows:

Education	£350,000
Community and welfare	£277,000
Medical and disability	£248,000
Arts and culture	£74,000
Religion	£45,000
Overseas aid	£16,000
General	£11,000

Beneficiaries included: Jewish Community Secondary School (£200,000); Jewish Care (£100,000); Great Ormond Street Hospital (£75,000); King David Schools (£55,000); Royal Opera House Foundation (£43,500); Action for Stammering Children (£30,000); and Young Epilepsy (£20,000). A number of grants are made to organisations with which the trustees have a connection.

Applications
In writing to the correspondent. 'The trust generally makes donations on a quarterly basis in June, September, December and March. In the interim periods, the Chair's Action Committee deals with urgent requests for donations which are approved by the trustees at the quarterly meetings.'

Information gathered from:
Accounts; Charity Commission record.

Mrs L. D. Rope Third Charitable Settlement

Education, religion, relief of poverty, general

£716,000 to organisations (2011/12)

Beneficial area
UK and overseas, with a particular interest in Suffolk.

Correspondent: Crispin Rope, Trustee, Crag Farm, Boyton, Near Woodbridge, Suffolk IP12 3LH (tel: 01473 333288)

Trustees: Crispin Rope; Jeremy Heal; Ellen Jolly; Catherine Scott; Paul Jolly.

CC Number: 290533

The charity takes the name of Lucy Rope, who died in 2003 aged 96. Mrs Rope engaged in many charitable endeavours throughout her life. The charity, administered by Mrs Rope's son, Crispin, is based near Ipswich, and takes a keen interest in helping people from its local area. Most of the funds are already committed to projects it has initiated itself, or to ongoing relationships. Unfortunately, only about one in ten applications to this trust can be successful.

Guidelines
The charity offers the following distinction between projects initiated by itself and unsolicited applications in its very detailed and informative accounts:

In practice, the work of the charity may be divided into two distinct categories. Firstly it initiates, supports and pursues certain specific charitable projects selected by the Founder or known to be generally in accordance with her wishes. Secondly, it approves grants to unsolicited applications that fall within the Founder's stated objectives and that comply with the set of grant-making policies outlined below, specifically for this second element of its work. The trustees devote more of the charity's resources to self-initiated projects as compared to pure grant making to unsolicited requests. In terms of grants funded during the year [2011/12], roughly £773,000 was given towards projects where the charity had either initiated the work or where a long-standing relationship over a number of years gave rise to new or continued assistance. In contrast roughly £336,000 of grant making arose from an increasing number of unsolicited applications for the charity's help.

Successful unsolicited applications to the charity usually display a combination of the following features, as outlined in the charity's 2011/12 accounts:

Size

The trustees very much prefer to encourage charities that work at 'grassroots' level within their community. Such charities are unlikely to have benefited greatly from grant funding from local, national (including funds from the National Lottery) or European authorities. They are also less likely to be as wealthy in comparison with other charities that attract popular support on a national basis. The charities assisted usually cannot afford to pay for the professional help other charities may use to raise funds.

Volunteers

The trustees prefer applications from charities that are able to show they have a committed and proportionately large volunteer force.

Administration

The less a charity spends on paying for its own administration, particularly as far as staff salaries are concerned, the more it is likely to be considered by the trustees.

Areas of interest

Charities with the above characteristics that work in any of the following areas:

- Helping people who struggle to live on very little income, including the homeless
- Helping people who live in deprived inner city and rural areas of the UK, particularly young people who lack the opportunities that may be available elsewhere
- Helping charities in our immediate local area of south east Suffolk
- Helping to support family life
- Helping disabled people
- Helping Roman Catholic charities and ecumenical projects

Grants made to charities outside the primary beneficial area of south east Suffolk are usually one-off and small in scale (in the range between £100 and £2,000).

Unlike many trusts, the charity can consider helping people on a personal basis. The trustees give priority, as they do with charities, to people struggling to live on little income, within the primary beneficial area. Grants are rarely made to individuals living outside the primary beneficial area. Of the individuals assisted, most are referred by field professionals such as housing or probation officers, on whose informed advice the trustees can place reliance [for further information, see *The Guide to Grants for Individuals in Need*, published by the Directory of Social Change].

Grantmaking in 2011/12

In 2011/12 the charity had assets of £51.9 million and an income of £1.3 million. Grants were made totalling £1.1 million, including £384,000 to individuals. Of the total disbursed to organisations, £336,000 was awarded in unsolicited grants while £389,000 was awarded to projects identified and selected by the trust itself. During the year the charity received over 2,200 applications for funding.

In 2011/12, the charity made grants in the areas shown in the displayed box below (including the amount given in grants to organisations).

Beneficiaries included: Mrs L D Rope Second Charitable Settlement (£100,000); CAFOD (£75,000); Disability Information and Advice, Lowestoft (£30,000); Ipswich CAB (£22,000); Kesgrave High School (£14,000); Juvenile Diabetes Research Foundation (£10,000); Buckingham Emergency Food Appeal (£8,000); and African Mission (£6,000).

Exclusions

The following categories of unsolicited applications will not be successful:

- Overseas projects
- National charities
- Requests for core funding
- Buildings
- Medical research/health care (outside of the beneficial area)
- Students (a very limited amount is available for foreign students)
- Schools (outside of the beneficial area)

- Environmental charities and animal welfare
- The arts
- Matched funding
- Repayment of debts for individuals

Applications

Send a concise letter (preferably one side of A4) explaining the main details of your request. Always send your most recent accounts and a budgeted breakdown of the sum you are looking to raise. The charity will also need to know whether you have applied to other funding sources and whether you have been successful elsewhere. Your application should say who your trustees are and include a daytime telephone number.

Information gathered from:

Accounts; annual report; Charity Commission record.

The Rose Foundation

General – grants towards building projects

£911,500 (2011/12)

Beneficial area

In and around London.

Correspondent: Martin Rose, Trustee, 28 Crawford Street, London W1H 1LN (tel: 020 7262 1155; website: www. rosefoundation.co.uk)

Trustees: Martin Rose; Alan Rose; John Rose; Paul Rose.

CC Number: 274875

Established in 1977, the foundation supports charities requiring assistance for their building projects, giving small grants to benefit as large a number of people as possible rather than large grants to small specific groups. The foundation applied to the Charity Commission to modernise its trust deed in 2002, which was to make it more applicable to how the foundation

---

MRS L. D. ROPE THIRD CHARITABLE SETTLEMENT

Charity's priorities for giving

General charitable purposes	£406,000	Public and other charitable purposes in the region of east Suffolk and in particular the parish of Kesgrave and the areas surrounding it, including Ipswich. Particular emphasis is placed on small grants to individuals in need in the charity's primary area.
Relief of poverty	£264,000	Support for a number of causes and individuals where the trustees have longer term knowledge and experience, particularly those both in the UK and in the Third World who are little catered for by other charities or by grants or benefits from governments or other authorities, or are in particularly deprived areas and, for overseas work, only through established links.
Advancement of education	£37,000	Support for educational projects connected with the founder's family. Support for an airship museum; support for Catholic and other schools in the general area of Ipswich; and projects relating to the interaction of mathematics and physical science with philosophy.
Advancement of religion	£18,000	Support for the Roman Catholic religion and ecumenical work, both generally and for specific institutions connected historically with the families of William Oliver Jolly and his wife, Alice and Dr Henry Rope and their descendants.

operates rather than to change how it works.

Grants are made towards small self-contained schemes (of generally less than £200,000) based in or around London and usually range from £5,000 to £10,000 each. Previously the trust has given up to £30,000, but has reduced this figure to keep to its spirit of giving a large number of smaller grants despite the decline of the stock market in recent years. Projects should commence between January and August or have started earlier but still be ongoing during that period.

The trustees' policy is to offer assistance where needed with the design and construction process, ensuring wherever possible that costs are minimised and the participation of other contributing bodies can be utilised to maximum benefit.

In 2011/12 the foundation had assets of £22 million and an income of £943,000. Grants were paid during the year to 72 organisations totalling £911,500.

As in previous years, the largest grant made during the year was given to St John Ambulance, which received £550,000 as part of a continuing programme of support. Other larger grants were made to the New Amsterdam Charitable Foundation (£87,000), a connected organisation based in the US and the Fred Hollows Foundation (£48,000), based in Australia.

Other beneficiaries included: University College School (£12,000); Jewish Care (£9,500); All Souls Church of England Primary School and Cancer Research UK (£7,000 each); Soho Theatre Company (£6,000); Cardinal Hume Centre, Flash Musicals and Zoological Society of London (£5,000 each); Regent's Park Open Air Theatre (£4,000); and Body and Soul (£3,000).

Exclusions

The foundation can support any type of building project (decoration, construction, repairs, extensions, adaptations) but not the provision of equipment (such as computers, transportation and so on). Items connected with the finishes, such as carpets, curtains, wallpaper and so on, should ideally comprise a part of the project not financed by the foundation. Funding will not be given for the purchase of a building or a site or for the seed money needed to draw up plans.

Applications

In writing to the correspondent including details of the organisation and the registered charity number, together with the nature and probable approximate cost of the scheme and its anticipated start and completion dates. Applications can be submitted anytime between 1 July and 31 March (the following year). The foundation hopes to inform applicants of its decision by the second week in July.

Information gathered from:

Accounts; Charity Commission record; funder's website.

Rosetrees Trust

Medical research
£1.5 million (2011/12)

Beneficial area

UK.

Correspondent: Sam Howard, Chief Executive, Russell House, 140 High Street, Edgware, Middlesex HA8 7LW (tel: 020 8952 1414; email: richard@rosetreestrust.co.uk; website: www.rosetreestrust.co.uk)

Trustees: Richard Ross; Clive Winkler; James Bloom; Lee Mesnick.

CC Number: 298582

Registered as the Teresa Rosenbaum Golden Charitable Trust, the trust was established in 1987 to support medical research leading to early improved treatments or new therapies covering many medical conditions. The trust is currently supporting over 100 research projects. The trust aims to find like-minded charities with which to co-fund valuable research projects. In 2009/10 a transfer of assets from the settlors' estate to the trust amounted to around £30 million. Richard Ross is the settlors' son and a well-known philanthropist. The trust is very keen to share the expertise it has developed over the years, which is available to co-donors at no cost. Organisations interested in sharing this knowledge should contact the trust directly.

The trust's main objectives are:

- Seed corn funding for outstanding research
- Encouraging outstanding young researchers with the potential to become professors and leaders in their field
- Diagnostic testing or testing of existing drugs for additional benefits to help or cure illnesses for relatively little cost
- Helping clinicians test bright ideas arising out of their everyday work to improve procedures and treatments

The trust usually starts with relatively small grants, but as the reporting progresses and a good working relationship develops between the trust and the researchers, these grants are steadily increased and over a period of years can build up to substantial sums.

The vast majority of grants are made through university and medical schools. During 2011/12 the trust had assets of £37.4 million and an income of £1.7 million. Grants were made totalling £1.5 million and were distributed to the following research institutes:

UCL and Royal Free	£400,000
King's College	£179,000
Hebrew University	£130,000
Royal College of Surgeons	£123,000
Imperial College	£101,000
Institute of Cancer Research	£51,000
University of Oxford	£41,000
University of Cambridge	£31,000
Barts and Queen Mary	£30,000
St George's Hospital	£30,000
University of Manchester	£16,000
Other centres	£276,000
Other grants	£109,000

Exclusions

No support for individuals or for non-medical research.

Applications

In writing to the correspondent. Applicants must complete a simple pro forma which sets out briefly in clear layman's terms the reason for the project, the nature of the research, its cost, its anticipated benefit and how and when people will be able to benefit. Proper reports in this form will be required at least six-monthly and continuing funding will be conditional on these being satisfactory.

The trust has previously stated:

The trustees are not medical experts and require short clear statements in plain English setting out the particular subject to be researched, the objects and likely benefits, the cost and the time-scale. Unless a charity will undertake to provide two concise progress reports each year, they should not apply as this is a vital requirement. It is essential that the trustees are able to follow the progress and effectiveness of the research they support.

Information gathered from:

Accounts; Charity Commission record; funder's website.

Rowanville Ltd

Orthodox Jewish
£670,000 (2011/12)

Beneficial area

UK and Israel.

Correspondent: Ruth Pearlman, Secretary, 8 Highfield Gardens, London NW11 9HB (tel: 020 8458 9266)

Trustees: Joseph Pearlman; Ruth Pearlman; Michael Neuberger; Montague Frankel.

CC Number: 267278

The objectives of the trust are 'to advance religion in accordance with the Orthodox Jewish faith'. The trust provides grants to charitable institutions and free accommodation for educational use.

In 2011/12 the trust had assets of £4.6 million and an income of £732,500. Grants were made totalling £670,000.

Beneficiaries included: Friends of Beis Yisrael Trust (£45,500); Yesamach Levav Trust (£30,000); North West Sephardish Synagogue (£22,000); Achisomoch Aid Co. Limited (£16,500); Sunderland Talmudical College (£15,000); Beth Jacob Grammar School for Girls (£9,000); Gateshead Talmudical College (£3,000); and Jewish Rescue and Relief Committee (£1,000).

Applications

The trust has previously stated that applications are unlikely to be successful unless one of the trustees has prior personal knowledge of the cause, as this charity's funds are already very heavily committed.

Information gathered from:

Accounts; Charity Commission record.

The Joseph Rowntree Charitable Trust

Equalities, rights and justice, power and accountability, peace and security, and sustainable future

£6.3 million (2012)

Beneficial area

Unrestricted, in practice mainly UK.

Correspondent: Nick Perks, Trust Secretary, The Garden House, Water End, York YO30 6WQ (tel: 01904 627810; fax: 01904 651990; email: jrct@jrct.org.uk; website: www.jrct.org.uk)

Trustees: Margaret Bryan, Chair; Peter Coltman; Christine Davis; Jenny Amery; Linda Batten; Helen Carmichael; Michael Eccles; Stan Lee; Emily Miles; Susan Seymour; Hannah Torkington; Imran Tyabji; Catriona Worrall.

CC Number: 210037

Background

The Joseph Rowntree Charitable Trust (JRCT) is established for general charitable purposes and benefits people and organisations mainly within Britain. Outside Britain, the trust makes grants for work towards peace, justice and reconciliation in both jurisdictions in the island of Ireland and, increasingly, in relation to influencing the policies of the European Union.

This is a Quaker trust and the value base of the trustees, as of the founder Joseph Rowntree (1836–1925), reflects the religious convictions of the Society of Friends. In the original founding trust deed of 1904 (from which the present deed is derived) Joseph Rowntree gave the trustees power to spend the trust fund and its income on any object which is legally charitable. In a memorandum written at the same time, which is not part of the trust deed and therefore not binding, he expressed a clear vision of how he hoped the fund would be used, while urging that 'none of the objects which I have enumerated, and which under present social conditions appear to me to be of paramount importance, should be pursued after it has ceased to be vital and pressing...'.

There are three Rowntree trusts, each of which is independent of the others. Joseph Rowntree Foundation (JRF) is one of the largest social policy research and development charities in the UK and seeks to better understand the causes of social difficulties, and to explore ways of overcoming them. The JRF is also involved in practical housing and care work through the Joseph Rowntree Housing Trust.

Joseph Rowntree Reform Trust Ltd (JRRT) promotes democratic reform, constitutional change and social justice, both in the UK and elsewhere. It is a non-charitable limited company and is therefore free to give grants for political purposes. The JRRT and JRCT have collaborated on various initiatives combating racism and encouraging democratic renewal, including research into voting behaviour in towns in the North of England, and the Power Inquiry.

Regular reviews are undertaken to reassess how it is appropriate to interpret the founder's vision in today's conditions. The trust continues to operate an ethical investment policy, aiming to ensure that, as far as possible, the trust's income is earned in ways which are compatible with its Quaker values and its grantmaking policy. As Quakers, they share a belief in the equal worth of all members of the human race, together with a recognition and appreciation of diversity.

Programmes

In October 2013 the trust released the following statement on its future activities:

> Over the past 18 months, JRCT has undertaken a strategic review. Many people fed into this process and we are grateful for these contributions.
>
> We reaffirm that our mission is to be a Quaker trust which seeks to transform the world by supporting people who address the root causes of conflict and injustice.

For the next 5 to 10 years we will continue to be a responsive grant making body, and will group our work into four themes:

- Equalities, rights and justice
- Power and accountability
- Peace and security
- Sustainable future

Under these four themes, we expect to continue to fund work in a number of areas where we have had a long-term commitment, including for example promoting human rights, racial justice, democratic and corporate accountability and challenging militarism, as well as strengthening work in the area of sustainability. We will also continue our funding programme focused on the transformation of the Northern Ireland conflict.

Sadly, we will be ending our funding in the Republic of Ireland, where we have supported some excellent work over the last two decades. We will also be closing our Quaker Concerns programme, although we will continue to consider applications from Quaker organisations under the above themes where they fit our published policies.

We are currently developing detailed guidance on our priorities within these new themes. This guidance will be published in May 2014, and the first deadline for applications under these new themes will be 1 September 2014. In the meantime, all our existing programmes are closed to applicants who are not current grantees, with the exception of our Northern Ireland programme which continues unchanged.

If you are a current grantee and are considering applying to the trust before September 2014, please contact the office first for further guidance.

We appreciate that it is always disruptive for organisations in the field when funders alter their priorities. We will aim to be as supportive and transparent as possible in relation to these changes.

In 2012 the trust had assets of £158 million and an income of just under £5.5 million. Grants were made totalling £6.3 million, and it is likely that this level of funding will continue when the trust resumes grantmaking under its revised programmes.

Exclusions

Generally, the trust does not make grants for:

- The personal support of individuals in need
- Educational bursaries
- Travel or adventure projects
- Medical research
- Building, buying or repairing buildings
- Business development or job creation schemes
- General appeals
- Providing care for elderly people, children, people with learning difficulties, people with physical

disabilities, or people using mental health services
▶ Work which has already been done
▶ Work in larger, older national charities which have an established constituency of supporters
▶ Work in mainstream education
▶ Academic research, except as an integral part of policy and campaigning work that is central to the trust's areas of interest
▶ Work on housing and homelessness
▶ The arts, except where a project is specifically concerned with issues of interest to the trust
▶ Work which the trust believes should be funded from statutory sources, or which has been in the recent past
▶ Work which tries to make a problem easier to live with, rather than getting to the root of it
▶ Local work in Britain (except Racial Justice work in West Yorkshire)

Further specific exclusions are included for individual programmes. Within its areas of interest, the trust makes grants to a range of organisations and to individuals. It is not necessary to be a registered charity to apply to the trust. However, it can only support work which is legally charitable as defined in UK law.

Applications

Note the information in the 'general' section. Potential applicants are advised to monitor the trust's website for current information or contact the trust directly.

Percentage of awards given to new applicants: between 20% and 30%.

Information gathered from:

Accounts; annual report; Charity Commission record; further information provided by the funder; funder's website.

The Joseph Rowntree Foundation

Research and development in social policy and practice

£5.3 million (2012)

Beneficial area

UK, with some preference for York and Bradford.

Correspondent: Julia Unwin, Chief Executive, The Homestead, 40 Water End, York YO30 6WP (tel: 01904 629241; fax: 01904 620072; email: info@jrf.org.uk; website: www.jrf.org.uk)

Trustees: Don Brand; Dr Ashok Jashapara; Bharat Mehta; Tony Stoller; Dame Mavis McDonald; Steven Burkeman; Graham Millar; Prof. Dianne Willcocks; Tony Stoller; Gillian Ashmore; Jas Baines.

CC Number: 210169

General

This is not a conventional grantmaking foundation. It supports research, of a rigorous kind, usually carried out in universities or research institutes, but also has a wide range of other activities not necessarily involving grants of any kind.

The Joseph Rowntree Foundation works in collaboration with the Joseph Rowntree Housing Trust to understand the root causes of social problems, identify ways of overcoming them, and show how social needs can be met in practice.

The purpose is to influence policy and practice by searching for evidence and demonstrating solutions to improve:
▶ The circumstances of people experiencing poverty and disadvantage
▶ The quality of their homes and communities
▶ The nature of the services and support that foster their well-being and citizenship

The foundation initiates, manages and pays for an extensive social research programme. It does not normally respond to unsolicited applications and many of its programmes issue formal and detailed requests for proposals. However modest proposals for minor gap-filling pieces of work in the foundation's fields of interest may sometimes be handled less formally and more rapidly.

They also make some grants locally in and around York, and directly manage or initiate housing schemes.

In 2012 the foundation had assets of £261.3 million and an income of £8.2 million. It spent over £5.3 million on grant commitments. The following information on the areas of work covered in the foundation's 2012–14 strategic plan is given on the foundation's website:

Areas of Work

Poverty in the UK

For over 100 years, we have investigated the root causes of poverty, monitoring its effects on people and places in the UK.

Current welfare reforms are a big challenge for anti-poverty work. Our poverty theme seeks to understand their impact on people and places in poverty. We also agree that the social security system can and should be improved to work better for them. We aim to understand the impacts of the recession on poverty and how employment really can become a sustainable route out of poverty.

We will search for the causes of and solutions to poverty in the UK. These include practical strategies to reduce poverty, and wider social and economic inequalities, focusing particularly on the

contribution of work, skills and economic growth.

We will be the place to get the facts about poverty and inequality.

Our key activities this year [2013] are:
▶ Progressing the anti-poverty strategy programme – effective ideas for reducing poverty in the UK
▶ Completing the Forced Labour and Future UK Labour Markets programmes, making policy and practice recommendations on employment and skills
▶ Updating our research on a Minimum Income Standard for the UK in 2013, showing the impacts of welfare reforms and changes in the costs of living
▶ Monitoring Poverty reports for Wales and the UK, and launching our JRF Data site – the place to get the facts on poverty trends
▶ New research from our poverty and ethnicity programme
▶ Evidence reviews about how much money matters to children's health and education

Place

Communities across the UK are feeling the effects of austerity measures, while demographic change and climate change add to the risk that disadvantaged people and places will suffer the most. We continue to look at how social, economic, environmental and policy changes affect housing, neighbourhoods and different places in the UK. We are focusing on four themes:
▶ Housing – how housing can be adapted to suit different types of household and the varying needs of people at different stages of life, including young people; and how it can reduce the impact of poverty in the UK
▶ Cities, growth and poverty – a new area of work looking at the relationship between economic growth and poverty in cities
▶ Climate change and social justice – how climate change will affect people and places facing poverty and disadvantage in the UK, including factors such as flooding, insurance, heatwaves and energy efficiency
▶ Deprived communities and neighbourhoods – many of our programmes include a focus on deprived areas, including: austerity in the UK; neighbourhood approaches to loneliness; dementia without walls; and anti-poverty strategies for the UK

At Derwenthorpe, our mixed-tenure development on the edge of York, we are working with the Joseph Rowntree Housing Trust to research and demonstrate how a socially and environmentally sustainable community can work in practice.

Ageing Society

By 2020, the Office for National Statistics (ONS) predicts that people over 50 will make up almost one-third (32%) of the workforce and almost half (47%) the adult population.

This requires us to think differently about ageing. The implications of an ageing society affect all of us, across generations and will touch every part of our lives. Our ageing society provides opportunities as well as challenges for individuals, families, communities, employers and government.

We're working to understand how these demographic changes will affect the way we live together, work together and support each other, whatever our age. We use evidence from research, practice and lived experience to share practical solutions and inspiring ideas that show how people and communities – now – are preparing and responding to ageing and old age. Much of our current work focuses on the local, practical, neighbourhood-based and the everyday.

We're focusing on four themes:

- Quality of life – later this year we'll be presenting key findings about what's important for a good quality of life in older age, especially if you need a high level of care or support. We're also looking at progressive housing models for older people
- Risk and relationships – we're exploring how risks and relationships are best managed in care homes and investigating risk and trust in everyday relationships where families, friends and neighbours might be part of an informal network of care and support
- Dementia – through our Dementia Without Walls work we will work in partnership to develop dementia-friendly communities in both York and Bradford. We will also be looking at how to ensure we become a dementia-friendly employer. People with dementia are central to this work, through local initiatives and the DEEP project
- Loneliness – affects anyone of any age. We've trained and supported local people in four neighbourhoods across Bradford and York to find out what causes loneliness where they live and how they, as individuals and communities, can contribute to the wellbeing of people who are at risk of, or are experiencing, loneliness

The focus and key objectives within each area of work are subject to change.

Research programmes
The foundation describes its programmes in considerable depth on its website. They all fall under a main area of work, or cover more than one.

How the foundation works
The foundation does not make grants: those supported are considered partners in a common enterprise. The foundation takes a close interest in each project from the outset, often bringing together an advisory group to give guidance on a project, and taking an active role in the dissemination of the project's findings to bring about policy and practice change. Foundation staff oversee the progress of individual projects within the programme and act as a point of contact throughout.

As a general rule, the foundation aims to provide full financial support rather than being one of a number of funders. However, where the involvement of another organisation would help the project achieve its aims, joint funding may be considered.

How work gets funded
The foundation is keen to fund a variety of different kinds of projects, depending on the state of knowledge about a particular topic.

- The majority of proposals are canvassed under broad programme themes, or through specific briefs using the JRF website, email notification, direct mail, and, occasionally, advertisements
- In addition, JRF sometimes commissions work directly
- Occasionally they will consider proposals arising from an unsolicited approach

The foundation does not have a preference for methodology but it must be appropriate for the question.

The foundation likes to be outward looking in its approach and encourages user groups and community-based groups to apply for funding where appropriate. If the proposal is for a research project the project team must include people with knowledge, experience and research skills to carry out a successful research project.

Who decides which projects are approved?
For proposals which have been received in response to a programme-based call for proposals:

1. Programme Manager and lead Assistant Director (Policy and Research) scrutinise all proposals to sift out proposals which are methodologically weak and which do not meet the foundation's brief.

2. Promising proposals are then further scrutinised by at least one independent external assessor who has relevant expertise, alongside the Programme Manager and lead Assistant Director, and the Director of Policy and Research.

3. Based on rigorous internal and external assessments, recommendations are made to the Director of Policy and Research (who makes the final decision for proposals which cost less than £100,000) and to the Trustee Board (who make the final decision for proposals which cost more than £100,000).

In some circumstances (e.g. when commissioning short evidence reviews or think-pieces, or commissioning pieces of work which are highly specialist and where the field is very limited), the foundation will use a 'limited competitive tender' or 'direct commission' approach.

Programmes and projects
Programmes use different approaches to secure the advice and scrutiny they require for good governance. Programmes often have a programme advisory group or network to draw in expertise from relevant fields, to advise on priorities and progress of the programme as a whole, and on issues concerning influence and impact. Programme advisory groups and networks do not make funding decisions.

York Committee
The York Committee makes grants to organisations to help improve the general quality of life in York, with particular regard for those who are in any way disadvantaged. Grants typically range from £100 to £5,000. trustees prefer to support specific needs rather than general running costs. Grants are given to charities and other not-for-profit organisations in the area covered by the City of York Council.

Funding in 2012
Funds committed to the main programmes during 2012:

Ageing Society	£1.54 million
Poverty	£1.35 million
Place	£735,000
Cross-theme work	£241,000
Bradford	£158,000
Other funding streams	£1.3 million

The foundation's excellent website gives full details of its work.

Exclusions
The foundation does not generally support:

- Projects outside the topics within its current priorities
- Development projects which are not innovative
- Development projects from which no general lessons can be drawn
- General appeals, for example from national charities
- Conferences and other events, websites or publications, unless they are linked with work which the foundation is already supporting
- Grants to replace withdrawn or expired statutory funding, or to make up deficits already incurred
- Educational bursaries or sponsorship for individuals for research or further education and training courses
- Grants or sponsorship for individuals in need

Grants from the York Committee are not given to:

- Animal welfare groups
- Archaeological work
- Individuals
- Routine maintenance or construction of buildings

- Medical research
- Overseas visits or overseas holidays

Applications

The foundation does not respond to unsolicited applications. Instead, it issues 'calls for proposals' and invites submissions to them. Detailed information, including guidance and a proposal registration form, is available from the foundation's website.

The York Committee has its own application guidelines and form, available on the foundation's website. Meetings to decide grants are held four times a year, usually February, May, August and November.

Information gathered from:

Accounts; annual report; Charity Commission record; funder's website.

Joseph Rowntree Reform Trust Ltd

Promoting political and democratic reform and defending of civil liberties

£1 million (2013)

Beneficial area

UK.

Correspondent: Tina Walker, Trust Secretary., The Garden House, Water End, York YO30 6WQ (tel: 01904 625744; fax: 01904 651502; email: info@ jrrt.org.uk; website: www.jrrt.org.uk)

Trustees: Dr Christopher Greenfield, Chair; Tina Day; Mandy Cormack; Dr Peadar Cremin; Alison Goldsworthy; Andrew Neal.

Joseph Rowntree was a Quaker businessman with a lifelong concern for the alleviation of poverty and the other great social ills of his day. He made a considerable fortune from the chocolate company which bore his name, and in 1904 transferred a large part of this wealth to three trusts, each designed to reflect and develop different aspects of his thinking about contemporary social problems. Known today as the Joseph Rowntree Foundation, the Joseph Rowntree Charitable Trust and the Joseph Rowntree Reform Trust (JRRT), all three continue to build upon the founder's original vision, applying it in their different ways to the problems of present-day society; however, they have always been separately administered and are totally independent of each other.

JRRT differs from the other Rowntree Trusts, and from almost every other trust in the UK, in that it is not a charity. Charities must not have political objectives and whilst they may engage in political activity in pursuit of their charitable aims, those aims must not in themselves be political. By contrast, this trust is a limited company which pays tax on its income. It is therefore free to give grants for political purposes; to promote political and democratic reform and defend civil liberties. It does so by funding campaigning organisations and individuals who have reform as their objective, and since it remains one of the very few sources of funds of any significance in the UK which can do this, it reserves its support for those projects which are ineligible for charitable funding.

The trust's main aims are to:

- Correct imbalances of power
- Strengthen the hand of individuals, groups and organisations who are striving for reform
- Foster democratic reform, civil liberties and social justice

The following is taken from the trust's website:

> The trust is not committed to the policies of any one political party although it has been a long-term funder of the Liberal Democrats (and predecessor parties) in order to redress the balance of financial inequality between parties and to foster political developments central to a healthy democratic process. It has also supported individual politicians or groups promoting new ideas and policies from all the major parties in the UK.
>
> The trust has also helped a large number of non-party pressure groups needing short-term assistance: however, the trust will not normally provide long-term funding. Such groups need not be national organisations, but the national relevance of local campaigns is a crucial factor that Directors will consider.

Currently, the trust has assets of around £30 million. Each year a potential grant budget of around £1 million is allocated which excludes administrative expenses and tax.

Information about grants is published on the trust's website once the grant has been ratified at a subsequent trust meeting. The list is not necessarily complete as the trust may decide that to achieve a particular grant's purpose or to protect the personal safety of those undertaking the work, it is not appropriate to make available the information.

Beneficiaries in 2013 included: Paladin National Stalking Advocacy (£70,000); Open Rights Group (£43,000); Privacy International (£40,000); MedConfidential (£38,000); Democratic Audit (£4,500); and Option A Team (£4,000).

Exclusions

The trust is not a registered charity and provides grants for non-charitable political and campaigning activities. Examples of work for which the trust does not make grants are:

- The personal support of individuals in need
- Educational bursaries
- Travel and adventure projects
- Building, buying or repairing properties
- Business development or job creation
- General appeals
- Academic research
- Work which the trust believes should be funded from statutory sources, or which has been in the recent past
- Administrative or other core costs of party organisations

Applications

Applicants should email a one page outline to the correspondent before making a formal application. If accepted, a full application can then be made.

The trust does not have a standard form, but applications should include:

- An application registration form (available to download from the website)
- Up to four pages setting out the proposal
- A full budget for the project
- The most recent audited accounts
- A CV, if applying as an individual

Trust staff make an initial assessment of applications and are authorised to reject those that are clearly inappropriate. All staff rejections are reported to the directors at their next meeting, when they consider all remaining applications. The meetings take place at quarterly intervals in March, July, October and December and the deadline for applications is approximately four or five weeks prior to the trust meeting. Applications for small grants of up to £5,000 can, however, be considered at any time and applicants should hear of the decision within two weeks.

Percentage of awards given to new applicants: between 30% and 40%.

Common applicant mistakes

'They do not heed warnings that we do not fund work which can be funded by charities.'

Information gathered from:

Information provided by the funder; funder's website.

Royal British Legion

Armed services

£7.7 million to organisations (2011/12)

Beneficial area

UK. Grants in Scotland are made by Poppyscotland.

Correspondent: The External Grants Officer, Haig House, 199 Borough High Street, London SE1 1AA (tel: 0845 772

5725; fax: 020 3207 2218; email: info@ britishlegion.org.uk; website: www. britishlegion.org.uk)

Trustees: John Crisford; Terry Whittles; Denise Edgar; Bill Parkin; Keith Prichard; Neil Salisbury; Martyn Tighe; Lt Col. David Whimpenny; Adrian Burn; Dr Diana Henderson; Maj. Gen. David Jolliffe; Anthony Macauley; Catherine Quinn; David Spruce; Wendy Bromwich.

CC Number: 219279

The Royal British Legion was formed in 1921 as a caring organisation for people in need from the Service and ex-Service community. It aims to safeguard the welfare, interests and memory of those who have served in the Armed Forces including, under certain circumstances, other support and defence organisations and the Mercantile Marine (beneficiaries). In June 2011 the Royal British Legion merged with Poppyscotland, which continues to operate a distinct charity and which makes grants in Scotland. The following information is provided by the charity:

> We can also give grants to any ex-Service charity that shares this aim.

> We may also give grants to non-ex-Service organisations provided that the grant will directly benefit ex-Service personnel.

> We give grants to any charitable organisation in England, Wales, Ireland and the Isle of Man that shares one or more of our objects, namely:

> ▪ To relieve need and to further the education of beneficiaries and their spouses, children and dependents
> ▪ To relieve need and protect the mental and emotional health of families left by those who have died in service
> ▪ To relieve suffering, hardship and distress to spouses and dependents caused by the absence of those serving in the Royal Navy, Army and Royal Air Force on Regular, Reserve or Auxiliary engagements and, under certain circumstances, other support and defence organisations and the Mercantile Marine
> ▪ To promote and support schemes for the resettlement, rehabilitation, retraining and sheltered employment, of beneficiaries and their spouses, children and dependents

> Grants may be for:

> ▪ Projects, for example, a particular time-limited activity that benefits ex-Service personnel
> ▪ Services, for example, to provide a support or welfare service
> ▪ Capital, for example, to build a facility or to purchase equipment

> Grants are awarded at the following levels:

> ▪ Level 1 – up to £25,000
> ▪ Level 2 – £25,000 – £500,000
> ▪ Level 3 – over £500,000.'

Detailed guidelines for each funding level are available on the trust's website.

In 2011/12 the trust had assets of £277.1 million and an income of £132.8 million. Total charitable expenditure was £110.1 million, most of which was spent on its own services. Grants to 57 organisations totalled £7.7 million, with a further £18.2 million given in grants to 25,333 individuals (further information can be found in *The Guide to Grants for Individuals in Need*, also published by the Directory of Social Change).

The largest organisational grants during the year were made to: The Officers' Association (£1.9 million); Imperial College of Science, Technology and Medicine (£1.7 million); Royal Commonwealth Ex-Service League (£654,000); Goodwin Trust (£500,000); Skill Force (£450,000); MediCinema (£410,000); Thrive (£205,000); Age Concern Liverpool and Sefton and Alabaré Christian Care Centres (£180,000 each); Stoll (£149,000); and Community Housing and Therapy (£105,000). Grants from Poppyscotland included: Citizens Advice Scotland (£183,000); and Scottish Veterans Garden City (£150,000).

Grants of less than £100,000 were made to 44 organisations totalling £944,000.

Exclusions

Grants are not made for:
▪ Memorials
▪ Commercial ventures, or any potential commercial ventures, for example clubs

Grants are not normally given for core costs, for example, administration or running costs of an organisation that is supporting ex-Service personnel. However, there may be exceptions to this, and the Royal British Legion aims to respond flexibly to applications, and is prepared to negotiate if there are special circumstances, for example, if the withholding of grant would harm the interests of ex-Service personnel.

Applications

In the first instance you should contact Scarlet Harris, External Grants Officer (Tel. 020 3207 2138 or email: externalgrants@britishlegion.org.uk) in order to explore whether you may be eligible for a grant, and at what level, so that you can be advised further on the detailed requirements.

Following this, you will be sent an application form which will explain on it the information you need to submit depending on the size of grant you are asking for.

Successful applicants, depending on the level of grant applied for, can expect to receive an award in between two and six months of sending in a correctly completed application form, available from the legion's website.

Information gathered from:

Accounts; annual report; Charity Commission record; funder's website.

The Rubin Foundation

Jewish charities, the arts, general

£375,000 (2011/12)

Beneficial area

UK and overseas.

Correspondent: Robert Rubin, Trustee, The Pentland Centre, Lakeside House, Squires Lane, Finchley, London N3 2QL (tel: 020 8346 2600)

Trustees: Alison Mosheim; Angela Rubin; Robert Rubin; Andrew Rubin; Carolyn Rubin.

CC Number: 327062

This foundation is closely connected with Pentland Group Ltd (*see The Guide to UK Company Giving, published by Directory of Social Change*), with three trustees being on the board of directors of that company. The foundation's income comes from donations from the company and interest on its bank deposits.

In 2011/12 the foundation had assets of £480,000 and an income of £309,500. Grants were made to organisations totalling £375,000.

Beneficiaries included: Chai Lifeline Cancer Care (£50,500); The Prince's Trust (£50,000); West London Synagogue and the International Business Leaders' Forum (£25,000 each); Parliamentary Committee against Anti-Semitism Foundation (£15,000); Children and The Arts and the Roundhouse Trust (£10,000 each); Chickenshed Theatre Company (£6,000); Cherie Blair Foundation for Women (£3,000); Footwear Benevolent Society (£2,000); and the Politics and Economic Research Trust (£1,000).

Applications

The foundation has previously stated that 'grants are only given to people related to our business', such as charities known to members of the Rubin family and those associated with Pentland Group Ltd. Unsolicited applications are very unlikely to succeed.

Information gathered from:

Accounts; Charity Commission record.

S. F. Foundation

Jewish, general

£1.7 million (2011/12)

Beneficial area
Worldwide.

Correspondent: Mrs Rivka Niederman, Secretary, 143 Upper Clapton Road, London E5 9DB (tel: 020 8802 5492)

Trustees: Hannah Jacob; Rivka Niederman; Miriam Schrieber.

CC Number: 1105843

Set up in 2004, this trust gives grants towards the 'advancement and furtherance of the Jewish religion and Jewish religious education and the alleviation of poverty amongst the Jewish community throughout the world.'

In 2011/12 the foundation had assets of £16.8 million and an income of £5.4 million. Grants were made totalling £1.7 million.

Charitable donations made by the foundation are detailed in a separate publication: *SF Foundation – Schedule of Charitable Donations*. The accounts stated that the publication is available by writing to the secretary. Despite requesting this publication, including an sae, no reply was received.

Applications

'The charity accepts applications for grants from representatives of various charities, which are reviewed by the trustees on a regular basis.'

Information gathered from:

Accounts; Charity Commission record.

The Saddlers' Company Charitable Fund

General, education

£361,000 (2011/12)

Beneficial area
UK.

Correspondent: Nigel Lithgow, Clerk to the Company, Saddlers' Hall, 40 Gutter Lane, London EC2V 6BR (tel: 020 7726 8661/6; fax: 020 7600 0386; email: clerk@ saddlersco.co.uk; website: www. saddlersco.co.uk)

Trustees: Campbell Pulley; D. J. Serrell-Wattes; David Hardy; David Snowden; Edward Pearson; Hugh Dyson-Laurie; Iain Pulley; John Vant; Jonathan Godrich; Michael Bullen; Michael Laurie; Peter Laurie; Peter Lewis; Tim Satchell; William Dyson-Laurie; Mark Farmar; David Chandler; Paul Farmar; Petronella

Jameson; Charles Barclay; John Robinson; Hugh Thomas; James Welch; Lt Col. G. E. Vere-Laurie.

CC Number: 261962

General

The Saddlers' Company Charitable Fund was formed in 1970. Over time, the objects of the fund have been refined to provide support for education, the British saddlery trade, the equestrian world, the City of London and general charitable activities. The decisions regarding the company's charities are taken by the Charities and Education Committee with regular reports back to the full trustee body.

The fund supports many of the same charities each year such as Alleyn's School and Riding for the Disabled. After making such allocations, and allowing for the agreed level of reserves, about one quarter of the remaining funds is allocated to major national charities working in all charitable sectors and the remaining three quarters are held for charitable appeals which are received throughout the year. The trustees have formulated a policy to focus on smaller charities assisting people with disabilities.

For grants targeted to be paid in July, members of the Livery are asked to visit a charity local to them and to report on the charity's suitability to receive a grant. The Liveryman prepares a report on the charity's purpose, budgetary and financial control, administration and general viability, together with a recommendation as to whether the charity should be supported and at what level. These reports are considered by a grant committee whose recommendations are passed to the trustees.

For grants targeted to be paid in January, a points-based system is used whereby a charity will accumulate points according to various criteria. The total amount of funds available is then distributed amongst the charities based upon how many points they have.

R M Sturdy Charitable Trust

A Past Master of the Worshipful Company of Saddlers and former trustee of the fund, Mr R M Sturdy, died in 2006. By a letter of wishes, he expressed the desire that the R M Sturdy Charitable Trust, of which he was the benefactor, be administered by the Worshipful Company of Saddlers after his death. The Court of Assistants, the governing body of the Worshipful Company of Saddlers, and whose members are the trustees of the fund, concluded that the most expeditious way of fulfilling this desire would be to create a restricted fund within the Saddlers' Company Charitable Fund. In 2007/08 a

transfer of £550,000 was made from the R M Sturdy Charitable Trust to the Saddlers Company Charitable Fund to establish the new fund.

Grantmaking in 2011/12

In 2011/12 the fund had assets of £9.1 million and an income of £411,000. Grants were made totalling £361,000, distributed in the following categories:

Education	£154,000
Support for the disabled and disadvantaged youth	£54,500
The equestrian world	£43,500
The Church	£21,500
General charitable activities	£16,500
Armed and Uniformed Services charities	£15,500
British saddlery and leathercraft trade	£7,000
City of London	£4,000

Beneficiaries across all categories included: Saddlers' Scholarships and Bursaries at Alleyn's School (£130,000); British Horse Society (£32,000); Riding for the Disabled Association (£27,500); City and Guilds of London Institute (£7,000); Birmingham Cathedral (£5,000); Royal Veterinary College and Leather Conservation Centre (£4,000 each); ABF – The Soldiers Charity and the Footsteps Foundation (£2,000 each); Centrepoint and Transport for All (£1,000 each).

Applications

In writing to the correspondent. Applications must be submitted by 31 May and 1 November. Grants are made in January and July, following trustees' meetings. Charities are asked to submit reports at the end of the following year on their continuing activities and the use of any grant received. Between 30% – 40% of grants are made to new applicants.

Percentage of awards given to new applicants: between 30% and 40%.

Common applicant mistakes

'Fail properly to describe the project they require funding for; lack of clarity and brevity.'

Information gathered from:

Accounts; annual report; Charity Commission record; further information provided by the funder.

Erach and Roshan Sadri Foundation

Education, welfare, homelessness, Zoroastrian religion, general

£427,500 (2011/12)

Beneficial area

Worldwide.

Correspondent: Mark Cann, Administrator, 10a High Street, Pewsey, Wiltshire SN9 5AQ (tel: 01672 569131; email: markcann@ersf.org.uk; website: www.ersf.org.uk)

Trustees: Margaret Lynch; Shabbir Merali; Darius Sarosh; Jehangir Sarosh; Sammy Bhiwandiwalla.

CC Number: 1110736

The main objects of the foundation are:

▶ Providing financial assistance for education and welfare purposes
▶ Relieving poverty by alleviating homelessness
▶ Assisting members of the Zoroastrian religious faith

The trustees also consider grant applications which fall outside the main criteria but have particular appeal to them. Grants are in the range of £2,000 and £100,000. 'Pump-priming' donations are offered – usually given to new organisations and areas.

In 2011/12 the foundation had assets of £3.6 million and an income of £84,500. Grants were made to 47 organisations during the year totalling £427,500, and were broken down as follows:

	Amount*
Education and welfare	£284,500
Zoroastrian	£90,000
Homelessness	£49,000
General	£7,000

* the figure also includes a grant of £3,500 to an individual.

One beneficiary was named in the 2011/12 accounts, the World Zoroastrian Organisation, which received £77,000. A summary of activities during the year is provided:

[The] money, as in previous years, has built houses, sheltered the homeless, rebuilt and equipped schools, sent positive welfare support to the armed services, employed key staff to prevent identified women slipping back into homelessness, assisted countless individuals with their education, helped the poor and vulnerable into work, supported social entrepreneurs in India, funded campaigns to educate about the threat of landmines and lifted lives through sport, to name just a few. The scope has been enormous and global. Funding has been sent to countries in five continents (though a majority of funding has been in UK and India) and spread amongst a number of religions aside from Zoroastrianism. The funding of a Muslim School, a Catholic Homeless project and Christian Housing in India are on-going examples.

The foundation's website details all of the organisations that have been awarded grants; beneficiaries in 2012/13 included: British Armed Forces Foundation (£28,000); On Course (£22,000); Children's Trust (£15,000); Honeypot and Prisoners Abroad (£10,000 each); Jessie May (£8,000); REACT (£5,000); and Mentoring+ (£2,000).

Exclusions

Applications are unlikely to be successful if they:

▶ Involve animal welfare or heritage
▶ Are a general appeal from large UK organisations

Applications

On a form which can be downloaded from the foundation's website, along with full and detailed guidelines. Forms can be returned by post or email. Meetings are held four times a year.

Note: 'Unsolicited material sent in addition to the clear and concise requirements of the application form is very likely to prove detrimental to your application. The trustees insist that additional items such as annual reports, glossy brochures, Christmas cards and accounts are not sent unless specifically requested.'

Information gathered from:

Accounts; annual report; Charity Commission record; funder's website.

The Alan and Babette Sainsbury Charitable Fund

General, with a focus on scientific and medical research, youth work, projects overseas and civil liberties

£414,000 (2011/12)

Beneficial area

UK and overseas.

Correspondent: Alan Bookbinder, Director, The Peak, 5 Wilton Road, London SW1V 1AP (tel: 020 7410 0330; fax: 020 7410 0332; website: www.sfct.org.uk)

Trustees: The Hon. Sir Timothy Sainsbury; Judith Portrait; John Julian Sainsbury; Lindsey M. H. Anderson.

CC Number: 292930

This is one of the Sainsbury Family Charitable Trusts, which share a joint administration and have a common approach to grantmaking. The settlor of the trust, Alan Sainsbury, was the grandson of the founders of J Sainsbury plc and former chair of the company. He established the trust in 1953, became Baron Sainsbury in 1962 and died in 1998.

The trust concentrates its resources on a small number of programmes, including:

▶ Arts and education projects which help young people to achieve their potential, particularly within Southwark, from where proposals are particularly encouraged
▶ Support for UK charities which defend civil liberties and human rights
▶ Projects in the developing world, especially Africa, which maximise educational and employment opportunities for young people
▶ Areas of scientific and medical research of particular interest to the trustees, especially multiple sclerosis and diabetes among young people

In 2011/12 the trust had assets of £13.3 million and an income of £408,000. Grants totalling £414,000 were paid during the year and were categorised as follows:

Scientific and medical research	2	£250,000
Youth work	5	£100,500
Overseas	7	£96,500
Civil liberties	3	£52,000
General	2	£11,500

The beneficiaries during the year included: Dose Adjustment for Normal Eating (£150,000 towards reducing waiting lists for the DAFNE course in West Essex); University of Oxford (£100,000, towards research into the beneficial effects of licensed drugs on multiple sclerosis); Salmon Youth Centre (£30,000 over two years towards core costs); Tsofen-High Technology Centre (£20,000, towards its new teacher training programme); Survivor's Fund (£12,000, towards the costs of establishing and running sewing co-operative for survivors of the Rwandan Genocide in Eastern Rwanda; Female Prisoners Welfare Project Hibiscus (£10,000, towards the completion of 'A Dangerous Journey', an educational anti-trafficking film aimed at women considered to be at risk from traffickers in West Africa); The Ashden Awards (£6,500, towards the organisation's core costs in 2012/13) and Toppesfield Village Hall Committee (£5,000, towards renovation costs of the community village and shop).

Exclusions

Grants are not normally made to individuals.

Applications

The trust states that: 'proposals are likely to be invited by the trustees or initiated at their request. Unsolicited applications will only be successful if they fall precisely within an area in which the trustees are interested'. A single application will be considered for support by all the trusts in the Sainsbury family group.

Information gathered from:

Accounts; annual report; Charity Commission record; funder's website.

The Sainsbury Family Charitable Trusts

See individual trusts
£114.5 million

Beneficial area

See individual trusts.

Correspondent: Alan Bookbinder, Director, The Peak, 5 Wilton Road, London SW1V 1AP (tel: 020 7410 0330; fax: 020 7410 0332; website: www.sfct. org.uk)

These trusts, listed below, each have their own entries. However they are administered together and it is said that 'an application to one is taken as an application to all'.

Their grantmaking ranges from the largest to the smallest scale, including massive long-term support for major institutions such as the National Gallery or the Sainsbury Centre for Mental Health as well as for a range of specific issues ranging from autism to the environmental effects of aviation. There is an office with over 30 staff and a large number of specialist advisers.

However, even collectively, the trusts do not form a generalist grantmaking organisation; though active in most fields of charitable activity, it is usually within particular and often quite specialised parts of each sector.

Most of the trusts use a similar formula to describe their grantmaking:

The trustees take an active role in their grant-making, employing a range of specialist staff and advisers to research their areas of interest and bring forward suitable proposals. Many of the trusts work closely with their chosen beneficiaries over a long period to achieve particular objectives. It should therefore be understood that the majority of unsolicited proposals we receive will be unsuccessful. As a rule the Gatsby, Glass-House, Linbury, Staples and Tedworth trusts do not consider unsolicited proposals.

A typical programme might have the following elements:

▷ Support for a major, long-term research initiative, whether academic or in the form of an action research programme

▷ Support for specialised national groups promoting good practice in the field concerned
▷ Grants for a few service delivery organisations, often small and local, and addressing the most severe aspects of the issues involved

In these editors' view, charities that are indeed developing new ideas and approaches would be most unwise to assume that the Sainsbury trusts will automatically get to hear of this.

'Applications' are probably not the best way forward and may perhaps be best avoided except where specifically requested. More sensible might be to write briefly and say what is being done or planned, on the assumption that, if one or more of the trusts is indeed interested in that area of work, they will want to know about what you are doing. A telephone call to do the same is fine. Staff are polite, but wary of people seeking to talk about money rather than issues.

More generally, the trusts are involved in a number of networks, with which they maintain long-term contact. Charities doing work relevant to the interests of these trusts may find that if they are not a part of these networks (which may not be inclusive and most of which are probably London-based) they may get limited Sainsbury attention.

The most inappropriate approach would often be from a fundraiser. Staff, and in many cases trustees, are knowledgeable and experienced in their fields, and expect to talk to others in the same position.

Most of the trusts do fund ongoing service delivery, but generally infrequently and usually on a modest scale. For such grants it is not clear how they choose this play scheme or that wildlife trust. To them, these may be small and relatively unimportant decisions, and they may rely on trustees or staff simply coming across something suitable, or on recommendations through what they have called their 'usual networks'.

The Sainsbury Family Trusts (with totals of grant payments or approvals for the most recent year available):

Gatsby Charitable Foundation	£42.7 million
Monument Trust	£45 million
Linbury Trust	£6.4 million
Kay Kendall Leukaemia Fund	£5.2 million
Headley Trust	£4.3 million
Jerusalem Trust	£2.6 million
True Colours Trust	£1.7 million
Ashden Trust	£1.3 million
Three Guineas Trust	£1 million
J J Charitable Trust	£929,000
Indigo Trust	£679,000
Mark Leonard Trust	£650,000
Staples Trust	£505,000
Glass-House Trust	£438,000
Tedworth Trust	£416,000

Alan and Babette Sainsbury Trust	£414,000
Woodward Charitable Trust	£243,000
Total	**£114.5 million**

Collective support

The trusts sometimes act collectively, with support for the same organisations from a number of the trusts. Organisations that occasionally appear in more than one grants list include the Royal Ballet School and National Portrait Gallery, and also Ashden Awards for Sustainable Energy.

It is not clear to the outsider whether such cross-trust support is the result of interaction at trustee or at officer level, or both. However it does seem that there is such a thing as being 'in' with the group of trusts as a whole – a cause of occasional resentment by those who see the Sainsbury trusts, perhaps entirely wrongly, as being something of a closed shop.

Exclusions

No grants are normally given to individuals by many of the trusts (though a number of them fund bursary schemes and the like operated by other organisations). Grants are not made for educational fees or expeditions.

Applications

The trusts' website provides the following information on how to apply:

The trusts only fund registered charities or activities with clearly defined charitable purposes.

The trustees take an active role in their grant-making, employing a range of specialist staff and advisers to research their areas of interest and bring forward suitable proposals. Many of the trusts work closely with their chosen beneficiaries over a long period to achieve particular objectives.

The trusts differ in their attitude to unsolicited proposals. As a rule Gatsby, Glass-House, Linbury, Mark Leonard, Staples, Tedworth and True Colours do not consider them, though several trusts have application forms for specific grant programmes in clearly defined areas:
▷ The Woodward Charitable Trust
▷ The Kay Kendall Leukaemia Fund
▷ The Headley Museums Archaeological Acquisition Fund
▷ The True Colours Trust

The Alan & Babette, Ashden, Headley, Indigo, Jerusalem, JJ, Monument and Three Guineas trusts will consider proposals, so long as they demonstrably and closely fit their specific areas of interest. However, it should be understood that the majority of unsolicited proposals are unsuccessful.

None of the trusts give direct support to:
▷ Individuals
▷ Educational fees
▷ Expeditions

Suitable applications to these trusts should be sent by post to [see

Correspondent], with a description (strictly no more than two pages please, as any more is unlikely to be read) of the proposed project, covering:

▶ The organisation explaining its charitable aims and objectives, and giving its most recent annual income and expenditure, and current financial position. Please do not send a full set of accounts.

▶ The project requiring funding - why it is needed, who will benefit and in what way

▶ The funding - breakdown of costs, any money raised so far, and how the balance will be raised.

Please do not send more than one application. It will be considered by all relevant trusts. There is no need to send supporting books, brochures, DVDs, annual reports or accounts.

All applications will receive our standard acknowledgement letter. If your proposal is a candidate for support from one of the trusts, you will hear from us within eight weeks of the acknowledgement. Applicants who do not hear from us within this time must assume they have been unsuccessful.

The Sandra Charitable Trust

Animal welfare and research, environmental protection, social welfare, health and youth development
£517,500 to organisations
(2011/12)

Beneficial area
UK with slight preference for south east England.

Correspondent: Keith Lawrence, Secretary, c/o Moore Stephens, 150 Aldersgate Street, London EC1A 4AB (tel: 020 7334 9191; fax: 020 7651 1953; email: keith.lawrence@moorestephens.com)

Trustees: Richard Moore; Michael Macfadyen.

CC Number: 327492

The trust was established in 1987 for general charitable purposes, with the main aim of the charity also being 'to support a wide variety of beneficiaries including nurses and charities involved in animal welfare and research, environmental protection, relief of poverty and youth development'.

In 2011/12 the trust has assets of £17.6 million and an income of £686,000. Grants were made totalling £606,000, of which £517,500 was donated to 117 organisations and £88,500 to 149 individuals.

Beneficiaries of the largest grants included: Kids (£50,000); The Florence Nightingale Foundation and Goring Health Charities (£30,000 each); Second Chance (£28,000); Arundel Castle Cricket Foundation (£25,000); Sparks (£17,000); and Project Rainbow and Vale House (£10,000 each).

More typical grants included those to: Barnardo's and the National Portrait Gallery (£5,000 each); Children with Cancer UK (£4,000); Changing Faces and the North Berwick Pipe Band (£3,000 each); Thames Valley Air Ambulance and the Pegasus School Trust (£2,000 each); and Alzheimer's Research UK, Families Against Neuroblastoma, Rotary Doctor Bank and Woodland Heritage (£1,000 each).

Exclusions
No grants to individuals other than nurses.

Applications
The trust states that 'unsolicited applications are not requested, as the trustees prefer to support charities whose work they have researched...the trustees receives a very high number of grant applications which are mostly unsuccessful'.

Information gathered from:
Accounts; annual report; Charity Commission record.

The Schreib Trust

Jewish, general
£445,000 (2011/12)

Beneficial area
UK.

Correspondent: Mrs Rivka Neiderman, Trustee, 147 Stamford Hill, London N16 5LG (tel: 020 8802 5492)

Trustees: Abraham Green; Rivka Niederman; Jacob Schreiber; Irene Schreiber.

CC Number: 275240

It is difficult to glean an enormous amount of information about this trust's grant-giving policies as only brief accounts were on file at the Charity Commission. Although the trust's objects are general, it lists its particular priorities as relief of poverty and the advancement of religion and religious education. In practice, the trust only supports Jewish organisations.

In 2011/12 the trust had assets of £430,500 and an income of £480,000. Grants were made totalling £445,000.

Previous beneficiaries have included: Lolev, Yad Eliezer, Ponovitz, Craven Walk Charity Trust, Shaar Hatalmud, Beis Rochel, Beth Jacob Building Fund, Toiras Chesed and Oneg Shabbos.

Applications
In writing to the correspondent.

Information gathered from:
Accounts; Charity Commission record.

The Schroder Foundation

General (see below)
£2.7 million (2011/12)

Beneficial area
Worldwide, in practice mainly UK.

Correspondent: Sally Yates, Secretary, 81 Rivington Street, London EC2A 3AY

Trustees: Bruno Schroder, Chair; Edward Mallinckrodt; Nicholas Ferguson; Charmaine Mallinckrodt; Leonie Fane; Claire Howard; Richard Robinson; Philip Mallinckrodt.

CC Number: 1107479

Set up in 2005, this foundation shares a common administration with Schroder Charity Trust (Charity Commission no. 214060). It does not respond to unsolicited applications.

The foundation's grantmaking policy, described in its 2011/12 accounts, reads as follows:

The objects of the foundation are to apply the income and capital for the benefit of any charitable object or purposes, in any part of the world, as the trustees think fit. The trustees have a policy of supporting a broad range of activities within the areas of the environment, education, arts, culture and heritage, social welfare, the community and international relief and development.

At their quarterly meeting the trustees consider what grants they will make and receive reports from grant recipients. The trustees travel widely in the UK and abroad and use the knowledge gained to support the work of the foundation and to inform grant-making policy. The foundation's policy is to focus on charitable causes with a previous track record or in organisations in which the foundation has a special interest. Organisations identified by the trustees for potential support are normally invited to submit a formal application outlining the project, its beneficiaries and how the funds will be applied according to the guidance for applicants to The Schroder Foundation. It is generally the trustees' policy to make only one-off grants. However, grants over a number of years are occasionally awarded.

In 2011/12 the foundation had assets of £10.6 million and an income of almost £1.6 million, most of which was in the form of donated assets. Grants were made to 39 organisations totalling almost £2.7 million.

The largest beneficiary during the year was the Schroder Fund at the University of Cambridge, which received £1.7 million. The donation is part of a long-standing relationship with the university and pays for the Schroder Professorship of German and the study of German there.

Other beneficiaries included: Freya van Moltke Stiftung (£88,000); Carbon Disclosure Project, Priors Court Foundation and Voluntary Services Overseas (£50,000 each); School Home Support (£35,000); London Youth Support Trust (£30,000); Fauna and Flora International (£25,000); West London Action for Children (£20,000); Cumberland Lodge – Windsor, One Voice Europe and the Royal National Institute for the Deaf (£10,000 each).

Applications

This trust **does not** respond to unsolicited applications. 'The trustees identify projects and organisations they wish to support and the foundation does not make grants to people or organisations who apply speculatively.'

Information gathered from:

Accounts; Charity Commission record.

Foundation Scotland

Community development, general

£6.9 million (2011/12)

Beneficial area

Scotland.

Correspondent: Tom Black, Community Engagement Manager, Empire House, 131 West Nile Street, Glasgow G1 2RX (tel: 01413 414960; fax: 01413 414972; email: nick@scottishcf.org; website: www.foundationscotland.org.uk)

Trustees: Bob Benson; Gillian Donald; Beth Edberg; Colin Liddell; Ian McAteer; Jimmy McCulloch; John Naylor; Ella Simpson; Lady Emily Stair; Tom Ward.

SC Number: SC022910

In common with other community foundations, Foundation Scotland (formerly the Scottish Community Foundation) makes grants from various sources – both public and private – as well as having its own endowment with which it distributes money. They provide administration and management support services to make charitable giving easy and tax-efficient. They also offer advice on charitable giving and a professional grantmaking service which links them to exceptional charities that are seeking funding. They aim 'to be the leading philanthropy organisation in Scotland for stronger communities [and] to inspire giving for Scotland – to improve lives.'

The foundation makes small grants, usually up to £5,000, for charities and community groups in Scotland, particularly those which are helping to build and sustain local communities.

There are two broad programmes, under which there are a range of different funds.

Scotland-wide programmes – includes express grants (up to £2,000); grants for women's projects; and comic relief local communities grants.

Local grants programmes – there are a variety of programmes which benefit people in specific areas of Scotland. Each has different grant levels, deadline dates and decision making practices. A list of local programmes is available on the foundation's website.

Note that grant schemes change frequently and potential applicants should consult the foundation's website, which is extremely comprehensive, for details of current programmes and their deadlines.

In 2011/12 the foundation held assets of £16.4 million and had an income of almost £8.8 million. Grants were made totalling £6.9 million (£2.7 million in 2010/11) with an additional £114,000 also given for community development.

Exclusions

The foundation does not usually fund:

▶ Individuals or groups which do not have a constitution
▶ Groups other than not-for-profit groups
▶ Groups whose grant request is for the advancement of religion or a political party (this means the foundation won't fund grant requests to support the core activities of religious or political groups)
▶ The purchase of second hand vehicles
▶ Trips abroad
▶ The repayment of loans, payment of debts, or other retrospective funding
▶ Payments towards areas generally understood to be the responsibility of statutory authorities
▶ Groups who will then distribute the funds as grants or bursaries
▶ Applications that are for the sole benefit to flora and fauna. Applicants are invited to demonstrate the direct benefit to the local community and/or service users in cases where the grant application is concerned with flora and fauna
▶ Projects which do not benefit people in Scotland

Note different grant programmes may have additional restrictions.

Applications

The foundation has a comprehensive website with details of the grant schemes currently being administered. Organisations are welcome to contact

the grants team to discuss their funding needs before making any application. Trustees meet at least four times a year.

Information gathered from:

Accounts; annual report; OSCR record; funder's website.

The Francis C. Scott Charitable Trust

Disadvantaged young people in Cumbria and North Lancashire

£872,000 (2012)

Beneficial area

Cumbria and north Lancashire (comprising the towns of Lancaster, Morecambe, Heysham and Carnforth).

Correspondent: Chris Batten, Director, Stricklandgate House, 92 Stricklandgate, Kendal, Cumbria LA9 4PU (tel: 01539 742608; fax: 01539 741611; email: info@fcsct.org.uk; website: www.fcsct.org.uk)

Trustees: Susan Bagot, Chair; Joanna Plumptre; Alexander Scott; Madeleine Scott; Don Shore; Clare Spedding; Peter Redhead; Melanie Wotherspoon.

CC Number: 232131

Summary

The trust was created in 1963 by Peter F Scott CBE, then Chair of the Provincial Insurance Company. Peter Scott, together with his parents Francis and Frieda Scott and his sister Joan Trevelyan, endowed the trust with a significant holding of Provincial Insurance Company shares.

It supports registered charities addressing community deprivation in Cumbria and north Lancashire, and is principally concerned with meeting the needs of young people from 0–21 years. It seeks to target its funds where they can be most effective and can make a real difference to people's lives.

General

The trust's helpful website gives the following overview of its grantmaking policy:

What we fund
The trust focuses on four main areas of work:

▶ Early years/family support work (0–5 year olds and those responsible for their care)
▶ Junior youth work (issues that attend the primary to secondary school transitions)
▶ Targeted youth work (adolescents' concerns re discrimination, pregnancy, homelessness, abuse and substance misuse)
▶ Transition to adulthood (prioritising those who are homeless and leaving

care/youth justice to go into training, employment and/or education)

The majority of our grants are multi-year revenue grants (i.e. salaries and running costs), however trustees will also fund capital projects that make a tangible difference to a local community.

Whilst we prefer to fund organisations that are registered charities, we will consider offering grants to organisations who are pursuing charitable objectives providing their aims/constitution are clearly not-for-profit. We will only consider applications from national organisations where the beneficiaries and project workers are based within our beneficial area.

Please note that trustees prefer to fund small to medium-sized organisations and it is therefore unlikely they will support applications from charities with a turnover in excess of £1 million. It is also worth noting that charities should not apply to both the Frieda Scott and Francis C Scott Charitable Trusts at the same time. We would encourage you to seek guidance from the staff if you are unsure.

Aspiring Leaders Programme
In partnership with Brathay Trust, the University of Cumbria and Common Purpose, we are currently sponsoring the Aspiring Leaders Programme which started in September 2011 and is due to run until 2014. This programme is an opportunity for local young adults to achieve a foundation degree, leadership development training and 1:1 mentoring support over a 3-year period. Our aim is to engender a step-change in the leadership capability of our local charity sector by investing in the talents of exceptional young adults who live within, and want to contribute to, the development of their own communities.

Small Grants
As funders we recognise that a one-off grant for a small charity run by volunteers is as important as a multi-year revenue grant is for a larger charity employing many staff. We therefore have a slightly different process for the consideration of small grants which is designed to give applicants a quicker decision – usually within 3–4 weeks of applying.

The criteria for small grants is exactly the same as for larger grants and the staff and trustees go through the same process of due diligence in assessing the merits of each application. Projects requiring either capital funding (e.g. equipment) or revenue funding (e.g. running costs) are welcome to apply.

As with all applications to FCSCT it is worth phoning the director for advice and guidance before filling in the application form. Once you have sent in your application form and accounts, the director will be in touch often with a few questions to better understand your project and/or to arrange a visit.

Following the meeting of the Small Grants Committee, the director will be in touch by email, letter or phone to let you know the outcome of your appeal. If successful, a cheque will usually be sent out within a week.

8-year Funding Model
The trustees have adopted the following approach to revenue funding for those projects/organisations they believe require extended investment in order to become established. Appeals for capital or bursary funding are considered separately.

Grants in 2012
In 2012 the trust had assets of £27.7 million and had an income of £774,000. There were 72 grants paid totalling £872,000, broken down as follows:

Grants were distributed into the following areas:

Young people	42	£420,000
Families and children, women and men	19	£233,000
Communities and charity support	7	£52,000
Disabled, chronically ill and elderly	2	£8,000
Other	2	£9,000

Beneficiaries across all categories included: Whitehaven Community Trust (£60,000); Whitehaven Foyer (£50,000); Safety Net Advice 8 Support Centre – Carlisle (£20,000); Walney Community Trust (£18,000); Aspatria Dreamscheme, Cumbria Starting Point and Self Injury Support in North Cumbria (£15,000 each); Distington Club for Young People (£10,000); Leonard Cheshire North West (£7,500); University of Cumbria (£5,000); New Rainbow Pre School (£4,000); Child and Family Connect (£2,000); and the Egremont Amenity Committee (£1,000).

It should be noted that these figures represent grants paid in the year, not the total committed to each beneficiary. As the trust funds many long-term projects many of these grants only represent one year of long-term funding.

Exclusions
The trust does not consider appeals:
- From individuals
- From statutory organisations
- From national charities without a local base/project
- From charities with substantial unrestricted reserves
- From medical/health establishments
- From schools/educational establishments
- From infrastructure organisations/second-tier bodies
- For projects principally benefiting people outside Cumbria/north Lancashire
- For retrospective funding
- For expeditions or overseas travel
- For the promotion of religion
- For animal welfare

Applications
The trust is always pleased to hear from charities that need help. If an organisation thinks that it may come within the trust's criteria it is encouraged to contact the director for an informal discussion before making an application.

Application forms are available to download from the trust's website or can be requested by phone, email or post. Applications should be completed and returned with the latest set of accounts (via email or post).

Applications for over £4,000 should be submitted at least four weeks before the trustee's meetings in late February, June, October and November. Check the website for the latest deadlines.

Applications for grants of less than £4,000 will be considered at small grants meetings every three to four weeks.

Applicants should refer to the trust's website which is very comprehensive and covers all aspects of the grantmaking process.

Percentage of awards given to new applicants: between 30% and 40%.

Common applicant mistakes
'Perhaps not reading the criteria on our website.'

THE FRANCIS C. SCOTT CHARITABLE TRUST

Phase	Year	Focus	Objective
1	up to one year	Research	Define area of need and then seek organisations to address it.
2	1–3	Core funding	Provide running costs (some or all) and actively support with staff time to ensure the project's early success.
3	4–6	Project funding	Foster a more strategic approach to funding and target project development.
4	7–8	Scale down funding	Withdraw funding over an agreed time period and attract other funders (especially statutory).
5	8+	Cease funding	Remain a background advocate for the project, but move on.

Information gathered from:

Accounts; annual report; Charity Commission record; further information provided by the funder; funder's website.

Seafarers UK (King George's Fund for Sailors)

The welfare of seafarers

£2.5 million (2012)

Beneficial area

UK and Commonwealth.

Correspondent: Dennis Treleaven, Head of Grants, 8 Hatherley Street, London SW1P 2YY (tel: 020 7932 5984; fax: 020 7932 0095; email: dennis.treleaven@ seafarers-uk.org; website: www.seafarers-uk.org)

Trustees: Peter Mamelok; Vice Admiral Peter Wilkinson; Michael Acland; Christian Marr; Simon Rivett-Carnac; Maj. Patrick Dunn; Capt. R. Barker; P. J. Buxton; T. Cadman; M. Carden; M. Dickinson; Jeffery Evans; J. Monroe; J. Saunders Watson; Ms D. Sterling.

CC Number: 226446

Summary

This trust supports people who have served at sea in the Royal Navy, Royal Marines, Merchant Navy and fishing fleets, their equivalents in the Commonwealth and their dependents. The fund makes grants, often recurrent, for a wide but little-changing range of seafarer's charities. Grants range from a few hundred pounds to several hundred thousand.

General

The charity gives grants to other charities that help with all aspects of seafarers' welfare including accommodation, medical services, disability services, financial aid, childcare, education and training and youth activities. They describe their four main objectives as:

 ▶ To ensure that all former UK and Commonwealth seafarers over normal retirement age and their dependents can live life free of poverty and with access to all reasonable health care and domestic assistance
 ▶ To ensure that serving UK and Commonwealth seafarers have access to reasonable shore amenities and communication with their families and financial help where appropriate
 ▶ To ensure that the dependent families of UK and Commonwealth seafarers can have access to a reasonable quality of life including adequate accommodation, clothing, education and holidays
 ▶ To assist those UK and Commonwealth citizens in maritime youth organisations

training for a seagoing careers, including the Sea Cadets, with the cost of facilities

The fund was set up in 1917 as a central fundraising organisation to support other seafarers' charities. Several years ago the charity underwent a structural overhaul to address its extremely high fundraising costs (35% of income). It succeeded in bringing this figure down to 21% in 2008 and in the process modernised the fund to make it more relevant, including adopting the operational name Seafarers UK. In 2011 fundraising costs were 27.9%; in 2012 they were 29.5%.

In future years they will be focusing on raising public awareness of seafarers and the hardship and danger that they face on a daily basis. They intend to do this by holding 'Seafarers Awareness Week'.

Main Grants

These are for over £5,000 and can be up to three years in length.

Small Grants

This scheme awards grants of up to £5,000, it is permanently open.

Marine Society and Sea Cadets

The trust makes a substantial contribution towards the Sea Cadets 'annual fund' which allocates money to units needing repairs, maintenance or new equipment. Any sea cadet unit should apply to that fund and will not be considered under the other programmes.

Emergency Grants

In exceptional circumstances, it may be possible for the trust to authorise payments of up to an agreed limit where applications from organisations or individuals are too urgent to wait for the normal cycle of distribution.

Grantmaking in 2012

In 2012 the trust had assets of £39.3 million and an income of just under £3.4 million. 73 grants were made to 67 organisations totalling £2.5 million (the charity informed us that this level of funding remained in place for 2013). Grants were made in the following areas:

Older and ex-seafarers	£929,000	37.2%
Seafarers of working age	£653,500	26.1%
Seafarers' dependents and families	£469,000	18.8%
Maritime youth groups	£387,500	15.5%
Improving efficiency	£70,000	2.8%

Beneficiaries included: Marine Society and Sea Cadets (£300,000 in total); Nautilus Welfare Funds (£178,000); Mission to Seafarers (£141,000); Seamen's Hospital Society (£121,000); Royal Navy and Royal Marines Children's Fund (£100,000); UK Sailing Academy (£82,500); Sailors' Children's Society (£75,000); Royal Liverpool Seamen's Orphan Institution (£60,000);

International Seafarers Assistance Network (£50,000); Combat Stress (£40,000); Community Network (£29,000); Queen Victoria Seamen's Rest (£22,000); Alabare Christian Care Centres (£15,000); Not Forgotten Association (£10,000); and the Falkland Islands Memorial Chapel Trust and Gardening Leave (£5,000 each).

Exclusions

The fund does not make any grants directly to individuals except in very exceptional cases but rather helps other organisations which do this. However, the fund may be able to advise in particular cases about a suitable organisation to approach.

Applications

Applications to the main grants scheme should download the form available on the trust's website and use the guidance notes also available. There is a deadline for this scheme each year which is published on the website.

Applications to the Marine Society and Sea Cadets scheme should use the specific form and guidelines available on the website.

Applications to the small grants scheme should download the small grants form and guidelines available on the website. There are no closing dates for the schemes that awards grants of up to £5,000. Only one application from an organisation can be considered in any 12 month period.

Percentage of awards given to new applicants: between 10% and 20%.

Common applicant mistakes

'Not reading the guidance notes that accompany the application form; trying to second guess the likely level of our support.'

Information gathered from:

Accounts; annual report; Charity Commission record; further information provided by the funder; funder's website.

The Samuel Sebba Charitable Trust

General, covering a wide range of charitable purposes with a preference for Jewish organisations

£2.3 million (2011/12)

Beneficial area

UK and Israel.

Correspondent: David Lerner, Chief Executive., 25–26 Enford Street, London W1H 1DW (tel: 020 7723 6028; fax: 020 7724 7412)

CC Number: 253351

This trust was established in 1967 for general charitable purposes. The trust's main areas of interest are: social welfare; palliative care; refugees; youth at risk; education; environment; human rights and social justice.

In 2011/12 the trust had assets of £58.5 million and an income of £6.3 million. There were 113 grants made totalling £2.3 million, which were categorised as follows:

Human rights and social justice	£522,500
Disability	£505,500
Education	£396,000
Welfare	£196,500
Youth at risk	£187,000
Environment	£134,500
Community	£107,500
Arts and culture	£70,000
Research	£61,000
Palliative care	£57,500
Health and medical	£42,000
Interfaith	£15,000

Beneficiaries across all categories included: Green Environment Fund (£93,000); King Solomon High School (£75,000); New Israel Fund (£55,000); Music of Remembrance (£33,000); Cystic Fibrosis Trust (£30,000); Deafblind UK (£25,000); Board of Deputies of British Jews and Brighton Voices in Exile (£20,000 each); Israeli Centre for Third Sector Research (£16,500); and Jewish Women's Aid (£15,000).

Exclusions

No grants to individuals.

Applications

Organisations applying must provide proof of need; they must forward the most recent audited accounts, a registered charity number, and most importantly a cash flow statement for the next 12 months. All applications should have a stamped addressed envelope enclosed. It is also important that the actual request for funds must be concise and preferably summarised on one side of A4. The trustees meet quarterly.

However, because of ongoing support to so many organisations already known to the trust, it is likely that unsolicited applications will, for the foreseeable future, be unsuccessful.

Information gathered from:

Accounts; annual report; Charity Commission record.

ShareGift (The Orr Mackintosh Foundation)

General, but see below
£887,000 (2011/12)

Beneficial area

UK.

Correspondent: Lady Mackintosh, 2nd Floor, 17 Carlton House Terrace, London SW1Y 5AH (tel: 020 7930 3737; fax: 020 7839 2214; email: help@ sharegift.org.uk; website: www.sharegift. org)

Trustees: Stephen Scott; Baroness Mary Goudie; Paul Killik.

CC Number: 1052686

Summary

Creating an entirely new flow of money to charities, this unique organisation is entirely unlike other trusts included in this book. ShareGift creates its income each year by pooling and selling donations of shares, principally those which are uneconomic to sell by normal methods because they are too small or otherwise inconvenient or unwanted. The funds released from this ongoing process are used to make donations, on a regular basis, to a wide range of other UK charities each year.

The charity makes donations at its own discretion, but is guided in doing so by information gathered in the course of its work about the charities and causes which are of interest to people who donate shares or help ShareGift in other ways. Since its inception, ShareGift has generated over £14 million for 1,700 charities, from major household names to tiny local initiatives, covering a vast area of national and international work.

Grants are normally made to the general funds of the charity concerned, rather than for specific projects. ShareGift is cause neutral and there are no restrictions on the kind of charitable work it can support, or where in the world it takes place, so long as the charity receiving the donation is UK-registered. No grants are given in response to applications by charities.

General

Launched in 1996, this charity was developed by Claire Nowak, a former city investment manager, now Viscountess Mackintosh of Halifax and Chief Executive of the charity, and Matthew Orr, a stockbroker whose firm, Killik and Co., provides free of charge many of the technical and support services required to operate ShareGift.

ShareGift's success as a charity is based on the fact that many people own small parcels of shares, for a variety of reasons, such as popularly advertised flotations of companies and as the result of take-overs and mergers. In what is still largely a paper-based share registration system, small shareholdings are often a considerable nuisance, needing some know-how to handle but being of too little value to justify paying professional fees to sell or manage. ShareGift's funds are mainly generated by working either directly with companies or with individual shareholders.

ShareGift accepts the relevant share certificates, with minimum hassle for the donor, transfers the shares into the charity's name, and, once sufficient shares in any given company have been collected by bulking together batches of similar donations from a number of donors, sells them. Donors who are UK taxpayers may also be able to claim tax relief on the gift.

Fundraising charities also work with ShareGift, primarily as a solution for donors who offer them small holdings of shares which are not viable for the charity to accept themselves. In the case of larger donations and major gifts, ShareGift generally encourages charities to accept and handle these themselves, as it is unable to act as a charitable stockbroker or as a direct conduit for donations to other charities. However, it will advise and assist charities which are having problems or are unfamiliar with dealing with a gift of shares, and, in some cases, may be able to facilitate a larger donation.

Grants in 2011/12

During the year the charity had assets of £284,500 and an income of nearly £1.3 million. Grants were made to 224 charities totalling £887,000. Individual donations of up to £50,000 were made across the spectrum of UK charities.

Beneficiaries included: Royal Society for the Protection of Birds (£50,000); the Prince's Trust (£30,000); Thomas Coram Foundation for Children (£26,000); Walking with the Wounded and CAFOD (£25,000 each); the James Trust (£20,000); Cable and Wireless Worldwide Foundation and the Daily Telegraph Christmas Appeal (£15,000 each); ICSA Education and Research Foundation (£10,000); Multiple Sclerosis Society and the British Red Cross (£7,500 each); Back-Up Trust, the Federation of Groundwork Trusts and Survival International Charitable Trust (£5,000 each); and Action for Prisoners' Families, Battersea Dogs' and Cats' Home, David Shepherd Wildlife Foundation and North West Air Ambulance (£1,000 each).

Exclusions

Grants to UK registered charities only.

Applications

Applications for funding are not accepted and no response will be made to charities that send inappropriate applications. ShareGift's trustees choose to support UK registered charities which reflect the broad range of charities which are of interest to the people and organisations that help to create the charity's income by donating their unwanted shares, or by supporting the charity's operation in other practical ways.

However, charities wishing to receive a donation from ShareGift's trustees can increase their chances of doing so by encouraging their supporters to donate unwanted shares to ShareGift and to make a note of their charitable interests when so doing, using the regular donation form provided by ShareGift.

In addition, ShareGift is willing to use its extensive experience of share giving philanthropically to help charities which wish to start receiving gifts of shares themselves. Charities are, therefore, welcome to contact ShareGift to discuss this further. ShareGift advises that, as basic training on share giving is now available elsewhere, charities wishing to benefit from their advice should ensure that they have first researched share giving generally and put some thought into how their charity intends to initiate and run a share giving appeal or strategy. Further information on this and other issues is available on the charity's website.

Information gathered from:

Accounts; annual report; Charity Commission record.

The Sheepdrove Trust

Mainly environment, education
£411,000 (2012)

Beneficial area

UK, but especially north Lambeth, London, where applicable.

Correspondent: Juliet E. Kindersley, Trustee, Sheepdrove Organic Farm, Lambourn, Berkshire RG17 7UN (tel: 01488 674726)

Trustees: Juliet E. Kindersley; Peter D. Kindersley; Harriet R. Treuille; Barnabas G. Kindersley.

CC Number: 328369

The trust is endowed with money made by the Dorling Kindersley publishing enterprise, but the trust's holding of shares in the company was sold in 2000, when the endowment was valued at £18 million. The trust has general

charitable purposes but has a particular interest in supporting initiatives involved in sustainability, biodiversity and organic farming. Grants are also made in other areas including educational research and spiritual care.

In 2012 the trust had assets of £18.7 million and an income of £444,000. Grants were made to organisations totalling £411,000.

Beneficiaries included: Wildlife Conservation Partnership (£74,000); GM Education Programme (£46,500); Slow Food UK Trust (£31,000); Friends of Kennington Park (£24,000); Watermill Theatre (£15,000); Mother Meera School – India and Vauxhall City Farm (£10,000 each); and the Pasture Fed Livestock Association and the Comedy School Charitable Trust (£5,000 each).

Applications

In writing to the correspondent.

Information gathered from:

Accounts; Charity Commission record.

The Archie Sherman Charitable Trust

Jewish charities, education, arts, general
£956,000 (2011/12)

Beneficial area

UK and Israel.

Correspondent: Michael Gee, Trustee, 27 Berkeley House, 15 Hay Hill, London W1J 8NS (tel: 020 7493 1904; email: trust@sherman.co.uk)

Trustees: Michael J. Gee; Allan H. S. Morgenthau; Eric A. Charles.

CC Number: 256893

Most of the funds go to Jewish causes, many of which receive ongoing support of typically more than £20,000 a year each. A few arts organisations are similarly supported, although the level of donation varies year to year.

The trust states that it reviews all commitments on a forward five-year basis so that a few new projects can be undertaken and income is made available.

In 2011/12 the trust had assets of £20 million and an income of £1.5 million. Grants were made to 28 organisations totalling £956,000, broken down as follows:

Arts, culture and general	14	£725,500
Health	5	£153,000
Education and training	3	£37,000
Overseas aid	2	£13,500

The largest grants were made to: the Jacqueline and Michael Gee Charitable Trust (£156,000); WIZO.UK (£141,000);

the Diana and Allan Morgenthau Charitable Trust (£131,000); and the Rosalyn and Nicholas Springer Charitable Trust (£125,000).

Other beneficiaries included: Jewish Child's Day (£60,000); Rabin Medical Centre (£47,000); Royal Academy of Arts (£41,000); Ben-Gurion University Foundation (£28,500); Norwood Ravenswood (£25,000); Community Security Trust (£15,000); Islington Community Theatre (£10,000); British Friends of the Jaffa Institute (£3,500); and Glyndebourne Arts Trust (£1,500).

Applications

In writing to the correspondent. Trustees meet every month except August and December.

Information gathered from:

Accounts; annual report; Charity Commission record.

The Shetland Charitable Trust

Social welfare, art and recreation, environment and amenity
£10.6 million (2011/12)

Beneficial area

Shetland only.

Correspondent: Michael Duncan, 22–24 North Road, Lerwick, Shetland ZE1 0NQ (tel: 01595 744994; fax: 01595 744999; email: mail@ shetlandcharitabletrust.co.uk; website: www.shetlandcharitabletrust.co.uk)

Trustees: Bobby Hunter, Chair; Jonathan Wills; Malcolm Bell; Allison Duncan; Betty Fullerton; Robert Henderson; Catherine Hughson; Ian Kinniburgh; Andrea Manson; Keith Massey; Stephen Morgan; Ian Napier; Drew Ratter; James Smith; Amanda Westlake.

SC Number: SC027025

The original trust was established in 1976 with 'disturbance receipts' from the operators of the Sullom Voe oil terminal. As a clause in the trust deed prevented it from accumulating income beyond 21 years from its inception, in 1997 most of its assets were transferred to a newly established Shetland Islands Council Charitable Trust, which is identical to the old trust except for the omission of the prohibition on accumulating income. This has now been renamed Shetland Charitable Trust. The trust was run by the Shetland Islands Council until 2002. From 2008 until mid-2013 the Office of the Scottish Charity Regulator closely monitored the activities of the trust following concerns raised by the public over conflicts of interest regarding the trustees and the local council. The trust underwent a restructure and recruited new trustees, which led the OSCR to end close scrutiny of the trust in June 2013.

The trust is generally a strategic funding body providing funding for other organisations to carry out their activities and only undertakes a small amount of 'direct' charitable activity in the Shetland community itself. The trust aims to provide public benefit to and improve the quality of life for the inhabitants of Shetland; ensure that people in need receive a high standard of service and care; protect and enhance Shetland's environment, heritage, culture and traditions; provide facilities that will be of long-term benefit to the inhabitants of Shetland; build on the energy and initiatives of local groups, maximise voluntary effort and input and assist them to achieve their objectives; support a balanced range of services and facilities to contribute to the overall fabric of the community; support facilities and services and jobs located in rural areas and maintain the value of the funds in the long term to ensure that future generations have access to similar resources in the post-oil era.

In 2011/12 the trust had assets of £216.9 million and an income of £9.5 million. Grants were made totalling £10.6 million.

The funds are used to create and sustain a wide range of facilities for the islands, largely by funding further trusts including: Shetland Recreational Trust (£2.6 million); Support to Rural Care Model (£2.5 million); Shetland Amenity Trust (£1 million); and Shetland Arts Development Agency (£732,000).

Other organisations and local projects receiving grants during the year included: Shetland Youth Information Service (£189,000); COPE Ltd (£155,000); Voluntary Action Shetland (£144,500); Shetland Churches Council Trust (£54,000); Swan Trust (£44,000); and Festival Grants (£30,000).

Exclusions

Funds can only be used to benefit the inhabitants of Shetland.

Applications

Applications are only accepted from Shetland-based charities. The trustees meet every two months.

The trust has different contact points for different categories of grant:

- Arts grants, development grants, senior citizens club grants and support grants – contact Michael Duncan on 01595 743828
- Social assistance grants – contact the duty social worker at: duty@shetland.gov.uk

Information gathered from:

Accounts; annual report; OSCR record; funder's website.

SHINE (Support and Help in Education)

Education of children and young people

£2.2 million (2011/12)

Beneficial area

Greater London and Manchester.

Correspondent: Paul Carbury, Chief Executive, 1 Cheam Road, Ewell Village, Surrey KT17 1SP (tel: 020 8393 1880; email: info@shinetrust.org.uk; website: www.shinetrust.org.uk)

Trustees: Jim O'Neill, Chair; David Blood; Mark Heffernan; Henry Bedford; Gavin Boyle; Mark Ferguson; Cameron Ogden; Dr Krutika Pau; Natasha Pope; Richard Rothwell; Stephen Shields; Bridget Walsh; Dr Caroline Whalley.

CC Number: 1082777

The following information is taken from the charity's website:

SHINE exists to help disadvantaged children and young people. We support programmes that concentrate on core educational subjects. Education provides choices. By funding best practice educational support projects SHINE is working to ensure that the participants can have choice and control in their lives.

SHINE operates as a business, rigorously evaluating the organisations and projects we fund to ensure the most effective intervention into young lives and the best possible value for money.

We want every penny of your donations to reach these projects so our trustees cover all our annual operating costs.

Current priorities

SHINE has spent the last 10 years researching, developing and testing our educational approach enabling us to identify areas where we can make a difference and find out what really works.

As a result, we are now concentrating our work on four funding strands:

SHINE on Saturday projects
We are particularly keen to fund clusters of primary schools in Greater London.

Serious Fun on Saturday projects
We would like to hear from independent schools in England that are interested in hosting a Serious Fun project and can identify potential partner schools in the state sector.

Other Saturday Programmes
Innovative projects, primarily those working with secondary school students.

Innovation
We are also interested in funding non-Saturday projects that take a fresh approach to closing the attainment gap.

We are particularly interested in projects that focus on science or maths and that have the potential for growth. We would also welcome enquiries from projects focusing on speech, language and communication at Key Stage One.

SHINE funds organisations to deliver education projects to 4–18 year olds in disadvantaged areas of London and Manchester with clearly defined outcomes concerned with raising academic achievement levels.

Keen to apply to us?
We do not accept unsolicited applications. If you are interested in applying to one of our funding streams please make sure you download and read the guidelines [on the charity's website] carefully before contacting us.

SHINE wishes to build long-term relationships with the organisations we fund. Therefore the majority of our grants are 2–3 years and are in excess of £20,000. We fund new start-ups, pilots and expansion or replication of projects. We will also fund core costs and staff posts.

Grants in 2011/12

During the year the charity had assets of £5.4 million and an income of £2.3 million. Grants were made totalling £2.2 million.

Beneficiaries included: SHINE @Chingford Hall (£180,000); SHINE @St Mary's Primary School (£165,000); Lift for Learning – DigiSmart (£150,000); London Bubble Theatre Company (£131,500); The Lyric – Hammersmith (£93,500); SHINE @ Clapham Park (£77,000); SHINE @ Axis (£60,000); Tutor Trust (£45,000); Serious Fun Kings School – Ely (£35,000); The Latin Programme (£25,000); Serious Fun Derrick Wood School (£20,000); Serious Fun Perse School (£12,000); Serious Fun Sheffield High School (£3,000).

Exclusions

Shine will not fund:

- Individuals
- Bursaries or any kind of student fees
- Projects outside of the UK
- Direct replacement of statutory funding
- Programmes where the primary aim is the personal development of young people rather than raising academic achievement levels
- Short-term or one-off projects
- Programmes narrowly targeted at specific beneficiary groups, with some exceptions
- Parenting programmes, where the primary focus is the parent rather than the child
- Activities promoting particular political or religious beliefs
- Projects taking place outside Greater London or Manchester (except for our Serious Fun strand and projects that are replicating on a national scale)

Applications

Potential applicants must check the charity's website for current guidelines and application criteria.

Information gathered from:

Accounts; annual report; Charity Commission record; funder's website.

The Shirley Foundation

Autism spectrum disorders with particular emphasis on medical research

£1.75 million (2011/12)

Beneficial area

UK.

Correspondent: Anne McCartney Menzies, Trustee, c/o James Cowper LLP, North Lea House, 66 Northfield End, Henley-on-Thames, Oxfordshire RG9 2BE (tel: 01491 579004; fax: 01491 574995; email: steve@steveshirley.com; website: www.steveshirley.com/tsf)

Trustees: Dame Stephanie Shirley, Chair; Prof. Eve Johnstone; Michael Robert Macfadyen; Anne McCartney Menzies.

CC Number: 1097135

The foundation, (formerly known as the Shirley Foundation Charitable Trust), was established in 1996 by Dame Stephanie Shirley, a business technology pioneer and the current Chair. Dame Stephanie is a highly successful entrepreneur turned ardent philanthropist. Having arrived in Britain as an unaccompanied child refugee from Germany in 1939, she started what is now Xansa on her dining room table with £6 in 1962. In 25 years as its chief executive she developed it into a leading business technology group, pioneering new work practices and changing the position of professional women (especially in hi-tech) along the way.

The following information is taken from the foundation's guidelines, available from its website:

> The mission of the Shirley Foundation is to facilitate and support pioneering projects with strategic impact in the field of autism spectrum disorder. Research projects should be innovative in nature with the potential to have a strategic impact and should ultimately be aimed at determining the causes of autism.

> It is desirable that applicants are investigators holding appointments at accredited academic, research or clinical institutions. Applicants who do not meet these criteria (e.g., postdoctoral fellows, clinical fellows, part-time faculty members, etc.) are eligible to apply if clear documentation is provided to show the support and commitment by the host institution.

In 2011/12 the foundation had assets of £1.8 million and an income of £69,500. Grants were made totalling £1.75 million to three organisations. They were: Edinburgh Development Trust – Autism Research Laboratories (£1 million); Autistica (£500,000); and Paintings in Hospitals – Autism and Disability Loan Scheme (£250,000).

The foundation appears to have developed a pattern of making a few substantial grants every other year.

Exclusions

No grants to individuals, or for non-autism-specific work. The foundation does not make political donations.

Applications

> Trustees meet twice yearly but applications for support are received throughout the year. Only those within the foundation's Mission are considered; applicants are reminded that projects should be innovative in nature with the potential to have a strategic impact in the field of Autism Spectrum Disorders. Research proposals should be aimed ultimately at determining causes of autism. Researchers should refer to the 'Guidance: Application for a medical research grant' available on the foundation's website.

> In the first instance a simple letter with outline proposal should be sent to Dame Stephanie Shirley at the registered address or emailed.

Percentage of awards given to new applicants: between 40% and 50%.

Information gathered from:

Accounts; Charity Commission record; further information provided by the funder; funder's website.

Shlomo Memorial Fund Ltd

Jewish causes

£1.4 million (2011/12)

Beneficial area

Unrestricted.

Correspondent: Channe Lopian, Secretary., Cohen Arnold and Co., New Burlington House, 1075 Finchley Road, London NW11 0PU (tel: 020 8731 0777; fax: 020 8731 0778)

Trustees: Amichai Toporowitz, Chair; Hezkel Toporowitz; Eliyah Kleineman; Channe Lopian; Chaim Y. Kaufman; Meir Sullam.

CC Number: 278973

This trust was established in 1978 to advance the Orthodox Jewish religion, relief of the poor and general charitable purposes.

In 2011/12 the trust had assets of £44 million and an income of

£11 million. Grants totalling £1.4 million were made to religious, educational and other charitable institutions. A list of grant beneficiaries was not included in the trust's accounts.

Previous beneficiaries include: Amud Haolam, Nachlat Haleviim, Torah Umesorah, Beit Hillel, ZSV Charities, Layesharim Tehilla, British Friends of Tashbar Chazon Ish, Chazon Ish, Mei Menuchos, Mor Uketsio, Shoshanat Hoamakim, Millennium Trust, and Talmud Torah Zichron Meir.

Applications

In writing to the correspondent.

Information gathered from:

Accounts; Charity Commission record.

Six Point Foundation

Welfare of Holocaust survivors and Jewish refugees

£911,000 to organisations

(2012/13)

Beneficial area

UK.

Correspondent: Susan Cohen, Executive Director, 25–26 Enford Street, London W1H 1DW (tel: 020 3372 8881; email: info@sixpointfoundation.org.uk; website: www.sixpointfoundation.org.uk)

Trustees: Frank Harding; Susan Grant; Vivienne Woolf; Julian Challis; Nigel Raine; Lionel Curry; Joanna Lassman.

CC Number: 1143324

The foundation was set up with and is funded by donations from the Otto Schiff Housing Association (OSHA). It aims to be a model spend out foundation that will distribute its funds by 2016. The objectives are to improve the quality of life of all financially disadvantaged Holocaust survivors and refugees of Jewish origin resident in the UK.

Grants of up to £30,000 are given for new or existing projects, usually for running costs but applications for capital costs may be considered. The foundation will fund projects up to the proportion of participants that meet its criteria. So for example, if 33% of total participants in a project meet the criteria, the foundation will contribute 33% of funds.

Grants are aimed at improving quality of life and welfare in an ageing population that experienced persecution rather than for Holocaust education projects. They are keen to find out where the gaps in existing health and social care provision lie.

In 2012/13 the foundation had assets of £4 million and an income of £830,000, mostly from donations from OSHA.

There were 41 grants made to organisations totalling £911,000.

Beneficiaries included: London Jewish Cultural Centre (£107,000 in two grants); London Association of Jewish Refugees (£98,000); The Holocaust Centre (£90,000); Birmingham Jewish Community Centre (£37,000); Ezra U'Marpeh (£25,000); Holocaust Survivors Centre/Shalvata (Jewish Care) (£23,000); Golden Years (£22,000); Senior N'Shei (£21,000); and North London Bikur Cholim and Bikur Cholim Ltd (£15,000 each).

There were an additional 123 grants given to individuals for welfare purposes totalling £88,000.

Exclusions

No grants for Holocaust education projects.

Applications

Applicants should firstly contact the foundation to discuss an application and agree a deadline for submission of an initial proposal. Guidance notes for this proposal are available to download from the foundation's website. If this initial proposal is successful, applicants will then be asked for more specific and detailed information. Applications will be acknowledged upon receipt and applicants should allow up to six months in total to complete the application process. Trustees meet five times a year to consider proposals and a site visit may be required.

Information gathered from:

Accounts; annual report; Charity Commission record; guidelines for applicants; funder's website; further information provided by the funder.

The Henry Smith Charity

Social welfare, older people, disability, health, medical research

£25.5 million to organisations (2012)

Beneficial area

UK. Specific local programmes in east and west Sussex, Hampshire, Kent, Gloucestershire, Leicestershire, Suffolk and Surrey.

Correspondent: Nick Acland, Director, Applications, 6th Floor, 65 Leadenhall Street, London EC3A 2AD (tel: 020 7264 4970; fax: 020 7488 9097; website: www. henrysmithcharity.org.uk)

Trustees: James Hambro, Chair; Rt Hon Claire Countes; Sir Richard Thompson; Gracia McGrath; Carola Godman-Law; Anna Scott; Merlyn Lowther; Noel Manns; Diana Barran; Marilyn Gallyer; Mark Newton; Patrick Maxwell; Peter Smallridge; Tristan Millington-Drake; Miko Giedroyc; Bridget Biddell; Vivian Hunt; James Hordern.

CC Number: 230102

The Henry Smith Charity was founded in 1628 with the objects of relieving and where possible releasing people from need and suffering. These objects continue in the grantmaking policy today. The Henry Smith Charity makes grants totalling around £25 million per annum for a wide range of purposes across the UK, funded from investments.

Grant programmes

The charity provides a number of grant programmes – the following information is taken from the charity's website:

THE HENRY SMITH CHARITY

Areas of funding

Black, Asian and Minority Ethnic (BAME)	Projects providing culturally appropriate services to Black, Asian and Minority Ethnic communities; including those that promote integration and access to mainstream services.
Carers	Projects providing advice and support; including respite services for carers and those cared for. Work can include educational opportunities for young carers.
Community Service	Projects providing support for communities in areas of high deprivation; including projects providing furniture recycling services, debt advice and community centres.
Disability	Projects providing rehabilitation, training or advocacy support to people who are disabled; this includes learning disabilities as well as physical disabilities.
Domestic and Sexual Violence	Projects providing advice, support and secure housing for families affected by domestic violence or sexual violence. Perpetrator programmes can be considered where organisations have secured, or are working towards, Respect accreditation.
Drugs, Alcohol and Substance Misuse	Projects supporting the rehabilitation of people affected by, or at risk of, drug and/or alcohol dependency, and projects supporting their families.
Ex-Service Men and Women	Projects providing services or residential care to ex-service men and women and their dependents.
Family Services	Projects providing support to families in areas of high deprivation.
Healthcare	Projects providing residential care, health care or outreach services, such as home care support. Services operated by the NHS will not normally be funded. In the case of applications from Hospices, priority is given to requests for capital expenditure.
Homelessness	Projects providing housing and services for homeless people and those at risk of homelessness.
Lesbian, Gay, Bisexual and Transgender	Projects providing advice, support and counselling for people who are Lesbian, Gay, Bisexual or Transgendered.
Mental Health	Projects promoting positive mental health or providing advice and support to people experiencing mental health problems.
Older People	Projects providing residential care, health care or emotional support, such as befriending services and day care centres. Priority will be given to projects in areas of high deprivation and those where rural isolation can be demonstrated.
Prisoners and Ex-offenders	Projects that help the rehabilitation and resettlement of prisoners and/or ex-offenders; including education and training that improve employability, and projects that support prisoners' families.
Prostitution and Trafficking	Projects that provide advice and support to sex industry workers; including advice on housing support and personal health, escaping exploitation and exiting prostitution.
Refugees and Asylum Seekers	Projects providing advocacy, advice and support to refugees and asylum seekers, and those promoting integration.
Young People	Projects maximising the potential of young people who experience educational, social and economic disadvantage; including young people in, or leaving, care.

We currently offer a range of grant programmes. Each has its own guidelines to help you apply. Please read the guidelines [on the charity's website] thoroughly before making your application.

The types of projects and services you can apply for a grant towards through our Main and Small Grants Programmes.

Main Grants Programme
Our main grants programme is for grants of £10,000 p.a. or over. There are two types of main grant:

Capital Grants
One-off grants for purchase or refurbishment of a building or purchase of specialist equipment.

Revenue Grants
Grants of up to three years for things like core costs (including salaries and overheads), or the running costs of a specific project (including staffing costs).

County Grants Programme
Our county grants programme supports the work of small organisations and charities in eight counties with which the Henry Smith Charity has a historical connection. The eight counties are Gloucestershire, Hampshire, Kent, Leicestershire, Suffolk, Surrey, East Sussex and West Sussex. To be eligible to apply for a county grant, your organisation's annual income must be below £250,000, unless you are working county-wide, in which case your income must be below £1 million.

Medical Research
Grants of up to three years for research undertaken by recognised 'Centres of Excellence.

Holiday Grants for Children
One-off grants of up to £3,000 for organisations, schools, youth groups etc specifically for holidays or outings for children under the age of 13 who are disabled or who live in areas of high deprivation.

Through the Main Grants Programme and Small and County Grants Programmes, grants are made in the categories shown in the box below (with examples of the type of work funded under each category).

Grantmaking in 2012
In 2012 the charity had assets of £715.7 million and an income of just over £10.5 million. Grants were made totalling over £26.6 million, broken down as displayed in the box below.

£463,000 worth of grants were withdrawn or returned in 2012, explaining the discrepancy between total grant figures and the category totals. *In 2012, this single major grant (see table below) was made towards a joint project with the Esmée Fairbairn Foundation in Northern Ireland.

The following is taken from the trust's 2012 chair's report:

> The bulk of our grant-making (£22.8 million) was spent on the 301 grants we made under our main grant programme for which we received 1,496 eligible applications. This, somewhat surprisingly, represented a modest reduction in the number of applications from 1,601 in 2011. The average grant size under the main scheme also reduced and was £76,000 compared to £79,000 the previous year.
>
> We have been expecting, but have not seen, an increase in applications as the economic situation becomes tougher and local authorities and governments reduce their funds going to charities which are supporting the most vulnerable in our society as this is where we also have our focus. While the number of applications has not increased we are generally seeing a marked reduction in the financial robustness of our applicants many of whom have dwindling reserves which is of concern for the future.

The following are a sample of organisations which received a grant in 2012:

Centre for Mental Health (£240,000), towards three years' running costs of an employability scheme for ex-offenders with mental health problems in Shropshire and Staffordshire; Care and Repair Neath Port Talbot (£117,500), towards three years' salary of the Operational Manager at a home repair project for older people in south Wales; Action Medical Research (£90,000), towards two years' medical research into finding a way to stop children with a

wheeze in early years developing asthma; Age UK Hammersmith and Fulham (£71,000), towards three years' salary and related core costs of a Resources and Publicity Assistant for an organisation that provides help and support to older people in the London Borough of Hammersmith and Fulham; Calderdale SmartMove (£56,500), towards three years' funding of the Volunteer Co-ordinator and the SmartSkills Co-ordinator at a project providing support to homeless people in West Yorkshire; Copenhagen Youth Project (£49,000), towards three years' continuation funding of the salary of the Finance and Admin Officer at a community youth project in the London Borough of Islington; Rhubarb Farm CIC (£40,500), towards three years' salary of a Finance and Volunteer Support Worker to provide volunteer placements and training to vulnerable adults in Derbyshire; Zone Youth Enquiry Service Plymouth (£22,500), towards two years' continuation funding of the salary of an Accreditation Youth Worker at a youth support project in Devon; Centre Project (£10,000), towards one year's running costs of a drop in service in Leicestershire for unaccompanied young asylum seekers; and the Deal Festival of Music and the Arts (£5,000), towards running costs of music and arts activities for disabled people in Kent.

Exclusions
The charity provides the following information:

> We do not make grants towards the following:
> - General appeals or letters requesting donations (full applications that follow our guidelines must be submitted)
> - Local authorities, or work usually considered a statutory responsibility
> - Schools, colleges or universities, except for independent special schools for pupils with disabilities or special educational needs
> - We will not fund the following unless they are in an area of high deprivation:
>   - Youth clubs
>   - Uniformed groups such as Scouts and Guides
>   - Community centres

THE HENRY SMITH CHARITY

Grant expenditure – organisations	2012	2011	2010	2009
Main grant programme (grants above £10,000)	£22.8 million	£24.2 million	£21.7 million	£19.4 million
Small grants (up to £10,000)	£1.6 million	£1.6 million	£1.7 million	£1.6 million
Major Grants	£250,000*	£417,000	£447,000	£210,000
Grant to historic parishes (Estates Fund distributions)	£620,000	£543,000	£468,000	£520,000
Grants for Christian projects	-	-	£460,000	£222,000
Holiday grants	£200,000	£150,000	£151,000	£94,000
Total grants to organisations	**£25.5 million**	£26.9 million	£24.9 million	£22 million

Grant expenditure – individuals	2012	2011	2010	2009
Grants to clergy	£825,000	£926,000	£518,000	£605,000
Grants to poor kindred	£736,000	£944,000	£520,000	£502,000
Total grants to individuals	**£1.5 million**	£1.9 million	£1 million	£1.1 million

- Counselling projects, except those that have a clearly defined client group and are in areas of high deprivation
- Pre-school projects, out of school hours play activities or holiday schemes, unless these are specifically for disabled children
- Community transport organisations or services
- Projects that promote religion
- Capital appeals for places of worship
- Organisations that do not provide direct services to clients (such as umbrella, second tier or grant-making organisations)
- Arts projects, unless able to evidence therapeutic or rehabilitative benefits to:
  - Older people
  - Disabled people
  - Vulnerable groups
  - Prisoners, or
  - Young people experiencing educational, social and economic disadvantage (such as young people in, or leaving, care)
- Education projects, except those able to evidence practical and rehabilitative benefits to:
  - Disabled people
  - Prisoners, or
  - Young people experiencing educational, social and economic disadvantage
- Leisure, recreation or play activities, unless they:
  - Are specifically for disabled people
  - Are able to evidence a significant rehabilitative benefit to people with mental health problems, or
  - Significantly improve opportunities and maximise the potential of young people who experience educational, social and economic disadvantage
- One-off events (such as festivals, conferences, exhibitions and community events)
- The core work of Citizens Advice Bureaux
- Projects that solely provide legal advice
- Core running costs of hospices
- Feasibility studies
- Professional associations, or training for professionals
- Organisations that do not have charitable aims (such as companies limited by shares and commercial companies)
- Start up costs, organisations that do not yet have a track record of service delivery, or that have not yet produced accounts
- Individuals, or organisations applying on their behalf
- Projects taking place or benefiting people outside the UK
- Overseas trips
- Residential holidays (except those that qualify under our Holiday Grants scheme)
- Heritage or environmental conservation projects
- Social research
- Campaigning or lobbying projects, or general awareness raising work
- Projects where the main focus is website development or maintenance
- IT equipment (unless related to a member of staff we are also being asked to fund)
- Capital projects that are solely to meet the requirements of the Disability Discrimination Act
- Organisations that have applied to us unsuccessfully within the previous 12 months

Applications

The charity provides the following information:

> Each of our grant programmes has a slightly different application and assessment process.
>
> You will find information about how to make your application in the guidelines for each type of grant. Some of our grants require you to fill in an application form. For others there is no application form; instead we provide guidance about to structure your application and what supporting documents you need to send us.
>
> Please ensure you send us all the supporting documents we ask you to include with your application. Incomplete applications will be returned unread.
>
> We strongly recommend that you download and read the guidelines of the relevant grant programme carefully before you start your application. It is important that you follow our guidance on how to apply.

Guidelines for each programme can be downloaded from the charity's website.

Common applicant mistakes

'Applicants do not clearly explain what services they provide and the difference that it makes to the lives of the people supported.'

Information gathered from:

Accounts; annual report; Charity Commission record; further information provided by the funder; funder's website.

The Sobell Foundation

Jewish charities, medical care and treatment, education, community, environment, disability, older people and young people

£3.5 million (2011/12)

Beneficial area

Unrestricted, in practice, England and Wales, Israel and the Commonwealth of Independent States (CIS).

Correspondent: Penny Newton, Administrator, PO Box 2137, Shepton Mallet, Somerset BA4 6YA (tel: 01749 813135; fax: 01749 813136; email: enquiries@sobellfoundation.org.uk; website: www.sobellfoundation.org.uk)

Trustees: Susan Lacroix; Roger Lewis; Andrea Scouller.

CC Number: 274369

The Sobell Foundation was established by the late Sir Michael Sobell in 1977 for general charitable purposes and is a grantmaking trust with which he was actively involved until shortly before his death in 1993. Grants tend to be made in line with the founder's interests which are principally causes benefiting children, the sick, elderly, needy and disabled. 'The trustees aim to achieve a reasonable spread between Jewish charities (operating principally in the UK and Israel) and non-Jewish charities operating in the UK.' Grants are made towards projects, items of equipment or general running costs.

The following information is taken from the foundation's website:

> As a grantmaking charity, we provide grants to fund projects and activities carried out by other charities. We receive many different applications for funding, from which our trustees make their funding decisions. For an application to be considered by the trustees, and for it to have the best chance of success, applicants should note the following guidelines.

Who may apply?
> We will only consider applications from charities registered with the Charity Commission, or charities that hold a Certificate of Exemption from the Inland Revenue. Overseas applicants must supply the details of a UK registered charity through which grants can be channelled on their behalf. We concentrate our funding on small national or local charities; the trustees are unlikely to support large national charities which enjoy wide support. We do not accept applications from individuals.

Which countries do we support?
> We restrict our funding on a geographical basis to the following countries: England, Wales, Israel, and Commonwealth of Independent States (CIS). We will only accept applications from charities based in these countries for projects and activities within these countries.

What type of work do we support?
> We restrict our funding to charities working in the following areas:
> - Medical care and treatment, including respite care and hospices
> - Care for physically and mentally disabled adults and children
> - Education and training for adults and children with physical and learning disabilities
> - Care and support of the elderly
> - Care and support for children
> - Homelessness
> - Immigrant absorption (Israel only)
> - Co-existence projects (Israel only)
> - Higher education (Israel only)

Unfortunately at the time of writing only the foundation's Summary Information Return was available, which contains limited information. In 2011/12 the foundation had an income of almost

£2 million; assets have previously stood at around £62 million. During the previous year, approximately 53% of grants made were to UK non-Jewish charities, 31% to Israeli charities and charities in the CIS, 15% to UK Jewish charities and 1% to other overseas charities. This allocation is within the ranges set by the trustees for grant allocation.

In 2011/12 grants were made to 428 organisations totalling £3.5 million.

Exclusions

No grants to individuals. Only registered charities or organisations registered with the Inland Revenue should apply.

Applications

Applications should be made in writing to the administrator using the application form obtainable from the foundation or printable from its website.

The application form should be accompanied by:
▶ Current year's summary income and expenditure budget
▶ Most recent annual report
▶ Most recent full accounts
▶ Inland Revenue certificate of exemption (if required)

The trustees receive a large number of applications for funding from registered charities during the year and support as many as possible of those which fall within the foundation's objectives. They aim to deal with requests within three months of receipt and to respond to each application received, whether or not a grant is made.

Trustees meet every three to four months and major grants are considered at these meetings. Requests for smaller amounts may be dealt with on a more frequent basis. Most applications are dealt with on an ongoing basis, and there are no deadlines for the receipt of applications. Organisations should wait 12 months before reapplying.

Information gathered from:

Charity Commission record; funder's website; Summary Information Return.

The Souter Charitable Trust

Christian evangelism, welfare
About £6 million (2011/12)

Beneficial area

UK, but with a preference for Scotland; overseas.

Correspondent: Dion Judd, Administrator, PO Box 7412, Perth PH1 5YX (tel: 01738 450408; email: enquiries@soutercharitabletrust.org.uk;

website: www.soutercharitabletrust.org.uk)

Trustees: Brian Souter; Betty Souter.

SC Number: SC029998

This trust is funded by donations from Scottish businessman Brian Souter, one of the founders of the Stagecoach transport company. The trust's website gives the following account of its policies:

> The trust supports projects engaged in the relief of human suffering in the UK and overseas – especially, but not exclusively, those with a Christian emphasis.
>
> We tend not to get involved with research or capital funding and we are much more likely to provide a contribution towards the revenue costs of a project.
>
> Grants are generally given to charitable organisations and not to individuals or in support of requests on behalf of individuals. Applications for building projects, personal educational requirements or personal expeditions are specifically excluded.

Most grants are one-off payments of £1,000 or less; a small number of projects receive support over three years. Previous grants indicate an interest in the support of marriage and parenting issues. There is a preference for funding revenue rather than capital costs.

In 2011/12 the trust had an income of almost £3.3 million and a total expenditure of £6.1 million, most of which is likely to have been given in grants. It should also be noted that during the previous year, 2010/11, the trust gave a total of £15.9 million in grants – further information is available on the trust's website.

Previous beneficiaries include: The Message Trust; Christians Against Poverty; Youth for Christ; Against Malaria Foundation; Mary's Meals; Chest Heart and Stroke Scotland; and Tearfund.

Exclusions

Building projects, individuals, personal education grants and expeditions are not supported.

Applications

In writing to the correspondent. Keep applications brief and no more than two sides of A4 paper: if appropriate, send audited accounts, but do not send brochures, business plans, DVDs and so on. The trust states that it will request more information if necessary. The trustees meet every two months or so, and all applications will be acknowledged in due course, whether successful or not. A stamped addressed envelope would be appreciated. Subsequent applications should not be made within a year of the initial submission.

Information gathered from:

OSCR record; funder's website. Accounts are available from the trust for £10.

The Sovereign Health Care Charitable Trust

Health, people with disabilities
£739,000 (2012)

Beneficial area

UK, with a preference for Bradford.

Correspondent: The Secretary, Royal Standard House, 26 Manningham Lane, Bradford, West Yorkshire BD1 3DN (tel: 01274 729472; fax: 01274 722252; email: charities@sovereignhealthcare.co.uk; website: www.sovereignhealthcare.co.uk)

Trustees: Mark Hudson, chair; Michael Austin; Dennis Child; Michael Bower; Russ Piper; Kate Robb-Webb; Robert Dugdale; Stewart Cummings.

CC Number: 1079024

The Sovereign Health Care Charitable Trust is funded by donations received under the Gift Aid scheme from Sovereign Health Care. The following information is given within the trust's guidelines, which are available from the company's website:

> Sovereign Health Care Charitable Trust funds work to do with health and well-being that is wholly charitable and usually undertaken either by registered charities or by organisations that have been established for charitable purposes, are properly constituted and have a bank account. In general the trust favours initiatives that touch people's lives and clearly make a difference. Grants are usually quite modest – a few thousand pounds at most. Large medical research initiatives where the trust's contribution would not be significant are unlikely to be a high priority.
>
> In terms of specific diseases and conditions, the charitable trust gives priority to those that are particularly prevalent in Bradford, especially: heart disease; chest/lung disease; lung cancer; stroke; diabetes; breast cancer; bowel cancer; prostate cancer; and oral cancer. Other priorities are: hospitals and hospices, disease prevention, healthy lifestyle and health promotion; deprivation, poverty or homelessness; disability; and mental health. The trust will also consider applications concerned with carers and with education and training where it relates to one of the other priority areas, though these do not have as high priority.
>
> The trust is prepared to consider applications from local charities, voluntary organisations and community groups. The majority of grants made are for services and activities within West Yorkshire, with a bias towards Bradford. Applications for the work of local groups, hospitals, hospices and other good causes that are

not from the Yorkshire area will not be supported.

The trust is prepared to consider applications from national charities if there is a clear benefit to people in the West Yorkshire area, preferably the delivery of services locally.

In 2012 the trust had assets of £281,500 and an income of £900,000. Grants were made to organisations totalling £739,000.

The main beneficiary during the year was Bradford Teaching Hospitals Foundation Trust (£221,000). Other beneficiaries included: Yorkshire Air Ambulance (£28,500); Marie Curie Cancer Care (£25,000); the Bradford Soup Run (£15,000); Leeds Rugby Foundation (£10,000); Calderdale and Huddersfield NHS Foundation Trust (£8,000); Deafblind UK (£7,500); Christians Against Poverty and Skipton Extended Learning For All (£5,000 each); Bradford Toy Library (£4,000); Barnardo's (£2,000); Clothing Solutions for Disabled People (£1,500); and Behind Closed Doors, Hope For Justice and SSAFA Forces Help (£1,000 each).

Exclusions
No grants to individuals.

Applications
The following information is given in the trust's guidelines:

> The charitable trust is keen not to burden the organisations it supports with too much paper work and 'jumping through hoops'. On the other hand, just sending a newsletter in the hope that this will trigger a cheque in return will not succeed.
>
> The trustees needs to know what you do, what you want money for, how much it's going to cost and, when appropriate, how you'll know that the money has made a difference. There is no application form; just write to the trust with the appropriate information. The kind of detail the trust expects from a local self-help group wanting a couple of hundred pounds will be different from the information it expects from a large charity wanting several thousand pounds for a new initiative.
>
> Trustees meet six times a year. From the trust receiving an application to the applicant receiving a cheque (or not) usually takes about two or three months. In the case of disasters and emergencies the trust may be able to act much more quickly. The trust notifies all applicants about the outcome of their request.
>
> The trust is likely to look at the copy of your latest report and accounts if it is available on the Charity Commission's website. If it's not available (you're a small charity or not a registered charity at all), then it would be helpful to have some figures about the organisation's finances, as well as figures about the work or activity you want the funding for. If you're in a difficult financial situation, explain what's going on and the steps you are taking to improve things. Conversely, if your accounts show huge 'free' reserves, you might want to explain why you still need a grant.

The deadlines for consideration at the following trustees' meeting are: 15 February; 15 April; 15 June; 15 August; 15 October; 15 December.

Percentage of awards given to new applicants: between 30% and 40%.

Common applicant mistakes
'They don't read the guidelines.'

Information gathered from:
Accounts; Charity Commission record; further information provided by the funder; funder's website.

Sparks Charity (Sport Aiding Medical Research For Kids)

Medical research
£2.4 million (2012/13)

Beneficial area
UK.

Correspondent: John Shanley, Chief Executive, 6th Floor, Westminster Tower, 3 Albert Embankment, London SE1 7SP (tel: 020 7091 7750; email: info@sparks.org.uk; website: www. sparks.org.uk)

Trustees: Sir Trevor Brooking; Hugh Emeades; Roger Uttley; Julian Wilkinson; Floella Benjamin; Jonathon Britton; Victoria Glaysher; Guy Gregory; David Orr; Frank van den Bosch; Robert Booker; Martin Jepson; Dr Simon Newell.

CC Number: 1003825

Sparks is one of the few charities that funds research into the wide range of conditions that can affect babies and children. It supports vital medical research that will:

- Increase the life expectancy of newborn babies
- Reduce the health risks for babies born prematurely
- Combat serious conditions such as spina bifida, cerebral palsy and childhood cancers, such as neuroblastoma
- Develop more effective treatments and diagnostic tools for life-limiting conditions affecting babies and young children

> The charity will only support research which is likely to have a clear clinical application in the near future. Therefore grant applications for routine basic research which is unlikely to have clinical application within ten years will not be considered.
>
> Sparks funded research takes the form of project grants of up to three years in length with a clearly definable subject area and outcome, equipment grants for use within a specific research proposal as previously defined, programme grants for researchers who have a sustained track record of successful grant awards from Sparks and fellowship grants. Pilot projects of short duration to test a concept in preparation for a full application will also be considered (see website). Grants are only made to projects where the principal applicant is in a tenured position at a university or research institution.
>
> Researchers who are making a substantial intellectual contribution to the project and require personal support from the grant may apply as co-applicants with a tenured member of staff as the principal applicant.

In 2012/13 the charity had assets of £435,000 and an income of £4.6 million, mainly from fundraising events. Research grants and other awards were made to institutions totalling £2.4 million.

Grants included those to: St Michael's Hospital, Bristol/Oslo University (£318,500); University of Manchester (£148,500); Cambridge University Hospitals (£115,500); University of Liverpool (£89,500); Chailey Heritage Clinical Services (£72,500); and Oxford University Hospitals (£66,500).

Exclusions
The charity is unable to consider:
- Grants for further education, for example, MSc/PhD course fees
- Grants towards service provision or audit studies
- Grants for work undertaken outside the UK
- Grants towards 'top up' funding for work supported by other funding bodies
- Grants to other charities

Applications
Sparks funds project grants up to the value of £150,000, Research Training Fellowships and Programme grants. Application forms and full guidelines are available on the charity's website.

Information gathered from:
Accounts; annual report; funder's website.

The Geoff and Fiona Squire Foundation

General, medicine, education, disability and the welfare and healthcare of children

£1.3 million (2011/12)

Beneficial area

UK.

Correspondent: Fiona Squire, Trustee, The Walton Canonry, 69 The Close, Salisbury, Wiltshire SP1 2EN

Trustees: Geoff W. Squire; Fiona Squire; B. P. Peerless.

CC Number: 1085553

Established in 2001, the foundation has general charitable purposes, with a particular interest in medicine, education, disability and the welfare and healthcare of children.

In 2011/12 the foundation had assets of £10.9 million and an income of £689,500. Grants were made to 23 organisations totalling £1.3 million.

The largest grants were made to: Salisbury Cathedral (£400,000); UCLH Charitable Foundation – Cancer Centre Appeal (£250,000); Teenage Cancer Trust (£207,000); SENSE Holiday Fund and Orpheus Centre (£100,000 each); and Lord's Taverners (£64,000).

Other beneficiaries included: Special Olympics Great Britain (£35,000); Starlight Children's Foundation (£30,000); Friends of Shepherds Down School (£20,000); Exeter House School (£10,000); Music for Youth (£7,500); Southern Spinal Injuries Trust (£5,000); NHMET Ark Annual Lecture (£3,500); and Deaf Blind UK and Brendoncare Club (£1,000 each).

Applications

The trust has previously stated: 'the trustees have in place a well-established donations policy and we do not therefore encourage unsolicited grant applications, not least because they take time and expense to deal with properly.'

Information gathered from:

Accounts; Charity Commission record.

St James's Place Foundation

Children and young people with special needs, hospices

£3.6 million (2013)

Beneficial area

UK.

Correspondent: Mark Longbottom, c/o St James's Place Wealth Management plc, St James's Place House, 1 Tetbury Road, Cirencester, Gloucestershire GL7 1FP (tel: 01285 878562; email: mark.longbottom@sjp.co.uk; website: www.sjpfoundation.co.uk)

Trustees: Malcolm Cooper-Smith, Chair; David Bellamy; Mike Wilson; Andrew Croft; Hugh Gladman; David Lamb.

CC Number: 1144606

This foundation was originally established in 1992, when it was known as the J. Rothschild Assurance Foundation. Following a strategic review, the foundation was wound up in 2012 and re-registered with the Charity Commission with a new registered charity number.

Employees and Partners (members of the St James's Place Partnership, the marketing arm of St James's Place) contribute to the foundation throughout each year and the sums raised are matched by the company. The combined amount is distributed each year to causes determined by the contributors.

The following information is taken from the foundation's website:

> We aim to make a significant difference to the lives of children and young people. Any small charity that meets the criteria can apply for a grant from the foundation, if it has a project in the UK that is for the direct benefit of economically disadvantaged or socially marginalised young people aged 25 years or younger, the physically disabled, or those suffering from a mental condition or life-threatening or degenerative illness. We also help people whose lives have been adversely affected by illness through the Hospice Movement. The foundation makes grants to hospices in the UK for things such as equipment, the cost of complementary therapy or specialist nursing staff.
>
> As well as the hundreds of smaller one-off grants that are made each year, the foundation makes significant, major, multi-year grants to charities both in the UK and overseas, whereby the cost of a salary or project will be funded over two to three years, providing greater stability for the charity.

The foundation makes grants under three main themes:

Cherishing the Children

This is our largest theme and is aimed at supporting disadvantaged and disabled young people under the age of 25.

Small grants of up to £10,000 are available to UK registered charities with an annual income of up to £750,000 (this restriction does not apply to Special Needs Schools or Mainstream Schools with a Special Needs Unit). A small number of major grants are also available to UK registered charities with an annual income of up to £8 million.

Who do we support?

▶ Young people (under the age of 25) with physical or mental health difficulties or life threatening or degenerative conditions
▶ Young carers (under the age of 25)
▶ Young people (under the age of 25) who are socially or economically disadvantaged

How do we help?

▶ Grants for small capital items
▶ Support for staff working directly or hands on with beneficiaries
▶ Support for projects of direct benefit to beneficiaries

Combating Cancer

The foundation is pleased to aid UK registered charities who support people with cancer.

Small Grants of up to £10,000 are available to UK registered charities with an annual income of up to £750,000 supporting individuals suffering from cancer, and their families.

Who do we support?

▶ Cancer patients of all ages.

How do we help?

▶ Grants for small capital items of direct benefit to cancer patients
▶ Support towards the salary of staff working directly with cancer patients
▶ Grants and support for projects aimed at increasing the quality of life for cancer patients

Supporting Hospices

The foundation is proud to support hospices in the United Kingdom. However, *we do not currently invite applications from individual hospices. Instead we will be working with Help the Hospices, the umbrella organisation supporting independent hospices in the UK and who will distribute funds to hospices on our behalf. Please visit the Help the Hospices website for updates on future grant programmes: www. helpthehospices.org.uk.*

Who do we support?

▶ Hospices working with all age ranges

Grants in 2013 totalled around £3.6 million.

Exclusions

The foundation has a policy of not considering an application from any charity within two years of giving a grant.

The foundation does not provide support for:

▶ Charities with reserves of over 50% of income
▶ Administrative costs
▶ Activities primarily the responsibility of statutory agencies
▶ Replacement of lost statutory funding
▶ Research
▶ Events
▶ Advertising
▶ Holidays
▶ Sponsorship
▶ Contributions to large capital appeals
▶ Single faith charities
▶ Social and economic deprivation

Charities that are raising funds on behalf of another charity

Applications

The following information is given on the foundation's website.

The foundation is only able to consider applications from UK registered charities as well as Special Needs Schools in the UK. We accept applications from national, regional and local charities operating in England, Scotland, Wales and Northern Ireland. Important note: we do not accept unsolicited applications from charities operating overseas.

The Small Grants Programme is available to smaller UK registered charities working nationally, regionally or locally in the UK with an annual income of up to £750,000. The amount applied for should be up to a maximum of £10,000 in any two-year rolling period. If an applicant is unsuccessful then a period of twelve months must elapse before re-applying.

If you believe that your application falls within the funding policy of the foundation, you are welcome to apply.

There are no deadlines or closing dates. Small Grants are considered on receipt and in rotation.

The whole procedure can take between four to six months (sometimes longer if many applications are received) so it is advisable to apply in good time if funds are required for a certain date.

Each application is considered on its merits based on the information provided in the online application form and the due diligence carried out by the foundation team. We will acknowledge receipt of your application by email.

Applications for a Small Grant will normally receive a visit from a representative of the foundation, who will subsequently report to the trustees. Following the trustees' decision, successful applicants will be notified.

Applications can be made online via the foundation's website.

Supporting Hospices

The foundation is proud to support hospices in the United Kingdom. However, we do not currently invite applications from individual hospices. Instead we will be working with Help the Hospices, the umbrella organisation supporting independent hospices in the UK, who will distributes funds to hospices on our behalf. For more information, visit the Help the Hospices website: www.helpthehospices.org.uk.

Major Grants Programme

The foundation's Major Grants Programme remains closed to unsolicited applications. Please check the foundation's website for up-to-date information.

Information gathered from:

Charity Commission record; funder's website.

The Staples Trust

Development, environment, women's issues
£505,000 (2011/12)

Beneficial area

UK and overseas.

Correspondent: Alan Bookbinder, Director, The Peak, 5 Wilton Road, London SW1V 1AP (tel: 020 7410 0330; fax: 020 7410 0332; website: www.sfct.org.uk)

Trustees: Jessica Frankopan; Peter Frankopan; James Sainsbury; Judith Portrait.

CC Number: 1010656

Summary

The Staples Trust is one of the Sainsbury Family Charitable Trusts, which share a joint administration. They have a common approach to grantmaking which is described in the entry for the group as a whole. The trust's main areas of interest are overseas development, environment, gender issues, the Frankopan Fund and general charitable purposes.

The trust is that of Jessica Frankopan (nee Sainsbury), and its trustees include her husband and her two brothers who lead the *Tedworth* and *Glass-House* trusts (see separate entries).

The trust offers the standard Sainsbury description of its grantmaking practice: 'Proposals are generally invited by the trustees or initiated at their request. Unsolicited applications are discouraged and are unlikely to be successful, even if they fall within an area in which the trustees are interested. The trustees prefer to support innovative schemes that can be successfully replicated or become self-sustaining'. There is a special interest in Croatia, with grants made to individuals via the Frankopan Fund, but this does not dominate grantmaking in central and Eastern Europe.

Grantmaking in 2011/12

During the year the trust had assets of almost £11.9 million and an income of £501,000. There were 37 new grants approved during the year amounting to £220,000, with payments made, including those approved in previous years, totalling £505,000. Grants paid during the year are categorised as displayed in the box below. This includes descriptions of where the trust focuses its efforts in each area.

Beneficiaries across all categories included: St Paul's Girls' School (£50,000); University of Cambridge – World Oral Literature Project (£20,000); Survival International Charitable Trust and Daughters of Eve (£15,000 each); First Story (£10,000); KickStart International (£7,500); Anthony Nolan Bone Marrow Trust and the Royal Society of Literature (£5,000 each); and Eagle House School (£2,000).

Exclusions

Normally, no grants to individuals.

Applications

See the guidance for applicants in the entry for the Sainsbury Family Charitable Trusts. A single application will be considered for support by all the trusts in the group.

THE STAPLES TRUST

Gender	£261,000	Trustees are committed to raising awareness of gender and how the diverse understanding and experiences of men and women have an impact on the structures of society. Trustees are willing to consider projects in the UK and overseas, focusing mainly on domestic violence and women's rights.
Overseas development	£45,000	Trustees' priorities in this category are projects which contribute to the empowerment of women, the rights of indigenous people, improved shelter and housing, income-generation in disadvantaged communities and sustainable agriculture and forestry. Trustees are particularly interested to support development projects which take account of environmental sustainability and, in many cases, the environmental and developmental benefits of the project are of equal importance.
Environment	£32,500	Projects are supported in developing countries, Central and Eastern Europe and the UK Grants are approved for renewable energy technology, training and skills upgrading and, occasionally, research.
Frankopan Fund	£24,000	Trustees have established a fund to assist exceptionally talented postgraduate students primarily from Croatia to further or complete their studies.
General	£142,500	

However, for this, as for many of the family trusts, 'proposals are generally invited by the trustees or initiated at their request. Unsolicited applications are discouraged and are unlikely to be successful, even if they fall within an area in which the trustees are interested'. See also the text above.

Information gathered from:

Accounts; annual report; Charity Commission record; funder's website.

The Peter Stebbings Memorial Charity

General charitable purposes
£464,000 (2011/12)

Beneficial area

UK, with a preference for London, and developing countries.

Correspondent: Andrew Stebbings, Trustee, Pemberton Greenish LLP, 45 Cadogan Gardens, London SW3 2AQ (tel: 020 7591 3349; fax: 020 7591 3412; email: charitymanager@pglaw.co.uk; website: peterstebbingsmemorialcharity. org)

Trustees: Andrew Stebbings; Nicholas Cosin; Jennifer Clifford.

CC Number: 274862

Registered in 1977, the charity was established in memory of Hedley Peter Stebbings, who was killed during active service during the Second World War. The following information is taken from the charity's website:

> The charity gives grants to registered charities in the UK, usually operating in London, and also in the developing world. Generally grants go to charities where the grant will make a difference and where the trustees can see how the money is being used.
>
> In the UK the grants are focused towards:
> ▷ Medical research and care, and
> ▷ Social welfare
>
> The main areas of interest are:
> ▷ Homelessness
> ▷ Hospices
> ▷ Mental health/counselling
> ▷ Drug & alcohol therapeutic support
> ▷ Offender support
> ▷ Community regeneration
> ▷ Vulnerable families, women and children, and
> ▷ The promotion of human rights
>
> The charity supports charities that operate in the developing world, including projects that support the community through:
> ▷ Education
> ▷ Basic skills and tools
> ▷ Health
> ▷ Sustainability
> ▷ Micro finance, and
> ▷ The promotion of human rights
>
> Grants are made at regular intervals during the year and the total level of

grants at present is approximately £350,000 a year. The trustees are concerned that their grant support will make a real difference to the work of applicant organisations.

> Generally, the trustees assist small to medium-sized charities with annual incomes of up to £5 million.
>
> The trustees fund projects, but are willing to consider core funding for organisations whose work they know. Local (London) charities have been helped where there is a link with the trustees' work or knowledge – this means London-based local charities, and not regional ones.

In 2011/12 the charity had assets of £7.3 million and an income of £238,500. Grants were made to 43 organisations totalling £464,000.

Beneficiaries included: Royal Marsden Hospital Project (£100,000); Liver Group (£59,500); The Maya Centre (£30,000); The Irene Taylor Trust (£20,000); St Christopher Hospice (£15,000); The AHOY Centre and Power International (£10,000 each); African Revival, Childreach International, Marylebone Project and the Sick Children's Trust (£5,000 each); The Rainbow Trust Children's Charity (£3,000); and Bart's City Life Saver (£2,000).

Exclusions

The charity will not assist:
▷ Individuals
▷ Large national or international charities
▷ Animal welfare
▷ Publications and journals (unless as part of a supported project)
▷ General appeals
▷ Any charity whose beneficiaries are restricted to particular faiths
▷ Educational institutions, unless for a particular project the trustees wish to support
▷ Arts organisations, unless there is a strong social welfare focus to the work (e.g. community arts projects)

Applications

An application form is available from the charity's website.

Information gathered from:

Accounts; Charity Commission record; funder's website.

The Steel Charitable Trust

Social welfare, culture, recreation, health, medical research, environment, and occasionally, overseas aid
£1 million (2011/12)

Beneficial area

Mainly UK with 30% of all grants made to organisations in the Luton and Bedfordshire areas.

Correspondent: Carol Langston, Administrator, Holme Farm, Fore Street, Bradford, Holsworthy, Devon EX22 7AJ (tel: 01409 281403; email: administrator@steelcharitabletrust.org. uk; website: www.steelcharitabletrust.org. uk)

Trustees: Nicholas E. W. Wright; John A. Childs, Chair; John A. Maddox; Anthony W. Hawkins; Wendy Bailey; Dr Mary Briggs; Philip Lawford.

CC Number: 272384

The trust was established in 1976 for general charitable purposes. Grants are made for social welfare, culture, recreation, health, medical research, environment, overseas aid and other general purposes. Grants are made at regular intervals during the year and the total level of grants is approximately £1 million per annum. Grants are generally made as single payments between £1,000 and £25,000. It is the trust's policy to distribute 30% of all grants in the Luton and Bedfordshire areas.

In 2011/12 the trust had assets of £21.6 million and an income of just over £1 million. There were 196 grants made totalling £1 million. This is broken down as displayed in the table opposite and includes the number of applications received within each category.

Beneficiaries included: North Devon Hospice (£50,000); Keech Hospice Care (£40,000); University of Bedfordshire – bursaries and Cancer Research UK (£25,000 each); National Deaf Children's Society (£20,000); SSAFA Forces Help (£15,000); London Youth Rowing Ltd and the People's Dispensary for Sick Animals (£10,000 each); Ilkeston School Specialist Arts College (£6,000); Caryl Jenner Productions Ltd and the British Federation of Brass Bands (£5,000 each); Familylives (£3,000); Royal Liverpool Philharmonic Society and Victim Support (£2,000 each); and South Northants Volunteer Bureau and the Bedford and District Society for People with Learning Disabilities (£1,000 each).

THE STEEL CHARITABLE TRUST

	No. of applications received	No. of grants made	Amount
Ill-health, disability or other disadvantage	458	73	£313,500
Health	128	22	£204,000
Arts, culture, heritage or science	229	25	£117,500
Education	167	16	£104,000
Citizenship or community development	104	13	£78,000
Poverty	72	15	£49,000
Armed forces, police or rescue services	10	6	£41,500
Animal welfare	15	5	£26,500
General charitable purposes	46	7	£19,500
Religion	26	6	£19,500
Amateur sport	10	1	£10,000
Human rights, racial harmony or equality	18	–	–
International aid	11	–	–

Exclusions

Individuals, students and expeditions are not supported.

Applications

All applicants must complete the online application form on the trust's website. Applications submitted by post will not be considered. There is no deadline for applications and all will be acknowledged. Trustees meet regularly during the year, usually in February, May, August and November. All successful applicants will be notified by email and will be required to provide written confirmation of the details of the project or work for which they are seeking a grant. Payment is then made in the following month.

To comply with the Data Protection Act 1998, applicants are required to consent to the use of personal data supplied by them in the processing and review of their application. This includes transfer to and use by such individuals and organisations as the trust deems appropriate. The trust requires the assurance of the applicant that personal data about any other individual is supplied to the trust with his/her consent. At the point of submitting an online application, applicants are asked to confirm this consent and assurance.

Percentage of awards given to new applicants: between 40% and 50%.

Information gathered from:

Accounts; annual report; Charity Commission record; further information provided by the funder; funder's website.

The Stewards' Company Ltd (incorporating the J. W. Laing Trust and the J. W Laing Biblical Scholarship Trust)

Christian evangelism, general
£4.85 million (2011/12)

Beneficial area

Unrestricted.

Correspondent: Brian Chapman, Secretary, 124 Wells Road, Bath BA2 3AH (tel: 01225 427236; fax: 01225 427278; email: stewardsco@stewards.co.uk)

Trustees: Brian Chapman; Alexander McIlhinney; Paul Young; Dr John Burness; William Adams; Andrew Griffiths; Prof. Arthur Williamson; Philip Page; Denis Cooper; Alan Paterson; Glyn Davies; Ian Childs; John Gamble; Philip Symons; William Wood; Andrew Street; Keith Bintley; John Aitken.

CC Number: 234558

The charity supports Christian evangelism, especially but not exclusively that of Christian Brethren assemblies. Its work is described as follows in their accounts:

> The principal activities of the charity are to act as owner or as custodian trustee of various charitable properties, mainly used as places of worship and situated either in the United Kingdom or overseas, and to act as administrative trustee of a number of Christian charitable trusts, including The J W Laing Trust and The J W Laing Biblical Scholarship Trust.

> The trust describes its objectives as being '] the advancement of the religion in any matter which shall be charitable, and in particular by the furtherance of the gospel of God and education in the Holy Scriptures as contained in the Old and New Testaments, and the relief of the poor.

Its grantmaking policy is described as follows:

> The trust takes into account the financial resources of the benefiting charities, the efforts made by members of such charities to maximise their own funding, including where appropriate sacrificial giving by themselves and their supporters, and the assessed value of the work of such charities consistent with the objective of the main grant-making charities [i.e. Stewards Company, Laing Trust and Laing Scholarship].

In 2011/12 the trust had assets of £125.2 million and an income of just over £2.1 million. Grants were made to organisations totalling £4.85 million and were broken down as follows:

| Home | £2.85 million |
| Overseas | £2 million |

The largest 50 grants were listed in the accounts. Beneficiaries included: Echoes of Service (£619,000); Beatrice Laing Trust (£466,000); UCCF – The Christian Unions (£393,000); Retired Missionary Aid Fund (£225,000); Interlink (£140,000); London School of Theology (£47,500); Langham Partnership (£35,000); Scripture Union (£20,000); and the Stapleford Centre (£17,000).

Applications

In writing to the correspondent.

Information gathered from:

annual report; Accounts; Charity Commission record.

Sir Halley Stewart Trust

Medical, social, educational and religious activities
£810,000 (2011/12)

Beneficial area

UK and some work in Africa.

Correspondent: Susan West, Administrator, 22 Earith Rd, Willingham, Cambridge CB24 5LS (tel: 01954 260707; email: email@sirhalleystewart.org.uk; website: www.sirhalleystewart.org.uk)

Trustees: Joanna Womack; Prof. Phyllida Parsloe; Dr Caroline Berry; Barbara Clapham; Dr Duncan Stewart; George Russell; Lord Stewartby; Prof. John Wyatt; Prof. John Lennard-Jones; Michael Collins; Prof. Philip Whitfield; W. Kirkman; Brian Allpress; Prof. Gordon Wilcock; Caroline Thomas; Theresa Bartlett; Louisa Elder; Amy Holcroft; Prof. Jane Gilliard.

CC Number: 208491

The trust was established in 1924 by Sir Halley Stewart who endowed the charity and established its founding principles.

During the course of his life Sir Halley Stewart was a non-conformist Christian minister, an MP, a pioneering industrialist and a philanthropist. When he founded the trust he specified four objects, to advance religion and education, to relieve poverty and to promote other charitable purposes beneficial to the community. He was concerned with the prevention and removal of human misery and in the realisation of national and worldwide brotherhood. He wished the trustees to have the fullest discretion in applying the income of the trust within its objects, but not for dogmatic theological purposes. A tradition of supporting medical research into the prevention of human suffering, not its relief, was established during his lifetime. He died in 1937.

The trust has a Christian basis and is concerned with the development of body, mind and spirit, a just environment, and international goodwill. To this end it supports projects in religious, social, educational and medical fields, mainly in the UK. The trust aims to promote and assist innovative research activities or pioneering developments with a view to making such work self-supporting.

As stated in the trustees' report for 2011/12, the three principles by which the trustees are guided in administering the trust are:

▷ Furthering for every individual such favourable opportunities of education, service and leisure as shall enable him or her most perfectly to develop the body, mind and spirit
▷ Securing a just environment in all social life whether domestic, industrial or national
▷ In international relationships to fostering good will between all races, tribes, peoples and nations to secure the fulfilment of hope of 'peace on earth'

Furthermore, grants are usually in the form of salary and there is a preference to support innovative and imaginative people, often 'promising young researchers, with whom they can develop a direct relationship.' Sometimes a contribution towards the expenses of a project is given, however trustees do not favour grant-giving to enable the completion of a project initiated by another body. Grants are normally limited to two or three years but are sometimes extended.

In 2011/12 the trust had assets of £23.9 million and an income of £919,000. Grants were made totalling £810,000, broken down as follows:

Medical	£366,000
Religious	£233,000
Social and Educational	£194,000

Note: this grant total was £17,000 less than stated in the accounts for 2011/12, as according to the administrator, 17 trustees 'had £1,000 to make small grants through individual CAF accounts. These are accounted for as 'personal grants.'

Beneficiaries include: Newcastle University, Institute of Health and Society (£27,500); Bail for Immigration Detainees (BID) and Bradford Court Chaplaincy Service (£25,000 each); RECOOP – Resettlement and Care for Older Ex-Offenders and Prisoners (£23,500); World Horizons Ltd (£20,000); Cardiff University, School of Biosciences (£19,500); and CO'DEC Research Centre, St John's College, Durham (£10,000).

Current priorities

The current priorities of the trust are in the form of three programmes, namely, medical, religious and social and educational. Details are taken from the trust's website:

Medical

Projects should be simple, not molecular, and capable of clinical application within 5 – 10 years. They may include a social or ethical element. Non-medical trustees should be able to understand the application and appreciate the value of the work. Projects may be of a type unlikely to receive support from research councils or large research-funding charities. Projects must obtain ethics committee approval where needed. The trustees welcome applications direct from researchers at UK medical institutions or university departments concerned with:

▷ Projects which aim to improve the quality of life of the elderly suffering from physical or psychological disorders
▷ The prevention of disease and disability in children
▷ The prevention, diagnosis and treatment of tropical infectious and parasitic diseases
▷ Innovative projects, involving any discipline, which are likely to improve health care
▷ Research focusing on developments in medical ethics
▷ Innovative medical projects caring for the needs of disadvantaged groups

Religious

The trust is committed to advancing the Christian religion. The trustees are particularly interested in innovative and practical ecumenical projects in the UK; and also those in countries outside the UK where there is special and specific need. The trustees seek to support ground-breaking projects proposed by inspirational individuals who have proven track records, or those evidencing energy, enthusiasm and imagination.

Current priorities are:

▷ To encourage Christian people to develop their skills in upholding and communicating their faith in the public domain

▷ To support and encourage the innovative teaching of Christianity within the United Kingdom
▷ To encourage specific groups of people to explore their experience of spirituality and their spiritual needs and strengths, and to help others to understand these
▷ To support innovative projects which aim to encourage a closer working relationship between Christian denominations; and/or, those that aim to improve inter-faith relationships by facilitating a better understanding between faiths

Social and educational

Applications are welcomed for the feasibility or piloting stage or the dissemination/practical implementation stage of projects that are likely to improve the conditions of a particular group of people, as well as having wider implications. Trustees will normally expect that the beneficiaries of a development project will have been involved in the design of the project and its continuing governance. They will also wish to see how the work will continue after a grant from the trust has finished (i.e. sustainability plans).

In the UK the trust seeks to support innovative projects, which attempt to:

▷ Prevent and resolve conflict, promote reconciliation and/or encourage re-connection between family members of all ages
▷ Help people 'move beyond disadvantage' – such projects might be concerned with the social and family aspects of unemployment, crime, imprisonment, homelessness, migration, mental health
▷ Address the needs of elderly people and those of all ages who may be vulnerable or exploited
▷ Accept responsibility for disseminating results to practitioners in a form which is likely to result in changes in their way of working

Overseas

The trust applies the same criteria as above to proposals from UK-based charities which operate through local organisations in the poorest politically stable African countries. (NB. for the foreseeable future the trust will fund overseas work in the field of education, water and healthcare through those organisations with which they have had previous partnerships or which trustees themselves identify. Please do not make general submissions.)

Exclusions

According to the trust's website, the trust will be unable to help with funding for any of the following:

▷ General appeals of any kind
▷ The purchase, erection or conversion of buildings
▷ Capital costs
▷ University overhead charges
▷ The completion of a project initiated by other bodies

The trust does not usually fund but may consider the following:

- Projects put forward indirectly through other 'umbrella' or large charities
- Educational or 'gap' year travel projects
- Running costs of established organisations or conferences
- Climate change issues
- Personal education fees or fees for taught courses-unless connected with research which falls within current priority areas. (Applications for such research work are normally made by a senior researcher seeking support for a student, or if coming directly from the student it should have project supervisor's written support; the trust does not favour grantmaking to enable the completion of a project or PhD.)

Grants are only ever paid to UK registered charities and never to individuals.

Applications

The following applicant guidelines are taken from the trust's website:

- Applications should be submitted from those directly involved in the project as opposed to fundraisers or development officers
- Applicants should make sure that their project fits the trust's objects and falls within its current priority areas
- Initial telephone enquiries to the trust's office are welcomed to discuss the suitability of an application

The trust does not have an application form. Applicants should write to the administrator always including a one-page lay 'executive' summary of the proposed work. The proposal should state clearly:

- What the aims of the project are and why it is believed to be innovative
- How the project fits the trust's objects and current priority areas
- What the overall budgeted cost of the project is and how much is being requested from the trust
- What the grant will be used for and how long the project will take to have practical benefits
- How the project/research results will be disseminated

Applications for young researchers should be accompanied by a letter of support from a senior colleague or research supervisor.

Development projects should indicate where they would hope to obtain future funding from. A CV of key individuals who will be responsible for the project should be provided and where appropriate; job description, set of audited accounts and annual report should also be provided.

There are no set application deadlines and applications are accepted anytime during the year. When the trust has received your application they will make contact (normally within two weeks) either to ask for further information; to tell you the application will be going forward to the next stage of assessment and what the timetable for a final decision will be; or to tell you that they are unable to help. The 2011/12 accounts also note: 'it is a deliberate policy of the trust to maintain as much personal and informal contact with applicants as possible, to keep paper work to the minimum consistent with efficient administration, and to make decisions on applications within four months.' Unsuccessful applicants are sent a personalised letter, or email, which explains the reason for rejection.

Percentage of awards given to new applicants: between 40% and 50%.

Common applicant mistakes

'Not realising our emphasis on "innovation"; asking for too much; fundraisers making applications from large charities; applying for ongoing running costs; wrong overseas continent; applications from individuals' needs.'

Information gathered from:

Accounts; annual report; Charity Commission record; further information provided by the funder; funder's website.

The Stobart Newlands Charitable Trust

Christian religious and missionary causes

£2.3 million (2012)

Beneficial area

UK.

Correspondent: Ronnie Stobart, Trustee, Mill Croft, Newlands, Hesket Newmarket, Wigton, Cumbria CA7 8HP (tel: 01697 478531)

Trustees: Richard Stobart; Ronnie Stobart; Peter Stobart; Linda Rigg.

CC Number: 328464

This family trust makes up to 50 grants a year, nearly all on a recurring basis to Christian religious and missionary bodies. Unsolicited applications are most unlikely to succeed.

The trustees are directors and shareholders of J Stobart and Sons Ltd, which is the source of almost all of the trust's income.

In 2012 the trust had assets of £211,500 and an income of almost £2.3 million from donations. Grants were made totalling £2.3 million (£1.5 million in 2011).

The largest grants during the year were made to: Caring for Life (£1 million); World Vision (£360,000); Mission Aviation Fellowship (£250,000); and Operation Mobilisation (£175,000). Other beneficiaries included: Every Home Crusade (£35,000); London City Mission (£28,000); Living Well Trust (£22,000); and Release International, Trans World Radio and Christian Aid (£10,000). Grants for less than £1,000 totalled £161,500.

Exclusions

No grants for individuals.

Applications

Unsolicited applications are most unlikely to be successful.

Information gathered from:

Accounts; annual report; Charity Commission record.

The Stone Family Foundation

Relief-in-need, social welfare, overseas aid

£4.4 million (2012)

Beneficial area

Worldwide.

Correspondent: The Clerk, Coutts and Co., 440 Strand, London WC2R OQS (tel: 020 7663 6825; email: sff@thinknpc. org; website: www.thesff.com)

Trustees: Coutts and Co.; John Kyle Stone; Charles H. Edwards.

CC Number: 1108207

Registered with the Charity Commission in February 2005, the foundation's objects are to relieve hardship or distress worldwide, particularly where this hardship is as a result of natural disasters or war.

> Since September 2010, the foundation's main focus has been on water, sanitation and hygiene (WASH). Our goal is to find and support lasting and effective ways to promote good sanitation, safe water and good hygiene across the world.

In 2012 the trust had assets of £43.6 million and an income of £4.2 million. Grants were made totalling almost £4.4 million.

Beneficiaries included: Opportunity International (£733,500); WaterAid (£591,000); Water and Sanitation for the Urban Poor (£508,000); IDE Cambodia (£469,000); Acumen Fund (£415,000); Rethink (£137,000); Room to Read (£100,000); Samaritans (£60,000); Hillside Clubhouse (£45,000); Paragon Charitable Trust (£28,000); University of Oxford Development Trust (£17,000); and Rainforest Saver Foundation (£6,500).

Loans are also available.

Exclusions

No grants to individuals.

Applications

The foundation is advised on potential grant recipients by New Philanthropy Capital, and states that it is not looking for new organisations to support at present. Check the foundation's website for up-to-date information.

Information gathered from:

Accounts; Charity Commission; funder's website.

Stratford-upon-Avon Town Trust

Education, welfare, general
£1.85 million (2012)

Beneficial area

Stratford-upon-Avon.

Correspondent: Helen Munro, Chief Executive, 14 Rother Street, Stratford-upon-Avon, Warwickshire CV32 6LU (tel: 01789 207111; fax: 01789 207119; email: admin@stratfordtowntrust.co.uk; website: www.stratfordtowntrust.co.uk)

Trustees: John Lancaster, Chair; Cllr Jenny Fradgley; Jean Holder; Rosemary Hyde; Cllr Juliet Short; Carole Taylor; Tim Wightman; Clarissa Roberts; Rob Townsend; Charles Bates; Cllr Ian Fradgley.

CC Number: 1088521

The Town Trust distributes the money generated by the Guild and College Estates in accordance with the Charity Commission Scheme of October 2001. The strategic objectives of the trust up to 2016 are:

▶ Distributing our discretionary grants in accordance with our grants strategy, making the most of the budget we have available

▶ Ensuring our assets – like our properties and investments – are managed and maintained effectively, maximising the income we get to fund grants

▶ Raising our profile in the community, so that more people know what we do and how we can help

▶ Practising good financial and resource management so that we get value for money and minimise our risks

▶ Making our £1 million Community Challenge a success by attracting plenty of good quality funding applications that will benefit the people of Stratford-upon-Avon

▶ Rejuvenating the Civic Hall to create an environment that can truly be a 'hall for all'

In achieving these objectives, the trust's priority areas are:

▶ Welfare and wellbeing – addressing need and suffering caused by poverty, sickness, disability, inequality, isolation or being left out. This includes projects and groups promoting physical, mental and spiritual wellbeing, healthy living

and improving opportunities for local people to live a full and active life

▶ Strengthening communities – helping to bring and bind people in Stratford-upon-Avon together to have a voice, help one another, get involved in their community and make it stronger

▶ Young people – projects that are led by young people for young people; helping them to access opportunities, grow into responsible citizens, fulfil their potential and deal with the challenges life sometimes throws at them

Our priorities are set by the trustees and reviewed regularly to make sure they fit the trust's mission and objectives. Projects and groups that don't tackle any of the three priorities are less likely to receive a grant from us.

We expect groups looking for funding from us to have other sources of project funding, volunteers, or support in kind. They should be sound and well run, and be inclusive. We also have special grants for schools, the college and people facing hardship.

In 2012 the trust had assets of £52.4 million and an income of £3.3 million. Grants were made totalling £1.85 million, which included £1.2 million in discretionary grants and £665,000 in non-discretionary grants. The non-discretionary grants were awarded to King Edward IV Grammar School (£625,500); almshouses (£33,000); and Holy Trinity Church (£7,000).

There were 187 discretionary grants made during the year. Those of £25,000 or more, listed in the accounts, were made to: Stratford-upon-Avon Christmas Lights (£60,000); Shakespeare Hospice (£50,000); Citizens Advice (£45,000); Warwickshire Police Authority (£43,500); Stratford-upon-Avon College (£30,500); Stratford High School (£28,500); and Stratford Methodist Church (£25,000).

Exclusions

No grants to organisations outside Stratford-upon-Avon.

Applications

Application forms can be completed online at the trust's website. Awards are made on a quarterly basis. The latest application deadlines are listed on the trust's website.

Percentage of awards given to new applicants: between 10% and 20%.

Common applicant mistakes

'Thinking Stratford district is the same as the town.'

Information gathered from:

Accounts; annual report; Charity Commission record; further information provided by the funder; funder's website.

The Bernard Sunley Charitable Foundation

General
£2.5 million (2011/12)

Beneficial area

Unrestricted, but a preference for southern England.

Correspondent: John Rimmington, Director, 20 Berkeley Square, London W1J 6LH (tel: 020 7408 2198; fax: 020 7499 5859; email: office@bernardsunley. org; website: www.bernardsunley.org)

Trustees: Joan Tice; Bella Sunley; Sir Donald Gosling; Dr Brian Martin; Anabel Knight; William Tice; Inigo Paternina.

CC Number: 1109099

The foundation was established in 1960 by Bernard and Mary Sunley. Bernard Sunley 'was a pioneer in the post-war reconstruction of Britain and an entrepreneur', and his son, John Sunley, was chair of the foundation until his death in 2011. John Sunley had significant business interests in the construction industry, as well as a concern for the welfare of younger people, older people and those facing disadvantage. He was also a keen sportsman and believed in the importance of local community life. All of these factors guide the foundation's charitable activities in supporting capital projects for registered charities and Community Amateur Sports Clubs (CASC).

Joan Tice, Bella Sunley, Anabel Knight and William Tice are all members of the founding family. The external trustees are Sir Donald Gosling, founder of NCP car parks and one of Britain's wealthiest men [see also the Gosling Foundation Ltd], and Dr Brian Martin, former director of the foundation.

Guidelines

The following guidelines are provided by the foundation to potential applicants, which detail the foundation's current priorities:

There are two criteria to fulfil before applying for a grant. Please ensure you read these carefully before making an application.

1 you must be a UK registered charity or a registered Community Amateur Sports Club to apply; and

2 you are applying specifically for assistance towards a capital project: new build, refurbishment, equipment or transport. Please note that we only fund capital projects. We do not fund running costs including salaries

Our grants are divided into the following categories.

Community

Trustees consider applications for two main themes under this category with the aim of creating cohesive and positive communities.

First, trustees are strong believers that every community needs a focus on which to build the cohesion of that community. They are therefore advocates of the 'village hall', particularly in isolated rural areas where facilities are often very limited.

Secondly, trustees aim to provide practical activities that help young people attain their full potential and take their place within society as responsible citizens. To this end, they support Youth Activity Centres, uniformed youth groups and youth clubs. They also help those who are young ex-offenders, 'at risk' or in danger of exclusion.

Types of application considered

▷ New build, refurbishment and improvements of village halls, scout huts, youth clubs, community centres and similar. This often includes access for the disabled, modernising kitchens, new storage space and updating toilets in line with health and safety regulations and the Disability Discrimination Act
▷ Equipment
▷ Specialised transport
▷ IT
▷ Playgrounds

Education

Trustees continue to focus on assisting those with special educational needs. They will not support projects in mainstream schools.

Types of application considered

▷ Building projects
▷ Specialised equipment
▷ Specialised transport

Arts

Trustees have built up a history of assistance to a small number of major art galleries, where grants are usually in support of capital building projects. They will not support small town museums, short-term festivals, theatre productions or touring ensembles.

Types of application considered

▷ Building and refurbishment of large national galleries, museums and theatres where there is an emphasis on education for the whole community

Health

The trustees' interests focus on building projects for hospices, residential care housing and treatment centres, and the provision of equipment to enhance medical treatment and care.

Types of application considered

▷ New build and improvements to hospices and treatment clinics
▷ Residential care for the elderly and those with special needs
▷ New equipment
▷ Research medical equipment
▷ Specialist transport
▷ Specialist mobility equipment

Social Welfare

Applications for capital projects are considered by trustees ranging from residential housing for the homeless, many of whom suffer from drug/alcohol abuse and mental health issues, to 'day centres' giving support, training and rehabilitation, with a view to people recovering their health and self esteem and resuming their place in society. Offender rehabilitation provision comes within this category.

Types of application considered

▷ New build and refurbishment of residential premises for rehabilitation and the relief of homelessness, and accommodation for young people 'at risk
▷ 'move on' support facilities
▷ Day care/Drop-in-centres
▷ Community household furniture recycling projects

Emergency & Armed Forces

Trustees support the welfare needs of those who serve or have served in the forces and their families, particularly ex-servicemen with health and mental issues resulting from their service to the Crown. Search and Rescue facilities will also be considered within this category.

Types of application considered

▷ Building and refurbishment of residential and rehabilitation centres, and emergency control centres, which do not qualify for statutory funding
▷ Specialised transport

Environment

Trustees support education and visitor centres at wildlife sites.

Types of application considered

▷ Building education and visitor centres
▷ Information and teaching aids

Animal Welfare

Trustees support the welfare of working and farm animals.

Types of application considered

▷ Facilities for working and farm animals

Amateur Sports

Please note that you must be a registered Community Amateur Sports Club or UK registered charity to apply. Sports clubs may apply for assistance with capital projects, thereby encouraging community participation in physical activities across all ages for health, well-being, teamwork and community cohesion.

Types of application considered

▷ Building and refurbishment of amateur sports facilities
▷ Sports equipment
▷ Equipment for grounds maintenance
▷ Specialised transport

Grantmaking in 2011/12

In 2011/12 the foundation had assets of almost £84.8 million and an income of £3.2 million. There were 424 grants made during the year totalling over £2.5 million.

Grants approved were classified as follows:

Category	2011/12	1960 to 2012
Community	£387,000	£16.5 million
Social welfare	£367,000	£2.3 million
Children and youth	£358,000	£11.2 million
Arts	£357,000	£9.2 million
Health	£277,000	£20.5 million
Education	£275,000	£17.9 million
Religion	£270,000	£4.7 million
Emergency and armed serviced	£120,000	£394,000
Amateur sport	£79,000	£171,000
Animal welfare	£40,000	£127,000
Older people	£23,000	£7.6 million
Environment	–	£3.2 million
Overseas	–	£2.4 million

Note: 'Social welfare' was added as a new category in 2002. 'Animal welfare' grants have been added as a separate category since 2007, leaving 'environment' as a separate category. 'Amateur sport' and 'emergency and armed services' have been added as categories since 2007. Overseas grants are now added to the relevant category.

Beneficiaries across all categories receiving £10,000 or more included: National Gallery – Sunley Room exhibitions (£240,000); Howard League for Penal Reform and Canterbury Cathedral Development Ltd (£100,000 each); Canterbury Christ Church University St Gregory's Development Project (£50,000); Country Trust (£36,000); Royal Academy of Arts (£25,000); Children's Hospice South West (£20,000); Off The Fence Trust (£15,000); and Factory Youth Zone (Manchester) Ltd, Sheltered Work Opportunities Project, Friends of Westfield School, Guildhall School Development Fund, Addaction, Parkinson's UK, St Andrew's House – Coventry, Combat Stress and Taverham Recreation Facility (£10,000 each).

Exclusions

The foundation states:

> We would reiterate that we do not make grants to individuals; we still receive several such applications each week. This bar on individuals applies equally to those people taking part in a project sponsored by a charity such as VSO, Duke of Edinburgh Award Scheme, Trekforce, Scouts and Girl Guides, and so on, or in the case of the latter two to specific units of these youth movements.

Applications

The foundation advises:

> There is no application form, but applicants should send a letter of application to the Director (see below) by post, enclosing the latest approved set of annual report and accounts (but only if these are not on the Charity Commission's website). Please give an email address, where possible, for subsequent correspondence.

> The letter should include the following:
> ▷ The purpose of the charity and its objectives

▶ The need and purpose of the project including who will benefit and how

▶ The cost of the project, including a breakdown of costs where appropriate

▶ The amount of money raised and from whom, and how it is planned to raise the shortfall

▶ If applicable, how the running costs of the project will be met once the project is established

▶ Any other documentation that the applicant feels will help to support or explain the appeal

Processing of grants is continuous so applications can be sent at any time. All applications will be acknowledged by email on receipt, and a decision made within three months, with an answer one way or the other.

Following an application, please do not reapply for at least twelve months (from the date of your original application) as it will be declined automatically.

Percentage of awards given to new applicants: over 50%.

Common applicant mistakes

'They fail to read the guidelines for making an application accurately, which are available on the foundation's website.'

Information gathered from:

Accounts; annual report; Charity Commission record; further information provided by the funder; funder's website.

Community Foundation for Surrey

Strengthening communities
£764,000 (2011/12)

Beneficial area
Surrey.

Correspondent: Stephen Blunt, Secretary, Surrey Community Foundation, 1 Bishops Wharf, Walnut Tree Close, Guildford, Surrey GU1 4RA (tel: 01483 409230; email: info@cfsurrey. org.uk; website: www.cfsurrey.org.uk)

Trustees: Prof. Patrick Dowling, Chair; Bridget Biddell; Stephen Blunt, Secretary; Matthew Bowcock; David Frank; Peter Hampson; Gordon Lee-Steere; Jim McAllister; Tracey Reddings; Andrew Wates; Richard Whittington; Graham Williams.

CC Number: 1111600

Part of the Community Foundation Network, this foundation was set up in 2005. Its trustees include representatives from local businesses, public sector and civic leaders.

Surrey Community Foundation works with donors who want to help local people in need and give something back to the community where they live or work.

Donations make a real and lasting difference to the quality of life in Surrey

and are targeted to where needs are greatest and lasting benefits are achieved.

Grant programmes

Surrey Community Foundation currently manages and funds 107 charities, funds and foundations, most of which are based in and benefit the people of Surry. Some examples of the larger funds are:

Memsnet Community Fund
The aim of the fund is to support community and voluntary groups that work with young people, especially those involved with training in technology, in Guildford, and the surrounding area.

Dunsfold Park Fund
The fund has been established to benefit local communities in the surrounding area of Dunsfold, Alfold, Cranleigh, Bramley and Hascombe with a priority on supporting projects which benefit children and young people.

Sanofi Health in the Community Fund
This fund supports projects that promote health and well-being in the Guildford community.

Central Surrey Health Community Fund
Supports groups in Epsom, Ewell, Mole Valley and Elmbridge who are concerned with the health and well-being of local people.

As with most community foundations, funds and programmes can change frequently. Potential applicants are advised to check the foundation's website for current information.

In 2011/12 the foundation had assets of £5.4 million and an income of £840,000, which was acquired through grants, donations and investments. The charity awarded 107 grants to community and voluntary groups during the year totalling £764,000.

Applications

An 'expression of interest form' is available at the foundation's website, which all individuals and groups are advised to check for more details, as all funds have their own criteria and closing dates.

Information gathered from:

Accounts; annual report; Charity Commission record and funder's website.

The Sussex Community Foundation

Community-based projects, education, disability, health, and the relief of poverty and sickness
£829,000 (2011/12)

Beneficial area

East Sussex, West Sussex or Brighton and Hove.

Correspondent: Kevin Richmond, Administrator, Suite B, Falcon Wharf, Railway Lane, Lewes BN7 2AQ (tel: 01273 409440; email: info@sussexgiving. org.uk; website: www.sussexgiving.org. uk)

Trustees: Neil Hart; Trevor James; Richard Pearson; Elizabeth Bennett; John Peel; Kathleen Gore; Steve Manwaring; Sharon Phillips; Mike Simpkin; Humphrey Price; Michael Martin; David Allam; Charles Drayson; Consuelo Brooke.

CC Number: 1113226

Sussex Community Foundation's mission is 'to inspire local giving to meet local needs.'

According to the trustees' report for 2011/12, the charitable objects of the foundation are:

The promotion of any charitable purposes for the benefit of the community in the counties of East Sussex, West Sussex and the City of Brighton and Hove and in particular the advancement of education, the protection of good health both mental and physical and the relief of poverty and sickness. Other exclusively charitable purposes in the United Kingdom and elsewhere which are in the opinion of the trustees beneficial to the community including those in the area of benefit.

The majority of grants are between £1,000 and £5,000. Small applications of less than £1,000 are encouraged.

In 2011/12 the foundation had assets of £4.7 million and an income of £2.2 million. 308 grants were awarded totalling £829,000. The average grant award during the year was £2,500.

The trust notes its success in reaching small, local organisations with 75% of the organisations funded having an annual turnover of less than £35,000. According to the application guidance notes, larger groups with an annual turnover of more than £500,000 are less likely to be funded.

123 grants were awarded in West Sussex, 90 in East Sussex and 66 in Brighton and Hove. Four Sussex-wide projects were supported and 23 grants were awarded to national charities working in the county. 16 individuals received grants

either the Paul Rooney Foundation Fund or the Westdene Fund. 100 grants (33%) were of £1,000 or less.

Grants were categorised according to the following themes, which the trustees intend to research and develop in future years in order to guide and inform donors:

Exclusion and Isolation	87	£225,000
Children and Young People	61	£185,000
Strengthening Communities	27	£103,000
Health and Medical	48	£102,500
Arts/Culture	13	£43,500
Older People	25	£32,500
Individuals	16	£20,000
Environment and Recycling	13	£19,500
Sports and Recreation	8	£15,500
Education and Training	4	£11,500
Animals	4	£7,500
Localgiving.com grants	–	£58,000
Other	2	£5,000

Beneficiaries include: Fletcher in Rye CIC (£25,500); Keep Out Crime Diversion Scheme (£20,000); Moulsecoomb Forest Garden and Wildlife Project and City Gate Community Projects (FareShare Project) (£15,000 each); AMAZE and Kent Community Foundation (£10,000 each); and Kaleidoscope, Fun in Action for Children and Central Sussex Citizens Advice – Horsham (£6,000).

Funds available

As with many community foundations, funds regularly open and close so it is worth consulting the foundation's website prior to embarking upon an application.

The types of funds available include small grants funds, endowment funds and grassroots grants, all of which are listed on the foundation's website. Check there for current availability.

Campaigns

According to the trustees' report for 2011/12, the foundation has launched two campaigns which aimed to encourage local giving from the general public:

▷ **Surviving Winter:** this campaign encouraged locals who received a winter fuel allowance but did not need it, to donate an equivalent amount to help others facing fuel poverty. The campaign raised £28,000 in 2011/12

▷ **Localgiving.com:** this website has been developed by the Community Foundation Network and aims to help small local charities and community groups raise funds online by encouraging the general public to support local causes. The foundation raised £58,000 in 2011/12

Exclusions

According to the foundation's guidance notes (obtained from the foundation's website August 2013):

Sussex Community Foundation will not support requests from or for:

▷ Organisations that are part of central, local or regional government
▷ Organisations that discriminate on the basis of race, religion, creed, national origin, disability, age, sexual orientation, marital status
▷ Individuals – including scholarships, sponsorships and other forms of financial assistance – apart from those applying to the Paul Rooney Foundation and to the Westdene Trust
▷ Fundraising activities such as benefits, charitable dinners, or sponsored events
▷ Goodwill advertising, dinner programmes, books, magazines or articles in professional journals
▷ Political activities
▷ Major capital appeals
▷ Small contributions to major campaigns
▷ Grants which will be used to make awards to a third party
▷ Sports sponsorships
▷ Projects which only benefit animals
▷ Projects seeking funds to improve the buildings or assets of the local authority e.g.; Friends or Parents of school groups looking for funds for playgrounds, school equipment etc
▷ Projects whose wider community appeal or benefit is limited
▷ Groups who have not returned monitoring from previous SCF awards

Applications

This information was obtained from the foundation's website, as well as its application guidance notes:

Applicants must have a hard copy of the signed application and supporting documents. Applicants have to be able to show that they are not-for-profit, but do not always have to be a charity. All applicants must be working for the benefit of the people of Sussex. Only one fund can be applied for at a time. There are four grants rounds a year, occasionally more. The deadline is approximately 8 weeks prior to the panel meeting.

The 'SCF General Application form' is used for most funds; however there are certain funds which have separate forms of their own. For more information please consult the foundation's website. Each of the funds listed under 'Download Available Funds' link, which is available on the 'Apply for Funding' page, are open to applications.

Application forms and guidance notes can be downloaded from the foundation's website. Alternatively applicants can request forms by post or email by ringing 01273 409440.

On receipt of the application, the foundation will contact applicants to advise them on when they are likely to hear back on the decision.

Percentage of awards given to new applicants: between 10% and 20%.

Common applicant mistakes

'Not evidencing need; not clearly showing benefit.'

Information gathered from:
Accounts; annual report; Charity Commission record; further information provided by the funder; funder's website.

Sutton Coldfield Charitable Trust

Relief of need, arts, education, building conservation, general
£860,500 to organisations
(2011/12)

Beneficial area

The former borough of Sutton Coldfield, comprising three electoral wards: New Hall, Vesey and Four Oaks.

Correspondent: Ernest Murray, Clerk to the Trustees, Lingard House, Fox Hollies Road, Sutton Coldfield, West Midlands B76 2RJ (tel: 01213 512262; fax: 01213 130651; website: www. suttoncoldfieldcharitabletrust.com)

Trustees: Dr Freddie Gick, Chair; Dr Stephen Martin; Neil Andrews; Susan Bailey; Malcolm Cornish; John Gray; Carole Hancox; Rodney Kettel; David Owen; Rob Pocock; Jane Rothwell; David Roy; Cllr Margaret Waddington; Michael Waltho; Linda Whitfield.

CC Number: 218627

The trust, which is one of the largest and oldest local trusts in the country, dates from 1528. Until 2012 the trust was called the Sutton Coldfield Municipal Charities.

The trust states that its objectives are:
▷ Relief of poverty
▷ Education
▷ Religion
▷ Health and the saving of lives
▷ Citizenship and community development
▷ Arts, culture, heritage and science
▷ Repair of historic buildings
▷ Amateur sport
▷ The advancement of education of persons under the age of 25 through grants to schools and individuals for fees, maintenance, clothing and equipment

Grantmaking to organisations is described as follows:

Priority is given to local organisations (large and small) that provide benefits for children and adults coping with the impact of disadvantage, sickness, old age or disability. Grants are made, for example, to local hospitals, hospices and charities. Some of these, such as St Giles Hospice, are large organisations with considerable clinical and care expertise. Others are locally organised support groups, dealing, for example, with complementary care therapies, eating disorders, prostate or breathing difficulties. Christmas lunches and summer trips are funded for local elderly groups.

Sutton's schools and colleges receive grants to purchase extra facilities and equipment that they cannot fund from their normal budgets. Charitable playgroups and nurseries are supported. SCMC does not fund independent schools and nurseries.

The charity makes awards to religious organisations, especially where these serve the wider community, for example through their centres. It also promotes art, music and drama (for example, concerts at the Town Hall and the local Theatres). Recreation and leisure are supported, including some amateur sport. Where there is significant public benefit, the charity makes grants to preserve historic buildings and improve the environment.

With a few exceptions, grants are not made to groups based outside Sutton.

In 2011/12 the trust had assets of £45.1 million and an income of £1.6 million. Grants were made totalling £906,000, which included £45,500 to individuals. Total grants were broken down as follows:

Education	£318,500
Relief of need	£142,000
Health or the saving of lives	£134,000
Citizenship or community development	£111,500
Religion	£53,000
Arts, culture, heritage or science	£45,500
Environment	£12,000

A recent list of beneficiaries was not available, although due to the amount of local charities that receive support, it is likely that the list remains fairly similar each year, with Good Hope Hospital and St Giles' Hospice receiving continued support.

Exclusions

No awards are given to individuals or organisations outside the area of benefit, unless the organisations are providing essential services in the area.

Applications

To make a grant application:

- Contact the trust, either by letter, or by telephoning: 01213 512262
- Outline your needs and request a copy of the trust's guidelines for applicants
- If appropriate, seek a meeting with a member of staff in making your application
- Ensure that all relevant documents, including estimates and accounts, reach the charity by the requested dates

Receipt of applications is not normally acknowledged unless a stamped addressed envelope is sent with the application.

Applications may be submitted at any time. The grants committee meets at least eight times a year. The board of trustees must approve requests for grants over £30,000.

At all stages, staff at the trust will give assistance to those making applications. For example, projects and applications can be discussed, either at the trust's office or on site. Advice about deadlines for submitting applications can also be given.

(There are application forms for individuals, who must obtain them from the trust.)

Percentage of awards given to new applicants: less than 10%.

Common applicant mistakes

'Pre-application visits by grants manager to applicants means that no mistakes occur.'

Information gathered from:

Accounts; annual report; Charity Commission record; further information provided by the funder; funder's website.

The Sutton Trust

Education

£1.1 million (2012)

Beneficial area

UK only.

Correspondent: The Trust Administrator, 9th Floor, Millbank Tower, 21–24 Millbank, London SW1P 4QP (tel: 020 7802 1660; fax: 020 7802 1661; email: info@suttontrust.com; website: www.suttontrust.com)

Trustees: Sir Peter Lampl; David Backinsell; Glyn Morris.

CC Number: 1067197

The Sutton Trust was established in 1997 with the aim of providing educational opportunities for children and young people from non-privileged backgrounds. It has funded a large number of access projects in early years, school and university settings, and now plans to focus primarily on research and policy work, as well as a small number of innovative pilot initiatives.

The following information is given on the trust's website:

> The Sutton Trust has a rich history in funding a wide range of projects and research in the early years, primary and secondary schooling and further and higher education.
>
> Our projects have a strategic importance: they might be particularly policy relevant, fill a gap in current provision or be bold and new in content or approach.
>
> The trust takes a proactive approach to the work it wishes to support and tends to develop programmes itself, contacting the organisations it wants to partner with. The vast majority of unsolicited proposals we receive are unsuccessful. We are however willing to consider exceptional proposals which fit closely with our specific areas of interest.
>
> If you feel your organisation has a programme which might interest us, please first complete a funding enquiry on the Contact Us page [on the trust's website], including a couple of paragraphs describing your idea. If the idea is in line with our current priorities you may be asked to submit a brief proposal.

The trust's programmes fall under the headings of

- Early years
- Schools
- University
- Professions

In 2012 the trust had assets of £383,000 and an income of £1.6 million, which included a substantial donation from Sir Peter Lampl. Grants were made totalling almost £1.1 million, and were broken down as follows:

University projects	£505,500
Schools/colleges	£385,500
Early years learning	£108,000
Research projects	£69,000

Individual grant amounts were not listed in the accounts. Beneficiaries included: Cambridge University (various projects); Durham University; Feltham School; Snapethorpe Primary School; and Policy Exchange.

Applications

The trust states that it, 'is now focusing on research and policy work, and will only be funding a select handful of small scale pilot projects. We envisage that most of these projects will be developed through existing contacts and partnerships'. As such, unsolicited applications are unlikely to be successful.

Information gathered from:

Accounts; Charity Commission record; funder's website.

The John Swire (1989) Charitable Trust

General charitable purposes

£1.8 million (2012)

Beneficial area

UK.

Correspondent: Michael Todhunter, Charities Administrator, Swire House, 59 Buckingham Gate, London SW1E 6AJ (tel: 020 7834 7717)

Trustees: Sir John Swire; J. S. Swire; B. N. Swire; Michael Robinson; Lady M. C. Swire.

CC Number: 802142

Established in 1989 by Sir John Swire of John Swire and Sons Ltd, merchants and ship owners, the trust supports a wide range of organisations including some in the area of arts, welfare, education, medicine and research.

In 2012 the trust had assets of £27.4 million and an income of £2.2 million. Grants were made totalling almost £1.8 million.

Beneficiaries included: The largest grant by far – University College Oxford (£1 million); Eton College (£213,000); Catching Lives, Kew Gardens and Selling Village Hall (£20,000 each); Kent Wildlife Trust and National Trust (£11,000 each); Mary Rose Museum and The Stroke Association (£10,000 each); Canterbury Festival and Royal British Legion (£6,000 each); Smile Support and Care and Stour Music (£5,000 each); Pilgrims Hospices in Kent, RAFT and Wildlife and Wetlands Trust (£2,000 each); Atlantic Salmon Trust and Deal Festival (£1,500 each); and 999 Club, British Heart Foundation, Canterbury Choral Society, Chatham Historic Dockyard Trust, Dover Boat Trust, Essex Yeomanry, Family Links Gurkha Welfare Trust, I CAN, Maggie's Centres, NSPCC, National Back pain Association, Prostate Research Campaign UK and Reeds School (£1,000 each).

Grants of less than £1,000 amounted to a total of £22,000.

Applications

In writing to the correspondent explaining how the funds would be used and what would be achieved.

Information gathered from:

Accounts; annual report; Charity Commission record.

The Charles and Elsie Sykes Trust

General, social welfare, medical research

£489,000 (2012)

Beneficial area

UK, with a preference for Yorkshire.

Correspondent: Judith Long, Secretary, Barber Titleys Solicitors, 6 North Park Road, Harrogate, Yorkshire HG1 5PA (tel: 01423 817238; fax: 01423 851112; website: www.charlesandelsiesykestrust.co.uk)

Trustees: John Ward, Chair; Anne Brownlie; Martin Coultas; Michael Garnett; Barry Kay; Dr Michael McEvoy; Peter Rous; Dr Rosemary Livingstone; Sara Buchan.

CC Number: 206926

Charles Sykes started his career as a twelve year old office boy, and became a successful businessman in the West Riding knitting wool trade with his own four-storey mill at Princeville, Bradford.

He achieved his life ambition in his eighty-second year when he launched the Charles Sykes Trust on 16 December 1954.

In 2012 it had assets of just over £12.8 million and an income of £456,000. There were 147 grants made during the year totalling £489,000.

A wide range of causes are supported, and the trust has subcommittees to consider both medical and non-medical grants.

The following is a breakdown of the total amounts awarded in each category:

Social and moral welfare	37	£152,500
Medical research	28	£73,000
Children and youth	20	£58,000
Hospices and hospitals	8	£43,000
Cultural and environmental heritage	8	£42,000
Disability	13	£36,000
Older people	9	£28,000
Blind and partially sighted	8	£20,000
Mental health and welfare	6	£17,000
Deaf and speech impaired	3	£5,500
Medical welfare	4	£5,000
Education	1	£3,000
Services and ex-services	1	£3,000
Animals and birds	1	£2,500

Beneficiaries included: Harrogate Citizens Advice (£51,500); Alzheimer's Research UK (£25,000); Association of the Friends of Connaught Court (£10,000); Caring for Life (£7,500); Bierley Community Association Ltd, British Heart Foundation, Doncaster Housing for Young People, Sheffield Mencap and Gateway and Swaledale Festival (£5,000 each); and Carers' Resource, Harrogate (£2,000).

Exclusions

Unregistered charities and overseas applications are not considered. Individuals, local organisations not in the north of England, and recently-established charities are unlikely to be successful.

Applications

To request funding you should download and fill in the application form [available on the trust's website]. Send it to the trust along with any other relevant information, particularly enclosing a copy of your latest audited or examined accounts to the present year, together with the annual report. It is more favourable for the application if the accounts are current. If the donation is required for any particular project, please provide full details and costings.

Your request will be considered by the appropriate subcommittee, which for medical projects currently includes two doctors. The subcommittee then makes a recommendation to the next full meeting of the trustees. Please note it is the trustees' policy only to support applications from registered charities with a preference for those in or benefiting the geographical area of Yorkshire.

Applications from schools, playgroups, cadet forces, scouts, guides, and churches must be for outreach programmes, and not for maintenance projects.

Each application will be answered by letter to state if they have been rejected, or put forward for further consideration. Those that are rejected after further consideration will be duly informed. The trustees are under no obligation to state the reasons why any particular application has been rejected, and will not enter into correspondence on the matter. Successful applications will receive a donation which may or may not be subject to conditions.

All applications are dealt with at the discretion of the trustees who meet quarterly.

Information gathered from:

Accounts; annual report; Charity Commission record; funder's website.

The Tajtelbaum Charitable Trust

Jewish, welfare

£456,000 (2011/12)

Beneficial area

Generally UK and Israel.

Correspondent: Ilsa Tajtelbaum, Trustee, PO Box 33911, London NW9 7ZX

Trustees: Ilsa Tajtelbaum; Jacob Tajtelbaum; Emanuel Tajtelbaum; Eli Jaswon.

CC Number: 273184

The trust makes grants in the UK and Israel to orthodox synagogues, Jewish educational establishments, homes for older people and hospitals.

In 2011/12 the trust had assets of £4.5 million and an income of £725,000. Grants were made totalling £456,000. A list of grant beneficiaries was not included in the trust's accounts.

Previous beneficiaries include: United Institutions Arad, Emuno Educational Centre, Ruzin Sadiger Trust, Gur Foundation, Before Trust, Beth Hassidei Gur, Comet Charities Ltd, Delharville, Kupat Gemach Trust, Centre for Torah and Chesed, Friends of Nachlat David and Friends of Sanz Institute.

Applications

In writing to the correspondent.

Information gathered from:

Accounts; Charity Commission record.

The Tedworth Charitable Trust

Parenting, child welfare and development, general

£416,000 (2011/12)

Beneficial area

Unrestricted, but UK in practice.

Correspondent: Alan Bookbinder, Director, The Peak, 5 Wilton Road, London SW1V 1AP (tel: 020 7410 0330; fax: 020 7410 0332; website: www.sfct. org.uk)

Trustees: Margaret Sainsbury; Jessica M. Sainsbury; Timothy J. Sainsbury; Judith S. Portrait.

CC Number: 328524

This is one of the Sainsbury Family Charitable Trusts, which share a joint administration and have a common approach to grantmaking.

This trust's main areas of interest are parenting, family welfare, child development, arts and the environment; the trust also makes grants for general charitable purposes.

'Proposals are generally invited by the trustees or initiated at their request. Unsolicited applications are discouraged and are unlikely to be successful, even if they fall within an area in which the trustees are interested. The trustees prefer to support innovative schemes that can be successfully replicated or become self-sustaining.'

In 2011/12 the trust had assets of £10.5 million and an income of £416,500. Grants were paid during the year to 21 organisations totalling £416,000, and were broken down as follows:

Arts and the environment	12	£183,000
Parenting, family welfare and child development	4	£125,000
General	5	£108,500

Beneficiaries included: Resurgence (£60,000); Home-Start (£40,000); Open Trust (£37,000); Foundation for Democracy and Sustainable Development (£35,000); Best Beginnings (£25,000); Family Links (£20,000); Women's Environmental Network (£12,500); and Vocal Futures (£9,000).

Exclusions

Grants are not normally made to individuals.

Applications

'Proposals are likely to be invited by the trustees or initiated at their request. Unsolicited applications are unlikely to be successful, even if they fall within an area in which the trustees are interested.' A single application will be considered for support by all the trusts in the Sainsbury family group. See the separate entry for the Sainsbury Family Charitable Trusts.

Information gathered from:

Accounts; annual report; Charity Commission record; funder's website.

Tees Valley Community Foundation

General

£807,000 (2011/12)

Beneficial area

The former county of Cleveland, being the local authority areas of Hartlepool, Middlesbrough, Redcar and Cleveland and Stockton-On-Tees.

Correspondent: Hugh McGouran, Chief Executive, Wallace House, Fallon Court, Preston Farm Industrial Estate, Stockton-on-Tees TS18 3TX (tel: 01642 260860; fax: 01642 313700; email: info@ teesvalleyfoundation.org; website: www. teesvalleyfoundation.org)

Trustees: Chris Hope, Chair; Brian Beaumont; Rosemary Young; Marjory Houseman; Neil Kenley; Alan Kitching; Keith Robinson; Peter Rowley; Wendy Shepherd; Jeff Taylor; Keith Smith; Eileen Martin.

CC Number: 1111222

The foundation's main aim is the promotion of any charitable purpose for the benefit of the community in the Tees Valley and neighbouring areas. Particular focus is given to the advancement of education, arts, the environment, the protection of good health (both mental and physical) and the relief of poverty and sickness.

Support is given to local registered charities and constituted community groups run for and by local people. The foundation always has a variety of grant programmes running and new ones are regularly added. In common with many other community foundations, funds and programmes can change frequently. Check the foundation's website for up-to-date information on current programmes.

Each scheme tends to have a different application procedure and size of award.

In 2011/12 it had assets of £11 million and an income of £926,000. Grants from all funds were made to 498 beneficiaries totalling almost £807,000

The foundation's annual report gives a flavour of its achievements during the year via various funds:

Endowment Funds
During the year, 417 recipients received grants totalling £473,500 made out of income generated by endowed funds held by the foundation. Significant categories are as follows:

Pursuit of Excellence
The Pursuit of Excellence programme, which supports gifted and talented young people who excel in sports or arts activities, awarded 30 grants totalling £18,500.

Tees Power Fund
A key partner of the foundation, Tees Power works as an exceptionally active donor and plays an integral role in the awarding of its grants. This year Tees Power supported 10 groups with grant value of £18,500.

Flow Through Funds
The most significant flow through funds managed by the Foundation during the year were:

ESF Community Grants
This is a programme of funding with County Durham Community Foundation acting as the accountable body, with the Tees Valley Community Foundation and Tyne & Wear Community Foundation acting as delivery agents. The fund is to support community based groups in their delivery of employability support and training. The foundation awarded 13 grants totalling £152,000 during the year ended 31 March 2012.

Grassroots Grants
Additional Grassroots funding was secured for three Top Tier Local Authority areas, Middlesbrough, Redcar and Cleveland and Hartlepool. Grants totalling £170,000 were awarded to 61 groups.

Fair Share
At 31 March 2012 there is a balance of £48,000 remaining which is being used to deliver a sustainability programme for groups already benefiting from Fair Share Trust (FST) funding as part of the funder's legacy strategy. This programme commenced 2010 and to date has taken the form of individual diagnostic sessions with all beneficiary organisations, resulting in individually tailored sustainability strategies. This is being delivered in tandem with a programme of Fair Share Workshops delivered through a combination of professional members and the more experienced FST participants, sharing knowledge with the less developed groups. During 2011/12 these workshops were opened to a wider Stockton Voluntary and Community Sector audience to increase the opportunity for skill sharing. This work [continued] until the end of the programme in June 2013. In one specific case, Hardwick in Partnership, we are linking the FST legacy directly to the new Transforming Local Infrastructure programme of which the foundation is a key partner. This will potentially enable a community asset transfer to take place to greatly improve Hardwick in Partnership's ability to become sustainable.

Making a Difference
Three grants totalling £3,750 were made to local community groups.

Easy Access
Three grants totalling £3,000 were made under the Easy Access scheme which was funded by both Middlesbrough and Redcar & Cleveland Primary Care Trusts. This funding has now ended.

Exclusions

No grants for:

- Major fundraising appeals
- Sponsored events
- Promotion of religion
- Retrospective funding
- Holidays or social outings
- Existing operating costs, e.g. salaries, rent, overheads
- Groups with excessive unrestricted or free reserves
- Groups in serious deficit
- Replacement of statutory funding
- Meeting any need which is the responsibility of central or local government
- Religious or political causes
- Fabric appeals
- Animal welfare

Each fund has separate exclusions which are available on the foundation's website.

Applications

Application forms are available on the trust's website. Applicants can received a maximum of £5,000 in any 12 month period from one or a combination of funds.

Information gathered from:

Accounts; annual report; Charity Commission record; funder's website.

The Thompson Family Charitable Trust

Medical, veterinary, education, general

£2.9 million (2011/12)

Beneficial area
UK.

Correspondent: Katherine P. Woodward, Trustee, Hillsdown Court, 15 Totteridge Common, London N20 8LR

Trustees: David B. Thompson; Patricia Thompson; Katherine P. Woodward.

CC Number: 326801

This trust has general charitable purposes. There appears to be preferences for educational, medical and veterinary organisations, particularly those concerned with horses and horseracing. It regularly builds up its reserves to enable it to make large donations in the future, for example towards the construction of new medical or educational facilities. 'It is the policy of the charity to hold reserves which will enable [it] to make major donations for capital projects in the near future (for example, to fund the construction and endowment of new medical or educational facilities) and appropriate projects are currently being investigated. In addition to such capital projects it is envisaged that grants to other charities will in future be made at a higher annual level than in recent years.'

In 2011/12 the trust had assets of £82.5 million and an income of £5.5 million. Grants were made to 38 organisations totalling £2.9 million.

The major beneficiary during the years was the Oracle Cancer Trust, which received £1 million. Other larger grants were made to: Macmillan Cancer Support (£500,000 in total); Great Ormond Street Children's Hospital Charity (£300,000 in total); Haberdashers' Aske's Boys' School Foundation (£200,000); Starlight Children's Foundation, Stroke Association, Prostate Cancer Charity, British Heart Foundation and Dementia UK (£100,000 each).

Other beneficiaries included: Parkinson's UK (£70,000); Changing Faces (£50,000); Cambridge Women's Aid (£40,000 in total); East Anglia's Children's Hospices (£10,000); Racing Welfare Charities (£9,500 in total); Leukaemia and Lymphoma Research (£5,000); and Gentleman's Night Out Child Sponsorship (£3,000).

Exclusions

No grants to individuals.

Applications

In writing to the correspondent.

Information gathered from:

Accounts; annual report; Charity Commission record.

The Sir Jules Thorn Charitable Trust

Medical research, medicine, small grants for humanitarian charities

£3 million (2012)

Beneficial area
UK.

Correspondent: David H. Richings, Director, 24 Manchester Square, London W1U 3TH (tel: 020 7487 5851; fax: 020 7224 3976; email: info@julesthorntrust.org.uk; website: www.julesthorntrust.org.uk)

Trustees: Elizabeth S. Charal, Chair; Prof. Sir Ravinder Maini; Sir Bruce McPhail; Nancy V. Pearcey; Christopher Sporborg; William Sporborg; John Rhodes; Prof. David Russell-Jones.

CC Number: 233838

The trust was established in 1964 for general charitable purposes and its primary interest is in the field of medicine. The founder of the trust, Sir Jules Thorn, made his fortune through his company Thorn Electrical Industries. Grants are awarded to universities and hospitals in the United Kingdom to support medical research, with modest donations provided also for medically related purposes. It is a member of the Association of Medical Research Charities. Outside of medicine small grants are also made for more general causes. The trust divides its work into five areas of interest:

- Medical science/medicine
- Serious illness
- Disability
- Disadvantage
- Overcoming adversity

Programmes

The trust has rationalised its grantmaking structure into three programmes:

Medical Research

The trust's main objective is to fund translational research which will bring benefit to patients through improved diagnosis or by assisting in the development of new therapies for important clinical problems. It recognises also the importance of encouraging young scientists to pursue a career in clinical research. Its two grant schemes have been designed with those objectives in mind. All areas of research other than Cancer and HIV/AIDS are considered.

(1) The Sir Jules Thorn Award for Biomedical Research

One grant of up to £1.5 million is offered annually to support a five year programme of translational biomedical research selected following a competition among applicants sponsored by the leading UK medical schools and NHS organisations.

UK medical schools and NHS organisations are eligible to submit one application annually.

Full guidance notes are available from the trust's website and potential applicants are encouraged to contact the trust before applying.

(2) The Sir Jules Thorn PhD Scholarship Programme

Three grants are available annually to support high quality postgraduate research training in UK medical schools under the supervision of a Senior Clinical Lecturer. A scholarship meets the cost of a stipend, tuition fees and consumables over a 3 year course of study leading to a PhD degree.

Scholarships are available only through medical schools invited to participate. Each November, selected medical schools are invited to apply for one scholarship to fund a three-year research project in the laboratory of a nominated Senior Clinical Lecturer who will supervise the PhD student. If the application is approved by the trust, the medical school is able to advertise the scholarship to postgraduate students. The successful applicant, chosen competitively, will commence the project in the following Summer.

The Ann Rylands small grants programme

Named after the daughter of the settlor and late chair of the trust, these small humanitarian grants are to encourage the work of smaller and medium sized charities. often operating within local communities, albeit that they may have a national reach.

Sir Jules Thorn was a great humanitarian and whilst his endowment was provided primarily for medicine and medical research, he was content for some funds to be allocated to charities in response to appeals of a humanitarian nature. Accordingly, the trustees earmark some resources each year for such purposes. The trust receives many more appeals than it can support with a grant. Each case is treated on its merits and the trustees' policy is to spread the funds as widely as possible.

Successful applicants are awarded grants of up to £1,500. Many charities have received grants over a number of years. Requests are considered for contributions to core funding or for specific projects, but this programme does not provide substantial sums for capital appeals.

Note that the Ann Rylands Special Project programme has been discontinued.

Medically-related donations

The trustees endeavour to allocate some funds each year for medicine generally, in addition to their primary commitment to medical research. They keep in mind Sir Jules Thorn's concern to alleviate the suffering of patients and to aid diagnosis.

The resources available are limited and depending on the appeals received the trustees may allocate the total fund in any one year to just one project, or divide it between several deserving appeals. Grants are awarded for a wide range of purposes. They may be linked to a very large appeal to expand important facilities for research in medical schools or to enhance patient care in hospitals. Other grants go to charities whose work is devoted to the care and comfort of patients with distressing clinical conditions. Grants under this programme are not provided for medical research and may only be used for capital projects (not operational funding).

Grantmaking in 2012

In 2012 the trust had assets of £105.6 million and an income of £2.5 million. There were 430 grants paid during the year totalling £3 million, with most grants by number (409) being small grants. Note that the following breakdown of grants refers to the old grant programmes:

Medical research grants	£1.7 million
Other medically-related grants	£790,000
Small grants	£329,000
Capital grants to hospitals and universities	£194,000

Newcastle University received the Sir Jules Thord Award for Biomedical research worth £1.5 million over a period of up to five years for a proposed study: 'Bringing the next generation sequencing to the next generation: early diagnosis of inherited immune deficiency'.

PhD scholarships totalling £244,500 were awarded to the universities of Liverpool, Dundee and Southampton.

Three capital grants to hospitals and universities were made: Southampton Hospital Charity 'Red and White' Appeal (£100,000) towards the creation of a specialist Day Case Treatment Unit for patients with leukaemia and other forms of life threatening blood cancer; Queen Elizabeth Hospital Birmingham (£50,000) towards the purchase of a CyberKnife robotic radiotherapy system to improve the treatment of cancer patients and Yeovil Hospital (£50,000) towards the Flying Colours appeal for a new Special Care Baby Unit at the Women's Hospital.

Other medically related grants included: North East Autism Society and Kirkwood Hospice (£100,000 each); Sunfield Children's Homes (£80,000); The Meath Epilepsy Trust, Sue Ryder Thorpe Hall Hospice, Bury Hospice and Tenovus (£50,000 each).

Small grants included: Willen Hospice (£5,000); Changing Faces, Ian Rennie Grove House Hospice Care, The Air Ambulance Service and The Rossendale Trust (£1,500 each); Bliss – The National Charity for the Newborn, Bolton Hospice, British Liver Trust, Friends of the Elderly, Scottish Huntington's Association and St Wilfred's Hospice Foundation (£1,250 each); Autism Bedfordshire, Beating Bowel Cancer, Dogs for the Disabled and British Refugee Council (£1,000 each); Guildford Action for Community Care, Launchpad Reading, Music in Hospitals (Scotland) and Relate Avon (£750 each); and Dyspraxia Foundation, East Bristol Advice and Information Centres, Sportability and Sailor's Society (£500 each).

Exclusions

The trust does not fund:

- Research which is considered unlikely to provide clinical benefit within five years
- Research which could reasonably be expected to be supported by a disease specific funder, unless there is a convincing reason why the trust has been approached
- Research into cancer or AIDS, for the sole reason that they are relatively well funded elsewhere
- Top up grants for ongoing projects
- Research which will also involve other funders
- Individuals – except in the context of a project undertaken by an approved institution which is in receipt of a grant from the trust
- Research or data collection overseas
- Research institutions which are not registered charities
- Third parties raising resources to fund research themselves

Applications

The Sir Jules Thorn Award

Applicants should first contact the trust to discuss their proposal before applying. Full guidance notes are available online and the deadline for applications is usually in the autumn.

The Sir Jules Thorn PhD Scholarship Programme

Scholarships are available only through medical schools invited to participate.

Medically related donations

Organisations seeking a medically related donation should download, complete and return the 'expression of interest form' as an email attachment to: donations@julesthorntrust.org.uk. Applicants should also attach an electronic copy of their latest trustee's report and financial statements. The trust chairman and director review all expressions of interest to decide whether a full application will be request for consideration by the board of trustees. The final decision as to whether an award is made and the amount rests with the trustees.

Ann Rylands Small donations programme

Applications are accepted, and preferred, online. However application forms can also be downloaded and sent to the trust by email or post. However, the trust does advise that online applications save both time and money.

Percentage of awards given to new applicants: between 30% and 40%.

Common applicant mistakes

'Not completing the small donations application form correctly, in full or at all. Not attaching required supporting information (budgets, trustees' report and financial statements etc.) in correct format or at all.'

Information gathered from:

Accounts; annual report; Charity Commission record; guidelines for applicants; further information provided by the funder; funder's website.

The Three Guineas Trust

Autism and Asperger's Syndrome, climate change
£1 million (2011/12)
Beneficial area
Worldwide, in practice mainly UK.

Correspondent: Alan Bookbinder, Director, The Peak, 5 Wilton Road, London SW1V 1AP (tel: 020 7410 0330; fax: 020 7410 0332; website: www.sfct. org.uk)

Trustees: Clare Sainsbury; Bernard Willis; Dominic Flynn.

CC Number: 1059652

This is one of the Sainsbury Family Charitable Trusts, which share a joint administration. They have a common approach to grantmaking which is described in the entry for the group as a whole.

Clare Sainsbury established the Three Guineas Trust in 1996 for general charitable purposes. The trust's focus is in the area of autism and the related Asperger's Syndrome, and more recently, significant grants have been awarded for research into climate change.

There is a specific fund to enable people in developing countries to hire autism practitioners from the UK to deliver practical, one-off training courses for professionals and parents in countries which have little current provision for autistic children and adults.

In 2011/12 the trust had assets of £14.9 million and an income of £1.5 million. Grants paid during the year, including commitments from previous years, totalled just over £1 million.

The trust regularly supports the University of Cambridge for a project to construct a new global economic model of a world free from dependence on carbon – this is currently the only climate change project the trust supports. During the year the university received £581,000.

Other beneficiaries included: Autism Cymru (£139,500); Turning the Red Lights Green (£72,000); Action for ASD (£45,000); and Resources for Autism (£25,000). The trust also awarded grants towards summer activity programmes for children with autistic spectrum disorders, with beneficiaries including: Blackpool Tiggers (£9,000); Killamarsh Autistic and PDA Support Group (£6,000); Disabilities and Self Help and Project Art Works (£5,000 each); and Helping Hands Autism Support Group (£3,500).

Exclusions
No grants for individuals or for research (except where it has an immediate benefit).

Applications
See the guidance for applicants in the entry for the Sainsbury Family Charitable Trusts. A single application will be considered for support by all the trusts in the group.

> The trustees do not at present wish to invite applications, except in the field of autism and Asperger's syndrome, where they will examine unsolicited proposals alongside those that result from their own research and contacts with expert individuals and organisations working in this field. The trustees prefer to support innovative schemes that can be successfully replicated or become self-sustaining. They are also keen that, wherever possible, schemes supporting adults and teenagers on the autistic spectrum should include clients/service users in decision-making.

Information gathered from:
Accounts; annual report; Charity Commission record.

The Tolkien Trust

General
£650,000 (2012/13)
Beneficial area
UK, with some preference for Oxfordshire, and overseas.

Correspondent: Cathleen Blackburn, Administrator, c/o Maier Blackburn LLP, Prama House, 267 Banbury Road, Oxford OX2 7HT (website: www. tolkientrust.org)

Trustees: Christopher Reuel Tolkien; Priscilla Mary Anne Reuel Tolkien; Michael Reuel Tolkien; Baillie Tolkien.

CC Number: 1150801

The trust's main assets are the copyrights in relation to certain works written by the late J. R. R. Tolkien including Smith of Wootton Major, Tree and Leaf, Roverandom and Mythopoeia. Although the trust has no permanent endowment, there should always be an income from book royalties during the period of copyright.

There are no specific guidelines for applicants. Grants are made to charities and charitable causes supporting children and young people, families, older people, the homeless and the socially disadvantaged, overseas aid and development, refugees, medical aid, research and education. Grants are also made to religious and arts organisations.

In September 2009 the trust reached an out-of-court settlement with New Line Cinema regarding the trust's entitlement to its share of the profits from the hugely successful Lord of the Rings trilogy of films. As a result, the trust's grantmaking capacity has increased in recent years. During 2010/11 the trust reviewed it policies and decide to give grants to fewer charities, but develop closer relationships with those charities, presumably with a view to making larger grants and/or supporting them over a number of years dependent on them demonstrating that they are spending their grants effectively.

In May 2013 the Tolkien Trust (Charity Commission no. 273615) ceased to exist, with funds being transferred to create this trust. No accounts were available for the new incarnation of the trust at the time of writing (December 2013), but for reference the previous trust held assets of around £27 million, with an annual income of around £1.7 million, mostly from royalties. The level of grantmaking was around £650,000 per year. Given the recent production of a new trilogy of films based on The Hobbit, it is likely that assets and income for this trust will increase.

The following information is taken from the trust's website:

> The trust is wholly discretionary, which means that its constitution does not impose any limitations on the charities it may benefit; it is therefore free to select those causes of interest to it.
>
> The trust does not publish any guidelines concerning the charities of interest to it but its filed accounts give an indication of the nature and number of causes benefited in recent years. Many of the chosen charities are benefited on an annual basis, and a large number have received support from the trust for many years.
>
> The trust has traditionally supported a wide spectrum of charitable causes throughout the world including:
> - Emergency and disaster relief
> - Overseas aid and development
> - The homeless and refugees
> - Healthcare charities, especially those focusing on illnesses of childhood and old age, the needs of disadvantaged communities and medical research
> - Religious causes promoting peace and reconciliation and work with impoverished communities
> - Environmental causes
> - Education and the arts

Previous beneficiaries include: Bodleian Library; Rebuilding Sri Lanka; Medical Foundation; Friends of the Connection at St Martin-in-the-Fields; Prisoners' Education Trust; Music in Lyddington; Cancer Active; Friends of Cardigan Bay; Shakespeare Link; and Marymount of Santa Barbara.

Exclusions
No grants to individuals.

Applications

In writing to the correspondent. Applications must be posted and email applications will not be accepted. The majority of donations are made to charities or causes selected by the trustees. There are no guidelines for applicants and the trust does not enter into correspondence with applicants in the interests of controlling administrative costs. It is left to the discretion of applicants how they feel they can best present their case for support. Decisions about donations annually at the end of March/beginning of April. Therefore, any applications should be timed to reach the trust by no later than 15 December in the preceding year.

Information gathered from:

Charity Commission record; funder's website.

The Tompkins Foundation

General

£345,500 (2011/12)

Beneficial area

UK, with a preference for the parishes of Hampstead Norreys, Berkshire and West Grinstead, West Sussex.

Correspondent: Richard Geoffrey Morris, Administrator, 7 Belgrave Square, London SW1X 8PH (tel: 020 7235 9322; fax: 020 7259 5129)

Trustees: Elizabeth Tompkins; Peter Vaines.

CC Number: 281405

The foundation was established in 1980 by Granville Tompkins, founder of Green Shield Stamps and the Argos retail chain, primarily for the advancement of education, learning and religion and the provision of facilities for recreation and other purposes beneficial to the community. However, most beneficiaries tend to be medical or health-related organisations. 'The trustees aim to respond to need and therefore consider that more specific plans [for the future] would be too restrictive.'

In 2011/12 the foundation had assets of £11 million and an income of £349,000. Grants were made to 20 organisations totalling £345,500, with 13 of the beneficiaries having received donations in the previous year.

The beneficiaries included: Arthroplasty for Arthritis (£50,000); Great Ormond Street Hospital Children's Charity (£30,000); Foundation of Nursing Studies and Chicken Shed Theatre (£25,000 each); Order of Malta Volunteers (£20,000); British Association

for Adoption and Fostering and Toynbee Hall (£10,000 each); Anna Freud Centre (£5,000); and Momentum Skills (£2,000).

Exclusions

No grants to individuals.

Applications

In writing to the correspondent, although unsolicited applications are unlikely to be successful as the trust has a regular list of charities which receive support.

Information gathered from:

Accounts; Charity Commission record.

The Constance Travis Charitable Trust

General

£1.2 million (2012)

Beneficial area

UK (national charities only); Northamptonshire (all sectors).

Correspondent: Ernest R. A. Travis, Trustee, Quinton Rising, Quinton, Northampton NN7 2EF

Trustees: Constance M. Travis; Ernest R. A. Travis; Peta J. Travis; Matthew Travis.

CC Number: 294540

Established in 1986, the trust has general charitable purposes, supporting local organisations in Northamptonshire as well as organisations working UK-wide and internationally.

In 2012 the trust had assets of £74.4 million and an income of £2.4 million. Grants were made during the year totalling almost £1.2 million, and were categorised as follows:

Medical, health and sickness	£251,500
Environment, conservation and heritage	£247,000
Arts and culture	£230,500
Community development	£206,500
Disability	£55,000
Religious activities	£46,000
Education and training	£37,000
Relief of poverty	£25,000
Accommodation and housing	£17,000
General	£14,000
Sport and recreation	£12,000
Overseas aid	£11,000
Animals	£6,000

Grants of £10,000 or more included those to: Royal Academy of Music (£210,000); Delapre Abbey Preservation Trust (£150,000); Northamptonshire Community Foundation (£115,000); Royal Albert Hall (£50,000); UCL Cancer Institute Research Trust (£20,000); Volunteer Reading Help (£15,000); and Alzheimer's Research Trust (£10,000).

Exclusions

No grants to individuals or non-registered charities.

Applications

In writing to the correspondent. Trustees meet at least quarterly. The trust's accounts note that 'though the trustees make grants with no formal application, they may invite organisations to submit a formal application'.

The trust does not welcome contact prior to applications.

Percentage of awards given to new applicants: between 10% and 20%.

Common applicant mistakes

'We only give to registered charities. We often get applications from unregistered charities.'

Information gathered from:

Accounts; annual report; Charity Commission record; further information provided by the funder.

The Triangle Trust (1949) Fund

Social welfare, health, people with disabilities, integration and general
£312,500 to organisations
(2012/13)

Beneficial area

Worldwide. In practice UK.

Correspondent: Dr Joanne Knight, Director, Foundation House, 2–4 Forum Place, Fiddlebridge Lane, Hatfield, Hertfordshire AL10 0RN (tel: 01707 707078; email: info@triangletrust.org.uk; website: www.triangletrust.org.uk)

Trustees: Melanie Burfitt, Chair; Dr Robert Hale; Mark Powell; Bruce Newbigging; Kate Purcell; Jamie Dicks; Helen Evans; Andrew Pitt.

CC Number: 222860

The trust was set up in 1949 by Sir Henry Jephcott, a pharmaceutical industrialist and former managing director of Glaxo Laboratories Ltd. In 2012 the trustees made the decision to become more focused and only support specialist organisations working with carers or the rehabilitation of ex-offenders.

The following information is taken from the trust's website:

What we fund
We offer funding for specialist community and voluntary organisations working with carers or the rehabilitation of offenders or ex-offenders within the UK.

Development Grants
The Triangle Trust recognises in the current economic climate, building a solid

foundation for long-term sustainability for your organisation can be of higher importance than starting a new project. We therefore offer development grants to provide funds towards your organisation's core costs.

We would like to see applicants use these grants to develop sustainable income sources, so that when our grant comes to end your organisation's income will not be reduced.

Grants are available for up to £40,000 or 50% of the organisation's current annual income, whichever is lowest, per year for 3 years. We would expect to see the amount requested each year tapering down as applicants develop other income streams to replace the grant income. The 50% of annual income limit is in place to discourage smaller organisations making an unrealistic step change in income that cannot be sustained when the grant ends.

Applicant criteria
Applicants must be a registered charity, not-for-profit social enterprise or community interest company working within the UK with a UK office. Social enterprise and community interest companies must have a governing document which shows the name, aim/purpose, objects of the group, including a dissolution clause – what happens if your group ceases to function. This clause should show that you are a not-for-profit group by confirming that any assets remaining after all debts are paid will be given to another voluntary group with similar aims. This document should also include details of your trustees or management committee.

The primary purpose of applicants' constitution must be to support unpaid carers or the rehabilitation of offenders or ex-offenders. (Organisations with a broader remit running a project to support unpaid carers or the rehabilitation of offenders or ex-offenders are not eligible to apply.) Applicants may be involved in providing direct practical support work, research projects or policy or campaigning work relevant to unpaid carers or the rehabilitation of offenders or ex-offenders.

Applicants must demonstrate in their application how they have expertise and a history of working with unpaid carers or offenders. Applicants must have some volunteer input, and annual income for the most recent financial year should be less than £2 million, although priority will be given to smaller organisations. Shortlisted applicants will be required to have a strategic plan in place ready to be presented during stage two of the application process.

Applicants must make a commitment to develop sustainable income streams during the grant period and should have evaluation systems for their work in place, and if not, part of the grant should be used to put a system in place. All previous successful and unsuccessful applicants to The Triangle Trust are welcome to apply.

Grant details
Any costs incurred by the applicant in undertaking its core business can be covered by the grant. We would expect to see the amount requested each year tapering down as applicants develop other sustainable income streams.

In 2012/13 the trust had assets of £17.7 million and an income of £630,000. Grants were made to organisations during the year totalling £312,500 – this included commitments from previous years within themes and purposes the trust no longer supports.

Exclusions
The trust will not fund the following:
▶ Overseas charities or projects outside the UK
▶ Charities for the promotion of religion
▶ Medical research
▶ Environmental, wildlife or heritage appeals

Also refer to the trust's eligibility criteria in the general section.

Applications
The following information was taken from the trust's website:

We will be holding one round of development grants per year for organisations working with carers, and one round per year for organisations working with the rehabilitation of offenders or ex-offenders. This will ensure applicants have a higher success rate and high quality applications are not rejected, compared to holding two or more rounds with lower success rates.

The application process will be two-stage. Following the submission of your initial online application, shortlisted applicants will be asked to host a visit from the Triangle Trust where they will be required to present their strategic plan for the next few years.

Only complete applications submitted using the online form by 5 pm on the published closing date [see the trust's website] will be accepted. Please ensure you meet all the criteria before deciding to apply.

Common applicant mistakes
'Applying when they are not eligible.'

Information gathered from:
Accounts; Charity Commission record; further information provided by the funder; funder's website.

The True Colours Trust

Special needs, sensory disabilities and impairments, palliative care, carers
£1.7 million (2011/12)

Beneficial area
UK and Africa.

Correspondent: Alan Bookbinder, Director, The Peak, 5 Wilton Road, London SW1V 1AP (tel: 020 7410 0330; fax: 020 7410 0332; email: truecolours@ sfct.org.uk; website: www. truecolourstrust.org.uk)

Trustees: Lucy Sainsbury; Dominic Flynn; Bernard Willis; Tim Price.

CC Number: 1089893

Established in 2001, this is one of the newest of the Sainsbury family charitable trusts. The following detailed information on the trust's interests and activities is taken from its 2011/12 annual report:

The True Colours Trust seeks to make a positive difference to the lives of children with special needs and their families and to support people with life limiting and/or life threatening illnesses. The Trustees grant-making continues to focus in the following three areas:
▶ Improving the service delivery and support offered to children and young people with complex disabilities and palliative care needs in the UK
▶ Strengthening the support offered to the families and siblings of children and young people with complex disabilities and palliative care needs in the UK
▶ Promoting and developing palliative care for adults and children in sub-Saharan Africa

The trust's work concentrates on the major barriers and challenges experienced by families, children and young people with complex disabilities and/or life limiting and life threatening conditions. The trust works closely with organisations that share its ambitions to provide imaginative, practical and often ground-breaking services in addition to delivering programmes that bring about sustained change whether at the level of policy or practice.

The trustees are advised by Joan Marston and Maggie Baxter on their work in Africa and by Christine Lenehan on their work in the UK.

Children and young people with complex disabilities in the UK
Research commissioned by the trust in 2004 showed that 55% of families with a disabled child live on the poverty line, primarily because of the costs of raising a disabled child. It also highlighted the emotional strain most families live with and the desperate need for respite care, appropriate childcare provision and accessible activities and services for disabled children. Although progress has

been made over the last eight years, there is still a long way to go.

The trustees remain committed to making life better for children and young people with profound disabilities and their families and to tackling the structural barriers which hinder these children, and their families, from living happy fulfilled lives.

The trustees' grant-making in this category is focused on the following areas:

- Support for organisations leading the way in developing services and opportunities for children and their families
- Raising the profile of disabled children and their families with central and local government
- Raising the profile of the siblings of disabled children and supporting services to meet their needs

The trustees were delighted by the achievements of the Every Disabled Child Matters Campaign which has been very successful in raising the profile of disabled children and securing additional Government funding. They have supported the campaign since its inception and continue to do so to ensure that national commitments to disabled children and their families are honoured.

The trustees have been particularly impressed by two other organisations in the sector: Heart n Soul, which gives training and performance opportunities to artists with learning disabilities, and Netbuddy, an on-line organisation which captures and shares parents' expertise in caring for a child with complex disabilities. In very different ways, both organisations give children, young people and their families unique resources and opportunities to live fulfilled lives.

Palliative care for children and young people in the UK

The trustees believe that all children and young people with a life limiting or life threatening illness have the right to quality palliative care. The trustees subscribe to the WHO definition of palliative care.

Palliative care improves the quality of life of patients and their families facing the problems associated with life limiting illnesses. It treats the patient's pain and symptoms and it is applicable early in the course of an illness, in conjunction with curative treatments, and at the end of life. Crucially palliative care also supports the patient's family through the illness and their bereavement.

The understanding and provision of palliative care for children and young people in the UK are inconsistent. Although there are some excellent service providers, too few families receive the help they need during a very difficult time in their lives. There should be a range of services available to allow children and families to choose how and where they receive support. There should also be specific support available to help parents and siblings through a very emotional and challenging time.

The trustees were delighted that children's services were included in the independent review into palliative care funding in England, commissioned by the Secretary of State for Health in 2010. They look forward to seeing the findings from the children's pilots next year and to a future in which there is a fair and transparent funding system, as the review set out to create.

The trustees continue to support the development of the children's palliative care sector through grants, which have been used for a variety of different purposes, from influencing national policy to demonstrating best practice at local, regional and national levels.

This year the trustees have focused on the following areas:

- Improving the quality and coverage of bereavement services for children and young people through a core grant to the Childhood Bereavement Network
- Supporting excellence and innovation at a local and regional level through grants to the Jessie May Trust in Bristol and St Oswald's Hospice in Newcastle
- Improving the sector's infrastructure by supporting the merger of the Association of Children's Palliative Care (ACT) and Children's Hospices UK to create a single national voice for children's palliative care – Together for Short Lives

Alongside these new grants, the trustees continue to support the UK's first Professorial Chair in Palliative Care for Children and Young People and a regional pilot of 24-hour support for children with palliative care needs.

Palliative care in sub-Saharan Africa

The need for palliative care is particularly acute in sub-Saharan Africa where it is estimated that there are 22 million people living with HIV, and that the number of people with cancer will double in the next twenty years. The lack of availability of opioids for the treatment of moderate to severe pain, as recommended by the WHO, means that people with life limiting illnesses suffer unnecessarily. In addition, the widespread introduction of anti-retroviral drugs has not decreased the need for palliative care; patients are living longer but are still ageing and suffering from symptoms of HIV as well as side effects of the medication.

The trustees are committed to improving access to affordable palliative care for adults and children in sub-Saharan Africa, prioritising the need for appropriate pain relief and the integration of palliative care services into established health systems.

This year the trust joined forces with five other organisations working on palliative care in Africa to form the 'Waterloo Coalition': a time-limited initiative to improve significantly access to palliative care in Malawi and Kenya between April 2011 and December 2012. The Coalition comprises The Diana, Princess of Wales Memorial Fund, the African Palliative Care Association, the Global Access to Pain Relief Initiative, the International Children's Palliative Care Network, the Worldwide Palliative Care Alliance and the True Colours Trust.

The Coalition worked pro-actively to identify and support in-country partners who could work alongside government providers to increase the number of patients accessing palliative care. This was done by replicating successful projects, training staff and ensuring access to essential drugs. In both Malawi and Kenya, there has been a significant increase in the number of people who have been able to access palliative care and appropriate pain relief as a result of funding from the Coalition. Health professionals have been trained and undertaken clinical placements, new palliative care units have been established in a number of hospitals and systems for ordering and supplying morphine have been strengthened significantly.

The trust also continues its work to:

- Increase awareness of palliative care and influence policy at a regional and international level through strategic grants to the African Palliative Care Association and the International Children's Palliative Care Network
- Improve access to palliative care services and opioids in Zambia
- Support palliative care services across the continent through a small grants programme, administered by the African Palliative Care Association

Small grants UK

The trustees are committed to supporting a large number of excellent local organisations and projects that work with disabled children and their families on a daily basis. This is done through the trust's small grants programme. It provides grants of up to £10,000 to help smaller organisations develop and deliver programmes for children, their siblings and families. It is open to applications at any time. Grants in this category are usually one-off contributions rather than multi-year grants for on-going revenue costs.

The trustees are particularly keen to support:

- Hydrotherapy pools
- Multi-sensory rooms
- Mini buses
- Young carers projects
- Sibling projects
- Bereavement support
- Specialised play equipment

Grantmaking in 2011/12

In 2011/12 the trust had assets of almost £9.9 million and an income of just over £1.7 million, mostly from donations. Grants were paid during the year totalling £1.7 million, and were broken down as follows:

Palliative care for children and young people in the UK	46%	£775,000
Palliative care in sub-Saharan Africa	29%	£483,500
Children and young people with complex disabilities in the UK	17%	£292,000
Small grants UK	7%	£123,500
General	1%	£1,300

Beneficiaries during the year (of both paid and approved grants) included: Childhood Bereavement Network (£405,000), towards the organisation's core costs over three years; Council for Disabled Children (£312,000), towards the core costs of the Every Disabled Child Matters campaign over three years and the development of resources to help parents understand Health and Safety legislation and their child's rights in this context; African Palliative Care Association (£200,000), towards the organisation's core costs over two years; Jessie May Trust (£150,000), towards the salary of a band 5 nurse and a contribution towards core costs over three years; Kenya Hospices and Palliative Care Association (£120,500), towards the costs of establishing integrated palliative care services in Kenya's 11 national referral hospitals and towards the development of a higher diploma in palliative care at Kenya Medical Training College; St Oswald's Hospice (£60,000), towards a two-year appointment of a part-time consultant in Paediatric Palliative Care to work across North East England; and Heart n Soul (£28,000), a one-off grant towards the organisation's core costs.

Small grants to UK organisations included those to: Julia's House (£11,500), towards its sibling support programme; Chicken Shed Theatre Company (£10,000), towards the purchase of a specially adapted minibus; Go Kids Go – Association of Wheelchair Children (£6,500), towards the cost of wheelchair training workshops; and Noah's Ark – The Children's Hospice (£5,000), towards its siblings support programme.

Exclusions

The trust does not give direct support for:

- Individuals
- Educational fees
- Expeditions

Applications

The following information is taken from the trust's website:

Programme Grants

The trust only funds registered charities or activities with clearly defined charitable purposes.

Trustees only consider unsolicited applications for their Small Grants Programmes (UK and Africa) and for their Individual Grants UK programme. Proposals for the trust's other programmes are invited by the trustees or initiated at their request. The trustees are keen to learn more about organisations whose work fits into the categories above but unsolicited applications are not encouraged and are unlikely to be successful.

Information about your organisation and project should be sent by post to The True Colours Trust, The Peak, 5 Wilton Road, London SW1V 1AP, please do not send more than 2 pages of A4 covering:

- The organisation – explaining its charitable aims and objectives, and giving its most recent annual income and expenditure, and current financial position. Please do not send a full set of accounts
- The project requiring funding – why it is needed, who will benefit and in what way
- The funding – breakdown of costs, any money raised so far, and how the balance will be raised
- At this stage please do not send supporting books, brochures, DVDs, annual reports or accounts

All correspondence will be acknowledged by post. If your organisation is a candidate for support, you will hear from us within 12 weeks of the acknowledgement. Applicants who do not hear from us within this time must assume they have been unsuccessful.

Small Grants – UK and Africa

The trustees welcome unsolicited applications for their small grants programmes, both in the UK and in Africa. Trustees are keen to make these programmes available to as many organisations as possible; it is therefore unlikely that they will fund any organisation in consecutive years.

UK

The trustees are committed to supporting a large number of excellent local organisations and projects that work with disabled children and their families on a daily basis. This is done through the trust's small grants programme. It provides grants of up to £10,000 to help smaller organisations develop and deliver programmes for children, their siblings and families. It is open to applications at any time. Grants in this category are usually one-off contributions rather than multi-year grants for on-going revenue costs.

Please note the following:

- This programme is for UK organisations and projects only
- The programme is unable to provide support to local authorities
- Trustees are keen to make the grant programme available to as many organisations as possible; it is therefore unlikely that they will fund organisations in consecutive years

Upon submission of your application you will receive an acknowledgement letter or email. If you do not hear from us within twelve weeks of the date of this acknowledgement please accept that the trustees, with regret, have not been able to make a grant in response to your appeal. You will not receive a letter explaining that your application has been unsuccessful.

Applications for small grants should be made using our online application form or alternatively you may complete the downloadable version of the form and either return to us by post or email.

Information gathered from:

Accounts; annual report; Charity Commission record; funder's website.

The Trusthouse Charitable Foundation

General
£2.1 million (2011/12)

Beneficial area
Unrestricted, but mainly UK.

Correspondent: Judith Leigh, Grants Manager, 6th Floor, 65 Leadenhall Street, London EC3A 2AD (tel: 020 7264 4990; website: www. trusthousecharitablefoundation.org.uk)

Trustees: Sir Jeremy Beecham; Baroness Sarah Hogg; The Duke of Marlborough; Anthony Peel; The Hon. Olga Polizzi; Sir Hugh Rossi; Lady Janet Balfour of Burleigh; Sir John Nutting; Howell Harris-Hughes; Revd Rose Hudson-Wilkin; Lady Hamilton.

CC Number: 1063945

The Trusthouse Charitable Foundation was formed out of a trust operated by the Council of Forte plc which inherited investments in the Granada Group. Its objects are such general charitable purposes as the trustees in their discretion may from time to time determine.

The foundation is administered on a day-to-day basis on behalf of the trustees by the Henry Smith Charity, although each charity is entirely independent.

The foundation's website gives the following information about its grantmaking objectives and policies:

Guidelines

Trusthouse gives grants for running costs or one-off capital costs to charities and not-for-profit organisations in accordance with criteria that are regularly reviewed and decided by the trustees.

In July 2008, the trustees reviewed its grants policy and decided to concentrate on projects addressing Rural Issues and Urban Deprivation.

Rural Issues

We accept applications from organisations which are addressing issues in rural areas. 'Rural' in this context means cities, towns, villages and areas with 10,000 or less inhabitants. We are interested in, for example, projects providing transport for the elderly, disabled or disadvantaged; contact networks for the young disabled; projects which encourage a sense of community such as community centres and village halls; employment training schemes especially those promoting local, traditional crafts; projects addressing issues such as drug/alcohol misuse or homelessness.

Urban Deprivation

We will accept applications from local or national charities or not-for-profit organisations which are working with residents of urban areas (i.e. more than 10,000 inhabitants) which are classified in the latest government Indices of Multiple Deprivation as being in the lowest 20%. We are interested in, for example, youth clubs; training schemes to help people out of unemployment; drop in centres for the homeless.

Applicants must clearly show in their appeal how their project fits into one or both of these categories.

Within these overarching themes, we are interested in three areas [displayed in the box below].

Types of Grant

What type of grant you apply for depends on:

- The annual income of your organisation
- The grant amount you are looking for
- Whether you are looking for capital costs or for running (i.e. core, salary or project) costs

Please note:
- All grants are for 1 year only. Trusthouse prefers not to make grants in successive years
- Organisations with an income over £500,000 are not eligible for Small Grants or Fast Track grants
- Organisations with an income over £5 million are not eligible under any of the grant schemes
- Capital projects are only eligible where the total cost is £1 million or less
- Hospices are eligible for capital grants even if their income is over £5 million and the total project cost is over £1 million

Grants in 2011/12

During the year the foundation had assets of £61.4 million and an income of £1 million. There were 284 grants paid totalling just under £2.1 million, distributed as follows (including support costs):

Youth	£338,500
Community centres	£279,000
Heritage	£236,000
Disabilities	£188,500
Community support services	£188,000
Overseas	£169,500
Arts	£117,500
Older people	£94,000
Homelessness	£79,500
Family support services	£50,500
Education	£45,000
Refugees and asylum seekers	£31,000
Medical	£24,500
Substance misuse	£23,000
Rehabilitation of Offenders	£20,500
Sport	£17,500
Domestic violence	£16,000
Churches	£11,500
Ethnic minorities	£11,000
Carers	£9,000
Counselling	£8,500
Other	£7,000
Hospices	£6,000
Themed grant	£4,000
Ex-services	£1,000

The foundation's annual report gives an interesting and informative summary of its achievements and activities during the year, and except of which is given here:

The trustees received 1,311 applications during the year, a noticeable decrease on the 1,543 applications received in 2010/11. Other funders have been experiencing a similar fall in numbers which appears surprising in the climate of statutory funding cuts and there is concern that the lack of applications may reflect the number of organisations which have had to close. In response to sector need, the trustees decided that with effect from 1 July 2012, the annual income level threshold for Small and Fast Track grants would rise from £300,000 to £500,000. This change enables medium sized organisations to apply for running/salary/project costs which they find especially hard to raise. It is also expected that this change will help to increase the number of applicants.

THE TRUSTHOUSE CHARITABLE FOUNDATION

Main category	Sub-category	Examples of projects supported
Community Support	Community	The support of carers; projects in deprived communities; projects addressing financial exclusion; the provision of sporting facilities or equipment in deprived areas.
	Drugs and alcohol	Rehabilitation of substance and alcohol mis-users.
	Elderly	Projects addressing isolation and loneliness (e.g. befriending schemes); domiciliary support (e.g. respite for carers), residential improvements/adaptations.
	Ex-offenders	Projects working with prisoners and ex-offenders to improve their life skills and reduce re-offending.
	Young people	Projects which build the confidence, life skills and employment skills of young people in need.
Disability and Healthcare	Physical and mental disability	Projects involving rehabilitation, (including related arts and sport programmes); projects particularly for ex-service men and women (including former employees of the emergency services); projects for children (including holidays); and respite care.
	Palliative care	The provision of domiciliary care; support for volunteers and carers; outreach services; the refurbishment of premises; the provision of equipment (excluding in all cases services or costs which are normally funded from statutory sources).
	Medicine	Special equipment (not available on the NHS) for the chronically or terminally ill at home. (Medical research projects are ineligible).
Arts, Education and Heritage	Arts	Projects which enable the disabled and people living in areas of need and poverty to participate in the performance arts and to experience artistic excellence in the performing arts; projects which encourage and give opportunities to young talented people whose circumstances might otherwise deny them (but not bursaries or fees).
	Education	Projects which help children at risk of exclusion or with exceptionally challenging behaviour to realise their educational potential; projects which encourage and give opportunities to young talented people whose circumstances might otherwise deny them access to further/higher education.
	Heritage	Smaller heritage projects, with a particular interest in industrial and maritime projects in areas of deprivation, which provide employment and/or volunteering opportunities for the local community and contribute to the regeneration of the area.

THE TRUSTHOUSE CHARITABLE FOUNDATION

Your organisation's annual income	Grant amount sought	What is the grant for?	Grants available
Under £500,000	£5,000 and under	Capital and/or running costs	Fast track
Under £500,000	£5,001 to £9,999	Capital and/or running costs	Small grant
Under £500,000	£10,000 to £30,000	Capital costs only	Large grant
Over £500,000, less than £5 million	£10,000 to £30,000	Capital costs only	Large grant

The quality of applications was variable throughout the year (e.g. applying for a disproportionate grant amount or lacking basic data such as details of achievements to date or user numbers). As a result, the trustees decided that with effect from 1 July 2012, the application system would move to a new completely form-based application system, consisting of specific questions covering the essential information required for assessment, but still giving space for applicants to describe and present the quintessential nature of their organisation. This is a first step towards the possibility of on-line applications in the longer term. The office continued through the year to provide comprehensive feedback on failed applications and to signpost applicants towards the website of the National Council of Voluntary Organisations, which has comprehensive advice of writing bids and potential sources of funding. A number of applicants, particularly those who are not professional fundraisers, commented on how helpful Trusthouse feedback and advice is.

By a curious coincidence the number of grants awarded was identical to the number in the previous year, 284, although the amount given was slightly less at £2.06 million (£2.1 million in 2010/11). A schedule at the back of this report gives details of every grant awarded during the year. Most of the grants were under £10,000, with an average value of £7,247 (£8,489 in 2010/11).

The current grants policy means that where possible, applications under the Large Grants scheme are awarded the full amount recommended by the assessor, with Small Grants being allotted funds from the remaining budget for each meeting of the Grants Committee. The average Large Grant in 2011/12 was £26,405 (£20,400 in 2010/11). This increase is accounted for by the fact that only 29 Large Grants were made as compared to 46 in 2010/11. A higher number of Large Grant applications were received this year but fewer met the funding criteria.

Seven grants of £30,000 were awarded under the Large Grants scheme as compared to nine in 2010/11. This year's grants of £30,000 included:

- KIND: towards the cost of creating a healthy living and wellbeing centre for disadvantaged children and their families in Toxteth, Liverpool
- Glasgow Building Preservation Trust: towards the cost of repairing a listed railway station building in Pollokshaws, Glasgow, to create a base for a charity recycling bikes and giving sporting/training opportunities to young people
- Daviot Village Hall: towards the cost of building a new hall at a small village in Aberdeenshire

Exclusions

The foundation will not normally consider supporting the following:

- Animal welfare
- Applications for revenue funding for more than one year
- Capital appeals for places of worship
- Grantmaking organisations or umbrella groups
- Grants for individuals (including bursaries through a third party organisation)
- Feasibility studies and evaluations
- Local authorities
- Local Education Authority schools or their Parent Teachers Associations, except if those schools are solely for students with Special Needs
- Medical research projects
- Office IT equipment including software costs
- Organisations that have received a grant for three consecutive years from the foundation
- Projects involving the start-up or piloting of new services
- Projects where the primary objective is environmental or conservation
- Projects where the primary objective is the promotion of a particular religion
- Renovation or alteration projects to make a building compliant with the Disability and Discrimination Act
- Revenue funding for organisations with an income of over £300,000 per annum
- Services operated by the NHS
- Social research
- Training of professionals within the UK
- Universities

Under normal circumstances, the foundation is not currently funding projects which are for:

- The purchase of computers, other electronic equipment or software for delivery of the charity's work (e.g. for an IT suite in a youth centre)
- PR or other awareness raising campaigns, including the publication of leaflets or events calendars, websites

Applications

On an application form available from the foundation's website, accessed following the completion of a brief eligibility questionnaire, which also identifies which type of grant may be most suitable. Details of additional information to be included with the application are given on the form. Applications must be made by post.

Percentage of awards given to new applicants: 74%.

Common applicant mistakes

'Not in a deprived area; not secured 50% of funding first; poor track record of compliance on Charity Commission website; no explanation of deficits on annual accounts; failure to explain what they do in practical terms; no evidence of results of work to date.'

Information gathered from:

Accounts; annual report; Charity Commission record; further information provided by the funder; funder's website.

The James Tudor Foundation

Relief of sickness, medical research, health education, palliative care
£573,500 (2011/12)

Beneficial area
UK and overseas.

Correspondent: Rod Shaw, Chief Executive, WestPoint, 78 Queens Road, Clifton, Bristol BS8 1QU (tel: 01179 858715; fax: 01179 858716; email: admin@jamestudor.org.uk; website: www.jamestudor.org.uk)

Trustees: Martin Wren, Chair; Richard Esler; Roger Jones; Cedric Nash.

CC Number: 1105916

The foundation was established in 2004. It makes grants for charitable purposes, usually in the UK, across six programme areas:

- Palliative care
- Medical research
- Health education, awards and scholarship
- The direct relief of sickness
- Overseas projects for the relief of sickness
- The fulfilment of the foundation's charitable objects by other means

In line with the principal objective, the foundation seeks to help small charities stay on their feet; to significantly improve the financial position of medium to large charities and to contribute to medical research where there is a probability of positive clinical outcomes.

Types of funding

Direct project support
This is the most successful area for funding requests.

Research
We will fund research where its aims match our objects and where we consider that it is likely to have a beneficial impact.

Awards and scholarships
We will occasionally fund awards and scholarships where they demonstrate that they contribute to the foundation's areas of benefit.

Building or refurbishment projects
The foundation is less likely to make grants towards capital projects (i.e. buildings and refurbishment costs). However, capital projects will be supported where clear benefit and good management are demonstrable.

Equipment
Items of equipment may be funded, particularly if part of a wider proposal. You should contact us first if your proposal includes requests for equipment funding.

Staffing
Staffing is occasionally supported. We would normally expect to see a proposal where self-financing is indicated within three years.

In 2011/12 the foundation had assets of £24.1 million and an income of £997,000. There were 71 grants made totalling £573,500, broken down as follows:

Relief of sickness	£150,500
Overseas	£99,500
Palliative care	£97,500
Medical research	£70,000
Health education	£44,000
Other	£112,500

The foundation gives the following analysis of the applications received during the year in its annual report:

274 full written applications were received (2011: 271), 49 of which were the product of the outline proposal step previously mentioned (2011: 53). Of the 274 received, 235 were eligible (2011: 221), maintaining the very high level of applications that fit the foundation's aims and objectives. At year-end 16 applications were in progress (2011: 36), 11 applications were held awaiting further information (2011: 52) and 122 were declined (2011: 95).

As a result of the foundation's excellent analysis of its grantmaking in its annual reports, it is possible to look at the figures for applications received over the past few years (as shown in the displayed box).

THE JAMES TUDOR FOUNDATION

	2006/07	2007/08	2008/09	2009/10	2010/11	2011/12
Applications received	226	386	288	309	271	274
No. of ineligible applications	63	87	50	53	50	39
No. of successful applications	36	43	56	63	70	71

Grantmaking in 2011/12

The foundation's annual report gives the following summary analysis of grantmaking during the year:

Palliative care
Palliative care is a major area of funding for the foundation. 10 grants (2011: 12) were awarded, all of which demonstrate clear benefits that match the foundation's objectives. Awards in this category show a wide distribution across the United Kingdom and have not been restricted geographically or by age of ultimate benefactor. The awards cover a spectrum of services.

£97,500 (2010: £102,000) was awarded in this category including £300 received as donations. The most significant grant was £30,000 awarded to the Children's Hospice South West to continue providing its sibling service. Support for the West Cumbria Hospice at Home continued with an award of £5,000 towards the core costs of the charity. Both are examples of continued support provided to those charities that have demonstrated excellence in their field, achieved positive outcomes and shown a desire for a meaningful and on-going relationship.

A further 8 awards were made; 6 awards individually of less than £10,000, including one discretionary award. These awards were provided for counselling, respite care, hospice at home provision, a cancer nurse and equipment.

Medical research
The directors continue to demonstrate support for medical research with an aim of ultimately providing benefit to the public. All applications in this category must have a high potential of positive clinical outcomes.

5 grants (2011: 8) were awarded in this category totalling £70,000 (2011: £216,000) and included an obligation to pay £10,750 that will fall due within twelve months of the year-end. A further £47,500 was paid in recognition of a constructive obligation made in a previous period to the University of Nottingham. The reduction in the total value of awards in this category is a reflection of the cyclical nature of research funding and does not indicate a lack of applications in this area.

The most significant award was to Islet Research. £21,500 was awarded for the continued funding of research into the prevention of transplant rejection; £10,750 was paid and a constructive obligation to pay a further £10,750 within 12 months of the year-end was created.

The University of Bath received an award of £19,500 as a contribution to their collaborative work with Frenchay Hospital, Bristol on 'smart' bandages that will potentially aid many burns victims; the award will fund a research nurse for the project for 12 months.

A further 3 awards were made; 2 awards individually of less than £10,000 and 1 discretionary award. These awards were provided for research into pre-term labour, juvenile lupus and recruitment for Alzheimer's trials.

Health education, awards and scholarships
This category attracts a broad spectrum of applications. In this year 6 grants (2011: 7) were made totalling £44,000 (2011: £79,000).

The most significant award was £16,500 granted to the British Liver Trust for the production of liver disease information booklets that achieved Department of Health accreditation. The Princess Alice Hospice was awarded £10,000 to provide an eLearning service and Youth Net received an award of £8,000 to provide health information about eating disorders on their extremely well-visited website for young people.

A further 3 discretionary awards were made for an eating programme for young people with autism, a sickle cell awareness campaign, and a booklet to encourage screening for heart defects in young people.

The direct relief of sickness
This is the most populous category. 25 (2011: 26) grants were approved representing a broad range of causes, both thematically and geographically. The total amount awarded in this category was £150,500 (2011: £204,000).

The largest single award was £18,500 granted to Special Effects to provide assessment for eye movement communication equipment for high-level spine-injured people. The Rainbow Trust was granted £15,000. This was the fourth occasion that support for a family support worker had been provided. BASIC received £12,000 for vocational services for people with brain injuries.

Headway, Cambridgeshire was paid £6,000 to support the community services manager and 2 constructive obligations were entered into; £6,000 falling due within twelve months of the year-end and £6,000 due for payment at a time greater than twelve months. South Lakes Society for the Blind (Sight Advice) was paid £5,000 for an assistive technology programme for the visually impaired and 2 constructive obligations were entered into; £5,000 falling due within twelve months of the year-end and £5,000 due for payment at a time greater than twelve months.

A further 20 awards were made individually of less than £10,000, including 11 discretionary awards. These awards were provided for: therapy, exercise and counselling services, items of equipment, helpline costs, helping older people, a support worker, a nurse for a day centre and a contribution towards disabled living.

Overseas work for the relief of sickness

This classification recognises the significance of work funded overseas and allows for additional controls that were put in place following the publication of guidance on this matter by the Charity Commission. In this year 10 grants were made totalling £99,500. As this is a new category no comparison with previous years is possible.

The most significant grant was a biennial award of £50,000 for continued support of the World Health Organisation to improving the position of unsafe abortion in Eastern Europe. Reproductive health remains the leading cause of ill-health and death for women of childbearing age worldwide. The Leprosy Mission received an award of £14,500 as on-going support for their leprosy and health related work in Nepal.

A further 8 awards were made individually of less than £10,000, including 3 discretionary awards. These awards were provided for maternal health (Sierra Leone and Nepal), HIV/AIDS (Tanzania and Malawi), health education (Rwanda), disability (Tanzania), immunisation (Guatemala), and outreach clinics (Nepal).

The achievement of the foundation's objects by other means

The directors recognise that not all applications which contribute to the fulfilment of the foundation's objects neatly fit into one of the previously mentioned categories. It was not intended to restrict applications by applying narrow criteria and therefore this additional category was provided. The inclusion of this category has enabled the directors of the foundation to approve an additional 15 (2011: 17) awards in the year under review.

The recipient of the highest amount was Aspire. £25,000 was granted as continued support of the assistive technology programme and a new grant of £25,000 was awarded for the Aspire Housing Programme, recognising the particular challenges to independent living faced by people with spinal injury.

The Meningitis Trust received £15,000 for the small grant programme they administer. This award recognises the long association with this charity that has consistently demonstrated excellent use of funds to support those who have been affected by meningitis. GivingWorldOnLine was awarded £13,500 for an income generation officer as the charity moves toward self-sufficiency.

A further 11 awards were made individually of less than £10,000, including 8 discretionary awards. These awards provided for a diverse range of equipment although grants for development and a fundraising event were also made.

Exclusions

The foundation will not accept applications for grants:
- That directly replace, or negatively affect, statutory funding
- For work that has already taken place
- For endowment funds
- For economic, community development or employment use
- For adventure or residential courses, expeditions or overseas travel
- For sport or recreation uses, including festivals
- For environmental, conservation or heritage causes
- For animal welfare
- From applicants who have applied within the last 12 months

Applications

On an application form available from the foundation's website. Comprehensive guidelines for applicant are also available from there. Potential applicants must first complete an initial eligibility check.

Percentage of awards given to new applicants: between 20% and 30%.

Common applicant mistakes

'Not reading our application guidelines fully before making their application.'

Information gathered from:

Accounts; annual report; Charity Commission record; further information provided by the funder; funder's website.

The Tudor Trust

General charitable purposes, social welfare

£17.5 million (2012/13)

Beneficial area

UK and sub-Saharan Africa.

Correspondent: Ms Nicky Lappin, Research and Information Manager, 7 Ladbroke Grove, London W11 3BD (tel: 020 7727 8522; email: general@ tudortrust.org.uk; website: www. tudortrust.org.uk)

Trustees: James Long; Dr Desmond Graves; Catherine Antcliff; Monica Barlow; Nell Buckler; Louise Collins; Elizabeth Crawshaw; Ben Dunwell; Helen Dunwell; Matt Dunwell; Christopher Graves; Mary Graves; Francis Runacres; Vanessa James; Rosalind Dunwell.

CC Number: 1105580

The trust meets a range of both capital and revenue needs for voluntary and community groups. Grants can be of all sizes, very often to be paid over a period of two or three years. There is no maximum or minimum grant amount. The trust supports work which addresses the needs of people at the margins of society. Grants for work outside the UK are targeted and proactive, and therefore applications are not sought for this aspect of the trust's work.

The trust was founded in 1955 by Sir Godfrey Mitchell who endowed it with shares in the Wimpey construction company for general charitable purposes.

The staffing is modest for an organisation spending this amount of money and giving around 340 grants a year. The 'support costs' of the grantmaking activity represent around 5% of the grant total. During the year, 32% of grants were made to new beneficiaries. The trust focuses on smaller forward-looking groups, led by capable and committed people. Characteristics that they look for in an organisation include:
- Organisations working directly with people who are on the margins of society
- A focus on building stronger communities by overcoming isolation and fragmentation and encouraging inclusion, connection and integration
- Organisations which are embedded in and have developed out of their community – whether the local area or a 'community of interest'
- High levels of user involvement, and an emphasis on self-help where this is appropriate
- Work which addresses complex and multi-stranded problems in unusual or imaginative ways
- Organisations which are thoughtful in their use of resources and which foster community resilience in the face of environmental, economic or social change

They are more likely to fund groups with an annual turnover of less than £1 million however do sometimes make grants to larger groups, particularly for work which could be influential or which a smaller organisation would not have the capacity to deliver.

Grants are made in four categories:
- Core funding
- Project grants
- Capital grants
- Grants to help strengthen an organisation

The trust may consider making a loan if this could be a helpful solution (two loans were made in 2012/13). There are no maximum or minimum grants and they can be made up to three years. They may fund over a longer period which usually involves a re-application. In order to tackle deep-rooted problems which can take time, their aim is to commit funding over a sustained period of time. In 2012/13, 32% of grants were being made over three years or via continuous funding.

In 2012/13 the trust had an income of £7.7 million and assets of £239.9 million. Grants were made to 342 organisations totalling £17.5 million, with the average amount being £56,000. Grants were distributed into the following areas:

Youth	42	£2.4 million
Older people	7	£229,000
Community	137	£6.7 million
Relationships	34	£2 million
Housing	20	£895,000
Mental health	22	£1.3 million
Substance misuse	10	£807,000
Learning	9	£342,000
Financial security	3	£163,000
Criminal justice	25	£1.6 million
Overseas	33	£1 million

The trust's annual report also included the distribution of grants by geographical spread:

East Midlands	15	£658,000
Eastern	10	£675,000
London	55	£2.7 million
North East	14	£799,000
North West	40	£2 million
Northern Ireland	7	£343,000
Scotland	20	£1.1 million
South East	20	£1 million
South West	30	£1.5 million
Wales	11	£655,000
West Midlands	12	£612,000
Yorkshire and the Humber	31	£1.3 million
National/multi-regional	44	£3 million
Overseas	33	£1 million

Grants for work outside the UK are targeted and proactive, and therefore applications are not sought for this aspect of the trust's work.

UK beneficiaries included: Gatwick Detainees Welfare Group (£160,000); Personal Support Unit (£150,000); Coalition for Independent Action and Female Prisoners Welfare Project Hibiscus (£120,000 each); Amber Foundation and Carefree Foster Independence – Cornwall (£105,000 each); Bankside Open Spaces Trust (£85,000); Be Attitude, Brighton Unemployed Centre Families Project and Latin Americas Women's Rights Service (£75,000 each); Alcohol Concern, Angelou Centre and Edinburgh Garden Partners (£60,000 each); Basement Studio, Broomhouse Centre and Green Light Trust (£50,000 each); Making Communities Work and Grow and Men's Action Network (£45,000 each); Age UK Haringey and Bath City Farm Ltd (£20,000 each); Plymouth Youth Sailing (£15,000); and Allsorts Youth Project (£6,500).

Overseas beneficiaries included: EMESCO Development Foundation (£90,000); Build It International (£70,000); Organic Agriculture Centre of Kenya – OACK (£40,000); Rammed Earth Consulting CIC and Youth Action for Rural Development (£20,000 each); Find Your Feet (£15,000); and Resources Orientated Development Initiatives – RODI (£2,000).

Exclusions

The trust does not make grants to:
- Individuals, or organisations applying on behalf of individuals
- Larger charities (both national and local) enjoying widespread support
- Statutory bodies
- Hospitals, health authorities or hospices
- Medical care, medical equipment or medical research
- Universities, colleges or schools
- Academic research, scholarships or bursaries
- Nurseries, playgroups or crèches
- One-off holidays, residential, trips, exhibitions, conferences, events, etc.
- Animal charities
- The promotion of religion
- The restoration or conservation of buildings or habitats (where there isn't a strong social welfare focus)
- Work outside the UK. The trust runs a targeted grants programme promoting sustainable agriculture in sub-Saharan Africa. They do not consider unsolicited proposals from groups working overseas
- Endowment appeals
- Work that has already taken place

Applicants are encouraged to call the information team for advice concerning applications.

Applications

According to the trust's website, the application process is made up of two stages. A first stage application must include the following:

1. A brief introductory letter
2. A completed organisation details sheet (available from the funding section of the trust's website)
3. A copy of your most recent annual accounts, and annual report if you produce one
4. Answers to the following questions, on no more than two sides of A4:
- What difference do you want to make, and how will your organisation achieve this?
- Why are you the right organisation to do this work?
- How do you know there is a need for your work, and who benefits from the work that you do?
- How would you use funding from Tudor?

The proposal should be addressed to the trustees and sent via post. Proposals will be acknowledged within a few days of being received. If the first-stage proposal is successful, applicants will receive an acknowledgement letter plus details about the second-stage of the process. The second stage will be conducted via telephone or a visit. The trust aims to let applicants know within a month whether or not they have progressed to the second stage application. The trust aims

to make a decision on most applications three months after progressing to the second stage. Trustees and staff meet every three weeks to consider applications.

More information is available on the trust's website.

Percentage of awards given to new applicants: 30%.

Common applicant mistakes

'Not including all information requested (e.g. accounts) or not answering our questions – just sending 'standard appeal'. Lack of detail on the basics, such as what they do, numbers helped, etc.'

Information gathered from:

Accounts; annual report; Charity Commission record; further information provided by the funder; funder's website.

Tuixen Foundation

General charitable purposes
£805,000 (2011/12)

Beneficial area
Worldwide.

Correspondent: Paul Clements, Trustee, c/o Coutts and Co., 27th Floor, St Mary Axe, London EC3 8BF (tel: 020 7649 2903)

Trustees: Peter D. Englander; Dr Leanda Kroll; Stephen M. Rosefield; Peter Clements.

CC Number: 1081124

Set up in 2000, this foundation spent its first few years of operation building up its assets. A number of charities are selected to receive a donation each year, and support may be ongoing over several years (likely to be for three years). International charities will also be considered, but the donations are mainly made to UK-based charities.

In 2011/12 the foundation had assets of £19.8 million and an income of just over £3 million. Grants were made totalling £805,000.

A list of grants was not available to view with the current accounts. Previous beneficiaries included: Impetus Trust (£175,500); University of Manchester (£100,000); Camfed (£50,000); Chance UK, Facing the World, School Home Support and Street League (£30,000 each); Sports Aid Trust (£25,000); First Step Trust (£20,000); and the Shannon Trust (£10,000).

Exclusions
No grants to individuals.

Applications
The foundation has previously stated that 'unsolicited applications are not

sought and correspondence will not be entered into'.

Percentage of awards given to new applicants: between 20% and 30%.

Information gathered from:

Accounts; Charity Commission record; further information provided by the funder.

The Douglas Turner Trust

General
£383,000 (2011/12)

Beneficial area

UK and overseas; however, in practice, there is a strong preference for Birmingham and the West Midlands.

Correspondent: Tim Patrickson, Administrator, 3 Poplar Piece, Inkberrow, Worcester WR7 4JD (tel: 01386 792014; email: timpatrickson@ hotmail.co.uk)

Trustees: John Del Mar, Chair; Peter Millward; David Pearson; Stephen Preedy; James Grindall.

CC Number: 227892

The trust was established in 1964 by Douglas Turner, a West Midlands industrialist who died in 1977. Grants are made to registered charities, mainly in the West Midlands, and around 50% by value of the grants awarded in 2011/12 were made to charities that are supported on an annual basis. These beneficiaries are visited every other year by the administrator and must satisfy the trustees of the need for continuing their support. Most of these charities are situated in, or working in, the West Midlands. The remaining grants are awarded to charities, principally in the same geographical area, many of which are seeking funds for single projects. The trustees also give consideration to national appeals, especially where these can show a local application, and to overseas appeals.

In 2011/12 the trust had assets of £14.8 million and an income of £395,000. Grants were made to 126 organisations totalling £383,000.

Disabled and health	35	£94,500
Youth and children	27	£76,000
Work in the community	29	£68,000
The arts	11	£34,500
Hospices	2	£33,000
International aid	6	£21,500
Social support	6	£20,000
Environment and heritage	4	£18,000
Work with the elderly	5	£16,500
Medical research	1	£1,000

The only beneficiaries listed in the 2011/12 accounts were charities with whom the trustees have a connection; these were: St Mary's Hospice Ltd

(£18,000); Birmingham Boys' and Girls' Union (£10,000); and Water Aid (£4,000 each).

Previous beneficiaries included: 870 House Youth Movement; Gingerbread; Listening Books; Dial Walsall; Compton Hospice; Gracewell Homes Foster Trust; Cotteridge Church Day Centre; Busoga Trust; Birmingham Botanical Gardens; Midlands Actors' Theatre; and Action Medical Research.

Exclusions

No grants to individuals or non-registered charities.

Applications

In writing to the correspondent, 'on applicant letterhead, two pages or less, and preferably not stapled together', with a copy of the latest annual report and accounts. There are no application forms. The trustees usually meet in February, May, August and December to consider applications, which should be submitted in the month prior to each meeting. All applications are acknowledged. Telephone or email enquiries may be made before submitting an appeal.

Percentage of awards given to new applicants: between 20% and 30%.

Common applicant mistakes

'Appeals too long; no accounts sent. Have not bothered to research our trust on our website.'

Information gathered from:

Accounts; annual report; Charity Commission record; further information provided by the funder.

Community Foundation Serving Tyne and Wear and Northumberland

Social welfare, education, religion, community benefit
£4.5 million to organisations (2011/12)

Beneficial area

Tyne and Wear and Northumberland.

Correspondent: Sonia Waugh, Deputy Chief Executive, Cale Cross House, 156 Pilgrim Street, Newcastle upon Tyne NE1 6SU (tel: 01912 220945; email: general@communityfoundation.org.uk; website: www.communityfoundation.org.uk)

Trustees: Prof. Christopher Drinkwater; Susan Winfield; Ashley Winter; Alastair Conn; Jamie Martin; Jo Curry; Colin Seccombe; Dean Higgins; Prof. Charles Harvey; Jane Robinson; John Clough; Gev Pringle; Fiona Cruickshank; Kate Roe.

CC Number: 700510

Established in 1988, the Community Foundation Serving Tyne and Wear and Northumberland is one of the largest community foundations in the UK. At the time of writing (August 2013), the foundation's website states that the 'core area of benefit is Tyne & Wear and Northumberland' and is fundamentally 'about this place, its people and its philanthropy, and seek to match local needs with donors' interests' with some work extending to cover County Durham and the Tees Valley. Grants are very occasionally made to other parts of the UK or the world.

The foundation was established for general charitable purposes but in particular towards the relief of poverty; the advancement of education (including training for employment or work); the advancement of religion and any other charitable purpose for the benefit of the community. Its helpful website contains comprehensive information on all of its activities and the programmes from which grants are available.

According to the foundation's 2013–16 strategy:

The foundation supports a wide range of causes and interests under three broad themes:
▸ Supporting people to overcome disadvantage
▸ Creating stronger communities
▸ Making the area a good place to live

Funds are set up by individuals, families and companies to help donors support their chosen interests. The majority of grants are made to groups, many of which are small and volunteer led, but the trust also funds larger organisations seeking smaller grants to support particular activities or developments. Applicants do not have to be registered charities but must be undertaking charitable work.

In common with other community foundations, the foundation administers a number of funds which are subject to change. The types of funds available include small grants funds, endowment funds and grassroots funds, all of which are listed on the foundation's website. Check there for current availability. Occasionally 'trademark grants' are made which are larger awards combining contributions from different funds. Some funds do support individuals. Individual grantmaking is almost always designed to nurture creative or athletic talent or to invest in education.

In 2011/12 the trust had assets of £47.9 million, an income of almost £5.4 million and made grants totalling just over £4.5 million, given in 1,695 grants broken down as follows:

271

Charities and voluntary organisations	1,461	£4.4 million
Individuals	234	£113,500

According to the trustees' report for 2011/12, 'the majority [of grants] continued to be for amounts of under £5,000 and to provide practical support for small voluntary and community groups'. Grants were distributed in the following categories:

Community foundation main funds	1,550	£3,200,000
ESF community grants	21	£194,000
Fair Share	9	£340,000
Grassroots grants	85	£168,000
The Henry Smith Charity	30	£659,000

Exclusions

The foundation supports applications for general running costs; specific projects or activities; and capital developments or equipment.

According to the trustees' report for 2011/12, 'the board has agreed certain exclusions for grants with its general funds and these are detailed in grant application materials available on request'.

Applications

There is one application form for the general Community Foundation grants and generally, separate forms for the other rolling grants programmes and one-off funds. Funds that support individuals are advertised separately. All of these plus application guidelines are available on the website.

Some of the programmes have deadlines and some do not; also, programmes change regularly so the trust's website should be checked for the most recent information.

If a grant is approved, there are terms and conditions that must be adhered to and a project report is to be submitted.

Organisations that are not registered charities can apply to get a grant, but grants can only be distributed for activities that are charitable in law. CICs or other social enterprises with a good business plan can apply for help with start-up or expansion, but help with general running costs is not usually supported.

Applicants must provide a copy of the bank statement; a copy of the latest annual accounts; constitution or set of rules; Child Protection or Vulnerable Adult Policy (if applicable); and copies of written estimates or catalogue pages if applying for grants regarding equipment or capital items.

Email this information where possible to: documents@communityfoundation.org.-uk and write the name of the organisation making the application in the subject line of the email.

Alternatively, send this information to the correspondent. Mark each of the documents clearly with the name of the organisation making the application.

Information gathered from:

Accounts; annual report; Charity Commission record; guidelines for applicants; funder's website.

Trustees of Tzedakah

Jewish charities, welfare
Around £450,000

Beneficial area

Worldwide, in practice mainly UK and Israel.

Correspondent: Michael Lebrett, Administrator, Brentmead House, Britannia Road, London N12 9RU (tel: 020 8446 6767)

Trustee: Trustees of Tzedakah Ltd.

CC Number: 251897

The objectives of this trust are the relief of poverty; advancement of education; advancement of religion; and general charitable purposes. The trust makes over 300 grants to organisations in a year ranging from around £25 to £35,000.

The charity has an income of around £500,000 each year, most of which is usually given in grants. Up-to-date information is usually unavailable as accounts are consistently filed late with the Charity Commission.

Previous beneficiaries include: Hasmonean High School Charitable Trust; Gertner Charitable Trust; Society of Friends of the Torah; Hendon Adath Yisroel Synagogue; Medrash Shmuel Theological College; Torah Temimoh; Willow Foundation; Tifferes Girls School; Sage Home for the Aged; Wizo; and Torah Movement of Great Britain.

Exclusions

Grants only to registered charities. No grants to individuals.

Applications

This trust states that it does not respond to unsolicited applications.

Information gathered from:

Charity Commission record.

The Underwood Trust

Medicine and health, social welfare, education, arts, environment and wildlife
£4.3 million (2011/12)

Beneficial area

Worldwide. In practice UK with a preference for Scotland and Wiltshire.

Correspondent: John Dippie, Trust Manager, c/o Tcp Atlantic Square Ltd, Fourth Floor South, 35 Portman Square, London W1H 6LR (tel: 020 7486 0100; website: www.theunderwoodtrust.org.uk)

Trustees: Robin Clark, Chair; Jack C. Taylor; Briony Wilson; Reg Harvey.

CC Number: 266164

The Underwood Trust was established in 1973. The name derives from Underwood Lane, Paisley, Scotland, which was the childhood home of one of the founders. It currently supports registered charities and other charitable organisations which benefit society nationally and locally in Scotland and Wiltshire.

The general aims of the trust are to cover a wide spectrum of activities so as to benefit as many charitable causes as possible and to make donations to organisations where its contribution really can be seen to make a difference. The trust does not wish to be the principal funder of a charity and medium sized bodies are more likely to receive grants than either very small charities or well-known large national ones.

Grants are categorised under the following headings:
▶ Medicine and health
▶ Social welfare
▶ Education and the arts
▶ Environment and wildlife

The allocation between these headings varies from year to year.

In 2011/12 the trust had assets of £25 million and an income of £372,000. A total of 48 grants were paid or committed amounting to £5.6 million; the amount actually paid in 2011/12 totalled £4.3 million. The trust provides the following summary of grantmaking during the year in its annual report:

> The following brief summary gives a flavour of the types of projects funded in the year.

> ### Restorative Solutions
> The largest commitment during the year was a donation of £1.35 million to Restorative Solutions. This organisation works on setting up Restorative Justice Programmes, in connection with the Neighbourhood Resolution Panels being set up by the Ministry of Justice. The funding from the trust, which will paid

over several years of this project, will be used to establish panels in several areas and train the facilitators.

Medicine and Health

The largest donation in the year in this category was £124,000 given to I Can for their telephone helpline service for the parents of children with problems with speaking, listening or understanding. A further donation of £50,000 was made to Shooting Star Chase to help fund a paediatric doctor in their children's hospice. A special donation of £50,000, in addition to a regular donation of £16,500, was made to the Living Paintings Trust to assist a funding crisis in their work with blind and partially sighted people. A donation of £25,000 was made to the Grand Appeal from Bristol Children's Hospital towards specialist equipment within The Underwood Trust Cardiology Department.

Six other donations totalling £76,000 were made during the year.

Education and the Arts

A special large donation was given in this category of £1 million to the One Degree More project run by the Community Foundation for Wiltshire & Swindon. This fund helps young people from disadvantaged backgrounds take up places in higher education.

Four other donations were made totalling £66,000.

Social Welfare

A further donation of £83,000 was made to Restorative Solutions for their Restorative Approaches in Neighbourhoods scheme addition to the large donation listed above.

The trust made emergency funding donations to Counsel & Care, the Maytree Respite Centre and Windmill Hill City Farm of £100,000, £50,000 and £25,000 respectively. Further donations of £50,000 were made to each of the NSPCC, for their Childline service, and Prisoners Abroad. The trustees had great sympathy for the East African Crisis Appeal and donated £25,000 to the Disasters Emergency Committee Appeal.

Twelve other donations totalling £140,000 were made. Seven of these were for £16,500 each to charities where the trust has given long-term support.

The Environment and Wildlife

Two special large donations were made in this category, the first a £1 million donation to the Game & Wildlife Conservation Trust which endowed the Underwood Trust Research Fellowship and secondly £850,000 to Wiltshire Wildlife Trust to fund the acquisition of Raines House on their Lower Moor Farm Nature Reserve.

Two donations of £50,000 and £203,000 were made to the Greenpeace Environmental Trust for their work on marine reserves and fisheries around the UK. Also the trust gave a further £50,000 to support the work of COAST working with marine reserves around the Isle of Arran. Friends of the Earth Trust received £50,000 towards their Land Use, Food and Water Programme.

Six other donations totalling £102,500 were made during the year.

In recent years the trust has been part of an informal networking group, the Environmental Funders Network and once again attended their conference in January 2012 held at Trafford Hall, Cheshire.

Exclusions

No grants are given to:
- Individuals directly
- Political activities
- Commercial ventures or publications
- The purchase of vehicles including minibuses
- Overseas travel, holidays or expeditions
- Retrospective grants or loans
- Direct replacement of statutory funding or activities that are primarily the responsibility of central or local government
- Large capital, endowment or widely distributed appeals

Applications

The trust provides the following information:

The resources of the trust are limited and inevitably there are many more good causes that it can possibly fund. All the available funds are allocated pro-actively by the trustees. We are keen that applicants do not waste both their own and our limited resources in applications which have little chance of success, and therefore please DO NOT apply to the trust. Currently the trust has no free funds.

Do not apply to the trust unless invited to do so.

The trust's website states that:

Due to the current economic situation and the reduction in interest rates our income has been greatly reduced. As such there are currently no free funds in the trust and therefore THE TRUST IS UNABLE TO ACCEPT UNSOLICITED APPLICATIONS. This position is expected to continue for the foreseeable future, but any changes to this will be posted on [its] website at the time.

Note: the trust is unable to deal with telephone or email enquiries about an application.

Information gathered from:

Accounts; annual report; Charity Commission record; funder's website.

The Michael Uren Foundation

General
£3 million (2011/12)

Beneficial area
UK.

Correspondent: Anne Gregory-Jones, Trustee, Haysmacintyre, Fairfax House, 15 Fulwood Place, London WC1V 6AY (email: agregory-jones@haysmacintyre. com)

Trustees: Michael Uren; Anne Gregory-Jones; Janis Bennett; Alastair McDonald.

CC Number: 1094102

The foundation was established in 2002 with general charitable purposes following an initial gift from Michael Uren.

'The trustees are particularly keen on making grants for specific large projects. This could mean that, to satisfy this objective, no significant grants are paid in one year. With the resultant reserves retained a large grant could be made in the following year.'

The trustees have set out the following primary objectives:
- Armed forces – support of charities relating to the armed forces, and the support of ex-service personnel
- Medical – support of advanced medical research, and expansion and modernisation of medical facilities
- Animal welfare – support of endangered species, regardless of location
- Education – supporting the furtherance of education, with a specific focus on the sciences, engineering and technology
- Historic buildings – the restoration and continued maintenance of historic buildings

In 2011/12 the trust had assets of £63.4 million and an income of £2.4 million. Grants were made to 13 organisations totalling just over £3 million.

The beneficiaries were: International Animal Rescue (£980,000); The Gurkha Welfare Trust and Moorfields Eye Charity (£500,000 each); Imperial College Trust (£300,000); Royal Naval Benevolent Fund (£250,000); WAVE Heritage Fund (£200,000); Royal British Legion (£111,000); City of London Royal Fusiliers Volunteers Trust (£100,000); Royal Society of Wildlife Trusts (£50,000); Magdalen and Lasher Trust and Afghan Appeal Fund (£20,000 each); Royal Navy Submarine Museum (£10,000); and Friends of St Mary's, Kenardington (£5,000).

Applications

In writing to the correspondent.

Information gathered from:

Accounts; Charity Commission record.

The Vail Foundation

General, Jewish

£1.4 million (2011/12)

Beneficial area

UK and overseas.

Correspondent: Michael S. Bradfield, Trustee, 5 Fitzhardinge Street, London W1H 6ED (tel: 020 7317 3000)

Trustees: Michael S. Bradfield; Paul Brett; Michael H. Goldstein.

CC Number: 1089579

This foundation was set up in 2001. 'The trustees receive applications for donations from a wide variety of charitable institutions including those engaged in medical ancillary services (including medical research), education, helping the disabled and old aged, relieving poverty, providing sheltered accommodation, developing the arts etc.'

In 2011/12 the foundation had assets of just over £7 million and an income of £243,000. There were 47 grants made to organisations totalling just over £1.4 million.

As in previous years, the organisations receiving the largest grants were: KKL Charity Ltd (£472,500 in total); United Jewish Israel Appeal (£270,000 in total); and the London School of Jewish Studies (£135,000 in total).

Other beneficiaries included: Community Security Trust (£60,000); Finchley Jewish Primary School Trust (£50,000); Jewish Leadership Council (£25,000); Kisharon Charitable Trust (£20,000); Chai Lifeline Cancer Care (£10,000); and the Chicken Soup Shelter (£5,000).

Applications

In writing to the correspondent. 'The trustees consider all requests which they receive and make such donations as they feel appropriate.'

Information gathered from:

Accounts; Charity Commission record.

The Valentine Charitable Trust

General charitable purposes

£532,000 (2011/12)

Beneficial area

Unrestricted, but mainly Dorset, UK.

Correspondent: Douglas Neville-Jones, Trustee, Preston Redman, Hinton House, Hinton Road, Bournemouth BH1 2EN (tel: 01202 292424)

Trustees: Douglas Neville-Jones; Patricia Walker; Peter Leatherdale; Susan Patterson; Roger Gregory; Diana Tory; Sheila Cox; Wing Cdr Donald Jack; Susan Ridley.

CC Number: 1001782

According to the 2011/12 trustees' report, the trust was founded by the late Miss Ann Cotton in 1990. The trust was established for general charitable purposes but in particular for the provision of amenities and facilities for the benefit of the public, the protection and safeguarding of the countryside and wildlife and the control and reduction of pollution. Miss Cotton lived most of her life in Dorset and involvement in local projects appealed to her.

The trust offers an interesting and informative insight into its grantmaking policy and the wishes of the trust's settlor in its annual report for 2011/12, which is reproduced here:

Grants to local charities: the trust particularly welcomes involvement in local projects in Dorset. There are no boundaries on what trustees consider local; however when charities have a limited area of interest, preference will be given to those which operate in Dorset.

Grants to charities which have traditionally received small grants: a pattern of making grants to relatively small charities has been made over the years and the trustees intend to continue these subject to an appropriate review. Many of these links originated in Miss Cotton's time or are a direct reflection of her thoughts. However, just because a charity has received grants on a regular basis does not guarantee an automatic decision for further grants in the future.

Grants to objects in other parts of the world: the charity supports a small number of initiatives in the third and developing world. The trustees particularly like to look for projects which offer sustainability to local communities.

Grants to one-off appeals: one-off appeals are regularly made to provide funding for specific projects, which are frequently made for local facilities.

However the trustees are not keen on funding village halls or the fabric of church buildings.

Grants for medical research and hospitals: as a matter of policy, when making regular donation to bodies or objects related to the NHS, the trust looks for assurance that any donations have no likelihood of being provided out of central funds in the future.

Grants for core funding: the trust makes donations towards core funding and makes such grants on a repeat basis. Recurring donations require a report from the applicant charity and a new application so that the position can be reviewed. If a particular charity has been supported once then the trust takes the stance that it will be supported again, unless there have been substantial changes that do not fit in with the trust's objectives since the last grant.

Matched funding and pledges: the trust offers funding to a project on the basis that the applicant can raise other funds. The other funds must be raised before the trust makes the donation. Donations are also made on the condition that the project goes ahead. All offers are subject to review until the time they are actually made.

Social investment funding: the trustee's report from 2011/12 stated that:

> Following Miss Cotton's death the charity's assets were invested in a very narrow range of investments. To assist with diversification, the trustees developed what they term social investment funding. This involves either the purchase of premises which are then leased to an operating charity for its use; the lease is usually at a modest or nominal rent and for a relatively limited term, or the provision of a loan with an interest rate of between 0% and base rate to an operating charity to allow it to acquire property.

In 2011/12 the trust had assets of £26.9 million and an income of £819,500. Grants were made to 112 organisations totalling £532,000.

Beneficiaries included: Lewis-Manning Cancer Trust (£20,000); Kerala India, Bournemouth Nightclub Outreach Work, Bournemouth Symphony Orchestra, Game and Wildlife Conservation Trust and St John of Jerusalem Eye Hospital (£10,000 each); Faithworks and National Coastwatch Institution (£7,500 each); Hope House Training and Support Ltd, St Philips Church Community Project and Vitalise (£6,000 each); Jubilee Sailing Trust, Parkstone Sports and Arts Centre, Shelter, Sports Forum for the Disabled and Tree Aid (£5,000 each); Poole Christian Fellowship, React and Smile Connect (£2,000 each); Traffic of the Stage (£1,000); Purbeck Strings (£300);

Youth Action for Holistic Development
(£200).

Exclusions

No grants to individuals. The trust
would not normally fund appeals for
village halls or the fabric of church
buildings.

Applications

In writing to the correspondent. The
trust provides the following insight into
its application process in its annual
report:

All applications will be acknowledged with
standard letters, even those that are not
appropriate for receiving a grant. This
responsibility is delegated to Douglas J E
Neville-Jones who then provides a report
to the next trustees' meeting.

The following general comments
summarise some of the considerations the
trustees seek to apply when considering
applications for funding.

The trustees look for value for money.
While this concept is difficult to apply in a
voluntary sector it can certainly be used
on a comparative basis and subjectively.
If the trustees have competing
applications they will usually decide to
support just one of them as they believe
that to concentrate the charity's donations
is more beneficial than to dilute them.

Regular contact with the charities to
which donations are made is considered
essential. Reports and accounts are also
requested from charities which are
supported and the trustees consider
those at their meetings.

The trustees take great comfort from the
fact that they employ the policy of only
making donations to other charities or
similar bodies. However they are not
complacent about the need to review all
donations made and the objects to which
those have been given.

The trustees are conscious that,
particularly with the smaller and local
charities, the community of those working
for and with the charity is an important
consideration.

The trustees regularly review the
classifications to which donations have
been made so that they can obtain an
overview of the charity's donations and
assess whether their policies are being
implemented in practice. They are
conscious that when dealing with
individual donations it is easy to lose sight
of the overall picture.

Information gathered from:

Accounts; annual report; Charity
Commission record.

The Vardy Foundation

Christian causes, education in
the north east of England,
young people and general
charitable purposes in the UK
and overseas

£1.12 million to organisations
(2011/12)

Beneficial area

UK and overseas, with a preference to
the north east of England.

Correspondent: Sir Peter Vardy,
Trustee, Venture House, Aykley Heads,
Durham DH1 5TS (tel: 01913 744744)

Trustees: Lady Margaret Vardy; Peter
Vardy; Richard Vardy; Sir Peter Vardy;
Victoria Vardy.

CC Number: 328415

The foundation was set up in 1989 with
general charitable objectives by Sir Peter
Vardy. Sir Peter Vardy made his fortune
in the motor retail business through his
company, Reg Vardy plc, founded by his
father. According to the trustees' report
for 2011/12, the foundation looks to
serve the public interest through
promoting the advancement of
education, religion, welfare, relief and
the arts.

According to the trustees' report for
2011/12:

The trustees have established two new
charities to provide services that do not
currently exist in the UK. Safe Families for
Children (SFFC) seeks to keep families
together and avoid children being taken
into the care system. Volunteer families
are recruited to offer short-term
residential care to children whose parents
are experiencing difficulties. A second
charity, The Jigsaw Foundation, will help
smaller charities in a wide range of ways
to work together, increase their
effectiveness and stimulate growth.

During 2011/12, the foundation also
purchased three homes in the north east
of England in collaboration with Betel
International. The homes house
approximately 200 men who suffer from
an alcohol or drug addiction with the
intention of reducing their chances of
reoffending and addiction relapse.

The trustees' report for 2011/12 states
that:

The foundation measures applications
against three main criteria:
 Projects should involve, help and
   encourage young people
 Projects, if in the UK, should ideally be
   based in the North of England
 Projects should be run against a
   backdrop of Christian values

In 2011/12 the foundation had assets of
£21.8 million and an income of almost
£1.1 million. Grants were made totalling

£1.36 million, of which £1.12 million
was distributed to 121 organisations and
£173,500 to 38 individuals.

Grants were categorised as follows:

Relief	4	£55,000
Education	6	£37,000
Religion	55	£506,000
Welfare	91	£725,000
Arts	3	£36,000

The largest beneficiaries during the year,
listed in the accounts, were: A Way Out
(£123,000); Reverend Norman
Drummond (£100,000); Betel
International (£97,000); Christians
Against Poverty (£50,000); and Premier
Radio (£40,000).

Exclusions

The foundation will not fund:
 Applications for more than a three
   year commitment
 Animal welfare projects
 Health related charities
 Projects normally provided by central
   or local government
 Individuals (including requests for
   educational support costs) (**Note:** the
   foundation does award grants to
   individuals, however these are likely
   to already be connected to the
   foundation or one of the educational
   institutions that receive funding from
   the foundation)
 Projects that do not demonstrate an
   element of self-funding or other
   funding
 Contribute to an organisation's
   healthy reserves or endowments

Applications

In writing to the correspondent.

Information gathered from:

Accounts; annual report; Charity
Commission record.

The Variety Club Children's Charity

Children's charities
£2.1 million to organisations
(2011/12)

Beneficial area

UK.

Correspondent: Stanley Salter, Trustee,
Variety Club House, 93 Bayham Street,
London NW1 0AG (email: info@
varietyclub.org.uk; website: www.
varietyclub.org.uk)

Trustees: Jarvis Astaire; Raymond
Curtis; Stanley Salter; Anthony Harris;
Anthony Hatch; Lionel Rosenblatt;
Pamela Sinclair; Ronald Nathan; Russell
Kahn; Trevor Green; Jonathan Shalit;
Laurence Davis; Norman Kaphan; Keith
Andrews; Malcolm Brenner; Lloyd Barr;
Jason Lewis; Ronald Sinclair; Nicholas

Shattock; William Sangster; Rodney Natkiel; Jane Kerner.

CC Number: 209259

Variety aims to improve the lives of disabled and disadvantaged children and young people throughout the UK. The club's website has the following interesting account of the origins of the charity:

> The roots of the Variety Club of Great Britain go back to 1927 when, in Pittsburgh, United States, a group of 11 men-all friends-and involved in show business set up a social club. They rented a small room in the William Penn Hotel for their new club, which they named the Variety Club, as all its members were drawn from various branches of the show business world.
>
> On Christmas Eve 1928 a one-month-old baby was abandoned on a seat in the Sheridan Square Theatre in Pittsburgh, Pennsylvania, with a note pinned to her dress, which read as follows:
>
> Please take care of my baby. Her name is Catherine. I can no longer take care of her. I have eight others. My husband is out of work. She was born on Thanksgiving Day. I have always heard of the goodness of show business people and pray to God that you will look after her' (signed, 'A heartbroken mother').
>
> When all efforts by the police and local newspapers failed to locate the parents, the theatre's 11 club members decided to underwrite the infant's support and education.
>
> The subsequent publicity surrounding Catherine and her benefactors attracted many other show business people anxious to help. Before long Catherine had more clothes and toys than any child could possibly need. Naturally the Club members had no trouble finding other disadvantaged children to benefit from the extra gifts and while the generous show business world donated presents to Catherine, the Club continued to supply a growing number of children with much-needed presents. As a result, by the time Catherine was adopted at the age of five, the Club that she had effectively started was well on the way to becoming a recognised children's charity.
>
> It was not long before the Variety Club decided to actively raise funds for its adopted cause of disadvantaged children. The first fundraising event of the Club was held under a Circus Big Top, which is why the circus vernacular is used within the Club structure world-wide.
>
> The Variety Club of Great Britain – or Tent 3 6- was set up by two Americans: Robert S Wolff, chairman of RKO, who became the club's first Chief Barker, and C J Latta of ABC Cinemas/Warner Brothers. It was formed at an inaugural dinner at the Savoy in October 1949 and by the end of 1950 had already raised nearly £10,000.
>
> From the start, Tent 36 – like the Variety Club as a whole – consisted of a group of charitable individuals and companies, the majority of whom were related to show business and were happy to give large sums of money for the cause-sometimes as straightforward cash donations and sometimes through their support for the Club's auctions and raffles with donated items. The Club numbered a formidable array of film producers, agents and celebrities within its ranks, all of whom were eager to give their time and services – free of charge – to help towards making the increasingly varied and wide ranging fundraising events as successful as possible.
>
> Variety Club of Great Britain, along with the other members of Variety Club International, has long been characterised as 'the Heart of Show Business'. Its membership over the years is drawn in large measure from the multi-faceted world of entertainment and the leisure industries.

Summary

According to the annual report for 2011/12, the charity's objectives are as follows:

- To promote and provide for the care and upbringing of sick, disabled and disadvantaged children within the United Kingdom
- The advancement of education and the relief of financial need of children within the United Kingdom
- To undertake, and to assist others to undertake, research into any illness or affliction affecting children which will advance knowledge and to publish the useful results of research
- The provision of facilities for recreation and other leisure time occupation for children in the interests of their social welfare with the object of improving the conditions of life for such children.

The three main areas of work cover:

- Mobility – coaches and wheelchairs, including sports wheelchairs
- Caring and health – specialist children's hospital wards and in-home care equipment
- Youth and education – youth clubs plus fun and educational days out

Grantmaking

In 2011/12 the charity had assets of £1 million and an income of £6.2 million. Grants and donations paid out during the year totalled just under £2.5 million. Of this total, just over £2.1 million was granted to organisations and £343,000 was granted to individuals.

The 2011/12 accounts provide an analysis of some of the services provided by the trust through the year:

The charity gave 125 electric wheelchairs; provided 139 grants for specialist disability equipment; made 30 grants to youth clubs for essential equipment; 63 sunshine coaches to schools, homes and other organisations and 34,000 children enjoyed days out.

Charitable expenditure was broken down as follows:

Sunshine coaches	£2 million
Wheelchairs	£225,000
Individual grants	£133,000
Grants to schools, hospitals, institutions	£61,000
Children's days out	£917,500

Organisations who received grants of over £5,000 included: Young Epilepsy – Surrey (£38,500); Oakfield School – Pontefract, Heritage House School – Buckinghamshire and Garth School – Lincolnshire (£37,000 each); Oak View School – Essex, The Village School – London and Milestone Academy – Kent (£32,000 each); Elmwood School – Somerset and Pennfields School – Wolverhampton (£27,000 each); Bradstow School – Kent and Waltham Forest Asian Mothers Group – London (£25,00 each); Wandle Valley School – Surrey (£24,000); and Wicksteed Leisure – Northants (£5,500).

A total of £45,500 was disbursed in grants of less than £5,000.

According to the 2011/12, the plans for 2013 involve 'initiating the equipping of playgrounds and parks around the UK to make them accessible to both disabled and able-bodied children and young people.'

Exclusions

Examples of grants outside the guidelines:

- Repayment of loans
- Garden adaptions
- Cost of a family/wheelchair adapted vehicle
- Administrative/salary costs
- Maintenance or on-going costs
- Distribution to other organisations
- Reimbursement of funds already paid out
- Hire, rental costs or down payments
- Computers
- Trips abroad or holiday costs
- Medical treatment or research
- Education/tuition fees

Applications

There are application forms for each programme available – with application guidelines – from the charity or through its website.

General application guidelines are as follows:

- Applications can be made on behalf of individual children, but these must be supported by a letter from an appropriately qualified professional, e.g. family doctor, occupational therapist, social worker, school teacher etc
- Applications can also be made from non-profit making groups and organisations working with children up to, and including, the physical age of 18 years. These include statutory bodies (schools and hospitals) and registered charities

- Applications can be made by parents, medical professionals, a school or organisation, hospitals and registered charities
- Applications for specialist items of equipment, i.e. walking frames, seating systems, specialist beds should be accompanied by a supporting letter from a physiotherapist or occupational therapist
- Quotations for equipment should accompany an application
- Applicants are advised to think carefully before submitting a more substantial request.

Variety will need to be convinced of the high quality and efficiency of your organisation before consideration is given to making a donation.

The grants committee meets six times per year; therefore, there is no deadline for applications to be made.

In some cases a member of the grants committee will contact you to discuss your application more fully.

Notification of the outcome of applications will be by letter, and the decision of the trustees is final.

Information gathered from:

Accounts; annual report; Charity Commission record; guidelines for applicants; funder's website.

Volant Charitable Trust

General charitable purposes, in particular women, children, the relief of poverty, the alleviation of social deprivation and the provision of social benefit to the community, in the UK and overseas

£1.17 million to organisations (2011/12)

Beneficial area

UK and overseas, with a preference for Scotland.

Correspondent: Christine Collingwood, Administrator, Box 8, 196 Rose Street, Edinburgh EH2 4AT (email: admin@ volanttrust.com; website: www. volanttrust.com)

Trustees: J. K. Rowling; Dr N. S. Murray; G. C. Smith; R. D. Fulton.

SC Number: SC030790

This trust was established in 2000 by the author J K Rowling for general charitable purposes. According to the trustees' report for 2011/12, 'the main aims of the trust are to support charitable organisations whose purpose is to alleviate poverty, suffering or social deprivation with particular emphasis on children's and women's issues.' The trust has two broad areas of funding:

- Charitable organisations involved in the support and protection of women, children, relief of poverty and alleviating social deprivation and the provision of social benefit to the community and the public at large
- Research and teaching related to the treatment, cure and nursing of Multiple Sclerosis and related conditions

Check the trust's website for up-to-date information on any changes to the above circumstances.

According to the trustees' report for 2011/12, the trust has simple guidelines:

- The trustees are particularly interested in supporting charitable organisations involved in the support and protection of women, children, relief of poverty and alleviating social deprivation and the provision of social benefit to the community and the public at large
- The trustees are prepared to support a charity by way of regular annual payments but generally not to exceed three years and will also support the general purposes of a charity or specific projects
- The trustees will, as and when appropriate, support disaster appeals but will not support applications from individuals who are seeking assistance, for a specific project or charitable work which that individual may be carrying out, or to relieve a need due to illness or similar circumstances

In 2011/12 the trust had assets of £51.3 million and an income of £2.6 million, a substantial amount of which included donations from the settlor. Grants were made during the year to 45 organisations totalling almost £1.17 million, and were broken down as follows:

Support and protection of women, children and young people	£791,000
Relief of poverty and social deprivation	£35,000
Provision of social benefit to the community	£150,000
International aid	£200,000

A £350,000 donation, which was allocated to Foundation Scotland subsequently awarded and committed 23 grants totalling £315,000 to charities (£35,000 was charged in fees). At the time of writing (August 2013), Foundation Scotland's website (www. foundationscotland.org.uk) provided the following information:

Foundation Scotland works with The Volant Charitable Trust to make awards of up to £10,000 p.a. on its behalf to charities and community groups in Scotland. Foundation Scotland manages that whole application process, and all enquiries should come through Foundation Scotland.

Beneficiaries of the largest grants were listed in the accounts. These were: Foundation Scotland (£350,000); Médecins Sans Frontières – Congo, Save

the Children – Ivory Coast (£100,000 each); The Place2Be (£90,000); The Roses Charitable Trust (£75,000); Women Onto Work (£60,000); and Kids Company (£50,000).

Exclusions

The trust will not provide grants to individuals or major capital projects.

Applications

Applications for funding requests of up to and including £10,000 per annum, for those projects based in Scotland only, are dealt with by the appointed agents, Foundation Scotland. According to Foundation Scotland's website:

The fund's primary focus is to support women, children and young people who are at risk and facing social deprivation. There is limited funding available, so only those projects that closely match the above criteria are likely to be considered for support.

Projects must demonstrate a strong focus on supporting women affected by hardship or disadvantage and on tackling the issues they face in order to make a lasting difference to their lives and life chances. Projects which tackle serious issues and help people to turn their lives around are given priority.

Organisations who are currently in receipt of a grant may not apply. Groups that will distribute funds as grants or bursaries to other groups may not apply.

An outline of the project using the enquiry form should be sent to: grants@foundationscotland.org.uk. Any questions should be directed towards Jane Martin on 01315 240301.

All other requests for funding are dealt with via an application form available from the Volant Trust's website.

Complete and return the application form, plus any supporting materials by post. Applications should not be hand delivered. If an application is hand delivered, management at mail boxes are not in a position to discuss applications and will not be expected to provide any form of receipt.

Information gathered from:

Accounts; annual report; OSCR record; funder's website.

Voluntary Action Fund (VAF)

General, social welfare and inclusion

£5.7 million (2011/12)

Beneficial area

Scotland.

Correspondent: Keith Wimbles, Chief Executive, Suite 3, Forth House, Burnside Business Court, North Road,

Inverkeithing, Fife KY11 1NZ (tel: 01383 620780; fax: 01383 626314; email: info@ voluntaryactionfund.org.uk; website: www.voluntaryactionfund.org.uk)

Trustees: Ron Daniel; Dorothy MacLauchlin; Michael Cunningham; Pam Judson; John McDonald; Douglas Guest; Shirley Grieve; Gail Edwards; Andrew Marshall-Roberts; Bridgid Corr; Sid Wales.

SC Number: SC035037

Formed in 2003 this organisation evolved from the former Unemployed Voluntary Action Fund (UVAF) which was established in 1982. In response to the changing nature of their work and the evolving economic and social environment in Scotland, the mission and objectives of the fund were updated and it became a charity called Investing in Social Change and Community Action: The Voluntary Action Fund (VAF).

The organisation is an independent grantmaking body which invests in voluntary and community based organisations across Scotland. Organisations and projects that challenge inequalities and overcome barriers to active participation in community life are supported.

According to the trustees' report for 2011/12, the fund's vision is for:

A fair society in which strong, resilient communities can flourish, and people can achieve their potential through active participation, volunteering and working together to tackle inequality and discrimination.

The principal objective of Voluntary Action Fund is the advancement of education, the protection of health and relief of poverty, sickness and distress, by the making of grants and the provision of financial support for projects and activities.

The fund's website states that

VAF manages funds that are open to application from eligible groups and organisations. The funding and support VAF provides enables community based organisations to involve volunteers, undertake projects that challenge inequalities and overcome barriers to being involved in community life.

In 2011/12 the fund had an income of £6.1 million, assets of £232,500 and made grants totalling £5.7 million, distributed through the following funds:

Equality Grants Programme	£4.7 million
Volunteering Scotland Grant Scheme	£806,500
Community Chest	£113,500
The European Year of Volunteering Grant Scheme	£102,500
Tackling Sectarianism	£13,500

Beneficiaries included: Scottish Equality Disability Forum – policy and information (£165,000); EHRC –

Independent Living in Scotland (£140,000); Scottish Transgender Alliance (£125,000); Scottish Alliance of Regional Equality Councils and Show Racism the Red Card (£120,000 each); Bridges Programme (£95,000); Maryhill CAB (£80,000); Positive Action in Housing (£60,000); Multi Ethnic Aberdeen Ltd (MEAL), Glasgow Wood Recycling and Faith in Community Scotland (£40,000 each); British Deaf Association – Building Capacity (£30,000); Homelink Family Support (£23,000); Alzheimer Scotland/Glasgow and E Dumbartonshire (£17,000); and Brighter Horizons – Banff (£9,000).

Exclusions

See the fund's website for details of any individual exclusions for each fund.

Applications

Application forms and guidance notes for open programmes are available on the fund's website. The fund recommends that interested parties contact them to discuss the project before making any application. Funds may open and close so applicants should check the website for the most recent updates. Different funds have different application guidance.

Information gathered from:

Accounts; annual review; OSCR record; funder's website.

The Community Foundation in Wales

Community, social inclusion, social welfare

£1.7 million (2011/12)

Beneficial area

Wales.

Correspondent: Liza Kellett, Administrator, St Andrews House, 24 St Andrews Crescent, Cardiff CF10 3DD (tel: 02920 379580; email: mail@cfiw.org.uk; website: www.cfiw.org. uk)

Trustees: Janet Lewis-Jones; David Dudley; Michael Westerman; Julian Smith; Frank Learner, Dr Caryl Cresswell; Jonathan Hollins; Henry Robertson; Lulu Burridge; Sheila Maxwell; Thomas Jones.

CC Number: 1074655

The Community Foundation in Wales promotes the cause of philanthropy in Wales by creating and managing relationships between donors and those who are running life-enhancing initiatives. We are dedicated to strengthening local communities by providing a permanent source of funding, building endowment and 'immediate impact' funds to link donors to local needs.

Our philanthropy advice and grant-making services are valued by individuals and families, businesses, and grant-making trusts within and outside Wales. Our clients and supporters include the Welsh Assembly Government, the Charity Commission in Wales, the Big Lottery Fund, and the BBC's Comic and Sport Relief Programmes.

We welcome applications from local charities, community groups and voluntary organisations that are engaged in tackling social need and economic disadvantage at a grass-roots level. Our clients are keen to match their giving to local needs and the following list, although not exhaustive, offers a flavour of the themes that our donors like to address.

▶ Community cohesion
▶ The environment
▶ Older people
▶ Minority groups
▶ Young people
▶ Economic disadvantage
▶ Social exclusion
▶ Rural isolation
▶ Crime reduction
▶ Substance misuse and addiction
▶ Skills development and confidence-building
▶ Education and lifelong learning
▶ Sport as a vehicle for social inclusion

In 2011/12 the foundation had assets of £8.4 million and an income of £2.6 million. Grants were made totalling £1.7 million and were divided as follows:

Improving physical and mental health	£687,000
Enabling young people and promoting education and life-long learning	£538,000
Building cohesion and confidence in communities	£368,000
Nurturing heritage and culture	£82,000
Protecting our environment	£22,000

The foundation manages a number of funds, many with their own individual criteria and some which relate to specific geographical areas of Wales.

Exclusions

The current focus of the foundation's clients is broad; however, it is unlikely to support:

▶ Political organisations and pressure groups
▶ Religious organisations, where the primary aim of the project is the promotion of faith
▶ Individuals, unless the specific focus of a fund
▶ General appeals
▶ Sports organisations where no obvious charitable element exists
▶ Medical research
▶ Statutory bodies e.g. schools, local authorities and councils, although the foundation will consider applications from school PTAs if the intended project is non-statutory in nature
▶ Animal welfare

- Arts and heritage projects unless there exists a clear, demonstrable community benefit
- Large capital projects
- Retrospective applications for projects that have taken place

Applications

The foundation manages a number of funds, many with their own individual criteria, and some which relate to specific geographical areas of Wales. Visit the foundation's website. If an organisation is uncertain about whether it meets the criteria for any of its named funds a general application may be completed at any time during the year. The foundation aims to match proposals to available funding and make contact if further information is required.

Information gathered from:

Accounts; Charity Commission record; funder's website.

Wales Council for Voluntary Action

Local community, volunteering, social welfare, environment, regeneration

£11.5 million (2011/12)

Beneficial area

Wales.

Correspondent: Tracey Lewis, Secretary, Baltic House, Mount Stuart Square, Cardiff CF10 5FH (tel: 02920 431734; email: help@wcva.org.uk; website: www.wcva.org.uk)

Trustees: Margaret McCarter; Catriona Williams; Pauline Young; Lydia Stephens; Peter Davies; Dilys Jackson; Eurwen Edwards; Fran Targett; Walter Dickie; Louise Bennett; Simon Harris; Michael Hewlett Williams; Philip Avery; Win Griffiths; Efa Jones; Chad Patel; John Jones; Anne Stephenson; Clive Wolfendale; Joy Kent; Paul Glaze; Janet Walsh; Rocio Cifuentes; Hilary Stevens; Liza Kellett; Martin Pollard; Mike Denman; Thomas Williams; Catherine Gwynant; Roy Norris; Moira Lockitt; Cherrie Galvin; Judy Leering.

CC Number: 218093

According to the trustees' report for 2011/12, 'Wales Council for Voluntary Action's (WCVA) mission is to provide excellent support, leadership and an influential voice for the third sector and volunteering in Wales.'

WCVA seeks to achieve change in the following areas:

- Economic participation: helping the sector to play its full part in tackling unemployment and economic activity
- Climate change: providing leadership and encouraging third sector organisations to take practical action to tackle both the causes and consequences of climate change
- Resources: helping to achieve a well-resourced sector where access to finance and other resources is maximised and diversified, and decision making is fair
- Public services: promoting the role the sector can play in commissioning, delivering and scrutinising public services, particularly through co-design

WCVA represents supports and campaigns for the voluntary sector in Wales by providing services, education, training, information, policy consultation, funding, advice and support to charities and other voluntary organisations in Wales.

WCVA administers a variety of grant programmes (12 in 2011/12) in a similar way to a community foundation. Check WCVA's website for up-to-date information on current programmes and deadlines.

In 2011/12 the charity had assets of £15.9 million and an income of just over £43 million, including £24.6 million from the Welsh Assembly (£16 million in 2010/11) and £5.8 million from European Structural Funds. Grants were made to 1,829 organisations across Wales totalling £11.5 million.

The following is a breakdown of the charity's grant distributions by programme during the year:

Communities First	1380	£4 million
Local Voluntary Services	19	£3 million
Goldstar	34	£115,000
Volunteering in Wales Fund	70	£906,000
Size of Wales	2	£2,100
Sustainable Living – Climate Change	12	£115,000
Environment Wales	106	£811,000
Biodiversity	27	£283,000
Volunteering Enhancement Initiative	19	£1.3 million
Wales Volunteering	3	£3,500
GwirVol	121	£704,500
Partnership Council	36	£130,500

Beneficiaries included: Gwent Association of Voluntary Organisations – Newport (£658,500); Powys Association of Voluntary Organisations (£403,000); Swansea Council for Voluntary Service (£246,000); Vale Centre for Voluntary Service (£127,500); British Trust for Conservation Volunteers (£42,500); RSPB Cymru (£37,500); CTC Challenge for Change (£25,500); Scope (£18,500); and the SAFE Foundation and Community First (£16,500 each).

Exclusions

Grants are made to constituted voluntary organisations only. Check the WCVA website for specific exclusions for individual funds.

Applications

There are separate application forms for each scheme. Contact WCVA on 0800 288 8329, or visit its website, for further information.

Information gathered from:

Accounts; annual report; Charity Commission record; funder's website.

Sir Siegmund Warburg's Voluntary Settlement

Arts

£2.2 million (2011/12)

Beneficial area

UK, especially London.

Correspondent: The Secretary, 19 Norland Square, London W11 4PU (email: applications@sswvs.org)

Trustees: Sir Hugh Stevenson; Doris Wasserman; Dr Michael Harding; Christopher Purvis.

CC Number: 286719

The trust was established in 1983 following the death of Sir Siegmund Warburg, founder of the S G Warburg and Co. investment bank. The trust is a general grant-maker, which is currently focused on providing support for the arts. Both revenue funding and capital projects will be considered. The trust states that it is 'likely to make only a small number of grants a year; the intention being to identify arts institutions and projects of the highest quality and to make grants which are likely to 'make a difference'. Therefore, while the trustees consider unsolicited applications, they are likely to be able to support only a small proportion of those received.'

In 2011/12 the trust had assets of £8.3 million and an income of £188,500. Following the trustees decision to start planning for the eventual wind-down of the trust, they have begun withdrawing larger amounts from the invested portfolio and distributing this in grants. During the year grants were made to 31 organisations totalling £2.2 million.

Beneficiaries included: British Museum, English National Opera and the National Gallery (£250,000 each); York Minster (£150,000); Bristol Old Vic (£100,000); Bush Theatre, Central School of Speech and Drama, Manchester Camerata and Salisbury and South Wiltshire Museum (£50,000 each); Hepworth Wakefield (£25,000); Cambridge Music Festival and the Sainsbury Institute for the Study of Japanese Art and Culture (£5,000 each); and St Paul's Girls' School (£2,000).

Exclusions

No grants to individuals.

Applications

Registered charities only are invited to send applications by email to: applications@sswvs.org. It is requested that initial applications should be no more than four sides of A4 and should be accompanied by the latest audited accounts.

Applications sent by post will not be considered.

Common applicant mistakes

'Failure to read instructions which are to be found in the charity's accounts.'

Information gathered from:

Accounts; annual report; Charity Commission record; further information provided by the funder.

The Waterloo Foundation

Children, the environment, developing countries and projects in Wales

£5.9 million (2012)

Beneficial area

UK and overseas.

Correspondent: Janice Matthews, Finance Manager, c/o 46–48 Cardiff Road, Llandaff, Cardiff CF5 2DT (tel: 02920 838980; email: info@ waterloofoundation.org.uk; website: www.waterloofoundation.org.uk)

Trustees: Heather Stevens; David Stevens; Janet Alexander; Caroline Oakes.

CC Number: 1117535

The foundation was established in early 2007 with a substantial endowment of £100 million in shares from David and Heather Stevens, co-founders of Admiral Insurance. The foundation states:

> We give grants to organisations in both the UK and worldwide. We are most interested in projects that help globally particularly in the areas of the disparity of opportunities and wealth and the unsustainable use of the world's natural resources. We want to help both the global community and the local community here in Wales.

The following information on the foundation's programmes is taken from its website:

World Development

The Waterloo Foundation (TWF) aims to support organisations which help the economically disadvantaged build the basis of sustainable prosperity. TWF is committed to providing support to developing countries which will be used in a sustainable way with lasting impact, and which avoids promoting a culture of aid-dependency. All grant applicants should be able to demonstrate the sustained impact of their programmes, and show how they meet the foundation's objectives.

TWF currently supports two principle themes of work to help achieve this goal:
- Improving an individual's ability to access a high-quality education
- Supporting communities to have access to clean drinking water, sanitation and hygiene

TWF has also supported enterprise development and income-generating activities, although this is not currently a main priority of our grant programme.

TWF supports organisations working in a variety of developing countries, in particular in Sub-Saharan Africa and South Asia. Further information on our geographical areas of priority can be found on the foundation's website.

What we will not fund

It is not our intention to fund projects with a principle aim to deliver increased access to improved health care. Whilst TWF recognises the importance of improving health outcomes in developing countries, we believe that there are already a number of very large trusts and foundations which have made this a priority of their work.

It is also not our intention to provide financial support to organisations seeking to alleviate the suffering resulting from high-profile natural or man-made disasters, including the delivery of food aid or shelter.

Environment

Through our environment fund we want to support projects which can help mitigate the damaging effects that humans are having on the environment and contribute to a positive change both now and in the future. The fund has two main themes:
- Marine – support for projects working to halt declining fish stocks
- Tropical Forests– support for projects protecting tropical rain forest, principally through avoided deforestation

What we will not fund

We are not able to offer funding for:
- Tree planting projects
- Projects focused solely on the use of fuel-efficient stoves – we have selected one partner to undertake forest-related efficient stove interventions
- Projects with animal conservation as the sole focus
- Projects focusing on environmental education

In addition, we are currently not accepting proposals for:
- REDD (Reducing Emissions from Deforestation and Degradation) projects, pending a review of projects already funded

Child Development

TWF is interested in the psychological and behavioural development of our children, and particularly in certain neuro developmental conditions and the factors that influence them. To that end we fund research as a main priority. We also fund some non-research projects, including dissemination of research, and to a lesser extent, intervention projects.

Research funding topic 2014: One Brain

In 2014, our funding will again focus on co-occurrences, and the fact that each child has one brain. We are interested in the common and co-occurring neurodevelopmental conditions of Dyslexia, Developmental Coordination Disorder (DCD) and ADHD, along with Rolandic Epilepsy and Developmental Trauma, and have a particular interest in factors under parents' influence.

Co-occurrence is a major issue for these children. Impairments in one domain are often accompanied by impairments in other domains. For example, a child identified as having Dyslexia is more likely to also have DCD and/or ADHD than a child who does not have Dyslexia. In this case, the main problem may be in the language domain, but the motor and attention domains are also affected, albeit perhaps to a lesser extent.

The medical community often refers to this as *comorbidity*. We are steadfastly refusing to use this term and refer instead to *co-occurrence*, which is surely more cheerful for children and their families. We do hope you will join us in using this terminology (indeed, we will prioritise those applications which refer to *co-occurrence* rather than to *comorbidity*).

The level of co-occurrence is perhaps unsurprising. After all, the same brain is responsible for all domains. The language domain, motor domain, and attention domain are all supported by the same brain. Moreover, the brain develops as a whole: each part of the brain grows together, uses the same mechanisms, and is influenced by the same factors. Although our diagnostic systems focus on separating problems according to the main domain of impairment, we now know that excluding other domains is to our peril. Our research strategy reflects this.

In 2014, our research funding will again support projects which account for the fact that these children are often affected in more than one domain. Successful applications will focus on two or more of the conditions or domains on our strategy. Projects focusing on, for example, a major deficit in the language domain must also identify how impairments in other domains will be addressed. Thus, an application concerned principally with children who have a problem in the language domain, must state how performance will be measured in the motor, attention, and/or social domains.

We prioritise projects which are closest to the point of making a difference to the lives of those affected by these conditions. As always, we are interested in factors which may alleviate these problems. We are particularly interested in those which are under families' influence, such as diet, sleep, and parenting behaviours.

The research we fund is clinically relevant, with clear benefit to those with these conditions and their family members. We fund both pure and applied research topics, prioritising those which are closest to direct patient benefit. Our pure research projects typically investigate the causal factors, core deficits and co-occurrences of particular disorders. Our applied research projects typically investigate factors relating to interventions for these disorders. We prioritise those which are cost-effective, would be easy to rollout, and directly involve parents and children (such as involving sleep and diet etc).

Dissemination Support

We love to support the dissemination of knowledge and best practice to children and their carers, and to related professionals. These grants are smaller than our research funding, and grants are typically up to £10,000, although can be up to £20,000. This dissemination can be either by researchers themselves or by support groups, and could take the form of:

- Website development
- Helplines
- Newsletters
- Conferences, either sponsorship of or attendance at

However, we are unlikely to wish to be the sole funder of any such support, so it will be important that you demonstrate what your own fundraising efforts have been and how we can augment your success. We will also consider how cost-effective your plans are.

Intervention Support

We are able to offer some support to projects in Wales which help families who are affected by one of the above conditions. We welcome such applications at any point through the year. We generally do not fund actual support for individual children with these conditions (e.g. homes, equipment or therapists for individuals etc) – sorry. However, we have limited capacity to fund a small number of intervention projects subject to the following criteria:

- In Wales
- High local need
- Low cost per intervention

Wales

Although the funding priorities for TWF are the Environment and World Development, the original founders of the Foundation live and work in Wales. To support our local community, we have allocated funding to three important issues:

Caring Wales

Why we want to help:

The 2011 Census showed that the number of people providing unpaid care for disabled, sick or elderly relatives and loved ones has risen substantially in the last decade. It reveals Wales still has the highest percentage of residents who are providing care compared with any region in England.

Census data released in early December 2012 reveals that the number of carers increased from 5.2 million to 5.8 million in England and Wales between 2001 and 2011. The greatest rise has been among those providing over 20 hours care – the point at which caring starts to significantly impact on the health and wellbeing of the carer, and their ability to hold down paid employment alongside their caring responsibilities.

What we will support:

The Caring Wales funding programme is open to applications from organisations working to support long-term carers, especially young carers, or carers of people with the conditions prioritised in our Child Development research fund. The strongest applications to this fund have been from organisations that:

- Provide a range of carer-centred support services
- Demonstrate strong links with other projects, interventions, organisations and services to ensure a holistic family support approach
- Reach a substantial number of individuals, whilst: proactively identifying and working with the most isolated and vulnerable carers; offering sufficient levels of support; proactively monitoring and evaluating their work to improve services and demonstrate impact; and, promoting participation of service users in shaping their services

Working Wales

Why we want to help:

When the UK economy was expanding, Wales continued to be the least prosperous region of the UK, with economic activity lower than the UK average. On top of this, the Welsh labour market has been affected slightly more by the recession than the rest of the UK, experiencing relatively large falls in its employment rate during the first third quarter of 2008 and second and third quarters of 2009 (source: *The Welsh Labour Market Following the Great Recession, WISERD*).

At the same time, any cushioning effect from the high level of public sector employment in Wales is rapidly diminishing due to central budget cuts with recent figures suggesting the loss of 10,000 jobs as a result.

We therefore provide funding to a small number of targeted initiatives that help people set up businesses or gain permanent paid employment. Please note that we are not currently accepting unsolicited applications to this fund.

Community Energy in Wales

Why we want to help:

The problems of climate change, and rising fuel and energy costs can be partly tackled using renewable energy systems. Wales has a wealth of natural resources with potential for clean, renewable energy generation. Communities that choose to produce their own energy can often generate a surplus, resulting in savings and income which can then be invested into community development projects.

What we will support:

We understand that different technologies have different benefits – communities need to be sure which is most appropriate and effective solution for them. We will therefore provide small amounts of funding for early-stages, feasibility studies, technical assistance etc. for renewable energy projects benefiting communities in Wales. The average grant available under this programme is £5,000–£10,000.

In 2012 the foundation had assets of £102.4 million and an income of just under £5 million. Grants were made totalling £5.9 million and were broken down as follows:

World Development	70	£2.4 million
Environment	36	£1.16 million
Size of Wales	9	£700,000
Other	66	£668,000
Child Development	34	£614,000
Wales	22	£371,500

The foundation's website provides detailed information on beneficiaries across all programmes.

Exclusions

The foundation will not support:

- Applications for grants for work that has already taken place
- Applications for grants that replace or subsidise statutory funding

The foundation will not consider applications for grants in the following areas:

- The arts and heritage, except in Wales
- Animal welfare
- The promotion of religious or political causes
- General appeals or circulars

It is unlikely to support projects in the following areas:

- From individuals
- For the benefit of an individual
- Medical charities (except under certain aspects of the foundation's 'Child Development' programme, particularly mental health)
- Festivals, sports and leisure activities
- Websites, publications, conferences or seminars, except under the foundation's 'Child Development' programme

Applications

The following information is available from the foundation's website:

We hope to make applying for a grant fairly painless and fairly quick. However it will help us a great deal if you could follow the simple rules below when sending in an application (there are no application forms).

Email applications to: applications@waterloofoundation.org.uk (nowhere else please!). Include a BRIEF description (equivalent to 2 sides of A4) within your email, but NOT as an attachment, of your project or the purpose for which you want the funding, detailing:

- Your charity's name, address and charity number
- Email, phone and name of a person to reply to
- A link to your website
- What it's for
- Who it benefits
- How much you want and when
- What happens if you don't get our help
- The programme under which you are applying

Don't write long flowery sentences – we won't read them.

Do be brief, honest, clear and direct. Use abbreviations if you like!

Don't send attachments to your email – your website will give us an introduction to you so you don't need to cover that.

Who can apply?

We welcome applications from registered charities and organisations with projects that have a recognisable charitable purpose. Your project has to be allowed within the terms of your constitution or rules and, if you are not a registered charity, you will need to send us a copy of your constitution or set of rules.

We make grants for all types of projects; start-up, initial stages and valuable ongoing funding. This can include running costs and overheads as well as posts; particularly under the World Development and Projects in Wales. We do not have any upper or lower limit on the amount of grant we offer but it is unlikely that we would offer a grant of more that £100,000.

If you are an organisation not based in the UK, then you must send us contact details for a named person, preferably from a UK registered entity, who is willing to provide us with a reference for your work. This could be:

- A current or former donor
- A partnership organisation
- A fundraising group
- An academic institution or think tank
- A government department or agency

They must have visited your organisation and be able to feed back on the quality of your work. Please state the name, contact details and relationship to the referee (i.e. past funder) at the beginning of your application. If you do not have a UK referee, please contact us to discuss a suitable alternative. Only applications with references will be considered.

Common applicant mistakes

'Not noting the required criteria for each of our funding programmes or combining some criteria from one programme and some from another but not fulfilling either one sufficiently.'

Information gathered from:

Accounts; annual report; Charity Commission record; further information provided by the funder; funder's website.

The Wates Foundation

Assisting organisations in improving the quality of life of the deprived, disadvantaged and excluded in the community

£1.2 million (2012/13)

Beneficial area

Berkshire; Bristol, Avon and Somerset; Buckinghamshire; Cambridgeshire; Dorset; Gloucestershire; Hampshire; Middlesex; Nottinghamshire; Oxfordshire; Surrey; Sussex; Warwickshire (not including the Greater Birmingham area) and the Greater London Metropolitan Area as defined by the M25 motorway.

Correspondent: Brian Wheelwright, Director, Wates House, Station Approach, Leatherhead, Surrey KT22 7SW (tel: 01372 861000; fax: 01372 861252; email: director@ watesfoundation.org.uk; website: www. watesfoundation.org.uk)

Trustees: Richard Wates; Emily King; Kate Minch; William Wates; Jonathan Heynes; Claire Spotwood-Brown.

CC Number: 247941

In 1966, three brothers Norman, Sir Ronald and Allan Wates of the Wates building firm (now the Wates Construction Group), amalgamated their personal charitable trusts into the single entity of The Wates Foundation.

In 2012/13 the foundation had assets of £17.1 million and an income of £493,000. Grants were made during the year totalling almost £1.2 million.

The foundation currently awards grants under the following programmes, although they may be subject to change after it reopens to new applicants in 2015:

- Building Family Values
- Community Health
- Safer Communities
- Life Transitions
- Strengthening the Charitable and Voluntary Sectors

Exclusions

See 'applications'.

Applications

Note the following statement from the foundation:

> The Wates Foundation reviewed its grant making policy in November 2011 in the light of a range of factors, including finance and levels of demand for support.
>
> As a result of this review, the foundation has adopted a wholly pro-active grant making strategy and will no longer take applications or bids for support from external organisations. Any unsolicited

applications or bids will be rejected automatically.

> This strategy will be in place until 31 March 2015.

Percentage of awards given to new applicants: 50%.

Common applicant mistakes

'Not reading our guidelines.'

Information gathered from:

Accounts; annual report; Charity Commission record; further information provided by the funder; funder's website.

The Wellcome Trust

Biomedical research, history of medicine, biomedical ethics, public engagement with science

£511.1 million (2011/12)

Beneficial area

UK and overseas.

Correspondent: Jonathan Best, Grants Operations Manager, Gibbs Building, 215 Euston Road, London NW1 2BE (tel: 020 7611 8888; fax: 020 7611 8545; email: grantenquiries@wellcome.ac.uk; website: www.wellcome.ac.uk)

Trustees: Sir William Castell; Prof. Dame Kay Davies; Prof. Richard Hynes; Baroness Eliza Manningham-Buller; Prof. Peter Rigby; Prof. Peter Smith; Prof. Anne Johnson; Damon Buffini; Prof. Michael Ferguson; Alan Brown.

CC Number: 210183

Summary

The Wellcome Trust is one of the world's leading biomedical research charities and is the UK's largest non-governmental source of funds for biomedical research. It is also the UK's largest charity.

The trust's mission is to foster and promote research with the aim of improving human and animal health.

Funding from the trust has supported a number of major successes including:

- Sequencing of the human genome
- Development of the antimalarial drug artemisinin
- Pioneering cognitive behavioural therapies for psychological disorders
- Establishing UK Biobank
- Building the Wellcome Wing at the Science Museum

The trust's major activities in 2011/12 are described by its chair, Sir William Castell, in its annual review as follows:

> The Wellcome Trust committed £701 million in grant funding and direct charitable activities this year, mostly in grants to scientists working in medical research, and most of them in the UK.

I was thrilled this October when the UK's strength in basic biomedical research was recognised by the 2012 Nobel Prize in Physiology or Medicine which was shared by a former governor of the trust, Professor Sir John Gurdon. His work showed that mature cells had the potential to be reprogrammed into stem cells. Subsequent decades of investment in stem cell research have brought us ever closer to realising the promise of stem cell therapies.

We saw again this year how sustained investment in research can bring real benefits. Genetics has been one of the trust's most focused areas of funding since the mid-1990s. First, we sought to decode the human genome; then we had to find ways to apply that knowledge. I think we are at a stage now when we can stop talking about genetics improving health in the future – it is improving health today. Looking forward, the trust is funding a clinical trial of a gene therapy for choroideraemia, a rare genetic disorder that slowly causes people to lose their eyesight. The therapy uses a benign virus to deliver a healthy copy of the defective gene into patients' eyes. The trial began in October 2011 and, this time next year, we should know whether it has been successful in halting loss of sight in the first 12 patients.

Central to much of the genetics research we fund is the Wellcome Trust Sanger Institute. We have invested more than £1 billion there over the last 18 years. The Sanger Institute was at the heart of the Human Genome Project, providing one third of the sequence decoded over ten years; today, it continues to lead the world in this field. With data capacity currently at 16 million gigabytes and a staff of 850, collaborating with the European Bioinformatics Institute on the same site and with thousands of other scientists around the world, the Sanger Institute now sequences dozens of genomes every day. Their work is driving the first wave of stratified medicine, improving cancer therapy for patients by examining the genetics of individual tumours, and revealing the genetic basis of the way specific cancers respond to different drugs.

At the same time, ever-improving technology is giving us an advantage against infectious diseases. A study published this summer demonstrated how modern genome sequencing could track methicillin-resistant Staphylococcus aureus (MRSA). Retrospective analysis of samples from a real outbreak of MRSA in a hospital showed that the outbreak could have been identified and stopped sooner with the new technology. This approach could help to control outbreaks of hospital-acquired infections more effectively than existing laboratory techniques.

Changing world
Britain was the workshop of the world 150 years ago. Today, we have a new role as one of the leading 'knowledge shops' in the world. Through partnerships with other funders, universities, businesses, charities and government agencies, we can facilitate creative interactions between researchers in all sectors. The Wellcome Trust continues to invest substantially in the UK's universities, but we are also ensuring that their scientific discoveries can be used to improve healthcare.

For example, together with GlaxoSmithKline and the UK government, the trust funds Stevenage Bioscience Catalyst, where academic and industry scientists work side by side in an ethos of 'open innovation'. The first tenants moved in this February. By working on the same site, researchers from different fields and sectors will be able to share expertise and exchange ideas. This should lead to new projects and the faster and more effective translation of research into patient benefit.

Investments
I am very pleased at the start made by Syncona, our new investment company set up this year specifically to invest in the health and biotechnology sectors. By investing in exciting opportunities in the translation of research into new treatments and patient care technologies, we expect it will make significant returns for the trust in the longer term. Syncona has already made its first investment and looks set to be a valuable catalyst to create value through new healthcare companies at an early stage of development.

Our investment returns drive our ability to make charitable commitments. In 2011/12, we returned £1.6 billion, bringing our investment return over ten years to 145% and over twenty years to 411%. These returns exceeded those from public equities but were achieved with considerably lower reported volatility. Our net portfolio value is £14.5 billion. Charitable cash payments in the year of £643 million are twice the level at the turn of the century and are 35% higher than in the year 2006/07 before the global financial crisis; steady growth in each subsequent year has provided useful stability to UK medical research as other funding sources have come under pressure.

Our macro-economic prognosis is not positive as fiscal austerity and debt deleveraging continues. However, we think that companies, focused on the opportunities created by ageing populations, the shift to disruptive knowledge-based industries, new Faster Growing Markets in Africa, Asia and Latin America and resource scarcity, with a global long-term horizon and patient investors, will be best placed in this environment.

A strong legacy
As governors, our responsibility is to use Sir Henry Wellcome's legacy to make a real difference to people's health around the world. While primarily supporting research towards achieving this goal, Henry's intention was always that science could also be understood and used by the public. We had a golden opportunity to bring science to the public as the London 2012 Olympic and Paralympic Games entertained and inspired the country. Our contribution to the Olympic spirit was In The Zone, providing over 30,000 UK schools with kits full of ideas for exciting classroom experiments focusing on the science of the body in motion. These will help teachers nurture a love of science in their students for years to come.

The popularity of science in schools continues to rise again, countering a decline in the numbers of students taking science and maths A Levels through most of the 1990s. The rise has coincided with the Wellcome Trust's support for the National Science Learning Centre in York, which provides continuing professional development training to teachers so that they can keep up with the latest developments in science and how best to teach it. Alongside this, in 2008 we launched Project ENTHUSE, a £27 million partnership between the trust, the UK government and industry, to provide bursaries that enable teachers to cover the full costs of attending these courses. Our 7000th bursary was awarded this year and the government has renewed its commitment to the scheme for a further five years.

The future of science really does depend on the quality of science education today. By supporting science teachers, we are fostering the next generation of researchers and a society that will cherish and support their work. It is an integral part of our long-term vision of funding the brightest minds to achieve extraordinary improvements in health.

Grantmaking
In 2011/12 the trust had assets of over £13.2 billion and an income of £222.6 million. Grants were made during the year totalling £511.1 million.

Amongst the many grants awarded during the year were those to universities and other institutions, mainly in the UK, but also elsewhere (these figures represent the total amount awarded during the year, and may comprise many grants):

University of Oxford	£56 million
University of Cambridge	£52.8 million
University College London	£47.1 million
University of Dundee	£34.9 million
Imperial College London	£30.9 million
Insight: Research for Mental Health	£20.7 million
King's College London	£19.4 million
London School of Hygiene and Tropical Medicine	£16 million
University of Kwazulu Natal, South Africa	£15.8 million
University of Edinburgh	£15.3 million
Newcastle University	£12.6 million
Myscience.Co Ltd	£10 million
University of York	£8.6 million
University of Glasgow	£7.5 million
University of Birmingham	£7.3 million
Wellcome Trust/Dept. of Biotechnology India Alliance, India	£7.3 million
Cardiff University	£6.9 million
Queen Mary, University of London	£5.9 million
University of Aberdeen	£5.8 million

University of Bristol	£5.4 million
Institute of Cancer Research	£5.4 million
Medical Research Council	£5.3 million
Diamond Light Source Ltd	£5.2 million
Cadila Pharmaceuticals Ltd, India	£5 million
Liverpool School of Tropical Medicine	£4.9 million
Birkbeck University of London	£4.8 million
University of Cape Town, South Africa	£4.8 million
University of Liverpool	£4.7 million
University of Exeter	£4.6 million
GlaxoSmithKline UK	£4.5 million
University of Manchester	£4.4 million
Summit Corporation plc	£4.1 million
UK Biobank Ltd	£4 million
University of Leeds	£3.9 million
Academy of Medical Sciences	£3.8 million
University of Ghana	£3.4 million
University of St Andrews	£3.3 million
Grants to other organisations	£55.4 million

Grantmaking Policy

The trust supports high-quality research across both the breadth of the biomedical sciences and the spectrum of proposals from 'blue skies' to clinical to applied research, and encourages the translation of research findings into medical benefits.

Although the majority of grants are awarded to United Kingdom recipients, there are also a number of schemes designed specifically for overseas applicants.

For the most part grant funding is channelled through a university or similar institution in response to proposals submitted by individual academic researchers. Applications are peer reviewed using referees selected by trust staff from the United Kingdom and international research

communities. Expert committees, which also include members from outside the United Kingdom, make most funding decisions, with external experts also brought into Strategic Award Committee meetings to assist in the decision-making process.

Grant awards are made to the employing institution, which is then required to take responsibility for administering a grant in accordance with its purpose and with the terms and conditions attached to the award. Only a limited number of small-scale awards are made directly to individuals. Grant funding is available via a range of schemes including:

▶ Short-term awards for between a few months and three years, and longer-term project and programme grants for research, usually for up to five years

▶ Awards for research training and career development where support is provided for individuals at all stages of their careers

▶ Strategic awards to provide outstanding research groups with significant levels of support

The trust is aware of the profound impact biomedical research has on society and in its grant making also seeks to raise awareness of the medical, ethical and social implications of research and to promote dialogue between scientists, the public and policy makers.

The trust also undertakes activities in and funds research into the history of medicine. The Wellcome Library, which forms part of Wellcome Collection, provides access to resources that support its activities, and the trust also provides grant funding for improved access to and preservation of other medical history collections in the United Kingdom.

In addition to the above, the trust funds its own research institute, the Wellcome Trust Sanger Institute, channelling support through a wholly-owned subsidiary, Genome Research Ltd. Led by Allan Bradley, the Director of the Sanger Institute, its researchers are engaged in research programmes using large-scale sequencing, informatics and analysis of genetic variation to further understanding of gene function in health and disease and to generate data and resources of lasting value to biomedical research.

Strategic Plan 2010–2020

For over 70 years, the Wellcome Trust has supported research of the highest quality with the aim of improving human and animal health. In our Strategic Plan for 2010–20, we present a vision that describes how we will work with our communities to evolve our support to be even more effective in achieving this aim. Our decision to develop a ten-year Plan reflects the long-term view we take in supporting research and the complex and global nature of the challenges that we face.

During the last five years, we have introduced several new approaches to our grant making. Strategic Awards enable outstanding research teams to take forward large and ambitious programmes of work. Our support for technology transfer to enable the practical applications of research has expanded, with the introduction of new schemes such as Seeding Drug Discovery. We have launched major initiatives to build individual and institutional research capacity in low- and middle-income countries. Wellcome Collection has opened as an innovative public venue for exploration and debate of medicine, life and art.

We have supported the work of thousands of individuals and teams leading to many important outcomes. Pioneering research at the Wellcome Trust Sanger Institute and in universities has transformed our understanding of the role of genetic variation in health and disease. The work at our Major Overseas Programmes has played a significant role in the fight against global diseases. Our support for the National Science Learning Centre in the UK has enhanced the professional development of science teachers in schools.

Looking ahead, we identify five major challenges for our partners in the research community. Each of these challenges contains many important research questions and opportunities. These range across the broadest spectrum of research, from structural biology to public health. We recognise that each of the

challenges is enormous and complex and will require ambitious approaches to make progress. We will work in partnership to provide the funding and support to tackle these challenges. We will build on our key at tributes; these are our scale, our long track record, our independence, our dedication to research excellence, our ability to work in partnership, and the unique breadth of our funding activities.

We will provide talented and innovative researchers with the freedom and resources that they need to generate the discoveries that are essential to overcome these challenges. Our funding philosophy is to support the brightest researchers at all stages of their careers and to create the environments that they need for their research. We will support a wide range of activities to accelerate the application of research that can benefit health. We will maximise opportunities to engage diverse audiences with medical science and the questions that science raises for society.

This Plan for the next decade provides the basis on which we will develop our funding strategies. It sets out how we will assess progress towards our goals, so that we can help to realise extraordinary improvements in health.

Our vision is to achieve extraordinary improvements in human and animal health.

Our mission is to support the brightest minds in biomedical research and the medical humanities.

Our funding focuses on:
1   Supporting outstanding researchers
2   Accelerating the application of research
3   Exploring medicine in historical and cultural contexts

Our five major challenges are:
1   Maximising the health benefits of genetics and genomics
2   Understanding the brain
3   Combating infectious disease
4   Investigating development, ageing and chronic disease
5   Connecting environment, nutrition and health

The full strategic plan is available from the trust's website. Extensive information is also available from the trust and is accessible through its excellent website.

Exclusions

The trust does not normally consider support for the extension of professional education or experience, the care of patients or clinical trials.

Contributions are not made towards overheads and not normally towards office expenses.

The trust does not supplement support provided by other funding bodies, nor does it donate funds for other charities to use, nor does it respond to general appeals.

Applications

The following text is taken from the trust's website:

eGrants: online application

The eGrants system enables applicants to apply for grants online. The system provides workflow to steer the application through head of department and university administration approval steps until final submission to the Wellcome Trust.

Most applicants for Science Funding and Medical Humanities grants are required to submit their applications via our eGrants system. However, Word forms are still available for:

- Preliminary applications
- Public Engagement grants
- Technology Transfer grants
- Applicants who have limited/unreliable access to the internet – please email the eGrants helpdesk – ga-formsupport@wellcome.ac.uk – if this is the case

If you haven't applied using eGrants before, here is what you need to do:

- Make sure your institution (or the institution that would be administering the grant, if you are not already based there) is registered with us and fill in a home page for yourself (this will include your personal details that can be downloaded onto future application forms)

Other people – such as coapplicants – will need to fill in details too.

The benefits of our eGrants system include:

- Better functionality
- Clear sign off process through the host institution
- Reduced administration at the trust
- Helping us to capture management information (useful for us and useful for you)

How to register

You can register with eGrants through the website, where full guidance and information is also available.

Information gathered from:

Accounts; annual report; Charity Commission record; funder's website.

The Welton Foundation

Principally supports projects in the health and medical fields. Other charitable purposes considered include education, welfare and arts organisations

£985,500 (2011/12)

Beneficial area

UK and overseas.

Correspondent: The Trustees, Old Waterfield, Winkfield Road, Ascot, Berkshire SL5 7LJ

Trustees: H. A. Stevenson; D. B. Vaughan; Dr Michael Harding.

CC Number: 245319

Registered in 1965, the trustees' report for 2011/12 states that the objective of the foundation:

Is to provide financial support to other charities at the absolute discretion of the trustees. As a discretionary trust the foundation has no fixed policy for making grants. The current policy of the trustees is in the main to support charitable causes in the fields of health and medicine, but they can exercise their discretion to make donations to any other charities.

In 2011/12 the foundation had assets of £5 million and an income of £202,000. According to the 2011/12 trustees' report, the foundation has decided to increase the level of grants that it provides. Grants were made to 26 organisations during the year totalling £985,500, categorised as follows:

Health and medicine	28	£930,000
Heritage	2	£10,000
Community development	3	£6,000
Culture and arts	5	£10,500
Disability	5	£15,000
Education and training	6	£14,000

Beneficiaries included: National Heart and Lung Institute (£450,000); Multiple System Atrophy Trust (£100,000); Psychiatry Research Trust (£79,500); University of Cape Town and Sheffield Institute for Translational Neuroscience (£50,000 each); National Society for Epilepsy (£20,000); Salisbury Cathedral Fund and Mary Rose Trust (£10,000 each); Aidis Trust and Combat Stress (£7,500 each); Tricycle Theatre (£5,000); and Cystic Fibrosis Trust (£500).

Exclusions

Grants only to registered charities and organisations with a charitable purpose.

Applications

The trustees meet regularly to review grant applications.

Information gathered from:

Accounts; annual report; Charity Commission record.

The Westminster Foundation

Social welfare, military charities, education, environment and conservation

£1.3 million (2012)

Beneficial area

Unrestricted, in practice mainly UK. Local interests in central London (SW1 and W1 and immediate environs), North West England, especially rural Lancashire and the Chester area, and the Sutherland area of Scotland.

Correspondent: Jane Sandars, Administrator, 70 Grosvenor Street, London W1K 3JP (tel: 020 7408 0988; fax: 020 7312 6244; email: westminster.foundation@grosvenor.com; website: www.westminsterfoundation.org.uk)

Trustees: The Duke of Westminster, Chair; Jeremy H. M. Newsum; Mark Loveday.

CC Number: 267618

The foundation was established in 1974 for general charitable purposes by the fifth Duke of Westminster and continues to make grants to a wide range of charitable causes. In 1987 the Grosvenor Foundation, a separately registered charity, transferred all its assets to The Westminster Foundation. This is assumed to be a largely personal trust, created by the present duke. He is well known in the charity world for his active personal involvement in many organisations, and no doubt a significant number of the regular beneficiaries are organisations with which he has developed a personal connection that goes beyond grantmaking.

The following information is taken from the foundation's website:

Our current grant-making strategy is focused on the issues around poverty in the UK.

Research we commissioned in 2012 highlighted several ways in which we could address some of these issues.

For 2013/14, the trustees have chosen to focus on two key themes:
- Youth homelessness
- Supporting communities

What do we mean by youth homelessness?
Homelessness amongst young people is an increasingly significant issue, both in London and across the UK.

In this programme, we are working with charitable organisations to prevent homelessness amongst young adults (in the age range 16–30). We are focusing on solutions that strengthen their self-sufficiency, improve well-being and assist with access to accommodation. Our Youth Homelessness Programme has two sub-themes: building self-sufficiency – equipping young people who are homeless, or at risk of becoming homeless, with the skills and support they need to obtain long-term economic stability and personal independence; supporting access to accommodation – this might include the provision of emergency shelters, hostels and support into longer-term accommodation to give people a chance to become independent young adults in society. Examples may include: emergency night shelters, housing advice services and innovative long-term approaches to breaking the cycle of homelessness in young people.

What do we mean by supporting communities?

Our Supporting Communities Programme targets issues of isolation, in both rural and urban contexts. We are working with charities and other voluntary organisations in our key locations: identifying the needs of residents in these communities and supporting local providers in addressing these needs.

Small Grants

▶ This fund is for one-off requests of up to £5,000
▶ Appeals are reviewed and decided on by our Small Grants Panel, which meets approximately every eight weeks

Major Grants

▶ £5,000 upwards
▶ This is our primary grant fund and the trustees distribute significant sums, often over more than one year
▶ Our Major Grants aim to address issues in a more targeted way and help bring about long-term change

In 2012 the foundation had assets of £38.8 million and an income of £2.8 million. There were 100 grants made totalling just over £1.3 million, with the average grant being £13,500.

Beneficiaries included: Community Foundation for Merseyside (£300,000), a multi-year grant towards the Liverpool ONE Fund, administered by the foundation, to provide grants to local community projects that meet the local priority needs; Veterans' Aid (£61,500), towards the rent of the charity's London offices over three years; Fine Cell Work (£54,500), towards the rent of the charity's London offices over three years; Richard House Hospice (£35,000), towards running costs; West Sutherland Fisheries Trust (£25,000), towards running costs; and Farms for City Children (£20,000), towards running costs.

Exclusions

Only registered charities will be considered. No grants to individuals, 'holiday' charities, student expeditions, or research projects.

Applications

The following information is given by the foundation on its website:

Before reading our guidelines in full and making an application for funding to the Westminster Foundation, we recommend you check your organisation against this brief eligibility test to ensure you do not spend time preparing an application that does not fit within our grant-making criteria. In order to apply to the Westminster Foundation:

▶ Your organisation needs to be a charity registered with the Charity Commission, or with exclusively charitable objectives (organisations that have exempt or excepted status such as educational establishments and churches may qualify under these criteria)

▶ Your funding request needs to benefit people within the UK, and specifically within: Westminster (parts of the old Metropolitan Borough of Westminster); Cheshire West and Chester; rural Lancashire (near the Forest of Bowland); North West Sutherland
▶ Your funding request cannot be for an individual person, trips or holidays, an animal charity or a medical research charity
▶ Your appeal should fall within one of our poverty-related funding programmes

Applications should be made via the foundation's website.

Percentage of awards given to new applicants: between 10% and 20%.

Common applicant mistakes

'Failure to check geographical guidelines; failure to consult our website before applying.'

Information gathered from:

Accounts; annual report; Charity Commission record; further information provided by the funder; funder's website.

The Garfield Weston Foundation

General charitable purposes, with preference to education, the arts, health (including research), welfare, environment, youth, religion and other areas of general benefit to the community

£46 million (2011/12)

Beneficial area

UK.

Correspondent: Philippa Charles, Director, Weston Centre, 10 Grosvenor Street, London W1K 4QY (tel: 020 7399 6565; email: gdarocha@garfieldweston. org; website: www.garfieldweston.org)

Trustees: Jana Khayat; Camilla Dalglish; Kate Hobhouse; Eliza Mitchell; Galen Weston; George Weston; Sophia Mason; Melissa Murdoch.

CC Number: 230260

The Garfield Weston Foundation was established in 1958 by Willard Garfield Weston, a Canadian businessman who moved to the UK with his family in 1932. He was the creator of Associated British Foods and the foundation was endowed with the donation of family-owned company shares.

Awards are regularly made in almost all fields except animal welfare. Grants are made in the general fields of arts, community, education, welfare, medical, youth, religion and environment. Requests for specific activities or programmes, capital projects and core costs are considered. Very large grants are considered.

According to the foundation's website:

The foundation aims to be responsive to where need is greatest. We therefore support a wide range of charitable activity rather than having specific priorities for funding or regional bias. The foundation appreciates how challenging it is for charities to raise funds and aims to keep the process of applying uncomplicated with a one-stage application. Despite the diversity of organisations and projects the foundation funds, the common themes are charities that demonstrate quality and excellence with projects that have clear outcomes and benefits, good leadership and sensible business plans.

The foundation has two streams of activity:

▶ Major grants: £100,000 and above
▶ Regular grants: £1,000 to £99,999

In 2011/12 the foundation had assets of £4.95 billion, an income of £42 million and gave grants totalling £46 million. Grants awarded in 2011/12 are as follows:

Arts	133	£4.4 million
Community	313	£2.1 million
Education	187	£12.7 million
Environment	73	£2.8 million
Health	149	£6.8 million
Religion	570	£7.4 million
Welfare	315	£6 million
Youth	292	£3.2 million
Other	27	£789,000

Grants over £20,000 included: Westminster Abbey (£3 million); Imperial War Museum, King's College London and the Foundation and Friends of the Royal Botanic Gardens – Kew (£1 million each); New Schools Network and Cancer Research UK (£500,000 each); the Outward Bound Trust (£375,000); Square Chapel Trust and Shakespeare's Globe (£300,000 each); Lyric Hammersmith and South Georgia Heritage Trust (£250,000 each); the Pennies Foundation, University of Hertfordshire and National Portrait Gallery (£150,000 each); the Whitworth Gallery and the New Marlowe Theatre Development Trust (£100,000 each); Welsh National Opera, Maidstone Museums' Foundation and the National Hospital Development Foundation (£75,000 each); Academy of Ancient Music, Asthma UK and the Public Catalogue Foundation (£50,000 each); Music for Youth, the Cartoon Museum and SANE (£30,000 each); and Norfolk Concerts and Eco Centre Wales (£20,000 each).

Beneficiaries under £20,000 included: Little Angel Theatre, the Hangleton and Knoll Project and British Stammering Association (£15,000 each); Sheffield Wildlife Trust, Hearts and Minds Ltd and Gracious Street Methodist Church (£10,000 each); the Actors' Workshop

Youth Theatre, the Solent Stream Packet Ltd and Prospects Kensington Ltd (£7,500 each); Rook Lane Arts Trust, Number One Community Trust and Life Education Centres Thames Valley (£5,000 each); Colliery Mission, the Temple Trust and Moyraverty HUB Playgroup (£1,000 each); and Shoestring (£500).

Exclusions

According to the foundation's guidelines, which can be found on its website, the foundation does not fund the areas indicated below:

- Any funding request made within 12 months of the outcome of a previous application, whether a grant was received or not
- UK registered charities only (unless it holds exempt status as a church, educational establishment, hospital or housing corporation)
- Overseas projects
- Individual applicants, individual research or study including gap year activities, study trips, fundraising expeditions and sponsorship
- Animal welfare charities
- One-off events such as galas or festivals, even if for fundraising purposes
- Specific salaries and positions, however core operating costs are supported where general salary costs are recognised
- Funding commitments over several years – grants made are typically for a single year
- Organisations who cannot demonstrate significant progress with fundraising

Applications

The trust's website states that applications are accepted at any time during the year and that there are no formal deadlines for the submission of applications. Organisations should allow approximately four months for a final outcome but acknowledgement of an application will be received within four weeks.

The trust asks that applications are sent as hard copies only through the post.

Information gathered from:

Accounts; annual report; Charity Commission record; funder's website.

The Will Charitable Trust

People with sight loss and the prevention and cure of blindness, cancer care, people with mental disability
£575,500 (2011/12)

Beneficial area

UK.

Correspondent: Christine Dix, Grants Administrator, Haysmacintyre, 26 Red Lion Square, London WC1R 4AG (email: admin@willcharitabletrust.org.uk; website: willcharitabletrust.org.uk)

Trustees: Alastair McDonald; Rodney Luff; Vanessa Reburn.

CC Number: 801682

According to the trustees' report for 2011/12, the trust provides financial assistance to charities, mainly in the UK, supporting the following categories:

- Care of and services for blind people, and the prevention and cure of blindness
- Care of people with learning disabilities in a way that provides lifelong commitment, a family environment and the maximum choice of activities and lifestyle
- Care of and services for people suffering from cancer, and their families

N.B. A small proportion of the trust's income may be allocated to assist in other fields, but this is rare and reserved for causes that have come to the attention of individual trustees. It is therefore only in very exceptional circumstances that the trustees will respond favourably to requests from organisations whose activities fall outside the categories listed above. It is unlikely that applications relating to academic research projects will be successful. The trustees recognise the importance of research, but lack the resources and expertise required to judge its relevance and value.

Larger exceptional grants are occasionally considered but this is unusual and generally confined to charities that are well known by the trust. There is no separate application process for and applicants will be identified from the normal grant round.

Grants are exclusive to UK registered or exempt charities. They must have proven track records of successful work in their field of operation or, in the case of newer charities, convincing evidence of ability. Charities of all sizes are considered and grants vary in amount accordingly. Grants generally fall within the range of £5,000 to £20,000.

The trustees' report for 2011/12 also states that:

In the current financial climate, commitments to make future payments are rarely given, with grants normally being one-off annual grants. Charities which have received a grant are encouraged to apply in the next and subsequent years, but should note that only rarely will grants be given to the same charity for four successive years. This does not however mean that a charity that has received three successive grants will not be eligible in future years, just that we would not generally award a grant in year four.

In 2011/12 the trust had assets of £17.6 million and an income of £644,000. There were 48 grants made during the year totalling £575,500, broken down as follows:

Cancer care	£250,500
Learning disabilities	£141,000
Blind people	£151,000
Conservation	£33,000

Note: Although 'conservation' has been included in this list, at the time of writing (August 2013) the trust's website states that it no longer supports this cause. According to the trust's website, 'a very large one-off grant to a conservation charity, followed by a much reduced spend in this field in recent years, led to the Trustees' decision in November 2012 to cease supporting this category completely.'

Beneficiaries included: Bury Hospice and St David's Foundation Hospice Care (£20,000 each); Cam Sight, L'Arche and CLIC Sargent Care for Children (£15,000 each); Weston Hospice Care and West Northumberland Citizens Advice (£12,000 each) County Durham Society for the Blind and FORCE Cancer Charity (£10,000 each); Mousetrap Theatre Projects and Livability (£8,000 each); Music in Hospitals and Talking Newspaper Association of the UK (£5,000 each).

Exclusions

Grants are only given to registered or exempt charities. 'It is unlikely that applications relating to academic or research projects will be successful. The trustees recognise the importance of research, but lack the resources and expertise required to judge its relevance and value.'

Applications

Applications in writing to the correspondent. There are no application forms; however the trust offers the following advice on its website on how applications should be presented:

We are not necessarily looking for glossy professional bids and understand that your application to us will vary according to the size of organisation you are, and the size of the proposed project. It can be a professionally prepared presentation pack, but can equally be a short letter with supporting information. Both will receive equal consideration.

Whatever the presentation, the following lists the areas that must be covered. Failure to do so will affect your chances of success:

1 **Organisation overview**. This paragraph/section must include a short background to the charity and a summary of activities. Please include relevant information regarding your clients/beneficiaries (this might include numbers helped, geographic location, age group etc.) and numbers of employees and volunteers. Please give us this information every time you apply

2 **Project description**. Tell us what you want a grant for/towards. Explain why it is necessary, what you hope to achieve, who will benefit and how

3 **Costs**. Tell us the total cost of your project and give us a breakdown including at least the main items of expenditure. Tell us how you intend to fund it, and how much you have raised so far. If the project is part of a larger one, please explain the wider context

4 **Contingency plan**. Explain what you intend to do if you fail to raise all the funds you need

5 **A timetable**. Tell us your timescale for raising funds and when you aim to have the project up and running

6 **Annual accounts.** Your latest audited accounts and Annual Review (if you have one) must be included

7 **Other information**. Please include any other information which you feel will assist us in judging your application. This could include for example a copy of your newsletter, or short promotional/advertising leaflets. Such publications often help give a flavour of an organisation

If you wish to discuss your application, or have other queries, please contact the Grants Administrator, Christine Dix, either by email or by telephone. Please note if you telephone that the office is open part-time and you may need to leave a message.

Deadlines

Blind people and Learning disabilities

▶ Applications should be submitted from November and by 31 January at the latest. Decisions are made in the following April and successful applicants will be notified by the end of the month

Cancer care

▶ Applications should be submitted from June and by 31 August at the latest. Decisions are made in the following November and successful applicants will be notified by the end of the month

Acknowledgement

Applications will normally be acknowledged within 3 weeks. Successful applicants will be notified before 30 April or 30 November as applicable. If you have not heard by those dates, you should assume that your application has been unsuccessful.

Reporting Requirements

We ask charities to whom we have awarded grants to submit a short update on their project by the application deadline the following year.

Information gathered from:

Accounts; annual report; Charity Commission record; funder's website.

The HDH Wills 1965 Charitable Trust

General charitable purposes with particular favour towards wildlife and conservation

£987,000 (2011/12)

Beneficial area

Mainly UK, occasionally overseas.

Correspondent: Wendy Cooper, Correspondent, Henley Knapp Barn, Fulwell, Chipping Norton, Oxon OX7 4EN (tel: 01608 678051; email: hdhwills@btconnect.com; website: www.hdhwills.org)

Trustees: Dr Catherine Wills; John Burrell Carson; Lord Victor Killearn; Charles Francklin; Martin Fiennes; Thomas Nelson.

CC Number: 1117747

The trust has been endowed by the family of Sir David Wills, from a fortune derived largely from the tobacco company of that name.

According to the trust's website, the trust has two principal funds:

▶ The general fund: donations totalling about £80,000 each year to general charities in grants of, typically, between £100 and £1,000- 90% of grants are for amounts of £500 or less

▶ The Martin Wills fund: donations totalling about £1 million in certain years to general, environmental and wildlife charities in grants of, typically, between £2,000 and £25,000. Grants from the Martin Wills fund are made in a seven year cycle. Check the trust's website for current priorities

In 2011/12 the trust had assets of £57.7 million and an income of £2.76 million. Grants were made from both funds during the year totalling £987,000.

Beneficiaries included: Salzburg Seminar and 21st Century Trust (£3,000 each); Countryside Learning, CMRF – Katie Nugent Fund and Break (£2,000 each); and Ashmolean Museum, First Story, Leonard Cheshire Disability and Refugee Resource (£1,000 each).

Exclusions

Registered or recognised charities only.

Applications

An online submission form is available from the trust's website. Only one application from a given charity will be considered in any 18-month period.

According to the trust's website:

On application you will be asked to supply the following information:

▶ Contact name, address, telephone number and email address

▶ Organisation's charitable status and charity registration number

▶ Brief description of the organisation and its work

▶ The organisation's most recent set of accounts

▶ A project document containing the following: a description of the project; a budget for the project; and how the project will be monitored and evaluated

According to the trust's website, the current grantmaking policy of the trust for the general fund is as follows:

▶ Charities only

▶ Generally no grants are made to an organisation that it has supported within the previous 18 months

▶ No support for individuals seeking personal support

▶ The fund seeks to make donations to charities which are small enough in size, or which apply for support for a modest project, to benefit substantially from a donation of £250 or £500, though it will consider grants of up to £5,000

▶ Grants may be made towards revenue, capital or project expenditure

▶ Grants are made on a rolling basis and there is no deadline for applications

The current grantmaking policy of the trust for the Martin Wills fund is as follows:

▶ Charities only

▶ Grants may be made towards revenue, capital or project expenditure

▶ Grants are distributed after the end of each financial year (the trust's financial year runs from 1 April to 31 March)

▶ Applications must be received by the trust before the end of the appropriate financial year

Information gathered from:

Accounts; annual report; Charity Commission record; funder's website.

The Community Foundation for Wiltshire and Swindon

Community welfare
£314,500 to organisations
(2011/12)

Beneficial area
Wiltshire and Swindon only.

Correspondent: Heidi Yorke, Grants Programme Director, Sandcliffe, 21 Northgate Street, Devizes, Wiltshire SN10 1JX (tel: 01380 729284; email: info@wscf.org.uk; website: www.wscf.org.uk)

Trustees: Richard Handover, Chair; Elizabeth Webbe; Denise Bentley; Christopher Bromfield; David Holder; Angus Macpherson; Dame Elizabeth Neville; Tim Odoire; Alison Radevsky; Ram Thiagarajah; John Woodget; Emma Gibbons; Helen Birchenough; Jason Dalley.

CC Number: 1123126

The Community Foundation was set up in 1991 and is 'dedicated to strengthening local communities by encouraging local giving'. Grant funding is placed where it will make a significant difference to those most in need. The primary focus is on disadvantage including, supporting community care, tackling isolation and investing in young people.

> The Community Foundation for Wiltshire and Swindon has particular strengths as a grant-making organisation. We are local. We understand what life is really like for the groups we support – especially the smaller 'grass-roots' groups. We can also offer help with problems, ideas for development, and regularly put groups in touch with other organisations that can offer specialist advice or assistance.

Grants range in size from £50 to £10,000 and are awarded for up to three years.

The foundation manages a wide range of grant programmes and can provide access to a range of funds.

Its two main programmes are:

Main Grants Fund
> At the heart of our grant making is the Main Grants Fund. Groups can apply to Main Grants to support a wide variety of project, core and ongoing costs.

> The Community Foundation for Wiltshire and Swindon will give grants to benefit local communities and to improve the lives of disadvantaged people in Wiltshire and Swindon.

> We aim to fund projects which:
> - Reduce isolation
> - Improve access to skills development
> - Provide access to social & recreational opportunities
> - Improve opportunities for employment
> - Help people move on with their lives

> We do not make contributions to large building projects under Main Grants, but can help where our grant will help increase accessibility and you cannot get the funding elsewhere.

We will fund
> - Core funding (normal running costs of a group)
> - New and established projects
> - Continuation funding
> - Training and other development activities that strengthen groups
> - Equipment
> - Building work that directly supports disabled access
> - Match funding

Small Grants Fund
> Grants of up to £750 are available to small projects. This is a fast track programme and applications can be turned around within a month.

Note: grant schemes can change frequently. Consult the foundation's website for full details of current programmes and their deadlines.

In 2011/12 the foundation had assets of £10 million and an income of £2.45 million. Grants were made to organisations totalling £314,500; individuals received grants totalling £169,500.

Exclusions
The foundation will not fund:
- Groups that have more than 12 months running costs in unrestricted (free) reserves
- Projects operating outside the County of Wiltshire/Borough of Swindon
- Organisations delivering services in Wiltshire or Swindon who do not have a local management structure
- Sponsored events
- General large appeals
- The advancement of religion
- Medical research and equipment
- Animal welfare
- Party political activities
- Schools
- Preschools
- CICs (apart from start-up funds)

Applications
The foundation describes its application process as follows:
1. To ensure that you do not waste time unnecessarily, we strongly recommend that you read the [exclusions] carefully before you start your expression of interest form
2. If after step 1, you feel that your project is eligible, fill in our 'expression of interest form'. We will let you know if you are eligible and send you an application pack. We make our application forms as straightforward and as short as possible. If your project is not eligible to apply to one of our funds, we will aim to put you in touch with someone who can help you
3. Complete the form and return it, within the deadline shown on the front of the pack. If you have any problems completing it, call us for assistance
4. A member of the grants team will assess your application and will either visit or telephone you. This meeting also provides the opportunity to discuss the application further and answer any questions
5. Your application and our assessment report go forward to the relevant Local Grants Committee. The committee then makes the decisions and these are ratified by our trustees
6. If we turn you down, you will get details in writing of the reason why. Contact us by telephone or email and we will let you know if you can re-apply
7. If you are awarded a grant, you will be asked to report back to us on how the money is spent and has been achieved

The foundation has told us: 'If people are in any doubt about any part of our process they should contact us to talk it through. We appreciate the amount of time which goes in making applications and want to do all that we can to make the process as straightforward as possible.'

Percentage of awards given to new applicants: between 20% and 30%.

Common applicant mistakes
'Incomplete applications. Not having read guidelines and not fitting criteria for the fund. Providing insufficient information in answer to questions.'

Information gathered from:
Accounts; annual report; Charity Commission record; further information provided by the funder; funder's website.

The Harold Hyam Wingate Foundation

Jewish life and learning, performing arts, music, education and social exclusion, overseas development, medical
£688,000 to organisations
(2011/12)

Beneficial area
UK and developing world.

Correspondent: Karen Marshall, Trust Administrator, 2nd Floor, 20–22 Stukeley Street, London WC2B 5LR (website: www.wingatefoundation.org.uk)

Trustees: Roger Wingate; Tony Wingate; Prof. Robert Cassen; Prof. David Wingate; Prof. Jonathon Drori; Daphne Hyman; Emily Kasriel; Dr Richard Wingate.

CC Number: 264114

The foundation was established in 1960 and aims to support Jewish life and learning, performing arts, music, education and social exclusion, developing countries and medical organisations. The trust also administers the Wingate Scholarships which makes grants to young people with outstanding potential for educational research. The foundation provides the following information on its website about its areas of interest:

Jewish Life and Learning

Jewish Life and Learning are subjects that account for a significant part of the foundation's annual budget.

By their selection of projects, institutions and activities which they would support, the trustees' aspiration is to encourage Jewish cultural, academic and educational life in a manner that enhances the Jewish contribution to the life of the wider community.

In particular, applications are invited from academic institutions specialising in Jewish subjects and from bodies promoting Jewish culture, including museums, libraries and literary publications.

Applications are also welcomed from organisations able to demonstrate a record in inter-faith dialogue, in the promotion of reconciliation between Jews in Israel and their Arab neighbours and the encouragement of liberal values in both communities.

Performing Arts (excluding music)

The foundation has been a consistent supporter of the performing arts. The trustees intend to maintain that policy with particular emphasis on financial support for not-for-profit companies with a record of artistic excellence that require additional funding, not available from public sources or commercial sponsorship, to broaden their repertoire or develop work of potentially outstanding interest which cannot be funded from usual sources.

Assistance will also be considered for training and professional development for creative talent or the technical professions.

Funding to stage productions is not available.

Music

The trustees recognise that music is seriously under-funded in the UK and will consider applications for support in those areas of music performance and education which do not readily attract backing from commercial sponsors or other funding bodies, or which are not eligible for public funding. Priority will be directed towards supporting the work or education of musicians based in, or wishing to study in, the UK, but by no means exclusively so. An important criterion will be whether, in the opinion of the trustees, the funding sought will make a significant difference to the applicant's prospects.

The foundation will be prepared to consider applications for support for on-going expenses and will be willing to consider such support for a period up to three years. Priority will be given to those organisations which give opportunities to young professionals and to education projects for young people as well as for new adult audiences. This would include direct assistance as well as funding for organisations which promote their work or performance, and support for Master Classes.

The foundation reserves the right to draw up particular priorities for a given year such as support for aspiring conductors, young composers, amateur choral work, or the musical education of young people and/or adults.

Education and Social Exclusion

The foundation recognises that there are already considerable public resources allocated to these two areas. However, it will be willing to consider support for projects which may not qualify for public funding or attract other major funding bodies. Contributions towards the running expenses of projects for a strictly limited period will be considered.

Eligible projects would ideally:
- Be innovative
- Focus on the disadvantaged
- Have lasting effects

Alternatively they should consist of work (e.g. action research, pilot schemes) that would lead to such projects, and preferably they should also be capable of replication if successful.

UK projects which the foundation has supported in the past include those providing for vulnerable and disturbed children, the education of the autistic, homeless children, deaf adults, disabled artists, outreach work of arts organisations and help for ex-offenders.

Please note that we do not fund school capital projects.

Developing Countries

Applications are welcome from organisations working in developing countries for projects in any of the foundation's priority fields, including music and the arts. It will be willing to consider support for projects which may not qualify for public funding or attract other major funding bodies. However the foundation would welcome applications which address the particular problem of water supply.

Projects supported in the past have included education for scheduled castes in India, training for classical musicians in South Africa and water supply in Africa.

In 2011/12 the foundation had assets of £8 million and an income of just over £248,000. Grants were made to 83 organisations totalling £688,000. It should also be noted that the foundation received 2,000 applications during the year. The ratio of the value of grants made to organisations during the year were categorised as follows:

Medical research	18%
Jewish life and learning	9%
Music	9%
Performing arts	9%
Education and social exclusion	7%
Development projects	7%
Literary prizes	1%

Beneficiaries of the largest grants were: Whitechapel Society for the Advancement of Knowledge of Gastroenterology (£100,000); Queen Mary and Westfield College (£96,000); and the World Ort Union (£30,000).

Other beneficiaries included: Donmar Warehouse (£15,000); Chichester Festival Theatre (£12,000); Jewish Community Centre London and the Young Vic (£10,000 each); FilmClubUK (£8,000); ReSurge Africa (£7,500); Tree Aid (£6,000); Cardboard Citizens, Computer Aid International and Village Water (£5,000 each); Arvon Foundation (£4,000); Classical Opera Company (£3,000); and the University of Glasgow (£1,000).

The Scholarship Fund awarded grants totalling £408,000 (40% of the foundation's total grants). For more information on the foundation's scholarship fund, visit: www.wingatescholarships.org.uk.

Exclusions

No grants to individuals (the scholarship fund is administered separately). The foundation will not normally make grants to the general funds of large charitable bodies, wishing instead to focus support on specific projects.

Applications

On an application form available from the foundation's website. Applications are only acknowledged if a stamped addressed envelope is enclosed or if the application is successful.

The administrator of the foundation only deals with enquiries by post and it is hoped that the guidelines and examples of previous support for successful applicants, given on the foundation's website, provides sufficient information. There is no email address for the foundation. Trustee meetings are held quarterly and further information on upcoming deadlines can be found on the foundation's website.

Percentage of awards given to new applicants: less than 10%.

Common applicant mistakes

'They don't read guidelines; they don't send an sae to acknowledge receipt then phone, email or write asking if their application has been received and always a day after the deadline or the day of the deadline. Make contact a few weeks later to ask if they have been successful. Asking why applications has failed previously. Asking for too much money.'

Information gathered from:
Accounts; annual report; Charity
Commission record; further information
provided by the funder; funder's website.

The Wixamtree Trust

General charitable purposes.
In particular, social welfare,
environment and conservation,
medicine and health, the arts,
education, sports and leisure
and training and employment
£958,000 (2011/12)

Beneficial area

UK and overseas, in practice mainly
Bedfordshire.

Correspondent: Paul Patten,
Administrator, 148 The Grove, West
Wickham, Kent BR4 9JZ (tel: 020 8777
4140; email: wixamtree@
thetrustpartnership.com; website: www.
wixamtree.org)

Trustees: Sir Samuel Whitbread; Lady
Whitbread; H. F. Whitbread; Charles
Whitbread; Ian Pilkington; Geoff
McMullen.

CC Number: 210089

The trust was established in 1949 for
general charitable purposes from a trust
deed rested with Humphrey Whitbread.
According to the trustees' report for
2011/12, the trust focuses most of its
support on organisations and projects
based or operating in Bedfordshire. A
small number of national charities with a
focus on family social issues are
supported. The trustees are also
sympathetic towards applications
received from organisations of which the
late Humphrey Whitbread was a
benefactor.

In 2011/12 the trust had assets of
£22.2 million and an income of
£762,500. Grants were made to 145
organisations totalling £958,000. They
were categorised as follows:

Medicine and health	£94,000
Social welfare	£362,500
Education	£17,000
The arts	£292,000
Environment and conservation	£146,000
Sports and leisure	£16,500
International	£30,000

Beneficiaries were not listed in the
accounts but could be viewed on the
trust's website. Beneficiaries included:
British Epilepsy Association; Narcolepsy
UK; Keech Hospice Care; Leighton
Linslade Homeless Service; Barton
Scouts and Guides Headquarters
Management Committee; Farms for City
Children; Bibles for Children; British
Association for Adoption and Fostering
(BAAF); Mitalee Youth Association;

Oakley Rural Day Care Centre;
Bedfordshire African Community
Centre; Dunstable and District Citizens
Advice; Luton West Indian Community
Association; Autism Bedfordshire;
Special Needs Out Of School Club in
Beds (SNOOSC); Whizz-Kidz; Child
Bereavement UK; Road Victims Trust;
Westminster College – Cambridge;
Bedford Creative Arts; Music First;
Bedfordshire Historical Record Society;
Bedfordshire Wildlife Rescue; European
Squirrel Initiative; Campaign to Protect
Rural England (CPRE); Fauna and Flora
International; Wheelchair Dance Sport
Association (UK); and Sandy Cricket
Club.

Exclusions

No grants to individuals.

Applications

Application forms can be downloaded
from the trust's website or requested via
email or post. The method of submission
must be via email at:
wixamtree@thetrustpartnership.com.
Future meeting dates and application
deadlines are also listed on the trust's
website.

Along with the application form,
applicants must provide a copy of their
latest audited report and accounts. If the
organisation is not a charity, then a copy
of its constitution must also be provided.
Applicants are permitted to provide
additional information to support their
application if they wish to do so.

According to the trust's website:

> The trustees have entered into an
> arrangement with the trustees of the Beds
> and Herts Historic Churches Trust
> (BHHCT) who consider applications from
> Bedfordshire churches which are seeking
> support for repairs to the fabric of their
> buildings. It was felt that the BHHCT had
> more expertise in this area and by using
> their network of assessors to decide what
> projects should be supported.
> Bedfordshire churches seeking such
> support should therefore complete a
> different application form and, once
> submitted to the administrator of the
> BHHCT, a site visit will be arranged to
> evaluate the project.

Successful applicants will be notified
within 14 days of the trustees' meeting
of the amount that has been approved.
Unsuccessful applicants will receive a
letter detailing the trustees' decision
within seven days of the meeting.

Before another application can be
submitted, the trust asks previously
successful organisations who already
hold grants to submit an annual report
on how the earlier grant has been used.

**Percentage of awards given to new
applicants:** less than 10%.

Common applicant mistakes

'Not meeting criteria.'

Information gathered from:
Accounts; annual report; Charity
Commission record; further information
provided by the funder; funder's website.

The Maurice Wohl Charitable Foundation

Jewish groups and health,
welfare and medical
organisations
£2 million (2011/12)

Beneficial area

UK and Israel.

Correspondent: Joseph Houri, Secretary,
Fitzrovia House, 2nd Floor, 153 – 157
Cleveland Street, London W1T 6QW
(tel: 020 7383 5111; email: josephhouri@
wohl.co.uk)

Trustees: Ella Latchman; Martin Paisner;
Prof. David Latchman; Sir Ian Gainsford;
Daniel Dover.

CC Number: 244519

The Maurice Wohl Charitable
Foundation was established in 1965. The
foundation's objectives are in
concurrence with Maurice Wohl's wishes
before his death. The trustees use a
memorandum prepared by Maurice
Wohl as guidance when making
donations.

Particular emphasis is given in the
following areas:
- Health, welfare and medical sciences,
  including the elderly
- Welfare and relief of poverty within
  the Jewish community, with a
  particular emphasis on children and
  young adults
- Jewish education
- Renovation of synagogues and
  yeshivas in London and Jerusalem

According to the trustees report for
2011/12:

> Through both capital projects and
> programme funding the foundation aims
> to achieve its objective of promoting
> health, welfare and the advancement of
> medical science for the benefit of the
> public. The foundation continues to fund
> local communal organisations within the
> Jewish community that research, identify
> and support those in urgent need The
> foundation recognises that a route out of
> poverty is through skills and employment.

In 2011/12 the foundation had assets of
£81.2 million and an income of
£1.7 million. Grants were made totalling
almost £2 million, broken down as
follows:

Welfare and relief of poverty	£74,000
Health, welfare and medical sciences	£1.3 million
Jewish education	£602,500

Beneficiaries included: King's College London Dental Institute (£861,000); King's College London (£245,000); The Interlink Foundation (£98,500); The University of Glasgow – Beatson Translational Research Centre (£64,000); Yad Harav Herzog (£45,000); The London School of Jewish Studies (£33,000); Bayis Sheli Ltd (£21,500); Friends of Ohel Torah (£15,000); Jewish Women's Aid and Helenslea Tsedoko Ltd (£10,000 each); Keren Shabbos and Michael Sobell Sinai School (£5,000 each); Spinal Research (£2,500); and Best Beginnings and Friends of Israel Educational Foundation (£945 each).

Exclusions

The trustees do not in general entertain applications for grants for ongoing maintenance projects. The trustees do not administer any schemes for individual awards or scholarships and they do not, therefore, entertain any individual applications for grants.

Applications

In writing to the correspondent. The trustees meet regularly throughout the year.

Information gathered from:

Accounts; annual report; Charity Commission record.

The Charles Wolfson Charitable Trust

Medical research, education and welfare

£6.5 million (2011/12)

Beneficial area

Unrestricted, mainly UK.

Correspondent: Cynthia Crawford, Administrator, 129 Battenhall Road, Worcester WR5 2BU

Trustees: Lord Simon Wolfson; Dr Sara Levene; The Hon Andrew Wolfson; Lord David Wolfson.

CC Number: 238043

The trust was established in 1960 for general charitable purposes. The intention of the trust is to make grants to organisations which fall within the areas of medicine, education and welfare, especially for capital or fixed term projects and the provision of rent free premises.

The bulk of the trust's income derives from grants received from Benesco, which is a registered charity whose investments are held in property. Benesco is in effect controlled by the trust and the annual accounts present both trust and consolidated financial statements including the combined assets, liabilities and income of the trust,

Benesco and its subsidiary companies as a group.

In 2011/12 the trust had assets of £156 million and an income of £7.9 million. Grants were made totalling £6.5 million and were categorised as follows:

Medicine	£2.6 million
Education	£1.6 million
Welfare	£2.3 million

Previous beneficiaries included: Addenbrookes Charitable Trust and Yavneh College Trust (£500,000 each); Jewish Care (£350,000); Cure Parkinson's Trust (£200,000); Huntingdon Foundation (£125,000); Royal Marsden Cancer Campaign (£50,000); Sir George Pinker Appeal (£30,000); Zoological Society of London (£25,000); Priors Court Foundation (£10,000); Tavistock Trust for Aphasia (£5,000); and the Roundhouse Trust (£1,000).

Exclusions

No grants to individuals.

Applications

In writing to the correspondent.

Information gathered from:

Accounts; annual report; Charity Commission record.

The Wolfson Family Charitable Trust

Jewish institutions and charities, particularly Jewish groups and Israeli institutions

£1.6 million (2011/12)

Beneficial area

UK; mostly Israel.

Correspondent: Paul Ramsbottom, Secretary, 8 Queen Anne Street, London W1G 9LD (tel: 020 7323 5730; fax: 020 7323 3241; website: www.wolfson.org.uk)

Trustees: Martin Paisner; Sir Ian Gainsford; Sir Bernard Rix; Sir Eric Ash; The Hon Laura Wolfson Townsley; The Hon Janet de Botton; Lord Turnberg; The Hon Elizabeth Wolfson Peltz.

CC Number: 228382

According to the trustees' report for 2011/12, 'the Wolfson Family Charitable Trust is a charitable foundation established by a trust deed in 1958 whose aims are the advancement of health, education, the arts and humanities.'

The trust gives a relatively small number of often very large grants, mostly to institutions in Israel, in the fields of science, medical research, health, welfare and arts and humanities. The trust's objectives are usually pursued by the

provision of buildings or equipment. Projects that help people with special needs (particularly physical and learning disabilities), provide high quality secondary education, or that improve access to culture and heritage are of particular interest to the trust.

The trustees' report states that grants are given to act as 'a catalyst, to back excellence and talent and to provide support for promising future capital projects which may currently be underfunded.'

In 2011/12 the trust had assets of £31.2 million and an income of £1.2 million. Grants were paid during the year totalling £1.6 million.

Science, technology and medical research	£900,000
Arts and humanities	£261,000
Health and welfare	£197,000
Education	£155,000

Most grants were paid to Israeli institutions, these included those to: Israel Museum (£200,000); Technion – Israel Institute of Technology and Weizmann Institute of Science (£171,000 each); Tel Aviv University (£162,000); The Hebrew University of Jerusalem (£126,000); The Academy of Medical Sciences (£100,000); Central Synagogue and Yemin Orde Wingate Academy (£50,000 each); Beit Issie Shapiro and Foundation for the Benefit of Holocaust Survivors (£20,000 each); The Langdon Foundation and Ezrra U'Marpeh (£15,000 each); Technoda Dorset (£7,500); Carmel Zvulun and Yuri Shtern Foundation (£5,000 each); and Min Ajliki (£2,500).

Exclusions

Exclusions, as stated on the trust's website, are as follows:

- Grants direct to individuals or through conduit organisations
- Overheads, maintenance costs, VAT and professional fees
- Non-specific appeals (including circulars) and endowment funds
- Costs of meetings, exhibitions, concerts, expeditions, etc
- The purchase of land or existing buildings (including a building's freehold)
- Film or promotional materials
- Repayment of loans
- Projects that have already been completed or will be by the time of award

Applications

According to the trust's website, awards are made once or twice a year. Awards for Israeli universities and hospitals are made in conjunction with designated programmes. Organisations should be charities or have a charitable purpose, generally have an income of above £50,000 and show evidence of long-term financial viability. Within the cultural field, organisations should have a national reputation for excellence. In the area of heritage, the trust is particularly interested in historic synagogues.

Funding is provided for capital projects and applicants should guarantee matched funding. Requests should generally be in the range of £5,000 to £25,000.

Applications can be made online via the trust's website.

Percentage of awards given to new applicants: between 40% and 50%.

Common applicant mistakes

'Submitting applications which are ineligible (e.g. from individuals or not for capital costs). Submitting applications which are circulars and not specifically focused towards the trust.'

Information gathered from:

Accounts; annual report; Charity Commission record; further information provided by the funder; funder's website.

The Wolfson Foundation

Medical and scientific research, education, health and welfare, heritage, arts

£49.7 million (2011/12)

Beneficial area

Mainly UK, but also Israel.

Correspondent: Paul Ramsbottom, Chief Executive, 8 Queen Anne Street, London W1G 9LD (tel: 020 7323 5730; fax: 020 7323 3241; website: www.wolfson.org.uk)

Trustees: Sir David Cannadine; Sir Eric Ash; Sir David Weatherall; Lord McColl of Dulwich; The Hon Janet De Botton; The Hon Laura Wolfson Townsley; Lord Turnberg; The Hon Deborah Wolfson Davis; Prof. Hermione Lee; Sir Michael Pepper.

CC Number: 206495

According to the trustees' report for 2011/12:

> The objective of the foundation is the support and promotion of excellence in the fields of science and technology, healthcare, education, the arts and humanities. Set up in 1955, it is endowed from the fortune created by Sir Isaac Wolfson through the Great Universal Stores Company.

Grants are for buildings and equipment, but not for revenue or project costs, in four main areas:

- Science and medicine
- Arts and humanities
- Education
- Health and welfare

Grants are given to act as a catalyst, to back excellence and talent and to provide support for promising capital

projects which may currently be underfunded. Details regarding grants are available at the foundation's website.

Funding is made through a number of programmes, including preventative medicine, people with special needs, historic buildings, libraries, the visual arts and education. Grants are made to universities for research equipment, new buildings and renovations. Awards for university research are normally made under the umbrella of designated programmes.

Scientific and medical research generally receives the highest proportion of the Wolfson Foundation's funding each year. The main share of 2011/12's funding was awarded to University College London to establish the Leonard Wolfson Experimental Neurology Centre (£20 million).

In 2011/12 the foundation had assets of £633 million and an income of £24.1 million. There were 291 grants made during the year totalling almost £49.7 million, broken down as follows:

Wolfson Neurology Initiative	1	£20 million
Science and medicine	22	£13.5 million
Arts and humanities	118	£6.9 million
Education	79	£5.8 million
Health and welfare	71	£3.7 million

The foundation provides more specific details about individual elements within its broader categories. This information can be found via the foundation's annual report. The following summary analysis provides a brief indication of the types of grants it pursues:

Medical research and health care: this area usually receives the highest proportion of funding through investment in infrastructure, which includes new and refurbished buildings and high value equipment. Projects funded also include smaller charities working in the fields of special needs and hospices.

Arts and humanities: the foundation aims to encourage merit in the cultural and academic spheres through capital projects at museum, galleries, educational institutions and performing arts organisations.

Education: open applications support teaching spaces at universities and secondary schools, as well as education spaces in cultural organisations, disability charities or those working in the area of public engagement with science. Pilot programmes have been established which look to improve access to high quality education. Large capital awards are also funded for higher education buildings, as well as funding for equipment and building projects for the teaching of science and technology at secondary schools.

Science education and research: the foundation has a long-standing interest in supporting public engagement with science. Grants are given for equipment, as well as research projects.

Health and disability: the foundation funds the improvement of facilities for organisations who address a variety of needs. Typical areas of interest are physical disability; learning disability; mental health; older people and end of life care.

Beneficiaries included: Wolfson Neurology Initiative (£20 million); University of Manchester – cancer research building (£2 million); Epilepsy Society – epilepsy research centre, Royal Botanic Gardens – Kew and National Theatre (£1 million each); English Heritage (£810,000); Design Museum (£500,000); University of Leicester – cardiovascular research laboratories and Royal College of Art – printmaking machine hall (£400,000 each); Rambert Dance Company (£250,000); The Hebrew University of Jerusalem (£210,000); Stroke Association (£150,000); Sutton Trust (£135,000); Manchester Historic Buildings Trust (£65,000); John Spendluffe Technology College and High Wycombe Royal Grammar School (£45,000 each); Old Castle Lachlan – Argyll and Sir William Turner's Alms-houses (£20,000 each); Mausolea and Monuments Trust (£10,000); and All Saints – Salop, On Course Foundation and St Peter – Brighton (£5,000 each).

Exclusions

The following are ineligible for funding:

- Individuals
- Conduit organisations
- Overheads, maintenance cost (including for software), VAT and professional fees
- VAT and professional fees
- Non-specific appeals (including circulars) and endowment funds
- Costs of meetings, exhibitions, concerts, expeditions, etc.
- Purchasing of land or existing buildings (including a building's freehold)
- Film or promotional materials
- Repayment of loans
- Completed projects
- Projects where the total cost is below £15,000

Applications

The foundation's website states:

> The Wolfson Foundation has a two stage application process. Details of eligibility and what we fund are contained within the various funding programme pages. Please note that, under some funding programmes, applicants are asked to submit via partner organisations, and so the application process and deadlines may vary from those described here. Such

cases are signposted within the relevant programme area pages.

We are committed to rigorous assessment in order to fund high quality projects. All applications undergo detailed internal review and assessment by external experts. As such, the time between submission of a Stage 1 application and a funding decision on a Stage 2 application will be a minimum of some five months (and may in some cases be substantially longer). As we do not make retrospective grants (i.e. your project will need to be on-going at the time that it is considered by our trustees), it is important to plan carefully the timing of your application.

Grants are generally given for capital infrastructure (new build, refurbishment and equipment) supporting excellence in the fields of science and medicine, health and disability, education and the arts and humanities.

The large majority of our funding is allocated through open programmes (i.e. programmes which are open for any applicant to apply, albeit within defined eligibility criteria). We also run a small number of closed programmes (i.e. programmes where the particular field being funded is tightly defined and where we work with a number of carefully selected organisations). Generally our capital infrastructure programmes are open programmes and our closed programmes are all bursary, scholarship or salary schemes focused on people rather than buildings or equipment. We welcome applications under our open programmes but do not accept unsolicited applications under our closed programmes.

The foundation is committed to working, where possible, in partnership with other funders and expert bodies. A number of our funding programmes are administered by other organisations and [the foundation's] website provides details of those programmes, including links to the relevant information on how to apply (which is generally via the partner organisation rather than direct to us). By partnership programmes we mean all programmes that are administered and/or co-funded by other organisations.

All stage applications should be submitted online through the foundation's website. For more information visit the website's funding pages.

Charities are encouraged to apply only once in a five year period.

Percentage of awards given to new applicants: between 40% and 50%.

Common applicant mistakes

'Submitting application which are ineligible (e.g. applications from individuals or projects which do not involve capital costs). Submitting applications which are circulars and not focused specifically towards the foundation. Applications where the timing is unsuitable as the project will be completed before the trustees' meeting.'

Information gathered from:

Accounts; annual report; Charity Commission record; further information provided by the funder; funder's website.

The South Yorkshire Community Foundation

General

£713,000 (2011/12)

Beneficial area

South Yorkshire wide, with specific reference to Barnsley, Doncaster, Rotherham, Sheffield.

Correspondent: Sue Wragg, Fund Manager, Unit 3 – G1 Building, 6 Leeds Road, Attercliffe, Sheffield S9 3TY (tel: 01142 424294; fax: 01142 424605; email: grants@sycf.org.uk; website: www.sycf.org.uk)

Trustees: Jonathan Hunt, Chair; David Moody; Sir Hugh Neill; Peter W. Lee; Martin P. W. Lee; Peter Hollis; Frank Carter; Jackie Drayton; Galen Ives; Christopher Jewitt; Michael Mallett; Sue Scholey; Maureen Shah; Allan Sherriff; Lady R. Sykes; R. J. Giles Bloomer; Timothy M. Greenacre; Allan Jackson; Jane Kemp; Jane Marshall; William Warrack.

CC Number: 1140947

The South Yorkshire Community Foundation, launched in 1986, specialises in funding small community and voluntary groups within the south Yorkshire area. Priority is given to small and medium-sized groups which find it hard to raise money elsewhere. Projects funded include those which help local people in need, such as people who may be homeless, ill, disabled or older, and community life, such as nursery care, arts and culture, nature and heritage and sport.

Applicants do not have to be a registered charity but do have to have a charitable purpose. As well as running its own programme, the foundation also makes grants on behalf of its donors.

The foundation is particularly interested in supporting groups or projects which:

- Support people in greatest need
- Are locally led and run
- Involve people who face particular discrimination or disadvantage e.g. young people, people with disabilities or facing mental health issues, black and minority ethnic communities and so on
- Respond to local communities' needs
- Work well with other local community initiatives
- Are innovative
- Will benefit from relatively small amounts of funding
- Give real value for money

In common with other community foundations, the South Yorkshire

Community Foundation administers a number of funds which are subject to change. The types of funds available include smalls grants funds, endowment funds and grassroots grants, all of which are listed on the foundation's website. Check there for current availability.

In 2011/12 the foundation had assets of just over £8.1 million and an exceptional income of £8.7 million due to incorporation and consolidation of other funds. In previous years income has typically been around £3.5 million. Grants were made during the year totalling £713,000, which were broken down geographically as follows:

Sheffield	29%	£206,500
Barnsley	26%	£193,500
Rotherham	20%	£148,000
Doncaster	18%	£130,500
Outside South Yorkshire	3%	£19,000
Deakin and Withers Fund	4%	£32,000

A wide range of organisations across all of the foundation's areas of operation were supported under various programmes, some of which may no longer be running. Many organisations received grants from more than one fund.

Exclusions

The following exclusions apply to all funds administered by the foundation:

- Groups that have substantial unrestricted funds
- National charities
- Activities promoting political or religious beliefs or where people are excluded on political or religious grounds
- Statutory bodies e.g. schools, local councils, colleges
- Projects outside of South Yorkshire
- Endowments
- Small contributions to large projects
- Projects for personal profit
- Minibuses or other vehicle purchases
- Projects that have already happened
- Animals
- Sponsorship and fundraising events

Applications

Applications are initiated online via the foundation's website. The foundation provides the following information there:

To apply online, click on the link [on the foundation's website] which asks for your email address. You will be emailed a unique link to your own application form which is Stage 1 of the process. Assistance with how to fill in the application form is available when you access that link and you will be able to save the application if you cannot complete it in one go. Once you have completed Part A and submitted it to us, you will also receive a copy by email for your records.

We will inform you within one month if you have been successful in moving to Stage

2 of our application process, when you will be invited to complete Part B of our standard application form and asked to submit supporting documents.

Part B requests your organisation's bank details and other information to back up what you told us in Part A. Two members of your organisation must also sign Part B to accept the Terms and Conditions if a grant is made.

Application Part B should then be posted to South Yorkshire Community Foundation together with the following documentation:

◗ A copy of your last year's accounts
◗ A photocopy of a bank statement no more than 3 months old
◗ Quotes (as appropriate)
◗ Any other material you consider relevant to your application (please do not send material you want returned) e.g. leaflets, flyers, press cuttings

Decision making

All applications are assessed against South Yorkshire Community Foundation's criteria and the criteria of the relevant funder(s). Those meeting eligibility will be invited to complete Part B of the application form. The complete application form is then assessed and then passed to a panel of independent volunteer decision makers that meets approximately every 12 weeks, and their decision is final.

Monitoring

We have to ensure that funding has been appropriately spent and therefore require monitoring information. A monitoring form will be posted or emailed to you with the letter confirming that your application has been successful. It will ask you to report on the difference the grant has made to your group and beneficiaries. This must be returned six weeks after the grant has been spent or the activity has finished.

Your project may also be subject to a monitoring visit and any audit requirements of the programme. You must retain and return with your monitoring copies of all receipts, invoices and all expenditure relating to your grants including any capital items.

South Yorkshire Community Foundation will only consider further applications if a satisfactory monitoring form is returned.

Feel free to contact the Grants team on 01142 424294, open Tuesday to Thursday during office hours, to discuss your application.

Information gathered from:

Accounts; annual report; Charity Commission website; funder's website.

The Yorkshire Dales Millennium Trust

Conservation and environmental regeneration
£801,000 (2011/12)

Beneficial area

The Yorkshire Dales.

Correspondent: Isobel Hall, Projects and Grants Manager, The Old Post Office, Main Street, Clapham, Lancaster LA2 8DP (tel: 01524 251002; fax: 01524 251150; email: info@ydmt.org; website: www.ydmt.org)

Trustees: Stephen Macare; Joseph Pearlman; Carl Lis; Colin Speakman; Dorothy Fairburn; Dorothy Fairburn; Hazel Cambers; David Sanders Rees-Jones; Jane Roberts; Peter Charlesworth; David Joy; Thomas Wheelwright; Margaret Billing; Andrew Campbell; David Shaw; Wendy Hull; Karen Cowley; Christine Leigh.

CC Number: 1061687

This trust's patron is HRH The Prince of Wales and the role of the trust is to distribute money to organisations, communities and individuals in the Yorkshire Dales. Grants are made towards the conservation and regeneration of the natural and built heritage and community life of the Yorkshire Dales. It supports, for example, planting new and restoring old woods, the restoration of dry stone walls and field barns, conservation of historical features and community projects.

The trust has adopted the following aims:

◗ To conserve or restore the natural, built, scenic and cultural heritage features which together make up the special landscape of the Dales
◗ To increase access for all by developing and promoting opportunities for wider access to and understanding of the Yorkshire Dales
◗ To support the economic life of the area, including enhancing the employable skills
◗ To support the people and communities of the Yorkshire Dales to live and work sustainably in this protected landscape
◗ To support and help to develop the social and community fabric of the Yorkshire Dales

The trust raises and distributes its own funds and manages programmes on behalf of external funders, such as the Heritage Lottery Fund and the Learning and Skills Council. Details of the trust's current funding schemes can be found on the trust's website.

The trust makes grants to applicants for up to 70% of their project costs. For every project it supports the trust can pull in matching funding from other sources.

In 2011/12 it had assets of £233,500 and an income of just over £1 million, made up almost entirely from grants and donations. Grants were made during the year totalling £801,000, including grants from the following restricted funds:

Yorkshire Dales National Park Authority Sustainable Development Fund	£199,500
North Yorkshire Aggregates Grant Scheme	£173,000
Settle Riverside	£159,000
Dales Woodland Restoration	£89,000

Applications

In writing to the correspondent.

Information gathered from:

Accounts; annual report; Charity Commission record; funder's website.

The Zochonis Charitable Trust

General, particularly youth education and welfare
£3.4 million (2011/12)

Beneficial area

UK, particularly Greater Manchester, and overseas, particularly Africa.

Correspondent: Ruth Barron, Administrator, DWF LLP, 1 Scott Place, 2 Hardman Street, Manchester M3 3AA (tel: 01618 380487; email: ruth.barron@dwf.co.uk)

Trustees: Sir John Zochonis; Christopher Nigel Green; Archibald G. Calder; Joseph J. Swift; Paul Milner.

CC Number: 274769

Established in 1977, this is the trust of Sir John Zochonis, former head of PZ Cussons, the soap and toiletries manufacturer. It has general charitable objectives but tends to favour local charities with a particular emphasis on education and the welfare of children. Grants do not appear to be ongoing, but local charities with an established relationship with the trust are supported intermittently, if not regularly, over many years.

In 2011/12 the trust had assets of £157.8 million and an income of almost £3.4 million. Grants were made to 207 organisations totalling £3.4 million.

Beneficiaries included: Cancer Research UK and Corpus Christi College Oxford (£150,000 each); VSO (£100,000); Police Foundation (£75,000); Manchester Art Gallery (£60,000); Gaddum Centre (£50,000); Mencap (£30,000); Missing

Foundation (£15,000); Royal Court
Liverpool Trust (£10,000); Centrepoint
(£5,000); Music and the Deaf (£3,000);
and Live Music Now North West
(£2,000).

Exclusions

No grants for individuals.

Applications

In writing to the correspondent.

Information gathered from:

Accounts; annual report; Charity
Commission record.

Community Foundation Network

Community foundations are charitable trusts which work in specific geographical areas as endowment builders, grant-makers and community leaders. They channel funds on behalf of individuals, organisations, companies and other agencies which recognise that their detailed knowledge of local needs puts them in an ideal position to distribute funding.

In England in particular, many community foundations have been the local agents for government programmes such as Grassroots Grants. They also manage large funds such as the Big Lottery-funded Fair Share Trust programme. The foundations are increasingly called on to help deliver short-term programmes and emergency assistance on behalf of other grantmakers.

There are currently 46 community foundations covering most parts of the UK, with new ones being established occasionally. In 2012/13 grants totalling £60 million were made by community foundations and the value of their endowed funds stood at £225 million, an increase of around 69% on the previous year. According to UK Community Foundations (the Community Foundation Network) website, community foundations made almost 20,000 grants in 2012/13, with the size of the average grant being £3,000.

A list of all current community foundations is available on the UK Community Foundations website, via an interactive map. This, and other useful information, can be found at ukcommunityfoundations.org.

Subject index

The following subject index begins with a list of categories used. The categories are very wide-ranging to keep the index as simple as possible. DSC's subscription website (www.trustfunding.org.uk) has a much more detailed search facility on the categories. There may be considerable overlap between the categories – for example, children and education, or older people and social welfare.

The list of categories is followed by the index itself. Before using the index, please note the following points.

How the index was compiled

1) The index aims to reflect the most recent grant-making practice. Therefore, it is based on our interpretation of which areas each trust has actually given to, rather than what its policy statement says or its charitable objects allow it to do in principle. For example, where a trust states that it has general charitable purposes, but its grants list shows a strong preference for welfare, we index it under welfare.

2) We have tried to ensure that each trust has given significantly in the areas under which it is indexed (usually at least £15,000). Thus small, apparently untypical grants have been ignored for index purposes.

3) The index has been complied from the latest information available to us.

Limitations

1) Policies may change, and some more frequently than others.

2) Sometimes there will be a geographical restriction on a trust's grantgiving which is not shown in this index, or the trust may not give to the area and the heading under which your specific purposes fall. It is important to read each entry carefully.

You will need to check that:

- the trust gives in your geographical area of operation
- the trust gives for the specific purposes you require
- there is no other reason to prevent you from making an application to this trust.

3) It is worth noting that one or two of the categories list almost half the trusts included in this guide.

Under no circumstances should the index be used as a simple mailing list. Remember that each trust is different and that the policies or interests of a particular trust often do not fit easily into the given categories. Each entry must be read individually before you send off an application. Indiscriminate applications are usually unsuccessful. They waste time and money and greatly annoy trusts.

The categories are as follows:

Arts, culture, sport and recreation *page 299*

This is a very wide category including: performing, written and visual arts; crafts; theatres, museums and galleries; heritage, architecture and archaeology; and sports.

Children and young people *page 300*

This is mainly for welfare and welfare-related activities.

Development, housing and employment *page 301*

This includes specific industries such as leather making or textiles.

Disability *page 302*

Disadvantaged people *page 302*

This includes people who are:

- socially excluded
- socially and economically disadvantaged
- unemployed
- homeless
- offenders
- educationally disadvantaged
- victims of social/natural occurrences, including refugees and asylum seekers.

Education and training *page 303*

Environment and animals *page 304*

This includes:

- agriculture and fishing
- conservation
- animal care
- environment and education
- transport
- sustainable environment.

General charitable purposes *page 305*

This is a very broad category and includes trusts that often have numerous specific strands to their programmes a well as those that will consider any application (subject to other eligibility criteria).

Arts, culture, sport and recreation

The 29th May 1961 Charitable Trust
Allchurches Trust Ltd
The H B Allen Charitable Trust
The Architectural Heritage Fund
The Ashden Trust
Backstage Trust
The Barcapel Foundation
The Baring Foundation
BBC Children in Need
BC Partners Foundation
The Big Lottery Fund
The Boltini Trust
The Liz and Terry Bramall Foundation
Edward Cadbury Charitable Trust
The William A Cadbury Charitable Trust
The Barrow Cadbury Trust and the Barrow Cadbury Fund
Calouste Gulbenkian Foundation – UK Branch
The Carpenters' Company Charitable Trust
The City Bridge Trust
The Clore Duffield Foundation
The Coalfields Regeneration Trust
The John S Cohen Foundation
The R and S Cohen Foundation
Colyer-Fergusson Charitable Trust
The Ernest Cook Trust
The Evan Cornish Foundation
The Peter Cruddas Foundation
The D'Oyly Carte Charitable Trust
The Daiwa Anglo-Japanese Foundation
The Davidson Family Charitable Trust
Peter De Haan Charitable Trust
The Djanogly Foundation
Dorset Community Foundation
The Drapers' Charitable Fund
The Dulverton Trust
Dunard Fund
The John Ellerman Foundation
The Eranda Foundation
Esmée Fairbairn Foundation
The February Foundation
The Fidelity UK Foundation
The Sir John Fisher Foundation
Fisherbeck Charitable Trust
The Fishmongers' Company's Charitable Trust
The Football Association Youth Trust

The Football Foundation
The Donald Forrester Trust
The Foyle Foundation
The Hugh Fraser Foundation
The Gannochy Trust
The Gatsby Charitable Foundation
Simon Gibson Charitable Trust
The Girdlers' Company Charitable Trust
The Glass-House Trust
The Golden Bottle Trust
The Goldsmiths' Company Charity
The Gosling Foundation Limited
The Great Britain Sasakawa Foundation
The Grocers' Charity
Paul Hamlyn Foundation
The Helen Hamlyn Trust
The Kathleen Hannay Memorial Charity
The Harbour Foundation
The Harpur Trust
The Peter Harrison Foundation
The Charles Hayward Foundation
The Headley Trust
The Hintze Family Charitable Foundation
Hobson Charity Limited
Jerwood Charitable Foundation
The Sir James Knott Trust
The Kohn Foundation
The Neil Kreitman Foundation
The Kirby Laing Foundation
The Leathersellers' Company Charitable Fund
The Leverhulme Trust
Lord Leverhulme's Charitable Trust
The Joseph Levy Charitable Foundation
The Linbury Trust
The Enid Linder Foundation
The George John and Sheilah Livanos Charitable Trust
Lloyds Bank Foundation for Northern Ireland
The London Marathon Charitable Trust
The Lord's Taverners
John Lyon's Charity
The Mackintosh Foundation
The MacRobert Trust
The Manifold Charitable Trust
The Manoukian Charitable Foundation
Marshall's Charity
The Mercers' Charitable Foundation
Milton Keynes Community Foundation
The Monument Trust
The Henry Moore Foundation

Children and young people

Development, housing and employment

The Pilgrim Trust
The Pilkington Charities Fund
Mr and Mrs J A Pye's Charitable
  Settlement
The Sigrid Rausing Trust
The Rayne Foundation
The Robertson Trust
Mrs L D Rope Third Charitable
  Settlement
The Joseph Rowntree Charitable
  Trust
The Saddlers' Company Charitable
  Fund
Foundation Scotland
Sir Halley Stewart Trust
The Sussex Community Foundation
Sutton Coldfield Charitable Trust
Community Foundation Serving
  Tyne and Wear and
  Northumberland
Volant Charitable Trust
Voluntary Action Fund (VAF)
Wales Council for Voluntary
  Action
The Waterloo Foundation
The Welton Foundation
The Wixamtree Trust

Disability

The 1989 Willan Charitable Trust
The 29th May 1961 Charitable
  Trust
The ACT Foundation
The Sylvia Adams Charitable Trust
Autonomous Research Charitable
  Trust
The Baily Thomas Charitable Fund
The Band Trust
The Barclay Foundation
The Big Lottery Fund
Percy Bilton Charity
The Bruntwood Charity
The William A Cadbury Charitable
  Trust
The Charities Advisory Trust
The City Bridge Trust
Colyer-Fergusson Charitable Trust
The Evan Cornish Foundation
The Crerar Hotels Trust
Cumbria Community Foundation
Dorset Community Foundation
The Drapers' Charitable Fund
The Charles Dunstone Charitable
  Trust
The EBM Charitable Trust
The John Ellerman Foundation
The Equitable Charitable Trust
The Eveson Charitable Trust
Esmée Fairbairn Foundation

The Fishmongers' Company's
  Charitable Trust
The Donald Forrester Trust
The Hugh Fraser Foundation
The Freemasons' Grand Charity
The Gatsby Charitable Foundation
Simon Gibson Charitable Trust
The Girdlers' Company Charitable
  Trust
The Goodman Foundation
The Gosling Foundation Limited
The Grocers' Charity
H C D Memorial Fund
The Hadley Trust
Hampton Fuel Allotment Charity
The Harbour Foundation
The Peter Harrison Foundation
The Headley Trust
Heart of England Community
  Foundation
The Hedley Foundation
Lady Hind Trust
The Jane Hodge Foundation
The Albert Hunt Trust
The J J Charitable Trust
The Jones 1986 Charitable Trust
Ernest Kleinwort Charitable Trust
The Sir James Knott Trust
The Kohn Foundation
Maurice and Hilda Laing Charitable
  Trust
The Kirby Laing Foundation
The Beatrice Laing Trust
The Leathersellers' Company
  Charitable Fund
The Joseph Levy Charitable
  Foundation
The Linbury Trust
The Enid Linder Foundation
Lloyds Bank Foundation for
  England and Wales
Lloyds Bank Foundation for
  Northern Ireland
Lloyds TSB Foundation for
  Scotland
The Trust for London
The Lord's Taverners
The R S Macdonald Charitable
  Trust
The MacRobert Trust
The Mercers' Charitable
  Foundation
Milton Keynes Community
  Foundation
John Moores Foundation
The Edith Murphy Foundation
Northamptonshire Community
  Foundation
The Northern Rock Foundation
The Northwood Charitable Trust
The Nuffield Foundation
The Parthenon Trust

The Peacock Charitable Trust
The Dowager Countess Eleanor
  Peel Trust
The Pilkington Charities Fund
Mr and Mrs J A Pye's Charitable
  Settlement
The Rank Foundation Limited
The Joseph Rank Trust
The Rayne Foundation
The Richmond Parish Lands
  Charity
The River Farm Foundation
The Robertson Trust
Mrs L D Rope Third Charitable
  Settlement
The Saddlers' Company Charitable
  Fund
The Francis C Scott Charitable
  Trust
The Shirley Foundation
The Henry Smith Charity
The Sobell Foundation
The Sovereign Health Care
  Charitable Trust
St James's Place Foundation
Sir Halley Stewart Trust
The Bernard Sunley Charitable
  Foundation
The Sussex Community Foundation
The Three Guineas Trust
The True Colours Trust
Community Foundation Serving
  Tyne and Wear and
  Northumberland
The Valentine Charitable Trust
The Variety Club Children's
  Charity
Volant Charitable Trust
Voluntary Action Fund (VAF)
The Welton Foundation
The Garfield Weston Foundation
The Will Charitable Trust
The HDH Wills 1965 Charitable
  Trust
The Wixamtree Trust
The Maurice Wohl Charitable
  Foundation
The Charles Wolfson Charitable
  Trust
The Wolfson Family Charitable
  Trust

Disadvantaged
people

The 1989 Willan Charitable Trust
The 29th May 1961 Charitable
  Trust
The Sylvia Adams Charitable Trust
The Alliance Family Foundation

Education and training

Environment and animals

General charitable purposes

The Wixamtree Trust
The Maurice Wohl Charitable
  Foundation
The Charles Wolfson Charitable
  Trust
The South Yorkshire Community
  Foundation
The Zochonis Charitable Trust

Illness

The Sylvia Adams Charitable Trust
Autonomous Research Charitable
  Trust
The Band Trust
The Big Lottery Fund
The City Bridge Trust
Colyer-Fergusson Charitable Trust
Roald Dahl's Marvellous Children's
  Charity
The John Ellerman Foundation
Esmée Fairbairn Foundation
The February Foundation
The Hugh Fraser Foundation
The Gatsby Charitable Foundation
The Girdlers' Company Charitable
  Trust
Global Charities
The Gosling Foundation Limited
The Hadley Trust
Hampton Fuel Allotment Charity
The Peter Harrison Foundation
Heart of England Community
  Foundation
The Hedley Foundation
The Hintze Family Charitable
  Foundation
The Albert Hunt Trust
The Elton John Aids Foundation
The Jones 1986 Charitable Trust
The Mary Kinross Charitable Trust
The Kohn Foundation
The Kirby Laing Foundation
The Beatrice Laing Trust
The Allen Lane Foundation
The LankellyChase Foundation
The Joseph Levy Charitable
  Foundation
The Linbury Trust
Lloyds Bank Foundation for
  Northern Ireland
Lloyds TSB Foundation for
  Scotland
John Lyon's Charity
The Mackintosh Foundation
The Mercers' Charitable
  Foundation
The Monument Trust
John Moores Foundation
The Edith Murphy Foundation

The Northern Rock Foundation
The Northwood Charitable Trust
The Pilgrim Trust
Mr and Mrs J A Pye's Charitable
  Settlement
The Robertson Trust
The Sovereign Health Care
  Charitable Trust
St James's Place Foundation
Sir Halley Stewart Trust
The Sussex Community Foundation
The True Colours Trust
The James Tudor Foundation
The Valentine Charitable Trust
The Variety Club Children's
  Charity
Volant Charitable Trust
Voluntary Action Fund (VAF)
The Welton Foundation
The Garfield Weston Foundation
The Will Charitable Trust
The HDH Wills 1965 Charitable
  Trust
The Wixamtree Trust
The Charles Wolfson Charitable
  Trust
The Wolfson Family Charitable
  Trust

Medicine and health

The 1989 Willan Charitable Trust
ABF The Soldiers' Charity
The ACT Foundation
Action Medical Research
Age UK
The AIM Foundation
The Al Fayed Charitable
  Foundation
The H B Allen Charitable Trust
The Alliance Family Foundation
The Arbib Foundation
The John Armitage Charitable
  Trust
Autonomous Research Charitable
  Trust
The Baily Thomas Charitable Fund
The Balcombe Charitable Trust
The Band Trust
The Barcapel Foundation
The Barclay Foundation
The Baring Foundation
BBC Children in Need
BC Partners Foundation
The Big Lottery Fund
The Liz and Terry Bramall
  Foundation
The Breadsticks Foundation
The Burdett Trust for Nursing

The William A Cadbury Charitable
  Trust
The Charities Advisory Trust
The Childwick Trust
The City Bridge Trust
The Clothworkers' Foundation
Richard Cloudesley's Charity
The Coalfields Regeneration Trust
The Colt Foundation
Colyer-Fergusson Charitable Trust
The Evan Cornish Foundation
The Crerar Hotels Trust
The Peter Cruddas Foundation
Cumbria Community Foundation
The D'Oyly Carte Charitable Trust
Roald Dahl's Marvellous Children's
  Charity
Baron Davenport's Charity
The Davidson Family Charitable
  Trust
The Djanogly Foundation
Dorset Community Foundation
The Royal Foundation of the Duke
  and Duchess of Cambridge and
  Prince Harry
The Dunhill Medical Trust
The James Dyson Foundation
The EBM Charitable Trust
The John Ellerman Foundation
The Eranda Foundation
The Eveson Charitable Trust
The Fidelity UK Foundation
The Sir John Fisher Foundation
The Fishmongers' Company's
  Charitable Trust
The Donald Forrester Trust
The Hugh Fraser Foundation
The Freemasons' Grand Charity
The Freshfield Foundation
The Gatsby Charitable Foundation
Simon Gibson Charitable Trust
The G C Gibson Charitable Trust
The Girdlers' Company Charitable
  Trust
The Golden Bottle Trust
The Goldsmiths' Company Charity
The Goodman Foundation
The Mike Gooley Trailfinders
  Charity
The Great Britain Sasakawa
  Foundation
The Grocers' Charity
H C D Memorial Fund
The Helen Hamlyn Trust
Hampton Fuel Allotment Charity
The Kathleen Hannay Memorial
  Charity
The Haramead Trust
The Maurice Hatter Foundation
The Charles Hayward Foundation
The Headley Trust
The Hedley Foundation

Older people

The Harbour Foundation
The Headley Trust
Heart of England Community
Foundation
The Jane Hodge Foundation
The Albert Hunt Trust
John James Bristol Foundation
The Jones 1986 Charitable Trust
Ernest Kleinwort Charitable Trust
The Sir James Knott Trust
The Beatrice Laing Trust
The Allen Lane Foundation
The Joseph Levy Charitable
Foundation
The Linbury Trust
Lloyds Bank Foundation for
England and Wales
Lloyds Bank Foundation for
Northern Ireland
Lloyds TSB Foundation for
Scotland
The Machkevitch Foundation
The Mercers' Charitable
Foundation
Milton Keynes Community
Foundation
The Edith Murphy Foundation
Nominet Charitable Foundation
Northamptonshire Community
Foundation
The Northern Rock Foundation
The Northwood Charitable Trust
The Nuffield Foundation
The Dowager Countess Eleanor
Peel Trust
The Pilkington Charities Fund
Mr and Mrs J A Pye's Charitable
Settlement
The Queen's Silver Jubilee Trust
The Rank Foundation Limited
The Joseph Rank Trust
The Rayne Foundation
The Sir James Reckitt Charity
The John and Sally Reeve
Charitable Trust
The Richmond Parish Lands
Charity
The Robertson Trust
The Henry Smith Charity
The Sobell Foundation
The Sovereign Health Care
Charitable Trust
Sir Halley Stewart Trust
The Bernard Sunley Charitable
Foundation
The Tolkien Trust
The Trusthouse Charitable
Foundation

Community Foundation Serving
Tyne and Wear and
Northumberland
Voluntary Action Fund (VAF)
Wales Council for Voluntary
Action
The Welton Foundation
The Garfield Weston Foundation
The HDH Wills 1965 Charitable
Trust
The Community Foundation for
Wiltshire and Swindon
The Wixamtree Trust
The Maurice Wohl Charitable
Foundation
The Charles Wolfson Charitable
Trust

Religion – Christianity

Allchurches Trust Ltd
The John Apthorp Charity
The Bosson Family Charitable Trust
The Bowland Charitable Trust
The Liz and Terry Bramall
Foundation
The William A Cadbury Charitable
Trust
The Carpenters' Company
Charitable Trust
Childs Charitable Trust
The Church and Community Fund
Church Urban Fund
Richard Cloudesley's Charity
The Dulverton Trust
Fisherbeck Charitable Trust
The Girdlers' Company Charitable
Trust
The Grace Charitable Trust
The Kathleen Hannay Memorial
Charity
Hexham and Newcastle Diocesan
Trust (1947)
The Jane Hodge Foundation
Sir Harold Hood's Charitable Trust
The Jerusalem Trust
Maurice and Hilda Laing Charitable
Trust
The Kirby Laing Foundation
The Beatrice Laing Trust
The Lancaster Foundation
The Leathersellers' Company
Charitable Fund
The William Leech Charity
Marshall's Charity
The Mercers' Charitable
Foundation
The George Müller Charitable Trust
The Rank Foundation Limited

The Sir James Reckitt Charity
Mrs L D Rope Third Charitable
Settlement
The Souter Charitable Trust
The Stewards' Company Limited
Sir Halley Stewart Trust
The Stobart Newlands Charitable
Trust
The Tolkien Trust
The Vardy Foundation
The Westminster Foundation

Religion – Hinduism

The Carpenters' Company
Charitable Trust

Religion – Inter-faith activities

Sir Halley Stewart Trust
The Carpenters' Company
Charitable Trust
The Community Foundation for
Northern Ireland
The Joseph Levy Charitable
Foundation

Religion – Islam

The Carpenters' Company
Charitable Trust

Religion – Judaism

4 Charity Foundation
A W Charitable Trust
Achisomoch Aid Company Limited
The Alliance Family Foundation
Amabrill Limited
The Bluston Charitable Settlement
Brushmill Ltd
The Carpenters' Company
Charitable Trust
Charitworth Limited
The Childwick Trust
The Clore Duffield Foundation
Itzchok Meyer Cymerman Trust
Ltd
The Davidson Family Charitable
Trust
The Debmar Benevolent Trust

Religious understanding

Rights, law and conflict

Science and technology

Social sciences, policy and research

Voluntary sector management and development

Women

Geographical index

The following geographical index aims to highlight when a trust gives preference for, or has a special interest in, a particular area: a county, region, city, town or London borough. Please note the following points.

1) Before using this index please read the following information and the introduction to the subject index on page 298. We must emphasise that this index:

   ▸ should not be used as a simple mailing list
   ▸ is not a substitute for detailed research.

   When you have identified trusts using this index, please read each entry carefully before making an application. Simply because a trust gives in your geographical area, this does not mean that it gives to your type of work.

2) Most trusts in this list are not restricted to one area; usually the geographical index indicates that the trust gives some priority for the area or areas.

3) Trusts which give throughout England or the UK have been excluded from the index, unless they have a particular interest in one or more locality.

4) Each section is ordered alphabetically according to the name of the trust. The categories for the overseas and UK indexes are as follows:

England

We have divided England into the following nine categories:

North East *page 314*

North West *page 314*

Yorkshire and the Humber *page 314*

East Midlands *page 314*

West Midlands *page 314*

Eastern England *page 314*

South West *page 314*

South East *page 314*

Greater London *page 314*

Some trusts may be found in more than one category due to them providing grants in more than one area, such as those with a preference for northern England.

Channel Islands *page 314*

Wales *page 314*

Scotland *page 315*

Northern Ireland *page 315*

Republic of Ireland *page 315*

Europe *page 315*

Overseas categories

Developing world *page 315*

This includes trusts which support missionary organisations when they are also interested in social and economic development.

Individual continents page 315

The Middle East has been listed separately. Please note that most of the trusts listed are primarily for the benefit of Jewish people and the advancement of the Jewish religion.

England

North East

The 1989 Willan Charitable Trust
The Coalfields Regeneration Trust
County Durham Community
Foundation
The Dulverton Trust
The Peter Harrison Foundation
Hexham and Newcastle Diocesan
Trust (1947)
The Sir James Knott Trust
The William Leech Charity
The Northern Rock Foundation
Tees Valley Community
Foundation
Community Foundation Serving
Tyne and Wear and
Northumberland

North West

The Bowland Charitable Trust
The Coalfields Regeneration Trust
Cumbria Community Foundation
The Dulverton Trust
Forever Manchester (The
Community Foundation for
Greater Manchester)
The Peter Harrison Foundation
The Helping Foundation
Community Foundation for
Merseyside
John Moores Foundation
The Morgan Foundation
The Northern Rock Foundation
Oglesby Charitable Trust
The Pilkington Charities Fund
The Francis C Scott Charitable
Trust
SHINE (Support and Help in
Education)
The Yorkshire Dales Millennium
Trust
The Zochonis Charitable Trust

Yorkshire and the Humber

Community Foundation for
Calderdale
The Coalfields Regeneration Trust
The Dulverton Trust
The Peter Harrison Foundation
The South Yorkshire Community
Foundation
The Yorkshire Dales Millennium
Trust

East Midlands

The Michael Bishop Foundation
The Coalfields Regeneration Trust
Derbyshire Community Foundation

The Dulverton Trust
The Maud Elkington Charitable
Trust
The Peter Harrison Foundation
The London Marathon Charitable
Trust
Northamptonshire Community
Foundation
The Wates Foundation

West Midlands

Birmingham & Black Country
Community Foundation
The Michael Bishop Foundation
The William A Cadbury Charitable
Trust
The Coalfields Regeneration Trust
Baron Davenport's Charity
The Dulverton Trust
The Eveson Charitable Trust
The Peter Harrison Foundation
Heart of England Community
Foundation
The Jordan Charitable Foundation
The London Marathon Charitable
Trust
Stratford upon Avon Town Trust
Sutton Coldfield Charitable Trust

Eastern England

The Dulverton Trust
Essex Community Foundation
The Harpur Trust
The Peter Harrison Foundation
The Hertfordshire Community
Foundation
The Jack Petchey Foundation

South West

The H B Allen Charitable Trust
Devon Community Foundation
Dorset Community Foundation
The Dulverton Trust
The Peter Harrison Foundation
John James Bristol Foundation
Quartet Community Foundation
The Valentine Charitable Trust
The Wates Foundation
The Community Foundation for
Wiltshire and Swindon

South East

The Arbib Foundation
The Coalfields Regeneration Trust
Colyer-Fergusson Charitable Trust
The Dulverton Trust
The Peter Harrison Foundation
Kent Community Foundation
Milton Keynes Community
Foundation
Community Foundation for Surrey
The Sussex Community Foundation
The Wates Foundation

Greater London

ABF The Soldiers' Charity
(formerly the Army Benevolent
Fund)
Amabrill Limited
The Campden Charities Trustee
Sir John Cass's Foundation
The City Bridge Trust
Richard Cloudesley's Charity
The R and S Cohen Foundation
Cripplegate Foundation
East End Community Foundation
The Glass-House Trust
The Goldsmiths' Company Charity
The M and R Gross Charities
Limited
Hampton Fuel Allotment Charity
The Harbour Foundation
The Helping Foundation
The Sir Joseph Hotung Charitable
Settlement
Hurdale Charity Limited
The J J Charitable Trust
The Jerusalem Trust
Jewish Child's Day
The Trust for London
The London Community
Foundation
The London Marathon Charitable
Trust
John Lyon's Charity
Nemoral Ltd
The Jack Petchey Foundation
The Richmond Parish Lands
Charity
The Rose Foundation
ShareGift (The Orr Mackintosh
Foundation)
SHINE (Support and Help in
Education)
Tuixen Foundation
The Wates Foundation

Channel Islands

The Freemasons' Grand Charity
Lloyds Bank Foundation for the
Channel Islands

Wales

The Baring Foundation
The Church and Community Fund
The Coalfields Regeneration Trust
The DM Charitable Trust
The Dulverton Trust
The James Dyson Foundation
Gwyneth Forrester Trust
The Freemasons' Grand Charity

The Daiwa Anglo-Japanese
   Foundation
The Debmar Benevolent Trust
The Djanogly Foundation
The DM Charitable Trust
The Dollond Charitable Trust
Euro Charity Trust
The Great Britain Sasakawa
   Foundation
Paul Hamlyn Foundation
The Helen Hamlyn Trust
Investream Charitable Trust
The Elton John Aids Foundation
Keren Association
The Neil Kreitman Foundation
The Kennedy Leigh Charitable
   Trust
The Leverhulme Trust
The Joseph Levy Charitable
   Foundation
Mayfair Charities Ltd
Melow Charitable Trust
Mercaz Torah Vechesed Limited
The Mittal Foundation
The Polonsky Foundation
Rowanville Ltd
The Samuel Sebba Charitable Trust
The Archie Sherman Charitable
   Trust
The Sobell Foundation
The Tajtelbaum Charitable Trust
Trustees of Tzedakah
The Vail Foundation
The Maurice Wohl Charitable
   Foundation
The Charles Wolfson Charitable
   Trust
The Wolfson Family Charitable
   Trust
The Wolfson Foundation

Mayfair Charities Ltd
Melow Charitable Trust
Mercaz Torah Vechesed Limited
The Polonsky Foundation
Rowanville Ltd
The Samuel Sebba Charitable Trust
The Archie Sherman Charitable
   Trust
The Sobell Foundation
The Tajtelbaum Charitable Trust
Trustees of Tzedakah
The Vail Foundation
The Maurice Wohl Charitable
   Foundation
The Charles Wolfson Charitable
   Trust
The Wolfson Family Charitable
   Trust
The Wolfson Foundation

Middle East

4 Charity Foundation
The Alliance Family Foundation
Charitworth Limited
Itzchok Meyer Cymerman Trust
   Ltd
The Debmar Benevolent Trust
The Djanogly Foundation
The DM Charitable Trust
The Dollond Charitable Trust
Investream Charitable Trust
Keren Association
The Neil Kreitman Foundation
The Kennedy Leigh Charitable
   Trust
The Leverhulme Trust
The Joseph Levy Charitable
   Foundation

Alphabetical index